America

The Essential Learning Edition

Second Edition

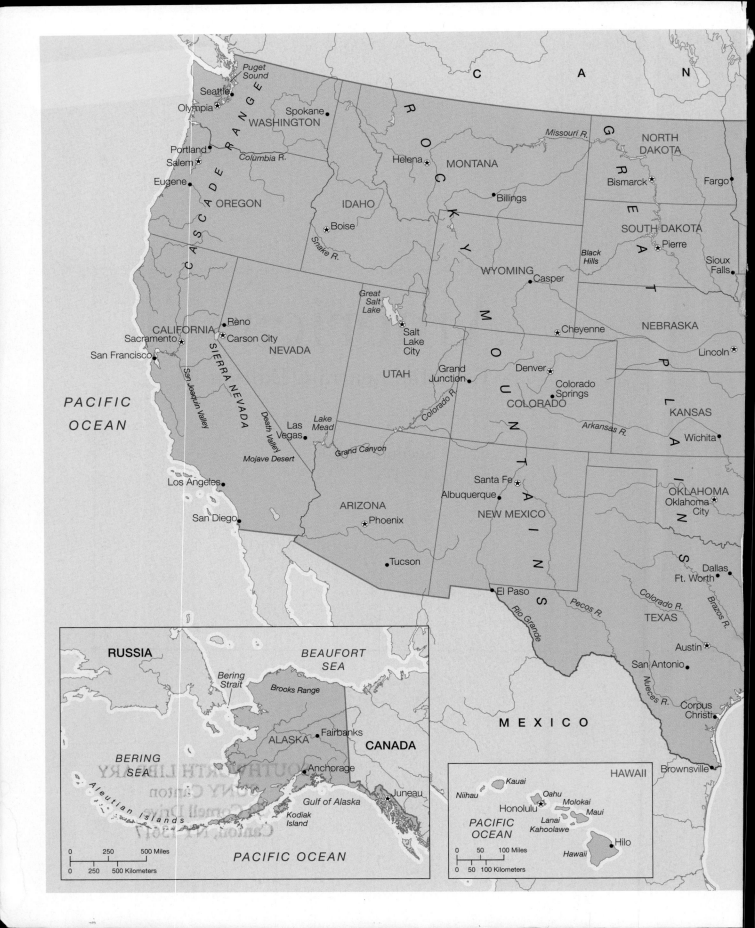

PACIFIC
OCEAN

CANADA

ROCKY

Puget
Sound

Seattle
Olympia
Spokane
WASHINGTON

Portland
Salem
Columbia R.
Helena
MONTANA

Eugene
OREGON
IDAHO
Billings

Boise
Snake R.

CASCADE RANGE

Missouri R.
NORTH
DAKOTA

Bismarck
Fargo

SOUTH DAKOTA
Black
Hills
Pierre
Sioux
Falls

WYOMING
Casper

Great
Salt
Lake
Salt
Lake
City

Reno
CALIFORNIA
Carson City
Sacramento
NEVADA

San Francisco

SIERRA NEVADA

San Joaquin Valley

Death Valley

Las
Vegas
Lake
Mead

Mojave Desert
Grand Canyon

Los Angeles

San Diego

UTAH

Grand
Junction
Colorado R.

Denver

Colorado
Springs
COLORADO

MOUNTAINS

Cheyenne
NEBRASKA

Lincoln

Arkansas R.
KANSAS

Wichita

Santa Fe
Albuquerque
ARIZONA
NEW MEXICO

Phoenix

Tucson

El Paso

Rio Grande

OKLAHOMA
Oklahoma
City

GREAT

PLAINS

Dallas
Ft. Worth

Colorado R.

Brazos R.

TEXAS

Austin
San Antonio

Pecos R.

Nueces R.

Corpus
Christi

Brownsville

MEXICO

PACIFIC
OCEAN

RUSSIA

Bering
Strait

BEAUFORT
SEA

Brooks Range

BERING
SEA

ALASKA
Fairbanks
CANADA

Anchorage

Aleutian Islands

Gulf of Alaska

Juneau

Kodiak
Island

PACIFIC OCEAN

0   250   500 Miles
0   250   500 Kilometers

HAWAII

Kauai
Niihau
Oahu
Honolulu
Molokai
Maui
Lanai
Kahoolawe

PACIFIC
OCEAN

Hawaii

Hilo

0   50   100 Miles
0   50   100 Kilometers

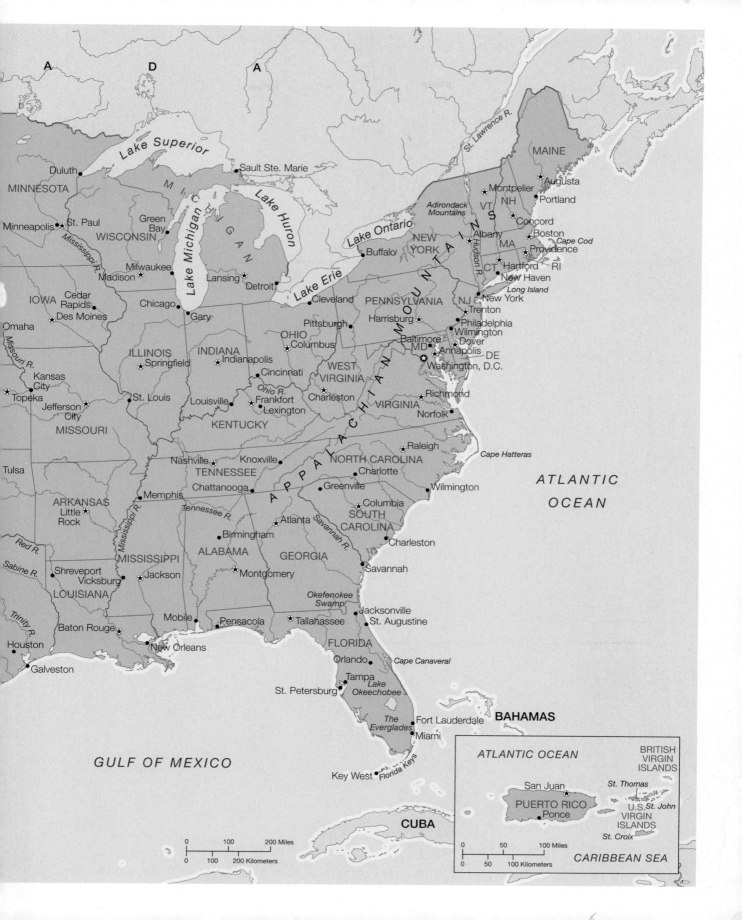

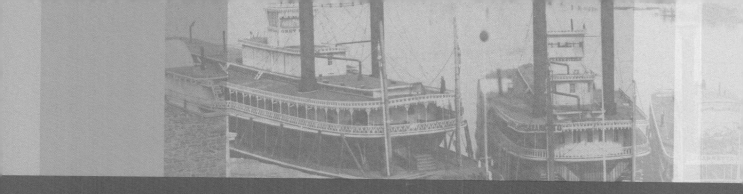

America
The Essential Learning Edition

VOLUME TWO

DAVID EMORY SHI

Second Edition

W. W. Norton & Company, Inc.
New York • London

W. W. Norton & Company has been independent since its founding in 1923, when William Warder Norton and Mary D. Herter Norton first published lectures delivered at the People's Institute, the adult education division of New York City's Cooper Union. The firm soon expanded its program beyond the Institute, publishing books by celebrated academics from America and abroad. By midcentury, the two major pillars of Norton's publishing program—trade books and college texts— were firmly established. In the 1950s, the Norton family transferred control of the company to its employees, and today—with a staff of four hundred and a comparable number of trade, college, and professional titles published each year—W. W. Norton & Company stands as the largest and oldest publishing house owned wholly by its employees.

Editor: Jon Durbin
Project Editor: Melissa Atkin
Editorial Assistant: Kelly Rafey, Lily Gellman
Marketing Manager, History: Sarah England Bartley
Manuscript Editor: Jude Grant
Managing Editor, College: Marian Johnson
Managing Editor, College Digital Media: Kim Yi
Production Manager: Andy Ensor, Elizabeth Marotta
Media Editor: Laura Wilk
Media Project Editor: Rachel Mayer
Media Associate Editor: Sarah Rose Aquilina
Associate Design Director: Hope Miller Goodell
Photo Editor: Stephanie Romeo
Permissions Manager: Megan Schindel
Permissions Specialist: Bethany Salminen
Composition: Graphic World
Manufacturing: LSC Communications—Kendallville

A catalogue record for the full edition is available from the Library of Congress.

This edition:
ISBN 978-0-393-61661-3 (pbk.)

W. W. Norton & Company, Inc., 500 Fifth Avenue, New York, NY 10110-0017
wwnorton.com
W. W. Norton & Company Ltd., 15 Carlisle Street, London W1D 3BS

1 2 3 4 5 6 7 8 9 0

For George Tindall, teacher, scholar, writer—gentleman

About the Author

DAVID EMORY SHI is professor of history and the president emeritus of Furman University in Greenville, South Carolina, an institution he led from 1994–2010. An Atlanta native, he earned degrees in history from Furman University and the University of Virginia before starting his academic career at Davidson College, where he won the Outstanding Teacher Award and chaired the history department. He is the author of several books on American cultural history, including the award-winning *The Simple Life: Plain Living and High Thinking in American Culture* and *Facing Facts: Realism in American Thought and Culture, 1850–1920*. More recently, he published a collection of speeches, newspaper columns, and essays titled *The Belltower and Beyond* and co-edited with Holly Mayer a book of primary sources called *For the Record: Documents in American History*. He lives in Brevard, North Carolina.

Contents
in Brief

Contents

Maps

Thinking Like A Historian

What's It All About?
(In the Norton Coursepack)

Preface

This second edition of *The Essential Learning Edition* continues to nurture *America*'s long-established focus on history as a storytelling art. It features colorful characters and anecdotes informed by balanced analysis and social texture, all guided by the unfolding of key events and imperfect but often fascinating human actors with an emphasis on the culture of everyday life. *The Essential Learning Edition* continues to provide a unique package of features to introduce students to the methods and tools used by historians to study, revise, and debate efforts to explain and interpret the past.

As always, the first step in my preparing a new edition is to learn from students and professors what can be improved, polished, added or deleted. The results of dozens of survey instruments provided a strong consensus: students want an inexpensive, visually interesting textbook written in lively prose that focuses on the essential elements of American history while telling the dramatic stories about the ways that individuals responded to and shaped events. Too many textbooks overwhelm them, students responded, either by flooding them with too much information or by taking too much for granted in terms of the knowledge that students bring to the introductory course. Students stressed that textbooks need to help them more readily identify the most important developments or issues to focus on (and remember) as they read.

To address these student concerns, I have continued to provide contextual explanations for events or developments that too often are taken for granted by authors. For example, this edition includes more material about the Native American experience, the nature and significance of the Protestant Reformation, the texture of daily life, the impact of the cotton culture on the global economy, and the march of capitalism.

When asked what they most wanted in an introductory text, instructors said much the same as their students, but they also asked for a textbook that introduced students to the nature of historical research, analysis, and debate. Many professors also mentioned the growing importance to them and their institutions of *assessing* the success of their students in meeting the learning goals established by their department. Accordingly, I have aligned *The Essential Learning Edition* with specific learning outcomes for the introductory American history survey course approved by various state and national organizations, including the American Historical Association. These learning outcomes also extend to the accompanying media package, enabling instructors to track students' progress towards mastery of these important learning goals.

These and other suggestions from students and professors have shaped this new version of *The Essential Learning Edition*. Each of the 30 chapters begins with a handful of **Core Objectives**, carefully designed to help students understand—and remember—the major developments and issues in each period. To make it easier for students to grasp the major developments, every chapter aligns the narrative with the learning objectives. Each Core Objective is highlighted at the beginning of each major section in the chapter for which it is relevant. **Core Objective flags** appear in the page margins to reinforce key topics in the narrative that are essential to understanding the broader Core Objectives. **Key terms**, chosen to reinforce the major concepts, are bolded in the text and defined in the margin, helping reinforce their significance. At the end of each chapter, review features continue to reiterate and review the Core Objectives, including pithy chapter summaries, lists of key terms, and chapter chronologies.

This book continues to be distinctive for its creative efforts to make every component—maps, images, etc.— a learning opportunity and teaching point. Maps, for example, include lists of questions to help students interpret the data embedded in them.

Interactive maps are but just one example of the innovative elements in this book designed to deepen student learning and get them more *engaged* in the learning dynamic. Chapters in *The Essential Learning Edition* also include a **What It's All About** feature, which visually summarizes in a graphical format major issues. These are now available exclusively in the Norton Coursepack for instructors to use in ways that are best suited for their courses. Some examples include:

- Chapter 3: Comparative examination of how different regions of the English colonies were settled and developed.
- Chapter 9: Analyzes sectional conflicts and the role the economic policies of Henry Clay and Andrew Jackson played in those conflicts.
- Chapter 12: Abolitionist versus pro-slavery arguments on slavery.
- Chapter 15: Tracing the legal and legislative road from slavery to freedom for African Americans in the former Confederate States.
- Chapter 23: The First New Deal compared to the Second New Deal.

Another unique new feature, called **Thinking Like a Historian,** helps students better understand—and apply—the research techniques and interpretive skills used by historians. Through carefully selected examples, the Thinking Like a Historian segments highlight the foundational role of primary and secondary sources as the building blocks of history and illustrates the ways in which historians have differed in their interpretations of the past. There is one Thinking Like a Historian feature for each of the seven major periods of American history; each feature takes on a major interpretive issue in that era. In Part I of the activity, students first read excerpts from two original secondary sources that offer competing interpretive views framing that period. In Part II, students then read some of the original primary sources that those same historians used to develop their arguments. Finally, students must answer a series of questions that guide their reading and analysis of the sources.

As always, this new edition also includes new content. As I created this new edition of *The Essential Learning Edition*, I have complemented the political narrative by incorporating more social and cultural history into the text. Key new discussions include:

- Chapter 1: Enriched coverage of pre-Columbian peoples, especially the Maya, Mexica (Aztecs), and Algonquians—and European explorations in North America. Additional material about the Renaissance and Reformation, especially Martin Luther and the Anglican Reformation.
- Chapter 2: Additional material on the social structure of European societies during the Age of Discovery, the crucially important and highly profitable Caribbean colonies, especially Barbados, and the process of enslaving Africans and shipping them to the Americas.
- Chapter 3: The everyday life of women and the role of women in evangelical revivals; enhanced treatment of Great Awakening; and, additional details on infant mortality and family dynamics in the colonial period.
- Chapter 4: New insights into the growing resistance to British authority in the colonies leading up to 1775.
- Chapter 5: Enriched treatment of Revolutionary War battles, the everyday life of soldiers, and the role of women revolutionaries and those who served as "camp followers" in support of the Continental armies.
- Chapter 6: Additional insights into Shays's Rebellion and the early stages of American capitalism.
- Chapter 7: Enhanced profile of Thomas Jefferson and his contradictory stance on slavery and women.
- Chapter 8: More information about the development of the cotton gin and its impact on the national economy. Added insights into the development of the textile mill system in New England and the daily life of Irish immigrants in seaboard cities as well as women in early labor unions.
- Chapter 10: A more robust portrait of Andrew Jackson and his distinctive life and personality as well as the Peggy Eaton Affair.
- Chapter 11: Delves more deeply into the economic significance and everyday dynamics of slavery and the culture of slave communities. More coverage of the "slave trail" from the Upper South to the Gulf coast states and of the nature of slave auctions. New details on the lives of plantation mistresses, their duties, double-standards, and systemic sexism they endured
- Chapter 12: Enriched treatment of the abolitionist movement and utopianism, especially the Shakers and the Oneida Community.

- Chapter 13: Additional color and texture about life on the Overland trails, Sutter's Fort, and the mining communities associated with the California Gold Rush. Also more in-depth treatment of the Fugitive Slave Act.
- Chapter 14: Enhanced attention to the everyday experience of Civil War soldiers—why they fought, what they ate, camp life, the horrors of battle and their sense of manly duty.
- Chapter 16: Deepened the discussion of the impact of the railroad boom on the Gilded Age economy and everyday life.
- Chapter 17: Reorganized the section on Native Americans in the West, including new sections on the Sand Creek Massacre, and Grant's Indian Policy, and expanded coverage on Custer, the Great Sioux War, and the Battle of the Little Big Horn. Added a profile of Ida Wells—African American woman who led the crusade against racial lynchings.
- Chapter 18: New section added that better frames the discussion of political life during the Gilded Age, including the balance between the two major parties, the surprising level of public participation in everyday politics, and the relationships between business & politics and industry & agriculture.
- Chapter 19: Details added about Theodore Roosevelt and the Rough Riders during the Cuba campaign.
- Chapter 20: Added a portrait of Walter Rauschenbusch and his role in promoting the social gospel.
- Chapter 21: More material about the everyday experience of soldiers in the Great War, especially the nature of trench warfare in the Western Front and the role of shellshock.
- Chapter 22: An enriched profile of Al Capone and more detailed treatment of the famous Democratic Convention of 1924.
- Chapter 23: A more textured account of the human effects of the Great Depression on the American people.
- Chapter 27: Enhanced treatment of John F. Kennedy, Lyndon B. Johnson, and Martin Luther King, Jr. And a profile of civil rights leader Medgar Evers.
- Chapter 30: New coverage of the Obama administration, the ongoing wars in Iraq and Afghanistan, the rise of voter populism, the surprising victory of Donald Trump in the 2016 election, and his tempestuous first year as president.

In sum, *The Essential Learning Edition* includes the most dramatic changes ever made in a resilient book that has been in print for more than thirty years.

Media Tools for Students and Instructors

America: The Essential Learning Edition, Second Edition, is supported by a robust collection of digital resources to support the core objectives and historical developments discussed in each chapter, while also building students' history "skills."

INQUIZITIVE

Norton InQuizitive uses interactive questions and guided feedback to motivate students to read and understand the key concepts, events, and historical developments. A variety of question types featuring images, maps, and sources prompt critical and analytical thinking on each of the chapter's Core Objectives. In a case study with *The Essential Learning Edition*, First Edition, 80% of history students said they think InQuizitive helped them learn the material from the textbook, 88% of students said they prefer InQuizitive to previous standard multiple-choice quizzes, and 92% of students would recommend that the instructor continue using InQuizitive.

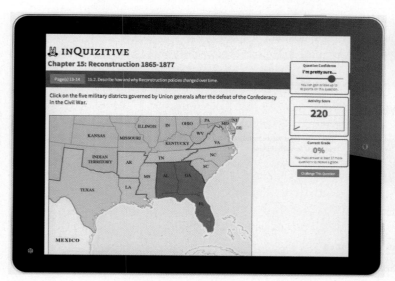

New! History Skills Tutorials

With the Second Edition we've expanded our digital resources to include a new series of tutorials to build students' critical analysis skills. The History Skills Tutorials combine video and interactive assessments to teach students how to analyze documents, images, and maps. By utilizing a three-step process, students learn a framework for analysis through videos featuring

David Shi, and then are challenged to apply what they have learned through a series of interactive assessments. The History Skills Tutorials can be assigned at the beginning of the semester to prepare students for analysis of the sources in the textbook and beyond, or integrated as remediation tools throughout the semester.

Student Site

This free site offers students access to additional resources to support student learning. Features include NEW! Chapter overview videos that prepare students for the reading by highlighting key events and themes that emerge in the chapter. In addition, there is a comprehensive collection of author videos exploring the core objectives from each chapter. Interactive iMaps, as well as an online reader featuring additional primary source documents, provide students with even more opportunities to engage with primary sources.

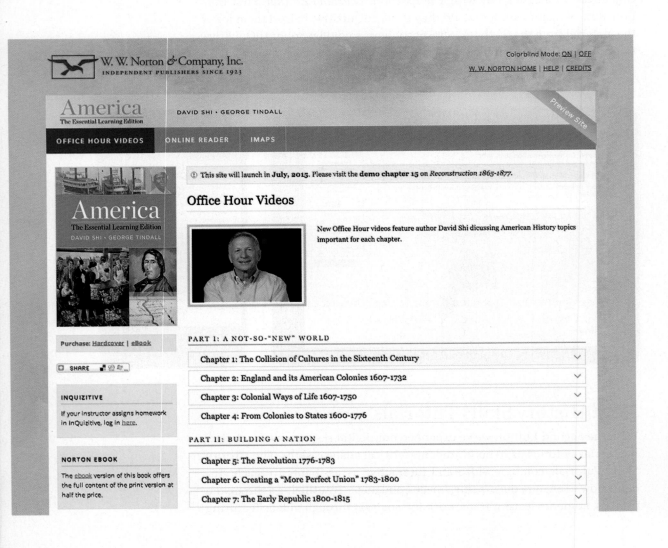

Norton Ebooks

Norton Ebooks give students and instructors an enhanced reading experience at a fraction of the cost of a print textbook. Students are able to have an active reading experience and can take notes, bookmark, search, highlight, and even read offline. As an instructor, you can even add your own notes for students to see as they read the text. Norton ebooks can be viewed on—and synced between—all computers and mobile devices.

Norton Coursepacks

Easily add high quality Norton digital media to your online, hybrid, or lecture course—all at no cost. Norton Coursepacks work within your existing learning management system; there's no new system to learn, and access is free and easy. Content is customizable and includes

- **Primary-Source Exercises** prompt students to compare documents and images with multiple-choice and short-answer questions for analysis.
- **Guided Reading Exercises** walk students through a three-step critical reading process: noting the important main points, summarizing in your own words, and answering short-answer questions to confirm understanding.
- **What's It All About** visually summarizes in a graphical format major issues. This feature from the First Edition has been fully revised for the Second Edition and can now be assigned directly to students through the Coursepack.
- **Online Reader** feature additional primary-source documents and images that go beyond what is in textbooks.
- **Chapter Review Quizzes** include multiple-choice, chronological matching, and true/false questions.
- **Author Videos,** including the NEW! Chapter Overview videos, illuminate key events, developments, and concepts in each chapter by bringing the narrative to life with additional context and anecdotes.
- **iMaps** are interactive versions of maps from the text that allow students to practice their map reading skills, with map worksheets for self-testing and labeling exercises.
- And all of the **Student Site** resources.

Classroom Presentation Tools

- **Lecture PowerPoints** (Bettye Hutchins, Vernon College) and **Art PowerPoints** feature photographs and maps from the book, retouched for in-class presentation.
- The **Norton American History Digital Archive** includes over 1,700 images, audio and video files that are arranged chronologically and by theme.

Instructor's Manual (Chad Garick, Jones County Junior College; Kenneth Howell, Blinn College)

The Instructor's Manual for *The Essential Learning Edition* has everything instructors need to prepare lectures and classroom activities: chapter summaries, suggestions for teaching Core Objectives, as well as lecture ideas, classroom activities, and lists of recommended books, films, and websites.

Test Bank (Thomas Born, Blinn College; Linda Coslett, Chattanooga State Community College)

The Test Bank features multiple-choice, true/false, and essay questions aligned with the chapter's Core Objectives and classified according to level of difficulty, and Bloom's Taxonomy, offering multiple avenues for content and skill assessment. All Norton test banks are available with ExamView Test Generator software, allowing instructors to easily create, administer, and manage assessments.

Acknowledgments

The quality and range of reviews on this project were truly exceptional. The book and its accompanying media components benefited from the insights of numerous instructors.

Milan Andrejevich, Ivy Tech College–South Bend
Carol A. Bielke, San Antonio Independent School District
April Birchfield, Asheville-Buncombe Technical Community College
Howard Bodner, Houston Community College
Matt Brent, Rappahannock Community College
Sharon J. Burnham, John Tyler Community College
Michael Collins, Texas State University
Scott Cook, Motlow State Community College
Carrie Coston, Blinn College
Nicholas P. Cox, Houston Community College
Carl E. Creasman Jr., Valencia College
Stephen K. Davis, Texas State University
Frank De La O, Midland College
Jim Dudlo, Brookhaven College
Robert Glen Findley, Odessa College
Brandon Franke, Blinn College
Chad Garick, Jones County Junior College
Mark S. Goldman, Tallahassee Community College
Devethia Guillory, Lone Star College–North Harris
Justin Hoggard, Three Rivers College
Andrew G. Hollinger, Tarrant County College

David P. Hopkins Jr., Midland College
Justin Horton, Thomas Nelson Community College
Theresa R. Jach, Houston Community College
Robert Jason Kelly, Holmes Community College
Nina McCune, Baton Rouge Community College
Richard Randall Moore, Metropolitan Community College–Longview
Ken S. Mueller, Ivy Tech College–Lafayette
Lise Namikas, Colorado State University–Global
Brice E. Olivier, Temple College
Candice Pulkowski, The Art Institutes
Carey Roberts, Liberty University
John Schmitz, Northern Virginia Community College–Annandale
Greg Shealy, University of Wisconsin–Madison
Thomas Summerhill, Michigan State University
Scott M. Williams, Weatherford College
Laura Matysek Wood, Tarrant County College Northwest
Crystal R.M. Wright, North Central Texas College

Once again, I thank my friends and colleagues at W. W. Norton for their consummate professionalism and good cheer, especially Jon Durbin, Laura Wilk, Sarah England, Melissa Atkin, Julie Sindel, Roy McClymont, Jonathan Mason, Kelly Rafey, Lily Gellman, Marian Johnson, Kim Yi, Rachel Mayer, Stephanie Romeo, Sarah Rose Aquilina, Hope Miller Goodell, Debra Morton-Hoyt, Andy Ensor, Liz Marotta, and Jude Grant.

Finally, I have dedicated this new version of *America* to George Brown Tindall, who died in 2006 at the age of eighty-five. When George and I first met in Manhattan in 1984 to discuss collaborating on this textbook project, we discovered that we shared an alma mater (Furman University), a passion for classroom teaching and student advising, and a commitment to exposing students to the color and drama of the past through lively narrative prose. George once told me that he taught not because his students needed him but because he needed them. Education was his calling; history was his passion. That so many of his former students became his closest friends testifies to his distinctive success as a professor.

A free-thinking, plain-speaking man, George was truly one of the nation's most distinguished historians. And, for over twenty years, he was my partner, mentor, and friend, but more than that, he was an inspiration. His love for language and for learning exercised a seductive charm on me. How bracing it was to be in the company of a gentleman for whom scholarship was a heroic enterprise. How refreshing it was to know someone for whom a perpetual bow-tie bespoke gentility and grace rather than pomposity. How beneficial it was to be challenged to become a better writer, a clearer thinker, and a more tenacious defender of one's own values and conclusions.

George Tindall remains a continuing influence on me. While few of his words and phrases remain in this latest edition, his robust spirit, pristine integrity, and refreshing humor live on—as they should.

***A VISIT FROM THE OLD MISTRESS* (1876)** This powerful painting by Winslow Homer depicts a plantation mistress visiting her former slaves in the postwar South. Although their living conditions are humble, these freedwomen stand eye-to-eye with the woman who kept them in bondage.

Reconstruction

1865–1877

In the spring of 1865, the Civil War was finally over. The United States was a "new nation," said an Illinois congressman, because it was now "wholly free." At a frightful cost of more than 730,000 lives and the destruction of the southern economy, the Union had won, and almost 4 million slaves had seized their freedom. No longer would enslaved workers be whipped, nor sold and separated from their families, nor prevented from learning to read and write or attending church. "I felt like a bird out of a cage," said former slave Houston Holloway from Georgia, who had been sold to three different owners during his first twenty years. "Amen. Amen. Amen. I could hardly ask to feel any better than I did that day." Eda Harper from Mississippi was even more ecstatic. Upon learning of the end of the war, she and her fellow slaves "danced all night long."

The ratification of the Thirteenth Amendment to the U.S. Constitution in December 1865 ended any doubt about the status of former slaves by abolishing slavery everywhere. Few owners, however, willingly freed their slaves until forced to by the arrival of Union soldiers. A North Carolina planter maintained that he and other whites "will never get along with the free negroes" because they were an "inferior race." Similarly, a Mississippi planter predicted that "these niggers will all be slaves again in twelve months." When a white man in South Carolina caught an enslaved mother and her children running toward freedom, he "drew his bowie-knife and cut her throat; also the throat of her boy, nine years old; also the throat of her girl, seven years of age; threw their bodies into the river, and the live baby after them."

Such brutal incidents illuminate the extraordinary challenges the nation faced in "reconstructing" and reuniting a ravaged and resentful South while

CORE
OBJECTIVES INQUIZITIVE

1. Identify the federal government's major challenges in reconstructing the South after the Civil War.

2. Describe how and why Reconstruction policies changed over time.

3. Assess the attitudes of white and black southerners toward Reconstruction.

4. Analyze the political and economic factors that helped end Reconstruction in 1877.

5. Explain the significance of Reconstruction to the nation's future.

helping to transform ex-slaves into free workers and equal citizens. It would not be easy. As a South Carolina planter threatened a federal official in the fall of 1865, "The war is not over." Rebels had been conquered, but they were far from being loyal Unionists.

The Reconstruction Era, from 1865 to 1877, witnessed a complex debate about the role of the federal government in ensuring civil rights. Some northerners wanted the former Confederate states returned to the Union with little or no changes. Others wanted Confederate leaders imprisoned or executed and the South rebuilt in the image of the rest of the nation. Still others cared little about reconstructing the South; they wanted the federal government to focus on promoting northern economic growth and westward expansion.

Although the Reconstruction Era lasted only twelve years, it was one of the most significant periods in U.S. history. The decisions made and policies enacted are still shaping American life nearly 150 years later.

CORE **OBJECTIVE**

1. Identify the federal government's major challenges in reconstructing the South after the Civil War.

The War's Aftermath in the South

In the spring of 1865, the former Confederacy presented a sharp contrast to the victorious North. Southerners were emotionally exhausted; fully a fifth of the southern white males had died in the war; many others had been maimed for life. In 1866, Mississippi spent 20 percent of the state's budget on artificial limbs for Confederate soldiers. Property values had collapsed. In the year after the war ended, eighty-one plantations in Mississippi were sold for less than a tenth of what they had been worth in 1860. Confederate money was worthless; personal savings had vanished; tens of thousands of horses and mules had been killed in the fighting, and many farm buildings and equipment destroyed. Burned-out Columbia, South Carolina was "a wilderness of ruins"; Charleston, the birthplace of secession, had become a place of "vacant houses, of widowed women, of rotting wharves, of deserted warehouses, of weed-wild gardens, of miles of grass-grown streets, of acres of pitiful and voiceless barrenness."

Confederate general Braxton Bragg returned to his "once prosperous" Alabama home to find "all was lost, except my debts." He and his wife, having been accustomed to prosperity, were forced to live in an abandoned slave cabin. South Carolina's Mary Chesnut was equally despondent at war's end: "We are scattered—stunned—the remnant of heart left alive with us, filled with brotherly hate" for the Union victors and devastated by her native region's "day of humiliation and sorrow" amid its "ruined homes and desolated country."

Emancipation wiped out $4 billion invested in slavery, which had enabled the explosive growth of the cotton culture. The heyday of the robust cotton economy was over, however. Not until 1879 would the cotton crop again equal the record harvest of 1860; tobacco production did not regain its prewar level until 1880; the sugar crop of Louisiana did not recover until

RICHMOND AFTER THE WAR
Before evacuating the capital of the Confederacy, Richmond, Virginia, local mobs set fire to warehouses and factories to prevent their falling into Union hands. Pictured here is one of Richmond's burnt districts in April 1865. Women in mourning attire walk among the shambles.

1893; and the rice economy along the coast of South Carolina and Georgia never regained its prewar levels of production or profit. In 1860, just before the Civil War, the South had generated 30 percent of the nation's wealth; in 1870, only ten years later, it produced but 12 percent.

Political turmoil accompanied the economic chaos. The process of forming new state governments first required deciding the official status of the seceded states: Were they now conquered territories? If so, then the Constitution assigned Reconstruction to Congress.

But what if, as Abraham Lincoln had argued, the Confederate states had never officially left the Union because secession was illegal? In that circumstance, the president would be responsible for Reconstruction. In either case, what would be the political, social, and economic status of the freed slaves? Were they citizens? If not, what was their status as Americans? There were no easy answers.

The Battle over Political Reconstruction

CORE **OBJECTIVE**
2. Describe how and why Reconstruction policies changed over time.

The Reconstruction of former Confederate states actually began during the war and went through several phases, the first of which was called Presidential Reconstruction. With Union forces advancing into the Confederacy during the fighting, President Lincoln in 1862 had named army generals to serve as temporary military governors for conquered areas. By the end of 1863, he had formulated a plan for regular governments in those states liberated from Confederate rule.

Lincoln's Wartime Reconstruction Plan

Presidential Reconstruction: Lincoln's Proclamation of Amnesty and Reconstruction

In late 1863, President Lincoln issued a Proclamation of Amnesty and Reconstruction, under which any former Rebel state could form a Union government whenever a number equal to 10 percent of those who had voted in 1860 took a formal oath of allegiance to the Constitution and the Union and received a presidential pardon acquitting them from treason charges.

Certain groups, however, were excluded from the pardon: Confederate government officials; senior officers of the Confederate army and navy; judges, congressmen, and military officers of the United States who had left their federal posts to join the rebellion; and those who had abused captured African American soldiers.

Northern politicians, however, disagreed over who had the authority to restore Rebel states to the Union. Most moderate Republicans supported Lincoln's program intended to quickly restore pro-Union southern governments. Many **Radical Republicans**, however, favored a drastic transformation of southern society. They wanted to make freed slaves citizens and grant them full civil rights. To do so, they argued, Congress, not the president, should supervise Reconstruction.

The Radicals also hoped to replace the white Democratic planter elite with a new generation of small farmers and middle-class Republicans, both black and white. "The middling classes who own the soil, and work it with their own hands," explained Radical leader Thaddeus Stevens, "are the main support of every free government."

In 1864, with the war still raging, the Radicals tried to take charge of Reconstruction by passing the Wade-Davis Bill, named for two leading Republicans in Congress. In contrast to Lincoln's 10 percent Reconstruction plan, the Wade-Davis Bill required that a *majority* of white male citizens declare their allegiance to the Union before a Confederate state could be readmitted.

Lincoln vetoes Wade-Davis Bill

The Wade-Davis Bill never became law, however, for Lincoln vetoed it as being too harsh. In retaliation, Radicals issued the Wade-Davis Manifesto, a public statement that accused Lincoln of exceeding his constitutional authority. Unfazed by the criticism, Lincoln continued his efforts to restore the Confederate states to the Union. He also rushed assistance to the freed slaves in the South.

The Freedmen's Bureau

The Thirteenth Amendment officially ended slavery, but what did freedom mean for the former slaves, most of whom had no land, no home, no food, and no education? "What is freedom?" asked Congressman James A. Garfield, a former Union general and a future U.S. president, in 1865. "Is it the bare privilege of not being chained? If this is all, then freedom is a bitter mockery, a cruel delusion." The debate over what freedom should entail for 4 million former slaves became the central issue of Reconstruction.

Radical Republicans Congressmen who identified with the abolitionist cause and sought swift emancipation of the slaves, punishment of the Rebels, and tight controls over former Confederate states.

FREEDMEN'S SCHOOL IN VIRGINIA As part of its effort to support former slaves in their transition to freedom, the Freedman's Bureau established schools for the freedpeople across the southern states. **What are the students learning in this Virginia school, and how might it help them become self-supporting?**

To address the complex issues raised by emancipation, Congress on March 3, 1865, created the **Freedmen's Bureau** to assist the suffering "freedmen and their wives and children." It was the first federal effort to provide assistance directly to people rather than to states. And its tasks were daunting. When General William T. Sherman learned that his friend, General Oliver O. Howard, had been appointed to lead the Freedmen's Bureau, he wrote him a letter in which he soberly warned that "It is not . . . in your power to fulfill one-tenth of the expectations of those who framed the Bureau." Undeterred by such realities, in May 1865, Howard declared that freed slaves "must be free to choose their own employers, and be paid for their labor."

Howard thereafter sent Freedmen's Bureau agents to the South to negotiate labor contracts between blacks and white landowners, many of whom resisted. The agents, never enough to fulfill their goals, also provided the former slaves with medical care, food, and clothing and helped set up schools and pay teachers. Northern missionary societies also established schools for the freedpeople across the South. As a Mississippi freedman explained, education "was the next best thing to liberty."

By 1870, the Freedmen's Bureau was supervising more than 4,000 new schools in the South serving almost 250,000 students, many of whose teachers were initially women volunteers from the North. The Freedmen's Bureau also helped former slaves reestablish connection with their family members and to legalize marriages that had been prohibited prior to the war.

Freedmen's Bureau Federal Reconstruction agency established to protect the legal rights of former slaves and to assist with their education, jobs, health care, and land ownership.

The Assassination of Lincoln

Lincoln assassinated (April 14, 1865)

Abraham Lincoln offered his last view of Reconstruction in the final speech of his life. On April 11, 1865, he rejected calls by Radicals for a vengeful Reconstruction. He wanted "no persecution, no bloody work," no hangings of Confederate leaders nor any extreme efforts to restructure southern social and economic life. Lincoln yearned for a peace "with malice toward none, with charity for all."

He did not get it.

On April 14, 1865, the president and his wife, Mary Todd, attended a play at Ford's Theatre in Washington, D.C. Lincoln was sitting defenseless as twenty-six-year-old John Wilkes Booth slipped into the unguarded presidential box. Booth, a famous actor and a rabid Confederate, fired his small pistol point-blank at the president's head. As Lincoln slumped forward, Booth pulled out a knife, stabbed Lincoln's military aide, and jumped from the box to the stage, breaking his leg in the process. He then mounted a waiting horse and fled the city. The president died nine hours later, leaving his widow "very pitiable—she has hysteria & has sometimes been very delirious."

The nation was suddenly leaderless. Vice President Andrew Johnson was sworn in as the new president, but for a time chaos reigned. Secretary of War Edwin Stanton, not knowing if the assassination was a prelude to a Confederate invasion, summoned General Ulysses Grant to defend the government in Washington, D.C. All roads into the city were closed, patrolled only by Union troops. Eleven days later, Union troops found Booth hiding in a northern

LINCOLN'S FUNERAL PROCESSION After Lincoln's assassination, his body was taken on a two-week long funeral procession through five different states, allowing millions of people the chance to see him. This photograph was taken on April 25, when the procession passed through New York City.

Virginia tobacco barn, where he was shot and killed. Booth whispered as he lay dying, "Tell my mother I died for my country."

Johnson's Plan

Lincoln's murder shocked and saddened the nation and propelled into the White House Vice President Andrew Johnson of Tennessee, a combative, stubborn man with a quick temper and fierce prejudices—he hated both the white southern elite and the idea of racial equality. Johnson was a pro-Union Democrat who had joined Lincoln's National Union ticket in 1864 as a gesture of wartime bipartisan unity.

Like Lincoln, Johnson was a self-made man. Born in 1808 into dirt-poor poverty in Raleigh, North Carolina, he lost his father when he was three and never attended school. His mother apprenticed him to a tailor to learn a trade. At thirteen he ran away and eventually landed in Greeneville, nestled in the mountains of east Tennessee, where he became a tailor. He taught himself to read, and his wife showed him how to write and do some basic arithmetic. A natural leader, he eventually served as the mayor, a state legislator, governor, congressional representative, and U.S. senator.

Johnson called himself a Jacksonian Democrat "in the strictest meaning of the term. I am for putting down the [Confederate] rebellion, because it is a war [of wealthy plantation owners] against democracy." While hating the "traitorous" planter elite, Johnson shared the racist attitudes of most southern whites. "Damn the negroes," he exclaimed to a friend during the war. "I am fighting those traitorous aristocrats, their masters."

President Johnson's plan to reconstruct the Confederate states closely resembled Lincoln's lenient terms. In May 1865, he issued a new Proclamation of Amnesty that excluded not only those ex-Confederates whom Lincoln had barred from a presidential pardon but also banned anyone with property worth more than $20,000. Johnson was determined to keep the wealthiest southerners from regaining political power. Surprisingly, however, he eventually pardoned most of the white "aristocrats" he claimed to despise. What brought about this change of heart? Johnson had apparently decided that he could buy the political support of prominent southerners by pardoning them, improving his own chances of reelection. His focus was on "restoring" rather than "reconstructing" the southern states.

Johnson's Restoration Plan included the appointment of a Unionist as provisional governor in each southern state, with authority to call a convention of men elected by "loyal" (that is, not Confederate) voters. Each state convention had to ratify the Thirteenth Amendment ending slavery. Johnson also encouraged the state conventions to consider giving a few blacks voting rights, especially those with some education or with military service so as to "disarm" the "Radicals who are wild upon" giving *all* African Americans the right to vote. Except for uncompromising Mississippi, each state of the former Confederacy held a convention that met Johnson's requirements but ignored his suggestion about giving voting rights to a few blacks.

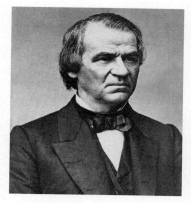

ANDREW JOHNSON
A Jacksonian Democrat from Tennessee, Johnson stepped into the role of president after Lincoln's assassination. He introduced a Restoration Plan that required southern states to ratify the Thirteenth Amendment and limited the political power of rich ex-Confederates.

Presidential Reconstruction: Johnson's Restoration Plan

Johnson's Restoration Plan
Plan to require southern states to ratify the Thirteenth Amendment, disqualify wealthy ex-Confederates from voting, and appoint a Unionist governor.

Freedmen's Conventions

Neither Lincoln nor Johnson saw fit to ask freedpeople in the South what they most needed. So the ex-slaves—men and women—took matters into their own hands. They met and marched, demanding not just freedom but citizenship and full civil rights, land of their own, and voting rights. Especially in and around large cities such as New Orleans, Mobile, Norfolk, Wilmington, Nashville, Memphis, and Charleston, former slaves, both men and women, mobilized to make their voices heard. They organized regular meetings, chose leaders, protested mistreatment by Confederates or federal officials, learned the workings of the federal bureaucracy, and sought economic opportunities as wage workers.

During the summer and fall of 1865, liberated slaves and free people of color from the North ("missionaries") and South organized freedmen's conventions (sometimes called Equal Rights Associations) across the South. Often led by ministers, they met in state capitals "to impress upon the white

FREEDMEN'S CONVENTION In this 1868 woodcut, a group of Southern freedpeople meet to discuss their political and social resolutions. **Who is participating in this freedmen convention, and how might the demographic diversity have contributed to the freedmen's initiatives?**

men," as the Reverend James D. Lynch told the Tennessee freedmen's convention, "that we are part and parcel of the American republic," and as such they were eager to counter the whites-only state conventions being organized under Johnson's Reconstruction plan. Virtually all the freedmen's conventions forged resolutions that stressed their desire for free public education, their need for wage-earning jobs and their own land, and their insistence on full civil rights, especially voting rights.

The North Carolina freedmen's convention elected as its president James Walker Hood, a free black from Connecticut. In his acceptance speech, he emphasized their goals: "We and the white people have to live here together. Some people talk of emigration for the black race, some of expatriation, and some of colonization. I regard this as all nonsense. We have been living together for a hundred years and more, and we have got to live together still; and the best way is to harmonize our feelings as much as possible, and to treat all men respectfully." Hood then demanded three constitutional rights for African Americans: the right to testify in courts, serve on juries, and "the right to carry [a] ballot to the ballot box."

In sum, the freedmen's conventions demanded that their voices be heard in Washington and southern state capitals. As the Virginia freedmen's convention asserted, "Any attempt to reconstruct the states . . . without giving to American citizens of African descent all the rights and immunities accorded to white citizens . . . is an act of gross injustice."

The Radical Republicans

Johnson's initial assault on the southern planter elite pleased Radical Republicans but not for long. Many Radicals who wanted Reconstruction to provide social and political equality for blacks resented Johnson's efforts to bring the South back into the Union as quickly as possible.

The most extreme Radical Republicans, Thaddeus Stevens of Pennsylvania and Charles Sumner of Massachusetts, wanted to deny former Confederates the right to vote in order to keep them from electing the old planter elite and to enable the Republican party to gain a foothold in the Democratic region. Stevens argued that the Civil War had been fought to produce a *radical revolution* in southern life: the "whole fabric of southern society must be changed" in order to "revolutionize southern institutions, habits, and manners." He had urged Lincoln to "free every slave—slay every traitor—burn every Rebel mansion!"

Stevens and other Radicals claimed they had the authority to confiscate the largest southern plantations, divide them into small farms, and give them to former slaves. The iron-willed Stevens, for example, viewed the Confederate states as "conquered provinces," subject to the absolute will of the U.S. Congress, not the president.

Andrew Johnson, however, balked at such an expansion of federal authority. At base, he was committed to the states' rights to control their affairs rather than to an intrusive federal government. "White men alone must manage the South," Johnson told a visitor.

Unreconstructed Southerners

After the war, most white southerners found their lives in turmoil. They could not forget the war or their defeat, and they resented and resisted the North's efforts to reconstruct their homeland. As a North Carolinian muttered in 1866, he felt the "bitterest hatred toward the North." He and others simply wanted to rebuild the new South as it had been before the war, the fabled "Old South," and they were determined to do so in their own way and under their own leadership. They saw no need for their beloved region to be "reconstructed" by outsiders.

So when the U.S. Congress met in December 1865, for the first time since the end of the war, the new southern state governments looked remarkably like the former Confederate governments. Southern voters had refused to extend voting rights to the newly freed slaves. Instead, they had elected former Confederate leaders as their new U.S. senators and congressmen. The outraged Republicans in Congress denied seats to all such "Rebel" officials.

Then, in May and July of 1866, white mobs murdered African Americans in Memphis and New Orleans. The massacres, Radical Republicans argued, resulted from Andrew Johnson's lenient policy toward white supremacists. "Witness Memphis, witness New Orleans," Senator Charles Sumner cried. "Who can doubt that the President is the author of these tragedies?" The race riots helped spur the Republican-controlled Congress to pass the Fourteenth Amendment (1866), extending federal civil rights protections to blacks.

> Black codes

The violence directed against southern blacks was triggered in part by black protests over restrictive laws passed by the new all-white southern state legislatures. These **black codes**, as a white southerner explained, would ensure "the ex-slave was not a free man; he was a free Negro." A northerner visiting the South explained that the black codes would ensure that "the blacks at large belong to the whites at large."

The black codes varied from state to state, but some provisions were in many of them. They recognized black marriages but prohibited interracial marriage. The Mississippi codes stipulated that "no white person could intermarry with a freedman, free negro, or mulatto." Violators faced imprisonment for life. The codes also prohibited blacks from voting, serving on juries, or testifying against whites. They could own property, but they could not own farmland in Mississippi or city property in South Carolina. In Mississippi, every black male over the age of eighteen had to be apprenticed to a white, preferably a former slave owner. Any blacks not apprenticed or employed by January 1866 would be jailed as "vagrants." If they could not pay the vagrancy fine—and most of them could not—they would be forced to work for whites as "convict laborers."

In other words, southern whites tried to restore slavery without using the word. The black codes infuriated Republicans. "We [Republicans] must see to it," Senator William Stewart of Nevada resolved, "that the man made free by the Constitution of the United States is a freeman indeed." And that is what they set out to do.

black codes Laws passed in southern states to restrict the rights of former slaves.

Johnson's Battle with Congress

Early in 1866, the Radical Republicans openly challenged Andrew Johnson over the control of Reconstruction policies. Johnson started the fight when he vetoed a bill renewing funding for the Freedmen's Bureau. The Republicans could not gather enough votes to overturn the veto. Then, on February 22, 1866, Johnson criticized the Radical Republicans for promoting black civil rights. Moderate Republicans thereafter deserted the president and supported the Radicals. President Johnson had become in their eyes "an alien enemy of a foreign state," Thaddeus Stevens declared.

In mid-March 1866, the Radical-led Congress passed the pathbreaking Civil Rights Act, which declared that "all persons born in the United States" (except Indians) were citizens entitled to "full and equal benefit of all laws." The new legislation infuriated President Johnson. Congress, he fumed, could not grant citizenship to blacks, who did not deserve it. Claiming that the proposed Civil Rights Act discriminated against the "white race," Johnson vetoed the bill, but this time, on April 9, 1866, Republicans overrode the presidential veto. It was the first time in history that Congress had overturned a presidential veto of a major bill. From that point on, President Johnson, a stubborn loner unable to accept criticism or embrace compromise, steadily lost both public and political support.

"SLAVERY IS DEAD (?)" Thomas Nast's 1867 cartoon argues that blacks were still being treated as slaves despite the passage of the Fourteenth Amendment. This detail illustrates a case in Raleigh, North Carolina: a black man was whipped for a crime despite federal orders specifically prohibiting such forms of punishment.

Congressional Reconstruction

To remove all doubt about the legality of the new Civil Rights Act, Congress passed the **Fourteenth Amendment** to the U.S. Constitution on June 16, 1866. It went far beyond the Civil Rights Act by guaranteeing citizenship to anyone born in the United States, except Native Americans. It also prohibited any efforts to violate the civil rights of "citizens," black or white; to deprive any person "of life, liberty, or property, without due process of law," or to "deny any person . . . the equal protection of the laws." With the Fourteenth Amendment, the federal government was assuming primary responsibility for protecting civil rights.

The fall 1866 congressional elections revealed the growing split between Andrew Johnson and the Radical Republicans. To win votes for his favored candidates, Johnson went on a speaking tour of the Midwest. His efforts backfired, however, when his speeches turned into ugly shouting contests between him and his critics. In Cleveland, Ohio, Johnson described the Radical Republicans as "factious, domineering, tyrannical" men, and he

Fourteenth Amendment (1866) Amendment to the U.S. Constitution guaranteeing equal protection under the law to all U.S. citizens, including former slaves.

exchanged hot-tempered insults with a heckler. Radical Republicans claimed that Johnson was behaving like a "drunken imbecile."

The 1866 congressional elections brought a devastating defeat for Johnson and the Democrats; in each house, Radical Republican candidates won more than a two-thirds majority, the margin required to override presidential vetoes. On March 2, 1867, the new Congress passed, over President Johnson's vetoes, three crucial laws creating what came to be called **Congressional Reconstruction**: the Military Reconstruction Act, the Command of the Army Act, and the Tenure of Office Act.

The Military Reconstruction Act was the capstone of the Congressional Reconstruction plan. It abolished the new governments "in the rebel States" established under President Johnson's lenient Reconstruction policies. In their place, Congress established military control over the defeated South. Congress exempted one state, Tennessee, because it had already ratified the Fourteenth Amendment. The Military Reconstruction Act, crafted by Thaddeus Stevens, divided the other ten ex-Confederate states into five military districts, each commanded by a general who acted as governor.

Yet only 10,000 federal troops, mostly African Americans, were expected to police those sprawling "military districts." There were never enough soldiers to enforce Congressional Reconstruction from Virginia to Texas. The entire state of Mississippi, for instance, had fewer than 400 soldiers to ensure compliance with the Reconstruction statutes.

The Military Reconstruction Act required each former Confederate state to create a new constitution that guaranteed the right of African American males to vote. (Women—black or white—did not yet have the vote and were not included in the discussions. The Radical Republicans were not so radical when it came to promoting the equality of women.) Once a majority of voters ratified the new state constitution, a newly elected state legislature had to ratify the Fourteenth Amendment before regaining its state's representation in Congress.

The Command of the Army Act directed that all army orders from the president go through the army's commanding general, Ulysses S. Grant. The Radical Republicans feared that President Johnson would appoint generals who would be too lenient. So they bypassed the president and entrusted General Grant to enforce Congressional Reconstruction in the South.

The Tenure of Office Act required Senate permission for the president to remove any federal official whose appointment the Senate had confirmed. Radicals intended this act to prevent Andrew Johnson from firing Secretary of War Edwin Stanton, the president's most outspoken critic in the cabinet. Stanton had openly criticized Johnson's lenient approach to the South and had allied himself with the Radicals.

Congressional Reconstruction thus sought to ensure that the freed slaves could participate in the creation of new state governments in the former Confederacy. As Thaddeus Stevens, a lifelong abolitionist inspired by the promise of "liberty, equality, and the rights of man," explained,

Congressional Reconstruction
Phase of Reconstruction directed by Radical Republicans through the passage of three laws: the Military Reconstruction Act, the Command of the Army Act, and the Tenure of Office Act.

the Congressional Reconstruction plan would create a "perfect republic" based on the principle of *equal rights* for all citizens. "This is the promise of America," he insisted. "No More. No Less."

Impeaching the President

The first two years of Congressional Reconstruction saw dramatic changes in the South. One by one, southern state legislatures rewrote their constitutions and ratified the Fourteenth Amendment. Radical Republicans now seemed fully in control of Reconstruction, but one person still stood in their way— Andrew Johnson. During 1867 and early 1868, Radicals decided that the defiant Democratic president must be removed from office.

TRIAL OF ANDREW JOHNSON In this *Harper's Weekly* illustration, Johnson is seated at the center of the foreground among his defense committee. The galleries of the Senate are packed with men and women watching the proceedings. **Why was Johnson's trial such a dramatic and contentious spectacle?**

Johnson himself opened the door to impeachment (the formal process by which Congress charges the president with "high crimes and misdemeanors") when he tried to fire Secretary of War Edwin Stanton. The sharp-tongued Stanton had refused to resign from the cabinet despite his harsh criticism of the president's Reconstruction policy. Radical Republicans had passed the Tenure of Office Act in 1866 to make it illegal for Johnson to remove Stanton for championing their cause. Johnson, who considered the Tenure of Office Act an illegal restriction of presidential power, fired Stanton on August 12, 1867, appointing General Ulysses S. Grant in his place.

The Radicals now saw their chance. By removing Stanton without congressional approval, Johnson had violated the law. On February 24, 1868, the Republican-dominated House passed eleven articles of impeachment (that is, specific charges against the president), most of which dealt with Stanton's firing and all of which were flimsy. In reality, the essential grievance against the president was that he had opposed the policies of the Radicals.

The first Senate trial of a sitting president began on March 5, 1868. It was a dramatic spectacle before a packed gallery of journalists, foreign dignitaries, and political leaders, all eager to watch the first effort to remove a president. As the trial began, Thaddeus Stevens warned the president: "Unfortunate, unhappy man, behold your doom!"

The five-week impeachment trial came to a stunning end on May 26, 1868, when the Senate voted 35 to 19 for conviction, only *one* vote short of the two thirds needed for removal. Senator Edmund G. Ross, a young Radical from Kansas, cast the deciding vote in favor of acquittal, knowing that his vote would ruin his political career. "I almost literally looked down into my open grave," Ross explained afterward. "Friendships, position, fortune, everything that makes life desirable . . . were about to be swept away by the breath of my mouth." Angry Radicals thereafter shunned Ross. He lost his reelection campaign and died in near poverty.

In the end, the effort by Radicals to remove Johnson was a grave political mistake, for it ended up weakening public support for Congressional Reconstruction. Nevertheless, the Radical cause did gain something: to avoid being ousted, President Johnson had privately agreed to stop obstructing Congressional Reconstruction.

Republican Rule in the South

In June 1868, Congressional Republicans agreed that eight former Confederate states—all but Virginia, Mississippi, and Texas—had met the tough new conditions for readmission to the Union. Congress readmitted those three states in 1870, with the added requirement that they ratify the **Fifteenth Amendment**, which gave voting rights to African American men.

The Fifteenth Amendment, submitted to the states in 1869 and ratified in 1870, prohibited states from denying a citizen's right to vote on grounds of "race, color, or previous condition of servitude." Susan B. Anthony and Elizabeth Cady Stanton, leaders of the movement to secure voting rights for women, demanded that the Fifteenth Amendment include women as well as black men. As Anthony stressed in a famous speech, the U.S. Constitution refers to "we, the people; not we, the white male citizens; nor yet we, the male citizens; but we, the whole people, who formed the Union—women as well as men." Most men, however, remained unreconstructed when it came to female voting rights. Radical Republicans tried to deflect the issue by declaring that it was the "Negro's hour," and women, both black and white, would have to wait—another fifty years, as it turned out.

CORE **OBJECTIVE**

3. Assess the attitudes of white and black southerners toward Reconstruction.

Reconstruction in Practice

When a federal official asked Garrison Frazier, a former Georgia slave, if he and others wanted to live among whites or among themselves, he said that they preferred "to live by ourselves, for there is a prejudice against us in the South that will take years to get over." In forging new lives in freedom, Frazier and many other former slaves then set about creating their own social institutions.

The Reconstruction of Black Social Life

The northern victory in the Civil War led to a striking transformation of African American religious life in the South. Before the war, slaves who attended white churches were forced to sit in the back. After the war, with the help of many northern Christian missionaries, both black and white, ex-slaves established their own African American churches.

Fifteenth Amendment (1870) Amendment to the U.S. Constitution forbidding states to deny any male citizen the right to vote on grounds of "race, color or previous condition of servitude."

Black churches quickly became the crossroads for African American community life. Ministers played dual roles: social and political leaders as well as preachers. One could not be a real minister, one of them claimed, without looking "out for the political interests of his people."

> African American churches

Many African Americans became Baptists or Methodists, in part because these were already the largest denominations in the South and in part because they reached out to the working poor. In 1866 alone, the African Methodist Episcopal (AME) Church gained 50,000 members. By 1890, over 1.3 million African Americans in the South had become Baptists, nearly three times as many as had joined any other denomination.

African American communities in the postwar South also rushed to establish schools. Getting an education, stressed one former slave, was the "first proof" of freedom. Most plantation owners kept blacks illiterate so they could not read abolitionist literature and organize uprisings. After the war, the white elite worried that education would encourage poor whites and poor blacks to leave the South in search of better social and economic opportunities. "They didn't want us to learn nothin'," one former slave recalled. "The only thing we had to learn was how to work."

> African American schools

The opposition of southern whites to education for blacks made public schools all the more important to African Americans. South Carolina's Mary McLeod Bethune, the fifteenth child of former slaves, rejoiced in the opportunity to gain an education: "The whole world opened to me when I learned to read." She walked five miles to school as a child, then earned a scholarship to college, and went on to become the first black woman to found a school that became a four-year college: Bethune-Cookman University, in Daytona Beach, Florida.

The Union League

The Fifteenth Amendment had enormous political consequences. No sooner was it ratified than northern Republicans, black and white, sought to convince freedmen to join the party of Lincoln. To do so, they organized Union Leagues throughout the former Confederacy. Republicans had founded the Union League (also called the Loyal League) in 1862 to rally voters behind Lincoln, the war, and the party. By late 1863, the league claimed over 700,000 members in 4,554 councils across the nation.

In the postwar South, these leagues were organized like fraternities, with formal initiations and rituals and secret meetings to protect the freed people from being persecuted by angry white Democrats. The leagues met in churches, schools, homes, and fields, often listening to northern speakers who traveled the South extolling the Republican party and encouraging blacks to register and vote. By the early 1870s, the Union League in the South had become one of the largest black social movements in history.

Through the help of the Union Leagues, some 90 percent of southern freedmen registered to vote, almost all of them as Republicans, and they voted in record numbers (often 80–90 percent). Their doing so often required great courage, for most white southerners were Democrats eager to deny freedmen the vote. "All the blacks who vote against my ticket shall walk the plank," threatened Howell Cobb, a Georgia Democrat who had been a Confederate general and former governor. Throughout the postwar South, angry whites persecuted, evicted, or fired African American workers who "exercised their political rights," as a Union officer reported from Virginia.

Black Republicans were at times equally coercive. "The Negroes are as intolerant of opposition as the whites," a white South Carolina Democrat observed. They shunned, expelled, and even killed any "of their own" who "would turn democrats." He added that freedwomen were as partisan as the men—and as intolerant of opposition: the "women are worse than the men, refusing to talk to or marry a renegade [black Democrat], and aiding [men] in mobbing him."

FREEDMEN VOTING IN NEW ORLEANS The Fifteenth Amendment, ratified in 1870, guaranteed at the federal level the right of citizens to vote regardless of "race, color, or previous condition of servitude." As this illustration from 1867 shows, however, former slaves had been registering to vote in some state elections—and voting in large numbers—since the 1860s, thanks in part to the community organizing efforts of Union Leagues.

Yet the net result of the Union Leagues was a remarkable mobilization of black voters who enabled men of color to gain elected offices for the first time in the states of the former Confederacy. Francis Cardozo, a black minister who served as president of the South Carolina Council of Union Leagues, declared in 1870 that South Carolina had "prospered in every respect" as a result of the enfranchisement of black voters enabled by the Union Leagues. "The fierce and determined opposition to us," he maintained, illustrated how powerful a force for equality the leagues had become.

African Americans in Southern Politics

Black military veterans formed the core of the first generation of African American political leaders in the postwar South. Participation in the Union army or navy had given many blacks their first opportunity to express their loyalty to the American nation. A Virginia freedman explained that the United States was "now *our* country," paid for "by the blood of our brethren" who died while serving in the Union military during the Civil War.

With many ex-Confederates denied voting rights, new African American voters helped elect some 600 blacks—most of them former slaves— as Republican state legislators under Congressional Reconstruction. In Louisiana, Pinckney Pinchback, a northern free black and former Union soldier, served as lieutenant governor. Two black senators served in Congress, Hiram Revels and Blanche K. Bruce, both Mississippi natives who had been educated in the North, while fourteen blacks were elected to the U.S. House of Representatives during Reconstruction.

African American vote

AFRICAN AMERICAN POLITICAL FIGURES OF RECONSTRUCTION As blacks gained the right to vote, many ex-Confederate whites were stripped of that right. As a consequence, several former slaves were elected to positions in government, such as Blanche K. Bruce (left) and Hiram Revels (right), who served in the U.S. Senate. Between them is Frederick Douglass, who was a major figure in the abolitionist movement.

White southern Democrats angrily resented "Negro rule"—the election of black Republicans. They complained that freed slaves were illiterate and had no civic experience or appreciation of political issues and processes. In this regard, of course, blacks were no different from millions of poor or immigrant white males who had been voting and serving in offices for years. Some freedpeople frankly confessed their disadvantages. Beverly Nash, an African American delegate to the South Carolina convention of 1868, told his colleagues: "We are not prepared for this suffrage [the vote]. But we can learn. Give a man tools and let him commence to use them, and in time he will learn a trade. So it is with voting."

Land, Labor, and Disappointment

Many former slaves stressed that what they needed most was their own land so that they could gain economic self-sufficiency. Emancipation, explained a black minister from Georgia, meant the freedom for blacks to "reap the fruit of our own labor, and take care of ourselves." Gaining their own farms, a Mississippi freedman named Merrimon Howard wrote, would enable "the poor class to enjoy the sweet boon of freedom."

In several southern states, Union armies during the war had given land to freedpeople. President Johnson, however, reversed such transfers of white-owned property to former slaves. In South Carolina, the Union general responsible for evicting former slaves urged them to "lay aside their bitter feelings, and become reconciled to their old masters." The former slaves, however, shouted "No, never!" and "Can't do it!" They knew that land ownership was the foundation of their freedom. Yes, they had no deeds or titles for the land, but it had been "earned by the sweat of *our* brows," said a group of

SHARECROPPERS This photograph, shot in 1899 by Frances Benjamin Johnston, one of the earliest female photojournalists, shows a sharecropping family outside their Virginia cabin. **How do the living conditions of sharecroppers compare to the life of slaves in the antebellum South?**

Alabama freedpeople. "Our wives, our children, our husbands, has been sold over and over again to purchase the lands we now locates on," a Virginia freedman noted. "Didn't we clear the land and raise de crops? We have a right to [that] land," he argued.

In the end, however, the federal government rescinded the wartime policy of land redistribution. It forced tens of thousands of former slaves to return their farms to white owners. The sense of betrayal among the former slaves was profound. An ex-slave in Mississippi forced to return his land to its white owner said that he and others were left with nothing: "no *land*, no *house*, not so much as a place to lay our head."

As former slaves were stripped of their own land, they had little choice but to revert to being farmworkers under a new system: sharecropping. In late June 1865, for example, Thomas Ferguson, a white plantation owner near Charleston, South Carolina, signed a contract with sixty-five of his former slaves. It called for them to "cultivate" his fields in exchange for "half of the crop raised."

> Sharecropping replaces slavery

This **sharecropping** system—whereby the landowner provided land, seed, and tools to a poor farmer in exchange for a *share* of the future crop—essentially reenslaved blacks because, as a federal army officer objected, no matter "how much they are abused, they cannot leave without permission of the owner." If they left, they would forfeit any right to a portion of the crop, and any workers who violated the terms of the contract could be evicted from the plantation, leaving them jobless and homeless—and thereby subject to arrest.

With little money or technical training, many freed blacks preferred sharecropping over working for wages, since it freed them from day-to-day supervision by white landowners. Over time, however, most sharecroppers, black and white, found themselves deeper in debt to the landowner, with little choice but to remain tied to the same discouraging system of dependence that, over the years, felt much like slavery. As a former slave acknowledged, he and others had discovered that "freedom could make folks proud but it didn't make 'em rich."

"Carpetbaggers" and "Scalawags"

Unreconstructed white southerners dismissed whites who served in the new Republican southern state governments as "carpetbaggers" and "scalawags." Carpetbaggers were allegedly opportunistic northerners who rushed to the South with all their belongings in cheap suitcases made of carpeting ("carpetbags") to grab political power. Some northerners were indeed corrupt opportunists. However, most of the northerners in the postwar South were Union military veterans who had arrived as early as 1865 or 1866, drawn back to the South by the desire to rebuild the region's devastated economy. Others were Union soldiers who never returned home after fighting in the South.

sharecropping A farming system developed after the Civil War by which landless workers farmed land in exchange with the landowner for farm supplies and a share of the crop.

CARPETBAGGER Many carpetbaggers were caricatured as opportunists taking advantage of the chaotic economic and political situation in the South. This cartoon is accompanied by the caption, "The bag in front of him, filled with others' faults, he always sees. The one behind him, filled with his own faults, he never sees."

Many other so-called carpetbaggers were teachers, social workers, or ministers motivated by a genuine desire to help free blacks and poor whites improve the quality of their lives. Union general Adelbert Ames, for example, stayed in the South after the war because he felt a "sense of Mission" to help the former slaves develop healthy communities. He served as the military governor of Mississippi before being elected as a Republican U.S. senator in 1870.

Most scalawags were southerners who had opposed secession but supported the Confederacy once the war started and then became Republicans after the war. Several distinguished figures became scalawags, including the former Confederate general James Longstreet, who decided that the Old South must change its ways. He became a successful cotton broker in New Orleans, joined the Republican party, and supported the Congressional Reconstruction program.

Southern Democrats especially hated the scalawags, or southern white Republicans, who they often called traitors to their region. A Nashville, Tennessee, newspaper editor dismissed them as the "merest trash."

Southern Resistance and White "Redemption"

> Reconstruction's final phase: Southern resistance and white "redemption"

Most southern whites viewed Reconstruction as a tragedy. They used all means possible—legal and illegal—to "redeem" their beloved South from northern control, Republican rule, and black assertiveness. An Alabama planter admitted that southern whites simply "can't learn to treat the freedmen like human beings."

> White violence against black political participation

With each passing year during Reconstruction, African Americans suffered increasing exploitation and abuse. The black codes created by white state governments in 1865 and 1866 were the first of many efforts to deny equality to African Americans. Southern whites used terror, intimidation, and violence to disrupt black Republican meetings; target black and white Republican leaders for beatings or killings; and, in general, to prevent blacks from exercising their political rights. Hundreds were killed across the South and many more injured in systematic efforts to "keep blacks in their place."

Such ugly incidents revealed a harsh truth: the death of slavery did not mean the birth of true freedom for many African Americans. For a growing number of southern whites, resistance to Congressional Reconstruction, military occupation, and "Radical rule" became more and more violent. Several secret terrorist groups—the White Leagues, the Red Shirts, the Knights of the White Camelia, and others—emerged to harass, intimidate, and even kill African Americans, especially those active in Union Leagues.

Ku Klux Klan A secret terrorist organization founded in Pulaski, Tennessee, in 1866 targeting former slaves who voted and held political offices, as well as people the KKK labeled as carpetbaggers and scalawags.

One such group, the **Ku Klux Klan** (KKK), was formed in 1866 in Pulaski, Tennessee. The name *Ku Klux* derived from the Greek word *kuklos* meaning "circle" or "band" (and *Klan* comes from the English word *clan*, or family).

The Klan, and other groups like it, began initially as a social club, with spooky costumes and secret rituals. At first a group of pranksters, its members soon turned to intimidation of blacks and white Republicans throughout the South. Their motives varied—anger over the Confederate defeat, resentment against federal soldiers occupying the South, complaints about having to pay black workers, and an almost paranoid fear that former slaves might seek violent revenge against whites. Klansmen rode about at night in white sheets and masks spreading horrendous rumors, issuing threats, and burning schools and churches. "We are going to kill all the Negroes," a white supremacist declared during one massacre intended to undermine and overthrow Republican rule.

The Legacy of Republican Rule

Yet for all the violent opposition directed against the Republican state governments, the new constitutions they created remained in effect for some years after the end of Radical Republican control. Among the most significant innovations brought about by the Republican state governments were those that increased participation in the political process: protecting black voting rights, restructuring legislatures to reflect shifting populations, and making more state offices elective to weaken the "good old boy" tradition of rewarding political supporters with state government jobs.

In South Carolina, former Confederate leaders opposed the Republican state legislature not simply because of its black members but because poor whites were also enjoying political clout for the first time, thereby threatening the traditional dominance of wealthy white plantation owners and merchants.

Given the hostile circumstances under which the Republican state governments operated in the South, their achievements were remarkable. They rebuilt an extensive railroad network and established public school systems—schools funded by state governments and open to all children but separated by race. Some 600,000 black pupils had enrolled in southern schools by 1877.

State governments under the Radicals also gave more attention to the poor and to orphanages, asylums, and institutions for the deaf and the blind of both races. Much-needed infrastructure—public roads, bridges, and buildings—was repaired or rebuilt. African Americans achieved rights and opportunities that would repeatedly be violated in coming decades but never completely taken away, at least in principle: equality before the law and the rights to own property, attend schools, learn to read and write, enter professions, and carry on business.

Yet several of the Republican state governments also suffered from corrupt practices. Bribes and kickbacks, whereby companies received

"WORSE THAN SLAVERY" This Thomas Nast cartoon condemns the Ku Klux Klan for promoting conditions "worse than slavery" for southern blacks after the Civil War.

Radical Republican achievements

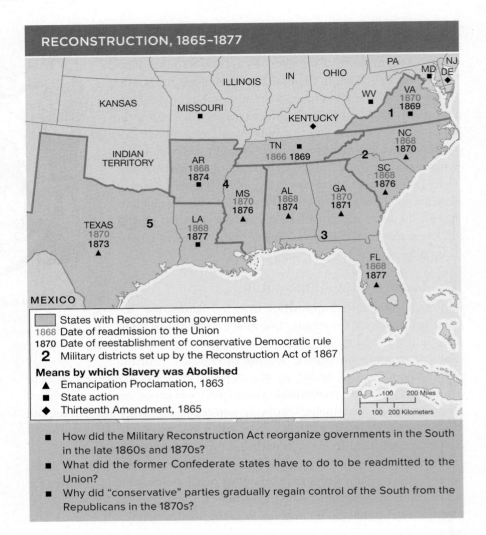

RECONSTRUCTION, 1865–1877

Legend:
- [ ] States with Reconstruction governments
- 1868 Date of readmission to the Union
- 1870 Date of reestablishment of conservative Democratic rule
- **2** Military districts set up by the Reconstruction Act of 1867

Means by which Slavery was Abolished
- ▲ Emancipation Proclamation, 1863
- ■ State action
- ◆ Thirteenth Amendment, 1865

- How did the Military Reconstruction Act reorganize governments in the South in the late 1860s and 1870s?
- What did the former Confederate states have to do to be readmitted to the Union?
- Why did "conservative" parties gradually regain control of the South from the Republicans in the 1870s?

government contracts and then secretly rewarded officials with cash, were commonplace. In Louisiana, the twenty-six-year-old Illinois carpetbagger, Henry Clay Warmoth, a Union war veteran and attorney, somehow turned an annual salary of $8,000 into a million-dollar fortune during his four years as governor (he was impeached and removed from office). "I don't pretend to be honest," he admitted. "I only pretend to be as honest as anybody in politics."

As was true in the North and the Midwest at the time, southern state governments awarded money to corporations, notably railroads, under conditions that invited shady dealings. In fact, some railroad executives received state funds but never built railroads. Bribery was rampant. The Radical Republican regimes did not invent such corruption, nor did it die with them. Governor Warmoth recognized as much: "Corruption is the fashion" in Louisiana, he explained.

The Grant Years and Northern Disillusionment

CORE **OBJECTIVE**

4. Analyze the political and economic factors that helped end Reconstruction in 1877.

Democrat Andrew Johnson's crippled presidency created an opportunity for Republicans to elect one of their own in 1868. Both parties wooed Ulysses S. Grant, the "Lion of Vicksburg," credited with spearheading the Union victory in the Civil War. His falling-out with President Johnson, however, had pushed him toward the Republicans.

The Election of 1868

The Republican party platform of 1868 endorsed Congressional Reconstruction. More important than the party platform, however, were the public expectations driving the election of Ulysses S. Grant, a heroic soldier whose campaign slogan was "Let us have peace."

African American votes help elect President Grant (1868)

The Democrats, not surprisingly, charged the Republican Congress with subjecting the South "to military despotism and Negro supremacy." They nominated Horatio Seymour, the wartime governor of New York and a passionate critic of Congressional Reconstruction. His vice presidential running mate, Francis P. Blair Jr., a former Union general from Missouri who had served in Congress, appealed directly to white bigotry when he denounced Republicans for promoting equality for "a semi-barbarous race" of black men who sought to "subject the white women to their unbridled lust."

A Democrat later said that Blair's egregiously "stupid and indefensible" remarks cost Seymour a close election. Grant swept the Electoral College, 214–80, but his popular majority was only 307,000 out of almost 6 million votes. More than 500,000 African American voters accounted for Grant's margin of victory.

Grant had proved himself a great military leader, but as the youngest president ever (forty-six years old), he was not nearly as bold a politician as he had been a general. He came to view the presidency more as a reward for his military leadership than as a profound responsibility. A political novice, he passively followed the lead of Congressional Republicans and was often blind to the corrupt political forces around him. Grant was awestruck by men of wealth who lavished gifts on him, including houses. He also showed poor judgment in his selection of cabinet members. During Grant's two terms in office, his seven cabinet positions changed twenty-four times. Some of his lieutenants were crooks who engaged in criminal behavior. His former comrade-in-arms, General William T. Sherman, felt sorry for his former commander because so many supposedly "loyal" Republicans used him for their own selfish gains.

"LET US HAVE PEACE" In the midst of the social and political turbulence of Reconstruction, Ulysses S. Grant's slogan, "Let us have peace"—as stamped on campaign coins like this one—struck a chord with the American voters.

Scandals

Corruption in the Grant administration

President Grant's administration soon fell into a cesspool of scandal. In the summer of 1869, two unprincipled financial schemers, Jay Gould and James Fisk Jr., infamous for bribing politicians and judges, plotted with the president's brother-in-law to create a public craze for gold by purchasing massive quantities of the precious yellow metal to drive up its value. The only danger to the scheme lay in the possibility that the federal Treasury would burst the bubble by selling large amounts of its gold supply, which would deflate the value of gold by putting more in circulation as coins. When journalists saw President Grant in public with Gould and Fisk, people assumed that he supported their gold scheme. As the rumor spread in New York City's financial district that the president endorsed the run-up in gold, its value soared.

On September 24, 1869—soon to be remembered as "Black Friday"—Gould and Fisk's scheme to drive up the price of gold worked as planned. Starting at a price of $150 an ounce, gold rose first to $160, then $165, leading more and more investors across the nation and around the world to join the stampede.

Then, around noon, President Grant and his Treasury secretary realized what was happening and began selling huge amounts of government gold. Within fifteen minutes, the bubble created by Fisk and Gould burst, and the price of gold plummeted to $138. Schemers who had bought gold lost fortunes. Their agony, said a New Yorker, "made one feel as if the Battle of Gettysburg had been lost and the Rebels were marching down Broadway." Soon the turmoil spread to the entire stock market, claiming thousands of victims. As Fisk noted, each man was left to "drag out his own corpse."

The plot to corner the gold market was only the first of several scandals that rocked the Grant administration. More disclosures of corruption followed, some involving members of the president's cabinet. The secretary

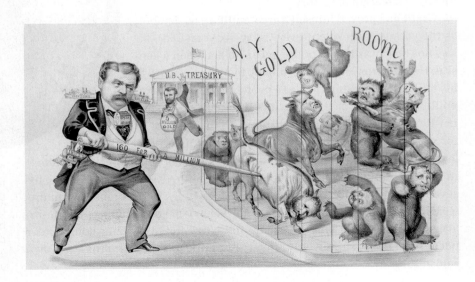

CORNERING THE GOLD MARKET In this political cartoon of the "Black Friday" gold scheme, Jay Gould attempts to control the gold market, represented by caged and enraged bulls and bears. In the background, President Grant dashes from the U.S. Treasury to the scene, frantically trying to bring down the soaring price of gold.

of war, it turned out, had accepted bribes from merchants who traded with Indians at army posts in the West. In St. Louis, whiskey distillers—dubbed the "whiskey ring" in the press—bribed federal agents to avoid paying taxes, bilking the government out of millions of dollars in revenue. Grant's personal secretary participated in that scheme, taking large sums of money and other valuables in return for inside information.

There is no evidence that Grant himself was involved in any of the frauds, but his poor choice of associates earned him widespread criticism. Democrats scolded Republicans for their "monstrous corruption and extravagance" and launched thirty-six investigations into supposedly corrupt acts during Grant's administration.

The Money Supply

Complex financial issues—especially monetary policy—dominated Grant's presidency. Prior to the Civil War, the economy operated on a gold standard. That is, state banks issued paper money that could be exchanged for an equal value of gold coins. So both gold coins and state bank notes circulated as the nation's currency. **Greenbacks** (because of the dye color used on the printed dollars) were issued by the federal government during the Civil War to help pay for the war.

> Greenbacks vs. gold coins

When a nation's supply of money grows faster than the economy itself, prices for goods and services increase (inflation). This is what happened during the Civil War when the greenbacks were issued. After the Civil War, the U.S. Treasury assumed that the greenbacks would be recalled from circulation so that consumer prices would decline and the nation could return to a "hard-money" currency—gold, silver, and copper coins—which had always been viewed as more reliable in value than paper currency.

The most vocal supporters of a return to hard money were eastern creditors (mostly bankers and merchants to whom others owed money) who did not want their debtors to pay them in paper currency. Critics of the gold standard tended to be farmers and other debtors. These so-called soft-money advocates opposed taking greenbacks out of circulation because shrinking the supply of money would bring lower prices (deflation) for their crops and livestock, thereby reducing their income and making it harder for them to pay their long-term debts. In 1868, congressional supporters of such a soft-money policy—mostly Democrats—had forced the Treasury to stop withdrawing greenbacks from circulation.

President Grant sided with the hard-money camp. On March 18, 1869, he signed the Public Credit Act, which said that the investors who purchased government bonds to help finance the war effort must be paid back in gold coins rather than paper currency. It was the first act of Congress that Grant signed, and it soon generated a decline in consumer prices (deflation) that hurt debtors, helped creditors, and in the process ignited a ferocious political debate over the merits of hard and soft money that would last throughout the nineteenth century—and beyond.

> Public Credit Act (1869)

greenbacks Paper money issued during the Civil War, which sparked currency debates after the war.

Financial Panic

Grant's effort to withdraw the greenbacks from circulation unintentionally helped cause a major economic collapse. During 1873, some twenty-five railroads stopped paying their bills, leading Jay Cooke and Company, the nation's leading business lender, to go bankrupt on September 18, 1873.

The resulting financial **Panic of 1873** triggered a deep depression. Thousands of businesses closed, and 3 million people lost their jobs. In the major cities, jobless, homeless Americans roamed the streets and formed long lines at charity soup kitchens.

The terrible contraction of the economy led the U.S. Treasury to reverse course and begin printing more greenbacks. For a time, the supporters of paper money celebrated, but in 1874 President Grant vetoed a bill to issue even more greenbacks. His efforts to remove paper money from circulation pleased his supporters but only prolonged what was then the nation's worst economic depression in its history.

Liberal Republicans

Reconstruction loses support

The sudden collapse of the nation's economy in 1873 also contributed to northerners' losing interest in Reconstruction. Liberal Republicans, a new faction in the Republican party, called for ending federal Reconstruction efforts in the South. They also promoted "civil service reforms" designed to end the "patronage system" whereby new presidents rewarded political supporters with federal government jobs.

In 1872, the Liberal Republicans held their own national convention, during which they accused the Grant administration of corruption, incompetence, and "despotism." They nominated an unlikely presidential candidate, Horace Greeley, the prominent editor of the *New York Tribune* and a longtime champion of a variety of causes, including abolitionism, socialism,

Panic of 1873 Financial collapse triggered by President Grant's efforts to withdraw greenbacks from circulation and transition the economy back to hard currency.

vegetarianism, and spiritualism. The Democrats also nominated Greeley as the only hope of beating Grant.

The result was predictable. Greeley, the shared candidate of the Liberal Republicans and Democrats, carried only six southern states and none in the North. Grant won thirty-one states and carried the national election by 3,598,235 votes to Greeley's 2,834,761. An exhausted Greeley confessed that he was "the worst beaten man who ever ran for high office." He died three weeks later.

White Terror

President Grant initially fought hard to enforce federal efforts to reconstruct the postwar South. But southern resistance to "Radical rule" increased and turned brutally violent. In Grayson County, Texas, a white man and two friends murdered three former slaves simply because they wanted to "thin the niggers out and drive them to their holes."

Klansmen focused their terror on prominent Republicans, black and white. In Mississippi they killed a black Republican leader in front of his family. Three white scalawag Republicans were murdered in Georgia in 1870. That same year an armed mob of whites assaulted a Republican political rally in Alabama, killing four blacks and wounding fifty-four. In 1871, some 500 masked men laid siege to South Carolina's Union County jail and eventually lynched eight black prisoners.

At the urging of President Grant, Republicans in Congress struck back at such racial violence with three Enforcement Acts (1870–1871). The first of these measures imposed penalties on those who interfered with any citizen's right to vote. The second dispatched federal election supervisors to monitor elections in southern districts where political terrorism flourished.

The third measure, called the Ku Klux Klan Act, outlawed the main activities of the KKK—forming conspiracies, wearing disguises, resisting officers, and intimidating officials. In 1871, the federal government singled out nine counties in upcountry South Carolina as a center of Klan-instigated violence and jailed several hundred people.

In general, however, the Enforcement Acts were not consistently applied. As a result, the violent efforts of southern whites to thwart Reconstruction escalated in the 1870s. On Easter Sunday in 1873 in Colfax, Louisiana, a mob of white vigilantes disappointed by local election results attacked a group of black Republicans, slaughtering eighty-one. It was the bloodiest racial incident during the Reconstruction period.

Southern "Redeemers"

The Klan's impact on southern politics varied from state to state. In the Upper South, it played only a modest role in helping Democrats win local elections. In the Lower South, however, Klan violence had more serious effects. In overwhelmingly black Yazoo County, Mississippi, vengeful whites used

| Violence against blacks escalates |

| Enforcement Acts (1870–1871) |

terrorism to reverse the political balance of power. In the 1873 elections, for example, the Republicans cast 2,449 votes and the Democrats 638; two years later the Democrats polled 4,049 votes, the Republicans 7.

Throughout the South, the activities of the Klan and other white supremacists disheartened black and white Republicans alike. "We are helpless and unable to organize," wrote a Mississippi scalawag. We "dare not attempt to canvass [campaign for candidates], or make public speeches." At the same time, northerners displayed a growing weariness with efforts to use federal troops to reconstruct the South and protect civil rights. "The plain truth is," noted the *New York Herald*, "the North has got tired of the Negro."

> **Resurgence of the southern white elite**

The erosion of northern interest in civil rights resulted from more than weariness, however. Western expansion, Indian wars, and political controversy over economic issues distracted attention from southern resistance to Republican rule and black rights. Given the violent intensity of diehard former Confederates' efforts to resist Reconstruction, it would have required far more patience, conviction, and resources for the federal government to protect the civil rights of blacks in the South.

Republican political control in the South gradually loosened during the 1870s as all-white "Conservative" parties mobilized the anti-Reconstruction vote. White Democrats—the so-called **redeemers** who supposedly "saved" the South from Republican control and "black rule"—used the race issue to excite the white electorate and intimidate black voters. They called themselves Conservatives rather than Democrats to distinguish themselves from northern Democrats. Where persuasion failed to work, Democrats used trickery to rig the voting. As one enthusiastic Democrat boasted, "The white and black Republicans may outvote us, but we can outcount them."

Republican political control collapsed in Virginia and Tennessee as early as 1869; in Georgia and North Carolina, it ended in 1870, although North Carolina had a Republican governor until 1876. Reconstruction lasted longest in the Deep South states with the largest black population; there, whites abandoned Klan masks for barefaced intimidation in paramilitary groups such as the Mississippi Rifle Club and the South Carolina Red Shirts. By 1876, Radical Republican regimes survived only in Louisiana, South Carolina, and Florida, and those collapsed after the elections of that year.

> **Democrats win control of Congress (1874)**

The white political elite's return to power in the South undermined the country's commitment to Congressional Reconstruction. The collapse of the economy and the much-publicized political scandals hurt Republicans in the 1874 congressional elections, in which the Democrats won control of the House of Representatives and gained seats in the Senate.

The Compromise of 1877

President Grant, despite the controversies swirling around him, wanted to run again in 1876, but many Republicans had lost confidence in his leadership. Others opposed the idea of his becoming the nation's first three-term

redeemers Postwar white Democratic leaders in the South who supposedly saved the region from political, economic, and social domination by northerners and blacks.

president. In the summer of 1875, Grant acknowledged defeat and announced his retirement, admitting that he had entered the White House with "no political training" and had made many "errors in judgment."

James Gillespie Blaine of Maine, former Speaker of the House, emerged as the Republican front-runner to succeed Grant, but he, too, bore the taint of scandal when newspapers reported that he had promised political favors to railroad executives in exchange for shares of stock in the company.

The scandal led the Republican Convention to pass over Blaine in favor of Ohio's favorite son, Rutherford B. Hayes. Elected governor of Ohio three times, most recently as a hard-money advocate of gold rather than greenbacks, Hayes had also made a name for himself as a civil service reformer by trying to reduce the number of government jobs subject to political appointment. His chief virtue, however, was that he offended neither Radicals nor reformers. As a journalist put it, he was "obnoxious to no one."

COMPROMISE OF 1877
This illustration represents the compromise between Republicans and southern Democrats that ended Radical Reconstruction.

The Democratic Convention was uncharacteristically harmonious from the start. The nomination went on the second ballot to Samuel J. Tilden, a wealthy corporate lawyer and reform governor of New York.

The 1876 campaign raised no burning issues. Both candidates favored relaxing federal authority in the South. As Hayes said privately, he did not approve of "bayonet rule" by federal troops in the South. In the absence of strong ideological differences, Democrats aired the Republicans' dirty linen. In response, Republicans waved "the bloody shirt," whereby they linked the Democratic party to secession, civil war, and the outrages committed against Republicans in the South. As Robert G. Ingersoll, the most celebrated Republican public speaker of the time, insisted: "The man that assassinated Abraham Lincoln was a Democrat. . . . Soldiers, every scar you have on your heroic bodies was given you by a Democrat!"

Despite the lack of major issues, the 1876 election generated the most votes in U.S. history up to that point. Early election returns pointed to a victory for the Democrat Tilden. Nationwide, he outpolled Hayes by almost 300,000 votes. By midnight following Election Day, Tilden had won 184 electoral votes—just 1 vote short of victory. Hayes went to bed that night convinced that he had lost.

Disputed election of 1876

During the night, however, Republican activists realized that the election hinged on nineteen disputed electoral votes from Florida, Louisiana, and South Carolina. The Democrats needed only one of the challenged votes to claim victory; the Republicans needed all nineteen. Republicans in those key states had engaged in election fraud while Democrats had used physical intimidation to keep black voters at home. Each of the three states, however, was then governed by a Republican who appointed the election boards, each of which reported narrow victories for Hayes. The Democrats immediately challenged the results.

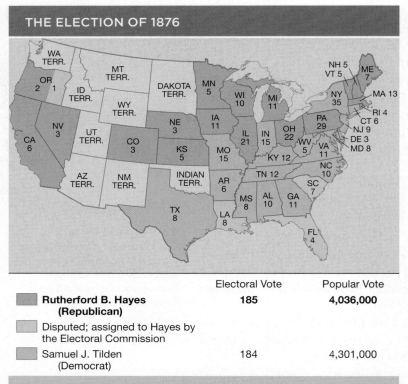

THE ELECTION OF 1876

	Electoral Vote	Popular Vote
Rutherford B. Hayes (Republican)	185	4,036,000
Disputed; assigned to Hayes by the Electoral Commission		
Samuel J. Tilden (Democrat)	184	4,301,000

- Why did the Republicans pick Rutherford Hayes as their presidential candidate?
- Why were the electoral votes of several states disputed?
- What was the Compromise of 1877?

In all three of the disputed southern states, rival election boards sent in conflicting counts. The nation watched and wondered as the politicians bickered about the contested election. The Constitution offered no guidance in this unprecedented situation. Days, then weeks, passed with no solution.

Finally, on January 29, 1877, the Congress set up a special Electoral Commission to settle the dispute. It met daily for weeks trying to verify the disputed vote counts in the three contested southern states. On March 1, 1877, the commission voted 8–7 along party lines in favor of Hayes. The House of Representatives declared Hayes president by an electoral vote of 185–184. Tilden decided not to protest the decision. His campaign manager explained that they preferred "four years of Hayes's administration to four years of civil war."

Hayes's victory hinged on the defection of key southern Democrats, who, it turned out, had made a number of secret deals with the Republicans. On February 26, 1877, prominent Ohio Republicans (including future president James A. Garfield) and powerful southern Democrats struck a private bargain—the **Compromise of 1877**—at Wormley's Hotel in Washington, D.C. The Republicans promised that if Hayes were named president, he would remove the last federal troops from the South.

The End of Reconstruction

In 1877, newly inaugurated President Hayes fulfilled his pledge: he withdrew federal troops from Louisiana and South Carolina, whose Republican governments collapsed soon thereafter. Over the next thirty years, the protection of black civil rights in the South crumbled under the pressure of restored white Democratic rule. As Henry Adams, a former Louisiana slave, observed in 1877, "The whole South—every state in the South—has got [back] into the hands of the very men that held us as slaves." New white state governments in the South rewrote their constitutions, rid their administrations of "carpetbaggers, scalawags, and blacks," and cut back spending on schools. "The Yankees helped free us, so they say," a former North Carolina slave named Thomas Hall remembered, "but [in 1877] they let us be put back in slavery again."

Compromise of 1877 Secret deal forged by congressional leaders to resolve the disputed election of 1876; Republican Rutherford B. Hayes, who had lost the popular vote, was declared the winner in exchange for his pledge to remove federal troops from the South, marking the end of Reconstruction.

Reconstruction's Significance

The collapse of Congressional Reconstruction in 1877 had tragic consequences, for it allowed the white South to renew long-standing patterns of discrimination against African Americans. Yet for all the unfulfilled promises of Congressional Reconstruction, it left an enduring legacy—the Thirteenth, Fourteenth, and Fifteenth Amendments—not dead in 1877 but dormant, waiting to be reawakened during the second reconstruction of civil rights in the 1950s and 1960s. The effort of the American government to "reconstruct" the former Confederacy represented the only instance of a society's granting citizenship to former slaves and electing freedmen to political offices within just a few years of emancipation.

If Reconstruction's experiment in interracial democracy did not provide true social equality or substantial economic opportunities for African Americans, it did create the essential constitutional foundation for future advances in the quest for equality and civil rights—not just for African Americans but for women and other minority groups as well.

Until the pivotal Reconstruction Era, the states were responsible for protecting citizens' rights. Thereafter, thanks to the Fourteenth and Fifteenth Amendments, blacks had gained equal rights (in theory), and the federal government assumed responsibility for ensuring that states treated blacks equally in terms of their basic civil rights. Congressional Reconstruction thus was a halfway revolution, sighed the former governor of North Carolina Jonathan Worth, and "nobody can anticipate the action of revolutions." A hundred years later, the cause of civil rights would be embraced again by the federal government—this time permanently.

Reviewing the
CORE OBJECTIVES | INQUIZITIVE

■ **Reconstruction Challenges** With the defeat of the Confederacy and the passage of the Thirteenth Amendment, the federal government had to develop policies and procedures to address a number of difficult questions: What was the status of the defeated states, and how would they be reintegrated into the nation's political life? What would be the political status of the former slaves, and what would the federal government do to integrate them into the nation's social and economic fabric?

■ **Reconstruction over Time** Abraham Lincoln and his successor, southerner Andrew Johnson, preferred a more lenient and faster *Restoration Plan* for the southern states. The *Freedmen's Bureau* attempted to educate and aid freed slaves, negotiate labor contracts, and reunite families. Lincoln's assassination led many northerners to favor the *Radical Republicans*, who wanted a more transformative plan designed to end the grasp of the old plantation elite on the South's society and economy. Southern whites resisted and established *black codes* to restrict the lives of former slaves. *Congressional Reconstruction* responded by stipulating that to reenter the Union, former Confederate states had to ratify the *Fourteenth* and *Fifteenth Amendments* to the U.S. Constitution in order to expand and protect the rights of African Americans.

■ **Views of Reconstruction** Many former slaves found comfort in their families and the independent churches they established, but land ownership reverted to the old white elite, reducing newly freed black farmers to *sharecropping*. African Americans enthusiastically participated in politics, with many serving as elected officials. Along with white southern Republicans (scalawags) and northern carpetbaggers, they worked to rebuild the southern economy. Many white southerners, however, blamed their poverty on freed slaves and Republicans, and they supported the *Ku Klux Klan's* violent intimidation of the supporters of these Reconstruction efforts and the goal of "redemption," or white Democratic control of Southern state governments.

■ **Political and Economic Developments and the End of Reconstruction** Scandals during the Grant administration involved an attempt to corner the gold market and the "whiskey ring's" plan to steal millions of dollars in tax revenue. In the face of these troubles and the economic downturn caused by both the *Panic of 1873* over railroad defaults and disagreement over whether to continue the use of *greenbacks* or return to the gold standard, northern support for Reconstruction eroded. Southern white *redeemers* were elected in 1874, successfully reversing the political progress of Republicans and blacks. In the *Compromise of 1877*, Democrats agreed to the election of Republican Rutherford B. Hayes, who put an end to the Radical Republican administrations in the southern states.

■ The Significance of Reconstruction

Southern state governments quickly renewed long-standing patterns of discrimination against African Americans, but the *Fourteenth* and *Fifteenth Amendments* remained enshrined in the Constitution, creating the essential constitutional foundation for future advances in civil rights. These amendments give the federal government responsibility for ensuring equal treatment and political equality within the states, a role it would increasingly assume in the twentieth century.

KEY TERMS

Radical Republicans *p. 536*

Freedmen's Bureau *p. 537*

Johnson's Restoration Plan *p. 539*

black codes *p. 542*

Fourteenth Amendment (1866) *p. 543*

Congressional Reconstruction *p. 544*

Fifteenth Amendment (1870) *p. 546*

sharecropping *p. 551*

Ku Klux Klan *p. 552*

greenbacks *p. 557*

Panic of 1873 *p. 558*

redeemers *p. 560*

Compromise of 1877 *p. 562*

CHRONOLOGY

1865	Congress sets up the Freedmen's Bureau
	Lincoln assassinated on April 14, 1865
	Johnson issues Proclamation of Amnesty
1865–1866	Southern state legislatures pass black codes
1866	Ku Klux Klan organized
	Congress passes Civil Rights Act
1867	Congress passes Military Reconstruction Act
	Freedmen begin participating in elections
1868	Fourteenth Amendment is ratified
	The U.S. House of Representatives impeaches President Andrew Johnson; the Senate fails to convict him
	Grant elected president
	Six former Confederate states readmitted to the Union
1869	Reestablishment of white Democratic rule ("redeemers") in former Confederate states
1870	Fifteenth Amendment ratified
	First Enforcement Acts passed
1872	Grant wins reelection
1873	Panic of 1873 triggers depression
1877	Compromise of 1877 ends Reconstruction

🐰 InQuizitive

InQuizitive Go to InQuizitive to see what you've learned—and learn what you've missed—with personalized feedback along the way.

DEBATING Reconstruction

Historians' interpretations of the past change over time. This happens for many reasons. Historians can revise their thinking in light of information from newly discovered *primary sources*. They can also interpret previously examined sources in new ways by applying new methodologies and theories. Finally, historians themselves are influenced by the values of their own society and times. Present-day events or particular personal interests can influence how historians think about the past. The study of how interpretations of history have changed is called *historiography*. It is the history of the field of history. For Part 4, *"A House Divided,"* the case study of debating Reconstruction demonstrates how the views of historians have changed dramatically over time.

For this exercise you have two tasks:

PART 1: Compare the two secondary sources on Reconstruction.

PART 2: Using primary sources, evaluate the arguments of the two secondary sources.

PART I Comparing and Contrasting Secondary Sources

Two *secondary sources*, the work of prominent historians from different eras, are included below for you to review. The first selection comes from William Dunning's (1857–1922) *Reconstruction, Political and Economic, 1865–1877*, written in 1907. Dunning was born on the eve of the Civil War to a well-to-do New Jersey family and enrolled at Columbia University soon after the end of Reconstruction. He lived during a time when racial segregation and white supremacy were the unchallenged law of the land, and he wrote some of the first books about Reconstruction.

Dunning was such a compelling force in the first half of the twentieth century that the many historians trained and influenced by him are referred to as the "Dunning School." He was particularly hostile to political idealists, a group that, in his mind, included abolitionists and Radical Republicans. Like many historians of his day, Dunning never questioned his own objectivity. However, later historians and activists have noted that his writings reflect the political beliefs and prejudices of his generation.

Interpretations of Reconstruction have undergone many changes since Dunning's time. The second excerpt, written 91 years later, is from Eric Foner's *The Story of American Freedom*. Born in 1943, Foner is the son of civil rights activists (one of them a historian) deeply concerned with the plight of African Americans. Foner completed his Ph.D. in 1969 during the height of the civil

rights movement. Widely regarded as the leading interpretation of Reconstruction, Foner's writing on the period brings together much of the scholarship that has revised "Dunning School" interpretations of Reconstruction, particularly as they described the role of African Americans in American society.

Before reading these excerpts, review Chapter 15 on the transition from President Andrew Johnson's Restoration Plan to Congressional Reconstruction.

Compare the work of these two historians by answering the following questions. Be sure to support your answers with specific examples drawn from the selections by Dunning and Foner.

■ What is the *topic* of each excerpt? What period of Reconstruction is the author writing about? What groups are examined?

■ Generally, how does each author portray the Reconstruction process? What in each author's writing reveals their attitude about Reconstruction? How do those feelings—whether positive or negative—affect each author's point of view?

■ What are the similarities in these two excerpts?

■ What are the major differences in interpretation between the excerpts?

- What is the main *argument* each historian makes?

- How do these interpretations compare to that presented in Chapter 15?

- These two excerpts were written 91 years apart. How might this have influenced the development of their arguments?

Secondary Source 1

William Dunning, *Reconstruction, Political and Economic, 1865–1877*

It was, indeed, no novelty for the people of the South to be subject to government by the United States army. . . . The reasoning by which the policy of Congress was justified in the North was regarded in the South as founded on falsehood and malice. So far as the "black codes" were concerned, it was pointed out that they could not be alleged as evidences of a tendency to restore slavery or introduce peonage [dependence], since the offensive acts had in many of the states been repealed by the legislatures themselves, and in all had been duly superseded by the civil rights act. The much-exploited outrages on freedmen and Unionists were declared to be exaggerated or distorted reports of incidents which any time of social tension must produce among the criminal classes. The rejection of the Fourteenth Amendment was considered as merely a dignified refusal by honorable men to be the instruments of their own humiliation and shame.

Under all these circumstances the southerners felt that the policy of Congress had no real cause save the purpose of radical politicians to prolong and extend their party power by means of negro suffrage [voting rights]. This and this alone was the purpose for which major-generals had been empowered to remodel the state governments at their will, to exercise through general orders the functions of executive, legislature, and courts, and to compel the white people to recognize the blacks as their equals wherever the stern word of military command could reach. It was as inconceivable to the southerners that rational men of the North should seriously approve of negro suffrage per se as it had been in 1860 to the northerners that rational men of the South should approve of secession per se. Hence, in the one case as in the other, a craving for political power was assumed to be the only explanation of an otherwise unintelligible proceeding.

Source: Dunning, William. *Reconstruction, Political and Economic, 1865–1877*. New York: Harper & Bros., 1907. 109–12.

Secondary Source 2

Eric Foner, *The Story of American Freedom*

Rejecting the idea that emancipation implied civil or political equality or opportunities to acquire property or advance economically, rights northerners deemed essential to a free society, most white southerners insisted that blacks must remain a dependent plantation workforce in a laboring situation not very different from slavery. During Presidential Reconstruction—the period from 1865 to 1867 when Lincoln's successor, Andrew Johnson, gave the white South a free hand in determining the contours of Reconstruction—southern state governments enforced this view of black freedom by enacting the notorious Black Codes, which denied blacks equality before the law and political rights and imposed on them mandatory year-long labor contracts, coercive apprenticeship regulations, and criminal penalties for breach of contract. Through these laws, the South's white leadership sought to ensure that plantation agriculture survived emancipation.

Thus, the death of slavery did not automatically mean the birth of freedom. But the Black Codes so flagrantly violated free labor principles that they invoked the wrath of the Republican North. Southern reluctance to accept the reality of emancipation resulted in a monumental struggle between President Andrew Johnson and the Republican Congress over the legacy of the Civil War. The result was the enactment of laws and constitutional amendments that redrew the boundaries of citizenship and expanded the definition of freedom for all Americans. . . .

Much of the ensuing conflict over Reconstruction revolved around the problem, as Senator Lyman Trumbull of Illinois put it, of defining "what slavery is and what liberty is." . . . By 1866, a consensus had emerged within the Republican Party that civil equality was an essential attribute of freedom. The Civil War had elevated "equality" to a status in the vocabulary of freedom it had not enjoyed since the Revolution. . . . In a remarkable, if temporary, reversal of political traditions, the newly empowered national state now sought to identify and protect the rights of all Americans.

Source: Foner, Eric. *The Story of American Freedom*. New York: W. W. Norton & Company, 1998. 103–105.

PART II **Using Primary Sources to Evaluate Secondary Sources**

When historians are faced with competing interpretations of the past, they often look at primary source material as part of the process of evaluating the different arguments. In the following selections, you'll find *primary sources* relating to the period of Reconstruction.

Carefully read the primary sources and answer the following questions. Decide how the primary source documents support or refute Dunning's and Foner's arguments about this period. You may find that some documents do both but for different parts of each historian's interpretation. Be sure to identify which specific components of each historian's argument the documents support or refute.

■ Which of the two historian's arguments is best supported by the primary source documents? If you find that both arguments are well supported by the evidence, why do you think the two historians produced such different interpretations?

■ Based on your comparison of the two arguments and your analysis of the primary sources, how has the interpretation of Reconstruction by historians shifted over time? What can you conclude about historiography from the work of these two historians?

Primary Source 1

Union Army general Carl Schurz, *Report on the Condition of the South*

A belief, conviction, or prejudice, or whatever you may call it, so widely spread and apparently so deeply rooted as this, that the negro will not work without physical compulsion, is certainly calculated to have a very serious influence upon the conduct of the people entertaining it. It naturally produced a desire to preserve slavery in its original form as much and as long as possible—and you may, perhaps, remember the admission made by one of the provisional governors, over two months after the close of the war, that the people of his State still indulged in a lingering hope slavery might yet be preserved—or to introduce into the new system that element of physical compulsion which would make the negro work. Efforts were, indeed, made to hold the negro in his old state of subjection, especially in such localities where our military forces had not yet penetrated, or where the country was not garrisoned in detail. Here and there planters succeeded for a limited period to keep their former slaves

in ignorance, or at least doubt, about their new rights; but the main agency employed for that purpose was force and intimidation. In many instances negroes who walked away from the plantations, or were found upon the roads, were shot or otherwise severely punished, which was calculated to produce the impression among those remaining with their masters that an attempt to escape from slavery would result in certain destruction. A large proportion of the many acts of violence committed is undoubtedly attributable to this motive.

Source: Schurz, Carl. *Report on the Condition of the South*. 39th Cong., 1st sess., Senate Executive Document 2, 1865. 19.

Primary Source 2

Mississippi Vagrant Law, 1865

All freedmen, free negroes and mulattoes in this State, over the age of eighteen years, found on the second Monday in January, 1866, or thereafter, with no lawful employment or business, or found unlawfully assembling themselves together, either in the day or night time, and all white persons so assembling themselves with freedmen, free negroes or mulattoes, or usually associating with freedmen, free negroes or mulattoes, on terms of equality, or living in adultery or fornication with a freed woman, free negro or mulatto, shall be deemed vagrants, and on conviction thereof shall be fined in a sum not exceeding, in the case of a freedman, free negro, or mulatto, fifty dollars, and a white man two hundred dollars, and imprisoned at the discretion of the court, the free negro not exceeding ten days, and the white man not exceeding six months. . . . All fines and forfeitures collected under the provisions of this act shall be paid into the county treasury for general county purposes, and in case any freedman, free negro or mulatto shall fail for five days after the imposition of any fine or forfeiture upon him or her for violation of any of the provisions of this act to pay the same, that it shall be, and is hereby, made the duty of the sheriff of the proper county to hire out said freedman, free negro or mulatto, to any person who will, for the shortest period of service, pay said fine and forfeiture and all costs. . . .

Source: Mississippi Vagrant Law, *Laws of Mississippi, 1865*, 90. In *Documentary History of Reconstruction: Political, Military, Social, Religious, Educational & Industrial, 1865 to the Present Time*. Edited by Walter Lynwood Fleming, 1:283 – 286. Cleveland, Ohio: The Arthur H. Clark Company, 1906.

Primary Source 3

Civil Rights Act of 1866

Be it enacted,... That all persons born in the United States and not subject to any foreign power, excluding Indians not taxed, are hereby declared to be citizens of the United States; and such citizens, of every race and color, without regard to any previous condition of slavery or involuntary servitude, except as a punishment for crime whereof the party shall have been duly convicted, shall have the same right, in every State and Territory in the United States, to make and enforce contracts, to sue, be parties, and give evidence, to inherit, purchase, lease, sell, hold, and convey real and personal property, and to full and equal benefit of all laws and proceedings for the security of person and property, as is enjoyed by white citizens, and shall be subject to like punishment, pains and penalties, and to none other, any law, statute, ordinance, regulation, or custom, to the contrary notwithstanding.

Source: Civil Rights Act of 1866, 14 Stat. 27 (April 9, 1866).

Primary Source 4

Radical Republican Thaddeus Stevens, "The Advantages of Negro Suffrage"

Unless the rebel States, before admission, should be made republican in spirit, and placed under the guardianship of loyal men, all our blood and treasure will have been spent in vain. . . . There is more reason why colored voters should be admitted in the rebel States than in the Territories. In the States they form the great mass of the loyal men. Possibly with their aid loyal governments may be established in most of those States. Without it all are sure to be ruled by traitors; and loyal men, black and white, will be oppressed, exiled, or murdered. . . . Have not loyal blacks quite as good a right to choose rulers and make laws as rebel whites? In the second place, it is a necessity in order to protect the loyal white men in the seceded States. The white Union men are in a great minority in each of those States. With them the blacks would act in a body; and it is believed that in each of said States, except one, the two united would form a majority, control the States, and protect themselves. Now they are the victims of daily murder. They must suffer constant persecution or be exiled. . . . Another good reason is, it would insure the ascendency of the Union party. . . . I believe . . . that on the continued ascendency of that party depends the safety of this great nation. If impartial suffrage is excluded in the rebel States, then every one of them is sure to send a solid rebel representative delegation to Congress, and cast a solid rebel electoral vote. . . . I am for negro suffrage in every rebel State. If it be just, it should not be denied; if it be necessary, it should be adopted; if it be a punishment to traitors, they deserve it.

Source: Stevens, Thaddeus. *Congressional Globe*, January 3, 1867, 252. In *Documentary History of Reconstruction: Political, Military, Social, Religious, Educational & Industrial, 1865 to the Present Time*. Edited by Walter Lynwood Fleming, 1:149–150. Cleveland, Ohio: The Arthur H. Clark Company, 1906.

Growing Pains

The defeat of the Confederacy in 1865 restored the Union and in the process helped accelerate America's transformation into an agricultural empire and an industrial powerhouse. A stronger sense of nationalism began to temper the regional conflicts of the prewar era. During and after the Civil War, the Republican-led Congress pushed through legislation to promote industrial and commercial development as well as western expansion at the same time that it was "reconstructing" the former Confederate states. In the process of settling the rest of the continent, ruthlessly forcing Indians onto reservations, and exploiting the continent's natural resources, the United States forged a dynamic new industrial economy serving an increasingly national and international market for American goods.

Fueled by innovations in mass production and mass marketing as well as advances in transportation and communications such as transcontinental railroads and transatlantic telegraph systems, huge corporations began to dominate the economy by the end of the nineteenth century. As the prominent social theorist William Graham Sumner remarked, the relentless process of industrial development "controls us all because we are all in it. It creates the conditions of our own existence, sets the limits of our social activity, and regulates the bonds of our social relations."

Late-nineteenth-century American life drew much of its energy from the mushrooming industrial cities. "This is the age of cities," declared midwestern writer Hamlin Garland. "We are now predominantly urban." Yet the transition from an economy made up of mostly small local and regional businesses to one dominated by large-scale national and international corporations affected rural life as well. For more and more Americans during the Gilded Age, their workday began with the shriek of a factory whistle rather than a crowing rooster.

As early as 1869, novelist Harriet Beecher Stowe reported that the "simple, pastoral" America "is a thing forever gone. The hurry of railroads . . . and the rush and roar of business" had displaced the Jeffersonian ideal of America remaining a nation of small farms and few cities. Stowe exaggerated, of course. Small farms and small towns survived the impact of the Industrial Revolution, but farm folk, as one New Englander stressed, must now "understand farming as a business; if they do not it will go hard with them."

The friction between the new forces of the national marketplace and the traditional folkways of small-scale family farming generated social unrest and political revolts (what one writer called "a seismic shock, a cyclonic violence") during the last quarter of the nineteenth century.

The clash between tradition and modernity, sleepy farm villages and bustling cities, peaked during the 1890s, one of the most strife-ridden decades in American history. A deep economic depression, political activism by farmers, and violent conflicts between industrial workers and employers transformed the presidential campaign of 1896 into a clash between rival visions of America's future.

The Republican candidate, William McKinley, campaigned on modern urban and industrial values. His opponent, William Jennings Bryan, the nominee of both the Democratic and the Populist parties, was an eloquent defender of America's rural past.

McKinley's victory proved to be a turning point in the nation's political and social history. By 1900, the United States had emerged as one of the world's greatest industrial powers, and it would thereafter assume a new leadership role in world affairs—for good and for ill.

CARNEGIE STEEL COMPANY Steelworkers operate the dangerous yet magnificent Bessemer converters at Andrew Carnegie's huge steel mill in Pittsburgh, Pennsylvania.

Big Business and Organized Labor

1860–1900

Although the Civil War devastated the South, it provided a powerful stimulant to the northern economy. The need to supply the massive Union armies with shoes, boots, uniforms, blankets, tents, weapons, food, wagons, and railroads ushered in an era of unprecedented industrial development. The scope of the war favored large-scale business enterprises and hastened the maturation of a truly national economy. An Indiana congressman told business leaders in 1864 that the war effort had sparked the development of the "resources and capabilities such as you never before dreamed you possessed."

During the war years, the number of manufacturing companies in the United States almost doubled. In 1865, Ohio's John Sherman, a powerful U.S. senator, wrote a letter to his brother, William T. Sherman, the celebrated Union general, in which he observed that the northern states had emerged from the war "unimpaired." The process of mass-producing mountains of goods for the war effort had given a widened "scope to the ideas of leading capitalists, far higher than anything undertaken in this country. They talk of millions as confidently as before [they talked] of thousands."

Between the end of the war and 1900, during the so-called Gilded Age, America experienced explosive growth. The nation's population tripled, farm production more than doubled, and manufacturing output grew *six* times over. In the thirty-five years

CORE
OBJECTIVES INQUIZITIVE

1. Explain the primary factors that stimulated unprecedented industrial and agricultural growth in the late nineteenth century.

2. Describe the entrepreneurs who pioneered the growth of Big Business, the goals they aimed to achieve, and the strategies they used to dominate their industries.

3. Evaluate the role of the federal government in the nation's economic development during this period.

4. Analyze the ways in which the social class structure and the lives of women changed in the late nineteenth century.

5. Assess the efforts of workers to organize unions to promote their interests during this era.

after the Civil War, the United States achieved the highest rate of economic growth in the world, more than double that of its closest rival, Great Britain. By 1900, American industries and corporate farms dominated global markets in steel and oil, wheat and cotton.

Such phenomenal growth caused profound social changes, the most visible of which was the sudden prospering of large industrial cities such as Pittsburgh, Chicago, and Cleveland. Millions of young adults left farms and villages to work in factories, mines, and mills and to revel in the energies of city life. In growing numbers, women left the "cult of domesticity" at home and entered the urban-industrial workplace as clerks, typists, secretaries, teachers, nurses, and seamstresses.

While a few people made enormous fortunes during the Gilded Age, most laborers remained in unskilled, low-wage jobs. Big Business was as untamed and reckless as the cow towns and mining camps of the West. New technologies and business practices outpaced the ability of the legal system to craft new laws and fashion rules of ethics to govern the rapidly changing economy. Business owners took advantage of this lawless environment to build fortunes, destroy reputations, exploit both workers and the environment, and gouge consumers. Yet out of the scramble for profits emerged phenomenal prosperity and a rising standard of living that became the envy of the world.

In generating wealth, capitalism fosters inequality. People with different talents, opportunities, and resources receive unequal rewards from their labors and innovations. In a capitalist democracy like America, the tensions between equal political rights and unequal economic status produce social instability. The overwhelming influence exercised by the business tycoons led to tensions that spurred the formation of labor unions and farm associations. Increasingly, those tensions erupted into violent clashes that demanded government intervention and produced class conflict.

CORE **OBJECTIVE**

1. Explain the primary factors that stimulated unprecedented industrial and agricultural growth in the late nineteenth century.

The Elements of Industrial Growth

Several factors converged after the Civil War to accelerate economic growth and industrial development. America's vast natural resources—land, rivers, forests, oil, coal, water, iron ore—created a huge advantage over other nations.

At the same time, a flood of immigrants provided an army of new low-wage workers and an expanding national market of consumers. Between 1865 and 1900, over 15 million newcomers arrived in the United States. In addition, inventors, research laboratories, and business owners developed labor-saving machinery and mass-production techniques that spurred dramatic advances in efficiency and productivity. Farms, canneries, factories, slaughterhouses, mines, mills, refineries, and other businesses turned out more products more cheaply, enabling more people to buy more of them. These technological advances created *economies of scale*, whereby larger business enterprises, including huge commercial farms, were able to afford expensive new machinery and large workforces that made them more productive than smaller enterprises.

Innovative business leaders (entrepreneurs) also spurred economic growth. A group of shrewd, determined entrepreneurs created huge new national corporations, some of which became virtual monopolies in industries like oil, steel, sugar, and meatpacking. As one wealthy investor said, a new breed of ruthlessly focused capitalists had emerged after the Civil War, driven by the "same all-pervading, all-engrossing anxiety to grow rich."

> Causes of industrial growth:
> (1) vast natural resources
> (2) flood of immigrants
> (3) technological innovations
> (4) entrepreneurs

The Second Industrial Revolution

The dramatic increases in economic productivity were spurred by the **Second Industrial Revolution**, which began in the mid–nineteenth century and was centered in the United States and Germany. This revolution resulted from three related developments. The first was the creation of modern transportation and communication systems, which gave farmers and factory owners access to national and international markets. The completion of transcontinental railroads and the development of larger, faster steamships helped expand markets worldwide, as did the laying of the telegraph cable under the Atlantic Ocean to connect the United States with Europe.

During the 1880s, a second major breakthrough—the creation of electrical power—accelerated the pace of change in industrial and urban development. Electricity dramatically increased the power, speed, and efficiency of machinery. It also spurred urban growth by making possible trolley and subway systems as well as elevators that enabled the construction of taller buildings.

> The Second Industrial Revolution: Modern transportation systems and electrical power

The third major catalyst for the Second Industrial Revolution was the systematic application of scientific research to industrial processes. In new laboratories staffed by graduates of new research universities and often funded by corporations or wealthy business owners, scientists (mostly chemists) and engineers discovered dramatic new ways to improve industrial processes. Researchers, for example, learned how to refine kerosene and gasoline from crude oil and how to make steel more efficiently and in much larger quantities.

> The Second Industrial Revolution: Improvement of industrial processes

Using these improved processes, inventors developed new products—telephones, typewriters, phonographs (record players), adding machines, sewing machines, cameras, zippers, farm machinery—which resulted in lower prices for an array of consumer items. These advances in turn expanded the scope and scale of industrial organizations. Capital-intensive industries, those requiring massive investments in specialized equipment, such as steel and oil, as well as processed food and tobacco, began emphasizing mass production and distribution across national and international markets.

Second Industrial Revolution Beginning in the late nineteenth century, a wave of technological innovations, especially in iron and steel production, steam and electrical power, and telegraphic communications, all of which spurred industrial development and urban growth.

Serving customers across the nation and around the world required more sophisticated strategies of marketing and advertising, thus expanding those industries. Between 1870 and 1900, expenditures on advertising increased more than tenfold. As early as 1867, a journalist complained that advertisements were invading "every department of life."

Corporate Farming

> Large-scale farming: "Bonanza farms"

At the same time that the industrial sector of the economy was experiencing rapid growth and an ever-increasing concentration of ownership and production into huge companies, the agricultural sector was also shifting quickly to a large-scale market model of operation. Corporations developed huge "bonanza farms" (growing mostly wheat and corn), which defied the nation's tradition of small-scale family farming. Bonanza farms appeared first in the Dakotas and Minnesota before spreading across the West. They were run like factories by professional, college-educated managers, who during harvest season would hire hundreds of migrant workers to bring in the crop.

Bonanza farms using the latest machinery and scientific management techniques became internationally famous for their productivity and efficiency. By 1870, America had become the world's leading agricultural producer, sending massive amounts of grain to foreign markets. In addition, with the start of the commercial cattle industry, the processes of slaughtering and packing meat became major industries, too. So the farm sector directly stimulated the industrial sector of the economy.

Technological Innovations

After the Civil War, technological innovations spurred phenomenal increases in industrial productivity. The U.S. Patent Office, which had recorded only 276 inventions during the 1790s, registered almost 235,000 new patents in the 1890s. The list of innovations was lengthy: barbed wire; mechanical harvesters, reapers, and combines; refrigerated rail cars; air brakes for trains; machine tools; steam turbines; typewriters; sewing machines; vacuum cleaners; electric motors; and countless others.

Few, if any, inventions could rival the importance of the telephone. In 1875, twenty-eight-year-old Alexander Graham Bell began experimenting with the concept of a "speaking telegraph," or talking through wires. The following year, he developed a primitive "electric speaking telephone" that enabled him to send a famous message to his assistant in another room: "Mr. Watson, come here, I want to see you." Bell then patented his device and started a company, the American Telephone and Telegraph Company (AT&T), to begin manufacturing telephones. Five years later, he

NEW TECHNOLOGIES A gaggle of businessmen watch Alexander Graham Bell at the New York end of the first long-distance telephone call to Chicago, in 1892.

OFFICE TYPISTS Newly entrusted with typewriters, women occupied the secretarial positions at many offices, such as the Remington Typewriter Company, pictured here.

perfected the long-distance telephone lines that revolutionized communication. By 1895, there were more than 300,000 telephones in use. Bell's patent became the most valuable one ever issued.

Technological innovations spur productivity

New inventions changed the nature of work. The development of typewriters, for example, brought a flood of women workers into business offices, which had been mostly all male. Because managers assumed that women had greater dexterity in their fingers and because women could be paid less than men, owners hired them to operate typewriters. Clerical positions soon became the fastest-growing job category for women.

New job options for women: Office work and sweatshops

Likewise, the introduction of sewing machines for the mass production of clothing and linens opened new doors to women—if not usually pleasant ones to walk through. So-called sweatshops emerged in the major cities, where large numbers of mostly young immigrant women worked long hours stitching clothes in cramped, stifling conditions.

Edison and electricity

Technological discoveries also transformed daily life, none more so than the creations of inventor Thomas Alva Edison. In the laboratory at his "science village" in Menlo Park, New Jersey, Edison promised to produce "a minor invention every ten days and a big thing every six months or so." He invented the phonograph in 1877 and the electric light bulb in 1879. Altogether he created or perfected hundreds of new devices and processes, including the storage battery, Dictaphone, mimeograph copier, electric motor, and motion-picture camera and projector.

Until the 1880s, flickering kerosene or gas lamps illuminated the nation. All that changed in 1882, when the Edison Electric Illuminating Company, later renamed General Electric, supplied electrical current to eighty-five customers in New York City, launching the electric utility industry. The invention of electric motors enabled factories to locate wherever owners wished; they no longer had to cluster around waterfalls or coal deposits for a ready supply of energy.

Railroads Leading the Way

More than any other industry, railroads illustrated the impact of innovative technologies on industrial development during the second half of the nineteenth century. Railroads were America's first truly *big business*, the first beneficiary of the great financial market known as Wall Street in New York City, the first industry to have operations in several states, and the first to develop a large-scale management bureaucracy. Railroads moved people and goods faster and farther than anything else could, and they did so in any weather. Towns that had rail stations thrived; those that did not died. A town's connection to a railroad, observed Anthony Trollope, a celebrated British writer touring the United States, was "the first necessity of life, and gives the only hope of wealth."

> Railroads' contributions to the economic boom

The railroad boom was the essential catalyst for America's transition to an urban-industrial economy. For a century, from the 1860s to the 1960s, most people entered or left a city through its railroad stations. Trains opened the West to economic development, enabled federal troops to suppress Indian resistance, ferried millions of European and Asian immigrants across the country, helped transform commercial agriculture into a major international industry, and transported raw materials to factories and finished goods to retailers.

Although the first great wave of railroad building had occurred in the 1850s, the most spectacular growth took place during the quarter century after the Civil War. Between 1865 and 1873, 35,000 miles of new track were laid across the nation, as much as had been built in the previous thirty years. The national rail network grew to nearly 200,000 miles by 1897, more than all of Europe combined.

Railroads were expensive enterprises that required huge capital investments to purchase engines and cars and construct track, trestles, and bridges. Railroads were also the largest consumers in the economy, stimulating other industries through their vast purchases of iron and steel, coal, timber, leather (for seats), and glass. In addition, railroad companies were the nation's largest employers. By the 1870s, the Pennsylvania Railroad alone had 55,000 employees, as many as the entire federal government.

But the railroads also brought problems. Many freewheeling developers cared more about making

CHINESE RAILROAD WORKERS Using horse-drawn carts, picks, shovels, and dynamite, Chinese laborers played a large role in constructing the transcontinental railroads.

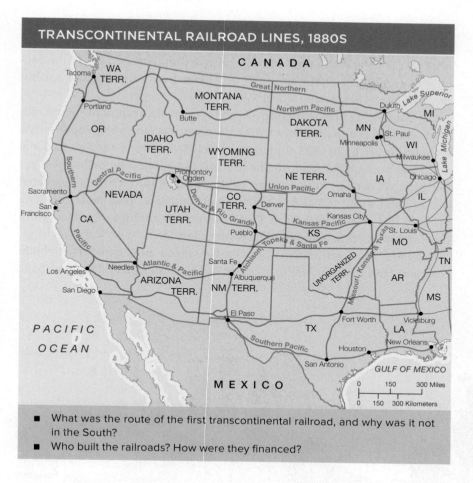

TRANSCONTINENTAL RAILROAD LINES, 1880S

- What was the route of the first transcontinental railroad, and why was it not in the South?
- Who built the railroads? How were they financed?

money than building good railroads. In their race to build new lines, companies overlooked dangerous working conditions that caused thousands of laborers to be killed or injured. Too many unneeded railroads were built; by the 1880s, there were twice as many railroad companies as the economy could support. Some railroads were poorly or even criminally managed and went bankrupt. Railroad lobbyists helped corrupt state and federal legislators, as the votes of politicians were "bought" with cash or shares of stock in the new railroad companies. As the head of the Union Pacific Railroad admitted, "Our method of doing business is founded upon lying, cheating, and stealing—all bad things."

Building the Transcontinentals

After the Civil War, railroad tracks in the South were gradually rebuilt and expanded. But the most spectacular achievements were the transcontinental lines built west of the Mississippi River across plains and deserts, over roaring rivers and deep canyons, and around and through the nation's tallest mountains, all the way to the Pacific coast.

The Pacific Railway Act (1862) authorized the construction of a rail line to be built by the Union Pacific Railroad Company westward from Omaha, Nebraska, and by the Central Pacific Railroad Company eastward from Sacramento, California. Both companies began construction during the war, but most of the work was done after 1865.

By connecting the nation from ocean to ocean, the transcontinental railroads enabled the creation of a truly national market for goods and services, including tourism. In 1872, Congress created Yellowstone, the first national park, and railroads began bringing tourists to the park in northwest Wyoming ten years later. Furthermore, as they pushed into sparsely populated western states and territories, the railroad companies became the region's primary real estate developers. They transported millions of settlers from the East, many of them immigrants eager to buy land.

The first transcontinental railroads were much more expensive to build compared with lines in the East. Because the routes passed through long

THE UNION PACIFIC MEETS THE CENTRAL PACIFIC The celebration of the first transcontinental railroad's completion took place in Promontory, Utah, 1869. **How did railroads transform industry? How did they impact people's everyday lives?**

stretches of unpopulated desert areas, construction materials as well as workers and their food and water had to be hauled long distances. Camps had to be built for housing. Crossing high mountains required extensive use of dynamite and costly tunnels and bridges. Harsh weather caused frequent work disruptions. The high costs made the railroad owners dependent on government financial support, which came in the form of substantial loans and cash subsidies as well as massive grants of "public" land taken from the Indians. The owners also relied on federal troops to crush the Native Americans whose ancestral lands were along the rail route.

The transcontinental railroads were, in the words of General William Tecumseh Sherman, the "work of giants." Their construction required heroic feats by workers and engineers who laid the rails, built the bridges, and gouged out the tunnels amid dangerous working conditions and severe weather. Some 10,000 men worked on the two railroads as they raced to connect with one another.

The Union Pacific crews were comprised of young, unmarried former Civil War soldiers, both Union and Confederate, along with ex-slaves and Irish and German immigrants. The Central Pacific crews were mainly Chinese workers lured to America either earlier by the California gold rush or more recently by railroad jobs. Most of these "coolie" laborers were single men eager to make money to take back to their homeland, where they could then afford to marry and buy a parcel of land. Their temporary status and dreams of a good life back in China made them more willing than American laborers to endure the low pay and dangerous working conditions.

The Union Pacific had built 1,086 miles of track compared with the Central Pacific's 689 miles when the race ended at Promontory Summit in the Utah Territory. There, on May 10, 1869, the president of the Central Pacific, Leland Stanford, drove a gold spike symbolizing the completion of the first transcontinental railroad. Others soon followed along routes to the north and south.

The Rise of Big Business

The emergence of "Big Business" in the late nineteenth century was one of the most significant developments in American history. Corporations grew much larger than ever before, transacting business across the nation and often around the world. They were also much more powerful politically and socially, forming a web of interconnected relationships with each other to influence governors, legislators, Congress, and presidents.

Before the Civil War, most businesses were small local enterprises run by their owners. After 1865, much of America suddenly got bigger—towns and cities, ships, locomotives, factories, machines, mines, and mills—and business organizations followed the same path in creating the most sweeping economic revolution in history. But the rapid expansion in the size and

CORE **OBJECTIVE**

2. Describe the entrepreneurs who pioneered the growth of Big Business, the goals they aimed to achieve, and the strategies they used to dominate their industries.

power of businesses created problems along with prosperity. "The growing wealth and influence of our large corporations," warned the *New York Times*, "is one of the most alarming phenomena of our time. Our public companies already wield gigantic power, and they use it like unscrupulous giants."

The Growth of Corporations

Rise of limited-liability corporations and elimination of competition

As businesses grew in size and scope, they took many forms. Some were owned by an individual, usually their founder; others were partnerships involving several owners. Increasingly during the late nineteenth century, however, large companies that served national and international markets were converted into "corporations"—legal entities that separate the *ownership* of an enterprise from the *management* of its operations. Once a corporation is registered ("chartered" or "incorporated") with a state government, it can raise money to operate ("capital") by selling shares of stock—representing partial ownership of the company—to people not otherwise involved with it, although those who found and manage a corporation usually own stock in it as well. Shareholders elect a board of directors who appoint and evaluate the corporation's executives ("management") and can replace them. One of the most important benefits of a corporation is "limited liability": stockholders share in the profits generated by a corporation, but they cannot be held personally liable for its debts if it fails.

Competition is supposed to be the great virtue of capitalism, since it forces businesses to produce better products and lower prices. As many American businesses grew larger and became giant corporations, however, some of them came to view competition as a burden. To try to eliminate it, competing companies selling similar products often formed secret "pools" whereby they agreed to keep their prices the same. Pools rarely lasted, however, because one or more of the participants usually violated the agreement by cutting prices. The more effective strategy for the most aggressive companies was to drive out or buy out their weaker competitors.

Strategies intended to eliminate competition aroused considerable controversy. In the process of forming huge companies, many business leaders cut ethical corners, bribed politicians, exploited workers, and broke laws. When asked how people might react to the shady methods he used to build his network of railroads, William Henry Vanderbilt famously replied: "The public be damned!"

The Barons of Business

Rise of industrial and financial giants

Most of the men (few women had such opportunities) who created big businesses and huge fortunes in the late nineteenth century were driven by a compulsive desire to become rich and influential. During and after the Civil War, becoming rich became a dominant ideal for many Americans. "To secure wealth is an honorable ambition," stressed Russell Conwell, a prominent Baptist minister from Philadelphia. "Money is power," he explained, and "every good man and woman ought to strive for power, to do good with it when obtained. I say, get rich! get rich!"

The richly varied industrial and financial giants who emerged after the Civil War were outsized men of grit and genius who found innovative—and occasionally illegal—ways to increase production, create efficiencies, and eliminate competition. Three entrepreneurs, in particular, stand out in this period for their shrewdness, ruthlessness, and remarkable achievements: John D. Rockefeller, Andrew Carnegie, and John Pierpont Morgan.

John D. Rockefeller Born in New York in 1839, John D. Rockefeller moved as a youth to Cleveland, Ohio. Soon thereafter, his father abandoned the family. Raised by his mother, a devout Baptist, Rockefeller developed a single-minded passion for systematic organization and self-discipline, and as a young man in the 1860s, he decided to bring order and rationality to the chaotic new boom-and-bust oil industry. Fiercely ambitious and a hard bargainer, he was obsessed with precision, efficiency, tidiness, and money. (A childhood friend recalled that he was "mad about money, though sane about everything else.") He said little, rarely smiled, and hardly ever laughed.

JOHN D. ROCKEFELLER The cofounder of Standard Oil Company, Rockefeller sought a monopoly over the oil industry.

The railroad and shipping connections around Cleveland made it a strategic location for serving the booming oil fields of nearby western Pennsylvania. The first oil well in the United States began producing in 1859 in Titusville, Pennsylvania, and led to the Pennsylvania oil rush of the 1860s. Because oil could be refined into kerosene, then widely used for lighting, heating, and cooking, the economic importance of the oil rush soon outstripped that of the California gold rush ten years earlier. Well before the end of the Civil War, oil refineries sprang up in Pittsburgh and Cleveland. Of the two cities, Cleveland had better rail service, so Rockefeller focused his energies there.

In 1870, Rockefeller teamed up with Henry M. Flagler, Samuel Andrews (inventor of an inexpensive means of refining crude oil), and his brother William Rockefeller to establish the **Standard Oil Company** of Ohio. Although the company quickly became the largest oil refiner in the nation, Rockefeller wanted more. His goal was to eliminate his competitors so as to gain control of the entire oil industry, for once he procured a near monopoly, he could raise oil prices as he saw fit.

> Strategy: Horizontal integration

During the 1870s, Rockefeller pursued a strategy of consolidating control called horizontal integration, in which a dominant corporation in a particular industry buys or forces out most of its competitors. In a few cases, Rockefeller hired former competitors as executives, but only "the big ones," he said, "those who have already proved they can do a big business. As for the others, unfortunately they will have to die." By 1879, Standard Oil controlled more than 90 percent of the oil refining in the nation. Still, that was not enough for Rockefeller, who intended "to secure the entire refining business of the world." His goal was a **monopoly**, a business that grows so large that it effectively controls an entire industry.

Standard Oil Company Corporation under the leadership of John D. Rockefeller that attempted to dominate the entire oil industry through horizontal and vertical integration.

monopoly Corporation so large that it effectively controls the entire market for its products or services.

THE RISE OF OIL Crowding this Pennsylvania farm are wooden derricks that extracted crude oil.

Rockefeller was ruthlessly efficient in his efforts to dominate the oil industry. He was adept at reducing expenses, incorporating the latest technologies, and eliminating waste while paying "nobody a profit." Because he shipped so much oil by rail, for example, he forced railroads to pay him secret cash "rebates" on his oil shipments, enabling him to pay less for shipping than his competitors paid.

Most important, instead of depending upon the products or services of other firms, known as middlemen, Standard Oil eventually owned everything it needed to produce, refine, and deliver oil, from wells to the finished product. The company had its own pipelines, built factories to make its own wagons and storage barrels, did its own hauling, and owned storage tanks and tanker ships. Essentially, Standard Oil did whatever it needed to produce crude oil; refine it into kerosene, gasoline, and lubricants; and then sell it. In economic terms, this business strategy is called vertical integration. A vertically integrated corporation owns all the different businesses needed to produce and sell its product.

During the 1870s, Standard Oil bought so many of its competitors that in an effort to limit its economic power, many state legislatures outlawed the practice of one corporation owning stock in competing ones. In 1882, Rockefeller tried to get around such laws by organizing the Standard Oil Trust, a new way of merging businesses. A **trust** is an arrangement that gives a person or corporation (the "trustee") the legal power to manage another person's money or another company. Instead of owning other companies

> Strategy: Vertical integration

trust Business arrangement that gives a person or corporation (the "trustee") the legal power to manage another person's money or another company without owning those entities outright.

outright, the Standard Oil Trust controlled more than thirty companies spread across several states by having their stockholders transfer their shares "in trust" to Rockefeller and eight other trustees. In return, the stockholders received "trust certificates," which paid them annual dividends from the Trust's earnings. The Standard Oil Trust gave Rockefeller a virtual monopoly over the American oil industry.

Strategy: Corporate trusts, e.g., the Standard Oil Trust

The formation of huge corporate trusts, a practice widely copied by the cattle, liquor, sugar, tobacco, salt, and leather industries, among others, generated intense criticism. In 1890, Congress responded by passing the Sherman Anti-Trust Act, which declared that efforts to monopolize industries and thereby "restrain" competition were illegal. The language of the new law was so vague and unclear, however, that it proved to be virtually toothless.

Sherman Anti-Trust Act

State laws against monopolies were initially more effective than the Sherman Act in controlling trusts. In 1892, Ohio's Supreme Court ordered the Standard Oil Trust dissolved because it was behaving like a monopoly. A furious Rockefeller then found another way of keeping control of his numerous companies: he created a **holding company**, a huge corporation that controls other companies by "holding" most or all of their stock certificates. A holding company produces nothing itself; it simply owns a majority of the stock in other companies.

holding company Corporation established to own and manage other companies' stock rather than to produce goods and services itself.

Rockefeller was convinced that ending competition among companies by creating a near monopoly was a good thing for the nation. Monopolies, he insisted, were the natural result of capitalism at work. "It is too late," he declared in 1899, "to argue about the advantages of [huge] industrial combinations. They are a necessity. The day of individualism is gone. Never to return." That year, Rockefeller brought his entire industrial empire under the direction of the Standard Oil Company of New Jersey, a gigantic holding company. By 1904, 318 holding companies in the United States controlled more than 5,300 factories.

Andrew Carnegie Like Rockefeller, Andrew Carnegie, who created the largest steel company in the world during the late nineteenth century, rose from boyhood poverty to fabulous riches in his adult life. Born in Scotland, he immigrated with his family in 1848 to Allegheny County, Pennsylvania. At age thirteen, he went to work in a textile mill. In 1853, he became personal secretary to Thomas Scott, then district superintendent of the Pennsylvania Railroad and later its president. When Scott moved up, Carnegie, driven by a fierce desire to succeed, took his place as superintendent. During the Civil War, when Scott became assistant secretary of war in charge of transportation, Carnegie went with him to Washington, D.C., and helped develop a military telegraph system.

Carnegie kept on moving—from telegraphy to railroading to bridge building and then to steelmaking. In the early 1870s, he

ANDREW CARNEGIE An immigrant from Scotland, Carnegie overcame childhood poverty and established the Carnegie Steel Company.

decided "to concentrate on the manufacture of iron and steel and be master in that." A tiny man (barely five feet tall) with giant ambitions, Carnegie wanted not simply to excel in the steel industry; he wanted to dominate it, just as John D. Rockefeller was doing with oil. Like Rockefeller, Carnegie accumulated vast wealth for the pure pleasure of the pursuit of it, and he often ruthlessly treated his workers and competitors.

Until the mid–nineteenth century, steel, which is stronger and more flexible than iron, could be made only from wrought iron—itself expensive since it had to be imported from Sweden—and only in small quantities. It took three tons of coke, a high-burning fuel derived from coal, to produce one ton of steel. As a result, steel was too costly to make in large quantities. That changed in the 1850s, when England's Sir Henry Bessemer invented what became known as the Bessemer converter, a process by which high-quality steel could be produced more quickly by blasting air (oxygen) through the molten iron in the furnace.

In the early 1870s, Carnegie decided to concentrate his operations on steel because Bessemer's process had made it so inexpensive to produce and the railroad industry needed massive amounts of it. As more steel was produced, its price dropped, and its industrial uses soared. In 1860, the United States produced only 13,000 tons of steel. By 1880, production had reached 1.4 million tons annually.

Between 1880 and 1900, Carnegie dominated the steel industry, expanding his own business by acquiring competitors or driving them out of business by cutting prices and taking their customers. Like Rockefeller, Carnegie focused on continuous innovation to reduce operating costs: "Cut the prices, scoop the market, run the mills full; watch the costs, and profits will take care of themselves."

Carnegie also expanded his industry by vertical integration, gaining control of every phase of the steelmaking business, including the raw materials needed to make steel. He owned coal mines in West Virginia, bought huge deposits of iron ore in Michigan and Wisconsin, and transported the ore in his own ships across the Great Lakes and then by rail to his steel mills in Pittsburgh.

The result was phenomenal. By 1900, the **Carnegie Steel Company** produced more steel each year than was produced in all of Great Britain. With 20,000 employees, it was the largest industrial company in the world. And Carnegie worked his people hard. His mills operated nonstop, with two-daily twelve-hour shifts, the only exception being the Fourth of July.

J. Pierpont Morgan Unlike Rockefeller and Carnegie, J. Pierpont Morgan was born to wealth. His father was a partner in a large English bank. After attending school in Switzerland and university in Germany, the younger Morgan was sent in 1857 to work in New York City for a new enterprise, **J. Pierpont Morgan and Company**. The firm, under various names, invested European money with American businesses and grew into a

---

Strategy: Continuous innovation, e.g., the Bessemer converter

Strategy: Mergers to eliminate competition, e.g., U.S. Steel Corporation

Carnegie Steel Company Corporation under the leadership of Andrew Carnegie that came to dominate the American steel industry.

J. Pierpont Morgan and Company An investment bank under the leadership of J. Pierpont Morgan that bought or merged unrelated American companies, often using capital acquired from European investors.

financial power by helping competing corporations merge and by purchasing massive amounts of stock in American companies and selling them at a profit, a process known as investment banking.

Morgan took over poorly run companies, appointed new executives, and supervised operations. Like Rockefeller and Carnegie, he believed in capitalism but hated the chaos of competition with other companies. In his view, high profits required order and stability, and stability required consolidating competitors into trusts that he would own and manipulate.

Morgan recognized early on the importance of railroads, and he acquired and reorganized one struggling rail line after another. By the 1890s, he controlled a sixth of the nation's railway system. But his crowning triumph was the consolidation of the steel industry. After a rapid series of mergers, he bought out Andrew Carnegie's huge steel and iron holdings in 1901. Morgan then added scores of related companies to form the new U.S. Steel Corporation, the world's first billion-dollar corporation, employing 168,000 people. It was the climactic event in the efforts of the great financial capitalists to reduce industrial competition.

J. PIERPONT MORGAN Despite his privileged upbringing and financial success, he was self-conscious about his deformed nose, caused by chronic skin diseases.

The "Gospel of Wealth"

However harsh the methods employed by the "captains of industry"—a term favored by their supporters—these aggressive entrepreneurs were convinced that they benefited the general public by accelerating the Industrial Revolution, creating jobs, and growing the economy. In his essay "The Gospel of Wealth" (1889), Carnegie argued that "not evil, but good, has come to the [Anglo-Saxon] race from the accumulation of wealth by those who have the ability and energy that produces it." Like other business barons, he accumulated a colossal personal fortune, but Carnegie—and Rockefeller—gave much of their money away, mostly to support education and medicine.

By 1900, Rockefeller had become the world's leading philanthropist. "I have always regarded it as a religious duty," he said late in life, "to get all I could honorably and to give all I could." He donated more than $500 million during his lifetime, including tens of millions to fund Baptist causes and $35 million to found the University of Chicago. His philanthropic influence continues today through the Rockefeller Foundation.

Philanthropy

As for Carnegie, after retiring from business at age sixty-five, he declared that the "man who dies rich dies disgraced." So he devoted himself to dispensing his $400 million fortune for the public good. Calling himself a "distributor" of wealth (he disliked the term *philanthropy*), he gave huge sums to numerous universities; built 2,500 public libraries around the country; and helped fund churches, hospitals, parks, and halls for meetings and concerts, including New York City's Carnegie Hall.

CORE **OBJECTIVE**

3. Evaluate the role of the federal government in the nation's economic development during this period.

The Alliance of Business and Politics

The big businesses developed by Rockefeller, Carnegie, Morgan, and others depended upon more than just their skills as entrepreneurs. Such corporations also developed cozy relationships with local, state, and federal government officials, a process of buying influence ("lobbying") that continues to this day. Big Business has legitimate political interests, but because of its size and resources, it also sometimes exercises a corrupt influence on government. Never was this conflicting role more evident than during the decades after the Civil War. The *New York Times* noted that the largest "unprincipled" corporations "control the Legislatures."

Federal and Republican Support for Business

High tariffs on imported goods

During and after the Civil War, the Republican party and the U.S. government grew increasingly allied with Big Business. A key element of this alliance was tariff policy, one of the most important political issues throughout the nineteenth century. Since 1789, the federal government had imposed tariffs—taxes on imported goods—both to raise revenue and to benefit American manufacturers, by forcing their foreign competitors to pay tariffs to get their products into American markets. Those tariffs, in turn, led foreign manufacturers to raise the prices on their products, thereby making them less competitive with American goods. In 1861, as the Civil War was starting, the Republican-dominated Congress enacted the Morrill Tariff, which doubled the tax rates on hundreds of imported items as a means of raising money for the war and of rewarding the businesses that supported Abraham Lincoln and the Republican party.

After the war, President Ulysses S. Grant and later Republican presidents and Congresses continued the party's commitment to high tariffs despite complaints that the tariffs increased consumer prices by restricting foreign imports and thereby relieving American manufacturers of the need to keep their prices down to be competitive. Farmers in the South and Midwest especially resented federal tariffs because they had to sell their crops in an open world market but had to buy manufactured goods whose prices were artificially high because of tariffs. Farmers and other advocates of "free world trade," including most southern Democrats, generally wanted Congress to lower or eliminate tariffs.

CELEBRATING BIG BUSINESS A lavish dinner celebrated the merger of the Carnegie and Morgan interests in 1901. The shape of the banquet table is meant to symbolize a steel rail.

During the Civil War, the Republican-dominated Congress also passed other key pieces of legislation related to the economy. The Legal Tender Act of 1862 for the first time authorized the federal government to issue paper money to help pay for the war. The new national paper currency was called "greenbacks" because of its green color. Having a uniform *national* paper currency rather than a hodgepodge of paper money issued by numerous state banks was essential to a modern economy. To that end, the National Banking Act (1863) created new national banks authorized to issue greenbacks, which discouraged state banks from continuing to issue their own paper money.

At the same time, Congress also took steps to tie the new states and territories of the West into the national economy. The U.S. government owned vast amounts of western land, most of it acquired from the Louisiana Purchase of 1803, the Oregon Treaty with Britain in 1846, and the lands taken from Mexico in 1848 after the Mexican-American War. In the Homestead Act of 1862, Congress provided free 160-acre homesteads to settlers on this western land. By encouraging widespread western settlement, the Homestead Act promoted economic growth by creating new markets for goods and services and spurring railroad construction to connect scattered frontier communities with major cities.

HOMESTEADERS An African American family poses outside their log and sod cabin in 1889. **Why did Congress adopt initiatives such as the Homestead Act, which offered settlers federally owned land for free?**

Introduction of national paper currency and land grants for homesteads and technical colleges

The Morrill Land-Grant College Act of the same year transferred to each state 30,000 acres of federal land for each member of Congress the state had. The sale of those lands provided funds for states to create colleges of "agriculture and mechanic arts," such as Iowa State University and Kansas State University. The new land-grant universities were created specifically to support economic growth by providing technical training needed by farmers as well as by rapidly growing industries such as mining, steel, petroleum, transportation, forestry, and construction (engineering). As already noted, congressional authorization for construction of the first transcontinental railroad and generous federal subsidies, loans, and land grants for the project provided additional boosts to the nation's economic development.

Laissez-Faire Theory and Corrupt Practices

Equally important in propelling the postwar economic boom was what government did *not* do. It did not regulate the activities of big businesses in any significant way or impose high corporate taxes, nor did it provide any meaningful oversight of business operations or working conditions for

Government's laissez-faire approach to business

laissez-faire An economic doctrine holding that businesses and individuals should be able to pursue their economic interests without government interference.

wage earners. In general, both Congress and the presidents in this period accepted the traditional economic doctrine of **laissez-faire**, a French phrase meaning "let them do as they will," which opposed government interference in the economy. Business leaders spent time—and money—ensuring that government officials did not regulate their businesses. For their part, members of Congress as well as state legislators were usually eager to help the new titans of industry and finance in exchange for campaign contributions and, often, direct bribes for looking the other way.

CORE **OBJECTIVE**

4. Analyze the ways in which the social class structure and the lives of women changed in the late nineteenth century.

A Changed Social Order

During the late nineteenth century, industrialization transformed not only the economy and the workplace; it also transformed social life. Tensions between the social classes became more visible. The growing gap between rich and poor was like "social dynamite," said the Reverend Josiah Strong in 1885. The Massachusetts reformer Lydia Maria Child noticed with alarm the growing class consciousness in America. The rich, she reported, "do not intermarry with the middle classes; the middle classes do not intermarry with the laboring class," nor did different classes "mix socially."

The Ways of the Wealthy

The Gilded Age

During the Gilded Age, the share of the nation's wealth owned by the richest 10 percent of families tripled, to more than three fourths in 1900. In 1861, there were only a few dozen millionaires in the United States. By 1900, there were over 4,000. Most of them were white Protestants who voted Republican, except for the small number of wealthy southern Democrats.

The financiers and industrialists who dominated social, economic, and political life in post–Civil War America amassed such fabulous wealth and showed it off so publicly that the period is still called the Gilded Age. The name came from a popular novel by Mark Twain and Charles Dudley Warner, *The Gilded Age: A Tale of Today* (1872), which mocked the crooked dealing of political leaders and the lavish wealth of the business elite, often called "robber barons" by their critics. To "gild" something is to cover it with a thin layer of gold, giving it the appearance of having greater value than it warranted.

Many of the *nouveaux riches* (French for "newly rich") indulged in what came

NOUVEAUX RICHES Upper-class members of New York City society pose for a photograph at the James Hazen Hyde Ball on January 31, 1905. **What were some common characteristics of the *nouveaux riches*?**

to be called "conspicuous consumption," competing with each other to host the fanciest parties and live in the largest and most extravagantly furnished houses. In 1869, E. L. Godkin, the editor of the *Nation* magazine, wrote that New York City was being flooded by rich "barbarians." One tycoon gave a lavish dinner honoring his dog and presented it with a $15,000 diamond necklace. At a party at New York's Delmonico's restaurant, the guests smoked cigarettes wrapped in $100 bills.

A Growing Middle Class

It was left to the fast-growing middle class to practice the traditional virtues of self-discipline and restraint, simplicity and frugality. The term *middle class* had first appeared in the 1830s and had become commonplace by the 1870s, as more and more Americans came to view themselves as members of a distinct social class between the ragged and the rich. The middle class, explained the Chicago writer George Ade in an 1895 essay, "The Advantage of Being 'Middle Class,'" meant those people who "are neither poverty-stricken nor offensively rich."

> Rise of white middle-class professionals

Most middle-class Americans working outside the home were salaried employees of large businesses, people making up a new class of "white-collar" professionals: editors, engineers, accountants, supervisors, managers, marketers, and realtors. Others, with women a growing share of the total, were clerks, secretaries, salespeople, and government employees, including teachers and librarians. At the same time, the number of attorneys, physicians, professors, journalists, nurses, and social workers rose dramatically. The number of women working for wages outside the home tripled between 1870 and 1900, when 5 million women (17 percent of all women) held full-time jobs. This development led one male editor to joke that he was being drowned "by the rising tide of femininity" in the workplace.

Middle-Class Women The growing middle-class female presence in the workforce partly reflected the increasing number of women who were gaining access to higher education. Dozens of women's colleges were founded after the Civil War, and many formerly all-male colleges became "co-ed" by admitting women. By 1900, in fact, a third of college students were women. To be sure, college women were often steered into home economics classes and "finishing" courses intended to perfect their housekeeping or social skills. Still, the doors of the professions—law, medicine, science, and the arts—were at least partially opened during the Gilded Age.

> Women admitted to colleges and professional jobs

In this context, then, the "woman question" that created so much public discussion and controversy in the second half of the nineteenth century involved far more than the issue of voting rights; it also concerned the liberation of at least some women from the home and from long-standing limits on their social roles. In addition to new jobs and professions, middle-class women took advantage of other, often new public venues for female interaction: charitable associations, women's clubs, literary societies, and church work. "If there is one thing that pervades and characterizes what is called the

> The "woman question"

COLLEGE WOMEN By the end of the century, women made up more than a third of all college students. Here, an astronomy class at New York's Vassar College is under way in 1880.

'woman's movement,'" E. L. Youmans, a prominent editor and writer, remarked, "it is the spirit of revolt against the home, and the determination to escape from it into the outer spheres of activity."

Neurasthenia Yet such determination to escape the cult of domesticity often came at a high price. Many women who wanted to play a more active role in the public world contracted a peculiar affliction called *neurasthenia*, an energy-draining psychological and physical disorder whose symptoms usually included insomnia, hysteria, headaches, depression, and a general state of fatigue. Although neurasthenia plagued both sexes, it most often affected college-educated middle-class women. Some prominent men tried to use this finding to force women back into the cult of domesticity. George M. Beard, a prominent neurologist who popularized the term *neurasthenia*, concluded—incorrectly—that women were "more nervous, immeasurably, than men" and that female neurasthenics tended to be women who had become "overly active" outside the home. This association of neurasthenia with independence led one doctor to insist that the malady provided the best "argument against higher education of women."

Many prominent women understandably objected to such self-serving male arguments. Charlotte Perkins Gilman, for instance, intended her short story "The Yellow Wallpaper" as a piece of "pure propaganda" to expose the horrors of the "rest cure" she was subjected to at age twenty-seven. A doctor had ordered her to "live as domestic a life as possible; have your child with you all the time; lie down an hour after each meal; have but two hours intellectual life a day; and *never touch pencil, brush, or pen as long as you live.*" This regimen, Gilman explained, took her "near lunacy."

Social worker Jane Addams also struggled with neurasthenia. After graduating in 1881 from Rockford College in Illinois, she found few opportunities to use her degree and lapsed into a state of depression during which she developed an intense "desire to live in a really *living* world." Middle-class women, she charged, were "so besotted with our [sentimental] novel reading that we have lost the power of seeing certain aspects of life with any sense of reality because we are continually looking for the possible romance."

Addams's intense desire to engage "real life" eventually led her to found Hull House, the famous "settlement house" in Chicago. There, she and other social workers helped immigrants make the transition to American life, and young women like herself "could learn of life from life itself" rather than from books.

The examples of Addams and others helped convince many middle-class women to enter the "real" world. By 1890, the *Arena* magazine could urge progressive-minded readers to recognize the traditional view of women as homebodies for what it was: "hollow, false, and unreal."

JANE ADDAMS The founder of Hull House, a settlement house to ease young women into the nondomestic world, Addams believed that social service requires a "scientific" observation of one's community in order to "see the needs" and provide "data for legislation" to reform abuses.

The Working Class

The continuing demand for unskilled workers by railroads, factories, mills, mines, slaughterhouses, and sweatshops attracted new groups to the workforce: immigrants above all but also growing numbers of women and children. In addition, millions of rural folk, especially young people, gave up farming and formed a fast-growing migratory stream from the agricultural regions of the South and Midwest to the cities.

Although wage levels rose overall during the Gilded Age, there was a great disparity between the pay for skilled and unskilled workers. During the economic recessions and depressions that occurred about every six years on average, the unskilled workers were the first to be laid off or to have their wages slashed. In addition, working conditions were difficult and often dangerous for those at the bottom of the occupational scale. The average workweek during the late nineteenth century was fifty-nine hours, or nearly six ten-hour days. Most steelworkers put in a twelve-hour day.

American industry had the highest rate of workplace accidents and deaths in the world, and there were virtually no safety regulations or government inspections. Few machines had safety devices; few factories or mills had fire escapes. Respiratory diseases were common in mines, textile mills, cigarette factories, and unventilated buildings. In the seven years between 1888 and 1894, 16,000 railroad workers were killed and 170,000 maimed in on-the-job accidents. The United States was the only industrial nation with no insurance program to cover medical expenses for on-the-job injuries.

Difficult, "unskilled" labor for working-class women

Working Women The Second Industrial Revolution transformed the nature of the workplace in ways that meant that mills, mines, factories, and large businesses needed far more unskilled workers than skilled ones. To fill these jobs, employers recruited women and children for many of the unskilled jobs because they were willing to work for lower wages than men. In addition to those laboring over typewriters, sewing machines, or textile looms, millions of women worked as maids, cooks, or other domestic laborers. In the manufacturing sector, women's wages averaged $7 a week, compared to $10 for unskilled men. A social worker sent to investigate working conditions for women reported that it was widely assumed in many factory settings that a married woman would accept lower wages because she "has a man to support her" (which was by no means always true).

Child labor

Child Labor After the Civil War, a growing number of wage laborers were children who worked full-time for meager wages in often unhealthy conditions. Most young people had always worked in America; farms required everyone to pitch in. After the Civil War, however, millions of children took up work outside the home or off the farm, sorting coal, stitching clothes, shucking oysters, peeling shrimp, canning food, blowing glass, tending looms in textile mills, and operating other kinds of machinery. By 1880, one of every six children under age fourteen in the nation was working full-time; by 1900, the United States had almost 2 million child laborers.

In New England and the South, thousands of children worked in dusty textile mills where, during the night shift, they had water thrown in

CHILDREN IN INDUSTRY These four young boys performed the dangerous work of mine helpers in West Virginia around 1900.

their faces to keep them awake. In the southern mills, a fourth of the employees were below the age of fifteen, and children as young as eight were laboring alongside adults, often working twelve hours a day, six days a week. As a result, they received little or no education. Factories, mills, mines, and canneries were especially dangerous places for children, who suffered three times as many accidents as adult workers and higher rates of respiratory diseases as well. A child working in a southern textile mill was only half as likely to reach the age of twenty as a child who did not work in a mill.

Organized Labor

CORE **OBJECTIVE**

5. Assess the efforts of workers to organize unions to promote their interests during this era.

During the Gilded Age, thousands of wage workers struggled to organize unions in an effort to force employers to recognize their needs and concerns. It was not easy, however. Most elected officials sided with business owners rather than workers. Another factor impeding the growth of labor unions was that much of the workforce was made up of immigrants who spoke different languages and often distrusted those from other ethnic groups.

Nonetheless, with or without unions, workers during the Gilded Age began to stage frequent strikes in response to wage cuts and other grievances. Strikes often turned violent. Perhaps at no time before or since have class tensions—both social and cultural—been as bitter as they were during the last quarter of the nineteenth century.

The Great Railroad Strike of 1877

After the financial panic of 1873, the major rail lines in the East cut the wages of their workers. In 1877, the companies announced another 10 percent wage cut, which led most of the railroad workers at Martinsburg, West Virginia, to walk off the job and block the tracks in order to shut down all traffic.

The Great Railroad Strike of 1877 spread quickly to hundreds of other cities and towns, and the resulting violence left more than 100 people dead and millions of dollars in damaged property. In Pittsburgh, thousands of striking workers burned thirty-nine buildings and destroyed more than 1,000 rail cars and locomotives. State militiamen called in from Philadelphia dispersed a crowd at the cost of twenty-six lives, but looting and burning continued until federal troops finally ended it. Eventually, the disgruntled workers, lacking organized bargaining power, had little choice but to drift back to work. The strike failed.

For many Americans, the Great Railroad Strike raised the possibility of what a Pittsburgh newspaper saw as "a great civil war in this country between labor and capital." Equally disturbing to those in positions of corporate and political power was the presence of many women among the protesters. A Baltimore journalist noted that the "singular part of the disturbances is the very active part taken by the women, who are the wives and mothers of the [railroad] firemen."

"THE CHINESE MUST GO"
In this advertisement for the Missouri Steam Washer, the American-made machine drives the stereotype of the Chinese laundryman back to China, playing on the growing anti-Chinese sentiments in the 1880s.

The Sandlot Incident

In California, the national railroad strike indirectly gave rise to a working-class political movement. In 1877, a meeting held in a vacant lot in San Francisco to express sympathy for the railroad strikers ended with attacks on passing Chinese workers. In the aftermath of the so-called Sandlot Incident, white mobs attacked Chinatown, home to 25,000 Chinese, mostly males, who experienced the worst forms of discrimination and segregation. The depression of the 1870s had hit the West Coast especially hard, and the Chinese were handy scapegoats for frustrated white laborers who believed the Asians had taken their jobs.

Soon an Irish immigrant, Denis Kearney, had organized the Workingmen's Party of California, whose platform called for the United States to stop Chinese immigration. A gifted agitator who had only recently become a naturalized American, Kearney lectured the "sand-lotters" about the "foreign peril" and blasted the rich railroad barons for exploiting the poor. The Workingmen's movement peaked in 1879, when its candidates were elected as state legislators and as mayor of San Francisco. Although Kearney failed to build a lasting movement, his anti-Chinese theme became a national issue. In 1882, Congress voted to prohibit Chinese immigration for ten years.

> The Workingmen's Party of California

Toward Permanent Unions

As the size and power of corporations increased during the second half of the nineteenth century, efforts to build a national labor union movement gained momentum. During the Civil War, because of the increased demand for skilled labor, so-called craft unions, made up of workers skilled in a particular handicraft or trade, grew in strength and number. Yet there was no overall connection among such groups until 1866, when the National Labor Union (NLU) convened in Baltimore.

The NLU was more interested in advocating for new state and local laws to improve workplace conditions than in bargaining with employers about wages and hours. It advocated improvements such as the eight-hour workday, workers' cooperatives (in which workers, collectively, would create and own their own large-scale manufacturing and mining operations), "greenbackism" (the printing of paper money to inflate the currency and thereby relieve debtors), and equal voting rights for women and African Americans. Like most such organizations in the nineteenth century, however, the NLU did not allow women as members. As one official explained the attitude of male unionists, "Woman was created to be man's companion," not his competitor in the workplace who would cause his wages to fall.

After William Sylvis, the head of the NLU, died suddenly in 1869 at the age of forty-one, its support fell away, and by 1872 the union had disbanded. The NLU was not a total failure, however. It was influential in persuading Congress to enact an eight-hour workday for federal employees and to repeal the 1864 Contract Labor Act, which was passed during the Civil War to encourage the importation of laborers through an arrangement, similar to the indentured servitude of colonial times, that allowed employers to pay for the passage of foreign workers to America; in exchange, the immigrants were committed to work for a specified number of years. Employers had taken advantage of the Contract Labor Act to recruit foreign laborers willing to work for lower wages than their American counterparts.

Knights of Labor A national labor organization with a broad reform platform; reached peak membership in the 1880s.

The Knights of Labor

In 1869, another labor group of national standing had emerged: the Noble Order of the **Knights of Labor**. The union grew slowly at first, but even as other unions collapsed during the depression of the 1870s, it spread more rapidly. The Knights of Labor endorsed the reforms advanced by previous workingmen's groups, including the creation of a bureau of labor statistics and mechanics' lien laws (to ensure payment of wages), the elimination of convict-labor competition, the establishment of the eight-hour work day and worker cooperatives, and greater use of paper currency. One plank in the platform, far ahead of the times, called for equal pay for equal work by men and women.

Throughout its existence, the Knights of Labor condemned violence, class warfare, and socialism, preferring boycotts to strikes as a

KNIGHTS OF LABOR This national union was the most egalitarian union during the Gilded Age.

way to pressure employers. The Knights allowed as members all who had ever worked for wages, except lawyers, doctors, bankers, and those who sold liquor. Theoretically, it was one big union of all workers, skilled and unskilled, men and women, immigrants and African Americans.

Rise of the Knights of Labor and Terence V. Powderly

In 1879, Terence V. Powderly, the thirty-year-old mayor of Scranton, Pennsylvania, became head of the Knights of Labor. Born of Irish immigrant parents, Powderly had started working for a railroad at age sixteen. Frail, sensitive to criticism, and indecisive at critical moments, he was in many ways unsuited to his new job. He was temperamentally opposed to strikes, and when they did occur, he did not always support the local groups involved. Yet the Knights owed their greatest growth to strikes that occurred under his leadership. In the early 1880s, the Knights increased their membership from about 100,000 to more than 700,000.

Anarchism

One of the many challenges facing the labor union movement was growing hostility from middle-class Americans who viewed unionized workers, especially those involved in clashes with police, as "radicals" or "anarchists." Anarchists believed that government—any government—was a device used by powerful capitalists to oppress the working poor. They dreamed of the eventual disappearance of government altogether, and some were willing to use bombs and bullets to achieve their revolutionary goal. Many European anarchists immigrated to the United States during the last quarter of the nineteenth century. Although most anarchists disavowed violence, the terrorists among them ensured that the label "anarchist" provoked frightening images in the minds of many Americans.

Labor-related violence increased during the 1880s as the gap between the rich and working poor widened. Between 1880 and 1900, 6.6 million hourly workers participated in more than 23,000 strikes nationwide. Chicago, the fastest-growing city in the nation, was a hotbed of labor unrest and a magnet for immigrants, especially German and Irish laborers, some of whom were socialists or anarchists who endorsed violence as a means of transforming the capitalist system. The Chicago labor movement's foremost demand was for an eight-hour workday, and what came to be called the **Haymarket Riot** grew indirectly out of prolonged agitation for this goal.

The Haymarket Riot

In May 1886, some 40,000 Chicago workers went on strike in support of an eight-hour workday. On May 3, violent clashes between strikers and "scabs" (nonunion workers who defied the strike) erupted outside the McCormick Harvesting Machine plant, where farm equipment was made. The police arrived, shots rang out, and two strikers were killed. The killings infuriated the leaders of the tiny anarchist movement in Chicago, which included many women. They printed leaflets demanding "Revenge!" and "Workingmen, to

Haymarket Riot (1886) Violent uprising in Haymarket Square, Chicago, where police clashed with labor demonstrators in the aftermath of a bombing.

Arms!" Calls went out for a mass protest the following night at Haymarket Square.

On the evening of May 4, after listening to long speeches complaining about low wages and long working hours, the crowd in Haymarket Square was beginning to break up when police arrived and ordered the workers to disperse. At that point, someone threw a bomb toward the police. The police then fired into the crowd, killing and wounding people, including other police. Throughout the night, police arrested scores of people. The next day, all labor meetings were banned in the city, and newspapers across the nation printed sensational headlines about anarchists terrorizing Chicago. One New York paper demanded stern punishment for "the few long-haired, wild-eyed, bad-smelling, atheistic, reckless foreign wretches" who promoted such unrest.

At trials during the summer of 1886, seven anarchist leaders, all but one of them German-language speakers, were sentenced to death despite the lack of any evidence linking them to the bomb thrower, whose identity was never established. In a statement to the court after being sentenced to be hanged, Louis Lingg declared that he was innocent of the bombing but was proud to be an anarchist who was "in favor of using force" to attack the abuses of the capitalist system.

Lawyers for the anarchists appealed the convictions to the Illinois Supreme Court. Meanwhile, petitions from around the world arrived at the Illinois governor's office appealing for clemency. One of the petitioners was Samuel Gompers, the founding president of the American Federation of Labor (AFL), which would soon replace the faltering Knights of Labor as the nation's leading union. "I abhor anarchy," Gompers stressed, "but I also abhor injustice when meted out even to the most despicable being on earth."

On November 10, 1887, Louis Lingg committed suicide in his cell. That same day, the governor commuted the sentences of two of the convicted conspirators to life imprisonment. The next day the four remaining condemned men were hanged. Two hundred thousand people lined the streets of Chicago as their caskets were taken for burial. To labor militants around the world, the executed anarchists were working-class martyrs; to the police and the economic elite in Chicago, they were demonic assassins. In his novel *The Titan*, Theodore Dreiser wrote that the Haymarket Riot "had brought to the

THE HAYMARKET RIOT A leaflet advertising the protest at Haymarket Square in Chicago, an event that would be remembered as the Haymarket Riot. **Why is the leaflet written in both English and German?**

American Federation of Labor
Founded in 1886 as a national federation of trade unions made up of skilled workers.

fore, once and for all, as by a flash of lightning, the whole problem of mass against class."

The Decline of the Knights of Labor

After the Haymarket Riot, tensions between workers and management reached a fever pitch across the nation. In 1886 alone, there were 1,400 strikes across the country involving 700,000 workers. But the violence in Chicago had triggered widespread public hostility to the Knights of Labor and labor groups in general. Despite his best efforts, Terence Powderly could never separate in the public mind the Knights from the anarchists, since one of those convicted of conspiracy in the bombing was a member of the union.

Powderly clung to leadership until 1893, but after that the union evaporated. Besides fear of its supposed radicalism and the failure of a railroad strike in 1886, membership in the Knights also declined because its leaders spent more time promoting national reforms than focusing on better wages and working conditions.

The Knights nevertheless attained some lasting achievements, among them an 1880 federal law providing for the arbitration of labor disputes and the creation of the federal Bureau of Labor Statistics in 1884 as well as several state labor bureaus. Another of their successes was the Foran Act of 1885, which, though poorly enforced, penalized employers who imported immigrant workers so that they could pay lower wages. And, by their example, the Knights also spread the idea of unionism and initiated a new type of union organization: the industrial union, which included all skilled and unskilled workers within a particular industry, such as railroad workers or miners.

Gompers and the AFL

The craft or trade unions, representing skilled workers, generally opposed efforts to unite with industrial unionism. Leaders of the craft unions feared that joining with unskilled laborers would mean a loss of their craft's identity and a loss of skilled workers' greater bargaining power. Thus, in 1886, delegates from twenty-five craft unions meeting in Columbus, Ohio, organized the **American Federation of Labor** (AFL). Its structure differed from that of the Knights of Labor in that it was a federation of many separate national unions, each of which was largely free to act on its own in dealing with business owners.

Samuel Gompers served as president of the AFL from its founding until his death, in 1924. Born in England of Dutch Jewish ancestry, Gompers came to the United States as a teenager, joined the Cigarmakers' Union in 1864, and became president of his New York City local union in 1877. Unlike Terence Powderly and the Knights of Labor, Gompers focused on concrete economic gains—higher wages, shorter hours, better working conditions—and avoided utopian ideas.

SAMUEL GOMPERS The head of the American Federation of Labor strikes an assertive pose.

The AFL at first grew slowly, but by 1890 it had surpassed the Knights of Labor in membership. By the turn of the century, it claimed 500,000 members in affiliated unions; in 1914, on the eve of World War I, it had 2 million; and in 1920 it reached a peak of 4 million. But even then the AFL embraced less than 15 percent of the nation's nonagricultural workers. In fact, all unions, including the railroad brotherhoods unaffiliated with the AFL, accounted for little more than 18 percent of those workers.

Formation of the American Federation of Labor (AFL)

Organized labor's strongholds were in transportation and the building trades. Most of the larger manufacturing industries—including steel, textiles, tobacco, and meatpacking—remained almost untouched. Gompers never opposed industrial unions and several became important affiliates of the AFL: the United Mine Workers, the International Ladies Garment Workers, and the Amalgamated Clothing Workers. But the AFL had its greatest success in organizing skilled workers.

Two incidents in the 1890s stalled the emerging industrial-union movement: the Homestead Steel Strike of 1892 and the Pullman Strike of 1894. These violent labor conflicts represented the climactic economic events of the Gilded Age. Each pitted workers in a bitter contest against one of the nation's largest and most influential corporations. The two strikes not only represented a test of strength for the organized labor movement but also served to reshape the political landscape.

The Homestead Steel Strike

The Amalgamated Association of Iron and Steel Workers, founded in 1876, was the largest craft union. At the massive iron and steel mill at Homestead, Pennsylvania, near Pittsburgh, the union had enjoyed friendly relations with Andrew Carnegie's company until the stern Henry Clay Frick became company chairman and chief executive in 1889. Frick prided himself on being the most anti-labor executive in the nation. A showdown was delayed until 1892, however, when the union contract came up for renewal. Carnegie, who had previously expressed sympathy for unions, went on a lengthy hunting trip in his native Scotland, leaving the rigid Frick to handle the difficult negotiations. Carnegie knew what was in the works: a cost-cutting reduction in the number of highly paid skilled workers through the use of labor-saving machinery. It was a deliberate attempt to smash the union. "Am with you to the end," he wrote to Frick after leaving for Scotland. He was "sure [Frick would] win."

As negotiations dragged on, the company announced on June 25 that it would stop negotiating with the union in four days unless an agreement was reached. The **Homestead Steel Strike**—or, more properly, a lockout of unionists, in which management closed down the mill to try to force the union to make concessions—began on that date. Frick told journalists that he was determined to have "absolute control of our plant and business." To that end, he built a twelve-foot-high fence around the plant and equipped it with watchtowers, searchlights, barbed wire, rifle slits, and high-pressure water cannons. He also hired a private army of 316 men from the Pinkerton

Homestead Steel Strike (1892) Labor conflict at the Homestead steel mill near Pittsburgh, Pennsylvania, culminating in a battle between strikers and private security agents hired by the factory's management.

HOMESTEAD STEEL STRIKE Three days before the Pinkertons arrived on barges, a Minnesota newspaper printed this biting satire of Carnegie, depicting him reclining on a stack of money atop his barricaded steel plant. In the caption below, Carnegie says to Frick, "Close the works and crush these people."

Detective Agency to protect what he called "Fort Frick." Before dawn on July 6, 1892, the "Pinkertons" floated up the Monongahela River on two barges pulled by a tugboat.

Thousands of unionists and supporters, many of them armed, were waiting on shore. A fourteen-hour gun battle broke out in which seven workers and four Pinkertons were killed and dozens wounded. Hundreds of women on shore shouted, "Kill the Pinkertons!" In the end, the Pinkertons surrendered, having agreed to be tried for murder, and were marched away to taunts from crowds lining the streets.

But the celebrations were short-lived. A week later, the Pennsylvania governor dispatched 8,000 state militiamen to Homestead, where they surrounded the steel mill and dispersed the picketing workers. Frick then hired strikebreakers to operate the mill. He refused to resume negotiations: "I will never recognize the union, never, never!"

The strike dragged on until November, but by then the union was dead and its leaders had been charged with murder and treason. The union cause was not helped when Alexander Berkman, a Lithuanian anarchist, tried to assassinate Frick in his office on July 23, shooting him twice in the neck and stabbing him three times. Despite his wounds, Frick fought back fiercely and, with the help of staff members, subdued the would-be assassin. Much of the local sympathy for the strikers evaporated. As a union leader explained, Berkman's bullets "went straight through the heart of the Homestead strike."

Penniless and demoralized, the defeated workers ended their walkout on November 20 and accepted the company's harsh wage cuts. Only a fifth of the strikers got their jobs back; the rest were "blacklisted" to prevent other steel mills from hiring them. Carnegie and Frick, with the support of local, state, and national government officials, had eliminated the union. But Carnegie's reputation was ruined. "Three months ago Andrew Carnegie was a man to be envied," wrote a St. Louis newspaper. "Today he is an object of mingled pity and contempt." The editor called him a "moral coward." A "single word from him [in Scotland] might have saved the bloodshed—but the word was never spoken."

The Pullman Strike

The **Pullman Strike** of 1894 was an even more notable confrontation between workers and management, as it paralyzed the economies of the twenty-seven states and territories making up the western half of the nation. It involved a dispute at Pullman, Illinois, a "model" industrial suburb of Chicago owned by the Pullman Palace Car Company, which made passenger train cars (called "Pullmans" or "sleeping cars").

Employees who built rail cars were required to live in the town's 1,400 cottages, which had been built to high standards, with gas heat and indoor plumbing. With 12,000 residents, the town of Pullman also boasted a library, theater, school, church, parks, playgrounds, and glass-roofed shopping mall owned by the company. There were no saloons, however, nor any social clubs, newspapers, or private property not owned by the company. No political activities, including election of local officials, were allowed.

During the terrible depression of 1893, George Pullman laid off 3,000 of his 5,800 employees and cut wages 25–40 percent for the rest, but he did not lower rents for housing or the price of food in the company store. In the spring of 1894, desperate workers joined the American Railway Union, founded the previous year by Eugene V. Debs.

The charismatic Debs was a child of working-class immigrants who had quit school at age fourteen to work for an Indiana railroad. By the early 1890s, he had become a tireless spokesman for labor radicalism, and he strove to organize all railway workers—skilled or unskilled—into the American Railway Union, which soon became a powerful labor organization. He quickly turned his attention to the Pullman controversy, urging the workers to obey the laws and avoid violence. After George Pullman fired

Pullman Strike (1894)
A national strike by the American Railway Union, whose members shut down major railways in sympathy with striking workers in Pullman, Illinois; ended with intervention of federal troops.

EUGENE V. DEBS Founder of the American Railway Union and later the presidential candidate for the Socialist Party of America, Debs mobilized the railroad workers to strike against Pullman.

THE PULLMAN STRIKE Federal troops guarding the railroads, 1894.

three members of a workers' grievance committee, the workers went on strike on May 11, 1894.

In June, after Pullman refused Debs's plea for a negotiated settlement, the Railway Union workers stopped handling trains containing Pullman rail cars. By the end of July, they had shut down most of the railroads in the Midwest, cutting off all traffic through Chicago. To keep the trains running, railroad executives hired strikebreakers, and the U.S. attorney general, a former lawyer for railroad companies, swore in 3,400 special deputies to protect them. Angry workers assaulted strikebreakers and destroyed property.

Finally, on July 3, President Grover Cleveland sent 2,000 federal troops into the Chicago area, claiming it was his duty to ensure delivery of the mail. Meanwhile, the attorney general convinced a federal judge to sign an "injunction," an official court decree, prohibiting the labor union from interfering with the delivery of mail and interstate commerce. On July 13, the union called off the strike. A few days later, a judge cited Debs for violating the injunction, and he served six months in jail.

The Supreme Court upheld the decree in the case of *In re Debs* (1895) on broad grounds of national sovereignty: "The strong arm of the national government may be put forth to brush away all obstructions to the freedom of interstate commerce or the transportation of the mails." Debs emerged from jail as a socialist who would later run for president. In 1897, George Pullman died of a heart attack, and the following year, the city of Chicago annexed the town of Pullman. A reporter for the *Nation* noted that despite the town's attractive features, what the workers wanted most was the chance to own a house of their own. "Mr. Pullman," he explained, "overlooked this peculiar American characteristic."

Economic Success and Excess

For all the stress and strain caused by the industrialization of the American economy, the nation's productivity soared in the late nineteenth century. By 1900, the United States was producing a third of the world's goods. The corporate empires developed by a generation of outsized business leaders created enormous fortunes for a few and real improvements in the quality of life of the many.

The majority of American workers for the first time now labored in factories and mines rather than on farms. "One can hardly believe," observed the philosopher John Dewey, "there has been a revolution in history so rapid, so extensive, so complete." The urban-industrial revolution had transformed the size, scope, and power of the American economy, for good and for ill. As the twentieth century dawned, an unregulated capitalist economy had gotten recklessly out of balance—and only government intervention could restore economic fairness and social stability.

Reviewing the
CORE OBJECTIVES | INQUIZITIVE

■ **The Causes of Industrial Growth**
During the late nineteenth century, agricultural and industrial production increased sharply. The national railroad network increased to nearly 200,000 miles, the most of any nation in the world. Farmers and industrialists expanded their production for both national and international markets. The *Second Industrial Revolution* saw the expanded use of electrical power, the application of scientific research to industrial processes, and other commercial innovations that brought new products to market and improved methods for producing and distributing them.

■ **The Rise of Big Business** Many businesses transformed themselves into limited-liability corporations and grew to enormous size and power in this period, often ignoring ethics and the law in doing so. Leading entrepreneurs like John D. Rockefeller, Andrew Carnegie, and J. Pierpont Morgan were extraordinarily skilled at organizing and gaining control of particular industries. Companies such as Rockefeller's *Standard Oil* and *Carnegie Steel* practiced both vertical and horizontal integration. To consolidate their holdings and get around laws prohibiting *monopolies*, they created *trusts* and eventually *holding companies* in an effort to bring "order and stability" to the marketplace. *J. Pierpont Morgan and Company*, the largest of the new "investment banks" focused on raising capital to enable mega-mergers of large companies.

■ **The Alliance of Business and Politics** The federal government encouraged economic growth after the Civil War by imposing high tariffs on imported products, granting public land to railroad companies and settlers in the West, establishing a stable currency, and encouraging the creation of land-grant universities to spur technical innovation and research. Equally important, local, state, and federal governments made little effort to regulate the activities of businesses. This *laissez-faire* policy allowed entrepreneurs to experiment with new methods of organization but also created the conditions for rampant corruption and abuses.

■ **A Changed Social Order** The huge fortunes of the Gilded Age flowed to a few prominent families, and social class tensions worsened as productivity increased. Business owners and managers showed little concern for workplace safety, and accidents and work-related diseases were common. Industrialization and the rise of Big Business also increased the number of people considering themselves part of the middle class. Middle-class women increasingly went to college, took business and professional jobs, and participated in other public activities despite male resistance.

■ **Organized Labor** It was difficult for unskilled workers to organize effectively into unions, in part because of racial and ethnic tensions among laborers, language barriers, and the efforts of owners and supervisors to undermine unionizing efforts. Business owners often hired strikebreakers, usually immigrant workers who were willing to take jobs at the prevailing wage because they were so desperate for a job. Business owners often relied on the support of political leaders, who would mobilize state and local militias and federal troops against strikers. Nevertheless, several unions did organize and advocate for workers' rights at a national level, including the National Labor Union and the *Knights of Labor*. After the violence associated with the *Haymarket Riot (1886)*, the *Homestead Steel Strike (1892)* and *Pullman Strike (1894)*, many Americans grew fearful of unions and viewed them as politically radical. Craft unions made up solely of skilled workers became more successful at organizing, such as the *American Federation of Labor*.

KEY TERMS

CHRONOLOGY

1859	First oil well is struck in Titusville, Pennsylvania
1861	Congress creates the Morrill Tariff
1869	First transcontinental railroad is completed
1876	Alexander Graham Bell patents his telephone
1876	Thomas A. Edison invents incandescent lightbulb
1880s	Widespread use of electrical power begins
1882	John D. Rockefeller organizes the Standard Oil Trust
1886	Haymarket Riot
1886	American Federation of Labor is organized
1892	Homestead Steel Strike
1894	Pullman Strike
1901	J. Pierpont Morgan creates the U.S. Steel Corporation

🐰 INQUIZITIVE

Go to InQuizitive to see what you've learned—and learn what you've missed—with personalized feedback along the way.

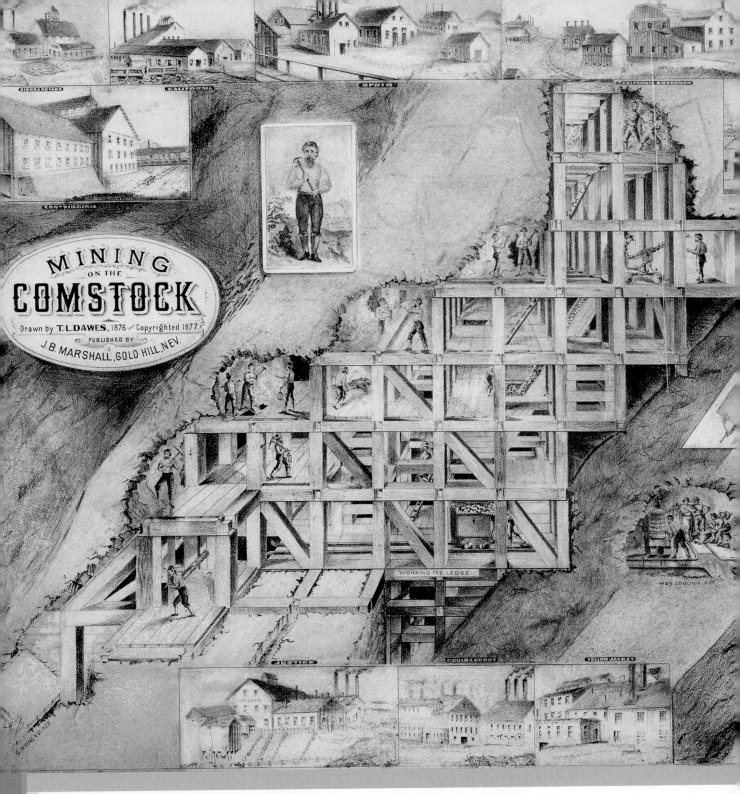

MINING ON THE COMSTOCK (1877) The Comstock Lode was one of the largest gold and silver mines to be discovered in America, yielding over $300 million over two decades. This illustration shows a cutaway of the Comstock Lode, revealing the complex network of shafts and supports as well as the various tasks of miners within its tunnels.

The South and the West Transformed

1865–1900

After the Civil War, the devastated South and the untamed West provided enticing frontiers for economic enterprise. The South had to be rebuilt, while the sparsely settled territories and states west of the Mississippi River were ripe for the development of farms, businesses, railroads, and towns. Banks and financiers in America and in Europe took advantage of these conditions to invest heavily in both regions but especially in the far western region between the Mississippi River and California.

Throughout the first half of the nineteenth century, people had viewed the Great Plains as a barren landscape suitable only for Indians. Half the state of Texas, for instance, remained unsettled at the end of the Civil War. After 1865, however, the federal government encouraged western settlement and economic development in what was then called "Indian Country." Two thirds of Native Americans in 1865 lived on the Great Plains, often warring with one another over rival "hunting rights" to the vast buffalo herds.

The construction of transcontinental railroads, the military conquest of the Indians, and the policy of distributing government-owned lands at low cost to settlers, ranchers, miners, and railroads combined to lure millions of pioneers and enterprising capitalists westward. Charles Goodnight, a Texas cattle rancher, recalled that "we were adventurers in a great land . . . fresh and full of the zest of darers." By 1900, a New West and a New South had emerged, and eleven new states had been created out of the western territories.

CORE OBJECTIVES InQuizitive

1. Analyze the ways in which a "New South" emerged in the late nineteenth century.

2. Describe the crop-lien system that emerged in the South, and explain how it shaped the region after the Civil War.

3. Explain how and why white southerners took away African Americans' right to vote and adopted "Jim Crow" segregation laws at the end of the nineteenth century.

4. Identify the various groups of migrants to the West after the Civil War and the reasons they went there.

5. Describe the experiences of miners, farmers, ranchers, and women in the West in the late nineteenth century.

6. Evaluate the impact on Native Americans of the federal government's policies in the West after the Civil War.

7. Describe how the South and West had changed by 1900.

CORE **OBJECTIVE**

1. Analyze the ways in which a "New South" emerged in the late nineteenth century.

The Myth of the New South

After the Civil War, the South fought an ideological civil war over the future of the region. Many white southerners embraced the "Lost Cause," a romanticized interpretation of the war that pictured the Confederates as noble, chivalrous defenders of the distinctive southern way of life against a tyrannical federal government headed by Abraham Lincoln. Southerners devastated by defeat found solace in a lingering nostalgia for the mythic Old South of white-columned plantations, white supremacy, and cotton-generated wealth produced by armies of enslaved blacks. As one southerner said, his native region remained "old-fashioned, medieval, provincial, worshipping the dead."

At the same time, no region has inspired a more tenacious *pride of place*, a localism anchored in family life enlivened by visions of a mythic past. Mississippi writer Eudora Welty once explained that in the South, "feelings are bound up with place." *Home* and *history* are two of the most revered words in southern life. Nineteenth-century southerners did not simply live in the present and dream of the future. They were forever glancing backward in the process of moving forward. As William Faulkner recognized in his novel *Intruder in the Dust* (1948), "The past isn't dead. It's not even past."

Other prominent southerners, however, looked more to the future. They called for a New South in which the region's predominantly agricultural economy would be diversified by an expanded industrial sector, and race relations would become harmonious.

The tireless champion of the New South ideal during the 1880s was Henry Woodfin Grady (1850–1889), the powerful editor of the *Atlanta Constitution* newspaper. In 1886, he told a New York City audience that there had been an Old South "of slavery and secession—that South is dead. There is now a New South of union and freedom—that South, thank God, is living, breathing, and growing every hour." The Old South, he added, "rested everything on slavery and agriculture, unconscious that these could neither give nor maintain healthy growth."

Grady saw the New South becoming "a perfect democracy" of small farms growing varied crops. This healthy agricultural sector would be complemented by new mills, factories, and cities. The postwar South, Grady claimed, held the promise of a real democracy, one no longer run by the planter aristocracy and no longer dependent upon cotton or slave labor. He imagined a New South with "a hundred farms for every plantation, fifty homes for every palace—and a diversified industry that meets the complex needs of this complex age."

Many southerners shared Henry Grady's vision of a New South dotted with new industries. The Confederacy, they concluded, had lost the war because it had relied too much upon King Cotton—and slavery. In the future, the New South must follow the North's example ("out-Yankee the Yankees")

A "New South"

and develop a strong industrial sector to go along with its agricultural foundation. Promoters of a New South also stressed that more-efficient farming, using the latest machinery and technical expertise, was essential in the still-backward South; that more widespread vocational training was urgently needed; and that racial harmony built upon the acceptance by blacks of white supremacy would provide a stable social environment for economic growth.

Developing a Textile Industry

The chief accomplishment of the New South was a dramatic expansion of the region's textile industry, which produced cotton thread, bedding, and clothing. From 1880 to 1900, the number of cotton mills grew from 161 to 400, the number of mill workers (most of whom were white, with women and children outnumbering men) increased fivefold, and the demand for cotton products went up eightfold.

Cotton fabrics

Thousands of dirt-poor farm folk—many of them children—rushed to take jobs in the new textile mills that blossomed after the war. Seventy percent of mill workers were under the age of twenty-one, and many were under the age of fourteen. A dawn-to-dusk job in a mill paying fifty cents a day "was much more interesting than one-horse farming," noted one worker, "because you can meet your bills." Those bills were usually paid to the mill owner, who provided ramshackle housing and basic supplies to the workers in his company village—for a fee. By 1900, the South had surpassed New England as the largest producer of cotton fabric in the nation.

The Tobacco Industry

Tobacco growing and cigarette production also soared. Essential to the revival of the tobacco industry was the Duke family of Durham, North Carolina. At the end of the Civil War, Washington Duke took his barnload of tobacco, dried it, and, with the help of his two sons, hitched two mules to his wagon and traveled across the state, selling tobacco in small pouches as he went. By 1872, the Dukes were producing 125,000 pounds of tobacco annually, and Washington Duke prepared to settle down and enjoy success.

Tobacco and cigarettes

Washington's son, James Buchanan "Buck" Duke, wanted even greater success, however. He spent lavishly on advertising schemes and perfected the mechanized mass production of cigarettes. Duke also undersold competitors in their own markets and cornered the supply of ingredients needed to make cigarettes. Eventually his primary competitors agreed to join forces with him, and in 1890 Duke brought most of them into the **American Tobacco Company**, which controlled nine tenths of the nation's cigarette production. A ferociously hard worker, Duke was well on his way to becoming one of the wealthiest and most powerful men in the nation. "I needed no vacation or time off," Duke explained. "There ain't a thrill in the world to compare with building a business and watching it grow before your eyes."

American Tobacco Company Business founded in 1890 by North Carolina's James Buchanan Duke, who combined the major tobacco manufacturers of the time, controlling 90 percent of the country's booming cigarette production.

SOUTHERN SMOKES Allen & Ginter was a major tobacco manufacturer that joined the American Tobacco Company. This advertisement, featuring black laborers in the tobacco fields, plays to the southern nostalgia for the "Old Dominion" before the Civil War.

Other New South Industries

Effective use of other natural resources helped revitalize the South along the Appalachian Mountain chain from West Virginia to Alabama. Coal production in the South (including West Virginia) grew from 5 million tons in 1875 to 49 million tons by 1900. At the southern end of the mountains, Birmingham, Alabama, sprang up during the 1870s in the shadow of Red Mountain, so named for its abundant iron ore, and boosters soon tagged the steelmaking city the "Pittsburgh of the South."

Urban and industrial expansion as well as rapid population growth created a need for housing, and after 1870 lumbering became the fastest growing industry in the South. Northern investors bought up vast forests of yellow pine and set about clear-cutting them and hauling the logs to new sawmills, where they were cut into lumber for the construction of homes and businesses. By 1900, lumber had surpassed textiles in annual economic value. Still, for all its advances, the South continued to lag behind the rest of the nation in industrial development.

The Redeemers

Henry Grady's vision of a New South celebrated the redeemers, the conservative, pro-business, white politicians in the Democratic party who had embraced the idea of industrial progress grounded in white supremacy. Their supporters referred to them as redeemers because they supposedly saved ("redeemed") the South from Yankee domination and "black rule" during Reconstruction.

The redeemers included a rising class of lawyers, merchants, railroad executives, and entrepreneurs who wanted a more diversified economy. They also sought cuts in state taxes and expenditures, including those for the public-school systems started after the war. "Schools are not a necessity," claimed a Virginia governor. Louisiana cut school funding so much that the percentage of its residents unable to read and write actually increased between 1880 and 1900. Black children in particular suffered from such cutbacks. The redeemers, however, did not want educated African Americans. "What I want here is Negroes who can make cotton," explained a white planter, "and they don't need education to help them make cotton."

The Failings of the New South

CORE **OBJECTIVE**

2. Describe the crop-lien system that emerged in the South, and explain how it shaped the region after the Civil War.

Despite the development of mills and factories, the South in 1900 remained the least industrial, least urban, least educated, and least prosperous region in the nation. Per capita income in the South in 1900 was only 60 percent of the national average. The typical southerner was less likely to be tending a textile loom or a steel furnace than, as the saying went, facing the eastern end of a westbound mule. The South was still dependent upon the North for investment capital and manufactured goods.

Cotton remained king after the Civil War, even though it never regained the huge profitability it had generated in the 1850s. By the 1880s, southern farmers were producing as much cotton as they had before the war but were earning far less money because the world price for cotton had declined.

Southern Poverty

Henry Grady also hoped that growing numbers of southern farmers would own their own land by the end of the nineteenth century, but the opposite occurred. Many southern farmers actually *lost* ownership of the land that they worked. A prolonged decline in crop prices during the last third of the nineteenth century made it more difficult than ever to buy and own land.

Because most southern communities had no banks after the Civil War, people had to find ways to operate with little or no cash. Many rural areas adopted a barter economy in which a local "crossroads" or "furnishing" merchant would provide food, clothing, seed, fertilizer, and other items to poor farmers "on credit" in exchange for a share (or "lien") of their crops when harvested.

Origins of the crop-lien system

The Crop-Lien System

Southern farmers, white and black, who participated in the **crop-lien system** fell into three distinct categories: small farm owners, sharecroppers, and tenants. The farms owned by most southerners were small; they did not generate much cash income. As a result, even owners had to pledge a portion of their future crop to the local merchant in return for supplies purchased on credit.

Sharecroppers, mostly blacks who had nothing to offer a landowner but their labor, worked the owner's land in return for shelter in a small cabin, seed, fertilizer, mules, supplies, and food—as well as a share of the crop, generally about half. Share tenants, mostly white farmers who were barely better off, might have their own mule or horse, a plow and tools, and a line of credit with the country store, but they still needed to rent land to farm. A few paid their rent in cash, but most, like sharecroppers, pledged a share of the harvested crops to the landowner. Usually, the tenant farmers were able to keep a larger share of the crop (about 60 percent) than the sharecroppers, which meant that landowners often preferred to rent to "croppers" rather than tenants.

Tenant farmers and sharecroppers

crop-lien system Credit system used by sharecroppers and share tenants who pledged a portion ("share") of their future crop to local merchants or landowners in exchange for farming supplies, food, and clothing.

"FREE SLAVES" African Americans painstakingly pick cotton while their white overseer observes them from atop his horse. **In what ways did sharecropping resemble slavery?**

Many African American sharecroppers worked for the same planter who had owned them as slaves. "The colored folks," said a black Alabama sharecropper, "stayed with the old boss man and farmed and worked on the plantations. They were still slaves, but they were free slaves." Eighty percent of southern blacks lived on farms in the late nineteenth century. African American Ned Cobb, an Alabama sharecropper, recalled that his father "put me to plowin' the first time at nine years old, right after my mother died." He plowed "barefoot" on rocky land.

The crop-lien system was self-destructive. The overwhelming focus on planting cotton or tobacco year after year stripped the soil of its fertility and stability, causing disastrous erosion as topsoil during storms washed into nearby creeks and rivers. In addition, landowners required croppers and tenants to grow only a "cash crop," so they usually could not have their own vegetable gardens but instead had to get their food from the local merchant in exchange for promised cotton.

Because most farmers did not own the land they worked, the cabins they lived in, or the tools they used, they had little incentive to enrich the soil or maintain buildings and equipment. "The tenant," explained a study of southern agriculture in 1897 written by Matthew B. Hammond, a South Carolina–born economist, "is interested only in the crop he is raising, and makes no effort to keep up the fertility of the land." The tenant system of farming,

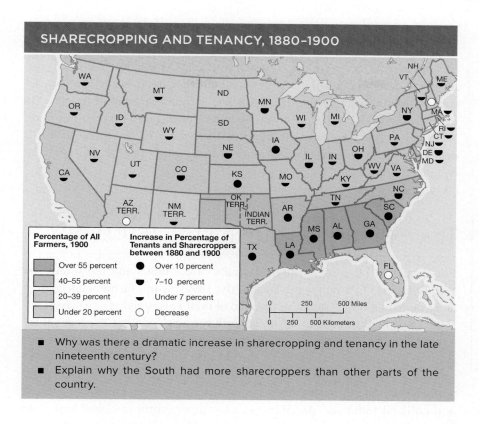

SHARECROPPING AND TENANCY, 1880–1900

Percentage of All Farmers, 1900

- Over 55 percent
- 40–55 percent
- 20–39 percent
- Under 20 percent

Increase in Percentage of Tenants and Sharecroppers between 1880 and 1900

- ● Over 10 percent
- ◐ 7–10 percent
- ◡ Under 7 percent
- ○ Decrease

■ Why was there a dramatic increase in sharecropping and tenancy in the late nineteenth century?

■ Explain why the South had more sharecroppers than other parts of the country.

Hammond concluded, had been "more wasteful and destructive than slavery was anywhere."

The crop-lien system was a post–Civil War version of economic slavery for poor whites as well as blacks. The landowner or merchant (often the same person) decided what crop would be planted and how it would be cultivated, harvested, and sold. In good times, croppers and tenants barely broke even; in bad times, they struggled to survive. Sharecroppers and share tenants were among the poorest people in the nation. Most of them had little or no education, rarely enough healthy food, and little hope for a better future.

Those who worked the farms developed an intense suspicion of their landlords, who often swindled workers by not giving them their fair share of the crops. Landlords kept the books, handled the sale of the crops, and gave the cropper or tenant his share of the proceeds after deducting for all the items supplied during the year, plus interest that ranged, according to one newspaper, "from 24 percent to grand larceny." Often, the cropper or tenant received nothing at the end of a harvest but a larger debt to be rolled over to the next year's crop. Over time, the high interest charged on the credit offered by the local store or landowner, coupled with sagging prices for cotton and other crops, created a hopeless cycle of debt among small farmers, sharecroppers, and share tenants.

Falling Cotton Prices

As cotton production soared during the last quarter of the nineteenth century, largely because of dramatic growth in Texas cultivation, the price paid for raw cotton fell steadily. "Have you all felt the effects of the low price of cotton," Mary Parham of Amite, Louisiana, wrote to her father in 1892. "It nearly ruined us. I did not get my house built. The farmers are very blue here. But [they are] getting ready to plant cotton again." As the price declined, desperate farmers planted even more cotton, which only accelerated the decline in price.

CORE **OBJECTIVE**

3. Explain how and why white southerners took away African Americans' right to vote and adopted "Jim Crow" segregation laws at the end of the nineteenth century.

Race Relations during the 1890s

The desperate plight of southern farmers in the 1880s and 1890s affected race relations—for the worse. During the 1890s, white farmers and politicians demanded that blacks be stripped of their voting rights and other civil rights as well. At the end of the nineteenth century, a violent "Negrophobia" swept across the South and much of the nation. In part, the new wave of racism was spurred by the revival of the old idea that the Anglo-Saxon "race" was intellectually and genetically "superior." Another reason was that many whites had come to resent any signs of African American financial success and political influence. An Alabama newspaper editor declared that "our blood boils when the educated Negro asserts himself politically."

Disenfranchising African Americans

By the 1890s, a new generation of African Americans born and educated since the end of the Civil War was determined to gain complete equality. They were more assertive and less patient than their parents. "We are not the Negro from whom the chains of slavery fell a quarter century ago, most assuredly not," a black editor announced. A growing number of young white adults, however, were equally determined to keep "Negroes in their place."

Mississippi took the lead in stripping blacks of their voting rights. The so-called **Mississippi Plan**, a series of state constitutional amendments in 1890, set the pattern of disenfranchisement that nine more states would follow. The disenfranchisement plan first instituted a residence requirement for voting—two years in the state, one year in a local election district. This was aimed at African American tenant farmers who were in the habit of moving yearly in search of better economic opportunities. Second, Mississippi disqualified blacks from voting if they had committed certain crimes. Third, in order to vote, people had to have paid all their taxes on time, including a so-called poll tax specifically for voting—a restriction that hurt both poor blacks and poor whites. Finally, all voters had to be able to read or at least "understand" the U.S. Constitution. White registrars decided who satisfied this requirement.

Mississippi Plan (1890) Series of state constitutional amendments that sought to disenfranchise black voters and was quickly adopted by nine other southern states.

Other states added variations on the Mississippi Plan. In 1898, Louisiana inserted into its state constitution the "grandfather clause," which allowed illiterate whites to vote if their fathers or grandfathers had been eligible to vote on January 1, 1867, when African Americans were still disenfranchised. By 1910, Georgia, North Carolina, Virginia, Alabama, and Oklahoma had incorporated the grandfather clause. Also in the Democratic "Solid South," every southern state created a Democratic primary process to select candidates, and most of these primaries excluded African American voters. When such "legal" means were not enough to ensure their political dominance, white candidates turned to fraud and violence.

The efforts to suppress the black vote succeeded. In 1896, Louisiana had 130,000 registered black voters. By 1900, it had only 5,320. In Alabama in 1900, 121,159 black men were literate, according to the census; only 3,742, however, were registered to vote. By 1900, black voting across the South had declined by 62 percent; the white vote, by 26 percent.

The Spread of Segregation

At the same time that whites were shoving blacks out of the political arena, they were also being segregated socially. The symbolic first target was railroad passenger cars. In 1885, novelist George Washington Cable noted that in South Carolina, blacks "ride in first-class [rail] cars as a right" and "their presence excites no comment." From 1875 to 1883, in fact, any local or state law requiring racial segregation violated the federal Civil Rights Act (1875).

By 1883, however, many northern whites endorsed the resegregation of southern life. In that year, the U.S. Supreme Court ruled that the Civil Rights Act of 1875 was unconstitutional. The judges explained that private individuals and organizations could engage in acts of racial discrimination because the Fourteenth Amendment specified only that "no State" could deny citizens equal protection of the law.

> Civil Rights Act of 1875 declared unconstitutional

SEGREGATION IN SCHOOLS
A group of African American elementary school students exercise at Howard University, a historically black university established in 1867.

THE LYNCHING OF HENRY SMITH Despite lack of evidence, Smith was convicted of murdering a white girl in Paris, Texas. A large crowd assembled to watch her family torture Smith from a platform labeled "Justice." After Smith was burned alive, the townspeople kept his charred teeth and bones as souvenirs.

Plessy v. Ferguson (1896): "separate but equal"

"Jim Crow" laws

separate but equal Underlying principle behind segregation that was legitimized by the Supreme Court ruling in *Plessy v. Ferguson* (1896).

The Court's interpretation in what came to be called the Civil Rights Cases (1883) left as an open question the validity of state laws requiring segregated public facilities under the principle of "separate but equal," a slogan popular in the South in the late nineteenth century. In the 1880s, Tennessee and Mississippi required railroad passengers to ride in racially segregated cars.

When Louisiana passed a similar law in 1890, African Americans challenged its constitutionality in *Plessy v. Ferguson* (1896). The case originated in New Orleans when Homer Plessy, an octoroon (a person having one-eighth African ancestry), refused to leave a whites-only railroad car and was convicted of violating the law.

In 1896, the Supreme Court ruled that states had a right to create laws segregating public places such as schools, hotels, and restaurants. Justice John Marshall Harlan, a Kentuckian who had once owned slaves, was the only member of the Court to dissent. He stressed that the Constitution is "color-blind, and neither knows nor tolerates classes among citizens. In respect of civil rights, all citizens are equal before the law." He feared that the Court's ruling would plant the "seeds of race hate" under "the sanction of law."

That is precisely what happened. The Court's ruling in the *Plessy* case legitimized the practice of racially **separate but equal** facilities in virtually every area of southern life. In 1900, the editor of the *Richmond Times* insisted that racial segregation "be applied in every relation of Southern life. God Almighty drew the color line, and it cannot be obliterated. The negro must stay on his side of the line, and the white man must stay on his side, and the sooner both races recognize this fact and accept it, the better it will be for both."

The new regulations came to be called "Jim Crow" laws. The name derived from "Jump Jim Crow," an old song-and-dance caricature of African Americans performed by white actor Thomas D. Rice in blackface makeup during the 1830s. Thereafter, the term *Jim Crow* became a satirical expression meaning "Negro." Signs reading "White Only" or "Colored Only" above restrooms and water fountains emerged as hallmarks of the Jim Crow system. Old racist customs dating back before the Civil War were revived. If whites walked along a sidewalk, blacks were expected to step aside and let them pass. There were even racially separate funeral homes, cemeteries, churches, and water fountains.

Widespread violence accompanied the creation of Jim Crow laws. From 1890 to 1899, the United States averaged 188 lynchings per year, 82 percent of which occurred in the South. Lynchings usually involved a black man (or men) accused of a crime, often rape. White mobs would seize, torture, and kill the accused, always in ghastly ways. Racial lynchings became so common that participating whites viewed them as forms of outdoor entertainment. Large crowds, including women and children, would watch the grisly event amid a carnival-like atmosphere. Photographs of gruesome lynchings surrounded by crowds of laughing and smiling whites were reproduced on postcards mailed across the nation. The governor of Mississippi declared that "if it is necessary that every Negro in the state will be lynched, it will be done to maintain white supremacy."

> Lynching

Mob Rule in North Carolina

White supremacy was violently imposed in the thriving coastal port of Wilmington, North Carolina, then the largest city in the state, with about 20,000 residents. In 1894 and 1896, black voters, by then a majority in the city, elected blacks to various municipal offices, infuriating the city's white elite. "We will never surrender to a ragged raffle of Negroes," warned a former congressman and Confederate colonel named Alfred Waddell, "even if we have to choke the Cape Fear River with [black] carcasses." It was not an idle threat.

On the morning of November 10, 1898, some 2,000 well-armed white men and teens rampaged through the streets of Wilmington. They first destroyed the offices of the *Daily Record*, the city's black-owned newspaper, then moved into the black neighborhoods, shooting African Americans and destroying homes and businesses. Almost a hundred blacks were killed. The mob then stormed the city hall, declared that Colonel Waddell was the new mayor, and forced the African American business leaders and elected officials to board northbound trains. The new self-appointed all-white city government issued a "Declaration of White Independence" that stripped blacks of their voting rights and their jobs. Desperate black residents appealed for help to the governor as well as President William McKinley but received none.

> Wilmington Insurrection

The Wilmington Insurrection marked the first time in history that a lawfully elected municipal government had been overthrown in the United States. Two years later, in the 1900 statewide elections, white supremacist Democrats vowed to cement their control of the political process. The night before the election, Colonel Waddell urged supporters to use any

WILMINGTON INSURRECTION A mob of white supremacists pose with their rifles before the demolished printing press of the *Daily Record*, an African American newspaper.

means necessary to suppress black voting: "You are Anglo-Saxons. You are armed and prepared and you will do your duty. . . . Go to the polls tomorrow, and if you find the negro out voting, tell him to leave the polls, and if he refuses, kill him, shoot him down in his tracks. We shall win tomorrow if we have to do it with guns." The Democratic party won by a landslide.

The Black Response

African Americans responded to the resurgence of racism in various ways. Some left the South in search of greater safety, equality, and opportunity, but the vast majority stayed in their native region and tried to adjust to the brutal realities of white supremacy. "Had to walk a quiet life," explained James Plunkett, a Virginian. "The least little thing you would do, they [whites] would kill ya."

Yet accommodation did not mean submission. Black southerners nurtured their own culture and racial pride. A young white visitor to Mississippi in 1910 noticed that nearly every black person he met had "two distinct social selves, the one he reveals to his own people, the other he assumes among the whites."

African American churches

African American churches continued to serve as hubs for black community life. Churches were used not only for worship but for social gatherings, club meetings, and political rallies. Churches enabled African Americans of all classes to interact and exercise roles denied them in the larger society. For men especially, churches offered leadership roles and political status. Serving as a deacon was often one of the most prestigious positions for an African American man.

Ida B. Wells One of the most outspoken African American activists of the time was Ida B. Wells. Born into slavery in 1862 in Mississippi, she attended a school staffed by white missionaries. She moved in 1880 to Memphis, where she taught in segregated schools and gained entrance to the social life of the city's African American middle class.

In 1883, after being denied a seat on a railroad car because she was black, Wells became the first African American to file suit against such discrimination. The circuit court decided in her favor and fined the railroad, but the Tennessee Supreme Court overturned the ruling. Wells thereafter discovered "[her] first and [it] might be said, my only love"—journalism—and, through it, a weapon with which to wage her crusade for justice. She became editor of *Memphis Free Speech*, a newspaper that focused on African American issues.

In 1892, when three of her friends were lynched by a white mob, Wells launched a crusade against lynching. Angry whites responded by destroying her office and threatening to lynch her. She moved to New York, where she continued to criticize Jim

IDA B. WELLS A journalist and outspoken advocate of racial equality, Wells was a cofounder of the National Association for the Advancement of Colored People.

Crow laws and demand that blacks have their voting rights restored. She helped found the National Association for the Advancement of Colored People (NAACP) in 1909 and worked for women's suffrage. In promoting racial equality, Wells often found herself in direct opposition to Booker T. Washington, the most influential African American leader of the time.

Booker T. Washington By the 1890s, Booker T. Washington, born a slave in Virginia in 1856, the son of a black mother and a white father, had become the foremost African American educator in the nation. At sixteen, he had enrolled at Hampton Normal and Agricultural Institute, one of several colleges for former slaves created during Reconstruction. Nine years later, the founder of Hampton Institute, Samuel Armstrong, a former Union general, received a request from a group in northern Alabama starting a black college called Tuskegee Institute. They needed a president of the new school. Armstrong urged them to hire Washington. Although only twenty-five, he was, according to Armstrong, "a very capable mulatto, clear headed, modest, sensible, polite, and a thorough teacher and superior man."

BOOKER T. WASHINGTON Founder of the Tuskegee Institute, a historically black university, Washington went on to become the nation's most prominent African American leader.

Young Washington got the job, and he quickly started building a school on a vacant lot. The first students had to help construct the first buildings, making the bricks themselves. As the years passed, bustling Tuskegee Institute became celebrated as a college dedicated to discipline and vocational training. Washington's recurring message to students was the importance of "practical knowledge." In part to please his white donors, he argued that blacks should not focus on fighting racial segregation. They should instead work hard, not complain, and not stir up trouble. At the same time that white southerners were preventing blacks from voting and imposing Jim Crow laws, Washington was urging African Americans to begin "at the bottom," as well-educated farmers, not as social activists.

Yet Washington's conservative approach emphasizing economic self-sufficiency did not satisfy many white racists. Thomas Dixon, a prominent North Carolina Baptist minister, state legislator, and novelist, complained that Washington was teaching his students "to be masters of men, to be independent, to own and operate their own industries," all of which would "destroy the last vestige of dependence on the white man for anything."

In a famous speech at the Cotton States and International Exposition in Atlanta in 1895, Washington urged the African American community, "Cast down your bucket where you are—cast it down in making friends . . . of the people of all races by whom we are surrounded. Cast it down in agriculture, mechanics, in commerce, in domestic service, and in the professions." Fighting for "social equality" and directly challenging white rule would be a huge mistake ("the extremest folly"). Any effort at "agitation" in

Atlanta Compromise (1895)
Speech by Booker T. Washington that called for the black community to strive for economic prosperity before demanding political and social equality.

the white-dominant South would, he warned, backfire. African Americans first needed to become self-sufficient economically. Civil rights would have to wait.

W. E. B. Du Bois By the start of the twentieth century, Booker T. Washington had become the most influential African American leader in the nation. Some younger black leaders, however, criticized him for sacrificing civil and political rights in his crusade for vocational education. W. E. B. Du Bois led this criticism.

A native of Massachusetts, Du Bois first experienced racial prejudice as a student at Fisk University in Nashville, Tennessee. Later he became the first African American to earn a doctoral degree from Harvard (in history and sociology). In addition to promoting civil rights, he left a distinguished record as a scholar, authoring more than twenty books. Trim and dapper, Du Bois had a flamboyant personality and a combative spirit. Not long after he began teaching at Atlanta University in 1897, he launched a public assault on Booker T. Washington's strategy for improving the quality of life for African Americans.

Du Bois called Washington's 1895 speech "the **Atlanta Compromise**" and the name stuck. Washington, he argued, was so determined to please powerful whites that he "accepted the alleged inferiority of the Negro" so blacks could "concentrate all their energies on industrial education, the accumulation of wealth, and the conciliation of the South."

Du Bois stressed that the priorities should be reversed—that African American leaders should adopt a strategy of "ceaseless agitation" directed at ensuring the right to vote and winning civil equality. The education of blacks, Du Bois maintained, should not be merely vocational but should develop bold leaders willing to challenge segregation and discrimination. He demanded that disenfranchisement and legalized segregation cease immediately and that the laws of the land be enforced.

For his part, Washington stressed that Du Bois never truly understood the brutal dynamics of southern racism. A more militant strategy in the South would only have gotten more blacks lynched. Nor did Du Bois or other critics know that Washington secretly financed legal efforts to oppose the Jim Crow laws. Such "quiet efforts," he noted, were more successful and realistic than the "brass band" approach championed by Du Bois.

The dispute between Washington and Du Bois came to define the tensions that would divide the twentieth-century civil rights movement: militancy versus conciliation, separatism versus assimilation, social justice versus economic opportunities. By 1915, when Washington died, the leadership of the nation's black community was passing to Du Bois and others whose uncompromising effort to gain true equality signaled the beginning of the civil rights century.

W. E. B. DU BOIS A fierce advocate for black education and civil rights.

The Settling of the New West

Like the South, the West has always been a region wrapped in myths and stereotypes. The vast land west of the Mississippi River contains remarkable geographic extremes: majestic mountains, roaring rivers, deep-sculpted canyons, searing deserts, grassy plains, and dense forests. For most western Americans, the Civil War and Reconstruction were remote events that hardly touched the lives of the Indians, Mexicans, Asians, farmers, ranchers, trappers, miners, and Mormons scattered through the plains, valleys, and mountains. There the relentless march of conquest, settlement, and exploitation continued, propelled by a special sense of "manifest destiny," a lust for land, a hope for quick fortunes, and a restless desire to improve one's lot in life.

Between 1870 and 1900, Americans settled more land in the West than in the centuries before 1870. By 1900, a third of the nation lived west of the Mississippi River. The post–Civil War West came to symbolize economic opportunity and personal freedom. On another level, however, the economic exploitation of the West was a story of irresponsible behavior and reckless abuse of nature that scarred the land, decimated its wildlife, and nearly exterminated much of Native American culture.

The Western Landscape

After mid-century, farmers and their families began spreading west to the Great Plains—western Kansas, Nebraska, Oklahoma, northern Texas, the Dakotas, eastern Colorado, Wyoming, and Montana. From California, miners moved eastward through the mountains to Utah and Nevada, drawn by one new strike after another. From Texas, nomadic cowboys annually migrated with herds of cattle northward onto the plains and even across the Rocky Mountains, into the Great Basin of Utah and Nevada.

The settlers in the West encountered challenges markedly different from those they had left behind. The Great Plains had little rainfall and few rivers. The scarcity of water and timber rendered useless the familiar trappings of the pioneer—the axe, the log cabin, the rail fence—as well as traditional methods of tilling the soil.

For a long time, the region was known as the Great American Desert, unfit for human habitation and therefore, in the minds of most Americans, the perfect refuge for Indians who refused to embrace the white way of life. That view changed in the last half of the nineteenth century, however. The discovery of gold, silver, copper, iron,

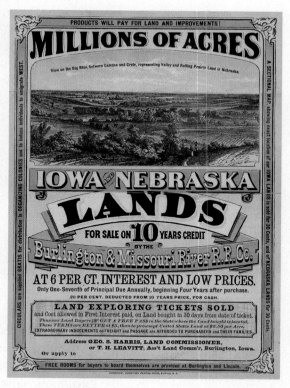

THE ALLURE OF THE WEST A circular from 1872 advertising westward emigration. The idyllic image of the Nebraska prairie captures the freedom symbolized by the West, and the financial details underneath are meant to persuade Americans to think of emigration as an economic opportunity.

THE NEW WEST

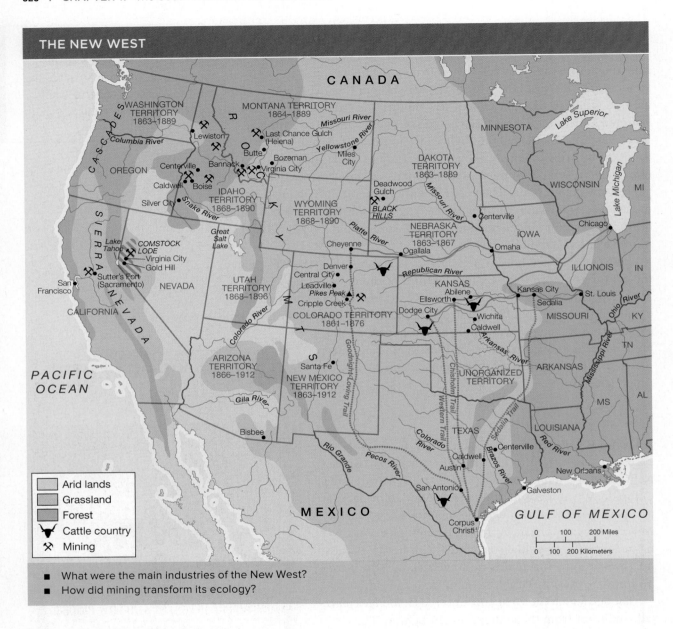

- What were the main industries of the New West?
- How did mining transform its ecology?

and coal; the completion of the transcontinental railroads; the collapse of Indian resistance; and the rise of the buffalo-hide and range-cattle industries convinced many Americans, as well as the federal government, that economic development of the West held the key to national prosperity. Capitalists made huge profits investing in western mines, cattle, railroads, and commercial farms. With the use of what water was available, new techniques of dry farming and irrigation could make the vast prairie lands fruitful after all.

The Migratory Stream

During the second half of the nineteenth century, an unrelenting stream of migrants flowed into what had been the largely Indian and Hispanic West. Millions of Anglo-Americans, African Americans, Mexicans, South Americans, and European and Chinese immigrants transformed the patterns of western society and culture. Most of the settlers were relatively prosperous white, native-born farm folk. Because of the expense of transportation, land, and supplies, the very poor could not afford to relocate. Three quarters of the western migrants were men.

The largest number of foreign immigrants came from northern Europe and Canada. In the northern plains, Germans, Scandinavians, and Irish were especially numerous. In the new state of Nebraska in 1870, a quarter of the 123,000 residents were foreign-born. In North Dakota in 1890, 45 percent of the residents were immigrants.

Canadian, northern European, and Chinese immigrants

Compared with European immigrants, those from China and Mexico were much less numerous but nonetheless significant. The Chinese were frequently discriminated against and denied citizenship rights. As perpetual outsiders, they became scapegoats whenever there was an economic downturn. In 1882, Congress passed the Chinese Exclusion Act, effectively banning further immigration from China.

The African American Migration

After the collapse of Radical Republican rule in the South, thousands of African Americans began migrating westward from Kentucky, Tennessee, Louisiana, Arkansas, Mississippi, and Texas. Some 6,000 southern blacks arrived in Kansas in 1879, and as many as 20,000 followed the next year. These African American migrants came to be known as **Exodusters**, because they were making their exodus from the South—in search of a haven from racism and poverty.

The foremost promoter of black migration to the West was Benjamin "Pap" Singleton. Born a slave in Tennessee in 1809, he escaped and made his way to Michigan. After the Civil War, he returned to Tennessee and decided that African Americans could never gain equal treatment if they stayed in the former Confederacy. When he learned that land in Kansas could be had for $1.25 an acre, he led a party of 200 colonists to the state in 1878, bought 7,500 acres that had been an Indian reservation, and established the Dunlop community.

Over the next several years, thousands of African Americans followed Singleton to Kansas, leading many southern leaders to worry about the loss of black laborers. In 1879, white southerners closed access to the Mississippi River and threatened to sink all boats carrying blacks to the West. An army officer reported to President Rutherford B. Hayes that "every river landing is blockaded by white enemies of the colored exodus; some of whom are mounted and armed, as if we are at war."

Exodusters African Americans who migrated west from the South in search of a haven from racism and poverty after the collapse of Radical Republican rule.

NICODEMUS, KANSAS By the 1880s, this colony had become a thriving town of Exodusters. Here, its residents are photographed in front of their First Baptist Church and general store.

By the early 1880s, however, the exodus of black southerners to the West had petered out. Many African American settlers were unprepared for the harsh living conditions on the plains. Their Kansas homesteads were often not large enough to be self-sustaining, and most of the black farmers were forced to supplement their income by hiring themselves out to white ranchers. Drought, grasshoppers, prairie fires, and dust storms led to frequent crop failures and bankruptcy.

The sudden influx of so many southern blacks also taxed resources and patience. There were not enough houses, stores, or construction materials, few government services, and rarely enough water. Disappointed and frustrated, many African American pioneers in Kansas soon abandoned their land and moved to the few cities in the state. The frontier was not the "promised land" that they had been led to expect, but it was better than what they had experienced in the South. As an Exoduster minister stressed, "We had rather suffer and be free."

By 1890, some 520,000 African Americans lived west of the Mississippi River. As many as 25 percent of the cowboys who participated in the Texas cattle drives were African Americans, and many federal horse soldiers in the West were black.

Western Mining

Prospectors and their followers

Valuable mineral deposits continued to lure people to the West after the Civil War. Every territory and state in the Far West developed a mining industry during the second half of the nineteenth century. The miners of the 1849 California gold rush (the forty-niners) had set the typical pattern, in which mobs of prospectors rushed to a new find, followed quickly by camp followers—a motley crew of peddlers, saloon keepers, prostitutes, gamblers, hustlers, and assorted desperadoes eager to "mine the miners." Lawlessness gave way first to vigilante rule as groups of miners created their own informal legal codes for the community and enforced penalties, including hangings, and, finally, to stable communities with municipal governments, sanitation, and law enforcement.

The drama of the 1849 gold rush was reenacted in the following three decades. Along the South Platte River, not far from Pikes Peak in Colorado, a prospecting party found gold in 1858, and stories of success brought perhaps 100,000 "fifty-niners" into the area by the next year. New discoveries in Colorado kept occurring: near Central City in 1859, at Leadville in the 1870s, and at Cripple Creek in 1891 and 1894—the last important strikes in the West, again gold and silver. During those years, farming and grazing had given the economy a stable base, and Colorado, the Centennial State, entered the union in 1876.

While the early miners were crowding around Pikes Peak in Colorado, the **Comstock Lode** was found near Gold Hill, Nevada, on the eastern slope of the Sierra Nevada Mountains near the California border. Henry Comstock, a Canadian-born fur trapper, had drifted to the Carson River diggings, which opened in 1856. He talked his way into a share of a new discovery made by two other prospectors in 1859 and gave it his own name. The lode produced massive amounts of gold and silver. Within twenty years, it had yielded more than $300 million from shafts that reached thousands of feet into the mountainside.

The growing demand for orderly government in the West led to the hasty designation of new territories and eventually the admission of a host of new states. After Colorado's admission in 1876, however, there was a long pause because of party divisions in Congress: Democrats were reluctant to create states out of territories that were heavily Republican. After the sweeping Republican victory in the 1888 legislative races, however, Congress admitted the Dakotas, Montana, and Washington in 1889 and Idaho and Wyoming in 1890. Utah entered the Union in 1896 (after the Mormons agreed to abandon the practice of polygamy) and Oklahoma in 1907, and in 1912 Arizona and New Mexico rounded out the forty-eight contiguous states. (The final two states, Alaska and Hawaii, were added fifty years later.)

Comstock Lode A mine in eastern Nevada acquired by Canadian fur trapper Henry Comstock that between 1860 and 1880 yielded almost $1 billion worth of gold and silver.

Life in the New West

In the 1880s, James H. Kyner, a railroad builder in Oregon, witnessed "an almost unbroken stream of emigrants from horizon to horizon." These "hardy, optimistic folk" traveled west in wagons, on horses, and on foot, "going west to seek their fortunes and to settle an empire." Most of them thought little about forcing out the Native Americans, Chinese workers, and Hispanic cowboys who were there first. Americans claimed a special "destiny" to settle, develop, and dominate the entire continent.

CORE **OBJECTIVE**

5. Describe the experiences of miners, ranchers, farmers, and women in the West.

To encourage new settlers in the West, the federal government generously helped finance the construction of four transcontinental railroads, dispatched federal troops to conquer and relocate Indians to designated reservations, and sold government-owned land at low prices—or gave it to railroad companies as a means of rapidly populating areas served by trains. The transcontinental railroads received some 200 million acres of government land. Over time, the railroads sold much of the land to create towns and ranches along the rail lines. The West of ranchers and farmers was in fact largely the product of the railroads; they were the lifeblood of the western economy.

The surge of western migration had many of the romantic qualities so often depicted in novels, films, and television shows. The people who braved harsh conditions to begin new lives in the West were indeed courageous and tenacious. Cowboys and Indians; outlaws and vigilantes; and farmers, ranchers, and herders populated the plains, while miners and trappers led more nomadic lives in the hills and backwoods.

These familiar images of western life tell only part of the story, however. Drudgery and tragedy were as commonplace as adventure and success. Droughts, locusts, disease, tornadoes, and the erratic fluctuations of commodities markets made life precarious and perilous.

In contrast to the Hollywood versions of the West, the people who settled the trans-Mississippi frontier were a diverse lot: they included women as well as men, African Americans, Hispanics, Asians, and European immigrants. The feverish quest for quick profits also helped fuel a boom/bust economic cycle that injected a chronic instability into the society and politics of the region. Ultimately, the massive western migrations would take a huge toll on the Native American tribes in the region.

The Cattle Boom

The cattle industry

When ranchers began herding cattle into the grasslands where the buffalo had roamed, they transformed the western landscape forever. For many years, wild cattle first brought to America by the Spanish had competed with buffalo in Texas and Arizona. Breeding them with Anglo-American domesticated cattle produced the hybrid Texas longhorns: tough, lean, and rangy, they were noted more for speed and endurance than for yielding lots of choice steaks. By 1865, millions of longhorns in Texas were wandering freely across the state. They had little value because the largest urban markets for beef were so far away—until the railroads arrived.

At the end of the Civil War, the Kansas Pacific railway crews were beginning to lay rails and ties in the buffalo country of the southern plains, between St. Louis and Kansas City. As buffalo hunters roamed the prairies, a few entrepreneurs began to imagine how the extension of the railroad might "establish a market whereas the Southern [cattle] drover and Northern buyer would meet upon an equal footing."

That junction was Abilene, Kansas, a "very small, dead place, consisting of about one dozen log huts." Once the rail lines reached Kansas from Missouri,

THE ORIGINAL COWBOYS Cowboys on horseback herd cattle into a corral beside the Cimarron River in Colorado in 1905. **How did the role of cowboys change in the final decades of the nineteenth century?**

Joseph G. McCoy, an Illinois livestock dealer, recognized the possibilities of driving vast herds of cattle raised in Texas northward to Kansas, where they would be loaded onto freight cars and sent to the rest of the nation.

In 1867, in tiny Abilene in eastern Kansas, McCoy bought 250 acres for a stockyard and built a barn, an office building, livestock scales, a hotel, and a bank. He then sent an agent to Texas to convince the owners of herds bound north on the Chisholm Trail to go through Abilene. Once the bellowing mass of Texas longhorns reached Abilene in August 1867, cattle by the thousands were loaded onto rail cars and shipped to Chicago stockyards where they were slaughtered and then sent (as sides of beef) to the cities around the nation.

Abilene flourished as the first successful cow town. By 1871, 700,000 steers were passing through it every year. The ability to ship huge numbers of cattle by rail transformed ranching into a major national industry and turned Kansas into a major economic crossroads. Other cattle towns sprouted along the rail line: Ellsworth, Wichita, Caldwell, Dodge City. None of them lasted more than a few years. Once people bought farms nearby, they lobbied successfully to stop the stampeding Texas herds from coming through their area. The cattlemen simply developed new routes north, to new cow towns and rail hubs in Colorado, Wyoming, and Montana. Soon those states had their own cattle ranches. By 1883, there were a half-million cattle in eastern Montana alone, as the disappearing buffalo herds gave way to steers and sheep.

Like miners, cattle ranchers met to develop their own code of laws and ways of enforcing them. As cattle often wandered onto other ranchers' land, cowboys would "ride the line" to keep the animals off the adjoining ranches. In the spring, they would "round up" the herds, which invariably got mixed up, and sort out ownership by identifying the distinctive ranch symbols "branded," or burned, into the cattle.

The end of the open range

All that changed in 1873, when Joseph Glidden, an Illinois farmer, developed the first effective and inexpensive form of barbed-wire fencing. Soon the "open range"—owned by all, where a small rancher could graze his cattle anywhere—was no more. Barbed-wire fences triggered "range wars," in which small ranchers, called fence cutters, fought to retain the open range.

Fencing converted prairie into pastures, which put many ranchers out of business; many of these former ranchers became cowboys working for wages. Cattle raising, like mining, evolved from a romantic adventure into a business dominated by "cattle barons" and large corporations. As one cowboy lamented, "Times have changed."

Farming on the Plains

Farming amid the unforgiving environment and harsh weather of the Great Plains was brutal. A New York newspaper publisher traveling to California described the Great Plains as a "land of starvation," "a treeless desert," scorching during daylight and "chill and piercing" cold at night. Still, people made the dangerous trek, lured by the inexpensive federal land and misleading advertisements celebrating life on the plains. One woman said she was "glad to be leaving" her farm in Missouri: "We were going to a new land and get rich." Few got rich, however. "In plain language," concluded a study by the Department of Agriculture, "a farmer's wife, as a general rule, is a laboring drudge."

The first homesteaders in the Great Plains were mostly landless folk eager to try their hand at farming. Many of them had never used a hoe or planted a seed. "I was raised in Chicago without so much as a back yard to play in," said a Montana homesteader, "and I worked 48 hours a week for $1.25. When I heard you could get 320 acres just by living on it, I felt that I had been offered a kingdom."

Though land was essentially free as a result of the Homestead Act (1862), horses, livestock, wagons, wells, lumber, fencing, seed, machinery, and fertilizer were not. Freight rates and interest rates on loans seemed criminally high. As in the South, declining crop prices produced chronic indebtedness, leading strapped western farmers to embrace virtually any plan to increase the money supply and thus pay off their debts with inflated currency. The virgin land itself, although fertile, resisted planting; the heavy sod woven with tough grass roots broke many a wooden plow. Since wood and coal were rare on the prairie, pioneer families initially had to use buffalo chips (dried dung from buffaloes and cattle) for fuel.

Farm families also fought a constant battle with the elements: tornadoes, hailstorms, droughts, prairie fires, blizzards, and pests. Swarms of locusts often clouded the horizon, occasionally covering the ground six inches deep. A Wichita newspaper reported in 1878 that the grasshoppers devoured "everything green, stripping the foliage off the bark and from the tender twigs of the fruit trees, destroying every plant that is good for food or pleasant to the eyes, that man has planted." In the late 1880s, a prolonged drought forced many homesteaders on the plains to give up. Thousands left, some in wagons whose canvas coverings read: "In God we trusted, In Kansas we busted."

Commercial Farming

Eventually, as the railroads brought piles of lumber from the East, farmers could leave their houses built of sod for more comfortable frame dwellings. New farm equipment, for those who could afford to buy it, greatly improved productivity. In 1868, James Oliver, a Scottish immigrant living in Indiana, made a successful chilled-iron "sodbuster" plow that greatly eased the task of plowing the plains. Improvements and new inventions in threshing machines, hay mowers, planters, manure spreaders, cream separators, and other devices lightened the burden of farm labor but added to the farmers' capital outlay. By 1880, a steam-powered combine could do the work of twenty men.

"Bonanza farms"

In Minnesota, the Dakotas, and central California, wealthy capitalists who could afford machinery for mass production created gigantic "bonanza farms" that became the marvels of the age. On one farm in North Dakota, 13,000 acres of wheat made a single field. Another bonanza farm employed over 1,000 migrant workers to tend 34,000 acres. Such agribusinesses were the wave of the future. Thomas Jefferson's dream of an America primarily made up of small farmers gave way to industrial agriculture.

While the overall value of farmland and farm products increased in the late nineteenth century, small farmers did not keep up. Their numbers grew in size but decreased in proportion to the population at large. Wheat in the Western states, like cotton in the South, was the great export crop that spurred economic

INNOVATIVE FARMING Powered by over a dozen horses and operated by two men, this early nineteenth-century machine boasted the ability of cutting, threshing, bagging, and weighing wheat all at the same time.

growth. For a variety of reasons, however, including an inability to afford new machinery, few small farmers prospered. By the 1890s, they were in open revolt against the "system" of corrupt processors (middlemen) and "greedy" railroads and bankers who they believed conspired against them.

Miners in the West

As ranchers and farmers settled the plains, miners played a crucial role in the economic and social development of the Far West. Throughout the region, mining camps and towns sprouted like mushrooms in the second half of the century. Initially, the miners lived in crude tents and shacks they built themselves. They worked a nine- to ten-hour day, six days a week, and usually took Sunday off. As a camp grew, it became a town with cabins, stores, and saloons providing modern services and conveniences.

> Effects of large-scale mining

The first wave of prospectors focused on "placer" (surface) mining, using metal pans to sift gold dust and nuggets out of riverbeds. But once the placer deposits were exhausted, miners had to use other methods, all of which required much larger operations and investments. As mining shifted from surface digging and panning to hydraulic mining, dredging, and deep-shaft hard-rock tunneling, mining ceased being an individual pursuit and became a big business. Only large-scale mining corporations financed by American and European investors could afford the expensive specialized power equipment and blasting dynamite needed for such operations. Many prospectors who had hoped to "strike it rich" turned into wage laborers working for mining corporations. Eventually, mine workers formed unions to represent their interests in negotiations with mine owners, in part because of low pay ($3 a day) and in part because deep-shaft mining was so dangerous. In the western hard-rock mines, on-the-job accidents disabled one out of every thirty miners and killed one out of eighty. Overall, some 7,500 workers were killed and 20,000 maimed in mine accidents during the late nineteenth century.

Mining and the Environment

Hydraulicking, dredging, and shaft mining transformed vast areas of landscape and vegetation. Massive stamping mills driven by steam engines crushed mountains of rock. Huge hydraulic cannons shot enormous streams of water under high pressure, stripping the topsoil and gravel from hillsides and creating steep-sloped canyons that could not sustain plant life. The massive amounts of dirt and debris unearthed by the water cannons covered rich farmland downstream and created sandbars that clogged rivers and killed fish. All told, some 12 billion tons of earth were blasted out of the Sierra Nevadas in California and washed into local rivers.

Mining Boomtowns

Tombstone, Arizona, only thirty miles from the Mexican border, was the site of substantial silver mining in the 1870s. By only its fourth year of existence, it was the fastest-growing boomtown in the Southwest. It boasted a bowling alley, four churches, an icehouse, a school, two banks, three newspapers, and an ice cream parlor along with 110 saloons, 14 gambling halls, and numerous dance halls and brothels. Miners and cowboys especially enjoyed shows at the Bird Cage Theatre, the "wildest, wickedest night spot between Basin Street [in New Orleans] and the Barbary Coast [in North Africa]," open twenty-four hours a day, 365 days a year.

Some of the other largest and most famous of the mining boomtowns included Virginia City in Nevada, Cripple Creek and Leadville in Colorado, and Deadwood in the Dakota Territory. They were male-dominated communities with a substantial population of immigrants: Chinese, Chileans, Peruvians, Mexicans, French, Germans, Scots, Welsh, Irish, and English. In terms of ethnic diversity, the western mining cities were the most cosmopolitan communities in America.

> Life in boomtowns

Mining towns were violent places. The small gold-mining town of Belleville, California, had fifty murders in one year. In 1871, a visitor to Corinne, Utah, a town only four years old with 2,000 residents, noted that the streets "are full of white men armed to the teeth, miserable-looking Indians dressed in the ragged shirts and trousers furnished by the federal government, and yellow Chinese with a business-like air and hard, intelligent faces."

Ethnic prejudice was as common as violence in mining towns. The Chinese, for example, were usually prohibited from working in the mines but were allowed to operate laundries and work in boardinghouses. Mexicans were often treated the worst. "Mexicans have no business in this country," a Californian insisted. "The men were made to be shot at, and the women were made for our purposes. I'm a white man—I am! A Mexican is pretty near black. I hate all Mexicans."

Most of the boomtowns, many of which were in remote mountainous areas, lasted only a few years. Once the mines played out, the people moved on, leaving ghost towns behind. In 1870, Virginia City, then called the richest city in America, hosted a population of 20,000. Today it has fewer than 1,000 residents.

Women in the West

The West remained a largely male society throughout the nineteenth century. Women in mining towns, most of whom worked as house cleaners, were as valued as gold. Many mining towns had a male-to-female ratio as high as 9 to 1. When four "respectable" women arrived in Nevada City, one of them reported that the men stood and gazed "at us with mouth and eyes wide open, every time we go out" in the streets.

In both mining towns and farming communities, women were prized as spouses, in part because farming required help. In 1900, 98 percent of the women in Nebraska were married. The women pioneers continued to face the traditional legal barriers and social prejudices prevalent in the East. A wife could not sell property without her husband's approval, for example.

> Pioneer women: Greater equality and independence

GATHERING "MEADOW MUFFINS" A pioneer woman collects dried buffalo dung to be used as fuel for cooking and warmth on cold prairie nights.

Texas women could not sue except for divorce, nor could they serve on juries, act as lawyers, or witness a will.

But the constant fight for survival west of the Mississippi made men and women more equal partners than in the East. Many women who lost their mates to the deadly toil of "sod busting" thereafter assumed complete responsibility for their farms. In general, women on the prairie became more independent than women leading domestic lives back east. A Kansas woman explained that "the environment was such as to bring out and develop the dominant qualities of individual character. Kansas women of that day learned at an early age to depend on themselves—to do whatever work there was to be done, and to face danger when it must be faced, as calmly as they were able."

It was not coincidental, then, that the new western territories and states were among the first to allow women to vote in local elections and hold office. Western territories and states also hoped that by allowing women to vote, they would attract more women settlers. In 1890, Wyoming was admitted to the Union as the first state that allowed women to vote in all elections. Utah, Colorado, and Idaho followed soon thereafter.

Western Indians

CORE OBJECTIVE

6. Evaluate the impact on Native Americans of the federal government's policies in the West after the Civil War.

As settlers spread across the continent, some 250,000 Native Americans, many of them originally from east of the Mississippi, were forced into what was supposed to be their last refuge, the Great Plains and mountain regions of the Far West. The 1851 Fort Laramie Treaty, in which the chiefs of the Plains Indians agreed to accept tribal boundaries and allow white emigrants to travel across their lands, worked for a while. Fighting resumed, however, as Indians continued their ancient practice of following the buffalo herds and as white (and black) emigrants began to settle on Indian lands rather than pass through them.

The Indian Wars

From the early 1860s until the late 1870s, the trans-Mississippi West raged with the so-called **Indian wars**. Although the U.S. government had signed numerous treaties with Indian nations giving them ownership of reservation lands for "as long as waters run and the grass shall grow," those commitments were repeatedly violated by buffalo hunters, miners, ranchers, farmers, railroad surveyors—and horse soldiers. In the 1860s, the federal government ousted numerous tribes from lands they had been promised "forever." A Sioux chieftain named Spotted Tail expressed the grieving anger felt by many Indians when he asked, "Why does not the Great Father [U.S. president] put his red children on wheels so that he can move them as he will?"

In the two decades before the Civil War, the U.S. Army's central mission in the West was to protect pioneers traveling on the major Overland Trails. During and after the war, the mission changed to ensuring that Native Americans stayed on the reservations and that Americans did not trespass on Indian lands.

Americans, however, repeatedly violated treaties with Native American peoples. The result was simmering frustration punctuated by outbreaks of tragic violence. In the summer of 1862, an uprising of Sioux warriors killed 644 white traders, settlers, government officials, and soldiers in the Minnesota Valley. It was the first of many clashes between the growing number of American settlers and miners and the Indians living on reservations in the Great Plains.

Two years later, a horrible incident occurred in Colorado as a result of the influx of white miners into the territory. After Indians murdered a white family near Denver, John Evans, the territorial governor, called on whites to "kill and destroy" the "hostile Indians on the plains." At the same time, Evans persuaded "friendly Indians" (mostly Cheyennes and Arapahos) to gather at "places of safety" such as Fort Lyon, in southeastern Colorado near the Kansas border, where they were promised protection.

Despite that promise, at dawn on November 29, 1864, Colonel John M. Chivington's 700 untrained militiamen attacked a camp of Cheyennes and Arapahos along Sand Creek, about forty miles from Fort Lyon. Black Kettle, the chief, frantically waved first an American flag and then a white flag, but the attacking soldiers paid no heed. Over seven hours, the Colorado militiamen slaughtered, scalped, and mutilated 165 peaceful Indians—men, women, children, and the elderly. Chivington, a former abolitionist and Methodist minister (the "Fighting Parson") who had preached against the brutalities of slavery, had told his men to "kill and scalp all [Indians], big and little, you come across."

Indian wars Bloody conflicts between U.S. soldiers and Native Americans that raged in the West from the early 1860s to the late 1870s, sparked by American settlers moving into ancestral Indian lands.

SAND CREEK MASSACRE Southern Cheyenne illustration of Chivington's devastating attack on the Cheyennes and Arapahos in 1864. A small group of warriors rides toward a line of armed militiamen, who are firing at will.

In his report on the lopsided bloodbath to army officials, Chivington lied, claiming a great victory against 1,000 entrenched Cheyenne warriors. The bloodthirsty colonel was greeted as a hero back in Denver. "Colorado soldiers have again covered themselves in glory," the *Rocky Mountain News* in Denver initially proclaimed.

Then the truth about Sand Creek began to come out. Captain Silas Soule, an abolitionist from Kansas who had joined the Union army at the start of the Civil War, witnessed the massacre but, along with his company of soldiers, had disobeyed orders to join the attack. "I refused to fire and swore [to my men] that none but a coward" would shoot unarmed women and children.

Sand Creek Massacre

Three weeks after the massacre, Soule wrote a letter to a superior officer revealing in graphic detail what had actually happened at Sand Creek: "Hundreds of women and children were coming toward us, and getting on their knees for mercy," he noted, only to be murdered and "have their brains beat out by men professing to be civilized." Far from being a hero, Soule added, Chivington encouraged the one-sided slaughter through his *lack* of leadership: "There was no organization among our troops, they were a perfect mob—every man on his own hook." Soule's company "was the only one that did not fire a shot." He predicted that "we will have a hell of a time with Indians this winter" because of what had happened at Sand Creek.

Congress and the army launched lengthy investigations into the tragedy at Sand Creek, and Captain Soule was among those called to testify in January 1865. The eventual congressional report concluded that Chivington had "deliberately planned and executed a foul and dastardly massacre," murdering "in cold blood" Indians who "had every reason to believe they were under [U.S.] protection." An army general described the Sand Creek Massacre as the "foulest and most unjustifiable crime in the annals of America."

Chivington resigned from the militia in disgrace in order to escape a military trial. He soon became the Denver sheriff. On April 23, 1865, Soule, the whistle-blower, was shot and killed in Denver. One of his murderers—never prosecuted—was identified as one of Chivington's soldiers.

Instead of helping to intimidate the remaining Indians, the public report on the **Sand Creek Massacre** ignited warfare that raged across the central plains for the next three years. Arapaho, Cheyenne, and Sioux war parties attacked scores of ranches and stagecoach stations, killing hundreds of white men and kidnapping many white women and children. More massacres were to come, on both sides. The federal government responded by authorizing the recruitment of soldiers from among Confederate military prisoners (called "white-washed Rebels") and the creation of African American cavalry regiments.

In 1866, Congress passed legislation establishing two "colored" cavalry units and dispatched them to the western frontier. The Cheyenne nicknamed them "buffalo soldiers" because they "fought like a cornered buffalo; who, like a buffalo, had suffered wound after wound, yet had not died; and who, like a buffalo, had a thick and shaggy mane of hair."

The buffalo soldiers were mostly Civil War veterans from Louisiana and Kentucky. They built and maintained forts, mapped vast areas of the Southwest, strung hundreds of miles of telegraph lines, protected railroad construction crews, subdued hostile Indians, and captured outlaws and rustlers. Eighteen of the buffalo soldiers won Congressional Medals of Honor for their service.

Indian Relocation

With other scattered battles erupting, a congressional committee in 1865 gathered evidence on the grisly Indian wars and massacres. Its 1867 "Report on the Condition of the Indian Tribes" led to the creation of an Indian Peace Commission charged with removing the causes of the Indian wars.

Congress decided that this would be best accomplished by persuading nomadic Indians yet again to move to out-of-the-way federal reservations where they would take up farming that would "civilize" them. They were to give up their ancestral lands in return for peace so that the whites could move in. The U.S. government had decided it had no choice but to gain control of the region—by purchase if possible, by force if necessary.

1867 Peace Commission

Sand Creek Massacre (1864) Colonel Chivington's unprovoked slaughter of the Cheyennes and Arapahos in Colorado, initially reported as a justified battle but soon exposed for the despicable massacre it was.

In 1867, a conference at Medicine Lodge, Kansas, ended with the Kiowas, Comanches, Arapahos, and Cheyennes reluctantly agreeing to move to land in western Oklahoma. The following spring, the western Sioux, called Lakotas, signed the Treaty of Fort Laramie (1868), in which they agreed to settle within the huge Black Hills Reservation in southwestern Dakota Territory, in part because they viewed the Black Hills as holy ground.

Grant's Indian Policy

In his inaugural address in 1869, President Ulysses S. Grant urged Congress to adopt more progressive policies toward Native Americans: "The proper treatment of *the original occupants of this land"* should enable the Native Americans to become *citizens* with all the rights enjoyed by every other American.

Grant's noble intentions, however, ran afoul of longstanding prejudices against Native Americans and the unrelenting efforts of miners, farmers, railroaders, and ranchers to trespass on Indian lands and reservations. The president recognized the challenges he faced. Indians, he admitted, "would be harmless and peaceable if they were not put upon by whites." Yet he also stressed that protecting the new transcontinental railroad across the plains was his top priority. In the end, however, Grant told army officers that "it is much better to support a peace commission than a [military] campaign against Indians."

Periodic clashes brought vengeful demands for military action. William T. Sherman, commanding general of the U.S. Army, directed General Philip Sheridan, who was in charge of the military effort in the West, to "kill and punish the hostiles [Indian war parties], capture and destroy the ponies" of the "Cheyennes, Arapahos, and Kiowas." Sherman then declared that "the more we kill this year, the less we will have to kill next year."

Neither Sherman nor Sheridan agreed with Grant's "peace policy." In their view, the president's naive outlook reflected the distance between the Great Plains and Washington, D.C. Fairness and understanding were not the correct weapons against Indian warriors. Sherman ordered Sheridan to force all "non-hostile" Indians onto federal reservations, where they would be provided land for farming, food, and supplies and equipment (a promise that was rarely kept).

Some Native Americans refused to be moved again. In the southern plains of New Mexico, north Texas, Colorado, Kansas, and Oklahoma, the Native Americans, dominated by the Comanches, the greatest horse-borne warriors in America, focused on hunting buffalo. Armed clashes occurred with increasing frequency until the Red River War of 1874–1875, when Sheridan's soldiers won a series of battles in the Texas Panhandle. He boasted that it was "the most successful of any Indian Campaign in this country since its settlement by the whites." The defeated Comanches, Cheyennes, Kiowas, and Arapahos were forced onto reservations.

Custer and the Sioux

Meanwhile, trouble was brewing again in the northern plains. White prospectors searching for gold were soon trespassing on Sioux hunting grounds despite promises that the army would keep them out. Ohio senator John Sherman warned that nothing would stop the mass migration of Americans across the Mississippi River: "If the whole Army of the United States stood in the way, the wave of emigration would pass over it to seek the valley where gold was found."

The massive gold rush in the Black Hills convinced some Indians to make a last stand. As Red Cloud, a Sioux chief, said, "The white men have crowded the Indians back year by year, and now our last hunting ground, the home of my people, is to be taken from us. Our women and children will starve, but for my part I prefer to die fighting rather than by starvation." Another prominent Sioux war chief, Sitting Bull, told Indians living on the Black Hills reservation that "the whites may get me at last, but I will have good times till then."

GEORGE A. CUSTER A reckless and glory-seeking lieutenant colonel of the U.S. Army, Custer led his troops to a catastrophic defeat against the Sioux in the Battle of Little Bighorn.

In 1875, Lieutenant Colonel George Armstrong Custer, a veteran Indian fighter driven by reckless ambition and courage, led a thousand soldiers in the Seventh Cavalry regiment into the Black Hills, where he announced the discovery of gold on French Creek near present-day Custer, South Dakota.

The news set off a massive gold rush, and within two years, the mining town of Deadwood overflowed with 10,000 miners. The undermanned army units in the area could not keep the miners from violating the rights guaranteed the Sioux by federal treaties. President Grant and federal authorities tried to convince the Sioux to sell the Black Hills to the government. Sitting Bull told the American negotiator to tell "the Great Father [Grant] that I do not want to sell any land to the government."

With that news, Custer was sent back to the Black Hills, this time to find roving bands of Sioux and Cheyenne warriors and force them back onto reservations. If they resisted, he was to kill them.

The colorful Custer, strikingly handsome with golden curly hair, stood out among his 600 horse soldiers. Having graduated last in his class at West Point, he was first in his class at gambling and socializing. Free-spirited and fun-loving, he studied and behaved just enough to graduate. He later urged cadets not to follow his own example. Custer loved war and the thrill of combat. An army officer said Custer was one of the few soldiers who fought for the fun of it; to him, war was "glorious." Custer was a natural warrior whose goal was "not to be wealthy, not to be learned, but to be great."

For all of Custer's flamboyant rebelliousness and lust for adventure, he was a bold, talented cavalry officer with remarkable endurance. During the Civil War, he had been promoted to general at the ripe age of twenty-three

BATTLE OF LITTLE BIGHORN, 1876 Amos Bad Heart Bull, an Oglala Sioux artist and historian, painted this scene from the Battle of Little Bighorn. **How did the Indians' victory at the Battle of Little Bighorn ultimately lead to their loss in the Great Sioux War?**

(reporters dubbed him the "Boy General") and had played an important role in the Union victory at Gettysburg, leading a gallant cavalry charge. Now he was in charge of an expedition to attack the wandering bands of Sioux hunting parties, even though he recognized that intruding Americans miners had caused the renewal of warfare. As Custer told newspaper reporters, "We are goading the Indians to madness by invading their hallowed [hunting] grounds."

The Great Sioux War

What became the **Great Sioux War** was the largest military campaign since the end of the Civil War. The war against the northern Indians lasted fifteen months and entailed fifteen battles in present-day Wyoming, Montana, South Dakota, and Nebraska. In June 1876, after several indecisive encounters, Custer found a large encampment of Sioux and their Northern Cheyenne and Arapaho allies on the Little Bighorn River in the southeast corner of the Montana Territory.

On June 25, Custer ordered his exhausted men to attack the Indian camp. "Hurrah boys, we've got them," he shouted, not realizing how vastly

Great Sioux War Conflict between Sioux and Cheyenne Indians and federal troops over lands in the Dakotas in the mid-1870s.

outnumbered they were. Within minutes, they were surrounded by as many as 2,500 warriors led by the fierce Crazy Horse ("A good day to fight, a good day to die!").

After a half hour of desperate fighting, Custer's 210 men, their ammunition exhausted, were all dead. Custer supposedly laughed as he fired his last bullet, for he knew his fate. Among the dead were two of Custer's brothers, a brother-in-law, and a nephew. Afterward, Cheyenne women pierced Custer's eardrums with sewing needles because he had failed to listen to their warnings to stay out of their ancestral lands. Custer's foolhardy tactics but brave death echoed a line from his favorite Shakespeare play, *Julius Caesar*: "I shall have glory by this losing day."

The Sioux had won their greatest battle, but in doing so they helped ensure that they would lose the war. Upon learning of the Battle of the Little Bighorn ("Custer's Last Stand"), President Grant and Congress abandoned the "peace policy" and dispatched more troops and supplies ("Custer's Avengers") to the plains. General Sheridan now planned for "total war" against the Sioux.

Under Sheridan's aggressive leadership, the army quickly regained the offensive and relentlessly pursued the Sioux and Cheyenne across Montana. Warriors were slain, villages destroyed, and food supplies burned. Iron Teeth, a Cheyenne woman, recalled an attack by "white soldiers" in November 1876. "They killed our men, women, and children." She ran away with her three daughters. Her husband and two sons remained to fight. "My husband," she remembered, "was walking, leading his horse, and stopping at times to shoot. Suddenly, I saw him fall. I started to go back to him, but my sons made me go on." The last time she saw her husband he was dead in the snow. "From the hilltops, we Cheyennes saw our lodges and everything in them burning."

Forced back onto reservations, the remaining Native Americans soon found themselves struggling to survive. Many of them died of starvation or disease. By the end of 1876, the chiefs living on the reservation agreed to sell the Black Hills to the U.S. government. In the spring of 1877, Crazy Horse and his people surrendered. The Great Sioux War was over.

The Last Resistance

In the Rocky Mountains and west to the Pacific Ocean, the same story of courageous yet hopeless resistance to masses of white intruders was repeated again and again. Indians were the last obstacle to white western expansion, and they suffered as a result. The Blackfeet and Crows had to leave their homes in Montana. In a war along the California-Oregon boundary, the Modocs held out for six months in 1871–1872 before they were overwhelmed. In 1879, the Utes were forced to give up their vast territories in western Colorado. In Idaho, the peaceful Nez Perce bands refused to surrender land along the Salmon River, and prolonged fighting erupted there and in eastern Oregon.

CHIEF JOSEPH Leader of the Nez Perce, Joseph was a strong, eloquent voice against the injustices suffered by the Native Americans.

In 1877, Joseph, a Nez Perce chief, led some 650 of his people on a 1,300-mile journey through Montana in hopes of finding safety in Canada. Just before reaching the border, they were caught by U.S. soldiers. As he surrendered, Joseph delivered an eloquent speech: "I am tired of fighting. Our chiefs are killed. . . . The old men are all dead. . . . I want to have time to look for my children, and see how many of them I can find. . . . Hear me, my chiefs! I am tired. My heart is sick and sad. From where the sun now stands I will fight no more forever." The Nez Perce asked to return to their ancestral lands in western Idaho, but they were forced to settle in the Indian Territory (Oklahoma), where many died of malaria.

A generation of Indian wars virtually ended in 1886 with the capture of Geronimo, a powerful chief of the Chiricahua Apaches, who had outridden, outwitted, and outfought the more numerous white soldiers in the Southwest for fifteen years. The fighting in Arizona and New Mexico was brutal. Once, the Apaches captured a group of settlers, tied them to their wagon wheels, and roasted them alive. U.S. Army units routinely lynched captured Apaches and treated women and children as combatants. Yet at times members of both sides expressed respect for the other. The general in charge of the soldiers who captured Geronimo called him "one of the brightest, most resolute, determined-looking men that I have ever encountered."

The Ghost Dance

The last major clash between Indians and American soldiers occurred in 1890. Late in 1888, Wovoka (or Jack Wilson), a Paiute in western Nevada, fell ill and in a delirium imagined being in the spirit world, where he learned of a deliverer coming to rescue the Indians and restore their lands. To hasten their deliverance, he said, the Indians must perform a ceremonial dance that would make them bulletproof against white soldiers. The Ghost Dance craze fed upon old legends of the dead reuniting with the living and bringing prosperity and peace.

The **Ghost Dance movement** spread rapidly. In 1890, the western Sioux adopted it with such passion that it alarmed white authorities. They banned the Ghost Dance on Lakota reservations, but the Indians defied the order and a crisis erupted. On December 29, 1890, a bloodbath occurred at Wounded Knee, South Dakota, after nervous soldiers fired into a group of Indians who had surrendered. Nearly 250 Indians and twenty-five soldiers died in the Battle of Wounded Knee.

The Indian wars had ended with characteristic brutality and misunderstanding. General Philip Sheridan, commander of U.S. troops in these conflicts, was acidly candid in summarizing how whites had treated the Indians: "We took away their country and their means of support, broke up their mode of living, their habits of life, introduced disease and decay among

Massacre at Wounded Knee

Ghost Dance movement
A spiritual and political movement among Native Americans whose followers performed a ceremonial "ghost dance" intended to connect the living with the dead and make the Native Americans bulletproof in battles intended to restore their homelands.

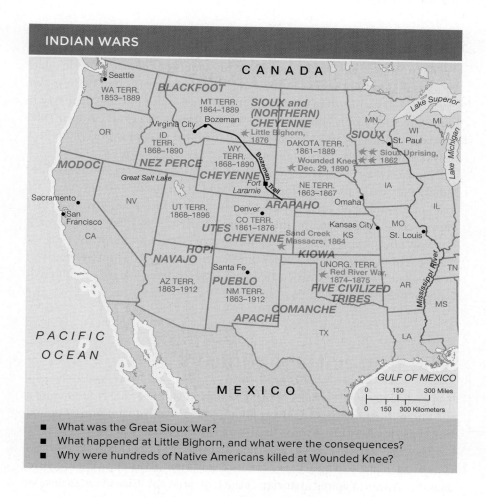

INDIAN WARS

- What was the Great Sioux War?
- What happened at Little Bighorn, and what were the consequences?
- Why were hundreds of Native Americans killed at Wounded Knee?

them, and it was for this and against this that they made war. Could anyone expect less?"

Attempts to Aid Indians

Indeed, many politicians and religious leaders condemned the persistent mistreatment of Indians. In his annual message of 1877, President Rutherford B. Hayes joined the protest: "Many, if not most, of our Indian wars have had their origin in broken promises and acts of injustice on our part." Helen Hunt Jackson, a novelist and poet, focused attention on the Indian cause in *A Century of Dishonor* (1881), a book that powerfully detailed the sad history of America's exploitation of Native Americans over the centuries.

In part as a reaction to Jackson's book, U.S. policies regarding Indians gradually improved, but they did little to improve the Indians' difficult living conditions and actually helped destroy remnants of their culture. The reservation policy inaugurated by the Peace Commission in 1867 did little more than extend a practice that dated from colonial Virginia. Partly humanitarian in motive, it also saved money: housing and feeding Indians on reservations cost less than fighting them.

Well-intentioned but biased white reformers sought to "Americanize" Indians by forcing them to become self-reliant farmers owning their own plots of land rather than members of bands or tribes holding property in common. Such reform efforts produced the **Dawes Severalty Act of 1887** (also called the General Allotment Act), the most sweeping policy directed at Native Americans in American history.

Sponsored by Senator Henry L. Dawes of Massachusetts, the act divided tribal lands and "allotted" them to individuals, granting 160 acres to each head of a family and lesser amounts to others. White Bear, a Kiowa chief, expressed a common complaint when he said that he did "not want to settle down in houses you [the federal government] would build for us. I love to roam over the wild prairie. There I am free and happy." His preferences were not heeded, however. Between 1887 and 1934, Indians lost an estimated 86 million of their 130 million acres.

CORE OBJECTIVE

7. Describe how the South and West had changed by 1900.

Turner's frontier thesis

Dawes Severalty Act of 1887 Federal legislation that divided ancestral Native American lands among the heads of each Indian family in an attempt to "Americanize" Indians by forcing them to become farmers working individual plots of land.

The End of the Frontier

The end of Native American resistance was one of several developments at the end of the nineteenth century that marked a transformation in the nation's history. Another involved a historical turning point.

The 1890 national census reported that the frontier era was over; Americans by then had spread across the entire continent. This news led Frederick Jackson Turner, a young historian at the University of Wisconsin, to develop his "frontier thesis." Published in 1893, it argued that more than slavery or any other single factor, "the existence of an area of free land, its continuous recession, and the advance of American settlement westward, explain American development." The experience of taming and settling the frontier, he added, had shaped the national character in fundamental ways. It was

> to the frontier [that] the American intellect owes its striking characteristics. That coarseness and strength combined with acuteness and acquisitiveness; that practical, inventive turn of mind, quick to find expedients; that masterful grasp of material things, lacking in the artistic but powerful to effect great ends; that restless, nervous energy; that dominant individualism, working for good and for evil, and withal that buoyancy and exuberance which comes with freedom— these are traits of the frontier, or traits called out elsewhere because of the existence of the frontier.

Now, however, Turner stressed, "the frontier has gone and with its going has closed the first period of American history."

Turner's view of the frontier—as the westward-moving source of the nation's democratic politics, open society, unfettered economy, and rugged individualism—gripped the popular imagination. But his frontier thesis left out much of the story of American development. The frontier experience that Turner described was in many respects a self-serving myth involving only Christian white men and devoid of towns and cities, which in fact grew along with the frontier, not after it had been tamed. He virtually ignored the role of women, African Americans, Native Americans, Hispanics, and Asians in shaping the human geography of the western United States. Moreover, Turner's frontier was always the site of heroism, triumph, and progress. He ignored the evidence of greed, exploitation, and failure in the settling of the West.

Turner also implied that America would be fundamentally different after 1890 because the frontier experience was essentially over. In many respects, however, the West has retained the qualities associated with the rush for land, gold, timber, and water rights. The mining frontier, as one historian has recently written, "set a mood that has never disappeared from the West: the attitude of every extractive industry—get in, get rich, get out."

By 1900, both the South and West were quite different from what they had been in 1865. What they had in common were dramatically changed economic conditions. In the West, the emergence of mechanized commercial agriculture changed the nature of farming. By the end of the nineteenth century, many homesteaders had been forced to abandon their farms and become wage-earning laborers, migrant workers often moving with the seasons to different states to harvest different crops. They were often treated as poorly as the sharecroppers in the South. One western worker complained that the landowner "looked at me, his hired hand, as if I was just another work horse."

As discontent rose among farmers and farmworkers in the South and the West, many of them joined the People's party, whose followers were known as Populists, a grassroots social and political movement that was sweeping the poorest rural regions of the nation. In 1892, a Minnesota farm spokesman named Ignatius Donnelly told Populists at their national convention that "we meet in the midst of a nation brought to the verge of moral, political, and material ruin." He affirmed that Populism sought "to restore the Government of the Republic to the hands of the 'plain people' with whom it originated."

| Birth of the Populist party |

The Populist movement would tie the South and West together in an effort to wrest control of the political system from the Republicans in the Northeast and Midwest. That struggle would come to define the 1890s and determine the shape of the twentieth century.

Reviewing the
CORE OBJECTIVES | INQUIZITIVE

■ **The New South** Many southerners embraced the vision of the New South promoted by Henry Grady and others, which called for a more diverse economy with greater industrialization, wider distribution of wealth, and more vocational training. The cotton textile industry grew to surpass that of New England, iron and steel manufacturing increased, and the *American Tobacco Company* became the world's largest manufacturer of cigarettes. But agriculture—and especially the growing of cotton—still dominated the southern economy, much as it had before the Civil War. Land remained concentrated in few hands, and the *crop-lien system* left much of the population, both black and white, with little choice but to cultivate cotton for these large landholders.

■ **Jim Crow policies in the South** During the 1890s, Southern states disenfranchised the vast majority of African American voters and instituted a series of policies known as Jim Crow laws segregating blacks and whites in all public facilities. Starting with the *Mississippi Plan (1890)*, state governments passed a series of comprehensive measures making it impossible for most African Americans and some poor whites to vote through poll taxes, grandfather clauses, literacy tests, and residency requirements. Disenfranchisement was followed by legalized segregation ("*separate but equal*"), ruled constitutional by the Supreme Court in the 1896 *Plessy v. Ferguson* decision. African Americans

who resisted were often the target of violence at the hands of whites, the worst form being organized lynching, or public torture, mutilation, and execution of African Americans, usually men. African Americans in the South responded by turning inward and strengthening their own social institutions. Their leading spokesman, Booker T. Washington, used a famous speech, called the *Atlanta Compromise* (1895), to encourage southern blacks to focus on vocational training and economic self-sufficiency rather than risking defeat by demanding the immediate restoration of their civil rights.

■ **Western Migrants** Life in the West was often harsh and violent, but the promise of cheap land or wealth from mining drew settlers from the East. Although most westerners were white Protestant Americans or immigrants from Germany and Scandinavia, Mexicans, African Americans (the *Exodusters*), and Chinese, as well as many other nationalities, contributed to the West's diversity. About three fourths of those who moved to the West were men.

■ **Miners, Farmers, Ranchers, and Women** Many migrants to the West were attracted to opportunities to mine, ranch, farm, or work on the railroads. Miners were drawn to the discovery of precious minerals such as silver at the *Comstock Lode* in Nevada in 1859. But most miners and cattle ranchers did not acquire wealth, because mining and raising cattle, particularly after the development of barbed wire and the end of the open range, became large-scale enterprises run by corporations. Because of the economic hardship and the rugged isolation of life in the West, women there achieved greater equality in everyday life, including voting rights, than did most women elsewhere in the country.

■ **Indian Wars and Policies** By 1900, Native Americans in the West were no longer free to roam the plains, as the influx of miners, ranchers, farmers, and soldiers had curtailed their traditional way of life. The prevailing attitude of most whites in the West was to displace or exterminate the Native Americans. In 1864, for example, Colorado militiamen decimated a group of Indians—men, women, and children—at the *Sand Creek Massacre.* Instances of armed resistance, such as the *Great Sioux War,* were crushed. Initially, Indian tribes were forced to sign treaties and were confined to reservations. Beginning in 1887 with the *Dawes Severalty Act,* the American government's Indian policy shifted. It now forced Indians to relinquish their traditional culture and adopt the "American way" of individual landownership.

KEY TERMS

American Tobacco Company *p. 613*

crop-lien system *p. 615*

Mississippi Plan (1890) *p. 618*

separate but equal *p. 620*

Atlanta Compromise (1895) *p. 624*

Exodusters *p. 627*

Comstock Lode *p. 629*

Indian wars *p. 637*

Sand Creek Massacre (1864) *p. 639*

Great Sioux War *p. 642*

Ghost Dance movement *p. 644*

Dawes Severalty Act of 1887 *p. 646*

CHRONOLOGY

1859	Comstock Lode is discovered
1862	Congress passes the Homestead Act
1864	Sand Creek Massacre in Colorado
1873	Joseph Glidden invents barbed wire
1876	Battle of Little Bighorn
1880s	Henry Grady spreads the New South idea
1886	Surrender of Geronimo marks the end of the Indian wars
1887	Congress passes the Dawes Severalty Act
1890	Battle of Wounded Knee
	James B. Duke forms the American Tobacco Company
1893	Frederick J. Turner outlines his "frontier thesis"
1900	South surpasses New England in production of cotton fabric

𝌀 INQUIZITIVE

Go to InQuizitive to see what you've learned—and learn what you've missed—with personalized feedback along the way.

WET NIGHT ON THE BOWERY (1911) This scene of early-twentieth-century life in New York City by John Sloan captures people of all walks of life converging on a rainy night: a smartly dressed society woman (left), a prostitute (center), and drunks stumbling about farther down the block. Running overhead is the elevated train, while an electric trolley gleams from the wet street.

Society and Politics in the Gilded Age

1865–1900

The period from the end of the Civil War to the beginning of the twentieth century was an era noted for the widening social, economic, and political gap between the powerful and the powerless, the haves and have-nots. It was sarcastically labeled the Gilded Age for its greed and vulgarity and was a time marked by conspicuous consumption by the newly rich as they flaunted their enormous personal wealth—the same wealth that financed extensive political and corporate corruption. While the Gilded Age brought dramatic changes to lives of citizens across all socioeconomic classes, the resulting transformations to social and cultural life could hardly be considered "gilded" to average Americans or recent immigrants.

Between 1865 and 1900, America's urban population skyrocketed from 8 million to 30 million. In 1865, there were fewer than twenty cities with populations over 50,000; by 1900, there were four times that many. Between 1865 and 1900, millions of European and Asian immigrants, as well as migrants from America's rural areas, streamed into cities, attracted by the jobs and excitements they offered. "We cannot all live in cities," cautioned Horace Greeley, the New York newspaper editor and Democratic presidential candidate in 1872, "yet nearly all seem determined to do so."

The growth of cities brought an array of problems, among them widespread poverty, unsanitary living conditions, and new forms of political corruption. How to feed, shelter, and educate the new city dwellers taxed

CORE OBJECTIVES INQUIZITIVE

1. Understand the effects of urban growth during the Gilded Age, including the problems it created.

2. Describe the "new immigrants" of the late nineteenth century and how they were viewed by American society.

3. Explain how urban growth and the increasingly important role of science influenced leisure activities, cultural life, and social policy in the Gilded Age.

4. Assess how the nature of politics during the Gilded Age contributed to political corruption and stalemate.

5. Evaluate the effectiveness of politicians in developing responses to the major economic and social problems of the Gilded Age.

6. Analyze why the money supply became a major political issue during the Gilded Age, especially among small farmers, and describe its impact on American politics.

Gilded Age (1860–1896)
An era of dramatic industrial and urban growth characterized by widespread political corruption and loose government oversight of corporations.

the imaginations and resources of government officials. Even more challenging was the development of neighborhoods divided by racial and ethnic background as well as social class.

At the same time, researchers were making discoveries that improved human health, economic productivity, and communications. Advances in modern science stimulated public support for higher education but also opened up doubts about many long-accepted "truths" and religious beliefs, doubts that led to conflicts over whether or how Charles Darwin's controversial theory of evolution could be applied to human society.

Political life during the **Gilded Age** was shaped by three main factors: the balance of power between Democrats and Republicans, the high level of public participation in everyday politics, and the often corrupt alliance between business and political leaders at all levels of government. In 1873, Job Stephenson, an Ohio congressman, claimed that members of the House of Representatives were so often selling their votes to big business lobbyists that the Capitol should have been renamed an "auction room."

The most important political issue of the Gilded Age, however, was the growing tension between city and country, industry and agriculture. Millions of financially distressed farmers felt ignored or betrayed by the political process. While industrialists and large commercial farmers prospered, small farmers struggled with falling crop prices, growing indebtedness to banks and railroads, and what they considered big-city greed and exploitation.

By the 1890s, discontented farmers would channel their frustrations into political form and enliven a growing movement to expand ("inflate") the nation's money supply as a way to relieve economic distress. The election of 1896 symbolized the central conflict of the Gilded Age: the clashing cultural and economic values of two Americas, one older, small-scale, and rural and the other newer, bigger, and urban.

CORE **OBJECTIVE**

1. Understand the effects of urban growth during the Gilded Age, including the problems it created.

America's Move to Town

Cities are perhaps the greatest human invention. Not only do they attract people in large numbers to live in close proximity but they also stimulate innovation and creativity, productivity and energy. "The greater part of our population must live in cities," announced Josiah Strong, a prominent Congregationalist minister, in 1898. "There was no resisting the trend."

After the Civil War, millions of Americans migrated from rural areas to cities. Many had been pushed off the land by new agricultural machinery that sharply reduced the need for farmworkers. Four men could now perform the farmwork that earlier had required fourteen.

Others were drawn by jobs and new opportunities. By the end of the nineteenth century, much of the settlement of the West was taking an urban form, with new towns forming around mines and railroad junctions. Still other migrants, bored by rural or small-town life, moved to cities in search of more excitement.

While the Far West had the greatest proportion of urban dwellers, concentrated in cities such as San Francisco and Denver, the Northeast and Midwest held far more people in huge cities—New York, Boston, Philadelphia, Pittsburgh, Chicago, Cincinnati, St. Louis, and others. More and more of these city dwellers had little or no money and nothing but their labor to sell. By 1900, more than 90 percent of the people in New York City's most densely populated borough, Manhattan, lived in rented houses or in congested, low-cost buildings called **tenements**, where residents, many of them immigrants, were packed like sardines in poorly ventilated and poorly lit apartments.

Growth in All Directions

Several advances in technology helped city buildings handle the surging populations. In the 1870s, heating innovations, such as steam radiators, enabled the construction of much larger apartment buildings, since coal-burning fireplaces and chimneys, expensive to build, were no longer needed in each apartment. In 1889, the Otis Elevator Company installed the first electric elevator, which made possible much taller buildings; before the 1860s, few structures had been more than five or six stories. During the 1880s, engineers also developed cast-iron and steel-frame construction techniques that allowed for taller structures—"skyscrapers."

> Skyscrapers and suburbs

Cities grew out as well as up, as horse-drawn streetcars and commuter railways let people live farther away from their downtown workplaces. In 1873, San Francisco became the first city to use cable cars that clamped onto a moving underground cable driven by a central power source. Some cities ran steam-powered trains on elevated tracks, but by the 1890s electric trolleys were preferred. Mass transit received an added boost from underground subway trains built in Boston, New York City, and Philadelphia.

The commuter trains and trolleys allowed a growing middle class of business executives and professionals (accountants, doctors, engineers, sales clerks, teachers, store managers, and attorneys) to retreat from crowded downtowns to quieter, tree-lined "streetcar suburbs." But the working poor, many of them immigrants or African Americans, could rarely afford to leave the inner cities. As their populations grew, cities became dangerously congested and plagued with fires, violent crimes, and diseases.

Crowds, Dirt, and Disease

The wonders of big cities—their glittering new electric lights, streetcars, telephones, department stores, theaters, and many other attractions—were magnetic lures for rural youth bored by the routine of isolated farm life. Millions of farm folk moved to the cities in search of economic opportunity and personal freedom. Yet in doing so they often traded one set of problems for

tenements Shabby, low-cost inner-city apartment buildings that housed the urban poor in cramped, unventilated apartments.

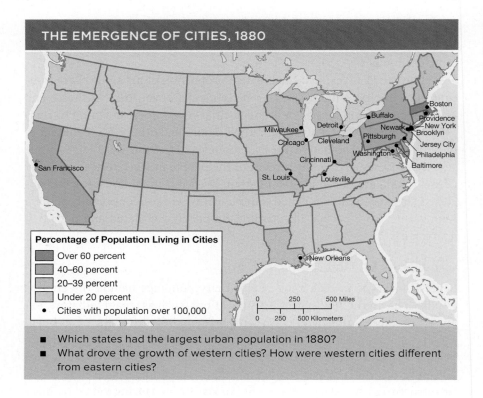

THE EMERGENCE OF CITIES, 1880

Percentage of Population Living in Cities

- Over 60 percent
- 40–60 percent
- 20–39 percent
- Under 20 percent
- Cities with population over 100,000

■ Which states had the largest urban population in 1880?

■ What drove the growth of western cities? How were western cities different from eastern cities?

another. In New York City in 1900, some 2.3 million people, two thirds of the city's entire population, were living in overcrowded and often filthy tenement housing.

> **Packed tenement housing**

Tenement apartment buildings were usually six to eight stories tall, lacking elevators, and jammed so tightly against one another that most of the apartments had little or no natural light or fresh air. Such buildings typically housed twenty-four to thirty-two families, usually with lots of children who had few places to play except in the streets. On average, there was only one toilet (called a *privy*) for every twenty people. In one New York tenement apartment, twelve adults slept in a room only thirteen feet square.

> **Unsanitary conditions and "sanitary reformers"**

Late-nineteenth-century cities were dirty, smelly, and disease-ridden. The child-mortality rate in many tenements was as high as 40 percent. Garbage and raw sewage were dumped into streets and waterways, causing epidemics of infectious diseases such as cholera, typhoid fever, and yellow fever. In one poor Chicago district at the end of the century, three of every five babies died before their first birthday.

So-called sanitary reformers—public health officials and engineers—eventually created cleaner conditions in tenements by creating regulations requiring more space per resident as well as more windows and plumbing facilities. Reformers also pushed successfully for modern water and sewage systems and for regular trash collection, which by 1900 had been adopted in nearly all American cities. The many animals in cities were a huge sanitary

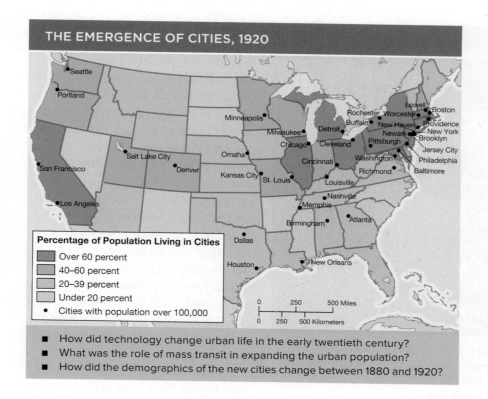

THE EMERGENCE OF CITIES, 1920

Percentage of Population Living in Cities

- Over 60 percent
- 40–60 percent
- 20–39 percent
- Under 20 percent
- Cities with population over 100,000

- How did technology change urban life in the early twentieth century?
- What was the role of mass transit in expanding the urban population?
- How did the demographics of the new cities change between 1880 and 1920?

challenge. Reformers lobbied to ban slaughterhouses as well as the raising of hogs and cattle within city limits and to replace horse-drawn trolleys with electric-powered streetcars or trolleys.

The New Immigration

America's roaring prosperity and the promise of political and religious freedom attracted waves of new immigrants from every part of the globe in the years after the Civil War. By 1900, nearly 30 percent of city residents were foreign-born. These newcomers provided much-needed labor, but their arrival in such huge numbers sparked racial and ethnic tensions.

A Surge of Newcomers from Europe

Immigration has always been one of the most powerful forces shaping American history. This was especially true between 1860 and 1920, as more and more foreigners, most of them young and poor, arrived from eastern and southern Europe in search of better living conditions and freedom from political and religious oppression. In 1890, four out of five New Yorkers were foreign-born, a higher proportion than in any other city in the world. Chicago was not far behind.

> CORE **OBJECTIVE**
> **2.** Describe the "new immigrants" of the late nineteenth century and how they were viewed by American society.

ELLIS ISLAND To accommodate the soaring numbers of immigrants passing through New York, Congress built a reception center on Ellis Island, near the Statue of Liberty. Pictured here is its registry room, where immigrants awaited close questioning by officials.

Rapidly growing industries seeking low-wage workers—including mines, railroads, mills, and factories—sent agents abroad to lure immigrants to the United States. Under the Contract Labor Act of 1864, the federal government helped pay for immigrants' travel expenses to America. The law was repealed in 1868, but not until 1885 did the government stop companies from importing foreign laborers, a practice that put immigrant workers under the control of their employers. The tide of immigration rose from just under 3 million annually in the 1870s to more than 5 million in the 1880s. It fell to a little over 3.5 million in the 1890s before rising to its record level of nearly 9 million per year in the first decade of the twentieth century.

The so-called old immigrants who came before 1880 were mainly Protestants and Roman Catholics from northern and western Europe. This pattern began to change, however, as the proportion of immigrants from southern and eastern Europe, especially Russia, Poland, Greece, and Italy, rose sharply. After 1890, these "**new immigrants**" made up a majority of the newcomers. Their languages and cultural backgrounds were markedly different from those of most old immigrants as well as most native-born Americans. The dominant religions of the new immigrants, for example, were Judaism, Eastern Orthodox, and Roman Catholicism, whereas Protestants still formed a large majority of the total U.S. population.

Strangers in a New Land

Employer exploitation of immigrants

Once on American soil, desperately poor immigrants needed to find jobs—quickly. Many were greeted at the docks by family and friends who had come over before them; others, by representatives of immigrant-aid societies or by company recruiters offering low-paying and often dangerous jobs in mines, mills, or sweatshops and on railroads. Since most immigrants knew little if any English and nothing about American employment practices, they were easy targets for exploitation. Many unwittingly lost a healthy percentage of their wages to unscrupulous hiring agents in exchange for a bit of whiskey and a job. Other companies eager for workers gave immigrants train tickets to inland cities such as Buffalo, Pittsburgh, Cleveland, Chicago, Milwaukee, Cincinnati, and St. Louis.

new immigrants Wave of newcomers from southern and eastern Europe, including many Jews, who became a majority among immigrants to America after 1890.

MULBERRY STREET, 1900 This photograph captures the many Italian immigrants who made Mulberry Street in downtown New York City their home at the turn of the century. Horse-drawn carts weave through people shopping, socializing, and people gazing.

The Nativist Response

Then, as now, many native-born Americans saw the wave of new immigrants as a threat to their way of life and their jobs. Many of these "**nativists**" were also racists who believed that "Anglo-Saxon" Americans—people of British or Germanic background—were superior to the Slavic, Italian, Greek, and Jewish newcomers. A Stanford University professor, for instance, called the immigrants from southern and eastern Europe "illiterate, docile, lacking in self-reliance and initiative, and not possessing the Anglo-Teutonic conceptions of law, order, and government."

Throughout American history, Congress has passed laws regulating immigration that have been inconsistent in their goals and frequently rooted in racial and ethnic prejudice. During the late nineteenth century, such prejudice took an especially ugly turn against the Chinese, who suffered discrimination even beyond that leveled at the new immigrants from Europe. By 1880, some 75,000 Chinese formed about a ninth of the population of California. Their visible differences made them easy targets for discrimination. They were not white, they were not Christian, and many could not read or write. Whites resented them for supposedly taking their jobs, although in

> Racism leads to restrictions on immigration

nativists Native-born Americans motivated by racial prejudice who blamed immigrants for social or economic problems and sought to restrict their access to America.

CHINESE EXCLUSION ACT The Chinese caricature of John Chinaman is escorted out of America by Lady Liberty with his ironing board and opium pipe, while other accepted minorities look on. **Why were Chinese immigrants targeted above other new immigrant populations?**

many instances the Chinese were willing to do the menial work that whites refused to do.

For these and other reasons, Congress in 1882 passed the **Chinese Exclusion Act**, the first federal law to restrict immigration on the basis of race. The act, which barred any more Chinese laborers from entering the country for the next ten years, was periodically renewed before being extended indefinitely in 1902. Not until 1943 were barriers to Chinese immigration finally removed.

The Chinese were not the only group targeted, however. In 1891, nativists formed the Immigration Restriction League to save the Anglo-Saxon "race" from being "contaminated" by "alien" immigrants. The league sought to convince Congress to ban illiterate immigrants, even though illiterate immigrants from Britain and Germany had been allowed into the United States in the past. Three presidents vetoed bills banning illiterate immigrants: Grover Cleveland in 1897, William H. Taft in 1913, and Woodrow Wilson in 1915 and 1917. The last time, however, Congress overrode the veto.

CORE **OBJECTIVE**

3. Explain how urban growth and the increasingly important role of science influenced leisure activities, cultural life, and social policy in the Gilded Age.

Chinese Exclusion Act (1882) Federal law that barred Chinese laborers from immigrating to America.

Changes in Popular and Intellectual Culture

The flood of people into cities brought changes in patterns of recreation and leisure. Middle- and upper-class families, especially those who had moved to streetcar suburbs, often spent free time together at home, singing around a piano, reading, or playing games—cards, dominoes, backgammon, chess, and checkers. In congested urban areas, politics as a form of public entertainment attracted ever larger crowds, saloons became even more popular social centers for working-class men, and new forms of mass entertainment—movie theaters, music halls, vaudeville shows, art museums, symphony orchestras, and circuses—appealed to a broad cross-section of city residents.

Urbanization and technological progress also contributed to the prestige of modern science, which increased enormously during the second half of the nineteenth century. By encouraging what one writer called a "mania for facts," scientists generated changes throughout social, intellectual, and cultural life. "I tell you these are great times," the writer and social critic Henry Adams wrote to his brother in 1862. "Man has mounted science and is now run away." Scientific research led to transformational technologies such as electrical power and lights, telephones, phonographs, motion pictures, bicycles, and automobiles.

Urban Leisure and Entertainment Options

Although only men could vote in most states, both men and women flocked to hear candidates speak at political party meetings. In the largest cities, membership in a political party offered many of the same benefits as belonging to a club or a college fraternity, as local political organizations provided social activities in addition to promoting new candidates. As labor unions became increasingly common, they, too, took on social roles for working-class men.

> Old and new forms of mass entertainment

The sheer number of city dwellers also helped generate new forms of mass entertainment, such as traveling Wild West shows, vaudeville shows featuring singers, dancers, and comedians; cycling; and spectator sports. In the last quarter of the nineteenth century, college football and basketball and professional baseball began attracting many fans. In large cities, the new streetcar transit systems helped people gather easily for sporting events, and rooting for the home team helped unify a city's ethnic and racial groups and social classes. By the end of the century, sports of all kinds had become a major part of American popular culture.

Still, the most popular leisure destinations for urban working-class men were not athletic stadiums but saloons, beer gardens, and dance halls. By 1900, the United States had more saloons (over 325,000) than grocery stores and meat markets. New York City alone had 10,000 saloons, or one for every 500 residents.

The saloon served as the workingman's social club, offering fellowship to men who often worked ten hours a day, six days a week. In cities such as New York, Boston, Philadelphia, and Chicago, the customers were disproportionately Irish, German, and Italian Catholics, who tended to vote Democratic partly because the "temperance" organizations that tried to close down saloons were led by Protestant Republicans.

VAUDEVILLE For as little as 1¢ a ticket, vaudeville shows aimed to please the tastes of their wildly diverse audience with a great range of entertainment.

The popularity of saloons

Politics was often the topic of discussion in saloons; in fact, in New York City in the 1880s, saloons doubled as polling places, where patrons could cast their votes in local elections. One journalist called the saloon "the social and intellectual center of the neighborhood."

Urban women and leisure

Besides drinking, socializing, and talking politics, men also went to saloons to check job postings, engage in labor union activities, cash paychecks, mail letters, read newspapers, and gossip. Patrons could play chess, billiards, darts, cards, dice, or even handball, since many saloons included gymnasiums. Although the main barroom was for men only, women and children were allowed to enter a side door to buy a pail of beer to carry home (a task called "rushing the growler"). Some saloons also provided "snugs," separate rooms for women customers. About a third of saloons, called "stall saloons," included "wine rooms" where prostitutes worked.

Married working-class women had even less leisure time than working-class men. As a social worker noted, "The men have the saloons, political clubs, trade-unions or [fraternal] lodges for their recreation . . . while the mothers have almost no recreation, only a dreary round of work, day after day, with occasionally doorstep gossip to vary the monotony of their lives." Married working-class women often used the streets as their public space. Washing clothes, supervising children at play, or shopping at the local market provided opportunities for socializing with other women.

CONEY ISLAND Even members of the working class could afford the inexpensive rides at the popular Steeplechase Park in Coney Island, Brooklyn, New York.

Single women, many of whom worked as domestic servants ("maids") and had more time than working mothers for leisure and recreation, flocked to dance halls, theaters, amusement parks, and picnic grounds. With the advent of movie theaters during the second decade of the twentieth century, the cinema became the most popular form of entertainment for working women. As an advertisement for a theater promised, "If you are tired of life, go to the movies."

The Impact of Darwinism

Virtually every field of thought during the Gilded Age felt the impact of English scientist Charles Darwin's controversial book *On the Origin of Species* (1859), whose first edition sold out in one day. Basing his conclusions on extensive field research, Darwin argued that most organisms produced many more offspring than could survive. Those offspring with certain favorable characteristics lived while others died from disease or predators. This process of "natural selection" over many millions of years, Darwin explained, had led to the evolution of modern species from less complex forms of life. As Darwin wrote, "The vigorous, the healthy, and the happy survive and multiply."

CHARLES DARWIN Darwin's scientific theories introduced and influenced more than a century of political and social debate.

The idea of biological evolution was shocking because most people in Europe and America still embraced a literal interpretation of the biblical creation story. Darwin's biological findings suggested to many, then and since, that there was no providential God controlling the universe and that people were no different from plants and animals, that they too evolved by trial and error rather than by God's purposeful hand.

These ideas generated heated arguments. Many Christians charged that Darwin's ideas led to atheism, a denial of the existence of God, while others found their faith severely shaken. Most of the faithful, however, came to reconcile science and religion. They decided that the process of evolutionary change occurring in nature must be God's doing.

Social Darwinism Although Darwin's complex theory of evolution applied only to biological phenomena, many drew broader implications from it, as the temptation to apply evolutionary theory to human society proved irresistible. Darwin's fellow Englishman Herbert Spencer, a leading social philosopher, was the first major prophet of what came to be called **social Darwinism**. Spencer argued that human society and its institutions, like the organisms studied by Darwin, evolved through the same process of natural selection. The "survival of the fittest," in Spencer's chilling phrase, was the engine of social progress.

Darwin himself dismissed Spencer's social theories, objecting in particular to his assumption that the evolutionary process in the natural world had any relevance to human social institutions. Others, however, eagerly endorsed

social Darwinism The application of Charles Darwin's theory of evolutionary natural selection to human society; social Darwinists used the concept of "survival of the fittest" to justify class distinctions, explain poverty, and oppose government intervention in the economy.

the notion of social Darwinism. If, as Spencer believed, society naturally evolved for the better through "survival of the fittest," then government interference with human competition in the marketplace was a serious mistake because it would help "unfit" people survive and thereby hinder progress.

Social Darwinism implied the need for hands-off, laissez-faire government policies; it argued against the regulation of business, for example, or of required minimum standards for sanitation and housing. To Spencer and his many followers, the only acceptable charity was voluntary, and even that was of dubious value. Spencer warned that "fostering the good-for-nothing [people] at the expense of the good, is an extreme cruelty" to the health of civilization.

For Spencer and his many American supporters, successful businessmen and corporations provided proof of the concept of "survival of the fittest." Oil tycoon John D. Rockefeller revealed his own embrace of social Darwinism when he told his Baptist Sunday-school class that the "growth of a large business is merely a survival of the fittest. . . . This is not an evil tendency in business. It is merely the working-out of a law of nature and a law of God."

Reform Darwinism The efforts on the part of Yale professor William Graham Sumner, Spencer's chief academic disciple, to use Darwinism to promote "rugged individualism" and oppose government regulation of business and efforts at social reform provoked strong criticism and inspired an alternative use of Darwinism in the context of human society. What came to be called reform Darwinism found its major advocate in Lester Frank Ward, a federal government employee who fought his way up from poverty and never lost his empathy for the underdog.

Ward's book *Dynamic Sociology* (1883) singled out one aspect of evolution that both Darwin and Spencer had neglected: the human brain. True, as Sumner claimed, people, like animals, compete, but as Ward explained, people also collaborate; unlike animals, people can plan for a distant future, and they have minds capable of shaping and directing social change. Far from being the helpless object of irresistible evolutionary forces, Ward argued, humanity could actively control the process of social evolution through long-range planning.

Ward's reform Darwinism thus posed a direct challenge to Sumner's conservative social Darwinism, holding that *cooperation*, not competition, would better promote social progress. Government, in Ward's view, could contribute to social progress by pursuing two main goals: alleviating poverty, which impeded the development of the mind, and promoting the education of the masses. "Intelligence, far more than necessity," Ward wrote, "is the mother of invention," and "the influence of knowledge as a social factor, like that of wealth, is proportional to the extent of its distribution."

As the intellectual justification for social progress, Ward's concept of reform Darwinism would prove to be one of the pillars of the "progressive" movement that would improve the quality of life in modern America during the late nineteenth century and after.

Gilded Age Politics

The Gilded Age was an era that saw more political corruption than political innovation. As a young college graduate in 1879, future president Woodrow Wilson described the state of the political system as "no leaders, no principles." The real movers and shakers of the Gilded Age were not the men who sat in the White House or Congress but those who owned the huge corporations. These "captains of industry," labeled "robber barons" by critics, regularly used their wealth to "buy" elections and favors from both major political parties and at all levels of government. Jay Gould, one of the most aggressive railroad giants, admitted that he elected "the [New York] legislature with [his] own money."

The activities of "special interests," those businesses that bought favors from government officials, dominated Gilded Age politics. As President Rutherford B. Hayes confessed, the "real difficulty" with the political system of his time was "the vast wealth and power in the hands of the few and unscrupulous who represent or control capital." By the end of the nineteenth century, however, new political movements and parties were pushing reforms to deal with the many excesses and injustices created by a political system that had grown corrupt in its support for the "special interests" of Big Business.

Local Politics and Party Loyalties

Perhaps the most important feature of Gilded Age politics was its local focus. Americans of the time expected little direct support from the federal government, and most political activity occurred at the state and local levels. Unlike today, the federal government was an insignificant force in the daily lives of most Americans, in part because it was so small. In 1871, the entire federal civilian workforce totaled 51,000 (most of them postal workers), of whom only 6,000 actually worked in Washington, D.C. Not until the twentieth century did the importance of the federal government begin to surpass that of local and state governments.

Americans during the Gilded Age were intensely loyal to their political party, which they joined as much for the social fellowship and networking connections as for its positions on issues. Attending political speeches and gatherings was a major form of public recreation, and party loyalists eagerly read newspaper coverage of political issues and joined in rallies, picnics, and parades.

Party members paid dues to join, and party leaders were so powerful in promoting their "special interests" that they demanded campaign contributions from the most powerful captains of industry and finance. Collis Huntington, a California railroad tycoon, admitted that bribery in the form of campaign contributions was regularly expected in Congress: "If you have to pay money to have the right thing done, then it is only just and fair to do it." Horatio Seymour, a Democratic governor of New York and a presidential

> **CORE OBJECTIVE**
> **4.** Assess how the nature of politics during the Gilded Age contributed to political corruption and stalemate.

> Corporate-funded corruption

> A local rather than federal focus

> Political parties as social networks and forms of recreation

> Bribery, patronage, and boss rule

WILLIAM "BOSS" TWEED A larger-than-life political boss was New York City's William "Boss" Tweed, whose powerful connections made "no prison big enough to hold the Boss." **How does the satirical portrayal of this party "boss" critique the political changes of the Gilded Age?**

party boss A powerful political leader who controlled a "machine" of associates and operatives to promote both individual and party interests, often using informal tactics such as intimidation or the patronage system.

patronage An informal system (sometimes called the "spoils system") used by politicians to reward their supporters with government appointments or contracts.

candidate in 1868, explained that "our people want men in office who will not steal, but who will not interfere with those who do."

In cities crowded with new immigrant voters, politics was usually controlled by "rings"—small groups of powerful insiders who shaped policy and managed the nomination and election of candidates. Each ring typically had a powerful **party "boss,"** an absolute ruler who used his "machine"—a network of neighborhood activists and officials—to govern local politics. Bosses staged election parades, fireworks displays, and free banquets—with alcoholic beverages—for voters. They helped settle local disputes, provided aid for the needy, and distributed government jobs and contracts to loyal followers and corporate donors. Throughout most of the nineteenth century, almost every government job—local, state, and federal—was subject to the latest election results. This meant that the party in power expected government employees to become campaign workers and to do the bidding of party bosses during elections.

Party bosses, often arrogant and dictatorial in their behavior, decided who the candidates would be, often determined the party's positions on significant issues, and commanded loyalty and obedience by rewarding and punishing their members. Once in power, the bosses excelled at **patronage**, the long-standing system whereby party leaders rewarded supporters with government jobs and contracts—the so-called spoils of office. It was—and remains—a system that invited abuse and corruption. As President Ulysses S. Grant's secretary told a Republican party boss, "I only hope you will distribute the patronage in such a manner as will help the Administration."

Partisan Politics at the National Level

Several factors gave national politics during the Gilded Age its distinctive texture. First, the national political parties were much more powerful forces than they are today. Party loyalty was intense, often extending over generations in many families. A second distinctive element of Gilded Age politics at the national level was the close division between Republicans and Democrats in Congress. Both parties avoided controversial issues or bold initiatives because neither was dominant. The third important aspect of post–Civil War politics was the intensity of voter involvement at all levels—local and state as well as national. Voter turnout during the Gilded Age was commonly 70–80 percent. (By contrast, the turnout for the 2016 presidential election was 55 percent.)

During the Gilded Age, most voters cast their ballots for the same party year after year, generation after generation, regardless of the candidates.

Party loyalty was often an emotional choice. In the 1870s and 1880s, for example, people in the North and South continued to fight the Civil War during political campaigns. Republican candidates regularly "waved the bloody shirt," encouraging war veterans to "vote like you shot," while accusing Democrats of having caused "secession and civil war."

Democrats, especially in the South, responded to such attacks by reminding voters that they stood for limited government, states' rights, and white supremacy. Republicans tended to favor high tariffs on imports, but Democrats also supported tariffs if they benefited businesses in their districts. Third parties, such as the Greenbackers, Populists, and Prohibitionists, appealed to specific interests and issues, such as currency inflation, railroad regulations, or legislation to restrict alcohol consumption.

Party loyalties reflected religious and ethnic divisions as well as geographic ones. After the Civil War, the Republican party remained strongest in the North and West and weakest in the South. It attracted mainly Protestants of British descent. As the party of Abraham Lincoln (the "Great Emancipator") and Ulysses S. Grant, Republicans could also rely upon the votes of African Americans in the South (until their right to vote was taken away late in the century) and of a large bloc of Union veterans of the Civil War, who were organized into a powerful national fraternal group called the Grand Army of the Republic.

The Democrats, by contrast, were a more diverse and often unruly coalition of southern whites, northern immigrants, Roman Catholics, Jews, freethinkers, and those repelled by the Protestant Republican "party of morality." As one Chicago Democrat explained, "A Republican is a man who wants you t' go t' church every Sunday. A Democrat says if a man wants to have a glass of beer on Sunday he can have it."

The mostly rural Republican Protestants considered saloons the central social evil around which all others revolved, and they associated these evils with the ethnic groups that frequented saloons. Carrie Nation, the most colorful member of the Women's Christian Temperance Union (WCTU), became nationally known for attacking saloons with a hatchet. Saloons, she argued, stripped a married woman of everything by turning workingmen into alcoholics, as had happened with Nation's first husband: "Her husband is torn from her, she is robbed of her sons, her home, her food, and her virtue."

Presidential Politics

Between 1869 and 1913, from the first term of President Ulysses S. Grant through the election of William Howard Taft, Republicans monopolized the White House except for the two nonconsecutive terms of New York Democrat Grover Cleveland.

Otherwise, however, national politics was remarkably balanced between the two major parties. Between 1872 and 1896, their strength was so closely divided that because of support for third-party candidates, *no* president won a majority of the popular vote. In each of those presidential elections, sixteen states invariably voted Republican and fourteen voted Democratic, leaving six states whose results determined the outcome. The swing-vote role played by two of those states, New York and Ohio, decided the election of eight presidents from 1872 to 1908.

No chief executive between Abraham Lincoln and Theodore Roosevelt could be described as a "strong" president. All believed that Congress, not the White House, should formulate major policies. As Senator John Sherman of Ohio stressed, "The President should merely obey and enforce the law."

CORE **OBJECTIVE**

5. Evaluate the effectiveness of politicians in developing responses to the major economic and social problems of the Gilded Age.

Corruption and Reform: Hayes to Harrison

Both Republicans and Democrats had their share of corrupt officials willing to buy and sell government jobs or legislative votes, yet as early as the 1870s, in response to the corruption uncovered in the Grant administration, each party also developed factions promoting honesty in government. The struggle for "clean" government became one of the foremost issues of the Gilded Age.

Hayes and Civil Service Reform

President Rutherford B. Hayes brought to the White House in 1877 both a lingering controversy over the disputed election results (critics called him "His Fraudulency") and a new style of uprightness in sharp contrast to the scandals of the Grant presidency. The son of an Ohio farmer, Hayes was wounded four times in the Civil War. He went on to serve in Congress and as governor of Ohio. Stubbornly honest and conservative, he was, said a Republican journalist, a "third-rate nonentity" whose only virtue was that he was "obnoxious to no one."

Hayes had been the compromise presidential nominee of the two factions fighting for control of the Republican party, the so-called Stalwarts and Half-Breeds, led, respectively, by Senators Roscoe Conkling of New York and James G. Blaine of Maine. The Stalwarts had been "stalwart" in their support of President Grant during the furor over the misdeeds of his cabinet members. Further, they had mastered the "spoils system" of distributing political jobs to party loyalists. The Half-Breeds were called such because they supposedly were only half-loyal to Grant and half-committed to reform of the spoils system. But the two warring Republican factions existed primarily to advance the careers of Conkling and Blaine, who detested each other.

Republican resistance to Hayes's reform efforts

To his credit, President Hayes tried to stay above the petty political bickering. He joined the growing public outrage over political corruption, admitting that his party "must mend its ways" by focusing on Republican principles rather than fighting over the spoils of office. Hayes announced that it was time "for **civil service reform**." He appointed a committee to consider a "merit system" for hiring government employees. In a dramatic gesture, Hayes also fired Chester A. Arthur, a Stalwart Republican who ran the New York Customs House, because Arthur had abused the patronage system in ways, according to Hayes, that promoted "ignorance, inefficiency, and corruption."

Hayes's commitment to cleaning up politics enraged Republican leaders. In 1879, Ohio congressman James Garfield warned Hayes that "if he wishe[d] to hold any influence" with fellow Republicans, he "must abandon some of his notions of Civil Service reform." For his part, Hayes confessed that he had little hope of success because he was "opposed by . . . the most powerful men in [his] party."

On economic issues, Hayes held to a conservative line that would guide his successors—from both parties—for the rest of the century. His answer to the growing demands for expansion of the nation's money supply (which would become one of the leading political issues of the late nineteenth century) was to veto the Bland-Allison Act (1878), which provided for a slight increase in the supply of silver coins. (More money in circulation—inflation—was generally believed to raise farm prices and help those trying to pay off debts.) When Congress, including many Republicans, overturned Hayes's veto, the bruised president confided in his diary that he had become a president without a party. In 1879, with a year still left in his term, Hayes was ready to leave the White House. "I am now in my last year of the Presidency," he wrote a friend, "and look forward to its close as a schoolboy longs for the coming vacation."

PASSING ALONG REFORM A cover of *Puck* magazine soon after Garfield's election of 1880 shows Hayes as a woman abandoning a child labeled "Civil Service Reform" on Garfield's front steps.

Garfield, Arthur, and the Pendleton Act

With Hayes choosing not to pursue a second term, the Republican presidential nomination in 1880 was up for grabs. In the end, the party's squabbling factions selected a compromise candidate, Congressman James A. Garfield. An early foe of slavery, the tall Garfield had served as a Union army general, like Grant and Hayes, before being elected to Congress in 1863. In an effort to please the Stalwarts and also win the crucial state of New York, Chester A. Arthur, whom Hayes had fired as head of the New York Customs House, was named the party's candidate for vice president.

The Democrats, as divided as the Republicans, selected their own compromise candidate: Winfield Scott Hancock, a retired Union general who had

civil service reform An extended effort led by political reformers to end the patronage system; led to the Pendleton Act (1883), which called for government jobs to be awarded based on merit rather than party loyalty.

distinguished himself at the Battle of Gettysburg but had done little since. In large part, Hancock was chosen to help deflect the Republicans' "bloody-shirt" attacks on Democrats as the party of the Confederacy. In an election marked by widespread bribery, Garfield eked out a popular-vote plurality of only 39,000, or 48.5 percent. He won a more comfortable margin of 214 to 155 in the Electoral College.

A Presidency Cut Short

In his inaugural address, President Garfield gave an impassioned defense of civil rights, arguing that the "elevation of the negro race from slavery to the full rights of citizenship is the most important political change we have known since the adoption of the Constitution of 1787." But he also confirmed that the Republicans had ended efforts to reconstruct the former Confederacy. Southern blacks were now on their own; they had been "surrendered to their own guardianship."

Garfield's potential as president was suddenly cut short on July 2, 1881, after only four months in office, when he was shot twice by Charles Guiteau, a former Republican who had been turned down for a federal job. One bullet grazed the president's arm; the other went into his back. As a policeman wrestled the assassin to the ground, Guiteau shouted: "Yes! I have killed Garfield! [Chester] Arthur is President of the United States. I am a Stalwart!"— a declaration that would eventually destroy the Stalwart wing of the Republican Party.

On September 19, after seventy-nine days, Garfield died of complications resulting from inept medical care. During a sensational ten-week trial, Guiteau explained that God had ordered him to kill the president. The jury refused to believe that he was insane and pronounced him guilty of murder. On June 30, 1882, Guiteau was hanged; an autopsy revealed that his brain was diseased.

The Civil Service Commission

Civil Service Commission: Merit system for government employees

In their grief over Garfield's death, Americans blamed Roscoe Conkling and the Stalwart Republicans for inciting Guiteau. One New York newspaper headline screamed: "Murdered by the Spoils System!" The new president, Chester A. Arthur, surprised most political observers by distancing himself from the Stalwarts and even becoming a civil service reformer himself.

In 1883, the momentum against the "spoils system" generated by Garfield's assassination enabled George H. Pendleton, a Democratic senator from Ohio, to convince Congress to establish a Civil Service Commission. Because of the Pendleton Civil Service Reform Act, a growing percentage of federal jobs would now be filled on the basis of competitive tests (the "merit system") rather than political favoritism. In addition, federal employees running for office were prohibited from receiving political contributions from other government workers.

The Pendleton Act was a limited first step in cleaning up the patronage process. It was sorely needed, in part because the federal government was expanding rapidly. By 1901, there would be 256,000 federal employees, five times the number in 1871. A growing number of these federal workers were women, who by 1890 held a third of the government's clerical jobs.

The Campaign of 1884

Chester Arthur's efforts to clean up the spoils system might have attracted voters, but they did not please Republican leaders. So in 1884, the Republicans dumped Arthur and chose as their presidential nominee James Gillespie Blaine of Maine, the handsome, colorful secretary of state, former senator, and longtime leader of the Half-Breeds.

Corruption and a Sex Scandal Blaine was the consummate politician. He inspired the party faithful with his electrifying speeches and knew how to wheel and deal in the back rooms, sometimes evading the law in the process. One critic charged that Blaine "wallowed in spoils like a rhinoceros in an African pool."

Newspapers soon uncovered evidence of Blaine's corruption in the so-called Mulligan letters. They revealed that as Speaker of the House, Blaine had secretly sold his votes on measures favorable to a railroad corporation. There was no proof that he had committed any crimes, but the circumstantial evidence was powerful: his senatorial salary alone could not have built either his mansion in Washington, D.C., or his palatial home in Augusta, Maine (which has since become the state's governor's mansion).

During the 1884 presidential campaign, more embarrassing letters surfaced linking Blaine to shady deal making. For the reform element of the Republican party, this was too much, and many Republicans refused to endorse Blaine's candidacy. Party regulars scorned such critics as "goo-goos"—the good-government crowd. The editor of a New York newspaper jokingly called the anti-Blaine Republicans **Mugwumps**, after an Algonquian Indian word meaning "big chief."

The Mugwumps, a self-appointed political elite dedicated to promoting honest government, saw the election as "moral rather than political." Centered in the large cities and major universities of the Northeast, they were mostly professors, editors, and writers who included in their number the most famous American of the time, Mark Twain. The Mugwumps generally opposed tariffs on imports and championed free trade. Their foremost goal was to reform the process of appointing people to government jobs by making *all* federal jobs nonpartisan. Their break with the Republican party testified to the depth of their convictions.

The rise of the Mugwumps, as well as growing national concerns about political corruption, prompted the Democrats to nominate New Yorker Grover Cleveland, a minister's son, as a reform candidate. Cleveland had first attracted national attention in 1881, when he was elected the mayor of Buffalo on an anti-corruption platform. In 1882, he was elected governor of New York, and he continued to build a reform record by fighting New York City's corrupt Tammany Hall ring. As mayor and as governor, he repeatedly

Mugwumps Reformers who bolted the Republican party in 1884 to support Democrat Grover Cleveland for president over Republican James G. Blaine, whose secret dealings on behalf of railroad companies had brought charges of corruption.

"ANOTHER VOICE FOR CLEVELAND" A political cartoon from 1884 depicts Cleveland, with the ironic label "Grover the Good" hanging from his jacket, plugging his ears to drown out the cry of his illegitimate child.

vetoed bills because in his view they served private interests at the expense of the public good. He supported civil service reform, opposed expanding the money supply, and preferred free trade to high tariffs, which tended to enrich big businesses at the expense of consumers.

Although Cleveland was known for his honesty and integrity, a juicy scandal erupted around him. A newspaper in Buffalo revealed that Cleveland, a bachelor, had befriended an attractive widow named Maria Halpin, who later named him the father of her baby born in 1874. Cleveland had discreetly provided financial support for the child.

The escapades of Blaine and Cleveland provided some of the most colorful battle cries in political history: "Blaine, Blaine, James G. Blaine, the continental liar from the state of Maine," Democrats chanted. Republicans countered with "Ma, ma, where's my pa?"

Blunders by the Blaine Campaign Near the end of the nasty campaign, Blaine and his supporters committed two fateful blunders. The first occurred at New York City's fashionable Delmonico's restaurant, where Blaine went to a private dinner with 200 of the nation's wealthiest business leaders to ask them to help finance his campaign. Accounts of the unseemly

event appeared in the newspapers for days afterward. One headline blared: "Blaine Hobnobbing with the Mighty Money Kings!" The article explained that the banquet was intended to collect contributions for a "Republican corruption fund."

The second Blaine blunder occurred when a Protestant minister visiting Republican headquarters in New York referred to the Democrats as the party of "rum, Romanism, and rebellion [the Confederacy]." Blaine, who was present, let pass the implied insult to Catholics—a fatal oversight, since he had always cultivated Irish American support with his anti-English talk and repeated references to his mother being a Catholic. Democrats claimed that Blaine was, at heart, anti-Irish and anti-Catholic.

The two incidents may have tipped the close 1884 presidential election. The electoral vote came in at 219 to 182 in Cleveland's favor, but the popular vote ran far closer: Cleveland's plurality was fewer than 30,000 votes out of 10 million cast. Cleveland won the key state of New York by only 1,149 votes out of 1,167,169 cast.

Cleveland's Reform Efforts

During his first few months in office, President Cleveland struggled to keep Democratic officials from reviving the patronage system. In a letter to a friend, the new president reported that he was living in a "nightmare," that "dreadful, damnable, office-seeking hangs over me and surrounds me" and that it made him "feel like resigning." Democratic newspapers heaped scorn on him for refusing to award federal jobs to his supporters. One accused Cleveland of "ingratitude" toward those who had "delivered the vote." Despite the president's best efforts to promote civil service reform, about two thirds of the 120,000 federal jobs went to Democrats as patronage during his administration.

GROVER CLEVELAND As president, Cleveland made the issue of tariff reform central to the politics of the late 1880s.

Democratic resistance to civil service reform

Cleveland also opposed federal favors to Big Business. "A public office is a public trust" was one of his favorite sayings. He held to a strictly limited view of government's role in both economic and social matters, a philosophy illustrated by his 1887 veto of a congressional effort to provide desperate Texas farmers with seeds in the aftermath of a drought. "Though the people support the government, the government should not support the people," Cleveland asserted. During his administration, he would veto more acts of Congress than any previous president.

Regulation of Railroad Rates For all of his genuine commitment to limited government intervention, Cleveland urged Congress to adopt an important new policy: federal regulation of the rates charged by interstate railroads (those whose tracks crossed state lines) to ship goods, crops, or livestock. He believed with many others that railroads were charging unfairly high freight rates, especially in communities served by only one railroad. States had adopted laws regulating railroads since the late 1860s, but in 1886 the Supreme Court declared in *Wabash, St. Louis, and Pacific Railroad Company v. Illinois* that no state could regulate the rates charged by railroads engaged in *interstate* traffic. Because most railroads did cross state lines, Cleveland urged Congress to close the loophole.

> **Creation of the Interstate Commerce Commission**

Congress followed through, and in 1887 Cleveland signed an act creating the **Interstate Commerce Commission** (ICC), the first federal agency designed to regulate business activities. The law empowered the ICC's five members to ensure that railroad freight rates were "reasonable and just." The commission's actual powers proved to be weak, however, when tested in the courts. Over time, the ICC came to be ignored, and the railroads continued their practice of charging high freight rates while making secret pricing deals with large shippers.

> **Cleveland's anti-tariff stance**

Tariff Reform and the Election of 1888 President Cleveland's most dramatic challenge to the corrupting power of Big Business focused on **tariff reform**. During the late nineteenth century, the government's high-tariff policies, shaped largely by the Republican party, had favored big businesses by effectively shutting out foreign imports, thereby enabling U.S. corporations to dominate their American markets and charge higher prices for their products.

In 1887, Cleveland argued that Congress should reduce both the tariff rates ("the vicious, inequitable and illogical source of unnecessary taxation . . . [and] a burden upon the poor") and the number of imported goods subject to tariffs (over 4,000 items), so as to enable European companies to compete in the American marketplace. His outspoken stance against high tariffs set the stage for his reelection campaign in 1888.

To oppose Cleveland, the Republicans, now calling themselves the GOP (Grand Old Party) to emphasize their longevity, turned to the obscure Benjamin Harrison, a Civil War veteran whose greatest attributes were his availability and the fact that he was from Indiana, a pivotal state in presidential elections. The grandson of President William Henry Harrison, he had a modest political record; he had lost a race for governor and had served one term in the U.S. Senate (1881–1887).

The Republicans accepted Cleveland's challenge to make tariffs the chief issue in the campaign. To fend off Cleveland's efforts to reduce the tariff, business executives contributed especially generously to the Republican cause. Still, the outcome was incredibly close. Cleveland won the popular vote by the thinnest of margins—5,540,329 to 5,439,853—but Harrison carried the Electoral College by 233 to 168. "Providence," said the new president, "has given us the victory." Matthew Quay, his campaign chairman, knew better. Harrison, he muttered, "ought to know that Providence hadn't a damned thing to do with it!" It was the distribution in key states of campaign money and promises of federal government jobs that won the election for Harrison.

Interstate Commerce Commission (ICC) (1887) An independent federal agency established in 1887 to oversee businesses engaged in interstate trade, especially railroads, but whose regulatory power was limited when tested in the courts.

tariff reform (1887) Effort led by the Democratic party to reduce taxes on imported goods, which Republicans argued were needed to protect American industries from foreign competition.

Republican Activism under Harrison

Harrison owed a heavy debt to Civil War veterans, whose votes had been critical to his election, and he paid it by signing the Dependent Pension Act, which doubled the number of Union war veterans (and their family members) receiving federal pensions. In addition, the Republicans took advantage of their control of the presidency and both houses of Congress to pass a cluster of other significant legislation in 1890: the Sherman Anti-Trust Act; the Sherman Silver Purchase Act; the McKinley Tariff Act; and the admission of Idaho and Wyoming as new states, which followed the admission of North and South Dakota, Montana, and Washington in 1889.

The Sherman Anti-Trust Act, named for Ohio senator John Sherman, was the first effort in the world to limit the size of businesses by prohibiting companies from "conspiring" to establish monopolies in their industries. Though badly needed, the new legislation was rarely enforced, in large part because of its vague definitions of "trusts" and "monopolies." From 1890 to 1901, only eighteen lawsuits were instituted, four of which were filed against labor unions rather than corporations.

As for tariff policy, Republicans viewed their victory over Cleveland in 1888 as a mandate to raise the tariff rates even higher. Piloted through Congress by Ohio representative William McKinley, the McKinley Tariff Act of 1890 raised duties on imported manufactured goods to their highest level ever. Its passage encouraged many American businesses to raise prices for their own goods, since they had no need to worry about European competitors, who were now effectively shut out of the American market.

"KING OF THE WORLD" Reformers targeted the growing power of monopolies, such as that of John D. Rockefeller's Standard Oil. **How did Congress attempt to curb Big Business in the 1890s?**

Inadequate Currency and Unhappy Farmers

Even more than tariffs, trusts, and efforts to clean up political corruption, national political life during the Gilded Age was preoccupied with complex monetary issues. In 1876, several farm organizations organized the independent "Greenback" party to promote the benefits of paper money over gold and silver coins; it won fifteen seats in Congress in 1878, illustrating the significance of currency issues to voters.

CORE **OBJECTIVE**

6. Analyze why the money supply became a major political issue during the Gilded Age, especially among small farmers, and describe its impact on American politics.

A shrinking money supply in a
growing economy

Behind many of these issues lay the fact that the nation's money supply had not grown along with the expanding economy of the late nineteenth century. From 1865 to 1890, the amount of money in circulation (both coins and paper currency) actually *decreased* about 10 percent at the same time that the economy and population were dramatically expanding. Such currency deflation raised the cost of borrowing money as the shrinking of the money supply enabled lenders to hike interest rates on loans. Creditors—bankers and others who loaned money—supported a "sound money" policy that limited the currency supply as a means of increasing their profits. By contrast, farmers, ranchers, and others who constantly had to borrow money to make ends meet claimed that the sound money policy had the deflationary effect of lowering prices for their crops and herds, driving them deeper into debt.

Increasing Unrest among Farmers

The 1890 congressional elections revealed a deep-seated unrest in the farming communities of the South and on the plains of Kansas and Nebraska, as well as in the mining towns of the Rocky Mountain region. People used the term *revolution* to describe the swelling grassroots support for the Populists, a new third party focused on the needs of miners and small farmers, many of whom did not own the land they worked. In drought-devastated Kansas, Populists won five congressional seats from Republicans. In early 1891, the newly elected Populists and Democrats took control of Congress just as an acute economic crisis appeared on the horizon: farmers' debts were mounting as crop prices plummeted.

A Vicious Cycle of Depressed Prices and Debt

Indebted farmers and falling
crop prices

Since the end of the Civil War, farmers in the South and the Great Plains had suffered from worsening economic conditions. The basic source of their problems was a decline in prices earned for their crops, a deflationary trend caused by overproduction and growing international competition in world food markets as well as the inadequate money supply.

The vast new lands brought under cultivation in the plains poured an ever-increasing supply of farm products into world markets, driving prices down. Meanwhile, farmers, especially small farmers in the South and West, had become increasingly indebted to "greedy" local banks or merchants who loaned them money to buy seed, fertilizer, tools, and other supplies. As prices for wheat, cotton, and corn dropped, however, so did the income the farmers received, thus preventing them from paying their debts on time.

In response, most farmers had no choice but to grow even more wheat, cotton, or corn, creating a vicious cycle: as still more grains and cotton were harvested and sold, the increased supply drove down prices and farmers' incomes even further. High tariffs on imported goods also hurt farmers because they blocked foreign competition, allowing U.S. companies to raise the prices of manufactured goods needed by farm families. Farmers, however, had to sell their crops in open world markets unprotected by tariffs, where competition lowered prices.

Besides bankers, merchants, and high tariffs, struggling farmers also blamed the railroads, warehouse owners, and food processors, the so-called middle men who helped get their products to market. They especially resented that railroads, most of which had a monopoly over the shipping of grains and livestock, charged such high rates to ship their farm products.

Silver and Inflation

Among all the factors distressing farmers, the nation's inadequate money supply emerged as the source of greatest frustration. In 1873, the Republican-controlled Congress had declared that only gold, not silver, could be used for coins. This decision (called "the Crime of '73" by critics) occurred just when silver mines in the western states had begun to increase their production. Hard-pressed farmers in the South and Midwest demanded increased coinage of silver, which would inflate the currency and thereby raise commodity prices, providing farmers with more income with which to pay their annual debts.

They found allies among legislators representing the new western states. All six states admitted to the Union in 1889 and 1890 had substantial silver mines, and their new congressional delegations—largely Republican—wanted the federal government to buy more silver for coins. The so-called silver delegates shifted the balance in Congress enough to pass the Sherman Silver Purchase Act (1890), which required the Treasury to purchase 4.5 million ounces of silver each month with new paper money. Such inflationary policies helped set the stage for the currency issue to eclipse all others during the financial panic that would sweep the country in 1893.

> The Sherman Silver Purchase Act (1890)

In the 1890 midterm elections, voters rebelled not only against the McKinley Tariff but also in support of the militant new farm protests. The result was that Democrats outnumbered Republicans in the new House of Representatives by almost 3 to 1; in the Senate, the Republican majority was reduced to eight. One of the election casualties was Congressman McKinley himself.

The Granger Movement

When the Department of Agriculture sent Oliver H. Kelley on a tour of the South in 1866, he regretted the social isolation of people living on small farms. To address the problem, Kelley in 1867 helped found the National Grange of the Patrons of Husbandry, better known as the Grange (an old word for places where crops were stored). In the next few years, the **Granger movement** mushroomed, reaching a membership of 1.5 million by 1874. It started out by offering social and educational activities for isolated farmers and their families, but as it grew, it also began to promote "cooperatives" where farmers could join together to buy, store, and sell their crops to avoid the high fees charged by brokers and other middlemen.

> "Granger laws"

Granger movement Began by offering social and educational activities for isolated farmers and their families and later started to promote "cooperatives" where farmers could join together to buy, store, and sell their crops to avoid the high fees charged by brokers and other middlemen.

"I FEED YOU ALL!" (1875) This Granger-inspired poster celebrates the farmer as the cornerstone of American society. Without the food he produces, no man in any occupation can do his job—including the very railroad magnate (left) and warehouse owners who try to exploit him.

In five midwestern states, Grangers persuaded legislatures to pass "Granger laws" to regulate the prices charged farmers by railroads and grain warehouses (called "elevators"). Railroads and warehouses challenged the new laws, but in *Munn v. Illinois* (1877), the Supreme Court ruled that states had the right to regulate property such as grain elevators and railroads that operated in a public interest. Nine years later, however, the Court threw out the *Munn* ruling, finding in *Wabash v. Illinois* (1886) that only Congress could regulate industries involved in interstate commerce.

Farmers' Alliances

The Granger movement gradually fizzled out as members directed their energies into political action. In the 1880s, **Farmers' Alliances** began growing in size and significance. Like the Grange, the Farmers' Alliances (divided at the national level into Northern, Southern, and Colored branches)

Farmers' Alliances Like the Granger movement, these organizations sought to address the issues of small farming communities; however, Alliances emphasized more political action and called for the creation of a third party to advocate their concerns.

organized social and recreational activities for farmers and their families, but they also emphasized political action. Struggling farmers throughout the South and Midwest, where most did not own their land, saw the Alliance movement as a way to address the hardships created by chronic indebtedness, declining crop prices, and devastating droughts.

The Alliance movement swept across the South and established strong support in Kansas and the Dakotas. In 1886, a white minister in Texas responded to the appeals of African American farmers by organizing the Colored Farmers' National Alliance. By 1890, the white Alliance movement had about 1.5 million members from New York to California, and the Colored Farmers' National Alliance claimed more than 1 million members.

In the farm states west of the Mississippi River, political activism intensified after a winter of record blizzards in 1887, which killed most of the cattle and hogs across the northern plains, and a prolonged drought two years later that destroyed millions of acres of corn, wheat, and oats. Distressed farmers lashed out against what they considered to be a powerful conspiracy of eastern financial and industrial interests, which they variously called "monopolies," "the money power," "Wall Street," or "organized wealth." The Alliance movement sponsored more than 1,000 rural newspapers and 40,000 lecturers to spread the word about the "tyrannical" forces arrayed against farmers.

New Third Parties

The Alliances, frustrated that few Democrats or Republicans embraced their cause, called for third-party political action to address their economic concerns. In 1890, farm activists in Colorado joined with miners and railroad workers to form the Independent party, and Nebraska farmers formed the People's Independent party. Across the South, however, white Alliance members hesitated to leave the Democratic party, seeking instead to influence or control it. Both the third-party and the southern approaches produced startling success.

In the Midwest, new third parties elected a U.S. senator and almost elected a governor under the banner of the new **People's party (Populists)** in Kansas, where a Populist won the governor's race in 1892. The Populists supported increased government intervention in the economy, for only the U.S. Congress could expand the money supply, counterbalance the power of Big Business, and provide efficient national transportation networks to support the agricultural economy. Third parties also took control of one house of the Kansas legislature and both houses in Nebraska. In the South Dakota and Minnesota legislatures, Populists won enough seats to control the balance of power between Republicans and Democrats.

In the South, the Alliance movement elected four Democratic supporters as governors, forty-four as congressmen, and several as U.S. senators, as well as seven state legislatures controlled by Alliance supporters.

Among the most respected of the southern Alliance leaders was red-haired Thomas E. Watson of Georgia. The son of prosperous slaveholders

> Populist successes in local and state elections and formation of a national party

People's party (Populists) Political party formed in 1892 following the success of Farmers' Alliance candidates; Populists advocated a variety of reforms, including free coinage of silver, a progressive income tax, postal savings banks, regulation of railroads, and direct election of U.S. senators.

MARY ELIZABETH LEASE
One of the first female attorneys in Pennsylvania, Lease was a charismatic leader in the farm protest movement.

who had lost everything after the Civil War, Watson became a successful lawyer and speaker on behalf of the Alliance cause. He took the lead in urging African American tenant farmers and sharecroppers to join white farmers in ousting the political elite. "You are kept apart," he told black and white farmers, "that you may be separately fleeced of your earnings."

In Kansas, Mary Elizabeth Lease emerged as a fiery speaker for the farm protest movement. Born in Pennsylvania, Lease migrated to Kansas, taught school, raised a family, and failed at farming in the mid-1880s. She then studied law, "pinning sheets of notes above her wash tub," and became one of the state's first female attorneys. A proud, tall, and imposing woman, she began giving public speeches on behalf of struggling farmers that drew attentive audiences. "The people are at bay," she warned in 1894; "let the bloodhounds of money beware." She urged angry farmers to obtain their goals "with the ballot if possible, but if not that way then with the bayonet."

The Election of 1892

The success of the Farmers' Alliances led to the formation of yet another new political party on the national level. In 1892, Alliance leaders organized a convention of the People's party, which opened on July 4 in Omaha, Nebraska. Delegates drafted a platform that called for unlimited coinage of silver, a "progressive" income tax whose rates would rise with personal income levels, and federal control of the railroads. The Populists also endorsed the eight-hour workday and new laws restricting immigration, for fear that foreigners were taking Americans' jobs.

The Populist party's platform turned out to be more exciting than its presidential candidate: Iowa's James B. Weaver, a former Union army officer who had headed the Greenback party ticket twelve years earlier. To attract southern voters, the Populists nominated a former Confederate general for vice president.

The major parties renominated the same candidates who had run in 1888: Democrat Grover Cleveland and Republican Benjamin Harrison. The tariff issue monopolized their attention. Each major candidate received more than 5 million votes, but Cleveland won a majority of the Electoral College. The Populists' Weaver received more than 1 million votes and carried Colorado, Kansas, Nevada, and Idaho. Alabama was the banner Populist state of the South, with 37 percent of its vote going to Weaver.

The Depression of 1893 and the "Free Silver" Crusade

While farmers were funneling their discontent into politics during the fall of 1892, a fundamental weakness in the economy was about to cause a major financial collapse and a social rebellion. Just ten days before Grover

Cleveland started his second presidential term, in the winter of 1893, the Philadelphia and Reading Railroad declared bankruptcy, setting off a national financial crisis, now called the **Panic of 1893**, that grew into the worst depression the nation had ever experienced.

Other overextended railroads collapsed, taking many banks with them. A quarter of unskilled urban workers lost their jobs, and by the fall of 1893 more than 600 banks had closed and 15,000 businesses had failed. Farm foreclosures soared in the South and West; between 1890 and 1894, more than 11,000 farmers lost their farms in Kansas alone. By 1900, a third of all American farmers rented their land rather than owned it. Kansans grimly joked: "In God we trusted, in Kansas we busted."

By 1894, the nation's economy had reached bottom. The grim depression, however, lasted another four years, with unemployment hovering at 20 percent. In New York City, the jobless rate was close to 35 percent, and 20,000 homeless people camped out at police stations and other makeshift shelters.

President Cleveland's response to the economic catastrophe was to convince Congress to return the nation's money supply to a solely gold standard by repealing the Sherman Silver Purchase Act of 1890, a move that only made the depression worse. The weak economy needed more money in circulation, not less. Investors rushed to exchange their silver for gold, thus further constricting the nation's money supply. A wave of violent labor unrest symbolized the fracturing of the social order; in 1894, some 750,000 workers went on strike.

In this climate of turmoil and anxiety, the 1894 congressional elections devastated President Cleveland and the Democrats. The Republicans gained 121 seats in the House, the largest increase ever. Only in the "Solid South" did the Democrats retain their advantage. The Populists emerged with six senators and seven representatives, and they expected the festering discontent in rural areas to carry them to national power in 1896. Their hopes would be dashed, however.

A PARTY OF PATCHES Printed on the cover of the satirical magazine *Judge* in 1891, this illustration portrays the People's party as a shoddy balloon full of hot air, carrying a basket labeled "platform of lunacy." The balloon is a patchwork of third-party groups, including the "Old" Granger party, the Knights of Labor, and the Farmers' Alliance. **What is this comic claiming about third-party politics?**

Panic of 1893 A major collapse in the national economy after several major railroad companies declared bankruptcy, leading to a severe depression and several violent clashes between workers and management.

WILLIAM JENNINGS BRYAN
Bryan's "Cross of Gold" speech at the 1896 Democratic Convention roused the delegates and secured him the party's presidential nomination.

Bryan's "Cross of Gold" speech

"money question"
Late-nineteenth-century national debate over the nature of U.S. currency; supporters of a fixed gold standard were generally moneylenders and thus preferred to keep the value of money high, while supporters of silver (and gold) coinage were debtors who owed money, so they wanted to keep the value of money low by increasing the currency supply (inflation).

Silverites versus Goldbugs

Cleveland's decision to repeal the Sherman Silver Purchase Act had created an irreparable division in his own party. One embittered pro-silver Democrat labeled the president a traitor. Politicians from western states with large silver mines increased their demands for the "unlimited" coinage of silver, presenting a strategic dilemma for Populists: should the party promote the long list of varied reforms it had originally advocated, or should it try to ride the silver issue into power?

The latter seemed more likely to succeed. Although flooding the economy with silver currency would probably not have provided the benefits its advocates claimed, the "free silver" crusade had taken on powerful symbolic overtones. Over the protests of more-radical members, Populist leaders decided to hold their 1896 nominating convention after the two major-party conventions, confident that the Republicans and Democrats would at best straddle the silver issue and enable the Populists to lure away pro-silver advocates from both.

Contrary to those expectations, the major parties took opposite positions on the currency issue. The Republicans, as expected, nominated William McKinley, a former congressman and governor of Ohio, on a platform committed to gold coins as the only form of currency. After the convention, a friend told McKinley that the **"money question"** would determine the election. He was right.

The Democratic convention in the Chicago Coliseum, the largest building in the world, was one of the great turning points in American political history. The pro-silver, largely rural delegates surprised the party leadership and the "Gold Democrats," or "goldbugs," by capturing the convention for their inflationary crusade.

Thirty-six-year-old William Jennings Bryan of Nebraska gave the final speech before the balloting began. A fiery evangelical moralist, Bryan was a two-term congressman who had lost a race for the Senate in 1894, when Democrats by the dozens were swept out of office. In the months before the convention, he had traveled throughout the South and West, speaking passionately for the unlimited coinage of silver and against Cleveland's "do-nothing" response to the depression.

Bryan was a magnetic public speaker with a booming voice, more a crusading preacher than a conventional politician. At the 1896 convention, he was only a "dark horse" candidate—that is, a little-known long shot—for the presidential nomination. So he chose to take a calculated risk: he would be intentionally provocative and disruptive.

In his now famous "Cross of Gold" speech, Bryan claimed to speak for the "producing masses of this nation" against the eastern "financial magnates" who had "enslaved" them by manipulating the money supply to ensure high interest rates for loans. He reminded the delegates that the "man who is employed for wages is as much a business man as his employer." As his melodramatic twenty-minute speech reached its peak, Bryan fused Christian imagery with Populist anger:

> I come to speak to you in defense of a cause as holy as the cause of liberty—the cause of humanity. . . . We have petitioned, and our petitions have been scorned. . . . We have begged, and they have mocked when our calamity came. We beg no longer; we entreat no more; we petition no more. We defy them!

Bryan then stretched his fingers across his forehead and reached his dramatic conclusion: "You shall not press down upon the brow of labor this crown of thorns. You shall not crucify mankind upon a cross of gold!"—at which point he extended his arms straight out from his sides, as if he were being crucified.

It was a riveting performance that worked better than even Bryan himself had anticipated. As he walked triumphantly off the stage, the delegates erupted in wild applause. "Everybody seemed to go mad at once," reported the *New York World*. For their part, the Republicans were not at all amused by Bryan's antics. A Republican newspaper observed that no political movement had "ever before spawned such hideous and repulsive vipers."

The day after his stirring speech, Bryan won the presidential nomination on the fifth ballot, but in the process the Democratic party split in two. Disappointed pro-gold, pro-Cleveland Democrats dismissed Bryan as a fanatic and a socialist. They were so alienated by both his positions and his rhetoric that they walked out of the convention and nominated their own candidate, Senator John M. Palmer of Illinois. "Fellow Democrats," Palmer announced, "I will not consider it any great fault if you decide to cast your vote for [the Republican] William McKinley."

When the Populists gathered in St. Louis for their presidential nominating convention two weeks later, they faced an impossible choice. They could name their own candidate and divide the pro-silver vote with the Democrats, or they could endorse Bryan and probably lose their identity as an independent party. In the end, they backed Bryan, but chose their own vice presidential candidate, Thomas E. Watson, and invited the Democrats to drop their vice presidential nominee. Bryan refused the offer.

> Pro-gold Democrats and pro-silver Populists

The Election of 1896

The election of 1896 was one of the most dramatic in American history, in part because of the striking contrast between the candidates and in part because the terrible depression made the stakes so high. Bryan, the nominee of both the Democrats and the Populists, was the first major candidate since Andrew Jackson to champion the poor, the discontented, and the oppressed

PRESIDENTIAL CAMPAIGN BADGES On the left wings of the "goldbug" and "silverite" badges are McKinley (top) and Bryan (bottom), with their running mates on the right. **Despite the similarity of these badges, how did McKinley's and Bryan's campaigns differ?**

against the financial and industrial elite. And he was the first leader of a major party to call for the expansion of the federal government to help the working and middle classes.

Candidate Bryan crisscrossed the country like a man on a mission, delivering hundreds of impassioned speeches on behalf of the "producing masses"—workers, farmers, miners, and small-business owners. His populist crusade was for whites only, however. Like so many otherwise progressive Democratic leaders, Bryan never challenged the practices of racial segregation and violence against blacks in the solidly Democratic South.

McKinley, meanwhile, stayed at home. He knew he could not compete with Bryan as a speaker, so he conducted a "front-porch campaign," welcoming delegations of Republican supporters at his home in Canton, Ohio, and giving only prepared statements to the press. McKinley's brilliant campaign manager, Marcus "Mark" Hanna, a wealthy business executive, shrewdly portrayed Bryan as a "Popocrat," a radical whose "communistic spirit" would ruin the capitalist system and stir up a class war. Hanna convinced the Republican Party to declare that it was "unreservedly for sound money"—meaning gold coins. Theodore Roosevelt, a rising Republican star, was horrified by the thought of Bryan becoming president. "The silver craze surpasses belief," he wrote a friend. "Bryan's election would be a great calamity."

By appealing to such fears, the Republican campaign raised vast sums of money from corporations and wealthy donors to finance an army of 1,400 speakers who traveled the country in McKinley's support. It was the most sophisticated—and expensive—presidential campaign in history. McKinley promoted himself as the "advance agent of prosperity" who would provide workers with a "full dinner pail." In the end, Bryan was overwhelmed by the better-organized and better-financed Republicans. McKinley won the popular vote by 7.1 million to 6.5 million and the Electoral College vote by 271 to 176. Two million more voters cast ballots than in 1892.

Bryan carried most of the West and the South but found little support in the East. In the critical Midwest, from Minnesota and Iowa eastward to Ohio, he did not carry a single state. His evangelical Protestantism repelled many Roman Catholic voters, who were normally drawn to the Democrats. Farmers in the Northeast, moreover, were less attracted to radical reform than were farmers in the wheat and cotton belts of the West and South. In the cities, workers found it easier to identify with McKinley's focus on reviving the industrial economy than with Bryan's farm-based free-silver evangelism.

McKinley defeats Bryan

Although Bryan lost, he began the Democratic party's shift from pro-business conservatism to its eventual twentieth-century role as a party of liberal reform. The Populist party, however, virtually disintegrated. Having won a million votes in 1896, it collected only 50,000 in 1900. Conversely, McKinley's victory climaxed a generation-long struggle for the political

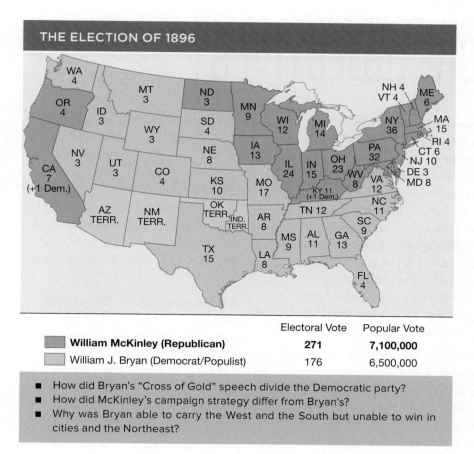

THE ELECTION OF 1896

	Electoral Vote	Popular Vote
William McKinley (Republican)	**271**	**7,100,000**
William J. Bryan (Democrat/Populist)	176	6,500,000

- How did Bryan's "Cross of Gold" speech divide the Democratic party?
- How did McKinley's campaign strategy differ from Bryan's?
- Why was Bryan able to carry the West and the South but unable to win in cities and the Northeast?

control of an industrialized America. The Republicans would be dominant—for a while.

By 1897, when McKinley was inaugurated as president, economic prosperity was returning. Part of the reason was inflation of the currency, which bore out the arguments of the Greenbackers and silverites that the money supply was inadequate. But the inflation came, in one of history's many ironies, not from more greenbacks or silver dollars issued by the federal government but from a flood of gold discovered in South Africa, northwest Canada, and Alaska. In 1900, Congress passed, and McKinley signed, a bill affirming that the U.S. money supply would be based only on gold.

Even though the Populist movement faded after William Jennings Bryan's defeat, most of the agenda promoted by Bryan Democrats and Populists, dismissed as too radical in 1896, would be implemented over the next two decades by a more diverse coalition of Democrats and Republicans who would call themselves "progressives."

> Economic recovery and new supplies of gold

Reviewing the
CORE OBJECTIVES |

■ **America's Move to Town**
America's cities grew in all directions during the *Gilded Age (1860–1896)*. Electric elevators and new steel-frame construction allowed architects to extend buildings upward, and mass transit both above- and below-ground enabled the middle class to retreat to suburbs. Crowded *tenements* bred disease and crime and created an opportunity for *party bosses* to gain power, in part by distributing to the poor the only relief that existed.

■ **The New Immigration** By 1900, 30 percent of Americans living in major cities were foreign-born, with the majority of *new immigrants* arriving from eastern and southern Europe rather than western and northern Europe, like most immigrants of generations past. Their languages, culture, and religion were quite different from those of native-born Americans. They tended to be Catholic, Eastern Orthodox, or Jewish rather than Protestant. Beginning in the 1880s, *nativists* advocated restrictive immigration laws and won passage of the *Chinese Exclusion Act (1882)*.

■ **Changes in Culture and Thought**
Many areas of American life underwent profound changes during the Gilded Age. The growth of large cities led to the popularity of vaudeville and Wild West shows and the emergence of football, baseball, and basketball as spectator sports. Saloons served as local social and political clubs for men, despite the disapproval of anti-liquor

groups. Charles Darwin's *On the Origin of Species* shocked people who believed in a literal interpretation of the Bible's account of creation. Herbert Spencer and William Graham Sumner were proponents of *social Darwinism*, which applied Darwin's theory of evolution to human society by equating economic and social success with the "survival of the fittest."

■ **Gilded Age Politics** The politics of the time was dominated by huge corporations and the money they used to buy political influence. Political power was still concentrated at the state and local levels. Americans were intensely loyal to the two major parties, whose local "bosses" and "machines" won votes by distributing *patronage* jobs and contracts to members as well as charitable relief. Party loyalties reflected regional, ethnic, and religious differences.

■ **Corruption and Reform: Hayes to Harrison** In addition to the *money question*, national politics in this period focused on *tariff reform (1887)*, the regulation of corporations, and *civil service reform*. The passage of the Pendleton Civil Service Reform Act in 1883 began the professionalization of federal workers. In the 1884 presidential election, Republicans favoring reform, the *Mugwumps*, helped elect Democrat Grover Cleveland. Cleveland signed the 1887 act creating the *Interstate Commerce Commission (ICC)*, intended to regulate interstate railroads. In 1890, under President Benjamin Harrison,

Republicans passed the Sherman Anti-Trust Act, the Sherman Silver Purchase Act, and the McKinley Tariff Act.

■ **Inadequate Currency Supply and Unhappy Farmers** Over the course of the late nineteenth century, the *money question* had become a central political issue. The supply of money had not increased as the economy had grown. This deflationary trend increased the value of money, which was good for bankers and creditors who could charge higher interest rates on loans, but bad for farmers who faced both more expensive mortgages and declining prices for their products, especially after the devastating *Panic of 1893* and the ensuing depression.

KEY TERMS

CHRONOLOGY

1859 Charles Darwin's *On the Origin of Species* is published

1873 San Francisco begins using cable cars for mass transit

1873 Congress ends silver coinage

1877 Rutherford B. Hayes is inaugurated president

1881 President James A. Garfield is assassinated

1882 Congress passes the Chinese Exclusion Act

1883 Congress passes the Pendleton Civil Service Reform Act

1886 Supreme Court issues *Wabash, St. Louis, and Pacific Railroad Company v. Illinois* decision

1887 Interstate Commerce Commission is created

1889 Otis Elevator Company installs the first electric elevator

1890 Congress passes the Sherman Anti-Trust Act, the Sherman Silver Purchase Act, and the McKinley Tariff Act

1891 Basketball is invented

⚎ INQUIZITIVE

Go to InQuizitive to see what you've learned—and learn what you've missed—with personalized feedback along the way.

THE CHARGE OF THE ROUGH RIDERS ON SAN JUAN HILL (1898) Before Frederic Remington pursued art professionally, he had unsuccessful forays into hunting, ranching, and even the saloon business in the West. His intimacy with the Western way of life, along with his technical skill and keen sense of observation, were not lost on Theodore Roosevelt, who invited Remington to travel with the Rough Riders during the Spanish-American War.

Seizing an American Empire

1865–1913

Throughout the nineteenth century, Americans displayed little interest in foreign affairs. The overriding priorities were at home: industrial development, western settlement, and domestic politics. After the Civil War, a mood of isolationism—a desire to stay out of conflicts elsewhere in the world, especially those among powerful European nations—dominated public opinion. America's geographic advantages encouraged this isolationist attitude: wide oceans to the east and west and militarily weak neighbors in the Western Hemisphere. That the powerful British navy protected the shipping lanes from the United States to the British Isles gave Americans a heightened sense of security.

Yet while wanting to stay out of Europe's conflicts, a growing number of Americans during the late nineteenth century urged U.S. officials to acquire territory outside North America. The old idea of "manifest destiny" from the 1840s—that the United States had been blessed by God ("destined") to expand its territory westward across the North American continent—now focused on expanding American control over other regions of the Western hemisphere and even in the Pacific and in Asia.

Armed with this concept of a destiny made manifest (revealed) to people by what they saw as the obvious superiority of their way of life, Americans embraced a new form of expansionism that sought distant territories as "colonies" with no intention of their becoming states.

CORE OBJECTIVES INQUIZITIVE

1. Describe the factors that motivated America's new imperialism after the Civil War.

2. Explain why and how America expanded its influence in the Pacific before the Spanish-American War (War of 1898).

3. Explain the causes of the Spanish-American War (War of 1898), and describe its major events.

4. Analyze the consequences of the Spanish-American War (War of 1898) for American foreign policy.

5. Describe the reasons for Theodore Roosevelt's rapid rise to the presidency, and evaluate the main elements of his foreign policies.

imperialism The use of diplomatic or military force to extend a nation's power and enhance its economic interests, often by acquiring territory or colonies and justifying such behavior with assumptions of racial superiority.

The new manifest destiny, in other words, became a justification for imperialism. For the United States to survive and prosper, expansionists argued, it had to keep pushing beyond its current borders. As historian Frederick Jackson Turner had proclaimed in 1893, the "frontier" in the West was gone, so Americans needed new frontiers in which to exercise their "expansive character" and to spread their democratic ideals and Christian beliefs. During the late nineteenth century, manifest destiny also took on racial meaning as many Americans agreed with Theodore Roosevelt that the United States needed to expand around the world "on behalf of the *destiny* of the [Anglo-Saxon] race."

In more practical terms, prominent political and business leaders argued that America's rapid industrial development required the addition of foreign territories—by conquest if necessary—in order to gain easier access to vital raw materials such as rubber, tin, copper, palm oil, and various dyes. At the same time, American manufacturers and commercial farmers had become increasingly dependent upon international trade, a dependence that required an expanded naval force to protect its merchant vessels as they crisscrossed the globe. And a modern, steam-powered navy needed bases in the Pacific where its ships could replenish their supplies of coal and water.

For these and other reasons, the United States during the last quarter of the nineteenth century expanded its military presence and territorial possessions both within and beyond the Western Hemisphere. During just a few crucial months in 1898, a nation born in a revolution against British colonial rule would itself become an imperial ruler of colonies around the world. Motivated by a mixture of moral and religious idealism, assumptions of "Anglo-Saxon" racial superiority, and naked greed, the expansionist push also generated strong opposition. But most Americans sided with future president Theodore Roosevelt, who in his 1896 book, *The Winning of the West*, declared that the conquest of the "backward peoples" of the world, like the defeat of the Indians in the American West, benefited "civilization and the interests of mankind."

CORE **OBJECTIVE**

1. Describe the factors that motivated America's new imperialism after the Civil War.

Toward the New Imperialism

Writing in 1902, the British economist J. A. Hobson announced that imperialism was "the most powerful factor in the current politics of the Western world." The United States was a latecomer to the **imperialism** long practiced by major Western nations. Beginning in the 1880s, the British, French, Belgians, Italians, Dutch, Spanish, and Germans had conquered most of Africa and Asia. Often competing with one another for particular territories, they had established colonial governments to rule over the native populations and exploited the colonies economically. Each of the imperial nations, including the United States, dispatched missionaries to convert conquered peoples to Christianity. By 1900, some 18,000 Protestant and Catholic evangelicals were scattered around the world.

During the late nineteenth century, a small yet influential group of American officials aggressively encouraged expansion beyond North America. They included powerful senators Albert J. Beveridge of Indiana and Henry Cabot Lodge of Massachusetts as well as the assistant secretary of the navy Theodore Roosevelt and naval captain Alfred Thayer Mahan, president of the U.S. Naval War College in Rhode Island.

In 1890, Mahan published ***The Influence of Sea Power upon History, 1660–1783***, in which he argued that Great Britain had demonstrated that national greatness flowed from naval power. Mahan insisted that modern economic development required a powerful navy centered on huge battleships, foreign commerce, colonies to provide raw materials and new markets for American products, and global naval bases. A self-described imperialist, he urged Americans to "look outward" beyond the continental United States. Mahan championed America's "destiny" to control the Caribbean Sea, build a Central American canal to connect the Atlantic and Pacific Oceans, and spread Christian civilization across the Pacific. His ideas were widely circulated within political and military circles in the United States as well as Great Britain and Germany, and by 1896 the United States had built eleven new steel battleships, making America's navy the third most powerful in the world behind Great Britain and Germany.

Claims of racial superiority reinforced the new imperialist spirit. During the late nineteenth century, many Americans readily assumed that the Anglo-Saxon race was dominant and others (Indians, Africans) were clearly inferior. Such traditional notions justifying racism were given new "scientific" authority by researchers at universities throughout Europe and America. Scholars at times went to absurd lengths to make racial distinctions—measuring facial angles, skull size, and brain weight. At the Johns Hopkins University in Baltimore, Professor James K. Hosmer claimed that "the primacy of the world will lie with us" because of the superior qualities of the Anglo-Saxon race.

Prominent Americans used the arguments of social Darwinism to justify economic exploitation and territorial conquest abroad and racial segregation at home. Among nations as among individuals, they claimed, only the strongest survive. John Fiske, a Harvard historian and popular lecturer on Darwinism, proclaimed in 1885 the superior character of "Anglo-Saxon" institutions and peoples. The English-speaking "race," he asserted, was destined to dominate the globe and transform the institutions, traditions, language—even the blood—of the world's "backward" races.

The Influence of Sea Power upon History, 1660–1783 Historical work in which Rear Admiral Alfred Thayer Mahan argued that a nation's greatness and prosperity comes from the power of its navy; the book helped bolster imperialist sentiment in the United States in the late nineteenth century.

FISKE FLYING THE EVOLUTION KITE This cartoon printed in the *Daily Graphic* in 1874 depicts John Fiske flying a kite labeled "The Doctrine of Evolution." Fiske and many of his contemporaries insisted that Anglo-Saxons were the superior "race," therefore justifiably dominant. **How did proponents of Anglo-Saxon superiority use social Darwinism as "scientific" proof of their claims?**

All these factors helped excite imperialist fervor in the United States during the late nineteenth century. As a Kentucky newspaper editor proclaimed in 1893, the United States was "the most advanced and powerful" nation in the world, an "imperial Republic" destined to shape the "future of the world." The *Washington Post* agreed, revealing that "the taste of Empire is in the mouth of the people."

CORE **OBJECTIVE**

2. Explain why and how America expanded its influence in the Pacific before the Spanish-American War (War of 1898).

Expansion in the Pacific

For John Fiske and other American imperialists, Asia offered an especially attractive target for expansion. In 1866, Secretary of State William H. Seward had predicted that the United States must inevitably impose its economic domination "on the Pacific Ocean, and its islands and continents." To take advantage of the huge Asian markets, Seward believed the United States first had to remove all foreign powers from the northern Pacific coast of North America and gain access to that region's valuable Pacific ports. To that end, he tried to acquire the British colony of British Columbia, sandwiched between Russian-owned Alaska and the Washington Territory.

"OUR NEW SENATORS" Mocking the Alaska Purchase, this political cartoon shows President Andrew Johnson and Secretary of State Seward welcoming two new senators from Alaska: an Eskimo and a penguin.

Late in 1866, while encouraging business leaders and civil authorities in British Columbia to consider becoming a U.S. territory, Seward learned of Russia's desire to sell Alaska. He leaped at the opportunity, in part because the purchase might influence British Columbia to join the union. In 1867, the United States bought Alaska for $7.2 million, thus removing Russia from North America as an imperial power. Critics scoffed at "Seward's folly" of buying the Alaskan "icebox," but it proved to be the biggest bargain since the Louisiana Purchase, in part because of its vast deposits of gold and oil—as well as ice.

Seward and other Americans promoting expanded trade with Asia also wanted the Hawaiian Islands. The islands, a unified kingdom since 1795, had a sizable population of American Christian missionaries and a single profitable crop, sugarcane. In 1875, Hawaii had signed a trade agreement with the United States that allowed Hawaiian sugar to enter the country duty-free in exchange for Hawaii's promise that none of its territory would be leased or granted to another nation. This agreement led to a boom in sugar production based on cheap immigrant workers, mainly Chinese and Japanese, and American sugar planters soon formed an economic elite. By the 1890s, the native Hawaiian population had been reduced to a minority by smallpox and other diseases, and Asian immigrants became the most numerous ethnic group.

Beginning in 1891, Queen Liliuokalani, the Hawaiian ruler, tried to restore "Hawaii for the Hawaiians" by restricting the political power exercised by U.S. planters in the islands. Two years later, however, Hawaii's white population (called *haoles*) revolted and overthrew the monarchy when John L. Stevens, the U.S. ambassador, brought in marines to support the coup in January 1893. The queen surrendered "to the superior force of the United States," leading Stevens to report to the secretary of state that the "Hawaiian pear is now fully ripe, and this is the golden hour for the United States to pluck it." Within a month, a committee representing the *haoles* asked the United States government to annex the islands, and President Benjamin Harrison sent an annexation treaty to the Senate just as he was leaving the presidency in early 1893.

QUEEN LILIUOKALANI The Hawaiian queen sought to preserve her nation's independence but was thwarted by the *haoles*, who pushed for annexation.

To investigate the situation, new president Grover Cleveland sent a special commissioner to Hawaii, who reported that the Americans there had acted improperly and that most native Hawaiians opposed annexation. Cleveland tried to restore the queen to power but met resistance from the *haoles*. On July 4, 1894, the government they controlled created the Republic of Hawaii, which included in its constitution a provision for American annexation.

In 1897, when William McKinley became president, he was looking for an excuse to annex the islands. "We need Hawaii," he claimed, "just as much and a good deal more than we did California. It is [America's] manifest destiny." The United States took control of Hawaii in the summer of 1898, over the protests of native Hawaiians who resented their nation being annexed without "the consent of the people of the Hawaiian Islands."

The Alaska Purchase and annexation of Hawaii

The Spanish-American War (War of 1898)

CORE **OBJECTIVE**

3. Explain the causes of the Spanish-American War (War of 1898), and describe its major events.

The annexation of Hawaii set in motion a series of efforts to create a much larger American presence in Asia. Ironically, this imperialist push originated not in Asia but in Cuba, a Spanish colony ninety miles south of Florida. Even more ironically, the chief motive for American intervention in Cuba was a sense of outrage at Spain's brutal imperialism.

"Free Cuba"

Throughout the second half of the nineteenth century, Cubans had repeatedly revolted against Spanish rule, only to be ruthlessly suppressed. As one of Spain's oldest colonies, Cuba was a major export market for Spanish goods. American sugar and mining companies had also invested heavily in Cuba. In fact, the United States traded more with Cuba than Spain did, and the American owners of sugar plantations in Cuba grew increasingly concerned about the security of their investments amid the rebellions.

On February 24, 1895, Cubans began another guerrilla war against Spanish troops, when uprisings erupted throughout the island. During what became the Cuban War for Independence (1895–1898), 95,000 Cuban peasants died of combat wounds as well as disease and starvation in Spanish detention camps.

Americans followed the conflict each day through the newspapers, the only source for international news. Two of the largest newspapers, William Randolph Hearst's *New York Journal* and Joseph Pulitzer's *New York World*, were then locked in a fierce competition for readers. Each strove to outdo the other with sensational headlines about every Spanish atrocity in Cuba, real or invented.

Editors sent their best reporters to Cuba and encouraged them to exaggerate the facts in their stories to attract more readers. Such sensationalist reporting came to be called **yellow journalism**. In addition to boosting the *Journal*'s circulation, Hearst wanted a war against Spain to propel the United States to world-power status. Once war was declared, he took credit for it; one of his headlines blared: "How do you like the Journal's War?" Many Protestant ministers and publications also campaigned for war in Cuba, in part because of antagonism toward Catholic Spain. A Catholic official in New York City criticized such "bloodthirsty preachers."

The Political Path to War

At the outset of the Cuban War for Independence in 1895, President Grover Cleveland tried to protect U.S. business interests in Cuba while avoiding military involvement. Mounting public sympathy for the rebel cause prompted growing concern in Congress, however. By concurrent resolutions on April 6, 1896, the House and Senate endorsed granting official recognition to the Cuban rebels. After his inauguration in March 1897, President William McKinley continued the policy of official neutrality but took a sympathetic stance toward the rebels. Later that year, Spain offered Cubans autonomy (self-government without formal independence) in return for ending the rebellion, but the Cubans rejected the offer.

Early in 1898, two events pushed Spain and the United States into a war that neither government wanted. On January 25, the **U.S. battleship *Maine*** docked in the harbor of Havana, the Cuban capital, supposedly on a courtesy call. On February 9, the *New York Journal* released the text of a letter from

> Yellow journalism, the de Lôme letter, and the sinking of the *Maine*

yellow journalism A type of news reporting, epitomized in the 1890s by the newspaper empires of William Randolph Hearst and Joseph Pulitzer, that intentionally manipulates public opinion through sensational headlines, illustrations, and articles about both real and invented events.

U.S. battleship *Maine* American warship that exploded in the Cuban port of Havana on February 15, 1898; though later discovered to be the result of an accident, the destruction of the *Maine* was initially attributed by war-hungry Americans to Spain, contributing to the onset of the Spanish-American War.

"$50,000 REWARD!" As if the news of the *Maine* sinking were not disturbing enough, the *New York Journal* sensationalized the incident by offering a $50,000 reward for the perpetrator—the equivalent of $1.3 million today. How did the sensationalized press and the resulting public opinion influence government action after the explosion of the *Maine*?

Depuy de Lôme, Spanish ambassador to the United States, to a friend in Havana. In the **de Lôme letter**, which had been stolen from the post office by a Cuban spy, de Lôme called McKinley "weak and a bidder for the admiration of the crowd, besides being a would-be politician who tries to leave a door open behind himself while keeping on good terms with the jingoes [aggressive nationalists] of his party." De Lôme resigned to prevent further embarrassment to his government.

Six days later, on February 15, the *Maine* exploded without warning and sank in Havana Harbor, with a loss of 266 men. Many years later, the sinking was ruled an accident resulting from an onboard coal explosion, but those eager for a war with Spain in 1898 were convinced the Spanish had destroyed the ship. The headline in the *New York Journal* screamed: "Whole Country Thrills with War Fever." The thirty-nine-year-old assistant secretary of the navy, Theodore Roosevelt, called the sinking "an act of dirty treachery on the part of the Spaniards" and told a friend that he "would give anything if President McKinley would order the fleet to Havana tomorrow." The United States, he claimed, "needs a war."

McKinley, however, assumed that the sinking was an accident and refused to be rushed into war. As the days passed and war did not come, Roosevelt, an unapologetic imperialist and war lover, told his friends that the president was too timid; he "has no more backbone than a chocolate éclair." With Roosevelt's encouragement, the public's outcry against Spain grew behind the saying "Remember the *Maine*!"

In the weeks following the sinking, the Spanish government agreed to every major demand by the American government regarding its rule over Cuba. But the weight of outraged public opinion and the influence of Republican "jingoists" such as Roosevelt and the president's closest friend, Senator Henry Cabot Lodge, eroded McKinley's neutrality.

de Lôme letter Private correspondence written by the Spanish ambassador to the United States, Depuy de Lôme, that described President McKinley as "weak"; the letter was stolen by Cuban revolutionaries and published in the *New York Journal* in 1898, deepening American resentment of Spain and moving the two countries closer to war in Cuba.

On April 11, President McKinley asked Congress for authority to use armed forces in Cuba to end the fighting there. On April 20, Congress declared Cuba independent and demanded the withdrawal of Spanish forces. Upon learning of the American actions, the Spanish government broke diplomatic ties with the United States and, after U.S. ships began blockading Cuban ports, declared war. Congress then passed its own declaration of war on April 25. The **Teller Amendment**, added on the Senate floor to the war resolution, denied any U.S. intention to annex Cuba.

President McKinley signed the war resolution and called for 125,000 volunteers to supplement the 28,000 men already serving in the U.S. Army. Among the first to enlist was the man who most lusted for war: Theodore Roosevelt, who resigned from his government post and told his tailor to make him a dashing army uniform. His political opponent, Democrat William Jennings Bryan, joined the ranks as a colonel in the Third Nebraska Volunteers.

Never has an American war, so casually begun and so enthusiastically supported, generated such unexpected and far-reaching consequences as did the conflict against Spain. Although McKinley had gone to war reluctantly, he soon saw it as an opportunity to acquire overseas territories. "While we are conducting war and until its conclusion," he wrote privately, "we must keep all we get; when the war is over we must keep what we want." A war to free Cuba thus became a way to gain an empire. (What had long been called the Spanish-American War has recently been renamed the War of 1898 because it involved not just Spanish and American combatants but also Cubans, Filipinos, and Puerto Ricans.)

"A Splendid Little War"

The war with Spain lasted only 114 days. The conflict was barely under way before the U.S. Navy produced a spectacular victory in the Pacific Ocean: Manila Bay in the Philippine Islands, a colony controlled by the Spanish for over 300 years. Just before war was declared, Roosevelt, still assistant secretary of the navy, ordered Commodore George Dewey, commander of the U.S. Asiatic Squadron, to engage Spanish forces in the Philippines in case of war on the other side of the world in Cuba.

Dewey arrived in Manila Bay on April 30 with six modern warships, which quickly destroyed or captured the outdated Spanish vessels there. Almost 400 Spaniards were killed or wounded in the lopsided battle. One overweight American sailor died of heatstroke. An English reporter called it "a military execution rather than a real contest." However lopsided the battle, the news of Dewey's victory set off wild celebrations in the United States.

Commodore Dewey was now in awkward possession of Manila Bay but without any soldiers to go onshore. Promised reinforcements, he stayed while German and British warships cruised offshore like watchful vultures, ready to seize the Philippines if the United States did not do so.

Teller Amendment Addition to the congressional war resolution of April 20, 1898, which marked the U.S. entry into the war with Spain; the amendment declared that the United States' goal in entering the war was to ensure Cuba's independence, not to annex Cuba as a territory.

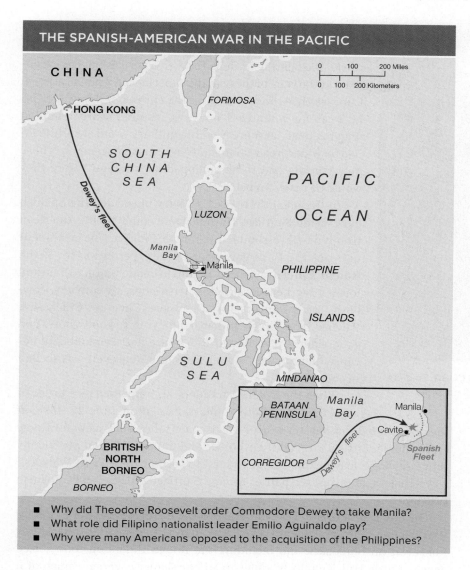

THE SPANISH-AMERICAN WAR IN THE PACIFIC

- Why did Theodore Roosevelt order Commodore Dewey to take Manila?
- What role did Filipino nationalist leader Emilio Aguinaldo play?
- Why were many Americans opposed to the acquisition of the Philippines?

In the meantime, Emilio Aguinaldo, the leader of the Filipino nationalist movement, declared the Philippines independent from Spain on June 12. With Aguinaldo's help, Dewey's forces entered Manila on August 13 and accepted the surrender of the Spanish troops there, who had feared revenge if they surrendered to the Filipinos.

News of the American victory sent President McKinley scurrying to find a map of Asia to locate "these darned islands" now occupied by U.S. soldiers and sailors. Senator Lodge was delighted with the news from the Philippines: "We hold the other side of the Pacific," he announced. "We must on no account let the [Philippine] Islands go."

AFRICAN AMERICAN TROOPS IN CUBA Soldiers stand in formation wearing old wool uniforms unsuited to Cuba's tropical heat.

Rough Riders The First Volunteer Cavalry, led in the Spanish-American War by Theodore Roosevelt; victorious in their only engagement, the Battle of San Juan Hill.

The Cuban Campaign

While these events were occurring halfway around the world, the fighting in Cuba reached a surprisingly quick climax. At the start of the war, the experienced Spanish army in Cuba was five times as large as the entire U.S. Army. McKinley's call for volunteers, however, inspired nearly a million men to enlist, far more than the military could absorb, leading to widespread confusion and mismanagement. Those new recruits had to be equipped and trained before they would be ready for battle.

In the meantime, the U.S. Navy blockaded the Spanish fleet inside Santiago Harbor while some 17,000 American troops hastily assembled at Tampa, Florida. One prominent unit was the First Volunteer Cavalry, better known as the **Rough Riders**, a special regiment made up of a thousand former Ivy League athletes, Irish cops, ex-convicts, cowboys, Texas Rangers, and Cherokee, Choctaw, Chickasaw, Pawnee, and Creek Indians—all "young, good shots, and good riders." The Rough Riders are best remembered because Lieutenant Colonel Theodore Roosevelt was second in command.

When the 578 Rough Riders, accompanied by a gaggle of reporters and photographers, landed on June 22, 1898, at the undefended southeastern tip of Cuba, chaos followed. Except for Roosevelt's horse, Little Texas, all their horses and mules had been mistakenly sent elsewhere, leaving the "Rough Riders" to become the "Weary Walkers." Nevertheless, land and sea battles around Santiago quickly broke Spanish resistance.

On July 1, about 7,000 U.S. soldiers took the fortified village of El Caney. While a much larger force attacked San Juan Hill, a smaller unit, led by Roosevelt on horseback and including the Rough Riders on foot, seized nearby Kettle Hill. Thanks to widespread newspaper coverage, much of it exaggerated, Roosevelt became a home-front legend for his headlong gallop toward the Spanish defenders wearing a blue polka-dot bandana. The *New York Times* reported that he had led the charge with "bulldog ferociousness," acting in a "grand drama for the world to watch and admire." With typical braggadocio, Roosevelt claimed that nobody "else could have handled this regiment quite as I handled it." He may have been bragging, but what he said was true.

Roosevelt loved being in the headlines, for being a military hero was his lifelong dream. According to the *New York World,* the young lieutenant colonel had become "more talked about than any man in the country." A friend reported to Roosevelt's wife that her husband was "revelling in victory and gore." He boasted that he had "killed a Spaniard with my own hand—like a jack rabbit." Unburdened by humility, Roosevelt requested a Congressional Medal of Honor for his much-publicized charge in Cuba. It did not come. (President Bill Clinton finally awarded the medal posthumously in 2001.)

While Colonel Roosevelt was basking in the glory of battle, other U.S. soldiers in Cuba were less enthusiastic about the terrors of modern warfare. Walter Bartholomew, a private from New York, reported that the war "in all its awfulness" was so "much more hideous than my wildest imagination that I have not yet recovered from the shock." A soldier standing beside him had "the front of his throat torn completely off" by a Spanish bullet.

COLONEL ROOSEVELT With one hand on his hip, Roosevelt rides with the Rough Riders in Cuba. Most of this regiment was culled from Arizona, New Mexico, and Texas because the southwestern climate resembled that of Cuba.

Spanish Defeat and Concessions

On July 3, the Spanish navy trapped at Santiago made a gallant run to evade the American fleet blockading the harbor. "The Spanish ships," reported Captain John Philip, commander of the U.S. warship *Texas*, "came out as gaily as brides to the altar." But the outgunned Spanish ships were quickly destroyed by the more modern American fleet. The casualties were as one-sided as those at Manila: 474 Spaniards were killed or wounded, while only one American was killed and one wounded. Spanish officials in Santiago surrendered on July 17. On July 25, an American force took control of Spanish-held Puerto Rico, meeting only minor resistance as it took control of that island.

American victories in Santiago and Puerto Rico

The next day, July 26, the Spanish government sued for peace. A cease-fire agreement was signed on August 12, the day before Americans entered Manila. In Cuba, the Spanish forces formally surrendered to the U.S. commander and then sailed for home; excluded from the ceremony were the Cubans, for whom the war had supposedly been fought.

On December 10, the United States and Spain signed the Treaty of Paris. Under its terms, Cuba was to become independent, and the United States was to annex Puerto Rico and continue to occupy Manila, pending a transfer of power in the Philippines. With the Treaty of Paris, the Spanish empire in the Americas, initiated by the voyages of Christopher Columbus some four centuries earlier, came to a humiliating end. Now the United States was ready to create its own empire.

Terms of the Treaty of Paris

In all during the four-month Spanish-American War (War of 1898), more than 60,000 Spanish soldiers and sailors died of wounds or disease—mostly

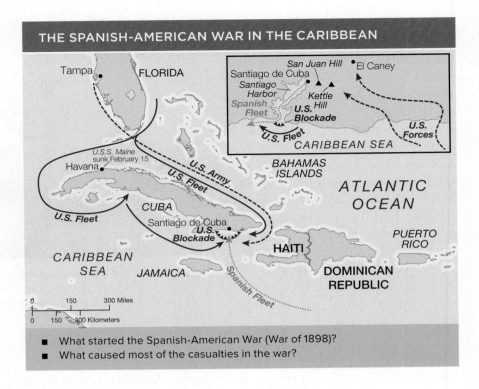

THE SPANISH-AMERICAN WAR IN THE CARIBBEAN

■ What started the Spanish-American War (War of 1898)?
■ What caused most of the casualties in the war?

malaria, typhoid, dysentery, or yellow fever. Among the 274,000 Americans who served in the war, 5,462 died, but only 379 in battle; most of the rest died from unsanitary conditions in the army camps. At such a cost, the United States was launched onto the world scene as a great power, with all the benefits—and burdens—of a new colonial empire of its own.

Halfway through the conflict in Cuba, John Hay, the U.S. ambassador to Great Britain, who would soon become secretary of state, wrote a letter to Roosevelt, his close friend. In acknowledging Roosevelt's trial by fire, Hay called the conflict "a splendid little war, begun with the highest motives, carried on with magnificent intelligence and spirit, favored by that fortune which loves the brave."

CORE **OBJECTIVE**

4. Analyze the consequences of the Spanish-American War (War of 1898) for American foreign policy.

Consequences of Victory

John Hay's enthusiastic language suggests how the War of 1898 boosted American self-confidence and reinforced the self-serving belief, influenced by racism as well as social Darwinism, that the United States had a "manifest destiny" to reshape the world in its own image.

In 1885, the Reverend Josiah Strong wrote a best-selling book titled *Our Country* in which he used a Darwinian argument to strengthen the appeal of manifest destiny. The "wonderful progress of the United States," he boasted, was itself an illustration of Charles Darwin's concept of "natural selection," since Americans had demonstrated that they were the world's "superior" civilization, "a race of unequaled energy" who represented "the largest liberty, the purest Christianity, the highest civilization" in the world, a race of superior people destined to "spread itself over the earth," to Central and South America, and "out upon the islands" in the Pacific and beyond to Asia.

Strong asserted that the United States had a Christian duty and economic opportunity to expand American influence around the world. A growing international trade, he noted, would grow directly out of America's missionary evangelism and racial superiority. "Can anyone doubt," he asked, "that this race . . . is destined to dispossess many weaker races, assimilate others, and mold the remainder until . . . it has Anglo-Saxonized mankind?"

Europeans agreed that the United States had now made an impressive entrance onto the world stage. The *Times* of London announced that the American victory over Spain must "effect a profound change in the whole attitude and policy of the United States. In the future America will play a part in the general affairs of the world such as she has never played before."

America ascends to the world stage and redefines "manifest destiny"

The United States had liberated most of Spain's remaining colonies, yet it soon substituted its own imperialism for Spain's. If war with Spain had saved many lives by ending the insurrection in Cuba, it would also lead the United States to take many lives in suppressing another anti-colonial insurrection, in the Philippines. The acquisition of America's first imperial colonies created a host of long-lasting moral and practical problems, from the difficulties of imposing U.S. rule by force on native peoples to those of defending far-flung territories around the globe.

Taking the Philippines

The Treaty of Paris destroyed the Spanish empire, leading Spaniards to call the U.S. victory "The Disaster." The treaty, however, had left the political status of the Philippines unresolved. American business leaders wanted the United States to keep the islands so that they could more easily penetrate the nearby China market, with its huge population. American missionary organizations, mostly Protestant, also favored annexation, since they viewed the Philippines as a useful base from which to bring Protestant Christianity to "the little brown brother" throughout Asia. Not long after the United States took control of the Philippines, American authorities ended the Roman Catholic Church's status as the islands' official religion and made English the new official language, thus opening the door for Protestant missionaries to begin evangelical activities across the region.

"WELL, I HARDLY KNOW WHICH TO TAKE FIRST!" With a growing appetite for foreign territory, Uncle Sam browses his options: Cuba Steak, Puerto Rico Pig, Philippine Floating Islands, and others. An expectant President McKinley waits to take his order.

American motives for annexation and further expansion in the Pacific

These factors were among the considerations that convinced President McKinley of the need to annex "those darned islands" in the Philippines. He explained that

one night late it came to me this way—I don't know how it was, but it came: (1) that we could not give them back to Spain—that would be cowardly and dishonorable; (2) that we could not turn them over to France or Germany—our commercial rivals in the Orient—that would be bad business and discreditable; (3) that we could not leave them to themselves—they were unfit for self-government—and they would soon have anarchy and misrule over there worse than Spain's was; and (4) that there was nothing left for us to do but to take them all, and to educate the Filipinos, and uplift and civilize and Christianize them, and by God's grace do the very best we could by them, as our fellowmen for whom Christ also died. And then I went to bed, and went to sleep and slept soundly.

In this one brief statement, McKinley had summarized the motivating ideas of American imperialism: (1) national glory, (2) expanding commerce, (3) racial superiority, and (4) Christian evangelism. American negotiators in Paris finally offered Spain $20 million for the Philippines, Puerto Rico, and Guam, a Spanish-controlled island in the western Pacific between Hawaii and the Philippines.

Meanwhile, the United States took other giant steps toward imperial expansion in the Pacific. In addition to annexing Hawaii in 1898, the United States had also claimed Wake Island, between Guam and Hawaii, which would become a vital link in a future transpacific telegraph cable. Then, in 1899, Germany and the United States agreed to divide the Samoa Islands. The United States annexed the easternmost islands; Germany took the rest.

By early 1899, the Senate had yet to ratify the Treaty of Paris ending the war with Spain. Anti-imperialists argued that annexing the Philippines would violate the long-standing American principle that people should be self-governing rather than colonial subjects. Opponents also noted the inconsistency of liberating Cuba and annexing the Philippines, as well as the danger that the Philippines would be impossible to defend if a foreign power such as Japan attacked.

The opposition might have killed the treaty had not the most prominent national Democratic leader, William Jennings Bryan, argued that ending the war would open the way for the future independence of the Philippines. His support convinced enough Democrats to enable Senate approval of the treaty on February 6, 1899, by the narrowest of margins: only one vote more than the necessary two thirds.

President McKinley, however, had no intention of granting independence to the Philippines. Although he privately told a friend that "if old Dewey had just sailed away when he smashed that Spanish fleet, what a lot of trouble he would have saved us," he publicly insisted that the United States take control of the islands as an act of "benevolent assimilation" of the native population. But a California newspaper gave a more candid explanation. "Let us be frank," the editor exclaimed. "WE DO NOT WANT THE FILIPINOS. WE WANT THE PHILIPPINES."

The Filipinos themselves had a different vision of their future. In January 1899, they declared their independence and named Emilio Aguinaldo the president of the first Philippine Republic. The following month, an American soldier outside Manila fired on soldiers in Aguinaldo's nationalist forces, called *insurrectos*, killing two. The next day, the U.S. army commander, without investigating the cause of the shooting, ordered his troops to assault the *insurrectos*, thus igniting a full-scale armed conflict that continued off and on for weeks. General Elwell S. Otis rejected Aguinaldo's proposals for a truce, saying that "fighting, having begun, must go on to the grim end." He would accept only the unconditional surrender of the Filipino forces.

On June 2, the Philippine Republic officially declared war against the United States, which now found itself in an even more costly conflict than the one with Spain, this one to suppress the Filipino independence movement.

EMILIO AGUINALDO As the first president of the Philippines, Aguinaldo led the *insurrectos* to war with the United States, who refused his appeal for a truce.

"THE WATER CURE" American soldiers torture a Filipino prisoner during the Philippine-American War. **How did the American soldiers' treatment of the Filipinos tie into the pseudoscientific notions of racial hierarchy?**

American Anti-Imperialist League Coalition of anti-imperialist groups united in 1899 to protest American territorial expansion, especially in the Philippine Islands; its membership included prominent politicians, industrialists, labor leaders, and social reformers.

Since the *insurrectos* more or less controlled the Philippines outside Manila, what followed was largely an American war of conquest at odds with the founding principle of the United States: that people should have the right to govern themselves.

The Philippine-American War

The American effort to crush Filipino nationalism lasted three years, involved some 126,000 U.S. troops, and took the lives of hundreds of thousands of Filipinos (most of them civilians) and 4,234 American soldiers. It was a brutal conflict, with massacres committed by both sides. Racism triggered numerous atrocities by the Americans, many of whom referred to the Filipinos as "niggers." U.S. troops burned villages, tortured and executed prisoners, and imprisoned civilians in overcrowded concentration camps.

Thus did the United States destroy a revolutionary movement modeled after America's own struggle for independence from Great Britain. Organized Filipino resistance had collapsed by the end of 1899. On April 1, 1901, at a ceremony in Manila, Aguinaldo swore an oath accepting the authority of the United States over the Philippines and pledging his allegiance to the U.S. government.

Against the backdrop of this nasty guerrilla war, the great debate over imperialism continued in the United States. In 1899, several groups combined to form the **American Anti-Imperialist League**. Andrew Carnegie footed the bills for the league and even offered $20 million to buy independence for the Filipinos. Other prominent anti-imperialists included union leader Samuel Gompers, who feared the competition of cheap Filipino labor, college presidents Charles Eliot of Harvard and David Starr Jordan of Stanford, and social reformer Jane Addams. Even former presidents Grover Cleveland and Benjamin Harrison urged President McKinley to withdraw U.S. forces from the Philippines.

The drive for imperialism, said the Harvard philosopher William James, had caused the United States to "puke up its ancient soul." Of the Philippine-American War, James asked, "Could there be any more damning indictment of that whole bloated ideal termed 'modern civilization'?" Senator George Frisbie Hoar, one of the few surviving founders of the Republican party, led the opposition to annexation in the Senate. Under the Constitution, he pointed out, "no power is given the Federal government to acquire territory to be held and governed permanently as colonies" or "to conquer alien people and hold them in subjugation."

Organizing the Former Spanish Territories

In the end, however, the imperialists won the debate over the status of the territories acquired from Spain. Senator Albert J. Beveridge boasted in 1900: "The Philippines are ours forever. And just beyond the Philippines are

U.S. INTERESTS IN THE PACIFIC

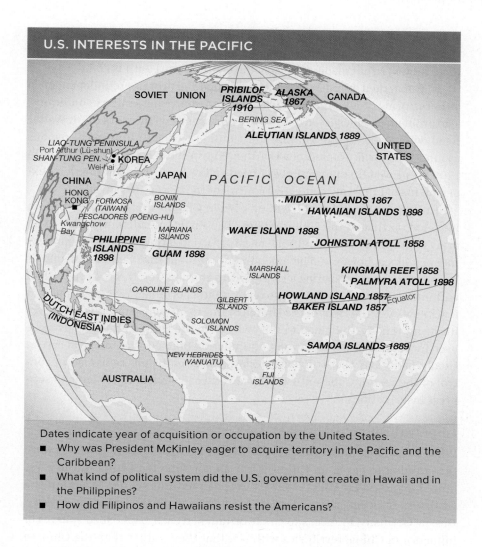

Dates indicate year of acquisition or occupation by the United States.

- Why was President McKinley eager to acquire territory in the Pacific and the Caribbean?
- What kind of political system did the U.S. government create in Hawaii and in the Philippines?
- How did Filipinos and Hawaiians resist the Americans?

China's illimitable markets. We will not retreat from either. . . . The power that rules the Pacific is the power that rules the world." He added that the American economy was producing "more than we can consume, making more than we can use. Therefore we must find new markets for our produce." And American-controlled colonies would make the best new markets. Without acknowledging it, Beveridge and others were using many of the same arguments that England had used in founding the American colonies in the seventeenth century.

On July 4, 1901, the U.S. military government in the Philippines came to an end, and Judge William Howard Taft became the civil governor. In 1902, Congress passed the Philippine Government Act, which declared the islands an "unorganized territory." In 1916, the Jones Act affirmed America's intention to grant the Philippines independence eventually, but that would not happen until 1946. Closer to home, Puerto Rico had been acquired in part to serve as a U.S. outpost guarding the Caribbean Sea. On April 12, 1900, the Foraker Act established a government on the island. The president appointed a governor and eleven members of an executive council, as well as an elected House of Delegates. Residents of the island were declared citizens of Puerto Rico; they were not made citizens of the United States until 1917.

In Cuba, the United States finally fulfilled the promise of independence after restoring order, organizing schools, and improving sanitary conditions. The problem of widespread disease in Cuba prompted the work of Dr. Walter Reed, who made an outstanding contribution to health in tropical regions around the world. Named head of the Army Yellow Fever Commission in 1900, he proved that mosquitoes carried yellow fever. The commission's experiments led the way to effective control of the disease worldwide.

In 1900, on President McKinley's order, Cubans drafted a constitution modeled on that of the United States. The Platt Amendment, added to an army appropriations bill in 1901, sharply restricted the Cuban government's independence, however. The amendment required that Cuba never impair its independence by signing a treaty with a third power, that it keep its debt within the government's power to repay it out of ordinary revenues, and that it acknowledge the right of the United States to intervene in Cuba whenever it saw fit. Finally, Cuba had to sell or lease to the United States lands to be used for coaling or naval stations, a stipulation that led to a U.S. naval base at Guantánamo Bay that still exists today. American troops remained in control of the rest of Cuba until 1902 and returned several times later to suppress insurrections.

Imperial Rivalries in East Asia

While the United States was conquering the Philippines, other nations were threatening to carve up China. After Japan defeated China in the First Sino-Japanese War (1894–1895), European nations set out to exploit the weakness of the huge, virtually defenseless nation. By the end of the century, Russia, Germany, France, and Great Britain had each established spheres of influence in China, territories within it that they (rather than the Chinese government) controlled but did not formally annex. In 1898 and again in 1899, the British asked the American government to join them in preserving the territorial integrity of China against further imperialist actions. Both times, however, the Senate rejected the request because the United States as yet had no strategic investment in the region.

The American outlook toward Asia changed with the defeat of Spain and the acquisition of the Philippines. Instead of acting jointly with Great Britain, though, the U.S. government decided to act alone. What came to be known as the **Open Door policy** was outlined in Secretary of State John Hay's Open Door Note, dispatched in 1899 to his European counterparts. Without consulting the Chinese, Hay announced that China should remain an "open door" to European and American trade and that other nations should not try to take control of Chinese ports or territory. As it turned out, none of the European powers except Britain accepted Hay's principles, but none rejected them, either. So Hay simply announced that all the major powers involved in China had accepted the policy.

Open Door policy Official U.S. assertion that Chinese trade would be open to all nations; Secretary of State John Hay unilaterally announced the policy in 1899 in hopes of protecting the Chinese market for U.S. exports.

The Open Door policy was rooted in the desire of American businesses to dominate Chinese markets. However, it also appealed to those who opposed imperialism because it pledged to keep China from being carved up by powerful European nations. But the much-trumpeted policy had little legal standing. When the Japanese became concerned about growing Russian influence in the disputed region of Manchuria in northeast China and asked how the United States intended to enforce the Open Door policy, Hay replied that America was "not prepared . . . to enforce these views." So the situation would remain for forty years, until continued Japanese military expansion in China would bring about a diplomatic dispute with America that would ignite into war in December 1941.

A new Asian crisis arose in 1900 when a group of Chinese nationalists known to the Western world as Boxers (they called themselves the "Fists of Righteous Harmony") rebelled against foreign involvement in China, especially Christian missionary efforts, and laid siege to foreign embassies in Peking (now known as Beijing). An international expedition of British, German, Russian, Japanese, and American soldiers rescued the international diplomats and their staffs. Hay, fearful that the intervention might become

INTERVENTION IN CHINA After quelling the Boxer Rebellion, U.S. troops march in the Forbidden Palace, the imperial palace in the Chinese capital of Peking.

an excuse for other nations to dismember China, took the opportunity to refine the Open Door policy. The United States, he said in a letter of July 3, 1900, sought a solution that would "preserve Chinese territorial and administrative integrity" as well as "equal and impartial trade with all parts of the Chinese Empire." Six weeks later, the foreign military expedition reached Peking and ended the Boxer Rebellion.

CORE **OBJECTIVE**

5. Describe the reasons for Theodore Roosevelt's rapid rise to the presidency, and evaluate the main elements of his foreign policies.

Theodore Roosevelt and "Big-Stick" Diplomacy

More than any other American of his time, Theodore Roosevelt transformed the role of the United States in world affairs. The nation had emerged from the War of 1898 a world power with major new international responsibilities. To ensure that Americans accepted their new global role, Roosevelt stretched both the Constitution and executive power to the limit. In the process, he pushed a reluctant nation onto the center stage of world affairs.

Rise to National Prominence

Roosevelt's "strenuous life" and early political success

Born in 1858, Roosevelt had grown up in New York City in a cultured, wealthy family. He visited Europe as a child, spoke German fluently, and graduated from Harvard with honors in 1880. From a sickly, nearsighted boy with chronic asthma, he built himself into a physical and intellectual athlete, a barrel-chested man of almost superhuman energy and hyperactivity who for the rest of his days lived and championed the "strenuous life."

A boxer, wrestler, mountain climber, hunter, and all-around outdoorsman, the robust Roosevelt also displayed extraordinary intellectual curiosity. He became a voracious reader in several languages, a natural scientist, a bird-watcher, a historian and essayist, and a zealous moralist. He wrote thirty-eight books on a wide variety of subjects. Within two years of graduating from Harvard, Roosevelt won election to the New York legislature. "I rose like a rocket," he later observed.

With the world seemingly at Roosevelt's feet, however, disaster struck. In 1884, his mother, Mittie, only forty-eight years old, died of typhoid fever. Eleven hours later, in the same house, his twenty-two-year-old wife, Alice, died in his arms of kidney failure, having recently given birth to their only child just two days earlier. The double funeral service for his wife and mother was so emotional that the officiating minister wept throughout his prayer.

Shaken by this "strange and terrible fate," Roosevelt turned his newborn daughter over to his sister, sold the family house, quit his political career, and moved west to the Dakota Territory, where he threw himself into roping and branding steers, shooting buffalo and bears, punching out bullies, capturing outlaws, fighting Indians (whom he called a "lesser race"), and reading novels by the campfire. He was, by his own admission, a poor shot, a bad roper, and an average horseman, but he loved every minute of his two years in the West; he never got over being a cowboy. "I owe more than I can express to the West," he emphasized in his memoirs.

Back in New York City, Roosevelt remarried and ran unsuccessfully for mayor in 1886. He later served six years as a federal civil service commissioner and two years as New York City's police commissioner. In 1896, Roosevelt campaigned energetically for William McKinley, and the new president was asked to reward him with the position of assistant secretary of the navy. McKinley resisted at first, saying that Roosevelt was too "hotheaded," but he eventually gave in.

Roosevelt lusted to be "one of the governing class," so he took full advantage of the celebrity he had gained with the Rough Riders in Cuba to win the governorship of New York in 1898. By then, he had become the most prominent Republican in the nation. "I have played it in bull luck this summer," the governor-elect wrote a friend about his recent streak of successes. "First, to get into the war; then to get out of it; then to get elected." Two years later, Republican leaders were urging him to become the vice presidential running mate for William McKinley, who was hoping for a second presidential term.

From Vice President to President

In the 1900 presidential contest, the Democrats turned once again to William Jennings Bryan, who wanted to make American imperialism the "paramount issue" of the campaign. The Democratic platform condemned the conflict against Filipino nationalists as "an unnecessary war" that had placed the United States "in the false and un-American position of crushing with military force the efforts of our former allies to achieve liberty and self-government."

The Republicans renominated McKinley and named Roosevelt, now known as "Mr. Imperialism," their candidate for vice president. Roosevelt, who despised Bryan as a dangerous "radical," crisscrossed the nation on behalf of McKinley, speaking in opposition to Bryan's "communistic and socialistic doctrines" promoting higher taxes and the unlimited coinage of silver. At one stop, Roosevelt claimed that Bryan's supporters were "all the lunatics, all the idiots, all the knaves, all the cowards." In the end, McKinley and Roosevelt won by 7.2 million to 6.4 million popular votes and 292 to 155 electoral votes. Bryan even lost Nebraska, his home state.

Less than a year later, however, McKinley's second term ended abruptly and tragically. On September 6, 1901, while the president was shaking hands with well-wishers at the Pan-American Exposition in Buffalo, New York, a twenty-eight-year-old unemployed anarchist named Leon Czolgosz (pronounced *CHOL-gosh*), the angry son of Polish immigrants, approached him with a gun concealed in a bandaged hand and fired twice at point-blank range. "I done my duty!" Czolgosz screamed. One bullet was deflected by the president's breastbone, but the other tore through his stomach and lodged in his back. On September 14, McKinley died, and the combustible Theodore

Roosevelt's election as vice president and McKinley's assassination

Roosevelt was suddenly the new president. "Now look," exclaimed Marcus "Mark" Hanna, the Ohio senator who had been McKinley's political manager, "that damned cowboy is President of the United States!"

McKinley's assassination marked the end of one political era and the beginning of another. Six weeks short of his forty-third birthday, Roosevelt was the youngest man to become president, but he had more experience in public affairs than most new presidents, and perhaps more vitality than any. One observer compared him to Niagara Falls—"both great wonders of nature." Roosevelt's glittering spectacles, glistening teeth, and overflowing enthusiasm were like divine gifts to political cartoonists, as was his famous motto, an old African proverb: "Speak softly, and carry a big stick."

Along with Roosevelt's boundless energy, ceaseless activity, and pugnacious personality went an unshakable sense of self-righteousness, which led

> "A great big boy" with a "bully pulpit"

BIG-STICK DIPLOMACY President Theodore Roosevelt wields "the big stick," symbolizing his aggressive diplomacy. As he stomps through the Caribbean, he drags a string of American warships behind him.

him to cast nearly every issue in moral and patriotic terms. He was the first truly activist president. The presidency was, as he put it, a "bully pulpit"—a wonderful platform for delivering fist-pumping speeches to the nation on the virtues of honesty, courage, and civic duty.

Nowhere was President Roosevelt's forceful will more evident than in his handling of foreign affairs. Like many of his political friends and associates, he was convinced that the "civilized" and "barbarian" people of the world faced inevitable conflict, not unlike the fate of the Native Americans pushed off their ancestral lands by Americans. In 1899, Roosevelt argued that the United States, as a "great civilized power," needed to take control of other regions of the world so as to bring "law, order, and righteousness" to "backward peoples."

The Panama Canal

After the War of 1898, the United States became more deeply involved in the Caribbean. One issue overshadowed every other in the region: the proposed Panama Canal. By enabling ships to travel from the Pacific Ocean directly into the Gulf of Mexico, such a canal would cut the travel distance between San Francisco and New York City by almost 8,000 miles.

From 1881 to 1887, a French company led by Ferdinand de Lesseps, who had engineered the Suez Canal in Egypt between 1859 and 1869, had spent nearly $300 million and some 20,000 lives to dig a canal a third of the way across Panama, which was still under the control of Colombia. The company convinced the United States to purchase its partially completed canal. In return for acquiring a canal zone six miles wide, the United States agreed to pay $10 million to Colombia.

The U.S. Senate ratified the Hay-Herrán Treaty in 1903, but the Colombian senate held out for $25 million. As President Roosevelt raged against the "foolish and homicidal corruptionists in Bogotá," the Panamanians revolted against Colombian rule. President Roosevelt aided the Panamanian rebels and signed a treaty with the newly independent nation that extended the Canal Zone from six to ten miles wide. For a $10 million down payment and $250,000 a year, the United States received "in perpetuity the use, occupation and control" of the Canal Zone. Roosevelt later explained that he "took the Canal Zone and let Congress debate; and while the debate goes on [about the legitimacy of his actions] the Canal does also." The Panama Canal opened on August 15, 1914.

Roosevelt's behavior in gaining control of the Panama Canal created ill will throughout Latin America that would last for generations. Equally upsetting to Latin

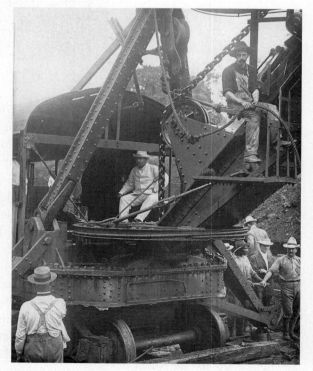

DIGGING THE LAND President Theodore Roosevelt operating a steam shovel during his 1906 visit to the Panama Canal.

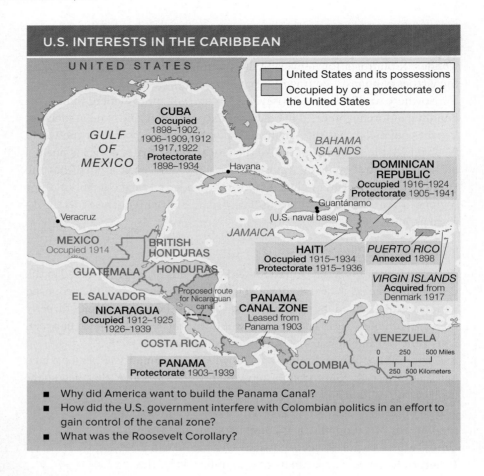

U.S. INTERESTS IN THE CARIBBEAN

■ Why did America want to build the Panama Canal?
■ How did the U.S. government interfere with Colombian politics in an effort to gain control of the canal zone?
■ What was the Roosevelt Corollary?

Roosevelt Corollary President Theodore Roosevelt's revision (1904) of the Monroe Doctrine (1823) in which he argued that the United States could use military force in Central and South America to prevent European nations from intervening in the Western Hemisphere.

Americans was constant interference by both the United States and European countries in the internal affairs of various Latin American nations. A frequent excuse for intervention in the early twentieth century was the collection of debts owed to U.S. or European banks. The Latin Americans responded to these actions with the Drago Doctrine (1902), named after the Argentinian foreign minister Luis María Drago, which prohibited armed intervention by other countries to collect debts.

In December 1902, however, German and British warships blockaded Venezuela to force repayment of debts owed to their nations' banks. Such an action defied not only the Drago Doctrine but also the Monroe Doctrine, the U.S. policy dating to 1823 that prohibited European intervention in the Western Hemisphere. Roosevelt decided that if the United States was going to keep European nations from intervening militarily in Latin America, "then sooner or later we must keep order [there] ourselves."

In 1904, a crisis over the debts of the Dominican Republic prompted Roosevelt to issue what came to be known as the **Roosevelt Corollary** to the Monroe Doctrine: the principle, in short, that in certain circumstances the United States was justified in intervening in Latin American nations to prevent outsiders from doing so. "Chronic wrongdoing," Roosevelt asserted, would justify U.S. exercise of "an international police power" in the region. Thereafter, Roosevelt and other U.S. presidents repeatedly used military force to ensure that Latin American nations paid their debts to U.S. and European banks.

Relations with Japan

While wielding a "big stick" in Latin America, Roosevelt was playing the role of peacemaker in East Asia. In 1904, the long-standing rivalry between Russia and Japan flared into warfare. The Japanese had decided that the Russians threatened Japan's ambitions to expand its influence in China and Korea. On February 8, Japanese warships devastated the Russian fleet; the Japanese then occupied the Korean peninsula and drove the Russians back into Manchuria.

> Negotiating an end to the Russo-Japanese War

When the Japanese signaled that they would welcome a negotiated settlement with Russia, Roosevelt sponsored a peace conference in Portsmouth, New Hampshire. In the Treaty of Portsmouth, signed on September 5, 1905, Russia acknowledged Japan's "predominant political, military, and economic interests in Korea" (Japan would annex the kingdom in 1910), and both powers agreed to leave Manchuria.

Japan's show of strength against Russia raised concerns among U.S. leaders about the security of the Philippines. During the Portsmouth talks, Roosevelt sent William Howard Taft to meet with the Japanese foreign minister in Tokyo. The two men negotiated the Taft-Katsura Agreement of July 29, 1905, in which the United States accepted Japanese control of Korea in exchange for Japan acknowledging U.S. control of the Philippines. Three years later, the Root-Takahira Agreement, negotiated by Secretary of State Elihu Root and the Japanese ambassador to the United States, reinforced the Open Door policy by supporting "the independence and integrity of China" and "the principle of equal opportunity for commerce and industry in China."

Behind the outward appearances of goodwill, however, lay mutual distrust. For many Americans, the Russian threat in East Asia now gave way to concerns about the "yellow peril" (a term apparently coined by Kaiser Wilhelm II of Germany). Racial conflict on the West Coast, especially in California, helped sour relations with Japan. In 1906, San Francisco's school board ordered students of

JAPANESE IMMIGRATION Japanese immigrants arrive at Angel Island, a major immigration station in the San Francisco Bay. By the early 1900s, ethnic tensions on the West Coast were escalating to the point of policy intervention.

THE GREAT WHITE FLEET In an act of pride and power, Roosevelt dispatched the entire U.S. Navy on a worldwide tour. No sooner had the "Great White Fleet" returned than the ships were all repainted in military gray. **What was Roosevelt communicating at home and abroad with this grand naval tour?**

Asian descent to attend a separate public school from "Americans." When the Japanese government sharply protested, President Roosevelt persuaded the school board to change its policy but only after making sure that Japanese authorities would stop encouraging unemployed Japanese "laborers" to immigrate to America. This "Gentlemen's Agreement" of 1907, the precise terms of which have never been revealed, halted what had become an influx of Japanese immigrants to California and brought some relief from racial tension there.

The Great White Fleet

After Roosevelt's election to a full term as president in 1904, he celebrated America's rise as a world power with a great flourish. In 1907, he sent the entire U.S. Navy, by then second in strength only to Britain's Royal Navy, on a grand fourteen-month tour around the world, announcing that he was ready for "a feast, a frolic, or a fight." At every port of call down the Atlantic coast of South America, up the Pacific coast, out to Hawaii, and down to New Zealand and Australia, the "Great White Fleet" of sixteen gleaming battleships received a rousing welcome. The triumphal procession continued to Japan, China, and the Philippines, then Egypt through the Suez Canal and across the Mediterranean Sea before steaming back to Virginia in early 1909, just in time to close Roosevelt's presidency on a note of triumph.

Roosevelt believed that the United States in the twentieth century must assume a much larger role in world affairs because of its international economic interests and its growing military power. America had become, he noted, the "balance of power of the whole globe."

Yet Roosevelt's success in expanding U.S. power abroad would have mixed consequences, since underlying it was a militantly racist view of the world shared by many other imperialists. In their view, the world included "civilized" nations such as the United States, Japan, and the nations of Europe and those they described as "barbarous," "backward," or "impotent" peoples unable to meet their basic obligations as organized societies. It was the responsibility of the "civilized" nations to exercise control of the "barbarous" peoples, by force if necessary. Roosevelt once called warfare the best way to promote "the clear instinct for race selfishness" and insisted that "the most ultimately righteous of all wars is a war with savages." Such belligerent, self-righteous bigotry defied American ideals of equality and would come back to haunt the United States in world affairs.

Taft's "Dollar Diplomacy"

Republican William Howard Taft, who succeeded Roosevelt as president in 1909, continued to promote America's economic interests abroad, practicing what Roosevelt called "**dollar diplomacy**." He used the State Department to help American companies and banks to invest in foreign countries, especially East Asia and the less developed nations of Latin America and the Caribbean. To ensure the stability of those investments, Taft, like Roosevelt, did not hesitate to intervene in nations experiencing political and economic turmoil. In 1909, Taft dispatched U.S. Marines to support a revolution in Nicaragua. Once the new government was formed, Secretary of State Philander C. Knox (a corporate attorney who had helped form the giant U.S. Steel Corporation) helped U.S. banks negotiate loans to prop it up.

Wilson's Interventionism

In 1913, the new Democratic president, Woodrow Wilson, attacked the "dollar diplomacy" practiced by Taft and Roosevelt, claiming that it was a form of economic imperialism. He promised to treat the Latin American nations "on terms of equality and honor." Yet Wilson, along with his secretary of state William Jennings Bryan, who called Latin Americans "our political children," dispatched American military forces to Latin America more often than Taft and Roosevelt.

Wilson argued that the United States must intervene to stabilize weak governments in the Western Hemisphere in order to keep European nations from doing so. He said it was "reprehensible" to allow European governments to take control of these "weak and unfortunate republics."

During his two presidential terms, Wilson sent U.S. troops into Cuba once, Panama twice, and Honduras five times. In 1915, when the Dominican Republic on the Caribbean island of Hispaniola refused to sign a treaty that would have given the United States a "special" role in governing the island nation, Wilson sent U.S. Marines, where they established a military government and fought a nasty guerrilla war against anti-American rebels.

dollar diplomacy Practice advocated by President Theodore Roosevelt in which the U.S. government fostered American investments in less developed nations and then used U.S. military force to protect those investments.

That same year, Wilson also intervened in Haiti, next door to the Dominican Republic. He admitted that his actions were "high-handed" but also justified because the "necessity for exercising control there is immediate, urgent, imperative." Others disagreed. As the *New York Times* charged, Wilson's frequent interventions made Taft's dollar diplomacy look like "ten cent diplomacy."

The United States in Mexico

Mexico was a much thornier problem for President Wilson's misguided meddling. In 1910, long-suffering Mexicans had revolted against the long-standing dictatorship of Porfirio Diaz, who had given foreign corporations a free rein in developing the nation's economy. After revolutionary armies occupied Mexico City in 1911, the victorious rebels began squabbling among themselves. The leader of the rebellion, Francisco Madero, was himself overthrown by his chief of staff, General Victoriano Huerta, who assumed power

INTERVENTION IN MEXICO American marines enter Veracruz, Mexico, in 1914. **How was American intervention greeted by Mexicans in Veracruz?**

in early 1913 and then had Madero and thirty other political opponents murdered.

Shocked by Madero's murder, President Wilson refused to recognize "a government of butchers." It was vital, he insisted, for the Latin American nations to have "fairly decent rulers." Huerta ignored Wilson's criticism and established a dictatorship. Wilson decided that Huerta must be removed. To do so, he ordered U.S. warships to halt shipments of foreign weapons to Huerta's new government. "I am going to teach the South American republics to elect good men," Wilson vowed to a British diplomat. Meanwhile, several rival revolutionary Mexican armies, the largest of which was led by a charming but ruthless bandit named Francisco Pancho Villa, began trying to unseat Huerta.

On April 9, 1914, nine American sailors were arrested in Tampico, Mexico, while trying to buy supplies. Mexican officials quickly released them and apologized to the U.S. naval commander. There the incident might have ended, but the imperious U.S. admiral demanded that the Mexicans fire a 21-gun salute to the American flag. After they refused, Wilson sent U.S. troops ashore at Veracruz on April 21, 1914. They occupied the city at a cost of nineteen American lives; at least 300 Mexicans were killed or wounded.

The use of military force in Mexico played out like many previous American interventions in the Caribbean and Central America. Congress readily supported the decision because American honor was at stake, and Wilson was sure that most Mexicans would welcome U.S. intervention since his intentions were so "unselfish."

But the arrival of U.S. troops in Veracruz backfired. Instead of welcoming the Americans as liberators, Mexicans viewed them as invaders. Newspapers in Mexico shouted for "Vengeance! Vengeance! Vengeance!" For seven months, the Americans governed Veracruz. They left in late 1914 after Huerta was overthrown by Venustiano Carranza.

Still, the troubles south of the border continued as various factions engaged in ongoing civil wars. In 1916, the colorful rebel leader, "Pancho" Villa, launched raids into Texas and New Mexico in a deliberate attempt to trigger U.S. intervention and to reinforce his anti-American credentials. On March 9, he and his men attacked Columbus, New Mexico, just three miles across the border. With Villa shouting "Kill all the Gringos!" his army of 500 peasant revolutionaries looted stores, burned the town, and killed seventeen Americans, men and women.

A furious Woodrow Wilson sent General John J. Pershing to Mexico with 6,000 U.S. soldiers to capture Villa and destroy his army. For nearly a year, with little success, Pershing's troops chased Villa's army through the rugged mountains of northern Mexico. As Pershing muttered, "It's like trying to chase a rat in a cornfield." In 1917, the American troops were ordered home. The elusive Villa, meanwhile, named his mule "President Wilson." By then, however, Wilson paid little notice, for he was distracted by a much greater threat: war in Europe.

Reviewing the
CORE OBJECTIVES | INQUIZITIVE

■ **Toward the New Imperialism**
Near the end of the nineteenth century,
the popular idea that America had
a "manifest destiny" to expand its
territory abroad and industrialists'
desire for new markets for their goods
helped to fuel America's new *imperialism*.
The racist ideology of social Darwinism
was used to justify the colonization of
less developed nations.

■ **Expansion in the Pacific** Business
leaders hoped to extend America's
commercial reach across the Pacific. The
United States purchased the vast Alaska
territory from Russia in 1867. In 1894,
Hawaii's minority white population,
led by American planters, overthrew
the native Hawaiian queen, declared a
republic, and requested that Hawaii be
annexed by the United States.

■ **The Spanish-American War
(The War of 1898)** When Cubans
revolted against Spanish colonial rule
in 1895, many Americans supported
their demand for independence. *Yellow
journalism* sensationalizing the harsh
Spanish suppression of the revolt
further aroused Americans' sympathy.
Early in 1898, the publication of the *de
Lôme letter*, followed by the mysterious
explosion sinking the *U.S. battleship
Maine* in Havana Harbor, helped propel
America into war with Spain. Under the
Treaty of Paris ending the war, Cuba
became independent and the United
States annexed Puerto Rico, which it
had occupied. In the Spanish colony of
the Philippine Islands, America's Pacific
naval fleet defeated the Spanish fleet

in the Battle of Manila Bay and took
control of the capital, Manila.

■ **Consequences of Victory**
A vicious guerrilla war in the Philippines
followed when Filipinos who favored
independence rebelled against U.S.
control. American soldiers eventually
suppressed the rebellion, and President
McKinley announced that the U.S.
would annex the Philippines. This
prompted a significant debate over
whether acquiring overseas territories
violated American principles of self-
determination and independence. But in
the end, the imperialists won the debate,
and Congress set up a government in the
Philippines as well as in Puerto Rico.
In Cuba, the United States imposed
significant restrictions on the new
government after U.S. forces left the
island. In the Pacific region, the United
States also annexed Hawaii, Guam,
Wake Island, and some of the Samoa
Islands during or shortly after the War
of 1898. In East Asia, Secretary of State
John Hay promoted the *Open Door policy
(1899)* of preserving China's territorial
integrity and equal access by all nations
to trade with China.

■ **Theodore Roosevelt and Big-
Stick Diplomacy** After succeeding
to the presidency upon McKinley's
assassination in 1901, Theodore
Roosevelt pursued an imperialist
foreign policy that confirmed the
United States' new role as a world
power. He helped negotiate the treaty
that ended the Russo-Japanese War,
oversaw diplomatic and military actions

leading to the U.S. construction and control of the Panama Canal, and sent the navy's fleet of new battleships around the world as a symbol of American might. He also proclaimed the *Roosevelt Corollary (1904)* to the Monroe Doctrine, asserting that the United States would intervene in Latin America as necessary in order to prevent European intervention.

■ **Taft and Wilson's Interventionism Abroad**
William H. Taft and Woodrow Wilson continued Roosevelt's pattern of intervening in the internal affairs of the other nations. What Roosevelt called *dollar diplomacy* involved the U.S. government fostering American investments in less developed nations and then using U.S. military force to protect those investments.

KEY TERMS

imperialism *p. 688*

The Influence of Sea Power upon History, 1660–1783 p. 689

yellow journalism *p. 692*

U.S. battleship *Maine p. 692*

de Lôme letter (1898) *p. 693*

Teller Amendment (1898) *p. 694*

Rough Riders *p. 696*

American Anti-Imperialist League *p. 702*

Open Door policy (1899) *p. 704*

Roosevelt Corollary (1904) *p. 710*

dollar diplomacy *p. 713*

CHRONOLOGY

1867	The United States purchases Alaska from Russia
1880s	European nations create colonial empires in Asia and Africa
1890	Alfred Mahan publishes *The Influence of Sea Power upon History, 1660–1783*
1894	Republic of Hawaii is proclaimed
1895	Cuban insurrection of Spanish rule
1898	U.S. battleship *Maine* explodes in Havana Harbor
	The Spanish-American War (War of 1898)
	United States annexes Hawaii
1899	U.S. Senate ratifies the Treaty of Paris, ending the Spanish-American War
1899–1902	Insurgents resist U.S. conquest of the Philippines
1903	Panamanians revolt against Colombia
1905	Russo-Japanese War
1907–1909	U.S. Great White Fleet circles the globe
1914	Panama Canal opens
1909–1917	U.S. military interventions in Mexico and Latin America

ᨑINQUIZITIVE

Go to InQuizitive to see what you've learned—and learn what you've missed—with personalized feedback along the way.

DEBATING the Annexation of the Philippines

Historians use different analytical methods to make sense of the past. Some focus on social and economic issues, such as class conflict or who profits from a particular policy choice. Other historians focus more on culture to understand how ideas, values, and beliefs have shaped the actions of historical figures. For Part 5, *"Growing Pains,"* we will examine how different analytical methods result in contrasting explanations for why the United States annexed and retained the Philippines following the defeat of Spain in 1898.

For this exercise you have two tasks:

PART 1: Compare the two secondary sources on why the United States annexed the Philippines.

PART 2: Using primary sources, evaluate the arguments of the two secondary sources.

PART I Comparing Secondary Sources

Two secondary sources from different analytical perspectives are included below. In *Standing at Armageddon: The United States, 1877–1919*, Nell Irvin Painter of Princeton University weaves together economic and foreign-policy concerns with the lives of ordinary Americans to explain the annexation of the Philippines. Kristin L. Hoganson of the University of Illinois, a gender historian, explores the question of why the United States annexed the Philippines in *Fighting for American Manhood: How Gender Politics Provoked the Spanish-American and Philippine-American Wars*. While both works contain elements of economic and cultural history, each historian emphasizes a particular analytical methodology.

Compare the views of these two scholars by answering the following questions. Be sure to find specific examples in the selections to support your answers.

■ According to each author, what problems in society did supporters of annexation think American control of the Philippines would solve?

■ Which author focuses on economic explanations, and which author focuses on cultural explanations, to explain imperialist support for annexation?

■ Do you think the authors' arguments are contradictory or complementary? In other words, can they both be correct?

Secondary Source 1

Nell Irvin Painter, "The White Man's Burden" (1989)

The foreign markets explanation sought the cause of depressions not in currency, distribution of wealth, or monopoly. The culprit, it seemed, was agricultural and industrial overproduction. Americans produced too much, it was said; it seemed to matter little that during the recent hard times thousands had run out of the very foodstuffs and manufactured goods reputedly overproduced. What was needed were new markets, especially in Asia, especially in the most populous country in the world, China. . . . While foreign markets had beckoned American businessmen for decades, this more urgent quest included the novel expectation that the government of the United States should play an active part in fostering exports. The Philippine Islands—like Hawaii—represented the perfect stepping-stones to China, stops along the way where coal burning ships bound for Asia could refuel. Expansionists saw the islands as the opportunity of the century. Manila might become an American version of Hong Kong, the British market city that tapped the markets and produce of South China. . . . For many Americans, expansion was the inevitable result of the machine age that had already filled up the continental United States and now seemed to demand the raw materials and foreign markets that overseas colonies promised. The vision of factories fuming nonstop and workers employed without interruption made this economic argument for annexation straightforward and persuasive.

Source: Painter, Nell Irvin. *Standing at Armageddon: The United States, 1877–1919.* New York: W. W. Norton & Company, 1989. 146–147.

Secondary Source 2

Kristin L. Hoganson, "The National Manhood Metaphor" (1998)

Whether they imagined the Filipinos as savages, children, or feminine figures, imperialists regarded them as a means for American men to develop their ability to govern. One adherent of imperialism summed up this belief when he averred that "the necessities involved in the unexpected annexation of strange dependencies will *call forth the governing faculty.*" The savage, childlike, and feminine stereotypes appealed to imperialists because they not only suggested the Filipinos' incapacity for self-government, but also enabled imperialists to cast themselves as civilizers and authoritative heads of household—that is, as men who wielded power. Heedful of British imperialists' claims that empire made men and interpreting colonial endeavors as unparalleled challenges, imperialists looked to the Philippines to turn white, middle- and upper-class American men into what they considered to be ideal citizens—physically powerful men who would govern unmanly subordinates with a firm hand, men accustomed to wielding authority, men who had overcome the threat of degeneracy. . . . In response to the accusations that their Philippine policies violated the nation's deepest convictions, imperialists brandished a national manhood metaphor. The youthful republic had become an adult, they declared, and should assume the responsibilities of a mature man. Rather than dwelling on its childish past, the nation should manfully shoulder its new obligations. . . . . Imperialists implied that failing to assume responsibility for dependents would reveal an unwillingness to advance from childlike dependency to paternalistic power. In short, it would reveal a lack of manhood in the nation.

Source: Hoganson, Kristin L. *Fighting for American Manhood: How Gender Politics Provoked the Spanish-American and Philippine-American Wars.* New Haven: Yale University Press, 1998. 155, 157.

PART II Using Primary Sources to Evaluate Secondary Sources

When historians are faced with competing interpretations of the past, they often look at primary source material to help evaluate the different arguments. Four speeches follow, each by an American politician who supported U.S. annexation and rule over the Philippines. The first is from President William McKinley's State of the Union speech following U.S. annexation of the Philippines and the start of the Philippine-American War. The second is from Henry Cabot Lodge, a Republican senator from Massachusetts who was a leading supporter of American imperialism. The third speech is from Albert Beveridge, senator from Indiana, who supported Lodge's imperialist policies. And the last speech, from Vice President Theodore Roosevelt, was delivered twelve days prior to assuming the presidency following McKinley's death. While these four politicians offer very different justifications for American annexation and rule over the Philippines, they were all prominent advocates of American imperialism. Your task is to understand their arguments and see how they might be used to support the analysis of the two historians.

Carefully read the primary sources and answer the following questions. Decide which of the primary source documents support or refute Painter's and Hoganson's argument about the annexation of the Philippines. You may find that some documents do both but for different parts of each historian's interpretation. Be sure to identify which specific components of each historian's argument the documents support or refute.

■ What arguments for U.S. retention of the Philippines does each senator offer?

■ Which of these sources would either Painter or Hoganson (or both) find most useful, and how might they use them to support their argument?

■ What might be the limitations on the usefulness of the sources for supporting their arguments?

■ After looking at the primary sources about annexation, which historian's argument do you find more compelling, and why do you find it so? If you find both arguments equally compelling, how could you combine the arguments?

Primary Source 1

William McKinley, "Annual Message of the President to Congress" (December 5, 1899)

The future government of the Philippines rests with the Congress of the United States. Few graver responsibilities have ever been confided to us. If we accept them in a spirit worthy of our race and our traditions, a great opportunity comes with them. The islands lie under the shelter of our flag. They are ours by every title of law and equity. They cannot be abandoned. If we desert them we leave them at once to anarchy and finally to barbarism. We fling them, a golden apple of discord, among the rival powers, no one of which could permit another to seize them unquestioned.... The suggestion has been made that we could renounce our authority over the islands and, giving them independence, could retain a protectorate over them. This proposition will not be found, I am sure, worthy of your serious attention. Such an arrangement would involve at the outset a cruel breach of faith....

No effort will be spared to build up the waste places desolated by war and by long years of misgovernment. We shall not wait for the end of strife to begin the beneficent work. We shall continue, as we have begun, to open the schools and the churches, to set the courts in operation, to foster industry and trade and agriculture, and in every way in our power to make these people whom Providence has brought within our jurisdiction feel that it is their liberty and not our power, their welfare and not our gain, we are seeking to enhance. Our flag has never waved over any community but in blessing. I believe the Filipinos will soon recognize the fact that it has not lost its gift of benediction in its world-wide journey to their shores.

Source: McKinley, William. "Message of the President." *Papers Relating to the Foreign Relations of the United States with Annual Message of the President to Congress, Transmitted to Congress, December 5, 1899.* Washington, D.C.: U.S. Government Printing Office, 1901. L–LII.

Primary Source 2

Henry Cabot Lodge, "The Retention of the Philippine Islands," Speech in the U.S. Senate (March 7, 1900)

I believe, we shall find arguments in favor of the retention of the Philippines as possessions of great value and a source of great profit to the people of the United States which cannot be overthrown. First, as to the islands themselves. They are over a hundred thousand square miles in extent, and are of the greatest richness and fertility. From these islands comes now the best hemp in the world, and there is no tropical product which cannot be raised there in abundance. Their forests are untouched, of great extent, and with a variety of hard woods of almost unexampled value.... It is sufficient for me to indicate these few elements of natural wealth in the islands which only await development.... A much more important point is to be found in the markets which they furnish. The total value of exports and imports for 1896 amounted in round numbers to $29,000,000, and this was below the average....

The Philippine Islands took from us imports to the value of only $94,000. There can be no doubt that the islands in our peaceful possession would take from us a very large proportion of their imports. Even as the islands are to-day there is opportunity for a large absorption of products of the United States, but it must not be forgotten that the islands are entirely undeveloped. The people consume foreign imports at the rate of only a trifle more than $1 per capita. With the development of the islands and the increase of commerce and of business activity the consumption of foreign imports would rapidly advance, and of this increase we should reap the chief benefit. We shall also find great profit in the work of developing the islands....

Manila, with its magnificent bay, is the prize and the pearl of the East. In our hands it will become one of the greatest distributing points, one of the richest emporiums of the world's commerce. Rich in itself, with all its fertile islands behind it, it will keep open to us the markets of China and enable American enterprise and intelligence to take a master share in all the trade of the Orient!

Source: Lodge, Henry Cabot. *The Retention of the Philippine Islands, Speech of Hon. Henry Cabot Lodge of Massachusetts, in the Senate of the United States, March 7, 1900.* Washington, D.C.: U.S. Government Printing Office, 1900. 37, 41.

Primary Source 3

Albert Beveridge, "Our Philippine Policy," Speech in the U.S. Senate (January 9, 1900)

But, Senators, it would be better to abandon the Philippines, and count our blood and treasure already spent a profitable loss, than to apply any academic arrangement of self-government to these children [the Filipino people]. They are not yet capable of self-government. How could they be? They are not a self-governing race; they are Orientals, Malays, instructed by Spaniards in the latter's worst estate. They know nothing of practical government, except as they have witnessed the weak, corrupt, cruel, and capricious rule of Spain. What magic will anyone employ to dissolve in their minds and characters those impressions of governors and governed which three centuries of misrule has created? What alchemy will change the oriental quality of their blood, in a year, and set the self-governing currents of the American pouring through their Malay veins? How shall they, in a decade, be exalted to the heights of self-governing peoples which required a thousand years for us to reach? . . .

Self-government is no cheap boon, to be bestowed on the merely audacious. It is the degree which crowns the graduate of liberty, not the reward of liberty's infant class, which has not yet mastered the alphabet of freedom. Savage blood, oriental blood, Malay blood, Spanish example—in these do we find the elements of self-government? . . .

The men we send to administer civilized government in the Philippines must be themselves the highest examples of our civilization. I use the word examples, for examples they must be in that word's most absolute sense. They must be men of the world and of affairs, students of their fellow-men, not theorists nor dreamers. They must be brave men, physically as well as morally. They must be men whom no force can frighten, no influence coerce, no money buy. Such men come high, even here in America. But they must be had. . . . Necessity will produce them. . . . Better abandon this priceless possession, admit ourselves incompetent to do our part in the world-redeeming work of our imperial race; better now haul down the flag than to apply academic notions of self-government to these children or attempt their government by any but the most perfect administrators our country can produce. I assert that such administrators can be found.

Source: Beveridge, Albert J. "Our Philippine Policy." In *The Meaning of the Times and Other Speeches*. Indianapolis: Bobbs-Merrill Company, 1908. 71–76.

Primary Source 4

Theodore Roosevelt, "National Duties," Speech at Minnesota State Fair (September 2, 1901)

Let me insist again, for fear of possible misconstruction, upon the fact that our duty is twofold, and that we must raise others while we are benefiting ourselves. In bringing order to the Philippines, our soldiers added a new page to the honor-roll of American history, and they incalculably benefited the islanders themselves. Under the wise administration of Governor Taft the islands now enjoy a peace and liberty of which they have hitherto never even dreamed. But this peace and liberty under the law must be supplemented by material, by industrial development. Every encouragement should be given to their commercial development, to the introduction of American industries and products; not merely because this will be a good thing for our people, but infinitely more because it will be of incalculable benefit to the people in the Philippines. We shall make mistakes; and if we let these mistakes frighten us from our work we shall show ourselves weaklings. . . . We gird up our loins as a nation, with the stern purpose to play our part manfully in winning the ultimate triumph; and therefore we turn scornfully aside from the paths of mere ease and idleness and with unfaltering steps tread the rough road of endeavor.

Source: Roosevelt, Theodore. "National Duties." In *The Strenuous Life: Essays and Addresses*. New York: Century Company, 1902. 295–297.

Modern America

The United States entered the twentieth century on a wave of unrelenting change, not all of it beneficial. In 1800, America was a predominantly rural, agrarian, Christian society largely unconcerned with international affairs. By 1900, the United States had become the world's most powerful economy, a highly industrialized and increasingly urban society with a growing involvement in world politics and international commerce. In other words, the nation was on the threshold of the modern era in which the United States emerged as a leading global power.

The prospect of modernity both excited and scared Americans. Old truths and beliefs clashed with unsettling new scientific discoveries and social practices. People debated the truth of Darwinism and the Bible, the existence of God, the dangers of jazz, and proposals to prohibit the sale of alcoholic beverages. The advent of automobiles and airplanes helped shrink distance between people, and communications innovations such as mass advertising, radio, and film helped strengthen a sense of unity or national consciousness.

In the process, the United States began to emerge from its isolationist shell. Throughout most of the nineteenth century, presidents and secretaries of state had sought to isolate America from the intrigues and conflicts of the great European powers. As early as 1780, in the midst of the Revolutionary War, future president John Adams had warned Congress against involving the United

States in the squabbles of Europe. "Our business with them, and theirs with us," he wrote, "is commerce, not politics, much less war."

With only a few exceptions, statesmen during the nineteenth century followed such advice. Noninvolvement in foreign wars and nonintervention in the internal affairs of foreign governments formed the pillars of American foreign policy until the end of the century. During the 1890s, however, expanding commercial interests around the world led Americans to broaden the horizons of their concerns. Imperialism, the acquisition by force of foreign colonies, was considered essential among the great European powers, and a growing number of American expansionists demanded that the United States join in the hunt for new territories and markets. Such motives helped spark the Spanish-American War of 1898 and helped to justify the resulting acquisition of colonies outside the continental United States.

The outbreak of the Great War in Europe in 1914 posed an even greater challenge to the tradition of isolation and nonintervention. The prospect of a

German victory over the French, the British, and the Russians threatened the European balance of power, which had long ensured the security of the United States. By 1917, it appeared that Germany might emerge triumphant and begin to menace the Western Hemisphere. Woodrow Wilson's crusade to transform international affairs in accordance with his idealistic principles during the Great War severed American foreign policy from its isolationist moorings. It also started a prolonged debate about the role of the United States in world affairs, a debate that the Second World War would resolve for a time on the side of internationalism.

While the United States was entering the world stage as a formidable military power, it was also settling into its role as a great industrial power. Cities and factories sprouted across the landscape. An abundance of new jobs and affordable farmland served as a powerful magnet attracting millions of immigrants from nearly every region of the world. They were not always welcomed, nor did they readily fit into American society. Ethnic and racial conflict, as well as clashes between workers and owners, increased at the turn of the century.

In the midst of such social turmoil and unparalleled economic development, reformers made their first serious attempts to adapt political and social institutions to the realities of the industrial age. The worst excesses and injustices of unregulated economic development—corporate monopolies, child labor, political corruption, hazardous working conditions, urban ghettos—were finally addressed in a comprehensive way. During the Progressive Era (1890–1917), local, state, and federal governments expanded their roles to rein in the excesses of industrial capitalism and develop more rational and efficient public policies.

A conservative Republican resurgence challenged the notion of the new regulatory approaches during the 1920s. Free enterprise and corporate capitalism witnessed a dramatic revival. But the stock market crash of 1929 helped propel the United States and the world into the worst economic downturn in history. The unprecedented severity of the Great Depression renewed public demands for expanded government programs to protect the general welfare and prevent more depressions in the future. "This nation asks for action," declared President Franklin Delano Roosevelt in his 1933 inaugural address. The many New Deal initiatives and agencies instituted by Roosevelt and congressional Democrats created the framework for a welfare state that has since served as the basis for public policy.

The New Deal helped revive public confidence and put people back to work, but it did not end the Great Depression. It took a second world war to restore full employment. The necessity of mobilizing the nation in support of the war against Germany and Japan also accelerated the growth of the federal government. And the vast scope of the war helped catapult the United States into a leadership role in world politics. The use of atomic bombs to end the war against Japan ushered in a new era of nuclear diplomacy that held the fate of the world in the balance. While relishing the new creature comforts associated with modern life, Americans in 1945 found themselves living amid an array of new anxieties as a chilling cold war emerged out of the world war.

"VOTES FOR US WHEN WE ARE WOMEN!" Parades organized by women's suffrage groups brought together women of all ages and classes. Here, from a patriotically outfitted automobile, some very young suffragists ask their many spectators for "votes for <u>us</u> when <u>we</u> are women."

The Progressive Era

1890–1920

Theodore Roosevelt's emergence as a national political leader coincided with the onset of what historians have labeled the Progressive Era (1890–1920), an extraordinary period of intense social activism and dramatic political innovation. Millions of "progressives" believed that America was experiencing a "crisis of democracy" that required bold action by churches, charitable organizations, experts, individuals—and an expanded role for governments. "Our country is going through a terrific period of unrest," explained Amos Pinchot, a leading progressive attorney and reformer from New York City. "Something is wrong," he said. Corruption was "destroying our respect for government, uprooting faith in political parties, and causing every precedent and convention of the old order to strain at its moorings."

Pinchot and other progressives argued that the United States had been changing so rapidly since the end of the Civil War that the nation was at risk of imploding. America had quickly become the world's fastest-growing industrial economy, but prosperity was not being evenly shared.

The widening gap between the rich and poor during the Gilded Age had become a major concern. Walter Weyl, a progressive economist, insisted that "we shall

CORE OBJECTIVES INQUIZITIVE

1. Explain the varied motives of progressive reformers.

2. Explain the various sources of thought and activism that contributed to the progressive movement.

3. Identify the specific goals of progressive reformers and how they advanced them.

4. Describe the contributions of Presidents Theodore Roosevelt and William Howard Taft to the progressive movement, and explain how and why the two men came to disagree.

5. Describe the progressive policies of President Woodrow Wilson, and explain why and how they differed from those of Presidents Roosevelt and Taft.

not advance far in working out our American ideals without striking hard at . . . inequality." Political equality, he added, "is a farce and a peril unless there is at least some measure of economic equality." The growth of new industries like railroading, steel, coal, and oil had attracted massive waves of poor farm folk and foreign immigrants to large cities whose basic social services—food, water, housing, education, sanitation, transportation, and medical care—could not keep pace with the rate of urban growth.

Between 1890 and 1920, progressive reformers attacked the pressing problems created by unregulated industrialization, unplanned urbanization, and the increasingly unequal distribution of wealth and power. But most of all, they insisted, something must be done to control the very large, very powerful corporations that dominated economic activity and corrupted its political life. As Amos Pinchot said, "We have permitted an uncontrolled industrial oligarchy to assume . . . tremendous and arrogant power."

By the beginning of the twentieth century, progressivism had become the most dynamic social and political force in the nation. In 1910, Woodrow Wilson, then serving as president of Princeton University, told a gathering of clergymen that progressivism had generated "an extraordinary awakening in civic consciousness" over the previous twenty years.

The Progressive Impulse

Progressives were liberals, not revolutionaries. They wanted to reform and regulate capitalism, not destroy it. Most progressives were civic-minded Christian moralists who felt that politics had become a contest between good and evil, honesty and corruption. What they all shared was the assumption that governments—local, state, and national—must take a more active role in addressing the huge problems created by rapid urban and industrial growth. Chicago's Jane Addams, a leading progressive reformer, reported that charities and churches were "totally inadequate to deal with the vast numbers of the city's disinherited." The "real heart of the [progressive] movement," declared another reformer, was to expand the role of government "as an agency of human welfare."

Progressivism was more a widespread impulse supported by elements of both major political parties than it was a single movement with a common agenda. Theodore Roosevelt called progressivism the "forward movement" because it generated positive changes led by people "who stand for the cause of progress, for the cause of the uplift of humanity and the betterment of mankind." Progressives, he stressed, "fight to make this country a better place to live in for those who have been harshly treated by fate."

Unlike Populism, whose grassroots appeal was largely confined to farming regions in the rural South and Midwest, progressivism was a wide-ranging national movement, centered in large cities but also popular in rural areas among what came to be called Populist progressives. Progressive activists, though mostly white, urban, middle-class professionals, were so numerous that they came in all stripes: men and women; Democrats, Republicans, Populists, and Socialists; labor unionists and business executives; teachers and professors; social workers and journalists; farmers and homemakers; whites and blacks; clergymen, atheists, and agnostics. Whatever their motives and methods, their combined efforts led to significant improvements at all levels of government and across all levels of society.

To make governments more "efficient" and businesses more honest and safer for workers and consumers, progressives drew upon the new "social sciences"—sociology, political science, psychology, public health, and economics—being developed at new research universities. The progressive approach to social problems was to "investigate, educate, and legislate." Florence Kelley, a tireless activist who fought to improve living conditions for the poor and to end child labor, voiced the era's widespread belief that once people knew "the truth" about social ills, "they would act upon it."

> Making government more responsive and efficient, and businesses more honest and safer places to work

Yet progressivism had its flaws and limitations, inconsistencies and hypocrisies. Progressives often armed themselves with Christian moralism, but their "do-good" perspective was limited by the racial and ethnic prejudices of the day as well as social and intellectual snobbery. The goals of white progressives rarely included racial equality; many otherwise "progressive" people, including Theodore Roosevelt and Woodrow Wilson, believed in the supremacy of the "Anglo-Saxon race." Many well-educated progressives also felt—and acted—superior to the working poor they wanted to help. They assumed that modern society was too complicated for the uninformed masses to understand, much less improve, without direction by those who knew better—progressives.

The Varied Sources of Progressivism

> CORE **OBJECTIVE**
> **2.** Explain the various sources of thought and activism that contributed to the progressive movement.

During the last quarter of the nineteenth century, political progressives at the local and state levels began to attack corrupt political bosses and irresponsible corporate barons. Their goals were more honest and efficient government, more effective regulation of big businesses ("the trusts"), and better living conditions for the majority of Americans who worked with their hands for wages. Only by expanding the scope of local, state, and federal governments, they believed, could these goals be attained.

Depression and Populism

More than any other factor, the devastating depression of the 1890s ignited the progressive spirit of reform. The worst economic downturn in American history to that point brought massive layoffs in factories, mines, railroads, and mills. Nearly a quarter of the adults in the workforce lost their jobs.

> The depression of the 1890s

Although the United States boasted the highest per capita income in the world, it also contained some of the highest concentrations of poverty among the industrialized nations. In 1900, an estimated 10 million of the 82 million Americans lived in desperate poverty, with annual incomes barely adequate to provide the minimum necessities of life. The devastating effects of the depression prompted many upper-middle-class urban people—lawyers, doctors, executives, social workers, teachers, professors, journalists, and college-educated women—to organize efforts to reform society.

The Populists

Populism was another thread in the fabric of progressivism. The Populist platforms of 1892 and 1896 included political reforms intended to give more power to "the people," such as the "direct" election of U.S. senators by the voters rather than by state legislatures. Although the defeat of William Jennings Bryan in the 1896 presidential campaign ended the Populist party as a serious political force, many of the reforms pushed by the Populists were implemented by progressives during the early twentieth century.

"Honest Government" Activism and Socialism

The Mugwumps and the Socialist party

The Mugwumps—"gentlemen" reformers who had fought the patronage system and insisted that government jobs be awarded on the basis of merit—supplied progressivism with another important element of its thinking: the "honest government" ideal. Over the years, the good-government movement expanded to include efforts not only to end political corruption but also to address persistent urban issues such as rising crime; access to electricity, clean water, and sewers; mass transit; and garbage collection.

Another significant "progressive" force was the growing influence of socialist ideas. In 1902, a pamphlet promoting working-class reforms claimed that "socialism is coming . . . and nothing can stop it. You can feel it in the air." The Socialist Party of America, supported mostly by militant farmers and immigrant Germans and Jews, served as the radical wing of progressivism. Unlike European socialists who followed the economic doctrines of Karl Marx, however, most American socialists did not call for the government to take ownership of large corporations. They focused instead on improving working conditions in factories and mills and on closing the widening income gap between rich and poor through "progressive" taxation. In any case, most progressives were capitalist reformers, not socialist radicals. They rejected the extremes of both socialism and laissez-faire individualism, preferring instead a regulated capitalism "softened" by humanitarianism. Labor leader Samuel Gompers, for example, dismissed socialists as unrealistic: "Economically you are unsound, socially you are wrong, industrially you are an impossibility!"

Muckraking Journalism

muckrakers Writers who exposed corruption and abuses in politics, business, consumer safety, working conditions, and more, spurring public interest in progressive reforms.

Progressivism depended upon newspapers and magazines to inform the public about political corruption and social problems. The so-called **muckrakers** were investigative journalists whose aggressive reporting educated the upper and middle classes about political and corporate wrongdoing and revealed "how the other half lives"—the title of Jacob Riis's pioneering work of photo-journalism about life in the slums of New York (1890). "The rich are farther from the poor than ever before," wrote a journalist in 1886, and muckrakers saw it as the responsibility of reporters to show people in comfortable circumstances the ugly realities of everyday poverty.

The muckrakers, who in addition to Riis included Ida Tarbell, Ray Stannard Baker, Lincoln Steffens, and William Allen White, got their nickname from Theodore Roosevelt, who said that crusading journalists were "often indispensable to . . . society, but only if they know when to stop raking the muck." By uncovering political corruption and writing about social ills in newspapers and popular monthly magazines such as *McClure's*, *Munsey's*, and *Cosmopolitan*, the muckrakers changed the face of journalism and gave it a new political role.

Muckrakers challenged readers to take action against political corruption and corporate wrongdoing. "We, the people of the United States, and nobody else," Tarbell insisted, "must cure whatever is wrong" with America. Roosevelt, both as governor of New York and as president, frequently used muckrakers to drum up support for his policies; he corresponded with them, invited them to the White House, asked their advice, and used their popularity with readers to help shape public opinion.

The golden age of muckraking began in 1902, when Samuel S. McClure, the owner of *McClure's*, began paying idealistic journalists to root out the rampant corruption in politics and corporations. McClure was determined to make his popular magazine a "power for good"; the "vitality of democracy," he insisted, depended upon journalists educating the public about "complex questions" involving the miserable conditions in which poor Americans lived and worked.

Ida Tarbell, one of the most dedicated muckrakers, loved "the sense of vitality, of adventure, of excitement" at *McClure's*. She spent years doggedly investigating the unethical and illegal means by which John D. Rockefeller had built his gigantic Standard Oil trust. At the end of her series of nineteen *McClure's* articles, she asked readers: "And what are we going to do about it?" McClure

COVER OF *McCLURE'S* MAGAZINE, 1902 This issue features the first of nineteen installments of Ida Tarbell's exposé on the Standard Oil Company, a seminal work of muckraking that influenced legislation and investigative reporting alike. **How did muckraking differ from the yellow journalism of the 1890s?**

told Tarbell that her campaign against monopolies had made her "the most famous woman in America."

Without the muckrakers, progressivism would never have achieved widespread popular support. During the early twentieth century, investigative journalism became such a powerful force for change that one editor said that Americans were benefiting from "Government by Magazine."

Religious Activism and Social Responsibility

Still another of the streams flowing into progressivism was religious activism directed at achieving social justice, the idea that society had an ethical obligation to help its poorest and most vulnerable members. A related ideal was the **social gospel**, the belief that religious institutions and individual Christians had an obligation to bring about the "Kingdom of God" on earth. In many respects, in fact, the progressive movement as a whole formed a new phase of Christian spiritual revival, an energetic form of public outreach focused not so much on individual conversion and salvation as on social reform. "We believe," as a social gospel organization explained, "that the age of sheer individualism is past, and the age of social responsibility has arrived."

> **The YMCA/YWCAs and Salvation Army**

During the last quarter of the nineteenth century, a growing number of churches and synagogues began emphasizing community service and the care of the unfortunate. New organizations also made key contributions to the movement. The Young Men's Christian Association (YMCA) and a similar group for women, the YWCA, both entered the United States from England in the 1850s and grew rapidly after 1870; the Salvation Army, founded in London in 1878, came to the United States a year later.

During the late nineteenth century, the YMCA and YWCA—both known as "the Y"—combined nondenominational religious evangelism with social services and fitness training in centers, segregated by race as well as gender, that were built in cities across the country. Intended to provide low-cost housing and healthful exercise in a "safe Christian environment" for young men and women from rural areas or foreign countries, the YMCA/YWCA centers often included libraries, classrooms, and kitchens. "Hebrew" counterparts—YMHAs and YWHAs—provided many of the same facilities in cities with large Jewish populations. Salvation Army centers offered "soup kitchens" to feed the poor and day nurseries for the children of working mothers.

> **Washington Gladden**

The major forces behind the social gospel movement were Christian activists who feared that churches had become too closely associated with the upper and middle classes and were losing their appeal to the working poor. In 1875, Washington Gladden, a prominent pastor in Springfield, Massachusetts, wrote a pathbreaking book, *Working People and Their Employers* (1876), which argued that true Christianity was based on the principle that "thou shalt love thy neighbor as thyself." Gladden rejected the view of the social Darwinists that the poor deserved their fate and should not be helped.

social gospel Mostly Protestant movement that stressed the Christian obligation to address the mounting social problems caused by urbanization and industrialization.

He argued that helping the poor was an essential element of the Christian faith. To that end, Gladden became the first prominent religious leader to support the rights of workers to form unions. He also spoke out against racial segregation and efforts to discriminate against immigrants.

Gladden's efforts helped launch a new era in religious life in which churches addressed the urgent problems created by a rapidly urbanizing and industrializing society. He and other "social gospelers" reached out to the working poor who labored long hours for low wages, lived in miserable slum housing, and lacked the legal right to form unions as well as insurance coverage for on-the-job accidents.

Walter Rauschenbusch, a German-born Baptist minister serving immigrant tenement dwellers in the Hell's Kitchen neighborhood of New York City, became the greatest champion of the social gospel. In 1907, he published a pioneering book, *Christianity and the Social Crisis*, in which he argued that "whoever uncouples the religious and social life has not understood Jesus." The Christian emphasis on personal salvation, he added, must be linked with an equally passionate commitment to social justice. Churches must embrace "the social aims of Jesus," he stressed, for Christianity was intended to be a "revolutionary" faith.

> Walter Rauschenbusch

In Rauschenbusch's view, religious life needed the social gospel to revitalize it and make it socially relevant: "We shall never have a perfect social life, yet we must seek it with faith." Like the muckrakers, Rauschenbusch sought to expose the realities of poverty in America and convince statesmen to deal with the crisis. His message resonated with Theodore Roosevelt, Woodrow Wilson, and many other progressives in both political parties. Years later, Rev. Martin Luther King Jr. spoke for three generations of radicals and reformers when he said that *Christianity and the Social Crisis* "left an indelible imprint on my thinking."

Rauschenbusch, Gladden, and other "social gospelers" sought to expand the "Kingdom of God" by following Christ's example and serving the poor and powerless. Rugged individualism may have been the path to wealth, they argued, but "Christian socialism" offered hope for unity among all classes. "Every religious and political question," said George Herron, a religion professor at Grinnell College, "is fundamentally economic." And the solution to economic tensions was social solidarity. As progressive economist Richard Ely put it, America could only truly thrive when it recognized that "our true welfare is not an individual matter purely, but likewise a social affair."

THE SOCIAL GOSPEL Jane Addams, the co-founder of Hull House, is photographed alongside a group of young women inside the settlement house. A champion of immigrants and the working class, Addams' social work expanded from the settlement house movement to political reform.

Jane Addams, Ellen Gates
Starr, and the settlement house
movement

Settlement Houses Among the most visible champions of the "social gospel" were those who volunteered in innovative community centers called settlement houses. At the Hull House settlement on Halsted Street in a working-class Chicago neighborhood, for instance, two women from privileged backgrounds, Jane Addams and Ellen Gates Starr, addressed the everyday needs of the working poor, especially newly arrived European immigrants.

Addams and Starr were driven by what Addams called an "impulse to share the lives of the poor" and to make social service "express the spirit of Christ." Their staff of two dozen women, most of whom lived at Hull House, served thousands of people each week. Besides a nursery for the infant children of working mothers, Hull House also sponsored health clinics, lectures, music lessons and art studios, men's clubs, an employment bureau, job training, a gymnasium, a coffeehouse, and a savings bank.

By the early twentieth century, there were hundreds of settlement houses in cities across the United States, most of them in the Northeast and Midwest. To Addams, the social gospel driving progressive reformers reflected their "yearning sense of justice and compassion." She and other settlement house leaders soon realized, however, that their work in the rapidly spreading immigrant slums was like bailing out the ocean with a teaspoon. They thus added political reform to their already lengthy agenda and began lobbying for new laws and regulations to improve the living conditions in poor neighborhoods.

As her influence in Chicago grew, Addams was appointed to prominent governmental and community boards, where she focused on improving

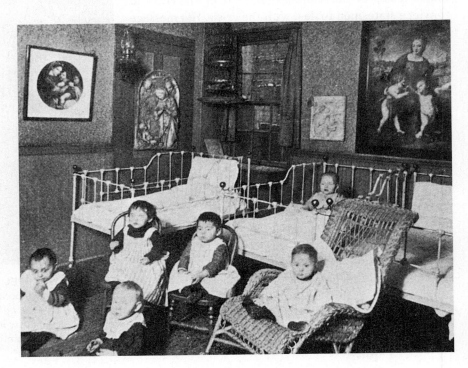

HULL HOUSE The nursery at Hull House, one of the many services offered by settlement houses to help new immigrants and the working poor.

public health and food safety, pushing for better street lighting and police protection, and reducing the use of narcotics. An ardent pacifist and outspoken advocate for suffrage (voting rights) for women, Addams would become the first American woman to win the Nobel Peace Prize.

The Woman Suffrage Movement

Jane Addams and other settlement house workers made up only a small share of the growing numbers of women working outside the home by the early twentieth century. The number of employed women tripled from 2.6 million in 1880 to 7.8 million in 1910. As women became more involved in the public world of work and wages, the women's rights movement also grew as it tirelessly pursued the right to vote.

After the Civil War, women in the suffrage (voting rights) movement had hoped that the Fifteenth Amendment, which guaranteed voting rights for African American men, would aid their own efforts to gain the vote. Such arguments made little impression on the majority of men, however, who still insisted that women stay out of politics. A Mississippi Democrat was blunt about his opposition: "I would rather die and go to hell," he claimed, "than vote for woman's suffrage."

In 1869, Susan B. Anthony and Elizabeth Cady Stanton had founded the National Woman Suffrage Association (NWSA) in New York City to promote a **woman suffrage** amendment to the Constitution. They condemned both the Fourteenth and Fifteenth Amendments for limiting "citizenship" and voting rights to males only. The NWSA considered the right to vote only one among many urgent feminist causes. For example, they also campaigned for new laws requiring higher pay for working women and making it easier for abused wives to get divorces.

Other suffrage activists insisted that pursuing multiple issues hurt their cause. In 1869, Julia Ward Howe and Lucy Stone formed the American Woman Suffrage Association (AWSA). Based in Boston, it focused single-mindedly on voting rights and included men among its leaders.

In 1890, the two rival groups united as the National American Woman Suffrage Association (NAWSA), the same year Wyoming was admitted as a state, the first that gave full voting rights for women. It was in the territories and states west of the Mississippi River that the suffrage movement had its earliest successes. In those areas, where Populism found its strongest support, women were more engaged in grassroots political activities than they were in the East. In addition, the early settlers in the western territories were mostly men, so they hoped that providing suffrage would encourage more women to settle in the new territories. Suffrage activists in the West also emphasized getting working women engaged in the effort, and they adopted many of the tactics used by labor unions in the West. For these reasons and others, the West was more supportive of women's rights. Between 1890 and 1896, the suffrage cause won three more victories in western states—Utah, Colorado, and Idaho.

> Western states' leadership on the suffrage issue

woman suffrage Movement to give women the right to vote through a constitutional amendment, spearheaded by Susan B. Anthony and Elizabeth Cady Stanton's National Woman Suffrage Association.

EAST MEETS WEST San Francisco suffragists marched across the country in 1915 to deliver an amendment petition with more than 500,000 signatures to Congress in Washington, D.C. Along the way, they were warmly received by other suffragists, like those of New Jersey, pictured here.

In the early twentieth century, however, the suffrage movement remained in the doldrums until proposals for voting rights at the state level easily won a Washington state referendum in 1910 and then carried California by a close majority in 1911. The following year three more western states—Arizona, Kansas, and Oregon—joined in to make a total of nine western states with full suffrage. In 1913, Illinois granted women voting rights in presidential and municipal elections. Yet not until New York acted in 1917 did a state east of the Mississippi River allow women to vote in all elections.

The advocates of women's suffrage put forth several arguments for their position. Many said that the right to vote and hold office was a matter of simple justice: women were just as capable as men of exercising the rights and responsibilities of citizenship. Others insisted that women were morally superior to men and therefore their participation would raise the quality of the political process and reduce the likelihood of future wars, corruption, and scandals. Women voters and politicians, advocates argued, would promote the welfare of society as a whole rather than partisan or selfish goals, so allowing women to participate in politics would create a great engine for progressive social change. One activist explicitly linked women's suffrage with the social gospel, declaring that women followed the teachings of Christ more faithfully than men; if they were elected to public office, they would "far more effectively guard the morals of society and the sanitary conditions of cities."

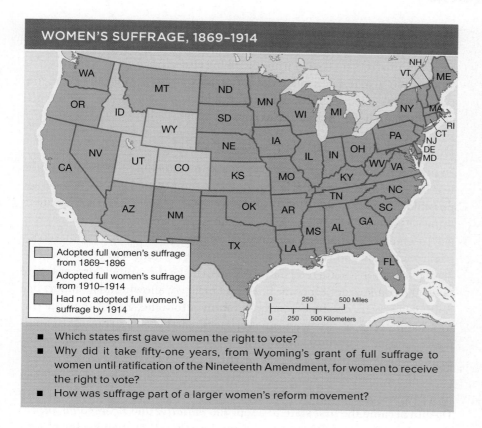

WOMEN'S SUFFRAGE, 1869–1914

Adopted full women's suffrage from 1869–1896

Adopted full women's suffrage from 1910–1914

Had not adopted full women's suffrage by 1914

- Which states first gave women the right to vote?
- Why did it take fifty-one years, from Wyoming's grant of full suffrage to women until ratification of the Nineteenth Amendment, for women to receive the right to vote?
- How was suffrage part of a larger women's reform movement?

Yet the woman suffrage movement was not free from the social, ethnic, and racial prejudices of its time. Carrie Chapman Catt, who became president of the National American Woman Suffrage Association in 1900, echoed the fears of many middle- and upper-class women when she warned of the danger that "lies in the votes possessed by the males in the slums of the cities, and the ignorant foreign [immigrant] vote." She added that the nation with "ill-advised haste" had given "the foreigner, the Negro and the Indian" the vote but still withheld it from white women. In the South, one suffragist claimed that giving white women the vote would help "insure immediate and durable white supremacy." Throughout the country, most suffrage organizations excluded African American women.

> The suffragists' arguments and prejudices

Progressives' Aims and Achievements

> CORE **OBJECTIVE**
> **3.** Identify the specific goals of progressive reformers and how they advanced them.

All the impulses and groups comprising the progressive movement grew out of what Theodore Roosevelt called the "fierce discontent with evil" that animated many Americans at the turn of the nineteenth century. Given their great diversity, however, progressives focused on many specific goals and used many different methods. They assaulted a wide array of social and political evils: from corrupt politicians to too-powerful corporations, from economic distress on small farms and in big cities to the general feeling that "the people" had lost control of the nation to what Roosevelt called "the special interests," selfish businesses and their leaders who were solely interested in "money-getting" at the expense of public welfare.

Reforms in the Political Process

In his monthly articles in *McClure's* magazine, Lincoln Steffens, one of the leading muckrakers, regularly asked: "Will the people rule? Is democracy possible?" Steffens and other progressives often answered that the way to improve America's democracy was to make it even more democratic.

> **Adoption of the direct primary, initiative, referendum, and recall**

To empower citizens to clean up a corrupt political system driven by backroom deals and rigged party conventions, Steffens and other progressives pushed for several reforms intended to make the political process more open and transparent. One was the direct primary, allowing all members of a political party to vote on the party's nominees for office rather than the traditional practice in which an inner circle of party leaders chose the candidates. In 1896, South Carolina became the first state to adopt a statewide primary, and within twenty years nearly every state had done so.

While urging states to adopt party primaries, progressives developed other ways to increase participation in the political process. In 1898, South Dakota became the first state to adopt the *initiative* and *referendum*, procedures that allowed voters to create laws directly rather than having to wait for legislative action. Citizens could sign petitions to have a proposal put on the ballot (the initiative) and could then vote it up or down (the referendum). Still another progressive innovation was the *recall*, first adopted in Oregon in 1910, whereby corrupt or incompetent elected officials could be removed by a public petition and vote. By 1920, nearly twenty states had adopted the initiative and referendum, and nearly a dozen had added the recall procedure.

> **Seventeenth Amendment: Direct election of U.S. senators**

Progressives also fought to change how U.S. senators were elected. Under the Constitution, state legislatures elected senators, a process that was frequently corrupted by lobbyists and vote buying. In 1900, for example, Senate investigators revealed that a Montana senator had given more than $100,000 in secret bribes to members of the legislature that chose him. In 1894, the House of Representatives passed a constitutional amendment to allow voters to elect senators directly, only to see it defeated in the Senate. In 1913, thanks to the efforts of progressives, the **Seventeenth Amendment**, providing for the direct election of senators, was ratified by enough states to become law.

Efficiency Movement in Business and Government

A second major theme of progressivism was the "gospel of efficiency." Its champion was Frederick Winslow Taylor, a Philadelphia-born engineer who during the 1890s became a celebrated business consultant, helping mills and factories operate more efficiently by practicing "scientific management." A

Seventeenth Amendment (1913) Constitutional amendment that provided for the public election of senators rather than the traditional practice allowing state legislatures to name them.

self-described progressive who became the nation's first "efficiency expert," Taylor showed employers how to cut waste and increase productivity. By breaking down work activities (filling a wheelbarrow, driving a nail, shoveling coal) into a sequence of mechanical steps and using stopwatches to measure the time it took each worker to perform each step in a task, Taylor established detailed performance standards (and cash rewards) for each job classification, specifying how fast people doing each job should work and when they should rest.

Taylorism in industrial management

The goal of what came to be called **Taylorism** was to improve both productivity and profits for employers and also raise pay for workers; as Taylor wrote, "Men will not do an extraordinary day's work for an ordinary day's pay." There would be no need for strikes by workers in such a system, he argued.

Many workers, however, resented Taylor's innovations, seeing them as just a tool to make people work faster. Yet Taylor's controversial system of industrial management became one of the most important contributions to capitalist economies in the twentieth century. It did bring concrete improvements in productivity. "In the future," Taylor predicted in 1911, "the system [rather than the individual workers] will be first."

Political progressives applied Taylorism to the operations of government by calling for the reorganization of state and federal agencies to eliminate overlap, the establishment of clear lines of authority, and the replacement of political appointees with trained specialists. By the early twentieth century, many complex functions of government had come to require specialists with technical expertise. As the young political scientist and future president Woodrow Wilson wrote, progressive ideals could be achieved only if government at all levels—local, state, and national—was "informed and administered by experts." Many cities set up "efficiency bureaus" to identify ways their governments were wasting money and to apply more cost-effective "best practices" from other cities.

The commission system and city-manager plan

Two Taylorist ideas for restructuring city and county governments also emerged in the first decade of the new century. One, the commission system, was first adopted in 1901 by the city of Galveston, Texas, after the local government collapsed following a devastating hurricane and tidal wave that killed over 8,000 people, the greatest natural disaster in American history. The commission system placed ultimate authority in a board composed of a small group of commissioners who combined both legislative and executive powers in heading up city departments—commissioners of sanitation, police, utilities, and so on. Houston, Texas, created a commission system in 1906; Dallas and Des Moines, Iowa, in 1907; and Memphis, in 1909.

Even more popular than the commission system was the city-manager plan, under which an appointed professional administrator ran a city or county government in accordance with policies set by the elected council and mayor. Staunton, Virginia, adopted the first city-manager plan in 1908. Five years later, the inadequate response of municipal officials to a flood led Dayton, Ohio, to become the first large city in the nation to adopt the plan.

Taylorism Labor system based on detailed study of work tasks, championed by Frederick Winslow Taylor, intended to maximize efficiency and profits for employers.

FRIENDS OF THE WORKINGMAN (*Left to right*) American labor leader Andrew Furuseth, Governor Robert M. La Follette, and muckraker Lincoln Steffens, ca. 1915.

Robert La Follette and the "Wisconsin idea"

Yet along with concrete benefits, the efforts to make local governments more "businesslike" and professional had a downside. Shifting control from elected officials representing individual neighborhoods to at-large commissioners and nonpartisan specialists separated local government from party politics, which for many working-class voters had been the main way they could have a voice in how they were governed locally. In addition, running a city like a business led commissioners and managers to focus on reducing expenses rather than expanding services, even when such expansion was clearly needed.

At the statewide level, this ideal of efficient government run by nonpartisan experts was pursued most notably by progressive Republican governor Robert M. La Follette of Wisconsin between 1901 and 1906. A small, wiry man with a huge head, "Fighting Bob" La Follette declared war on "vast corporate combinations" and political corruption by creating a nonpartisan state government that would become a "laboratory for democracy." To do so, he worked closely with professors from the University of Wisconsin to establish a Legislative Reference Bureau, which provided elected officials across the state with nonpartisan research, advice, and help in the drafting of legislation.

La Follette used the bureau's reports to enact such reforms as the direct primary, stronger railroad regulation, the conservation of natural resources, and workmen's compensation programs to support people injured on the job. "If it can be shown that Wisconsin is a happier and better state to live in," declared La Follette, "that its institutions are more democratic, that the opportunities of all its people are more equal, that social justice more nearly prevails . . . then I shall rest content in the feeling that the Progressive movement has been successful." The "Wisconsin idea" of more efficient government run by experts was widely publicized and copied by other progressive governors.

Regulation of Business

Of all the problems facing American society at the turn of the century, one towered above all: the regulation of giant corporations, a third major theme of progressivism. The threat of corporate monopolies increased during the depression of the 1890s as struggling companies were gobbled up by larger ones. Between 1895 and 1904, 157 new holding companies gained control of 1,800 different businesses. Almost fifty of these giant holding companies controlled over 70 percent of the market in their respective industries. In 1896, fewer than a dozen companies other than railroads were worth $10 million or more. By 1903, that number had soared to 300. The explosive growth of big business changed the nature of business life. "We have come upon a very different age from any that preceded us," New Jersey governor Woodrow Wilson observed. People now worked "not for themselves" but "as employees of great corporations."

Concerns over the concentration of economic power in "trusts" and other forms of monopolies had led Congress to pass the Sherman Anti-Trust Act in 1890, but its language about what constituted a monopoly was so vague that it proved ineffective. In addition, government agencies responsible for regulating businesses often came under the influence of those they were supposed to regulate. Congress, for instance, appointed retired railroad executives to the Interstate Commerce Commission (ICC), which had been created to regulate railroads. The issue of regulating the regulators has never been fully resolved.

> Little success in regulating Big Business

Promotion of Social Justice

A fourth important focus of the progressive movement was the effort to promote greater *social justice* for the working poor and for jobless and homeless people. In addition to their work in settlement houses and other religiously inspired efforts, many progressives formed new advocacy organizations such as the National Consumers' League, which educated consumers about harsh working conditions in factories and mills as well as companies' widespread use of child workers as a means of lowering labor costs.

> Campaigns for social justice by advocacy organizations and women's clubs

Other grassroots progressive organizations, such as the General Federation of Women's Clubs, founded in 1890, insisted that the nation's civic life needed the humanizing effect of female leadership. Caroline Brown started the Chicago Women's Club to help women address the "live issues of this world we live in." Women's clubs across the country sought to clean up filthy city slums by educating residents about personal and household hygiene ("municipal housekeeping"), urging construction of sewer systems, and launching public-awareness campaigns about the connection between unsanitary conditions and disease. Women's clubs also campaigned for childcare centers; kindergartens; government inspection of food processing plants; stricter housing codes; laws protecting women in the workplace; and more social services for the poor, sick, disabled, and abused. Still others addressed the widespread problems related to prostitution and alcohol abuse.

The Campaign against Drinking

Middle-class women reformers, most of them motivated by strong religious convictions, were the driving force behind efforts to stop the sale and consumption of alcoholic beverages. Founded in Cleveland, Ohio, in 1874, the Women's Christian Temperance Union (WCTU) was the largest women's group in the nation, boasting 300,000 members. By attacking drunkenness and closing saloons, such reformers hoped to: (1) prevent domestic violence

> Temperance, abstinence, and prohibition: The WCTU and the Anti-Saloon League

FRANCES WILLARD The founder and president of the WCTU, Willard lobbied for a range of progressive reforms, prohibition chief among them.

by husbands and fathers, (2) reduce crime in the streets, and (3) remove one of the worst tools of corruption—free beer on election days—used by political bosses to "buy" votes among the working class. As a Boston sociologist concluded, the saloon had become "the enemy of society because of the evil results produced upon the individual."

Frances Willard, the dynamic president of the WCTU between 1879 and 1898, greatly expanded the goals and scope of the organization. Under her leadership, it moved beyond moral persuasion of saloonkeepers and drinkers and began promoting legislation to ban alcohol ("prohibition") at the local, state, and federal levels. Willard also pushed the WCTU to lobby for other progressive reforms important to women, including a nationwide eight-hour workday, the regulation of child labor, government-funded kindergartens, the right to vote for women, and federal inspections of the food industry. More than anything else, however, the WCTU stayed true to its original mission and continued to campaign against drinking.

Opposition to alcohol abuse was one of the most widely popular of the many progressive reforms. What came to be called the prohibition or temperance movement was national in scope but especially popular in the Midwest and South, where conservative Protestants were most numerous.

The battle against alcoholic beverages took on new strength in 1893 with the formation of the Anti-Saloon League, an organization based in local churches that pioneered the strategy of the single-issue political pressure group. Describing itself as "the Protestant church in action against the saloon," the bipartisan league, like the WCTU, initially focused on closing down saloons rather than abolishing alcohol. Eventually, however, it decided to force the prohibition issue into the forefront of state and local elections. At its "Jubilee Convention" in 1913, the league endorsed the nineteenth amendment to the Constitution. It prohibited the manufacture, sale, and consumption of alcoholic beverages. Congress finally approved the Prohibition amendment in 1917.

Labor Legislation

In addition to the efforts to reduce alcohol consumption, other progressive reformers pushed legislation to improve working conditions in mills, mines, and factories—and on railroads. In 1890, almost half of wage workers toiled up to twelve hours a day—sometimes seven days a week—in unsafe, unsanitary, and unregulated conditions. Legislation to ensure better working conditions and limit child labor was perhaps the most significant reform to emerge from the drive for progressive social justice.

Efforts to regulate children's and women's work

At the end of the nineteenth century, fewer than half of working families lived solely on the husband's earnings. Everyone in the family who could work did so. Many married women engaged in "homework"—making clothes, selling flower arrangements, preparing food for others, and taking in boarders. Parents in poor families also frequently took their children out of school in order to put them to work outside the home—in factories, shops, mines, mills, and canneries, and on farms. In 1900, some 1.75 million children between the ages of ten and fifteen were working outside the home.

Many progressives argued that children, too, had rights in a democracy. The National Child Labor Committee, organized in 1904, sought to prohibit the employment of young children. Within ten years, the committee convinced most state legislatures to ban the hiring of children below a certain age (varying by state from twelve to sixteen) and limiting the hours children might work.

Progressives who focused on improving the lives of children also demanded that cities build more parks and playgrounds. Further, reformers made a concerted effort to regulate the length of the workday for women, in part because some working mothers were pregnant and others had children at home with inadequate supervision. Spearheaded by Florence Kelley, the first president of the National Consumers' League, progressives convinced many state governments to ban the hiring of children below a certain age and to limit the hours that women and children could work.

CHILD LABOR Children shuck oysters in 1913 at the Varn & Platt Canning Company in Bluffton, South Carolina. **What reforms were put in place in the early 1900s to protect children in the workforce?**

It took a tragic disaster to spur meaningful government regulation of dangerous workplaces. On March 25, 1911, a fire broke out at the Triangle Shirtwaist factory (called a "sweatshop" because of its cramped and unventilated work areas) in New York City. Escape routes were limited because the owner kept the stairway door locked to prevent theft, and 146 workers trapped on the upper floors of the ten-story building died in the fire or leaped to their deaths.

The victims of the Triangle Shirtwaist fire were mostly young, foreign-born women in their teens, almost all of whom were Jewish, Italian, or Russian immigrants. In the aftermath of the gruesome deaths, dozens of new city and state regulations dealing with fire hazards, dangerous working conditions, and child labor were enacted across the nation.

PRODUCTS OF THE TENEMENT WORKSHOP

Glove Finishing

Chiffon Applique

Infants Dress (D)

NATIONAL CONSUMERS' LEAGUE EXHIBIT To raise awareness about labor reform, everyday objects are displayed at a New York exhibition in 1908 alongside descriptions of the poor working conditions and exploitation that went into their manufacture.

The Supreme Court followed an inconsistent course in its rulings on state labor laws. In *Lochner v. New York* (1905), the Court ruled that a law limiting the workday to no more than ten hours was unconstitutional because it violated workers' right to accept any jobs they wanted, no matter how bad the working conditions or how low the pay.

Three years later, however, in *Muller v. Oregon* (1908), the Court upheld a ten-hour-workday law for women, largely on the basis of research showing the ill effects of long working hours on women's health. In *Bunting v. Oregon* (1917), the Court accepted a state law allowing no more than a ten-hour workday for both men and women. For twenty more years, however, the nation's highest court held out against state laws requiring a minimum wage.

The "Progressive" Income Tax

Progressives also promoted social justice by addressing America's growing economic inequality. One way to redistribute wealth was through the creation of a "progressive" federal income tax—so called not because of the idea's association with the progressive movement, but because the tax rates are based on a sliding scale—that is, the rates "progress" or rise as income levels rise, thus forcing the rich to pay more. Such a "graduated" or "progressive" tax system was the climax of the progressive movement's commitment to a more equitable distribution of wealth.

The progressive income tax was an old idea. In 1894, William Jennings Bryan had persuaded Congress to create a 2 percent tax on annual incomes over $4,000. When millionaires responded by threatening to leave America, Bryan exclaimed, "If some of our 'best people' prefer to leave the country rather than pay the tax . . . let them depart." Soon after the tax became law, however, the Supreme Court declared it unconstitutional on a technicality.

The idea of a "graduated" federal income tax refused to die, however. Progressives believed that such a tax would help slow the concentration of wealth in the hands of the richest Americans, who between 1890 and 1910 had nearly doubled their share of the national income, chiefly at the expense of the middle class. In 1907, President Theodore Roosevelt announced his support for the tax. Two years later, his successor, William Howard Taft, endorsed a constitutional amendment allowing such a tax, and Congress agreed. Finally, in 1913, this **Sixteenth Amendment** was ratified by enough states to become a national law.

Sixteenth Amendment: Authorization of an income tax

Sixteenth Amendment (1913) Constitutional amendment that authorized the federal income tax.

Progressivism under Roosevelt and Taft

CORE **OBJECTIVE**
4. Describe the contributions of Presidents Theodore Roosevelt and William Howard Taft to the progressive movement, and explain how and why the two men came to disagree.

In the late nineteenth century, most progressive policies originated at the state and local levels. Federal reform efforts began in earnest only when Theodore Roosevelt became president in 1901 after the assassination of William McKinley. During his rapid rise to national fame and leadership, Roosevelt had grown more progressive with each passing year. Unlike McKinley, who was patient and cautious, "T.R." was relentlessly energetic, and, in the words of one journalist, "impetuous, impatient, and wholly lacking in tact." He could not stand indecision or inaction. And he loved what he called "strenuosity." In the White House, the ever-boyish Roosevelt invited male guests to wrestle and box with him or to fight with wooden swords or climb trees. "His personality," said a friend, "so crowds the room that the walls are worn thin and threaten to burst outward."

Like Andrew Jackson, Roosevelt greatly increased the power of the presidency in the process of enacting his progressive agenda. His friend and successor, William Howard Taft, continued Roosevelt's "progressive" effort to regulate corporate trusts, but he proved neither as energetic nor as wide-ranging in his role as a reformer president—a difference that led to a fateful break between the two men.

Roosevelt's Taming of Big Business

Roosevelt accomplished more by aggressive executive action than by convincing Congress to pass legislation. As president, he believed he could do anything not expressly forbidden by the Constitution. Mark Twain, the most popular writer in America, said that Roosevelt was willing to "kick the Constitution into the backyard whenever it gets in his way."

In outlining his progressive agenda, Roosevelt applauded the growth of industrial capitalism but declared war on corruption and on cronyism—the awarding of political appointments, government contracts, and other favors to politicians' personal friends and donors. He endorsed a "**Square Deal**" for "every man, great or small, rich or poor."

The Square Deal program featured what was called the "Three Cs": greater government *control* of corporations, enhanced *conservation* of natural resources, and new regulations to protect *consumers* against contaminated food and medicines.

Roosevelt began by calling for more rigorous government enforcement of the Sherman Anti-Trust Act against huge corporations engaged in illegal activities. In his view, some big businesses were bad not because they were big but because their executives acted unethically or unfairly. From his youth, Roosevelt had developed a firm commitment to "fair play" in sports, in business, and in politics, and his version of progressivism centered on a commitment to equal opportunity. "A great democracy," he insisted, "has got

Square Deal Roosevelt's progressive agenda of the "Three Cs": *control* of corporations, *conservation* of natural resources, and *consumer* protection.

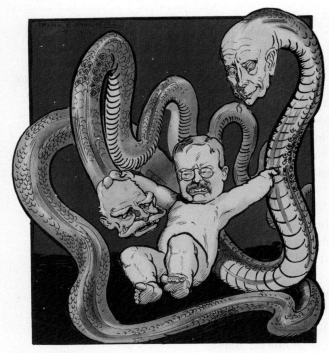

SQUARE DEAL This 1906 cartoon likens Roosevelt to the Greek legend Hercules, who as a baby strangled snakes sent from hell to kill him. Here, the serpents are pro-corporation senator Nelson Aldrich and Standard Oil's John D. Rockefeller.

to be *progressive* or it will soon cease to be great or a democracy."

In 1902, only five months into his presidency, Roosevelt stunned financiers when he ordered the U.S. attorney general to break up the Northern Securities Company, a vast network of railroads and steamships run by J. Pierpont Morgan that monopolized transportation in several regions of the country. Shocked that Roosevelt would try to dismantle his corporation, Morgan rushed from New York to the White House and told the president: "If I have done anything wrong, send your man to my man and they can fix it up." But the attorney general, who was also at the meeting, told Morgan: "We don't want to 'fix it up.' We want to stop it." Morgan then asked Roosevelt if he planned to attack his other trusts, such as U.S. Steel and General Electric. "Certainly not," Roosevelt replied, "unless we find out that . . . they have done something wrong." In 1904, the Supreme Court ruled 5–4 that the Northern Securities Company was indeed a monopoly and must be dismantled.

Altogether, Roosevelt approved about twenty-five anti-trust suits against oversized corporations. He also sought stronger regulation of the railroads. In 1903, Congress passed the Elkins Act, making it illegal for railroads to give secret rebates (cash refunds) on freight charges to favored high-volume customers. That same year, Congress created a Bureau of Corporations to monitor the activities of big businesses. When the Standard Oil Company refused to turn over its records, the government brought an anti-trust suit that led to the breakup of the powerful company in 1911. The Supreme Court also ordered the American Tobacco Company dismantled because it had monopolized the cigarette industry.

The 1902 Coal Strike

> Roosevelt as a referee between management and labor

In everything Roosevelt did, he acted forcefully. On May 12, 1902, for example, some 150,000 members of the United Mine Workers (UMW) walked off the job at coal mines in Pennsylvania and West Virginia. The miners were seeking a 20 percent wage increase, a reduction in daily working hours from ten to nine, and official recognition of the union by the mine owners, who refused to negotiate. Instead, the owners, mostly railroad corporations, shut down the mines to starve out the miners, many of whom were immigrants from eastern Europe. One owner expressed the ethnic prejudices shared by many other owners when he proclaimed, "The miners don't suffer—why, they can't even speak English."

By October, the lengthy shutdown of the mines had caused the price of coal to soar, and hospitals and schools reported empty coal bins as winter approached. In many northern cities, the poor had run out of coal for heating. "The country is on the verge of a vast public calamity," warned Walter Rauschenbusch.

Washington Gladden led a petition drive urging Roosevelt to step in to mediate the strike. The president decided upon a bold move: he invited leaders of both sides to a conference in Washington, D.C., where he appealed to their "patriotism, to the spirit that sinks personal considerations and makes individual sacrifices for the public good." The mine owners in attendance, however, refused even to speak to the UMW leaders.

Roosevelt was infuriated by what he called the "extraordinary stupidity and temper" of the "wooden-headed" owners, saying he wanted to grab their spokesman "by the seat of his breeches" and "chuck him out" a window. Instead, he threatened to take over the mines and send in soldiers to run them. When a congressman questioned the constitutionality of such a move, Roosevelt roared, "To hell with the Constitution when the people want coal!"

The president's threat worked: the strike ended on October 23. The miners won a reduction to a nine-hour workday and a 10 percent wage increase but failed to gain union recognition by the owners. Roosevelt had become the first president to use his authority to referee a dispute between management and labor.

Roosevelt's Election to a Second Term

Roosevelt's forceful leadership won him the Republican nomination for election in his own right in 1904. The Democrats, having lost twice with William Jennings Bryan, turned to the more conservative and virtually unknown Alton B. Parker, chief justice of the New York Supreme Court. His only distinction was being the dullest—and most forgettable—presidential candidate in history. One journalist dubbed the colorless Parker as "the enigma from New York." The most interesting item in Parker's official campaign biography was that he had trained his pigs to come when called by name.

> A reelection mandate for Roosevelt and progressivism

In the election, the Democrats suffered their worst defeat in thirty-two years. After sweeping to victory by an electoral vote of 336 to 140, Roosevelt told his wife that he was "no longer a political accident." He now had a popular mandate to do great things. On the eve of his inauguration in March 1905, Roosevelt announced: "Tomorrow I shall come into office in my own right. Then watch out for me!" He was ready to become the leader of the progressive movement.

Regulation of the Railroad, Food, and Drug Industries

Roosevelt launched his second term with an even stronger commitment to regulating corporations and their corrupt owners (the "criminal rich") who exploited workers and tried to eliminate competition. In his efforts to

> The Hepburn Act and ICC

promote the "moral regeneration of business," he took aim at the railroads first. In 1906, he persuaded Congress to pass the Hepburn Act, which for the first time gave the federal ICC the power to set maximum freight rates for the railroad industry.

Under Roosevelt's Square Deal programs, the federal government also assumed oversight of key industries affecting public health: meat-packers, food processors, and makers of drugs and patent medicines. Muckraking journalists had revealed all sorts of unsanitary and dangerous activities in the preparation of food and drug products by many companies.

Perhaps the most powerful blow against these abuses was struck by Upton Sinclair's novel *The Jungle* (1906), which told the story of a Lithuanian immigrant working in a filthy Chicago meatpacking plant:

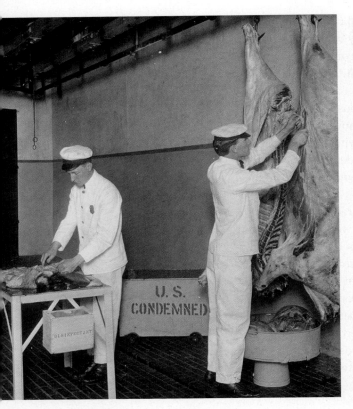

BAD MEAT Government inspectors closely examine tainted sides of beef at a meatpacking plant.

> It was too dark in these storage places to see well, but a man could run his hand over these piles of meat and sweep off handfuls of the dried dung of rats. These rats were nuisances, and the packers would put poisoned bread out for them, they would die, and then rats, bread, and meat would go into the hoppers [to be ground up] together.

After reading *The Jungle*, Roosevelt urged Congress to pass the Meat Inspection Act of 1906. It required the Department of Agriculture to inspect every animal whose carcass crossed state lines—both before and after slaughter. The Pure Food and Drug Act (1906), enacted the same day, required producers of food and medicines to host government inspectors, too.

> The Meat Inspection Act and the Pure Food and Drug Act

Environmental Conservation

One of the most enduring legacies of Roosevelt's leadership was his energetic support for environmental conservation, one of the pillars of his Square Deal programs. Roosevelt, an avid outdoorsman, naturalist, and amateur scientist, championed efforts to manage and preserve the nation's natural resources (which he called "wild places") for the benefit of future generations. He created fifty federal wildlife refuges, approved five new national parks and fifty-one federal bird sanctuaries, and designated eighteen national monuments, including the Grand Canyon.

> Roosevelt and Gifford Pinchot: Preserving natural resources

In 1898, Roosevelt had endorsed the appointment of his friend Gifford Pinchot, Amos's brother and the nation's first professionally trained forest manager, as the head of the U.S. Department of Agriculture's Division of Forestry. A handsome, wealthy man who devoted his life to forestry, Pinchot, like Roosevelt, was a pragmatic conservationist; he believed in economic growth as well as environmental preservation. Pinchot said that the conservation movement promoted the "greatest good for the greatest number for the longest time."

Roosevelt and Pinchot used the Forest Reserve Act (1891) to protect 172 million acres of federally owned forests from being logged. Lumber companies were furious, but Roosevelt held firm, declaring, "I hate a man who skins the land." Overall, Roosevelt set aside more than 234 million acres of federal land for conservation purposes and created 45 national forests in 11 western states. As Pinchot recalled late in life, "Launching the conservation movement was the most significant achievement of the T.R. Administration, as he himself believed."

Roosevelt and Race

Roosevelt's most significant failure as a progressive was his refusal to confront racism. Like Populists, progressives worked to empower "the people" against the entrenched "special interests." In the view of most of them, however, "the people" did not include African Americans, Native Americans, or some immigrant groups. Most white progressives shared the prevailing racist attitudes of the time. They ignored or even endorsed the passage of Jim Crow laws in the South that prevented blacks from voting and subjected them to rigid racial separation in schools, housing, parks, and playgrounds.

By 1901, nearly every southern state had successfully prevented almost all African Americans from voting or holding political office by disqualifying or terrorizing them. During the Progressive Era, hundreds of African Americans were lynched each year across the South, where virtually no blacks were allowed to serve on juries or work as sheriffs or policemen. A white candidate for governor in Mississippi in 1903 announced that he believed "in the divine right of the white man to rule, to do all the voting, and to hold all the offices, both state and federal."

At the same time, few progressives questioned the many informal and private patterns of segregation and prejudice in the North and West. "The plain fact is," the muckraking journalist Ray Stannard Baker admitted in 1909, "most of us in the North do not believe in any real democracy between white and colored men."

Theodore Roosevelt himself shared such prejudices. He confided to a friend in 1906 his belief that "as a race and in the mass" African Americans "are altogether inferior to whites." Yet on occasion the president made exceptions. On October 16, 1901, soon after becoming president, Roosevelt invited Booker T. Washington, then the nation's most prominent black leader, to the White House for dinner. Upon learning of the meeting, white Southerners exploded with fury. The *Memphis Scimitar* newspaper screamed that Roosevelt's allowing a "nigger" to dine with him was "the most damnable outrage that has ever been perpetrated by a citizen of the

THEODORE ROOSEVELT AND BOOKER T. WASHINGTON
Roosevelt addresses the National Negro Business League in 1900 with Washington seated to his left.

United States." South Carolina senator Benjamin R. Tillman was even angrier. He threatened that "a thousand niggers in the South will have to be killed to teach them 'their place' again."

Roosevelt found such violent reactions "inexplicable," but in the end he gave in to the criticism. Never again would he host an African American leader. During a tour of the southern states in 1905, he pandered to whites by highlighting his own southern ancestry (his mother was from Georgia) and expressing his admiration for the Confederacy and Robert E. Lee. His behavior, said a black leader, was "national treachery to the Negro."

Worse was to come, however. The following year, 1906, witnessed a violent racial incident in Brownsville, Texas, where a dozen or so members of an African American army regiment got into a shootout with whites who had been harassing them outside a saloon. One white bartender was killed and a police officer seriously wounded. Both sides claimed the other started the shooting. An investigation concluded that the soldiers were at fault, but no one could identify any of the shooters, and none of the soldiers was willing to talk about the incident.

Roosevelt responded to their silence by dishonorably discharging the entire regiment of 167 soldiers, several of whom had been awarded the Congressional Medal of Honor for their service in Cuba during the War of 1898. None of them received a hearing or a trial.

Critics of Roosevelt's harsh action flooded the White House with angry telegrams. Roosevelt, however, refused to show any mercy to "murderers, assassins, cowards, and comrades of murderers." (Sixty years later, the U.S. Army "cleared the records" of all the black soldiers.) Disheartened African Americans predicted that Roosevelt's harsh language would ignite "race hatred and violence" against innocent African Americans. "We shall oppose the re-nomination of Theodore Roosevelt," said the *Washington Bee*, a black-owned newspaper.

The Transition from Roosevelt to Taft

In fact, after his 1904 victory Roosevelt had decided not to run for president again, in part because he did not want to be the first president to serve the equivalent of a third term. It was a noble gesture but a political blunder he would later regret. His pledge to serve only four more years would have momentous political consequences. For now, however, he urged Republicans to nominate his longtime friend and secretary of war, William Howard Taft, whom the Republican Convention endorsed on its first ballot in 1908. The

Democrats decided to give William Jennings Bryan one more chance. Although Roosevelt dismissed Bryan as a "quack," he retained a faithful following, especially in the South.

Taft, who had no stomach for political campaigning, reluctantly agreed to run and promised to continue Roosevelt's policies. The Democratic platform echoed the Republican emphasis on needed regulation of business but called for lower tariffs. Bryan struggled to attract national support and was defeated for a third time, as Taft swept the Electoral College, 321–162.

William Howard Taft had superb qualifications to be president. Born in Cincinnati in 1857, he was the son of a prominent attorney who had served in President Grant's cabinet. He had graduated second in his class at Yale, where he had studied under the famous social Darwinist William Graham Sumner and gone on to become a leading legal scholar, serving on the Ohio Supreme Court. In 1900, President McKinley had appointed him the first American governor-general of the Philippines, and three years later Roosevelt named him secretary of war.

Unlike the robust, athletic Roosevelt, Taft struggled most of his life with obesity, topping out at 332 pounds and earning the nickname "Big Bill." One newspaper said that he looked "like an American bison—a gentle, kind one." Roosevelt, he explained, "loves the woods, he loves hunting; he loves roughing it, and I don't." His primary sin, he confessed, was laziness. He often fell asleep at public events. Although good-natured and easygoing, Taft as president never managed to escape the shadow of his charismatic predecessor. "When I hear someone say 'Mr. President,'" he confessed, "I look around expecting to see Roosevelt."

WILLIAM HOWARD TAFT The twenty-seventh president, Taft served in the shadow of Roosevelt, and freely admitted his dislike of politics.

Taft was a cautious and conservative progressive who vowed to preserve capitalism by protecting "the right of property" and the "right of liberty." In practice, this meant that he was even more determined than Roosevelt to support "the spirit of commercial freedom" against monopolistic trusts, but he was not interested in pushing for additional reforms. Taft was no crusader; he viewed himself as a judge-like administrator, not an innovator. He said he "hated politics" and was reluctant to exercise presidential authority (after leaving the White House, he got the job he had always wanted most, chief justice of the U.S. Supreme Court).

> Taft as president: Highly qualified, judge-like administrator

Taft and Tariffs

After taking office, Taft displayed his credentials as a progressive Republican by supporting lower tariffs on imports; he even called a special session of Congress to address the matter. But he proved less skillful than Roosevelt in

> Taft's failure to gain real tariff reform

dealing with Congress. He discontinued Roosevelt's practice of holding weekly press conferences during which he would influence congressmen by using his "big stick through the press." Taft confessed that he did not know how to use the "bully pulpit," which Roosevelt had perfected. In the end, the Payne-Aldrich Tariff (1909) made little change in federal tariff policies. Some rates went down while others went up, but overall, tariff policies continued to favor the industrial Northeast over the rest of the nation. Taft's failure to gain real reform and his lack of a "crusading spirit" like Roosevelt's angered the progressive, pro-Roosevelt wing of the Republican party, whom Taft dismissed as "assistant Democrats."

The Ballinger-Pinchot Controversy

Taft's commercial "giveaway" of federal lands

In 1910, the split between the conservative and progressive Republicans grew into a chasm because of what came to be called the Ballinger-Pinchot controversy, which made Taft appear to be abandoning Roosevelt's environmental conservation policies. Taft's new secretary of the interior, Richard A. Ballinger, threw open to commercial use millions of acres of federal lands that Roosevelt had ordered protected. As chief of forestry, the quarrelsome Gifford Pinchot expressed concerns to Taft about the "giveaway," but the president refused to intervene. When Pinchot made his opposition public early in 1910, Taft fired him, labeling him a "fanatic." In doing so, Taft set in motion a feud with Roosevelt that would eventually end their friendship—and cost him his reelection.

The Taft-Roosevelt Feud

Taft's progressive record

In 1909, soon after Taft had become president, Roosevelt and his son Kermit sailed to Africa, where they would spend nearly a year shooting big-game animals. (When he heard about the extended safari, J. Pierpont Morgan, still angry at Roosevelt for breaking up the Northern Securities Company, expressed the hope that "every lion would do its duty.") Roosevelt had left the White House assuming that his chosen successor would continue to pursue a progressive agenda. Instead, in his view, by filling the cabinet with corporate lawyers and firing Gifford Pinchot, Taft had failed to "carry out my work unbroken." Taft means well, Roosevelt would say, "but he means well *feebly*." He was "utterly helpless as a leader."

Roosevelt's rebuke of Taft was in many ways undeserved. Taft had at least attempted tariff reform, which Roosevelt had never dared. Yes, he had fired Pinchot, but he had replaced him with other conservationists. In the end, Taft's administration preserved more federal land in four years than Roosevelt's had in nearly eight. Taft's administration also filed twice as many anti-trust suits as did Roosevelt's, including the one that led to the breakup of the Standard Oil Company in 1911.

Taft advanced other progressive causes as well. He strengthened federal control over railroad freight rates, an issue long promoted by farmers and farm organizations. In 1910, with his support, Congress passed the

Mann-Elkins Act, which extended the authority of the ICC beyond railroads to telephone and telegraph companies. Taft established a federal Children's Bureau (1912) to promote children's welfare and a Bureau of Mines (1910) to oversee that huge industry. Taft also supported giving women the right to vote and workers the right to join unions.

But none of that satisfied Roosevelt. During the fall of 1910, the former president, still furious at Taft and eager to return to the political spotlight, gave a speech at Osawatomie, a small town in eastern Kansas, in which he gave a catchy name to his latest progressive principles and proposals, calling his sweeping agenda the New Nationalism. Roosevelt explained that he wanted to go beyond ensuring a "Square Deal" in which corporations were forced to "play by the rules"; he now promised to "change the rules" to force large corporations to promote social welfare and to serve the needs of working people. To save capitalism from the threat of a working-class revolution, he called for tighter federal regulation of "arrogant" corporations ("the great special business interests") that too often tried to "control and corrupt" politics, for a federal income tax (the Sixteenth Amendment had still not been ratified by the states), and for federal laws regulating child labor. It was a sweeping agenda that would greatly expand the power of the federal government over economic and political life. "What I have advocated," he explained, "is not wild radicalism. It is the highest and wisest kind of conservatism."

> **Roosevelt's New Nationalism**

Then, on February 24, 1912, Roosevelt abandoned his earlier pledge and announced his entry into the race for the 1912 Republican presidential nomination. He dismissed Taft as a "hopeless fathead" and "flubdub" who had "sold the Square Deal down the river." Taft responded to his friend's attacks by calling Roosevelt a "dangerous egotist" and a "demagogue." The two friends now began a bitter war in which Roosevelt had the better weapons, not the least of which was his love of a good fight. Elihu Root, a Republican leader,

POLITICAL GIANTS This cartoon depicts Roosevelt charging through the air at Taft, who is seated on a mountaintop.

SIDESHOW TED This 1912 cartoon criticizes the Bull Moose Party for being just a sideshow (with suffragists selling lemonade outside) and points out the menacing ego of Roosevelt himself.

Progressive party Political party founded by Theodore Roosevelt to support his bid to regain the presidency in 1912 after his split from the Taft Republicans.

described Roosevelt as "essentially a fighter, and when he gets into a fight he is completely dominated by the desire to destroy" his opponent.

By 1912, a dozen or so "progressive" states were letting citizens vote for presidential candidates in party primaries rather than the traditional practice whereby party leaders chose the nominee. Roosevelt decided that if he won big in the Republican primaries, he could claim to be "the people's choice" for the nomination. But even though he won all but two of the primaries, including the one in Taft's home state of Ohio, his personal popularity was no match for Taft's authority as party leader. In the thirty-six states that still chose candidates by conventions dominated by party bosses, the Taft Republicans prevailed, and at the Republican National Convention Taft was easily nominated for reelection.

An outraged Roosevelt denounced Taft and his supporters as thieves and walked out of the convention along with his delegates—mostly social workers, teachers, professors, journalists, and crusaders for women's suffrage, along with a few wealthy business executives who loved Roosevelt.

Six weeks later the breakaway faction reconvened in Chicago to create a **Progressive party** with Roosevelt as its candidate. While speaking to the delegates, he assured them that he felt "fit as a bull moose," leading journalists to nickname the Progressives the "Bull Moose party." When Roosevelt closed his acceptance speech by saying that "[w]e stand at Armageddon [the climactic encounter between Christ and Satan], and we battle for the Lord," the delegates began singing the hymn "Onward, Christian Soldiers." One reporter wrote that the "Bull Moose" movement was not so much a political party as it was a religious crusade.

The Progressive party platform revealed Roosevelt's growing liberalism. It supported a minimum "living wage" for hourly workers; women's suffrage; campaign finance reform; and a federal system of social insurance to protect people against sickness, unemployment, and disabilities. It also pledged to end the "boss system" governing American politics. Most of all, however, Roosevelt promised "to dissolve the unholy alliance between corrupt business and corrupt politics." Conservative critics now called Roosevelt "a socialist," a "revolutionist," and "a virtual traitor to American institutions."

Once nominated as a third-party candidate, Roosevelt repeatedly declared that Taft was not a progressive because he had tried to "undo" efforts at environmental conservation and had failed to fight either for social justice or against the "special interests." Instead, the former president charged, Taft had aligned himself with the "privileged" political and business leaders who steadfastly opposed "the cause of justice for the helpless and the wronged."

Woodrow Wilson's Progressivism

CORE **OBJECTIVE**

5. Describe the progressive policies of President Woodrow Wilson, and explain why and how they differed from those of Presidents Roosevelt and Taft.

The Republican fight between Taft and Roosevelt gave hope to the Democrats, whose presidential nominee, New Jersey governor Woodrow Wilson, had enjoyed remarkable success in his brief political career. Until his nomination and election as governor in 1910, Wilson had been a college professor and then president of Princeton University; he had never run for any political office or worked in business. Instead, he was a man of ideas with extraordinary abilities: a keen intellect, an analytical temperament, a fertile imagination, a tireless work ethic, and an inspiring speaking style. As the son and grandson of Presbyterian ministers, he was convinced that God had chosen him for greatness as a statesman. Wilson convinced himself that only he knew what was best for the nation. People often "call me an idealist," he explained. "Well, that is the way I know I am an American."

Wilson's Dramatic Rise

Born in Staunton, Virginia, in 1856, Thomas Woodrow Wilson grew up in Georgia and the Carolinas during the Civil War and Reconstruction. Tall and slender with a long, chiseled face, he developed an unquestioning religious faith. He prayed and read the Bible daily all his life. Driven by a consuming sense that God had selected him to "serve" humanity, he often displayed an unbending self-righteousness and a fiery temper, qualities that would prove to be his undoing as president. Over the course of his presidency, he would sometimes mutter, "God save us from compromise."

Wilson graduated from Princeton in 1879. After law school at the University of Virginia, he briefly practiced law in Atlanta, but he found legal work "dreadful drudgery" and soon enrolled at Johns Hopkins University to study history and political science, earning one of the nation's first doctoral degrees. He became an expert in constitutional government and preferred the British prime-minister system over the American presidential model because it enabled a leader to accomplish more. He then taught at several colleges before serving as the president of Princeton.

WOODROW WILSON The only president to date to hold a Ph.D. degree, Wilson's intellect and idealism compensated for his little political experience.

Eight years later, New Jersey Democrats offered Wilson their support for the 1910 gubernatorial nomination. He accepted the offer but already harbored higher ambitions. If he could become governor, he reflected, "I stand a very good chance of being the next President of the United States." Like Theodore Roosevelt, Wilson was an intensely ambitious and idealistic man who felt destined to preside over America's emergence as the greatest world power.

Although Wilson called himself an "amateur" politician, he proved a surprisingly effective campaigner and won the New Jersey governor's race by a landslide victory. The professor-turned-governor then persuaded the state legislature to adopt an array of progressive reforms to curb the power of political party bosses and corporate lobbyists. "After dealing with college politicians," Wilson joked, "I find that the men who I am dealing with now seem like amateurs."

Governor Wilson soon attracted the attention of national Democratic leaders. At the 1912 Democratic convention, less than two years after beginning his political career, he faced stiff competition from several veteran party leaders for the presidential nomination, but with the support of William Jennings Bryan, he won on the forty-sixth ballot. It was, Wilson said, a "political miracle."

The Election of 1912

The 1912 presidential campaign was one of the most exciting in history. It involved four capable candidates: Democrat Woodrow Wilson, Republican William Howard Taft, Socialist Eugene V. Debs, and Progressive Theodore Roosevelt. For all their differences in personality and temperament, the candidates shared a basic progressive assumption that modern social problems could be resolved only through active governmental intervention.

As the contest unfolded, it settled down to a running debate between Roosevelt's New Nationalism and Wilson's **New Freedom**, a program designed by Louis D. Brandeis, a progressive Boston lawyer and future justice of the U.S. Supreme Court. The New Freedom aimed to restore competition in the economy by eliminating *all* trusts rather than simply regulating the ones that misbehaved. Whereas Roosevelt admired the power and efficiency of law-abiding corporations, no matter how large, Brandeis and Wilson were convinced that huge, "heartless" industries needed to be broken up.

On election day, Wilson won handily in the Electoral College, collecting 435 votes; Roosevelt received 88, and Taft, the only Republican nominee for president ever to finish third, garnered just 8. After learning of his election, the self-righteous Wilson told the chairman of his campaign committee that "I owe you nothing. God ordained that I should be the next president of the United States. Neither you nor any other mortal could have prevented that."

Had the Republicans not divided their votes between Taft and Roosevelt, however, Wilson would have lost. His was the victory of a minority candidate

> New Freedom: Eliminating rather than regulating trusts

New Freedom Program championed in 1912 by the Woodrow Wilson campaign that aimed to restore competition in the economy by eliminating all trusts rather than simply regulating them.

THE ELECTION OF 1912

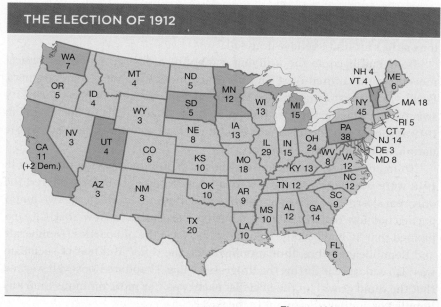

	Electoral Vote	Popular Vote
Woodrow Wilson (Democratic)	**435**	**6,300,000**
Theodore Roosevelt (Progressive)	88	4,100,000
William H. Taft (Republican)	8	3,500,000

- Why was Taft so unpopular?
- How did the division between Roosevelt and Taft give Wilson the victory?
- Why was Wilson's victory in 1912 especially significant?

over a divided opposition. Since all four candidates called themselves progressives, however, the president-elect expressed his hope "that the thoughtful progressive forces of the nation may now at last unite."

The election of 1912 profoundly altered the character of the Republican party. The defection of the Bull Moose Progressives had weakened the party's progressive wing. As a result, when Republicans returned to power in the 1920s, they would be more conservative in tone and temperament than Roosevelt and his progressive supporters.

The real surprise of the 1912 election, however, was the strong showing of the Socialist party candidate, Eugene V. Debs, running for the fourth time. The tall, lanky, blue-eyed idealist had devoted his life to fighting the "monstrous system of capitalism" on behalf of the working class, first as a labor union official, then as a socialist promoting government ownership of railroads and other key industries and the sharing of profits with workers. Debs voiced a brand of socialism that was flexible rather than rigid, Christian rather than Marxist, democratic rather than totalitarian. He believed in political transformation, not violent revolution. As one of his supporters said,

Eugene V. Debs and the "Rising Tide of Socialism"

"That old man with the burning eyes actually believes that there can be such a thing as the brotherhood of man. And that's not the funniest part of it. As long as he's around I believe it myself."

Debs had become the unifying symbol of a diverse American radical movement that united West Virginia coal miners, Oklahoma sharecroppers, Pacific Northwest lumberjacks, and immigrant workers in New York City sweatshops. One newspaper highlighted the "Rising Tide of Socialism" in 1912 as some 1,150 Socialists won election to local and state offices across the nation, including eighteen mayors.

To many voters, the Socialists, whose 118,000 dues-paying members in 1912 were double the number compared with the year before, offered the only real alternative to a stalemated political system in which the two major parties had few real differences. A business executive in New York City explained that he had become a Socialist "because the old parties [Democrats and Republicans] were flimflamming us all the time." But fear of socialism was also widespread during the Progressive Era. Theodore Roosevelt warned that the rapid growth of the Socialist party was "far more ominous than any Populist or similar movement in the past."

In 1912, with very few campaign funds, Debs crisscrossed the nation giving fiery speeches that frequently announced: "Comrades, this is our year!" He dismissed Roosevelt as "a fraud" whose progressive promises were nothing more than "the mouthings of a low and utterly unprincipled self-seeker and demagogue." Debs's untiring efforts brought him over 900,000 votes, an astonishing total for a Socialist, more than twice as many as he had received four years earlier.

A Burst of Reform Bills

On March 4, 1913, a huge crowd surrounded the Capitol in Washington, D.C., to watch Woodrow Wilson's inauguration. At the White House, President Taft told his successor that "I'm glad to be going—this is the lonesomest place in the world."

The new president with the long nose and spectacles declared that it was not "a day of triumph" but "a day of dedication." He promised to lower "the stiff and stupid" Republican tariffs, create a new national banking system, strengthen anti-trust laws, and establish an administration "more concerned about human rights than about property rights."

President Wilson: An expert on government, an activist, and a "fierce" reformer

Wilson worried about people comparing him to the colorful, hyperactive Roosevelt: "He appeals to their imagination; I do not. He is a real, vivid person. . . . I am a vague, conjectural [philosophical] personality, more made up of opinions and academic prepossessions than of human traits and red corpuscles." Roosevelt had been a strong president by force of personality; Wilson became a strong president by force of conviction.

Despite their differences, the two progressive presidents shared a belief that national problems demanded national solutions. Together they set in motion the modern presidency, expanding the scope of the executive branch at the expense of Congress. They both shared Wilson's view that the U.S. president "is at liberty in both law and conscience to be as big as he can."

Like Roosevelt, Wilson was an activist president; he was the first to speak to the nation over the radio and to host weekly press conferences. He was also unusual among presidents in that he frequently spoke to Congress and visited legislators in their offices in the Capitol. As a political scientist, Wilson was an expert at the processes of government. During his first two years, he pushed through Congress more new bills than any previous president. Like "most reformers," however, Wilson, commented the president of Harvard University, "had a fierce and unlovely side." The new president found it hard to understand—much less work with—people who disagreed with him.

Wilson's victory, coupled with Democratic majorities in the House and Senate, gave his party effective national power for the first time since the Civil War. It also gave southerners a significant role in national politics for the first time since 1860. In addition to the president himself, five of Wilson's ten

BRINGING DOWN MONOPOLIES Published in Puck Magazine one week before the 1912 election, this cartoon depicts a small, bespectacled Woodrow Wilson wielding an ax labeled "Tariff Revision" to cut down a vine labeled "Excessive Protection." A giant, symbolizing the monopolies, tumbles to the ground. How did Woodrow Wilson keep his campaign promise to combat monopolies?

cabinet members were born in the South. At his right hand was "Colonel" Edward M. House of Texas, who held no official government position but was Wilson's most trusted adviser. The president described House as "my second personality. He is my independent self. His thoughts and mine are one." House helped steer Wilson's proposals through a Congress in which southerners, by virtue of their seniority, held the lion's share of committee chairmanships. As a result, much of the progressive legislation of the Wilson era would bear the names of southern Democrats.

The Tariff and the Income Tax

Wilson's new administration faced its first big test on the complex issue of tariff reform. By 1913, the federal tariff included hundreds of taxes on different imported goods, from oil to nails, all designed to benefit American manufacturers. The president believed that U.S. corporations were misusing the tariff to keep out foreign competitors and create monopolies that kept consumer prices artificially high. To lower tariff rates, Wilson summoned Congress to a special session that lasted eighteen months, the longest in history, and he addressed its members in person—the first president to do so since John Adams. The new tariff bill passed the House easily. The crunch came in the Senate, the traditional graveyard of tariff reform, where swarms of industry lobbyists grew so thick, Wilson said, that "a brick couldn't be thrown without hitting one of them." By publicly criticizing the "industrious and insidious" tariff lobby, Wilson finally convinced Congress to support his approach.

The first income tax for most Americans

The Underwood-Simmons Tariff (1913) lowered average tariff rates on imports—from about 40 percent to 25 percent—for the first time since the Civil War. To compensate for the government's reduced tariff revenue, the bill created the first income tax allowed under the newly ratified Sixteenth Amendment: the initial tax rates were 1 percent on income more than $3,000 ($4,000 for married couples) up to a top rate of 7 percent on annual income of $50,000 or more. Most Americans (99 percent) paid no income tax at all because they earned less than $3,000 a year.

The Federal Reserve Act

Creation of the Federal Reserve System

Before the new tariff had cleared the Senate, the administration proposed the first major banking reform since the Civil War. Ever since Andrew Jackson had killed the Second Bank of the United States in the 1830s, the nation had been without a central bank to manage its currency. Instead, the money supply was chaotically "managed" by thousands of local and state banks. Such a decentralized system produced instability and inefficiency. During financial panics, fearful depositors, eager to get their money, would create panicked "runs" on banks that caused many of them to go bankrupt. In fact, the primary reason for a new central bank was to prevent more such panics, which had occurred five times since 1873. The most recent crisis, in 1907, had prompted the creation of a congressional commission to decide whether the United States needed a centralized banking system.

By 1913, Wilson agreed that the nation's banking system needed a central reserve agency that, in a crisis, could distribute emergency cash to banks threatened by runs. Any new national banking system, however, must be overseen by the government rather than by bankers themselves (the "money power"). He wanted a new central bank that would benefit the entire economy, not just the large banks headquartered on Wall Street in New York City.

After much dickering, Congress finally passed the **Federal Reserve Act** on December 23, 1913. It created a new national banking system with twelve regional districts, each of which had its own Federal Reserve Bank that was owned by member banks in the district. Nationally chartered banks had to be members of the Federal Reserve System. But state-chartered banks—essentially unregulated—did not (and, indeed, two thirds of the nation's banks chose not to become members of the Federal Reserve System).

The purpose of the new Federal Reserve System was to adjust the nation's currency supply to match the needs of the economy and to ensure the stability and integrity of member banks. When banks were short of cash,

Federal Reserve Act (1913) Legislation passed by Congress to create a new national banking system in order to regulate the nation's currency supply and ensure the stability and integrity of member banks that made up the Federal Reserve System across the nation.

they could borrow from the Federal Reserve. Each of the new regional Federal Reserve banks issued Federal Reserve notes (currency) to member banks in exchange for their loans. By doing so, "the Fed," as the system came to be called, promoted economic growth and helped preserve the stability of banks during panics. A conservative Republican called the Federal Reserve Act "populistic, socialistic, half-baked, destructive, and unworkable." The new system soon proved its worth, however, and the criticism eased as the years passed. The Federal Reserve Act was the most significant new program of Wilson's presidency.

Anti-Trust Actions

While promoting tariff and banking reforms, Wilson made "trust-busting" the central focus of his New Freedom program. Giant corporations had continued to grow despite the Sherman Anti-Trust Act and the Bureau of Corporations, the federal watchdog agency created by Theodore Roosevelt. Wilson decided to make a strong **Federal Trade Commission** (FTC) the cornerstone of his anti-trust program. Created in 1914, the five-member FTC defined "unfair trade practices" and issued "cease-and-desist" orders when it found evidence of such practices.

Like Roosevelt, Wilson also supported efforts to strengthen and clarify the Sherman Anti-Trust Act. Henry D. Clayton, a Democrat from Alabama, drafted an anti-trust bill in 1914. The **Clayton Anti-Trust Act** declared that labor unions were not to be viewed as "monopolies in restraint of trade," as courts had done since 1890. It also prohibited directors from serving on the boards of competing companies and further clarified the meaning of various "monopolistic" activities.

> A new Federal Trade Commission and Anti-Trust Act

Progressives' Disappointments with Wilson

In November 1914, just two years after his election, President Wilson announced that he had accomplished the major goals of progressivism. He had fulfilled his bold promises to lower the tariff, create a national banking system, and strengthen the anti-trust laws. The New Freedom was now complete, he wrote, for he had no desire to continue increasing the power of the federal government. "The history of liberty," he stressed, "is the history of the limitation of governmental power, not the increase of it."

Wilson's announcement bewildered many progressives, especially those who had long advocated additional federal social-justice legislation that Wilson had earlier supported. Herbert Croly, the influential editor of the *New Republic* magazine, was dumbfounded by Wilson's conservative turn. He wondered how the president could assert "that the fundamental wrongs of a modern society can be easily and quickly righted as a consequence of [passing] a few laws." Wilson's about-face, he concluded, "casts suspicion upon his own sincerity [as a progressive] or upon his grasp of the realities of modern social and industrial life."

Federal Trade Commission (1914) Independent agency created by the Wilson administration that replaced the Bureau of Corporations as an even more powerful tool to combat unfair trade practices and monopolies.

Clayton Anti-Trust Act (1914) Legislation that served to enhance the Sherman Anti-Trust Act (1890) by clarifying what constituted "monopolistic" activities and declaring that labor unions were not to be viewed as "monopolies in restraint of trade."

NEW FREEDOM, OLD RULES
Wilson and the First Lady ride in a carriage with African American drivers.

Progressivism for Whites Only

Wilson's support for racial segregation

African Americans were also disappointed by Wilson's racial conservatism. Like many other progressives, Wilson showed little interest in addressing the racial discrimination and violence that African Americans faced. In fact, he shared many of the racist attitudes common at the time. As a student at Princeton, he had dismissed African Americans as "an ignorant and inferior race." Later, as a politician, Wilson rarely consulted black leaders and largely avoided associating with them in public or expressing support for them. That he refused to create a National Race Commission was a great disappointment to the black community, as were his cabinet appointments of white southerners who were outspoken racists.

Josephus Daniels, a North Carolina newspaper editor who became Wilson's secretary of the navy, was a white supremacist who wrote that "the subjection of the negro, politically, and the separation of the negro, socially, are paramount to all other considerations in the South." For Daniels and other southern progressives, "progress" was possible only if blacks were "kept in their place."

Daniels and other cabinet members racially segregated the employees in their agencies; Secretary of State William Jennings Bryan supported such efforts to create separate offices, dining facilities, restrooms, and water fountains. Wilson claimed that racial segregation "is not humiliating but a benefit." He was the first president since the Civil War who openly endorsed discrimination against African Americans, arguing that segregation in government buildings was in "their best interests." His administration also reduced the number of African American appointees to federal offices.

After visiting Washington, D.C., in 1913, Booker T. Washington reported that he had "never seen the colored people so discouraged and bitter." In November 1914, a delegation of African American leaders met with Wilson in the White House to ask how a "progressive" president could adopt such "regressive" racial policies. Wilson responded that both races benefited from the policies because they eliminated "the possibility of friction." William Trotter, a Harvard-educated African American newspaper editor who had helped found the National Association for the Advancement of Colored People (NAACP), scolded the president: "Have you a 'new freedom' for white Americans, and a new slavery for 'your Afro-American fellow citizens' [a phrase Wilson had used in a speech]? God forbid." A furious Wilson then told Trotter and the other visitors to leave, saying, "Your tone, sir, offends me."

The Vote for Women

Activists for women's suffrage also were disappointed in President Wilson (as they had been in President Roosevelt). Despite having two daughters who were suffragists, he insisted that the issue of women's voting rights should be left to the states rather than embodied in a constitutional amendment.

Wilson's lack of support led some leaders of the suffrage movement to revise their tactics. In 1910, Alice Paul, a New Jersey–born Quaker social worker who had earned a doctoral degree in political science from the University of Pennsylvania, urged activists to picket state legislatures, target and "punish" politicians who failed to endorse suffrage, chain themselves to public buildings, incite police to arrest them, and undertake hunger strikes. In March 1913, Paul organized 5,000 suffragists to march in protest at Wilson's inauguration.

Four years later, Paul formed the National Woman's Party after deciding that suffragists must do something even more dramatic to force Wilson to support their cause: picket the White House. Beginning on January 11, 1917, Paul and her followers took turns carrying signs there all day, five days a week, for six months, until the president ordered their arrest. Some sixty suffragists were jailed. For her leadership role, Paul was sentenced to seven months in prison. She then went on a hunger strike, leading prison officials to force-feed her through a tube inserted in her nose. Under an avalanche of press coverage and public criticism, Wilson finally pardoned her and the other jailed activists.

ALICE PAUL In this photo Paul sews a suffrage flag—orange and purple, with stars—that she and other suffragists often waved at strikes and protests.

Progressive Resurgence

By 1916, the need to create a winning political coalition in the upcoming presidential election—which required courting Republican as well as Democratic progressives—had pushed Wilson back onto the road of reform. The president scored progressive points when he nominated Louis D. Brandeis to the Supreme Court, making him the Court's first Jewish member when he was confirmed by the Senate. Wilson also won congressional approval for a broad program of legislation to help farmers and workers.

Farm Legislation

Because farmers continued to suffer from a shortage of capital available for lending, Wilson supported a proposal to set up special rural banks to provide long-term farm loans. The Federal Farm Loan Act became law in 1916. Under the control of the Federal Farm Loan Board, twelve Federal Land banks offered loans to farmers for five to forty years at low interest rates. Under the act, farmers could borrow up to 50 percent of the value of their land.

At about the same time, a dream long advocated by Populists—federal loans to farmers on the security of their crops stored in warehouses—finally came to fruition when Congress passed the Warehouse Act of 1916. These crop-security loans were available to sharecroppers and tenant farmers as well as to farmers who owned the land that they worked.

Farmers were also pleased by the passage of the Smith-Lever Act of 1914 and the Smith-Hughes Act of 1917. The Smith-Lever Act provided federal programs to educate farmers about new farm machinery and new ideas related to agricultural efficiency. The Smith-Hughes Act funded agricultural and mechanical education in high schools. Farmers with the newfangled automobiles had more than a passing interest as well in the Federal Highways Act of 1916, which helped finance new highways, especially in rural areas.

Labor Legislation

The progressive resurgence of 1916 broke the logjam on workplace reforms as well. One of the long-standing goals of many progressive Democrats was a federal child-labor law. When Congress passed the Keating-Owen Act in 1916, banning products made by child workers under fourteen from being shipped across state lines, Wilson expressed doubts about its constitutionality but eventually signed it. The act was later ruled unconstitutional by the Supreme Court on the grounds that child labor was outside the bounds of Congress's authority to regulate interstate commerce. Effective action against child labor abuses had to wait until the New Deal of the 1930s.

Another landmark law was the eight-hour workday for railroad workers, a measure that the Supreme Court upheld. The Adamson Act of 1916 resulted from a threatened strike by railroad unions demanding an eight-hour day and other concessions. Wilson, who objected to some of the unions' demands, nevertheless asked Congress to approve the Adamson Act. It required time-and-a-half pay for overtime work beyond eight hours and appointed a commission to study working conditions in the railroad industry.

The Limits of Progressivism

Progressivism reached its peak during Wilson's two terms as president. People grew optimistic about the economy and an improving society. After two decades of political upheaval and social reform (three if the Populists in the 1890s are counted), progressivism had shattered the traditional *laissez-faire* notion that government had no role in regulating the economy or in improving the quality of life. The courage and compassion displayed by progressives of all stripes demonstrated that people of good will could make a difference in improving social conditions for all. Progressivism awoke people to the evils and possibilities of modern urban-industrial life. Most important, progressives established the principle that governments—local, state, and federal—had a responsibility to ensure that Americans were protected from abuse by powerful businesses and corrupt politicians. As a Texas progressive said in 1910, most Americans now acknowledged that governments must protect "the weak against the encroachments of the strong."

Yet even though it had succeeded in accomplishing most of its goals—and its racial, ethnic, and class biases are more obvious today than they were at the time—progressivism still fell short of its supporters' hopes and ideals. Child labor would not be addressed on a national level until the Great Depression in the 1930s. It would also take the shock of the Depression to gain passage of a national minimum wage and the creation of a government-administered pension program for retirees and disabled workers (Social Security).

Finally, progressivism faded because international relations pushed aside domestic concerns. By 1916, the optimism of a few years earlier disappeared in the face of the distressing slaughter occurring in Europe in the Great War. The twentieth century, which had dawned with such bright hopes for social progress, held in store episodes of unprecedented brutality that led people to question whether governments could be trusted to serve the "public interest" or that "progress" was even possible anymore.

Reviewing the
CORE OBJECTIVES |

■ **The Progressive Impulse**
Progressives believed that
industrialization and urbanization
were negatively affecting American life.
They were mostly middle-class idealists
who promoted reform and government
regulation in order to ensure social
justice. They also called for legislation
to end child labor, promote safety in
the workplace, ban the sale of alcoholic
beverages, regulate or eliminate trusts
and other monopolies, and grant *woman
suffrage*.

■ **The Varied Sources of
Progressivism** Progressivism grew
out of many sources going back several
decades. The depression in the 1890s
led many urban middle-class people to
pursue reforms to aid the working class
and the poor. Many religious reformers,
such as those involved in the *social
gospel* movement, had urged their fellow
Christians to reject social Darwinism
and do more to promote a better life
for the urban poor. The settlement
house movement spread through urban
America as educated middle-class
women formed community centers
in poverty-stricken neighborhoods.
Muckrakers—investigative journalists
who exposed significant political and
corporate corruption—further fueled
the desire of progressive reformers to
address abuses of power in American
society.

■ **Progressives' Aims and
Achievements** To address corruption
in politics, progressives implemented
political reforms such as the direct
primary; initiative, referendum, and

recall at the state level; and the direct
election of senators through the
Seventeenth Amendment (1913). They
also focused on incorporating new
modes of efficiency into government
administration through *Taylorism*.

Many middle-class women reformers
targeted what they saw as the social evils
of alcohol consumption, prostitution,
and poor living and working conditions.
Social justice reformers also fought
successfully for a progressive income
tax with the passage of the *Sixteenth
Amendment (1913)*.

■ **Progressivism under Roosevelt
and Taft** The administrations of
Theodore Roosevelt and William H. Taft
increased the power of the president
and the federal government to regulate
corporate power. Roosevelt promoted his
progressive *Square Deal* program, which
included the arbitration of the 1902 coal
strike, and Pure Food and Drug Acts.
After severe criticism of his White House
meeting with Booker T. Washington, he
made no further gestures toward racial
harmony or equality.

Choosing not to seek reelection in
1908, Roosevelt endorsed Taft, who easily
won the election. But Taft's inability to
bring about major tariff reduction with
the Payne-Aldrich Tariff Act, among
other failings, led Roosevelt to run
again for president, promoting his New
Nationalism vision. Unable to defeat Taft
for the Republican nomination, Roosevelt
formed a *Progressive party*. This split
the Republican vote, allowing Democrat
Woodrow Wilson, another progressive
reformer, to win the office.

■ **Woodrow Wilson's Progressivism** Wilson's *New Freedom* program promised less federal intervention in business and a return to traditional Democratic policies that supported low tariffs and anti-trust regulation. He followed through on his promises with the Underwood-Simmons Tariff Act and the *Federal Reserve Act (1913)* and by beginning a rigorous anti-trust program with the passage of the *Clayton Anti-Trust Act (1914)* and the creation of the *Federal Trade Commission (1914)*. To rally Republican progressives to his side for the 1916 reelection, he endorsed greater regulation of child labor and railroad corporations, particularly through the Adamson Act. He also successfully sponsored two bills to allow farmers to get federal loans, a longtime goal of the Populist movement.

KEY TERMS

muckrakers *p. 730*

social gospel *p. 732*

woman suffrage *p. 735*

Seventeenth Amendment (1913) *p. 738*

Taylorism *p. 739*

Sixteenth Amendment (1913) *p. 744*

Square Deal *p. 745*

Progressive party *p. 754*

New Freedom *p. 756*

Federal Reserve Act (1913) *p. 760*

Federal Trade Commission (1914) *p. 761*

Clayton Anti-Trust Act (1914) *p. 761*

CHRONOLOGY

1889	Hull House opens in Chicago
1901	William McKinley is assassinated; Theodore Roosevelt becomes president
	Governor Robert La Follette creates the "Wisconsin idea"
1902	Roosevelt attempts to arbitrate a coal strike
	Northern Securities Company break up
1903	Congress passes the Elkins Act
1904	National Child Labor Committee formed
1906	Upton Sinclair's *The Jungle* is published
	Congress passes the Meat Inspection Act and the Pure Food and Drug Act
1909	William Howard Taft inaugurated
1911	Triangle Shirtwaist fire
1912	Woodrow Wilson elected president
1913	5,000 suffragists protest Wilson's inauguration
	Sixteenth and Seventeenth Amendments ratified
	Underwood-Simmons Tariff and Federal Reserve Act passed
1914	Congress passes the Clayton Anti-Trust Act
1916	Congress passes the Adamson Act

🐰 INQUIZITIVE

Go to InQuizitive to see what you've learned—and learn what you've missed—with personalized feedback along the way.

MAKE AMERICAN HISTORY In this poster for a U.S. Navy recruiting station in New York City, a sailor encourages a young man to play a patriotic role in the Great War and gestures toward warships in the distance.

America and the Great War

1914–1920

Throughout the nineteenth century, the Atlantic Ocean had protected America from the major land wars on the continent of Europe. During the early twentieth century, however, the nation's century-long isolation from European wars ended. Ever-expanding world trade meant that American interests were more deeply entwined with the economies of Europe. In addition, the development of steam-powered ships and submarines meant that foreign navies could directly threaten American security.

At the same time, the election of Woodrow Wilson in 1912 brought to the White House a self-righteous moralist determined to impose his standards for proper conduct on what he saw as renegade nations. This combination of circumstances made the outbreak of the "Great War" in Europe in 1914 a profound crisis for the United States, a crisis that would become the defining event of the early twentieth century and force America to accept its role and responsibilities as a dominant world power.

For almost three years, President Wilson maintained America's stance of "neutrality" toward the war while providing increasing amounts of food and supplies to Great Britain and France. In 1917, however, German submarine attacks on U.S. ships forced Congress into declaring war.

CORE OBJECTIVES INQUIZITIVE

1. Describe the outbreak of the Great War and the distinctive nature of the fighting on the Western Front, and explain why the United States entered the conflict.

2. Explain how the Wilson administration mobilized the home front, and analyze how mobilization efforts shaped American society.

3. Describe the major events of the war after U.S. entry, and explain the U.S. contribution to the defeat of the Central Powers.

4. Evaluate Woodrow Wilson's efforts to promote his plans for a peaceful world order as outlined in his Fourteen Points.

5. Analyze the consequences of the war at home and abroad.

Once America entered the war, almost 5 million men entered the military. As new jobs opened up, African Americans living in the South flocked to northern cities in search of industrial work to support the war effort. With victory in hand in 1919, America would find itself as the reluctant leading world power divided over whether to approve the Treaty of Versailles while facing substantial social and economic challenges at home with the return of legions of soldiers entering the workforce.

CORE **OBJECTIVE**

1. Describe the outbreak of the Great War and the distinctive nature of the fighting on the Western Front, and explain why the United States entered the conflict.

An Uneasy Neutrality

Never burdened by humility, Woodrow Wilson once declared that he had "a first-class mind." He was indeed highly intelligent, thoughtful, principled, and courageous. Upon learning of death threats against him, for example, he refused to change his schedule of public appearances. "The country," he explained, "cannot afford to have a coward for President."

For all his accomplishments and abilities, however, Wilson had no experience or expertise in international relations before his election as president. The former college professor admitted before taking office that "it would be an irony of fate if my administration had to deal chiefly with foreign affairs"—a topic he did not even mention in his 1913 inaugural address. But from the summer of 1914, when a terrible war erupted in Europe, foreign relations increasingly overshadowed all else, including Wilson's ambitious New Freedom program of progressive reforms.

Although inexperienced in international affairs, Wilson did not lack ideas or convictions about global issues. He saw himself as directed by God to help create a new world order governed by morality and ideals rather than by selfish national interests. Both Wilson and William Jennings Bryan, his secretary of state, believed that America had a duty to promote democracy and Christianity around the world. "Every nation of the world," Wilson declared, "needs to be drawn into the tutelage [guidance] of America."

The Outbreak of War

Woodrow Wilson confronted his greatest challenge beginning in the summer of 1914, when a war that few wanted yet no one could stop broke out in Europe. The "dreadful conflict" erupted suddenly, like "lightning out of a clear sky," a North Carolina congressman said. Wilson was shocked by "this incredible European eruption." Unfortunately, it coincided with a sharp decline in the health of his wife, Ellen, who died on August 6. "God has stricken me almost beyond what I can bear," the president wrote a friend.

Wilson would also have trouble bearing the accelerating horrors of the war in Europe. Its scope and destruction were unprecedented. Lasting for more than four years, from 1914 to 1918, the Great War would involve more nations and cause greater destruction than any previous conflict. The appalling slaughter would cost 20 million military and civilian deaths, and 21 million more were wounded. The Great War would topple monarchs and destroy empires, create new nations, and set in motion a series of events that would lead to an even greater war in 1939—one that led to the retroactive renaming of the Great War as the First World War, or World War I.

Wars are much easier to start than to control. The Great War resulted from long-simmering and extremely complex national rivalries and ethnic conflicts in Central Europe that second-rate statesmen and war-hungry generals allowed to spin out of control. At the core of the tensions was the Austro-Hungarian Empire, an unstable collection of eleven nationalities whose leaders were determined to stop the aggressive expansionism of its neighbor and long-standing enemy, Serbia. At the same time, a recklessly militaristic Germany, led by Kaiser (Emperor) Wilhelm II, was eager to assert its dominance on the European continent against its old enemies, the Russian Empire and France, at the same time that it was expanding its navy to challenge the British Empire's supremacy on the seas.

War erupted just five weeks after Gavrilo Princip, a nineteen-year-old Serbian nationalist in Sarajevo (the capital of present-day Bosnia-Herzegovina), shot and killed the heir to the Austro-Hungarian throne, fifty-year-old Archduke Franz Ferdinand, and his pregnant wife, Sophie, on June 28, 1914.

> Assassination in Sarajevo

The killings in Sarajevo set Europe on fire. To avenge the murders, Austria-Hungary, with Germany's approval, bullied and humiliated Serbia by demanding a say in its internal affairs. Serbia gave in to virtually all the demands, but Austria-Hungary declared war anyway. In turn, Russia mobilized its army to defend Serbia, an action that triggered chain reactions by a complex system of European military alliances: the **Central Powers** (Germany, Austria-Hungary, Bulgaria, and Turkey [the Ottoman Empire]), and the **Allied Powers** (France, Great Britain, and Russia).

Germany declared war on Russia on August 1, 1914, and on France two days later. Germany, hoping to defeat France before Russia could mobilize its armies in the east, invaded neutral Belgium to get at France, murdering hundreds of civilians in the process. The "rape of Belgium" brought Great Britain into the war against Germany on August 4 on the **Western Front**, the line of fighting in northern France and Belgium. Despite being a member of the Triple Alliance, Italy at first declared its neutrality in the war and then joined the Allies in return for a promise of territory taken from Austria-Hungary.

On the sprawling Eastern Front, Russian armies clashed with German and Austro-Hungarian forces as well as those of the Turkish (Ottoman) Empire. Within five weeks of the assassination in Sarajevo, a "great war" had erupted.

An Industrial War

The Great War was the first industrial war, fought between nations using new weapons that dramatically increased the war's scope and destruction. Machine guns, submarines, aerial bombing, poison gas, flame throwers, land mines, mortars, long-range artillery, and armored tanks changed the nature of warfare and produced appalling casualties and widespread destruction, a

Central Powers One of the two sides during the Great War, including Germany, Austria-Hungary, Bulgaria, and Turkey (the Ottoman Empire).

Allied Powers Nations fighting the Central Powers during the Great War, including France, Great Britain, and Russia; later joined by Italy and, after Russia quit the war in 1917, the United States.

Western Front Contested frontier between the Central and Allied Powers that ran along northern France and across Belgium.

THE GREAT WAR IN EUROPE, 1914

- Central Powers (Triple Alliance)
- Allied Powers (Triple Entente)
- Neutral countries

- How did the European system of military alliances spread conflict across Europe?
- How was World War I different from previous wars?
- How did the war in Europe lead to ethnic tensions in the United States?

slaughter on a scale unimaginable to this day. An average of 900 Frenchmen and 1,300 Germans died *every* day on the Western Front. It was the mechanized weaponry that made possible such mass killing on an "industrial" scale—the same scale on which items were mass-produced in an industrial economy.

The early weeks of the war involved fast-moving assaults as German armies swept westward across Belgium and northeastern France. Then mistakes piled up on both sides. What began as a war of quick movement in August 1914 bogged down into a prolonged stalemate during September and thereafter.

Nightmarish **trench warfare** came to symbolize a brutal war of futility, as both sides bogged down. They then built a series of zigzagging trenches, some of them forty feet deep and swarming with rats, traversing the Western Front from the coast of Belgium some 450 miles across northeastern France to the border of Switzerland. "When all is said and done," grumbled an English infantry officer, "the war was mainly a matter of holes and ditches."

trench warfare A form of prolonged combat between the entrenched positions of opposing armies, often with little tactical movement.

TRENCH WARFARE German soldiers prepare for attack, their main defense the deep trenches and their main offense a set of machine guns. **What were the living conditions like in the trenches?**

Soldiers often ate, slept, lived, and died without leaving their crowded underground homes. A French soldier described life in the trenches as a "physical, almost animal" existence in which "the primitive instincts of the race have full sway: eating, drinking, sleeping, fighting—everything but loving."

The object in such a war of attrition was not so much to gain ground as to keep inflicting death and destruction on the enemy until its manpower and resources were exhausted. In one assault against the Germans at Ypres in Belgium, the British lost 13,000 men in three hours of fighting—during which time they gained 100 meaningless yards. As the war ground on, nations on both sides found themselves using up their available men, resources, courage, and cash.

Robert W. Service, a British Canadian poet serving as a volunteer ambulance driver on the front lines, tried to express in verse their miserable lives in the trenches:

> Oh, the rain, the mud, and the cold,
> The cold, the mud, and the rain;
> With weather at zero it's hard for a hero
> From language that's rude to refrain.
> With porridgy muck to the knees,
> With sky that's a-pouring a flood,
> Sure the worst of our foes
> Are the pains and the woes
> Of the RAIN,
> THE COLD,
> AND THE MUD.

Commanders soon realized that troops could not stand such woeful conditions for long, so they began rotating troops on the line to keep their morale from collapsing.

From 1914 to 1918, the opposing armies in northeastern France attacked and counterattacked along the Western Front, hardly gaining any ground one way or another despite casualties in the millions. Time and again, inept generals sent masses of mud-streaked, steel-helmeted soldiers "over the top," meaning climbing up and out of waterlogged trenches. They then had to slog across "no-man's-land" between the opposing entrenchments, soon running into webs of entangling barbed wire and devastating fire from machine guns and high-powered rifles overlaid by constant artillery shelling.

It was not the kind of warfare anyone had expected or wanted. Words cannot convey the scale of the carnage. During the Battle of Verdun, in northeastern France, which lasted from February to December 1916, some 32 million artillery shells streaked across the landscape—1,500 shells for *every* square yard of the battlefield.

The hellish nature of trench warfare posed extraordinary psychological challenges for the combatants. In 1916, a British officer ordered his unit to "fix bayonets" and prepare to charge out of the trenches when he sounded his whistle. One of his men recalled standing "beside a young chap called Lucas, and he was a bundle of nerves. He was simply shivering and shaking like a leaf. He could hardly hold his rifle, never mind fix [attach] his bayonet. So I fixed mine and then I said, 'Here you are, Lucas,' and I fixed it for him." They then clambered out of the trench and began moving forward. "There were shell-holes everywhere . . . and there were lads falling all over the place" as German machine guns mowed them down. "Lucas went down."

Thousands of soldiers on both sides fell victim to "shell shock," now known as post–traumatic stress disorder. "It was a horrible thing," explained a nurse. "They became quite unconscious, with violent shivering and shaking." Victims of shell shock were often hysterical and could neither eat nor sleep. An English private tried to explain in a letter to his mother what he had experienced during the Battle of the Somme: "We had strict orders not to take prisoners, no matter if wounded. My first job . . . was to empty my magazine on three Germans that came out of one of their deep dugouts, bleeding badly [in order] to put them out of their misery. They cried for mercy, but I had my orders. . . . It makes my head jump to think about it."

The unprecedented firepower deployed during the Great War ravaged the land, obliterating nine villages and turning farmland and forests into cratered wastelands. Some 162,000 French soldiers died at Verdun; the Germans lost 143,000. Charles de Gaulle, a young French lieutenant who forty years later would become his nation's president, said the conflict had become a "war of extermination." Its horrific butchery seemed especially pointless, since neither side was capable of gaining the advantage. A British army chaplain described the war as a senseless "Waste of Muscle, Waste of Brain, Waste of Patience, Waste of Pain . . . Waste of Glory, Waste of God."

TOTAL RUIN German soldiers stand before the French fort Souville during a pause in the Battle of Verdun in September of 1916. The constant artillery fire scoured out huge craters and destroyed all traces of the forest that stood there before.

There was no precedent for such a ghastly war. Throughout 1914, both sides talked about the "glory" and "glamour" of war, notions that the British poet Wilfred Owen called "the old Lie." (Owen would be killed in combat in 1918, just a week before the war ended.)

An end to innocence about war

The old-fashioned romantic concepts of war were forever changed as masses of soldiers died like cattle in a slaughterhouse, killed often at such long distances that they never saw the enemy. Amid the senseless killing in the mucky trenches, the innocence about the true nature of warfare died, too. "Never such innocence again," wrote the English poet Philip Larkin. "I am cured of ever wishing to be a soldier again," wrote one young veteran.

In 1917, George Barnes, a British official whose son had been killed in the war, went to speak at a military hospital in London where injured soldiers were being fitted with artificial limbs. At the appointed hour, the wounded men, in wheelchairs and on crutches, all with empty sleeves or pant legs, arrived to hear the speaker. Yet when Barnes was introduced and rose to talk, he found himself speechless—literally. As the minutes passed in awkward silence, tears rolled down his cheeks. Finally, without having said a word, he simply sat down. What the mutilated soldiers heard was not a war-glorifying speech but the muted sound of grief. The war's mindless horrors had come home. Britain's King George V called it a "horrible and unnecessary war."

Initial American Reactions

When war erupted in Europe, American officials were stunned. One of Wilson's cabinet members recorded that "the end of things had come. I stopped in my tracks, dazed and horror-stricken." Shock in the United States over the bloodbath in Europe mingled with gratitude that a wide ocean stood between America and the killing fields. President Wilson maintained that the United States "was too proud to fight" in Europe's war, "with which we have nothing to do, whose causes cannot touch us." He repeatedly urged Americans to remain "neutral in thought as well as in action." Privately, however, Wilson was not neutral. He sought to provide Great Britain and France with as much financial assistance and supplies as possible.

Ethnic divisions in American public opinion

That was more easily said than done. More than a third of the nation's citizens were "hyphenated Americans"—first- or second-generation immigrants who retained strong ties to their native countries. Eight million German Americans lived in the United States in 1914, and many among the 4 million Irish Americans felt a deep-rooted hatred toward Britain, which had ruled the Irish for centuries. These groups instinctively leaned toward the Central Powers. But most other white Americans, largely of British origin, supported Britain and France.

By the spring of 1915, the Allied Powers' desperate need for food and supplies had generated an economic boom for American businesses, bankers, and farmers. U.S. exports to France and Great Britain quadrupled from 1914 to 1916. To finance their record-breaking purchases of American supplies, the Allies, especially Britain and France, needed loans from U.S. banks and "credits" from the U.S. government that would allow the Allies to pay for their American purchases later.

Early in the war, Secretary of State Bryan, a strict pacifist, took advantage of Wilson's absence from Washington after the death of his wife to declare that loans and credits to any warring nation were "inconsistent with the true spirit of neutrality." Upon his return, a furious Wilson reversed Bryan's policy by removing all restrictions on loans to the warring nations ("belligerents"). American banks and other investors would eventually advance more than $2 billion to the Allies before the United States entered the war and only $27 million to Germany.

Despite the disproportionate financial assistance provided to the Allies, the Wilson administration clung to its official stance of neutrality through two and a half years of warfare. Wilson tried valiantly to uphold the age-old principle of "freedom of the seas." As a neutral nation, the United States, according to international law, should have been able to continue its trade with all the

"THE SANDWICH MAN" To illustrate America's hypocritical brand of neutrality, this political cartoon shows Uncle Sam wearing a sandwich board that advertises the nation's conflicting desires.

belligerents. On August 6, 1914, Secretary of State Bryan called upon the warring nations to respect the rights of all neutral nations to ship goods across the Atlantic. The Central Powers promptly accepted, but the British refused. In November 1914, the British ordered the ships of neutral nations like the United States to submit to searches to discover if cargoes were bound for Germany. A few months later, they announced that they would seize any ships carrying goods to Germany.

Neutral Rights and Submarine Attacks

With the German naval fleet bottled up by a British blockade, the German government proclaimed a war zone around the British Isles. All ships in those waters would be attacked by submarines, the Germans warned, and "it may not always be possible to save crews and passengers." The German decision, based upon the fact that surprise was the chief advantage of the submarine or **U-boat** (*Unterseeboot* in German), violated the long-established wartime custom of stopping an enemy vessel and allowing the passengers and crew to board lifeboats before sinking it. During 1915, German U-boats sank 227 British ships in the Atlantic Ocean and the North Sea.

> German U-boats and the sinking of the *Lusitania*

The United States called the German submarine policy "an indefensible violation of neutral rights," and Wilson warned Germany that he would hold it to "strict accountability" for any destruction of American lives and property. Then, on May 7, 1915, a German submarine sank an unarmed British luxury liner off the Irish coast. Only as it tipped into the waves was the German commander able to make out the name **Lusitania** on the ship's hull. Of the 1,198 persons on board who died, 128 were Americans.

Americans were outraged. The sinking of the *Lusitania*, asserted ex-president Theodore Roosevelt, was an act of piracy and mass murder that called for a declaration of war. Wilson disagreed; he at first urged patience: "There is such a thing as a man being too proud to fight. There is such a thing as a nation being so right that it does not need to convince others by force that it is right."

Critics scolded Wilson for his timid response, with Roosevelt dismissing it as "unmanly," calling the president a "jackass," and threatening to "skin him alive if he doesn't go to war." Wilson himself privately admitted that he had misspoken. "I have a bad habit of thinking out loud," he confessed to a friend the day after his "too proud to fight" speech. The timid language, he said, had "occurred to me while I was speaking, and I let it out. I should have kept it in."

Wilson's previous demand for "strict accountability" now forced him to make a stronger response. On May 13, Secretary of State Bryan signed a letter demanding that the Germans abandon unrestricted submarine warfare and pay reparations to the families of those killed in the sinking of the *Lusitania*. The Germans responded that the ship was armed (which was false) and secretly carried a cargo of rifles and ammunition (which was true). A second letter, on June 9, repeated the American demands in stronger terms. The

U-boat German military submarine used during the Great War to attack warships as well as merchant ships of enemy and neutral nations.

Lusitania British ocean liner torpedoed and sunk by a German U-boat; the deaths of nearly 1,200 of its civilian passengers, including many Americans, caused international outrage.

REMEMBERING THE *LUSITANIA* The sinking of the *Lusitania* in 1915 sparked widespread anger, which was expressed in propaganda posters such as this, urging Americans to join the Allied forces. **How might this poster have motivated Americans to fight in World War I and influenced their understanding of what they were fighting for?**

United States, Wilson asserted, was "contending for nothing less high and sacred than the rights of humanity."

Bryan, a pacifist, resigned as secretary of state in protest of Wilson's pro-British stance. Upon learning of Bryan's departure, Edith Bolling Galt, soon to be Wilson's second wife, shouted: "Hurrah! Old Bryan is out!" She called the former secretary of state an "awful Deserter." The president confided that he, too, viewed Bryan as a "traitor." He complimented Edith on her vindictiveness: "What a dear partisan you are . . . and how you can hate, too!" Bryan's successor, Robert Lansing, signed the second "*Lusitania* Note."

Stunned by the global outcry over the *Lusitania*, the German government told its U-boat captains to quit attacking passenger vessels. Despite the order, however, a German submarine sank the British liner *Arabic*, and two Americans on board were killed. The Germans paid a cash penalty to their families and issued what came to be called the *Arabic* Pledge on September 1, 1915: "Liners will not be sunk by our submarines without warning and without safety of the lives of noncombatants, provided that the liners do not try to escape or offer resistance."

During early 1916, Wilson's most trusted adviser, Colonel Edward M. House, visited London, Paris, and Berlin but found neither side ready to begin serious negotiations to end the war. So the killing continued. On March 24, 1916, a U-boat torpedoed the French ferry *Sussex*, killing eighty passengers and injuring two Americans. When Wilson threatened to break off diplomatic relations, Germany renewed its pledge that U-boats would not torpedo merchant and passenger ships. The *Sussex* Pledge was far stronger than the German promise after the *Arabic* sinking the year before and implied the virtual abandonment of submarine warfare.

The Debate over "Preparedness"

The growing scope of the Great War and the quarrels over trading with belligerent nations contributed to a growing demand in the United States for a stronger army and navy. On December 1, 1914, champions of the "preparedness" movement, including Theodore Roosevelt, had organized the National Security League to promote more military spending. After the *Lusitania* sinking, Wilson asked the War and Navy Departments to develop plans for a $1 billion military expansion. Many Americans—pacifists, progressives, and midwestern Republicans—opposed the "preparedness" effort, seeing it as simply a propaganda campaign to benefit businesses that made weapons and other military equipment. Some of them charged that Wilson was secretly plotting to get the nation into the war. A popular song in 1916 reflected such views: "I Didn't Raise My Boy to Be a Soldier."

Despite such opposition, Congress passed the National Defense Act in 1916, which provided for the expansion of the U.S. Army from 90,000 to 223,000 men over the next five years. While former secretary of state Bryan complained that Wilson wanted to "drag this nation into war," the reverse was actually true. Wilson told an aide that he was determined not to "be rushed into war, no matter if every damned congressman and senator stands up on his hind legs and proclaims me a coward."

> National Defense Act (1916) expands army

Opponents of "preparedness" insisted that the expense of military expansion should rest upon the wealthy people who they believed were promoting it in order to profit from trade with the Allies. The income tax became their weapon. The Revenue Act of 1916 doubled the income tax rate from 1 to 2 percent, created a 12.5 percent tax on munitions makers, and added a new tax on "excessive" corporate profits. The new taxes were the culmination of the progressive legislation that Wilson approved to strengthen his chances in the upcoming presidential election. Fearing that Theodore Roosevelt would be the Republican presidential candidate challenging Wilson, Colonel House believed that the "Democratic Party must change its historic character and become the progressive party in the future."

The Election of 1916

As the 1916 election approached, Republicans hoped to reunify the party so as to regain the White House, and Theodore Roosevelt hoped to become their leader again. But he had committed the deadly political sin of abandoning his party to run as a Progressive in 1912. His eagerness for America to enter the European war also scared many voters. Needing a candidate who would draw Roosevelt progressives back into the fold, the Republicans turned to Supreme Court Justice Charles Evans Hughes, who had led New York as a progressive governor from 1907 to 1910.

The Democrats, staying with Wilson, adopted a platform that endorsed social-welfare legislation and prudent military preparedness. The peace theme, refined in the slogan "He kept us out of war," became the rallying cry of the Wilson campaign, although the president at the same time dismissed isolationism as outdated. The United States, he stressed, could no longer refuse to play the "great part in the world which was providentially cut out for her. . . . We have got to serve the world."

> Wilson's reelection slogan: "He kept us out of war"

The candidates were remarkably similar. Both Wilson and Hughes were sons of preachers, both were attorneys and former professors, both had been progressive governors, and both were known for their integrity. A disgusted Roosevelt called the bearded Hughes a "whiskered Wilson." Wilson, however, proved to be the better campaigner—barely. By midnight on election night, the president went to bed assuming that he had lost his bid for a second term. Roosevelt was so sure Hughes had won that he sent him a congratulatory telegram. At 4:00 A.M., however, the results from California were tallied, and Wilson had eked out a victory in that deciding state by only 4,000 votes, becoming the first Democrat to win a second consecutive term since Andrew Jackson in 1832.

America Goes to War

After his reelection, Wilson again urged the warring nations in Europe, in the "name of our Lord and Savior," to stop fighting and negotiate a "peace without victory" but to no avail. As a French official scoffed, peace without victory was like "bread without yeast."

On January 31, 1917, desperate German military leaders announced the resumption of unrestricted submarine warfare in the Atlantic. All vessels from the United States headed for Britain, France, or Italy would be sunk without warning. "This was practically ordering the United States off the Atlantic," said an angry William McAdoo, Wilson's secretary of the treasury. "Freedom of the seas," said the *Brooklyn Eagle*, "will now be enjoyed [only] by icebergs and fish."

The German decision to unleash its submarines in the Atlantic, Colonel House wrote in his journal, left Wilson "sad and depressed," for the president knew it would mean war. For their part, the German leaders greatly underestimated the American reaction. The United States, the German military newspaper proclaimed, "not only has no army, it has no artillery, no means of transportation, no airplanes, and lacks all other instruments of modern warfare." When his advisers warned that German submarines might cause the United States to enter the war, Kaiser Wilhelm scoffed, "I don't care."

On February 3, President Wilson told a joint session of Congress that the United States had broken diplomatic relations with the German government in order to preserve the "dignity and honor of the United States." Three weeks later, on February 25, Wilson learned that the British had intercepted an important telegram from a German official, Arthur Zimmermann, to the Mexican government, urging the Mexicans to invade the United States. In exchange, Germany would give Mexico "lost territory in Texas, New Mexico, and Arizona." On March 1, news of the so-called **Zimmermann telegram** broke in the press, infuriating Americans and intensifying calls for war against Germany. A New York newspaper said the telegram was "final proof that the German government has gone stark mad."

In March 1917, German submarines sank five U.S. ships in the North Atlantic. That was the last straw for President Wilson, who on April 2 asked Congress to declare war on the German empire for its "cruel and unmanly" actions. He insisted that "the world must be made safe for democracy" and

Unrestricted submarine warfare, the Zimmermann telegram, and the U.S. declaration of war

Zimmermann telegram Message sent by a German official to the Mexican government urging an invasion of the United States; the telegram was intercepted by British intelligence agents and angered Americans, many of whom called for war against Germany.

PEACE WITH HONOR A car decked out in pro-Wilson advertisements proclaims Woodrow Wilson's promise of peace, prosperity, and preparedness. Wilson's neutrality policies proved popular in the 1916 campaign.

free from war. Wilson said the United States was entering the war, not so much to defend the nation or its honor as to lead a "great crusade" to end wars forever—an unattainable goal that would eventually lead to great disillusionment. For now, however, the Congress erupted into a roar of approval. Two days later, the Senate passed the war resolution by a vote of 82–6. The House of Representatives followed, 373–50, and Wilson signed the measure on April 6.

Jeanette Rankin of Montana, the first woman elected to the House of Representatives, was one of the few members who voted against war. "You can no more win a war than you can win an earthquake," she explained. "I want to stand by my country, but I cannot vote for war."

Wilson had doubts of his own. The president feared—accurately, as it turned out—that mobilizing the nation for war and stamping out dissent would destroy the ideals and momentum of progressivism: "Every reform we have made will be lost if we go into this war." Yet he saw no choice.

America's long embrace of isolationism was over. The nation had reached a turning point in its relations with the world that would test President Wilson's political and diplomatic skills—and his stamina.

Mobilizing a Nation

In April 1917, the U.S. Army remained small and untested, armed with outdated weapons or none at all. With only 107,000 men, it was only the seventeenth-largest army in the world. Now the Wilson administration needed to recruit, equip, and train an army of millions and transport them across an ocean infested with German submarines.

Mobilizing the nation for war led to an unprecedented expansion of federal government authority. Millions of men between the ages of twenty-one and thirty were drafted into the armed services. The government also forced the conversion of industries and farms to wartime needs, took over the railroads, and in many other respects assumed control of national life.

Soon after the U.S. declaration of war, President Wilson acknowledged that "it is not the army we must train and shape for war, it is a nation." He called for complete economic mobilization on the home front and created new federal agencies to coordinate this effort. The War Industries Board (WIB), established in 1917, soon became the most important of all the federal mobilization agencies. Bernard Baruch, a brilliant financier, headed the WIB, which had the unprecedented authority to allocate raw materials, order construction of new factories, and set prices.

Wilson appointed Republican Herbert Hoover, the celebrated engineer and business leader and future president, to head the new Food Administration, whose slogan was "Food will win the war." Its purpose was to increase agricultural production while reducing civilian food consumption, since Great Britain and France needed massive amounts of American corn and wheat. Hoover organized a huge group of volunteers who fanned out across the country to urge housewives and restaurants to participate in "Wheatless" Mondays, "Meatless" Tuesdays, and "Porkless" Thursdays and Saturdays.

Fighting in the Great War cost the U.S. government $30 billion, which was more than thirty times the entire federal budget in 1917. In addition to raising taxes to finance the war effort, the Wilson administration launched a nationwide campaign to sell "Liberty Bonds," government certificates that guaranteed the purchaser a fixed rate of return. The government recruited dozens of celebrities to promote bond purchases, arguing that a Liberty bond was both a patriotic investment in the nation and a smart investment in one's own financial future. People who refused to buy bonds were branded as traitors. Even the Boy Scouts and Girl Scouts sold bonds,

THE IMMIGRANT EFFORT This Food Administration poster emphasizes that "wheat is . . . for the allies," an important message to immigrants who hailed from the nations making up the Central Powers. **Describe the patriotic imagery in this poster and how it ties into popular American ideals.**

AT THE MUNITIONS FACTORY Women on both sides played crucial roles in the war effort, from building airplanes to cooking for soldiers overseas. Here, American women use welding torches to make bombs.

using advertising posters that said "Every Scout to Save a Soldier." By war's end, the government had sold over $20 billion in bonds, most of which were purchased by banks and investment houses rather than individuals.

A New Labor Force

Removing millions of men from the workforce for service in the armed forces created an acute labor shortage across the United States during 1917. To meet it, women were encouraged to take jobs previously held mostly by men. One government poster shouted: "Women! Help America's Sons Win the War: Learn to Make Munitions." Another said, "For Every Fighter, a Woman Worker."

Initially, women had supported the war effort mostly in traditional ways. They helped organize fund-raising drives, donated canned food and war-related materials, volunteered for the Red Cross, and joined the army nurse corps. But as the scope of the war widened, both government and industry recruited women to work on farms, loading docks, and railway crews as well as in the armaments industry, machine shops, steel and lumber mills, and chemical plants. "At last, after centuries of disabilities and discrimination," noted a speaker at a Women's Trade Union League meeting in 1917, "women are coming into the labor [force] and festival of life on equal terms with men."

The changes in female employment turned out to be limited and brief, however. About 1 million women participated in "war work," but most of them were young and single and already working outside the home, and most returned to their previous jobs once the war ended. In fact, male-dominated unions encouraged women to go back to domestic roles. The Central Federated Union of New York insisted that "the same patriotism which induced women to enter industry during the war should induce them to vacate their positions after the war."

The Great Migration northward

The Great War also generated dramatic changes for many members of minority groups, both women and men. Hundreds of thousands of African American men entered the military, where they were required to serve in racially segregated units commanded by white officers, as in the Civil War a half century earlier. On the home front, northern businesses sent recruiting agents into the southern states, which were still largely rural and agricultural, to find workers for their factories and mills. For the first time, such efforts were directed at African Americans as well as whites. More than 400,000 southern blacks, mostly farmers, joined what came to be known as the **Great Migration** northward, a mass movement that would continue through the 1920s and change the political and social chemistry of northern cities such as St. Louis, Chicago, Detroit, New York, Philadelphia, and Washington, D.C. By 1930, the number of African Americans living in the North was triple that of 1910.

Recruiting agents and newspaper editors, both black and white, portrayed the North as the "land of promise" for southern blacks suffering from their region's depressed agricultural economy and rising racial intimidation and violence. Northern factory jobs were plentiful and high-paying by southern standards, and racism was less obvious and violent—at least at first. A black migrant from Mississippi wrote home from Chicago in 1917 that he wished he had moved north twenty years earlier. "I just begin to feel like a man [here]," he explained. "It's a great deal of pleasure in knowing that you have some privilege. My children are going to the same school with the whites, and I don't have to be humble to no one."

Many Mexican Americans found similar opportunities to improve their status during the war and after. Some joined the military. David Barkley Hernandez had to drop his last name when he enlisted in San Antonio, Texas, because the local draft board was not accepting Mexicans. In 1918, just two days before the war ended, he died in France while returning from a dangerous mission behind German lines. Hernandez became the first person of Mexican descent in the U.S. Army to win the Congressional Medal of Honor.

Even more Latinos pursued economic opportunities created by the war effort. Between 1917 and 1920, some 100,000 Mexicans crossed the border into the United States. The economic expansion caused by the war enabled migrant farmworkers already living in states such as Texas, New Mexico, Arizona, and California to take better jobs in factories and mills in rapidly

Great Migration Mass exodus of African Americans from the rural South to the Northeast and Midwest during and after the Great War.

growing cities such as Phoenix, Los Angeles, and Houston, where they moved into Spanish-speaking neighborhoods called *barrios*.

But the newcomers, whether Latinos or blacks, were often resented rather than welcomed. J. Luz Saenz, a Mexican American from Texas, noted in his diary that it took only three days after he was discharged from the army to have whites "throw us out from restaurants and deny us service as human beings." In 1917, more than forty African Americans and nine whites were killed during a riot in a weapons plant in East St. Louis, Illinois. Two years later, a Chicago race riot left twenty-three African Americans and fifteen whites dead.

A Loss of Civil Liberties

Once the United States entered the war, patriotic emotions often took a negative turn, as Americans equated anything German with disloyalty. Many quit drinking beer because German Americans owned most of the breweries. Symphonies refused to perform classical music by Bach and Beethoven, schools dropped German-language classes, and patriots renamed *sauerkraut* as "liberty cabbage," *German measles* as "liberty measles," and *dachshunds* as "liberty pups." President Wilson had predicted as much. "Once [we] lead this people into war," he said, "they'll forget there ever was such a thing as tolerance." What Wilson did not say was that he himself would lead the effort to suppress civil liberties, for, as he claimed, subversive forces in a nation at war must be "crushed out."

Under the Espionage and Sedition Acts, Congress outlawed public criticism of government leaders and war policies. The Espionage Act of 1917

The Espionage and Sedition Acts (1917–1918)

DON'T TALK

THE WEB IS SPUN FOR YOU WITH INVISIBLE THREADS

KEEP OUT OF IT HELP TO DESTROY IT

STOP = THINK

ASK YOURSELF IF WHAT YOU WERE ABOUT TO SAY MIGHT HELP THE ENEMY

SPIES ARE LISTENING

KEEP OUT OF IT In this 1918 war poster, the kaiser—with his famous moustache and spiked German helmet—is characterized as a spider, spinning an invisible web to catch the stray words of Allied civilians.

imposed penalties of up to $10,000 and twenty years in prison for anyone who gave aid to the enemy; tried to incite insubordination, disloyalty, or refusal of duty in the armed services; or interfered with the war effort in other ways. To root out "vicious spies and conspirators," Wilson recruited 250,000 informers—the American Protective League—to turn in those suspected of treason. He was convinced that newly arrived immigrants had "poured the poison of disloyalty into the very arteries of our national life."

During the war, 1,055 people were convicted under the Espionage Act, not one of whom was a spy. Most of them were simply critics of the war. The Socialist leader Eugene V. Debs, a militant pacifist, was convicted under the Espionage Act simply for opposing the war and was sentenced to ten years in prison. He told the court he would always criticize wars imposed by the "master" class: "While there is a lower class, I am in it. While there is a criminal element, I am of it. While there is a soul in prison, I am not free."

The Sedition Act of 1918 extended the penalties to those who did or said anything to obstruct government sales of war bonds or to advocate cutbacks in production and—in case something had been overlooked—for saying, writing, or printing anything "disloyal, profane, scurrilous, or abusive" about the American form of government, the Constitution, or the army and navy.

In two important decisions just after the war, the Supreme Court upheld the Espionage and Sedition Acts. *Schenck v. United States* (1919) reaffirmed the conviction of Charles T. Schenck, the head of the Socialist party, for circulating anti-draft leaflets among members of the armed forces. Justice Oliver Wendell Holmes wrote the unanimous court opinion that freedom of speech did not apply to words that represented "a clear and present danger to the safety of the country." In *Abrams v. United States* (1919), the Court upheld the conviction of a man who had distributed pamphlets opposing American military intervention in Russia to remove the Bolsheviks who had seized power in 1917. Here, Justices Holmes and Brandeis dissented from the majority view. The "surreptitious publishing of a silly leaflet by an unknown man," they argued, posed no danger to government policy.

CORE **OBJECTIVE**

3. Describe the major events of the war after U.S. entry, and explain the U.S. contribution to the defeat of the Central Powers.

The American Role in the War

In 1917, America's war strategy focused on helping the struggling French and British armies on the Western Front. On December 21, 1917, French premier Georges Clemenceau urged the Americans to rush their army, called the American Expeditionary Force (AEF), to France. "A terrible blow is imminent," he told an American journalist about to leave Paris. "Tell your Americans to come quickly." Clemenceau was referring to the likelihood of a massive

German attack, made more probable by the end of the fighting on the Eastern Front following the Bolshevik Revolution in Russia in November 1917.

The Bolshevik Revolution

Among the many casualties of the Great War, none was greater in scale than the Bolshevik Revolution and the destruction of the Russian Empire and its monarchy. On March 15, 1917, bumbling tsar Nicholas II, having presided over terrible losses in a war that also ruined the Russian economy, had turned the nation over to the "Provisional Government" of a new Russian republic committed to continuing the war. The fall of the tsar gave Americans the illusion that all the major Allied powers were now fighting for the ideals of constitutional democracy—an illusion that was shattered after the Germans in April helped exiled radical Vladimir Lenin return to Russia from Switzerland in a secret, sealed train, hoping that he would cause turmoil in his homeland. He did much more than that.

> Communist revolution in Russia

As Lenin observed, power in war-weary Russia was lying in the streets, waiting to be picked up. To do so, he mobilized the Bolsheviks, a small but determined group of Communist revolutionaries, who during the night of November 6–7 seized power from the Provisional Government, established a dictatorship, and called for a quick end to Russian involvement in the European war. Lenin banned political parties and organized religions (atheism became the official belief); eliminated civil liberties and the free press; and killed or imprisoned opposition leaders, including the tsar and his family.

The Bolshevik Revolution triggered a prolonged civil war throughout Russia in which the United States and its allies worked to overthrow the Communists. Wilson sent 20,000 American soldiers to Siberia to support the anti-Communist Russian forces, an effort that proved unsuccessful.

Lenin declared that the world would be freed from war only by a global revolution in which capitalism would be replaced by communism. To that end, he wanted to get Russia out of the Great War as soon as possible. On March 3, 1918, Lenin signed a humiliating peace agreement with Germany, the Treaty of Brest-Litovsk. The treaty forced Russia to transfer vast territories to Germany and its ally Turkey and to recognize the independence of the Ukraine region. In addition, Russia had to pay $46 million to Germany. Lenin was willing to accept such a harsh peace because he needed to concentrate on his many internal enemies in the civil war.

VLADIMIR LENIN A Russian Communist revolutionary, Lenin led the Bolsheviks in overthrowing the monarchy and ultimately established the Soviet Union.

Crucial U.S. Contribution on the Western Front

Less than three weeks later, on March 21, the Germans began the first of several spring offensives in France and Belgium designed to win the war before the AEF arrived in force. By May, the German armies had advanced to the Marne River, within fifty miles of Paris.

> American forces help repel the Germans in 1918

That was as far as they got, however, for in June, at the monthlong Battle of Belleau Wood, U.S. forces commanded by General John J. Pershing joined

MEUSE-ARGONNE OFFENSIVE (1918) American soldiers of the 23rd Infantry, 2nd Division, fire machine guns at the Germans from what was left of the Argonne Forest in France.

the French in driving the Germans back. During the ferocious fighting, a French officer urged an American unit to retreat. In a famous exchange, U.S. Marine captain Lloyd W. Williams refused the order, saying: "Retreat? Hell, we just got here."

The crucial American role in the fighting occurred in a great Allied offensive, begun on September 26, 1918. With the French commander urging "everyone to battle," the American troops joined British and French armies in a drive toward Sedan, France, and its strategic railroad, which supplied the German army. With 1.2 million U.S. soldiers involved, including some 180,000 African Americans, it was the largest American action of the war, and it resulted in 117,000 U.S. casualties, including 26,000 dead.

Along the entire French-Belgian front, however, the outnumbered Germans were in desperate retreat eastward across Belgium during the early fall of 1918. "America," wrote German general Erich Ludendorff, "became the decisive power in the war."

The End of the War

Woodrow Wilson was determined to ensure that the Great War would be the last world war. To that end, during 1917, he appointed a group of American experts, called the Inquiry, to draft a peace plan. With their advice, Wilson developed what would come to be called the **Fourteen Points**, a comprehensive list of provisions intended to shape the peace treaty and the postwar world. He presented his Fourteen Points in a dramatic speech to a joint session of Congress on January 8, 1918, describing his proposal "as the only

Fourteen Points President Woodrow Wilson's proposed plan for the peace agreement after the Great War, which included the creation of a "league" of nations intended to keep the peace.

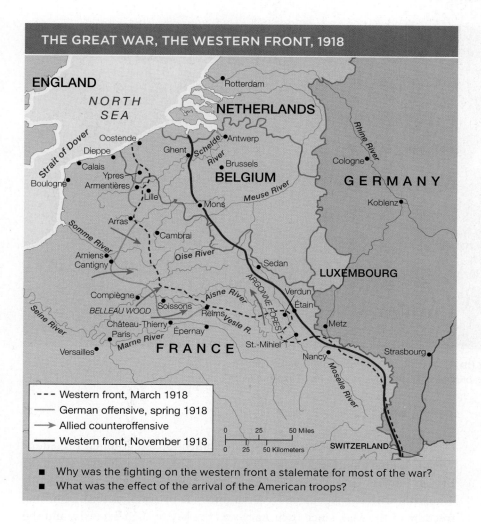

THE GREAT WAR, THE WESTERN FRONT, 1918

- - - Western front, March 1918
—— German offensive, spring 1918
→ Allied counteroffensive
—— Western front, November 1918

0   25   50 Miles
0   25   50 Kilometers

■ Why was the fighting on the western front a stalemate for most of the war?
■ What was the effect of the arrival of the American troops?

possible program" for peace. The first five points called for the open conduct of diplomacy, the recognition of neutral nations' right to continue maritime commerce in time of war ("freedom of the seas"), the removal of international trade barriers ("free trade"), the reduction of armaments, and the transformation of colonial empires into independent nations.

Most of the remaining points dealt with territorial claims: they called on the Central Powers to evacuate occupied lands and urged the victors to follow the difficult principle of "self-determination" in redrawing the map of Europe, allowing overlapping nationalities and ethnic groups to develop their own independent nations. Point 13 created a new nation for the Poles, a people long dominated by the Russians on the east and the Germans on the west. Point 14, the capstone of Wilson's postwar scheme, called for a "league" of nations to preserve global peace. When the Fourteen Points were made public, African American leaders asked the president to add a fifteenth point: an end to racial discrimination. Wilson did not respond.

ARMISTICE NIGHT IN NEW YORK (1918) George Luks, known for his vivid paintings of urban life, captured the unbridled outpouring of patriotism and joy that extended into the night of Germany's surrender.

On October 3, 1918, a new German chancellor telegraphed President Wilson, asking for an end to the fighting on the basis of his Fourteen Points. British and French leaders accepted the Fourteen Points as a basis of negotiations but with two significant reservations: the British insisted on limiting freedom of the seas, since their navy was the key to their security, and the French demanded reparations (payments) from Germany and Austria for war damages.

Meanwhile, by the end of October 1918, Germany was on the verge of collapse. Millions were fed up with the war, and thousands were starving. Revolutionaries rampaged through the streets. Sailors mutinied. Germany's allies dropped out of the war: Bulgaria, on September 29, 1918; Turkey, on October 30; and Austria-Hungary, on November 3. On November 9, the German kaiser resigned, and a republic was proclaimed. Then, on November 11 at 5:00 A.M., an armistice (cease-fire agreement) was signed by which the Germans were assured that Wilson's Fourteen Points would be the basis for the peace conference.

Six hours later, at the eleventh hour of the eleventh day of the eleventh month, and after 1,563 days of terrible warfare, the guns fell silent. From Europe, Colonel House sent a telegram to President Wilson: "Autocracy [government by an individual with unlimited power] is dead; long live democracy and its immortal leader."

The end of fighting led to wild celebrations throughout the world as fear and grief gave way to hope. "The nightmare is over," wrote African American activist W. E. B. Du Bois. "The world awakes. The long, horrible years of dreadful night are passed. Behold the sun!" Wilson was not as joyful. The Great War, he said, had dealt a grievous injury to civilization "which can never be atoned for or repaired."

Cease-fire and celebrations

During its nineteen months of combat in the Great War, the United States had lost 53,000 servicemen in combat. Another 63,000 died of various diseases, especially the influenza epidemic that swept through Europe and around the world in 1918. Germany's war dead totaled more than 2 million, including civilians. France lost nearly 1.4 million combatants; Great Britain, 703,000; and Russia, 1.7 million. The new Europe would be very different from the prewar version: much poorer, more violent, more polarized, more cynical, less sure of itself, and less capable of decisive action. The United States, for good or ill, emerged from the war as the world's dominant power.

The Politics of Peace

In the making of a peace agreement to end the war, Woodrow Wilson showed himself both at his best and worst. The Fourteen Point peace program embodied his vision of a better world governed by fairer principles. For a glorious moment at the end of 1918, the idealistic American president was the world's self-appointed prophet of peace. He felt guided "by the hand of God." Wilson's godlike vision of creating a peacekeeping "League of Nations" promised that henceforth all nations would live in harmony. If the diplomats gathering to draft the peace treaty failed to follow his ambitious plans to reshape the world in America's image, he warned, "there will be another world war" within a generation. In the end, however, Wilson's grand efforts at global peacemaking failed—at home, not abroad, and because of his own faults.

CORE **OBJECTIVE**

4. Evaluate Woodrow Wilson's efforts to promote his plans for a peaceful world order as outlined in his Fourteen Points.

Wilson's Key Errors

Whatever the merits of Wilson's peace plan, his efforts to implement it proved clumsy and self-defeating. He made several key decisions at war's end that would come back to haunt him. First, against the advice of his staff and of European leaders, he decided to attend the peace conference in Paris that opened on January 18, 1919. Never before had an American president visited Europe or left the nation for such a prolonged period (six months). During his months abroad, Wilson lost touch with political developments at home.

Wilson's prolonged absence in Europe

Second, in the congressional election campaign during the fall of 1918, Wilson defied his advisers as well as political tradition by urging voters to elect a Democratic Congress to support his policies. Prior to that time, presidents had remained neutral during congressional elections. Republicans, who for the most part had backed Wilson's war measures, were not pleased.

Wilson's disregard for Republicans at home

FIT FOR A MESSIAH A triumphant Wilson rode down the Champs-Élysées as the crowds showered him with flower petals and cheered, "*Vive Wilson! Vive l'Amérique! Vive la liberté!*"

Nor were voters, especially western farmers upset with government price ceilings placed on wheat. In the elections, the Democrats lost control of both houses of Congress, leading Theodore Roosevelt to claim that Wilson could no longer claim "to speak for the American people."

Wilson further weakened support for his peacemaking efforts when, in a deliberate slight, he declined to include a prominent Republican to the American delegation headed to the peace conference. Although House had urged him to appoint Theodore Roosevelt or Senator Henry Cabot Lodge, the president's most prominent critics, Wilson refused. In the end, he appointed Harry White, an obscure Republican. Former president William Howard Taft groused that Wilson's real intention in going to Paris was "to hog the whole show."

When Wilson reached Europe in December 1918, the cheering crowds in London, Paris, and Rome verged on hysteria. Millions of grateful Europeans greeted him as their hero, even a savior. An Italian mayor described Wilson's visit as the "second coming of Christ." Others hailed him as the "God of peace." The adoration went to Wilson's head; he privately admitted that he was now "at the apex of my glory in the hearts of these people."

From such a height, however, there could only be a fall. Although popular with the European people, they would not be drafting the peace treaty. Instead, Wilson had to deal at the peace conference with tough-minded European statesmen who shared neither his lofty goals nor his American ideals. In fact, they resented his efforts to forge a peace settlement modeled on American values. In the end, the European leaders would force him to abandon many of his objectives and become a horse trader—not a messiah.

The Paris Peace Conference

The Paris Peace Conference lasted from January to June 1919. The participants had no time to waste. The German, Austro-Hungarian, and Ottoman Empires were in ruins. Across much of the European continent, food was scarce and lawlessness flourished. The threat of revolution hung over Central Europe as Communists in the defeated nations threatened to take control of governments in chaos.

As the most significant world event of the era, the peace conference dealt with immensely complex and controversial issues (including the need to create new nations, such as Yugoslavia and Iraq, and redrawing the maps of Europe and the Middle East) that required both political statesmanship and technical expertise. The British delegation alone included almost 400 members, many of them specialists in political geography or economics.

THE BIG FOUR David Lloyd George, Vittorio Orlando, Georges Clemenceau and President Woodrow Wilson (from left to right) stand outside the palace at Versailles in the midst of the treaty negotiations.

From the start, the Paris Peace Conference was controlled by the "Big Four" who met together some 140 times: the prime ministers of Britain, France, and Italy and the president of the United States. The seventy-seven-year-old French premier Georges Clemenceau, known as "The Tiger," was a stern realist who had little patience with President Wilson's idealistic preaching. In response to Wilson's declaration that "America is the only idealistic nation in the world," Clemenceau grumbled that talking with the American leader was like talking to Jesus Christ. "God gave us the Ten Commandments and we broke them," the French leader sneered. "Wilson gave us the Fourteen Points—we shall see."

The Big Four fought not only in private but in public as well. The French and the British, led by Prime Minister David Lloyd George, insisted that Wilson agree to their proposals to weaken Germany economically and militarily, while Vittorio Orlando, prime minister of Italy, focused on gaining territories from defeated Austria.

Wilson, suffering from poor health, lectured them all about the need to craft a peace treaty without revenge and to embrace his beloved **League of Nations**, which he insisted must be the "keystone" of any peace settlement. Whatever compromises he might have to make and whatever mistakes might result, Wilson believed that his proposed world peace organization— the League of Nations— would abolish war—forever.

Article X of the League of Nations charter, which Wilson called "the heart of the League," pledged member nations to impose military and economic sanctions, or penalties, against those that engaged in aggression. The League,

The Big Four: Wilsonian idealism vs. European realism

League of Nations Organization of nations formed in the aftermath of the Great War to mediate disputes and maintain international peace; despite President Wilson's intense lobbying for the League of Nations, Congress did not ratify the Versailles Treaty, and the United States failed to join.

Wilson assumed, would exercise enormous moral influence, making military action unnecessary. These unrealistic expectations became, for Wilson, a self-defeating crusade.

On February 14, 1919, Wilson presented the finished draft of the League covenant to the Allies and left Paris for a visit home, where he already faced growing opposition among Republicans. The League of Nations, Theodore Roosevelt complained, would revive German militarism and undermine American morale. "To substitute internationalism for nationalism," Roosevelt argued, "means to do away with patriotism." His close friend Henry Cabot Lodge, the powerful chairman of the Senate Foreign Relations Committee, also scorned Wilson and his idealism. He confessed to Roosevelt the violent "hatred I feel toward Wilson." Lodge opposed the League of Nations because, he claimed, it would potentially involve sending U.S. troops to foreign conflicts without Senate approval.

The Treaty of Versailles

> The Treaty of Versailles: Wilson's concessions on territory, reparations, and "war guilt"

Back in Paris in the spring of 1919, Wilson lost his leverage with the British and French because it was increasingly uncertain that the U.S. Senate would approve any treaty he endorsed. Wilson also gave in on many controversial issues solely to ensure that the Europeans would approve his League of Nations. For example, Wilson yielded to French demands that Germany transfer vast territories on its western border to France and on its eastern border to Poland. In other territorial matters, Wilson had to abandon his lofty but impractical and ill-defined principle of national self-determination, whereby every ethnic group would be allowed to form its own nation. As Secretary of State Robert Lansing correctly predicted, preaching self-determination would only "raise hopes which can never be realized." (Wilson himself later told the Senate that he wished he had never said that "all nations have a right to self-determination.")

In their efforts to allow for at least some degree of ethnic self-determination in multiethnic regions, the statesmen at Versailles created the newly independent countries of Austria, Hungary, Poland, Yugoslavia, and Czechoslovakia in Central Europe and four new nations along the Baltic Sea: Finland, Estonia, Lithuania, and Latvia. The victorious Allies, however, did not create independent nations out of the colonies of the defeated and now defunct European empires. Instead, they assigned the former German colonies in Africa and the Turkish colonies in the Middle East to France and Great Britain to govern for an unspecified time while Japan took control of the former German colonies in east Asia.

The bitterest arguments among the diplomats in Paris focused on efforts to make Germany pay for the expenses of the war (reparations). The British and especially the French (on whose soil much of the war had been fought) wanted Germany to pay the *entire* financial cost of the war, including the lifetime pensions they would pay to their veterans. On this point, Wilson made perhaps his most fateful concessions. He agreed to a clause in the

EUROPE AFTER THE TREATY OF VERSAILLES, 1919

Legend:
- ·········· 1914 boundaries
- New nations
- Plebiscite areas
- Occupied area

0   250   500 Miles
0   250   500 Kilometers

- Why was self-determination so difficult to apply in Central Europe?
- How did territorial concessions weaken Germany?

peace treaty that forced Germany to accept responsibility for the war and its entire expense. The "war guilt" clause so offended Germans that it became a major factor in the rise of the Adolf Hitler and the Nazi party during the 1920s. Wilson himself privately admitted that if he were a German he would refuse to sign the treaty.

On May 7, 1919, the victorious powers presented the treaty to the German delegates, who returned three weeks later with 443 pages of criticism. A few changes were made, but when the Germans still refused to sign, the French threatened to launch a new military attack. Finally, on June 28, the Germans gave up and signed the treaty in the glittering Hall of Mirrors at Versailles, the magnificent palace built by King Louis XIV in the late seventeenth century. Thereafter, it was called the **Treaty of Versailles**.

When Adolf Hitler, a young German soldier, learned of the treaty's provisions, he vowed revenge. "It cannot be that two million Germans have fallen in vain," he screamed during a speech in Munich in 1922. "We demand vengeance!" In the end, Wilson and the Allies were better at winning the war than making a lasting peace.

Treaty of Versailles Peace treaty that ended the Great War, forcing Germany to dismantle its military, pay immense war reparations, and give up its colonies around the world.

The Debate over Ratification

On July 8, 1919, Wilson returned home to urge the U.S. Senate to ratify the Paris treaty. Before leaving Paris, he had assured a French diplomat that he would not allow any changes to it. "I shall consent to nothing," he vowed. "The Senate must take its medicine." Thus began one of the most brutally partisan and bitterly personal disputes in American history.

On July 10, Wilson became the first president to enter the Senate and deliver a treaty to be voted on. He called upon the senators of both parties to accept their "great duty" and ratify the treaty, which had been guided "by the hand of God." Breathing defiance, Wilson then grew needlessly confrontational. He dismissed critics of the League of Nations as "blind and little provincial people." The whole world, Wilson claimed, was relying on the United States to sign the Versailles Treaty: "Dare we reject it and break the heart of the world?"

> The U.S. Senate debate over the Treaty of Versailles

Yes, answered Senate Republicans who had decided that Wilson's commitment to the League of Nations was a reckless threat to America's independence. Henry Cabot Lodge denounced the treaty's "scheme of making mankind suddenly virtuous by a statute or a written constitution." Lodge's strategy was to stall a vote on the treaty in hopes that public opposition to the president would grow. To do so, he took six weeks to read aloud the lengthy text of the treaty to his Foreign Relations committee. He then organized a parade of expert witnesses, most of them opposed to the treaty, to appear at the committee's hearings on ratification.

In the Senate, a group of "irreconcilables," fourteen Republicans and two Democrats, refused to support U.S. membership in the League. They were mainly western and midwestern isolationists who feared that such sweeping international commitments would threaten domestic reforms. The irreconcilables would prove useful to Lodge's efforts to defeat the treaty, but he himself belonged to a larger group called the "reservationists," who insisted upon limiting American participation in the League of Nations in exchange for approving the rest of the treaty.

The only way to get Senate approval was for Wilson to meet with Lodge and others and agree to revisions, the most important of which was the requirement that Congress authorize any American participation in a League-approved war. As Republican senator Frank B. Kellogg of Minnesota stressed, the proposed changes were crafted not by enemies of the treaty but by friends who wanted to save it. Republican senator James Watson of Indiana told Wilson that he must accept some revisions: "Mr. President, you are licked. There is only one way you can take the United States into the League of Nations." The inflexible president, who assumed that his opponents were both misguided and morally wrong, lashed back: "Lodge's reservations? Never!"

> Wilson takes treaty to the American people

In September 1919, facing defeat after a summer of fruitless debate, an exhausted Wilson decided to bypass his Senate opponents by speaking

GOING TO TALK TO THE BOSS After failing to convince Congress to ratify the Treaty of Versailles, Wilson set out on a national tour to win over the American people, as shown in this cartoon printed in 1919. **What was the result of Wilson's efforts to have the treaty ratified?**

directly to voters. On September 2, against his doctor's orders and his wife's advice, he left Washington for a grueling transcontinental railroad tour through the Midwest to the West Coast, intending to visit twenty-nine cities. No president had ever made such a strenuous effort to win over public support. In St. Louis, Wilson said that he had returned from Paris "bringing one of the greatest documents of human history," which was now in danger of being rejected by the Senate. He pledged to "fight for a cause . . . greater than the Senate. It is greater than the government. It is as great as the cause of mankind, and I intend, in office or out, to fight that battle as long as I live."

Onward through Nebraska, South Dakota, Minnesota, North Dakota, Montana, Idaho, and Washington, Wilson traveled by rail and spoke, sometimes as many as four times a day, despite suffering from pounding headaches. It did not help his morale to learn that his secretary of state, Robert Lansing, had said during the president's absence from Washington, D.C., that the League of Nations was "entirely useless." By the time Wilson's train reached Spokane, Washington, the president was visibly fatigued. But he kept going, heading south through Oregon and California. Some 200,000 people greeted him in Los Angeles. By then, he had covered 10,000 miles in twenty-two days and given thirty-two major speeches.

Physical Breakdown and Political Failure

Then disaster struck. After delivering an emotional speech on September 25 in Pueblo, Colorado, Wilson collapsed from his headaches and had to admit that he could not finish the trip ("I am going to pieces"). With tears rolling down his cheeks as he looked out the train's window, he told his doctor that he had suffered the "greatest disappointment of [his] life."

Back in Washington, D.C., a week later, the president suffered a crushing stroke (cerebral hemorrhage) that almost killed him. The episode left him paralyzed on his left side; he could barely speak or see. Only his secretary, his doctor, and his wife, Edith, knew his true condition. For five months, Wilson lay in bed while his doctor issued reassuring medical bulletins to reporters. The president "lived on, but oh, what a wreck of his former self!" sighed a White House staffer. "He had changed from a giant to a pygmy." If a document needed Wilson's signature, his wife guided his trembling hand, leading a senator to complain that the nation now had a "petticoat government."

Secretary of State Lansing urged the president's aides to declare him disabled and appoint the vice president in his place; they angrily refused. "I hate Lansing," Edith Wilson told Secretary of the Navy Josephus Daniels. Soon thereafter, Lansing was replaced.

The stroke made Wilson even more arrogant and stubborn. He became emotionally unstable, at times crying uncontrollably and behaving oddly. For the remaining seventeen months of his presidential term, his protective wife, along with aides and trusted cabinet members, kept him isolated from all but the most essential business. When a group of Republican senators visited the White House, one of them said, "Well, Mr. President, we have all been praying for you." Wilson replied, "Which way, Senator?"

Such presidential humor was rare, however. Wilson's hardened arteries seemed to have hardened his political judgment as well. His outspoken wife reinforced his prejudices, calling Lodge a "stinking snake." For his part, Lodge pushed through the Senate fourteen changes (the number was not coincidental) in the draft of the Versailles Treaty. Wilson rejected the proposed changes, and as a result, his supporters in the Senate were thrown into an unlikely alliance with the irreconcilables, who opposed the treaty under any circumstances.

The Senate voted 55–39 against Lodge's revised treaty. On the question of approving the original treaty without changes, the irreconcilables and the reservationists, led by Lodge, combined to defeat ratification again, 53–38. Lodge said that if the president "had been a true idealist, in regard to the covenant of the League of Nations, he would have . . . secured its adoption by the Senate of the United States by accepting some modification of its terms."

With the treaty defeated, Woodrow Wilson's grand effort at global peacemaking had failed miserably. Congress tried to declare an official end to American involvement in the war by a joint resolution on May 20, 1920, which Wilson vetoed in a fit of spite. It was not until July 2, 1921, four months

> **Wilson's stroke and the treaty's defeat**

after he had left office and almost eighteen months after the fighting had stopped, that another joint resolution officially ended America's war with Germany and Austria-Hungary. Separate peace treaties with Germany, Austria, and Hungary were ratified on October 18, 1921, but by then Warren G. Harding was president of the United States.

The failure of the United States to ratify the Versailles Treaty and exercise strong world leadership would have long-range consequences. With Great Britain and France too exhausted and too timid to keep Germany weak and isolated, a dangerous power vacuum would emerge in Europe that Adolf Hitler and the Nazis would fill.

Lurching from War to Peace

CORE **OBJECTIVE**
5. Analyze the consequences of the war at home and abroad.

The Versailles Treaty, for all the time the Senate spent on it, was but one of many issues demanding attention in the turbulent period after the war. The year 1919 began with joyous victory parades, but celebration soon gave way to widespread labor unrest, socialist and Communist radicalism, race riots, terrorist bombings, and government crackdowns. With millions of servicemen returning to civilian life, war-related industries shutting down, and wartime price controls ending, unemployment and prices for consumer goods spiked.

President Wilson's leadership was missing during the postwar crisis. Bedridden by his stroke, the president became increasingly grim, distant, and depressed. Wilson, observed David Lloyd George, the British prime minister, was "as much a victim of the war as any soldier who died in the trenches."

The Spanish Flu

Beginning in 1918, many Americans confronted an infectious enemy that produced far more casualties than the war itself. It became known as the Spanish flu (although its geographic origins are debated), and its contagion spread around the globe and altered the course of world history. The disease appeared suddenly in the spring of 1918, and its initial outbreak lasted a year and killed millions of people worldwide, twice as many as had died in the war. In the United States alone, it accounted for 675,000 deaths, over ten times the number of U.S. combat deaths in France. A fifth of the nation's population caught the flu, so many that the public health system was strained to the breaking point. Hospitals ran out of beds, and funeral homes ran out of coffins. By the spring of 1919, the pandemic had finally run its course, ending as suddenly—and as inexplicably—as it had begun. Although another outbreak occurred in the winter of 1920, people had grown more resistant to it. No disease in human history had killed so many people worldwide, and no war, famine, or natural catastrophe had killed so many people in such a short time.

THEIR FIRST VOTES Women of New York City's East Side vote for the first time in the presidential election of 1920.

Suffrage at Last

> Women's suffrage: Ratification of the Nineteenth Amendment

As the first outbreak of the Spanish flu was ending, women finally gained a constitutional guarantee of their right to vote. After six months of delay, debate, and failed votes, Congress finally passed the **Nineteenth Amendment** in the spring of 1919 and sent it to the states for ratification. Tennessee's legislature was the last of thirty-six state assemblies to approve the amendment, and it did so in dramatic fashion. The initial vote was 48–48. Then a twenty-four-year-old Republican legislator named Harry T. Burn changed his no vote to yes at the insistence of his strong-willed mother, the widow of a farmer. She had written him a note admonishing him to be a "good boy" and vote for suffrage. He did, and the Nineteenth Amendment became official on August 18, 1920, making the United States the twenty-second nation in the world to allow women to vote in national elections. It was the climactic achievement of the Progressive Era. Suddenly, 9.5 million women became voters; in the 1920 presidential election, they would make up 40 percent of the electorate.

The Economic Transition

> A surge of labor strikes and public reaction against them

As consumer prices continued to rise, discontented workers, released from wartime controls on wages, grew more willing to go out on strike for their demands. In 1919, more than 4 million hourly wage workers, 20 percent of the total in the U.S. workforce, participated in 3,600 strikes against management. Most of them wanted nothing more than higher wages and shorter workweeks, but their critics linked striking workers with the worldwide Communist movement.

After a general strike in Seattle, the mayor, Ole Hanson, claimed the strikers were seeking a "revolution" under Bolshevik influence, and a Seattle

Nineteenth Amendment (1920) Constitutional amendment that granted women the right to vote in national elections.

newspaper declared that "this is America—not Russia." Such charges of a Communist conspiracy were greatly exaggerated. In 1919, fewer than 70,000 Americans nationwide belonged to the Communist party. The Seattle strike lasted only five days, but public resentment of the strikers damaged the cause and image of unions across the country.

The most controversial postwar labor dispute was in Boston, where most of the police went on strike on September 9, 1919. The furious Massachusetts governor Calvin Coolidge, mobilized the National Guard. After four days, the striking policemen offered to return, but instead they were all fired. When labor leaders appealed for their reinstatement, Coolidge responded in words that made him an instant national hero: "There is no right to strike against the public safety by anybody, anywhere, any time."

Race Riots

The summer of 1919 also sparked a wave of deadly race riots across the nation. As more and more African Americans, including many of the 367,000 who were war veterans, moved out of the rural South to different parts of the country, developed successful careers, and asserted their civil rights in the face of deeply embedded segregationist practices, resentful whites reacted with an almost hysterical racism.

What African American leader James Weldon Johnson called the Red Summer (*red* signifying blood) began in July, when a mob of whites invaded a black neighborhood in Longview, Texas, angry over rumors of interracial dating. They burned shops and houses and ran several African Americans out of town. A week later, in Washington, D.C., exaggerated or even false reports of black assaults on white women stirred up white mobs, and gangs of white and black rioters waged a race war in the streets until soldiers and driving rains ended the fighting.

"Red Summer" of race riots

The worst was yet to come. In late July, 38 people were killed and 537 injured in five days of race rioting in Chicago, where some 50,000 African Americans, mostly from the rural South, had moved during the war, leading

SAFE, BRIEFLY Escorted by a police officer, an African American family moves its belongings from their home, likely destroyed by white rioters, into a protected area of Chicago.

to tensions with local whites over jobs and housing. White unionized workers especially resented blacks who were hired as strikebreakers. Altogether, twenty-five race riots erupted in 1919, and there were eighty lynchings of African Americans, eleven of them war veterans.

The Red Scare

With so much of the public convinced that the strikes and riots were inspired by Communists and anarchists (two very different groups who shared a hatred for capitalism), a New York journalist reported that Americans were "shivering in their boots over Bolshevism, and they are far more scared of [Vladimir] Lenin than they ever were of the [German] Kaiser. We seem to be the most frightened victors the world ever saw."

Fears of revolution in America were fueled by the violent actions of a few scattered militants. In early 1919, the Secret Service discovered a plot by Spanish anarchists to kill President Wilson and other government officials. In April 1919, postal workers intercepted nearly forty homemade mail bombs addressed to government officials. One slipped through and blew off the hands of a Georgia senator's maid. In June, another bomb destroyed the front of U.S. attorney general A. Mitchell Palmer's house in Washington, D.C.

J. EDGAR HOOVER Fresh out of law school, Hoover joined the Justice Department and rose the ranks to become the first director of the FBI.

Palmer, who had ambitions to succeed Wilson as president, concluded that a "Red Menace," a Communist "blaze of revolution," was "sweeping over every American institution of law and order." In August 1919, Palmer appointed a twenty-four-year-old attorney named J. Edgar Hoover to lead a new government division created to collect information on radicals. Hoover and others in the Justice Department worked with a network of 250,000 informants in 600 cities, all of them members of the American Protective League, which was founded during the war to root out "traitors" and labor radicals.

On November 7, 1919, while Wilson lay incapacitated in the White House, federal agents rounded up 450 alien "radicals," most of whom were law-abiding Russian immigrants looking for work. All were deported to Russia without a court hearing. On January 2, 1920, police raids in dozens of cities swept up 5,000 more suspects, many taken from their homes without arrest warrants.

First Red Scare (1919–1920)
Outbreak of anti-Communist hysteria that included the arrest without warrants of thousands of suspected radicals, most of whom (especially Russian immigrants) were deported.

What came to be called the **First Red Scare** (after another outbreak of anti-Communist hysteria occurred in the 1950s) represented one of the largest violations of civil liberties in American history. In 1919, novelist Katharine Fullerton Gerould announced in *Harper's Magazine* that, as a result of the government crackdown, America "is no longer a free country in the old sense." Civil liberties that had long been protected were being violated with abandon.

Panic about possible foreign terrorists erupted in communities across the nation as vigilantes took matters into their own hands. At a patriotic pageant in Washington, D.C., a sailor shot a spectator who refused to rise for "The Star-Spangled Banner"; the crowd cheered. In Hammond, Indiana, a jury took only two minutes to acquit a man who had murdered an immigrant for yelling "To hell with the U.S." In Waterbury, Connecticut, a salesman was sentenced to six months in jail for saying that Lenin was "one of the brainiest" of the world's leaders.

By the summer of 1920, the Red Scare had begun to subside. Although Attorney General Palmer kept predicting more foreign-inspired terrorism, it never came. Bombings tapered off; the wave of strikes and race riots receded. By September 1920, when a bomb at the corner of Broad and Wall Streets in New York City killed thirty-eight people, Americans were ready to take it for what it was: the work of a crazed mind and not the start of a revolution. The Red Scare nonetheless left a lasting mark on American life. It strengthened the conservative crusade for "100 percent Americanism" and new restrictions on immigration.

Effects of the Great War

The extraordinary turbulence in 1919 and 1920 was an unmistakable indication of how the Great War had changed the shape of modern history: the world war was a turning point after which little was the same. It had destroyed old Europe—not only many of its cities, people, empires, and economies but also its self-image as the admired center of civilized Western culture. Winston Churchill, the future British prime minister, called postwar Europe "a crippled, broken world." Peace did not bring stability; the trauma of the war lingered long after the shooting stopped. Most Germans and Austrians believed they were the victims of a harsh peace, and many wanted revenge, especially a hate-filled German war veteran named Adolf Hitler. At the same time, the war had hastened the already simmering Bolshevik Revolution, which caused Russia to exit the war and abandon its western European allies and, in 1922, to reemerge on the world stage as the Union of Soviet Socialist Republics (USSR). Thereafter, Soviet communism would be one of the most powerful forces shaping the twentieth century.

Postwar America was a much different story. For the first time, the United States had decisively intervened in a major European war. The American economy had emerged from the conflict largely unscathed, and bankers and business executives were eager to fill the vacuum created by the destruction of the major European economies. The United States was now the world's dominant power. In 1928, ten years after the end of the Great War, a British official in London explained that Great Britain now faced "a phenomenon for which there is no parallel in our modern history." The United States, he added, was "twenty-five times as wealthy, three times as populous, twice as ambitious, almost invulnerable, and at least our equal in prosperity, vital energy, technical equipment, and industrial strength." What came to be called the "American Century" was at hand.

CORE OBJECTIVES |

■ **An Uneasy Neutrality** In 1914, a system of military alliances divided Europe in two. Britain, France, and the Russian Empire had formed the Triple Entente, later called the *Allied Powers*. The *Central Powers* were comprised of Germany, Austria-Hungary, Bulgaria, and Turkey (Ottoman Empire). Italy would switch sides in 1915 and join the Allied Powers. In the summer of 1914, the assassination of the heir to the Austro-Hungarian throne by a Serbian nationalist triggered a chain reaction involving these alliances that erupted into the Great War.

On the *Western Front*, troops primarily engaged in *trench warfare*. New weapons such as machine guns, long-range artillery, and poison gas resulted in unprecedented casualties.

The Wilson administration initially declared the nation neutral but allowed American businesses to extend loans to the Allies. Americans were outraged by the German *U-boat* warfare, especially after the 1915 sinking of the British passenger liner *Lusitania*. In 1917, the publication of the *Zimmermann telegram* led the United States to enter the Great War.

■ **Mobilizing a Nation** The Wilson administration drafted millions of young men and created new agencies, such as the War Industries Board and the Food Administration, to coordinate industrial and agricultural production. As white workers left their factory jobs to join the army, hundreds of thousands of African Americans migrated from the rural South to the urban North, known as the *Great Migration*. Many southern whites and Mexican Americans also migrated to industrial centers. One million women worked in defense industries. The federal government severely curtailed civil liberties during the war. The Espionage and Sedition Acts of 1917 and 1918 criminalized public opposition to the war.

■ **The American Role in the War** In 1918, the arrival of millions of fresh American troops turned the tide of the war, rolling back a final desperate German offensive. German leaders sued for peace, and an armistice was signed on November 11, 1918.

Woodrow Wilson insisted that the war aim of the United States was the emergence of a new, democratic Europe. His *Fourteen Points (1918)* speech outlined his ideas for smaller, ethnically based nation-states to replace the empires. A *League of Nations*, he believed, would promote peaceful resolutions to future conflicts.

■ **The Politics of Peace** At the Paris Peace Conference, Wilson was only partially successful in achieving his goals. The *Treaty of Versailles (1919)* did create the *League of Nations* but included a "war guilt" clause that forced Germany to pay massive reparations for war damages to France and Britain. In the United States, the fight for Senate ratification of the treaty pitted supporters and those who wanted certain revisions against those who feared that involvement in a league of nations would hinder domestic reforms and require U.S. participation in future wars. Wilson's refusal to compromise and alienation of Republican senators resulted in the failure of Senate ratification.

■ **Lurching from War to Peace** The Bolsheviks established a Communist regime in the old Russian Empire in 1917. The German and Austro-Hungarian Empires were dismantled and replaced by smaller nation-states. The "war guilt" clause fostered German bitterness and contributed to the subsequent rise of the Nazis.

The United States struggled with its new status as the leading world power and with changes at home. As wartime industries shifted to peacetime production, wartime wage and price controls were ended, and millions of former soldiers reentered the workforce. Unemployment rose and consumer prices increased, provoking labor unrest in many cities. Many Americans believed the labor strikes were part of a Bolshevik plot to gain power in the United States. Several incidents of domestic terrorism fueled these fears and provoked the *First Red Scare (1919–1920)*. Race riots broke out as resentful white mobs tried to stop African Americans from exercising their civil rights. The summer of 1919 also saw the passage of the *Nineteenth Amendment*; ratified in 1920, it gave women throughout the country the right to vote.

KEY TERMS

Central Powers *p. 771*

Allied Powers *p. 771*

Western Front *p. 771*

trench warfare *p. 772*

U-boat *p. 777*

Lusitania *p. 777*

Zimmermann telegram *p. 780*

Great Migration *p. 784*

Fourteen Points *p. 788*

League of Nations *p. 793*

Treaty of Versailles *p. 795*

Nineteenth Amendment (1920) *p. 800*

First Red Scare *p. 802*

CHRONOLOGY

1914	The Great War (World War I) begins in Europe
1915	The British liner *Lusitania* is torpedoed by a German U-boat; 128 Americans are killed
1916	Congress passes the National Defense Act and the Revenue Act
Apr. 1917	United States enters the Great War
Nov. 1917	Bolshevik Revolution in Russia
Jan. 1918	Woodrow Wilson delivers his Fourteen Points
Nov. 11, 1918	Representatives of warring nations sign armistice
1919	Paris Peace Conference convenes
	Germany signs the Treaty of Versailles
	Race riots break out during the Red Summer
1919–1920	First Red Scare leads to arrests and deportations of suspected radicals
	Boston police strike ends by firing strikers
1920	Senate rejects the Treaty of Versailles
	Nineteenth Amendment is ratified

⚇ INQUIZITIVE

Go to InQuizitive to see what you've learned—and learn what you've missed—with personalized feedback along the way.

NIGHTCLUB (1933) With all its striking sights and sounds, the roar of the twenties subsided for some at the heart of it all. In this painting by American artist Guy Pène du Bois, flappers and their dates crowd into a fashionable nightclub, yet no one is dancing.

A Clash of Cultures

1920–1929

The decade between the end of the Great War and the onset of the Great Depression at the end of 1929 was perhaps the most dynamic in American history, a period of rapid urbanization, technological innovation, widespread prosperity, social rebelliousness, cultural upheaval, and political conservatism.

The decade's two most popular labels—the Jazz Age and the Roaring Twenties—describe a turbulent period that was, as a writer in the *New York Times* declared in 1923, "the greatest era of transition the human race has ever known. Old institutions are crumbling, old ideals are being battered into dust; the shock of the most cataclysmic war in history has left the world more disorganized than ever."

Among the most obvious changes during the twenties was an economic boom fueled by the spread of transformational technologies (automobiles, trucks, tractors, airplanes, radios, movies, electrical appliances, indoor plumbing) that greatly improved the standard of living for most Americans. At the same time, major social and political changes signaled what many people called a "New Era" in American life. The Eighteenth Amendment (1919) outlawed alcoholic beverages ("Prohibition"), setting off an epidemic of lawbreaking as thirsty Americans defied the law throughout the twenties. The Nineteenth Amendment (1920) allowed women to vote (although most African American women—and men—in the South were prevented from doing so) and to experience many freedoms previously limited to men.

CORE OBJECTIVES INQUIZITIVE

1. Assess the impact of the consumer culture that emerged in America during the 1920s, and explain the factors that contributed to its growth.

2. Describe other major new social and cultural trends and movements that became prominent during the twenties, and explain how they challenged traditional standards and customs.

3. Explain what "modernism" means in intellectual and artistic terms and how the modernist movement influenced American culture in the early twentieth century.

4. Identify important examples of reactionary conservatism in the decade, and analyze their impact on government policies.

5. Trace the Republican party's dominance of the federal government during the twenties, and analyze the extent to which its policies were a rejection of progressivism.

Another disruptive force was growing public awareness of the scientific discoveries of Albert Einstein in physics and Sigmund Freud in psychology, findings that undermined many traditional assumptions about God, the universe, and human behavior while profoundly affecting social and cultural life. Such controversial new ideas and sweeping social changes created what one historian called a "nervous generation" of Americans "groping for what certainty they could find." Mabel Dodge Luhan, a leading promoter of modern art and literature, said that the generation of young literary and artistic rebels that emerged during and after the war was determined to overthrow "the old order of things."

Much of the cultural conflict during the 1920s grew out of tension between rural and urban ways of life. For the first time, more Americans lived in cities than in rural areas after the Great War. While urban economies prospered, farmers suffered from the end of the wartime boom in food exports to Europe. As the rural economy remained depressed throughout the twenties, 4 million people moved from farms to cities, bringing their different cultural values with them. Amid this population shift, bitter fights erupted between supporters and opponents of evolutionary theory, Prohibition, and the increasing ethnic and religious diversity of America, among other charged issues.

In the political arena, both major parties still included "progressive" wings, but they were shrinking. Woodrow Wilson's losing fight with the Republican-led Senate over the Treaty of Versailles, coupled with his administration's savage crackdown on dissenters and socialists during and after the war, had weakened an already fragmented progressive movement. As the tireless reformer Amos Pinchot bitterly observed, President Wilson had "put his enemies in office and his friends in jail." By 1920, many disheartened progressives had withdrawn from public life. The prominent reformer Jane Addams lamented that the twenties, dominated politically by a Republican party devoted to the interests of big business, were "a period of political and social sag."

CORE **OBJECTIVE**

1. Assess the impact of the consumer culture that emerged in America during the 1920s, and explain the factors that contributed to its growth.

A "New Era" of Consumption

During the twenties, the thriving U.S. economy became the envy of the world. Following the brief postwar recession in 1920–1921, Americans benefited from the fastest economic growth in history. Jobs were plentiful, inflation was low, and income rose throughout the decade. The nation's total wealth almost doubled between 1920 and 1930, while wage workers enjoyed a whopping 30 percent increase in income, the sharpest rise in history. By 1929, the United States had the highest standard of living in the world.

Construction led the way. By 1921, a building boom was under way that would last the rest of the decade. At the same time, the remarkable growth of the automotive industry created an immediate need for roads, highways, service stations, and motels that stimulated other industries such as steel, concrete, and furniture. Technology also played a key role in the prosperity of the twenties by enabling mass production through the assembly-line process. New machines (electric motors, steam turbines, dump trucks, tractors, bulldozers, steam shovels) and more efficient ways of operating farms, factories, plants, mines, and mills generated dramatic increases in productivity.

In the late nineteenth century, the U.S. economy had been driven by commercial agriculture and large-scale industrial production—the building of railroads and bridges, the manufacturing of steel, and the construction of housing and businesses in cities. During the twenties, such industrial production continued, but the dominant aspect of the economy involved an explosion of new consumer goods made available through a national marketplace.

A Growing Consumer Culture

Perhaps the most visible change during the twenties was the emergence of a powerful, urban-dominated **"consumer culture"** in which the mass production and consumption of nationally advertised products came to dictate much of social life and social status. A 1920 newspaper editorial insisted that the American's "first importance to his country is no longer that of citizen but that of consumer. Consumption is a new necessity." The U.S. economy had entered what many called a "New Era" in which the consumption of goods became a national obsession. To keep factory production humming required converting people into carefree shoppers. "People may ruin themselves by saving instead of spending," warned one economist.

In the twenties, old virtues such as hard work, plain living, and frugal money management were challenged by a new system of values celebrating leisure, self-expression, and self-indulgence, all achieved through the purchase of "name-brand" products. "During the war," a journalist noted in 1920, "we accustomed ourselves to doing without, to buying carefully, to using economically. But with the close of the war came reaction. A veritable orgy of extravagant buying is going on. Reckless spending takes the place of saving, waste replaces conservation."

To keep people buying, executives focused their resources on two crucial innovations: marketing and advertising campaigns to increase consumer demand and new ways for buyers to finance purchases over time ("layaway") rather than having to pay cash up front. Installment buying promised instant gratification for consumers ("Buy Now, Pay Later"). Paying with cash and staying out of debt came to be seen as needlessly "old-fashioned"

A MODERN HOME This 1925 Westinghouse advertisement urges homemakers to buy its "Cozy Glow, Jr." heater and "Sol-Lux Luminaire" lamp, among other electrical appliances that "do anything for you in return."

Rise of mass culture: New emphasis on spending, advertising, credit, and conveniences

consumer culture A society in which mass production and consumption of nationally advertised products comes to dictate much of social life and status.

practices. Consumer debt almost tripled during the twenties. Mass advertising, first developed in the late nineteenth century, grew into a huge enterprise driving the mass-production/mass-consumption economy. (Popular new weekday radio programs, for example, were sponsored by national companies trying to sell laundry detergent and hand soap—hence the term *soap operas*.) Because women purchased two thirds of consumer goods during the twenties, advertisers aimed commercials at them. An ad in *Photoplay* magazine targeted the "woman of the house" because "she buys most of the things which go to make the home happy, healthful, and beautiful. Through her slim, safe fingers goes most of the family money."

Perhaps no decade in American history witnessed such dramatic changes in everyday life. Electricity during the twenties was a revolutionary new force. In 1920, only 35 percent of homes had electricity; by 1930, the number was 68 percent. Similar increases occurred in the number of households with indoor plumbing, washing machines, and automobiles. Moderately priced creature comforts and conveniences, such as flush toilets, electric irons and fans, handheld cameras, wristwatches, cigarette lighters, vacuum cleaners, and linoleum floors, became more widely available, especially among the rapidly growing urban middle class.

The Rise of Mass Culture

Mass advertising and marketing campaigns increasingly led to a mass culture: Americans now not only saw and heard the same advertisements and shopped at the same companies' stores, but they also read the same magazines, listened to the same radio programs, and watched the same movies. Through these media, they could follow the lives and careers of the nation's first celebrities and superstars. At the same time, Americans were increasingly on the move: automobiles enabled more people to travel easily, exposing them to new values and different viewpoints. America in the twenties, explained the celebrated New York journalist Walter Lippmann, was experiencing "a vast dissolution of ancient habits" as more and more Americans embraced the New Era's consumer culture.

A Love Affair with Movies

In 1896, a New York City audience viewed the first moving-picture show. By 1924, there were 20,000 movie theaters (the largest of which were called "motion picture palaces") across the nation, showing 700 new "silent" films a year that used captions to show the dialogue. By 1930, even most small towns had theaters, and movies had become the nation's chief form of mass entertainment. Movie attendance during the 1920s averaged 80 million people a week, more than half the national

CHARLIE CHAPLIN An English-born actor who rose to international fame as the "Tramp," Chaplin is pictured above in the 1921 silent film *The Kid*.

population, and attendance surged even more after 1928, when "talking" movies appeared. Americans spent ten times as much on movies as they did on tickets to baseball and football games.

The Radio Craze

Radio broadcasting experienced even more spectacular growth. Between 1922 and 1930, the number of families owning a radio soared from 60,000 to nearly 14 million. The widespread ownership of radios changed the patterns of everyday life. At night after dinner, families gathered around the radio to listen to music, speeches, news broadcasts, weather forecasts, and comedy shows. One ad claimed that the radio "is your theater, your college, your newspaper, your library."

Taking to the Air

Advances in transportation were as significant as the impact of radio and movies. In 1903, Wilbur and Orville Wright, owners of a bicycle shop in Dayton, Ohio, had built and flown the first airplane at Kitty Hawk, North Carolina. The first flight went only a few hundred feet at 34 miles per hour. Airplane technology advanced slowly until the outbreak of war in 1914, after which Europeans rapidly adapted the airplane as a military weapon. When the United States entered the war, it had no combat planes—American pilots flew British or French planes. An American aircraft industry arose during the war but collapsed in the postwar demobilization. Under the Kelly Act of 1925, however, the federal government began to subsidize the industry through the awarding of airmail contracts. The Air Commerce Act of 1926 provided federal funds for the advancement of air transportation and navigation, including the construction of airports.

> Charles Lindbergh's and Amelia Earhart's boost to the new aviation industry

The aviation industry received a huge psychological boost in 1927 when twenty-six-year-old Charles A. Lindbergh Jr. made the first *solo* transatlantic flight, traveling from New York City to Paris in thirty-three and a half hours. The heroic feat, which won him $25,000 and a Congressional Medal of Honor, was truly dramatic: already exhausted from lack of sleep when he took off, Lindbergh flew through severe storms as well as blinding fog for part of the way. When he landed in France, more than 100,000 people greeted him with thunderous cheers, and a New York City parade celebrating Lindbergh's accomplishment surpassed even the celebration of the end of the Great War. Youngsters developed a new dance step in his honor, called the Lindy Hop. Five years after Lindbergh's famous flight, New York City celebrated another pioneering aviator—Amelia Earhart, who became the first woman to fly solo across the Atlantic.

AMELIA EARHART The pioneering aviator would tragically disappear in her 1937 attempt to fly around the world.

The Car Culture

By far the most significant economic and social development of the early twentieth century was the widespread ownership of automobiles. The first motorcar had been manufactured for sale in 1895, but the founding of the Ford Motor Company in 1903 revolutionized the infant industry, for Henry Ford vowed to democratize the automobile. "When I'm through," he predicted, "everybody will be able to afford one, and about everyone will have one."

Ford's Model T, the celebrated "Tin Lizzie," cheap and long-lasting, appeared in 1908 at a price of $850 (about $22,000 at today's prices). By 1924, Ford's increasingly efficient production techniques enabled him to sell the same car for $290 (less than $4,000 today). The Model T changed little from year to year, and it came in only one color: black. Ford ads assured buyers that they "could have any color [they] want, as long as it is black."

In 1916, the total number of cars in the United States passed 1 million; by 1920, more than 8 million were registered, and in 1929 there were more than 23 million. The automobile revolution benefited from the discovery of vast oil fields in Texas, Oklahoma, Wyoming, and California. By 1920, the United States was producing two thirds of the world's oil and gasoline.

Henry Ford and the automotive revolution

The automobile industry became the leading example of modern mass-production techniques and efficiency. Ford's Highland Park plant outside Detroit increased output dramatically by creating a moving assembly line rather than having a crew of workers assemble each car in a fixed position. With conveyors pulling the parts along feeder lines and the chassis moving steadily down an assembly line, each worker performed a single particular task, such as installing a fender or a wheel. This system could produce a new car in ninety-three minutes.

Such efficiency enabled Ford to lower the price of his cars, thereby increasing the number of people who could afford them. For the workers, however, producing cars this way made for a monotonous, mind-numbing experience, especially since Ford prohibited them from talking, sitting, smoking, or singing on the job. But his efficient methods accomplished his goal. During the twenties, the United States built ten times more automobiles than did all of Europe.

Just as the railroad helped transform the pace and scale of life in the second half of the nineteenth century, the mass production of automobiles changed social life during the twentieth century. During the 1920s, Americans literally developed a love affair with cars. In the words of one man, young people viewed the car as "an incredible engine of escape" from parental control and a safe place to "take a girl and hold hands, neck, pet, or . . . go the limit."

Cars helped fuel the economic boom of the 1920s by creating tens of thousands of new jobs and a huge demand for steel, rubber, leather, oil, and gasoline. The ever-expanding car culture stimulated road construction (financed in large part by gasoline taxes), sparked a real estate boom in

HIGHLAND PARK PLANT, 1913 The Ford Motor Company led the way in efficient and cost-cutting production methods. Here, gravity slides and chain conveyors move each automobile down the assembly line. **What was it like to work in one of Ford's factories?**

Florida and California, and dotted the landscape with gasoline stations, traffic lights, billboards, and motor hotels ("motels"). By 1929, the federal government was constructing 10,000 miles of paved highways each year.

Spectator Sports

The widespread ownership of automobiles as well as rising incomes changed the way people spent their leisure time. City dwellers could easily drive into the countryside; visit friends and relatives; and go to ballparks, stadiums, or boxing rings to see baseball or football games and prizefights. During the 1920s, Americans fell in love with mass spectator sports.

Created in the 1870s in rural areas, baseball had, by the 1920s, gone urban and earned its label of "the national pastime." With larger-than-life heroes such as New York Yankee stars George Herman "Babe" Ruth Jr. and Henry Louis "Lou" Gehrig, professional baseball teams attracted huge crowds.

In 1922, the Yankees built a new stadium, called the "house that Ruth built," and they went on to win World Series championships in 1923, 1927, and 1928. More than 20 million people attended professional baseball games in 1927, the year that Ruth, the "Sultan of Swat," set a record by hitting sixty home runs and leading the league in most other hitting categories. Because baseball was still a racially segregated sport, so-called Negro leagues provided leagues for African Americans to play in and watch.

> Mass popularity of baseball, football, and boxing

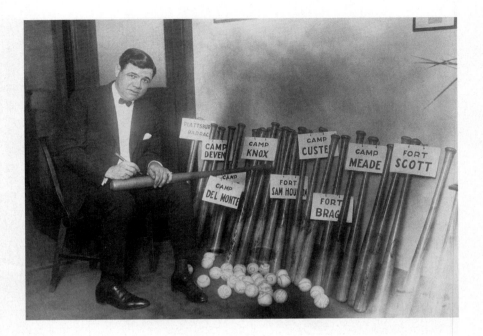

BABE RUTH This star pitcher and outfielder won the hearts of Americans with the Boston Red Sox, New York Yankees, and finally the Boston Braves. Here, he autographs bats and balls for military training camps.

Football, especially at the college level, also attracted huge crowds. It, too, benefited from superstars such as Harold Edward "Red" Grange, the phenomenal running back for the University of Illinois and the first athlete to appear on the cover of *Time* magazine. In a 1924 game against the University of Michigan, the bruising "Galloping Ghost" scored a touchdown each of the first four times he carried the ball; after Illinois won, students carried Grange on their shoulders for two miles across the campus. "What a football player," a sports writer marveled. "He is melody and symphony. He is crashing sound. He is brute force." When Grange signed a contract with the Chicago Bears in 1926, he single-handedly made professional football competitive with baseball as a spectator sport.

What Ruth and Grange were to their sports, William Harrison "Jack" Dempsey was to boxing. In 1919, he won the world heavyweight title from Jess Willard, a giant of a man weighing 300 pounds and standing six and a half feet tall. Dempsey knocked him down seven times in the first round. After Willard, his face bruised and bloodied, threw in the towel in the fourth round, Dempsey became a national celebrity and a wealthy man.

Like Babe Ruth, the brawling Dempsey was especially popular with working-class men, for he too had been born poor and lived for years as a "hobo," wandering the rails in search of work and challenging toughs in bars to fight for money. In 1927, when James Joseph "Gene" Tunney defeated Dempsey, more than 105,000 people attended, including a thousand reporters, ten state governors, and numerous Hollywood celebrities. Some 60 million people listened to the fight over the radio. Dempsey was more than a champion; he was a hero to millions. A leading sportswriter stressed that he was "warm and generous, a free spender when he had it and a soft touch for anybody down on his luck."

The "Jazz Age"

While most Americans of all ages became devoted to spectator sports, radio programs, and movies during the twenties, many young people focused their energies on social and cultural rebellion—daring new fads and fashions, new music, new attitudes, and new ways of having fun. F. Scott Fitzgerald, a boyishly handsome Princeton University dropout, became "the voice of his generation" after his best-selling first novel, *This Side of Paradise* (1920), re-created the unadulterated hedonism of student life at Princeton. Fitzgerald made famous the "**Jazz Age**" as the evocative label for the spirit of rebelliousness and spontaneity he saw welling up among young Americans. As one of the most popular songs of the twenties proclaimed, "In the meantime, in between time, ain't we got fun!"

The Birth of Jazz

Fitzgerald's celebration of the "Jazz Age" referred to the raging popularity of jazz music, a dynamic blend of several musical traditions. It had first emerged as piano-based "ragtime" at the end of the nineteenth century. Thereafter,

CORE **OBJECTIVE**

2. Describe other major new social and cultural trends and movements that became prominent during the twenties, and explain how they challenged traditional standards and customs.

Jazz Age Term coined by writer F. Scott Fitzgerald to characterize the spirit of rebellion and spontaneity among young Americans in the 1920s, a spirit epitomized by the hugely popular jazz music of the era.

DUKE ELLINGTON Jazz emerged in the 1920s as an especially American expression of the modernist spirit. African American artists bent musical conventions to give freer rein to improvisation and sensuality. **What were some of the critiques levied against the Jazz movement, and who made them?**

African American musicians such as Jelly Roll Morton, Duke Ellington, Louis Armstrong, and Bessie Smith (the "Empress of the Blues") combined the energies of ragtime with the emotions of the blues to create *jazz*, originally an African American slang term meaning sexual intercourse. With its constant improvisations and variations and its sensual spontaneity, jazz appealed to many people of all ethnicities and ages because it celebrated pleasure and immediacy, letting go and enjoying the freedom of the moment. In 1925, an African American journalist announced that jazz had "absorbed the national spirit, that tremendous spirit of go, the nervousness, lack of conventionality and boisterous good-nature characteristic of the American, white or black."

The culture of jazz quickly spread from its origins in New Orleans, Kansas City, Memphis, and St. Louis to the African American neighborhoods of Harlem in New York City and Chicago's South Side. Large dance halls met the swelling demand for jazz music and the dance craze that accompanied it, including new dances like the Charleston and the Black Bottom whose sexually provocative movements shocked traditionalists.

Many Americans were not fans of jazz. In 1921, the *Ladies' Home Journal* discouraged jazz dancing because of its "direct appeal to the body's sensory centers," and Princeton professor Henry van Dyke dismissed jazz as "merely an irritation of the nerves of hearing, a sensual teasing of the strings of physical passion." Such criticism, however, failed to stem the frenzied popularity of jazz, which swept across Europe as well as America.

A Revolution in Manners and Morals

Much of the shock to old-timers during the Jazz Age came from the revolution in manners and morals among young people, especially those on college campuses. From novels such as *This Side of Paradise* as well as dozens of magazine articles, middle-class Americans learned about the hidden world of "flaming youth" (the title of another popular novel): wild parties, free love, speakeasies, skinny-dipping, and "petting" in automobiles on lovers' lanes. A promotional poster for the 1923 silent film *Flaming Youth* asked: "How Far Can a Girl Go?" Other ads claimed the movie appealed especially to "neckers, petters, white kisses, red kisses, pleasure-mad daughters, [and] sensation-craving mothers."

The increasingly frank treatment of sex during the twenties resulted in part from the spreading influence of Sigmund Freud, the founder of modern psychoanalysis. Freud, an Austrian trained as a physician, changed the way people understood their behavior and feelings by insisting that the mind is essentially and mysteriously "conflicted" by unconscious efforts to control or repress powerful irrational impulses and sexual desires ("libido").

By 1909, when Freud first visited the United States to lecture at Clark University in Massachusetts, he was surprised to find

SIGMUND FREUD The founder of modern psychoanalysis, Freud's writings on the subconscious, dreams, and latent sexual yearnings captured the attention of many Americans, especially young adults.

himself famous "even in prudish America." It did not take long for his ideas to penetrate society at large. Psychoanalysis soon became the most celebrated—and controversial—technique for helping troubled people come to grips with their psychic demons. Through "talk therapy," patients discussed their inner frustrations and revealed their repressed fears and urges. By 1916, there were some 500 psychoanalysts in New York City alone.

For many young Americans, Freud provided scientific justification for rebelling against social conventions and indulging in sex. Some oversimplified his theories by claiming that sexual pleasure was essential for emotional health, that all forms of sexual activity were good, and that all inhibitions—feelings of restraint—about sex were bad. Traditionalists, on the other hand, were shocked at the scandalous behavior of rebellious young women who claimed to be acting out Freud's theories. "One hears it said," complained a Baptist magazine, "that the girls are actually tempting the boys more than the boys do the girls, by their dress and conversation."

Young women emboldened by gaining the right to vote sought other freedoms as well. The empowered "new woman" of the twenties eagerly discarded the confining wardrobe of their "frumpy" mothers—pinched-in corsets, choking girdles, layers of petticoats, and floor-length dresses—in favor of more daring attire.

In 1919, skirts were typically six inches above the ground; by 1927, they were at the knee. The shortest ones were worn by the so-called **flappers**, young women who—in defiance of proper prewar standards—drove automobiles; "bobbed" their hair (cut it short, requiring the invention of the "bobby pin"); and wore minimal underclothing, gauzy fabrics, sheer stockings, and plenty of makeup, especially brightly colored rouge and lipstick and smoky mascara. They also often joined young men in smoking cigarettes, (illegally) drinking and gambling, and shaking and shimmying to the sensual energies of jazz music.

Self-consciously outrageous and outlandish, flappers wanted more out of life than marriage and motherhood. Their carefree version of feminism was fun-loving, defiant, and self-indulgent. The flappers aroused furious criticism. A Catholic priest in Brooklyn complained that the feminism of the 1920s had provoked a "pandemonium of powder, a riot of rouge, and a moral anarchy of dress." In discussing the flapper phenomenon, a newspaper columnist reported that "the world is divided into those who delight in her, those who fear her, and those who try pathetically to take her as a matter of course."

THE BEAUTIFUL AND THE DAMNED The wayward daughter of a strict Alabama judge, Zelda Fitzgerald famously lived up to husband Scott's description of her as the "First American Flapper." In an outfit typical of flappers, Zelda Fitzgerald poses with her husband on the Riviera in 1926.

flappers Young women of the 1920s whose rebellion against prewar standards of femininity included wearing shorter dresses, bobbing their hair, dancing to jazz music, driving cars, smoking cigarettes, and indulging in illegal drinking and gambling.

Women in the 1920s

Most women in the 1920s were not flappers, however. Lillian Symes, a long-time activist in the women's movement, stressed that her "generation of feminists" had little in common with the "spike-heeled, over-rouged flapper of today. We grew up before the postwar disillusionment engulfed the youth of the land."

The conservative political mood of the twenties helped to steer many women back into their traditional roles as homemakers, and college curricula began to shift accordingly. At New York's Vassar College, an all-women's school, students took domesticated courses such as "Husband and Wife," "Motherhood," and "The Family as an Economic Unit." At the same time, fewer college-educated women pursued careers outside the home: the proportion of physicians who were women fell from 6 to 4 percent during the twenties, with similar reductions among dentists, architects, and chemists. A student at all-female Smith College expressed frustration "that a woman must choose between a home and her work, when a man may have both. There must be a way out, and it is the problem of our generation to find the way."

As before, most women who worked outside the home labored in unskilled, low-wage jobs. Only 4 percent of working women in the 1920s were salaried professionals; the vast majority worked for hourly wages. Some women moved into new vocations created by the growing consumer culture, such as accounting assistants and department-store clerks. The number of beauty shops soared from 5,000 in 1920 to 40,000 in 1930, creating new jobs for hair stylists, manicurists, and cosmeticians.

The majority of women, however, remained either full-time wives and mothers or household servants. Fortunately, the advent of electricity and electrical appliances—vacuum cleaners, toasters, stoves, washing machines, irons—made housework quicker and easier than it had been for their mothers and grandmothers. African American and Mexican American women faced the greatest challenges. As a New York City newspaper observed, they did the "work which white women will not do." Women of color usually worked as maids, laundresses, or seamstresses, or on farms.

The Harlem Renaissance

As their Great Migration from the South continued into the twenties, African Americans found new freedom of speech and action in northern settings; they also gained leverage as voters by settling in states with many electoral votes. With these new opportunities came a bristling spirit of protest known as the **Harlem Renaissance**, the nation's first self-conscious black literary and artistic movement.

The movement started among the fast-growing African American community in the Harlem neighborhood of northern Manhattan in New York City. In 1890, one in seventy people in Manhattan had been African American; by 1930, it was one in nine. The "great, dark city" of Harlem, as poet

Harlem Renaissance
The nation's first self-conscious black literary and artistic movement; centered in New York City's Harlem district, which had a largely black population in the wake of the Great Migration from the South.

Langston Hughes called it, contained more blacks per square mile than any other urban neighborhood in the nation. Their numbers generated a sense of common identity, growing power, and distinctive self-expression that soon made Harlem the cultural capital of African American life. Dotted with raucous nightclubs where writers and painters discussed literature and art while listening to jazz and drinking bootleg alcohol, Harlem became what journalists called the "Nightclub Capital of the World."

The Harlem Renaissance writers celebrated African American culture, especially jazz and the blues. As Langston Hughes wrote, "I am a Negro—and beautiful. . . . The night is beautiful. So [are] the faces of my people." He loved Africa and its cultural heritage but declared, "I was not Africa. I was Chicago and Kansas City and Broadway and Harlem."

James Weldon Johnson, a poet, lawyer, and civil rights activist, coined the term *Aframerican* to designate Americans with African ancestry, whom he called "conscious collaborators" in the creation of American society and culture. By 1930, the Harlem Renaissance writers had produced dozens of

AUGUSTA SAVAGE Shown here with her statue *Realization* (1938), Savage found success in America and abroad, though after much struggle with racism.

novels and volumes of poetry; several Broadway plays; and a flood of short stories, essays, and films. A people capable of producing such great art and literature, Johnson declared, should never again be "looked upon as inferior."

Garveyism

The celebration of African American culture also found expression in what came to be called Negro nationalism, which promoted black separatism from mainstream American life. Its leading spokesman was the flamboyant Marcus Garvey. In 1916, Garvey brought to Harlem the headquarters of the Universal Negro Improvement Association (UNIA), which he had started in his native Jamaica two years before.

Garvey insisted that blacks had *nothing* in common with whites—and that was a good thing. He therefore called for racial separation instead of integration. "The black skin," he stressed, "is not a badge of shame, but rather a glorious symbol of national greatness." In passionate speeches and in editorials in his newspaper, the *Negro World*, Garvey urged African Americans to separate themselves from the surrounding white culture. He saw every white person as a "potential Klansman" and endorsed the "social and political separation of all peoples to the extent that they promote their own ideals and civilization."

MARCUS GARVEY Founder of the Universal Negro Improvement Association and leading spokesman for "Negro nationalism," Garvey's ideas of racial separation and pride resonated with many African Americans in the 1920s and beyond.

The NAACP: Progressive interracial activism on racial issues

National Association for the Advancement of Colored People (NAACP) Organization founded in 1910 by black activists and white progressives that promoted education as a means of combating social problems and focused on legal action to secure the civil rights supposedly guaranteed by the Fourteenth and Fifteenth Amendments.

The UNIA grew rapidly amid the racial tensions of the postwar years. By 1923, Garvey claimed to have as many as 4 million UNIA members served by 800 offices across the country. Garvey's goal was to build an all-black empire in Africa: "We will let white men have America and Europe, but we are going to have Africa." To that end, he began calling himself the "Provisional President of Africa," raising funds to send Americans to Africa, and expelling any UNIA member who married a white.

Garvey's message of black nationalism and racial solidarity appealed to many African Americans living in slums in northern cities, but it appalled other black leaders. W. E. B. Du Bois, for example, labeled Garvey "the most dangerous enemy of the Negro race.... He is either a lunatic or a traitor." An African American newspaper pledged to help "drive Garvey and Garveyism in all its sinister viciousness from the American soil."

Garvey's crusade collapsed in 1923 when a court convicted him of mail fraud related to overselling shares of stock in a steamship corporation intended to transport American blacks to Africa. Sentenced to five years in prison, he was pardoned in 1927 by President Calvin Coolidge on the condition that he be deported to Jamaica. Garvey died in obscurity in 1940, but the memory of his movement kept alive an undercurrent that would reemerge in the 1960s under the slogan "black power."

The NAACP

A more lasting force for racial equality during the twenties was the **National Association for the Advancement of Colored People (NAACP)**, founded in 1910 by black activists and white progressives. African American NAACP leaders came mainly from the Niagara Movement, a group that had met each year since 1905 at places associated with the anti-slavery movement (Niagara Falls; Oberlin, Ohio; Boston; Harpers Ferry) and issued defiant statements against discrimination. Within a few years, the NAACP had become a broad-based national organization. It embraced the progressive idea that the solution to social problems begins with education, by informing people about the harsh realities of social problems. W. E. B. Du Bois became the organization's director of publicity and research and the editor of its journal, *Crisis*.

The NAACP focused its political strategy on legal action to bring the Fourteenth and Fifteenth Amendments back to life. One early victory came with *Guinn v. United States* (1915), in which the Supreme Court struck down Oklahoma's efforts to deprive African Americans of the vote. In *Buchanan v. Warley* (1917), the Court invalidated a residential segregation ordinance in Louisville, Kentucky. In 1919, the NAACP launched a national campaign against lynching, still a common form of vigilante racist violence. An anti-lynching bill to make mob murder a federal crime passed the House in 1922 but lost to a filibuster by white southerners in the Senate.

The Modernist Revolt

CORE **OBJECTIVE**

3. Explain what "modernism" means in intellectual and artistic terms and how the modernist movement influenced American culture in the early twentieth century.

"The world broke in two in 1922 or thereabouts." So said the celebrated American writer Willa Cather. She meant that during the twenties a civil war erupted between cultural modernists and their traditionalist critics. Modernists were rebellious intellectuals, writers, and artists who engaged in a relentless search for new and scandalous modes of expression and behavior. They saw the start of the twentieth century as a historical hinge opening the way for a new worldview that rejected traditional values (progress, reason, and even God) and notions of reality.

To represent the disorienting changes associated with modernity, they adopted radical new forms of artistic expression. In 1922, the Irish modernist James Joyce published his pathbreaking novel *Ulysses* and the Anglo-American poet T. S. Eliot wrote "The Waste Land." Critics charged that Eliot, Joyce, and others were "ruining" literature. One said that Eliot's impenetrable writing was "a gash at the root of our poetry." Modernists fought back, claiming that they were simply acknowledging the arrival of an unsettling new way of viewing life and expressing its raucous energies.

Modernism, as much a state of mind as a movement, did not simply drop out of the sky in 1922. It had been years in the making. During the early twentieth century, people were both inspired and terrified by an explosion of new scientific and technical knowledge that unveiled troubling mysteries of the universe. Since the eighteenth-century Enlightenment, conventional wisdom had held that the universe was governed by basic laws of time and energy, light and motion. This rational world of order and certainty disintegrated in the early twentieth century, thanks to the discoveries of European physicists.

Science and Modernism: Einstein and Relativity

In the first decade of the twentieth century, Albert Einstein, a young German physicist, published several research papers that changed science forever. The first paper, for which he was later awarded the Nobel Prize, described how light was not only a wave of energy but also a stream of tiny particles, called quanta or photons.

This wave-particle duality became the foundation of what is known as quantum physics and would later provide the theoretical basis for such developments as television, laser beams, and semiconductors used to make computers. Einstein's second paper confirmed the existence of molecules and atoms by showing statistically how their random collisions explained the jerky motion of tiny particles in water.

Yet it was Einstein's third paper that truly upended traditional notions of the universe. It grew out of one of his favorite thought experiments: if you

ALBERT EINSTEIN One of the most influential scientists of the twentieth century, Einstein was awarded a Nobel Prize in 1921.

Modernism and science: Einstein's breakthroughs and impact

were in a train that neared the speed of light, would you see time and space differently? Einstein's reflections led to his special theory of relativity (1905), which explains that no matter how fast one is moving toward or away from a source of light, the speed of that light beam will appear the same, a constant 186,000 miles per second. But as a train accelerates to near the speed of light, time on the train will slow down from the perspective of a stationary observer, and the train itself will get shorter and heavier.

The most important of Einstein's shocking ideas was his general theory of relativity (1916), which maintained that the fundamental concepts of space, time, matter, and energy were not distinct, independent things with continuous dimensions, as Sir Isaac Newton had assumed in the eighteenth century. Instead, they were interacting elements in constant flux as the result of gravity's effects on them.

Nothing is fixed or absolute in Einstein's bewildering universe; everything is *relative* to the location and motion of the observer and the effects of gravity, which warps space and time. Things are big or little, long or short, slow or fast, light or heavy only by comparison to something else. So, for example, the particular spot on earth on which we are positioned at any given moment is not fixed but is, relative to the sun, moving through space at 18.5 miles per second. Einstein also revealed that objects shrink as they approach the speed of light, that beams of light are bent by gravity, and that all physical matter is simply stored energy.

Einstein revolutionized time, space, and light. Although few understood the details of his theories, many began to embrace the idea that there were no absolute standards or fixed points of reference in the world. During the twenties, the idea of "relativity" gradually emerged in popular discussions of decidedly nonscientific topics such as sexuality, the arts, and politics; there was less faith in absolutes, not only of time and space but also of truth and morality. Just as Darwinism became not just a biological theory but also a social, economic, and political force, so too did Einstein's concept of relativity shape many of the intellectual, cultural, and social currents of the twentieth century. In 1920, the year before Einstein was awarded the Nobel Prize, an American journalist said that his theories had moved physics into the region of "metaphysics, where paradox and magic take the place of solid fact . . . and common sense." The farther scientists reached out into the universe and into the microscopic world of the atom, the more traditional certainties dissolved.

Modernist Art and Literature

modernism An early-twentieth-century cultural movement that rejected traditional notions of reality and adopted radical new forms of artistic expression.

The scientific breakthroughs associated with Freud, Einstein, and others helped to inspire a "modernist" cultural revolution among intellectuals and creative artists. **Modernism** as a recognizable movement in the arts and ideas had appeared first in the capitals of Europe—London, Paris, Berlin, and

Vienna—in the 1890s. By the second decade of the twentieth century, cultural modernism had spread to the United States, especially New York City and Chicago. It arose out of a widespread recognition that Western civilization was experiencing bewildering changes as new technologies, modes of transportation and communication, and startling scientific discoveries transformed the nature of everyday life and the way people "saw" the world.

The shocking horrors of the Great War expanded the appeal of modernism—and helped explain why modernists cared little for established standards of good taste or for history. To be "modern" in the early twentieth century was to break free of tradition, by taking chances, violating artistic rules and moral restrictions, and behaving in deliberately shocking ways, including treating sexuality with a startling frankness. "Art," said a modernist painter, "is meant to disturb."

As an experimental cultural impulse, full of astonishing energy and contradictions, surprise and scandal, modernism manifested three unsettling assumptions: (1) God did not exist; (2) "reality" was not rational, orderly, or obvious; and (3) in the aftermath of the Great War, social progress could no longer be taken for granted.

These modernist premises led writers, painters, musicians, dancers, and architects to risk poverty and humiliation by rudely rebelling against good taste, old-fashioned morals, and old-time religion. In its simplest sense, modernism was a disrespectful war of new values against old ones. Experimental poet Ezra Pound provided the slogan for modernism when he exclaimed, "Make It New!"

Like many previous cultural movements, modernism involved a new way of *seeing* the world by a new intellectual and cultural elite determined to capture and express the hidden realm of imagination and dreams. Doing so, however, often made their experimental writing, art, music, and dance vague and obscure, famously difficult to understand, interpret, or explain. "The pure modernist is merely a snob," explained a British writer. For many modernists, being misunderstood by the general public was a badge of honor. The American experimentalist writer Gertrude Stein, for example, declared that a novel "which tells about what happens is of no interest." Instead of depicting "real" life or telling recognizable stories, she was interested in playing with language. Words, not people, are the characters in her writings.

Modernism provoked, perplexed, and upset people. Until the twentieth century, most writers and artists had taken for granted an accessible "real" world that could be readily observed, scientifically explained, and accurately represented in words or paint or music. The young generation of modernist rebels, however, applied Einstein's ideas about relativity to a world in which "reality" no longer had an objective or recognizable basis. They agreed wholeheartedly with Freud that reality was subjective, something to be imagined and expressed by one's innermost being rather than reproduced from the visible world. Walter Pach, an early American champion of modern art, explained that modernism resulted from the discovery by Freud and others of "the role played by the unconscious in our lives."

> Modernism as a cultural movement

***RUSSIAN BALLET* (1916)** Jewish American artist Max Weber's painting is a modernist take on a traditional subject. Splicing the scene of the performance into planes of jarring colors, this painting exemplifies the impact of psychoanalysis and the theory of relativity on the arts.

For modernists such as the Spanish painter Pablo Picasso and the Irish writer James Joyce, then, art involved an unpredictable journey into the realm of individual fantasy and dreams, exploring and expressing the personal, the unknown, the primitive, the abstract. In the early-twentieth-century art world, modernists discarded literal representation of recognizable subjects in favor of vibrant color masses, simplified forms, or geometric shapes. American artist Marsden Hartley reported from Paris that his reading of Freud and other "new psychologists" had led him to quit painting objects from "real life" and instead paint "intuitive abstractions."

The Armory Show

Modernism and art: The Armory Show of 1913

The crusade to bring European-inspired modernism to the United States reached a climax in the Armory Show of 1913, the most scandalous event in the history of American art. Mabel Dodge, one of the organizers, wrote that the exhibition would cause "a riot and revolution and things will never be the same afterwards."

To house the 1,200 modernist works of art collected from more than 300 painters and sculptors in America and Europe, the two dozen young painters who organized the show leased the vast 69th Army Regiment Armory in New York City. The Armory Show, officially known as the International Exhibition of Modern Art, opened on February 17, 1913. As Dodge had predicted, it created an immediate sensation.

For many who toured the Armory Show, modern art became the thing that they loved to hate. Modernism, growled a prominent art critic, "is nothing else than the total destruction of the art of painting." The *New York Times* warned visitors who shared the "old belief in reality" that they would enter "a stark region of abstractions" at the "lunatic asylum" show that was "hideous to our unaccustomed eyes." The experimentalist ("*avant-garde*") artists whose works were on display (including paintings by Vincent Van Gogh, Paul Gaugin, and Henri Matisse as well as Cezanne and Picasso) were "in love with science but not with objective reality," the *Times* critic complained, adding that they had produced paintings "revolting in their inhumanity." Former president Theodore Roosevelt dismissed the show as "repellent from every standpoint"—an indication of the gap separating political progressivism from artistic modernism.

THE ARMORY SHOW, 1913 Celebrated by some and hated by others, the Armory Show brought widespread attention to the modernist movement. **What elements of modernism were commonly criticized by the show's visitors?**

Yet the Armory Show also generated excitement. "A new world has arisen before our eyes," announced an art magazine. "To miss modern art," a critic stressed, "is to miss one of the few thrills that life holds." From New York, the show went on to Chicago and Boston, where it aroused similarly strong responses and attracted overflow crowds. A quarter-million people viewed the exhibition in the three cities.

After the Armory Show, modern art became one of the nation's favorite topics of debate. Many artists, writers, and critics adjusted to the shock of modernism and found a new faith in the disturbing powers of art. "America in its newness," predicted Walt Kuhn, a painter who helped organize the exhibition, "is destined to become the coming center" of modernism. Indeed, the Museum of Modern Art, founded in New York City in 1929, came to house the world's most celebrated collection of avant-garde paintings and sculpture.

The "Lost Generation"

In addition to modernism, the arts and literature of the twenties were also greatly influenced by the horrors of the Great War. F. Scott Fitzgerald wrote in *This Side of Paradise* (1920) that the younger generation of Americans, the "sad young men" who had fought in Europe to "make the world safe for democracy," had "grown up to find all Gods dead, all wars fought, all faiths in man shaken." Cynicism had displaced idealism in the wake of the war's

Modernism and literature: The Lost Generation

horrific senselessness. As Fitzgerald asserted, "There's only one lesson to be learned from life anyway. . . . That there's no lesson to be learned from life."

Fitzgerald, Ernest Hemingway, and other self-conscious young modernists came to be labeled the Lost Generation—those who had lost faith in the values and institutions of Western civilization and were frantically looking for new gods to worship. It was Gertrude Stein who in 1921 told Hemingway that he and his friends who had served in the war were "a lost generation." When Hemingway objected, she held her ground. "You are [lost]. You have no respect for anything. You drink yourselves to death."

In his first novel, *The Sun Also Rises* (1926), Hemingway used the phrase "lost generation" as the book's opening quotation. The novel centers on Jake Barnes, a young American journalist castrated by a war injury. His despairing impotence leads him to wander the cafes and nightclubs of postwar Europe with his unhappy friends, who acknowledge that they are all wounded and sterile in their own way: they have lost their innocence, their illusions, and their motivation to do anything with their lives in a world that had lost its meaning through the disorienting discoveries of modern science and the horrors of world war.

CORE **OBJECTIVE**

4. Identify important examples of reactionary conservatism in the decade, and analyze their impact on government policies.

The Reactionary Twenties

The self-indulgent excesses of the "lost generation" made little sense to the vast majority of Americans during the twenties, many of whom aggressively defended established values, old certainties, and the comfort of past routines. The reactionary conservatism of the twenties fed on the energies provided by militant traditional Protestantism and a revival of **nativism**.

Nativism

The Red Scare of 1919 and a postwar surge of immigration helped generate a new wave of anti-immigrant hysteria. From June 1920 to June 1921, more than 800,000 foreigners arrived in the United States, 65 percent of them from southern and eastern Europe. In the early 1920s, more than half of the white men and a third of the white women working in mines, mills, and factories were European immigrants, some of whom had brought with them to America a passion for socialism or anarchism. The foreign connections of so many political radicals triggered efforts by "nativists" to close the door to immigrants. Many nativists also tried to stir up hatred of immigrants already in the United States and of their "un-American" religions and ideas.

nativism Reactionary conservative movement characterized by heightened nationalism, anti-immigrant sentiment, and laws setting stricter regulations on immigration.

Sacco and Vanzetti

The most celebrated criminal case of the 1920s reinforced the connection between European immigrants and political radicalism. On May 5, 1920, two Italian immigrants who described themselves as revolutionary anarchists eager to topple the American government, shoemaker Nicola Sacco and fish peddler Bartolomeo Vanzetti, were arrested outside Boston, Massachusetts. They were charged with stealing $16,000 from a shoe factory payroll and killing the paymaster and a guard. Both men were armed with loaded pistols when arrested, both lied to police about their activities, and both were identified by eyewitnesses. But the stolen money was never found.

The **Sacco and Vanzetti case** occurred at the height of Italian immigration to the United States and against the backdrop of numerous terror attacks by anarchists, some of which Sacco and Vanzetti had participated in. Such a charged atmosphere ensured that their 1921 trial would become a huge public spectacle. The presiding judge openly revealed his biases, referring to the defendants as "anarchist bastards." Amid such a heated

SACCO AND VANZETTI The trial and conviction of these working-class Italian immigrants became a public spectacle amid the growing mood of nativism.

atmosphere, Sacco and Vanzetti were convicted and sentenced to death: their appeals lasted seven years before they were executed on August 23, 1927, still claiming their innocence. By then, Sacco and Vanzetti had become martyrs, victims of American injustice to millions around the world. The case remains passionately disputed today.

Immigration Restriction

Concerns about an invasion of foreign radicals led a reactionary Congress to pass the Emergency Immigration Act of 1921, which restricted annual immigration from each European country to 3 percent of the total number of that nationality represented in the 1910 census. The **Immigration Act of 1924** reduced the number to 2 percent and changed the standard to the 1890 census, which had included fewer "new" immigrants from southern and eastern Europe. The law also set a permanent overall limitation, effective in 1929, of slightly over 150,000 new arrivals per year.

The purpose of the new quotas was clear: to favor immigrants from northern and western Europe and reduce those from southern and eastern Europe. A Kansas congressman expressed the prejudices felt by many rural American Protestants: "On the one side is beer, bolshevism, unassimilating settlements and perhaps many flags—on the other side is constitutional government; one flag, stars and stripes."

The new immigration laws excluded anyone from Japan or China. On the other hand, the Immigration Act of 1924 left the gate open to new arrivals from countries in the Western Hemisphere, so that an unintended result of the law was a substantial increase in the Hispanic Catholic population of the

Sacco and Vanzetti case (1921)
Trial of two Italian immigrants that occurred at the height of Italian immigration and against the backdrop of numerous terror attacks by anarchists; despite a lack of clear evidence, the two defendants, both self-professed anarchists, were convicted of murder and were executed.

Immigration Act of 1924
Federal legislation intended to favor northern and western European immigrants over those from southern and eastern Europe by restricting the number of immigrants from any one European country to 2 percent of the total number of immigrants per year, with an overall limit of slightly over 150,000 new arrivals per year.

United States. People of Latin American descent (chiefly Mexicans, Puerto Ricans, and Cubans) became the fastest-growing ethnic minority in the country.

The New Klan

A revived Ku Klux Klan

The most violent of the reactionary movements during the twenties was a revived Ku Klux Klan, the infamous post–Civil War group of anti-black racists that had re-created itself in 1915. The old Klan had died out in the 1870s once white Democrats regained control of the former Confederate states after Reconstruction. Now, no longer simply a southern group intent on terrorizing African Americans, the new Klan was a nationwide organization devoted to "100 percent Americanism"; only "natives"—white Protestants born in the United States—could be members.

With its secret signs and codes, weird rituals, and its costumes featuring white sheets and spooky hats, the Klan promoted strict personal morality, opposed bootleg liquor, and preached hatred against not only African Americans but Roman Catholics, Jews, immigrants, Communists, and atheists. The United States was no melting pot, shouted Imperial Wizard William J. Simmons, a traveling salesman turned Methodist preacher: "It is a garbage can! . . . When the hordes of aliens walk to the ballot box and their

KU KLUX KLAN RALLY In 1925, the KKK held an expansive march down Pennsylvania Avenue in Washington, D.C. **What contributed to the resurgence of the KKK during the 1920s, and how did the organization's ideology shift with the times?**

votes outnumber yours, then that alien horde has got you by the throat." The new Klan included a women's auxiliary group called the Kemellia, and whole families attended Klan gatherings, "klasping" hands while listening to inflammatory speeches, watching fireworks, and burning crosses.

The reborn Klan, headquartered in Atlanta and calling itself the "Invisible Empire," grew rapidly in cities and small towns across the nation. It was no longer simply a southern organization. During the 1920s, 40 percent of Klan members were in three midwestern states (Illinois, Indiana, and Ohio), and Connecticut had more Klan members than Mississippi. Recruiters, called Kleagles, played "upon whatever prejudices were most acute in a particular area." In Texas, the Klan fed on prejudice against Mexicans. In California, it focused on Japanese Americans, and in New York the enemy was primarily Jews and Catholics. The new Klan also benefited from the war on alcohol. Klansmen declared war on bootleggers and moonshiners.

Most Klan members were small farmers, sharecroppers, or wage workers, but the organization also attracted doctors, lawyers, accountants, business leaders, teachers, and even politicians. As a prominent southern journalist observed, the new Klan was "anti-Negro, anti-alien, anti-red, anti-Catholic, anti-Jew, anti-Darwin, anti-Modern, anti-Liberal; Fundamentalist, vastly Moral, militantly Protestant." By 1923, the Klan had more than 4 million members, including judges, mayors, sheriffs, state legislators, six governors, and three U.S. senators.

The Grand Dragon of Indiana, a con man named David C. Stephenson, grew so influential in electing local and state officials (the "kluxing" of America, as he called it) that he boasted, "I am the law in Indiana!" Klan-endorsed candidates won the Indiana governorship and controlled the state legislature. At the 1924 Republican State Convention, Stephenson patrolled the aisles with a pistol and later confessed that he "purchased the county and state officials." Stephenson, who had grown wealthy by skimming from the dues he collected from Klan members as well as selling robes and hoods, planned to run for president of the United States.

But the Klan's influence, both in Indiana and nationwide, crumbled after Stephenson was sentenced to life in prison in 1925 for kidnapping and raping a twenty-eight-year-old woman who then committed suicide. At the same time, several states passed anti-Klan laws and others banned the wearing of masks. By 1930, nationwide membership had dwindled to 100,000, mostly southerners. Yet the bigoted impulse underlying the Klan lived on, fed by deep-seated fears and hatreds that have yet to disappear.

Fundamentalism

While the Klan saw a threat mainly in the "alien menace," many defenders of "old-time religion" felt threatened by ideas circulating in "progressive" Protestant churches, especially the idea that the Bible should be studied in the light of modern scholarship (the "higher criticism") or that it should

SCOPES MONKEY TRIAL
In this snapshot of the courtroom, Scopes (far left) clasps his face in his hands and listens to his attorney (second from right). Darrow (far right) listens, too, visibly affected by the sweltering heat and humidity.

accommodate Darwinian theories of biological evolution. In response to such "modern" notions, conservative Protestants embraced a militant new fundamentalism, which was distinguished less by a shared faith than by a posture of hostility toward "liberal" beliefs and its insistence on the literal truth of the Bible.

Fundamentalist hostility toward Darwinism: The Scopes Trial

Among national leaders, only the "Great Commoner," William Jennings Bryan, the former congressman, secretary of state, and three-time presidential candidate, had the support, prestige, and eloquence to transform fundamentalism into a popular crusade. He passionately denounced Charles Darwin's theory of evolution, insisting that "all the ills from which America suffers can be traced back to the teaching of evolution." Bryan supported anti-evolution bills in numerous state legislatures, but the only victories came in the South. Governor Miriam "Ma" Ferguson of Texas outlawed school textbooks that included sections on Darwinism. "I am a Christian mother," she declared, "and I am not going to let that kind of rot go into Texas schoolbooks."

The dramatic climax of the fundamentalist war on Darwinism came in Tennessee, where in 1925 the legislature outlawed the teaching of evolution in public schools and colleges. In the tiny mining town of Dayton, in eastern Tennessee, civic leaders eager for publicity persuaded John T. Scopes, a twenty-four-year-old high-school science teacher and part-time football coach, to become a test case against the new law. Scopes used a textbook that taught Darwinian evolution, and police arrested him for doing so. The town boosters succeeded beyond their wildest hopes: the **Scopes Trial** received worldwide publicity—but it was not flattering to Dayton.

Scopes Trial (1925) Highly publicized trial of a high-school teacher in Tennessee for violating a state law that prohibited the teaching of evolution; the trial was seen as the climax of the fundamentalist war on Darwinism.

Before the start of the twelve-day "monkey trial" on July 10, 1925, the narrow streets of Dayton swarmed with evangelists, atheists, hot-dog and soda-pop peddlers, and hundreds of newspaper and radio reporters. A man tattooed with Bible verses preached on a street corner while a live monkey was paraded about town.

The stars of the show pitting science against fundamentalism were both national celebrities: Bryan, a true believer in the literal Bible, volunteered his services to the prosecution, and Clarence Darrow, the nation's most famous trial lawyer, a tireless defender of hopeless causes who championed the rights of the working class, offered to defend Scopes and evolution.

Bryan insisted that the trial was not about Scopes but about a state's right to determine what was taught in the public schools, and he announced that the "contest between evolution and Christianity is a duel to the death." Darrow countered: "Scopes is not on trial. Civilization is on trial." His goal was to prevent "bigots and ignoramuses from controlling the education of the United States" by proving that America was "founded on liberty and not on narrow, mean, intolerable and brainless prejudice of soulless religio-maniacs."

On July 20, Scopes's defense team called Bryan to the stand as an "expert" witness on biblical interpretation. Under Darrow's aggressive cross-examination, Bryan repeatedly revealed his ignorance of biblical history and scholarship and gradually conceded that he had never worried that many of the Bible's stories conflicted with common sense and basic scientific truths. At one point, he claimed that Darrow was insulting Christians. Darrow, his thumbs clasping his colorful suspenders, shot back: "You insult every man of science and learning in the world because he does not believe in your fool religion." At one point, Darrow and Bryan, their patience exhausted in the broiling summer heat, lunged at each other, prompting the judge to adjourn court.

As the trial ended, the judge ruled that the only issue before the jury was whether John T. Scopes had taught evolution, and no one had denied that he had done so. Eager to get on with their lives and get the peach harvest in, the jurors did not even sit down before deciding that Scopes was guilty. But the Tennessee Supreme Court, while upholding the anti-evolution law, waived Scopes's $100 fine on a technicality. Both sides claimed victory.

Five days after the trial ended, William Jennings Bryan died of a heart condition aggravated by heat and fatigue. Scopes left Dayton to study geology at the University of Chicago; he became a petroleum engineer. Meanwhile, the Scopes Trial only sharpened the national debate between fundamentalism and evolution that continues today.

Prohibition

William Jennings Bryan died knowing that one of his other religious crusades had succeeded: alcoholic beverages had been outlawed nationwide. The movement to prohibit beer, wine, and liquor forged an unusual alliance

> Challenges and side effects of banning booze

Prohibition (1920–1933)
National ban on the manufacture and sale of alcohol, though the law was widely violated and proved too difficult to enforce effectively.

between rural and small-town Protestants and urban political progressives—between believers in "old-time religion," who considered drinking sinful, and social reformers, mostly women, who were convinced that **Prohibition** would reduce divorces, prostitution, spousal abuse, and other alcohol-related violence. "There would not be any social evil," insisted Ella Boole of the Women's Christian Temperance Union, "if there was no saloon evil." Elizabeth Tilton, a Bostonian active in efforts to ban alcohol, claimed that alcohol was "directly and indirectly responsible for 42 percent of broken homes, 45 percent of children cruelly deserted, 50 percent of crime, 25 percent of our poverty, not to mention feeble mindedness and insanity."

What connected the two groups to each other and to nativist movements were the ethnic and social prejudices that many members shared. The head of the Anti-Saloon League, for example, declared that German Americans "eat like gluttons and drink like swine." For many anti-alcohol crusaders, in fact, the primary goal of Prohibition seemed to be policing the behavior of the foreign-born, the working class, the poor, and blacks.

During the Great War, both houses of Congress had finally responded to the efforts of the Anti-Saloon League and the Women's Christian Temperance Union. The wartime need to use grain for food rather than for making booze, combined with a grassroots backlash against beer brewers because of their German background, transformed the cause of Prohibition into a virtual test of American patriotism. On December 18, 1917, Congress sent to the states the Eighteenth Amendment. Ratified on January 16, 1919, it banned "the manufacture, sale, and transportation of intoxicating liquors," effective one year later.

Prohibition was thus the law during the 1920s—but it was not widely followed. As the most ambitious social reform ever attempted in the United States, it proved to be a colossal and costly failure. It was too sweeping for the government to enforce and too frustrating for most Americans to respect, and it had many consequences not widely foreseen. The loss of liquor taxes, for example, cost the federal government almost 30 percent of its annual revenue. The closing of breweries, distilleries, and saloons eliminated thousands of jobs. Even more troubling was the huge number of Americans who broke the law and the enormous

ALL FAIR IN DRINK AND WAR Torpedoes filled with malt whiskey were discovered in the New York harbor in 1926, an elaborate attempt by bootleggers to smuggle alcohol during Prohibition. Each "torpedo" had an air compartment so it could be floated to shore.

boost that Prohibition during the twenties gave to police corruption and to organized crime.

The Volstead Act (1919), which outlined the rules and regulations needed to enforce the Eighteenth Amendment, had so many loopholes that it virtually guaranteed failure. For example, the law allowed individuals and organizations to keep and use any liquor owned on January 16, 1919, when the amendment was officially ratified. Not surprisingly, people stocked up before the law took effect. The Yale Club in Manhattan stored enough liquor to supply itself for the entire thirteen years that Prohibition was enforced.

An even greater weakness of Prohibition was that Congress never supplied adequate funding to enforce it. In 1920, the United States had only 1,520 federal agents in the Prohibition Bureau to police 100 million Americans. Given the public thirst for alcohol and the profits to be made in making and selling it illegally, called "bootlegging," it would have taken vast armies of agents to police the nation. Even so, police jailed more than a half-million people for violating the Volstead Act. In the South, police targeted blacks and poor whites.

Many of the activities associated with the Roaring Twenties were fueled by bootleg liquor supplied by organized crime and sold in illegal saloons called "speakeasies," which were often ignored by local police corrupted by bribes. New York City's police commissioner estimated that there were 32,000 speakeasies in the city in 1929, compared to 15,000 saloons in 1919. Popular singer Bessie Smith openly proclaimed, "Any bootlegger sure is a pal of mine."

President Warren G. Harding and members of Congress displayed the ironies and hypocrisies associated with Prohibition. At the same time that the president was lambasting the "national scandal" of noncompliance with Prohibition, he regularly drank and served bootleg liquor in the White House, explaining that he was "unable to see this as a great moral issue."

The largest bootlegger in Washington, D.C., reported that "a majority of both houses" of Congress were regular customers. Although total national alcohol consumption did decrease during the twenties, in many parts of the nation drinking actually *increased*. As the popular humorist Will Rogers quipped, "Prohibition is better than no liquor at all."

Prohibition turned many Americans into criminals and supplied organized crime with a source of enormous new income. The most ruthless Prohibition-era gangster was Alphonse Gabriel "Al" Capone. Born in Brooklyn in 1899, the son of Italian immigrants, he was expelled from school for hitting a female teacher. Capone then aligned himself with organized crime gangs. During a fight at a brothel, he suffered a knife wound on his cheek that gave him his lifelong nickname: "Scarface."

Capone moved to Chicago in his early twenties and worked his way up in the city's most notorious organized crime family. By age twenty-six, Capone was in charge. In 1927, his Chicago-based bootlegging, prostitution, and

"AL" CAPONE In this photo from 1931, Capone (right) meets with his attorney, Abraham Teitelbaum, unfazed in the face of federal imprisonment.

gambling empire involved 700 gangsters, extended from Canada to Florida, and brought in $60 million a year (over $1 billion in today's dollars), much of which he spent bribing police officials, judges, and politicians.

Capone loved flashy clothes, gaudy jewelry, and fancy cars yet fancied himself a modern "Robin Hood," a friend of the poor and jobless, dispensing wads of cash to soup kitchens throughout Chicago. Yet he was also utterly ruthless. When he learned that two of his henchmen were planning to turn him in to the police, Capone invited them to dinner and then bludgeoned them to death with a baseball bat. Capone frequently insisted that he was merely giving the public the goods and services it demanded: "They say I violate the Prohibition law. Who doesn't?" He neglected to add that he had ordered the execution of dozens of rival criminals.

Capone's Mafia empire grew so large that he attracted the attention of President Herbert Hoover, who in March 1929, asked Andrew Mellon, his Treasury secretary, "Have you got this fellow Capone yet? I want that man in jail." Mellon decided that the best hope for prosecuting the notorious mobster was to prove that he never paid taxes on his ill-gotten gains.

Federal law-enforcement officials, led by a dynamic agent named Eliot Ness, smashed Capone's bootlegging operations in 1929. Soon thereafter, Ness, having refused bribes from Capone, charged the crime boss with tax evasion. Tried and found guilty in 1931, Capone spent most of the next thirteen years in federal prison. Bankrupt and helpless, he died in 1947 of degenerative syphilis contracted years before in one of his own brothels.

Republican Resurgence

CORE OBJECTIVE

5. Trace the Republican party's dominance of the federal government during the twenties, and analyze the extent to which its policies were a rejection of progressivism.

In national politics, the small-town backlash against modern city life—whether represented by immigrants plotting revolution, liberal churches accepting evolution, or jazzed-up flappers swilling cocktails—mirrored Republican efforts to reverse the progressivism of Theodore Roosevelt and Woodrow Wilson. By 1920, the progressive political coalition that had reelected Wilson in 1916 had fragmented. The growing middle class had become preoccupied less with reform than with enjoying the general prosperity based on the miracles of mass production, mass consumption, and labor-saving electrical appliances.

Progressivism did not simply disappear, of course. The impulse for honest, efficient government and regulation of business remained strong, especially at the state and local levels, where movements for better roads, education, public health, and social-welfare programs gained momentum. At the national level, however, Republican conservatives returned to power.

Harding and "Normalcy"

After the Great War, most Americans had had enough of Woodrow Wilson's crusading idealism and questioned any leader who promoted sweeping reforms. Wilson himself recognized the shifting public mood. "It is only once in a generation," he remarked, "that a people can be lifted above material things. That is why conservative government is in the saddle two-thirds of the time."

The Election of 1920

In 1920, Republican party leaders, unable to settle on a nationally prominent figure as their presidential candidate, turned in the end to Warren G. Harding, an easygoing, silver-haired senator from Ohio. A Republican leader explained that Harding was selected not for his abilities or experience (which were limited) but because he looked presidential. Harding, he said, was "the best of the second-raters." After learning that Harding had been nominated, his wife told a journalist, "I can see but one word written over the head of my husband if he is elected—and that word is tragedy." The savage journalist H. L. Mencken was less sympathetic in his assessment of Harding: "No other such complete and dreadful nitwit is to be found in the pages of American history."

Harding set the conservative tone of his campaign when he told a Boston audience that it was time to end Wilsonian progressivism: America needed "not heroics, but healing; not nostrums, but normalcy; not revolution, but restoration; not agitation, but adjustment; not surgery, but serenity; not the dramatic, but the dispassionate." In contrast to Wilson's internationalism, Harding, like Donald Trump almost a century later, promised to "safeguard America first . . . to exalt America first, to live for and revere America first."

Harding's victorious "return to normalcy"

Harding's vanilla promise of a "**return to normalcy**" reflected his unexceptional background and personality. A farmer's son and newspaper editor, he described himself as "just a plain fellow" who was "old-fashioned and even reactionary in matters of faith and morals." In his personal life, however, Harding was hardly "old-fashioned": he drank illegal liquor in the White House, smoked and chewed tobacco, loved twice-weekly poker games with his buddies in the White House library, and had numerous extramarital affairs and even fathered children with women other than his domineering wife, Florence, whom he called "the Duchess." One of the president's mistresses blackmailed him, demanding money for her silence—which she received.

The public, however, was unaware of Harding's escapades. Voters saw him as a handsome, charming politician who looked the part of a leader yet recognized his own limitations. "I am not fit for this office and should never have been here," he once admitted. "I cannot hope to be one of the great presidents, but perhaps I may be remembered as one of the best loved."

The Democrats, meanwhile, had to contend with the breakup of the Wilsonian coalition and the conservative postwar mood. At the 1920 Democratic convention, another Ohioan, James Cox, a former newspaper publisher and former governor of the state, won the nomination of his increasingly divided party on the forty-fourth ballot. For vice president, the convention chose New Yorker Franklin Delano Roosevelt, only thirty-eight years old, who as assistant secretary of the navy occupied the same position his Republican cousin Theodore Roosevelt had once held.

The country voted overwhelmingly for the Republican party's promised return to normalcy. Harding's victory led a crestfallen Clarence Darrow to quip that he had grown up hearing that "anybody can become president. I'm beginning to believe it."

Harding polled 16 million votes to 9 million for Cox, who won no state outside the South. The Republican majority in both houses of Congress increased. Franklin Roosevelt predicted that his Democratic party could not hope to return to national power until the Republicans led the nation "into a serious period of depression and unemployment." He was right.

Harding's Associates and Personality

Harding in office had much in common with Ulysses S. Grant. His cabinet, like Grant's, mixed some of the "best minds" in the party, whom he had promised to seek out, with some of its worst characters. Charles Evans Hughes, like Grant's Hamilton Fish, became a distinguished secretary of state. Herbert Hoover in the Commerce Department, Andrew W. Mellon in the Treasury Department, and Henry C. Wallace in the Agriculture Department were dedicated public servants. Other cabinet members and Harding appointees, however, were not so conscientious. The secretary of the interior landed in prison, and the attorney general narrowly escaped serving time.

Harding loved hobnobbing and "bloviating" (a favorite word of his, meaning "speaking in a pompous, long-winded way") at public events and

return to normalcy Campaign promise of Republican presidential candidate Warren G. Harding in 1920, meant to contrast with Woodrow Wilson's progressivism and internationalism.

THE OHIO GANG President Warren Harding (third from right) surrounded himself with a network of questionable friends, often appointing them to public office despite inferior credentials.

joking around with his political buddies behind the scenes. As president, however, he was in over his head and knew it. "I don't think I'm big enough for the Presidency," he confided to a friend. He much preferred to relax with the "Ohio gang," his closest friends, who shared his taste for whiskey, poker, and women. Still, Harding and his social friends did have a political agenda.

Andrew Mellon and the Economy

The Harding administration inherited a slumping economy still burdened by high wartime taxes and a national debt that had ballooned from $1 billion in 1914 to $27 billion in 1920 because of the expenses associated with the war. Unemployment was at nearly 12 percent. To address these challenges, the new president established a pro-business tone, vetoing a bill to provide war veterans with a cash bonus, arguing that it would increase the federal budget deficit.

To generate economic growth, Secretary of the Treasury Andrew Mellon, the third richest man in the world behind John D. Rockefeller and Henry Ford, set out reducing federal spending and lowering tax rates. Mellon persuaded Congress to pass the landmark Budget and Accounting Act of 1921, which created a Bureau of the Budget to streamline the process of preparing an annual federal budget. The bill also created a General Accounting Office to audit spending by federal agencies. This act fulfilled a long-held progressive desire to bring greater efficiency and nonpartisanship to the budget preparation process.

> The Mellon Plan: Economic growth through low taxes and spending and high tariffs

The brilliant but cold Mellon (his son described him as a "thin-voiced, thin-bodied, shy and uncommunicative man") also proposed a series of sweeping tax reductions. By 1918, the tax rate on the highest income bracket had risen to 73 percent because of the extraordinary expense of the war. Mellon believed that such high rates were pushing wealthy Americans to avoid paying taxes by investing their money in foreign countries or in tax-free government bonds.

Throughout the twenties, with the support of Congress and Presidents Harding and Coolidge, Mellon's policies systematically reduced tax rates while increasing tax revenues. The top annual tax rate was cut from 73 percent in 1921 to 24 percent in 1929. Rates for the people with the lowest annual incomes were also cut substantially, thereby helping the working poor.

The Mellon Plan worked. By 1926, 65 percent of federal income tax revenue came from people with incomes of $300,000 or more. In 1921, less than 20 percent had come from this group. During this same period, the overall income tax burden on those with incomes of less than $10,000 dropped from $155 million to $32.5 million. By 1929, barely 2 percent of American workers earned enough income to pay any tax at all.

THE MELLON PLAN In this 1924 political cartoon, President Coolidge and Andrew Mellon speed down a hill in the direction of tax reduction, while the Democrats and U.S. Chamber of Commerce heckle from the sidelines, encouraging them to go even faster.

At the same time, Mellon helped Harding reduce the federal budget. Government expenditures fell, as did the national debt, and the economy soared. Unemployment plummeted to 2.4 percent in 1923. Mellon's admirers tagged him the greatest secretary of the Treasury since Alexander Hamilton in the late eighteenth century. In addition to tax cuts, Mellon promoted the long-standing Republican policy of high tariffs on imported goods. The Fordney-McCumber Tariff of 1922 increased rates on chemical and metal products to help prevent the revival of German corporations that had dominated those industries before the Great War. To please commercial farmers, who historically had benefited little from tariffs, the new act further extended duties on agricultural imports.

Reduced Regulation and Racial Progressivism

The Republican economic program of the 1920s also featured reduced regulation of corporations. Neither Harding nor his successor, Calvin Coolidge, could dismantle the federal regulatory agencies created during the Progressive Era, but they named as commissioners of those agencies people who generally promoted regulation "friendly" to business interests. Republican senator Henry Cabot Lodge boasted that "we have torn up Wilsonism by the roots."

> Commission and court appointments friendly to business; policies and speeches opposed to racism

In addition, Harding's four Supreme Court appointments were all conservatives, including Chief Justice William Howard Taft, the former president, who announced that he had been "appointed to reverse a few decisions." During the 1920s, the Taft court struck down a federal child-labor law and a minimum-wage law for women and issued numerous injunctions against striking unions as well as rulings limiting the powers of federal regulatory agencies.

In one area, however, Harding proved to be more progressive than Woodrow Wilson. He reversed the Wilson administration's policy of excluding African Americans from federal government jobs and spoke out against the vigilante racism that had flared up across the country during and after the war.

In his first speech to Congress in 1921, Harding insisted that the nation deal with the "race question." He attacked the Ku Klux Klan for fomenting "hatred and prejudice and violence" and urged Congress "to wipe the stain of barbaric lynching from the banners of a free and orderly, representative democracy." Southern Democrats in the Senate, however, stopped an anti-lynching bill from becoming law.

Setbacks for Unions

Organized labor suffered under Republican rule in the 1920s. Although President Harding endorsed collective bargaining and tried to reduce the twelve-hour workday and the six-day workweek to give the working class "time for leisure and family life," he ran into stiff opposition in Congress. After the war, the Red Scare and the violent strikes of 1919 led many people to equate labor unions with radicalism.

> A corporate campaign against organized labor

The brief postwar depression further weakened the unions, and in 1921 business groups in Chicago designated the **open shop** to be the "American plan" of employment. Although the open shop in theory implied only an employer's right to hire anyone, whether a union member or not, in practice it meant discrimination against unionists and a refusal by companies to negotiate with unions even when most of the workers belonged to one.

To suppress unions, employers often required new workers to sign "yellow-dog" contracts, which forced them to agree not to join a union. Owners also used spies, blacklists, and intimidation to keep their workers from organizing unions. Some employers, such as Henry Ford, tried to kill the unions with kindness by introducing programs of "industrial democracy" guided by company-sponsored unions or various schemes of "welfare capitalism," such as profit sharing, bonuses, pensions, health programs, recreational activities, and the like.

All these anti-union efforts paid off. Union membership dropped from about 5 million in 1920 to 3.5 million in 1929. But the anti-union movement, led by businesses that wanted to keep wages low, unwittingly helped to create a "purchasing crisis" whereby the working poor were not making enough money to buy the huge volume of goods being churned out by America's ever more productive industries.

Isolationism in Foreign Affairs

> Isolationist foreign policy and expanding global economic interests

In addition to the Senate's rejection of American membership in the League of Nations, the postwar spirit of isolation from world affairs found other expressions: the Red Scare, the higher tariff rates on imports, and the restrictive immigration laws with which the nation all but shut the door to newcomers.

Yet the desire to stay out of foreign wars did not mean that the United States could ignore its own expanding global interests. American businesses now had worldwide connections. As a result of the Great War, the United States had become the world's chief banker, and American investments and loans enabled foreigners to purchase U.S. exports.

Probably nothing did more to heighten American isolationism—or anti-American feeling in Europe—than the complex challenge facing Great Britain and France: paying off their huge war debts to the United States. Beginning in 1917, when France and Great Britain ran out of money for military supplies, the U.S. government had advanced them massive loans, first for the war effort and then, after the war, for reconstruction projects. Most Americans, including Treasury secretary Mellon, expected the debts to be repaid, but the Europeans thought otherwise. The British noted that after the American Revolution, the newly independent United States had refused to pay old debts to British merchants. The French likewise pointed out that they had never been repaid for helping the Americans win the Revolutionary War.

Throughout the 1920s, the British and French were in a complex financial bind. To get U.S. dollars to use to pay their war-related debts, European

open shop Business policy of not requiring union membership as a condition of employment; such a policy, where legal, has the effect of weakening unions and diminishing workers' rights.

nations had to sell their goods to the United States. However, rising American tariff rates made imported European goods more expensive and less competitive with U.S. products, thus making it even harder for the Allies to repay their war-related debts. The French and British insisted that they could repay only by collecting the $33 billion in war reparations due them from defeated Germany, whose economy was devastated after the war by hyperinflation of consumer prices. Twice during the 1920s, the financial strain on the German economy forced American bankers to intervene with more loans so that Germany could pay its reparations to Britain and France, thereby enabling them to pay their debts to the United States—and in the process weakening the global economy.

Attempts at Disarmament

After the Great War, many Americans decided that excessive armed forces and weaponry had been the principal causes of the terrible conflict. The best way to keep the peace, they argued, was to limit the size of armies and navies. The United States had no intention of maintaining a large army after 1920, but under the shipbuilding program begun in 1916, it had constructed a powerful navy second only to that of Great Britain. Although neither the British nor the Americans wanted a naval armaments race, both were worried about the growth of Japanese power in Asia and the Pacific.

To address the problem, President Harding in 1921 invited diplomats from eight nations to a conference in Washington, D.C., at which Secretary of State Charles Evans Hughes made a blockbuster proposal. The only way to avoid an expensive naval arms race, he declared, "is to end it now" by eliminating scores of existing warships and prohibiting the construction of new ones. It was one of the most dramatic moments in diplomatic history. In less than fifteen minutes, one journalist reported, Hughes had destroyed more warships "than all the admirals of the world have sunk in a cycle of centuries." His daring proposal was greeted by a "tornado of cheering" among the delegates.

Following Hughes's lead, delegates from the United States, Britain, Japan, France, and Italy signed the Five-Power Treaty (1922), which limited the size of their navies. It was the first disarmament treaty in history. The five major powers also agreed to refrain from strengthening their military forces in the Pacific. The agreement in effect partitioned the world into spheres of influence: U.S. naval power became supreme in the Western Hemisphere, Japanese power in the western Pacific, and British power from the North Sea to Singapore.

With these disarmament agreements in hand, Harding could boast of what seemed to be a brilliant diplomatic coup. But the Five-Power Treaty set limits only on "capital" ships (battleships and aircraft carriers); the race to build cruisers, destroyers, submarines, and other smaller craft continued. Japan withdrew from the agreement in 1934, and by then the Soviet Union and Germany, which had been excluded from the conference, were building

> The Five-Power Treaty provides for naval disarmament

WASHINGTON NAVAL CONFERENCE International powers convene in Washington, D.C. to negotiate the world's first disarmament treaty.

up their navies as well. Thus, twelve years after the Washington Conference, the dream of naval disarmament died.

The Harding Scandals

Teapot Dome, other scandals, and Harding's death and historical reputation

Republican conservatives such as Henry Cabot Lodge, Andrew W. Mellon, Calvin Coolidge, and Herbert Hoover operated out of a philosophical conviction designed to benefit the nation. Members of Harding's Ohio gang, however, used their White House connections to line their own pockets. Early in 1923, for example, Harding learned that the head of the Veterans Bureau was systematically looting medical and hospital supplies. A few weeks later, the legal adviser to the bureau committed suicide, leaving a note for Harding, which the president refused to read. Not long afterward, a close friend of Attorney General Harry M. Daugherty, who had set up an office in the Justice Department from which he illegally sold paroles, pardons, and judgeships, was found shot dead in a hotel room after he had threatened to "quit the racket." Finally, the attorney general himself was implicated in the fraudulent handling of German assets seized after the war. These were but the most visible of the many scandals that touched federal agencies under Harding.

One major scandal rose above all, however. The "**Teapot Dome**," like "Watergate" fifty years later, would become the catchphrase for the climate of corruption surrounding a presidential administration. The Teapot Dome was a government-owned oil field in Wyoming managed by the Department of the Interior. Interior secretary Albert B. Fall, deeply in debt and eight years overdue in paying his taxes, began signing overly generous federal contracts with close friends who were executives of petroleum companies that wanted access to Teapot Dome. It turned out that he had taken bribes of about $400,000 (which came in "a little black bag") from an oil tycoon. Fall was convicted of conspiracy and bribery and sentenced to a year in prison, the first former cabinet official to serve time for misconduct in office.

Teapot Dome (1923) Harding administration scandal in which Secretary of the Interior Albert B. Fall profited from secret leasing of government oil reserves in Wyoming to private oil companies.

How much Harding knew of the scandals was unclear, but he knew enough to be troubled. "My God, this is a hell of a job!" he confided to a journalist. "I have no trouble with my enemies; I can take care of my enemies all right. But my damn friends, my God-damn friends. . . . They're the ones that keep me walking the floor nights!"

In 1923, Harding left on what would be his last journey, a speaking tour to the West Coast and a trip to the Alaska Territory. He suffered an attack of food poisoning in Seattle, recovered briefly, then died in a San Francisco hotel. He was fifty-seven years old.

Because of Harding's sexual misbehavior and his corrupt associates, his administration came to be viewed as one of the worst in history. Even Herbert Hoover, his loyal secretary of commerce, admitted that Harding was not "a man with either the experience or the intellectual quality that the position needed" and that he was unable to admit or resolve the "terrible corruption by his playmates."

TEAPOT DOME SCANDAL In this 1924 political cartoon, Washington officials attempt to outrun the Teapot Dome scandal, represented by a giant steamrolling teapot, on an oil-slicked highway.

More recent assessments suggest, however, that the scandals obscured Harding's accomplishments. He led the nation out of the turmoil of the postwar years and helped create the remarkable economic boom of the 1920s. He also promoted diversity and civil rights, appointing Jews to key federal positions and becoming the first president to criticize racial segregation in a speech before a white audience in the South. No previous president had promoted women's rights as forcefully as he did. Yet even Harding's foremost scholarly defender admits that he lacked good judgment and "probably should never have been president."

Coolidge Conservatism

The news of Harding's death reached Vice President Calvin Coolidge when he was visiting his father in the isolated mountain village of Plymouth Notch, Vermont, his birthplace. There, at 2:47 A.M. on August 3, 1923, by the light of a kerosene lamp, Colonel John Coolidge, a farmer and merchant, administered the presidential oath of office to his son.

Calvin Coolidge, born on the Fourth of July in 1872, was a throwback to an earlier era. A puritan in his personal life, he was, unlike Harding, horrified by the jazzed-up Roaring Twenties, whose rebellious social and cultural forces he could not understand. But he sincerely believed in the ideals of personal integrity and devotion to public service. He was also a virtuous evangelist for capitalism who would bring stability to the White House and prosperity to the economy.

CALVIN COOLIDGE "Silent Cal" was so reticent that when he died in 1933, American humorist Dorothy Parker remarked, "How could they tell?"

Coolidge: "The chief business of the American people is business."

A Modest, Upright, and Tight-Lipped Evangelist for Capitalism

Although Coolidge had won every political race he had entered, he had never loved the limelight. Shy and awkward, he was a man of famously few words—hence, his nickname, "Silent Cal." After being reelected president of the Massachusetts State Senate in 1916, he gave a four-sentence inaugural address that concluded with "above all things, be brief." He later explained that he had "never been hurt by what he had not said." Voters liked Coolidge's uprightness, his straight-talking style, and his personal humility. He was a simple, direct man of strong principles and intense patriotism who championed self-discipline and hard work.

As a Massachusetts state senator, Coolidge had often aligned himself with Republican progressives. He voted for women's suffrage, a state income tax, a minimum wage for female workers, and salary increases for public-school teachers. By the time he entered the White House, however, he had abandoned most of those causes.

Coolidge was determined *not* to be an activist president. He noted that his greatest accomplishment was "minding [his] own business." Unlike Theodore Roosevelt and Woodrow Wilson, he had no exaggerated sense of self-importance; he knew he was "not a great man." Nor did he have an ambitious program to push through Congress. "Four-fifths of our troubles," Coolidge professed, "would disappear if we would sit down and keep still." Following his own logic, he insisted on twelve hours of sleep *and* an afternoon nap. The irreverent journalist H. L. Mencken claimed that Coolidge "slept more than any other president." His idea of a great day was one during "which nothing happened."

Even more than Harding, Coolidge sought to reduce the size and scope of the federal government. "If the federal government were to go out of existence," he predicted, no one would notice. He also linked the nation's welfare with the success of big business. "The chief business of the American people is business," he preached. "The man who builds a factory builds a temple. The man who works there worships there." Where Harding had tried to balance the interests of labor, agriculture, and industry, Coolidge focused on promoting industrial development. He reduced federal regulations of business and, with the help of Treasury secretary Mellon and Republican congresses, continued to lower income tax rates.

Coolidge was also "obsessed" with reducing spending, even to the point of issuing government workers only one pencil at a time—and only after they turned in the stub of the old pencil. "I am for economy" in government spending, he stressed. "After that, I am for more economy." When a South African mayor sent the president two lion cubs as a present, Coolidge named them

"Tax Reduction" and "Budget Bureau." His fiscal frugality and pro-corporate stance led the *Wall Street Journal* to rejoice: "Never before, here or anywhere else, has a government been so completely fused with business."

America also had too many laws, Coolidge insisted, and it was "much more important to kill bad bills than to pass good ones." True to his word, he vetoed fifty acts of Congress. As a journalist said, "In a great day of yes-men, Calvin Coolidge was a no-man."

The Election of 1924

Coolidge easily gained the party's 1924 presidential nomination. Meanwhile, the Democrats again fell to fighting among themselves, prompting humorist Will Rogers's classic statement, "I am a member of no organized political party. I am a Democrat."

The party's nominating convention in New York City's Madison Square Garden illustrated the deep divisions between urban and rural America during the 1920s. One of the leading presidential contenders, William McAdoo, Woodrow Wilson's son-in-law, won the endorsement of the Ku Klux Klan. Some 20,000 Klansmen rallied across the Hudson River in New Jersey, burning crosses to show their support for McAdoo. The other front-runner, New York City mayor Al Smith, was an Irish Catholic who led the party's anti-Klan, anti-Prohibition wing.

Neither McAdoo nor Smith could gain the nomination. The hopelessly fragmented Democrats took a record 103 ballots over 16 broiling summer days to decide on a compromise candidate: John W. Davis, a little-known corporate lawyer from West Virginia who could nearly outdo Coolidge in his conservatism.

The marathon Democratic convention prompted journalist H. L. Mencken of the *Baltimore Evening Sun* to describe the gathering as being as "fascinating as a revival or a hanging. It is vulgar, it is ugly, it is stupid, it is tedious . . . and yet it is somehow charming. One sits through long sessions wishing heartily that all the delegates were dead and in hell—and then suddenly there comes a show so gaudy and hilarious, so melodramatic and obscene, unimaginably exhilarating and preposterous, that one lives a gorgeous year in an hour."

While the Democrats bickered, rural populists and urban progressives again decided to abandon both major parties, as they had done in 1912. Reorganizing the old Progressive party, they nominated Robert M. "Fighting Bob" La Follette for president. The Wisconsin Republican senator (and former governor) had voted against the 1917 declaration of war against Germany.

In the 1924 campaign, the voters preferred to "Keep Cool with Coolidge," who decisively swept both the popular and the electoral votes. Davis took only the solidly Democratic South, and La Follette carried only Wisconsin. The popular vote went 15.7 million for Coolidge, 8.4 million for Davis, and

Coolidge landslide: The height of postwar conservatism

4.8 million for La Follette—the largest vote ever for a third-party candidate up to that time.

Coolidge's landslide victory represented the height of postwar political conservatism. The Democratic party was in disarray, and the Republicans were triumphant. Business executives interpreted the Republican victory as an endorsement of their leading influence on government, and Coolidge saw the economy's surging prosperity as confirmation of his support of the interests of business. In fact, the prosperity and technological achievements of the New Era did have much to do with Coolidge's victory.

The Rise of Herbert Hoover

During the twenties, the drive for industrial efficiency, which had been a prominent theme among progressives, powered the wheels of mass production and consumption and became a cardinal belief of Republican leaders. Herbert Hoover, who served as secretary of commerce in the Harding and Coolidge cabinets, was himself a remarkable success story.

Born into an Iowa farm family in 1874, Hoover was orphaned by age nine. He thereafter became a shy but industrious "loner" who would gain international prestige as a mining engineer, oil tycoon, financial wizard, and multimillionaire before the age of forty. His meteoric success and genius for managing difficult tasks bred a self-confidence that bordered on conceit. Famously short-tempered and quick to take offense, Hoover had to have complete control of any project he managed. "I have insisted on having my own way," he admitted, and in his twenties, he was already planning to be the president of the United States.

Hoover the "Wonder Boy"

After applying his managerial skills to the Food Administration during the Great War, Hoover served with the U.S. delegation at the Versailles peace conference. He idolized Woodrow Wilson and supported American membership in the League of Nations. A young Franklin Roosevelt, then assistant secretary of the navy, stood in awe of Hoover, the man he would eventually defeat in the presidential election of 1932. In 1920, Roosevelt said that Hoover was "certainly a wonder [boy], and I wish we could make him President of the United States."

Hoover soon disappointed Roosevelt, however, by declaring himself a Republican "progressive conservative." In a book titled *American Individualism* (1922), Hoover promoted an "ideal of *service*" that went beyond "rugged individualism." He wanted government to encourage business leaders to forgo "cutthroat competition" and called instead for them to engage in "voluntary cooperation" by forming trade associations that would share information and promote standardization and efficiency—all in an effort to increase productivity.

As secretary of commerce during the 1920s, Hoover transformed the small department into the government's most dynamic agency. He looked

Hoover and Republicans as champions of industrial efficiency

for new markets for business, created a Bureau of Aviation to promote the new airline industry, and established the Federal Radio Commission.

The 1928 Election: Hoover versus Smith

On August 2, 1927, while on vacation in the Black Hills of South Dakota, President Coolidge suddenly announced, "I do not choose to run for President in 1928." His decision surprised the nation and cleared the way for Hoover to win the 1928 Republican nomination. The party's platform took credit for the nation's longest period of sustained prosperity, the government's cost cutting, debt and tax reduction, and the high tariffs ("as vital to American agriculture as . . . to manufacturing") designed to "protect" American businesses from foreign competition.

The Democratic nomination went to four-term New York governor Alfred E. Smith, the "Happy Warrior." The two candidates presented sharply different images: Hoover, the successful businessman and bureaucratic manager from an Iowa farm, versus Smith, a professional politician from a Lower East Side neighborhood of New York City. To working-class Democrats in northern cities, Smith was a hero, the poor grandson of Irish immigrants who had worked himself up to being governor of the most populous state. His outspoken criticism of Prohibition also endeared him to the Irish, Italians, Germans, and others in the North who enjoyed beer or wine.

On the other hand, as the first Roman Catholic nominated for president by a major party, a product of big-city machine politics, and a "wet" on Prohibition (in direct opposition to his party's platform), Smith represented all that was hateful to southern and western rural Democrats—as well as most rural and small-town Republicans. A powerful Kansas newspaper editor declared that the "whole puritan civilization, which has built a sturdy, orderly nation, is threatened by Smith." The Ku Klux Klan issued a "Klarion Kall for a Krusade" against him, mailing thousands of postcards proclaiming that "Alcohol" Smith, the Catholic New Yorker, was the Antichrist. While Hoover stayed above the fray, reminding Americans of their unparalleled prosperity, Smith was forced to deal with constant criticism. He denounced his opponents for injecting "bigotry, hatred, intolerance and un-American sectarian division" into the campaign. But it did little good.

> A third straight Republican presidential landslide

On Election Day, Hoover won in the third consecutive Republican presidential landslide, with 21 million popular votes to Smith's 15 million and an Electoral College majority of 444–87. Hoover even cracked the Democrats' Solid South, leaving Smith only six Deep South states plus Massachusetts and Rhode Island. Republicans kept control of both houses of Congress.

The election was a clear indication that voters appreciated the prosperity generated during the Harding and Coolidge administrations. Coolidge, however, was skeptical that Hoover could sustain the good times. He quipped that the "Wonder Boy" had offered him "unsolicited advice for six years, all of it bad." Coolidge's skepticism about Hoover's political abilities would prove all too accurate, as the talented new president would confront an economic earthquake that would test all his skills—and more.

Reviewing the
CORE OBJECTIVES | INQUIZITIVE

■ **A "New Era" of Consumption**
During the 1920s, the American economy grew at the fastest rate in history, while consumer debt tripled. Innovations in production, advertising, and financing, combined with a jump in the use of electricity, enabled and encouraged millions of Americans to purchase automobiles, radios, and other electrical household appliances. The new *consumer culture* valued leisure, self-expression, and self-indulgence. More and more Americans purchased national brand-name items from retail chain stores, listened to the same radio shows, and watched the same movies.

■ **The Jazz Age** New social and cultural movements challenged the traditional order. The carefree attitude of the 1920s, perhaps best represented by the frantic rhythms of jazz music, led writer F. Scott Fitzgerald to call the decade the *Jazz Age*. Though *flappers* emerged to challenge gender norms, the majority of women remained full-time housewives or domestic servants. As the Great Migration continued, African Americans in northern cities felt freer to speak out against racial injustice and express pride in their race. The *Harlem Renaissance* gave voice to African American literature and arts. Racial separatism and black nationalism grew popular under Marcus Garvey, while the *National Association for the Advancement of Colored People (NAACP)* made efforts to undo racism through education and legislation.

■ **The Modernist Revolt** Many artists and intellectuals were attracted to *modernism*, which drew upon Einstein's theory of relativity and Freud's psychological explorations. For modernists, the world was no longer governed by reason, but rather something created and expressed through one's highly individual consciousness. To be "modern" meant to break free of tradition, to violate restrictions, and to shock and confuse the public.

■ **The Reactionary Twenties**
Retaliating against these challenges to convention, various movements fought to uphold their traditional ideas of what America was and how it should remain. In reaction to a renewed surge of immigration after the Great War and the Red Scare, Americans again embraced *nativism*. The 1921 *Sacco and Vanzetti case*, which resulted in the conviction and death sentence of two Italian immigrants who were self-professed anarchists, reinforced the fear that immigrants were too often troublemakers. Nativists persuaded Congress to restrict future immigration with the *Immigration Act of 1924*. A revived Ku Klux Klan gained a large membership and considerable political influence across the nation. Fundamentalist Protestants campaigned against teaching evolution in public schools, arguing instead for the literal truth of the Bible. Their efforts culminated in the 1925 *Scopes Trial*. Progressive reformers and conservative Protestants supported the nationwide *Prohibition* of alcoholic beverages that started in 1920. Union membership declined as businesses adopted new techniques like the *open shop*.

■ **Republican Resurgence** Disillusionment with the Great War turned the public against progressivism and in favor of disarmament and isolationism. The Republican Party benefited from this shift in the public mood. Warren G. Harding's call for a *return to normalcy* brought about his landslide presidential victory in 1920.

His administration followed the Mellon Plan, which succeeded in reviving the economy. Despite numerous scandals that plagued the Harding administration, including the *Teapot Dome (1923)*, the progressive goal of efficiency through better management remained a part of many Republican initiatives, such as the Budget and Accounting Act.

KEY TERMS

consumer culture *p. 809*

Jazz Age *p. 815*

flappers *p. 817*

Harlem Renaissance *p. 818*

National Association for the Advancement of Colored People (NAACP) *p. 820*

modernism *p. 822*

nativism *p. 826*

Sacco and Vanzetti case (1921) *p. 827*

Immigration Act of 1924 *p. 827*

Scopes Trial (1925) *p. 830*

Prohibition (1920–1933) *p. 832*

return to normalcy *p. 836*

open shop *p. 840*

Teapot Dome (1923) *p. 842*

CHRONOLOGY

1903	Wright Brothers fly first motorized airplane
	Ford Motor Company is founded
1910	National Association for the Advancement of Colored People (NAACP) is founded
1913	Armory Show brings modern art to America
1916	Marcus Garvey brings Universal Negro Improvement Association to New York
1920	Prohibition begins
	Warren G. Harding is elected president
1921	Sacco and Vanzetti trial
	Five-Power Treaty
	Congress passes Emergency Immigration Act
1923	Teapot Dome scandal
	Harding dies
1924	Congress passes Immigration Act
	Calvin Coolidge is reelected president
1925	Scopes "monkey trial"
1927	Charles A. Lindbergh Jr. makes first solo transatlantic airplane flight
	Sacco and Vanzetti are executed
1928	Herbert Hoover is elected president

⬛ INQUIZITIVE

Go to InQuizitive to see what you've learned—and learn what you've missed—with personalized feedback along the way.

CONSTRUCTION OF A DAM (1939), DETAIL One of the most famous and controversial of the artists commissioned by the New Deal's Works Progress Administration was William Gropper, who painted this mural in the Department of the Interior building in Washington, D.C. Based on his observations of dam construction on the Columbia and Colorado Rivers, Gropper illustrates the triumph and brotherhood that emerged from America's grand undertakings during the Great Depression.

New Deal America

1929–1939

The milestone year 1929 dawned with high hopes. Rarely had a new president entered office with greater expectations. In fact, Herbert Hoover, the "Great Engineer," was worried that people viewed him as "a superman; that no problem is beyond my capacity." Hoover was right to be concerned. People did consider him a superman—"the man who had never failed"—a dedicated public servant whose engineering genius and business savvy would ensure continued prosperity. In 1929, more Americans were working than ever before and earning record levels of income. But that was about to change in unexpected ways.

The Great Depression, which began at the end of 1929, brought with it widespread human misery. No other business slump had been so deep, so long, or so painful. One out of four Americans in 1932 was unemployed; in many large cities, nearly half the adults were out of work. Some 500,000 people had lost homes or farms because they could not pay their mortgages. Thousands of banks had failed; millions of people lost their life savings.

Jobless, homeless, and hungry people grew desperate. A man noted in his diary that "hold-ups and killings are becoming more frequent, and it becomes dangerous to walk the streets." Worst of all, many Americans lost hope. As former president Coolidge acknowledged in 1932, "In other periods of depression, it has always been possible to see some things which were solid and upon which you could base hope . . . but as I look about, I now see nothing to give ground to hope."

What made the Great Depression so severe and so enduring was its global nature. In 1929, the economies of Europe were still reeling from the Great War. Once the American economy tumbled, it sent shock waves throughout Europe and elsewhere.

The suffering was worldwide when Franklin Delano Roosevelt was elected in 1932 to lead an anxious nation mired in the third year of an unprecedented economic downturn. Within days of becoming president, Roosevelt, often called FDR, took dramatic steps that forever transformed the scope and role of the federal government. He and a supportive Congress adopted bold measures to relieve the human suffering and promote economic recovery.

Roosevelt was not an ideologue; rather, he was a pragmatist willing to try different approaches. As he once explained, "Take a method and try it. If it fails, admit it frankly and try another." Roosevelt's program for recovery, the New Deal, was therefore a series of trial-and-error actions rather than a comprehensive scheme. None of these well-intentioned but often poorly planned initiatives worked perfectly, and in fact some of them failed miserably. But their combined effect was to restore hope and energy to a nation paralyzed by fear and uncertainty.

CORE **OBJECTIVE**

1. Identify the major causes of the Great Depression.

The Causes of the Great Depression

Herbert Hoover's election in 1928 boosted the hopes of investors in what had come to be called the "Great Bull Market." Since 1924, the prices of stock shares invested in U.S. companies had steadily risen. Beginning in 1927, prices soared further on wings of reckless speculation. In 1929, President Hoover voiced concern about the "orgy of mad speculation" in the stock market, and he urged investors to be more cautious—but to no avail. Treasury secretary Andrew W. Mellon's tax reductions had given people more money to spend or invest, much of which went into the stock market. The nation's foremost economist, Irving Fisher of Yale University, assured investors in 1929 that "stock prices have reached what looks like a permanently high plateau."

The Stock Market during the Twenties

Margin loans, reckless stock speculation, and slowing economy

What made it so easy for hundreds of thousands of people to invest in stocks during the twenties was the common practice of buying stock "on margin"— that is, an investor could make a small cash down payment (the "margin") on shares of stock and borrow the rest from a stockbroker, who held the stock certificates as security in case the stock price plummeted. If stock prices rose, as they did in 1927, 1928, and most of 1929, the investor made enough profits to pay for the "margin loan" and reinvest the rest. But if the stock price declined and the buyer failed to meet a "margin call" for cash to pay off the broker's loan, the broker could sell the stock at a much lower price to cover the loan. By August 1929, stockbrokers were lending investors more than two thirds of the face value of the stocks they were buying. Yet few people seemed concerned, and stock prices kept rising.

But despite the soaring stock market, there were signs that the economy was weakening. By 1927, steel production, residential construction, and automobile sales were slowing, as was the rate of consumer spending. By mid-1929, industrial production, employment, and other measures of economic activity were also declining. Still, the stock market rose.

Then, in early September 1929, the speculative bubble burst when the stock market fell sharply. By the middle of October, world markets were in a steep decline. Still, most investors remained bullish. On October 22, 1929, a leading bank president assured reporters that there was "nothing fundamentally wrong with the stock market or with the underlying business and credit structure."

The Crash

The next week, however, stock market values tumbled, triggering a wild scramble as terrified investors tried to sell stocks whose values were falling. Then, on Black Tuesday, October 29—the worst day in the stock market's history to that point—widespread panic set in. Stock prices went into free fall. By the end of the month, stocks on the New York Stock Exchange had dropped an average of 37 percent. An atmosphere of gloom settled over the financial community. "Life would no longer be, ever again, all fun and games" the comedian Harpo Marx sighed, as he anticipated the onset of the worst depression in history.

> Black Tuesday

After the catastrophic drop in the stock market, fear and uncertainty spread like a virus across the nation and around the world. Investors who had borrowed heavily to buy stocks were now forced to sell their holdings at huge losses in order to pay their debts. Several stockbrokers and investors who had lost everything committed suicide. The president of a cigar company that had gone bankrupt jumped off the ledge of a New York hotel. A Seattle man shot himself. Two men, business partners, joined hands and jumped to their deaths from the Ritz Hotel in New York City. Room clerks in Manhattan hotels began asking guests at registration if they wanted a room for jumping or sleeping.

> Financial panic

During 1930, the national economy sputtered and stumbled. Some 26,355 businesses shut down; even more failed the following year. Half the textile workers in New England mills were jobless. The resulting slowdown in economic growth, called a *recession*, became so severe and long-lasting that it came to be called the **Great Depression**. The collapse of the stock market did not *cause* the Great Depression. Rather, it revealed that the prosperity of the 1920s had been built on weak foundations.

Of course, the stock market crash had the added effect of creating a psychological panic that accelerated the economic decline. Frightened that they

Great Depression (1929–1941) Worst economic downturn in American history; it was spurred by the stock market crash in the fall of 1929 and lasted until the Second World War.

BLACK TUESDAY On October 29, 1929, the stock market fell lower than it ever had before. In this photo, a crowd of shareholders and investors gather outside Wall Street in a panic, many of them facing enormous debt.

were at risk of losing everything, people rushed to get their money out of banks and out of the stock market. Such panicky behavior only made things worse. By 1932, more than 9,000 banks had closed their doors. The nation's formerly robust economy experienced a shocking collapse that would last over ten years.

Why the Economy Collapsed

> Stagnant wages, slow consumer spending, drop in GDP, and widespread unemployment

What were the underlying *causes* of the Great Depression? Economists still debate the relative importance of the various factors, but most scholars emphasize a combination of interrelated elements that triggered the profound economic downturn. The economy had actually begun to fall into a recession in the summer of 1929, months *before* the stock market crash. Too many business owners during the twenties had taken large profits while providing minimal wage increases to employees. And by plowing profits into business expansion, executive salaries, and stock dividends rather than wage increases for hourly workers, employers created a growing imbalance: factories and mills were producing more goods but the purchasing power of consumers was declining because of stagnant wages.

During the twenties, industrial productivity had increased 43 percent, but the wages of factory workers had gone up only 11 percent, in part because labor unions had declined in power and had lost their ability to ensure that wages for their workers were fair. In 1920, there were 5 million union members in the United States; by 1929, there were only 3.4 million. Two thirds of American families in 1929 earned less than $2,000 in annual income, an amount said by economists to provide "only basic necessities." In essence, the economy was producing more and more products that consumers could not afford to buy, and too many people had been borrowing too much money for unproductive purposes, such as speculating in the stock market.

As panic set in, factories cut back production or shut down altogether. From 1929 to 1933, U.S. economic output (called *gross domestic product*, or GDP) dropped almost 27 percent. By 1932, one quarter of the workforce was out of work. Businesses posted signs that read, "We Are Firing, Not Hiring."

At the same time that the financial and industrial sectors were collapsing in the early 1930s, the farm sector remained feeble. Increasing production during the twenties had led to lower prices for grains and livestock, in part because the spreading use of tractors to replace horses and mules made farmers much more productive. As more corn and wheat were grown, however, the prices farmers earned for their crops began a relentless decline. To make matters worse, record harvests in the summer and fall of 1929 caused prices for corn, wheat, and cotton to fall even faster, pinching the income of struggling farmers. A bushel of wheat that brought a farmer $2.94 in 1920 brought only 30 cents by 1932.

> Weak agricultural sector worsens

Government Actions and the Economy

Government policies also contributed to the Depression. High tariffs hurt the economy by reducing foreign trade. Like most Republican presidents, Herbert Hoover supported congressional efforts to raise tariffs on imported goods in order to keep out foreign competition. The Smoot-Hawley Tariff of 1930, authored by two leading Republicans, Reed Owen Smoot and Willis C. Hawley, was intended to help the farm sector by raising tariff barriers on farm products imported into the United States. But a swarm of corporate lobbyists convinced Congress to add hundreds of new imported manufactured items to the tariff bill.

> Government policies: High tariffs, shrinking trade, and an inadequate money supply

More than 1,000 economists urged Hoover to veto the tariff bill because its logic was flawed: by trying to "protect" American farmers from foreign competition, the bill would actually raise prices on most raw materials and consumer products by impeding imports. Hoover signed the bill anyway, causing another steep drop in the stock market. The new Smoot-Hawley Tariff also prompted other countries to retaliate by passing tariffs of their own, thereby making it more difficult for American farms and businesses to sell their products abroad. U.S. exports plummeted, worsening the depression.

Another factor contributing to the Great Depression was the stance of the Federal Reserve (known as "the Fed"), the government agency responsible for serving as a "central bank" by managing the nation's money supply and interest rates. Instead of expanding the nation's money supply in an effort to generate growth, the Federal Reserve did the reverse, reducing the money supply out of concern for possible inflation in consumer prices. Between 1929 and 1932, the nation's money supply shrank by a third, leading almost

BANK RUN As news of the Great Crash spread across the world, people rushed to their banks to withdraw their deposits, and some banks, such the American Union Bank in New York City, were forced to close their doors. **How did this panicked reaction contribute to the already declining economy?**

10,000 small banks to close their doors and in turn taking millions of their depositors with them into bankruptcy.

The Impact of Europe's Economy

European nations default on paying war debts

A final cause of the Depression was the chaotic state of the European economy, which had never fully recovered from the shock of the Great War. During the late 1920s, nations such as Great Britain, France, Spain, and Italy slowed their purchases of American goods as their shattered economies, slowly recovering from the devastation of the war, were finally able to produce more goods of their own. Meanwhile, the important German economy continued to flounder. A related factor was the continuing inability of European nations to pay their debts to each other—and to the United States—that they had incurred during the war. The American government insisted that the $11 billion it loaned to the Allies be repaid, but nations such as Great Britain and France had no money to send to Washington, D.C. They were forced to borrow huge sums ($5 billion) from U.S. banks, which only increased their overall indebtedness.

After the stock market crash in October 1929, American banks could no longer prop up the European economies. The Federal Reserve's tighter monetary policy also drastically slowed the amount of American capital (money) going abroad. The economies of nations like Germany, which had grown dependent upon loans from American banks during the twenties, were devastated as American money dried up. Then the Smoot-Hawley Tariff made it even more difficult for European nations to sell their products in the United States, which meant that those countries had less money with which to buy American goods. So as the European economy sputtered, it dragged the American economy deeper into depression.

The Human Toll of the Depression

The Depression of the 1930s came to be called "Great" because its effects were so severe and long-lasting. It generated record levels of unemployment and widespread human distress. By 1932, perhaps a quarter of the entire population could not afford housing or adequate food. The carefree optimism of the twenties disappeared as the suffering spread. Grassroots protests erupted as the Depression worsened. In many cities, hungry people looted grocery stores. Angry mobs stopped local sheriffs from foreclosing on farms; others threatened to lynch judges at bankruptcy hearings. In Harlan, Kentucky, coal miners went on strike to protest a cut in their wages. The mine owners called in the National Guard, which routed the union.

In 1931, Socialists recruited 45,000 people to join the Unemployed Citizens' League in Seattle, Washington, which helped people avoid eviction and bankruptcy, found them part-time jobs, and lobbied for more government assistance. Some people talked of revolution. "Folks are restless," Mississippi governor Theodore Bilbo told reporters in 1931. "Communism is gaining a foothold. . . . In fact, I'm getting a little pink myself." Yet for all the radical talk, few Americans embraced communism during the early 1930s. "There was anger and rebellion among a few," recounted an Iowa farmer, but most people lived in "helpless despair and submission."

Unemployment and "Relief"

As the economy spiraled downward between 1930 and 1933, growing numbers of workers were fired or saw their wages cut. National unemployment soared to 4 million in 1930, 8 million in 1931, and 12 million by 1932. Some 6,000 jobless New Yorkers sold apples on street corners.

Many struggling business executives and professionals—lawyers, doctors, dentists, accountants, stockbrokers, teachers, nurses, and engineers—went without food and stopped going to doctors and dentists in order to save money and to avoid the humiliation of "going on relief." A dentist in New York City and his wife committed suicide, explaining in a note, "We want to get out of the way before we are forced to accept relief money." The sense of shame cut across class lines. In *The Grapes of Wrath* (1939), John Steinbeck's best-selling novel about the Depression, a poor but proud woman is disgraced by accepting "charity" from the Salvation Army: "We was hungry. They made us crawl for our dinner. They took our dignity."

Hunger

Hard-pressed families went without fruit and most vegetables, eating mostly beans and soup. Surveys of children in the nation's public schools in 1932 showed that one quarter suffered from

THE GRAPES OF WRATH **(1939)** A first edition of John Steinbeck's best seller, which told the story of a family of tenant farmers struggling to survive during the Great Depression.

malnutrition. In a rural school in Appalachia, a teacher told a sickly child to go home and get something to eat. "I can't," she replied. "It's my sister's turn to eat." In 1931, New York City hospitals reported about 100 cases of actual starvation, where people died solely from the lack of food. Hungry people by the millions lined up at soup kitchens where minimal amounts of food and water were distributed; others rummaged through trash cans behind restaurants. In Detroit, "we saw the city at its worst," wrote Louise V. Armstrong. "One vivid, gruesome moment of those dark days we shall never forget. We saw a crowd of some fifty men fighting over a barrel of garbage which had been set outside the back door of a restaurant. American citizens fighting over scraps of food like animals!"

Homelessness

The contraction of the economy especially squeezed debtors, who had monthly mortgages or installment debts to pay. A thousand Americans per day lost their homes to foreclosure. At first, the poor made homeless by the Depression were usually placed in *poorhouses* or *workhouses*. By 1933, however, the numbers of homeless overwhelmed the small number of public facilities. People were forced to live under bridges, on park benches, and in doorways and police stations. To make matters worse, the poor were degraded as a class of outsiders and subject to frequent abuse and arrest. The constitutions of fourteen states even banned paupers from voting.

Millions of homeless people, mostly men, simply took to living on the road or the rails. These hobos, or tramps, as they were called, walked, hitchhiked in cars, or sneaked onto empty railway cars and rode from town to town. One railroad, the Missouri Pacific, counted 200,000 people living in its empty boxcars in 1931. The following year, the Southern Pacific Railroad reported that it had evicted 683,457 people from its freight trains. A black military veteran recalled life as a freight train hobo: "Black and white, it didn't make any difference who you were, 'cause everybody was poor. . . . They didn't have no mothers or sisters, they didn't have no home; they were dirty, they had overalls on, they didn't have no food, they didn't have anything."

Desperate Responses

As always, those hardest hit were the most disadvantaged groups—immigrants, women, farmers, the urban unemployed, Native Americans, and African Americans. Desperate conditions did lead desperate people to do desperate things. Crime soared during the 1930s, as did street-corner begging, homelessness, and prostitution.

CHICAGO SHANTYTOWN In response to the economic devastation of the Great Depression, numerous shantytowns emerged in cities across the country to house the recently homeless; here, a man reads a newspaper outside his makeshift dwelling in Chicago.

A Pennsylvania man wrote the governor in 1931, explaining that he did not "want to steal, but I won't let my wife and boy cry for something to eat. . . . How long is this going to keep up? I cannot stand it any longer."

Although the divorce rate dropped during the decade, in part because couples could not afford to live separately or pay the legal fees to obtain a divorce, many jobless husbands simply deserted their wives and children. Some 1.5 million husbands left home during the thirties. "You don't know what it's like when your husband's out of work," a woman told a reporter. "He's gloomy and unhappy all the time. Life is terrible. You must try all the time to keep him from going crazy." With their future so uncertain, married couples often decided not to have children; birth rates plummeted during the 1930s. Many struggling parents sent their children to live with relatives or friends. Some 900,000 children simply left home and joined the growing army of homeless tramps. During the Great Depression, for the first time ever, more people left the United States than arrived as immigrants.

> Families in distress: Crime, desertion, and declining birth rates

The Plight of Married Working Women

Women were placed in a peculiar position by the Depression. By 1932, 20 percent of working women were unemployed, a slightly lower percentage than men. On the one hand, because women held a disproportionate number of the lowest-paying jobs, they were often able to keep their jobs as employers laid off the higher-paid men. Even if they kept their jobs, however, many women also had the added burden of keeping their families together emotionally when their husbands lost jobs. Many magazines during the thirties published articles about the challenge of maintaining households when the husband had been "unmanned" by losing his job as breadwinner. One of the most famous Broadway show tunes during the early thirties was "Remember My Forgotten Man."

As the Depression deepened, however, married women in the workforce became the primary targets of layoffs. Some twenty-six states passed laws prohibiting the employment of married women. The reasoning behind such laws was that a married woman—who presumably had a husband to take care of her—should not "steal" a job from a man. It was acceptable for single women to find jobs because these were usually lower-paying jobs considered "women's work": sales clerks, beauticians, schoolteachers, secretaries, and nurses.

The job market for African American women was even more restricted, with most black women working as maids, cooks, or laundresses. In a desperate attempt

APPLYING FOR A JOB In October 1938, the government advertised six custodian positions and 15,000 African American women started lining up overnight to turn in their applications. Pictured here is a policeman leaping over a hedge to administer some crowd control.
What legislative barriers did some states institute to regulate employment opportunities?

to create jobs for unemployed men, many employers adopted policies barring married women from employment. For example, three fourths of the public school systems across the nation during the Great Depression fired women teachers who got married. As a legislator commented, the working woman in Depression-era America was "the first orphan in the storm."

African Americans, Mexicans, and Asians

Most African Americans during the Depression still lived in the eleven southern states of the former Confederacy, where the southern economy, still farm-dominated, was already depressed. Most African Americans who lived in the South earned their livelihood from farming as tenants and share-croppers. Pervasive racial discrimination kept blacks out of the few labor unions in the South and consigned them to the most-menial, lowest-paying jobs. Most blacks were still excluded from voting, segregated from whites in public places like hotels and trains, and limited mostly to farmwork. Already living in poverty, they were among the hardest hit by the Depression. As a blues song called "Hard Times Ain't Gone Nowhere" revealed, "Hard times don't worry me; I was broke when it first started out." Some 3 million rural blacks in the South lived in cramped cabins without electricity, running water, or bathrooms.

In many mills, factories, mines, and businesses, the philosophy of "last hired, first fired" meant that the people who could least afford to be jobless were fired first. Blacks who had left the poverty-stricken South to take factory jobs in the North were among the first to be laid off. African Americans across the nation had the highest rate of joblessness in the early years of the Great Depression. "At no time in the history of the Negro since slavery," reported the Urban League, "has his economic and social outlook seemed so discouraging." Churches and other charity organizations gave aid, but some only assisted whites and refused to provide support for blacks, Mexicans, and Asians.

Impoverished whites found themselves competing with local Hispanics and Asians for seasonal farmwork in the cotton fields or orchards of large corporate farms. Many Chinese, Japanese, and Filipino farm laborers moved to cities. Mexicans were also mostly migrant farmworkers, traveling from farm to farm to work during harvest and planting seasons of different crops. They settled in California, New Mexico, Arizona, Colorado, Texas, and the midwestern states. As economic conditions worsened, government officials called for the deportation of Mexican-born Americans in order to avoid the cost of providing them with public services. By 1935, over 500,000 Mexican Americans and their American-born children were deported to Mexico. The state of Texas alone returned over 250,000 people.

Deportation of Mexican-born Americans

Dust Bowl Migrants

In the southern plains of the Midwest and the Mississippi Valley, a terrible drought during the 1930s created a catastrophe known as the **Dust Bowl**. Colorado, New Mexico, Kansas, Nebraska, Texas, Arkansas, and Oklahoma were

Dust Bowl Vast area of the Midwest where windstorms blew away millions of tons of topsoil from parched farmland after a long drought in the 1930s, causing great social distress and a massive migration of farm families.

the states hardest hit. Crops withered and income plummeted. Strong winds swept across the treeless plains, scooping up millions of tons of parched topsoil into billowing dark clouds that floated east across entire states, engulfing farms and towns in what were called black blizzards. By 1938, over 25 million acres of prairie land had lost their topsoil.

Human misery paralleled the environmental devastation. Parched farmers could not pay their debts, and banks foreclosed on their property. Suicides soared. With each year, millions of people abandoned their farms. Many uprooted farmers and their families from the South and the Midwest headed toward California, where jobs were said to be plentiful. So off they went on a cross-country trek in pursuit of new

OKIES ON THE RUN A sharecropping family reaches its destination of Bakersfield, California, in 1935, after they "got blowed out in Oklahoma."

opportunities. Frequently lumped together as "Okies" or "Arkies," most of the dust bowl refugees were from cotton belt communities in Arkansas, Texas, Missouri, and Oklahoma. During the 1930s and 1940s, some 800,000 people, mostly whites, left those four states and headed to the Far West in a migration powerfully described in Steinbeck's *The Grapes of Wrath* as well as in the folk songs of Woody Guthrie, a musician who traveled the nation during the thirties, singing about people down on their luck.

Most people uprooted by the dust bowl went to California's urban areas—Los Angeles, San Diego, or San Francisco. Others moved into the San Joaquin Valley, the agricultural heartland of California. There they discovered that rural California was no paradise. Only a few of the dust bowl migrants could afford to buy land. Living in tents or crude cabins and frequently on the move, the migrant workers suffered from exposure to the elements, poor sanitation, and social abuse. As an Okie reported, when the big farmers "need us they call us *migrants*, and when we've picked their crop, we're *bums* and we got to get out."

From Hooverism to the New Deal

CORE **OBJECTIVE**
3. Explain the response of the Hoover administration to the Great Depression.

The initial response of government officials to the Great Depression was denial: there was no crisis, they insisted. All that was needed, President Hoover and others argued, was to let the sick economy cure itself. The best policy, Treasury secretary Andrew Mellon advised, would be to "liquidate labor, liquidate stocks, liquidate the farmers, liquidate real estate." Letting events run their course, he insisted, would "purge the rottenness out of the system. High costs of living and high living will come down. People will work harder, live a more moral life."

Mellon's do-nothing approach did not work, however. Falling wages and declining land and home values made it harder for farmers, businesses, and households to pay their debts. With so many people losing jobs and income, consumers and businesses simply could not buy enough goods and services to get the economy growing again.

Hoover's Efforts at Recovery

Hoover's efforts to end the Depression: Government construction projects and private cooperation

President Hoover was less willing than Andrew Mellon to sit by and let events take their course. As the "Great Engineer," he in fact did more than any president had ever done before in such dire economic circumstances. Hoover, for example, invited business, labor, government, and agricultural leaders to a series of White House conferences in which the president urged companies to maintain employment and wage levels, asked union leaders to end strikes, and pleaded with states to follow through on planned construction projects. None of these efforts worked. Unemployment continued to rise, and wage levels continued to fall.

In speech after speech, the bland Hoover tried to become a cheerleader for American capitalism. In early May 1930, the president told the U.S. Chamber of Commerce that he was "convinced we have passed the worst and with continued effort we shall rapidly recover." A few weeks later, Hoover assured a group of bankers that the "depression is over." The Hoover administration also circulated upbeat slogans such as "Business IS Better" and "Keep Smiling." But uplifting words were not enough. More and more people kept losing their jobs and homes. Hoover never felt comfortable giving comfort to a desperate nation. His recurring statement—"No one has yet starved"—was hardly reassuring or, as it turned out, accurate, for millions of Americans were desperately hungry.

Shortsighted Tax Increases

The Revenue Act of 1932

The Great Depression was the greatest national emergency since the Civil War, and the nation was woefully unprepared to deal with it. As personal income plummeted, so too did government tax revenues. Despite the Depression, President Hoover insisted on trying to balance the federal budget. To do so, he pushed through Congress the Revenue Act of 1932, the largest—and most poorly timed—peacetime tax increase in American history. By taking money out of consumers' pockets, the higher taxes accelerated the economic slowdown. People had less money to spend when what the depressed economy most needed was increased consumer spending.

Hoover's Reaction to the Social Crisis

By the fall of 1930, many city governments were buckling under the strain of lost revenue and growing human distress. The federal government had no programs to deal with homelessness and joblessness. State and local

HOOVERVILLE Left: Of the many Hoovervilles set up in Seattle alone, this particular shantytown near the shipyards was the largest and lasted nine years. Right: A toddler begs for change in one of the Bonus Army camps.

governments cut spending, worsening the economic situation. All across the country, shantytowns sprouted in vacant lots where people erected shacks out of cardboard and scrap wood and metal. There they shivered and suffered, calling their makeshift villages *Hoovervilles* in criticism of the president. To keep warm during the winter, the homeless wrapped themselves in newspapers, calling them *Hoover blankets*. As the number of suffering people rose, more and more people called for governments to step in to deal with the emergency of homeless, starving people. Frustrated by his critics, Hoover dismissed the concerns of "calamity mongers and weeping men."

President Hoover refused to provide any federal programs to help the needy for fear that the nation would be "plunged into socialism" if the government provided direct support to the poor. His governing philosophy, rooted in America's commitment to rugged individualism, self-reliance, and free enterprise, set firm limits on emergency government action, and he was unwilling to set that philosophy aside even to meet an unprecedented national emergency. The president still trumpeted the virtues of "self-reliance" and individual initiative, claiming that government assistance would be the very worst thing for a nation in crisis, for it would rob people of the desire to help themselves.

> Hoover rejects federal intervention

Hoover hoped that the "natural generosity" of the American people and local charitable organizations would be sufficient to handle the crisis, and he believed that volunteers (the backbone of local charity organizations) would relieve the social distress caused by the Depression. But Hoover's faith in traditional "voluntarism" was misplaced. Although most Americans tried to

> Voluntarism

get jobs to earn a living, there simply were no jobs, even for industrious people. The magnitude of the social crisis overwhelmed the resources of local and state relief agencies. Churches and charitable organizations like the Salvation Army and the Red Cross were swamped with needy people.

Rising Criticism of Hoover

As always, a depressed economy hurt the political party in power—and its president. The *New York Times* reported in the summer of 1930 that public opinion "is turning rather heavily against the Hoover administration." One wit claimed that "if you put a rose in Hoover's hand, it would wilt."

The Democrats shrewdly exploited Hoover's predicament. In November 1930, they gained their first national election victory since 1916, winning a majority in the House and a near majority in the Senate. Hoover refused to see the elections as a warning signal. Instead, he grew more resistant to calls for federal intervention in the struggling economy. By 1932, almost 25 percent of the workforce—15 million people—were unemployed. Still, a defiant Hoover resisted calls for federal assistance. The *New York Times* concluded that Hoover had "failed as a party leader. He has failed as an economist. . . . He has failed as a business leader. . . . He has failed as a personality because of [his] awkwardness of manner and speech and lack of mass magnetism."

Congressional Initiatives

Reconstruction Finance Corporation

With a new Congress in session in 1932, demands for federal action forced Hoover to do more. That year, the new Congress set up the **Reconstruction Finance Corporation** (RFC) to make emergency loans ("bailouts") to struggling banks, life-insurance companies, and railroads. Yet if the federal government could help huge banks and railroads, asked New York Democratic senator Robert F. Wagner, why not "extend a helping hand to that forlorn American, in every village and every city of the United States, who has been without wages since 1929?" Democrats like Wagner called for federal help for the people hit hardest by the economic collapse. But Hoover held back and only signed the Emergency Relief Act (1932), which authorized the RFC to make loans to the states for construction projects.

Farmers and Veterans in Protest

Meanwhile, desperate farmers across the nation took matters into their own hands. The average *annual* income of families working the land during the early 1930s was $240. Prices for agricultural products fell so low that farmers lost money if they took them to market. Thousands of midwestern farmers joined the Farmers' Holiday Association to protest the low prices by dumping milk, vegetables, and fruits on the highways.

Fears of organized revolt arose when thousands of unemployed military veterans converged on the nation's capital in the spring of 1932. The **Bonus Expeditionary Force**, made up of veterans of the American Expeditionary

Reconstruction Finance Corporation (1932) Federal program established under President Hoover to loan money to banks and other corporations to help them avoid bankruptcy.

Bonus Expeditionary Force (1932) Protest march on Washington, D.C., by thousands of military veterans and their families, calling for immediate payment of their service bonus certificates; violence ensued when President Herbert Hoover ordered their tent villages cleared.

Force that fought in Europe in the Great War, pressed Congress to pay the cash bonus owed to nearly 4 million veterans. The House passed a bonus bill, but when the Senate voted it down to avoid a tax increase, most of the veterans went home. The rest, along with their wives and children, having no place to go, camped in vacant federal buildings and in a shantytown at Anacostia Flats, within sight of the nation's Capitol building.

Eager to remove the homeless veterans, Hoover persuaded Congress to pay for their train tickets home. More left, but others stayed even after Congress adjourned, hoping at least to meet with the president. Late in July, President Hoover ordered the government buildings cleared. In doing so, a policeman panicked, fired into the crowd, and killed two veterans. The secretary of war then dispatched 700 soldiers to remove the "Bonus Army." Using horses, tanks, tear gas, and bayonets, the soldiers dispersed the unarmed veterans and their families and burned their makeshift camp. Fifty-five veterans were injured and 135 arrested.

> Bonus Army

The Democratic governor of New York was horrified as he read newspaper accounts of the army's violent assault on the Bonus Army. "Well," Franklin Roosevelt told an aide, "this elects me" as the next president. (The military veterans of the war were finally paid their "bonus" in 1936).

The disheartened, angry mood of the Bonus Army matched the sour mood of the country, as well as that of President Hoover himself. He worked hard, seven days a week, but the stress of dealing with the Great Depression sapped his health and morale. "I am so tired," he said, "that every bone in my body aches." When aides urged Hoover to be more of a public leader, he replied, "I have no Wilsonian qualities." The man who in 1928 had seemed to be an organizational genius and had promised Americans "permanent prosperity" was now the laughingstock of the nation. *Time* magazine reported that "two years have destroyed the Hoover legend." In the end, Hoover's efforts to

ASSAULT ON THE BONUS ARMY
Unemployed military veterans of the Bonus Expeditionary Force clash with Washington, D.C., police at Anacostia Flats in July 1932. **What brought the Bonus Expeditionary Force to the capital, and why did some of the veterans stay?**

THE ELECTION OF 1932

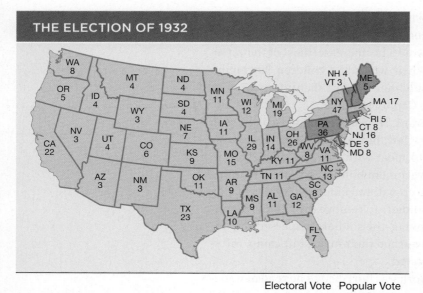

		Electoral Vote	Popular Vote
	Franklin D. Roosevelt (Democratic)	**472**	**22,800,000**
	Herbert Hoover (Republican)	59	15,800,000

- Why did Roosevelt appeal to voters struggling during the Depression?
- What were Hoover's criticisms of Roosevelt's New Deal?
- What policies defined Roosevelt's New Deal during the presidential campaign?

restore prosperity were simply not enough, in large part because he never understood or acknowledged the seriousness of the economic problems that he and the nation faced.

The 1932 Election

In June 1932, glum Republicans gathered in Chicago to nominate Hoover for a second presidential term. The delegates went through the motions in a mood of defeat but felt they had no choice. By contrast, the Democrats arrived in Chicago for their nominating convention a few weeks later confident that they would nominate the next president.

Fifty-year-old New York governor Franklin Delano Roosevelt won the nomination on the fourth ballot. In a bold gesture, Roosevelt flew for nine hours to Chicago to accept the nomination in person instead of awaiting formal notification. No nominee had ever done so. Roosevelt had broken with tradition, he told the delegates, because the stakes were so high. Hoover and the Republicans, he stressed, had failed to address the terrible economic disaster. "I pledge you, I pledge myself to a *new deal* for the American people," he declared. It would be one that would "break foolish traditions" and create a new government "of competence and courage."

But first Roosevelt would have to defeat Herbert Hoover. His race against the Republican president would be "more than a political campaign; it [was] a call to arms." It was a vague but self-assured and uplifting message of hope at a time when many people were slipping into despair. Roosevelt's upbeat personality communicated joy, energy, and confidence. His campaign song was "Happy Days Are Here Again."

Throughout the campaign, Roosevelt blamed the Great Depression on the Republicans. He attacked Hoover for his "extravagant government spending" and repeatedly promised a "New Deal" for the American people. Like Hoover, Roosevelt pledged to balance the federal budget, but he was willing to create short-term deficits to prevent starvation and revive the economy. Perhaps most important, he recognized that a revitalized economy would require new ideas and aggressive action. "The country needs, and, unless I mistake its temper, the country demands bold, persistent experimentation," he said. "Above all, try something." There were "many ways of going forward," Roosevelt explained, but "only one way of standing still."

In contrast to Roosevelt, the bewildered Hoover lacked vitality and vision. Roosevelt's proposals, he warned, "would destroy the very foundations of our American system." The election, he stressed, was a battle "between two philosophies of government" that would decide "the direction our nation will take over a century to come." On Election Day, Hoover lost that battle. Voters swept Roosevelt into office with 23 million votes to Hoover's 16 million.

Roosevelt's New Deal

CORE **OBJECTIVE**

4. Assess the goals and accomplishments of the early New Deal.

Roosevelt had promised voters a "New Deal," and within hours of being inaugurated he and his aides set about changing the role of government in American life. The new president had been in a hurry all his life.

Born in 1882, the adored only child of wealthy, aristocratic parents, young Franklin Roosevelt had enjoyed a pampered life. He was educated by tutors at Hyde Park, his father's Hudson River estate north of New York City. Young Roosevelt attended Harvard College and Columbia University Law School. While a law student, he married Anna Eleanor Roosevelt, a niece of his fifth cousin, Theodore Roosevelt, then president of the United States.

In 1910, Franklin Roosevelt won a Democratic seat in the New York State Senate. Tall, handsome, and athletic, blessed with a sparkling personality and infectious smile, Roosevelt seemed destined for greatness. In 1913, Woodrow Wilson appointed him assistant secretary of the navy. In 1920, Roosevelt became James Cox's vice presidential running mate on the Democratic ticket.

Then a tragedy occurred. In 1921, at age thirty-nine, Roosevelt contracted polio, leaving him permanently disabled, unable to stand without braces. For seven years, aided by his remarkable wife, Eleanor, Roosevelt strengthened his body to compensate for his disability. The long battle for recovery transformed the young aristocrat. He became less arrogant, less superficial, more focused, and more interesting. A friend recalled that Roosevelt emerged from his struggle with polio "completely warm-hearted, with a new humility of spirit" that led him to identify with the poor and the suffering.

In 1928 and 1930, Roosevelt won the governorship of New York. The aristocrat had developed the common touch as well as a great talent for public relations, but he also was vain and calculating, a clever manipulator of others. In other words, he was a master politician.

FRANKLIN DELANO ROOSEVELT This photo captures Roosevelt preparing to deliver the first of his popular radio "fireside chats," in which he would discuss measures to reform the American banking system.

Launching the New Deal

Roosevelt was neither an efficient administrator nor a deep thinker. One of his closest aides said the president never "read a serious book." But Roosevelt had courage, a charming personality, strong instincts, unrelenting optimism, and a willingness to experiment with different ways to address problems. He would support a balanced budget and complain about a "bloated bureaucracy," for example, only to incur more budget deficits than all his predecessors combined and dramatically expand the scope of federal government. His inconsistencies reflected his distinctively flexible personality as he launched his presidency and the New Deal.

The 1933 Inauguration

Inaugurated as president in March 1933, Franklin Delano Roosevelt assumed leadership during one of the greatest crises in modern history, a crisis that threatened the very fabric of American capitalism. "The situation is critical, Franklin," the prominent journalist Walter Lippmann warned President-elect Roosevelt. "You may have to assume dictatorial powers"—as had already happened in Germany, Italy, and the Soviet Union.

Roosevelt did not become a dictator, but he did take extraordinary steps to address the Depression while assuring Americans "that the only thing we have to fear is fear itself." Roosevelt confessed in his inaugural address that he did not have all the answers, but he did know that "this nation asks for action, and action now." To deal with the crisis, he asked Congress for "a broad Executive power to wage a war against the emergency" just as "if we were in fact invaded by a foreign foe." Roosevelt's uplifting speech won rave reviews. Nearly 500,000 Americans wrote letters to the new president after his inauguration.

The First Hundred Days

New Deal goals: Relief, recovery, and reform

In March 1933, President Roosevelt confronted four major challenges: reviving the industrial economy, relieving the widespread human misery, rescuing the ravaged farm sector and its desperate families, and reforming those aspects of the capitalist system that had helped cause the Depression. His goal in providing "relief, recovery, and reform" was to save the nation's capitalist system, not destroy it, while also providing help to those in great distress.

The new president admitted that he planned to try several different "experiments" to solve the Great Depression. Eleanor Roosevelt said her husband and his top advisers were "going at it blindly, because we're in a tremendous stream, and none of us knows where we are going to land." To advise him about options, the new president assembled a "brain trust" of brilliant specialists, many of them college professors, who feverishly developed fresh ideas to address the nation's urgent problems. "I'm not the smartest fellow in the world," Roosevelt admitted, "but I sure can pick smart colleagues."

Roosevelt and his advisers initially settled on a three-pronged strategy to revive the economy and help those in need. First, they addressed the banking crisis and provided short-term emergency relief for the jobless. Second, the New Dealers encouraged agreements between management and unions designed to keep businesses from failing. Third, they attempted to raise depressed commodity prices by paying farmers "subsidies" to shrink the size of their crops and herds. By reducing the supply of grain, cattle, and pigs, prices would rise and thereby increase farm income. From March 9 to June 16, the so-called First Hundred Days, a cooperative Congress approved fifteen major pieces of legislation proposed by the president. Several of these programs composed what came to be called the **First New Deal (1933–1935)**.

Shoring Up the Financial System

Money is the lubricant of capitalism, and money was fast disappearing from circulation by 1933. Ever since the stock market crash of 1929, panicky depositors had been withdrawing their money from banks and the stock market for fear that the banks and corporations would fail. Taking so much money out of circulation, however, worsened the Depression and brought the banking system to the brink of collapse.

Banking Regulation

Soon after taking office, Roosevelt called Congress into emergency session to pass the Emergency Banking Relief Act, which declared a week-long bank holiday to allow the financial panic to subside. (A sulking Herbert Hoover called it a "move to gigantic socialism.") For the first time in history, all banks closed their doors to stop the panic. Roosevelt's financial experts worked all night drafting a bill to restore confidence in the nation's banks. On March 12, in the first of his radio "fireside chats" to the American people, the president assured the 60 million listeners that it was safer to "keep your money in a reopened bank than under the mattress." His reassurances soothed a nervous nation. The following day, people took their money back to banks. "Capitalism was saved in eight days," said one of Roosevelt's advisers.

A few weeks later, on June 16, 1933, Roosevelt signed the Banking Act of 1933, part of which created the **Federal Deposit Insurance Corporation** (FDIC), which guaranteed customer saving accounts up to $2,500, thus reducing the likelihood of future panics. In addition to insuring savings accounts, the Glass-Steagall Act, part of the Banking Act of 1933, called for the separation of commercial banking from investment banking in order to prevent banks from investing the savings of depositors in the risky stock

> Emergency Banking Relief Act and "fireside chats"

First New Deal (1933–1935) Franklin D. Roosevelt's ambitious first-term cluster of economic and social programs designed to combat the Great Depression.

Federal Deposit Insurance Corporation (1933) Independent government agency, established to prevent bank panics, that guarantees the safety of deposits in citizens' savings accounts.

THE GALLOPING SNAIL
A vigorous Roosevelt drives Congress to action in this *Detroit News* cartoon from March 1933. **What steps did Roosevelt take to bring about immediate relief from the banking crisis?**

market; only banks that specialized in investment could trade in the stock market after 1933. In addition, the Federal Reserve Board was given more authority to intervene in future financial emergencies. These steps ended the banking crisis.

Regulating Wall Street

Before the Great Crash in 1929, there was very little government oversight of the securities (stocks and bonds) industry, popularly known as "Wall Street," the financial district in Manhattan where the largest banks and brokerage houses were centered. In 1933, the Roosevelt administration developed two important pieces of legislation intended to regulate the operations of the stock market to eliminate fraud and abuses. The first, the Securities Exchange Act of 1933, was the first major federal legislation to regulate the sale of stocks and bonds. It required corporations that issued stock for public sale to "disclose" all relevant information about the operations and management of the company so that investors could know what they were buying. The second bill, the Securities Exchange Act of 1934, established the **Securities and Exchange Commission**, a federal agency to enforce the new laws and

Securities and Exchange Commission (1934) Federal agency established to regulate the issuance and trading of stocks and bonds in an effort to avoid financial panics and stock market crashes.

regulations governing the issuance and trading of stocks and bonds. The act also required that all stockbrokers be licensed.

The Federal Budget and the End of Prohibition

Roosevelt next convinced Congress to pass the Economy Act (1933), allowing him to cut government workers' salaries, reduce payments to military veterans for non-service-connected disabilities, and reorganize federal agencies—all in order to reduce government expenses.

> Economy Act and end of Prohibition

Roosevelt then took the dramatic step of ending Prohibition, in part because it was being so widely violated, in part because most Democrats wanted it ended, and in part because he wanted to regain the federal tax revenues from the sale of alcoholic beverages. The Twenty-First Amendment, ratified on December 5, 1933, ended Prohibition.

Helping the Unemployed and Homeless

Another urgent priority in 1933 was relieving the widespread human distress caused by the Great Depression. Herbert Hoover had stubbornly refused to help the unemployed and homeless, since he assumed that individual acts of charity (what he called *voluntarism*) and the efforts of local service organizations (churches and charities) would be sufficient to get people clothed, fed, and housed. Roosevelt had a much greater sense of urgency than Hoover. The new president developed a series of programs that created what came to be called the "welfare state." He did not believe that individuals should be given cash (a "dole"), but he did want the government to help people get jobs. For the first time, the federal government took primary responsibility for assisting the most desperate Americans, because the number of people in need far exceeded the capacity of charitable organizations and local government agencies.

> Creation of the welfare state

Putting People to Work

The Federal Emergency Relief Administration (FERA), headed by Harry Hopkins, was Roosevelt's first effort to deal with massive unemployment. It sent money to the states to spend on the unemployed and homeless. After the state-sponsored programs funded by the FERA proved inadequate, Congress created the Civil Works Administration (CWA) in November 1933. It was the first large-scale *federal* experiment with work relief, hiring people directly on the government payroll at competitive wages. Several states had done so before but never the national government. The CWA provided 4 million federal jobs during the winter of 1933–1934. The agency organized a variety of useful projects: repairing 500,000 miles of roads, laying sewer lines, constructing or improving more than a thousand airports and 40,000 public schools, and providing 50,000 teaching jobs that helped keep small rural public schools open. When the program's costs skyrocketed to over $1 billion, Roosevelt dissolved the CWA early in 1934. By April, some 4 million workers were again unemployed.

> Federal work relief

FEDERAL RELIEF PROGRAMS Civilian Conservation Corps enrollees in 1933, on a break from work. Directed by army officers and foresters, the CCC adhered to a semimilitary discipline.

The CCC

The most successful of the New Deal jobs programs was the Civilian Conservation Corps (CCC), managed by the War Department. It built 2,500 rustic camps in forty-seven states to house 3 million unemployed, unmarried young men aged eighteen to twenty-five. The CCC also recruited 150,000 jobless military veterans and 85,000 Native Americans, housing them in separate camps.

CCC workers, called "soil soldiers," built roads, bridges, campgrounds, fire towers, fish hatcheries, and 800 parks; planted 3 *billion* trees in national forests; taught farmers how to control soil erosion; and fought fires. Roosevelt believed that a "nation that destroys its soils destroys itself. Forests are the lungs of our land, purifying the air and giving fresh strength to our people." Over the next nine years, the 2.5 million CCC enrollees, supervised by soldiers, were given shelter, clothing, and food, as well as a small wage of $30 a month ($25 of which had to be sent home to their families). The CCC workers could also earn high-school diplomas at their camps.

Saving Homes

Federal Housing Administration (FHA) and the National Industrial Recovery Act (NIRA)

During 1933, a thousand homes or farms were being foreclosed upon each day because people could not afford to pay their mortgages. To address the problem, Roosevelt established the Home Owners' Loan Corporation, which helped homeowners refinance their mortgages at lower interest rates to avoid bankruptcy. In 1934, Roosevelt created the Federal Housing Administration (FHA), which offered home mortgages of much longer duration (twenty years) in order to reduce their monthly payments.

Reviving the Industrial Sector

The centerpiece of the New Deal's efforts to revive the industrial economy was the National Industrial Recovery Act (NIRA) of 1933. One of its two major sections dealt with economic recovery by creating massive public-works construction projects funded by the federal government. The NIRA created the Public Works Administration (PWA), granting $3.3 billion for the construction of government buildings, highways, bridges, dams, port facilities, and sewage plants.

The second, and more controversial, part of the NIRA created the **National Recovery Administration** (NRA), headed by Hugh S. Johnson, a hard-drinking retired army general known for his administrative expertise, a "blustering, dictatorial, and appealing" bureaucrat. The NRA represented a radical shift in the federal government's role in the economy. Never before in peacetime had Washington bureaucrats taken charge of setting prices, wages, and standards for working conditions.

The primary purpose of the NRA was to promote economic growth by temporarily waiving the anti-trust laws and allowing large corporations to create detailed "codes of fair competition" among themselves for 500 different industries, including the setting of prices on an array of products. At the same time, the NRA codes also included "fair-labor" policies long sought by unions and social progressives: a national forty-hour workweek, minimum weekly wages of $13 ($12 in the South, where living costs were lower), and a ban on the employment of children under the age of sixteen. The NRA also guaranteed the right of workers to organize unions.

Yet the NRA experiment had left an enduring mark. The NRA codes set new workplace standards, such as the forty-hour workweek, a minimum wage, and the abolition of child labor. The NRA's endorsement of collective bargaining between workers and owners spurred the growth of unions. Yet as 1934 ended, economic recovery was still nowhere in sight.

Agricultural Assistance

In addition to rescuing the banks and providing jobs to the unemployed, Roosevelt and his advisers promoted the long-term recovery of agriculture. Roosevelt created the Farm Credit Administration to help farmers deal with their crushing debts. Like the Home Owners' Loan Corporation, the Farm Credit Administration helped farmers refinance their mortgages at lower interest rates and lower monthly payments to avoid bankruptcy.

The **Agricultural Adjustment Act** of 1933 created a new federal agency, the Agricultural Adjustment Administration (AAA), which sought to raise prices for crops and herds by paying farmers to cut back production. The money for such payments came from a tax levied on the "processors" of certain basic commodities—cotton gins, flour mills, and slaughterhouses. By the time the AAA was created, however, the spring growing season was already under way. The prospect of another bumper cotton crop forced the AAA to sponsor a "plow-under" program in which farmers were paid to kill the sprouting seeds in their fields.

To destroy a growing crop was a "shocking commentary on our civilization," Agriculture secretary Henry A. Wallace admitted. "I could tolerate it only as a cleaning up of the wreckage from the old days of unbalanced production." Moreover, in an effort to raise pork prices, some 6 million baby pigs were slaughtered and buried. By the end of 1934, the AAA efforts had worked: wheat, cotton, and corn production had declined and prices for those commodities had risen. Farm income increased by 58 percent between 1932 and 1935.

The National Recovery Act (NRA): Creation of fair labor standards and recognition of the right to unionize

Farm Credit Association and the Agricultural Adjustment Act (1933)

National Recovery Administration (1933) Controversial federal agency that brought together business and labor leaders to create "codes of fair competition" and "fair-labor" policies, including a national minimum wage.

Agricultural Adjustment Act (1933) Legislation that paid farmers to produce less in order to raise crop prices for all; the AAA was later declared unconstitutional by the U.S. Supreme Court in the case of *United States v. Butler* (1936).

NORRIS DAM The massive dam in Tennessee, completed in 1936, was essential to creating jobs and expanding power production under the TVA.

Regional Planning: The TVA

One of the most innovative programs of the First New Deal created the Tennessee Valley Authority (TVA), an ambitious venture designed to bring electrical power, flood control efforts, and jobs to Appalachia, the desperately poor mountainous region that included West Virginia, western Virginia and North Carolina, Kentucky, eastern Tennessee, and northern Georgia and Alabama.

By 1940, the TVA, a multipurpose public corporation, had constructed twenty-one electricity-generating dams, which created the "Great Lakes of the South." The agency, moreover, dredged rivers to allow for boat and barge traffic, promoted soil conservation and scientific forestry management, experimented with fertilizers, drew new industries to the region, encouraged the formation of labor unions, improved schools and libraries, and provided 1.5 million farms with access to electricity and indoor plumbing.

During Roosevelt's first year in office, his flurry of new programs and his personal charm generated widespread support. A former CCC worker remembered that Roosevelt "restored a sense of confidence and morale and hope—hope being the greatest of all." The First New Deal programs—as well as Roosevelt's leadership—had given Americans a sense of renewed faith in the future. Voters showed their appreciation in the congressional elections of 1934: the Democrats increased their dominance in Congress with an almost unprecedented midterm victory for a party in power.

Eleanor Roosevelt

One of the reasons for Franklin Roosevelt's popularity was his energetic wife, Eleanor Roosevelt, who had become an enormous political asset and would prove to be one of the most influential leaders of the time. Never had a first lady been so engaged in public life.

Born in 1884 in New York City, the niece of Theodore Roosevelt, Eleanor married her distant cousin Franklin in 1905. During the 1920s, Eleanor Roosevelt began a lifelong crusade on behalf of women, blacks, and youth. Her tireless compassion resulted in part from the loneliness she had experienced as she was growing up and in part from the sense of betrayal she felt upon learning in 1918 that her husband had fallen in love with Lucy Mercer, her personal secretary. "The bottom dropped out of my own particular world," she recalled.

Eleanor and Franklin decided to maintain their marriage, but as their son James said, it became an "armed truce." Eleanor later observed that she could "forgive, but never forget." Alice Roosevelt Longworth—the daughter of Theodore Roosevelt and a cousin of Eleanor's—actually nurtured the affair, hosting Mercer and Franklin for secret dinners. She later explained that Roosevelt "deserved a good time . . . he was married to Eleanor."

Eleanor Roosevelt redefined the role of the First Lady. She was not content to host social events in the White House. Instead, she became an outspoken activist: the first woman to address a national political convention; to write a nationally syndicated newspaper column; and to hold regular press conferences, over 300 of them.

The tireless Eleanor crisscrossed the nation, speaking in support of the New Deal, meeting with African American leaders, supporting women's causes and organized labor, and urging Americans to live up to their humanitarian ideals. In 1933, she convened a White House conference on the emergency needs of women, which urged the Federal Emergency Relief Administration (FERA) to ensure that it "pay particular attention to see that women are employed wherever possible." Within six months, some 300,000 women were at work on various federal government projects.

Eleanor Roosevelt, said a journalist, had become "the most influential woman of our times." A popular joke in Washington claimed that President Roosevelt's nightly prayer was in the form of an urgent plea: "Dear God, please make Eleanor a little tired." In fact, however, he was deeply dependent upon his industrious wife. She was the agitator dedicated to what *should* be done; he was the practical politician concerned with what *could* be done.

ELEANOR ROOSEVELT
Intelligent, principled, and a political figure in her own right, she is pictured here addressing the Red Cross Convention in 1934.

The New Deal under Fire

CORE OBJECTIVE
5. Analyze the major criticisms of the early New Deal.

By 1934, Franklin Roosevelt had become the best loved and most hated president of the twentieth century. Although a child of wealth and prestige, he was loved because he believed in and fought for the common people, for the "forgotten man" (and woman). The president, said a southern white tenant farmer, "is as good a man as ever lived," and a textile-mill worker reinforced the point by declaring that Roosevelt "is the biggest-hearted man we ever had in the White House." Fans also loved what one French leader called his "glittering personality." Roosevelt radiated personal charm, joy in his work, courage in a crisis, and optimism for the future. "Meeting him," said the British prime minister Winston Churchill, "was like uncorking a bottle of champagne."

New Deal criticized by those on the Left and Right

But Roosevelt was hated, too, especially by business leaders and political conservatives who believed the New Deal and the higher taxes it required were moving America toward socialism. Others, on the Left, hated Roosevelt for not doing enough to end the Depression. By the mid-1930s, the early New Deal programs had helped stop the economy's downward slide, but prosperity remained elusive. "We have been patient and long suffering," said a farm leader. "We were promised a New Deal. . . . Instead, we have the same old stacked deck."

Continuing Hardships

Although the programs making up the First New Deal helped ease the devastation caused by the Depression, the Depression continued to exact a terrible toll as the shattered economy slowly worked its way back to health. As late as 1939, some 9.5 million workers (17 percent of the labor force) remained unemployed.

African Americans and the New Deal

New Deal discrimination, the NAACP, and the "Black Cabinet"

The New Deal also had its blind spots. However progressive Franklin Delano Roosevelt was on social issues, he showed little interest in the plight of African Americans, even as black voters, by 1936, were shifting from the Republicans (the "party of Lincoln") to the Democrats. President Roosevelt, like Woodrow Wilson before him, failed to address long-standing patterns of racism and segregation in the South for fear of angering conservative southern Democrats in Congress.

As a result, many of the New Deal programs discriminated against blacks. As Mary White Ovington, the treasurer of the National Association for the Advancement of Colored People (NAACP), stressed, the racism in any agency "varies according to the white people chosen to administer it, but always there is discrimination."

For example, the payments from the AAA to farm owners to take land *out* of production in an effort to raise the prices for farm products forced hundreds of thousands of tenant farmers and sharecroppers, both blacks and whites, off the land. Meanwhile, the FHA refused to guarantee mortgages on houses purchased by blacks in white neighborhoods. In addition, both the CCC and the TVA practiced racial segregation.

The NAACP waged an energetic legal campaign against racial prejudice throughout the 1930s, as did Eleanor Roosevelt. The First Lady convinced the president to appoint more African Americans to government positions than ever before. One of the most visible of the new appointees was Mary McLeod Bethune, the child of former slaves from South Carolina, who had founded Bethune-Cookman College in Florida and had served as the head of the NAACP in the 1920s. In 1935, Roosevelt approved her appointment as the director of the Division of Negro Affairs within the National Youth Administration, an agency that provided jobs to unemployed young Americans.

Court Cases and Civil Liberties

The continuing prejudice against blacks in the South was vividly revealed in a controversial case in Alabama that attracted national attention. In 1931, an all-white jury, on flimsy evidence, hastily convicted nine black males, ranging in age from thirteen to twenty-one, of raping two young white women while riding a freight train. Eight of the "Scottsboro Boys" were sentenced to death as whites in the courtroom cheered.

"Scottsboro Boys"

The injustice of the Scottsboro case sparked protests throughout the nation and around the world. The two white women, it turned out, had been selling sex to white and black teens on the train. One of the women eventually recanted the rape charges and began appearing at rallies on behalf of the black defendants.

No case in American legal history had ever produced as many trials, appeals, reversals, and retrials as the much-publicized Scottsboro case. Further, it prompted two important legal interpretations. In *Powell v. Alabama* (1932), the U.S. Supreme Court overturned the original convictions in the case because the judge had not ensured that the accused were provided adequate defense attorneys. The Court ordered new trials.

In another case, *Norris v. Alabama* (1935), the Court ruled that the systematic exclusion of African Americans from Alabama juries had denied the Scottsboro defendants equal protection under the law—a principle that had widespread impact on state courts by opening up juries to blacks. Eventually, but too late to help the defendants, whose lives were ruined, the state of Alabama dropped the charges against the four youngest of the "Scottsboro

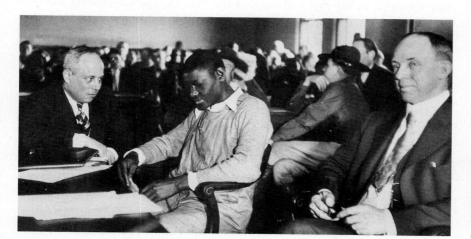

SCOTTSBORO CASE Heywood Patterson (center), one of the defendants in the case, is seen here with his attorney, Samuel Leibowitz (left) in Decatur, Alabama, in 1933.

Boys" and granted paroles to the others; the last one was released from prison in 1950.

Native Americans and the Depression

The "Indian New Deal"

The Great Depression also ravaged Native Americans. They were initially encouraged by Roosevelt's appointment of John Collier as the commissioner of the Bureau of Indian Affairs (BIA). Collier steadily increased the number of Native Americans employed by the BIA and ensured that Native Americans gained access to the various federal relief programs. Collier's primary objective, however, was passage of the Indian Reorganization Act. Designed to reinvigorate Native American cultural traditions by restoring land to tribes, the proposed law would grant them the right to start businesses and establish self-governing constitutions, and provide federal funds for vocational training and economic development. The act that Congress finally passed, however, was a much-diluted version of Collier's original proposal, and the "Indian New Deal" brought only a partial improvement to the lives of Native Americans. Yet it did spur the various tribes to revise their constitutions so as to give women the right to vote and hold office.

Critics Assault the New Deal

For all their criticisms of the inadequacy of New Deal programs, Native Americans and African Americans still voted in large majorities for Franklin Roosevelt. Other New Deal critics, however, despised Roosevelt as much as they hated his policies.

Huey Long

The most potent political threat to Roosevelt came from Louisiana's Democratic senator Huey P. Long. A short, colorful man with wild curly hair, Long, known as the "Kingfish," was a theatrical political performer (a "demagogue") who appealed to the raw emotions of the masses. The swaggering son of a backwoods farmer, he sported pink suits and pastel shirts, red ties, and two-toned shoes. He claimed to serve the poor, arguing that his Louisiana would be a place where "every man [is] a king, but no one wears a crown."

First as Louisiana's governor, then as its most powerful U.S. senator, Long came to view the state as his personal empire. Reporters called him the "dictator of Louisiana." True, he reduced state taxes, improved roads and schools, built charity hospitals, and provided better public services, but in the process, he became a bullying dictator who used bribery, intimidation, and blackmail to get his way.

In 1933, Senator Long arrived in Washington as a supporter of Roosevelt and the New Deal, but he quickly grew suspicious of the NRA's efforts to cooperate with big business. Having developed his own presidential aspirations, he also grew jealous of "Prince Franklin" Roosevelt's popularity.

To launch his own presidential candidacy, Long devised a simplistic plan for dealing with the Great Depression, which he called the Share-the-Wealth Society. Long wanted to raise taxes on the wealthiest Americans and redistribute the money raised to "the people"—giving every poor family $5,000 and every wage worker an annual income of $2,500, providing pensions to retirees, reducing working hours, paying bonuses to military veterans, and enabling every qualified student to attend college.

It did not matter that Long's plan would have spent far more dollars than would have been raised by his proposed taxes. As he told a group of Iowa farmers, "Maybe somebody says I don't understand it [government finance]. Well, you don't have to. Just shut your damn eyes and believe it. That's all." By early 1935, the outspoken Long claimed to have enough support to unseat Roosevelt. "I can take him," he bragged. "He's a phony. . . . He's scared of me. I can outpromise him, and he knows it. People will believe me, and they won't believe him."

HUEY LONG As the powerful governor of Louisiana, Long was a shrewd lawyer and consummate politician.

The Townsend Plan

Another popular critic of Roosevelt was a retired California doctor, Francis E. Townsend. Outraged by the sight of three elderly women digging through garbage cans for food scraps, Townsend began promoting the Townsend Recovery Plan in 1934. It called for the federal government to pay $200 a month to every American over sixty who agreed to quit working. The recipients had to spend the money each month; it could not be saved. Townsend claimed that his plan would create new jobs for young people by forcing older people to retire, and it would energize the economy by enabling retirees to buy more every month.

Like Huey Long's "Share Our Wealth" scheme, the numbers in Townsend's crackpot scheme did not add up: the Townsend Plan, which would serve only 9 percent of the population, would have paid those retirees more than half the *total* national income. Yet Townsend, like Long, didn't care about the numbers adding up. "I'm not in the least interested in the cost of the plan," he blandly told a congressional committee. Not surprisingly, however, the Townsend Plan attracted great support among Americans aged sixty and older. Thousands of Townsend Clubs sprang up across the nation to mobilize support for the scheme, and advocates of the plan flooded the White House with letters urging Roosevelt to enact it.

Townsend Plan and Father Coughlin

Father Coughlin

A third outspoken critic of Roosevelt was Father Charles E. Coughlin, the Roman Catholic "radio priest" in Detroit who founded the National Union for Social Justice in 1935. In fiery weekly broadcasts over the CBS radio network that attracted as many as 40 million listeners, he assailed Roosevelt as

ROOSEVELT'S CRITICS Dr. Francis E. Townsend, Rev. Gerald L. K. Smith, and Father Charles E. Coughlin (left to right) attend the Townsend Recovery Plan convention in Cleveland, Ohio.
What were the main features of the Townsend Recovery Plan, and how would they have played out if put into effect?

"anti-God" and claimed that the New Deal was a Communist conspiracy.

During the 1930s, Coughlin became openly anti-Semitic, claiming that Roosevelt was a tool of "international Jewish bankers." He charged that the New Deal was in fact the "Jew Deal." He praised Hitler and the Nazis for killing Jews because he believed that all Jews were Communists who must be hunted down. "When we get through with the Jews in America," the thuggish Coughlin bragged, "they'll think the treatment they received in Germany was nothing."

Coughlin, Townsend, and Long were Roosevelt's most prominent critics. Of the three, Long had the largest political following. A 1935 survey showed that he could draw over 5 million votes as a third-party candidate for president in 1936, perhaps enough to prevent Roosevelt's reelection. Roosevelt decided to "steal the thunder" from his most vocal critics by instituting an array of new programs. "I'm fighting Communism, Huey Longism, Coughlinism, Townsendism," Roosevelt told a reporter in early 1935. He explained that he must fight even harder "to save our system, the capitalist system," from such "crackpot ideas."

Opposition from the Court

The growing opposition to the New Deal came from all directions. Among the most powerful was the Supreme Court. By the mid-1930s, businesses were filing lawsuits against various elements of the New Deal, and some of them made their way to the Supreme Court.

The Supreme Court versus The New Deal

Supreme Court overturns some New Deal programs

On May 27, 1935, the U.S. Supreme Court killed the NIRA by a unanimous vote. In *Schechter Poultry Corporation v. United States* (1935), the justices ruled that Congress had given too much of its authority to the president when the NIRA gave the NRA the power to bring business and labor leaders together to create "codes of fair competition" for their industries. In a press conference soon after the Court announced its decision, Roosevelt fumed: "We have been relegated to the horse-and-buggy definition of interstate commerce."

By 1935, however, the NRA had developed more critics than friends. While the NRA had worked for a time, and the downward spiral of wages and prices subsided, as soon as economic recovery began, small business owners complained that the larger corporations dominated the NRA, whose price-fixing ability robbed small producers of the chance to compete. And because the NRA wage codes excluded agricultural and domestic workers (at the insistence of southern Democrats), three out of every four African Americans derived no direct benefit from the program.

Then, on January 6, 1936, in *United States v. Butler*, the Supreme Court declared the AAA's tax on the companies that processed food crops and commodities like cotton unconstitutional. In response to the Court's decision, the Roosevelt administration passed the Agricultural Adjustment Act of 1938, which reestablished the earlier crop-reduction payment programs but left out the tax on processors. Although the AAA helped boost the overall farm economy, conservatives criticized its sweeping powers. By the end of its 1936 term, the Supreme Court had ruled against New Deal programs in seven of nine major cases. The same line of conservative judicial reasoning, Roosevelt warned, might endanger other New Deal programs—if he did not act swiftly to prevent it.

The Second New Deal

Roosevelt refused to let his critics derail the New Deal. To rescue his legislative program from judicial and political challenges, he launched in January 1935 the second, more radical phase of the New Deal, explaining that "social justice, no longer a distant ideal, has become a definite goal" of his administration.

In his effort "to steal Huey Long's thunder," the president called on Congress to pass a cluster of "must" legislation that included a new federal construction program to employ the jobless; banking reforms; increased taxes on the wealthy; and programs to protect people during unemployment, old age, and illness. Roosevelt's closest aide, Harry L. Hopkins, told the cabinet: "Boys—this is our hour. We've got to get everything we want—a [public-]works program, social security, wages and hours, everything—now or never."

The WPA

In the first three months of 1935, dubbed the Second Hundred Days, Roosevelt used all his considerable political skills to convince the Democratic-controlled Congress to pass most of the **Second New Deal**'s "must" legislation. The results changed the face of American life.

The first major initiative, the $4.8 billion Emergency Relief Appropriation Act, sailed through the new Congress. Roosevelt called it the "Big Bill" because it was the largest peacetime spending bill in history up to that point. It included an array of federal job programs managed by a new government agency, the **Works Progress Administration** (WPA).

The WPA quickly became the nation's largest employer, hiring an average of 2 million people annually over four years. Federal WPA workers built New York's LaGuardia Airport; restored the St. Louis riverfront; and managed the bankrupt city of Key West, Florida. The WPA also employed a wide range of talented writers, artists, actors, and musicians in new cultural

> **CORE OBJECTIVE**
> **6.** Evaluate the ways the New Deal changed and how it transformed the role of federal government.

Second New Deal (1935–1938) Expansive cluster of legislation proposed by President Roosevelt that established new regulatory agencies, strengthened the rights of workers to organize unions, and laid the foundation of a federal social welfare system through the creation of Social Security.

Works Progress Administration (1935) Government agency established to manage several federal job programs created under the New Deal; it became the largest employer in the nation.

programs: the Federal Theatre Project, the Federal Art Project, the Federal Music Project, and the Federal Writers' Project.

The National Youth Administration (NYA), also under the WPA, provided part-time employment to students and aided jobless youths. Twenty-seven-year-old Lyndon B. Johnson directed an NYA program in Texas, and Richard M. Nixon, a struggling Duke University law student, found work through the NYA at 35¢ an hour. Although the WPA took care of only 3 million of some 10 million jobless at any one time, in all it helped some 9 million people weather desperate circumstances before it expired in 1943.

FEDERAL ART PROJECT A group of WPA artists at work on *Building the Transcontinental Railroad*, a mural celebrating the contributions of immigrants that appears in the immigrants' dining hall on Ellis Island.

The Wagner Act

Another major element of the Second New Deal was the National Labor Relations Act, often called the **Wagner Act** in honor of the New York senator, Robert Wagner, who drafted it and convinced Roosevelt to support it. The Wagner Act was one of the most important pieces of labor legislation in history, guaranteeing workers the right to organize unions and bargain directly with management about wages and other issues. It also prohibited employers from interfering with union activities. The Wagner Act created a National Labor Relations Board to oversee union activities across the nation.

Social Security

Wagner Act (1935) Legislation that guaranteed workers the right to organize unions, granted them direct bargaining power, and barred employers from interfering with union activities.

Social Security Act (1935) Legislation enacted to provide federal assistance to retired workers through tax-funded pension payments and benefit payments to the unemployed and disabled.

As Francis Townsend stressed, the Great Depression hit the oldest Americans and those with disabilities especially hard. To address the problems faced by the elderly, blind, and disabled, Roosevelt proposed the **Social Security Act** of 1935. Social Security was, he announced, the "cornerstone" and "supreme achievement" of the New Deal.

The basic concept of government assistance to the elderly was not new. Progressives during the early 1900s had proposed a federal system of social security for the aged, poor, disabled, and unemployed. Other nations had already enacted such programs, but not the United States. The hardships caused by the Great Depression revived the idea of a social security program, however, and Roosevelt masterfully guided the legislation through Congress.

The Social Security Act, designed by Secretary of Labor Frances Perkins, the first woman cabinet member in history, included three major provisions. Its centerpiece was a self-financed federal retirement fund for people over sixty-five. Beginning in 1937, workers and employers contributed payroll taxes to establish the fund. Most of the collected taxes went toward pension payments to retirees; the rest went into a trust fund for the future.

Roosevelt stressed that Social Security would not guarantee everyone a comfortable retirement. Rather, it would supplement other sources of income and protect the elderly from some of the "hazards" of life. Only during the 1950s did voters and politicians come to view Social Security as the *primary* source of retirement income for working-class Americans.

The Social Security Act also set up a shared federal-state unemployment-insurance program, financed by a payroll tax paid by employers. In addition, the new legislation committed the national government to a broad range of social-welfare activities based upon the assumption that "unemployables"—people who were unable to work—would remain a state responsibility while the national government would provide work relief for the able-bodied. To that end, the Social Security Act provided federal funding for three state-administered programs—old-age assistance, aid to dependent children, and aid for the blind—and further aid for maternal, child-welfare, and public health services.

SOCIAL SECURITY The federal government distributed posters such as this one to educate the public about the new Social Security Act.

When compared with similar programs in Europe, the new U.S. Social Security system was conservative. It was the only government-managed retirement program in the world financed by taxes on the earnings of workers; most other countries funded such programs out of general government revenues.

The Social Security payroll tax was also a regressive tax because it used a single withholding tax *rate* for everyone, regardless of income level. It thus pinched the poor more than the rich. It also hurt Roosevelt's efforts to revive the economy because it removed from circulation a significant amount of money: the new Social Security tax took money out of workers' pockets and placed it into a retirement fund, worsening the shrinking money supply that was one of the main causes of the Depression.

In addition, the Social Security system, at the insistence of southern Democrats determined to maintain white supremacy in the region, excluded 9.5 million workers who most needed the new program: farm laborers, domestic workers (maids and cooks), and the self-employed, a disproportionate percentage of whom were African Americans.

Roosevelt regretted the limitations of the Social Security Act, but he saw them as necessary compromises in order to gain congressional approval and to withstand court challenges. As he replied to an aide who criticized funding the pension program out of employee contributions: "I guess you're right on the economics, but those taxes were never a problem of economics. They are politics all the way through. We put those payroll contributions there to give the contributors a moral, legal, and political right to collect their pensions and their unemployment benefits. With those taxes in there, no damn politician can ever scrap my Social Security program."

> Second New Deal: Social Security and Wealth-Tax Act

Roosevelt also preferred workers to fund their own Social Security pensions because he wanted Americans to view their retirement checks not as a welfare payment but as an *entitlement*—as something that they had paid for, something they deserved. On the other hand, conservatives condemned the Social Security Act as another example of Roosevelt's tyrannical expansion of government power. Former president Herbert Hoover was among a few Americans who refused to apply for a Social Security card because of his opposition to the "radical" program. He received a Social Security number anyway.

Taxing the Rich

Another major bill making up the second phase of the New Deal was the Revenue Act of 1935, sometimes called the "Wealth-Tax Act" but popularly known as the "soak-the-rich" tax. The Revenue Act raised tax rates on annual income greater than $50,000, in part because of stories that many wealthy Americans were not paying taxes. The powerful banker J. P. Morgan confessed to a Senate committee that he had created fictitious sales of stock to his wife that enabled him to pay no taxes.

Morgan and other business leaders fumed over Roosevelt's tax and spending policies. The newspaper editor William Randolph Hearst growled that the wealth tax was "essentially communism." Roosevelt countered: "I am fighting communism. . . . I want to save our system, the capitalistic system." Yet he added that saving capitalism and "rebalancing" its essential elements required a more equal "distribution of wealth." Like his cousin Theodore, Franklin Roosevelt did not hate capitalism; he hated capitalists who engaged in "unfair" or illegal behavior.

A New Direction for Unions

The New Deal helped revive the labor union movement. When the NIRA demanded that every industry code affirm workers' rights to organize, alert unionists quickly translated it to mean "the president wants you to join the union." John L. Lewis, head of the United Mine Workers (UMW), was among the first to capitalize upon the pro-union spirit of the NIRA. He rebuilt the UMW from 150,000 members to 500,000 within a year.

Spurred by Lewis's success, Sidney Hillman of the Amalgamated Clothing Workers and David Dubinsky of the International Ladies Garment

Workers organized laborers in the clothing industry. As leaders of industrial unions (composed of all types of workers in a particular industry, skilled or unskilled), which were in the minority by far, they found the smaller, more restrictive craft unions (comprising skilled male workers only, with each union serving just one trade) to be obstacles to organizing workers in the country's basic industries.

In 1935, with the passage of the Wagner Act, industrial unionists formed a Committee for Industrial Organization (CIO), and craft unionists (skilled workers) began to fear submergence by the mass unions made up mainly of unskilled workers. Jurisdictional disputes divided them, and in 1936 the American Federation of Labor (AFL) expelled the CIO unions, which then formed a permanent structure, called after 1938 the Congress of Industrial Organizations (also known by the initials CIO). The rivalry spurred both groups to recruit more members.

The CIO's major organizing drives in the automobile and steel industries began in 1936, but until the Supreme Court upheld the Wagner Act in 1937, companies failed to cooperate with its pro-union provisions. Employers used various forms of intimidation to fight the efforts of workers to form unions. Early in 1937, automobile workers spontaneously adopted a new tactic, the "sit-down strike," in which workers refused to leave a workplace until employers had granted collective-bargaining rights to their union.

"Sit-down strikes"

Led by the fiery young union organizer Walter Reuther, thousands of employees at the General Motors assembly plants in Flint, Michigan, occupied the factories and stopped all production. Female workers supported their male counterparts by picketing at the plant entrances. Company officials called in police to harass the strikers, sent spies to union meetings, and

LABOR UNION VIOLENCE
This 1935 photograph captures unionized strikers fighting "scabs," or nonunion replacement employees, as the scabs attempt to pass the picket line and enter the factory.

threatened to fire the workers. They also pleaded with President Roosevelt to dispatch federal troops. He refused, while expressing his displeasure with the sit-down strike, which the courts later declared illegal. The standoff lasted over a month. Then, on February 11, 1937, the company relented and signed a contract recognizing the fledgling United Automobile Workers (UAW) as a legitimate union.

Roosevelt's Second Term

On June 27, 1936, Franklin Delano Roosevelt accepted the Democratic party's nomination for a second term. The Republicans chose Governor Alfred M. Landon of Kansas, a progressive Republican who had endorsed many New Deal programs. The Republicans hoped that the followers of Long, Coughlin, Townsend, and other Roosevelt critics would combine to draw enough Democratic votes away from Roosevelt to throw the election to them. That possibility faded, however, when an assassin, the son-in-law of a Louisiana judge whom Huey Long had sought to remove, shot and killed the forty-two-year-old senator in 1935.

In the 1936 election, Roosevelt carried every state except Maine and Vermont, with a popular vote of 27.7 million to Landon's 16.7 million, the largest margin of victory up to that point. Democrats would also dominate Republicans in the new Congress, 77–19 in the Senate and 328–107 in the House.

In winning another landslide election, Roosevelt forged in 1936 a new electoral coalition that would affect national politics for years to come. While holding the support of most traditional Democrats, North and South, the president made strong gains in the West among beneficiaries of New Deal agricultural programs. In the northern cities, he held on to the ethnic groups helped by New Deal welfare policies. Many middle-class voters who had benefited from New Deal measures flocked to support Roosevelt, as did intellectuals stirred by the ferment of new ideas coming from the government. The revived labor union movement threw its support to Roosevelt. And, in the most profound departure of all, African American voters for the first time cast the majority of their ballots for a Democratic president. "My friends, go home and turn Lincoln's picture to the wall," a Pittsburgh journalist told black voters. "That debt has been paid in full."

The Court-Packing Plan

Roosevelt's landslide victory emboldened him to make even more radical efforts to end the Great Depression. In his second inaugural address, delivered on January 20, 1937, he promised even greater reforms. The challenge to democracy, he maintained, was that millions lacked "the necessities of life. . . . I see one-third of a nation ill-housed, ill-clad, ill-nourished." Roosevelt argued that his reelection demonstrated that the nation wanted even more extensive government action to revive the economy. The 3 to 1 Democratic majorities in Congress ensured he could pass new legislation. Yet a major roadblock stood in the way: the conservative Supreme Court.

Suits challenging the constitutionality of the Social Security and Wagner Acts were pending. Given the conservative bent of the Court, the Second New Deal seemed in danger of being nullified by judges, just as much of the original New Deal had been.

For that reason, Roosevelt hatched a plan to change the Court's conservative stance by increasing its members. Congress, not the Constitution, determines the size of the Supreme Court, which over the years had numbered between six and ten justices. In 1937, the number was nine. On February 5, 1937, Roosevelt, without consulting congressional leaders or even his own advisers, asked Congress to name up to six new Supreme Court justices, explaining that the aging justices then on the Court were falling behind in their work and needed help.

The clumsy "Court-packing" plan, as opponents labeled the president's scheme, backfired. It was too manipulative and far too political. A leading journalist said that Roosevelt had become "drunk with power." Others compared him to the European dictators, Hitler and Stalin. Roosevelt's plan aroused fears even among Democrats that the president was seeking dangerous new powers.

As it turned out, unforeseen events blunted Roosevelt's blundering effort to change the Court. To everyone's surprise, a sequence of Court decisions during the spring of 1937 upheld disputed provisions of the Wagner and Social Security Acts. In addition, a conservative justice resigned, and Roosevelt replaced him with one of the most consistent New Dealers, Senator Hugo Black of Alabama.

Despite criticism from both parties, however, Roosevelt insisted on forcing his Court-packing bill through the Congress. On July 22, 1937, the Senate overwhelmingly voted it down. It was the biggest political blunder of Roosevelt's career. The episode fractured the Democratic party and damaged the president's prestige. For the first time, Democrats in large numbers, especially southerners, opposed Roosevelt, and the momentum of his 1936 landslide victory was lost. As Secretary of Agriculture Henry A. Wallace later remarked, "The whole New Deal really went up in smoke as a result of the Supreme Court fight."

COURT-PACKING PLAN
The Democratic Congress (represented by a donkey) kicks up its heels at Roosevelt in opposition to his court-packing plan.

A Slumping Economy

During the years 1935 and 1936, the depressed economy was finally showing signs of revival. By the spring of 1937, industrial output had finally moved above the 1929 level. In 1937, however, Roosevelt, worried about federal

"Roosevelt's recession" in 1937

budget deficits and rising inflation, ordered sharp cuts in government spending. As a result, the economy suddenly stalled and slid into a business slump deeper than that of 1929. In only three months, unemployment rose by 2 million people. When the spring of 1938 failed to bring economic recovery, Roosevelt asked Congress to adopt a new large-scale federal spending program, and Congress voted $3.3 billion in new expenditures. The increase in government spending helped, but only during World War II would employment reach pre-1929 levels.

Setbacks for the President

Democrats divided over New Deal

During the late 1930s, the Democrats in Congress increasingly split into two factions, with conservative southerners on one side and liberal northerners on the other. Many southern Democrats balked at the national party's growing dependence upon the votes of northern labor unions and African Americans. Senator Ellison "Cotton Ed" Smith of South Carolina, the powerful chair of the Committee on Agriculture, and several other southern delegates walked out of the 1936 Democratic convention, with Smith declaring that he would not support any party that views "the Negro as a political and social equal." Other critics believed that Roosevelt was exercising too much power and spending too much money. Some disgruntled southern Democrats began to work with conservative Republicans to veto any additional New Deal programs.

Roosevelt now headed a divided party, and the congressional elections of November 1938 handed the administration another setback when the Democrats lost seven seats in the Senate and eighty in the House. In his State of the Union message in 1939, Roosevelt for the first time proposed no new reforms. The conservative coalition of Republicans and southern Democrats had stalemated the once-unstoppable Roosevelt. As one observer noted, the New Deal "has been reduced to a movement with no program, with no effective political organization, with no vast popular party strength behind it."

A Halfway Revolution

The New Deal's political momentum petered out in 1939 just as a new world war was erupting in Europe and Asia. Many of the New Deal programs had failed or were poorly conceived and implemented, victims of bureaucratic infighting and inefficient management, but others were changing American life for the better: Social Security, the federal regulation of stock markets and banks, minimum-wage levels for workers, federally insured bank accounts, government-sanctioned labor unions.

The greatest triumph of the New Deal, however, was not its successful programs but its demonstration that American democracy could, through governmental lawmaking and presidential leadership, cope with the collapse of capitalism. A self-proclaimed "preacher President," Roosevelt raised the nation's spirits and its income through his relentless optimism and unprecedented activism.

Roosevelt changed the role of the federal government and the presidency in national life. During the 1930s, for the first time in peacetime, the federal government assumed responsibility for planning and managing the economy and intervening to ensure social stability. By the end of the 1930s, the power and scope of the national government were vastly larger than in 1932. Landmark laws expanded the powers of the national government by establishing regulatory agencies and laying the foundation of a social welfare system. Most important of all, however, the New Deal restored a sense of hope to many people who had grown discouraged and desperate.

Foundation for social welfare system

The enduring reforms of the New Deal entailed more than just a bigger federal government, an activist president, and revived public confidence; they also constituted a significant change from the progressivism of Theodore Roosevelt and Woodrow Wilson. Those reformers had assumed that the function of progressive government was to use aggressive *regulation* of industry and business to ensure that people had an equal opportunity to pursue the American dream.

Franklin Roosevelt and the New Dealers went beyond the progressive concept of regulated capitalism by insisting that the government provide at least a minimal level of support for all Americans. The enduring protections afforded by bank-deposit insurance, unemployment benefits, a minimum hourly wage, the Wagner Act, and Social Security pensions provided people with a sense of security as well as a safeguard for the nation against future economic crises (there has not been a similar depression since the 1930s).

Federal regulation of business and banking

The greatest failure of the New Deal was its inability to restore prosperity and end record levels of unemployment. In 1939, 10 million Americans—nearly 17 percent of the workforce—remained jobless. Only the prolonged crisis of the Second World War would finally produce full employment—in the military as well as in factories making things for the military.

Roosevelt's energetic pragmatism was his greatest strength—and weakness. He was flexible in developing new policies and programs; he kept what worked and discarded what failed. The result was both profoundly revolutionary and profoundly conservative. Roosevelt sharply increased the regulatory powers of the federal government and laid the foundation for what would become an expanding system of social welfare programs. Roosevelt, however, was no socialist, as Republican critics charged; he sought to preserve the basic capitalist economic structure while providing protection to the nation's most vulnerable people. In this sense, the New Deal represented a "halfway revolution" that permanently altered the nation's social and political landscape. In a time of peril, Roosevelt created for Americans a more secure future.

Reviewing the
CORE OBJECTIVES |

■ **The Great Depression** The 1929 stock market crash revealed the structural flaws in the economy, but it was not the only cause of the *Great Depression (1929–1941)*. During the twenties, business owners did not provide adequate wage increases for workers, resulting in the overproduction of many goods by the end of the decade. The nation's agricultural sector also suffered from overproduction. Government policies—such as high tariffs and the reduction of the nation's money supply—further reduced the nation's consumption and exacerbated the emerging economic depression.

■ **The Human Toll of the Depression** Thousands of banks and businesses closed, while millions of homes and jobs were lost. By the early 1930s, many people were homeless and hopeless. The *Dust Bowl* of the 1930s compounded the hardship for rural Americans. Discrimination against married women, African Americans, Native Americans, Hispanics, and Asian Americans in hiring was widespread.

■ **Hoover's Failure** The first phase of federal response to the Great Depression included President Hoover's attempts at increasing public works and exhorting unions, businesses, and farmers to revive economic growth. In 1932, Congress created the *Reconstruction Finance Corporation* to help banks and corporations avoid bankruptcy, but Hoover's philosophy of voluntary self-reliance prevented him from using federal intervention to relieve the suffering of American citizens. When

thousands of out-of-work veterans of the Great War, the *Bonus Expeditionary Force*, protested in Washington, D.C., their efforts ended in violence. In March 1933, the economy was shattered. Millions more Americans were without jobs, basic necessities, and hope.

■ **The First New Deal** During his early months in office, Congress and President Roosevelt enacted the *First New Deal (1933–1935)*, which propped up the banking industry with the *Federal Deposit Insurance Corporation (1933)*, provided short-term emergency work relief, promoted industrial recovery with the *National Recovery Administration (1933)*, raised agricultural prices with the *Agricultural Adjustment Act (1933)*, and enforced new laws and regulations on Wall Street with the *Securities and Exchange Commission (1934)*. In this second phase of the federal response, most of the early New Deal programs helped end the economy's downward spiral but still left millions unemployed and mired in poverty.

■ **New Deal under Fire** The Supreme Court ruled that several of the First New Deal programs were unconstitutional violations of private property and states' rights. Many conservatives criticized the New Deal for expanding the scope and reach of the federal government so much that it was steering the nation toward socialism. By contrast, other critics did not think the New Deal went far enough. African American critics decried the widespread discrimination in New Deal policies and agencies.

The Second New Deal and the New Deal's Legacy Roosevelt responded to the criticism and the continuing economic hardship with a third phase, the *Second New Deal (1935–1938)*, which sought to reshape the nation's social structure by expanding the role of the federal government. Many of its programs, such as the *Works Progress Administration (1935)*, *Social Security Act (1935)*, and the *Wagner Act (1935)*, aimed to achieve greater social justice by establishing new regulatory agencies and laying the foundation of a federal social welfare system. The Second New Deal reformed business, industry, and banking with provisions such as unemployment pay, a minimum hourly wage, old-age pensions, and bank-deposit insurance. The New Deal established the idea that the federal government should provide a baseline quality of life for all Americans.

KEY TERMS

Great Depression (1929–1941) *p. 853*

Dust Bowl *p. 860*

Reconstruction Finance Corporation (1932) *p. 864*

Bonus Expeditionary Force (1932) *p. 864*

First New Deal (1933–1935) *p. 869*

Federal Deposit Insurance Corporation (1933) *p. 869*

Securities and Exchange Commission (1934) *p. 870*

National Recovery Administration (1933) *p. 873*

Agricultural Adjustment Act (1933) *p. 873*

Second New Deal (1935–1938) *p. 881*

Works Progress Administration (1935) *p. 881*

Wagner Act (1935) *p. 882*

Social Security Act (1935) *p. 882*

CHRONOLOGY

1929	Herbert Hoover inaugurated as president in March, and stock market crashes in late October
1930	Congress passes the Smoot-Hawley Tariff
1932	Congress sets up the Reconstruction Finance Corporation
	Bonus Expeditionary Force heads to Washington, D.C.
	Franklin D. Roosevelt is elected president
March–June 1933	First One Hundred Days of Roosevelt's presidency
December 1933	Twenty-First Amendment repeals Prohibition
1935	Roosevelt creates the Works Progress Administration
	Supreme Court finds National Industrial Recovery Act unconstitutional
	Congress passes the Wagner Act
1936	President Roosevelt is reelected in a landslide
1937	Social Security goes into effect
	Roosevelt attempts Court-packing scheme

📖 INQUIZITIVE

Go to InQuizitive to see what you've learned—and learn what you've missed—with personalized feedback along the way.

***RAISING THE FLAG ON IWO JIMA* (FEBRUARY 23, 1945)** Six members of the U.S. Marine Corps raise the flag on Mount Suribachi during the Battle of Iwo Jima. Three of these marines would die within days of this photograph, which later earned photographer Joe Rosenthal the Pulitzer Prize. A bronze statue of this scene is the centerpiece of the Marine Corps War Memorial in Virginia.

The Second World War

1933–1945

When Franklin Roosevelt became president in 1933, he shared with most Americans a determination to stay out of international disputes. His focus was on combating the Great Depression. While the United States had become deeply involved in global trade during the twenties, it had remained aloof from global conflicts. So-called isolationists insisted that there was no justification for America to become embroiled in international affairs. With each passing year during the thirties, however, Germany, Italy, and Japan threatened the stability of Europe and Asia.

Roosevelt strove mightily to keep the United States out of what he called the "spreading epidemic of world lawlessness," as brutal fascist dictatorships in Germany and Italy and ultranationalist militarists in Japan violated international law by invading neighboring countries.

By the end of the decade, Roosevelt had decided that the only way for the United States to avoid another war was to offer all possible assistance to its allies, Great Britain and France. His efforts to make the United States the "arsenal of democracy" ignited a fierce debate between isolationists and interventionists, a debate that ended with shocking suddenness on December 7, 1941, when Japan staged a surprise attack against U.S. military bases at Pearl Harbor in Hawaii. The

CORE OBJECTIVES INQUIZITIVE

1. Assess how German and Japanese actions led to the outbreak of war in Europe and in Asia.

2. Evaluate how President Roosevelt and Congress responded to the outbreak of wars in Europe and Asia between 1933 and 1941.

3. Analyze the effects of the Second World War on American society.

4. Explain the major factors that enabled the United States and its allies to win the war in Europe.

5. Describe how the Japanese were defeated in the war in the Pacific.

6. Evaluate the efforts of President Roosevelt and the Allies to shape the postwar world.

Second World War that Americans had struggled for years to avoid had arrived at last. It would become the most significant event of the twentieth century, engulfing five continents and leaving few people untouched.

The Japanese attack unified the American people as never before. Men and women rushed to join the armed forces. Eventually, 16.4 million Americans would serve in the military during the war, including 350,000 women. To win the war against Japanese imperialism and German and Italian fascism, the United States mobilized all its economic resources; total war required massive government spending that boosted industrial production and wrenched the economy out of the Great Depression.

Four years after the Japanese attack on Pearl Harbor, the United States and its allies emerged victorious in the costliest and most destructive war in history. Whole cities were destroyed, nations dismembered, and societies transformed. More than 50 million people were killed in the war between 1939 and 1945—perhaps 60 percent of them civilians, including millions of Jews and other ethnic minorities murdered in Nazi death camps and Soviet concentration camps.

The global scope and scale of the Second World War transformed America's role in the world. Isolationism gave way to internationalism. By 1945, America was the world's most powerful nation, with new international interests and global responsibilities. Instead of bringing peace, however, the end of the fighting led to a new "cold war" between two former allies, the United States and the Soviet Union.

<table>
<tr><td>

CORE **OBJECTIVE**

1. Assess how German and Japanese actions led to the outbreak of war in Europe and in Asia.

</td></tr>
</table>

The Rise of Fascism in Europe

In 1917, Woodrow Wilson had led the United States into the Great War in order to make the world "safe for democracy." In fact, though, democracy was in retreat after 1919. Soviet communism was on the march during the twenties and thirties. So, too, was its ideological opponent, **fascism**, a radical form of totalitarian government in which a dictator uses propaganda and brute force to seize control of all aspects of national life—the economy, the armed forces, the legal and educational systems, and the press.

Fascism in Germany and Italy thrived on a violent ultranationalist patriotism and almost hysterical emotionalism built upon claims of racial superiority and the simmering resentments that grew out of defeat in the Great War. At the same time, halfway around the world, the Japanese government fell under the control of militarist expansionists eager to conquer China and all of south Asia. Japanese leaders were convinced that they were a "master race" with a "mission" to conquer and lead a resurgent Asia, just as Hitler claimed that Germany's "mission" on behalf of the superior "Aryan" race was to dominate Europe. By 1941, there would be only a dozen or so democratic nations left on earth.

fascism A radical form of totalitarian government that emerged in 1920s Italy and Germany in which a dictator uses propaganda and brute force to seize control of all aspects of national life.

Italy and Germany

In 1922, political journalist Benito Mussolini and his black-shirted supporters had seized control in Italy, taking advantage of an inept government incapable of dealing with widespread unemployment and runaway inflation. By 1925, he was wielding dictatorial power as "Il Duce" (the Leader). Mussolini eliminated all opposition political parties and approved the killing of several political opponents. "Mussolini Is Always Right," screamed propaganda posters. Yet there was something almost comical about the strutting, chest-thumping Mussolini, who claimed, "My animal instincts are always right." Italy, after all, was a declining industrial power whose pitiful performance in the Great War was a national embarrassment.

Germany was another matter, however. There was nothing amusing about Mussolini's German counterpart, the Austrian-born Adolf Hitler, whom Mussolini privately described as "an aggressive little man . . . probably a liar, and certainly mad."

Hitler's remarkable transformation during the 1920s from social misfit to head of the National Socialist German Workers' (Nazi) party startled the world. Hitler and the Nazis claimed that they represented a German ("Aryan") master race whose "purity and strength" were threatened by liberals, Jews, Communists, homosexuals, and other "inferior" peoples. Hitler promised to make Germany strong again by uniting all the German-speaking peoples of Europe into a vast empire that would give fast-growing Germany "living space" to expand, dominate the "lesser" races, and rid the continent of Jews.

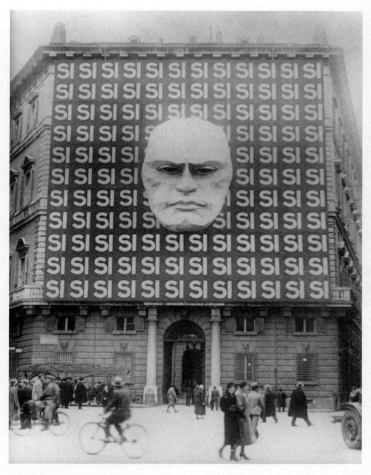

FASCIST PROPAGANDA Mussolini's headquarters in Rome's Palazzo Braschi, which bore an oversized reproduction of his leering face and 132 *si's* (Italian for "yes") in 1934.

Hitler had little patience with conventional political processes. "Democracy must be destroyed," he shouted. To enforce his rise to power, Hitler recruited 2 million street-brawling thugs ("storm troopers") to intimidate his opponents. "We are barbarians!" Hitler shouted. "We want to be barbarians! It is an honorable title. We shall rejuvenate the world!" Hitler also urged Germany to defy the restrictions on its armed forces imposed by the hated Treaty of Versailles after the Great War.

Hitler was appointed chancellor on January 30, 1933, five weeks before Franklin Roosevelt was first inaugurated. Like Mussolini, he declared himself absolute leader, or *Führer*, banned all political parties except the Nazis, created a secret police force known as the *Gestapo*, and stripped people of

> Mussolini seizes power in Italy (1922); Hitler becomes head of Nazi party in Germany

> Hitler becomes German chancellor and creates Nazi police state (1933)

ADOLF HITLER Hitler performs the Nazi salute at a rally. The majestic banners, triumphant music, powerful oratory, and expansive military parades were both hypnotic and alluring to the public.

Military buildup begins in Japan (1934)

voting rights. There would be no more elections, labor unions, or strikes. During the mid-1930s, Hitler's brutal Nazi police state cranked up the engines of tyranny and terrorism, propaganda and censorship. Brown-shirted Nazi storm troopers fanned out across the nation, burning books and persecuting, imprisoning, and murdering Communists, Jews, and their sympathizers.

The Expanding Axis

As the 1930s unfolded, a catastrophic series of events in Asia and Europe sent the world hurtling toward disaster. In 1931–1932, some 10,000 Japanese troops had occupied Manchuria, a province in northeast China blessed with valuable deposits of iron ore and coal. At the time, China was fragmented by civil war between Communists led by Mao Zedong and Nationalists led by Chiang Kai-shek. The Japanese took advantage of China's weakness to proclaim Manchuria's independence, renaming it the "Republic of Manchukuo." This was the first major step in Japan's eventual effort to control all of China.

In 1935, Mussolini launched Italy's reconquest of Ethiopia, a weak nation in eastern Africa that Italy had controlled until 1896 (Mussolini dismissed it as "a country without a trace of civilization"). When the League of Nations branded Mussolini as an aggressor and imposed economic sanctions on Italy, the Italian ruler expressed surprise that European leaders would prefer a "horde of barbarian Negroes" in Ethiopia over Italy, the "mother of civilization."

In 1935, Hitler, in flagrant violation of the Versailles Treaty, began rebuilding Germany's armed forces. The next year, 1936, he sent 35,000 soldiers into the Rhineland, the demilitarized buffer zone between France and Germany. In a staged vote, 99 percent of the Germans living in the Rhineland approved Hitler's action. The failure of France and Great Britain to counter his bold moves convinced Hitler that the western democracies were weak and frightened.

The year 1936 also witnessed the outbreak of the Spanish Civil War, which began when Spanish troops loyal to General Francisco Franco, with the support of the Roman Catholic Church, revolted against the fragile new republican government. Hitler and Mussolini rushed troops ("volunteers"), warplanes, and massive amounts of military and financial aid to support Franco's fascist insurgency.

While peace in Europe was unraveling, the Japanese government fell under the control of aggressive militarists. In 1937, a government official announced that the "tide ha[d] turned against the liberalism and democracy that once swept over the nation."

On July 7, 1937, Japanese and Chinese soldiers clashed at China's Marco Polo Bridge, west of Beijing. The incident quickly developed into a full-scale conflict, the Sino-Japanese War. From Beijing, the Japanese army swept northward toward Nanjing, home of the Nationalist Chinese government.

In 1937, Japan joined Germany and Italy in establishing the Rome-Berlin-Tokyo **"Axis" alliance**. Hitler and Mussolini vowed to create a "new order in Europe" that would end the domination of Great Britain and France, while the Japanese imperialists pursued their "divine right" to control all of east Asia by creating what they called the Greater East Asia Co-Prosperity Sphere.

Anschluss and the Munich Pact (1938)

Hitler was equally aggressive. In March 1938, he forced the *Anschluss* (union) of Austria with Germany. German armies marched into Austria, followed by Hitler, whose triumphant return to his homeland delighted pro-German crowds waving Nazi flags and tossing flowers. When Mussolini congratulated Hitler for his daring move, the German dictator told his Italian partner that he would "never forget him for this. Never, never, never—whatever happens."

> Germany annexes Austria (1938) and takes control of Czechoslovakia (1938–1939)

A month later, after arresting over 70,000 opponents of the Nazis, German leaders announced that a remarkable 99.75 percent of Austrian voters had "approved" the German takeover. Again, no nation stepped up to oppose Hitler's aggressive actions, and soon the new Nazi government in Austria began adopting Hitler's policies of arresting or murdering opponents and imprisoning or exiling Jews, including the famed psychiatrist Sigmund Freud.

Hitler's appetite for conquest was voracious. He turned next to the Sudeten territory (or Sudetenland), a mountainous region in western Czechoslovakia along the German border where more than 3 million ethnic Germans lived. Paralyzed by fear of another world war, British and French leaders tried to "appease" Hitler, hoping that if they agreed to his demands for the Sudeten territory he would stop his aggressions.

On September 30, 1938, the British prime minister, Neville Chamberlain, the French prime minister, Édouard Daladier, Italian dictator Benito Mussolini, and Hitler signed the notorious Munich Pact, which transferred the Sudetenland to Germany, leading the Czechoslovakian president to resign in protest.

Chamberlain claimed that the Munich treaty provided "peace for our time. Peace with honor." Winston Churchill, a member of the British Parliament who would himself become prime minister in May 1940, strongly disagreed. In a speech to the House of Commons, Churchill claimed, "England has been offered a choice between war and shame. She has chosen shame, and will get war." The Munich Pact, he predicted, would not end Hitler's aggression. "This is only the beginning of the reckoning."

"Axis" alliance Military alliance formed in 1937 by the three major fascist powers: Germany, Italy, and Japan.

Churchill was right. Hitler never intended to honor the Munich Pact: "That piece of paper is of no further significance whatever." Although Hitler had promised that the Sudetenland would be his last territorial demand, he violated his pledge in March 1939, when he sent German tanks and soldiers to conquer the remainder of Czechoslovakia. The European democracies, having shrunk their armies after the Great War, continued to cower in the face of Hitler's ruthless behavior and seemingly unstoppable military forces.

After German troops seized all of Czechoslovakia on March 15, 1939, Hitler called it "the greatest day of my life." President Roosevelt was not amused. He decided that Hitler and Mussolini were "madmen" who "respect force and force alone." Throughout late 1938 and 1939, he tried to convince Americans, as well as British and French leaders, that the growing menace of fascism must be stopped. He also persuaded Congress to increase military spending in anticipation of a possible war.

The Conquest of Poland

Later in 1939, the insatiable Hitler turned his sights to Poland, Germany's eastern neighbor. In part, he wanted to regain German territory taken to form Poland after the Great War, but he also wanted to conquer Poland so as to give the German army a clear path to invade the Soviet Union. To ensure that the Soviets did not interfere with his plans, Hitler camouflaged his intentions on August 23, 1939, when he signed the German-Soviet Nonaggression Pact with the Soviet premier, Josef Stalin.

The announcement of the treaty stunned a world that had understood fascism and communism to be eternal enemies. By the terms of the treaty, the two tyrants secretly agreed to divide northern and eastern Europe between them. Just nine days later, at dawn on September 1, 1939, 1.5 million German troops invaded Poland from the north, south, and west. Hitler ordered his armies "to kill without mercy men, women, and children of the Polish race or language."

This was the final straw for the western democracies. Having allowed Austria and Czechoslovakia to be conquered by Hitler's war machine, the leaders of Great Britain and France now did an about-face. On September 3, 1939, they honored their commitment to defend Poland. Europe, the world's smallest continent, was again embroiled in what would soon become another world war. The nations making up the British Empire and Commonwealth around the world—Canada, India, Australia, New Zealand—joined the war against Nazi Germany.

Sixteen days after German troops stormed across the Polish border, the Soviet Union invaded Poland from the east. Pressed

JOSEF STALIN The leader of the Soviet Union, Stalin rose to power in the mid-1920s after the death of Vladimir Lenin.

from all sides by its old enemies, 700,000 poorly equipped Polish soldiers (many Poles fought on horseback) surrendered, having suffered 70,000 deaths and many more wounded.

On October 6, 1939, the Nazis and Soviets divided conquered Poland between them and then set about systematically destroying it. Hitler's goal was to obliterate Polish civilization, especially the Jews, and Germanize the country. For his part, Stalin wanted to recapture Polish territory lost by Russia during the Great War. Over the next five years, the Nazis and Soviets arrested, deported, enslaved, or murdered millions of Poles.

In late November 1939, the Soviets invaded neighboring Finland, leading President Roosevelt to condemn Russia's "wanton disregard for law." Outnumbered 5 to 1, Finnish troops held off the Soviet invaders for three months but were forced to negotiate a surrender in March 1940 that gave the Soviet Union a tenth of Finland.

The Outbreak of War in Europe

After the quick German conquest of Poland, the war on the ground in Europe settled into a three-month stalemate during early 1940 as Hitler's generals waited out the winter. Then, in the early spring, Germany suddenly attacked again. At dawn on April 9, without warning, Nazi armies invaded Denmark and landed along the Norwegian coast. German paratroopers, the first used in warfare, seized Norway's airports. Denmark fell in a day, Norway within a few weeks. On May 10, German forces invaded the Low Countries—Belgium, Luxembourg, and the Netherlands (Holland). Luxembourg fell the first day, the Netherlands four days later. Belgium lasted until May 28.

A few days later, German tanks roared into northern France. "The fight beginning today," Hitler declared, "decides the fate of the German nation for the next thousand years!" Hitler's brilliant **blitzkrieg** ("lightning war") strategy centered on speed. Fast-moving columns of tanks, motorized artillery, and truck-borne infantry, all supported by warplanes and paratroopers, moved so quickly that they paralyzed their stunned opponents.

A British army sent to help the Belgians and the French fled along with French troops toward the coast, with the Germans in hot pursuit. On May 26, Great Britain organized a desperate weeklong evacuation of battle-weary British and French soldiers from the beaches at Dunkirk, on the northern French coast. Despite attacks from German warplanes, some 338,000 soldiers escaped to England on more than a thousand ships and small boats, barges, and ferries, leaving behind vast stockpiles of vehicles, weaponry, and ammunition. "Wars are not won by evacuations,"

blitzkrieg (1940) The German "lightning war" strategy characterized by swift, well-organized attacks using infantry, tanks, and warplanes.

WINSTON CHURCHILL The prime minister of Great Britain, Churchill led the nation during the Second World War.

AGGRESSION IN EUROPE, 1935–1939

■ Keeping in mind the terms of the Treaty of Versailles, explain why Hitler began his campaign of expansion by invading the Rhineland and the Sudetenland.

■ Why did the attack on Poland begin World War II, whereas Hitler's previous invasions of his European neighbors did not?

observed Prime Minister Churchill, "but there was a victory inside this deliverance."

While the miraculous evacuation at Dunkirk was unfolding, German forces decimated the remaining French armies. The crumbling French war effort prompted Italy's dictator, Mussolini, to declare war on France and Great Britain, which he dismissed as "the reactionary democracies of the West." Roosevelt characterized Mussolini's action as a "stab in the back."

On June 14, 1940, German soldiers marched unopposed through the streets of Paris. Eight days later, French leaders surrendered. The war was but ten months old, yet Germany ruled most of Europe. Great Britain now stood alone facing Hitler's relentless military power. "The war is won," an ecstatic Hitler bragged to Mussolini. "The rest is only a matter of time." He spoke too soon.

The United States: From Isolationism to Intervention

During the 1930s, most Americans responded to the mounting crises in Europe and Asia by deepening their commitment to isolationism. A prominent Senate inquiry into the role of bankers and businesses in the American decision to enter the Great War reinforced the isolationist sentiment. Chaired by Senator Gerald P. Nye of North Dakota, the "Nye Committee" began its hearings in 1934 and lasted until early 1936. The committee concluded that weapons makers and bankers (the "merchants of death") had spurred U.S. intervention in the European war in 1917 and were continuing to "help frighten nations into military activity."

U.S. Neutrality

In 1935, in response to Italy's invasion of Ethiopia and the Nye Committee hearings, President Roosevelt signed the first of several "neutrality laws" intended to avoid the mistakes that had led the nation into the Great War. However, the president did not, as Woodrow Wilson had done in 1914, ask Americans to remain neutral in their hearts because "even a neutral has a right to take account of the facts," which in his view, unlike in 1914, made it clear to all that Germany was the aggressor.

The Neutrality Act of 1935 prohibited Americans from selling weapons or traveling on ships owned by nations at war. The law reflected the desire of most Americans to stay out of Europe's conflicts. As a Minnesota senator declared in 1935, "To hell with Europe and the rest of those nations!" In 1936, Congress revised the Neutrality Act by banning loans to warring nations.

Roosevelt, however, was not so sure that the United States could or should remain neutral in a world of growing conflict. In October 1937, he delivered a speech in Chicago, the heartland of isolationism, in which he called for international cooperation to "quarantine the aggressors" responsible for disturbing world peace, especially the Japanese who had assaulted China. But his appeal for a more active American role in world affairs fell flat in Congress and across the nation.

The Neutrality Act of 1937 allowed the president to require that nonmilitary American goods bought by warring nations be sold on a cash-and-carry basis (that is, a nation would have to pay cash and then carry the American-made goods away in its own ships). This would preserve America's profitable trade with warring nations without running the risk of being drawn into the fighting.

In September 1939, Roosevelt decided that the United States must do more to stop "aggressor" nations. He summoned Congress into special session to revise the Neutrality Act. "I regret the Congress passed the Act," the president said. "I regret equally that I signed the Act."

> CORE **OBJECTIVE**
>
> **2.** Explain how President Roosevelt and Congress responded to the outbreak of wars in Europe and Asia between 1933 and 1941.

> 1937 Neutrality Act: Nonmilitary goods for warring nations

> 1939 Neutrality Act: Military supplies for Britain and France

U-BOATS After the Treaty of Versailles set limits on the size of the German navy, Germany developed military submarines of unprecedented size and power. Here, a row of Nazi U-boats are on display in the German port of Kiel in 1938. **How did Germany's military preparations compare with those of the United States and Great Britain?**

After six weeks of debate, the Congress passed the Neutrality Act of 1939, which allowed Britain and France to send their own ships to the United States to bring back American military supplies. It was, said Roosevelt, the best way "to keep us out of war."

Preparing America for War

U.S military buildup, increased aid to Great Britain, and peacetime conscription

As Hitler's armies continued their conquest of Europe, the United States found itself in no condition to wage war. After the Great War, the U.S. Army was reduced to a small force; by 1939, it numbered only 175,000. By contrast, Germany had almost 5 million soldiers. In promoting "military prepared-ness," President Roosevelt in May 1940 called for increasing the size of the army and producing 50,000 combat planes in 1942, a seemingly outlandish goal, since Germany was producing only 15,000 warplanes that year. Roos-evelt also increased military aid to Great Britain, promising to provide all possible "aid to the Allies short of war."

As had occurred during the Great War, German submarines destroyed many of the ships carrying supplies from America to Great Britain. To ad-dress the challenge, Roosevelt and Prime Minister Churchill, whose mother was an American, negotiated in early September 1940 the Destroyers for

Bases Agreement, by which fifty old U.S. warships went to the British Royal Navy in return for allowing the U.S. to build military bases on British island colonies in the Caribbean.

Two weeks later, on September 16, 1940, Roosevelt made an even more controversial decision, opposed even by his wife, Eleanor, when he pushed through a reluctant Congress the first peacetime conscription (military draft) in history, requiring the registration of all 16 million men aged twenty-one to thirty-five.

The world crisis transformed Roosevelt. For much of his second term, he had been stalemated by congressional opposition to the New Deal. Now he was revitalized by the urgent need to stop the spread of Nazism across Europe.

Adding to Roosevelt's concerns was the possibility that Germany might have a secret weapon. The famous physicist Albert Einstein, an Austrian Jew who had fled Nazism, had alerted Roosevelt in the fall of 1939 that the Germans were trying to create atomic bombs. In June 1940, the president set up the National Defense Research Committee to coordinate military research, including a top-secret effort to develop an atomic bomb—the Manhattan Project—before the Germans did.

Almost 200,000 people worked on the Manhattan Project, including Dr. J. Robert Oppenheimer, who led the team of distinguished scientists scattered among several secret facilities across the country. The Manhattan Project was so secret that Vice President Harry Truman knew nothing about it.

> The Manhattan Project

The Battle of Britain

Having conquered western Europe, Hitler began planning the invasion of Great Britain ("Operation Sea Lion"). The Germans first sought to destroy Britain's Royal Air Force (RAF) before invading the island nation. In what came to be known as the Battle of Britain, the Nazis deployed some 2,500 warplanes, outnumbering the RAF 2 to 1. "Never has a nation been so naked before its foes," Winston Churchill admitted.

> German bombers attack Great Britain: The Blitz

The feisty prime minister became the symbol of Britain's determination to stop Hitler. With his bulldog face, ever-present cigar, and "V for Victory" gesture, he urged the British citizenry to make the defense of their homeland "their finest hour." He breathed defiance while preparing the nation for a German invasion. The British, he pledged, would confront Hitler's invaders with "blood, toil, tears, and sweat." They would "never surrender."

In July and August 1940, the German air force (*Luftwaffe*) launched day and night bombing raids against military targets across southeast England. The Royal Air Force, with the benefit of radar, a

THE LONDON "BLITZ" An aerial photograph of London set aflame by the heavy German bombing raids in 1940. Winston Churchill responded, "We shall never surrender."

secret new technology, surprised the world by fending off the German assault. Hitler then ordered his bombers to target civilians and cities (especially London) in nighttime raids designed to terrorize the nation. During September and October of 1940, the Germans caused massive destruction in Britain's major cities.

The air raids killed some 43,000 civilians, wounded thousands more, and left 2 million homeless. But the German bombing campaign enraged rather than demoralized the British people. A London newspaper headline summarized the nation's defiant mood: "Is That the Best You Can Do, Adolf?"

At the same time, British fighter pilots were destroying 1,300 German warplanes. The British success in the air was a decisive turning point in the war, for in October 1940 Hitler scrapped his planned invasion of the British Isles. It was the first battle he had lost.

Debate over America's Role

During the Battle of Britain, Franklin Roosevelt began a long, urgent, and eloquent campaign to convince Americans that isolationism was impractical and even dangerous. His actions to aid Great Britain and prepare America for war outraged isolationists. A prominent Democrat remembered that the dispute between isolationists and "interventionists" was "the most savage political debate during my lifetime."

Isolationists, mostly midwestern and western Republicans who believed that Roosevelt was systematically drawing the United States into another European war, formed the America First Committee to oppose "military preparedness." Charles Lindbergh, the first man to fly solo across the Atlantic Ocean, led the isolationist effort. He claimed that Jews who owned "our motion pictures, our press, our radio, and our government" were behind Roosevelt's efforts to help Britain, which, he argued, was doomed.

Roosevelt's Third Term

Roosevelt reelected (1940)

Lindbergh and the other isolationists sought to make the 1940 presidential campaign a debate about the European war. In June, just as France was falling to Germany, the Republicans nominated a dark-horse candidate, Wendell L. Willkie of Indiana, a plainspoken corporate lawyer who as a former Democrat had voted for Roosevelt in 1932 and had remained registered as a Democrat until 1938. In his acceptance speech, Willkie clumsily referred to "you Republicans."

Once the campaign started, Willkie warned that Roosevelt was a "warmonger" and predicted that "if you reelect him you may expect war in April, 1941." Roosevelt responded that he had "said this before, but . . . shall say it again and again and again: Your boys are not going to be sent into any foreign wars." In November 1940, Roosevelt won an unprecedented third term by a comfortable margin of 27 million votes to Willkie's 22 million and by an even more decisive margin, 449–82, in the Electoral College.

The Lend-Lease Bill

Once reelected, Roosevelt found an ingenious way to provide more military aid to Britain, whose cash was running out. The **Lend-Lease Bill**, introduced in Congress on January 10, 1941, allowed the president to lend or lease military equipment to "any country whose defense the President deems vital to the defense of the United States." It was a bold challenge to the isolationists, prompted by Roosevelt's conviction that "no nation can appease the Nazis. No man can turn a tiger into a kitten by stroking it." The United States, he added, would provide everything the British needed to fend off a German invasion while doing the same for China in its war against Japan. "We must be the great arsenal of democracy," Roosevelt explained.

Between 1941 and 1945, the Lend-Lease program would ship $50 billion worth of supplies to Great Britain, the Soviet Union, France, China, and other Allied nations. Lend-Lease was Roosevelt's most aggressive effort to move America from isolationism to interventionism. Winston Churchill called it the most generous "act in the history of any nation."

Germany Invades the Soviet Union

While Americans continued to debate Roosevelt's efforts to help Great Britain, the European war expanded. In the spring of 1941, German troops joined Italian forces in Libya, forcing the British army in North Africa to withdraw to Egypt. In April 1941, invading Nazi armies overwhelmed Yugoslavia and Greece. With Hungary, Romania, and Bulgaria also under Nazi control, Hitler ruled nearly all of Europe. His maniacal ambition was unbounded, however.

On June 22, 1941, without warning, massive German armies invaded their supposed ally, the Soviet Union, in "Operation Barbarossa." Hitler's objective in turning on Stalin was his long-standing dream to destroy communism, enslave the vast population of the Soviet Union, and exploit its considerable natural resources.

Hitler's decision to attack the Soviet Union was the defining moment of the European war, for the Germans eventually would be worn down and thrown back by the Soviets. At first, however, the largest invasion in history seemed a great success as German armies raced across the vast plains of western Russia; entire Soviet armies and cities were surrounded and destroyed. During the second half of 1941, 3 million Soviet soldiers were captured, many of whom were then murdered or starved to death. For four months, the Soviet armies retreated in the face of the German blitzkrieg. By December 1941, German units had reached the suburbs of Moscow, a thousand miles east of Berlin.

To American isolationists, Germany's invasion of Russia confirmed that America should stay out of the war and let two dreadful dictatorships bleed each other to death. Roosevelt, however, included the Soviet Union in the Lend-Lease agreement, for along with Winston Churchill, he was determined to keep the Soviets fighting Hitler rather than see them surrender. In 1941

Lend-Lease Bill (1941)

Lend-Lease Bill (1941) Legislation that allowed the president to lend or lease military equipment to any country whose own defense was deemed vital to the defense of the United States.

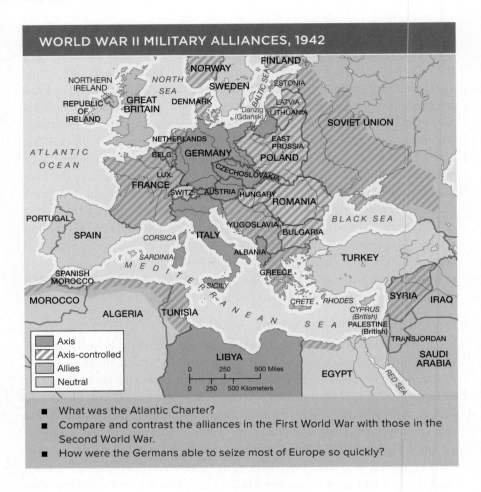

WORLD WAR II MILITARY ALLIANCES, 1942

- What was the Atlantic Charter?
- Compare and contrast the alliances in the First World War with those in the Second World War.
- How were the Germans able to seize most of Europe so quickly?

| United States sends massive aid to Soviet Union |

alone, America sent thousands of trucks, tanks, guns, and warplanes to the Soviet Union, along with food (especially Spam), and enough cotton, blankets, shoes, and boots to clothe every Soviet soldier.

Gradually, Stalin used his dictatorial powers to slow the Nazi advance by forcing people to fight—or be killed. During the Battle of Moscow, Russian defenders showed their pitiless resolve by executing 8,000 civilians charged with "cowardice." Slowly the tide started to turn against the once-unbeatable Germans. By the winter of 1941–1942, Hitler's generals were learning the same bitter lesson that the Russians had taught Napoleon and the French army in 1812. Invading armies must contend not only with Russia's ferocious fighters and enormous population but also vast distances, deep snow, and subzero temperatures.

The Atlantic Charter

| The Atlantic Charter (1941) and German U-boats |

By the late summer of 1941, the United States was no longer a "neutral" nation. In August, Roosevelt and Churchill met on a U.S. warship off the Canadian coast, where they drew up a joint statement of "common principles"

JAPANESE EXPANSION BEFORE THE ATTACK ON PEARL HARBOR

Territory under Japanese control, Dec. 7, 1941

Dates of acquisition or occupation
- 1870–1899
- 1900–1929
- 1930–1940

- Why did the Japanese want to control French Indochina and the Dutch East Indies?
- Why did Japan sign the Tripartite Pact with Germany and Italy?

known as the **Atlantic Charter**. The agreement pledged that after the "final destruction of the Nazi tyranny" the victors would promote certain shared values: the self-determination of all peoples, economic cooperation, freedom of the seas, and a new system of international security to be called the United Nations. Within weeks, eleven anti-Axis nations, including the Soviet Union, had endorsed the idealistic principles of the Atlantic Charter.

No sooner had Roosevelt signed the Atlantic Charter than U.S. ships in the North Atlantic were attacked. On October 17, 1941, a German submarine ("U-boat") sank the American warship *Kearny*. Eleven seamen died. Two weeks later, the destroyer *Reuben James* went down, with a loss of 115 seamen. The sinkings spurred Congress to change the 1939 Neutrality Act by allowing merchant vessels to be armed and to enter combat zones and the

Atlantic Charter (1941) Joint statement crafted by Franklin D. Roosevelt and British prime minister Winston Churchill that listed the war goals of the Allied Powers.

ports of nations at war ("belligerents"). Roosevelt ordered U.S. warships to "shoot on sight" any German submarines.

Step by step, the United States had given up neutrality and now was engaging in naval warfare against Nazi Germany. Still, Americans hoped to avoid taking the final step into all-out war.

The Storm in the Pacific

Japanese in Indochina and the Export Control Act (1940)

Hitler's efforts to conquer Great Britain and the Soviet Union stalled by late 1941, but U.S. relations with Japan were worsening. In 1940, Japan and the United States began a series of moves that pushed them closer to war. Japan built airfields in northern Indochina and cut the railroad into south China. The United States responded with the Export Control Act of July 2, 1940, which authorized President Roosevelt to restrict the export of military supplies and other strategic materials crucial to Japan.

The Tripartite Pact

The Tripartite Pact (1940) signed, Japan takes control of French Indochina, and United States freezes its assets

On September 27, 1940, the Tokyo government signed a Tripartite Pact with Germany and Italy, by which each pledged to declare war on any nation that attacked any of them. In July 1941, Japan announced that it was taking complete control of French Indochina. Roosevelt responded by freezing all Japanese financial assets in the United States and restricting oil exports to Japan (the United States was then producing half the world's oil). *Time* magazine claimed that Roosevelt was "waging the first great undeclared war in U.S. history." Without access to American oil, iron, steel, and other products, Japan's expansionist plans were stalled. Japanese military leaders responded by invading French Indochina and the Dutch East Indies to acquire the strategic raw materials cut off by the United States.

The Attack on Pearl Harbor

On October 16, 1941, War Minister Hideki Tōjō became the Japanese prime minister. Viewing war with the United States as inevitable, he ordered a powerful fleet of Japanese warships to prepare for war. The Japanese naval commander, Admiral Isoroku Yamamoto, knew that his country could not defeat the United States in a long war; its only hope was "to decide the fate of the war on the very first day" by launching a "fatal attack" on the U.S. Navy.

On November 5, 1941, the Japanese asked the Roosevelt administration to end its embargo of oil and other products or "face conflict." The American secretary of state, Cordell Hull, responded on November 26 that Japan must remove all its troops from China before the United States would lift its embargo. The

HIDEKI TŌJŌ Serving simultaneously as prime minister and war minister of Japan, Tōjō led Japan until 1944, one year before the country's unconditional surrender.

EXPLOSION OF THE U.S.S. *SHAW* The destroyer exploded at Pearl Harbor after Japanese warplanes pummeled it with three bombs. The *Shaw* was repaired shortly thereafter and went on to earn eleven battle stars in the Pacific campaign.

Japanese government then secretly ordered a fleet of warships to begin steaming toward Hawaii.

The U.S. Navy Department in Washington, D.C., sent an urgent message to all its commanders in the Pacific: "Negotiations with Japan . . . have ceased, and an aggressive move by Japan is expected within the next few days." During the morning of Sunday, December 7, 1941, 360 Japanese planes began bombing the unsuspecting U.S. fleet at **Pearl Harbor** and the planes at the nearby airfield.

Of the eight American battleships, all were sunk or disabled, along with eleven other ships. Japanese bombers also destroyed 180 American warplanes. The raid, which lasted less than two hours, killed more than 2,400 American servicemen (mostly sailors) and civilians and wounded nearly 1,200 more. At the same time that the Japanese were attacking Pearl Harbor, they were also assaulting U.S. military facilities in the Philippines and on Guam and Wake Islands in the Pacific, as well as British bases in Singapore, Hong Kong, and Malaysia.

Pearl Harbor (1941) Surprise Japanese attack on the U.S. fleet at Pearl Harbor on December 7, which prompted the immediate American entry into the war.

Pearl Harbor attacked and United States enters the war

The attack on Pearl Harbor surprised Americans but fell short of military success in two important ways. First, the Japanese warplanes ignored the maintenance facilities and oil storage tanks in Hawaii that supported the U.S. fleet, without which the surviving ships would have been forced back to California. Second, the Japanese bombers missed the U.S. aircraft carriers that had luckily left port a few days earlier. In the naval war to come, aircraft carriers, not battleships, would prove to be the decisive weapon.

In a larger sense, the Japanese attack on Pearl Harbor was a spectacular miscalculation, for the surprise attack aroused Americans to wage total, vengeful war and brought the isolationist movement to an abrupt end. Even the Japanese admiral who planned the attack had misgivings amid his officers' celebrations: "I fear that we have only succeeded in awakening a sleeping tiger." The British leader Winston Churchill, however, was delighted at the news, for he desperately wanted the United States to enter the war against Germany and Japan. After learning of the Japanese attack, he went to bed and "slept the sleep of the saved and thankful."

On December 8, President Roosevelt, composed and determined, delivered his war message to Congress: "Yesterday, December 7, 1941—a date which will live in infamy—the United States of America was suddenly and deliberately attacked by naval and air forces of the Empire of Japan." Three days later, on December 11, Germany and Italy declared war on what Hitler called the "half Judaized and the other half Negrified" United States, which he insisted "was not dangerous to us." The separate wars raging in Asia, Europe, and Africa had now become one global conflict. President Roosevelt predicted in a radio address that "we are going to win, and we are going to win the peace that follows." Privately, however, he knew that it would be a long, tough war against the "forces of savagery and barbarism."

CORE **OBJECTIVE**

3. Analyze the effects of the Second World War on American society.

War Powers Act (1941)

Mobilization at Home

Waging war against Germany and Japan required harnessing all of America's immense industrial capacity for military purposes. On December 18, 1941, Congress passed the War Powers Act, which gave the president far-reaching authority to reorganize government agencies and create new ones, regulate business and industry, and even censor mail and other forms of communication.

With the declaration of war, men between the ages of eighteen and forty-five were drafted. Some 16 million men and several hundred thousand women served in the military during the war. Many teens lied about their age in order to enlist. The average American soldier or sailor in the Second World War was twenty-six years old, stood five feet eight, and weighed 144 pounds, an inch taller and eight pounds heavier than the typical recruit in the First World War. Only one in ten had attended college and only one in four had graduated from high school.

Arsenal of Democracy

In 1940, Adolf Hitler had scoffed at the idea that the United States could produce 50,000 warplanes a year, claiming that America was nothing but "beauty queens, millionaires, and Hollywood." His ignorance of America's industrial potential proved fatal to Germany's war plans. By the end of 1942, U.S. war production had already exceeded the *combined* output of Germany, Japan, and Italy. At an Allied planning conference in Iran in 1943, Josef Stalin raised a glass to toast "American production, without which this war would have been lost."

The **War Production Board**, created by Roosevelt in 1942, directed the conversion of industries to war production. In 1941, more than 3 million automobiles were manufactured in the United States; only 139 were built during the next four years. Instead of cars, automobile plants produced huge numbers of tanks, jeeps, trucks, and warplanes. "Something is happening that Hitler doesn't understand," announced *Time* magazine in 1942. "It is the miracle of production."

In making the United States the "great arsenal of democracy," the Roosevelt administration transformed the economy into the world's most efficient military machine. By 1945, the year the war ended, plants in the United States, many of them running twenty-four hours a day, seven days a week, produced 300,000 warplanes, 89,000 tanks, 3 million machine guns, and 7 million rifles.

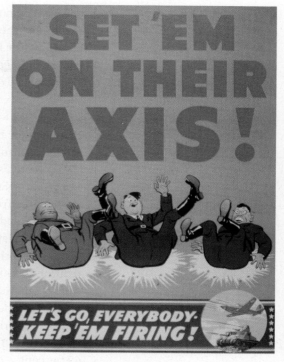

WAR PRODUCTION BOARD This 1942 poster features caricatures of Mussolini, Hitler, and Tōjō, who—according to the poster—will fall on their "axis" if American civilians continue their relentless wartime production.

Financing the War

To cover the war's huge cost (some $3 trillion in today's values), Congress passed the Revenue Act of 1942 (also called the Victory Tax). It raised tax rates and increased the number of taxpayers. In 1939, only 4 million people (about 5 percent of the workforce) filed tax returns; the new act made most workers (75 percent) taxpayers. By war's end, 90 percent of workers were paying income tax.

Tax revenues covered about 45 percent of military costs from 1939 to 1946; the government borrowed the rest, mostly by selling $185 billion worth of government war bonds, which paid interest to purchasers. In all, by the end of the war, the national debt was six times what it had been at the start.

The size of the federal government soared during the war. Over a dozen new federal agencies managed the shift to a war economy. The number of civilian federal workers quadrupled, from 1 million to 4 million. Jobs were suddenly plentiful as millions of people quit work to join the military. The nation's unemployment rate plummeted from 14 percent in 1940 to 2 percent in 1943.

People who had long lived on the margins of the economic system, especially women, entered the labor force in large numbers. Stubborn pockets of

> U.S. employment soars

War Production Board Federal agency created by Roosevelt in 1942 that converted America's industrial output to war production.

poverty did not disappear, but for most civilians, especially those who had earlier lost their jobs and homes in the Depression, the war spelled a better life than ever before. Some 24 million Americans moved during the war to take advantage of new job opportunities. Many of them headed to the West Coast, where shipyards and airplane factories were hiring nonstop.

Economic Controls

Office of Price Administration (1942)

The need for the United States not only to equip and feed its own military forces but also provide massive amounts of food, clothing, and weapons to its allies created shortages of many consumer goods and rising prices. In 1942, Congress ordered the Office of Price Administration to set price ceilings. With prices frozen, basic goods had to be allocated through rationing, with coupons doled out for limited amounts of sugar, coffee, gasoline, automobile tires, and meat.

The government promoted patriotic conservation with a massive public relations campaign that circulated posters with slogans such as "Use it up, wear it out, make it do, or do without." Businesses and workers often grumbled about the wage and price controls. Yet government efforts to stabilize wages and prices succeeded. By the end of the war, consumer prices had risen about 31 percent, a record far better than the World War I rise of 62 percent.

The War at Home

The Second World War transformed life at home as it was being fought abroad. The dramatic changes required by the conflict transformed many areas of social life, the impact of which would last long after the war's end.

Women in the War

Millions of women join workforce and military

The war marked a watershed in the status of women. With millions of men going into military service, the demand for civilian workers shook up old prejudices about gender roles in the workplace—and in the military. During the war, nearly 200,000 women served in the **Women's Army Corps** (WAC) and the navy's equivalent, Women Accepted for Volunteer Emergency Service (WAVES). Others joined the Marine Corps, the Coast Guard, and the Army Air Force.

More than 6 million women entered the civilian workforce during the war, an increase of more than 50 percent overall (110 percent in manufacturing alone). To help recruit women, the government launched a promotional campaign featuring the story of "Rosie the Riveter," a woman named Rosina Bonavita, who excelled as a riveter at an airplane factory.

Many men opposed women taking traditionally male jobs. A disgruntled male legislator asked who would handle traditional household tasks if women flocked to factories: "Who will do the cooking, the washing, the mending, the humble homey tasks to which every woman has devoted her-

Women's Army Corps
Women's branch of the U.S. Army; by the end of the Second World War, nearly 150,000 women had served in the WAC.

WOMEN OF THE WORKFORCE, 1942 At the Douglas Aircraft Company in Long Beach, California, three women assemble the tail fuselage of a Boeing B-17 Flying Fortress bomber. **How did World War II open up new opportunities for women?**

self; who will rear and nurture the children?" Many women, however, were eager to escape the bland routine of domestic life and earn good wages. A female welder remembered that her wartime job "was the first time I had a chance to get out of the kitchen and work in industry and make a few bucks. This was something I had never dreamed would happen."

African Americans

More than a half-million African Americans left the South for better opportunities during the war years, and more than a million blacks nationwide joined the industrial workforce for the first time. Lured by jobs and higher wages in new military-related plants and factories, African Americans from Texas, Oklahoma, Arkansas, and Louisiana headed west, where the dramatic expansion of defense-related jobs had significant effects on the region's population. During the war years, the number of African Americans rose sharply in western cities such as Seattle, Portland, and Los Angeles.

Rural poor take manufacturing jobs

At the same time, the construction of military bases and the influx of new personnel provided a boon to southern textile mills responding to the war effort through the manufacture of military uniforms and blankets. Manufacturing jobs led tens of thousands of "dirt poor" sharecroppers and tenant farmers, many of them African Americans, to leave the land for steady work in new mills and factories. Sixty of the hundred new army camps created during the war were in southern states, further transforming local economies. Throughout the United States during the Second World War, the rural population decreased by 20 percent.

Racial Tension at Home

Racial discrimination and race riots at home

Although Americans found themselves fighting against the racial bigotry celebrated by fascism and Nazism, the war did not end racism in the United States. The Red Cross, for example, initially refused to accept blood donated by blacks, and the president of North American Aviation announced that "we will not employ Negroes." Blacks who were hired were often limited to the lowest-paid, lowest-skilled jobs.

Some courageous black leaders fought back. In 1941, A. Philip Randolph, head of the Brotherhood of Sleeping Car Porters, planned a march on Washington, D.C., to demand an end to racial discrimination in defense industries. To fend off the march, the Roosevelt administration struck a bargain. Randolph called off the demonstration in return for a presidential order requiring equal treatment in the hiring of workers.

Throughout the war, African Americans noted the irony of the United States fighting against racism abroad while tolerating it at home. "The army is about to take me to fight for democracy," a black Detroit draftee said, "but I would [rather] fight for democracy right here." During the summer of 1943 alone, there were 274 race-related incidents in almost fifty cities. In Detroit, growing racial tensions escalated into a full-fledged riot. Fighting raged for two days until federal troops arrived. By then, twenty-five blacks and nine whites had been killed, and more than 700 people had been injured.

African Americans in Uniform

African Americans serve in segregated military units

The most volatile social issue ignited by the war was African American participation in the military. Although the armed forces were still racially segregated in 1941, African Americans rushed to enlist after the Japanese attack on Pearl Harbor. As Joe Louis, the world heavyweight boxing champion, explained, "Lots of things [are] wrong with America, but Hitler ain't going to fix them."

African American soldiers and sailors, assigned to racially segregated units, were initially excluded from combat. Black officers could not command white soldiers or sailors. Henry L. Stimson, the secretary of war, claimed that "leadership is not embedded in the negro race." Every army

HOME FRONT VERSUS FRONTLINES Left: Though tasked with protecting the African American man from further violence in the Detroit Riots of 1943, the police officers do nothing when a member of the white mob reaches out to strike him. Right: The Tuskegee Airmen were the first African American military pilots. Here, the first graduates are reviewed at Tuskegee, Alabama, in 1941. **How did racial tensions in America impact the military's organization and actions abroad?**

camp and navy base had segregated facilities—and experienced frequent racial "incidents."

Altogether, about a million African Americans—men and women—served in the armed forces during the war. Among the most famous African American servicemen were some 600 pilots trained in Tuskegee, Alabama. The so-called **Tuskegee Airmen** ended up flying more than 15,000 missions. Their unquestionable excellence spurred military and civilian leaders to desegregate the armed forces after the war.

Mexicans and Mexican Americans

As rural dwellers moved to western cities, many farm counties experienced a labor shortage. In an ironic about-face, local and federal government authorities who before the war had forced migrant laborers back across the Mexican border now recruited them to harvest crops on American farms. The Mexican government would not consent to provide the needed workers, however, until the United States promised to ensure decent working and living conditions for the migrant workers. The result was the creation of the **bracero program** in 1942, whereby Mexico agreed to provide seasonal farmworkers on yearlong contracts. Under the bracero program, some 200,000 Mexican farmworkers entered the western United States. At least that many more crossed the border as undocumented workers.

The rising tide of Mexican Americans in Los Angeles prompted a stream of anti-Mexican editorials and ugly racial incidents. Even though

Tuskegee Airmen U.S. Army Air Corps unit of African American pilots whose combat success spurred military and civilian leaders to desegregate the armed forces after the war.

bracero program (1942) System that permitted seasonal farmworkers from Mexico to work in the United States on yearlong contracts.

OFF TO COURT Latinos dressed in zoot suits are chained and escorted onto a Los Angeles County sheriff's bus for a court appearance in June of 1943.

some 300,000 Mexican Americans served in the war and earned a higher percentage of Congressional Medals of Honor than any other minority group, racial prejudices still prevailed. Southern California saw constant conflict between Anglo servicemen and Mexican American gang members and teenage "zoot-suiters" (zoot suits were flamboyant clothing worn by some young Mexican American men). In 1943, several thousand off-duty sailors and soldiers, joined by hundreds of local whites, rampaged through the streets of Los Angeles, assaulting Hispanics, African Americans, and Filipinos. The weeklong violence came to be called the "Zoot Suit Riots."

Native Americans in the Military

Indians supported the war effort more fully than any other group in American society. Almost a third of eligible Native American men served in the armed forces. Many others worked in defense-related industries, and thousands of Indian women volunteered as nurses or joined the WAVES. As was the case with African Americans, Indians benefited from the experiences afforded by the war. Those who left reservations to work in defense plants or to join the military gained new vocational skills.

Why did so many Native Americans fight for a nation that had stripped them of their land and ravaged their heritage? Some felt that they had no choice. Mobilization for the war effort ended many New Deal programs that had provided Indians with jobs. At the same time, many viewed the Nazis and the Japanese warlords as threats to their own homeland.

Whatever their motivations, Indians distinguished themselves in the military. Unlike their African American counterparts, In-

NAVAJO CODE TALKERS The complexity of the Navajo language made it impossible for the Axis Powers to decode American messages. Here, a code talker relays messages for the marines in the Battle of Bougainville in the South Pacific in 1943.

dian servicemen were integrated into regular units with whites. Perhaps their most distinctive role was serving as "code talkers": every military branch used Indians, especially Navajos, to encode and decipher messages using Indian languages unknown to the Germans and Japanese.

Discrimination against Japanese Americans

The attack on Pearl Harbor ignited an irrational hunger for vengeance against the Nisei—people of Japanese descent living in the United States. As Idaho's governor declared, "A good solution to the Jap problem would be to send them all back to Japan, then sink the island." Such hysteria helps explain why the U.S. government sponsored one of the worst violations of civil liberties during the twentieth century when it forcibly removed more than 112,000 Nisei from their homes along the West Coast and transported them to ten "**war relocation camps**."

President Roosevelt initiated the incarceration of Japanese Americans (whom he called "Japs") when he issued Executive Order 9066 on February 19, 1942. More than 60 percent of those "relocated" were U.S. citizens; a third were under the age of nineteen. Forced to sell their farms and businesses at great loss, the Nisei lost not only their property but also their liberty. Few if any were disloyal (in fact, 39,000 Japanese Americans served in the armed forces during the war), but all were victims of fear and racial prejudice. Not

war relocation camps Detention camps housing thousands of Japanese Americans from the West Coast who were forcibly interned from 1942 until the end of the Second World War.

A FAREWELL TO CIVIL RIGHTS American troops escorted Japanese Americans by gunpoint to remote internment camps, many of which were horse racing tracks, whose stables served as housing. **What international and domestic tensions led to the executive order to intern the Japanese Americans?**

until 1983 did the government acknowledge the injustice of the internment policy. Five years later, it granted those Nisei still living $20,000 each in compensation, a tiny amount relative to what they had lost during four years of confinement.

CORE **OBJECTIVE**

4. Explain the major factors that enabled the United States and its allies to win the war in Europe.

The Allied Drive toward Berlin

By mid-1942, Americans began to hear good news from the war in Europe. U.S. naval forces were increasingly successful at destroying German U-boats off the Atlantic coast. This was all the more important because the Grand Alliance—Great Britain, United States, and the Soviet Union—called for the defeat of Germany first. Defeating the Japanese in the Pacific could wait.

War Aims and Strategy

The Russian Front

A major consideration for Allied military strategy was the massive fighting in the Soviet Union, where, in fact, the outcome of the war against Hitler was largely decided. During 1941–1942, the Nazis and the Soviets waged colossal battles. The Soviet population—by far—bore the brunt of the war against the Nazis, leading Josef Stalin to insist that the Americans and British attack the Germans in western Europe, thereby forcing Hitler to pull units away from the Russian Front.

Meanwhile, with most of the German army deployed on the Russian Front, the British and American air forces, flying from bases in England, would bomb military and industrial targets in German-occupied western Europe, and especially in Germany itself, while the American and British strategists prepared plans to attack Nazi troops in North Africa, Italy, and France.

Roosevelt and Churchill agreed that they needed to create a second front in western Europe, but they could not decide on the timing or the location of an attack on German forces. U.S. military planners wanted to attack the Germans in France before the end of 1942. The British, however, were wary of moving too fast. An Allied defeat on the French coast, Churchill warned, was "the only way in which we could possibly lose this war." Finally, Roosevelt told U.S. military planners to accept Churchill's compromise proposal for a joint Anglo-American invasion of North Africa, then controlled by German and Italian armies.

The North Africa Campaign

Allied armies take North Africa

On November 8, 1942, British and American forces landed in Morocco and Algeria on the North African coast ("Operation Torch"). A little-known U.S. general, Dwight D. Eisenhower, led the assault. Farther east, British armies were pushing the Germans and Italians back across Libya.

The Americans were beaten badly in early battles. During the winter and spring of 1943, however, Eisenhower, soon known by his nickname, "Ike," found a brilliant field commander in General George Patton. Armed with ivory-handled pistols and brimming with bravado, he showed American troops how to fight a war of speed and daring. Hammered from all sides and unable to retreat, some 250,000 Germans and Italians surrendered on May 12, 1943, leaving all of North Africa in Allied control.

The Casablanca Conference

Five months earlier, in January 1943, Roosevelt, Churchill, and the Anglo-American military chiefs met at Casablanca, the largest city in Morocco. Stalin chose to stay in the Soviet Union, but he again urged the Allies to invade Nazi-controlled western Europe in order to relieve the pressure on the Russians.

At the Casablanca Conference, Churchill and Roosevelt made several key decisions. After intense debates, the British convinced the Americans that they should follow up the anticipated victory in North Africa with an assault on German and Italian forces on the Italian island of Sicily. Roosevelt and Churchill also decided to step up the bombing of Germany and to increase shipments of military supplies to the Soviet Union and the Nationalist Chinese forces fighting the Japanese.

Before leaving the Casablanca conference, Roosevelt announced that the war would end only with the "unconditional surrender" of all enemy nations. This decision was designed to quiet Soviet suspicions that the United States and its Allies might negotiate separately with Hitler to end the war. The announcement also reflected Roosevelt's determination that "every person in Germany should realize that this time Germany is a defeated nation."

The Battle of the Atlantic

While fighting raged in North Africa, the Battle of the Atlantic reached its climax. Great Britain desperately needed more food and military supplies from the United States, but German submarines were sinking the British vessels transporting American goods faster than British shipyards could replace them. By July 1942, some 230 Allied ships and almost 5 million tons of war supplies had been lost. "The only thing that ever frightened me during the war," recalled Churchill, "was the U-boat peril."

By the end of 1942, however, the British and Americans discovered ways to defeat the U-boats. A key breakthrough occurred when British experts cracked the German naval radio codes, enabling Allied convoys to steer clear of U-boats or to hunt them down with warplanes (called "subchasers") and new anti-submarine weapons deployed on warships. New technology also helped. Sonar and radar allowed Allied ships to track submarines. In May 1943, the Allies destroyed forty-one U-boats. Thereafter, the U-boats were on the defensive, and Allied shipping losses fell significantly.

New military technologies: Sonar and radar

Sicily and Italy

Allied forces reclaim Sicily and Italy: Mussolini flees

On July 10, 1943, following the Allied victory in North Africa, about 250,000 British and American troops landed on the coast of Sicily in the first effort to reclaim European territory since the war began. The entire island was in Allied hands by August 17, bringing to an end Benito Mussolini's twenty years of fascist rule in Italy. On July 25, 1943, the Italian king had dismissed Mussolini as prime minister and had him arrested. The new Italian government startled the Allies when it offered to switch sides in the war. To prevent them from doing so, Hitler sent German armies into Italy. Mussolini, plucked from prison by a daring German airborne raid, became head of a puppet fascist government in northern Italy as Allied forces took control of the rest of the country. On June 4, 1944, the U.S. Fifth Army entered Rome.

The Tehran Conference

Late in the fall of 1943, in Tehran, Iran, Churchill and Roosevelt had their first joint meeting with Josef Stalin. Their discussions focused on the planned invasion of Nazi-controlled France and a simultaneous Russian offensive westward across eastern Europe. The three leaders agreed to create an international organization—the United Nations—to maintain peace after the war.

Upon arriving back in the United States, Roosevelt confided to Churchill his distrust of Stalin, stressing that it was a "ticklish" business keeping the "Russians cozy with us" because of the tension between communism and capitalism. As General Eisenhower stressed, however, the fate of Britain and the United States depended upon the Soviets' survival as an ally against Nazi Germany. "The prize we seek," he said in 1942, "is to keep 8 million Russians [soldiers] in the war."

The Strategic Bombing of Europe

Allied air supremacy over Europe

Behind the long-anticipated Allied invasion of German-occupied France lay months of preparation. While waiting for D-day (the day the invasion would begin), the U.S. Army Air Forces tried to pound Germany into submission. The air campaign against Germany, carried out night and day, killed some 350,000 civilians and displaced many others.

Yet the strategic air offensive failed to shatter either German morale or war production; many bombs missed their targets because of thick clouds, high winds, and inaccurate navigational systems. The massive Allied bombing campaign, however, did force the Germans to commit precious resources to air-raid defense and eventually wore down their air force. With Allied air supremacy over Europe assured by 1944, the much-anticipated invasion of Hitler's "Fortress Europe" could move forward.

Planning an Invasion

In early 1944, General Dwight D. Eisenhower arrived in London with a new title: Supreme Commander of the Allied Expeditionary Force (AEF) that would invade Nazi-controlled western Europe. Eisenhower faced the daunting task of planning "Operation Overlord," the daring assault on Hitler's

"Atlantic Wall," a formidable array of fortifications, mines, machine guns, barbed wire, and jagged beach obstacles along the French coastline. An attack by sea against heavily fortified defenders was the toughest of military operations. The planned invasion of France gave Churchill nightmares: "When I think of the beaches . . . choked with the flower of American and British youth . . . I see the tides running red with their blood. I have my doubts. I have my doubts."

As D-day approached in early June 1944, Eisenhower's chief of staff predicted only a 50–50 chance of success. The seaborne invasion was the greatest gamble and most complex military operation in history. "I am very uneasy about the whole operation," admitted Sir Alan Brooke, the head of British forces. "It may well be the most ghastly disaster of the whole war." Eisenhower was so concerned about the invasion that he carried in his wallet a note to be circulated if the Allies failed. It read: "If any blame or fault attaches to the attempt, it is mine alone."

D-day and After

Operation Overlord succeeded in part because it surprised the German defenders. The Allies made elaborate efforts—including the positioning of British decoy troops and making misleading public statements—to fool the Nazis into believing that the invasion would come at Pas-de-Calais, on the French-Belgian border, where the English Channel was narrowest. Instead, the landings would occur along 50 miles of shoreline in northern Normandy, a French coastal region almost 200 miles south.

Operation Overlord

On the evening of June 5, General Eisenhower visited some of the 16,000 American paratroopers preparing to drop behind the German lines in France to seize key bridges and roads. The tough soldiers noticed Eisenhower's concern and tried to lift his spirits. "Now quit worrying, General," one of them said, "we'll take care of this thing for you." Another said, "We ain't worried. It's Hitler's turn to worry." After the planes took off, Eisenhower returned to his car with tears in his eyes. "Well," he said quietly to his driver, "it's on."

As the planes carrying the paratroopers arrived over France, thick clouds and German anti-aircraft fire disrupted the formations. Some soldiers were dropped miles from their landing sites, some were dropped far out at sea, some were dropped so low that their parachutes never opened. Yet the U.S. 82nd and 101st Airborne Divisions, although badly scattered, outfought three German divisions during the chaotic night and prepared the way for the main invasion by destroying bridges and capturing artillery positions and key road junctions.

GENERAL DWIGHT D. EISENHOWER Eisenhower instructing paratroopers before they launch the D-day assault in Operation Overlord.

THE LANDING AT NORMANDY Before they could huddle under a seawall and begin to root out the region's Nazi defenders, soldiers landing on the Normandy coast on June 6, 1944 had to cross a fifty-yard stretch that exposed them to machine guns housed in concrete bunkers. **What made the Normandy invasion a turning point for the Allied forces?**

The Normandy Landings

D-day: The Normandy Landings

As the gray, misty light of dawn broke on D-day morning, June 6, 1944, the largest invasion fleet in history—some 5,300 Allied ships carrying 370,000 soldiers and sailors—filled the horizon off the Normandy coast. Sleepy German soldiers guarding the beaches awoke to see Allied ships of every size. A French boy said he saw "more ships than sea."

When Hitler learned of the Allied landings, he boasted that "the news couldn't be better. As long as they [the Allied armies] were in Britain, we couldn't get at them. Now we have them where we can destroy them." In the United States, word that the long-anticipated liberation of Nazi Europe had begun captured the nation's attention. Businesses closed, church bells tolled, and traffic stopped so that people could pray in the streets. Churchill called the D-day invasion "undoubtedly the most complicated and difficult" military operation in history.

During the first day of the Normandy landings, rough seas caused injuries and nausea and capsized dozens of landing craft. Indeed, many of them never managed to land at all, and over a thousand men, weighed down by their packs and equipment, drowned as they stepped off landing craft into water over their heads. Some of the landing craft delivered their often sea-sick troops to the wrong locations. "We have landed in the wrong place," shouted Brigadier General Theodore Roosevelt Jr. (son of the former president), who would receive the Medal of Honor for his courage that day. "But we will start the war from here."

The noise was deafening as shells exploded across the beach and in the surf. The bodies of the killed, wounded, and drowned piled up amid wrenching cries for help. "As our boat touched sand and the ramp went down," Private Harry Parley remembered, "I became a visitor to Hell."

The first U.S. units ashore at Omaha Beach, beneath 130-foot-tall cliffs defended by German machine guns and mortars, lost more than 90 percent of their men. Officers struggled to rally the exhausted, bewildered men pinned down on the beach. "Two kinds of men are staying on this beach," shouted Colonel George Taylor on Omaha Beach. "The dead and those who are going to die. Get up! Move in! Goddammit! Move in and die!"

Inch by inch, the U.S. soldiers pushed across the beach and up the cliffs. By nightfall, 156,000 Allied soldiers—57,000 of them Americans—were scattered across fifty miles of Normandy coastline. So, too, were the bodies of some 5,000 dead or wounded Allied soldiers.

On June 13, a week after the Normandy landings, Erwin Rommel, the German commander, told his wife that the "battle is not going at all well for us." Within three weeks, the Allies had landed more than 1 million troops, 566,000 tons of supplies, and 171,000 vehicles. "Whether the enemy can still be stopped at this point is questionable," German headquarters near Paris warned Hitler. "The enemy air superiority is terrific and smothers almost every one of our movements. . . . Losses in men and equipment are extraordinary."

Operation Overlord was the greatest seaborne invasion in the annals of warfare, but it was small when compared with the offensive launched by the Soviets a few weeks after D-day. Between June and August 1944, the Soviet army killed, wounded, or captured more German soldiers (350,000) than were stationed in all of western Europe.

Still, the Normandy invasion was a turning point in the war. With the beachhead secured, the Allied leaders knew that victory was in their grasp. "What a plan!" Churchill exclaimed to the British Parliament. For all the Allied success, however, Eisenhower privately struggled with the daily casualty reports. "How I wish this cruel business of war could be completed quickly," he wrote his wife.

The Liberation of Paris

It would take seven more weeks and 37,000 more lives for the Allied troops to gain control of Normandy; the Germans lost more than twice as many. Some 19,000 French civilians died in the carnage. Then, on July 25, 1944, American armies broke out from Normandy and headed east toward Paris. On August 15, a joint American-French invasion force landed on the French Mediterranean coast and raced up the Rhone Valley in eastern France.

The path to victory in France was anything but smooth; German resistance collapsed only after ten weeks of ferocious fighting. A division of the

WORLD WAR II IN EUROPE AND AFRICA 1942–1945

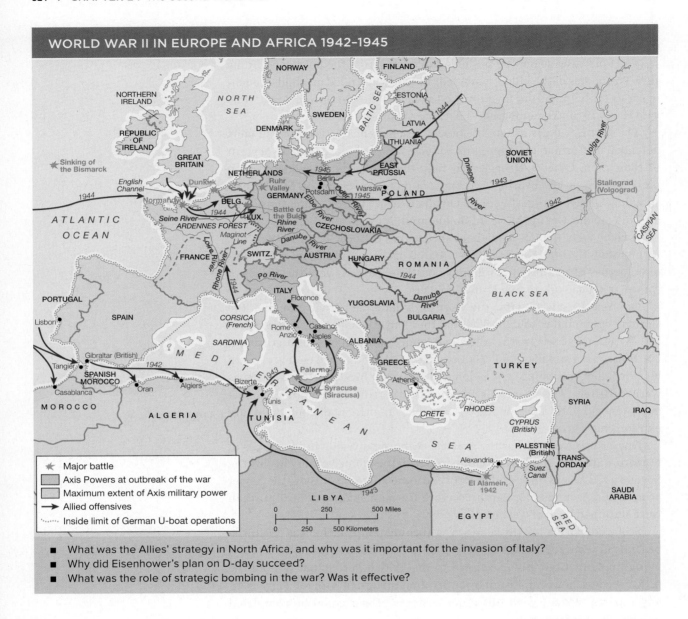

- Major battle
- Axis Powers at outbreak of the war
- Maximum extent of Axis military power
- Allied offensives
- Inside limit of German U-boat operations

■ What was the Allies' strategy in North Africa, and why was it important for the invasion of Italy?

■ Why did Eisenhower's plan on D-day succeed?

■ What was the role of strategic bombing in the war? Was it effective?

Free French Resistance, aided by American units, had the honor of liberating Paris on August 25. As American soldiers marched through the city's cheering crowds, a reporter said that he had never "seen in any place such joy as radiated from the people of Paris this morning."

By mid-September, most of France and Belgium had been cleared of German troops; meanwhile, the Soviet army moved relentlessly westward along a 1,200-mile front, pushing the fleeing Germans out of Russia. Between D-day until the end of the war in Europe a year later, 1.2 million Germans were killed and wounded.

Roosevelt's Fourth Term

In 1944, war or no war, the calendar required another presidential election. This time the Republicans nominated New York governor Thomas E. Dewey, who argued that it was time for a younger man to replace the "tired" Democratic leader. Nevertheless, on November 7, 1944, Franklin Roosevelt won yet again, this time by a popular vote of 25.6 million–22 million and an electoral vote of 432–99.

Roosevelt elected to fourth term (1944)

The End of the War in the European Theater

By the time Roosevelt won his fourth presidential term, Allied armies were approaching the German border from the east and west. Churchill worried that if the Soviets arrived first in shattered Berlin, the German capital, Stalin would control the postwar map of Europe. He urged Eisenhower to beat the Soviets to Berlin. Eisenhower, however, decided it was not worth the estimated 100,000 American casualties to liberate Berlin before the Soviets did.

The Yalta Conference

Anticipating victory in Germany, the Soviets hosted the Allied leaders at a seaside resort on the Black Sea. At the **Yalta Conference** (February 4–11, 1945), the "Big Three" agreed that once Germany surrendered, the Soviets would control eastern Germany, and the Americans and British would take charge of the industrial areas in the west. Berlin, the German capital within the Soviet zone, would be subject to joint occupation.

THE YALTA CONFERENCE Churchill, Roosevelt, and Stalin (with their respective foreign ministers behind them) confer on plans for the postwar world in February 1945.

Stalin's goals at Yalta were both defensive and expansive: he wanted to retrieve former Russian territory ceded to Poland after World War I and to impose Soviet control over the countries of eastern and central Europe. Roosevelt, exhausted and in failing health, agreed to most of Stalin's demands because he needed the Soviets to help defeat Japan. Military analysts estimated that Japan could hold out for eighteen months after the defeat of Germany.

The Collapse of Nazi Germany

By early 1945, Nazi Germany was on the verge of defeat, but President Roosevelt would not live to join the victory celebrations. In the spring of 1945, he went to the "Little White House" in Warm Springs, Georgia. On the morning of April 12, 1945, he complained of a headache but seemed to be in good

Yalta Conference (1945)
Meeting of the "Big Three" Allied leaders—Franklin D. Roosevelt, Winston Churchill, and Joseph Stalin—to discuss how to divide control of postwar Germany and eastern Europe.

spirits, pleasantly distracted by his beloved stamp collection. At midday he told an artist painting his portrait that "we've got just about 15 minutes more to work." Then, as she watched him reading some documents, he groaned, saying that he had "terrific pain" in the back of his head. Then he slumped over and fell into a coma. He died two hours later.

Roosevelt's death shocked and saddened people all over the world. Even his sharpest critics were devastated. Ohio senator Robert Taft, known as "Mr. Republican," called Roosevelt's death one of the worst tragedies in American history. "The President's death removes the greatest figure of our time at the very climax of his career. . . . He dies a hero of the war, for he literally worked himself to death in the service of the American people." By contrast, a desperate Adolf Hitler saw in Roosevelt's death a "great miracle" for the besieged Germans. "The war is not lost," he told an aide. "Read it. Roosevelt is dead!"

> **Soviet troops enter Berlin; Germany surrenders**

Hitler's shrinking Nazi empire collapsed less than a month later. In Berlin, as Soviet troops entered the German capital, Adolf Hitler married his mistress, Eva Braun, in an underground bunker on the last day of April. She then poisoned herself, and he killed himself with a pistol shot. Two days later, on May 2, Berlin fell. Five days later, on May 7, the chief of staff of the German armed forces signed a treaty agreeing to unconditional surrender. So ended the Nazi domination of Europe, little more than twelve years after Hitler had come to power proclaiming his "Thousand-Year Reich."

On May 8, V-E Day (Victory in Europe) generated massive celebrations. In New York City, 500,000 people celebrated in the streets. Yet the elation was tempered by the ongoing war against Japan and the immense challenges of helping war-torn Europe rebuild. The German economy had to be revived; a new democratic government had to be formed; and the Germans and millions of other Europeans had to be clothed, housed, and fed.

The Holocaust

The end of the war in Europe revealed the horrific extent of the **Holocaust**, Hitler's systematic efforts to destroy the Jews of Europe, for whom he harbored an obsessive hatred. Reports of the Nazis' methodical slaughter of Jews had appeared as early as 1942, but the ghastly stories of millions killed in gas chambers seemed beyond belief until the Allied armies liberated the death camps in central and eastern Europe. There the Germans had imposed their "Final Solution" to what Hitler called the "Jewish problem": the wholesale extermination of some 6 million Jews, along with more than 1 million other captured peoples.

In 1945, Allied troops were horrified at what they discovered in the concentration camps. Bodies were piled as high as buildings; survivors were virtually skeletons. General Eisenhower reported to his wife that the evidence of "starvation, cruelty, and bestiality were so overpowering as to leave me a bit sick."

Holocaust Systematic efforts by the Nazis to exterminate the Jews of Europe, resulting in the murder of over 6 million Jews and more than a million other "undesirables."

HOLOCAUST SURVIVORS
American troops encounter survivors of the Mauthausen concentration camp in their barracks in May of 1945. The Nazis tattooed their prisoners with identification numbers on their wrists or chests, as seen on the man at left.

American officials, even some Jewish leaders, had dragged their feet in acknowledging the Holocaust during the war for fear that relief efforts for Jewish refugees might stir up anti-Semitism at home. Under pressure, President Roosevelt had set up a War Refugee Board early in 1944. It managed to rescue about 200,000 European Jews and some 20,000 others. Overall, however, the Allied response to the Nazi atrocities was inept at best and disgraceful at worst. In 1944, Churchill called the Holocaust the "most horrible crime ever committed in the history of the world."

Fighting in the Pacific

For months after the attack on Pearl Harbor, the news from the Pacific was "all bad," as President Roosevelt confessed. The Japanese captured numerous territories in Asia, including the British colonies of Hong Kong, Burma, Malaysia, and Singapore as well as the French colony of Indochina. "Everywhere in the Pacific," said Winston Churchill, "we were weak and naked." In the Philippines, U.S. forces and their Filipino allies, outmanned, outgunned, and malnourished, surrendered in the early spring of 1942. Within six months, Japan had seized control of a vast new Pacific empire.

Coral Sea and Midway

During the spring of 1942, U.S. forces finally had some success in two key naval battles. The Battle of the Coral Sea (May 7–8, 1942) stopped a Japanese fleet headed toward the enormous island of New Guinea. Planes from the *Lexington* and the *Yorktown* sank one Japanese carrier, damaged another, and destroyed several smaller ships. American losses were greater, but the Japanese threat against Australia was stopped.

> CORE **OBJECTIVE**
> **5.** Describe how the Japanese were defeated in the war in the Pacific.

Battles of Coral Sea and Midway (1942)

Less than a month later, Admiral Yamamoto steered his main Japanese battle fleet toward Midway, the westernmost of Hawaii's inhabited islands, from which he hoped to strike again at Pearl Harbor. This time it was the Japanese who were surprised. Americans had broken the Japanese military radio code, allowing Admiral Chester Nimitz, commander of the U.S. central Pacific fleet, to learn where Yamamoto's fleet was heading. Nimitz then reinforced the air base at tiny Midway Island with planes and aircraft carriers.

The first Japanese attack against Midway, on June 4, 1942, severely damaged the island's defenses but at the cost of about a third of the Japanese planes. American bombers then struck back. In the strategic Battle of Midway, U.S. warplanes sank three Japanese aircraft carriers and crippled a fourth; it was the first major defeat for the Japanese navy in 350 years and the turning point of the Pacific war.

The American victory at Midway blunted Japan's military momentum, eliminated the threat to Hawaii, and bought time for the United States to organize its massive industrial productivity for a wider war. Japanese hopes for a short, decisive war were dashed.

MacArthur's Pacific Strategy

American and Australian forces were under the command of General Douglas MacArthur, an egotistical military genius who constantly irritated his superiors in Washington with his "unpleasant personality" and his relentless efforts at self-promotion. Yet MacArthur was indeed a brilliant strategist. In 1942, his forces began to dislodge the Japanese from islands in the southwest Pacific.

Guadalcanal (1943) and Pacific leapfrogging

After first pushing the Japanese back in New Guinea, on August 7, 1942, 19,000 U.S. Marines landed on Guadalcanal Island, where the Japanese had built an air base. Savage fighting on Guadalcanal lasted through February 1943, but it resulted in the Japanese army's first defeat, a loss of 20,000 men compared to 1,752 Americans.

The Japanese were skilled defensive fighters who rarely surrendered, and they controlled most of the islands in the Pacific. Their suicidal intensity in battles in New Guinea and on Guadalcanal led MacArthur and American military planners to adopt a brilliant "leapfrogging" strategy whereby they focused on the most important islands and bypassed the others, leaving the isolated Japanese bases to "wither on the vine," as Admiral Nimitz put it.

Battles in the Central Pacific

On June 15, 1944, U.S. forces liberated Tinian, Guam, and Saipan, three Japanese-controlled islands in the Mariana Islands. Saipan was strategically important because it allowed the new American B-29 "Superfortress" bombers to strike Japan itself. General MacArthur's forces then invaded the Japanese-held Philippines on October 20. The Japanese, knowing that the loss of the Philippines would cut them off from essential raw materials, brought in warships from three directions to battle the U.S. fleet.

GENERAL DOUGLAS MACARTHUR MacArthur theatrically coming ashore at the island of Leyte in the Philippines, October 1944. **What was MacArthur's strategy for pushing the Japanese out of the Pacific islands?**

The four sea battles fought in the Philippine Sea from October 23 to October 26, 1944, known collectively as the Battle of Leyte Gulf, was the largest naval engagement in history and the worst Japanese defeat of the war. By the end of the last day, thirty-six Japanese warships, including four aircraft carriers, had been destroyed. The battle included the first Japanese *kamikaze* ("divine wind") attacks—suicide pilots deliberately crashing their bomb-laden planes into American warships.

Battle of Leyte Gulf (1944)

A Grinding War against Japan

The closer the Allied forces got to Japan itself, the fiercer the resistance they encountered. While fighting continued in the Philippines, 30,000 U.S. Marines landed on Japanese-held Iwo Jima island, a speck of volcanic rock 760 miles from Tokyo that the Americans needed as a base for fighter planes to

Iwo Jima (1945)

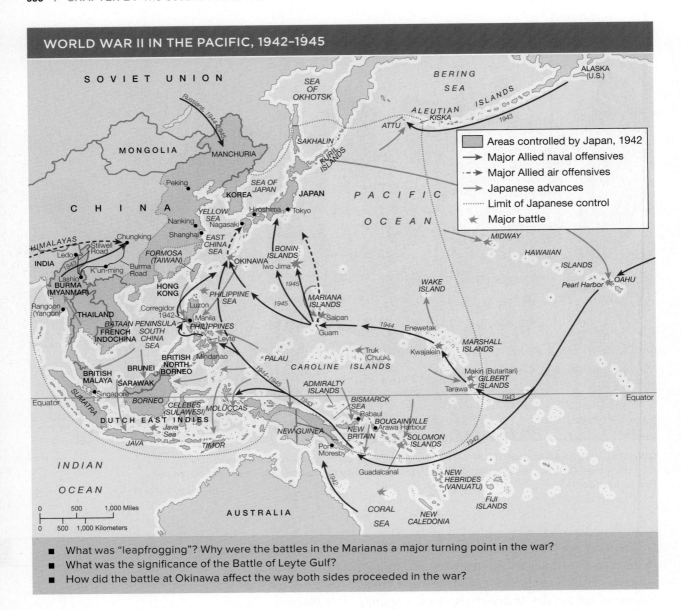

WORLD WAR II IN THE PACIFIC, 1942–1945

Legend:
- Areas controlled by Japan, 1942
- Major Allied naval offensives
- Major Allied air offensives
- Japanese advances
- Limit of Japanese control
- ★ Major battle

- What was "leapfrogging"? Why were the battles in the Marianas a major turning point in the war?
- What was the significance of the Battle of Leyte Gulf?
- How did the battle at Okinawa affect the way both sides proceeded in the war?

escort bombers over Japan. It took nearly six weeks to secure the tiny island at a cost of about 7,000 American lives.

Battle of Okinawa

The fight for the Japanese island of Okinawa, which began on April 1, 1945, was even bloodier. The Americans needed Okinawa as a staging area for the invasion of Japan. The conquest of Okinawa was the largest amphibious operation of the Pacific war, involving some 300,000 troops and almost three months of brutal fighting. More than 110,000 Japanese were killed; the remaining 7,871 were either captured or surrendered.

Preparations for the Invasion of Japan

Even as the fighting still raged on Okinawa, Allied commanders began planning Operation Downfall—the invasion of Japan itself. To weaken the Japanese defenses, destroy many of their war-related industries, and erode civilian morale, the Allied command launched massive bombing raids over Japan in the summer of 1944. Then, in early 1945, General Curtis Lemay, head of the U.S. Bomber Command, ordered devastating "firebomb" raids upon Japanese cities. On March 9, for example, some 300 B-29 bombers incinerated sixteen square miles of Tokyo, killing 85,000 people.

THE AFTERMATH OF "LITTLE BOY" A photograph of the wasteland that remained after the atomic bomb "Little Boy" decimated Hiroshima, Japan, on August 6, 1945.

The Atomic Bomb

Still, the Japanese refused to surrender. In early 1945, new president Harry S. Truman learned of the first successful test explosion of an atomic bomb in New Mexico. Once military planners knew the bomb would work, they selected two Japanese cities as targets. The first was **Hiroshima**, a port city and army headquarters on the island of Honshu.

> Atomic bomb dropped on Hiroshima

In mid-July 1945, the Allied leaders met in Potsdam, Germany, near Berlin. There they issued the Potsdam Declaration, which demanded that Japan surrender or face "prompt and utter destruction."

On July 25, 1945, Truman ordered that the atomic bomb be dropped if Japan did not surrender before August 3. Although an intense debate has emerged over the decision to drop the bomb, Truman said that he "never had any doubt that it should be used." He explained that "we faced half a million casualties trying to take Japan by land. It was either that or the atom bomb, and I didn't hesitate a minute, and I've never lost any sleep over it since."

To Truman and others, the use of atomic bombs seemed a logical next step to end the war. As it turned out, scientists greatly underestimated the bomb's power. They predicted that 20,000 people would be killed, an estimate that proved much too low.

Hiroshima (1945) Japanese port city that was the first target of the newly developed atomic bomb on August 6, 1945. Most of the city was destroyed.

The deadline passed, and on August 6, 1945, a B-29 bomber named the *Enola Gay* (after the pilot's mother) took off at 2:00 A.M. from the island of Tinian and headed for Hiroshima. At 8:15 A.M., flying at 31,600 feet, the *Enola Gay* released the five-ton, ten-foot-long uranium bomb nicknamed "Little Boy." Forty-three seconds later, as the *Enola Gay* turned sharply to avoid the blast, the bomb tumbled to an altitude of 1,900 feet where it exploded, creating a blinding flash of light followed by a fireball towering to 40,000 feet. The tail gunner on the *Enola Gay* described the scene: "It's like bubbling molasses down there . . . the mushroom is spreading out . . . fires are springing up everywhere . . . it's like a peep into hell."

The mighty bomb's shock wave and firestorm killed some 78,000 people, including thousands of Japanese soldiers and twenty-three American prisoners of war. By the end of the year, the death toll would reach 140,000, as more people died of injuries or radiation poisoning. In addition, the bomb destroyed 70,000 buildings, and turned four square miles of the city into rubble.

President Truman was aboard the battleship *Augusta* returning from the Potsdam Conference when he learned that the atomic bomb had been dropped. "This is the greatest thing in history!" he exclaimed. Americans greeted the news with similar joy, for the atomic bomb promised a quick end to the long nightmare of war. "No tears of sympathy will be shed in America for the Japanese people," the *Omaha World-Herald* predicted. "Had they possessed a comparable weapon at Pearl Harbor, would they have hesitated to use it?" Others reacted more soberly when they considered the implications of atomic warfare. "Yesterday," journalist Hanson Baldwin wrote in the *New York Times*, "we clinched victory in the Pacific, but we sowed the whirlwind."

Two days after the Hiroshima bombing, an opportunistic Soviet Union, hoping to share in the spoils of victory, entered the war in the Pacific by sending Russian troops into Japanese-occupied Manchuria along the border between China and the Soviet Union.

Truman and his aides, frustrated by the stubborn refusal of Japanese leaders to surrender and fearful that the Soviet Union's entry would complicate negotiations, ordered a second atomic bomb ("Fat Man") to be dropped on Japan. On August 9, the city of Nagasaki, a shipbuilding center, experienced the same nuclear devastation that had destroyed Hiroshima. Five days later, on August 14, 1945, the Japanese emperor finally accepted the terms of surrender.

BOMBING OF NAGASAKI A 20,000-foot-tall mushroom cloud swallowed the city of Nagasaki after the atomic bombing on August 9, 1945.

A New Age Is Born

CORE **OBJECTIVE**

6. Evaluate the efforts of President Roosevelt and the Allies to shape the postwar world.

Thus ended the costliest war in human history. The Soviet Union suffered 20 million deaths, China 10 million, Germany 5.6 million, and Japan 2.3 million. The Second World War (1939–1945) was more costly for the United States than any other foreign war: 292,000 battle deaths and 114,000 noncombat deaths. In proportion to its population, however, the United States suffered far fewer losses than did the other Allied nations or their enemies. For every American killed in the Second World War, for example, some 59 Soviets died.

The Second World War was the pivotal event of the twentieth century; it reshaped entire societies, transformed international relations, and destroyed German and Italian fascism as well as Japanese militarism. The colonial empires in Africa and Asia governed by European nations rapidly crumbled as the changes wrought by the war unleashed independence movements. In 1947, for example, the new nations of India and Pakistan liberated themselves from British control. The Soviet Union emerged from the war as a new global superpower, while the United States, as Winston Churchill told the House of Commons, stood "at the summit of the world."

The end of colonial empires and the emergence of the Soviet Union as a global power

Why Did the Allies Win?

Many factors contributed to the Allied victory in the Second World War. The American and British leaders—Roosevelt and Churchill—were better at coordinating military efforts and maintaining national morale than were Hitler, Mussolini, and the Japanese emperor, Hirohito. By 1944, Hitler had grown increasingly unstable and unpredictable in his decision making and more withdrawn from the German people, especially after a failed attempt by high-ranking officers to assassinate him in July.

In the end, however, what turned the tide of war was the awesome productivity of American industry and the ability of the Soviet Union to absorb the massive German invasion and then push the Nazis back all the way to Berlin. By the end of the war, Japan had run out of food and Germany had run out of fuel. By contrast, the United States was churning out more of everything at war's end. As early as 1942, just a few weeks after the Japanese attack on Pearl Harbor, Fritz Todt, a Nazi engineer, told Hitler that the war against the United States was already lost because of America's ability to outproduce all the other warring nations combined.

Yalta's Legacy and the Postwar World

Franklin Roosevelt viewed the Yalta meeting as a test of whether the wartime alliance between the United States and the Soviet Union would survive once the conflict ended. Like Woodrow Wilson before him, Roosevelt staked his hopes for postwar cooperation on the creation of a new international

The United Nations (1945)

peacekeeping organization, the United Nations. At Yalta, the "Big Three" agreed to hold organizational meetings in the United States beginning on April 25, 1945. In order to get Stalin's approval of the United Nations, Roosevelt gave in to the Soviet dictator's demands for territory held by Japan in northeast Asia.

Soviet domination of eastern Europe

Stalin also signed the Yalta Declaration of Liberated Europe, which called for open elections in the liberated nations of eastern Europe. Nevertheless, the wily Stalin would fail to live up to the promises he made at Yalta. When the Red Army "liberated" Hungary, Romania, Bulgaria, Czechoslovakia, Poland, and eastern Germany, it plundered and sent back to Russia anything of economic value, dismantling thousands of factories and mills and rebuilding them in the Soviet Union. To ensure control over the nations of eastern Europe, the Soviets shipped off to prisons anyone who questioned the new Communist governments they created.

Republicans later savagely attacked Roosevelt for "giving" eastern Europe over to Soviet domination at Yalta. Some blamed his behavior on his declining health. But even a robust Roosevelt could not have dislodged the Soviet army from its control of eastern Europe. The course of the war shaped the outcome at Yalta, not Roosevelt's failed diplomacy. The United States had no real leverage when it came to eastern Europe; the huge Soviet army controlled Poland and its neighbors. As a U.S. diplomat admitted, "Stalin held all the cards" at Yalta.

The Transformation of American Life

The Second World War had far-reaching social effects. The war transformed American life by ending the Great Depression and launching a period of unprecedented prosperity. Big businesses during the war grew into gigantic corporations as a result of huge government contracts for military weapons and supplies. New technologies and products developed for military purposes—radar, computers, electronics, plastics and synthetics, jet engines, rockets, atomic energy—began to transform the private sector, as did new consumer products resulting from war-related innovations. And new opportunities for women as well as for African Americans, Mexican Americans, and other minorities set in motion major social changes that would culminate in the civil rights movement and the feminist movement two decades later.

The postwar United States: Global superpower

The expansion of the federal government spurred by the war effort continued after 1945. Presidential authority increased enormously at the expense of congressional and state power. The isolationist sentiment in foreign relations that had been so powerful in the 1920s and 1930s evaporated, as the United States assumed new global responsibilities and economic interests.

In August 1945, President Truman told the nation that the United States had "emerged from this war the most powerful nation in this world—the most powerful nation, perhaps, in all history." But the Soviet Union, despite its profound human losses and physical destruction, had gained much new territory, built massive armed forces, and enhanced its international influence, making it the greatest power in Europe and Asia. A little over a century after Frenchman Alexis de Tocqueville had predicted that Europe would eventually be overshadowed by the United States and Russia, his prophecy had come to pass.

■ **Fascism and the Start of the War**
In Italy, *fascism* took hold under Benito Mussolini, who assumed control in 1922 by promising law and order. Adolf Hitler rearmed Germany in defiance of the Treaty of Versailles and aimed to unite all German speakers in a "Greater Germany." Civil war in Spain and the growth of the Soviet Union under Josef Stalin contributed to a precarious balance of power in Europe. By March 1939, Nazi Germany had annexed Austria and seized Czechoslovakia. Hitler then invaded Poland with the *blitzkrieg* strategy in September 1939, after signing a nonaggression pact with the Soviet Union. At last, the British and French governments declared war.

■ **America Goes to War** The United States issued "neutrality laws" to keep it out of war, but with the fall of France in 1940, Roosevelt accelerated military aid to Great Britain through the *Lend-Lease Bill (1941)*. In 1941, the United States and Great Britain signed the *Atlantic Charter*, announcing their aims in the war. After Japan joined with Germany and Italy to form the *"Axis" alliance* and Japan announced its intention to take control of French Indochina, President Roosevelt froze Japanese assets in the United States and restricted oil exports to Japan. The frustrated Japanese decided to launch a surprise attack at *Pearl Harbor*, Hawaii, in hopes of destroying the U.S. Pacific Fleet.

■ **The Second World War and American Society** The war ended unemployment and the Great Depression. Farmers, too, recovered from hard times, supported by Mexican labor through the *bracero program*. The federal government, through agencies like the *War Production Board*, took control of managing the economy for the war effort. Many women took nontraditional jobs, some in the *Women's Army Corps*. About 1 million African Americans served in the military in segregated units such as the *Tuskegee Airmen*. More than 100,000 Japanese Americans were forced into *war relocation camps*.

■ **Road to Allied Victory in Europe** By 1943, the Allies had defeated the German and Italian armies occupying North Africa, then launched attacks on Sicily and the mainland of Italy. Stalin demanded an Allied attack on the Atlantic coast of France, but Operation Overlord was delayed until 1944. Invaded from the west and the east, German resistance slowly crumbled. Allied leaders Roosevelt, Churchill, and Stalin met at the *Yalta Conference* in February 1945, where they decided to divide a conquered Germany into occupation zones. In May, Soviet forces captured Berlin and Germany surrendered. After the war, Allied forces discovered the extent of the *Holocaust*— the Nazis' systematic attempt to exterminate the Jews.

■ **The Pacific War** The Japanese advance across the Pacific was halted in June 1942 when the U.S. Navy destroyed much of the Japanese fleet in the Battle of Midway. The United States fought costly battles in New Guinea and Guadalcanal before dislodging the Japanese from the Philippines in 1944. Fierce Japanese resistance at Iwo Jima and Okinawa and refusal to surrender led the new president, Harry S. Truman, to drop atomic bombs on the Japanese cities of *Hiroshima* and Nagasaki.

■ **Postwar World** The Soviet Union and the United States emerged from the war as global superpowers. Military production had brought America out of the Great Depression, and new military technologies changed industrial and private life. The opportunities for women and minorities during the war also increased their aspirations and would contribute to the emergence of the civil rights and feminist movements.

KEY TERMS

fascism *p. 894*

"Axis" alliance *p. 897*

blitzkrieg (1940) *p. 899*

Lend-Lease Bill (1941) *p. 905*

Atlantic Charter (1941) *p. 907*

Pearl Harbor (1941) *p. 909*

War Production Board *p. 911*

Women's Army Corps *p. 912*

Tuskegee Airmen *p. 915*

bracero program (1942) *p. 915*

war relocation camps *p. 917*

Yalta Conference (1945) *p. 925*

Holocaust *p. 926*

Hiroshima (1945) *p. 931*

CHRONOLOGY

1933	Hitler becomes chancellor of Germany
1935	Italy invades Ethiopia
1936–1939	Spanish Civil War
1937	Japan launches war against China
1938	Hitler forces the *Anschluss* (union) of Austria and Germany
1939	Soviet Union agrees to a non-aggression pact with Germany
September 1939	German troops invade Poland
1940	Battle of Britain
September 1940	Germany, Italy, and Japan sign the Tripartite Pact
June 1941	Germany invades Soviet Union
August 1941	United States and Great Britain sign the Atlantic Charter
December 7, 1941	Japanese launch surprise attack at Pearl Harbor, Hawaii
June 1942	Battle of Midway
July 1943	Allied forces land on Sicily
June 6, 1944	D-day in France
February 1945	Yalta Conference
May 8, 1945	Nazi Germany surrenders unconditionally; V-E Day
August 1945	Atomic bombs dropped on Hiroshima and Nagasaki

INQUIZITIVE

Go to InQuizitive to see what you've learned—and learn what you've missed—with personalized feedback along the way.

DEBATING the United States' Response to the Holocaust

One of the more difficult tasks that historians face is assessing the actions and beliefs of historical figures within an ethical framework. Should individuals be judged by the standards of their own time or by those of today? Should we hold celebrated historical figures to a higher ethical standard? For Part 6, "*Modern America*," President Franklin D. Roosevelt's and the U.S. government's response to the Holocaust during the Second World War demonstrates how historians can disagree when they attempt to evaluate individuals from an ethical perspective.

For this exercise you have two tasks:

PART 1: Compare the two secondary sources on the United States and the Holocaust.

PART 2: Using primary sources, evaluate the arguments of the two secondary sources.

PART I Comparing Secondary Sources

The first secondary source is from David Wyman, chair of the David S. Wyman Institute of Holocaust Studies. The second is coauthored by Holocaust historian Richard Breitman, editor of the journal *Holocaust and Genocide Studies*, and historian Allan J. Lichtman. Both teach at American University in Washington, D.C. In the following selections, these scholars explore President Franklin Roosevelt's response to the challenges posed by the Holocaust.

Compare the views of these scholars by answering the following questions. Use specific examples from the selections to support your answers.

■ How do the authors characterize and explain the American response to the Holocaust?

■ What role does each author ascribe to Franklin D. Roosevelt?

■ How does each author assess the morality of the response to the Holocaust of both the U.S. government and President Roosevelt? What ethical standards do the authors use in making their assessments?

■ What ethical standard would *you* use to evaluate the conduct of President Roosevelt and the U.S. government?

Secondary Source 1

David S. Wyman, *The Abandonment of the Jews* (1985)

Why did America fail to carry out the kind of rescue effort that it could have?

The American State Department . . . had no intention of rescuing large numbers of European Jews. On the contrary, they continually feared that Germany or other Axis nations might release tens of thousands of Jews into Allied hands. Any such exodus would have placed intense pressure on Britain to open Palestine [then under British control] and on the United States to take in more Jewish refugees, a situation the two great powers did not want to face. Consequently, their policies aimed at obstructing rescue possibilities and dampening public pressures for government action.

Authenticated information that the Nazis were systematically exterminating European Jewry was made public in the United States in November 1942. President Roosevelt did nothing about the mass murder for fourteen months, then moved only because he was confronted with political pressures he could not avoid and because his administration stood on the brink of a nasty scandal over its rescue policies. The War Refugee Board, which the President then established to save Jews and other victims of the Nazis, received little power, almost no cooperation from Roosevelt or his administration, and grossly inadequate government funding.

Strong popular pressure for action would have brought a much fuller government commitment to rescue and would have produced it sooner. Several factors hampered the growth of public pressure. Among them were anti-Semitism and anti-immigration attitudes, both widespread in American society in that era. . . . In 1944 the United States War Department rejected several appeals to bomb the Auschwitz gas chambers and the railroads leading to Auschwitz, claiming that such actions would divert essential airpower from decisive operations elsewhere. . . . Franklin Roosevelt's indifference to so momentous an historical event as the systematic annihilation of European Jewry emerges as the worst failure of his presidency.

Source: Wyman, David S. *The Abandonment of the Jews: America and the Holocaust, 1941–1945.* New York: The New Press, 1984 xiv–xv.

Secondary Source 2

Richard Breitman and Allan J. Lichtman, *FDR and the Jews* (2013)

Some scholars have condemned Franklin Delano Roosevelt, the president of the United States from 1933 to 1945, for callously standing by while Hitler persecuted German Jewry and then exterminated nearly two-thirds of Europe's Jews. . . . Others claim that Roosevelt did everything feasible to rescue European Jews and saved millions of potential victims by orchestrating the defeat of Nazi Germany in World War II. . . .

For most of his presidency Roosevelt did little to aid the imperiled Jews of Germany and Europe. He put other policy priorities well ahead of saving Jews and deferred to fears of an anti-Semitic backlash at home. He worried that measures to assist European Jews might endanger his political coalition at home and then a wartime alliance abroad. FDR usually avoided singling out the Jews in public. When he engaged Jewish issues, he maneuvered, often behind the scenes. When he hesitated,

other American officials with far less sympathy for Jews set or carried out policies. Still, at times Roosevelt acted decisively to rescue Jews, often withstanding contrary pressures from the American public, Congress, and his own State Department. Oddly enough, he did more for the Jews than any other world figure, even if his efforts seem deficient in retrospect. He was a far better president for Jews than any of his political adversaries would have been. Roosevelt defied most Republican opponents and some isolationist Democrats to lead political and military opposition to Nazi Germany's plans for expansion and world domination. . . .

Unlike other authors, we examine FDR's decision-making as president from the perspective of his life experiences and full political career. Roosevelt's handling of the crisis of European Jewry may offer the best opportunity to understand the political dynamics of American responses to persecution and genocide in foreign lands. FDR was a man of faith. He recognized both moral issues across the globe and the practical concerns of governing a great nation. . . . How he responded, and why, reveals much about the strengths and limitations of the American presidency.

The story of FDR and the Jews is ultimately a tragic one that transcends the achievements and failures of any one leader. Even if FDR had been more willing to override domestic opposition and twist arms abroad, he could not have stopped the Nazis' mass murder of some six million Jews. For Hitler and his followers, the annihilation of Jews was not a diversion from the war effort, but integral to its purpose. For America and Britain, the rescue of Jews, even if practical, was ultimately subordinate to the overriding priorities of total war and unconditional surrender of the enemy. "Action expresses priorities," Mahatma Gandhi said while engaged in a freedom struggle of his own.

Source: Breitman, Richard, and Allan J. Lichtman. *FDR and the Jews.* Cambridge, Mass.: The Belknap Press of Harvard University Press, 2013. 2, 6–7.

PART II Using Primary Sources to Evaluate Secondary Sources

When historians confront competing interpretations of the past, they often look at primary source material as part of the process of evaluating the different arguments. A selection of primary source materials relating to the United States and the Holocaust follows. The first document is a 1942 letter to the president from the leaders of the American Jewish community. The second selection comes from a State Department memorandum to the British

government regarding refugees from Nazi-occupied territories. The third document is an excerpt from a letter from Secretary of State Cordell Hull to the president regarding the Bermuda conference of April 1943, in which the United States and Great Britain discuss the issue of Jewish refugees. The fourth document is a 1944 memorandum written by John Pehle, an assistant to Treasury secretary Henry Morgenthau Jr., following a meeting with President

Roosevelt. Morgenthau was the highest-ranking Jewish member of FDR's cabinet and the leading advocate for U.S. intervention in stopping the Holocaust. The fifth document is a draft statement by President Roosevelt regarding crimes against humanity that was distributed to Axis forces in Europe in 1944. The final document is a July 4, 1944, letter from Assistant Secretary of War John J. McCloy to John W. Pehle outlining reasons why the War Department rejected Pehle's request to bomb the rail lines used to transport Jews and other prisoners to the Nazi death camps.

Carefully read each of the primary sources and answer the following questions. Decide which of the primary source documents support or refute Wyman's and Breitman and Lichtman's arguments about the U.S. response to the Holocaust. You may find that some documents do both but for different parts of each historian's interpretation. Be sure to identify which components of each historian's argument the documents support or refute.

■ Based on these primary sources, how would you characterize the U.S. government's response to the Holocaust?

■ Judging from these primary sources, what role did President Roosevelt play in formulating U.S. policy toward the Holocaust?

■ Which of the primary sources do you think Wyman and Breitman and Lichtman would find most useful, and how might they use them to support their argument?

■ Which of the secondary sources do you think is best supported by the primary source evidence?

■ Based on the ethical standard you would use to evaluate the conduct of President Roosevelt and the U.S. government (see the previous questions for comparing secondary sources), how do you assess what these primary sources reveal about the U.S. government's and the president's response to the Holocaust?

Primary Source 1

Representatives of the Jewish Community of the United States, "Letter to the President" (December 8, 1942)

Dear Mr. President:

We come to you as representatives of all sections of the Jewish community of the United States. Within recent months all Americans have been horrified by the verification of reports concerning the barbarities against the inhabitants of countries over-run by Hitler's forces.

To these horrors has now been added the news of Hitler's edict calling for the extermination of all Jews in the subjugated lands.

Already almost two million Jews, men, women and children, have been cruelly done to death, and five million more Jews live under the threat of a similar doom.

The record of these heinous crimes against the Jews in East Europe is detailed in the attached memorandum. . . .

In the midst of their suffering, however, the peoples of Europe are sustained by a hope that the victory of the Democracies will destroy the Nazi scourge and restore freedom to the world. European Jews share that hope. But will they live to see the dawn of this day of freedom? Unless action is taken immediately, the Jews of Hitler's Europe are doomed.

In this hour of deepest anguish and despair we turn to you, Mr. President. . . .

We ask you now once again to raise your voice—in behalf of the Jews of Europe. We ask you once again to warn the Nazis that they will be held to strict accountability for their crimes. We ask you to employ every available means to bring solemn protest and warning to the peoples of the Axis countries so that they may be deterred from acting as the instruments of the monstrous designs of their mad leaders. . . .

Maurice Wertheim, President, American Jewish Committee
Dr. Stephen Wise, President, American Jewish Congress
Adolph Held, President, American Jewish Labor Committee
Henry Monsky, President, B'nai B'rith
Israel Goldstein, President, Synagogue Council of America
Rabbi Israel Rosenberg, Chairman, Union of Orthodox Rabbis in the United States

---

Source: Wertheim, Maurice, Adolph Held, Israel Goldstein, Stephen Wise, Henry Monsky, and Rabbi Israel Rosenberg. "Letter to the President, December 8, 1942." Selected Digitized Documents Related to the Holocaust and Refugees, 1933–1945. Official File 76—Church Matters: 76c—Jewish, October–December 1942. Franklin D. Roosevelt Presidential Library & Museum.

Primary Source 2

U.S. Department of State, Response to British Embassy on Assisting Jewish Refugees (February 25, 1943)

Since the entry of the United States into the war, there have been no new restrictions placed by the Government of the United States upon the number of aliens of any nationality permitted to proceed to this country under existing laws, except for the more intensive examination of aliens required for security reasons. . . . In affording asylum to refugees, however, it is and must be bound by legislation enacted by Congress [in] determining the immigration policy of the United States.

Source: United States Department of State. "Refugees from Nazi-Occupied Territory: Reception in the United Kingdom and British Colonial Territory [February 25, 1943]." President's Secretary's File, Box 71, State Department—Summary of Consular Reports Relating to Conditions in Occupied Countries, January 1942–May 1943, July 8, 1941. Franklin D. Roosevelt, Papers as President: The President's Secretary's File (PSF), 1933–1945. Franklin D. Roosevelt Presidential Library & Museum.

Primary Source 3

Secretary of State and the President's Correspondence, Abstract (May 7, 1943)

Writes at length to the President re the recent Bermuda Conference on Refugees, and in this connection encloses a copy of the summary or outline of the recommendations, which have been unanimously made by the American and British Delegates. . . . The most important of the items recommended at Bermuda concerns the evacuation of some 5,000 persons from Bulgaria via Turkey to Palestine, another important recommendation requires action by the U.S. Government as well as by the British Government relates to the movement of some 20,000 refugees from Spain to North Africa, "not only to relieve the Spanish authorities of the present burden, but also to make it possible for Spain to receive more and more refugees who in turn may be evacuated to North Africa." . . . . The President made certain suggestions . . . as follows: that we do not give unlimited promise but that we undertake with Britain to share the cost of financing from time to time any specific cases—in connection with the providing for refugees; that we can do nothing but comply strictly with the present immigration laws. . . . he agrees that we cannot open the question of our immigration laws, and he agrees with Sec'y. Hull as to bringing in temporary visitors, stating: "We have already brought in a large number." The President returned the above-mentioned cablegram with his O.K.

Source: "Abstract, Letter to President Franklin Delano Roosevelt from Secretary of State Cordell Hull, May 7, 1943." Selected Digital Documents Related to the Holocaust and Refugees, 1933–1945. Series 1, Official File 76—Church Matters: 76c—Jewish—Abstracts, 1943–1945. Franklin D. Roosevelt Presidential Library & Museum. Accessed at FRANKLIN, FDR Library's Digital Collections.

Primary Source 4

U.S. State Department's Efforts to Rescue European Jews, Memorandum (January 16, 1944)

Secretary Morgenthau advised the President that he was deeply disturbed about the failure of the State Department to take any effective action to save the remaining Jews in Europe. He explained that the Treasury Department . . . had uncovered evidence indicating that not only were the people in the State Department inefficient in dealing with this problem, but that they were actually taking action to prevent the rescue of the Jews. . . . The President listened attentively and seemed to grasp the significance of the various points. . . . The President said he agreed that some effective action could be taken. . . . The President seemed disinclined to believe that Long [Assistant Secretary of State Breckinridge Long] wanted to stop effective action from being taken, but said that Long had been somewhat soured on the problem when Rabbi Wise got Long to approve a long list of people being brought into this country, many of whom turned out to be bad people. Secretary Morgenthau reminded the President that at a Cabinet meeting Biddle [identify] had indicated that only three Jews of those entering the United States during the war had turned out to be undesirable. The President said that he had been advised that the figure was considerably larger. In any event he felt that Long was inclined to be soured on the situation. . . . The Secretary told Mr. Stettinius in plain words that he was convinced that people in the State Department, particularly Breckinridge Long, were deliberately obstructing the execution of any plan to save the Jews and that forthright immediate action was necessary if this Government was not going to be placed in the same position as Hitler and share the responsibility for exterminating all the Jews of Europe.

Source: Pehle, John. "Memorandum for the Secretary's Files, January 16, 1944." Eleanor Roosevelt Papers—Henry Morgenthau Jr. Diary. Vol. 694, Acquiescence Memo, Personal Report to the President, and related documents, January 13–16, 1944. Selected Digitized Documents Related to the Holocaust and Refugees, 1933–1945. Franklin D. Roosevelt Presidential Library & Museum. Accessed at FRANKLIN, FDR Library's Digital Collections.

Primary Source 5

Franklin D. Roosevelt, "The Blackest Crimes of All History" (April 3, 1944)

[O]ne of the blackest crimes of all history—begun by the Nazis in the days of peace, and multiplied by them a hundred fold in time of war—the wholesale systematic murder of the Jews of Europe—goes on unabated every hour. It is therefore fitting that we should again proclaim our determination that none who participate in any of these acts of savagery shall go unpunished. The United Nations have made it clear that they will pursue the guilty and deliver them up in order that justice be done. That warning applies not only to the leaders but also to their functionaries and subordinates in Germany and in the satellite countries. All who knowingly take part in the deportation of Jews to their death in Poland, or Norwegians and French to their death in Germany, are equally guilty with the executioner. All who share the guilt shall share the punishment.

Source: "Draft Press Release, Statement by the President re: the Holocaust, April 3, 1944." Series 1: Franklin D. Roosevelt Significant Documents, Box 1, FDR-63. Significant Documents Collection. Franklin D. Roosevelt Presidential Library & Museum.

Primary Source 6

U.S. War Department to Treasury Department, On Bombing Death Camp Railways (July 4, 1944)

I refer to your letter of June 29 . . . proposing that certain sections of railway lines between Hungary and Poland be bombed to interrupt the transportation of Jews from Hungary. The War Department is of the opinion that the suggested air operation is impracticable. It could be executed only by the diversion of considerable air support essential to the success of our forces now engaged in decisive operations and would in any case be of such very doubtful efficacy that it would not amount to a practical project. The War Department fully appreciates the humanitarian motives which prompted the suggested operation, but for the reasons stated above, the operation suggested does not appear justified.

Source: McCloy, John J. "Letter, John J. McCloy to John W. Pehle re: bombing of railway lines transporting Jews to death camps, July 4, 1944." Series 1: Franklin D. Roosevelt Significant Documents, Box 1, FDR-63. Significant Documents Collection. Franklin D. Roosevelt Presidential Library & Museum.

The American Age

As the Second World War was ending in 1945, President Franklin D. Roosevelt, like Woodrow Wilson before him, staked his hopes for a peaceful future on a new international organization, the United Nations. On April 25, 1945, two weeks after Roosevelt's death and two weeks before the German surrender, delegates from fifty nations at war with Germany and Japan met in San Francisco to draw up the Charter of the United Nations. The charter gave the UN Security Council "primary responsibility for the maintenance of international peace and security." The Security Council included five *permanent* members: the United States, the Soviet Union (replaced by the Russian Federation in 1991), Great Britain, France, and the Republic of China (replaced by the People's Republic of China in 1971). Each permanent member could *veto* any proposed action by the United Nations. It quickly became evident, however, that two members of the Security Council, the United States and the Soviet Union, had such intense differences of opinion about international policies that the United Nations was largely impotent in dealing with the cold war that dominated postwar politics. As a consequence, the postwar period was one of neither war nor peace but a constant state of tension.

The United States emerged from the Second World War as the world's preeminent military and economic power, the only nation in possession of atomic weapons. While much of Europe and Asia struggled to recover from the human

misery and physical devastation of the war, including an acute shortage of men, the United States was virtually unscathed, its economic infrastructure intact and operating at peak efficiency. Jobs that had been scarce in the 1930s were now available for the taking. By 1955, the United States, with only 6 percent of the world's population, was producing half the world's goods. American capitalism became a dominant cultural force around the world, too. In Europe, Japan, South Korea, and elsewhere, American products, fashion, and forms of entertainment attracted excited attention. Henry Luce, the publisher of *Time* and *Life* magazines, proclaimed that the twentieth century had become the "American century."

Yet a deepening "cold war" between the democratic and Communist nations cast a cloud of concern over the postwar world. The combative ideological contest with the Soviet Union produced numerous foreign crises and sparked a domestic witch hunt for Communists in the United States. After 1945, Republican and Democratic presidents aggressively sought to "contain" the spread of communism around the world.

This containment strategy embroiled the United States in costly wars in Korea and in Southeast Asia. A backlash against the Vietnam War (1964–1973) also inflamed a youth rebellion at home in which militant young idealists not only opposed the war but also provided much of the energy for many overdue social reforms, including racial equality, gay rights, feminism, and environmentalism. The anti-war movement destroyed Lyndon Johnson's presidency in 1968 and provoked a conservative counterattack. President Richard Nixon's paranoid reaction to his critics led to the Watergate affair and the destruction of his presidency.

Through all this turmoil, however, the expanding role of the federal government that Franklin Roosevelt and his New Deal programs had initiated remained essentially intact. With only a few exceptions, both Republicans and Democrats after 1945 acknowledged that the federal government must assume greater responsibility for the welfare of individuals. Even President Ronald Reagan, a sharp critic of federal social-welfare programs during the 1980s, recognized the need for the government to provide a "safety net" for those who could not help themselves.

Yet this fragile consensus on public policy and the cold war had collapsed by the late 1980s amid stunning international developments and social changes at home. The surprising implosion of the Soviet Union in 1989 and the disintegration of European communism left the United States the only superpower. After forty-five years, U.S. foreign policy was no longer focused on a single adversary. During the early 1990s, East and West Germany reunited, racial segregation (*apartheid*) in South Africa ended, and Israel and the Palestinians, long-standing foes, signed a treaty ending hostilities—at least for a while.

The end of the cold war and the dissolution of the Soviet Union into Russia and fourteen separate nations lowered the threat of nuclear war and reduced public interest in foreign affairs. Yet numerous ethnic, nationalist, and separatist conflicts brought constant tensions and instability at the end of the twentieth century and into the twenty-first. The United States found itself drawn into political and military crises in faraway lands such as Bosnia, Somalia, Afghanistan, Iraq, Ukraine, and Syria.

Throughout the 1990s, the United States waged a difficult struggle against many groups engaged in organized terrorism. The challenges facing intelligence agencies in tracking the movements of foreign terrorists became tragically evident in 2001. At 8:46 on the morning of September 11, 2001, the world watched in horror as a hijacked commercial airplane slammed into the North Tower of the World Trade Center in New York City. Seventeen minutes later, a second hijacked plane hit the South Tower. While the catastrophe was unfolding in New York City, a third hijacked airliner crashed into the Pentagon in Washington, D.C., while a fourth, presumably headed for the White House or the Capitol, missed its mark when passengers assaulted the four terrorists, sending the plane out of control and crashing to the ground near Shanksville, Pennsylvania, killing all 45 people on board.

Within hours of the hijackings, officials identified the nineteen hijackers as members of Al Qaeda (Arabic for "the Base"), a well-financed worldwide network of Islamic terrorists, led by a wealthy Saudi renegade, Osama bin Laden. The new president, Republican George W. Bush, responded by declaring a "war on terror." With the passage of the so-called Patriot Act, Congress gave the president new authority to track down and imprison terrorists at home and abroad. The war on terror began with assaults first on terrorist bases in Afghanistan and then on Saddam Hussein's dictatorship in Iraq ("Operation Iraqi Freedom"). Yet terrorism proved to be an elusive and resilient foe, and the war in Iraq and the ensuing U.S. military occupation was much longer, more expensive, and less successful than Americans had expected.

The 9/11 terror attacks generated a wave of patriotism in the United States, but divisive issues remained. A huge federal debt, rising annual budget deficits, and soaring health-care costs threatened to bankrupt an America that was becoming top-heavy with retirees as the baby boom generation born during and after the Second World War entered its sixties. The "graying of America" had profound social and political implications. It made the tone of political debate more conservative (because older people tend to be more conservative) and exerted increasing stress on health-care costs, nursing-home facilities, and the Social Security system.

The surprising victory of Barack Obama in the 2008 presidential election resulted from people embracing his theme of "hope and change." He pledged to end the wars in Iraq and Afghanistan, unite a divided nation, create a health-care system directed at the uninsured, and provide jobs to the growing numbers of unemployed. As the first African American president, Obama symbolized the societal changes transforming national life in the twenty-first century. Yet no sooner was Obama inaugurated than he inherited the worst economic slowdown since the Great Depression of the 1930s. What came to be called the Great Recession dominated the Obama presidency and, indeed, much of American life, bringing with it a prolonged sense of uncertainty and insecurity. For all its economic power and military might, the United States in the twenty-first century has not eliminated the threat of terrorism or unlocked the mystery of sustaining prosperity in an era of globalization.

DUCK AND COVER The familiar duck-and-cover drill that was practiced in many schools across the country was first implemented in 1949, when the Soviet Union set off its first nuclear explosive and the cold war arms race. Pictured above are American schoolchildren practicing in February 1951 how to react to a nuclear attack.

The Cold War and the Fair Deal

1945–1952

No sooner did the Second World War end than a prolonged "cold war" began between East and West. The awkward wartime alliance between the capitalist United States and the communist Soviet Union collapsed during the spring and summer of 1945. With the elimination of Nazism, their common enemy, the two strongest nations to emerge from the war became intense ideological rivals who could not bridge their differences over basic issues such as human rights, individual liberties, democratic elections, and religious freedom. Mutual suspicion and a race to gain influence over the "non-aligned" nations of the world in Asia, Africa, the Middle East, and Central and South America further distanced the two former allies. The defeat of Japan and Germany had created power vacuums in Europe and Asia that sucked the Soviet Union and the United States into an unrelenting war of words fed by clashing strategic interests and political ideologies.

The postwar era also saw an eruption of anti-colonial liberation movements in Asia, Africa, and the Middle East that would soon strip Great Britain, France, the Netherlands, and the United States of their global empires. The Philippines, for example, gained its independence from America in 1946. The next year, Great Britain withdrew from Hindu-dominated India after carving out two new Islamic nations, Pakistan and Bangladesh

CORE OBJECTIVES INQUIZITIVE

1. Explain why and how the cold war between the United States and the Soviet Union developed after the Second World War.

2. Analyze the impact of American efforts to contain the Soviet Union and the expansion of communism during Truman's presidency.

3. Describe Truman's efforts to expand the New Deal, and evaluate the effectiveness of his own "Fair Deal" agenda.

4. Assess the major international developments during 1949–1950, including the outbreak of the Korean War, and explain how they altered U.S. foreign policy.

5. Examine the emergence of the Red Scare after the Second World War, and explain its impact on American politics and society.

(originally called East Pakistan). The emergence of Communist China (the People's Republic) in 1949 further complicated global politics and the dynamics of the cold war.

The postwar world was thus an unstable one in which international tensions shaped domestic politics as well as foreign relations. The advent of atomic weapons was both a blessing and curse. Such weapons of mass destruction made the very idea of warfare unthinkably horrific, which in turn made national leaders more cautious to avoid letting disputes get out of hand. Yet even the mere possibility of nuclear holocaust cast a cloud of anxiety over the postwar era.

CORE **OBJECTIVE**

1. Explain why and how the cold war between the United States and the Soviet Union developed after the Second World War.

The Cold War

Less than three months after Harry S. Truman had begun his new role as vice president, Eleanor Roosevelt calmly told him, "Harry, the President is dead." When Truman asked what he could do to help her, the First Lady replied: "Is there anything we can do for *you*? For you are the one in trouble now." She knew full well that Truman was filling the shoes of a larger-than-life statesman beloved by most of the nation and that each of his major decisions would be compared to "what Roosevelt would have done." In fact, Truman often called Eleanor to ask her what Franklin would have done.

President Truman had no experience in foreign relations, had rarely traveled abroad, and had been kept out of Roosevelt's strategy sessions. He had never even visited the War Room in the White House. His weaknesses were many. He was a clumsy public speaker, frequently stumbling over long words and sentences. He also lacked Roosevelt's dash and charm, his brilliance and creativity.

The plain-speaking man from Missouri had virtues of his own, however. Truman resembled Andrew Jackson in his decisiveness, bluntness, folksy manner—and raw courage. A common man who became president at an uncommon time, Truman was a feisty leader who rose above his limitations to do extraordinary things. His challenges were enormous: he was expected to lead America into a postwar era complicated by the cold war against communism and the need to rebuild a devastated Europe and Asia. And Truman was supposed to do all that while managing the complex conversion to peacetime at home. He ended up doing better than anyone expected. While visiting Truman at the end of his presidency in 1952, the British leader Winston Churchill confessed that he initially had "held [Truman] in very low regard," telling him, "I loathed your taking the place of Franklin Roosevelt. I misjudged you badly. Since that time, you, more than any other man, have saved Western civilization."

HARRY S. TRUMAN The successor to Franklin Roosevelt who led the United States out of World War II.

Origins of the Cold War

Historians have long debated the unanswerable question: Was the United States or the Soviet Union more responsible for the onset of the cold war? The conventional view argues that the Soviets, led by Joseph Stalin, a ruthless Communist dictator ruling a traditionally insecure nation, set out to dominate the globe after 1945. The United States had no choice but to stand firm in defense of democratic capitalist values.

By contrast, revisionist historians insist that President Truman was the primary culprit. Instead of continuing Roosevelt's efforts to collaborate with Stalin and the Soviets, Truman's behavior aggravated the tensions between the two countries with his confrontational foreign policies. Yet such an interpretation fails to recognize that the president inherited a deteriorating relationship with the Soviets. East and West in the postwar world were captives of a nuclear nightmare of fear, suspicion, competition, and posturing.

In retrospect, the onset of the cold war seems to have been unavoidable. America's traditional commitment to free-enterprise capitalism, political self-determination, and religious freedom conflicted dramatically with the Soviet Union's preference for controlling its neighbors, enforcing ideological conformity, and prohibiting religions. Insecurity, as much as Communist ideology, drove much of Soviet behavior after the Second World War. Russia, after all, had been invaded by Germany twice in the first half of the twentieth century, and Soviet leaders wanted loyal nations on their borders. As had often happened before, the peoples of Eastern Europe found themselves caught in the middle.

> U.S.–Soviet fears and suspicions; conflicting visions for postwar Europe

Differences with the Soviets

The wartime military alliance against Nazism disintegrated after 1945 as the Soviet Union violated the promises it had made at the Yalta Conference and imposed its military control and Communist political system on the nations of Eastern Europe. On May 12, 1945, four days after victory in Europe, Winston Churchill asked Truman: "What is to happen about [Eastern] Europe? An **iron curtain** is drawn down upon [the Russian] front. We do not know what is going on behind [it]." Churchill and Truman wanted to lift the "iron curtain" and help those nations develop democratic governments. They still hoped that Stalin's promise of democratic elections would be carried out, but events during the second half of 1945 dashed those expectations and ruptured U.S.-Soviet relations.

> Iron curtain

As early as the spring of 1945 and continuing for the next two years, the Soviet Union installed new "puppet" governments in Central and Eastern Europe (Bulgaria, Czechoslovakia, East Germany, Poland, Romania, and Yugoslavia). In each nation, one by one, the Soviets eliminated all political parties except the Communists. They then created secret police forces; took control of intellectual and cultural life, including the mass media (especially the radio networks); undermined the Roman Catholic Church; and organized a process of "ethnic cleansing" whereby millions of Germans, Poles,

iron curtain Term coined by Winston Churchill to describe the cold war divide between Western Europe and the Soviet Union's Eastern European satellite nations.

and Hungarians were relocated from Eastern Europe, usually to West Germany or to prisons. Anyone who opposed the new Soviet regime was exiled, silenced, executed, or imprisoned. Stalin intended the postwar reign of terror to make people better Communists by locking up or killing those who refused to be Communists.

Stalin's promises at the Yalta Conference to allow open elections in the nations controlled by Soviet armies had turned out to be lies. A frustrated James F. Byrnes, U.S. secretary of state, tried to use America's atomic bombs as leverage to pressure the Soviets to abide by the Yalta accords. In April 1945, he had suggested to President Truman that nuclear weapons "might well put us in position to dictate our own terms [with the Soviets] at the end of the war." The Soviets, however, had paid little notice to such "atomic diplomacy," in part because their spies had kept them informed of what American scientists had been doing and in part because they were quickly developing their own atomic bombs.

Throughout the spring of 1945, the Soviets created new "friendly governments" in Eastern Europe, arguing that the United States had done the same in Italy and Japan after those nations had surrendered. The difference was the Soviets violated their pledges at the Yalta Conference by preventing non-Communists from participating in the political process.

A few days before the opening of the San Francisco conference to organize the United Nations in April 1945, Truman met with Soviet foreign minister Vyacheslav Molotov at the White House. The Soviets had just put in place a pro-Communist government in Poland in violation of Stalin's pledge at Yalta to allow free elections. Truman directed Molotov to tell Stalin that the United States expected the Soviet leader to live up to his agreements. "I have never been talked to like that in my life," Molotov angrily replied. "Carry out your agreements," Truman snapped, "and you won't get talked to like that."

Later, in July 1945, when Truman first met Stalin at the Potsdam Conference, he wrote his mother that he had never seen "such pig-headed people as are the Russians." He described himself as "an innocent idealist" surrounded by wolves. He later acknowledged that the Soviets broke their promises "as soon as the unconscionable Russian Dictator [Stalin] returned to Moscow!" Truman added, with a note of embarrassment, "And I liked the little son of a bitch."

POTSDAM CONFERENCE The Big Three, (from left to right) British Prime Minister Clement Atlee, President Truman, and Josef Stalin, sit side by side at the Potsdam Conference in Germany, 1945.

The Containment Policy

By the beginning of 1947, relations with the Soviet Union had grown ice cold. A year before, in February 1946, Stalin had declared that peace was impossible "under the present capitalist development of the world economy." His provocative statement led the State Department to ask for an analysis of Soviet communism from forty-two-year-old George F. Kennan, the best-informed expert on the Soviet Union working in the U.S. embassy in Moscow.

Kennan responded on February 22, 1946, with a famous 8,000-word "Long Telegram" in which he described the roots of Russian history, the pillars of Soviet policy, Stalin's "neurotic view of world affairs," and Russia's historic determination to protect its western border with Europe. Kennan explained that the Soviet Union was founded on a rigid ideology (Marxism-Leninism) that saw a fundamental conflict between the communist and capitalist nations. Stalin and other Soviet leaders, he added, could not imagine "permanent peaceful coexistence" with the capitalist nations. The Soviet goal was to build military strength while promoting tensions between the capitalist democracies and subverting their stability by all possible means.

The best way for the United States to deal with such an ideological foe, Kennan advised, was not military confrontation. Instead, he called for patient, persistent, and firm "strategic" efforts to "contain" Soviet expansionism over the long term, without resorting to war. Creating such "unalterable counterforce," he predicted, would eventually cause "either the breakup or the gradual mellowing of Soviet power" because communism, in Kennan's view, was an unstable system that would eventually collapse if Americans were patient and helped postwar Europe rebuild its economies.

Kennan's analysis so impressed new secretary of state George C. Marshall that he put him in charge of the State Department's Policy Planning office. No other American diplomat at the time forecast so accurately what would happen to the Soviet Union some forty years later.

In its broadest dimensions, Kennan's call for the "firm and vigilant **containment** of Russian expansive tendencies" echoed the outlook of Truman and his advisers and would guide U.S. foreign policy for decades. Kennan's careful analysis, however, was vague on several key issues: How exactly were the United States and its allies to "contain" the Soviet Union's expansionist tendencies? How should the United States respond to specific acts of Soviet aggression around the world? Kennan was an analyst, not a policy maker. He left the task of "containing" communism to President Truman and his advisers, most of whom, unlike Kennan, viewed containment as a *military* doctrine rather than a

CORE **OBJECTIVE**

2. Analyze the impact of American efforts to contain the Soviet Union and the expansion of communism during Truman's presidency.

George Kennan's "Long Telegram" and containment policy

containment U.S. cold war strategy to exert political, economic, and, if necessary, military pressure on global Soviet expansion as a means of combating the spread of communism.

GEORGE F. KENNAN A keen expert on Soviet ideology and author of the "Long Telegram," Kennan authored the doctrine of containment.

political strategy. As Truman insisted, "Unless Russia is faced with an iron fist and strong language, another war is in the making." In his view, Stalin and the Soviets only understood one language: the language of military power. "I'm tired of babying the Soviets."

In 1946, civil war broke out in Greece between an undemocratic, authoritarian government backed by the British and a Communist-led insurgency supported by the Soviets that held the northern part of the nation. On February 21, 1947, the British informed the U.S. government that they could no longer provide economic and military aid to Greece; they would withdraw their 40,000 troops in five weeks and end all economic aid. Truman quickly conferred with congressional leaders, one of whom, Republican senator Arthur Vandenberg of Michigan, warned the president that he would need to "scare the hell out of the American people" about the urgent necessity to stop the menace of spreading communism in order to gain public support for his aid program.

> Communist threat abroad: Civil war in Greece

The Truman Doctrine

> Truman Doctrine

On March 12, 1947, President Truman responded to the crisis in the eastern Mediterranean by asking Congress for $400 million to assist Greece and Turkey. More important, the president announced what came to be known as the **Truman Doctrine**. He declared that since the Communist challenge was worldwide, it had to be confronted everywhere around the globe. Like a row of dominoes, he predicted, the fall of Greece to communism would spread to the other nations of the Middle East, then to Western Europe. To prevent such a catastrophe, the United States must "support free peoples who are resisting attempted subjugation by armed minorities or by outside pressures." In this single sentence, the president established the foundation of U.S. foreign policy for the next forty years. In Truman's view, shared by later presidents, the assumptions of the "domino theory" made an aggressive "containment" strategy against communism a necessity.

At the State Department, George Marshall thought the "flamboyant anti-communism" in Truman's speech was unnecessarily provocative, and George F. Kennan cringed at the president's "grandiose" commitment to "contain" communism *everywhere*. In his view, Truman's "militarized view of the cold war" was a foolish crusade that knew no limits. Efforts to "contain" communism needed to be selective rather than universal, political and economic rather than military in nature. For all its power, he noted, the United States could not intervene in every "hot spot" around the world. Kennan saw no need to provide military aid to Turkey, where no Communist threat existed. And he preferred that economic assistance, not weapons, be provided to Greece. In his view, the Soviet threat was primarily political, not military, in nature.

Truman and his advisers rejected Kennan's concerns. In 1947, Congress approved the president's request for economic and military assistance to Greece and neighboring Turkey. The Truman Doctrine marked the begin-

Truman Doctrine (1947) President Truman's program of "containing" communism in Eastern Europe and providing economic and military aid to any nations at risk of Communist takeover.

ning of a contest that the former presidential adviser Bernard Baruch named in a 1947 speech to the legislature of South Carolina: "Let us not be deceived—today we are in the midst of a *cold war*." Only a few observers at the time questioned the implications of the Truman Doctrine. Walter Lippmann, the nation's leading political journalist, characterized Truman's new policy as a "strategic monstrosity" that would entangle the United States in endless international disputes and force it to partner with right-wing dictatorships—as turned out to be the case.

Marshall Plan (1948) Secretary of State George C. Marshall's post–World War II program providing massive U.S. financial and technical assistance to war-torn European countries.

The Marshall Plan

In the spring of 1947, most of postwar Europe remained broke, shattered, and desperate. Factories had been bombed to rubble; railroads and bridges had been destroyed. People were starving for food and for jobs, and political unrest was growing. By 1947, Socialist and Communist parties were emerging in many European nations struggling to recover after the war, including Italy, France, and Belgium. The crisis in postwar Europe required bold action.

Marshall Plan

While giving a graduation speech at Harvard University in May, Secretary of State George C. Marshall, building upon suggestions given to him by George Kennan and other members of the State Department, called for massive financial and technical assistance to rescue war-ravaged Europe, including the Soviet Union. What came to be known as the **Marshall Plan** was "directed not against country or doctrine, but against hunger, poverty, desperation, and chaos."

It was intended to reconstruct the European economy, neutralize Communist insurgencies, and build up secure foreign markets for American products. As Truman said, "The American [capitalist] system can survive only if it is part of a world system." The Marshall Plan was about more than economics, however. It was also part of Truman's effort to contain the expansionist tendencies of the Soviet Union by building up a strong Western Europe. The Americans, said a British official, "want an integrated Europe looking like the United States of America."

In December 1947, Truman submitted Marshall's proposal to a special session of Congress. Initially, Republican critics dismissed it as "New Dealism" for Europe. However, two months later, on February 25, 1948, a Communist-led coup in Czechoslovakia, the last nation in Eastern Europe with

"THE WAY BACK" The Marshall Plan, which distributed economic aid throughout Europe, is represented in this 1947 cartoon as a thin rope that is Europe's only hope for climbing to safety.

a democratic government, ensured congressional passage of the Marshall Plan, for it seemed to confirm the immediate Communist threat to Western Europe.

The Marshall Plan exceeded the hopes of its founder. From 1948 until 1951, the plan provided $13 billion to sixteen European nations to help revive their war-ravaged economies. The Soviet Union, however, refused to participate, calling it "dollar imperialism." The Marshall Plan returned prosperity to Europe. The British foreign minister called the plan "a lifeline to sinking men." By 1951, Western Europe's industrial production had soared to 40 percent above prewar levels, and its farm output was larger than ever. England's *Economist* magazine called the Marshall Plan "an act without peer in history."

Divided Germany

The Marshall Plan drew the nations of Western Europe closer together, but it increased tensions with the Soviet Union, for Stalin saw the American effort to rebuild the European economy as a way to weaken Soviet influence in the region. The breakdown of the wartime alliance between the United States and the Soviet Union also left the problem of postwar Germany unsettled.

In 1945, Berlin, the German capital, had been divided into four sectors or zones, each governed by one of the four principal Allied nations, the United States, France, Great Britain, and the Soviet Union. The German economy languished, requiring the U.S. Army to provide food and supplies to millions of civilians. Slowly, the Allied occupation zones evolved into functioning governments. In 1948, the British, French, and Americans united their three administrative zones into one and developed a common currency for West Germany. The West Germans also organized state governments and began drafting a federal constitution.

FAMILY REUNION A girl gives her grandmother a kiss through the barbed-wire fence that divides the Dutch-German frontier in 1947.

THROUGH THE IRON CURTAIN German children greet a U.S. cargo plane with waves and cheers as it prepares to land in West Berlin to drop off much-needed food and supplies. **In what way was the Berlin airlift a "victory" for the United States and Great Britain?**

The political unification of West Germany infuriated Stalin, who was determined to keep Germany weak. And the status of divided Berlin, located a hundred miles inside the Soviet occupation zone (East Germany), had become a powder keg. In March 1948, Stalin forced the issue of Berlin's status by preventing the new West German currency from being used in the city. Then, on June 23, he ordered the Soviet army occupying eastern Germany to stop all road, rail, and water traffic into West Berlin, hoping the blockade would force the United States and its allies to leave the divided city.

The Americans interpreted Stalin's aggressive blockade as a tipping point in the cold war. "When Berlin falls," predicted General Lucius D. Clay, the iron-willed U.S. Army commander in Germany, "western Germany will be next. Communism will run rampant." The United States thus faced a dilemma fraught with dangers: risk a third world war by using force to break the Soviet blockade or begin a humiliating retreat from West Berlin.

> Soviet blockade of Berlin and the Berlin Airlift

Truman, who prided himself on his decisiveness, made clear his stance: "We stay in Berlin—period." In response to the Soviet blockade, the United States announced an embargo against all goods exported from Soviet-controlled eastern Germany, and it began organizing a massive airlift to provide needed food and supplies to the 2.5 million West Berliners. The whole world watched as the two superpowers teetered on the edge of conflict. Truman noted solemnly in his diary: "We are very close to war."

By October 1948, the U.S. and British air forces were landing cargo planes every few minutes at the Berlin airport, flying in 7,000 tons of food, fuel, medicine, coal, and equipment each day to keep the 2.25 million Berliners

THE OCCUPATION OF GERMANY AND AUSTRIA

- How did the Allies divide Germany and Austria at the Yalta Conference?
- What was the "iron curtain"?
- Why did the Allies airlift supplies to Berlin?

alive. To support the Berlin airlift and prepare for a possible war, thousands of former military pilots were called back into service, Truman revived the military draft, and Congress provided emergency funds to increase military spending. Almost fifty airmen died in various accidents.

For all the threats and harsh words, however, the **Berlin airlift** went on daily for 321 days without any shots being fired. Finally, on May 12, 1949, the Soviets lifted the blockade, in part because bad Russian harvests made them desperate for food grown in western Germany.

The Berlin airlift was the first major "victory" for the West in the cold war. The unprecedented efforts of the United States and Great Britain to supply West Berliners transformed most of them into devoted allies. In May 1949, as the Soviet blockade was ending, the Federal Republic of Germany (West Germany) was founded. Six months later, in October, the German Democratic Republic (East Germany) came into being.

Berlin airlift (1948–1949) Effort by the United States and Great Britain to fly massive amounts of food and supplies into West Berlin in response to the Soviet land blockade of the city.

Forming Alliances

The Soviet blockade of Berlin convinced the United States and its allies that they needed to act together to stop further Communist expansion into Western Europe. On April 4, 1949, a month before the blockade ended, twelve nations signed the North Atlantic Treaty: the United States, Great Britain, France, Belgium, the Netherlands, Luxembourg, Canada, Denmark, Iceland, Italy, Norway, and Portugal. Greece and Turkey joined the alliance in 1952, West Germany in 1955, and Spain in 1982.

The **North Atlantic Treaty Organization (NATO)**, the largest collective defense alliance in the world, declared that an attack against any one of the members was an attack against all. The creation of NATO marked the high point of efforts to "contain" the Soviets from expanding into Western Europe. By joining NATO, the United States—for the first time since its alliance with France during the Revolutionary War—committed itself to go to war on behalf of its allies. Isolationism was dead.

Reorganizing the Military

The onset of the cold war and the emergence of nuclear weapons led Truman to sign the **National Security Act (1947)**, which centralized control of the military establishment. It created a Department of Defense to oversee the three separate military branches—the army, navy, and air force—and the National Security Council (NSC), a group of the government's top specialists in international relations who advised the president. The act made permanent the Joint Chiefs of Staff, a wartime innovation bringing together the leaders of the military branches, and it established the Central Intelligence Agency (CIA) to coordinate global intelligence-gathering activities.

A New Jewish Nation: Israel

At the same time that the United States was helping form new alliances, it was also helping form a new nation. Palestine, the biblical Holy Land, had been a British protectorate since 1919. For hundreds of years, Jews throughout the world had dreamed of returning to their ancestral homeland of Israel and its ancient capital Zion, a part of Jerusalem. Many Zionists, Jews who wanted a separate Jewish nation, had migrated there. More arrived during and after the Nazi persecution of European Jews, and they received energetic support from American Jews and worldwide Jewish organizations. Hitler's gruesome effort to kill millions of Jews convinced many that their only hope for a secure future was to create their own nation.

Late in 1947, the United Nations voted to divide ("partition") Palestine into separate Jewish and Arab states. The Jews readily agreed, but the Arabs fiercely opposed the UN partition. Palestine was their ancestral home, too. Jerusalem was as holy to Muslims as it was to Jews and Christians. Arabs viewed the creation of a Jewish nation in Palestine as an act of war, and they attacked Israelis in early 1948. Hundreds of people died before the Haganah (Jewish militia) won control of most of Palestine. When the

Israel joins the United Nations

North Atlantic Treaty Organization (NATO) Defensive political and military alliance formed in 1949 by the United States, Canada, and ten Western European nations to deter Soviet expansion in Europe.

National Security Act (1947) Congressional legislation that created the Department of Defense, the National Security Council, and the Central Intelligence Agency.

British administration of Palestine officially expired on May 14, 1948, David Ben-Gurion, the Jewish leader in Palestine, soon to be elected prime minister, proclaimed the independence of Israel. President Truman, who had been in close touch with American Jewish leaders, officially recognized the new Israeli state within minutes, as did the Soviet Union.

One million Jews, most of them European immigrants, now had their own nation. Early the next morning, however, the Arab League nations—Lebanon, Syria, Iraq, Jordan, and Egypt—invaded Israel, beginning a period of nearly constant warfare in the Holy Land. UN mediators gradually worked out a truce agreement, restoring an uneasy peace by May 11, 1949, when Israel joined the United Nations. Israel kept all its conquered territories, including the whole Palestine coast. The Palestinian Arabs lost everything. Most of them became stateless refugees who scattered into the neighboring nations of Lebanon, Jordan, and Egypt.

Expanding the New Deal

> CORE **OBJECTIVE**
>
> **3.** Describe Truman's efforts to expand the New Deal, and evaluate the effectiveness of his own "Fair Deal" agenda.

For the most part, Republicans and Democrats in Congress cooperated with President Truman on issues related to the cold war. They were not as unified in dealing with domestic policies. The cost-cutting Republicans in Congress hoped that they could end the New Deal as the war itself ended. As a brand-new president, Truman thought otherwise as he guided the nation's "complicated and difficult" transition from war to peace.

From War to Peace

> Conversion to a peacetime economy

With the end of the wars in Europe and Asia, Truman in September 1945 called Congress into a special emergency session at which he presented a twenty-one-point program to guide the nation's "reconversion" effort from wartime back to peacetime. Truman's postwar challenge was to ensure that the peacetime economy absorbed the millions of men and women who had served in the armed forces and were now seeking civilian jobs. That would not be easy. The day after the war in Asia ended, the Springfield Armory, which had made weapons for the army, fired every worker. As other military-dependent companies announced layoffs, the nation faced a crisis as some 12 million men and women in uniform eager to leave military service and find civilian jobs confronted a postwar economy careening into recession.

Truman's program to ensure a smooth transition to a peacetime economy included proposals for unemployment insurance to cover more workers, a higher minimum wage, the construction of massive low-cost public housing projects, regional development projects modeled on the Tennessee Valley Authority to put military veterans to work, and much more. A powerful Republican congressman named Joseph W. Martin was stunned by the scope of Truman's proposals. "Not even President Roosevelt," he gasped, "ever asked for so much at one sitting."

Truman's primary goal was to "prevent prolonged unemployment" while avoiding the "bitter mistakes" made after the First World War that had produced a wild inflation in consumer prices and a recession. To do so, he also wanted to retain, for a while, the wartime controls on wages, prices, and rents as well as the rationing of scarce food items. Most of all, Truman wanted to minimize unemployment.

Congress responded by approving the Employment Act of 1946, which authorized the federal government "to promote maximum employment, production, and purchasing power." Republicans and conservative southern Democrats in Congress balked at most of Truman's efforts to revive or expand New Deal programs. One called Truman's proposals "creeping socialism." The Great Depression was over, critics stressed. Different times demanded different programs—or none at all.

The end of the war caused short-term economic problems but not the postwar depression that many had feared. Many women working in defense industries were shoved out as men took off uniforms and looked for jobs. At a shipyard in California, the foreman gathered all the women workers and told them to go welcome the troop ships as they pulled into port. "We were thrilled. We all waved," recalled one of the women. Then, the next day, the women working at the shipyard were let go to make room for male veterans.

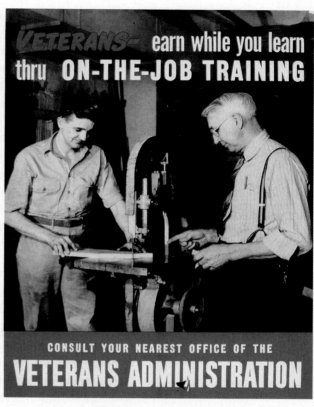

ON-THE-JOB TRAINING An advertisement aimed at young veterans promotes the G.I. Bill's professional resources, intended to help military veterans enter the workforce.

Still, several shock absorbers cushioned the economic impact of demobilization: federal unemployment insurance and other Social Security benefits; the Servicemen's Readjustment Act of 1944, known as the GI Bill of Rights, under which the federal government provided $13 billion for military veterans to use for education, vocational training, medical treatment, unemployment insurance, and loans for building houses and starting new businesses.

> Peacetime: Women return home, the GI Bill, and a "baby boom"

With the war over, military veterans eagerly returned to colleges, jobs, wives, and babies. Marriage rates soared at war's end. So, too, did population growth, which had dropped off sharply in the 1930s. Americans born during this postwar period (roughly 1946–1964) composed what came to be called the "baby boom generation," a disproportionately large group that would shape the nation's social and cultural life throughout the second half of the twentieth century and after.

Wages, Prices, and Labor Unrest

The most acute economic problem Truman faced was the postwar spike in prices for consumer goods. During the war, the government had frozen all wages and prices—and banned strikes by labor unions. When wartime economic controls on the economy ended, prices for consumer goods shot

> Inflation spikes after the war

up, which led labor unions to demand pay increases for workers. When management balked, a series of postwar strikes at automobile plants, steel mills, coal mines, and railroads erupted across the nation in 1945–1946.

Like Theodore Roosevelt before him, Truman grew frustrated with the stubbornness of both management and labor leaders. He took federal control of the coal mines, whereupon the mine owners agreed to union demands. Truman also seized control of the railroads and won a five-day postponement of a strike. When the union leaders refused to make further concessions, however, the president decried their "obstinate arrogance" and threatened to draft striking railroad workers into the armed forces. A few weeks later, the unions backed down and returned to work, having won healthy improvements in wages and benefits. By taking such a hard line, however, Truman lost the support of a key constituency within the Democratic party coalition: unionists.

Widespread union strikes

Political Cooperation and Conflict

As congressional elections approached in the fall of 1946, Republicans used a simple campaign slogan: "Had Enough? Vote Republican!" Public discontent ran high, especially among the 5 million workers who had gone out on strike. A union leader tagged Truman the "No. 1 Strikebreaker," while much of the public, upset at the unions, price increases, and food shortages, blamed the strikes on the White House.

Labor unions emerged from the war with more power than ever before. Some 14.5 million workers, over a third of the workforce, were unionized. Union members had tended to vote Democratic but not in the 1946 elections, which gave Republicans majorities in both houses of Congress for the first time since 1928. "The New Deal is kaput," one newspaper editor crowed. That so many congressional Democrats had lost disheartened Truman. "To be president of the United States," he complained, "is to be lonely, very lonely. . . . Melancholy goes with the job."

The new Republican Congress curbed the power of unions by passing the **Taft-Hartley Labor Act** of 1947 (officially called the Labor-Management Relations Act), which prohibited "unfair labor practices" such as the "closed shop" (in which nonunion workers could not be hired by a unionized company). The Taft-Hartley Act also required union leaders to take "loyalty oaths" declaring that they were not members of the Communist party. It also banned strikes by federal employees and imposed a "cooling-off" period of eighty days on any strike that the president deemed dangerous to the public welfare. Yet the most troubling element of the new bill was a provision that allowed state legislatures to pass "right-to-work" laws that ended the practice of forcing all workers to join a union once a majority voted to unionize.

Taft-Hartley Labor Act (1947)

Truman vetoed the Taft-Hartley bill, denouncing the "shocking" bill as "unworkable," "burdensome," and "disruptive." Working-class Democrats were delighted. Many blue-collar unionists who had gone over to the Republicans in 1946 now returned to the Democrats. Congress, however, over-

Taft-Hartley Labor Act (1947)
Congressional legislation that banned "unfair labor practices" by unions, required union leaders to sign anti-Communist "loyalty oaths," and prohibited federal employees from going on strike.

FIGHT FOR DESEGREGATION Demonstrators led by activist A. Philip Randolph (left) picket the Democratic National Convention on July 12, 1948, calling for racial integration of the armed forces.

turned the president's veto and the Taft-Hartley Act became law. By 1954, fifteen states, mainly in the South and West, had used the Taft-Hartley Act to enact right-to-work laws forbidding union shops. Those states thereafter recruited industries to relocate because of their low wages, low state taxes, and nonunion policies. As the Republicans celebrated their victory, however, they took little notice of the fact that the Taft-Hartley Act would cause most union members to vote Democratic in 1948.

Civil Rights during the 1940s

Another of Truman's challenges in postwar labor relations was the bigotry faced by returning African American soldiers. When one black soldier arrived home in a uniform decorated with combat medals, a white neighbor yelled: "Don't you forget . . . that you're still a nigger." Another black veteran was yanked off a bus in South Carolina and beaten so badly in a jail cell that he was blinded.

The Second World War, however, did improve America's overall racial landscape. As a *New York Times* editorial explained in early 1946, "This is a particularly good time to campaign against the evils of bigotry, prejudice, and race hatred because we have witnessed the defeat of enemies who tried to found a mastery of the world upon such cruel and fallacious policy."

African American veterans had fought in large numbers to overthrow the Nazi regime of government-sponsored racism, and returning veterans were unwilling to put up with continuing racial abuse at home. In addition, the cold war confrontation with the Soviet Union gave American leaders added incentive to improve race relations. In the ideological contest with communism for influence among the newly emerging nations of Africa, the Soviets often compared racism in the South to the Nazis' treatment of the Jews.

Black veterans who spoke out against racial bigotry often risked their lives. In 1946, a white mob gunned down two African American couples in rural Georgia. One of the murderers explained that George Dorsey, one of the victims, was "a good nigger" until he went into the army. "But when he came out, he thought he was as good as any white people."

In the fall of 1946, a delegation of civil rights activists urged President Truman to condemn the Ku Klux Klan and the lynching of African Americans. The delegation graphically described incidents of torture and intimidation against blacks in the South.

Such horrific racial incidents so shocked Truman that he appointed a Committee on Civil Rights to investigate violence against African Americans. Southern Democrats were infuriated. A Mississippi congressman claimed that Truman "had seen fit to run a political dagger into our backs" by intervening in southern race relations. A South Carolina legislator said his friends and neighbors were now "more afraid of Truman than of Russia." A Mississippi newspaper reflected the prevailing sentiment among southern whites when it ran the following front-page headline: "Mississippi Is Through with Truman."

> Truman appoints Committee on Civil Rights and desegregates the military

Such harsh criticism only inspired Truman to do more for African Americans. On July 26, 1948, he took a bolder step when he banned racial discrimination in the federal government. Four days later, he issued an executive order ending racial segregation in the armed forces. The air force and navy quickly complied, but the army dragged its feet until the early 1950s. By 1960, however, the armed forces were the most racially integrated of all national organizations. Desegregating the military was, Truman claimed, "the greatest thing that ever happened to America." Southerners did not think so. Democrat Mendel Rivers, the powerful South Carolina congressman, boasted that Truman "is a dead bird" as far as being reelected. "We in the South are going to see to that."

Jackie Robinson

Meanwhile, racial segregation was being dismantled in a much more public field of endeavor: professional baseball. In April 1947, as the baseball season opened, the Brooklyn Dodger roster included the first African American to play major-league baseball: Jackie Robinson. The Dodgers chose Robinson in part because of his baseball abilities and in part because of his personality: he was a strong, quiet warrior of incomparable courage who would not fight back when provoked. And he was often provoked. During his first season with the Dodgers, teammates and opposing players viciously baited Robinson, pitchers threw at him, base runners spiked him, and spectators booed him, even as he led the team to win the National League championship. Hotels refused him rooms, and restaurants denied him service. Hate mail arrived by the bucketful. One sportswriter called the trailblazing Robinson "the loneliest man I have ever seen in sports." On the other hand, black spectators loved Robinson's courageous example; they turned out in droves to watch him play. As time passed, Robinson won over many fans and players with his courage, wit, and talent, and other teams soon began signing black players. Racial attitudes were changing—slowly.

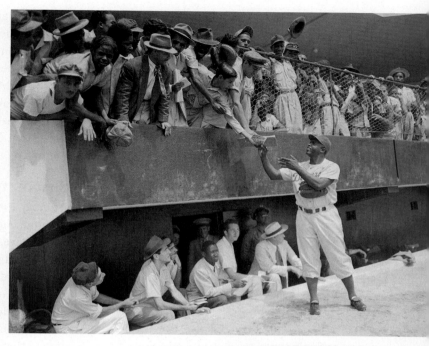

JACKIE ROBINSON Robinson's unfaltering courage and skill diversified baseball, drawing African American and Latino spectators to the games. Here, he greets his Dominican fans at Trujillo High School in Santo Domingo.

Mexican Americans

In the Far West, Mexican Americans (often grouped together with other Spanish-speaking immigrants as *Hispanics* or *Latinos*) continued to experience ethnic prejudice after the war. Schools in Arizona, New Mexico, Texas, and California routinely segregated Mexican American children from whites. After the war, the 500,000 Latino military veterans were especially frustrated that their efforts in the armed forces did not bring equality at home. "We had paid our dues," said one war veteran, yet nothing had changed. Latinos were frequently denied access to the educational, medical, and housing benefits made available to white veterans. In fact, some mortuaries even denied funeral services to Mexican Americans killed in combat. As a funeral director in Texas explained, "The Anglo people would not stand for it."

To fight such prejudicial treatment, Mexican American war veterans led by Dr. Hector Perez Garcia, a decorated U.S. Army major, organized the American GI Forum in Texas in 1948. Soon there were branches throughout Texas and across the nation. Garcia, born in Mexico in 1914 and raised in Texas, stressed the importance of formal education to Mexican Americans. The new organization's motto proclaimed: "Education Is Our Freedom and Freedom Should Be Everybody's Business." At a time when Mexican Americans in Texas averaged no more than a third-grade education, Garcia and five of his siblings were exceptional, each having completed medical school and become physicians. Yet upon Major Garcia's return from the war, he encountered "discrimination everywhere. We had no opportunities. We had to pay [poll taxes] to vote. We had segregated schools. We were not allowed to go into public places."

: done

HECTOR PEREZ GARCIA Photographed alongside President Reagan, Garcia attends the American GI Forum in El Paso, Texas. Garcia advocated education and equal treatment of all Americans, eventually earning the Presidential Medal of Freedom.

Garcia and the GI Forum initially focused on veterans' issues but soon expanded the organization's scope to include fostering equal treatment for all people. The GI Forum lobbied to end poll taxes, sued for the right of Latinos to serve on juries, and developed schools for jobless veterans. In 1984, President Ronald Reagan presented Garcia with the Presidential Medal of Freedom, the nation's highest civilian honor.

Shaping the Fair Deal

By early 1948, after three years in the White House, Truman had yet to shake the widespread impression that he was a hapless successor to the magisterial FDR. Most political analysts assumed that the president would lose his reelection effort in November. The *New York Times* reported in April 1948 that Truman's "influence is weaker than any president's in modern history." Journalist Walter Lippmann observed that Truman's decision to seek reelection was simply a function of his "stubborn pride." That the Democratic party was splitting in two did not help his reelection chances: southern conservatives resented Truman's outspoken support of civil rights, while the left wing of the party criticized his firing of Secretary of Commerce Henry A. Wallace in September 1946 for openly criticizing the administration's anti-Soviet policies.

Virtually everyone predicted a Truman defeat in 1948. "Never was there such a mess," the president told his mother. "The President," predicted the *United States News*, "is a one-termer." When asked how he planned to deal with an Eightieth Congress dominated by Republicans, the feisty Truman said he intended to do "as I damn please for the next two years and to hell with them."

Truman's "Fair Deal"

Predictions of a Truman defeat in 1948 did not faze the combative president, however. He mounted an intense campaign. His first step was to shore up the major elements of the New Deal coalition of working-class voters: farmers, labor unionists, and African Americans. In his 1948 State of the Union message, Truman announced that the programs that he would later call his "**Fair Deal**" (to distinguish his new domestic program from Roosevelt's New Deal) would build upon the New Deal by offering something to nearly every group the Democrats hoped to attract as voters. The first goal, Truman said, was to ensure civil rights for all Americans. He added proposals to increase federal aid to education, expand unemployment and retirement benefits, create a comprehensive system of national health insurance, enable more rural people to connect to electricity, and increase the minimum wage.

Fair Deal (1949) President Truman's proposals to build upon the New Deal with national health insurance, the repeal of the Taft-Hartley Act, new civil rights legislation, and other initiatives; most were rejected by the Republican-controlled Congress.

The Surprise Election of 1948

The Republican-controlled Congress dismissed Truman's proposals—and their doing so would backfire on them. At the Republican Convention, New York governor Thomas E. Dewey won the presidential nomination on the third ballot. The platform endorsed most of the New Deal reforms and approved the administration's bipartisan foreign policy; Dewey promised to run things more efficiently, however.

Upset victory: Truman reelected

In July, a glum Democratic Convention gathered in Philadelphia. Delegates who expected to do little more than go through the motions, however, were doubly surprised: first by the battle on the convention floor over civil rights and then by President Truman's acceptance speech. Liberal Democrats called on Congress to end segregation in the South and commended Truman "for his courageous stand on the issue of civil rights." White segregationist delegates from Alabama and Mississippi walked out of the convention in protest.

On July 17, a group of rebellious southern Democrats met in Birmingham, Alabama. While waving Confederate flags and singing "Dixie," they nominated South Carolina's segregationist governor, Strom Thurmond, on a States' Rights Democratic ticket, quickly dubbed the "Dixiecrat party." The **Dixiecrats** denounced Truman's "infamous" civil rights initiatives and championed states' rights against any federal efforts to change the tradition of white supremacy in the South. The award-winning Atlanta newspaper editor, Ralph McGill, pointed out that the Dixiecrat organization was actually "the anti-Negro party."

Dixiecrats Breakaway faction of white southern Democrats who defected from the national Democratic party in 1948 to protest the party's increased support for black civil rights and to nominate their own segregationist candidates for elective office.

A few days later, on July 23, the left wing of the Democratic party gathered in Philadelphia to form a new Progressive party and nominate for president Henry A. Wallace, Roosevelt's former secretary of agriculture and vice president—whom Truman had fired as secretary of commerce. Wallace charged that both major parties were recklessly provoking a confrontation with the Soviet Union. The choice, announced a speaker at the Progressive party convention, was between "Wallace or war."

The splits in the Democratic ranks seemed to spell the final blow to Truman, but the feisty president pledged to "win this election and make the Republicans like it!" He then set out on a 31,000-mile "whistle-stop" train tour, making 271 speeches scolding the "do-nothing" Republicans in Congress. Friendly audiences loved his fighting spirit and dogged courage, shouting, "Pour it on, Harry!" and "Give 'em hell, Harry." Truman responded: "I don't give 'em hell. I just tell the truth and they think it's hell."

BIRTH OF THE DIXIECRATS Alabama delegates stand to boo Truman's announcement of his civil rights platform before walking out of the 1948 Democratic National Convention. **What social and political factors contributed to the formation of the Dixiecrats?**

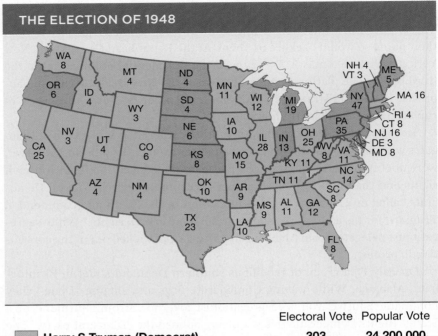

THE ELECTION OF 1948

	Electoral Vote	Popular Vote
Harry S Truman (Democrat)	**303**	**24,200,000**
Thomas E. Dewey (Republican)	189	22,000,000
J. Strom Thurmond (States' Rights Democrat)	39	1,200,000

- Why did the political pundits predict a Dewey victory?
- Why was civil rights a divisive issue at the Democratic Convention?
- How did the candidacies of Thurmond and Wallace help Truman?

The polls predicted a sure win for Dewey and the Republicans, but on election day Truman won the biggest upset in history to that point, taking 24.2 million votes (49.5 percent) to Dewey's 22 million (45.1 percent) and winning a thumping margin of 303–189 in the Electoral College. Thurmond and Wallace each received more than a million votes, but the Dixiecrat rebellion backfired by angering black voters, who turned out in droves to support Truman, while the Progressive party's radicalism made it hard for Republicans to tag Truman as soft on communism.

The Fair Deal Rejected

Truman viewed his surprising victory as a mandate for expanding the social welfare programs established by Franklin Roosevelt. "Every segment of our population and every individual," he declared, "has a right to expect from our government a *fair deal*." Truman's Fair Deal proposals promised "greater economic opportunity for the mass of the people."

Yet there was little new in Truman's Fair Deal proposals. Most of them were simply extensions or enlargements of earlier New Deal programs: a higher minimum wage, expansion of Social Security coverage to 10 million

> Congress rejects Fair Deal legislation

workers not included in the original 1935 bill, and a sizable slum-clearance and public-housing program for 800,000 poor Americans. Despite enjoying Democratic majorities in Congress, however, Truman ran up against the same alliance of conservative southern Democrats and Republicans who had allied against Roosevelt in the late 1930s. The bipartisan conservative coalition nixed most of Truman's new Fair Deal programs. Congress rejected several civil rights bills, national health insurance, federal aid to education, and a new approach to subsidizing farmers. Congress also turned down Truman's requested repeal of the anti-union Taft-Hartley Act. Yet the Fair Deal was not a complete failure. It laid the foundation for programs that the next generation of reformers would promote in the sixties and after.

The Cold War Heats Up

As was true during Truman's first term, global concerns during his second term would again distract the president's attention from domestic issues. In his 1949 inaugural address, President Truman called for a vigilant anti-Communist foreign policy resting on three pillars: the United Nations, the Marshall Plan, and NATO. None of those pillars could help resolve the civil war in China, however.

CORE **OBJECTIVE**

4. Assess the major international developments during 1949–1950, including the outbreak of the Korean War, and explain how they altered U.S. foreign policy.

"Losing" China

One of the thorniest postwar problems, the Chinese civil war, was fast coming to a head in 1949. The Chinese Nationalists, led by Chiang Kai-shek, had been fighting Mao Zedong and the Communists since the 1920s. After the Second World War, the Nationalists were put on the defensive as the Communists won over most of the peasants. By the end of 1949, the Nationalist government was forced to flee to the island of Formosa, which it renamed Taiwan. Truman's critics—mostly Republicans—now asked bitterly, "Who lost China to communism?" What they did not explain in attacking Truman was how he could have prevented a Communist victory without a massive U.S. military intervention, which would have been risky, unpopular, and expensive. After 1949, the United States continued to recognize the Nationalist government on Taiwan as the official government of China, delaying formal relations with "Red China" (the People's Republic of China) for thirty years.

Communist victory in China

The Soviets Develop Atomic Bombs

As the Communists were gaining control of China, the Soviets were developing their own atomic bombs. News that the Soviets had detonated a nuclear weapon in 1949 frightened people around the world and led Truman to speed up the construction of a hydrogen "superbomb," a weapon far more powerful than the atomic bombs dropped on Japan. That the Soviets now possessed

MAO ZEDONG Chairman of the Chinese Communist Party and founder of the People's Republic of China, Mao led in a Communist victory against the Chinese Nationalists in 1949.

SHELTER FOR SALE On display in a 1950s showroom is a basement bomb fallout shelter, complete with a television, library, and exercise bike. **What does the prevalence of fallout shelters like this one during the cold war show about the American mentality at the time?**

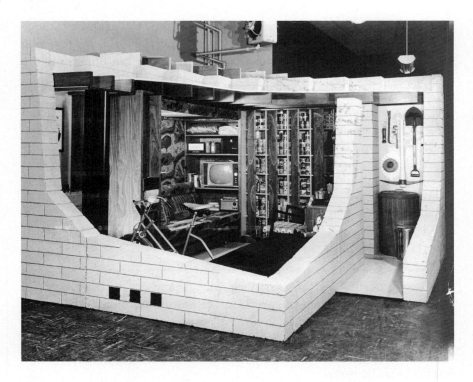

atomic weapons greatly heightened every cold war confrontation between East and West. "There is only one thing worse than one nation having an atomic bomb," said Nobel Prize–winning physicist Harold C. Urey. "That's two nations having it."

NSC-68

In January 1950, President Truman, concerned about the Soviets possessing atomic weapons, asked the NSC to assess America's changing role in the cold war world. Four months later, the council submitted to the president a top-secret report called **NSC-68**. The document, officially approved by Truman in September, laid out in alarmist tones the major assumptions of U.S. foreign policy for the next twenty years: "The issues that face us are momentous, involving the fulfillment or destruction not only of this Republic but of civilization itself." NSC-68 endorsed George Kennan's "containment" strategy, but where he had focused on political and economic counterpressure against the Soviets, its tone was global and militaristic, calling for "a policy of calculated and gradual coercion" against Soviet expansionism—everywhere.

Hawkish Paul Nitze, Kennan's successor as director of policy planning for the State Department, wrote NSC-68. He claimed that the Soviets, driven by their "fanatical faith" in their destiny to impose their will "on the rest of the world," were becoming increasingly "reckless" in their international behavior and would invade Western Europe by 1954, by which time they would have enough nuclear weapons to destroy the United States.

NSC-68 (1950) Top-secret policy paper approved by President Truman that outlined a militaristic approach to combating the spread of global communism.

By signing NSC-68, Truman endorsed its assumptions about a perpetual struggle with Soviet communism in which there could be only victory or defeat. "It meant," he pledged, "doubling or tripling the [defense] budget, increasing taxes heavily, and imposing various kinds of economic controls. It meant a great change in our normal peacetime way of doing things." NSC-68 became the guidebook for future American policy, especially as the United States became involved in an unexpected war in Korea that ignited into open combat the smoldering animosity between East and West, communism and capitalism.

War in Korea

By mid-1950, tensions between the United States and the Soviet Union in Europe had temporarily eased into a stalemate. In Asia, however, the situation remained turbulent. The Communists had gained control of mainland China and were threatening to destroy the Chinese Nationalists, who had taken refuge on the island of Taiwan. Japan, meanwhile, was experiencing a dramatic recovery from the devastation of defeat and the destruction caused by U.S. bombing raids during the Second World War. Douglas MacArthur showed deft leadership as the consul in charge of U.S.-occupied Japan. He oversaw the disarming of the Japanese military, the drafting of a democratic constitution, and the nation's economic recovery, all of which were turning Japan into America's friend.

To the east of Japan, however, tensions between North Korea and South Korea threatened to erupt into civil war. The Japanese had occupied the Korean peninsula since 1910, and after their defeat and withdrawal in 1945, the victorious Allies had faced the difficult task of creating a new independent Korean nation. Complicating that effort was the presence of Soviet troops in northern Korea. They had accepted the surrender of Japanese forces above the 38th parallel, which divides the Korean peninsula, while U.S. forces had overseen the Japanese surrender south of that line. The Soviets quickly organized a Communist government called the Democratic People's Republic of Korea (North Korea) in the industrial north. The Americans countered by helping establish a democratic government in the agricultural and more populous south, the Republic of Korea (South Korea). By the end of 1948, separate regimes had appeared in the two sectors, Soviet and American forces had withdrawn, and some 2 million North Koreans had fled to South Korea.

On June 25, 1950, with the encouragement of the Soviet Union and Communist China, the Soviet-equipped North Korean People's Army—135,000 strong—invaded the Republic of South Korea and sent the South Korean army reeling in a headlong retreat. Within three days of fighting, the North Korean army had captured Seoul, the South Korean capital.

When asked how he would respond to the invasion, President Truman declared: "By God, I'm going to let them have it!" He then made a critical decision: without consulting the Joint Chiefs of Staff or Congress, Truman

FIGHT AND FLIGHT American soldiers brush shoulders with Korean refugees as they march into the Nakdong River region in the south.

decided to wage war through the backing of the United Nations rather than seeking a declaration of war from Congress.

An emergency meeting of the UN Security Council in New York City in late June 1950 censured the North Korean "breach of peace." By sheer coincidence, the Soviet delegate, who held a veto power, was at the time boycotting the council because it would not seat Communist China in place of Nationalist China. On June 27, the Security Council took advantage of his absence to call on UN members to "furnish such assistance to the Republic of Korea as may be necessary to repel the armed attack and to restore international peace and security in the area." With this UN endorsement, Truman ordered U.S. air, naval, and ground forces to defend South Korea. He then appointed seventy-year-old Douglas MacArthur as the supreme commander of the UN forces.

U.S. "police action" in Korea

The Korean conflict was the first military action fought under the banner of the United Nations, only five years old, and some twenty other nations participated. The United States provided the largest contingent of non-Korean forces by far, some 330,000 troops. The American military defense of South Korea set a worrisome precedent: war by order of a president rather than by a vote of Congress, which the U.S. Constitution requires. Truman dodged the constitutional issue by officially calling the conflict in Korea a "police action" rather than a war.

Turning the Tables

For the first three months, the fighting in Korea went badly for the Republic of Korea and the UN forces. By September 1950, the decimated South Korean troops were barely hanging on to the southeast corner of the Korean peninsula. Then, in a brilliant maneuver on September 15, General MacArthur staged a surprise amphibious landing behind the North Korean lines at Inchon, the port city for Seoul. UN troops drove a wedge through the North Korean army; only a quarter of the North Koreans, some 25,000 soldiers, managed to flee across the border. Days later, South Korean troops recaptured Seoul.

At that point, an overconfident MacArthur persuaded Truman to allow the U.S. troops to push north and eliminate the Communists in Korea. Containment of communism was no longer enough; MacArthur now hatched a grandiose plan to rid North Korea of the "red menace," even if this meant expanding the war into China in order to prevent the Chinese from resupplying their North Korean allies. Truman foolishly approved MacArthur's request to advance into North Korea so as to destroy its armies and enable the unification of both Koreas.

The Chinese Intervene

By October 1950, UN forces were on the verge of capturing the North Korean capital, Pyongyang. President Truman, concerned that MacArthur's move into North Korea would provoke Communist China to enter the war, flew 7,000 miles to Wake Island for a conference with MacArthur on October 15 (the haughty general had refused to travel to the United States). At his meeting with Truman, MacArthur dismissed Chinese threats to intervene, even though they had massed troops on the Korean border. That same day, the Communist government in Beijing announced that China "cannot stand idly by" as their North Korean allies were humiliated. Five days later, UN forces entered the North Korean capital, and on October 26, advance units had reached Ch'osan, on the Yalu River, North Korea's border with China.

The brash MacArthur predicted total victory by Christmas. He could not have been more wrong. On the night of November 25, some 500,000 Chinese "volunteers" crossed into Korea and surprised MacArthur, sending the U.S. forces in desperate retreat just at the onset of winter. A frantic Truman wrote in his diary that it "looks like World War III is here." By January 15, the Communist Chinese and North Koreans had recaptured Seoul, the South Korean capital. "We ran like antelopes," said one American soldier. "We lost everything we had."

Chinese intervention in Korea

MacArthur Pushes the Limit

The Chinese intervention forced MacArthur to admit that the conflict had become "an entirely new war." He asked for thirty-four atomic bombs and proposed air raids on China. MacArthur's plans to use nuclear weapons and attack China horrified Truman and the military leadership in Washington,

THE KOREAN WAR, 1950 AND 1950–1953

1950

Vladivostok

CHINA
MANCHURIA

Yalu River

Ch'osan

U.S.S.R

NORTH
KOREA

North Korean
offensive,
June – Sept. 1950

P'yŏngyang

SEA
OF
JAPAN

38°

Inch'ŏn · Seoul

SOUTH
KOREA

YELLOW
SEA

UN position,
Sept. 1950

Pusan

0   50   100 Miles
0   50   100 Kilometers

KOREA STRAIT   JAPAN

1950–1953

Vladivostok

CHINA
MANCHURIA

Yalu River

Chinese attack, Nov. 1950

NORTH
KOREA

Ch'osan

Farthest
UN advance,
Nov. 1950

U.S.S.R

SEA
OF
JAPAN

P'yŏngyang

Truce line,
July 27, 1953

P'anmunjŏm · Chorwon

Seoul

Inch'ŏn

UN retreat,
Jan. 1951

YELLOW
SEA

MacArthur
Sept. 15, 1950

UN
forces

SOUTH
KOREA

UN position,
Sept. 1950

Pusan

38°

0   50   100 Miles
0   50   100 Kilometers

KOREA STRAIT   JAPAN

- How did the surrender of the Japanese in Korea set up the conflict between Soviet-influenced North Korea and U.S.-influenced South Korea?
- What was General MacArthur's strategy for retaking Korea?
- Why did President Truman remove MacArthur from command?

D.C. It would be, explained General Omar Bradley, chairman of the Joint Chiefs of Staff, "the wrong war at the wrong place at the wrong time with the wrong enemy."

In late 1950, the UN forces rallied. By January 1951, they finally secured their lines below Seoul and then launched a counterattack. When Truman began negotiations with the North Koreans to restore the prewar boundary, General MacArthur undermined the president by issuing an ultimatum for

China to make peace or suffer an attack on their own country. His contempt for Truman became a public issue when on April 5, on the floor of Congress, the Republican minority leader read a letter from MacArthur that criticized the president and said that "there is no substitute for victory." Such a reckless act of insubordination left Truman only two choices: he could either accept MacArthur's aggressive demands or fire him.

Sacking a Hero

On April 11, 1951, with civilian control of the military at stake, Truman removed the brilliant but bullheaded MacArthur (Truman called him "Mr. Prima Donna") and replaced him with jut-jawed General Matthew B. Ridgway. "I believe that we must try to limit the war to Korea," Truman explained. "A number of events have made it evident that General MacArthur did not agree with that policy. I have therefore considered it essential to relieve General MacArthur so that there would be no doubt or confusion as to the real purpose and aim of our policy."

MacArthur controversy

Truman's sacking of MacArthur divided a shocked nation into two emotional camps. "Seldom had a more unpopular man fired a more popular one," *Time* magazine reported. Senator Joseph McCarthy called the president a "son of a bitch" for sacking MacArthur, and an editorial in the *Chicago Tribune* demanded that Truman "be impeached and convicted." In his diary, Truman acknowledged the ferocious backlash against him: "Quite an explosion. . . . Letters of abuse by the dozens." Sixty-six percent of Americans surveyed initially opposed Truman's relieving MacArthur of command.

The man Truman fired was a larger-than-life military hero. Republicans in Congress protested MacArthur's removal, but Truman stood firm, claiming the decision was an obvious one: "I fired him because he wouldn't respect the authority of the President. I didn't fire him because he was a dumb son of a bitch, although he was, but that's not against the law for generals. If it was, half to three-quarters of them would be in jail." The fact that all the top military leaders supported Truman's decision deflated much of the criticism.

FIRING OF MACARTHUR In this 1951 cartoon by L. J. Roche, President Harry Truman, Secretary of State Dean Acheson, and the Pentagon dance in the American public's proverbial frying pan for the removal of General Douglas MacArthur from his post as the supreme commander of UN forces in Korea. **How did Americans react to Truman's decision to fire MacArthur?**

A Cease-Fire

38th parallel divided North and South Korea

On June 24, 1951, the Soviet representative at the United Nations proposed a cease-fire in Korea along the 38th parallel, the original dividing line between North and South. Secretary of State Dean Acheson accepted the cease-fire (armistice) a few days later with the consent of the United Nations. China and North Korea responded favorably. Truce talks started on July 10, 1951, only to drag on for two years while sporadic fighting continued. The chief snags were exchanges of prisoners (many captured North Korean and Chinese soldiers did not want to go home) and South Korea's insistence on unification of the two rival Koreas.

By the time a truce agreement was reached, on July 27, 1953, however, Truman had retired and Dwight D. Eisenhower was president. No peace treaty was ever signed, and Korea, like Germany, remained divided. The inconclusive war cost the United States more than 33,000 battle deaths and 103,000 wounded or missing. South Korean casualties, all told, were about 2 million, and North Korean and Chinese casualties an estimated 3 million.

The Impact of the Korean War

U.S. military buildup worldwide

The Korean War influenced U.S. foreign policy in significant ways. To most Americans, the North Korean attack on South Korea provided concrete proof that there was an international Communist conspiracy to control the world guided by the Soviet Union.

Truman's assumption that Stalin and the Soviets were behind the invasion of South Korea prompted three far-reaching decisions. First, Truman mistakenly viewed the Korean conflict as actually a diversion for a Soviet invasion of Western Europe, so he ordered a major expansion of U.S. military forces in Europe—and around the world. Second, the president increased assistance to French troops fighting a Communist independence movement in the French colony of Indochina (which included Vietnam), starting America's deepening military involvement in Southeast Asia. Third, the Korean War demonstrated how important a role Japan would play in America's military presence in Asia.

Another Red Scare

CORE **OBJECTIVE**

5. Examine the emergence of the Red Scare after the Second World War, and explain its impact on American politics and society.

The Korean War excited another Red Scare at home, as in 1919, as people grew fearful that Soviet-directed Communists were infiltrating American society. Since 1938, the **House Committee on Un-American Activities (HUAC)** had claimed that Communist agents had infiltrated the federal government. On March 21, 1947, just nine days after he announced the Truman Doctrine, the president signed an executive order (also known as the Loyalty Order) requiring federal government workers to go through a background investigation to ensure they were not Communists or even associated with Communists (as well as other "subversive" groups).

The president knew that the "loyalty program" violated the civil liberties of government workers, but he felt he had no choice. He was responding to pressure from FBI director J. Edgar Hoover and Attorney General Tom Clark, both of whom believed that there were numerous spies working inside the federal government. Truman was also eager to blunt criticism by Republicans that he was not doing enough to ensure that Soviet sympathizers were not working in government.

The president himself thought that fears about Communist subversives were exaggerated. "People are very much wrought up about the communist 'bugaboo,'" he wrote to Pennsylvania governor George Earle, "but I am of the opinion that the country is perfectly safe so far as Communism is concerned." By early 1951, the federal Civil Service Commission had cleared over 3 million government workers, while only 378 had been dismissed for doubtful loyalty. In 1953, President Dwight D. Eisenhower revoked the Loyalty Order.

House Committee on Un-American Activities (HUAC) Committee of the U.S. House of Representatives formed in 1938; originally tasked with investigating Nazi subversion during the Second World War and later focused on rooting out Communists in the government and the motion-picture industry.

The Hollywood Ten

In May 1947, charges that the movie industry in Hollywood was a "hotbed of communism" led the HUAC to launch a full-blown investigation. The HUAC subpoenaed dozens of prominent actors, producers, and directors to testify at its hearings, held in Los Angeles in October. Ten witnesses refused to answer questions about their political activities, arguing that such questions violated their First Amendment rights. When asked if he were a member of the Communist party, screenwriter Ring Lardner Jr. replied: "I could answer, but I would hate myself in the morning." Another member of the so-called Hollywood Ten, screenwriter Dalton Trumbo, shouted as he left the hearings, "This is the beginning of an American concentration camp." All ten were cited for contempt of Congress, imprisoned, and blacklisted (banned) from the film industry.

The HUAC witch hunt inspired playwright Arthur Miller, who himself was blacklisted, to write *The Crucible* (1953), a dramatic account of the notorious witch trials in Salem, Massachusetts, at the end of the seventeenth century, intended to alert Americans to the dangers of the anti-Communist hysteria.

THE VERGE OF VERDICT A few courageous movie stars attended the HUAC hearings to support their friends and colleagues who were accused of being Communists. Left to right: Danny Kaye, June Havoc, Humphrey Bogart, and Lauren Bacall (seated).

Alger Hiss

The spy case most damaging to the Truman administration involved Alger Hiss, president of the Carnegie Endowment for International Peace, who had earlier served in several government agencies, including the State Department. Whittaker Chambers, a former Soviet spy and later an editor of *Time* magazine, told the HUAC in 1948 that Hiss had given him secret documents ten years earlier, when Chambers was spying for the Soviets and Hiss was working in the State Department.

Hiss sued Chambers for libel, and Chambers produced microfilms of the State Department documents that Hiss had passed to him. Hiss denied the accusation, whereupon he was indicted and, after one mistrial, convicted in 1950. The charge was perjury, but he was convicted of lying about espionage, for which he could not be tried because the statute of limitations on that crime had expired.

More cases of Communist infiltration surfaced. In 1949, eleven top leaders of the Communist party of the United States were convicted under the Smith Act of 1940, which outlawed any conspiracy to advocate the overthrow of the government. The Supreme Court upheld the law under the doctrine of a "clear and present danger," which overrode the right to free speech.

Atomic Spying

Julius and Ethel Rosenberg

In 1950, the FBI unearthed the existence of a British-American spy network that had secretly passed information about the development of the atomic bomb to the Soviet Union. These disclosures led to the widely publicized arrest of Klaus Fuchs, a German-born English physicist who had worked in the United States during the war, helping develop the atomic bomb.

As it turned out, a New York couple, former Communists Julius and Ethel Rosenberg, were part of the same Soviet spy ring. Their claims of innocence were undercut by the confession of Ethel's brother, who admitted he was a spy along with his sister and brother-in-law.

The convictions of Fuchs and the Rosenbergs fueled Republican charges that Truman's administration was not doing enough to hunt down Communist agents who were stealing American military secrets. The Rosenberg case, called the crime of the century by J. Edgar Hoover, also heightened fears that a vast Soviet network of spies and sympathizers was operating in the United States—and now had "given" Stalin the secret of building atomic weapons. Irving Kaufman, the federal judge who sentenced the Rosenbergs to death, explained that "plain, deliberate murder is dwarfed . . . by comparison with the crime you have committed." They were the first Americans ever executed for spying.

McCarthy's Witch Hunt

Evidence of Soviet spying encouraged politicians to exploit fears of the Communist menace at home. Early in 1950, a little-known Republican senator, Joseph R. McCarthy of Wisconsin, suddenly surfaced as the most ruthless manipulator of the nation's anti-Communist anxieties.

An intelligent, determined, but unethical man thirsty for media attention, McCarthy took up the cause of anti-Communism with a fiery speech to a Republican women's club in Wheeling, West Virginia, on February 9, 1950. He claimed that the State Department was infested with Communists—and he claimed to have their names, although he never provided them.

"Joe" McCarthy's reckless charges created a media sensation and, over the next four years, led the senator to make more irresponsible accusations, initially against Democrats, whom he attacked as "dupes" or "fellow travelers" of the "Commies," then against just about everyone, including the U.S. Army.

Truman privately denounced McCarthy as "just a ballyhoo artist who has to cover up his shortcomings with wild charges," but McCarthy grew into a formidable figure. He enjoyed the backing of fellow Republicans eager to hurt Democrats in the 1950 congressional elections by claiming they were "soft on Communism." Senator Lyndon B. Johnson of Texas said McCarthy was "the sorriest senator" in Washington, "but he's riding high now, he's got people scared to death."

By the summer of 1951, what had come to be called **McCarthyism** had gotten out of control. McCarthy outrageously accused George Marshall, the former secretary of state and war hero, of making "common cause with Stalin." Concerns about the truth or fair play did not faze him. He refused to answer critics or provide evidence; his goal was to use groundless accusations to create a reign of terror.

Despite his outlandish claims and bullying style, McCarthy never uncovered a single Communist agent in the government. Yet his smear campaign, which tarnished many lives and reputations, went largely unchallenged until the end of the Korean War—and he attracted millions of fans. During the Red Scare, thousands of left-wing Americans were "blacklisted" from employment because of past political associations, real or rumored. Movies with titles like *I Married a Communist* fed the hysteria, and stories in popular magazines warned of "a Red under every bed."

Fears of Soviet spies led Congress in 1950 to pass the McCarran Internal Security Act over President Truman's veto, making it unlawful "to combine, conspire, or agree with any other person to perform any act which would substantially contribute to . . . the establishment of a totalitarian dictatorship." Communist organizations had to register with the attorney general. Would-be immigrants who had belonged to totalitarian parties in their home countries were denied entry to the United States. And during any future national emergencies, Communists were to be herded into concentration camps as the Japanese had been during World War II. The McCarran Internal Security Act, Truman said in his veto message, would "put the government into the business of thought control."

JOSEPH R. MCCARTHY
A photo from 1954 of McCarthy, the senator with a mission to sweep the Communists from the government and beyond.

McCarran Internal Security Act

McCarthyism Anti-Communist hysteria led by Senator Joseph McCarthy's witch hunts attacking the loyalty of politicians, federal employees, and public figures, despite a lack of evidence.

Assessing the Red Scare and the Cold War

The Red Scare ended up violating the civil liberties of innocent people. President Truman may have erred in 1947 by creating a government loyalty program that aggravated the anti-Communist hysteria. His attorney general, Tom Clark, contended that there were "so many Communists in America" that they "were everywhere—in factories, offices, butcher shops, on street corners, in private businesses—and each carries with him the germs of death for society."

Truman also overstretched American resources when he pledged to "contain" communism everywhere. Containment itself proved hard to contain amid the ideological posturing of Soviet and American leaders. Its chief theorist, George F. Kennan, later confessed that he had failed to spell out the limits of the containment policy and to stress that the United States needed to prioritize its responses to Soviet adventurism.

The years after the Second World War were unlike any other postwar period. Having taken on global burdens, the nation became committed to a permanently large national military establishment, along with the attendant creation of shadowy new government agencies such as the NSC, the National Security Agency, and CIA. The federal government—and the presidency—continued to grow larger, more powerful, and more secretive during the cold war, fueled by the actions of both major political parties as well as by the intense lobbying efforts of what Dwight D. Eisenhower would later call the *military-industrial complex*—defense contractors, lobbyists, and so on.

Fears of communism at home grew out of legitimate concerns about a Soviet spy network in the United States but mushroomed into politically motivated paranoia. As had been true during the First Red Scare, after the First World War, long-standing prejudices against Jews fed the anti-Communist hysteria; indeed, many Communist sympathizers were Jews from Eastern Europe. The Red Scare also provided a powerful tool for Republicans eager to attack the Truman administration and the Democratic party, claiming that the Democrats were "soft on Communism." One of the worst effects of the Red Scare was to encourage widespread conformity of thought and behavior in the United States. By 1950, it had become dangerous to criticize anything associated with the American way of life.

On March 30, 1952, Harry Truman announced he would not seek another presidential term, in part because it was unlikely he could win. Less than 25 percent of voters surveyed said that he was doing a good job, the lowest presidential approval rating in history. Although Americans applauded Truman's integrity and courage, they were disheartened that members of his administration were inept and even corrupt. The unrelenting war against communism, at home and abroad, led people to question Truman's strategy. Negotiations to end the war in Korea had bogged down for many months, the "red-baiting" of McCarthyism was expanding across the nation, and conservative southern Democrats, members of Truman's own party, had defeated

Violations of civil liberties and overstretched foreign policy

Creation of the "military-industrial complex"

most of the president's Fair Deal proposals in Congress. The war in Korea had brought higher taxes and higher prices for consumers, many of whom blamed Truman for their frustrations. Only years later would people (and historians) fully appreciate how effective Truman had been in dealing with so many complex problems.

To the end of his presidency, Truman, a plainspoken man who made decisions based on his "gut-feeling" about what was "right," viewed himself as an ordinary person operating amid extraordinary times. "I have tried my best to give the nation everything I have in me," Truman told reporters at one of his last press conferences. "There are a great many people . . . who could have done the job better than I did it. But I had the job and had to do it." And it was not a simple job, by any means. At the end of one difficult day in the White House, Truman growled while sipping bourbon: "They [his critics] talk about the power of the President, how I can just push a button to get things done. Why, I spend most of my time kissing somebody's . . . [butt]."

By the time a frustrated Truman left the White House in early 1953, the cold war against communism had become an accepted part of the American way of life. But fears of Soviet and Chinese communism were counterbalanced by the joys of unexpected prosperity. Toward the end of Truman's presidency, during the early fifties, the economy began to grow at the fastest rate in history, transforming social and cultural life, and becoming the marvel of the world. The booming economy brought with it the "nifty" fifties.

Reviewing the
CORE OBJECTIVES | <small>INQUIZITIVE</small>

■ **The Cold War** The cold war was an ideological contest between the Western democracies (especially the United States) and the Communist nations (especially the Soviet Union). At the end of the Second World War, the Soviet Union established "friendly" governments in the Eastern European countries it occupied behind an *iron curtain*, violating promises that Stalin had made at the Yalta Conference. The United States and the Soviet Union, former allies, differed openly on issues of human rights, individual liberties, self-determination, and religious freedoms. As mutual hostility emerged, the two nations and their allies competed to shape the postwar global order.

■ **Containment** President Truman responded to the Soviet occupation of Eastern Europe with *containment*, a policy to halt the spread of communism by opposing it wherever it emerged around the world. With the *Truman Doctrine (1947)*, the U.S. provided economic and military aid to countries facing Communist insurgencies, such as Greece and Turkey. The *National Security Act (1947)* reorganized the U.S. armed forces and created the Central Intelligence Agency. The *Marshall Plan (1948)* offered postwar redevelopment aid to all European nations. In 1948-1949, the United States withstood a Soviet blockade of supplies to West Berlin with the *Berlin airlift* and, in 1949, became a founding member of the *North Atlantic Treaty Organization (NATO)*.

■ **Truman's Fair Deal** The *Fair Deal (1949)* sought to expand the New Deal in the face of intense Republican opposition in Congress. While he could not stop the Republican-backed, anti-union *Taft-Hartley Labor Act (1947)*, Truman successfully expanded Social Security, desegregated the military, and banned racial discrimination in the hiring of federal employees. In his second term, he proposed a civil rights bill, national health insurance, federal aid to education, and new farm subsidies. However, conservative majorities of Republicans and southern Democrats (*Dixiecrats*) defeated most of these proposals.

■ **The Korean War** While containment policies halted Soviet expansion in Europe, they proved less effective in East Asia as Communists won a long civil war in China in 1949 and ignited a war in Korea. In response, Truman authorized *NSC-68 (1950)*, a study that proposed a dramatic increase in military spending and nuclear arms. When North Korean troops invaded South Korea in June 1950, Truman quickly decided to go to war under the auspices of the United Nations, thus bypassing Congress's authority to declare war. After three years of war, a truce established a demilitarized zone in Korea on either side of the 38th parallel. Truman also began assisting French efforts to subdue a Communist insurgency in its Southeast Asian colony of Indochina.

■ **The Red Scare** The onset of the cold war inflamed another Red Scare. After the Second World War, investigations by the *House Committee on Un-American Activities (HUAC)* sought to find "subversives" within the federal government. Starting in 1950, Senator Joseph R. McCarthy exploited American fears of Soviet infiltration of the U.S. government. *McCarthyism* flourished in the short term because the threat of a world dominated by Communist governments seemed all too real to many Americans.

KEY TERMS

iron curtain *p. 953*

containment *p. 955*

Truman Doctrine (1947) *p. 956*

Marshall Plan (1948) *p. 957*

Berlin airlift (1948–1949) *p. 960*

North Atlantic Treaty Organization (NATO) *p. 961*

National Security Act (1947) *p. 961*

Taft-Hartley Labor Act (1947) *p. 964*

Fair Deal (1949) *p. 968*

Dixiecrats *p. 969*

NSC-68 (1950) *p. 972*

House Committee on Un-American Activities (HUAC) *p. 979*

McCarthyism *p. 981*

CHRONOLOGY

1944	Congress passes the GI Bill of Rights
April 1945	Fifty Allied nations sign the UN Charter
	Soviet Union begins installing "puppet" Communist regimes in Eastern Europe
February 1946	State Department official George Kennan issues his "Long Telegram"
March 1947	President Truman announces the Truman Doctrine
May 1947	Secretary of State George Marshall proposes the Marshall Plan
June 1947	Congress passes Taft-Hartley Labor Act
July 1947	National Security Council is established
May 1948	Israel is proclaimed an independent nation
July 1948	Truman issues an executive order ending segregation in the U.S. armed forces
August 1948	Alger Hiss accused of having been a Soviet spy before the HUAC
October 1948	Berlin airlift begins
April 1949	NATO is created
October 1949	China "falls" to communism
	Soviet Union tests an atomic bomb
February 1950	McCarthy's Red Scare begins
June 1950–July 1953	The Korean War

⚉ INQUIZITIVE

Go to InQuizitive to see what you've learned—and learn what you've missed—with personalized feedback along the way.

AMERICAN CONSUMERISM The United States experienced tremendous prosperity after the Second World War, giving many Americans the unprecedented opportunity of carefree consumption in the 1950s—and personal indebtedness.

Affluence and Anxiety in the Atomic Age

1950–1959

I n the summer of 1959, two newlyweds spent their honeymoon in an underground bomb shelter in their backyard. *Life* magazine showed the couple in their twenty-ton steel-and-concrete bunker stocked with enough food and water to survive an atomic attack. The image of the newlyweds seeking sheltered security in a new age of nuclear terror symbolized how America in the 1950s was awash in contrasting emotions. The deepening cold war with the Soviet Union cast a frightening shadow over the nation's traditional sunny optimism. In 1959, two out of three Americans listed the possibility of atomic war as the nation's most urgent threat.

Despite the fears of nuclear destruction, however, Americans emerged from the Second World War proud of their military strength, international stature, and industrial might. It was a time rich with possibilities, and people were eager to seize their destinies. As the editors of *Fortune* magazine proclaimed in 1946, "This is a dream era. . . . The Great American Boom is on."

So it was, at least for the growing number of white middle-class Americans. During the late 1940s and throughout the 1950s, the United States enjoyed unprecedented economic growth and technological innovation that created a dazzling array of new consumer products. Amid the insecurities of the cold war, most people were remarkably content with the improving quality of their lives. Divorce and homicide rates fell and people

CORE OBJECTIVES INQUIZITIVE

1. Explain President Eisenhower's political philosophy and priorities.

2. Identify the factors that contributed to postwar prosperity, and analyze to what extent all Americans benefited from it.

3. Examine the criticism of postwar American society and culture, and describe the various forms of dissent and anxiety.

4. Evaluate the goals, strategies, and impact of the civil rights movement that emerged in the 1950s.

5. Assess President Eisenhower's priorities in conducting the nation's foreign policy and his influence on global affairs.

moderate Republicanism
Promise to curb federal government and restore state and local government authority, spearheaded by President Eisenhower.

lived longer, on average, thanks in part to miraculous medical breakthroughs such as new antibiotics and the vaccine invented by Dr. Jonas Salk that ended the menace of polio. The "happy days" image of America in the fifties as an innocent, prosperous nation awash in good times and enlivened by teenage energies has a kernel of truth, but life in the fifties was much more complicated than that, hugely varied and even contradictory and hypocritical at times, with many Americans worried about an uncontrollable future.

CORE **OBJECTIVE**

1. Explain President Eisenhower's political philosophy and priorities.

Moderate Republicanism— The Eisenhower Years

Dwight David Eisenhower dominated the political landscape during the 1950s. The military hero of World War II, the "savior of Europe," was a model of moderation, modesty, stability, and optimism. Eisenhower's commitment to what he called **moderate Republicanism** promised to restore the authority of state and local governments and restrain the federal government from engaging in any more political and social "engineering." In the process, he sought to renew traditional virtues and inspire Americans with a vision of a brighter future despite the continuing cold war.

"Time for a Change"

By 1952, the Truman administration had piled up a heavy burden of political liabilities. Its bold stand in Korea had resulted in a bloody stalemate in the war, renewed wage and price controls at home, and the embarrassing exposure of corrupt lobbyists who rigged military contracts. The disclosure of corruption within several federal agencies led Truman to fire nearly 250 employees of the Internal Revenue Service, but doubts lingered that the president would ever finish the housecleaning.

It was, Republicans claimed, "time for a change," and public sentiment turned their way as the 1952 election approached. Beginning in the late 1940s, both Republican and Democratic leaders, including President Truman, recruited General Eisenhower to be their presidential candidate. Born in Texas but raised in Kansas, the son of a storekeeper, Eisenhower, known as "Ike," had displayed remarkable organizational and diplomatic abilities in coordinating the Allied invasion of Nazi-controlled Europe. In 1952, after serving as president of Columbia University, he moved to Paris to become the supreme commander of NATO forces in Europe. His decision to run for president as a Republican was wildly popular. Bumper stickers announced: "I Like Ike."

Eisenhower won the nomination on the first ballot. Republican leaders then tried to reassure conservatives by balancing the ticket with a youthful,

DWIGHT D. EISENHOWER
Eisenhower's many supporters wore "I Like Ike" hats, pins, and even nylon stockings, speaking to the consumer culture's impact on politics.

fiercely ambitious running mate: Richard M. Nixon, a thirty-nine-year-old California senator whose dogged insistence on pursuing the Alger Hiss spying case in congressional hearings had brought him national prominence.

Nixon built his early political career as an anti-Communist bent on exposing left-wing "subversives" holding government posts in the Truman administration. The Republican party platform declared that the Democratic emphasis on "containing" communism was a "negative, futile, and misguided" form of appeasement. The Eisenhower administration, if elected, would roll back the Communist threat by bringing "genuine independence" to the "captive peoples" of Eastern Europe.

> Rolling back communism

The Election of 1952

The 1952 presidential campaign matched two contrasting personalities. Eisenhower, though a political amateur, had been in the public eye for a decade. Illinois governor Adlai Stevenson, the Democratic candidate, was hardly known outside his home state. Eisenhower pledged to clean up "the mess in Washington." To this he added a promise to secure "an early and honorable" end to the conflict in Korea.

> An end to the Korean War

Stevenson was outmatched. Although a brilliant man whose witty speeches charmed liberals, he came across to most voters as too aloof and intellectual. The Republicans labeled him an "egghead" (meant to suggest a balding professor with more intellect than common sense). Even Truman questioned Stevenson's decisiveness, grumbling that the Democratic candidate "was too busy making up his mind whether he had to go to the bathroom or not."

On election night, the affable Eisenhower with a radiant smile triumphed in a landslide, gathering nearly 34 million votes to Stevenson's 27 million. The electoral vote was much more lopsided: 442–89. The hapless Stevenson even failed to win his home state of Illinois.

More important, the election marked a turning point in Republican fortunes in the South. For the first time in more than a century, the Democratic "Solid South" was moving toward a two-party system. By winning four Democratic southern states, Eisenhower had made it respectable, even fashionable, to vote for a Republican presidential candidate in the South.

THE ELECTION OF 1952

	Electoral Vote	Popular Vote
Dwight D. Eisenhower (Republican)	442	33,900,000
Adlai E. Stevenson (Democrat)	89	27,300,000

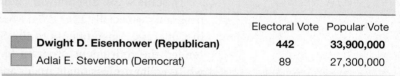

- Why was the contest between Adlai Stevenson and Dwight D. Eisenhower lopsided?
- Why was Eisenhower's victory in the South remarkable?

Voters liked Eisenhower's folksy charm and battle-tested poise better than they liked his political party. In the 1952 election, Democrats retained most of the governorships, lost control of the House by only eight seats, and broke even in the Senate, where only the vote of the vice president gave Republicans the slimmest possible majority. The congressional elections two years later would further weaken the Republican grip on Congress, and Eisenhower would have to work with a Democratic Congress throughout his last six years in office.

A "Middle Way" Presidency

Consensus and compromise between conservatism and liberalism

Eisenhower was the first professional soldier elected president since Ulysses S. Grant in 1868 and the last president born in the nineteenth century. He promised to pursue a "middle way" between conservatism and liberalism. He saw no need to dismantle all the New Deal and Fair Deal programs. Instead, he wanted to end the "excesses" that had resulted from twenty years of Democratic control of the White House. Eisenhower's cautious personality and genial public face fit perfectly with the prevailing mood of most voters. He was a unifier, not a divider; he inspired trust and sought consensus and compromise; he avoided confrontation. Eisenhower also championed the nineteenth-century view that Congress should make policy and the president should carry it out. A journalist noted in 1959 that "the public loves Ike. The less he does, the more they love him."

"Dynamic Conservatism" at Home

Eisenhower called his domestic program "dynamic conservatism," by which he meant being "conservative when it comes to money and liberal when it comes to human beings." His administration set out to reduce defense spending and military personnel, lower tax rates, weaken government regulation of business, and restore power to the states. The new president warned repeatedly against the dangers of "creeping socialism," "huge bureaucracies," and budget deficits.

In the end, however, Eisenhower kept intact the basic structure of the New Deal, much to the chagrin of conservative Republicans. He told his brother Edgar in 1954 that if the "stupid" right wing of the Republican party tried "to abolish Social Security and eliminate labor laws and farm programs, you would not hear of that party again in our political history."

In some ways, Eisenhower's administration actually expanded New Deal programs, especially after 1954, when it had the help of Democratic majorities in Congress. Amendments to the Social Security Act in 1954 and 1956 extended the retirement program to millions of workers formerly excluded: white-collar professionals, maids and sales clerks, farmworkers, and members of the armed forces. Eisenhower also approved increases in the minimum wage and additional public-housing projects for low-income occupants.

Under Eisenhower, the federal government launched two massive construction projects: the St. Lawrence Seaway and the National System of Interstate and Defense Highway Systems, both of which resembled the huge public-works projects constructed under the New Deal during the 1930s. The St. Lawrence Seaway project (in partnership with Canada) opened the Great Lakes to oceangoing ships.

The **Federal-Aid Highway Act** (1956) created a national network of interstate highways to serve the needs of commerce and defense, as well as the convenience of citizens. The interstate highway system, funded by gasoline taxes, took twenty-five years to construct and was the largest federal project in history. It stretched for 47,000 miles and required 55,512 bridges. The vast project created jobs; stimulated the economy; and spurred the tourism, motor hotel ("motel"), and long-haul trucking industries. Interstate highways transformed the way people traveled and where they lived, and they even created a new form of middle-class leisure, the family vacation by car.

The second great age of the automobile had arrived after the war. In 1948, only 60 percent of families had owned a car; by 1955, 90 percent owned a car and many households had two. "The American," the Mississippi writer William Faulkner observed in 1948, "really loves nothing but his automobile." Americans had always cherished personal freedom and mobility, rugged individualism and masculine force, and automobiles embodied all these qualities and more. Cars in the fifties were much more than a form of transportation; they provided social status and personal freedom. The "car culture" soon transformed social behavior, prompting the creation of "convenience stores," drive-in movies, and fast-food restaurants.

**Federal-Aid Highway Act
(1956)** Largest federal project
in U.S. history, which created a
national network of interstate
highways.

The End of McCarthyism

Republicans thought their presidential victory in 1952 would curb the often-unscrupulous efforts of Wisconsin senator Joseph R. McCarthy to ferret out Communist spies in the federal government. Instead, the publicity-seeking senator grew even more outlandish in his behavior. McCarthy finally over-reached when he made the absurd charge that the U.S. Army itself was "soft" on communism. On December 2, 1954, the Senate voted 67–22 to "condemn" the crusading senator for his reckless tactics. Soon thereafter, his political influence collapsed. His savage crusade against Communists in government had catapulted him into the limelight and captured the nation's attention, but in the process he had trampled upon civil liberties. McCarthy's political demise helped the Democrats capture control of both houses of Congress in the 1954 elections. In 1957, at the age of forty-eight, he died of a liver inflammation brought on by years of alcohol abuse.

A People of Plenty

CORE **OBJECTIVE**
2. Identify the factors that contributed to postwar prosperity, and analyze to what extent all Americans benefited from it.

What most distinguished the United States from the rest of the world after the Second World War was what one journalist called America's "screwball materialism." After a brief postwar recession in 1945–1946, the economy soared to record heights as businesses shifted from wartime production to the construction of new housing and the manufacture of an array of mass-produced consumer goods. In 1957, *U.S. News and World Report* magazine declared that "never had so many people, anywhere, been so well off." By 1960, some 90 percent of American families owned a car and 87 percent had a television set.

Postwar Prosperity

Global arms race

Several factors created the nation's tremendous prosperity. First, huge federal expenditures during the Second World War and the Korean War had catapulted the economy out of the Great Depression. High government spending at all levels—federal, state, and local—continued in the 1950s, thanks to the global arms race unleashed by the cold war and the relentless construction of new highways, bridges, airports, and ports. The still-large military budget after 1945 represented 60 percent of the national budget and was by far the single most important stimulant to the economy.

Robust manufacturing and dramatic new technologies

The superior productivity of American industries also contributed to dramatic economic growth. No sooner was the war over than the federal government turned over to civilian owners many of its defense plants, giving them a boost as they retooled for peacetime manufacturing. Military-related research also helped stimulate new glamour industries: chemicals (including plastics), electronics, and aviation. By 1957, the aircraft industry was the nation's largest employer. The extraordinary increase in productivity benefited from new technologies, including the first generation of computers. Factories and industries became increasingly "automated." At the same time, the oil boom in Texas, Wyoming, and Oklahoma continued to provide the United States with low-cost fuel to heat buildings and drive cars and trucks.

Another reason for the record-breaking growth of the U.S. economy was the lack of foreign competition. Most of the other major industrial nations—Great Britain, France, Germany, Japan, and the Soviet Union—had been physically devastated during the Second World War, leaving American manufacturers with a virtual monopoly on international trade that lasted well into the 1950s.

> U.S. dominance in international trade

The Consumer Culture

What differentiated the postwar era from earlier periods of prosperity was the large number of people who shared in the rising standard of living—not just corporate executives and salaried managers but also hourly wage workers. Between 1947 and 1960, the average income for the working class increased by as much as it had in the previous *fifty* years. More and more blue-collar Americans, especially automotive and steel workers, moved into the middle class. George Meany, the leading union spokesman during the 1950s, declared in 1955 that his members "never had it so good." That same year, three out of every four American adults categorized themselves as "middle class."

> Increased income across classes

POSTWAR CONSUMERISM
Booming chain stores, such as this Super Giant Supermarket, began to dot the suburbs of 1950s America, offering an outlet for the pent-up consumerism of the postwar years.

Americans had money to spend during the fifties, and they did so with gusto, becoming famous around the world for their carefree consumption. In 1955, a marketing consultant stressed that the nation's "enormously productive economy demands that we make *consumption* a way of life, that we convert the buying and use of goods into [religious] rituals, that we seek our spiritual satisfaction, our ego satisfaction, in consumption." The consumer culture, he explained, demanded that things be "consumed, burned up, worn out, replaced, and discarded at an ever-increasing rate."

> Increased consumer spending: Credit cards, homeownership, and television

Americans engaged in a prolonged buying spree aided by financing innovations that made it easier to buy things. The first credit card appeared in 1949; by the end of the decade, "buying with plastic" had become the new norm for tens of millions of people. Personal indebtedness doubled during the fifties, in part because people were so confident about their economic future. Frugality became unpatriotic. As television personality Hugh Downs remembered, "Those were exciting days . . . of hope and optimism . . . when the sky was the limit."

A Buying Spree

What most Americans wanted to buy after the Second World War was a new house. In 1945, only 40 percent of Americans owned homes; by 1960, the number had increased to 60 percent. And those new homes featured the latest electrical appliances—refrigerators, dishwashers, washing machines, vacuum cleaners, electric mixers, carving knives, even shoe polishers.

The use of electricity tripled during the decade, in part because of the popularity of television. Watching television quickly displaced listening to the radio or going to the movies as the most popular way to spend free time. Between 1948 and 1952, the number of homes with TV sets jumped from 172,000 to 15.3 million. In 1954, grocery stores began selling frozen "TV

FAMILY, MODIFIED The fantasy of the American family changed with the onslaught of new, affordable products. In this 1959 advertisement for TV dinners, the family eats out of disposable containers in front of the television.

dinners" to be heated and consumed while watching popular shows such as *Father Knows Best*, *I Love Lucy*, and *The Adventures of Ozzie and Harriet*, all of which idealized the child-centered world of suburban white families. The popularity of television provided a formidable medium for advertisers to promote a powerful new phase of the consumer culture that reshaped the contours of postwar life: the nature of work, where people lived and traveled, how they interacted, and what they valued. It also affected class structure, race relations, and gender roles. Jack Metzgar, the son of a Pennsylvania steelworker, remembered that in 1946 "we did not have a car, a television set, or a refrigerator. By 1952, we had all those things."

The GI Bill of Rights

As World War II came to an end, fears that the sudden influx of war veterans into the civilian workforce would disrupt the economy and produce widespread unemployment led Congress to pass the Servicemen's Readjustment Act of 1944, nicknamed the **GI Bill of Rights** (*GI* meaning "government issue," a phrase stamped on military uniforms and equipment that became slang for "serviceman").

Between 1944 and 1956, the GI Bill boosted upward social mobility in postwar America. It included a package of crucial benefits to veterans: unemployment pay for one year, preference to those applying for federal government jobs, loans for home construction or starting a business, access to government hospitals, and generous subsidies for education. Some 5 million veterans bought new homes with the assistance of GI Bill mortgage loans, which required no down payment. Almost 8 million veterans took advantage of $14.5 billion in GI Bill benefits to attend college or enroll in job-training programs. Before the Second World War, approximately 160,000 Americans had graduated from college each year. By 1950, the figure had risen to 500,000. In 1949, veterans accounted for 40 percent of college enrollments, and the United States could boast the world's best-educated workforce, largely because of the GI Bill.

Overall, the GI Bill was one of the most successful federal programs in history. Many African American veterans, however, could not take advantage of its benefits. Most colleges and universities remained racially segregated and refused to admit blacks. Those that enrolled blacks often discriminated against them. African Americans attending white colleges or universities were barred from playing on athletic teams, attending social events, and joining fraternities or sororities. In addition, black veterans could not buy homes in white neighborhoods.

The Suburban Frontier

The second half of the twentieth century witnessed a mass migration to a new frontier—the suburbs. The acute housing shortage after the war (98 percent of cities reported shortages of houses and apartments in 1945) sparked the suburban revolution. Of the 13 million homes built between 1948 and

GI Bill of Rights (1944) Provided unemployment, education, and financial benefits for World War II veterans to ease their transition back to the civilian world.

suburbia Communities formed from mass migration of middle-class whites from urban centers.

Sunbelt migration, suburban development, and the car culture

1958, 11 million were in suburbs. Rural America continued to lose population during the 1950s (and after), as many among the exploding middle-class white population moved to what were called the Sunbelt states—California, Arizona, Florida, Texas, and the southeastern region, where rapid population growth generated an economic boom. As air-conditioning became a common household fixture in the Sunbelt states, it greatly enhanced the appeal of living in warmer climates.

Suburbia met an acute need—affordable housing—and fulfilled a common dream—personal freedom and familial security within commuting distance of cities. In the half century after the Second World War, the suburban good life for middle-class white families included a big home with a big yard on a big lot accessed by a big car—or two. The widespread ownership of cars enabled the suburban revolution during the fifties. During the 1950s, suburbs grew six times as fast as cities, and by 1970 more people lived in suburbs than in cities.

A brassy New York real estate developer, William Levitt, led the suburban revolution. Between 1947 and 1951, on 6,000 acres of Long Island farmland near New York City, he built 17,447 small, look-alike homes (essentially identical in design) to house more than 82,000 people. The planned community, called Levittown, included schools, swimming pools, shopping centers, and playing fields.

LEVITTOWN Identical mass-produced houses in Levittown, New York, and other suburbs across the country provided veterans and their families with affordable homes. **In what ways did Levittown reflect a shift in American culture toward consumerism and conformity?**

Levitt encouraged and even enforced uniformity and conformity in Levittown. The houses all sold for the same price—$6,900, with no down payments for veterans—and featured the same floor plan and accessories. Each had a picture window, a living room, a bathroom, a kitchen, and two bedrooms. Trees were planted every twenty-eight feet in the former potato fields, and homeowners were required to cut their grass once a week.

Levitt soon built three more Levittowns, in Pennsylvania, New Jersey, and Puerto Rico. They and other planned suburban communities benefited greatly from government assistance. Federal and state tax codes favored homeowners over renters, and local governments paid for the infrastructure required by new Levittown-style suburban subdivisions: roads, water and sewer lines, fire and police protection. By insuring loans for up to 95 percent of the value of a house, the

Federal Housing Administration made it easy for builders to construct low-cost homes and for people to buy them.

Levitt and other suburban developers created lily-white communities. Initially, the contracts for houses in Levittown specifically excluded "members of other than the Caucasian race," since Levitt believed that whites would not want to buy a house in Levittown if blacks were living there. As he explained, "We can solve a housing problem or we can try to solve a racial problem. But we can't combine the two."

Suburbia, Levittowns, and racial segregation

A year later, however, the U.S. Supreme Court ruled in *Shelley v. Kraemer* (1948) that such racial restrictions were illegal. The court ruling, however, did not end segregated housing practices; it simply made them more discreet. In 1953, when Levittown, New York's population reached 70,000, it was the largest community in the nation without a single African American resident. Although Jewish himself, Levitt discouraged Jews from living in his communities. "As a Jew," he explained, "I have no room in my heart for racial prejudice. But the plain fact is that most whites prefer not to live in mixed communities. This attitude may be wrong morally, and someday it may change. I hope it will."

Other developers across the country soon mimicked Levitt's efforts, building suburban communities with rustic names such as Lakewood, Streamwood, Elmwood, Cedar Hill, Park Forest, and Deer Park. In 1955, *House and Garden* magazine could declare that suburbia had become the "national way of life."

Minorities on the Move

African Americans were not part of the initial wave of suburban development, but they began moving in large numbers after 1945. The mass migration of rural southern blacks to the urban North, Midwest, and West after the Second World War was much larger than the similar trend after the First World War, and its social consequences were even more dramatic. After 1945, more than 5 million southern blacks formed a new "great migration" out of the South in search of better jobs, higher wages, decent housing, and greater civil rights.

A new "great migration"

By 1960, for the first time in history, more African Americans were living in urban areas than in rural areas. As blacks moved into northern cities, however, many white residents moved to the suburbs, leaving behind racial ghettos. Nine of the nation's ten largest cities lost population to the suburbs during the 1950s. Between 1950 and 1960, some 3.6 million whites left the nation's largest cities for new suburban neighborhoods while 4.5 million blacks moved into those same cities, most of them coming from the rural South.

Deeply entrenched racial attitudes outside the South forced blacks to organize their own efforts to counter the hostility they confronted in communities across the nation. Through organizations such as the National Association for the Advancement of Colored People (NAACP), the Congress

Anti-discrimination legislation in the North

THE SECOND GREAT MIGRATION African American families, such as the New Jersey–bound family pictured here, moved to northern cities in droves following the end of World War II.

of Racial Equality, and the National Urban League, they sought to change the hearts and minds of their white neighbors. However, for all the varied forms of racism that black migrants to the North and West encountered, most of them preferred their new lives to the enforced segregation and often violent racism that they had left behind in the South. Southern blacks still faced voting discrimination and segregation in theaters, parks, schools, colleges, hospitals, buses, cinemas, libraries, restrooms, beaches, bars, and prisons. By the late 1950s, black leaders had convinced most northern states to adopt some form of anti-discrimination legislation.

Hispanic migration to the United States

Just as African Americans were on the move, so, too, were Mexicans and Puerto Ricans. Congress renewed the bracero program, begun during the Second World War, which enabled Mexicans to work as wage laborers in the United States, often as migrant workers moving from farm to farm as needed for the planting and harvest seasons. Mexicans streamed across the nation's southwest border, and by 1960 Los Angeles had the largest concentration of Mexican Americans in the nation.

Like African Americans who served in the war, Mexican Americans, Puerto Ricans, and other Hispanic/Latino minorities benefited, in theory at least, from the GI Bill. Between 1940 and 1960, nearly a million Puerto

Ricans, mostly small farmers and agricultural workers, moved into mainland American cities, especially New York City. In fact, by the late 1960s more Puerto Ricans lived in New York City than in San Juan, the capital of Puerto Rico. The popular Broadway musical drama *West Side Story* (1957) high-lighted the tensions generated by the influx of Puerto Ricans into tradition-ally white neighborhoods.

Shifting Women's Roles

During the Second World War, millions of women had responded to patriotic appeals and assumed traditionally male jobs in factories and mills to help the war effort. After the war, those same women were encouraged to return to their traditional roles as loving wives, caring mothers, and happy homemak-ers. A 1945 article in *House Beautiful* magazine lectured women on their domestic duties. The returning war veteran, it said, was "head man again. . . . Your part in the remaking of this man is to fit his home to him, understand-ing why he wants it this way, forgetting your own preferences."

Advertisements in popular magazines often targeted middle-class women, depicting them happily bound to the house, at work in the kitchen in dresses adorned with jewelry (usually pearl necklaces) and high heels, con-versing with children, serving dinner, cleaning, and otherwise displaying the joy of a clean home or the latest kitchen appliance. The prevailing images of middle-class life in the fifties featured tree-lined suburban streets, kids

"The happy homemaker"

HOLLYWOOD HOMEMAKERS TV shows and films were outlets for homemakers' anxieties and fantasies. Top: *Leave it to Beaver* (1957) was a popular comedy about a young boy and his happy-go-lucky family living in suburban America. Bottom: Domestic bliss was never in reach for African American characters. In *Porgy and Bess* (1959), Dorothy Dandridge plays an addict so lost in the vice of New Orleans that even her self-sacrificing disabled lover (Sidney Poitier) cannot save her.

riding their bikes through beautiful neighborhoods, and women as devoted servants to their husbands.

During the fifties, the U.S. marriage rate reached an all-time high, and the average age of marriage for women plummeted to nineteen. There was enormous social pressure on teenage girls to get married quickly; if a woman wasn't engaged or married by her early twenties, she was in danger of becoming an "old maid." Getting married during high school or while in college became the norm. In 1956, one-fourth of all white college women wed while still enrolled in school, and most dropped out before receiving a degree. A common joke of the time was that women went to college to get an "M.R.S. degree"—that is, a husband.

Despite this modern version of the nineteenth century's "cult of domesticity," in which women's roles were largely confined to the home and family duties, many women did work outside the home during the fifties, usually out of necessity. In 1950, women made up 29 percent of the workforce, and that percentage rose steadily throughout the decade. Some 70 percent of employed women worked in clerical positions—secretaries, bank tellers, or sales clerks—or on assembly lines in factories or in the service industry (as waitresses, laundresses, maids, etc.).

The Child-Centered Fifties

The fifties witnessed a record number of marriages—and births. The decade was an ideal time to be a child. The horrors of the Second World War were over, the economy was surging, and social life became centered on the needs of children—because there were so many of them. Between 1946 and 1964, the birth of 76 million Americans reversed a century-long decline in the nation's birth rate and created a demographic upheaval whose repercussions are still being felt.

The "**baby boom**" peaked in 1957, when a record 4.3 million births occurred, one every seven seconds. Most brides during the fifties were pregnant within seven months of their wedding, and they didn't stop at just one child. Large families were typical. From 1940 to 1960, the number of families with three children doubled and the number of families having a fourth child quadrupled. Dr. Benjamin Spock's *The Common Sense Book of Baby and Child Care* sold more than a million copies a year during the fifties.

> Demands of a "baby boom"

The unusually large baby boom generation has since shaped social history and economic development. Postwar babies initially created a surge in demand for diapers, washing machines, and baby food, then required the construction of thousands of new schools—and the hiring of teachers to staff them.

As the so-called baby boomers became children and then adolescents, their needs drove much of the economy's growth, creating a huge market for toys, candy, gum, records, clothes, and other items. The powerful forces promoting conformity in American social life during the cold war influenced the role of women.

baby boom Markedly high birth rate in the years following World War II, leading to the biggest demographic "bubble" in U.S. history.

A special issue of *Life* magazine in 1956 featured the "ideal" middle-class woman: a thirty-two-year-old "pretty and popular" white suburban housewife, mother of four, who had married at age sixteen. She was described as an excellent wife, mother, volunteer, and "home manager" who preferred marriage and child rearing to a career outside the home. She made her own clothes, hosted dozens of dinner parties each year, sang in her church choir, and was devoted to her husband. "In her daily round," *Life* reported, "she attends club or charity meetings, drives the children to school, does the weekly grocery shopping, makes ceramics, and is planning to study French." The soaring birth rate reinforced the deeply embedded notion that a woman's place was in the home. "Of all the accomplishments of the American woman," the *Life* cover story proclaimed, "the one she brings off with the most spectacular success is having babies."

A Religious Nation

After the Second World War, Americans, unlike Europeans, joined churches and synagogues in record numbers. In 1940, less than half the adult population belonged to a church; by 1960, over 65 percent were members of churches or synagogues. Sales of Bibles soared, as did the demand for books, movies, and songs with religious themes. The cold war provided a direct stimulant to Christian evangelism. Communism, explained the Reverend Billy Graham, the most famous evangelist of the fifties, was "a great sinister anti-Christian movement masterminded by Satan" that must be fought wherever it emerged around the world.

President Eisenhower promoted a patriotic religious crusade during the fifties. "Recognition of the Supreme Being," he declared, "is the first, the most basic, expression of Americanism. Without God, there could be no American form of government, nor an American way of life." In 1954, Congress added the phrase "one nation under God" to the Pledge of Allegiance and in 1956 made the statement "In God We Trust" the nation's official motto. Eisenhower ordered that the motto be displayed on all currency. A godly nation, it was widely assumed, would better withstand the march of "godless" communism.

The prevailing tone of the popular religious revival of the 1950s was upbeat and soothing. As the Protestant Council of New York City explained to its radio and television presenters, their on-air broadcasts "should project love, joy, courage, hope, faith, trust in God, goodwill. Generally avoid condemnation, criticism, controversy. In a very real sense we are 'selling' religion, the good news of the Gospel."

ROADSIDE SERVICE Drive-in churches offered its members the comfort of listening to Sunday Mass from their cars. Here, the pastor of New York's Tremont Methodist Church greets a member of his car-centered congregation.

CORE **OBJECTIVE**

3. Examine the criticism of postwar American society and culture, and describe the various forms of dissent and anxiety.

Cracks in the Picture Window

In contrast to the "happy days" image of the fifties, there was growing anxiety, dissent, and diversity. In *The Affluent Society* (1958), for example, economist John Kenneth Galbraith attacked the prevailing notion that sustained economic growth was solving chronic social problems. He reminded readers that despite America's vaunted prosperity, the nation had yet to eradicate poverty, especially among minorities in inner cities; female-led households; Mexican American migrant farmworkers; Native Americans; and rural southerners, both black and white.

Poverty amid Prosperity

Chronic poverty; income gap widens between whites and minorities

Uncritical praise for the "throwaway" culture of consumption during the 1950s masked the chronic poverty amid America's much-celebrated plenty. In 1959, a quarter of the population had *no* financial assets, and more than half had no savings accounts or credit cards. Poverty afflicted nearly half the African American population, compared to only a quarter of whites. True, by 1950, blacks were earning on average more than four times their 1940 wages. But African Americans and members of other minority groups lagged well behind whites in their *rate* of improvement, and the gap between the average yearly income of whites and minorities widened. At least 40 million people remained "poor" during the 1950s, but their plight was largely ignored amid the wave of middle-class white consumerism.

Literature

Many social critics, writers, and artists rejected America's worship of consumerism during the fifties. One of the most striking aspects of the decade was the sharp contrast between the happy public mood and the increasingly bitter social criticism coming from intellectuals, theologians, novelists, playwrights, poets, and artists. A growing number of writers and artists questioned the prevailing complacency about the goodness and superiority of the American way of life. Writer Norman Mailer, for instance, said the 1950s was "one of the worst decades in the history of man."

Mailer was one of many social critics who challenged what they viewed as the decade's moral complacency and bland conformity. Despite America's mythic devotion to rugged individualism, the nation during the cold war celebrated conformity. As novelist John Updike observed, he and other writers felt estranged "from a government that extolled business and mediocrity." The most

RALPH ELLISON Best remembered for his 1952 novel, *Invisible Man*, Ellison's writings were critical of the social and cultural changes sweeping through post-war America.

enduring novels of the postwar period emphasized the individual's struggle for survival amid the smothering forces of mass society. The characters in books such as James Jones's *From Here to Eternity* (1951), Ralph Ellison's *Invisible Man* (1952), Saul Bellow's *Seize the Day* (1956), J. D. Salinger's *Catcher in the Rye* (1951), William Styron's *Lie Down in Darkness* (1951), and Updike's *Rabbit, Run* (1961) are restless, tormented souls who can find neither contentment nor respect in an uninterested world.

The upper-middle-class white suburbs and the culture of comfortable conformity they created were frequent literary targets during the fifties. Writer John Cheever located most of his often brilliant short stories in suburban neighborhoods outside of New York City—"cesspools of conformity," where life was mindless and hollow. The typical suburban dweller, as one critic charged in 1956, did everything like the neighbors: "buys the right car, keeps his lawn like his neighbor's, eats crunchy breakfast cereal, and votes Republican."

> **Beats** Group of bohemian writers, artists, and musicians who flouted convention in favor of liberated forms of self-expression.

> Social criticism: Complacency and conformity in the suburbs

The Beats

A small but highly visible and controversial group of young writers, poets, painters, and musicians rejected the materialism of the consumer culture as well as the traditional expectations and responsibilities of middle-class life. They were known as the **Beats**, a term with multiple meanings: to be "beat" was likened to being "upbeat" and even "beatific," as well as being "on the beat" in "real cool" jazz music. But the rebellious Beats also liked the name because it implied "weariness," being "exhausted" or "beaten down," qualities that none of them actually exhibited.

Jack Kerouac, Allen Ginsberg, William Burroughs, Neal Cassady, Gary Snyder, and other Beats were cultural outlaws who rebelled against conventional literary and artistic expression and excelled at outrageous behavior. Intensely self-absorbed, they celebrated, even embodied, lives of breathtaking risk and originality, fueled by spontaneity and energy. They pursued rebellious and reckless lives of alcohol- and drug-induced ecstasies and sexual excesses (many of them were gay or bisexual during an era when homosexuality was considered a form of deviance requiring psychotherapy). The mostly male Beats viewed women as second-class accessories; Carolyn Cassady said her husband Neal's approach to making love was "rape." She added that Neal and the "boys didn't know where they were going. . . . They just knew they wanted to *go*."

ART ACHE The Beat community fostered in its members a frenzied desire to create. In this 1959 photograph, poet Tex Kleen reads in a bathtub at Venice Beach, California, while artist Mad Mike paints trash cans. **How did the Beat movement relate to the mainstream push toward cultural conformity?**

The Beats (bohemians) reject middle-class values

The Beat hipsters grew out of the bohemian underground in New York City's Greenwich Village and in San Francisco. Undisciplined and often unkempt, they were essentially apolitical, more interested in transforming themselves than in reforming the world. They sought personal rather than social solutions to their needs and anxieties; they wanted their art and literature to change consciousness rather than address social ills.

As Kerouac insisted in his remarkable novel *On the Road* (1957), the first draft of which he typed almost nonstop during three feverish weeks, his rootless, reckless friends were not beat in the sense of beaten down; they were "mad to live, mad to talk, mad to be saved, desirous of everything at the same time, the ones who never yawn or say a commonplace thing, but burn, burn, burn like fabulous yellow roman candles exploding like spiders across the stars."

The Beats nursed an urge to "go, go, go" and not stop until they got there, wherever "there" might be. Their road to salvation lay in hallucinogenic drugs and lots of alcohol, casual sex, petty crime, gratuitous violence, a passion for up-tempo jazz ("bebop"), fast cars, the street life of urban ghettos, an affinity for Buddhism, and a restless, vagabond spirit that took them racing back and forth across the country between San Francisco and New York. At heart, the Beats were romantics searching for an authentic sense of self in a nation absorbed in consumerism, conformism, and anti-communism. The tortured rebelliousness of the Beats set the stage for the more widespread youth revolt of the 1960s.

Rock 'n' Roll

The millions of children making up the first wave of the baby boomers born during and just after the Second World War became adolescents in the 1950s. A distinctive teen subculture began to emerge, and a wave of juvenile delinquency swept across middle-class society. By 1956, over a million teens were being arrested each year. One contributing factor was access to automobiles, which enabled teens to escape parental control and, in the words of one journalist, provided "a private lounge for drinking and for petting [embracing and kissing] or sex episodes."

Many concerned observers blamed teen delinquency on rock 'n' roll, a new form of music that emerged during the 1950s. Alan Freed, a Cleveland disc jockey, coined the term rock 'n' roll in 1951. He had noticed that white teenagers buying rhythm and blues (R&B) records preferred the livelier recordings by African Americans and Hispanic Americans. Freed began playing R&B records on his radio show, but he called the music "rock 'n' roll" (a phrase used in African American communities to refer to dancing and sex). Freed's popular program helped bridge the gap between "white" and "black" music. African American singers such as Chuck Berry, Little Richard, and Ray Charles, as well as Hispanic American performers such as

Ritchie Valens (Richard Valenzuela), captivated young, white, middle-class audiences eager to claim their own cultural style.

At the same time, Elvis Presley, the lanky son of a poor Mississippi farm family who moved to a public housing project in Memphis, Tennessee, began experimenting with "rockabilly" music, a unique blend of gospel, country-and-western, and R&B. At the same time, Sam Phillips, a local radio disc jockey, was searching for a particular type of pop singer. "If I could find a white man with a Negro sound," Phillips said, "I could make a billion dollars."

Then he found Elvis. In 1956, the twenty-one-year-old Presley, by then a regional star famous for his long, unruly hair, his sensual sneer, and his wildly swiveling hips, released his smash-hit recording "Heartbreak Hotel." Over the next two years, he emerged as the most popular musician in American history. Presley's gyrating, sensual stage performances (his nickname was "Elvis the Pelvis") and his incomparably rich and raw baritone voice drove teenagers (a word that came into use during the fifties) wild and earned him millions of fans around the world. His movements, said one music critic, "suggest, in a word, sex."

ELVIS PRESLEY Hysterical girls grab at him from all angles, but the "King of Rock and Roll" stays cool, crooning into the camera while performing in Miami, 1956.

Cultural conservatives were outraged by Presley's antics. Critics urged parents to destroy his records because they promoted "a pagan concept of life." A Roman Catholic official denounced Presley as a vile symptom of a teenage "creed of dishonesty, violence, lust and degeneration." Patriotic groups claimed that rock 'n' roll music was part of a Communist plot to corrupt America's youth. Writing in the *New York Times*, a psychiatrist characterized rock 'n' roll as a "communicable disease." A U.S. Senate subcommittee investigating juvenile delinquency warned that Elvis was threatening "to rock-n-roll the juvenile world into open revolt against society. The gangster of tomorrow is the Elvis Presley type of today."

Yet rock 'n' roll flourished amid such opposition, in part because it was so controversial. It gave teenagers a self-conscious sense of belonging to a tribal social group. More important, it brought together, on equal terms, musicians (and their audiences) of varied races and backgrounds. In doing so, it helped dispel the racial prejudices that conflicted with the nation's ideals.

CORE **OBJECTIVE**
4. Evaluate the goals, strategies, and impact of the civil rights movement that emerged in the 1950s.

The Early Years of the Civil Rights Movement

Soon after the cold war began, Soviet diplomats began to use America's racial discrimination against African Americans as a propaganda tool to illustrate the supposed defects of the American way of life. Under the Jim Crow system in the southern states, blacks still risked being lynched if they registered to vote. They were forced to use separate facilities in public—water fountains, restrooms, hotels, theaters, parks—and to attend segregated schools. In the North, discrimination was not as "official," but it was equally real, especially in housing and employment. During the mid-1950s, the ongoing tragedy of race relations in the United States offered President Eisenhower an opportunity to exercise transformational leadership; his unwillingness to do so was his greatest failure. As *Time* magazine noted in 1958, Eisenhower "overlooked the fact that the U.S. needed [his] moral leadership in fighting segregation."

Eisenhower and Race

Eisenhower had entered the White House committed to civil rights in principle, and he pushed for improvements in some areas. During his first three years as president, for example, public facilities (parks, playgrounds, libraries, restaurants) in Washington, D.C., were desegregated, and he intervened to end discrimination at military bases in Virginia and South Carolina. Beyond that, however, Eisenhower refused to make civil rights for African Americans a moral crusade. Pushing too hard against segregation in the South, he believed, would "raise tempers and increase prejudices," doing more harm than good.

Eisenhower's civil rights record

Two aspects of Eisenhower's political philosophy limited his commitment to racial equality: his preference for state or local action over federal involvement and his doubt that laws could change attitudes. "I don't believe you can change the hearts of men with laws or decisions," he insisted. His passive attitude toward racial issues meant that governmental leadership on civil rights would come from the judiciary more than from the executive or legislative branch.

In 1953, Eisenhower appointed former Republican governor Earl Warren of California as chief justice of the U.S. Supreme Court, a decision he later said was the "biggest damn fool mistake I ever made." Warren, who had seemed safely conservative while in elected office, displayed a social conscience and a streak of libertarianism that was shared by another Eisenhower appointee to the Court, William J. Brennan Jr. Under Warren's leadership (1953–1969), the Supreme Court became one of the most powerful forces for social and political change through the 1960s.

FOUNTAINS OF TRUTH An Alabama day-hotel offers its white clientele chilled water from a cooler, while its African American guests must use a rudimentary drinking fountain.

African American Activism

However, the most crucial leaders of the civil rights movement came from the long-suffering people whose rights were most often violated: African Americans, Hispanic Americans, Asian Americans, and other minorities. Rural and urban, young and old, male and female, courageous blacks led what would become the most important social movement in twentieth-century American history. With brilliance, bravery, and dignity, they fought on all fronts—in the courts, at the ballot box, and in the streets—against the deeply entrenched system of racial segregation and discrimination. Although many African Americans moved to the North and West during and after the Second World War, a majority remained in the South, where they had to attend segregated public schools, accept the least desirable jobs, and operate within a rigidly segregated society that restricted their civil rights. In the 1952 presidential election, for example, only 20 percent of eligible African Americans were registered to vote.

In the mid-1930s, the National Association for the Advancement of Colored People (NAACP) challenged the "**separate but equal**" judicial doctrine that had upheld racial segregation since the *Plessy* decision by the Supreme Court in 1896. Yet it took almost fifteen years to convince the

NAACP's legal efforts

separate-but-equal Principle that formed the basis for legal racial segregation.

courts that racial segregation must end. Finally, in *Sweatt v. Painter* (1950), the Supreme Court ruled that a separate black law school in Texas was *not* equal in quality to the state's whites-only schools. The Court ordered the state to remedy the situation. It was the first step toward dismantling America's tradition of racial segregation.

The Brown Decision

Brown v. Board of Education: The separate-but-equal doctrine overturned

By the early 1950s, challenges to state laws mandating racial segregation in the public schools were rising through the court system. Five such cases, from Kansas, Delaware, South Carolina, Virginia, and the District of Columbia—usually cited by reference to the first, **Brown v. Board of Education** *of Topeka, Kansas*—came to the Supreme Court for joint argument by NAACP attorneys in 1952. President Eisenhower told the attorney general that he hoped the justices would postpone dealing with the explosive case "until the next Administration took over." When it became obvious that the Court was moving forward, Eisenhower invited Earl Warren to a White House dinner during which he urged the chief justice to side with segregationists. Warren was not swayed: "You mind your business," he told the president, "and I'll mind mine."

Brown v. Board of Education (1954) Landmark Supreme Court case that struck down racial segregation in public schools and declared "separate-but-equal" unconstitutional.

Warren himself wrote the pathbreaking opinion, handed down on May 17, 1954, in which a unanimous Court declared that "in the field of public education the doctrine of 'separate but equal' has no place." In support of its opinion, the Court cited sociological and psychological findings demonstrating that even if racially separate schools were equal in quality, the very practice of separating students by race caused feelings of inferiority among black children. A year later, the Court directed that the process of racial *integration* should move "with all deliberate speed."

Eisenhower refused to endorse or enforce the Court's ruling. Privately, he grumbled "that the Supreme Court decision set back progress in the South at least fifteen years." Anyone who thinks "you can do these things by force is just plain nuts," he said. While token racial integration began as early as 1954 in Kentucky and Missouri, hostility mounted in the Lower South and Virginia. The Alabama State Senate and the Virginia legislature both passed resolutions "nullifying" the Supreme Court's decision.

SEPARATE, BUT NOT EQUAL African American children pose outside their segregated schoolhouse in Selma, Alabama, in 1965.

Opponents of court-ordered integration of schools and other public places were defiant. In 1956, 101 members of Congress signed a Declaration of Constitutional Principles ("Southern Manifesto") denouncing the Supreme Court's decision in the *Brown* case as "a clear abuse of judicial power" that had created an "explosive and dangerous condition" in the South. Only three southern Democrats in Congress refused to sign. One of them, Senator Lyndon B. Johnson of Texas, would become president seven years later. In six southern states at the end of 1956, two years after the *Brown* ruling, not a single black child attended school with whites.

The Montgomery Bus Boycott

The *Brown* case did much more than mobilize white resistance in the South. It inspired many blacks (and white activists) by suggesting that the federal government was finally beginning to confront racial discrimination. Yet the essential role played by the NAACP and the courts in providing a legal lever for the civil rights movement often overshadows the courageous contributions of individual African Americans who took great personal risks to challenge segregation in their communities.

For example, in Montgomery, Alabama, on December 1, 1955, Mrs. Rosa Parks, a forty-two-year-old black seamstress, civil rights activist, and secretary of the local NAACP chapter, refused to give up her seat on a city bus to a white man. Like many southern communities, Montgomery, the "Cradle of the Confederacy," required blacks to sit in the rear seats of buses or trains. They could sit in the front seats designated for whites only if there were empty seats. If a white rider asked for a black to move, they were expected to go "to the back of the bus."

Parks, however, was "tired of giving in" to the humiliating practice. When the bus driver told her that "niggers must move back" or he would have her arrested, she replied, with quiet courage and fierce determination, "You may do that." Police then arrested her. The next night, black community leaders met in the Dexter Avenue Baptist Church to organize a long-planned boycott of the city's bus system, 75 percent of whose riders were African Americans. Student and faculty volunteers from Alabama State University stayed up all night to distribute 35,000 flyers denouncing the arrest of Rosa Parks and urging support for the **Montgomery bus boycott**.

In the Dexter Avenue church's twenty-six-year-old pastor, Martin Luther King Jr., the boycott movement found a brave and charismatic leader. Born in Atlanta, the grandson of a slave and son of a prominent minister, the short, stocky King was intelligent and courageous. He also was an eloquent and passionate speaker. "We must use the weapon of love," King told his supporters. "We must realize so many people are taught to hate us that they are not totally responsible for their hate." To his foes, the self-controlled King warned, "We will soon wear you down by our capacity to suffer, and in winning our freedom we will so appeal to your heart and conscience that we will

Montgomery bus boycott Boycott of bus system in Montgomery, Alabama, organized by civil rights activists after the arrest of Rosa Parks in 1955.

NONVIOLENT CIVIL DISOBEDIENCE Left: Rosa Parks is fingerprinted by a Montgomery policeman on February 22, 1956, along with about 100 others who joined the bus boycott. Right: Martin Luther King, Jr. is roughly arrested for loitering in 1958. He would be arrested thirty times in his life for defying racist laws.

win you in the process." King preached **nonviolent civil disobedience**, the tactic of defying unjust laws through peaceful actions, but he also valued militancy, for without confrontation with those in power there would be no negotiation or progress.

The Montgomery bus boycott achieved remarkable unity. For 381 days, African Americans, women and men, used carpools, called black-owned taxis; hitchhiked; or simply walked. White supporters also provided rides. A few boycotters rode horses or mules to work. The unprecedented mass protest infuriated many whites; police harassed and ticketed black carpools, and white thugs attacked black pedestrians. Ku Klux Klan members burned black churches and bombed houses owned by King and other boycott leaders. King himself was arrested twice. In trying to calm an angry black crowd eager for revenge against their white tormentors, he urged restraint: "Don't get panicky. Don't get your weapons. We want to love our enemies."

On December 20, 1956, the Montgomery boycotters won a federal case they had initiated against racial segregation on public buses. The Supreme Court affirmed that "the separate but equal doctrine can no longer be safely followed as a correct statement of the law." The next day, King and other African Americans boarded the buses. The success of the boycott showed that well-coordinated, nonviolent black activism could trigger major changes in public policy. Among African Americans, hope replaced resignation during the bus boycott, and action supplanted passivity. The boycott also catapulted

nonviolent civil disobedience
Tactic of defying unjust laws through peaceful actions championed by Dr. Martin Luther King Jr.

King into the national spotlight. And what of Rosa Parks? She and her husband lost their jobs, and hate mail as well as death threats forced them to leave Alabama. They moved to Detroit, where they remained fully engaged in the evolving civil rights movement.

The Civil Rights Acts of 1957 and 1960

President Eisenhower's timidity in the field of race relations emerged again when he was asked to protect the right of African Americans to vote. In 1956, hoping to exploit divisions between northern and southern Democrats and to reclaim some of the black vote for Republicans, congressional leaders agreed to support what became the Civil Rights Act of 1957. The first civil rights law passed since 1875, it finally got through the Senate, after a year's delay, with the help of majority leader Lyndon B. Johnson, a Texas Democrat who knew that he could never be elected president if he was viewed as just another racist white southerner. The bill was intended to ensure that all Americans, regardless of their race or ethnicity, were allowed to vote. Although Johnson believed that the civil rights bill was just and necessary, he won southern acceptance of the bill by watering down its enforcement provisions. Eisenhower assured Johnson that the final version represented "the mildest civil rights bill possible."

The Civil Rights Act established the Civil Rights Commission and a new Civil Rights Division in the Justice Department intended to prevent interference with the right to vote. Yet by 1959, the Civil Rights Act had not resulted in a single southern black voter being added to the rolls. Neither did the Civil Rights Act of 1960, which provided for federal courts to register African Americans to vote in districts around the country where there was a "pattern and practice" of racial discrimination. This bill, too, lacked teeth and depended upon vigorous presidential enforcement to achieve any tangible results.

Desegregation in Little Rock

A few weeks after the Civil Rights Act of 1957 was passed, Arkansas's Democratic governor, Orval Faubus, a rabid segregationist eager to win a third term, called out the state's National Guard to prevent nine black students from entering Little Rock's Central High School under a federal court order. The National Guard commander's orders were explicit: "No niggers in the building."

> Eisenhower sends federal troops to Little Rock

When one of the students, fifteen-year-old Elizabeth Eckford, tried to enter the school, a surging mob of jeering whites shrieked, "Lynch her! Lynch her!" Local authorities removed the students from the school in an effort to protect them, and the mayor frantically called the White House to request federal troops to stop the violence.

At that point, President Eisenhower reluctantly dispatched a thousand army paratroopers to Little Rock to protect the brave black students as they entered the school. It was the first time since the 1870s that federal troops

"LYNCH HER!" Fifteen-year-old Elizabeth Eckford endures the hostile screams of future classmates as she enters Central High School in Little Rock.

had been sent to the South to protect the rights of African Americans. Dunbar Ogden, a Presbyterian minister in Little Rock, found a ray of hope in the ugly confrontation: "This may be looked back upon by future historians as the turning point—for good—of race relations in this country."

The soldiers stayed in Little Rock through the school year. Unyielding southern segregationists lashed out at the president, charging that Eisenhower was violating states' rights. In 1954, Virginia senator and former governor Harry F. Byrd had supplied a rallying cry for white diehards when he called for "**massive resistance**" against federal efforts to enforce integration in the South.

Eisenhower denied that he was making any moral judgment about the situation in Little Rock. His use of federal troops had little to do with "the integration or segregation question" and everything to do with maintaining law and order. Although Eisenhower favored equality of opportunity, he privately retained the racial prejudice of his generation. Equality, he explained to an aide, did not mean "that a Negro should court my daughter."

Martin Luther King Jr. forced Eisenhower out of his comfort zone. He had earlier criticized Eisenhower's tepid support of civil rights; now he told the president that the "overwhelming majority of southerners, Negro and white, stand behind your resolute action to restore law and order in Little Rock." Southern politicians had a different view. Many called for the president's impeachment and removal.

In the summer of 1958, Governor Faubus, supported by the state legislature, closed the Little Rock high schools rather than allow racial integration. The governor of Virginia did the same in his state. Their actions led Jonathan Daniels, editor of the Raleigh, North Carolina, *News & Observer*, to write that closing public schools in order to avoid integration is "something beyond secession from the Union; [it] is secession from civilization."

Court proceedings in Arkansas dragged into 1959 before the schools reopened. Resistance to integration in Virginia collapsed when both state and federal courts struck down state laws that had cut off funds to integrated public schools. Thereafter, massive resistance to racial integration occurred mostly in the Lower South, where five states—from South Carolina westward through Louisiana—still opposed even token integration. Not a single pupil in those states attended an integrated school. Faubus, who continued to spew his racist hate, went on to serve six terms as governor of Arkansas.

massive resistance White rallying cry for disrupting federal efforts to enforce racial integration in the South.

Southern Christian Leadership Conference

After the confrontation at Little Rock, progress toward greater civil rights seemed agonizingly slow. Frustrated African Americans began blaming the NAACP for relying too much on the courts to end segregation. "The Negro masses are angry and restless, tired of prolonged legal battles that end in paper decrees," reported black journalist Louis Lomax. "The organizations that understand this unrest and rise to lead it will survive; those that do not will perish."

The widespread sense of disappointment after the Little Rock incident gave Martin Luther King's nonviolent civil rights movement even greater visibility. As King explained, "We were confronted with blasted hopes, and the dark shadow of a deep disappointment settled upon us. So we had no alternative except that of preparing for direct action, whereby we would present our very bodies as a means of laying our case before the conscience of the local and national community."

On January 10, 1957, following the Montgomery bus boycott victory, Dr. King invited about sixty black ministers and leaders to Ebenezer Church in Atlanta. Their goal was to form an organization to coordinate and support nonviolent direct action as a method of desegregating bus systems across the South. Influential African American civil rights activists Ella Baker and Bayard Rustin, the Reverend Fred Shuttlesworth of Birmingham, the Reverend Joseph Lowery of Mobile, the Reverend Ralph Abernathy of Montgomery, and the Reverend C. K. Steele of Tallahassee all played key roles in this meeting.

On February 15, a follow-up meeting convened in New Orleans. Out of these two meetings came a new organization called the **Southern Christian Leadership Conference (SCLC)**, with Dr. King as its president. Unlike the NAACP, which recruited individual members, SCLC coordinated activities on behalf of a cluster of organizations, mostly individual churches or community groups such as the Montgomery Improvement Association. Because Dr. King pushed SCLC and its member churches to take direct action against the segregated white South, only a few African American ministers were initially willing to affiliate with SCLC, for fear of a white backlash.

King persisted, however, and over time SCLC grew into a powerful organization at the center of the growing civil rights movement. The civil rights activists knew that violence awaited them. Roy Wilkins, the head of the NAACP, noted that "the Negro citizen has come to the point where he is not afraid of violence. He no longer shrinks back. He will assert himself, and if violence comes, so be it."

Thus began the second phase of the civil rights movement, a phase that would come to fruition in the 1960s as King and other African American activists showed the nation the courage to resist injustice, the power to love everyone, and the strength to endure discouragement and opposition. And they did so without the support of President Eisenhower. As the

Southern Christian Leadership Conference (SCLC) Civil rights organization formed by Dr. Martin Luther King Jr. that championed nonviolent direct action as a means of ending segregation.

NAACP chief Roy Wilkins asserted: "President Eisenhower was a fine general and a good, decent man, but if he had fought World War II the way he fought for civil rights, we would all be speaking German today."

CORE **OBJECTIVE**

5. Assess President Eisenhower's priorities in conducting the nation's foreign policy and his influence on global affairs.

Foreign Policy in the 1950s

The Truman administration's commitment to "contain" communism had focused on the Soviet threat to Western Europe. During the 1950s, the Eisenhower administration, especially Secretary of State John Foster Dulles, expanded America's objective in the cold war. "Containment" was no longer enough; communism must be "rolled back" around the world. The Eisenhower administration soon discovered, however, that the complexities of world affairs and the realities of Soviet and Communist Chinese power made the commitment to manage the destiny of the world unrealistic—and costly.

Concluding an Armistice

A truce in Korea (1953)

To break the stalemate in the Korean peace talks, Eisenhower took the bold step in mid-May 1953 of intensifying the aerial bombardment of North Korea. The president let it be known that he would use nuclear weapons if a truce were not forthcoming. Thereafter, negotiations moved quickly toward a cease-fire agreement (called an armistice) on July 26, 1953, affirming the established border between the two Koreas just above the 38th parallel. Other factors in bringing about the armistice were China's rising military losses in the conflict and the spirit of uncertainty and caution felt by the Soviet Communists after the death of Joseph Stalin on March 5, 1953, six weeks after Eisenhower's inauguration.

Dulles and Massive Retaliation

The architect of the Eisenhower administration's efforts to "roll back" communism was Secretary of State John Foster Dulles. Like Woodrow Wilson, Dulles was a minister's son, a self-righteous statesman with immense energy and intelligence who believed that the United States was "born with a sense of destiny and mission" to lead the world. His British counterparts, however, were not impressed with his sermonizing speeches, calling them "dull, duller, Dulles."

Dulles insisted that the Democratic policy of "containing" communism was "immoral" because it did nothing to free people from oppression. America, he argued, should instead work toward the "liberation" of the "captive peoples" of Eastern Europe and China. When George F. Kennan, the leading Soviet analyst in the State Department who had first suggested the containment doctrine, dismissed such hollow rhetoric as lunacy, Dulles fired him. For his part, Eisenhower was quick to explain that the "liberation" doctrine would not involve military force. He would promote the removal of Communist control "by every peaceful means, but only by peaceful means."

Dulles and Eisenhower knew that the United States could not win a ground war against the Soviet Union or Communist China, both of whose armies had millions more soldiers than the United States. Nor could the administration afford—politically or financially—to sustain military expenditures at the levels required during the Korean War. So in an effort to get "more bang for the buck," Dulles and Eisenhower crafted a new military strategy growing out of the Korean experience. It came to be called "**massive retaliation**," which meant using the threat of nuclear warfare ("massive retaliatory power") to prevent Communist aggression. The massive retaliation strategy, Eisenhower, Dulles, and the military chiefs argued, would provide a "maximum deterrent at bearable cost."

The strategy of threatening "massive retaliation" had major weaknesses, however. By the mid-1950s, both the United States and the Soviet Union had developed hydrogen bombs, which were 750 times as powerful as the atomic bombs dropped on Japan in 1945. The use of a single hydrogen bomb would have a devastating global impact, yet war planners envisioned using hundreds of them. "The necessary art," Dulles explained, was in the brinksmanship, "the ability to get to the verge without getting into war.... If you are scared to go to the brink, you are lost." Yet the massive retaliation strategy meant that it escalated every global dispute into a possible war of annihilation.

"DON'T BE AFRAID – I CAN ALWAYS PULL YOU BACK" In this political cartoon, Secretary of State John Foster Dulles pushes a reluctant America to the brink of war. **Why might the cartoonist have portrayed Dulles as a small, round Superman?**

The CIA and Foreign Interventions

At the same time that Eisenhower and Dulles were publicly promoting the "liberation" of Communist nations in Europe and Asia and "massive retaliation" as a strategy against the Soviets, they were secretly using the new **Central Intelligence Agency (CIA)** to influence world politics.

The anti-colonial independence movements unleashed by the Second World War placed the United States in the awkward position of watching nationalist groups around the globe revolt against British and French rule. In Iran in May 1951, the parliament seized control of the nation's British-run oil industry. The following year, a newly elected prime minister, European-educated Mohammed Mossadegh, an elderly attorney, cut all diplomatic ties with Great Britain.

Secretary of State John Foster Dulles decided that Mossadegh was a "madman" who had to go in order to safeguard the Persian Gulf for oil exports and prevent a Communist takeover. The CIA and the British intelligence service, MI6, then launched "Operation Ajax," designed, in the words of the agency's head, Allen Dulles (the secretary of state's brother), to "bring

CIA intervention in the Middle East and Latin America

massive retaliation Strategy that used the threat of nuclear warfare as a means of combating the global spread of communism.

Central Intelligence Agency (CIA) Intelligence-gathering government agency founded in 1947; under President Eisenhower's orders, it secretly undermined elected governments deemed susceptible to communism.

about the fall of Mossadegh." The man who planned the coup was Kermit Roosevelt, the Middle East expert at the CIA and the grandson of Theodore Roosevelt.

The CIA bribed Iranian army officers with hundreds of thousands of dollars and hired Iranian agents to arrest Mossadegh, who was then convicted of high treason. Thereafter, in return for access to Iranian oil, the U.S. government provided massive support for the anti-Communist and increasingly authoritarian regime of the shah (king) of Iran, Mohammad Reza Pahlavi, who seized power after the removal of Mossadegh. The Iranians did not forget that the Americans had put the hated shah in power. Nearly a half century later, in 2000, Secretary of State Madeleine Albright recognized how easy it was to see "why many Iranians continue to resent the intervention by America in their internal affairs."

The success of the CIA-engineered coup in Iran emboldened Eisenhower to authorize other secret operations to undermine "unfriendly" government regimes. In 1954, the target was Guatemala, a desperately poor Central American country led by Colonel Jacobo Arbenz Guzman. Arbenz's decision to take over U.S.-owned property and industries in Guatemala convinced John Foster Dulles that Guatemala was falling victim to "international communism." He persuaded Eisenhower to approve a CIA operation to organize a secret Guatemalan army in Honduras. On June 18, 1954, aided by CIA-piloted warplanes, the 150 paid "liberators" crossed the border into Guatemala and forced Arbenz Guzman into exile in Mexico. The United States then installed a new ruler in Guatemala who eliminated all political opposition.

The CIA operations revealed that the United States was secretly overthrowing elected governments around the world to ensure that they did not join the Soviet bloc. The illegal operations succeeded in toppling rulers, but in doing so they destabilized Iran and Guatemala and created resentments in the Middle East and Central America that would come back to haunt the United States decades later.

Indochina: Background to America's Longest War

During the fifties, the United States also became embroiled in the complex region of Southeast Asia. Indochina, created by French imperialists in the nineteenth century out of the old kingdoms of Cambodia, Laos, and Vietnam, offered a distinctive case of anti-colonial nationalism. During the Second World War, after Japanese troops had occupied the region, the Viet Minh (League for the Independence of Vietnam) waged a guerrilla resistance movement led by Ho Chi Minh, a seasoned revolutionary and passionate nationalist. Mild-mannered and soft-spoken, "Uncle Ho," a wispy man weighing barely a hundred pounds, worked sixteen hours each day toward a single goal: independence for his country. "You must give the people an example of poverty, misery, and denial," he explained. At the end of the war against Japan, the Viet Minh controlled part of northern Vietnam. On

September 2, 1945, Ho Chi Minh proclaimed the creation of a Democratic Republic of Vietnam, with its capital in Hanoi.

The French, like the Americans would later, underestimated the determination of Ho and the Vietnamese nationalists to maintain their independence. In 1946, the First Indochina War erupted when Ho's fighters resisted French efforts to restore the colonial regime. French forces quickly regained control of the cities, while the Viet Minh controlled the countryside. When the Korean War ended, the United States continued its efforts to strengthen French control of Vietnam. By the end of 1953, the Eisenhower administration was paying nearly 80 percent of the cost of the French military effort, and the United States found itself at the brink of military intervention.

In December 1953, some 12,000 French soldiers parachuted into **Dien Bien Phu**, a cluster of villages in a valley ringed by mountains in northern Vietnam near the Laotian border. The French military plan, which Eisenhower deemed foolish, was to build a well-fortified base to lure Viet Minh guerrillas into the open and then overwhelm them with superior firepower. The French assumed that the surrounding forested hills were impassable. The French strategy, however, backfired because it underestimated the determination of the Viet Minh. Slowly, in single file, over 55,000 Viet Minh fighters equipped with Chinese Communist weapons took up positions atop the ridges overlooking the French military base. They laboriously dismantled cannons and carried them in pieces up the hills, then dug trenches and tunnels down into the valley. By March 1954, the French garrison at Dien Bien Phu was surrounded.

HO CHI MINH Though a ruthless leader, Ho cultivated a humble, proletarian version of himself as Uncle Ho, a man of the people.

As the weeks passed, the French government pleaded with the United States to use its warplanes to relieve the pressure on Dien Bien Phu, which a French journalist called "Hell in a very small place." The National Security Council—Dulles, Vice President Nixon, and the chairman of the Joint Chiefs of Staff—urged Eisenhower to use atomic bombs to aid the trapped French force. Eisenhower snapped back: "You boys must be crazy. We can't use those awful things against Asians for the second time in less than ten years. My God!"

The president opposed any U.S. intervention unless the British joined the effort. When they refused, Eisenhower told the French that U.S. military action in Vietnam was "politically impossible." As Eisenhower stressed, "No one could be more bitterly opposed to ever getting the U.S. involved in a hot war in that region than I am." On May 7, 1954, the Viet Minh fighters overwhelmed the last French resistance at Dien Bien Phu. The catastrophic defeat signaled the end of French colonial rule in Asia.

On July 20, 1954, representatives of France, Britain, the Soviet Union, the People's Republic of China, and the Viet Minh signed the Geneva Accords.

Dien Bien Phu Cluster of Vietnamese villages and site of a major Vietnamese victory over the French in the First Indochina War.

DIEN BIEN PHU Viet Minh soldiers march French captives to a prisoner camp in Dien Bien Phu on May 7, 1954.

The complex agreement gave Laos and Cambodia their independence and divided Vietnam in two at the 17th parallel. The Geneva Accords gave the Viet Minh Communists control in the North; the French would remain south of the line until nationwide elections would be organized in 1956 to reunify all of Vietnam.

The Geneva Accords, South Vietnam, and the Viet Cong

American and South Vietnamese representatives, however, refused to sign the Geneva Accords, arguing that the treaties legitimized the Communist victory. After 1954, Ho Chi Minh took complete control of the government in North Vietnam, executing thousands of Vietnamese he deemed opponents.

In South Vietnam, power gravitated to a new premier chosen by the French at American urging: Ngo Dinh Diem, a Catholic nationalist who had opposed both the French and the Viet Minh. In 1954, Eisenhower began providing military and economic aid to Diem. The U.S. president remained opposed to the use of U.S. combat troops, believing that military intervention would lead to a costly stalemate—as indeed it eventually did.

Diem's autocratic efforts to eliminate all opposition played into the hands of the Communists, who found eager recruits among the discontented

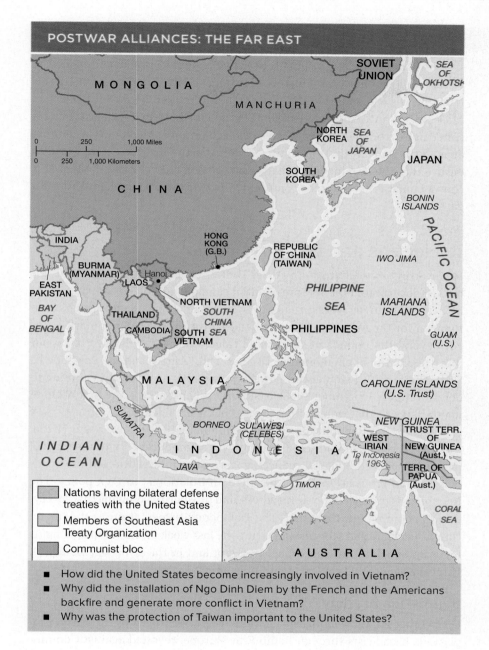

POSTWAR ALLIANCES: THE FAR EAST

Legend:
- Nations having bilateral defense treaties with the United States
- Members of Southeast Asia Treaty Organization
- Communist bloc

- How did the United States become increasingly involved in Vietnam?
- Why did the installation of Ngo Dinh Diem by the French and the Americans backfire and generate more conflict in Vietnam?
- Why was the protection of Taiwan important to the United States?

South Vietnamese. By 1957, Communist guerrillas known as the **Viet Cong** were launching attacks on the Diem government. As the warfare intensified, the Eisenhower administration concluded that its only option was to "sink or swim with Diem."

In 1954, Eisenhower had used what he called the **"falling domino" theory** to explain why the United States needed to fight communism in Vietnam: "You have a row of dominos set up, you knock over the first one, and what will happen to the last one is the certainty that it will go over very

Viet Cong Communist guerrillas in South Vietnam who launched attacks on the Diem government.

"falling domino" theory Theory that if one country fell to communism, its neighboring countries would necessarily follow suit.

quickly." If South Vietnam were to fall to communism, he predicted, the rest of Southeast Asia would soon follow.

The domino analogy, originally used by President Truman and echoed by presidents Eisenhower, Kennedy, Johnson, and Nixon, assumed that Communism was a monolithic global movement directed by Soviet leaders in Moscow. Yet anti-colonial insurgencies such as those in Southeast Asia resulted more from nationalist motives than communist ideology. The domino analogy also meant that the United States must police the entire world to ensure that the dominoes, no matter how small, did not begin falling. As a consequence, every insurgency around the world mushroomed into a strategic crisis.

Reelection and Foreign Crises

While Secretary of State John Foster Dulles was trying to intimidate Communist governments, a new presidential campaign unfolded in 1956. Eisenhower still enjoyed widespread public support. James Reston, a political reporter for the *New York Times*, noted that the president's popularity "has got beyond the bounds of reasonable calculation and will have to be put down as a national phenomenon, like baseball." Americans had developed a "love affair" with Eisenhower, but the president's health was beginning to deteriorate. In September 1955, he suffered a heart attack, the first of three major illnesses that would affect the rest of his presidency.

In 1956, the Republicans eagerly renominated Eisenhower and Nixon. The party platform endorsed Eisenhower's "moderate Republicanism," meaning balanced budgets, reduced government intervention in the economy, and an internationalist rather than an isolationist foreign policy. The Republicans promised "peace, progress, and prosperity," crowing that "everything's booming but the guns." The Democrats turned again to the liberal Illinois leader, Adlai Stevenson. During the last week of the campaign, fighting erupted along the Suez Canal in Egypt and in the streets of Budapest, Hungary, events that caused major international crises.

Repression in Hungary

On October 23, 1956, Hungarian nationalists, encouraged by American propaganda broadcasts through Radio Free Europe, revolted against Communist troops in Budapest. The Soviets responded by sending 500,000 soldiers and 4,000 tanks into Hungary, where they killed thousands of Hungarian "freedom fighters" before installing a new puppet government.

Eisenhower offered his sympathy to the Hungarian people but nothing more. His strategy in dealing with such crises was, as he later said, "Take a hard line—and bluff." Although he avoided war over the Soviet suppression of democracy in Hungary, Eisenhower had allowed administration officials, especially Secretary of State Dulles, to make reckless pledges about "rolling back" communism and "liberating" the nations of Eastern Europe. "To all

HUNGARIAN UPRISING A crowd of Hungarian freedom fighters mount a Soviet tank in Budapest in November, 1956. Despite Eisenhower's sympathetic attitude toward the Hungarians, he offered no American aid, and the rebellion was quashed by the Soviets.

those suffering under Communist slavery," Dulles promised, "let us say you can count on us."

In Hungary, the Soviets called the Eisenhower administration's bluff. The Hungarian freedom fighters, having been led to expect U.S. support, paid with their lives. Vice President Richard Nixon cynically reassured Eisenhower that the Soviet crackdown on the rebellion would be beneficial in showing the world the ruthlessness of communism. The president, however, felt pangs of guilt, telling Dulles that "we have excited Hungarians for all these years" and are "now turning our backs on them when they are in a jam." Dulles showed little concern, reminding the president that "we always have been against violent rebellion."

The Suez War

Eisenhower was more successful in handling an unexpected international crisis in Egypt, which occurred at the same time as the revolt in Hungary. In 1952, an Egyptian army officer, Gamal Abdel Nasser, had overthrown King Farouk. Once in power, Nasser set out to become the leader of the entire Arab world. To do so, he promised to destroy the new Israeli nation, created in 1948.

Nasser, with Soviet support, first sought control of the Suez Canal, the crucial international waterway in Egypt connecting the Mediterranean and Red Seas. The canal had opened in 1869 as a joint French-Egyptian venture, and from 1882 on, British troops had protected the canal as the British Empire's "lifeline" to India and its other Asian colonies. When Nasser's nationalist regime pressed for the withdrawal of the British forces, an Anglo-Egyptian treaty provided for British withdrawal within twenty months.

In 1955, Nasser, adept at playing both sides in the cold war, announced a huge arms deal with the Soviet Union. The United States countered by offering to help Egypt finance a massive hydroelectric dam at Aswan on the Nile River. In 1956, when Nasser increased trade with the Soviet bloc and recognized the People's Republic of China, Dulles abruptly canceled the offer to fund the Aswan Dam.

Unable to retaliate directly against the United States, Nasser seized control of the Suez Canal Company and denied access to Israel-bound ships. The British and French were furious. On October 29, 1956, while Hungarian rebels were battling Soviet tanks, Israeli, British, and French forces invaded Egypt. Nasser responded by sinking all forty of the international ships then in the Suez Canal. A few days later, Anglo-French commandos and paratroopers took control of the canal.

The attack on Egypt by Britain, France, and Israel almost destroyed the NATO alliance. Eisenhower criticized the military action as a revival of the "old-fashioned gunboat diplomacy" associated with colonial imperialism: "How could we possibly support Britain and France," he asked, "if in doing so we lose the whole Arab world?" He worried that Soviet leaders would use the incident to deepen their influence in the region.

Cease-fire in Suez crisis

To defuse the crisis, Eisenhower adopted a bold stance. He put America's armed forces on alert around the world and warned Soviet diplomats that the United States would go to war if the Communist superpower tried to intervene. Then the president shocked Americans by demanding that the British and French withdraw their troops from the Suez Canal and that the Israelis evacuate the Sinai Peninsula—or face severe economic sanctions. That the three aggressor nations grudgingly complied with a cease-fire agreement on November 7 testified to Eisenhower's strength, influence, and savvy in dealing with military matters.

The **Suez crisis** and the Hungarian revolt led Adlai Stevenson to declare the administration's foreign policy "bankrupt." Most voters, however, decided that the foreign turmoil spelled a poor time to switch leaders, and they handed Eisenhower an even more lopsided victory than the one in 1952. In carrying Louisiana, Eisenhower became the first Republican to win a Lower South state since Reconstruction; nationally, he carried all but seven states and won the electoral vote by 457–73. Eisenhower's decisive victory, however, failed to swing a congressional majority for his party in either house.

Reactions to *Sputnik*

On October 4, 1957, the Soviets shocked the world when they announced the launch of the first communications satellite, called *Sputnik* ("traveling companion"). Americans panicked at the news. The Soviet success in space dealt a severe blow to the prestige of American science and technology, which had

Suez crisis (1956) British, French, and Israeli attack on Egypt after Nasser's seizure of the Suez Canal; President Eisenhower interceded to demand the withdrawal of the British, French, and Israeli forces from the Sinai Peninsula and the strategic canal.

POSTWAR ALLIANCES: EUROPE, NORTH AFRICA, THE MIDDLE EAST

- Members of NATO
- Members of Middle East Trade Organization
- Arab League
- Communist bloc (Warsaw Pact)

- How did General Nasser try to play the United States and the Soviet Union against each other?
- Why did the Israelis, French, and British attack Egypt?
- How was the Suez War resolved?

seemed unquestionably preeminent since the Second World War. It also changed the military balance of power. If the Soviets had such advanced rocketry, many people reasoned, then perhaps they could hit U.S. cities with nuclear missiles. Democrats charged that the Soviets had "humiliated" the United States; they launched a congressional investigation to assess the new threat to the nation's security.

"*Sputnik* mania" led the United States to increase defense spending and establish a crash program to enhance science education. In 1958, Congress created the National Aeronautics and Space Administration to coordinate research and development related to outer space. The same year, Congress, with Eisenhower's support, enacted the National Defense Education Act (NDEA), which authorized massive federal grants to colleges and universities to enhance education and research in mathematics, science, and modern languages, as well as for student loans and fellowships. The NDEA provided more financial aid to higher education than any other previous legislation.

The Eisenhower Doctrine

In the aftermath of the Suez crisis, Eisenhower decided that the United States must replace Great Britain and France as the guarantor of Western interests in the Middle East. In 1958, Congress approved what came to be called the Eisenhower Doctrine, a resolution that promised to extend economic and military aid to Arab nations and to use armed force if necessary to assist any such nation against Communist aggression. When Lebanon appealed to the United States to help fend off an insurgency, Eisenhower dispatched 5,000 marines into the country. In October 1958, once the situation had stabilized, U.S. forces (up to 15,000 at one point) withdrew.

Crisis in Berlin

The unique problem of West Berlin, an island of Western capitalism deep in Soviet-controlled East Germany, boiled over in the late 1950s. Since the Second World War, West Berlin had served as a "showplace" of Western democracy and prosperity, a listening post for Western intelligence gathering and a funnel through which news and propaganda from the West penetrated what British leader Winston Churchill had labeled the "iron curtain."

Although East Germany had sealed its western frontiers, refugees could still pass from East to West Berlin. On November 10, 1958, however, Nikita Khrushchev, the unpredictable Soviet leader who had earlier boasted that "history is on our side. We will bury you," threatened to give East Germany control of East Berlin and of the air lanes into West Berlin unless the U.S. and its Allies withdrew from West Berlin. After the deadline he set (May 27, 1959), Western occupation authorities would have to deal with the Soviet-controlled East German government, in effect recognizing it or facing the possibility of another blockade.

Eisenhower refused to budge from his position on Berlin but sought a settlement. There was little hope of resolving the conflicting views on Berlin and the possibility of reuniting East and West Germany into one nation, but the negotiations distracted attention from the May 27 deadline, which passed almost unnoticed. In September 1959, Khrushchev and Eisenhower agreed that the time was ripe for a summit meeting of the two leaders.

The U-2 Summit

The summit meeting blew up in Eisenhower's face, however. On Sunday morning, May 1, 1960, he learned that a Soviet rocket had brought down a U.S. spy plane (called the U-2) flying at 70,000 feet some 1,200 miles inside the Soviet border. Khrushchev, embarrassed by the ability of U.S. spy planes to enter Soviet airspace,

NIKITA KHRUSHCHEV The Soviet premier speaks on the problem of the divided city of Berlin, 1959.

sprang a trap on Eisenhower. At first the Soviets announced only that the plane had been shot down. The U.S. government, not realizing that the Soviets had captured the downed pilot, lied about the incident, claiming that it was missing a weather-monitoring plane over Turkey. Khrushchev then disclosed that the Soviets had American pilot Francis Gary Powers "alive and kicking." Now the world knew that Eisenhower had lied. On May 11, he abandoned U.S. efforts to cover up the incident, acknowledging that "we will now just have to endure the storm." Rather than blame others, Eisenhower took personal responsibility for the spying, explaining that such illegally obtained intelligence information was crucial to national security. At the testy summit meeting in Paris five days later, Khrushchev lectured Eisenhower for forty-five minutes before walking out. The U-2 incident set back efforts to reduce cold war tensions in Berlin and worldwide. Later, in 1962, Francis Gary Powers would be exchanged for a captured Soviet spy.

U.S.-Soviet setback: The U-2 conflict; diplomatic relations with Cuba suspended

Castro's Cuba

Yet Eisenhower's greatest embarrassment was not the U-2 incident but Fidel Castro's new Communist regime in Cuba, which came to power on January 1, 1959, after two years of guerrilla warfare against the brutal U.S.-supported dictator, Fulgencio Batista. The bearded, cigar-smoking Castro, always dressed in military fatigues, readily embraced Soviet support as he systematically imprisoned hundreds of opponents, canceled elections, and staged public executions. His tyrannical communism led a CIA agent to

FIDEL CASTRO Castro (center) became Cuba's Communist premier in 1959 after three years of guerrilla warfare.

predict, "We're going to take care of Castro just like we took care of Arbenz [in Guatemala]." The Soviets warned that any American intervention in Cuba would trigger a military response.

One of Eisenhower's last acts as president, on January 3, 1961, was to suspend diplomatic relations with Castro's Cuba. Eisenhower also authorized a secret CIA operation to train a force of Cuban refugees to oust Castro. Yet the final decision on the use of the anti-Castro invasion force would rest with the next president, John F. Kennedy.

Assessing the Eisenhower Presidency

During President Eisenhower's second term, Congress added Alaska and Hawaii as the forty-ninth and fiftieth states (1959), while the nation experienced its worst economic slump since the Great Depression. Volatile issues such as civil rights; defense policy; and corrupt aides, including White House chief of staff Sherman Adams, Eisenhower's most trusted and influential adviser, compounded the administration's troubles. The president's desire to avoid divisive issues and maintain public goodwill led him at times to value harmony and popularity over justice. One observer called the Eisenhower years "the time of the great postponement," during which the president left domestic and foreign policies "about where he found them in 1953."

Opinion of Eisenhower's presidency has improved with time, however. After all, Eisenhower fulfilled his pledge to end the war in Korea, refused to intervene militarily in Indochina, and maintained the peace in the face of explosive global tensions.

Perhaps Ike's greatest decisions were the wars he chose to avoid. After the truce in Korea, not a single American soldier died in combat during his two administrations, something no president since has achieved. For the most part, he acted with poise, restraint, and intelligence in managing an increasingly complex cold war that he predicted would last for decades.

If Eisenhower did little to address social and racial problems, he did balance the budget while sustaining the major reforms of the New Deal. If he tolerated unemployment of as much as 7 percent, he saw to it that inflation remained minimal. Even Adlai Stevenson, defeated twice by Eisenhower, admitted that Ike's victory in 1952 had been good for America. "I like Ike, too," he said. Still, it is fair to ask what might have happened if Eisenhower had chosen to invest his enormous prestige and popularity in the civil rights movement. His passivity meant that the next presidents would be forced to improve race relations in a much more volatile political and social climate.

Eisenhower's January 17, 1961, farewell address to the American people focused on a topic never before addressed by a public official: the threat posed to government integrity by "an immense military establishment and a large arms industry." As a much-celebrated military leader, it was all the more striking for Eisenhower to highlight the dangers of a huge "military-industrial complex" exerting "unwarranted influence" in Congress and the White House. "The potential for the disastrous rise of misplaced power exists and will persist," he warned. Eisenhower confessed that his greatest disappointment was that he could affirm only that "war has been avoided," not that "a lasting peace is in sight." Despite the combative language of Secretary of State John Foster Dulles, Eisenhower never promoted warfare as an instrument of foreign policy. Instead, he pledged to "do anything to achieve peace within honorable means. I'll travel anywhere. I'll talk to anyone." His successors would not be as successful in keeping war at bay.

Reviewing the
CORE OBJECTIVES |

■ **Eisenhower's Dynamic Conservatism** As president, Dwight Eisenhower promoted what he called *moderate Republicanism* or "dynamic conservatism." He expanded Social Security coverage and launched ambitious public-works programs, such as the *Federal-Aid Highway Act (1956)*, which constructed the Interstate Highway System. He opposed large budget deficits, however, and cut spending on national defense and an array of domestic programs.

■ **Growth of the U.S. Economy** High levels of federal government spending, begun before the war, continued during the postwar period. The *GI Bill of Rights (1944)* boosted home buying and helped many veterans attend college and enter the middle class. Consumer demand for homes, cars, and household goods that had been unavailable during the war; additional product demand created by the *baby boom*; and the new ability to finance purchases with credit cards all fueled the economy. After the Second World War, with the growth of *suburbia*, corporations, and advertising, America's mass culture displayed what critics called a bland sameness. A large majority of Americans, including many in the working class, experienced unprecedented rising living standards during the 1950s. But discrimination continued against African Americans, Hispanics, and women.

■ **Critics of Mainstream Culture** The *Beats* rebelled against what they claimed was the suffocating conformity of middle-class life in the fifties, as did many other writers and artists. Adolescents rebelled through acts of juvenile delinquency and a new form of sexually provocative music called rock 'n' roll. Pockets of chronic poverty persisted despite record-breaking economic growth, and minorities did not prosper to the extent that white Americans did.

■ **Civil Rights Movement** During the early 1950s, the NAACP mounted legal challenges in federal courts to states requiring racially segregated public schools. In the most significant case, *Brown v. Board of Education* (1954), the U.S. Supreme Court nullified the *separate-but-equal* doctrine. Many white southerners adopted a strategy of *massive resistance* against court-ordered desegregation. In response, civil rights activists, both blacks and whites, used *nonviolent civil disobedience* to force local and state officials to allow integration, as demonstrated in the *Montgomery bus boycott* in Alabama and the forced desegregation of public schools in Little Rock, Arkansas. Martin Luther King organized the *Southern Christian Leadership Conference (SCLC)* to rally civil rights opposition after white violence against activists in Little Rock. In 1957, the U.S. Congress passed a Civil Rights Act intended to stop discrimination against black voters in the South, but it was rarely enforced.

■ **American Foreign Policy in the 1950s** Eisenhower's first major foreign-policy accomplishment was to end the fighting in Korea. Thereafter, Eisenhower relied on *Central Intelligence Agency (CIA)* intervention, financial and military aid, and threats of *massive retaliation* to stem the spread of Communism. Though American aid was not enough to save the French at *Dien Bien Phu*, Eisenhower's belief in the *"falling domino" theory* deepened U.S. support for the government in South Vietnam in its war with North Vietnam and the communist *Viet Cong* insurgents. He came closest to ordering military intervention in the *Suez crisis (1956)* but was able to mediate a solution. Closer to home, however, he approved a secret CIA operation to overthrow Fidel Castro, Cuba's Communist leader.

KEY TERMS

CHRONOLOGY

1949	The first credit card is introduced
1952	Eisenhower wins the presidency
July 1953	Armistice is reached in Korea
	CIA organizes the overthrow of Mohammed Mossadegh in Iran and Jacobo Arbenz Guzman in Guatemala
1954	*Brown v. Board of Education*
July 1954	Geneva Accords adopted
December 1955	Montgomery, Alabama, bus boycott begins
1956	Elvis Presley releases "Heartbreak Hotel"
	Congress passes the Federal-Aid Highway Act
	Soviets suppress Hungarian revolt
	In Suez War, Israel, Britain, and France attack Egypt
1957	Desegregation of Central High School in Little Rock, Arkansas
	Soviet Union launches *Sputnik 1* satellite
	Baby boom peaks
1959	Fidel Castro seizes power in Cuba
1960	The U-2 incident

⏦ INQUIZITIVE

Go to InQuizitive to see what you've learned—and learn what you've missed—with personalized feedback along the way.

***SKYWAY* (1964)** With new frontiers came new fears. Artist Robert Rauschenberg's collage encapsulates the turbulence of the sixties: the stark collisions of the old and the new and the total disorder of it all. John F. Kennedy, early manned space flights, and the Vietnam War are suspended within the childish form of the collage, making Rauschenberg's message all the more foreboding.

New Frontiers

1960–1968

For those who considered the social and political climate of the fifties dull, the following decade provided a striking contrast. The sixties were years of extraordinary social turbulence and liberal activism, tragic assassinations and painful trauma, cultural conflict and youth rebellion. Assassins killed four of the most important leaders of the time: John F. Kennedy, Malcolm X, Martin Luther King Jr., and Robert F. Kennedy. The "politics of expectation" that a British journalist said shone brightly in Kennedy's short tenure as president did not die with the president in November 1963. Instead, Kennedy's idealistic commitment to improving America's quality of life—for everyone—was given new meaning and energy by his very different successor, Texan Lyndon B. Johnson, whose War on Poverty and Great Society programs outstripped Franklin Roosevelt's New Deal in their scope and promises, expense and controversy.

Johnson's remarkable energy and legislative savvy resulted in a blizzard of new federal programs. At the same time, many social issues that had been ignored or postponed for decades—civil rights for minorities, equality for women, gay rights, federal aid to the poor—forced their way to the forefront of national concerns.

In the end, however, Lyndon Johnson promised too much. The elaborate Great Society programs fell victim to unrealistic hopes, poor execution, and the nation's expanding involvement with the war in Vietnam. The deeply entrenched assumptions of the cold war against global communism led the nation into the longest, most controversial, and least successful war in its history.

CORE OBJECTIVES INQUIZITIVE

1. Assess President John F. Kennedy's efforts to contain communism abroad and pursue civil rights and other social programs at home.

2. Describe the strategies and achievements of the civil rights movement in the 1960s, and explain the divisions that emerged among its activists during the decade.

3. Analyze Lyndon B. Johnson's War on Poverty and Great Society initiatives, and evaluate their impact on American society.

4. Explain Presidents Kennedy's and Johnson's motivations for deepening America's military involvement in the Vietnam War, and appraise their efforts to preserve a non-Communist South Vietnam.

5. Examine the presidential election of 1968, and explain the issues that propelled Richard Nixon to victory.

CORE **OBJECTIVE**

1. Assess President John F. Kennedy's efforts to contain communism abroad and pursue civil rights and other social programs at home.

The New Frontier

In his 1960 speech accepting the Democratic presidential nomination, John F. Kennedy showcased the muscular language that would stamp the rest of his campaign and his presidency: "We stand today on the edge of a **New Frontier**—the frontier of unknown opportunities and perils—a frontier of unfulfilled hopes and threats." Kennedy and his staff fastened upon the frontier metaphor as the label for their proposed domestic program because they believed that Americans had always been adventurers, eager to conquer and exploit new frontiers. Kennedy promised that he would get the country "moving again" and be a more aggressive cold warrior than Eisenhower.

Kennedy versus Nixon

In 1960, the presidential election pitted against each other two candidates—Vice President Richard M. Nixon and Massachusetts senator John F. Kennedy (JFK)—of similar ages and life experiences. Both were elected to Congress in 1946, both were navy veterans, and both preferred foreign affairs over domestic issues. In fact, however, they were more different than alike.

As the popular Eisenhower's partner over successive terms, Nixon was assured the Republican nomination for president in 1960. A native of California, the ambitious son of a shopkeeper, he had fought tenaciously to be a success, first as an attorney, then as a congressman. He had come to Washington eager to reverse the tide of New Deal liberalism. His visibility among Republicans benefited from his leadership of the anti-Communist hearings in Congress during the McCarthy hysteria.

All his life, Nixon had had to claw and struggle to the top. Now he had the presidency within his grasp. But Nixon, graceless, awkward, and stiff, proved to be one of the most complicated and most interesting political figures in American history.

By 1960, Vice President Nixon had developed the reputation for being a cunning deceiver, the "Tricky Dick" who concealed his real ideas and bigoted attitudes. Kennedy told an aide that "Nixon doesn't know who he is . . . so every time he makes a speech he has to decide which Nixon he is, and that will be very exhausting."

The forty-three-year-old Kennedy had not distinguished himself in the House or the Senate, but he was tall and youthful, handsome and charming, and he had the energy and wit to match his grace and ambition. He also had a bright, agile mind; a quick wit; a Harvard education; a record of heroism in the Second World War; a rich and powerful Roman Catholic family; and a beautiful, accomplished, and young wife, only thirty-two years old.

In the words of a southern senator, Kennedy fused "the best qualities of Elvis Presley and Franklin D. Roosevelt"—a combination that played well in the first-ever televised presidential debate. Some 70 million people tuned in and saw an obviously uncomfortable Nixon, still weak from a recent illness,

New Frontier Proposed domestic program championed by the incoming Kennedy administration in 1961 that aimed to jump-start the economy and trigger social progress.

THE KENNEDY-NIXON DEBATES Nixon's decision to debate his less prominent opponent on television backfired.

perspiring heavily and looking pale, haggard, and even sinister before the camera. Kennedy, on the other hand, appeared tanned and calm, projected a cool poise, and offered crisp answers that made him seem Nixon's equal, if not superior, in his fitness for the nation's highest office.

John Kennedy's political rise owed much to the effective public relations campaign engineered by his father, Joseph Kennedy, a self-made tycoon with a genius for promotion. "Can't you get it into your head," the elder Kennedy told John, "that it's not important what you *really* are? The only important thing is what people *think* you are." To ensure that people thought well of his son, the elder Kennedy hired writers to produce his son's two books, paid a publisher to print them, purchased thousands of copies to make them "best sellers," and helped engineer his son's elections to the Congress and Senate.

The momentum that Kennedy gained from the first debate with Nixon was not enough to ensure his victory. The Democratic candidate became a relentless campaigner—traveling 65,000 miles, visiting twenty-five states, and making over 350 speeches—including an address to Protestant ministers in Texas in which he neutralized concerns about his being a Roman Catholic by stressing that the pope in Rome would never "tell the President—should he be a Catholic—how to act."

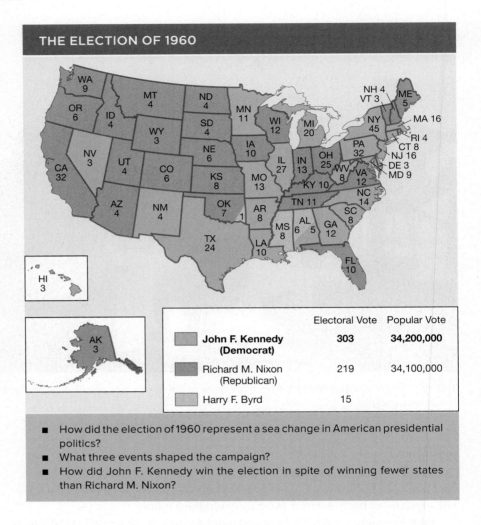

THE ELECTION OF 1960

	Electoral Vote	Popular Vote
John F. Kennedy **(Democrat)**	**303**	**34,200,000**
Richard M. Nixon (Republican)	219	34,100,000
Harry F. Byrd	15	

- How did the election of 1960 represent a sea change in American presidential politics?
- What three events shaped the campaign?
- How did John F. Kennedy win the election in spite of winning fewer states than Richard M. Nixon?

Kennedy also worked to increase the registration of African American voters across the nation, and he won the hearts of many black voters by helping to get Martin Luther King Jr. out of a Georgia jail after being arrested for "trespassing" in an all-white restaurant. "I've got a suitcase of votes," explained King's appreciative father, "and I'm going to take them to Mr. Kennedy and dump them in his lap." On the Sunday before Election Day, a million leaflets about Kennedy's enabling King's release from prison were distributed in African American churches across the nation.

When the votes were counted, Kennedy and his running mate, the powerful Texas senator Lyndon B. Johnson, had won the closest presidential election since 1888. The winning margin was only 118,574 votes out of more than 68 million cast. Nixon had carried more states than Kennedy, sweeping most of the West and holding four of the six southern states that Eisenhower had carried in 1956. But Kennedy won 70 percent of the black vote, which proved decisive in at least three key states. Nixon convinced himself that the Democrats had stolen the election through chicanery in Illinois and Texas. Nursing an inflated sense of grievance, he resolved never again to be outdone by a rival's dirty politics.

A Vigorous New Administration

John F. Kennedy was the first Roman Catholic elected president and the youngest man ever elected. His inauguration ceremony on a cold, clear, blustery January day set the tone of youthful elegance, charm, and energy that would signify the *Kennedy style*. In his inaugural speech, the president quite intentionally spoke as the leader of "a new generation of Americans," implying that Eisenhower had come to represent older Americans. Kennedy dazzled listeners with uplifting words: "Let every nation know, whether it wishes us well or ill, that we shall pay any price, bear any burden, meet any hardship, support any friend, oppose any foe, to assure the survival and success of liberty. And so, my fellow Americans: ask not what your country can do for you—ask what *you* can do for your country."

Such inspiring language heralded a presidency of fresh promise and new beginnings, an activist administration committed to bringing together the "best and the brightest" minds in the nation to fashion a dazzling new era in political achievement. Yet much of the glamour surrounding Kennedy was cosmetic. Despite his athletic interests and robust appearance, he suffered from serious medical problems: Addison's disease (a withering of the adrenal glands), venereal disease, chronic back pain resulting from a birth defect, and fierce fevers. He took powerful prescription medicines or injections daily, sometimes hourly, to manage a degenerative bone disease, to deal with anxiety, to help him sleep, and to control his allergies.

Kennedy and his associates hid his physical ailments—as well as his sexual dalliances in the White House with a galaxy of women, including actress Marilyn Monroe and Judith Campbell Exner, the girlfriend of a Chicago mob boss. The handsome president was a compulsive womanizer. When Kennedy met British prime minister Harold Macmillan, he left him speechless by asking, "I don't know about you, Harold, but if I don't have a woman every three days, I get terrible headaches. How about you?"

Kennedy had a difficult time launching his New Frontier domestic program. Conservative southern Democrats joined with Republicans to block his efforts to increase federal aid to education, provide medical insurance for the aged, and create a cabinet-level department of urban affairs and housing to address poverty in the inner cities. Legislators did approve the Peace Corps, created in 1961 to recruit idealistic young volunteers who would provide educational and technical service abroad. The Kennedy administration also persuaded Congress to

> Kennedy's New Frontier

JACK AND JACKIE Young, refined, and fabulous, the Kennedys were instant celebrities. Women teased their hair into the First Lady's famous hairdo, while men craved JFK's effortless cool.

increase the minimum wage and pass a Housing Act that earmarked nearly $5 billion for new public-housing projects in poverty-stricken inner-city areas. And Kennedy won support for an accelerated space program with the audacious goal of landing astronauts on the moon before the end of the decade.

Kennedy and Civil Rights

The most important development in domestic life during the sixties occurred in civil rights. Throughout the South, racial segregation remained firmly in place. Signs outside public restrooms distinguished between "whites" and "colored"; signs in restaurants declared "Colored Not Allowed," or "Colored Served Only in Rear." Stores prohibited African Americans from trying on clothes before buying them. Witnesses in courtrooms were sworn in with their hands placed on different Bibles, depending on their race. Despite the *Brown v. Board of Education* ruling in 1954, many public schools across the South remained segregated and unequal in quality.

Like Franklin D. Roosevelt and Dwight Eisenhower, John F. Kennedy celebrated racial equality but did little to promote it until events forced him to do so. He was reluctant to challenge conservative southern Democrats on the explosive issue of segregation. His caution reflected his narrow election margin in 1960. He and his brother Robert ("Bobby"), the attorney general as well as the president's closest adviser, had to be forced into actively supporting the civil rights movement.

Catastrophe in Cuba

Kennedy's record in foreign relations, as in domestic affairs, was mixed but more spectacularly so. Although he had told a reporter that he wanted to "break out of the confines of the Cold War," he quickly found himself reinforcing its restrictive assumptions. While still a senator, Kennedy had blasted Eisenhower for not being tough enough with the Soviets and for allowing Fidel Castro and his Communist followers to take over Cuba in 1959.

Soon after his inauguration, Kennedy learned that a secret CIA operation, approved by Eisenhower, was training 1,500 anti-Castro Cubans for an invasion of their homeland. U.S. military leaders assured Kennedy that the invasion plan ("Operation Trinidad") was feasible; CIA analysts naively predicted

WALK OF SHAME Captured anti-Castro Cubans at the Bay of Pigs. **Why was Kennedy's involvement at the Bay of Pigs so disastrous?**

that news of the invasion would inspire anti-Castro Cubans to rebel against their Communist dictator. In reality, the covert operation had little chance of succeeding. Indeed, it became one of the rarest of historical events: a total failure.

When the ragtag force, transported on American ships, landed before dawn at the **Bay of Pigs** on Cuba's south shore on April 17, 1961, Castro's forces were waiting for them. Kennedy panicked when he realized the operation was failing and refused desperate pleas from the rebels for "promised" support from U.S. warplanes. General Lyman Lemnitzer, chair of the Joint Chiefs of Staff, said that Kennedy's "pulling out the rug [on the Cuban invaders] was . . . absolutely reprehensible, almost criminal." Some 1,200 rebels were captured; the rest were killed. (Kennedy later authorized the payment of $53 million to ransom the rebels).

The clumsy effort to overthrow the Cuban government was a catastrophe. It humiliated Kennedy and elevated Castro in the eyes of the world. A *New York Times* columnist reported that the Americans involved in the botched invasion "looked like fools to our friends, rascals to our enemies, and incompetents to the rest." In Moscow, Nikita Khrushchev asked if Kennedy could "really be that indecisive?" To his credit, Kennedy admitted that the Bay of Pigs invasion was a "colossal mistake" and "the worst experience of my life." While pacing back and forth, he kept muttering to himself, "How could I have been so stupid?" Kennedy never again trusted his trigger-happy military and intelligence advisers.

The Vienna Summit

Just six weeks after the Bay of Pigs fiasco, Kennedy, heavily medicated because of chronic back pain, met Khrushchev at a summit conference in Vienna, Austria. Khrushchev bullied the young president and threatened to limit American access to Berlin, the divided city inside Communist East Germany. Kennedy confided to a journalist that the summit "was awful. Worst thing of my life. He rolled right over me—he thinks I'm a fool—he thinks I'm weak. . . . He treated me like a little boy." When asked what he planned to do next, Kennedy replied: "I have to confront them [the Soviets] someplace to show that we're tough." Desperate to show his mettle, Kennedy responded by calling up Army Reserve and National Guard units to protect West Berlin. When military advisers told him that he would have to use nuclear weapons to protect Berlin, Kennedy lost his temper: "God damn it . . . use your head. What we are talking about is seventy million dead Americans."

Then, on August 13, 1961, the Soviets stopped all traffic between East and West Berlin and erected the twenty-seven-mile-long **Berlin Wall**, made of concrete and topped with barbed wire. For the United States, the wall became a powerful propaganda weapon. As Kennedy said, "Freedom has many difficulties and democracy is not perfect, but we have never had to put up a wall to keep our people in."

> Berlin Wall

Bay of Pigs (1961) Failed CIA operation that deployed Cuban rebels to overthrow Fidel Castro's Communist regime.

Berlin Wall Twenty-seven-mile-long concrete wall constructed in 1961 by East German authorities to stop the flow of East Germans fleeing to West Berlin.

SEVERED TIES Two West Berliners climb the newly constructed Berlin Wall to communicate with a family member at an open window.

| Green Berets |

The Berlin Wall demonstrated the Soviets' willingness to challenge American resolve in Europe. Kennedy and Secretary of Defense Robert McNamara responded by embarking upon the most intensive arms race in history, increasing the number of nuclear missiles fivefold, adding 300,000 men to the armed forces, and creating the U.S. Special Forces (Green Berets), an elite group of commandos specializing in guerrilla warfare who could provide a "more flexible response" than nuclear weapons to "hotspots" around the world and enable the United States to wage small wars in faraway lands. In contrast to the Eisenhower-Dulles emphasis on "massive retaliation," Kennedy sought more flexibility: "We intend to have a wider choice than humiliation or all-out war."

The Cuban Missile Crisis

| Soviet missiles in Cuba |

In the fall of 1962, Nikita Khrushchev and the Soviets posed another challenge to Kennedy, this time only ninety miles off the Florida coast. To protect Communist Cuba from another American-backed invasion, Khrushchev approved the secret installation of Soviet missiles on the island nation. The Soviets felt they were justified in doing so because the United States had earlier installed missiles with nuclear warheads in Turkey, along the Soviet border.

On October 16, 1962, photos taken by U.S. spy planes revealed the Soviet missile sites in Cuba. Although the Soviet actions violated no law or treaty, Kennedy decided that the forty or so missiles had to be removed. But how? As the air force chief of staff told Kennedy, "You're in a pretty bad fix, Mr. President."

Over the next thirteen days, perhaps the most dangerous two weeks in history, Kennedy and the National Security Council (NSC) discussed several possible responses, ranging from doing nothing to invading Cuba. The commander of the marines at one point reminded the group that the missiles in Cuba were not a true threat. The Soviet Union "has a hell of a lot better way to attack us than to attack us from Cuba." Yet the group insisted that the missiles be removed for symbolic reasons.

At that point, the world came closer to a war involving the exchange of nuclear weapons than it ever has before or since. Kennedy and the NSC discussed in some detail the unthinkable possibility of a nuclear war, even estimating the damage that atomic bombs might inflict on major cities. Eventually, however, the group narrowed the options to a choice between a "surgical" air strike on the missiles and a naval blockade of Cuba. Although the military advisers urged bombing the missile sites followed by an invasion of the island, Kennedy chose the naval blockade, which was carefully disguised by calling it a *quarantine*, since a *blockade* is technically an act of war.

On Monday night, October 22, President Kennedy delivered a solemn speech to the world, announcing that the U.S. Navy was establishing a naval quarantine of Cuba to prevent Soviet ships from delivering the goods and weapons that the island nation depended upon. He urged the Soviets to "move the world back from the abyss of destruction."

Tensions grew as Khrushchev replied that Soviet ships would ignore the quarantine. He accused Kennedy of "an act of aggression propelling

> Naval quarantine of Cuba

> Soviets remove missiles under nuclear threat

THE CUBAN MISSILE CRISIS Photographs taken from a U.S. surveillance plane on October 14, 1962, revealed both missile launchers and missile shelters near San Cristóbal, Cuba. **What were the implications of this discovery on America's international relations?**

humankind into the abyss of a world nuclear-missile war." Despite such rhetoric, however, on Wednesday, October 24, five Soviet ships, presumably with more missiles aboard, stopped well short of the quarantine line. Two days later, Khrushchev, knowing that the U.S. still enjoyed a 5 to 1 advantage in nuclear weapons, offered a deal. Neither he nor Kennedy wanted to be the first president to launch nuclear missiles. The Soviets would remove the missiles in return for a *public* pledge by the United States not to invade Cuba—and a *secret* agreement to remove U.S. missiles from Turkey. Kennedy agreed. Secretary of State Dean Rusk stressed to a newscaster, "Remember, when you report this, [say] that eyeball to eyeball, they [the Soviets] blinked first."

In the aftermath of the **Cuban missile crisis**, tensions between the United States and the Soviet Union subsided, in part because of several symbolic steps: an agreement to sell the Soviet Union surplus American wheat, the installation of a "hotline" telephone between Washington and Moscow to provide instant contact between the heads of government, and the removal of aging U.S. missiles from Turkey, Italy, and Britain.

Controlling Atomic Weapons

Going to the edge of nuclear war over Soviet missiles in Cuba led Kennedy and others in the administration to soften their cold war rhetoric and pursue other ways to reduce the threat of atomic warfare. As Kennedy told his advisers at a White House meeting, "It is insane that two men, sitting on opposite sides of the world, should be able to decide to bring an end to civilization." In June 1963, the president began discussions with the Soviets to reduce the risk of nuclear war. "If we cannot end our differences," he said, "at least we can help make the world a safe place for diversity." After two months of difficult negotiations, those discussions resulted in the Test Ban Treaty with the Soviet Union and Great Britain, ratified in September 1963, which banned the testing of nuclear weapons in the atmosphere. It was an important move toward improved relations with the Soviet Union. As Kennedy put it, using an ancient Chinese proverb, "A journey of a thousand miles begins with one step."

> Test Ban Treaty: Bans testing of nuclear weapons in the atmosphere

Kennedy and Vietnam

As tensions with the Soviet Union eased, a new crisis was growing in Southeast Asia, where events were moving toward what would eventually become the greatest American foreign-policy calamity of the century. The situation in South Vietnam had worsened under the corrupt leadership of Premier Ngo Dinh Diem and his family. He had backed away from promised social and economic reforms, and his repressive tactics, directed not only against Communists but also against the Buddhist majority and other critics, played into the hands of his enemies.

> Military advisers in Vietnam

Kennedy continued to dispatch military "advisers" to South Vietnam in the hope of stabilizing the situation (they were called advisers to avoid the impression that U.S. troops were doing the fighting). When he took office, the

Cuban missile crisis (1962)
Thirteen-day U.S.-Soviet standoff sparked by the discovery of Soviet missile sites in Cuba; closest the world has come to nuclear war since 1945.

United States had 900 troops in Vietnam; by the end of 1963, there were 16,000, all of whom were officially classified as advisers rather than combatants. "If I tried to pull out," Kennedy explained, "we would have another Joe McCarthy red scare on our hands," with cold war hawks accusing him of "losing" Vietnam to communism. "We must be patient, we must persist."

By 1963, Kennedy was receiving sharply conflicting reports from South Vietnam. U.S. military analysts expressed confidence in the Army of the Republic of Vietnam. Journalists, however, predicted civil turmoil as long as Diem remained in power. By midyear, frequent Buddhist demonstrations against Diem ignited widespread discontent. The spectacle of Buddhist monks setting themselves on fire in public squares to protest government tyranny stunned Americans.

By the fall of 1963, the Kennedy administration had decided that the autocratic Diem was "out of touch with his people" and had to go. On November 1, U.S.-backed army generals seized the South Vietnamese government but then took a step that Kennedy had neither intended nor expected: they murdered Diem and his brother.

> United States backs coup in South Vietnam

The rebel generals, however, provided no more political stability than had Diem, and successive coups set the fragile country spinning from one military leader to another. Thereafter, unstable South Vietnam essentially became an American colony. The United States put the generals in power, gave the orders, and provided massive financial support, much of which was diverted into the hands of corrupt politicians. During that tumultuous fall of 1963, Kennedy seemed to have developed doubts about the ability of the United States to prop up the South Vietnamese government. When asked about the South Vietnamese effort to hold off Communist insurgents, he replied: "In the final analysis it's their war. They're the ones who have to win it or lose it. We can help them as advisers but they have to win it."

Kennedy's Assassination

By the fall of 1963, John F. Kennedy had matured a great deal as president. Not only had he come to understand the urgency and momentum of the civil rights movement, he also had come to see the cold war as a more complex issue than he had believed during his first year in office. In October 1963, he announced his intention to withdraw U.S. forces from South Vietnam by the end of 1965.

What Kennedy would have done thereafter in Vietnam has remained a matter of endless discussion, because on November 22, 1963, while riding at noon in an open car through Dallas, Texas, he was shot and killed by Lee Harvey Oswald, a twenty-four-year-old ex-marine turned Communist who worked in the Texas School Book Depository, from which he fired at Kennedy with a rifle. Kennedy seemed to have had a premonition of his death. "We're heading into nut country today," he warned his wife Jackie that morning. "But Jackie, if somebody wants to shoot me from a window with a rifle, nobody can stop it, so why worry about it?"

PRESIDENT SHOT DEAD Commuters read the news of President Kennedy's assassination on November 22, 1963.

Debate still swirls about whether Oswald, who had lived in the Soviet Union for a time, acted alone or was part of a conspiracy to assassinate the president, in part because Oswald did not live long enough to tell his story. As Oswald was being transported to a court hearing, Jack Ruby, a Dallas nightclub owner distraught over Kennedy's death, shot and killed a handcuffed Oswald as a nationwide television audience watched.

Kennedy's shocking assassination and his heartrending funeral enshrined the young president in the public imagination as a martyred leader cut down in the prime of his life. His short-lived but drama-filled presidency had flamed up and out like a comet hitting the earth's atmosphere. Americans wept in the streets, and the world was on edge as the wounded nation welcomed a new and very different president.

CORE **OBJECTIVE**

2. Describe the strategies and achievements of the civil rights movement in the 1960s, and explain the divisions that emerged among its activists during the decade.

Expansion of the Civil Rights Movement

After the Montgomery bus boycott of 1955–1956, Martin Luther King Jr.'s philosophy of militant nonviolence stirred others to challenge the deeply entrenched patterns of racial segregation in the South. During the sixties, King became the face and heart of the civil rights movement. His goal was integration and equality, and he was an uplifting example of fortitude and dignity in confronting brutality and oppression. By nature, he was inspirational and courageous, with an astonishing capacity for forgiveness and a deep understanding of the dynamics of political power and social change. Yet he was also immensely complicated and contradictory, even hypocritical, as the FBI discovered by subjecting him to relentless electronic surveillance and even blackmail.

King was neither a genius nor a saint, but his shortcomings pale into insignificance when compared to his achievements. He was one of the world's most inspiring examples of courage, conviction, and dignity in the face of violent prejudice and persecution. With the help of those he led and inspired, King changed the trajectory of American history—for the better. Alas, he did not live to see the promised land made possible by his actions.

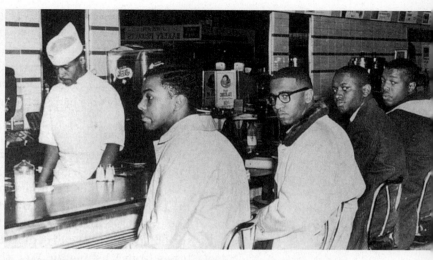

CIVIL RIGHTS AND ITS PEACEFUL WARRIORS The Greensboro Four—(from left) Joseph McNeil, Franklin McCain, Billy Smith, and Clarence Henderson—await service on day two of their sit-in at the Woolworth's.

Sit-Ins

The civil rights movement gained added momentum when four polite, well-dressed black college students sat down and ordered coffee and doughnuts at an "all-white" Woolworth's lunch counter in Greensboro, North Carolina, on February 1, 1960. The clerk refused to serve them, explaining that blacks had to eat standing up or take their food outside. The Greensboro Four, as the students came to be called, waited for forty-five minutes and then returned the next day with two dozen more students. Along with others, they returned every day for a week, patiently tolerating being jeered at, jostled, and spat upon by white hooligans.

The "sit-in" movement spread quickly to six more towns in the state, and within two months similar sit-ins—involving 50,000 blacks and whites, men and women, young and old—had occurred in over a hundred cities in thirteen states. Some 3,600 people had been arrested. Black comedian Dick Gregory participated in several sit-ins at whites-only restaurants. When the managers told him, "We don't serve Negroes," he replied: "No problem, I don't eat Negroes." By the end of July 1960, officials in Greensboro lifted the whites-only policy at the Woolworth's lunch counter. The civil rights movement had found an effective new tactic: nonviolent sit-ins against segregation.

In April 1960, some 200 college student activists, black and white, had converged in Raleigh, North Carolina, to form the **Student Nonviolent Coordinating Committee** (**SNCC**—pronounced "snick"). The goal of what they came to call "the movement" was to intensify the effort to dismantle segregation. SNCC broadened the sit-ins, which began at restaurants, to

> The Greensboro Four: Lunch counter "sit-ins"

Student Nonviolent Coordinating Committee (SNCC) Interracial organization formed in 1960 with the goal of intensifying the effort to end racial segregation.

Freedom Riders Activists who, beginning in 1961, traveled by bus through the South to test federal court rulings that banned segregation on buses and trains.

include "kneel-ins" at all-white churches and "wade-ins" at segregated public swimming pools. In many communities, demonstrators were pelted with rocks, burned with cigarettes, subjected to unending verbal abuse, and even killed by white racists. As a Florida hog farmer named Holstead "Hoss" Manucy explained to a journalist, "I ain't got no bad habits. Don't smoke. Don't cuss. My only bad habit is fightin' niggahs."

Freedom Rides

In 1961, civil rights leaders decided to put "the movement on wheels" by integrating public transportation: buses and trains. Their larger goal was to force the Kennedy administration to engage the cause of civil rights in the Democratic South. On May 4, the New York–based Congress of Racial Equality (CORE), led by James Farmer, sent a courageous group of eighteen black and white **Freedom Riders**, as they were called, on two public buses from Washington, D.C., through the Lower South to New Orleans. They wanted to test a federal court ruling that banned racial segregation on buses and trains, and in terminals. Farmer warned Attorney General Robert F. Kennedy that the bus riders would probably be attacked as they traveled through the South.

The warning was well founded, for on May 14, a mob of white racists in rural Alabama, many of them members of the Ku Klux Klan, surrounded the Greyhound bus carrying the Freedom Riders. After throwing a firebomb into

FREEDOM RIDERS On May 14, 1961, a white mob assaulted a Freedom Bus, flinging fire bombs into its windows and beating the activists as they emerged. Here, the surviving Freedom Riders pause outside the burnt shell of their bus.

the bus, angry whites barricaded the bus's door. "Burn them alive," one of them yelled. "Fry the damned niggers." After the gas tank exploded, the riders were able to escape the burning bus, only to be battered by metal pipes, chains, and clubs.

A few hours later, Freedom Riders on a second bus were beaten by whites armed with bats and chains after entering whites-only waiting rooms at the bus terminal in Birmingham. The police, as it turned out, had encouraged the beatings. Alabama's governor complained that the Freedom Riders were violating "our law and customs." The next day, the Freedom Riders wanted to continue their trip, but the bus drivers refused.

When Diane Nash, a fearless black college student and SNCC leader in Nashville, Tennessee, heard about the violence in Birmingham, she recruited new riders. President Kennedy called her, warning that she would "get killed if [she did] this," but she refused to back down. "It doesn't matter if we're killed," she told the president. "Others will come—others will come."

On May 17, Nash and ten students took a bus to Birmingham, where they were arrested. While in jail, the students sang "freedom songs": "We'll Never Turn Back," "Ain't Gonna Let Nobody Turn Me Around," "We Shall Overcome." Eugene "Bull" Connor, the notoriously racist police chief, grew so frustrated at their joyous rebelliousness that he drove them in the middle of the night to the Tennessee state line and dropped them off to walk, saying, "I couldn't stand your singing." Instead of going to Nashville, however, the gutsy students returned to Birmingham.

President Kennedy was not inspired by the courageous Freedom Riders. To him, they were a "pain in the ass," threatening to embarrass him and the United States on the eve of his summit meeting with Soviet leader Nikita Khrushchev. The president and his brother Bobby dismissed the Freedom Riders as "publicity seekers." The Kennedys had no intention of promoting any civil rights legislation.

The demonstrators persisted, finally forcing the president to provide another bus, which enabled them to renew the journey to New Orleans. When the new group of Freedom Riders reached Montgomery, the capital of Alabama, white racists attacked them. The next night, civil rights activists gathered at a Montgomery church to honor the Freedom Riders, but their meeting was interrupted by a rampaging mob of whites armed with rocks and fire bombs. Ministers made frantic appeals to the White House. President Kennedy responded by urging the Alabama governor to intervene. After midnight, National Guardsmen arrived to disperse the mob. The Freedom Riders continued into Mississippi, where they were imprisoned. They never made it to New Orleans.

Still, they succeeded in their larger goal. The courage and principled resistance of the Freedom Riders—and of federal judges across the nation whose rulings supported integration efforts—led the Interstate Commerce Commission in September 1961 to order that all interstate transportation facilities be integrated. The Freedom Riders had worked and were a turning

Integration of interstate transportation facilities

point in the civil rights movement. Widespread media coverage showed the nation that the nonviolent protesters were prepared to die for their rights rather than continue to endure racist assaults on their dignity.

James Meredith

Desegregating the University of Mississippi

In the fall of 1962, James Meredith, an African American student and U.S. Air Force veteran whose grandfather had been a slave, tried to enroll at the all-white University of Mississippi in Oxford. Ross Barnett, the governor of Mississippi, described by *Time* magazine as "as bitter a racist as inhabits the nation," refused to allow Meredith to register for classes. The militantly stubborn Barnett breathed scorching defiance: he vowed "to rot in jail before he will let one Negro ever darken the sacred threshold of our white schools."

Robert Kennedy then dispatched federal marshals to enforce the law. When the marshals were assaulted by a white mob shouting "Go to Hell, JFK," President Kennedy sent National Guard troops (all white). The arrival of soldiers on the campus ignited rioting that left two dead and dozens injured. Once the violence subsided, however, James Meredith was registered at the university. "Only in America," a reporter noted, "would the federal government send thousands of troops to enforce the right of an otherwise obscure citizen to attend a particular university."

Birmingham

Several months later, in early 1963, in conjunction with the celebration of the hundredth anniversary of Abraham Lincoln's Emancipation Proclamation, Martin Luther King Jr. announced that he and other civil rights activists were fed up "with tokenism and gradualism and see-how-far-you've-comeism. We can't wait any longer. Now is the time." He then defied the wishes of President Kennedy by organizing a massive series of demonstrations against segregation in Birmingham, Alabama, a state presided over by a feisty new racist governor—George Wallace—who had vowed to protect "segregation now, segregation tomorrow, segregation forever!" King knew that demonstrations in Birmingham would likely provoke violence, but a hard-won victory there, he felt, would build national support and "break the back of segregation all over the nation" by revealing southern "brutality openly—in the light of day—with the rest of the world looking on" through television cameras.

The Birmingham campaign began with sit-ins at restaurants, picket lines at segregated businesses, and a march on city hall. The police arrested and jailed the activists. Each day, however,

BULL'S DOGS Eugene "Bull" Connor ordered Birmingham police to unleash their dogs on civil rights demonstrators in May of 1963.

more demonstrators, black and white, joined in the efforts. As King and others led demonstrations through Birmingham streets in April, the all-white police force led by Bull Connor used snarling dogs, tear gas, electric cattle prods, and fire hoses on the protesters. Millions of Americans across the nation were outraged when they saw the ugly confrontations on television. "The civil rights movement," President Kennedy observed, "owes Bull Connor as much as it owes Abraham Lincoln." It also owed a lot to the power of television, which brought the savagery of racism into millions of American homes.

More than 3,000 demonstrators were arrested in Birmingham, including Dr. King. While in jail, he wrote a "Letter from Birmingham Jail," a stirring defense of "**nonviolent civil disobedience**," which has since become a classic document of the civil rights movement. "One who breaks an unjust law," King stressed, "must do so openly, lovingly, and with a willingness to *accept the penalty*." King's efforts prevailed when Birmingham officials finally agreed to end their segregationist practices. White racists did not change overnight, however. One angry Alabaman sent a letter to King: "This isn't a threat but a promise—your head will be blown off as sure as Christ made green apples."

Throughout the Lower South, whites defied efforts at racial integration. On June 11, 1963, Alabama governor George Wallace personally blocked the door at the University of Alabama as African American students tried to register for classes. Wallace finally stepped aside in the face of insistent federal marshals and army troops. That night President Kennedy told the nation that he was urging Congress to pass a major new civil rights bill.

Four hours later, in Mississippi, a thirty-seven-year-old African American civil rights activist, Medgar Evers, listened to the president's speech in his car. Kennedy's new commitment to civil rights so excited him that he turned the car around and went home so that he could discuss the speech with his children. When Evers arrived at his house in Jackson at midnight, he was shot in his driveway by a white racist lying in ambush. He staggered to the carport and collapsed in front of his horrified wife and children. He died before reaching a hospital.

Such violence aroused the nation's indignation and reinforced Kennedy's commitment to make civil rights America's most pressing social issue. The killing of Medgar Evers led the president to host his first meeting of civil rights leaders in the White House and helped spur plans for a massive demonstration on the Mall in Washington, D.C. Yet southern Democrats in Congress blocked Kennedy's civil rights bill.

"I Have a Dream!"

The standoff in Congress led African American leaders to take a bold step. On August 28, some 250,000 blacks and whites of all ages, many of them schoolchildren transported on buses for the occasion, marched arm in arm down the Mall in Washington, D.C., chanting "Equality Now!" and singing "We Shall Overcome."

> Nonviolent civil disobedience: King's "Letter from Birmingham Jail"

nonviolent civil disobedience The principled tactic that Martin Luther King Jr. advocated: peaceful lawbreaking as a means of ending segregation.

"I HAVE A DREAM" Martin Luther King Jr. is photographed before delivering his now-famous speech at the March on Washington while the crowd of protesters watches, captivated. **How did the March on Washington differ from previous nonviolent protests in Southern cities like Birmingham?**

Nonviolent civil disobedience: March on Washington

The **March on Washington** for Jobs and Freedom was the largest political demonstration in American history. The organizers, primarily civil rights veterans Bayard Rustin and A. Philip Randolph, never imagined that so many people would participate. "When you looked at the crowd," remembered a U.S. Park Service ranger, "you didn't see blacks or whites. You saw America." Prominent entertainers Mahalia Jackson; Marian Anderson; Joan Baez; Bob Dylan; Odetta; and Peter, Paul, and Mary sang protest songs, and civil rights activists gave speeches calling for racial justice.

Then something remarkable happened. Standing on the steps of the Lincoln Memorial, thirty-four-year-old Martin Luther King Jr., who in recent years had been attacked four times, had seen his home bombed three times, and had been arrested fourteen times, spoke to the huge crowd. The crowd roared with anticipation. He began awkwardly. Noticing his nervousness, someone on stage urged him to "tell 'em about the dream."

As if suddenly inspired, King set aside his prepared remarks and delivered an extraordinary sermon in the form of a speech, using righteousness and fiery passion to inspire his listeners to action. He started slowly and picked up speed, as if he were preaching at a revival, giving poetic voice to the hopes of millions as he stressed the "fierce urgency of now" and the unstoppable power of "meeting physical force with soul force." President Kennedy,

March on Washington (1963) Civil rights demonstration on the National Mall, where Martin Luther King Jr. gave his famous "I Have a Dream" speech.

who earlier had tried to convince organizers to call off the march, was watching King's speech on TV at the White House, just a mile away. As King spoke, the president told an aide that "he's damn good."

Dr. King then shared his dream of an America in which racism would be put on a path to extinction and the ideal of equality would be realized:

> In spite of the difficulties and frustrations of the moment, I still have a *dream*. It is a *dream* deeply rooted in the American dream. I have a *dream* that one day this nation will rise up and live out the true meaning of its creed: 'We hold these truths to be self-evident; that all men are created equal.' I have a *dream* that one day . . . the sons of former slaves and the sons of former slaveowners will be able to sit together at the table of brotherhood.

As if at a massive church service, many in the crowd began shouting "Amen!" as King summoned a flawed nation to justice: "So let freedom ring!" he shouted, for "when we allow freedom to ring from every town and every hamlet, from every state and every city, we will be able to speed up the day when *all* God's children—black men and white men, Jews and Gentiles, Protestants and Catholics—will be able to join hands and sing in the words of the old Negro spiritual, *"Free at last, free at last, thank God Almighty, we are free at last!"*

As King finished, there was a startling hush, then a deafening ovation. The crowd spontaneously began singing "We Shall Overcome," holding hands and swaying as if at a prayer meeting.

King's dream of ending racial violence remained just that—a dream deferred. Eighteen days after the March on Washington, four Klansmen in Birmingham detonated a bomb in a black church, killing four young girls. The awful murders sparked indignation across the country—and around the world. The editors of the *Milwaukee Sentinel* stressed that the Birmingham bombing "should serve to goad the conscience. The deaths . . . in a sense are on the hands of each of us."

The Warren Court

The civil rights movement depended as much upon the courts as it did upon the leadership of Dr. King and others, and federal judges kept forcing states and localities to integrate schools and other public places. Under Chief Justice Earl Warren, the U.S. Supreme Court also made landmark decisions in other areas of American life.

Federal Courts force integration in schools and public places

In 1962, the Court ruled that a school prayer adopted by the New York State Board of Regents violated the constitutional prohibition against government-supported religion. In *Gideon v. Wainwright* (1963), the Court required that every felony defendant be provided a lawyer regardless of the defendant's ability to pay. In 1964, the Court ruled in *Escobedo v. Illinois* that a person accused of a crime must be allowed to consult a lawyer before being interrogated by police. Two years later, in *Miranda v. Arizona,* the Court issued a bitterly criticized ruling when it ordered that an accused person in police custody be informed of certain basic rights: the right to remain silent; the right to know that anything said to authorities can be used against the individual in court; and the right to have a defense attorney present during interrogation; since then, these requirements have been known as "Miranda rights." In addition, the Court established rules for police to follow in informing suspects of their legal rights before questioning could begin.

Freedom Summer

During late 1963 and throughout 1964, in the aftermath of President Kennedy's assassination, the civil rights movement grew in scope, visibility, and power. Racism, however, remained entrenched in the Lower South. Blacks continued to be excluded from the political process. For example, in 1963 only 6.7 percent of Mississippi blacks were registered to vote, the lowest percentage in the nation. White officials in the South kept African Americans from voting through a variety of means: charging them expensive poll taxes; forcing them to take difficult literacy tests; making the application process inconvenient; and intimidating them through the use of arson, beatings, and lynchings.

African American voter registration drives

In early 1964, Harvard-educated Robert "Bob" Moses, a thin, bespectacled, black New Yorker who had resigned from Martin Luther King Jr.'s Southern Christian Leadership Conference (SCLC) to head up the SNCC office in Mississippi, decided it would take "an army" to force the state to give voting rights to blacks. So he set about recruiting an army of black and white volunteers who would live with rural African Americans, teach them in "freedom schools," and help them register to vote.

Most of the recruits for what came to be called "Freedom Summer" were idealistic white college students, and many were Jewish. Mississippi's white leaders prepared for "the nigger-communist invasion" by doubling the state police force and stockpiling tear gas, electric cattle prods, and shotguns. The famous writer Eudora Welty reported from her hometown of Jackson, Mississippi, that she had heard that "this summer all hell is going to break loose."

It did. In mid-June, the volunteer activists met at an Ohio college to learn about southern racial history, nonviolent civil disobedience, and the likely abuses they would suffer. On the final evening of the training session, Moses pleaded with anyone who feared heading to Mississippi to go home; several of them did. The next day, the remaining volunteers boarded buses and headed south, fanning out across the state. In

FREEDOM SCHOOL A volunteer from Brooklyn, New York, instructs young black students on the arts, African American history, and civil rights at a freedom school in Jackson, Mississippi, as part of the "Mississippi Summer Project" in August 1964.

all, forty-one "freedom schools" that summer taught thousands of children math, writing, and history. They also tutored black adults about the complicated process of voter registration.

Forty-six-year-old Fannie Lou Hamer was one of the local blacks who worked with the SNCC volunteers during Freedom Summer. The youngest in a household of twenty children, she had spent most of her life working on local cotton plantations. During the Freedom Summer of 1963 and after, she led gatherings of volunteers in freedom songs and excelled as a lay preacher. "God is not pleased," she said, "at all the murdering, and all of the brutality, and all the killings for no reason at all. God is not pleased at the Negro children in the State of Mississippi, suffering from malnutrition. God is not pleased because we have to go raggedy each day. God is not pleased because we have to go to the field and work from ten to eleven hours for three lousy dollars."

In response to Freedom Summer, the Ku Klux Klan, local police, and other white racists harassed, arrested, and assaulted many of the young volunteers. Hamer was brutally beaten by jail guards in Winona. Then, in June 1964, Klan members abducted and murdered three young civil rights workers: James Earl Chaney, Andrew Goodman, and Michael "Mickey" Schwerner. Their decomposed bodies were found two months later in a cattle pond. In the process of searching for the missing men, authorities found the bodies of eight black males in rivers and swamps. The murders, said one volunteer, were "the end of innocence," after which "things could never be the same."

"Freedom schools"

From Civil Rights to Black Power

Racism was never limited solely to the South. In retrospect, it was predictable that the civil rights movement would shift its focus from the rural South to the very different plight of urban blacks. By the mid-sixties, about 70 percent of the nation's African Americans were living in urban areas, most of them in central-city ghettos bypassed by prosperity. Though the majority of African Americans continued to identify with the nonviolent, Christian-centered integration movement promoted by Martin Luther King Jr. and organizations such as the NAACP, SCLC, CORE, and the Urban League, King and others acknowledged privately that many young blacks, especially those in large cities, were losing faith in the strategy of nonviolence.

The fragmentation of the civil rights movement was tragically evident on August 11, 1965, when Watts, the largest black ghetto in Los Angeles, exploded in a frenzy of rioting and looting. When the uprising ended, 34 were dead, almost 4,000 were in jail, and property damage exceeded $35 million. Chicago and Cleveland, along with forty other American cities, experienced similar race

WHITE TERROR Young men cruise through a riot zone in Chicago in 1966, brandishing a Confederate flag and racist signs.

MALCOLM X The black power movement's most influential spokesman, Malcolm X's militant message conflicted with Martin Luther King Jr.'s emphasis on nonviolence.

riots in the summer of 1966. The following summer, Newark, New Jersey, and Detroit, Michigan, burst into flames. Between 1965 and 1968, nearly 300 racial uprisings shattered the peace of urban America.

The racial violence in northern cities revealed the civil war within the civil rights movement. As Gil Scott-Heron, a black musician, sang: "We are tired of praying and marching and thinking and learning / Brothers want to start cutting and shooting and stealing and burning." What came to be called "Black Power" began to compete with the integrationist, nonviolent philosophy espoused by Dr. King and the SCLC.

The most articulate spokesman for the **black power movement** was Malcolm X (formerly Malcolm Little, the X denoting his lost African family name). His parents were courageous supporters of Marcus Garvey's 1920s crusade for black nationalism, and his childhood home in Lansing, Michigan, was burned to the ground by white racists. Malcolm quit school during ninth grade and began to display what would become a lifelong ability to reinvent himself. By age nineteen, now known as Detroit Red, he had become a thief, drug dealer, and pimp. He spent seven years in Massachusetts prisons, where he experienced a conversion and joined a small Chicago-based religious sect, the Nation of Islam (NOI), whose members were called Black Muslims.

The organization had little to do with Islam and everything to do with its domineering leader, Elijah Muhammad, and the cultlike devotion he required. Muhammad dismissed whites as "devils" and championed black nationalism, racial pride, self-respect, and self-discipline. By 1953, a year after leaving prison, Malcolm X was a full-time NOI minister famous for his electrifying speeches attacking white racism and black powerlessness.

Malcolm X dismissed mainstream civil rights leaders such as Martin Luther King Jr. as being "nothing but modern Uncle Toms" who "keep you and me in check, keep us under control, keep us passive and peaceful and nonviolent." His militant speeches inspired thousands of mostly urban blacks to join NOI. "Yes, I'm an extremist," Malcolm acknowledged in 1964. "The black race in the United States is in extremely bad shape. You show me a black man who isn't an extremist and I'll show you one who needs psychiatric attention." More than most black leaders, Malcolm X expressed the emotions and frustrations of the inner-city African American working poor. Yet at the peak of his influence, Malcolm X became embroiled in a conflict with Elijah Muhammad that proved fatal; NOI assassins killed Malcolm X in Manhattan on February 21, 1965.

Black militancy did not die with Malcolm X, however. By 1966, "black power" had become a rallying cry for young extremists. When Stokely Carmichael, a twenty-five-year-old graduate of Howard University, became head of SNCC, he enforced the separatist philosophy of black power by ousting whites

black power movement Militant form of civil rights protest focused on urban communities in the North that emerged as a response to impatience with the nonviolent tactics of Martin Luther King Jr.

from the organization. "When you talk of black power," Carmichael shouted, "you talk of bringing this country to its knees, of building a movement that will smash everything Western civilization has created."

Where Dr. King spoke to white America's moral conscience, Carmichael spoke to the seething rage of the young black underclass impatient with non-violent protest. Soon he would move on to the Black Panther party, a group of leather-jacketed black revolutionaries founded in Oakland, California, attracting recruits with its incendiary strategies. H. Rap Brown, who succeeded Carmichael as head of SNCC in 1967, was equally committed to a strategy of violence. He urged blacks to "get you some guns" and "kill the honkies [whites]."

Black Power in Retrospect

Although widely covered in the media, the black power movement never attracted more than a small minority of African Americans. Dr. King dismissed black separatism and the promotion of violent social change, reminding his followers that "we can't win violently."

Still, the emphasis on black power had two positive effects upon the civil rights movement. First, black power advocates forced King and other mainstream black leaders and organizations to shift their focus from the rural South to poverty-stricken inner-city ghettos in the North and West. Legal access to restaurants, schools, and other public accommodations, King pointed out, meant little to people mired in chronic poverty. They needed jobs and decent housing as much as they needed access to all-white facilities. To this end, King began to emphasize the economic needs of the black

Black Panther party

PANTHER POWER Black Panthers display the black power salute outside of a San Francisco Liberation School, where activists raised awareness and appreciation of African American history, a topic often ignored by white, mainstream curriculums.

urban underclass, launching his own war on poverty. The time had come, he declared while launching his "Poor People's Campaign" in December 1967, for radical new measures "to provide jobs and income for the poor." Yet as King and others stressed, the hugely expensive war in Vietnam was taking funds away from federal programs serving the poor, and black soldiers were dying in disproportionate numbers in Southeast Asia.

Second, the controversial black power movement also motivated African Americans to take greater pride in their racial heritage by pushing for black studies programs in schools and colleges, the celebration of African cultural and artistic traditions, the organizing of inner-city voters to elect black mayors, laws forcing landlords to treat blacks fairly, and the creation of grassroots organizations and community centers in black neighborhoods. It was Malcolm X who insisted that blacks call themselves *African Americans* as a symbol of pride in their roots and as a spur to learn more about their history. As the popular singer James Brown urged, "Say it loud—I'm black and I'm proud."

CORE **OBJECTIVE**

3. Analyze Lyndon B. Johnson's War on Poverty and Great Society initiatives, and evaluate their impact on American society.

Lyndon B. Johnson and the Great Society

Growing federal support for civil rights came from an unlikely source: a drawling white Texan who succeeded John F. Kennedy in the White House. Lyndon B. Johnson, the towering Texan known as "LBJ," a graduate of Southwest Texas State Teachers College, took the presidential oath on board the plane that brought Kennedy's body back to Washington from Dallas. Jacqueline Kennedy, still in her blood-soaked suit, stood beside him. Fifty-five years old and six feet four inches tall, Johnson had spent twenty-six years in Washington and served nearly a decade as one of the most powerful Democratic leaders ever in the Senate. Now he was the first southern president since Woodrow Wilson, a legislative magician who had excelled as Senate majority leader.

Johnson's transition to the presidency was not easy. The Kennedy brothers despised him and his hardscrabble background. They had excluded him from key decisions, often dismissing the rural Texan with the deep southern drawl and coarse manners as "Rufus Cornpone." JFK had warned his aides that Johnson was "a very insecure, sensitive man with a huge ego."

Johnson brought to the White House a dramatically different personality and style from that of his predecessor. Unlike Kennedy, who was born to great wealth, Johnson was a rags-to-riches story. With almost superhuman energy and crushing ambition, he had worked his way out of poverty during the Great Depression to become one of the Senate's most dominating figures.

LBJ had none of the Kennedy elegance. His ego and insecurities were as massive as his vanity and ambition. He could not stand being alone; he insisted on being the center of attention wherever he went. Johnson personalized the presidency. At press conferences, he referred to "my Security Council," "my Cabinet," "my legislation," and "my boys" fighting in Southeast Asia.

George Reedy, the president's press secretary, said that Johnson was a "man of too many paradoxes." Ruthless and often bullying, needy and warmhearted, he was a whirlwind of workaholic energy and inspiring hopes, a crude idealist and a brutal optimist so thin-skinned that he took all criticism personally. In his view, people were either with him or against him. There was no middle ground.

THE OATH OF OFFICE Less than an hour and a half after Kennedy's death, Johnson took the presidential oath aboard Air Force One between his wife, Lady Bird (left), and Jacqueline Kennedy (right), before flying out of Dallas for Washington, D.C.

At bottom, Johnson was a narcissistic manic-depressive. Being respected was not enough; he needed to be adored. Famous for his dramatic mood swings, brooding discontent, and private insecurities, he often berated his aides with raw outbursts of cutting profanity and belittling humor. Yet he was also a man capable of "roaring energy" and surprising passions, compassionate and generous toward the poor, and sincerely committed to attacking racism. Most of all, Johnson yearned to be loved and recognized as a transformational leader.

Like the Kennedy brothers, LBJ displayed a lifelong weakness for attractive women. He often bragged about how many women he had bedded and ordered that none of his secretaries be "tired old maids." Early in his presidency, he alerted reporters that they should ignore him "coming in and out of a few women's bedrooms while in the White House." (His devoted yet long-suffering wife, Lady Bird, acknowledged that "Lyndon loved the human race, and half of the human race are women.")

Those who viewed Johnson as a stereotypical southern conservative failed to appreciate his long-standing admiration for Franklin D. Roosevelt, the depth of his concern for the poor, and his bold support for the cause of civil rights (in part because he needed to win over the northern wing of the Democratic party). "I'm going to be the best friend the Negro ever had," Johnson bragged to a member of the White House staff soon after becoming president. His commitment to civil rights was in part motivated by politics, in part by his desire to bring the South into the mainstream of American life, and in part by his life experiences. His first teaching job after college was at an elementary school in Texas serving Mexican American children. The experience created in him a lifelong desire to help "those poor little kids. I saw hunger in their eyes and pain in their bodies. Those little brown bodies had so little and needed so much." He grew determined to "fill their souls with ambition and interest and belief in the future."

Unlike the politically cautious Kennedy, Johnson had Texas-sized ambitions. Few presidents had ever dreamed as big as Lyndon Johnson. He was determined to be the greatest American president, the one who did the most good for the most people. He promised to "help every child get an education, to help every Negro and every American citizen have an equal opportunity, to help every family get a decent home, and to help bring healing to the sick and dignity to the old."

Politics and Poverty

LBJ's first legislative acts: Revenue Act (1964), Civil Rights Act (1964), and Economic Opportunity Act (1964)

Johnson managed legislation through Congress better than any president in history, including Franklin Roosevelt, his idol. LBJ was the consummate wheeler-dealer. "It is the politician's task," Johnson asserted, "to pass legislation, not to sit around saying principled things." In 1964, he set about doing just that, taking advantage of widespread public support to push through Congress Kennedy's stalled measures for tax reductions and civil rights. He later said that he wanted to take Kennedy's incomplete program "and turn it into a martyr's cause." The Revenue Act of 1964 provided a 20 percent reduction in tax rates (the top rate was then a whopping 91 percent, compared to 39.6 today). It was intended to give consumers more money to spend so as to boost economic growth and create new jobs, and it worked as planned. Unemployment fell from 5.2 percent in 1964 to 4.5 percent in 1965, and 3.8 percent in 1966.

Civil Rights Act of 1964

Long thwarted by southern Democrats who had held it up in Congress, the **Civil Rights Act of 1964** finally became law on July 2 after eighty days of congressional debate. President Johnson played a crucial role in its passage. He used his experience as a power broker in the Senate to launch his own risky crusade for racial justice as president. One senator who survived the "Johnson treatment," as it came to be called, said that the president would "twist your arm off at the shoulder and beat your head with it" if you did not agree to vote as he wanted.

Soon after becoming president, Johnson hosted his close friend and arch-segregationist, Senator Richard Russell of Georgia, for lunch at the White House and warned him, in order to pass the Civil Rights Act: "You've got to get out of my way. I'm going to run over you." "You may do that," Russell replied. "But by God, it's going to cost you the South and cost you the

Civil Rights Act of 1964
Legislation that outlawed discrimination in public accommodations and employment, passed at the urging of President Lyndon B. Johnson.

election of 1964." Johnson answered: "If that's the price I've got to pay, I'll pay it gladly." Soon thereafter, Johnson told Congress that "we have talked long enough in this country about equal rights. . . . It is time now to write the next chapter, and to write it in the book of law."

Many others (called the "coalition of conscience" by labor leader Walter Reuther) helped Johnson convince Congress to pass the Civil Rights Act—congressional committee chairs, both Republicans and Democrats; labor unions; church leaders; and civil rights organizations. Their collective efforts produced what is arguably the single most important piece of legislation created in the twentieth century. The passage of the Civil Rights Act after more than a year of congressional delays marked one of those extraordinary moments when the ideals of democracy, equal opportunity, and human dignity were affirmed by action.

The Civil Rights Act of 1964 banned racial segregation in public places such as bus terminals, restaurants, theaters, and hotels. It also gave new powers to the federal government to bring lawsuits against organizations or businesses that violated constitutional rights, and it established the Equal Employment Opportunities Commission to ensure that employers treated job appli-

DOWN WITH SEGREGATION A worker removes a sign from a public restroom at Montgomery Municipal Airport that reads: "WHITE MEN."

cants equally, regardless of race, gender, or national origin. On the night after signing the pathbreaking Civil Rights Act, Johnson knew that many conservative white southerners would be outraged. He correctly predicted that "we have just delivered the South to the Republican party for a long time to come." Instead of being elated, he was glum, for he feared that his commitment to civil rights would cost him the election of 1964.

The War on Poverty

In addition to fulfilling Kennedy's legislative priorities that had been stalled in Congress, Johnson launched a much more elaborate legislative program of his own by declaring "unconditional war on poverty in America." Americans had "rediscovered" poverty in 1962 when the social critic Michael Harrington published a powerful exposé, *The Other America*. Harrington revealed that more than 40 million people were mired in an invisible "culture of poverty" that held them hostage in a vicious cycle. Poverty led to poor housing conditions, which in turn led to poor health, poor attendance at school or work, alcohol and drug abuse, unwanted pregnancies, single-parent families, and so on. Harrington added that poverty was much more extensive in the United States than people realized because much of it was hidden from view in isolated rural areas or inner-city slums. He urged the United States to launch a "comprehensive assault on poverty."

Economic Opportunity Act (1964) Key legislation in President Johnson's "War on Poverty" that created the Office of Economic Opportunity and programs like Head Start and the work-study financial-aid program for low-income college students.

President Kennedy had read Harrington's book and had asked his advisers in the fall of 1963, just before his assassination, to investigate the poverty problem and suggest solutions. Upon taking office as president, Johnson announced that he wanted an anti-poverty legislative package that was "big and bold, that would hit the nation with real impact." He was determined to help the "one-fifth of all American families with incomes too small to even meet their basic needs." They needed better homes, better schools, better medical care, and better job training. Money for the program would come from the tax revenues generated by corporate profits made possible by the tax reduction of 1964, which had led to one of the longest sustained economic booms in history. By the mid-1960s, unemployment had dropped, consumer spending had increased, and corporate profits were soaring.

Economic Opportunity Act of 1964

The **Economic Opportunity Act of 1964** was the primary weapon in Johnson's much-trumpeted "War on Poverty." It created an Office of Economic Opportunity to administer eleven new community-based programs, many of which still exist. They included a Job Corps training program for inner-city youths aged sixteen to twenty-one; a Head Start educational program for disadvantaged preschoolers; a Legal Services Corporation to provide legal assistance for low-income Americans; work-study financial-aid programs for low-income college students; grants to small farmers and rural businesses; loans to businesses that hired the chronically unemployed; the Volunteers in Service to America program that recruited volunteers to combat inner-city poverty; and the Community Action Program, which would allow the poor "maximum feasible participation" in organizing and directing their own

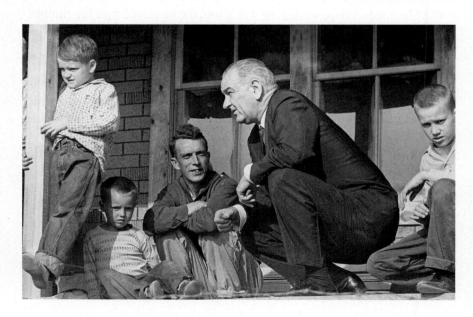

WAR ON POVERTY In 1964, Johnson visited Tom Fletcher, a father of eight children living in a tar-paper shack in rural Kentucky. Fletcher became a "poster father" for the War on Poverty, though, as it turned out, his life improved little from its programs.

neighborhood programs designed for their benefit. In 1964, Congress also approved the Food Stamp Act, a program run by the Department of Agriculture to help poor people afford to buy groceries.

The Election of 1964

Johnson's successes in creating an array of new federal social-welfare programs triggered a Republican counterattack. Arizona senator Barry Goldwater, a wealthy department-store owner, emerged as the blunt-talking leader of the growing conservative wing of the Republican party. In his best-selling book *The Conscience of a Conservative* (1960), Goldwater had called for ending the income tax and drastically reducing federal entitlement programs such as Social Security. Conservatives controlled the Republican Convention when it gathered in San Francisco in the early summer of 1964, and they ensured Goldwater's nomination. "I would remind you," Goldwater told the delegates, "that extremism in the defense of liberty is no vice." He later explained that his objective was like that of Calvin Coolidge in the 1920s: "to reduce the size of government. Not to pass laws, but repeal them."

In his memoirs, Goldwater admitted that he knew he had no chance to win the presidency: "I just wanted the conservatives to have a real voice in the country." As a candidate, he frightened many voters when he urged wholesale bombing of North Vietnam and even suggested using atomic weapons. He criticized Johnson's War on Poverty as a waste of money, told students that the federal government should not provide any assistance for education, and opposed the nuclear test ban treaty and the Civil Rights Act of 1964, having been one of only six Republican senators to vote against it. To Republican campaign buttons that claimed "In your heart, you know he's right," Democrats responded, "In your guts, you know he's nuts."

Johnson portrayed himself as a responsible centrist in contrast to Goldwater's "extreme" conservatism. He chose as his running mate Hubert H. Humphrey of Minnesota, a prominent liberal senator who had long promoted civil rights. In contrast to Goldwater's aggressive rhetoric on Vietnam, Johnson pledged that he was "not about to send American boys nine or ten thousand miles from home to do what Asian boys ought to be doing for themselves."

The result was a landslide. Johnson polled 61 percent of the vote; Goldwater carried only Arizona and five states in the Lower South. Johnson won the electoral vote by a whopping 486–52. In the Senate, the Democrats increased their majority by two (68–32) and in the House by thirty-seven (295–140). Goldwater's success in the Lower South, however, accelerated the region's shift to the Republican party, and his candidacy proved to be a turning point in the development of the national conservative movement, inspiring a generation of young activists and the formation of

CAMPAIGN BUTTONS, 1964
A button for and against Barry Goldwater from the election campaigns of 1964. **What were the main issues in Goldwater's platform?**

conservative organizations that would transform the dynamics of American politics during the 1970s and 1980s. Their success would culminate in the presidency of Ronald Reagan, the Hollywood actor who co-chaired the California for Goldwater campaign in 1964.

The Great Society

Lyndon Johnson interpreted his lopsided victory as a mandate for massive changes. He knew, however, that his popularity would quickly fade. "Every day I'm in office," he told his aides, "I'm going to lose votes. I'm going to alienate somebody. . . . We've got to get this legislation fast. You've got to get it during my honeymoon."

As Johnson's War on Poverty gathered momentum, his already-outsized ambitions grew even more. In May 1964, he announced his intention to launch an array of new programs intended to create a "Great Society" that would end poverty and racial injustice and provide "abundance and liberty for all." That was a magisterial goal, but it "was just the beginning," Johnson insisted, given that the United States had the resources to do much more than assault poverty. "We have the opportunity to move not only toward the rich society and the powerful society, but upward to the Great Society." He did not explain precisely what he meant by a "great society," but it soon became clear that Johnson viewed the federal government as the magical lever for raising the quality of life for all Americans—rich and poor. He would surpass his hero Franklin Roosevelt in expanding the goals and scope of the federal government to ensure that Americans were a people of plenty.

When Johnson became president in November 1963, Social Security was America's only nationwide social program. That soon changed. In 1965, Johnson began flooding Congress with waves of Great Society legislation that he said would end poverty, revitalize decaying cities, provide every young person the chance to attend college, protect the health of the elderly, enhance the arts and humanities, clean up the nation's polluted air and water, and make the highways safer and prettier. The scope of Johnson's Great Society programs exceeded Franklin D. Roosevelt's New Deal, in part because of the nation's extraordinary prosperity during the mid-1960s. "This country," Johnson proclaimed, "is rich enough to do anything it has the guts to do and the vision to do and the will to do." That proved *not* to be the case, however.

Health Insurance, Housing, and Higher Education

Johnson's Great Society: Medicare and Medicaid (1965), the Higher Education Act (1965), and the Housing and Urban Development Act (1965)

Johnson's first priority was federal health insurance and aid to help young people pursue higher education, "liberal" proposals that had languished since President Truman had proposed them in 1945. For twenty years, the steadfast opposition of the physicians making up the American Medical Association (AMA) had stalled a comprehensive medical-insurance program. Now that Johnson and the Democrats had the votes to pass the measure, however, the AMA joined Republicans in supporting a bill serving those over age sixty-five. The act that finally emerged went well beyond the original proposal. It created not just a **Medicare** health-insurance program for the elderly but also a **Medicaid** program of federal grants to states to help cover medical expenses for the poor. Johnson signed the bill on July 30, 1965, in Independence, Missouri, with eighty-one-year-old Harry Truman looking on.

The Higher Education Act of 1965 increased federal grants to universities, created scholarships for low-income students, provided low-interest loans for students, and established a National Teachers Corps. "Every child," Johnson asserted, "must be encouraged to get as much education as he has the ability to take."

The momentum generated by the Higher Education and Medicare acts helped carry 435 more Great Society bills through Congress. Among them was the Appalachian Regional Development Act of 1966, which allocated $1 billion for programs in remote mountain areas that had long been pockets of desperate poverty. The Housing and Urban Development Act of 1965 provided $3 billion for urban renewal projects. Funds to help low-income families pay their rent followed in 1966, and the same year a new Department of Housing and Urban Development appeared, headed by Robert C. Weaver, the first African American cabinet member.

In implementing his Great Society programs, Lyndon Johnson had, in the words of one Washington reporter, "brought to harvest a generation's backlog of ideas and social legislation." People were amazed by Johnson's energy, drive, and legislative skills. He never seemed to stop or slow down. A woman in Hawaii noted that Johnson "is a mover of men. Kennedy could inspire men, but he couldn't move them."

The Immigration Act

Little noticed in the stream of Great Society legislation was a major new immigration bill, the **Immigration and Nationality Services Act of 1965**, which Johnson signed in a ceremony held on Liberty Island in New York Harbor. Both Democrats and Republicans supported the new act in an era when bipartisan cooperation was still possible. In his speech, Johnson stressed that the law would redress the wrong done to those "from southern and eastern Europe" and the "developing continents" of Asia, Africa, and Latin America. The old system, dating back to 1924, greatly favored immigrants from Great Britain and the countries of western and northern Europe over those from southern and eastern Europe, Asia, and Africa. The new law abolished the discriminatory annual quotas based upon an immigrant's national origin and treated all nationalities and races equally. In place of nationality quotas, it created hemispheric ceilings on visas issued: 170,000 for persons from outside the Western Hemisphere, 120,000 for persons from within. It also stipulated that no more than 20,000 people could come from any one country each year.

Medicare and Medicaid Health-care programs designed to aid the elderly and disadvantaged, respectively, as part of President Johnson's Great Society initiative.

Immigration and Nationality Services Act of 1965 Legislation that abolished discriminatory quotas based upon immigrants' national origin and treated all nationalities and races equally.

VOTING RIGHTS ACT Johnson signs the Voting Rights Act of 1965, flanked by Martin Luther King Jr. and other civil rights supporters.

During the sixties and since, Asians and Latin Americans became the largest contingent of new Americans. Over 60 million immigrants have come to America since 1965, and most of them were natives of Latin America and Asia. Significant numbers of them joined the armed forces, making the military much more diverse than ever.

Voting Rights Legislation

Building upon the successes of "Freedom Summer," Martin Luther King Jr. organized an effort in early 1965 to register the 3 million unregistered African American voters in the South. In Selma, Alabama, where only 250 of the 15,000 blacks of voting age were registered voters, hundreds of black and white civil rights protesters began a march to Montgomery, about fifty-four miles away, only to be assaulted by 500 state troopers using clubs, tear gas, and bullwhips. "The news from Selma," reported the *Washington Post*, "will shock and alarm the whole nation."

A federal judge agreed to allow the marchers to continue, and President Johnson provided troops for their protection. Still, two white marchers—a mother of five from Detroit and a Boston minister—were murdered. By March 25, when the demonstrators reached Montgomery, some 25,000 people were with them, and Dr. King delivered a rousing address on the steps of the state capitol in which he said, "The battle is in our hands. And we can answer with creative nonviolence the call to higher ground to which the new directions of our struggle summons us."

Several days earlier, Johnson had urged Congress to "overcome the crippling legacy of bigotry and injustice" by making the cause of civil rights "our cause too." He then concluded by slowly speaking the words of the movement's hymn: "And we *shall* overcome."

The resulting **Voting Rights Act of 1965** ensured all citizens the right to vote. It authorized the attorney general to send federal officials to register voters in areas that had long experienced racial discrimination. In states or counties where fewer than half the adults had voted in 1964, the act banned the various ways, like literacy tests, that local officials used to keep blacks and Hispanics from voting. By the end of the year, some 250,000 African Americans were newly registered to vote in several southern states. By 1968, an estimated 53 percent of blacks in Alabama were registered to vote compared to only 14 percent in 1960. In this respect, the Voting Rights Act was even more important than the Civil Rights Act

Voting Rights Act of 1965 Legislation ensuring that all Americans were able to vote; ended literacy tests and other means of restricting voting rights.

because it empowered black voters in the South, thereby transforming the white-dominated politics in the region and enabling, for the first time, the election of black public officials.

Assessing the Great Society

As an accidental president following a tragic assassination, Lyndon B. Johnson sought to give Americans a sense of forward movement in troubled times and show them that he could overcome their fears of a divided America and create a "Great Society" whereby people would be "more concerned with the quality of their goals than the quantity of their goods."

Yet the Great Society and War on Poverty programs never lived up to Johnson's grandiose goals, in part because the Vietnam War soon took priority and siphoned away funding and in part because neither Johnson nor his congressional supporters understood the stubborn complexity of chronic poverty.

The Great Society, however, did include several triumphs for low-income Americans. Infant mortality has dropped, college completion rates have soared, malnutrition has virtually disappeared, and far fewer elderly Americans are living below the poverty line. The federal guarantee of civil rights and voting rights remains in place to this day. Medicare and Medicaid have become two of the most appreciated government programs. Consumers now have a federal agency protecting them. Head Start programs providing preschool enrichment activities for poor students have produced long-term benefits. The federal food stamp program has improved the nutrition and health of children living in poverty. Finally, the scholarships provided to low-income college students have been immensely valuable in enabling young people to gain access to higher education.

Several of Johnson's most ambitious programs, however, were ill conceived, others were vastly underfunded, and many were mismanaged and even corrupt. Some of the problems they were meant to address actually worsened. As Joseph Califano, one of Johnson's senior aides, confessed: "Did we legislate too much? Were mistakes made? Plenty of them." Medicare, for example, removed incentives for hospitals to control costs, so medical bills skyrocketed—for everyone. In addition, food stamp fraud soared as people took advantage of a program intended to ensure healthy nutrition.

Overall, Great Society programs helped reduce the percentage of the population living in poverty from 19 percent in 1964 to 10 percent in 1973, but it did so largely by providing federal welfare payments, not by finding people decent jobs. By 1966, middle-class resentment over the cost and excesses of the Great Society programs had generated a conservative backlash that fueled a Republican resurgence in Congress. By then, however, the Great Society had transformed public expectations of the power and role of federal government.

Conservative backlash over Great Society programs

CORE **OBJECTIVE**

4. Explain Presidents Kennedy's and Johnson's motivations for deepening America's military involvement in the Vietnam War, and appraise their efforts to preserve a non-Communist South Vietnam.

Tonkin Gulf Resolution (1964)
Congressional action that granted the president unlimited authority to defend U.S. forces abroad after an allegedly unprovoked attack on American warships off the coast of North Vietnam.

The Tragedy of Vietnam

In foreign affairs, Lyndon Johnson was, like Woodrow Wilson, a novice. And, again like Wilson, his presidency would become a victim of his crusading idealism abroad. During early 1965, a frequently haggard LBJ confided to friends that the "Vietnam thing" was "wearing him down." As racial violence erupted in America's cities, the war in Vietnam reached new levels of intensity and destruction. With weapons supplied by China and the Soviet Union, North Vietnam provided massive support to the Viet Cong (VC), the Communist guerrillas fighting in South Vietnam to overthrow the U.S.-backed government and unify the divided nation under Communist control.

When he became president, Johnson inherited a long-standing U.S. commitment to prevent a Communist takeover in Vietnam. Beginning with Harry S. Truman, U.S. presidents had done just enough to avoid being charged with having "lost" Vietnam to communism. Johnson initially sought to do the same, fearing that any other course of action would undermine his political influence and jeopardize his Great Society programs in Congress. His path, however, took the United States into a deeper military commitment in Southeast Asia.

In November 1963, when President Kennedy was assassinated, there were 16,000 U.S. military "advisers" in South Vietnam. Early in his presidency, Johnson doubted that Vietnam was worth more extensive military involvement. In May 1964, he told his national security adviser, McGeorge Bundy, that he had spent a sleepless night worrying about Vietnam: "It looks to me like we are getting into another Korea. . . . I don't think it's worth fighting for. And I don't think we can get out. It's just the biggest damned mess that I ever saw."

Yet Johnson's fear of appearing weak abroad outweighed his misgivings. By the end of 1965, there were 184,000 U.S. troops in Vietnam; in 1966, there were 385,000; and by 1969, at the height of the American war effort, 542,000.

Escalation in Vietnam

The official justification for the military "escalation"—a Defense Department term favored in the Vietnam era—was the **Tonkin Gulf Resolution**, passed by the Senate on

U.S. AIR STRIKES Sustained bombing of Vietnam left thirty- to fifty-foot-wide craters that can still be seen today.

August 7, 1964. On that day, President Johnson told a national television audience that on August 2 and 4, North Vietnamese torpedo boats had attacked two destroyers, the U.S.S. *Maddox* and the U.S.S. *C. Turner Joy,* in the Gulf of Tonkin, off the coast of North Vietnam. Johnson's description of "naked aggression on the high seas" was later shown to be false and misleading; the U.S. ships had actually fired first. They had been supporting South Vietnamese attacks against two North Vietnamese islands—attacks planned by American advisers.

The Tonkin Gulf Resolution authorized the president to "take all necessary measures" to protect U.S. forces and "to prevent further aggression." Senator Wayne Morse of Oregon, who had learned that Johnson's account of the incident in the Tonkin Gulf was false, argued that American warships were in fact engaged in "acts of war rather than acts of defense." His efforts to oppose Johnson failed, however. Only Morse and one other senator voted against the Tonkin Gulf Resolution, which Johnson thereafter interpreted as equivalent to a congressional declaration of war. Aware of frenzied meetings and hushed tones in the White House, Lady Bird Johnson concluded that "we might have a small war on our hands."

HIDDEN A Vietnamese mother hides her son and herself in the bushes near the village of Le My in 1965 after U.S. Marines clear the area of Viet Cong forces.

It would be no small war, however. Soon after Johnson's landslide victory over Goldwater in November 1964, he made the crucial decisions that committed the United States to a full-scale war in Vietnam. On February 5, 1965, VC guerrillas killed 8 and wounded 126 at a U.S. base near Pleiku, in South Vietnam. More attacks later that week led Johnson to order "Operation Rolling Thunder," the first sustained bombing of North Vietnam, which was intended to stop the flow of soldiers and supplies into the south. Thereafter, there were essentially two fronts in the expanding war: one, in North Vietnam, where U.S. warplanes continued a massive bombing campaign, and the other, in South Vietnam, where nearly all the ground combat occurred.

In March 1965, the new U.S. commander in Vietnam, General William C. Westmoreland, greeted the first American combat troops in Vietnam. By the summer, U.S. forces were engaged in "search-and-destroy" operations against VC guerrillas throughout South Vietnam. It was a frustrating war for the Americans. The Viet Cong, made up of both men and women, wore no uniforms and dissolved by day into the villages, hiding among Vietnamese civilians. Their elusiveness exasperated American soldiers, most of whom were not trained for such unconventional warfare in dense jungles and intense heat and humidity.

As combat operations increased, so did casualties (the number of killed, wounded, and missing) announced each week on the nightly television news, along with the "body count" of alleged VC dead. "Westy's war," although fought with helicopter gunships, chemical defoliants (Agent Orange), and highly flammable napalm, became like the trench warfare of World War I—a war of attrition, whereby each side hoped to outlast the other by causing so much loss of life as to force a surrender. "We will not be defeated," Johnson told the nation in April. "We will not grow tired. We will not withdraw."

The Context for Policy

Commitment to "containing" communism

President Johnson's decision to "Americanize" the Vietnam War, so mistaken in retrospect, was consistent with the foreign-policy principles pursued by all presidents after the Second World War. The idea of "containing" communism, articulated first in the 1947 Truman Doctrine, endorsed by President Eisenhower, and reaffirmed by President Kennedy, included a pledge to oppose the advance of communism anywhere in the world. "Why are we in Vietnam?" Johnson asked during a speech in 1965. "We are there because we have a promise to keep. . . . To leave Vietnam to its fate would shake the confidence of all these people in the value of American commitment."

Military intervention was thus a logical culmination of the assumptions that had long been shared by the foreign-policy establishment and the leaders of both political parties. At the same time, Johnson and his advisers believed that military efforts in Vietnam must not reach levels that would cause the Chinese or Soviets to become involved—which meant, in effect, that a military victory was never possible. As a practical matter, the United States was not fighting to "win" the war but to prevent the North Vietnamese and the Viet Cong from winning and, eventually, thereby force them to sign a negotiated settlement. This meant that the United States would have to maintain a military presence as long as the Vietnamese Communists retained the will to fight.

The Vietnam War was the defining event for the baby boomers, the largest generation of Americans ever, and it divided that generation in lasting ways. As it turned out, American support for the war eroded faster than the will of the North Vietnamese leaders to tolerate devastating casualties and destruction.

Widespread opposition to the war on college campuses began in 1965 with "teach-ins" at the University of Michigan. The following year, Senator J. William Fulbright of Arkansas, chairman of the Senate Foreign Relations Committee, began congressional investigations into American policy in Vietnam. George F. Kennan, the author of the containment doctrine, told the committee that the containment doctrine was appropriate for Europe but not for Southeast Asia, a region that was not essential to U.S. security. In addition, a respected military leader testified that America's strategy had no chance of achieving victory.

Such opposition to the war effort brought out the worst in Johnson. He labeled his political critics and anti-war protesters "Communists" and used government agencies to punish them.

Still, the resistance to the escalating war grew. By 1967, anti-war demonstrations were attracting massive support, and Americans were dividing themselves into "hawks" who supported the war and "doves" who opposed it. Nightly television accounts of the fighting—Vietnam was the first war to receive extended television coverage and hence was dubbed the "living-room war"—called into question the accuracy of statements by military and government officials claiming the Americans were winning. Journalists called it a "credibility crisis."

> Mounting opposition to the Vietnam War

By May 1967, even Secretary of Defense Robert McNamara was wavering: "The picture of the world's greatest superpower killing or injuring 1,000 civilians a week, while trying to pound a tiny backward nation into submission on an issue whose merits are hotly disputed, is not a pretty one." Between 1965 and 1968, U.S. warplanes dropped more bombs on Vietnam than had fallen on all enemy targets in the Second World War. Yet there was "no light at the end of the tunnel."

On a personal level, Johnson was determined not to be the first president to lose a war. Yet as American military involvement deepened and criticism of the war mounted, Johnson grew more frustrated, depressed, and irritable as his doubts about the war turned to despair. "I can't get out [of Vietnam]. I can't finish it with what I got. So what the hell can I do?" His wife recalled that Vietnam became a "hell of a thorn stuck in his throat. It wouldn't come up; it wouldn't go down. . . . It was pure hell."

Johnson and his advisers badly underestimated the strength of the North Vietnamese and Viet Cong commitment to unify Vietnam and expel American forces. While the United States fought a limited war for limited objectives, the Vietnamese Communists, aided by the Soviets and Chinese, fought an all-out war for their very survival. Just as General Westmoreland was assuring Johnson and the public in early 1968 that his troops were on the verge of gaining the upper hand, the Communists organized widespread assaults that jolted American confidence and resolve.

The Turning Point

On January 31, 1968, the first day of the Vietnamese New Year (Tet), some 70,000 Viet Cong and North Vietnamese soldiers defied a holiday truce by launching well-coordinated assaults on American and South Vietnamese forces throughout South Vietnam. The old capital city of Hué fell to the Communists, and VC fighters temporarily occupied the U.S. embassy in Saigon, the capital of South Vietnam. Within a few days, however, superior American firepower turned the tables. General Westmoreland proclaimed the **Tet offensive** a major defeat for the Viet Cong, and most military strategists later agreed with him.

Tet offensive (1968) Surprise attack by Viet Cong guerrillas and North Vietnamese army on U.S. and South Vietnamese forces that shocked the American public and led to widespread sentiment against the war.

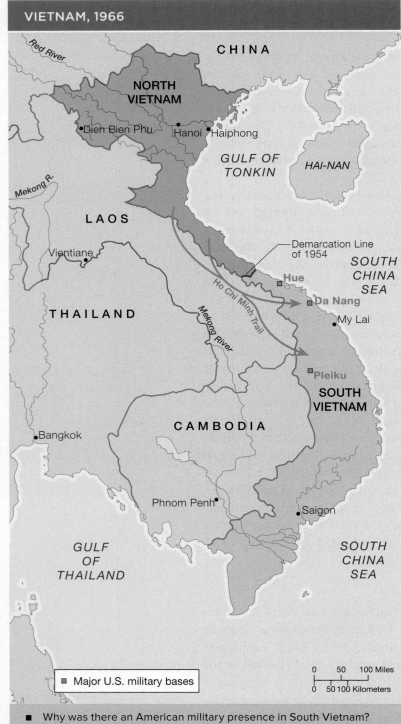

VIETNAM, 1966

■ Major U.S. military bases

0   50   100 Miles

0   50 100 Kilometers

■ Why was there an American military presence in South Vietnam?
■ What was the Ho Chi Minh Trail?
■ What was the Tet offensive?

The Viet Cong had hoped the Tet offensive would ignite a general uprising in the countryside. In that, they failed. Yet while VC casualties were enormous, the *political* impact of the surprise attack was dramatic, for it decisively turned Americans against the war. The scope and intensity of the Tet offensive contradicted upbeat claims by U.S. commanders that the war had been going well. "What the hell is going on?" CBS newscaster Walter Cronkite demanded when he heard about the offensive. "I thought we were winning this war." *Time* and *Newsweek* magazines soon ran antiwar editorials urging the withdrawal of U.S. forces. President Johnson's popularity plummeted.

Equally disturbing to LBJ was General Westmoreland's unexpected request for more than 200,000 additional U.S. troops. The request stunned Clark Clifford, the new defense secretary. He told the president that the military leaders "don't know what they're talking about." Instead of winning the war, he added, the United States had become mired in a sinkhole with "no end in sight." America's involvement in Vietnam was a "bottomless pit," reported another presidential adviser.

Civil rights leaders and social activists felt betrayed as they saw federal funds earmarked for the War on Poverty gobbled up by the ever-expanding war. By 1967, the United States was spending some $2 billion each month in Vietnam, about $322,000 for every VC killed; anti-poverty programs at home received only $53 per person. As Martin Luther King Jr. pointed out, "The bombs in Vietnam explode at home—they destroy the hopes and possibilities for a decent America."

President Johnson, under constant assault by critics of "Johnson's War," grew increasingly embittered, isolated, and exhausted. He suffered from depression and bouts of paranoia as he realized that the Vietnam War ("that bitch of a war") was undermining his Great Society programs and threatening his reelection.

Senator Eugene McCarthy took advantage of the consternation caused by the Tet Offensive to ramp up his anti-war challenge to Johnson in the Democratic primaries. With anti-war students rallying to his "Dump Johnson" candidacy, McCarthy polled a stunning 42 percent of the vote to Johnson's 48 percent in New Hampshire's March Democratic primary. "Dove bites Hawk," a reporter quipped.

McCarthy's success convinced Robert F. Kennedy, now a New York senator, to launch his own challenge to Johnson's reelection. Johnson now seemed mortally wounded, and he hated Kennedy, dismissing him as a "grandstanding little runt." Being challenged for reelection by members of his own party devastated Johnson. The growing opposition to the Vietnam War was an even worse blow. During a private meeting with military leaders, the president acknowledged that "the country is demoralized. . . . Most of the press is against us. . . . We have no support for the war." Johnson had also grown concerned about his own health. His wife, Lady Bird, told him to think about retiring after one term.

WHOSE WAR? Johnson lowers his head in disappointment as he listens to a commander's report from Vietnam in 1968.

On March 31, 1968, a haggard and solemn Johnson appeared on national television to announce a limited halt to the bombing of North Vietnam and renewed efforts for a negotiated cease-fire. Then he added a shocking postscript: "I shall not seek, and I will not accept, the nomination of my party for another term as your President." As his daughter explained, the "agony of Vietnam" had engulfed her father.

Johnson, a flawed giant overflowing with contradictions, had promised far more than he could accomplish, raising false hopes and stoking violent resentments. He ended up losing two wars—the one in Vietnam and the one against poverty. Although U.S. troops would remain in Vietnam for five more years, the quest for military victory ended with Johnson's presidency. America had tried to fight a "limited war" in Vietnam. The problem with such a strategy was that the Vietnamese Communists fought an absolute war.

Among other things, Johnson's presidency revealed that the resources of the United States, including its military power, were vast but limited; the nation could not do everything it wanted, which was a disheartening realization for many Americans used to getting their way.

CORE **OBJECTIVE**

5. Examine the presidential election of 1968, and explain the issues that propelled Richard Nixon to victory.

Sixties Crescendo

By the late 1960s, traditional notions of authority were everywhere under attack. An angry spirit of rebelliousness among disaffected youth who were "beyond your command," according to singer Bob Dylan, expanded into a multidimensional attack, not only on the Johnson administration and the war in Vietnam but on virtually every aspect of mainstream life, including the family, the middle-class work ethic, universities, religion, and the integrationist philosophy underpinning the nonviolent civil rights movement led by Martin Luther King Jr. Many alienated young Americans during the sixties, often lumped together as "hippies," felt that they were part of "the Revolution," a magical force of history that would overthrow a corrupt and outdated way of life.

A Traumatic Year

All the turbulent elements affecting American life came to a head in 1968, the most traumatic year in a traumatic decade. As *Time* magazine reported, "Nineteen sixty-eight was a knife blade that severed past from future." It was "one tragic, surprising, and perplexing thing after another."

Martin Luther King assassinated

On April 4, only four days after Lyndon Johnson's shocking withdrawal from the presidential race, a white racist named James Earl Ray shot and killed Martin Luther King Jr. as the black leader stood outside the Lorraine Motel in Memphis, Tennessee. Ray had earlier vowed that he was going "to get the big nigger."

King's murder set off a wave of violence. The prominent African American writer James Baldwin said that whites would never understand the depth of black grief. Riots occurred in over a hundred cities, but the damage was especially devastating in Chicago, Baltimore, and Washington. Forty-six people were killed, all but five of them black. Some 20,000 U.S. Army troops and 34,000 National Guardsmen eventually helped stop the violence across the country.

The night that Martin Luther King died, Senator Robert Kennedy was in Indianapolis, Indiana. Upon hearing the sad news, he stood on a flatbed truck to speak to a grieving crowd of African Americans. "Those of you who are black can be filled with hatred, with bitterness and a desire for revenge," he said. "We can move toward further polarization. Or we can make an effort, as Dr. King did, to understand, to reconcile ourselves and to love."

Love was hard to find in 1968. Two months after King's death, after midnight on June 6, 1968, Robert Kennedy appeared at the Ambassador Hotel in Los Angeles to celebrate his victory over Senator Eugene McCarthy in the California Democratic presidential primary. Kennedy closed his remarks by pledging that "we can end the divisions within the United States, end the violence."

After the applause subsided, Kennedy walked through the kitchen on his way to the press room for interviews. Along the way, a Jordanian Arab named Sirhan Sirhan, resentful of the senator's strong support of Israel, pulled out a pistol and fired eight shots, hitting Kennedy in the head and wounding three others. Kennedy died the next morning.

Only forty-two years old, the father of ten children with another on the way, Kennedy was buried beside his brother John in Arlington National Cemetery outside of Washington, D.C. The assassinations of Robert Kennedy, Martin Luther King Jr., Malcolm X, and John Kennedy came to frame the sixties. With their deaths, a wealth of idealism died, too—the idealism that Bobby Kennedy had hoped would put a fragmented America back together again. A growing number of young people felt orphaned from the political system. Having lost the leading voices for real change in the political process, many of them lost hope in democracy and turned to radicalism and violence.

> Robert F. Kennedy assassinated

Chicago and Miami

In the summer of 1968, the social unrest came to a head at the Democratic National Convention. In August, delegates gathered inside a Chicago convention hall to nominate Johnson's faithful vice president, Hubert H. Humphrey, as the party's contender for the presidency. LBJ had endorsed Humphrey as his successor despite criticizing him in private as a lightweight. Humphrey, he told an aide, was "all heart and no balls."

> Riots at the 1968 Democratic National Convention

Outside the Chicago convention hall, almost 20,000 police officers, National Guard troops, and television reporters stood watch over a large gathering of scruffy, passionate anti-war protesters herded together miles away in a public park. Their youthful energy had been converted to electrical fury as they taunted the police with obscenities. Richard J. Daley, Chicago's gruff Democratic mayor, warned that he would not tolerate disruptions. Nonetheless, ugly riots broke out and were televised nationwide. It was war in the streets. As police used tear gas and clubs to pummel anti-war demonstrators, others chanted, "The whole world is watching." As the *New York Times* reported, "Those were our children in the streets, and the Chicago police beat them up."

Three weeks before the Chicago riots, the Republicans had gathered in Miami Beach to nominate Richard Nixon. Only six years earlier, after he had lost the California governor's race, Nixon had vowed never again to run for public office. By 1968, however, he had changed his mind and become a self-appointed spokesman for the values of "middle America." He and the Republicans offered a vision of stability ("law and order") that appealed to what Nixon called the "**silent majority**" of working-class and middle-class Americans. In accepting the nomination, Nixon promised to listen to "the voice of the great majority of Americans, the forgotten Americans, the non-shouters, the non-demonstrators, that are not racists or sick, that are not guilty of the crime that plagues the land."

silent majority Term popularized by President Richard Nixon to describe the great majority of American voters who did not express their political opinions publicly; "the non-demonstrators."

THE ELECTION OF 1968

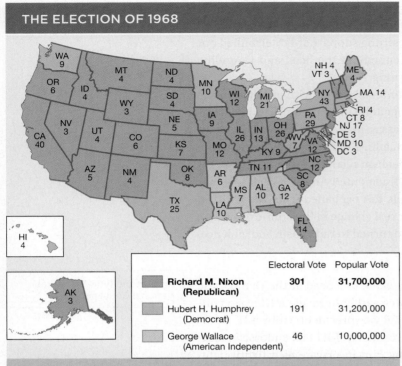

	Electoral Vote	Popular Vote
Richard M. Nixon (Republican)	**301**	**31,700,000**
Hubert H. Humphrey (Democrat)	191	31,200,000
George Wallace (American Independent)	46	10,000,000

- How did the riots at the Chicago Democratic Convention affect the 1968 presidential campaign?
- What does the electoral map reveal about the support base for each of the three major candidates?
- How was Nixon able to win enough electoral votes in such a close three-way presidential race?
- What was Wallace's appeal to 10 million voters?

George Wallace, the governor of Alabama and an outspoken segregationist, dismissed both Democrats and Republicans as too liberal ("owned by the Eastern Establishment") and ran on the American Independent party ticket, a party he formed to defend racial segregation. Wallace also promised to get tough on "scummy anarchists" and bring stability to the nation. He appealed even more forcefully than Nixon to voters' disgust with anti-war protesters, the mushrooming federal welfare system, the growth of the federal government, forced racial integration, and rioting in urban ghettos.

Wallace displayed a savage wit on the campaign trail, once saying that the "only four-letter words that hippies did not know were w-o-r-k and s-o-a-p." Wallace predicted that on Election Day, the nation would realize that "there are a lot of rednecks in this country." His candidacy generated considerable appeal outside his native South, especially among white working-class communities, where resentment of Johnson's Great Society liberalism flourished. Although never likely to win, Wallace hoped to deny Humphrey and Nixon an electoral majority and thereby throw the choice into the House of Representatives, which would have provided a fitting climax to a chaotic year.

Nixon resolved to do anything to win the election, including violating the Logan Act, which prohibits citizens from communicating with foreign governments about controversial issues. Just weeks before the voters went to the polls, Nixon ordered one of his aides to "monkey wrench" President Johnson's last-minute efforts to win a negotiated settlement to the Vietnam War. When Johnson learned of Nixon's efforts through CIA surveillance, he was furious, shouting that the Republican presidential candidate had committed "treason." While it remains an open question whether Johnson could have negotiated a deal to end the war before the election, Nixon's most recent biographer concluded that "of all of Richard Nixon's actions in a lifetime of politics, this was the most reprehensible," for he chose winning an election over the possibility of ending a war that he knew was unwinnable.

Nixon Triumphant

On November 5, 1968, voters gave Nixon what he had been lusting for since 1960, when he and Governor Spiro Agnew of Maryland, his acid-tongued running mate, eked out a narrow victory of some 500,000 votes, a margin of about 1 percentage point. The electoral vote was more decisive: 301 for Nixon, 191 for Hubert Humphrey. George Wallace received 10 million votes, 13.5 percent of the total, while all but one of Wallace's 46 electoral votes were from the Lower South. Nixon swept all but four of the states west of the Mississippi. By contrast, Humphrey's support came almost exclusively from the Northeast.

So at the end of a turbulent year, near the end of a traumatic decade, a society divided between sharply hostile points of view on the right and left looked to combative Richard Nixon to bring "peace with honor" in Vietnam and to "bring us together" as a nation. Nixon privately admitted that he was a polarizing figure, not a harmonizer. In his first week in the White House, he told an aide: "I've got to put on my nice-guy hat . . . but let me make it clear that's not my nature."

Reviewing the
CORE OBJECTIVES | INQUIZITIVE

■ **Kennedy's New Frontier**
President John F. Kennedy promised a *New Frontier* in 1961, but many of his domestic policies stalled in Congress. He inherited a CIA plan to topple Fidel Castro's regime in Cuba, which resulted in the *Bay of Pigs (1961)* fiasco. Soviet premier Nikita Khrushchev tested American resolve by erecting the *Berlin Wall* and installing missiles in Cuba, provoking the *Cuban missile crisis (1962)*. Kennedy ordered a naval "quarantine" of Cuba and succeeded in forcing Khrushchev to withdraw the missiles. During his presidency, Kennedy also deepened America's anti-Communist commitment in Vietnam.

■ **Civil Rights' Achievements** At the beginning of the sixties, growing numbers of African Americans and whites staged acts of *nonviolent civil disobedience* to protest discrimination in the South. In 1960, student activists formed the *Student Nonviolent Coordinating Committee (SNCC)* to intensify efforts to dismantle segregation. In 1961, courageous *Freedom Riders* attempted to integrate Southern bus and train stations. Martin Luther King Jr. delivered his famous "I Have a Dream" speech at the *March on Washington (1963)*. But King and other leaders did little to address the concerns of the inner cities. The *black power movement* emphasized militancy, black pride, separatism, and, often, violence.

■ **Johnson's Great Society** Early in his presidency, Johnson shepherded through Congress the *Civil Rights Act of 1964* and, as part of his "war" on poverty, the *Economic Opportunity Act (1964)*. After his resounding presidential victory in 1964, he pushed his vision for a Great Society through Congress—hundreds of initiatives that expanded federal social-welfare programs, such as the *Voting Rights Act, Medicare,* and *Medicaid.* Yet Johnson's massive expansion of the Vietnam War eventually siphoned resources away from the war on poverty while failing to prevent a Communist takeover in the South.

■ **The Vietnam War** In 1964, President Johnson used the Tonkin Gulf incident off the coast of Vietnam to push through Congress the *Tonkin Gulf Resolution (1964)*, which gave the administration the power to wage war in southeast Asia without a Congressional declaration of war. By 1968, over 500,000 U.S. military personnel were in South Vietnam. Claims that the American effort was winning the war were upended by the North Vietnamese *Tet Offensive (1968)*. The Tet Offensive led many Americans to decide that the war could not be won. Resistance to "Johnson's War" thereafter steadily increased.

■ **1968 Presidential Election** Johnson shockingly chose not to seek reelection in early 1968. Anti-war Democrats rallied around Senators Eugene McCarthy and Robert Kennedy. In April, Martin Luther King Jr. was assassinated, setting off a series of violent riots in urban ghettos across the country. Robert Kennedy was assassinated in June. Ultimately, the Democrats selected Johnson's loyal vice president, Hubert Humphrey, as their nominee, provoking angry protests by anti-war demonstrators. Republicans nominated former candidate Richard Nixon, who claimed to represent... t majority. The segregationist 1968 Chicago Democratic Party Convention. former governor of Alabama, George Wallace, ran as an independent candidate and also appealed to the silent majority. In the end, Nixon narrowly beat Humphrey and Wallace.

TERMS

CHRONOLOGY

February 1960	Greensboro Four stage a sit-in
April 1960	Student Nonviolent Coordinating Committee (SNCC) formed
November 1960	John F. Kennedy elected president
April 1961	Bay of Pigs invasion fails
May 1961	Freedom Rides begin
August 1961	Soviets erect the Berlin Wall
October 1962	Cuban missile crisis
August 1963	March on Washington for Jobs and Freedom
November 1963	John F. Kennedy assassinated in Dallas, Texas
June 1964	Congress passes the Civil Rights Act
August 1964	Congress passes the Tonkin Gulf Resolution
November 1964	Lyndon B. Johnson elected to a full term
February 1965	Malcolm X assassinated
June–August 1965	Congress passes immigration reform, Medicare and Medicaid, the Voting Rights Act
August 1965	Race riots in Watts, California
January 1968	Viet Cong stage the Tet offensive
April 1968	Martin Luther King Jr. assassinated
June 1968	Robert Kennedy assassinated
November 1968	Richard Nixon elected president

INQUIZITIVE

Go to InQuizitive to see what you've learned—and learn what you've missed—with personalized feedback along the way.

REBELS WITH A CAUSE Established in 1967, the Vietnam Veterans against the War grew quickly during the sixties and seventies. Here, a former marine throws his service uniform jacket and medals onto the steps of the Capitol on April 23, 1971, as part of a five-day protest against the U.S. invasion of Laos, an outgrowth of the Vietnam War.

Rebellion and Reaction

THE 1960s AND 1970s

As Richard M. Nixon entered the White House in early 1969, he took charge of a nation whose social fabric was in tatters. Everywhere, it seemed, institutions and notions of authority were under attack. The traumatic events of 1968 had been like a knife blade cutting the past away from the future, revealing how deeply divided America had become and how difficult a task Nixon faced in carrying out his campaign pledge to restore social harmony.

In the end, the stability and harmony he promised proved elusive. His controversial policies and his combative temperament heightened rather than reduced societal tensions. Ironically, many of the same forces that had enabled the complacent prosperity of the fifties—the baby boom, the Cold War, and the growing consumer culture—helped generate the social upheaval of the sixties and early seventies. The civil rights movement promoting equality for African Americans inspired efforts to ensure equal treatment for other minorities—women, gays, Native Americans, Hispanics, and others. It was one of the most turbulent and significant periods in American history—exciting, threatening, explosive, and transformative.

Despite President Nixon's promise to restore the public's faith in the integrity of government leaders, he ended up aggravating the growing cynicism about the motives and methods of government officials. "The press is the enemy," he told his staff. During 1973 and 1974, the Watergate scandal resulted in the greatest constitutional crisis since the impeachment of President Andrew Johnson in 1868, and it ended with the first resignation in history of a U.S. president.

CORE OBJECTIVES InQUIZITIVE

1. Explore the origins of the youth revolt, and compare the responses of the New Left and the counterculture.

2. Assess the influence of the youth revolt and the early civil rights movement on other protest movements and how new protest movements affected social attitudes and public policy.

3. Analyze how Richard Nixon's election strategy and domestic policies were affected by the political environment of the late sixties.

4. Analyze how and why Richard Nixon and Henry Kissinger changed military and political strategies to end America's involvement in the Vietnam War.

5. Examine the world order that evolved after the Vietnam War from Richard Nixon's and Henry Kissinger's diplomacy and foreign policies.

6. Explain how the Watergate scandal unfolded, and assess its political significance.

CORE **OBJECTIVE**

1. Explore the origins of the youth revolt, and compare the responses of the New Left and the counterculture.

"Forever Young": The Youth Revolt

The Greensboro sit-ins in 1960 not only launched a decade of civil rights activism but also signaled an end to the carefree inertia that had enveloped many college campuses and much of social life during the fifties. Rennie Davis, a sophomore at Ohio's Oberlin College in 1960, remembered that the young Greensboro civil rights militants inspired him and many others to become political and social activists. "Here were four students from Greensboro who were suddenly all over *Life* magazine. There was a feeling that they were us and we were them, and a recognition that they were expressing something we were feeling as well."

The sit-ins, marches, protests, ideals, and sacrifices associated with the civil rights movement inspired other minority groups—women, Native Americans, Hispanics, gays, and the disabled—to demand justice, freedom, and equality as well. As Bob Dylan sang in 1963, "How many times can a man turn his head / And pretend that he just doesn't see?" He and many other idealistic young people decided that they could no longer turn a blind eye to the growing evidence of widespread injustice and inequality staining the American dream.

Youth disillusionment with the U.S. government and "authority"

A full-fledged youth revolt erupted during the mid-1960s. "Your sons and your daughters / Are beyond your command," sang Dylan in "The Times They Are a-Changin'." By 1970, more than half of Americans were under thirty years old, and almost 8 million of them were attending college. The baby boomers, who unlike their parents had experienced neither an economic depression nor a major war during their young lives, were now attending colleges and universities in record numbers; enrollment quadrupled between 1945 and 1970.

Many universities had become gigantic institutions dependent upon huge research contracts from corporations and the federal government, especially the Defense Department. As these "multiversities" grew larger and more bureaucratic, they became targets for a generation of students wary of involvement in what President Dwight D. Eisenhower had labeled "the military-industrial complex." As criticism of U.S. military involvement in Vietnam mounted, young people disillusioned with the government and "authority" of all kinds flowed into two distinct yet frequently overlapping movements: the New Left and the counterculture.

The New Left

Students for a Democratic Society (SDS)

The political arm of the youth revolt originated in 1960 when Tom Hayden and Alan Haber, two University of Michigan students, formed Students for a Democratic Society (SDS), a campus-based organization influenced by the tactics of the civil rights movement. In 1962, Hayden and Haber convened a meeting of sixty young men and women activists at Port Huron, Michigan.

Their goal was outrageously ambitious: to design a strategy to remake the United States into a more democratic society.

At the Michigan gathering, Hayden, a member of SNCC and a veteran of the civil rights struggle in the South, drafted an impassioned document known as the Port Huron Statement. It began: "We are the people of this generation, bred in at least moderate comfort, housed in universities, looking uncomfortably to the world we inherit." Only by giving power to "the people," the manifesto insisted, could America restore its founding principles. Inspired by the example of African American civil rights activists in the South, Hayden declared that college students should engage in "participatory democracy" by snatching "control of the educational process from the administrative bureaucracy."

Hayden and others adopted the term **New Left** to distinguish their efforts at grassroots democracy from those of the Old Left of the thirties, which had embraced an orthodox Marxism. "We have no sure formulas, no closed theories," Hayden explained. The New Left was determined to let the people decide what form the new society would take. SDS grew quickly during the sixties, forming chapters on more than a thousand campuses.

In the fall of 1964, students at the University of California at Berkeley took Hayden's New Left program to heart. Several had returned to the campus after spending the summer working with the Student Nonviolent Coordinating Committee's (SNCC) voter-registration project in Mississippi (Freedom Summer), where three volunteers had been killed by Klansmen and many others arrested or harassed. Their idealism and activism had been aroused, and they were now eager to bring changes to campus life as well. When the university's chancellor announced that campus political demonstrations were banned, thousands of students staged a sit-in. After a tense thirty-two-hour standoff, the administration relented. Student groups then formed the free-speech movement (FSM).

Led by Mario Savio, a philosophy major who had participated in Freedom Summer in Mississippi, the FSM initially protested on behalf of students' rights, but it quickly mounted a more general criticism of the university and what Savio called the "depersonalized, unresponsive bureaucracy" smothering many campuses. In 1964, Savio led hundreds of students into UC Berkeley's administration building and organized a sit-in. The university president was not amused. In the early-morning hours, 600 police arrested the protesters. But their example lived on.

> **New Left** Term coined by the Students for a Democratic Society to distinguish their efforts at grassroots democracy from those of the 1930s Old Left, which had embraced orthodox Marxism and admired the Soviet Union under Stalin.

> Student free-speech movement

THE FREE-SPEECH MOVEMENT Mario Savio, a founder of the FSM, speaks at a rally at the University of California at Berkeley.

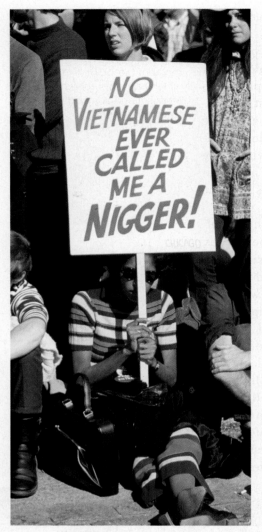

ALL THAT RISES MUST CONVERGE
This protester's sign at a Washington, D.C., demonstration bridged the civil rights and anti-war movements, which called for many of the same racial and political reforms. **How did race and socioeconomic background factor into the military draft?**

Anti-War Protests

The goals and tactics of FSM and SDS soon spread to colleges across the country. By 1965, however, the growing U.S. involvement in Vietnam changed the New Left's agenda. With the dramatic expansion of the war after 1965, millions of young men during the late sixties faced the grim prospect of being drafted to fight in an increasingly unpopular conflict.

In fact, however, the Vietnam War, like virtually every other, was primarily a poor man's fight. Most college students were able to postpone military service until they received their degree or reached the age of twenty-four; in 1965–1966, college students made up only 2 percent of all military inductees. African Americans and Hispanics were twice as likely to be drafted as whites.

As the war dragged on, Americans divided into two bitter factions, hawks and doves, those who supported the war and those who opposed it. Some 200,000 young men ignored their draft notices during the sixties, and some 4,000 served prison sentences for doing so. Another 56,000 qualified for conscientious objector status during the Vietnam War, compared with only 7,600 during the Korean conflict. Others ceremoniously burned their draft cards in front of television cameras. Still others fled the United States altogether—several thousand moved to Canada or Sweden—to avoid military service.

The most popular way to escape the draft was to use a variety of creative techniques to flunk the physical examination. Whatever the preferred method, many college students succeeded in avoiding military service. Of the 1,200 men in Harvard's class of 1970, only 56 served in the military, and just 2 of them went to Vietnam.

Rising Violence

Throughout 1967 and 1968, the anti-war movement grew more violent as inner-city ghettos in Cleveland, Detroit, Newark, and other large cities were exploding in flames fanned by racial injustice. Frustration over deeply entrenched patterns of discrimination in employment and housing, as well as staggering rates of joblessness among inner-city African American youths, ignited rage in scores of urban ghettos. "There was a sense everywhere, in 1968," journalist Garry Wills wrote, "that things were giving way. That man had not only lost control of his history, but might never regain it."

During the eventful spring of 1968—when Lyndon Johnson announced that he would not run for reelection and Martin Luther King Jr. and Robert F. Kennedy were assassinated—campus unrest boiled over across the country. The turmoil reached a climax at Columbia University, where SDS student radicals and black militants occupied the president's office and classroom buildings. Mark Rudd, the campus SDS leader, called his parents to report that "we took a building." His father, Jacob Rudd, a retired army officer, replied: "Well, give it back." He did not, and after a failed attempt by professors to negotiate an end to the takeover, the university's president canceled classes and called in the New York City police. President Nixon declared that the rebellion at Columbia was "the first major skirmish in a revolutionary struggle to seize the universities." The university's president said that May 1968 was the "most disastrous month in the history of American higher education."

COLUMBIA RIOTS Mark Rudd, leader of SDS at Columbia University, speaks to the media during student protests in April 1968.

The events at Columbia inspired similar clashes among students, administrators, and police at Harvard, Cornell, and San Francisco State, among others. Vice President Spiro Agnew, famous for his colorful language, dismissed the young militants as "impudent snobs who characterize themselves as intellectuals." He also condemned the "circuit-riding, Hanoi-visiting . . . caterwauling, riot-inciting, burn-America-down" anti-war protesters, whom he labeled "thieves and traitors" and "nattering nabobs of negativism."

The Counterculture

Looking back over the 1960s, Tom Hayden, the founder of SDS, recalled that most rebellious young Americans did not join SDS. They "were not narrowly political. Most were not so interested in attaining [elected] office but in changing lifestyles." Hayden acknowledged that the shocking events of 1968 led disaffected young rebels—so-called hippies—to abandon conventional political activism and campus protests in favor of joining the **counterculture**, an unorganized rebellion against mainstream institutions, values, and behavior. Hippies focused on changing lifestyles rather than changing politics. In pursuing personal liberation, they rejected the pursuit of wealth and careers and instead embraced simple living, authenticity, friendship, peace, and especially, *freedom*.

Counterculture: Hippies and Yippies and communes and Title IX

The counterculture and the New Left both fiercely rejected the status quo, but the hippies preferred to "drop out" rather than try to change the political system. Their preferred anti-war slogan was "Make Love, Not War." Like the Beats of the fifties, hippies celebrated personal freedom from virtually all traditional constraints. In all their colorful variety, they were at once defiant, innocent, optimistic, and indulgent as they rejected the authority of

counterculture Unorganized youth rebellion against mainstream institutions, values, and behavior that more often focused on cultural radicalism rather than political activism.

the nation's core institutions: the family, government, political parties, corporations, the military, and colleges and universities.

The colorful lifestyle of those embracing the counterculture included an array of popular ideals and activities: peace, love, harmony, rock music, mystical religions, mind-altering drugs, casual sex, and communal living arrangements. Many hippies practiced meditation and yoga. Hippie fashion featured defiantly long hair for both women and men (prompting the derisive label *long hairs*), flowing cotton dresses, ragged bell-bottom blue jeans, tie-dyed T-shirts, love beads, peace symbols, and sandals. Young men grew beards and women discarded makeup as badges of difference (or indifference, as it were).

The countercultural rebels were primarily middle-class whites alienated by the Vietnam War, racism, political corruption, and parental authority. In their view, a superficial materialism had settled over mainstream life, which they defied by embracing the tactics recommended by the drug-promoting former Harvard psychology professor Timothy Leary: "Tune in, turn on, drop out." Illegal drugs—marijuana, amphetamines, cocaine, peyote, hashish, heroin, and LSD—were commonplace within the counterculture. Said Todd Gitlin, a former SDS president, "More and more, to get access to youth culture" in the late 1960s, "you had to get high." The Byrds sang about getting "Eight Miles High," and singer/songwriter Bob Dylan proclaimed that "everybody must get stoned."

In fact, getting stoned was the motivation behind the 1967 "Summer of Love" centered in San Francisco when over 100,000 hippies ("flower children") from around the country converged on the city's hip Haight-Ashbury district and other enclaves around northern California. The loosely organized "Council for the Summer of Love" intended the gathering to be the first step in a grassroots revolution celebrating alternative lifestyles, especially those "of compassion, awareness, and love, and the revelation of unity for all mankind." That same summer, the Beatles issued one of their all-time best-selling songs, "All You Need Is Love"—a number-one hit worldwide.

The countercultural alternative to SDS and the New Left was the zany Youth International Party, better known as the Yippie movement, founded by two irreverent pranksters, Jerry Rubin and Abbie Hoffman. The Yippies were

FLOWER POWER Hippies let loose at a 1967 love-in, gatherings that celebrated peace, free love, and nontheological spirituality, often as a gesture of protest.

YIPPIES Author Ken Kesey and his posse, the Merry Pranksters, held Acid Test Graduation parties throughout the San Francisco, California, area that celebrated the psychedelic drug LSD (also known as "acid"). **How did the Yippie movement reimagine a revolution against capitalist values?**

countercultural comedians, wacky mischief-makers bent on thumbing their noses at conventional laws and behavior and mocking capitalism as well as the consumer culture. Hoffman explained that their "conception of revolution is that it's fun." The Yippies were the jokesters in the generational revolution, a clownish force of history that, they believed, would overthrow the power structure. Rubin claimed that the widespread use of "psychedelic" drugs among young Americans "signifies the total end of the Protestant ethic: screw work, we want to know ourselves," and that meant rejecting America's "sick notion of work, success, reward, and status."

The anarchistic Yippies specialized in scandalous theatrical gestures and pranks intended to generate media coverage. They organized marijuana "smoke-ins," threw pies in the faces of political figures, nominated a pig named Pigasus for the presidency, urged voters to cast their ballots for "None of the Above," and threatened to put LSD in Chicago's water supply during the Democratic National Convention in 1968. When asked what being a Yippie meant, Hoffman replied: "Energy–fun–fierceness–exclamation point!" He had no interest in making the Yippies a traditional political organization. "We shall not defeat *Amerika* by organizing a political party," he declared. "We shall do it by building a new nation—a nation as rugged as the marijuana leaf."

For some, the counterculture involved experimenting with alternative living arrangements, especially "intentional communities" or "communes." Communal living in urban areas such as San Francisco's Haight-Ashbury district, New York's Greenwich Village, Chicago's Uptown, and Atlanta's Fourteenth Street neighborhood were popular for a time, as were rural communes. Thousands of inexperienced hippie romantics flocked to the countryside during the late 1960s, eager to liberate themselves from parental and institutional restraints, live in harmony with nature, and coexist in an atmosphere of love and openness.

Like Henry D. Thoreau, those participating in the back-to-the-land movement were seeking a path to more *authentic* living, which would deepen their sense of self and forge genuine community ties. "Out here," one of the rural communalists reflected, "we've got the earth and ourselves and God above. . . . We came for simplicity and to rediscover God."

Yet all but a handful of the back-to-the-land experiments collapsed within a few months or years. Almost none of those attracted by rural life actually knew how to sustain a farm. And in many cases they were not willing to do the hard work that living off the land required. "The hippies will not change America," a journalist predicted, "because change means pain, and the hippie subculture is rooted in the pleasure principle." A resident of Paper Farm in northern California, which started in 1968 and collapsed a year later, said of its participants: "They had no commitment to the land—a big problem. All would take food from the land, but few would tend it. . . . We were entirely open. We did not say no [to anyone]. We felt this would make for a more dynamic group. But we got a lot of sick people."

The sixties counterculture thrived on music—initially folk "protest" songs and later psychedelic or "acid rock" music. During the early years of the decade, Pete Seeger; Joan Baez; Peter, Paul and Mary; and Bob Dylan, among others, produced powerful songs of social protest and reform. In Dylan's "The Times They Are a-Changin'," first sung in 1963, he warned: "There's a battle outside and it's ragin' / It'll soon shake your windows and rattle your walls / For the times, they are a-changin'."

Within a few years, however, the hippies' favorite performers were those under the influence of mind-altering drugs, especially the San Francisco–based "acid rock" bands: Jefferson Airplane, Big Brother and the Holding Company (Janis Joplin), and the Grateful Dead.

BOB DYLAN Born Robert Allen Zimmerman, Dylan came to the New York folk music scene by way of northern Minnesota, penning the antiwar movement anthem "Blowin' in the Wind."

Huge outdoor music concerts were wildly popular events among the counterculture. The largest of these was the sprawling Woodstock Music and Art Fair ("Aquarian Exposition"). In mid-August 1969, more than 400,000 mostly young people converged on a 600-acre farm near the tiny rural town of Bethel, New York, for the world's "largest happening," three days "of peace and music."

Woodstock festival (1969)

The powerful lure of the festival was the all-star cast of musicians: Jimi Hendrix, Jefferson Airplane, Janis Joplin, Santana, the Who, Joan Baez, and Crosby, Stills & Nash, among many others. For three days amid summer heat, rain storms, and rivers of mud, the assembled flower children "grooved" on good music, beer and booze, cheap marijuana, and casual sex. Drug use was rampant, but there were no robberies, assaults, or rapes. Reflecting on the scene, a long-haired teen said: "People are finally getting together."

The carefree "spirit of love" that blossomed at the Woodstock festival was short-lived, however. Just four months later, when other concert promoters tried to replicate the "Woodstock Nation" experience at the Altamont Speedway Free Festival near San Francisco, the counterculture fell victim to the criminal culture. The Rolling Stones hired the Hells Angels motorcycle gang to provide "security" for their show. During the band's performance of "Under My Thumb," a drunken Hells Angel stabbed to death an eighteen-year-old African American man wielding a gun in front of the stage. Three other spectators died of accidents that night, and much of the vitality and innocence of the counterculture died with them. After 1969, the hippie phenomenon began to fade as the counterculture became counterproductive. The spirit of liberation ran up against the hard realities of growing poverty, drug addiction, crime, and mental and physical illness among the flower children.

At the same time, the New Left was also self-destructing as an organized political movement. In large measure, SDS committed suicide when it abandoned the pacifist principles that had originally inspired participants and given the movement moral legitimacy. The Weathermen, a violent SDS splinter group named for a line in a Bob Dylan song, took to the streets of Chicago in October 1969 to assault police and trash the city. Almost 300 were arrested. During the so-called Days of Rage between September 1969 and May 1970, there were 250 bombings of draft board offices, ROTC buildings on university campuses, federal government facilities, and corporate headquarters. In March 1970, three Weathermen died when a bomb they were making in New York City exploded prematurely.

Decline of the New Left

SDS and other radical groups also suffered internal disputes and were forced underground by the aggressive efforts of federal law enforcement agencies. The energy behind the youth revolt waned as the Vietnam War began to wind down. There would be a resurgent wave of student protests against the Nixon administration in 1970–1971, but thereafter campus unrest diminished as Nixon ended the military draft and withdrew U.S. troops from Vietnam, which greatly defused the resistance movement.

CORE **OBJECTIVE**

2. Assess the influence of the youth revolt and the early civil rights movement on other protest movements and how new protest movements affected social attitudes and public policy.

Social Activism Spreads

The same liberationist ideals that prompted young people to revolt against mainstream American values and to protest against the Vietnam War also led many to embrace other causes. The success of the civil rights movement inspired other groups to demand equal opportunities and equal rights as well—women; Mexican Americans, Native Americans, and other ethnic groups; gays; the elderly; and the physically and mentally disabled. Still others joined the emerging environmental movement or groups working on behalf of consumers, led by the crusading Ralph Nader.

The New Feminism

Like the New Left, the new feminism drew much of its inspiration and many of its tactics from the civil rights movement. The women's movement in the late nineteenth and early twentieth centuries had focused on gaining the right to vote. The feminist movement of the 1960s and '70s was much more comprehensive in its goals, seeking equal rights in virtually every area of life. Its aim was to challenge the conventional ideal of female domesticity and ensure that women gained equal treatment in the workplace.

Most women in the early sixties, however, did not yet view gender equality as possible or even desirable. In 1962, more than two thirds of women surveyed agreed that the most important family decisions "should be made by the man of the house." Although the Equal Pay Act of 1963 had made it illegal to pay women less than men for doing the same job, varied forms of discrimination and harassment continued in the workplace and throughout society. Women, who were 51 percent of the nation's population in the sixties and held 37 percent of the jobs, earned overall salaries that were 42 percent less than those for men.

The Feminine Mystique (1963)

Betty Friedan, a forty-two-year-old journalist and mother of three from Peoria, Illinois, emerged as the leader of the **women's movement** during the mid-1960s. Her influential book _The Feminine Mystique_ (1963) helped launch a new phase of female protest. Friedan claimed that "something was very wrong with the way American women are trying to live their lives today." Her generation of white, college-educated women (she did not discuss working-class or African American women) had actually lost ground after the Second World War, when many left wartime employment and settled in suburbia as full-time wives and mothers, only to suffer from the "happy homemaker" syndrome that undermined their intellectual capacity and public aspirations while tying them to household duties. "A century earlier," she wrote, "women had fought for higher education; now girls went to college to get a husband."

women's movement Wave of activism sparked by Betty Friedan's _The Feminine Mystique_ (1963); it argued for equal rights for women and fought against the cult of domesticity that limited women's roles to the home as wife, mother, and homemaker.

Friedan blamed a massive propaganda campaign by advertisers and women's magazines for brainwashing women to embrace the "feminine mystique" of blissful domesticity in which fulfillment came only with marriage and motherhood. Underemployed women, Friedan claimed, "were being duped into believing homemaking was their natural destiny."

The Feminine Mystique, an immediate best seller, forever changed American society by defining "the problem that has no name." Friedan's analysis of the "feminine mystique" that limited women's lives to being bored housewives and tired mothers inspired many well-educated, unfulfilled middle- and upper-class white women who felt trapped by a suffocating suburban ideal of household drudgery. Moreover, Friedan discovered that there were far more women working outside the home (a third of the workforce) than she had assumed. Many of these working women were frustrated by the demands of holding "two full-time jobs instead of just one—underpaid clerical worker and unpaid housekeeper." Perhaps most important, Friedan helped the emerging women's movement to focus on empowering women to achieve their "full human capacities"—in the home, in schools, in offices, on college campuses, and in politics.

In 1966, Friedan and other activists founded the National Organization for Women (NOW). They chose the acronym NOW because it was part of a popular civil rights chant: "What do you want?" protesters yelled. "FREEDOM!" "When do you want it?" "NOW!"

BETTY FRIEDAN Author of *The Feminine Mystique* and the first president of NOW, Friedan's feminism was directed mainly at middle- and upper-class white women and aimed to empower them to aspire beyond female domesticity.

Initially, NOW sought to end gender discrimination in the workplace and went on to spearhead efforts to legalize abortion and obtain federal and state support for child-care centers. In August 1970, Friedan organized a march for women's equality in New York City that involved 50,000 people walking down Fifth Avenue. Change came slowly, however. By 1970, there was still only one woman in the U.S. Senate, ten in the House of Representatives, and none on the Supreme Court or in the president's cabinet.

In the early seventies, members of Congress, the Supreme Court, and NOW advanced the cause of gender equality. Title IX of the Educational Amendments of 1972 barred discrimination on the basis of gender in any "education program or activity receiving federal financial assistance." Most notably applied to athletics, Title IX spurred female participation in high school sports to increase nearly tenfold and almost double at the college level.

National Organization for Women (NOW) and Title IX

Congress also overwhelmingly approved an equal-rights amendment (ERA) to the federal constitution, which, if ratified by the states, would have required equal treatment for women throughout society and politics. By mid-1973, twenty-eight states had approved the amendment, still ten short of the thirty-eight states needed for approval.

In 1973, the Supreme Court, in its ***Roe v. Wade*** decision, made history by striking down state laws forbidding abortions during the first three months of pregnancy. The majority on the Court ruled that women have a fundamental "right to choose" whether to bear a child or not, since pregnancy necessarily affects a woman's health and well-being. The *Roe v. Wade*

Roe v. Wade **(1973)** Landmark Supreme Court decision striking down state laws that banned abortions during the first trimester of pregnancy.

decision and the ensuing success of NOW's efforts to liberalize local and state abortion laws generated a powerful conservative backlash, especially among Roman Catholics and evangelical Protestants, who mounted a potent "right-to-life" crusade that helped fuel the conservative political resurgence in the seventies and thereafter.

Meanwhile, all-male colleges, including Yale, Princeton, and the U.S. Military Academy, led a movement for coeducation that swept the country. "If the 1960s belonged to blacks," said one feminist, "the next ten years are ours."

Radical Feminism

Radical feminism: Direct action and social transformation

During the late sixties, a new wave of younger and more radical feminists emerged to challenge everything from women's economic, political, and legal status to sexual double standards for men and women. They sought "women's liberation" from all forms of "sexism" (also called "male chauvinism" or "male oppression"), not simply equality in the workplace.

The new generation of feminists, often called "women's libbers," was more militant than Betty Friedan and others who had established NOW. Many younger feminists were veterans of the civil rights movement and the anti-war crusade who had come to realize that male revolutionaries could be sexists, too. They began meeting in small groups to discuss their opposition to the war and racism, only to discover at such "consciousness-raising" sessions that what bound them together were their shared grievances as women operating in a "man's world."

To gain true liberation, many of them decided, required exercising "sexual politics" whereby women would organize themselves into a political movement based on women's common problems and goals. The writer Robin Morgan captured this newly politicized feminism in the slogan "The personal is political," a radical notion that Betty Friedan rejected. When lesbians demanded a public role in the women's movement, Friedan deplored the "lavender menace" of lesbianism as a divisive distraction that would only enrage their opponents. By 1973, however, NOW had endorsed gay rights.

Friedan failed to dampen or deflect the younger generation of women activists, just as Martin Luther King Jr. had failed to suppress the Black Power movement. The goal of the women's liberation movement, said Susan Brownmiller, a self-described "radical feminist," was to "go beyond a simple concept of equality. NOW's emphasis on legislative change left the radicals cold." She dismissed Friedan as "hopelessly bourgeois." For women to be truly equal, Brownmiller and others believed, required transforming *every* aspect of society: child rearing, entertainment, domestic duties, business, and the arts. Lesbianism, she and others argued, should be celebrated rather than hidden.

Radical feminists also took direct action, such as picketing the 1968 Miss America Pageant, burning copies of *Playboy* and other men's magazines, tossing their bras and high-heeled shoes into "freedom cans," and assaulting gender-based discrimination in all its forms.

WHAT WOMEN WANT Left: The Women's Strike for Equality brought tens of thousands of women together on August 26, 1970, to march for gender equality and celebrate the fiftieth anniversary of the Nineteenth Amendment, which gave voting rights to women. Right: The anti-feminist campaign, STOP ERA ("Stop Taking Our Privileges, Equal Rights Amendment"), found its most outspoken activist in Phyllis Schlafly, a constitutional lawyer and staunch conservative. **How did this new wave of radical feminism differ from earlier feminist movements?**

Fractured Feminism

By the end of the seventies, sharp disputes between moderate and radical feminists had fractured the women's movement in ways similar to the fragmentation experienced by civil rights organizations a decade earlier. The movement's failure to broaden its appeal much beyond the confines of the white middle class also caused reform efforts to stall. Ratification of the ERA, which had once seemed a straightforward assertion of equal opportunity ("Equality of rights under the law shall not be denied or abridged by the United States or by any State on account of sex"), was bogged down in several state legislatures. By 1982, it had finally died, three states short of passage. Conservatives saw the defeat of the ERA as a triumph, for they drew much of their strength from the backlash against changing social attitudes about women's roles.

> Successes and failures of feminism: Gains in education, employment, and politics; conservative backlash; and failure of the ERA

Yet the successes of the women's movement endured. Whether young or old, conventional or radical, those women fighting for equal rights focused on several basic issues during the sixties and seventies: gender discrimination in the workplace, equal pay for equal work, an equal chance at jobs traditionally reserved for men, the availability of high-quality, government-subsidized child-care centers, and easier access to birth control devices, prenatal care, and abortion. Feminists helped win improvements in divorce laws and gained easier access for women seeking clinical abortions.

It was also the feminist movement that called attention to issues long hidden or ignored in American society. In 1970, for example, 36 percent of the nation's "poor" families were headed by women, as were most urban families dependent upon federal welfare services. Nearly 3 million poor children needed access to day-care centers, but there were only places for 530,000. It was the feminist movement that helped women achieve mass entry into the labor market and enjoy steady improvements toward equal pay and treatment in the workplace. In 1960, some 37 percent of women were working outside the home; by 1980, 52 percent were doing so.

A growing presence in the labor force brought women a greater share of economic and political influence. By 1976, more than half of married women, and nine of ten female college graduates, were employed outside the home, a development that one economist called "the single most outstanding phenomenon of this century." Women also enrolled in graduate and professional schools in record numbers. During the 1970s, women began winning elected offices at the local, state, and national levels.

The Sexual Revolution and the Pill

Birth control and changing sexual attitudes

The feminist movement coincided with the so-called sexual revolution, a much-discussed loosening of traditional restrictions on social behavior. During the sixties and after, Americans became more tolerant of premarital sex, and women became more sexually active. Between 1960 and 1975, the number of college women engaging in sexual intercourse doubled, from 27 percent to 50 percent. Enabling this change, in large part, was a scientific breakthrough in contraception: the birth-control pill, approved for public use by the Food and Drug Administration in 1960.

BIRTH CONTROL To spread the word about birth-control options, Planned Parenthood in 1967 displayed posters like this one in New York City buses.

Widespread access to the pill fundamentally changed social life by giving women a greater sense of sexual freedom. The pill also led to more open discussion of birth control, reproduction, and sexuality in general. By 1990, the world would have 400 million fewer people because of the pill. Although the birth-control pill also contributed to a rise in sexually transmitted diseases, many women viewed it as a godsend—an inexpensive, nonintrusive way for them to gain better control over their bodies and their futures. "It was a savior," recalled Eleanor Smeal, president of the Feminist Majority Foundation. "The whole country was waiting for it. I can't even describe to you how excited people were."

Hispanic Rights

The activism of student revolts, the civil rights movement, and the crusade for women's rights soon spread to various ethnic minority groups. The word *Hispanic*, referring to people who trace their ancestry to Spanish-speaking Latin America or Spain, came into increasing use after 1945 in conjunction with growing efforts to promote economic and social justice. (Although frequently used as a synonym for *Hispanic*, the term *Latino* technically refers only to people of Latin American descent.) Labor shortages during World War II had led defense industries to offer Hispanic Americans their first significant access to skilled-labor jobs. And as was the case with African Americans, service in the military during the war years helped heighten an American identity among Hispanic Americans, increasing their desire for equal rights and social opportunities.

Social equality, however, remained elusive for Hispanics who were wanted in the United States for their labor but not for their culture. After World War II, Hispanic Americans still faced widespread discrimination in hiring, housing, and education. Poverty was rampant. In 1960, for example, the median income of a Mexican American family was only 62 percent of the national average. Hispanic American activists denounced segregation; called for improved public schools serving their children; and struggled to increase Hispanic political influence, economic opportunities, and visibility in the curricula of schools and colleges.

Hispanic civil rights leaders faced an awkward dilemma: what should they do about the continuing stream of undocumented Mexican workers flowing across the border into the United States? Many Mexican Americans argued that their hopes for economic advancement and social equality were put at risk by the daily influx of Mexican laborers willing to accept low-paying jobs. Mexican American leaders thus helped end the bracero program in 1964 (which trucked in contract day laborers from Mexico during harvest season).

In the early sixties, Mexican American workers formed their own civil rights organization, the **United Farm Workers (UFW)**. Its founder was the charismatic Cesar Chavez. Born in 1927 in Yuma, Arizona, the son of Mexican immigrants, Chavez moved with his family to California in 1939. There they joined thousands of other poor migrant farmworkers moving from job to job, living in tents, cars, or ramshackle cabins. After serving in the U.S. Navy during the Second World War and then working as a migrant laborer, Chavez became a community organizer focused on registering Latinos to vote.

Then, along with Dolores Huerta, a talented organizer, Chavez created in 1965 the UFW, a union for migrant lettuce workers and grape pickers, many of them undocumented immigrants who could be deported at any time. Up and down California, Chavez led nonviolent mass protest marches that had the energy of religious pilgrimages; he staged hunger strikes like those of his hero, India's Mahatma Gandhi; and he managed nationwide boycotts.

> Nonviolent Protest: Marches, boycotts, and *la huelga* (strike against California grape growers)

United Farm Workers (UFW) Organization formed in 1962 to represent the interests of Mexican American migrant workers.

CESAR CHAVEZ The usually energetic Chavez is visibly weakened from a twenty-five-day hunger strike in support of the United Farm Workers Union in March of 1968. Robert F. Kennedy, a great admirer of Chavez, is seated to his right.

The UFW gained national attention in September 1965 when the union organized a strike (*la huelga*) against the corporate grape growers in California's San Joaquin Valley. As Huerta explained, "We have to get farmworkers the same type of benefits, the same type of wages, and the respect that they deserve because they do the most sacred work of all. They feed our nation every day."

Chavez's relentless energy and deep Catholic faith, his insistence upon nonviolent tactics, his reliance upon college-student volunteers, his skillful alliance with organized labor and religious groups, and the life of poverty he chose for himself—all combined to attract media interest and popular support. In 1968, Chavez began a twenty-five day hunger strike to raise national attention for his efforts. On the day when he broke his fast, the first to greet him with bread was Robert F. Kennedy, then campaigning for the Democratic presidential nomination. "The world must know, from this time forward, that the migrant farm worker, the Mexican-American, is coming into his own rights," Kennedy declared. He added that the farmworkers were gaining "a special kind of citizenship. . . . You are winning it for yourselves—and therefore no one can ever take it away."

However, the chief strength of the Hispanic rights movement lay less in the tactics of sit-ins and protest marches than in the rapid growth of the Hispanic American population. In 1970, Hispanics in the United States numbered 9 million (4.8 percent of the total population); by 2000, their numbers had increased to 35 million (12.5 percent); and in 2012, they numbered 53 million, making them the nation's largest minority group (17 percent). The voting power of Hispanics and their concentration in states with key electoral votes has helped give the Hispanic point of view significant political clout.

Native American Rights

American Indians—many of whom had begun calling themselves *Native Americans*—also emerged as a political force in the late 1960s. Two conditions combined to make Indian rights a priority. First, many whites felt guilty for the way their ancestors had taken the lands of people who had, after all, been here first. Second, the plight of Native Americans was more desperate than that of any other group in the country. Indian unemployment was ten times the national rate, life expectancy was twenty years lower than the national average, and the suicide rate was a hundred times higher than the rate for whites.

Although President Lyndon Johnson funneled federal anti-poverty-program funds into reservations, militants within the Indian community grew impatient with the pace of change. Those promoting "**Red Power**" organized protests and demonstrations against local, state, and federal agencies. On November 20, 1969, fourteen Red Power activists occupied Alcatraz Island near San Francisco, which until 1963 had hosted an infamous federal prison. Over the next several months, hundreds of others, mostly students, joined the protest. The Nixon administration responded by cutting off electrical service and telephone lines. Stranded without electrical power and fresh water, most of the protesters left the island. Finally, on June 11, 1971, the government removed the remaining fifteen Native Americans from the island.

In 1968, the year before the Alcatraz occupation, two Chippewas (or Ojibwas) living in Minneapolis, George Mitchell and Dennis Banks, founded the American Indian Movement (AIM). In October 1972, AIM organized the Trail of Broken Treaties caravan, which traveled by bus and car across the nation from the West Coast to Washington, D.C., drawing attention to the history of the federal government's broken treaties and promises. When officials in the Nixon administration refused to meet with the protesters, they occupied the federal Bureau of Indian Affairs on November 3. The sit-in ended when federal negotiators agreed to renew discussions of Native American grievances about the administration of government programs intended to improve their quality of life.

In 1973, AIM led 200 Sioux in the occupation of the tiny village of Wounded Knee, South Dakota, where the U.S. Seventh Cavalry had massacred a Sioux village in 1890. Outraged by the light sentences given a group of local whites who had killed a Sioux in 1972, the organizers sought to draw attention to the plight of the Indians living on the reservation there. After the militants took eleven hostages, federal marshals and FBI agents surrounded the encampment.

The occupation of Wounded Knee captured more media attention in its first few days than the Indian rights movement had received in the decade up to that point. For ten weeks the two sides engaged in a tense standoff. When AIM leaders tried to bring in food and supplies, a shoot-out erupted, with one Indian killed and another wounded. Soon thereafter, the confrontation ended with a government promise to reexamine Indian treaty rights.

Indian protesters subsequently discovered a more effective tactic than direct

> **Red Power** Activism by militant Native American groups to protest living conditions on Indian reservations through demonstrations, legal action, and at times, violence.

STANDOFF AT WOUNDED KNEE After occupying Wounded Knee and taking eleven hostages, members of the American Indian Movement and the Oglala Sioux stand guard outside of the town's Sacred Heart Catholic Church. **Why might the occupation of Wounded Knee have generated so much media attention?**

Legal recognition of historic Native American treaties and tribal rights

action and sit-ins: they went into federal courts armed with copies of old treaties and demanded that the documents become the basis for financial restitution for the lands taken from them over the centuries. In Alaska, Maine, South Carolina, and Massachusetts, they won substantial settlements that officially recognized their tribal rights and awarded monetary compensation at levels that upgraded the standard of living on several reservations.

Gay Rights

The liberationist impulses of the sixties also encouraged homosexuals to assert their right to equal treatment. Throughout the decade, gay men and lesbians continued to confront disgust, cruelty, and violence. On Saturday night, June 28, 1969, New York City vice police raided the Stonewall Inn, a popular gay bar in Greenwich Village, because it lacked a liquor license. Instead of dispersing, the diverse patrons fought back, and the struggle spilled into the streets. Hundreds of other gays and their supporters joined the fracas.

The **Stonewall riots** lasted throughout the weekend, during which the Stonewall Inn caught fire and burned down. When the turmoil ended, gays had forged a new sense of solidarity embodied in two new organizations, the Gay Liberation Front and the Gay Activists' Alliance, both of which focused on ending discrimination and harassment against gays and transvestites. "Gay is good for all of us," proclaimed one of its members. "The artificial categories 'heterosexual' and 'homosexual' have been laid on us by a sexist society."

As news of the Stonewall rebellion spread, the gay rights movement grew in its numbers and its demands. By 1973, almost 800 gay organizations had emerged across the country, and every major city had a visible gay community and cultural life. That year, the American Psychiatric Association removed homosexuality from its official manual of "mental illnesses." Colleges

Stonewall riots (1969) Violent clashes between police and gay patrons of New York City's Stonewall Inn, seen as the starting point of the modern gay rights movement.

GAY PRIDE IN THE SEVENTIES Gay rights activists march in the Fifth Annual Gay Pride Day demonstration, commemorating the anniversary of the Stonewall riots that jump-started the gay rights movement in the United States.

and universities began offering courses and majors in Gay Studies (also called Queer Studies), and grassroots movements as well as national organizations began pushing for official government recognition of same-sex marriages. As was the case with the civil rights and women's movements, however, the campaign for gay rights soon suffered from internal divisions and a conservative counterattack.

Nixon and the Revival of Conservatism

CORE **OBJECTIVE**

3. Analyze how Richard Nixon's election strategy and domestic policies were affected by the political environment of the late sixties.

By the end of the 1960s, Americans were engaged in a cultural civil war. The turmoil of the decade spawned a backlash from what Richard Nixon called the "great silent majority" of middle-class Americans that propelled him to a narrow election victory in November 1968, in large part because he promised to bring "law and order" to a nation overflowing with "violence, lawlessness, and permissiveness." Nixon was no friend of the civil rights movement, the youth revolt, or spreading social activism. He had been elected president as the representative of middle America, those voters fed up with liberal politics; countercultural hippies; radical feminism; gay rights; and **affirmative action**, government programs giving preferential treatment to minorities and women to atone for past injustices.

The Conservative Backlash

Alabama's Democratic governor, George Wallace, led the conservative counterattack. "Liberals, intellectuals, and long hairs," he shouted, "have run the country for too long." Wallace repeatedly lashed out at "welfare queens," unmarried women who he claimed "were breeding children as a cash crop" in order to receive federal child-support checks. Wallace's support was not limited to the South. He became the popular voice for many working-class whites across the nation fed up with political liberalism and social radicalism.

All in the Family, the most popular TV show in the 1970s, was created to showcase the decade's cultural wars. In the much-celebrated sitcom (situation comedy), the Bunker family lived in a state of perpetual conflict in a working-class borough outside of New York City. Semiliterate Archie Bunker (played by Carroll O'Connor), a loading-dock worker, was the gruff but lovable head of the family, a proud Republican, Nixon supporter, and talkative member of the "silent majority" who was a bundle of racial, ethnic, gender, and political prejudices. Enthroned in his easy chair, he railed each week against blacks, Jews, Italians, Poles, gays, feminists, hippies, and liberals (including his live-in daughter and her hippie husband, both "bleeding-heart" liberals). At one point, Archie declares: "I ain't no bigot. I'm the first guy to say, 'It ain't your fault that youse are colored.'"

The producer of the series, Norman Lear, intended Archie's raging intolerance as a satire to provoke viewers to question their own prejudices. In

The "silent majority"

affirmative action Programs designed to give preferential treatment to women and people of color as compensation for past injustices.

fact, however, many of the 50 million people watching each Saturday night identified *with* the narrow-minded values of Archie Bunker, who in 1973 was "the most recognized face in America."

At a grassroots level, conservatives in the early seventies used the courts to fight preferential treatment for historically disadvantaged groups, arguing that government-mandated affirmative-action programs were neither fair nor efficient ways to address the problems of historic inequality. In supporting such efforts, Nixon appealed to the working- and middle-class whites who feared that America was being corrupted by permissiveness, anarchy, and the tyranny of the rebellious minority. He promised to return "law and order" to a nation on the verge of chaos.

In 1952, the powerful senator Robert A. Taft of Ohio, known as "Mr. Republican," had characterized young Senator Richard Nixon as a "little man in a big hurry" with "a mean and vindictive streak." A grocer's son from Whittier, California, Nixon was a humorless man of fierce ambition and extraordinary perseverance. Raised in a family that struggled with poverty, he had to claw and struggle to the top his whole life, and he nursed a deep resentment of people who had an easier time of it (the "moneyed class").

Nixon was much more than persistent, however. He was also smart, shrewd, cunning, and doggedly determined to succeed in politics. A cold, calculating man who saw enemies around every corner, Nixon feasted on his fears, allowing his paranoia and vengefulness to isolate him from political reality. Republican senator Barry Goldwater described Nixon as "the most complete loner I've ever known." Throughout his career, Nixon displayed violent mood swings punctuated by raging temper tantrums, vulgar profanity, and anti-Semitic outbursts. He was nicknamed "Tricky Dick" because he was a good liar. In his speech accepting the Republican nomination in 1968, Nixon pledged "to find the truth, to speak the truth, and to live the truth." In fact, however, he often did not speak the truth. One of his presidential aides admitted that "we did often lie, mislead, deceive, try to use [the media], and to con them."

Nixon's Appointments

In his first term, Nixon selected for his cabinet and White House staff only white men who would carry out his orders with blind obedience. John Mitchell, the gruff attorney general who had been a senior partner in Nixon's New York law firm, was the new president's closest confidant. H. R. (Bob) Haldeman, a former advertising executive, served as chief of staff. As Haldeman explained, "Every President needs a son of a bitch, and I'm Nixon's. I'm his buffer, I'm his bastard." John Ehrlichman, a Seattle attorney and college schoolmate of Haldeman's, was Nixon's chief domestic-policy adviser. Nixon called him his "chief executioner." John W. Dean III, an associate deputy in the Office of the U.S. Attorney General, became the White House legal counsel.

Nixon tapped as secretary of state his old friend William Rogers, who had served as attorney general under Dwight D. Eisenhower, but the president had no intention of making Rogers the nation's chief diplomat. Instead, Nixon virtually ignored Rogers and the State Department while forging an unlikely partnership with Dr. Henry Kissinger, a brilliant German-born Jew and Harvard political scientist who had become the nation's leading foreign-policy expert. His thick German accent, owlish appearance, and outsized ego had helped make him an international celebrity, courted by presidents of both parties. In 1969, Nixon named Kissinger his national security adviser, and in 1973 Kissinger became secretary of state, although in private Nixon called him "my Jew-boy."

Nixon and Kissinger, the politician and the professor, formed an odd but effective diplomatic team. Both were loners and outsiders who preferred operating in secret; both were defensive and even paranoid at times; and both mistrusted and envied the other's power and prestige. Nixon would eventually grow tired of Kissinger's efforts at self-promotion and his frequent threats to resign if he did not get his way.

For his part, Kissinger lavished praise on Nixon in public, while in private he dismissed the president as an insecure man with a "meatball mind" who went on frequent stress-induced drinking binges. Yet for all their differences, they worked well together, in part because they both loved secrecy and intrigue, power politics and diplomatic flexibility, and in part because of their shared vision of a new multipolar world order beginning to replace the bipolar Cold War.

The Southern Strategy

A major reason for Nixon's election victories in 1968 and 1972 was his shrewd southern strategy, designed to win over white southern Democrats angered by the civil rights revolution. The majority of white southern voters were religious and patriotic, fervently anti-Communist and anti-union, and skeptical of social-welfare programs directed at minorities. For a century, whites in the "Solid South" had steadfastly voted for Democrats in national elections. Their doing so reflected lingering southern resentments, dating back to the Civil War and Reconstruction, that demonized Abraham Lincoln and his Republican successors for imposing northern ways of life on the South, including racial integration.

During the late 1960s and '70s, however, a surging economy and a spurt of population growth began to transform the South. The region's warm climate, low cost of living, absence of labor unions, low taxes, and government incentives for economic development convinced waves of businesses, workers, professionals, and retirees to relocate to the region.

CAMPAIGNING IN THE SOUTH, 1968 Nixon's presidential campaigns relied on his southern strategy, which capitalized on the changing demographics of the so-called Solid South. **How did Nixon craft his message to appeal to southern voters?**

Between 1970 and 1990, the South's population grew by 40 percent, more than twice the national average. During the seventies, the rate of job growth in the South was seven times greater than in New York and Pennsylvania. In the 1960s and '70s, southern "redneck" culture suddenly became all the rage, as people across the nation embraced stock-car racing, cowboy boots, pickup trucks, barbecue, and country music.

Rapid population growth—and the continuing spread of air-conditioning—brought the Sunbelt states of the South, the Southwest, and California more congressional seats and more electoral votes. Every president elected between 1964 and 2008 had roots in the Sunbelt, the region that spearheaded the backlash against 1960s radicalism. Nixon's favorite singer, country star Merle Haggard, crooned in his smash hit, "Okie from Muskogee": "We don't smoke marijuana in Muskogee / We don't take our trips on LSD / We don't burn our draft cards down on Main Street / We like livin' right and bein' free."

Haggard's conservative working-class fans bristled at anti-war protesters, hippies, rising taxes, social-welfare programs, and civil rights activism. The alienation of many blue-collar whites from the liberalism of the Democratic party, as well as the demographic changes transforming Sunbelt states and the white backlash against court-ordered integration, created a fertile opportunity for the Republican party to exploit, which Richard Nixon cleverly seized.

| Political realignment in a conservative South

In the 1968 presidential campaign, Nixon's southern strategy took advantage of the backlash against liberalism and civil rights in the region to win over traditionally Democratic white voters to the Republican party, welcoming the segregationist white South into the party of Lincoln. Nixon cleverly "played the race card," assuring white conservatives that he would appoint justices to the Supreme Court who would undermine federal enforcement of civil rights laws, such as mandatory school busing to achieve racial integration and affirmative action, which gave minorities priority in hiring decisions and the awarding of government contracts. Nixon also appealed to the economic concerns of middle-class southern whites by promising lower tax rates and less government regulation. Finally, like George Wallace, he used hard-hitting, polarizing rhetoric pledging to restore "law and order" in the streets of America.

In the 1972 election, it was Nixon's southern strategy that won the day: he carried every southern state by whopping majorities. The Republican takeover of the once Democratic "Solid South" was the greatest realignment in American politics since Franklin D. Roosevelt's election in 1932. It was also an unlikely coalition, for it brought together traditional "country-club" Republicans—corporate executives, financiers, and investors—with poor, rural, fundamentalist southerners who had always voted for Democrats. What they shared was a simmering hatred for what the Democratic party had become.

Nixon's Domestic Agenda

As president, Nixon was less a rigid conservative ideologue than he was a crafty politician forced to deal with a Congress controlled by Democrats. He therefore chose his battles carefully and showed surprising flexibility, leading political journalist Tom Wicker to describe him as "at once liberal and conservative, generous and begrudging, cynical and idealistic, choleric and calm, resentful and forgiving."

During his first term, Nixon focused on developing policies and programs that would please conservative Republicans and recruit conservative Democrats. He touted his New Federalism, which sent federal monies to the states and local governments for them to spend as they saw fit. He also disbanded the core agency of Lyndon Johnson's War on Poverty program—the Office of Economic Opportunity—and cut funding to several Great Society programs.

New Federalism and Democratic legislation

At the same time, the Democrats in Congress passed significant new legislation that Nixon did sign: the right of eighteen-year-olds to vote in national elections (1970) and in all elections under the Twenty-Sixth Amendment (1971); increases in Social Security benefits and food-stamp funding; the Occupational Safety and Health Act (1970) to ensure safer workplace environments; and the Federal Election Campaign Act (1971), which modified the rules governing corporate financial donations to political campaigns.

Nixon and Civil Rights

During his first term, President Nixon followed through on his campaign pledges to conservative white southerners to blunt the momentum of the civil rights movement. He appointed no African Americans to his cabinet and refused even to meet with the all-Democratic Congressional Black Caucus. "We've had enough social programs: forced integration, education, housing," he told his chief of staff. "People don't want more [people] on welfare. They don't want to help the working poor, and our mood needs to be harder on this, not softer."

Nixon also launched a concerted effort to block congressional renewal of the Voting Rights Act of 1965 and to delay implementation of federal court orders requiring the racial desegregation of school districts in Mississippi. Sixty-five lawyers in the U.S. Justice Department signed a letter protesting Nixon's stance. The Democratic-controlled Congress then extended the Voting Rights Act over Nixon's veto.

The Supreme Court also thwarted Nixon's efforts to slow desegregation. Above the entrance to the Supreme Court building in Washington, D.C., are inscribed four words: "Equal justice under law." In its first decision under the new chief justice, Warren Burger—a Nixon appointee—the Court ordered the racial integration of the Mississippi public schools in *Alexander v. Holmes County Board of Education* (1969). During Nixon's first term, more schools were desegregated under court orders than in all the Kennedy-Johnson years combined.

Nixon's efforts to block desegregation in urban areas were also failures. The Burger court ruled unanimously in *Swann v. Charlotte-Mecklenburg Board of Education* (1971) that school systems must bus students out of their neighborhoods if necessary to achieve racially integrated schools. Protests over

OFF TO SCHOOL Because of violent protests against desegregation, school buses in South Boston are escorted by police in October of 1974.

ENVIRONMENTAL AWARENESS
An Earth Day demonstration dramatizing the dangers of air pollution, April 1972.

busing desegregation thereafter erupted in the North, the Midwest, and the Southwest, as white families in Boston, Denver, and other cities denounced the destruction of "the neighborhood school." Angry white parents in Pontiac, Michigan, were so determined to stop mandatory busing to achieve racial integration that they firebombed empty school buses.

Nixon and Environmental Protection

Dramatic increases in the price of oil and gasoline during the seventies fueled a major energy crisis in the United States. Natural resources grew limited—and increasingly precious. Bowing to pressure from both parties, as well as polls showing that 75 percent of voters supported stronger environmental protections, President Nixon told an aide, "Keep me out of trouble on environmental issues"—he was "bored" by them. Yet he recognized that the public mood had shifted in favor of greater federal environmental protections, especially after two widely publicized environmental events in 1969.

The first was a massive oil spill off the coast of Santa Barbara, California. Within ten days, an enormous slick of crude oil contaminated 200 miles of California beaches, killing thousands of sea birds and marine animals. Six months later, on June 22, 1969, the Cuyahoga River, an eighty-mile-long stream that slices through the center of Cleveland, Ohio, spontaneously caught fire. Fouled with oil and grease, bubbling with subsurface gases, and littered with debris, the chocolate-colored river ignited and burned for five days, its flames leaping fifty feet into the air. Like the Santa Barbara oil spill, the images of the burning river became an important catalyst in the raising of environmental awareness across the nation. A 1969 survey of college campuses by the *New York Times* revealed that many young people were transferring their idealism from the anti-war movement to the environmental movement.

President Nixon knew that if he vetoed legislative efforts to improve environmental quality, the Democratic majorities in Congress would overrule him, so he chose not to stand in the way. In late 1969, Nixon signed the amended Endangered Species Preservation Act and the National Environmental Policy Act. The latter became effective on January 1, 1970, the year that environmental groups established an annual Earth Day celebration that would involve millions nationwide.

Environmental Protection Agency (EPA) Federal environmental agency created by Nixon to appease the demands of congressional Democrats for a federal environmental watchdog agency.

In 1970, Nixon by executive order created two new federal environmental agencies, the **Environmental Protection Agency (EPA)** and the National Oceanic and Atmospheric Administration (NOAA). Why he did so remains a subject of debate, for Nixon had little love for the environment.

The most plausible explanation is that he hoped to mollify leftists associated with the antiwar movement. Whatever the case, the same year, he signed the Clean Air Act to reduce air pollution on a national level. Two years later, however, Nixon vetoed a new clean water act, only to see Congress override his effort. He also undermined many of the new environmental laws by refusing to spend money appropriated by Congress to fund them.

> Nixon approves Environmental Protection Agency (EPA)

"Stagflation"

The major domestic development during the Nixon administration was a floundering economy. The accumulated expense of the Vietnam War and the Great Society programs helped quadruple the annual inflation rate from 3 percent in 1967 to 12 percent in 1974. Meanwhile, unemployment, at only 3.3 percent when Nixon took office, nearly doubled to 6 percent by the end of 1970. Economists coined the term **stagflation** to describe the unprecedented situation of stalled economic growth (stagnation), rising inflation, and high unemployment all occurring at the same time. Consumer prices usually rose with a rapidly growing economy and rising employment. Now it was just the reverse, and there were no easy ways to fight the unusual combination of recession and inflation.

stagflation Term coined by economists during the Nixon presidency to describe the unprecedented situation of stagnant economic growth and consumer price inflation occurring at the same time.

Stagflation had at least three deep-rooted causes. First, the Johnson administration had financed both the Great Society social-welfare programs and the Vietnam War without a major tax increase, thereby generating larger federal deficits, a major expansion of the money supply, and price inflation. Second, and more important, U.S. companies were now facing stiff international competition from West Germany, Japan, and other emerging industrial powers around the world. Third, America's prosperity since 1945 had resulted in part from the ready availability of cheap sources of energy. No other nation was more dependent than the United States upon the automobile and the automobile industry, and no other nation was more wasteful in its use of fossil fuels in factories and homes. During the seventies, however, oil and gasoline became scarcer and costlier. High energy prices and oil shortages took their toll on the economy.

> The "Nixon recession": Federal deficits, international competition, new workers, and an oil crisis

Just as America's domestic petroleum reserves began to dwindle and dependence upon foreign sources increased, the Organization of Petroleum Exporting Countries (OPEC) decided to use its huge oil supplies as a political and economic weapon. In 1973, the United States sent massive aid to Israel after a devastating Syrian-Egyptian attack that was launched on Yom Kippur, the holiest day on the Jewish calendar. OPEC responded by

OIL CRISIS, 1973 The scarcity of oil forced the rationing of gasoline. Service stations, such as this one in Oregon, would close early because of the gas shortage, leaving Americans like this suited businessman to find other means of transportation.

announcing that it would not sell oil to the United States and other nations supporting Israel in the so-called Yom Kippur War and that it was raising its oil prices by 400 percent.

President Nixon alerted Americans to a stark new fact: "We are heading toward the most acute shortage of energy since the Second World War." He asked the airlines to reduce their flights, lowered the maximum speed limit on federal highways to 55 mph, halted plans to convert electricity-generating plants from coal to oil, and urged all Americans to conserve energy.

The Arab oil embargo, called by some an "economic Pearl Harbor," caused gasoline shortages and skyrocketing prices. American motorists suddenly faced mile-long lines at gas stations. "These people are like animals foraging for food," said a gas station owner. "If you can't sell them gas, they threaten to beat you up, wreck your station, or run you over with a car." To manage the crisis, the federal government created a gas-rationing program: service stations would be open on alternate days to drivers with license plates ending in odd or even numbers.

Another condition leading to stagflation was the flood of new workers—mainly baby boomers and women—into the labor market. From 1965 to 1980, the workforce grew by almost 30 million workers, a number greater than the total labor force of France or West Germany. The number of new jobs could not keep up with the growth of the workforce, leaving many unemployed.

The Nixon administration responded erratically and ineffectively to stagflation, trying old remedies for a new problem. First, the president sought to reduce the federal deficit by raising taxes and cutting the budget. When the Democratic Congress refused to cooperate, he encouraged the Federal Reserve Board to reduce the nation's money supply by raising interest rates. The stock market immediately nosedived, and the economy plunged into the "Nixon recession."

A sense of desperation about the stagnant economy seized the White House. In 1969, when asked about the possibility of imposing government caps on wages and prices, Nixon had been clear: "Controls. Oh, my God, no! . . . We'll never go to controls." In 1971, however, he reversed himself. He froze all wages and prices for ninety days, arguing that doing so would generate a "new prosperity: more jobs, more incomes, more profits, without inflation and without war." It did not work out that way as the economy remained sluggish.

CORE **OBJECTIVE**

4. Analyze how and why Richard Nixon and Henry Kissinger changed military and political strategies to end America's involvement in the Vietnam War.

"Peace with Honor": Ending the Vietnam War

By the time Nixon entered the White House in January 1969, he and Henry Kissinger had developed a comprehensive vision of a new world order. The result of their collaboration was a dramatic transformation of U.S. foreign policy. Since 1945, the United States had lost its monopoly on nuclear weapons, its overwhelming economic dominance, and much of its geopolitical influence. The rapid rise of competing power centers in Europe, China, and Japan complicated the Cold War as well as international relations in general.

Nixon and Kissinger envisioned defusing the Cold War by pursuing peaceful coexistence with the Soviets and Chinese. After a "period of confrontation," Nixon explained in his 1969 inaugural address, "we are entering an era of negotiation." Preoccupied with secrecy, Nixon and Kissinger bypassed the State Department, including Secretary of State Rogers, and the Congress in their efforts to take advantage of quickly shifting world events.

The immediate task for Nixon and Kissinger was to end the war in Vietnam, which one presidential aide called a "bone in the nation's throat." Until the war ended and all troops had returned home, the social harmony that President Nixon had promised would remain elusive. Privately, he had decided that "there [was] no way to win the war" in Vietnam, so instead he sought what he called "peace with honor." That is, the United States could not simply cut and run; it needed to withdraw in a way that upheld the credibility of its military alliances around the world. Peace, however, was long in coming, not honorable, and shockingly brief.

> **"Peace with honor"**

Gradual Withdrawal

The Vietnam policy implemented by Nixon and his national security adviser Henry Kissinger moved along three fronts. First, U.S. negotiators in Paris demanded the withdrawal of Viet Cong forces from South Vietnam and the preservation of the U.S.-backed government of President Nguyen Van Thieu. The North Vietnamese and Viet Cong negotiators, for their part, insisted on retaining a Communist military presence in the south and reunifying the Vietnamese people under a government dominated by the Communists. There was no common ground. Hidden from public awareness and from America's South Vietnamese allies were secret meetings between Kissinger and the North Vietnamese.

On the second front, Nixon tried to quell domestic unrest. He labeled the anti-war movement a "brotherhood of the misguided, the mistaken, the well-meaning, and the malevolent." He sought to defuse the anti-war movement by steadily reducing the number of U.S. troops in Vietnam, justifying the reduction as the natural result of "**Vietnamization**"—the equipping and training of South Vietnamese soldiers and pilots to assume the burden of combat. From a peak of 560,000 troops in 1969, U.S. combat forces returned home at a steady pace. By 1973, only 50,000 troops remained in Vietnam.

> **"Vietnamization" and ending the military draft**

In 1969, Nixon also established a draft lottery whereby the birth dates of nineteen-year-old men were randomly selected and assigned a number between 1 and 366 in order of their selection. Those with low lottery numbers, from 1 to 160, would be the first drafted into military service. (My number was 83.)

The lottery system eliminated many inequities and clarified the likelihood of being drafted. Four years later, in 1973, the president ended the draft altogether by creating an all-volunteer military.

Vietnamization Nixon-era policy of equipping and training South Vietnamese forces to take over the burden of combat from U.S. troops.

Those initiatives, coupled with the troop withdrawals from Vietnam, defused the anti-war movement. Opinion polls showed strong public support for Nixon's policies related to the Vietnam War. "We've got those liberal bastards on the run now," the president gloated, "and we're going to keep them on the run." Nixon had much less success in forcing concessions from the North Vietnamese negotiators.

On the third front, while steadily reducing the number of U.S. combat troops in Southeast Asia, Nixon and Kissinger greatly expanded the U.S. bombing of North Vietnam in hopes of pressuring the Communist leaders to end the war. Kissinger felt that "a fourth-rate power" like North Vietnam must have a "breaking point" at which it would decide it was suffering too much damage. Nixon agreed, suggesting that they let the North Vietnamese leaders know that he was so "obsessed about Communism" that he might use the "nuclear button" if necessary.

| Three fronts: Negotiation, troop reduction, and air strikes

In March 1969, Nixon approved a secret fourteen-month-long bombing campaign aimed at Communist Vietnamese forces that were using neighboring Cambodia as a base for raids into South Vietnam. Congress did not learn of the air strikes until 1970, although the total tonnage of bombs dropped was four times that dropped on Japan during World War II.

Still, Hanoi's leaders did not flinch; they decided to let Nixon's domestic critics undermine his presidency. Then, on April 30, 1970, Nixon announced an "incursion" into "neutral" Cambodia by U.S. troops to "clean out" hidden Vietnamese Communist military bases. Privately, Nixon told Kissinger, who strongly endorsed the decision to extend the fighting into Cambodia, "If this doesn't work, it'll be your ass, Henry." Nixon knew that sending troops into Cambodia would reignite the anti-war movement. Secretary of State William Rogers predicted, "This will make the [anti-war] students puke."

Divisions at Home

| Escalation of anti-war riots over the invasion of Cambodia

Just as Nixon had expected, the escalation of the air war in Vietnam and the extension of the war into Cambodia triggered widespread anti-war demonstrations. In the fall of 1969, two massive daylong rallies in hundreds of cities across the nation and around the world brought millions of protesters into the streets. Nixon, however, was unmoved by the behavior of such "bums." As he gruffly explained, "We expect it; however, under no circumstances will I be affected whatever by it."

In the spring of 1970, news of the secret Cambodian "incursion" by U.S. forces set off explosive protests on college campuses and across the nation. In Ohio, the governor sent the National Guard to Kent State University to control campus rioting. The poorly trained guardsmen panicked and opened fire on rock-throwing demonstrators, killing four student bystanders.

The widely publicized killings at Kent State added new fury to the anti-war and anti-Nixon movement. That spring, demonstrations occurred on more than 350 campuses. A presidential commission charged with investigating the shootings concluded that they were "unnecessary and unwarranted." Not all agreed, however. A resident of Kent told a reporter, "Anyone

who appears on the streets of a city like Kent with long hair, dirty clothes, or barefooted deserves to be shot. . . . It would have been better if the Guard had shot the whole lot of them." Singer Neil Young had a different view. Shortly after the killings, he composed a song called "Ohio":

> Tin soldiers and Nixon's coming.
> We're finally on our own.
> This summer I hear the drumming.
> Four dead in Ohio.

The Ohio governor banned radio stations from playing the song, which only made it more popular.

Eleven days after the Kent State tragedy, on May 15, Mississippi highway patrolmen riddled a dormitory at predominantly black Jackson State College with bullets, killing two student protesters and wounding twelve others. In New York City, anti-war demonstrators who gathered to protest the student deaths and the invasion of Cambodia were attacked by conservative "hard-hat" construction workers, many of them shouting "All the way, USA" and "America: Love It or Leave It." They forced the protesters to disperse and then marched on City Hall to raise the U.S. flag, which had been lowered to half-staff in mourning for the Kent State victims. "Thank God for the hard hats," Nixon exclaimed.

The following year, in June 1971, the *New York Times* began publishing excerpts from *The History of the U.S. Decision-Making Process of Vietnam Policy*, a secret Defense Department study commissioned by Robert McNamara before his resignation as Lyndon Johnson's secretary of defense in 1968. The so-called Pentagon Papers, leaked to the press by Daniel Ellsberg, a former marine and thereafter a Defense Department official,

The Pentagon Papers published (1971)

confirmed what many critics of the war had long suspected: Congress and the public had not received the full story on the Gulf of Tonkin incident of 1964. Plans for U.S. entry into the war were being drawn up even as President Johnson was promising that combat troops would never be sent to Vietnam. Although the Pentagon Papers dealt with events only up to 1965, the Nixon administration blocked their publication, arguing that release of the classified information would endanger national security and would prolong the war. By a vote of 6–3, the Supreme Court ruled against the government. Newspapers throughout the country began publishing the controversial documents the next day.

War without End

During 1972, mounting social divisions at home and the approach of the presidential election influenced the negotiations in Paris between the United States and representatives of North Vietnam. In the summer of 1972, Henry Kissinger renewed private meetings with the North Vietnamese negotiators, and he now dropped his insistence upon the removal of all North Vietnamese troops from South Vietnam before the withdrawal of the remaining U.S. troops. On October 26, only a week before the U.S. presidential election, a jubilant Kissinger announced that "peace is at hand."

Christmas bombings of North Vietnam (1972)

As it turned out, however, this was a cynical ploy to win votes for Nixon's reelection bid. Several days earlier, the Thieu regime in South Vietnam had rejected the Kissinger plan for a cease-fire, fearful that allowing North Vietnamese troops to remain would virtually guarantee a Communist victory.

The Paris peace talks broke off on December 16, and two days later the newly reelected Nixon ordered massive bombings of Hanoi and Haiphong, the two largest cities in North Vietnam. "The bastards have never been bombed like they're going to be bombed this time," Nixon pledged. Over just twelve days, U.S. pilots dropped some 36,000 tons of bombs on Hanoi. These so-called Christmas bombings and the simultaneous U.S. mining of North Vietnamese harbors aroused worldwide protest.

Paris Peace Accords (1973)

Yet the bombings also made the North Vietnamese more willing to negotiate. The air strikes stopped on December 29, and the talks in Paris soon resumed. A month later, on January 27, 1973, the United States, North and South Vietnam, and the Viet Cong signed an "agreement on ending the war and restoring peace in Vietnam," known as the Paris Peace Accords.

In fact, however, the accords represented a carefully disguised U.S. surrender that enabled Nixon to end the nation's combat role. While Nixon and Kissinger claimed that the bombings had brought North Vietnam to its senses, in truth the North Vietnamese never altered their basic stance; they kept 150,000 troops in South Vietnam and remained committed to the reunification of Vietnam under one government.

What had changed was the willingness of the South Vietnamese leaders, who were not allowed to participate in the negotiations, to accept the agreement, however reluctantly, on the basis of Nixon's personal promise that the United States would respond "with full force" to any Communist violation of the agreement. Kissinger had little confidence that the treaty provisions would enable South Vietnam to survive on its own. He told a White House staffer, "If they're lucky, they can hold out for a year and a half."

By the time the Paris Peace Accords were signed in 1973, another 20,000 American troops had died since Nixon had taken office in 1969, the morale of the U.S. military had been shattered, hundreds of thousands of Southeast Asians had been killed or wounded, and fighting soon broke out again in both Vietnam and Cambodia. In the end, Nixon and Kissinger's diplomatic efforts gained nothing the president could not have accomplished in 1969 by ending the war on similar terms.

The Collapse of South Vietnam

On March 29, 1973, the last U.S. combat troops left Vietnam. The same day, the North Vietnamese released almost 600 American prisoners of war, most of them downed pilots. Within months of the U.S. withdrawal, however, the cease-fire in Vietnam collapsed, the war between North and South resumed, and the Communist forces gained the upper hand. In Cambodia (renamed the Khmer Republic after a 1970 military coup) and Laos, where fighting had been more sporadic, a Communist victory seemed inevitable.

In 1975, the North Vietnamese launched a full-scale invasion, sending the South Vietnamese army into headlong panic, followed by ragged swarms of terrified civilians. South Vietnamese president Nguyen Van Thieu desperately appealed to Washington for the promised U.S. assistance to which he was entitled by the Paris Peace Accords—and to which South Vietnam had grown addicted. But the U.S. Congress, long since weary of spending more dollars and lives in Vietnam, refused. On April 21, President Thieu resigned and flew to Taiwan, carrying with him three and a half tons of gold to ease his sorrow.

"Peace with honor" had proven to be, in the words of one CIA official, only a "decent interval"—enough time for the United States to remove itself before the collapse of the South Vietnamese government. On April 30, 1975, Americans watched on television as North Vietnamese tanks rolled into Saigon, soon to be renamed Ho Chi Minh City, and military helicopters lifted desperate U.S. embassy and South Vietnamese officials and their families to warships offshore.

The longest, most controversial, and least successful war in American history up to that point was finally over, leaving a bitter legacy. During the period of U.S. involvement, the combined death count for combatants and

LEAVE WITH HONOR Hundreds of thousands of South Vietnamese tried to flee the Communist forces with evacuating Americans. Here, a U.S. official punches a Vietnamese man attempting to join his family in an overflowing airplane at Nha Trang in April 1975.

civilians reached nearly 2 million. North Vietnam absorbed incredible losses—some 600,000 soldiers and countless civilians killed. South Vietnam lost 240,000 soldiers, and over 500,000 Vietnamese became refugees in the United States. More than 58,000 Americans died in Vietnam, 300,000 were wounded, 2,500 were declared missing, and almost 100,000 returned missing one or more limbs. The United States spent over $158 billion on the war.

The Vietnam combat veterans (average age nineteen, compared to twenty-six, the average age of servicemen in World War II) faced a unique ordeal. They had "lost" a war in which their country had lost interest. When they returned, many found that even their families were unwilling to talk about what the soldiers had experienced or were embarrassed about their involvement in the war. "I went over there thinking I was doing something right and came back a bum," said Larry Langowski from Illinois. "I came back decked with medals on my uniform, and I got spit on by a hippie girl."

The Vietnam War, initially described as a crusade on behalf of democratic ideals, instead revealed that American democracy was not easily transferable to regions of the world that lacked any historical experience with democratic government. Fought to show that the United States would be steadfast in containing the spread of communism, the war instead sapped the national will and fragmented the national consensus that had governed foreign affairs since 1947, when President Truman developed policies to "contain" communism around the world. It also changed the balance of power in domestic politics.

As opposition to the war undermined Lyndon B. Johnson's presidency, it also created enduring fractures within the Democratic party. Said George McGovern, the anti-war senator and 1972 Democratic presidential nominee, "The Vietnam tragedy is at the root of the confusion and division of the Democratic party. It tore up our souls."

Not only had a decade of American effort in Vietnam proved costly and futile, but the Khmer Rouge, the insurgent Cambodian Communist movement, had also won a resounding victory over the government of the U.S.-backed Khmer Republic, plunging that country into a horrific bloodbath. The maniacal Khmer Rouge leaders renamed the country Kampuchea and organized a genocidal campaign to destroy all their opponents, killing almost a third of the total population.

The Nixon Doctrine and a Thawing Cold War

CORE **OBJECTIVE**

5. Examine the world order that evolved after the Vietnam War from Richard Nixon's and Henry Kissinger's diplomacy and foreign policies.

Despite the frustrations associated with his efforts to end the Vietnam War, Richard Nixon, like John F. Kennedy, greatly preferred foreign policy over domestic policy (which he compared to building "sewer projects"), and his greatest successes were in international relations. Nixon was an expert in foreign affairs, and he benefited greatly from the expertise and strategic vision of Henry Kissinger. Their grand design for U.S. foreign policy after the Vietnam War centered on developing friendly relations with the Soviet Union and Communist China. Kissinger said they wanted to "improve the possibilities of accommodations with each as we increase our options with both," enabling all three superpowers to reduce the cost of the arms race while minimizing the possibility of nuclear war.

The CIA in Chile

Kissinger pressed for a return to an Eisenhower-era approach to foreign policy that entailed using the CIA to pursue America's strategic interests covertly and reducing large-scale military interventions. Ever since Fidel Castro and his Communist supporters gained control of Cuba in 1959, American presidents had been determined to prevent any more Communist insurgencies in the Western Hemisphere.

In 1970, Salvador Allende, a Marxist, a Socialist party leader, a friend of Fidel Castro's, and a rabid critic of the United States, was a leading presidential candidate in Chile, a thousand-mile-long nation on the southwest coast of South America. Allende's candidacy caused President Nixon and Henry Kissinger great concern, for they knew that, if elected, Allende planned to "nationalize" Chilean industries, including those owned by U.S. corporations. They did not want "another Castro" in Latin America. Chile "could end up being the worst failure of the Nixon administration," Kissinger warned.

In September 1970, Nixon told the head of the CIA that an Allende government in Chile was "unacceptable," and he authorized $10 million to prevent an Allende presidency, urging the CIA to do anything "[its] imagination [could] conjure" up to stop Allende. Nevertheless, although CIA agents provided campaign funds to Allende's opponents, he was elected on October 24, 1970. Within a few months, Allende had taken over dozens of U.S.-owned enterprises in Chile.

> U.S. foreign policy in Latin America: Anti-communism and the CIA

The CIA then encouraged Chilean military leaders to oust him. In September 1973, the army took control, Allende either committed suicide or was murdered, and General Augusto Pinochet, a ruthless military dictator supposedly friendly to the United States, declared himself the head of the government.

After Pinochet assumed power, he ordered the assassination of thousands of political opponents. Kissinger, now secretary of state, told Nixon that the CIA "didn't do it," but "we helped" put him in office by creating the conditions that made the coup possible. It was yet another example of the United States being so obsessed by anti-communism and protecting American business interests that it was willing to interfere in the democratic process of other nations and help remove elected officials through covert operations.

The Nixon Doctrine

In July 1969, while trying to get America out of the war in Vietnam, President Nixon unveiled what came to be called the Nixon Doctrine, a new approach to America's handling of international crises. Unlike John F. Kennedy, who

> Nixon recognizes Communist China (1972)

had declared that the United States would "pay any price, bear any burden" to win the Cold War, Nixon explained that "America cannot—and will not—conceive *all* the plans, design *all* the programs, execute *all* the decisions, and undertake *all* the defense of the free nations of the world." Those nations experiencing Communist insurgencies must in the future assume primary responsibility for their own defense. The United States under the Nixon Doctrine would provide weapons and money but not soldiers.

At the same time that Nixon was reducing the likelihood of U.S. military interventions, he announced that he would pursue partnerships with Communist countries in areas of mutual interest. That Nixon, a Republican with a history of rabid anti-communism, would embrace such a policy of **détente** (a French word meaning "easing of relations") with America's Communist archenemies shocked many observers and demonstrated yet again his pragmatic flexibility.

NIXON GOES TO CHINA President Nixon and Chinese premier Zhou Enlai raise a toast to each other at the lavish farewell banquet in Shanghai that rounded off the historic visit. **What was the international reaction to Nixon's visit to China?**

détente Period of improving relations between the United States and Communist nations, particularly China and the Soviet Union, during the Nixon administration.

The People's Republic of China

Nixon had a genius for surprise, an exquisite gift for defying expectations and doing the unexpected. In 1971, without even informing Secretary of State Rogers, Nixon sent Henry Kissinger on a secret trip to Beijing to explore the possibility of U.S. recognition of Communist China. Since 1949, when Mao Zedong's revolutionary movement established control in China, the United States had refused to recognize the People's Republic of China, preferring to regard Chiang Kai-shek's exiled regime on the island of Taiwan as the legitimate Chinese government. Now, however, the time seemed ripe for a bold renewal of ties. Both the United States and Communist China were exhausted from intense domestic strife (anti-war protests in America, the Cultural Revolution in China), and both were eager to resist Soviet expansionism.

Nixon's bombshell announcement on July 15, 1971, that Kissinger had just returned from Beijing and that the president himself would be going to China the following year sent shock waves around the world. Nixon became the first U.S. president to use the term *People's Republic of China*, an important symbolic step in his efforts to normalize relations with the most populous nation in the world. The Nationalist Chinese on Taiwan felt betrayed, and the Japanese, historic enemies of China, were furious at the American news. What they called "Nixon shock" played a major role in the collapse of the Japanese government. In October 1971, the United Nations voted to admit the People's Republic of China and expel Taiwan.

On February 21, 1972, during the "week that changed the world," Americans who had lived amid the intense anti-Communist atmosphere of the Cold War were stunned to turn on their televisions and see President Nixon shake hands and drink toasts in Beijing with Prime Minister Zhou Enlai and Communist party chairman Mao Zedong. In one simple but astonishing stroke, Nixon and Kissinger had ended two decades of diplomatic isolation of the People's Republic of China. They had seen a geopolitical opportunity and seized it.

During the president's weeklong China visit, the two nations agreed to scientific and cultural exchanges, steps toward the resumption of trade, and the eventual reunification of Taiwan with the mainland. As a conservative anti-Communist, Nixon had accomplished a diplomatic feat that his Democratic predecessors could not have attempted for fear of being branded "soft on Communism." Nixon and Kissinger's bold move in China had the added benefit of giving them leverage with the Soviet Union, which was understandably nervous about a U.S.-Chinese alliance.

> Nixon recognizes Communist China (1972)

Embracing the Soviet Union

In truth, China welcomed the breakthrough in relations with the United States because of tensions with its neighbor, the Soviet Union, with which it shared a long but contested border. By 1972, the Chinese leadership had become more fearful of the Soviet Union than the United States. The Soviet leaders, in turn troubled by the agreements between China and the United States, were also eager to ease tensions with the Americans.

> The Moscow summit: Trade agreements, arms reductions, and the easing of Cold War tensions

Once again, President Nixon surprised the world by announcing that he would visit Moscow in 1972 for discussions with Leonid Brezhnev, the Soviet premier. The high drama of the China visit was repeated in Moscow, with toasts and elegant dinners attended by world leaders who had previously regarded each other as incarnations of evil.

What became known as détente with the Soviets offered the promise of less intense competition between the superpowers. Nixon and Brezhnev signed the pathbreaking **Strategic Arms Limitation Talks (SALT I)** treaty, which negotiators had been working on since 1969. The SALT agreement did not end the nuclear arms race, but it did limit the number of missiles with nuclear warheads and prohibited the construction of missile-defense systems. The Moscow summit also produced new trade agreements, including an arrangement whereby the United States sold almost a quarter of its wheat crop to the Soviets at a favorable price (critics called it the Great Grain Robbery).

The Moscow summit resulted in the dramatic easing of tensions between the two Cold War superpowers. As Nixon told Congress upon his return, "Never before have two adversaries, so deeply divided by conflicting ideologies and political rivalries, been able to limit the armaments upon which their survival depends."

For Nixon and Kissinger, the agreements with China and the Soviet Union represented monumental changes in the global order that would have lasting consequences. Over time, the détente policy with the Soviet Union would help end the Cold War altogether by lowering Soviet hostility to

Strategic Arms Limitation Talks (SALT I) Agreement signed by President Nixon and Premier Leonid Brezhnev prohibiting the development of missile defense systems in the United States and Soviet Union and limiting the quantity of nuclear warheads for both.

Western influences penetrating their closed society, which in turn slowly eroded Communist rule from the inside.

Shuttle Diplomacy

U.S.-negotiated cease-fire in the Middle East

The Nixon-Kissinger initiatives in the Middle East were less dramatic and less conclusive than the agreements with China and the Soviet Union, but they did show that the United States at long last recognized the legitimacy of Arab interests in the region and its own dependence upon Middle Eastern oil, even though the Arab nations were adamantly opposed to the existence of Israel. In the Six-Day War of 1967, Israeli forces had routed the armies of Egypt, Syria, and Jordan and seized territory from all three nations. Moreover, the number of Palestinian refugees, many of them homeless since the creation of Israel in 1948, increased after the Israeli victory.

The Middle East remained a tinderbox of tensions. On October 6, 1973, the Jewish holy day of Yom Kippur, Syria and Egypt, backed by money from Saudi Arabia and armed with Soviet weapons, attacked Israel, igniting what became the Yom Kippur War. It created the most dangerous confrontation between the United States and the Soviet Union since the Cuban missile crisis. When the Israeli army, with weapons supplied by the United States, launched a fierce counterattack that appeared likely to overwhelm Egypt, the Soviets threatened to intervene militarily.

Nixon was bedridden because he was drunk, according to Henry Kissinger and other aides, so Kissinger, as secretary of state, presided over a National Security Council meeting that placed America's military forces on full alert to keep the Soviets out of the Middle Eastern war.

On October 20, Kissinger flew to Moscow to meet with Soviet premier Leonid Brezhnev. Kissinger skillfully negotiated a cease-fire agreement and exerted pressure on the Israelis to prevent them from taking additional Arab territory. In an attempt to broker a lasting settlement, Kissinger made numerous flights among the capitals of the Middle East. His "shuttle diplomacy" won acclaim from all sides, though he failed to find a comprehensive formula for peace. He did, however, lay the groundwork for an important treaty between Israel and Egypt in 1977.

Watergate

CORE **OBJECTIVE**
6. Explain how the Watergate scandal unfolded, and assess its political significance.

Nixon's foreign policy achievements allowed him to stage the presidential campaign of 1972 as a triumphal procession. Early on, the main threat to his reelection came from George Wallace, who had the potential as a third-party candidate to deprive the Republicans of conservative southern votes and thereby throw the election to the Democrats. That threat ended, however, on May 15, 1972, when Wallace was shot in an assassination attempt. Although he survived, he was left paralyzed below the waist and had to withdraw from the campaign. Nixon sought to take political advantage of the shooting by ordering aides to plant a false story that Democrats had orchestrated Wallace's assassination.

Meanwhile, the Democrats nominated Senator George McGovern of South Dakota, an anti-war liberal known for his integrity. "George is the most decent man in the Senate," said Robert Kennedy. "As a matter of fact, he is the only decent man." Decency does not win elections, however. McGovern was a poor campaigner who was viewed by many Americans as a left-wing extremist, and he never had a chance of winning, for Nixon had defused the Vietnam War as the central issue in the campaign. The president highlighted in his speeches that he had brought over 500,000 veterans home from Vietnam. The remaining U.S. troops were no longer in combat roles, and draftees were no longer going to Vietnam. In August 1972, Nixon disbanded the Selective Service; the draft was no longer an issue as the nation transitioned to an all-volunteer military. And by Election Day, only 20,000 U.S. military personnel remained in South Vietnam.

In the 1972 election, Nixon won the greatest victory of any Republican presidential candidate in history, capturing 520 electoral votes to only 17 for McGovern. The popular vote was equally decisive: 46 million to 28 million, a proportion of the total vote (60.8 percent) that was second only to Lyndon Johnson's victory over Barry Goldwater in 1964. The only downside to Nixon's triumph was that the Democrats maintained control of Congress.

For all his abilities and accomplishments, however, Nixon remained a chronically insecure person. More than most presidents, he nursed grudges and took politics personally, and he could be ruthless—even criminal—in attacking his opponents. As president, he began keeping a secret "enemies list" and launched numerous efforts to embarrass and punish those on the list. He also approved illegal plans to break into the offices of his opponents. Little did Nixon know that such behavior would bring his second term crashing down around him.

"Dirty Tricks"

By the spring of 1972, senior Nixon aide John Ehrlichman was overseeing a secret team of agents who performed various bumbling acts of sabotage against leading Democrats, such as falsely accusing Democratic senators Hubert H. Humphrey and Henry Jackson of sexual improprieties, forging press releases, setting off stink bombs at Democratic campaign events, and planting spies on McGovern's campaign plane.

During the campaign, McGovern had complained about the numerous "dirty tricks" orchestrated by members of the Nixon administration. Nixon, it turned out, had ordered illegal wiretaps on his opponents (as well as on his own aides), tried to coerce the Internal Revenue Service to intimidate Democrats,

JOHN EHRLICHMAN Ehrlichman, aide to President Nixon, addresses the Senate Watergate committee on July 24, 1973.

and told his chief of staff, Bob Haldeman, to break into the safe at the Brookings Institution, a Washington research center with Democratic ties. "Goddamnit," he told Haldeman, "get in and get those files. Blow the safe and get [them]." Charles "Chuck" Colson, one of the most active "dirty tricksters," admitted that "we did a hell of a lot of things and never got caught." But he had no regrets. He said he would "walk over his grandmother" if it would help Nixon stay in power.

> **The Watergate break-in (1972)**

McGovern expressed great concern over an incident on June 17, 1972, when Washington, D.C., police caught five burglars breaking into the Democratic National Committee headquarters in the exclusive Watergate hotel-apartment-office complex. The burglars were all former CIA agents, four of whom were Miami-based Cuban exiles; the other, James W. McCord, was the Nixon campaign's security director. The police also arrested two other men—G. Gordon Liddy and E. Howard Hunt—who were directing the break-in from a hotel across the street. The police found wads of hundred-dollar bills on the burglars. At the time, McGovern's complaints about the bungled **Watergate** break-in seemed like sour grapes from a candidate running far behind in the polls.

Nixon and his staff did their best to dismiss the news of the "third-rate burglary." The president denied any involvement in this "very bizarre incident." But he was lying. A worried Nixon told Alexander Haig, his national security adviser, "We will cover up [the Watergate burglary] until hell freezes over." (Nixon had selected Haig, an army general, as his national security adviser because he was "the meanest, toughest, most ambitious son of a bitch [Nixon] ever knew.")

In a frantic effort to protect Nixon, his White House aides secretly provided $350,000 in "hush money" to the jailed burglars, only to learn that they wanted $1 million. Nixon and his aides also discussed using the CIA to derail the Justice Department's investigation of the burglary. White House spokesmen lied to journalists and destroyed evidence related to the case. Bob Haldeman wanted the jailed Cubans to take the fall, suggesting that they claim they acted solely on their own. He also told the FBI to quit investigating the incident, falsely claiming that it involved a super-secret CIA operation.

Nixon encouraged such cover-up efforts, stressing that his "main concern [was] to keep the White House out of it." In August 1972, the cornered president told reporters that his own investigation into the Watergate incident had confirmed that no one in the White House or the administration was involved with the burglary. In fact, however, there was no such investigation. Nixon was by then thoroughly enmeshed in the efforts to cover-up the Watergate burglary.

Watergate (1972–1974)
Scandal that exposed the criminality and corruption of the Nixon administration and ultimately led to President Nixon's resignation in 1974.

Uncovering the Cover-up

During the trial of the accused Watergate burglars in January 1973, the relentless questioning of federal judge John J. Sirica, who was a Republican, a Nixon supporter, and a hard-nosed jurist nicknamed "Maximum John," led one of the accused to tell the full story of the Nixon administration's involvement. James W. McCord, security chief of the Committee to Re-Elect the President (CREEP), was the first in what would become a long line of informers to reveal the systematic efforts of Nixon and his aides to create an "imperial presidency" above the law. By the time of the Watergate break-in, the money to finance such "dirty tricks" was being illegally collected through CREEP and controlled by the White House staff.

> CREEP: Committee to Re-Elect the President

The trail of evidence pursued first by Judge Sirica, then by a grand jury, and then by a Senate committee headed by Democrat Samuel J. Ervin Jr. of North Carolina, led directly to what White House legal counsel John Dean called a "cancer close to the Presidency." By now, Nixon was personally leading the cover-up, using his presidential powers to block the investigation. He even coached his aides how to lie under oath. Most alarming, as it turned out, the Watergate burglary was merely one small part of a larger pattern of corruption and criminality sanctioned by the Nixon White House.

> The Watergate cover-up

The Watergate cover-up crumbled as various people began to cooperate with prosecutors. One of the burglars, James McCord, told Judge Sirica that the White House had provided them with "hush money" and that witnesses had lied at the trial. He then "named names" in testifying before the Ervin committee. His doing so led other White House aides to confess their role in the burglary and the cover-up. At the same time, two reporters for the *Washington Post*, Carl Bernstein and Bob Woodward, relentlessly pursued the story, eventually making it a compelling topic of national conversation. Still, Nixon continued to lie, telling Americans that he condemned "any attempt to cover up this case."

The cover-up unraveled further in 1973 when L. Patrick Gray, acting director of the FBI, resigned after confessing that he had destroyed incriminating documents at the behest of the president. On April 30, Ehrlichman and Haldeman resigned (they would later serve time in prison), as did Attorney General Richard Kleindienst. A few days later, Nixon nervously assured the public in a television address, "I am not a crook." Then John Dean, the White House legal counsel, whom Nixon had dismissed because of his cooperation with prosecutors, shocked the nation by telling the Ervin committee that there had been a White House cover-up approved by the president.

Nixon thereafter behaved like a cornered lion. Preoccupied with frantic efforts at self-defense and survival, he refused to provide Senator Ervin's committee with documents it requested, citing "executive privilege" to protect national security. Then, in another shocking disclosure, a White House aide told the Ervin committee that Nixon had installed a secret taping system in the White House and that many of the conversations about the Watergate burglary and cover-up had been recorded.

> The "Nixon tapes" and the Saturday Night Massacre

The bombshell news about the recording system in the Oval Office set off a yearlong legal battle for the "Nixon tapes." Harvard law professor Archibald Cox, whom Nixon's new attorney general, Elliot Richardson, had appointed as special prosecutor to investigate the Watergate case, took the president to court in October 1973 to obtain the tapes. Nixon refused to release the recordings and ordered Cox fired.

On October 20, in what became known as the "Saturday Night Massacre," Richardson and his deputy, William Ruckelshaus, resigned rather than follow Nixon's orders to fire the special prosecutor. (Solicitor General Robert Bork finally fired Cox.)

Nixon's dismissal of Cox produced a firestorm of public indignation. Numerous newspaper and magazine editorials, as well as a growing chorus of legislators, called for the president to resign or be impeached for obstructing justice. A Gallup poll revealed that Nixon's approval rating had plunged to 17 percent, the lowest in history.

Cox's dismissal failed to end Nixon's legal troubles. The new special prosecutor, Leon Jaworski, a prominent Texas attorney, also took the president to court. In March 1974, the Watergate grand jury indicted John Ehrlichman, Bob Haldeman, and former attorney general John Mitchell for obstruction of justice and named Nixon an "unindicted co-conspirator."

On April 30, Nixon, still refusing to turn over the actual tapes, released 1,254 pages of transcribed recordings that he had edited himself, often substituting the phrase "expletive deleted" for the vulgar language and anti-Semitic rants he had frequently unleashed in the Oval Office ("People said my language was bad," Nixon later rationalized, "but Jesus, you should have heard LBJ!"). At one point in the transcripts, the president told his aides that they should have frequent memory lapses when testifying about the cover-up.

The transcripts provoked widespread anger and disgust, for they revealed a president behaving in disgracefully unpresidential ways. His Oval Office conversations were so self-serving, bigoted, and profane that they degraded the stature of the presidency—"shabby, disgusting, immoral," said Republican senator Hugh Scott. The release of the transcripts only fueled the growing demands for Nixon to resign.

By the summer of 1974, Nixon was in full retreat. He became alternately combative, melancholy, and petty. The besieged president's efforts to orchestrate the cover-up obsessed him, unbalanced him, and unhinged him. Haldeman said he was the "weirdest man ever to live in the White House." During White House visits, Henry Kissinger found Nixon increasingly unstable and drinking heavily. After meeting with the president, Senator Barry Goldwater reported that Nixon "jabbered incessantly, often incoherently." He seemed "to be cracking."

The Watergate drama transfixed Americans, who watched the daily Ervin committee hearings as if they were episodes in a soap opera. On July 24, 1974, the Supreme Court ruled unanimously, in *United States v. Richard M. Nixon*, that the president must surrender *all* the tape recordings. A few days later, the House Judiciary Committee voted to recommend three articles of impeachment: obstruction of justice through the payment of "hush money" to witnesses and the withholding of evidence; abuse of power through the

Calls for Nixon's impeachment

United States v. Richard M. Nixon (1974)

WATERGATE SCANDAL A demonstration outside the White House calls on Congress to impeach Nixon for his illegal actions. **How did the American populace learn about Watergate and what were some of their reactions to the news?**

use of federal agencies to deprive citizens of their constitutional rights; and defiance of Congress by withholding the tapes. The president, Alexander Haig, now Nixon's chief of staff, confided to White House aides, was "guilty as hell." He then told Nixon, his boss, that he did not "see how we [could] survive this one."

Before the House of Representatives could meet to vote on impeachment, Nixon grudgingly handed over the complete set of White House tapes. The drama continued, however, when investigators learned that segments of several recordings were missing, including eighteen minutes of a key conversation in June 1972 during which Nixon first mentioned the Watergate burglary. The president's loyal secretary took the blame for the erasure, claiming that she had accidentally pushed the wrong button, but technical experts later concluded that the missing segments had in fact been intentionally deleted.

The other White House tape recordings, however, provided more than enough evidence of Nixon's involvement in the cover-up. At one point, the same president who had been the architect of détente with the Soviet Union and the recognition of Communist China had yelled at aides who were asking what they and others should say to Watergate investigators, "I don't give a shit what happens. I want you all to stonewall it, let them plead the Fifth Amendment, cover up or anything else."

V FOR "VICTORY" Before boarding the White House helicopter following his resignation, Nixon flashes a bright smile and his trademark V-sign to the world on August 9, 1974.

The incriminating tape recordings led Republican leaders to urge Nixon to quit rather than face an impeachment trial in the Senate. "There are only so many lies you can take and now there has been one too many," Senator Barry Goldwater concluded. "Nixon should get his ass out of the White House—today."

On August 9, 1974, the embattled president did just that: he resigned from office, the only president ever to do so. In 1969, he had begun his presidency hoping to heal a fractured America, to "bring people together." Now he left the White House to begin a self-imposed exile at his home in San Clemente, California, having deeply wounded the nation. A London newspaper explained that over the course of two centuries, America had digressed "from George Washington, who could not tell a lie, to Richard Nixon, who could not tell the truth."

Nixon never understood why the Watergate affair could have ended his presidency; in his view, his only mistake was getting caught. Nixon claimed that a president's actions could not be "illegal." He was wrong. The Watergate affair's clearest lesson was that not even a president is above the law.

> Nixon the first president to resign in office

Watergate and the Presidency

If there was a silver lining in the dark cloud of Watergate, it was the vigor and resilience of the institutions that had brought a rogue president to justice—the press, Congress, the courts, and aroused public opinion.

Congress responded to the Watergate revelations with several pieces of legislation designed to curb executive power. Already nervous about possible efforts to renew U.S. military assistance to South Vietnam, in 1973 the Democratic Congress passed the **War Powers Act**, which requires a president to inform Congress within forty-eight hours if U.S. military forces are deployed in combat abroad and to withdraw them after sixty days unless Congress specifically approves their stay.

Then, in an effort to correct abuses in the use of campaign funds, Congress enacted legislation in 1974 that set new ceilings on campaign contributions and expenditures. And, in reaction to the Nixon claim of "executive privilege" as a means of withholding evidence, Congress strengthened the 1966 Freedom of Information Act to require prompt responses to requests for information from government files and to place on government agencies the burden of proof for classifying information as secret.

War Powers Act (1973)
Legislation requiring the president to inform Congress within forty-eight hours of the deployment of U.S. troops abroad and to withdraw them after sixty days unless Congress approves their continued deployment.

An Unelected President

During Richard Nixon's last year in office, the Watergate crisis so dominated national politics that major domestic and foreign problems received little attention. Vice President Spiro Agnew had himself been forced to resign in October 1973 for accepting bribes from Maryland contractors before and during his term in office.

The vice president at the time of Nixon's resignation was Gerald Ford, a congenial former House minority leader from Michigan whom Nixon had appointed to succeed Agnew under the provisions of the Twenty-Fifth Amendment, which had been ratified in 1967. On August 9, 1974, Ford was sworn in as the nation's first politically appointed chief executive, the only person in history to serve as both vice president and president without having been elected to those offices. "I am acutely aware that you have not elected me as your president by your ballots," he said in a national speech. "So I ask you to confirm me as your president with your prayers."

President Ford reassured the nation, "Our long nightmare is over." He pledged to preside over the government with "openness and candor." But restoring public confidence in political leaders was not easy. Only a month after taking office, on September 8, 1974, Ford reopened the wounds of Watergate by issuing a "full, free, and absolute pardon" to Richard Nixon for any federal crimes he may have committed.

Many Americans were not in a forgiving mood when it came to Nixon, and Ford's pardon unleashed a storm of controversy. "Jail Ford!" yelled protesters outside the White House. Others wondered why a pardon should be given to someone who had not yet been charged with a crime. The *Washington Post* charged that Ford's decision was "nothing less than the continuation of a cover-up," while the *New York Times* dismissed the pardon as "profoundly unwise, divisive, and unjust."

A congressional subcommittee grilled Ford about the pardon, asking if Nixon had made a secret deal in exchange for resigning. Ford vigorously denied the charge, adding that nothing was to be gained by putting Nixon in prison. Ford was probably right, but the pardon thereafter hobbled his presidency. His approval rating plummeted from 71 percent to 49 percent in one day, the steepest drop ever recorded. Even Ford's press secretary resigned in protest of his boss's decision. The accidental president never fully recovered the public's confidence.

The Ford Years

As president, Gerald Ford adopted the posture he had developed as the minority leader in the House of Representatives: naysaying leader of the opposition who believed that the federal government exercised too much power. In his first fifteen months as president, Ford vetoed thirty-nine bills passed by Congress, thereby outstripping Herbert Hoover's all-time veto record in less than half the time.

GERALD FORD The thirty-eighth president listens apprehensively to news of rising rates of unemployment and inflation in 1974.

By far the most important development during Ford's brief presidency was the struggling economy. During the fall of 1974, the nation had entered the deepest recession since the Great Depression. Unemployment jumped to 9 percent in 1975, the annual rate of inflation reached double digits, and the federal deficit soon hit a record.

President Ford announced that inflation had become "Public Enemy No. 1," but instead of taking bold action, he launched a timid public relations campaign featuring lapel buttons that simply read "WIN," symbolizing the administration's determination to "Whip Inflation Now." The government distributed 12 million WIN buttons, but they became a national joke and a symbol of Ford's ineffectiveness in the fight against stagflation. He himself later admitted that it was a failed "gimmick."

By 1975, when Ford delivered his State of the Union address, he conceded that "the state of the union [was] not good." The economic recession, not inflation, was now his greatest concern. In March 1975, Ford signed a tax-reduction bill that failed in its goal of stimulating economic growth. Instead it was the federal budget deficit that grew from $53 billion in 1975 to $74 billion in 1976.

In foreign policy, Ford retained Henry Kissinger as secretary of state and pursued Nixon's goals of stability in the Middle East, friendly relations with China, and détente with the Soviet Union. In addition, Kissinger's tireless Middle East diplomacy produced an important agreement: Israel promised to return to Egypt most of the Sinai territory captured in the 1967 war, and the two nations agreed to rely upon negotiations rather than force to settle future disagreements. These limited but significant achievements should have enhanced Ford's image, but they were drowned in the sea of criticism over the collapse of the South Vietnamese government in the face of the North Vietnamese invasion.

The Election of 1976

Both political parties were in disarray as they prepared for the 1976 presidential election. At the Republican Convention, Gerald Ford had to fend off a powerful challenge from Ronald Reagan, a former two-term California governor and Hollywood actor who had become the darling of the party's growing conservative wing. At one point, Ford told reporters, "Ronald Reagan and I have one thing in common—we both played football. I played for Michigan. He played for Warner Brothers."

The Democrats chose an obscure dark horse candidate: James (Jimmy) Earl Carter Jr., who had served just one term as governor of Georgia. When Carter told his mother he was running for president, she replied: "President of *what*?" Tip O'Neill, the Democratic Speaker of the House, dismissed Carter as "a complete unknown."

Yet the long shot Carter had several assets. A former naval officer and engineer turned peanut farmer, Carter was one of several Democratic southern governors who sought to move their party away from its traditional "tax and spend" liberalism. The federal government, he charged, was a "horrible, bloated, confused . . . bureaucratic mess." The many Great Society social welfare programs created by LBJ were a "failure" that were in "urgent need of a complete overhaul."

Carter insisted that he was neither a liberal nor a conservative but a pragmatic "engineer" who would be able to get the "right thing" done in the "right ways." In addition, he capitalized on post-Watergate cynicism about politicians by promising that he would "never tell a lie to the American people." He also trumpeted his status as a political "outsider" whose inexperience in Washington politics would in fact be an asset. Carter was certainly different from conventional candidates. Political reporters covering the campaign marveled at a Southern Baptist candidate who was a "born-again" Christian and Sunday school teacher who claimed that he "would never tell a lie" to the people.

A poll taken during the campaign found that voters viewed Ford as "a nice guy," but "not . . . very smart about the issues the country is facing." Ford reinforced that impression during a televised debate with Carter when he mistakenly claimed that "there is no Soviet domination of Eastern Europe." Viewers realized that Ford knew little about foreign policy and that he seemed to be "soft" on communism.

To the surprise of many, the little-known Carter revived the New Deal voting alliance of southern whites, blacks, urban labor unionists, and ethnic groups like Jews and Hispanics to eke out a narrow win, receiving 41 million votes to Ford's 39 million. A heavy turnout of African Americans in the South enabled Carter to sweep every state in the region except Virginia. He also benefited from the appeal of Minnesota senator Walter F. Mondale, his liberal running mate and a favorite among blue-collar workers and the urban poor. Ford was the first president to lose his bid for a second term since Herbert Hoover in 1932.

The significant story of the election was not so much Carter or Ford but the low voter turnout. "Neither Ford nor Carter won as many votes as Mr. Nobody," said one reporter, commenting on how almost half the eligible voters, apparently alienated by Watergate, the stagnant economy, and the two lackluster candidates, chose to sit out the election. In explaining why he had not voted, a man noted that he was "a three-time loser. In 1964 I voted for the peace candidate—Johnson—and got war. In '68 I voted for the law-and-order candidate—and got crime. In '72 I voted for Nixon again, and we got Watergate." Such an alienated voter was not a good omen for a new Democratic president about to begin his first term.

Reviewing the
CORE OBJECTIVES | INQUIZITIVE

■ **Youth Revolt** Civil rights activism inspired a heightened interest in a number of social causes during the 1960s, especially among the youth. Students for a Democratic Society (SDS) embodied the *New Left* ideology and helped spur the free-speech movement (FSM) starting at the University of California, Berkeley, and spreading to many campuses across the nation. By 1970, a distinctive *counterculture* also emerged among disaffected youth and attracted hippies, many of whom used mind-altering drugs, lived on rural communes, and refused conventional life, which they viewed as corrupt and constricting.

■ **The Inspirational Effects of the Civil Rights Movement** The energy, ideals, tactics, and courage of the civil rights movement inspired many other social reform movements, including the *women's movement*, the *Red Power* movement and the *United Farm Workers (UFW)*. In 1973, women's lives were transformed when the Supreme Court in *Roe v. Wade* struck down state laws banning abortions during the first trimester of a pregnancy, ruling that women had a "right to choose" whether to bear a child. The 1969 *Stonewall riots* marked a militant new era in the crusade for gay rights.

■ **Reaction and Domestic Agenda** Richard Nixon took advantage of the backlash against these liberal politics and cultural movements to win election in 1968. His "southern strategy" drew large numbers of conservative southern white Democrats into the Republican party for the first time. As president, he sought to slow the momentum of *affirmative-action* programs intended to benefit minorities, but in 1970 he created the *Environmental Protection Agency (EPA)*. Both the Nixon and Ford administrations were unable to overcome *stagflation*.

■ **End of the Vietnam War** In his 1968 campaign, Nixon pledged to secure "peace with honor" in Vietnam, but years would pass before the war ended. He did change the military strategy in Vietnam by implementing *Vietnamization*: increasing aid to South Vietnam and aggressively bombing North Vietnam, while attempting to negotiate a cease-fire with North Vietnam. North and South Vietnam agreed to a cease-fire called the Paris Peace Accords. Democrats in Congress passed the *War Powers Act (1973)* designed to limit the ability of presidents to wage war in the absence of a Congressional declaration of war. In 1975, the South Vietnamese government collapsed after a massive North Vietnamese invasion. The Communist victors forcibly reunited the North and South.

■ **Détente** Nixon's greatest accomplishments were in foreign policy. As an aggressive anti-Communist, he shocked the world by opening diplomatic relations with Communist China and pursuing *détente* with the Soviet Union, focusing on areas of shared agreement with the 1972 *Strategic Arms Limitation Talks (SALT I)* treaty.

■ **Watergate** During the 1972 presidential campaign, the Committee to Re-Elect the President (CREEP) was implicated in the *Watergate* burglary. In *United States v. Richard M. Nixon* (1974), the Supreme Court ruled that Nixon had to surrender the recordings of White House meetings dealing with the scandal. Nixon resigned in 1974 to avoid impeachment.

KEY TERMS

New Left *p. 1079*

counterculture *p. 1081*

women's movement *p. 1086*

Roe v. Wade (1973) *p. 1087*

United Farm Workers (UFW) *p. 1091*

Red Power *p. 1093*

Stonewall riots (1969) *p. 1094*

affirmative action *p. 1095*

Environmental Protection Agency (EPA) *p. 1100*

stagflation *p. 1101*

Vietnamization *p. 1103*

détente *p. 1110*

Strategic Arms Limitation Talks (SALT I) *p. 1111*

Watergate (1972–1974) *p. 1114*

War Powers Act (1973) *p. 1118*

CHRONOLOGY

1960	Students for a Democratic Society (SDS) founded
1963	Betty Friedan's *The Feminine Mystique* published
1965	United Farm Workers (UFW) established
	Forced integration of Mississippi schools
1966	National Organization for Women (NOW) founded
1967–1968	Inner-city riots; student sit-ins on college campuses
1968	Riots at the Democratic National Convention
	American Indian Movement (AIM) founded
March 1969	U.S. warplanes bomb Cambodia
June 1969	Stonewall riots in New York City
August 1969	Woodstock music festival attracts more than 400,000 people
1970	Kent State and Jackson State shootings
1971	*Pentagon Papers* published
1972	Nixon visits China and the Soviet Union, signs the Strategic Arms Limitation Talks (SALT I) treaty
1972–1974	Watergate scandal unfolds
1973	Sioux occupation of Wounded Knee, South Dakota
	U.S. troop withdrawal from Vietnam begins
	Roe v. Wade
1974	Nixon resigns; Gerald Ford becomes president
April 1975	Saigon falls to the North Vietnamese

🐰 INQUIZITIVE

Go to InQuizitive to see what you've learned—and learn what you've missed—with personalized feedback along the way.

FEELS GOOD TO BE RIGHT This proud Republican and Reagan supporter lets her decorated top hat adorned with campaign buttons speak for her at the 1980 Republican National Convention. Held in Detroit, Michigan, the convention nominated former California governor Ronald Reagan, who promised to "make America great again."

Conservative Revival

1977–1990

During the seventies, the United States lost much of its self-confidence. The failed Vietnam War; the sordid revelations of the Watergate scandal; and the spike in oil prices, interest rates, and consumer prices revealed the limits of the nation's power, prosperity, and virtue. Surveys showed that Americans felt defensive and dispirited about their nation and its prospects in what journalists were calling a new "age of limits." For a nation long accustomed to economic growth and spreading prosperity, the persistence of stagflation and gasoline shortages exasperated Americans. Even in July 1976, as the United States celebrated the bicentennial of its independence, many people were downsizing their expectations of the American dream.

Jimmy Carter took office promising a government that would be "competent" as well as "decent, open, fair, and compassionate." After four years as president, however, Carter had little to show for his efforts. The economy remained sluggish, consumer prices continued to increase at historic levels, and failed efforts to free Americans held hostage in Iran prompted critics, including Democrats, to denounce the administration as being indecisive and inept. In the end, Carter's call for "a time of national austerity" revealed both his ineffective legislative skills and his misreading of the public mood.

CORE OBJECTIVES InQuizitive

1. Analyze why Jimmy Carter had such limited success as president.

2. Identify the key factors that led to the election of Ronald Reagan, the rise of the conservative movement, and the resurgence of the Republican party.

3. Define "Reaganomics," and evaluate its effects on American society and economy.

4. Explain how Reagan's Soviet strategy helped end the Cold War.

5. Characterize the social and economic issues and innovations that emerged during the 1980s.

6. Appraise the impact of the end of the Cold War and the efforts of President George H. W. Bush to create a post–Cold War foreign policy.

The Republicans capitalized on the public frustration by electing Ronald Reagan president in 1980. Where Jimmy Carter had denounced the evils of unregulated capitalism, Reagan promised to revive the capitalist spirit, restore national pride, and regain international respect. He did all that and more. During his two-term presidency in the 1980s, he transformed the political landscape. Reagan accelerated the conservative resurgence in politics and set in motion the forces that would cause the collapse of the Soviet Union and the end of the Cold War.

CORE **OBJECTIVE**

1. Analyze why Jimmy Carter had such limited success as president.

The Carter Presidency

James (Jimmy) Earl Carter Jr. won the close 1976 election over the incumbent Gerald Ford because he convinced voters that he was an incorruptible political "outsider," a born-again Christian of pure motives who would restore integrity and honesty to the presidency in the aftermath of the Watergate scandal. He also promised that he was committed to restraining "big government" spending.

In his 1977 inaugural address, Carter confessed that he had no grand "vision" of the future. Unlike his predecessors, he highlighted America's limitations rather than its potential: "We have learned that 'more' is not necessarily 'better,' that even our great nation has its recognized limits, and that we can neither answer all questions nor solve all problems." That may have been true, but retrenchment was not what many voters wanted to hear. Carter later admitted that his remarks about dialing back national expectations were "politically unpopular," for "Americans were not accustomed to limits—on natural resources or on the power of our country to . . . control international events."

Jimmy Who?

Like Gerald Ford before him, Jimmy Carter was an honest, forthright man. Yet his charming modesty in public masked a complex and at times contradictory personality. "Jimmy's a hard person to get to know," admitted his top aide, Hamilton Jordan. No modern president was as openly committed to his Christian faith as Carter was. At the same time, few other presidents were as tough on others as Carter was. He once called the lovable Democratic leader Hubert Humphrey "a loser."

The former governor of Georgia who came out of nowhere to win the presidential campaign ("Jimmy Who?") never lacked self-confidence. All his life he had displayed a fierce determination to succeed and expected those around him to show the same tenacity. "I am pretty rigid," Carter admitted. Carter and his closest aides, all of whom he brought with him from Georgia, arrived in Washington, D.C., in early 1977 convinced that they were going to clean up the "mess" made by politicos and bureaucrats within the federal government. Congress, Carter noted in his diary, "was disgusting." Yet his naive dismissal of Congress would prove to be his downfall, as he himself later admitted.

Carter, the former naval officer, nuclear engineer, efficiency expert, and business executive, the first president to have been born in a hospital, wanted to be a "strong, aggressive president," an incorruptible outsider who would use his technical expertise to clean up the "Washington mess." He would make the federal government run more smoothly at less expense to the taxpayers by eliminating waste and providing expert management. Yet he had little ability to inspire people to follow his lead. Democratic senator Eugene McCarthy described Carter as an "oratorical mortician" while a journalist stressed that "there's no music in him." Carter was, as he himself acknowledged, a manager rather than a visionary.

In 1977, Carter needed to summon all his intelligence and conviction ("I like to run things," he said), for he faced difficult economic problems and formidable international challenges. Americans expected him to restore U.S. stature abroad and to cure the stubborn economic recession and reduce both unemployment and inflation at a time when all industrial economies around the world were struggling.

THE CARTERS After his inauguration, President Jimmy Carter forgoes the traditional limousine and walks down Pennsylvania Avenue with his wife, Rosalynn.

Early Success

During the first two years of his presidency, Carter enjoyed several successes, both symbolic and real. In a sign of his frugality, he sold the presidential yacht, reduced the size of the White House staff by a third, and told cabinet officers to give up their government cars and drive their own. His new administration included more African Americans and women than any before. He fulfilled a controversial campaign pledge by offering amnesty (forgiveness) to the thousands of young men who had fled the country rather than serve in the U.S. military in Vietnam. He reorganized the executive branch and created two new cabinet-level agencies, the Departments of Energy and Education. He also pushed through Congress several significant environmental initiatives, including stricter controls over the strip-mining of coal, the creation of a $1.6-billion "Superfund" to clean up toxic chemical waste sites, and a bill protecting more than 100 million acres of Alaskan land from development. He also deregulated the trucking, airline, and financial industries in an effort to restore competition. At the end of his first hundred days in office, Carter enjoyed a 75 percent public approval rating.

Carter's Limitations

Carter's successes were short-lived, however. By nature, he was less a compelling leader than a rigid bureaucrat and compulsive micromanager (he even insisted on scheduling the use of the White House tennis court). For his first two years in the White House, Carter chose to serve as his own chief of staff, with disastrous results, for he was so busy with mundane activities that he failed to establish an uplifting vision for the nation's future. Instead of focusing on a few priorities, Carter tried to do too much too fast, and his inexperienced team of senior aides was often more a burden than a blessing. The chief of staff he finally appointed, Hamilton Jordan, spent much of his time drinking, chasing women, and alienating members of Congress. Worst of all, the self-proclaimed "outsider" president saw little need to consult with Democratic leaders, which helps explain why many of his legislative requests got nowhere.

A deepening recession

Ultimately, however, Carter's inability to revive the economy doomed his presidency. Stagflation continued to defy easy solutions. Carter first tried to attack unemployment, authorizing some $14 billion in federal spending to trigger job growth while cutting taxes by $34 billion. His actions helped generate new jobs but in doing so caused a spike in inflation. Annual inflation (increases in consumer prices) jumped from 5 percent when he took office to as much as 13 percent during 1980. The result was a deepening recession, rising unemployment, and growing criticism of the president. Liberals complained that Carter was doing nothing to address spreading poverty and inner-city decline. He responded with a lecture that sounded more like a Republican president: "Government cannot solve our problems. It cannot eliminate poverty, or provide a bountiful economy, or reduce inflation, or save our cities, or cure illiteracy, or provide energy."

The "energy crisis"

What made Carter's efforts to restore prosperity more challenging was the worsening "energy crisis." Since the Arab oil embargo in 1973, the price of imported oil had doubled, while U.S. dependence upon foreign oil had grown from 35 to 50 percent of its annual needs. In April 1977, Carter presented Congress with a comprehensive energy proposal designed to cut oil consumption, charging that America was the "most wasteful nation on earth." Legislators, however, turned down most of the bill's key elements, in part because of Carter's poor relationship with Democrats in Congress. The final energy bill, the National Energy Act of 1978, was so gutted by oil, gas, and automobile industry lobbyists that one presidential aide said it looked like it had been "nibbled to death by ducks."

In 1979, the energy crisis grew even more troublesome when Islamic fundamentalists took over the government in oil-rich Iran. The revolutionaries shut off the supply of Iranian oil to the United States, creating gasoline shortages and much higher prices. Warning that the "growing scarcity in energy" would paralyze the U.S. economy, Carter asked Congress for a new and much more comprehensive energy bill, but again the legislators rejected its energy conservation measures. In a symbolic gesture, Carter had thirty-two solar panels installed on the White House roof to draw attention to the nation's need to become energy independent.

A "Crisis of Confidence"

By July 1979, Carter had grown so discouraged that he took an unusual step: for eleven days he holed up at Camp David, the presidential retreat in the Maryland mountains. There, he met privately with some 150 representatives from business, labor, education, politics, religion, even psychiatrists—all the while keeping the media at bay.

Loss of congressional support and public confidence

Then, on July 15, the president returned to the White House and delivered a televised speech in which he sounded more like an angry preacher than a charismatic president. He claimed that a "crisis of confidence" was paralyzing the nation. The people had lost confidence in his leadership and America had become rudderless, with no "sense of purpose." He then made a crucial mistake when he seemingly blamed Americans for the problems facing the nation. "All the legislation in the world can't fix what's wrong with America," Carter stressed. He chastised Americans for having become preoccupied with "owning and consuming things" at the expense of "hard work, strong families, close-knit communities, and our faith in God."

The nation was at a crossroads, Carter concluded. Americans could choose continued self-indulgence and political stalemate, or they could revive traditional values, such as thrift, mutual aid, simple living, and spirituality. "We can take the first step down that path as we begin to solve our energy problem. Energy will be the immediate test of our ability to unite this nation."

Carter failed that test, however. An Arizona newspaper grumbled that "the nation did not tune in Carter to hear a sermon. It wanted answers. It did not get them." Even Democrats lambasted the president's speech. Arkansas governor Bill Clinton said that Carter was behaving more like a "17th-century New England Puritan than a 20th-century Southern Baptist." Carter's new energy proposals got nowhere in Congress. By the fall of 1979, his ratings in public polls were the lowest in history, leading former president Gerald Ford to observe that if Nixon had created "an imperial presidency," Carter had fashioned "an imperiled presidency."

Carter's Foreign Policy

Carter's crowning achievement, which even his most bitter critics applauded, was his dogged effort to work out a 1978 peace agreement between Prime Minister Menachem Begin of Israel and President Anwar el-Sadat of Egypt. When the two foreign leaders arrived at the presidential retreat at Camp David, Maryland, they refused to be in the same room together, so Carter shuttled back and forth with various versions of a settlement. His strenuous

Carter's foreign policy controversies: Human rights, the Panama Canal Treaty, responses to the Soviet invasion of Afghanistan

THE CAMP DAVID ACCORDS
Egyptian president Anwar
el-Sadat (left), Jimmy Carter
(center), and Israeli prime minister
Menachem Begin (right) at the
announcement of the Camp David
Accords, September 1978.

efforts paid off. It was the first time that an Arab nation (Egypt) had officially recognized the existence of Israel. However, this historic agreement, dubbed the **Camp David Accords** for the presidential retreat where the negotiations took place, created only a "framework for peace," not a true settlement of differences. In the wake of the Camp David Accords, most Arab nations condemned Sadat as a traitor, and Islamic extremists assassinated him in 1981. Still, Carter's high-level diplomacy made another war between Israel and the Arab world less likely.

Human Rights

Carter stumbled again, however, when he vowed that "the soul of our foreign policy" should be an absolute "commitment to human rights" abroad, drawing a direct contrast between his international "idealism" and the geopolitical "realism" practiced by Richard Nixon and Henry Kissinger. Carter created an Office of Human Rights within the State Department and selectively cut off financial assistance to some repressive governments around the world (Chile, El Salvador, Rhodesia, and South Africa) while maintaining support of brutal governments in places like Argentina, Ethiopia, Pakistan, and Uruguay. Carter's inconsistent moralism led critics to argue that he was sacrificing America's national interests in order to promote an impossible standard of international moral purity.

Panama Canal

Similarly, Carter's controversial decision to turn over control of the Panama Canal Zone to the Panamanian government aroused intense criticism. The president argued that Panama's deep resentment of America's having taken control of the Canal Zone during the presidency of Theodore Roosevelt left

Camp David Accords (1978)
Peace agreement facilitated by
President Carter between Prime
Minister Menachem Begin of
Israel and President Anwar
el-Sadat of Egypt, the first Arab
head of state to officially recognize the state of Israel.

him no choice but to transfer management of the canal to Panama. Conservatives blasted Carter for surrendering U.S. control of such a strategic asset. Ronald Reagan claimed the canal was America's forever: "We bought it, we paid for it, it's ours."

Afghanistan

In 1979, Carter faced another crisis when the Soviet army invaded Afghanistan, where Islamist *jihadists* ("holy warriors") were rebelling against a faltering Communist government. Carter responded with a series of steps, some of which provoked intense criticism: he refused to sign a new Strategic Arms Limitation Talks (SALT II) treaty with the Soviets, suspended grain shipments to the Soviet Union, began supplying Afghan "freedom fighters" with weapons smuggled through Pakistan, requested large increases in military spending, required all nineteen-year-old men to register for the military draft, and called for an international boycott of the 1980 Olympic Games, which were to be held that summer in Moscow.

The Soviet invasion of Afghanistan also prompted the president to announce what came to be called the Carter Doctrine, in which the president threatened to use military force to prevent any nation from gaining control of the Persian Gulf waterways, through which most of the oil from the Middle East made its way to foreign ports, including American cities.

Crisis in Iran

Then came the **Iranian hostage crisis**, a series of dramatic events that illustrated the inability of the United States to control world affairs. In January 1979, Islamic revolutionaries in Iran ousted the pro-American government led by the shah of Iran, Mohammad Reza Pahlavi, who owed his rule to secret CIA intervention in 1953. The turmoil in Iran led to a sharp drop in oil production, driving gasoline prices up worldwide. By the spring of 1979, Americans were again waiting in long lines to pay record prices for limited amounts of gasoline.

In October, the United States allowed the deposed shah to receive medical treatment at an American hospital. This "humanitarian" decision enraged Iranian revolutionaries. On November 4, 1979, a frenzied mob of several thousand Iranian youths stormed the U.S. embassy in Tehran, chanting "Death to Carter, death to the shah." They seized sixty-six diplomats and staff, including fifty-two American citizens.

The Iranian leader, Ayatollah Ruhollah Khomeini, endorsed the mob action and demanded the return of the hated shah of Iran from the United States (along with all his wealth) in exchange for the release of the hostages. Angry Americans, including many in Congress, demanded a military response to the kidnappings in Iran. Carter, however, appealed to the United

Iranian hostage crisis (1979) Storming of the U.S. embassy in Tehran by Iranian revolutionaries, who held fifty-two Americans hostage for 444 days, despite President Carter's appeals for their release and a botched rescue attempt.

AYATOLLAH KHOMEINI Religious figure and leader of the Iranian Revolution that overthrew the Iranian monarchy in 1979.

A KING'S RANSOM An Iranian militant holds a group of U.S. embassy staff members hostage in Tehran, Iran, in 1979. **How did the Iranian hostage crisis reflect on Carter's leadership and American authority?**

Nations, but Iran scoffed at UN requests for release of the hostages. Carter then froze all Iranian financial assets in America and asked Europe to join the United States in a trade embargo of Iran, including its oil. The trade restrictions were only partially effective because America's allies were not willing to lose access to Iranian oil.

As the hostage crisis continued and gasoline prices rose to record levels, a frustrated Carter authorized a risky rescue attempt by U.S. commandos on April 24, 1980 (his decision caused his secretary of state, Cyrus Vance, to resign in protest). The raid had to be aborted when three of the eight helicopters developed mechanical problems; it ended with eight U.S. deaths when a helicopter collided with a transport plane at a remote staging site in the Iranian desert.

For fourteen months, the frustrating Iranian hostage crisis paralyzed Carter's ability to lead the nation. Like a black cloud, it loomed over every decision he made. For many, the prolonged standoff with Iran became a symbol of his failed presidency. "For the first time in its history," *Business Week* magazine observed, "the United States is no longer growing in power and influence among the nations of the world." A Democrat in Congress reported that Carter "hasn't a single friend up here. Not one soul." The hostage stand-off finally ended after 444 days, on January 20, 1981, when Carter, just hours before leaving office, released several billion dollars of Iranian assets to ransom the hostages.

The Rise of Ronald Reagan

No sooner had Carter been elected in 1976 than conservative Republicans (the "New Right") had mobilized to defeat him. Their plans for a Republican revival centered on the popularity of tall, square-shouldered, plain-speaking Ronald Reagan, the handsome Hollywood actor, two-term California governor, and prominent political commentator. Reagan was not a deep thinker, but he was a superb reader of the public mood, an outspoken emotional patriot, and a committed champion of conservative principles.

CORE **OBJECTIVE**

2. Identify the key factors that led to the election of Ronald Reagan, the rise of the conservative movement, and the resurgence of the Republican party.

The Actor Turned President

Born in the drab prairie town of Tampico, Illinois, in 1911, the son of an often-drunk shoe salesman and a devout, Bible-quoting mother, Ronald Reagan graduated from tiny Eureka College in 1932 during the depths of the Great Depression. He first worked as a radio sportscaster before starting a movie career in Hollywood in 1937. He served three years in the army during the Second World War, making training films. At that time, as Reagan recalled, he was a Democrat, "a New Dealer to the core" who voted for Franklin D. Roosevelt four times. After the war, Reagan became president of the acting profession's union, the Screen Actors Guild, where he honed his negotiating skills and fended off Communist efforts to infiltrate the union.

Reagan supported Democrat Harry S. Truman in the 1948 presidential election, but during the 1950s he decided that federal taxes were too high. In 1960, he campaigned as a Democrat for Richard Nixon, and two years later he abandoned the Democrats and joined the Republican party. Reagan achieved political stardom in 1964 when he delivered a rousing speech on national television on behalf of Barry Goldwater's presidential candidacy. Soon thereafter, wealthy admirers convinced him to run for governor of California in 1966, and he won by a landslide.

Now, as the Republican presidential nominee in 1980, Reagan set about drawing a vivid contrast between his optimistic vision of America's future and Jimmy Carter's bleak outlook and "mediocre leadership." President Carter, he claimed, kept saying, that "our nation has passed its zenith. My fellow citizens, I utterly

RONALD REAGAN The "Great Communicator" flashes his charming, trademark smile.

reject that view." Unlike Carter, Reagan insisted that there was "nothing wrong with the American people" and that there were "simple answers" to the complex problems facing the United States, though they were not *easy* answers. He pledged to end many of the federal social-welfare programs, increase military spending to "win" the Cold War, dismantle the "bloated" federal bureaucracy, reduce taxes and government regulations of business ("get the government off our backs"), and appoint conservative judges to the Supreme Court and federal courts across the nation. He also promised to affirm old-time religious values by banning abortions and reinstituting prayer in public schools. (He ended up doing neither.)

Reagan's popularity resulted from his remarkable skill as a public speaker (journalists dubbed him the "Great Communicator") and his steadfast commitment to a few basic principles and simple themes. Blessed with a baritone voice and a wealth of entertaining stories, he charmed audiences with his folksy stories and captivating smile. Reagan rejected Carter's assumption that Americans needed "to start getting along with less, to accept a decline in our standard of living." He instead promised boundless economic expansion. By reducing taxes and easing government regulations of businesses, he pledged, the engine of free enterprise capitalism would spread prosperity to everyone.

The Rise of the "New Right"

Population growth in conservative Sun Belt states

By 1980, social developments had made Reagan's anti-liberal stance a major asset. An increase in the number of senior citizens, a group that tends to be more politically and socially conservative, and the steady migration of people—especially older Americans—to the conservative Sunbelt states was shifting the political balance of power toward Reagan's philosophy. Fully 90 percent of the nation's total population growth during the 1980s occurred in southern or western Sun Belt states, while the Northeast and industrial states of the Midwest—Ohio, Michigan, Illinois, Michigan, Pennsylvania, and West Virginia (called the "Rust Belt")—experienced economic decline, factory closings, and mass migration to the Sunbelt. The population shifts triggered a massive redistricting of the House of Representatives, with Florida, California, and Texas gaining seats and northern states such as New York losing them.

Tax revolts

A related development during the seventies was a growing grassroots tax revolt. As consumer prices and the value of houses rose, so too did property taxes. In California, Ronald Reagan's home state, skyrocketing property taxes threatened to force many working-class people from their homes. This spurred grassroots efforts to cut back on the size and cost of state government to enable reductions in property taxes.

In June 1978, tax rebels in California, with Reagan's support, succeeded in putting an initiative known as Proposition 13 on the state ballot. An overwhelming majority of voters—both Republicans and Democrats—approved the measure, which slashed property taxes by 57 percent and amended the state constitution to make it more difficult for local and state governments to raise taxes. The "Prop 13" tax revolt in California soon spread across the nation, leading the *New York Times* to call it a "modern Boston Tea Party."

The Christian Right

The California tax revolt fed into a national conservative resurgence led by the rapidly growing "**Christian Right**." Religious conservatives promoting a faith-based political agenda formed the strongest grassroots movement of the late twentieth century. By the 1980s, Catholic conservatives and Protestant evangelicals owned powerful television and radio

LOOK ON THE RIGHT SIDE The rise of the Christian Right saw protests against Supreme Court rulings that reinforced the separation of church and state. Here, in a 1984 protest organized by the Moral Majority, students chant "Kids want to pray!" in support of an amendment to reinstate prayer in public schools.

stations, operated their own schools and universities, and organized "megachurches" from which such "televangelists" as the Reverend Jerry Falwell launched a cultural crusade against the "demonic" forces of liberalism at home and communism abroad.

In 1979, Falwell formed the Moral Majority (later renamed the Liberty Alliance) to campaign for the major political and social goals of the religious right: the economy should operate without "interference" by the government, which should be reduced in size; the Supreme Court decision in *Roe v. Wade* (1973) legalizing abortion should be reversed; Darwinian evolution should be replaced in school textbooks by the biblical story of creation; daily prayer should return to public schools; women should submit to their husbands; and Soviet communism should be opposed as a form of pagan totalitarianism.

> A crusade against liberalism, feminism, and abortion

That Ronald Reagan became the hero of the Christian Right reflected the candidate's rare communication skills, for he himself rarely attended church services and had no strong religious affiliations. However, white evangelical Christians—alienated by the "liberal social agenda" of the Democratic party, especially policies regarding abortion and endorsement of gay rights—became a crucial element in Reagan's electoral strategy.

Anti-Feminist Backlash

By the late seventies, a well-organized and well-financed backlash against the feminist movement reinforced the rise of the Christian Right. Antifeminist activists like Phyllis Schlafly, a conservative Catholic attorney and Republican activist from Alton, Illinois, stopped the Equal Rights Amendment (ERA) from being ratified by the required thirty-eight states.

Christian Right Christian conservatives with a faith-based political agenda that includes prohibition of abortion and allowing prayer in public schools.

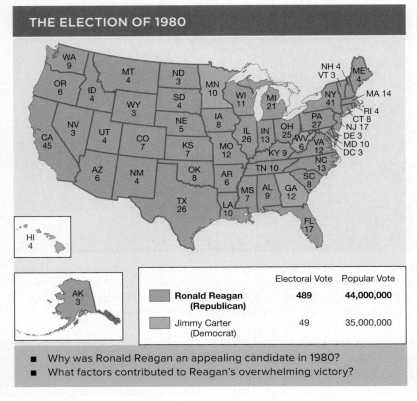

THE ELECTION OF 1980

	Electoral Vote	Popular Vote
Ronald Reagan (Republican)	**489**	**44,000,000**
Jimmy Carter (Democrat)	49	35,000,000

- Why was Ronald Reagan an appealing candidate in 1980?
- What factors contributed to Reagan's overwhelming victory?

Schlafly's STOP (Stop Taking Our Privileges) ERA organization, founded in 1972, warned that the ERA would allow husbands to abandon their wives, force women into military service, and give gay "perverts" the right to marry. She and others also stressed that the gender equality promised by the proposed amendment violated biblical teachings about women's "God-given" roles as nurturers and helpmates. By the end of the decade, the national effort to gain ratification of the ERA had stalled, largely because no states in the conservative South and West had ratified it.

Many of Schlafly's anti-ERA supporters also participated in the growing anti-abortion, or "pro-life," movement. The National Right to Life Committee, supported by the National Conference of Catholic Bishops, denounced abortion as murder, and the emotional intensity of the issue made it a powerful political force. Reagan highlighted his support for traditional "family values," gender roles, and the "rights" of the unborn, which helped persuade many northern Democrats—mostly working-class Catholics—to switch parties and support Reagan.

Financing Conservatism

The business community as well had become a source of revitalized conservative activism. In 1972, the leaders of the nation's largest corporations formed the Business Roundtable to promote business interests in Congress. Within a few years, many of those corporations had created political action committees (PACs) to distribute money to pro-business political candidates. Corporate donations also helped fund conservative "think tanks," such as the American Enterprise Institute, the Cato Institute, and the Heritage Foundation, all of which opposed "liberal" legislation. By 1980, the national conservative insurgency had become a powerful political force with substantial financial resources, carefully crafted ideas, and grassroots energy, all of which helped explain Ronald Reagan's presidential victory.

The Election of 1980

Reagan's supporters during the 1980 campaign loved his simple solutions, upbeat personality, and genial humor, and they responded passionately to his recurring question at campaign stops: "Are you better off than you were four years ago?" Their answer was a resounding "No!" Carter had not been able to gain the release of the Americans held hostage in Iran, nor had he improved the economy. His approval ratings had sunk below those of Richard Nixon.

On election day, Reagan swept to a lopsided victory, with 489 electoral votes to 49 for Carter, who carried only six states. The popular vote was 44 million (51 percent) for Reagan to Carter's 35 million (41 percent), with 7 percent going to John Anderson, a moderate Republican who ran on an independent ticket. Reagan's thumping of Carter signaled a major realignment of voters in which many so-called Reagan Democrats—conservative white southern Protestants and blue-collar northern Catholics crossed over to the Republican party.

The Reagan Revolution

CORE OBJECTIVE
3. Define "Reaganomics," and evaluate its effects on American society and economy.

Those Democrats who dismissed sixty-year-old Ronald Reagan, the oldest man to assume the presidency, and the first to have been divorced, as a mental lightweight famously inattentive to the details of policy and management, underrated his many virtues, including the importance of his years in front of a camera. Politics is a performing art, all the more so in the age of television, and few politicians had Reagan's stage presence—or confidence. His remarkable ability to make voters again believe in American greatness won him two presidential elections, in 1980 and 1984, and ensured the victory of his chosen successor, Vice President George H. W. Bush, in 1988. Just how revolutionary the "Reagan era" was remains a subject of intense debate, but what cannot be denied is that Reagan's actions and beliefs set the tone for the decade's political and economic life.

Reagan's First Term

"Fellow conservatives," new-president Ronald Reagan said in a speech in 1981, "our moment has arrived." Eventually, he succeeded as president where Jimmy Carter failed for three main reasons. First, Reagan focused on a few essential priorities (lowering tax rates, reducing the scope of the federal government, increasing military spending, and conducting an anti-Soviet foreign policy), and he pursued those goals with what an aide called a "warmly ruthless" intensity. Second, Reagan, unlike Carter, was a shrewd negotiator with congressional leaders and foreign heads of state. Reagan also recognized early on that governing a representative democracy requires compromises. He thus combined the passion of a revolutionary with the pragmatism of a diplomat. Third, Reagan's infectious optimism, like that of Franklin Roosevelt before him, gave people a sense of common purpose and renewed confidence. "We have every right," he stressed, "to dream heroic dreams."

Reaganomics President Reagan's "supply-side" economic philosophy combining tax cuts with the goals of decreased government spending, reduced regulation of business, and a balanced budget.

Reagan's first step as the new president was to freeze hiring for the federal government. A larger government, he declared, "is not the solution to our problems. Government *is* the problem." To drive home that theme, he ordered that the portrait of Harry Truman in the Cabinet Room be replaced with one of Calvin Coolidge, the most anti-government president of the twentieth century—and, like Reagan, a man who loved afternoon naps.

Public affection for Reagan spiked just two months into his presidency when an emotionally disturbed man eager for notoriety fired six shots at the president, one of which punctured a lung and lodged near his heart. The witty Reagan told doctors as they prepared for lifesaving surgery: "Please tell me you're Republicans." Reagan's gritty response to the assassination attempt created an outpouring of support that gave added momentum to his presidency. The Democratic Speaker of the House, Tip O'Neill, told colleagues that Reagan "has become a hero. We can't argue with a man as popular as he is."

Reaganomics

Economic Recovery Tax Act (1981)

On August 1, 1981, the president signed the Economic Recovery Tax Act (ERTA), which cut personal income taxes by 25 percent, lowered the maximum rate from 70 to 50 percent for 1982, and offered a broad array of other tax concessions. The tax-cut bill was the centerpiece of what Reagan called his "commonsense" economic plan. While theorists called the philosophy behind the plan "supply-side economics," journalists dubbed the president's proposals **Reaganomics**.

Simply put, Reaganomics argued that the stagflation of the seventies had resulted from excessive taxes, which weakened incentives for individuals and businesses to increase productivity, save money, and reinvest in economic expansion. The supply-side, or Reaganomics, solution to stagflation was to slash tax rates on companies and individuals, especially on the wealthy, in the belief that they would spend their tax savings on business expansion and consumer goods (the supply side of the economy). By generating economic growth, Reaganomics promised to generate enough new tax revenues from rising corporate profits and personal incomes to pay for the cuts in tax rates.

In the short term, however, ERTA did not work as planned. The federal budget deficit grew rather than shrank. By November 1981, the economy was officially in recession, "a slight one," explained the president.

Budget Cuts

Failure to curb "liberal" social-welfare programs

To offset the loss of government tax revenues, thirty-four-year-old David Stockman, Reagan's budget director, a former Michigan congressman, proposed sharp reductions in federal spending, including Social Security and Medicare, the two most expensive—and most popular—federal social-welfare programs. Liberal Democrats howled at Stockman's efforts to slash social-welfare budgets. Reagan responded that he was committed to maintaining the "safety net" of government services for the "truly needy."

For all of Reagan's bold talk about shrinking the government, he was not a true revolutionary in that regard. In the end, the president and Congress agreed to cut "food stamps" (government subsidies to help poor people buy groceries) only 4 percent from what the Carter administration had planned to spend. The Reagan administration also continued huge federal subsidies to corporations and agribusinesses—what critics called "welfare for the rich." In the end, Reagan never dismantled the major federal social-welfare programs that he had savagely criticized.

Within a year, David Stockman realized that the cuts in domestic spending approved by Reagan had fallen far short of what the president had promised. Massive increases in military spending greatly complicated the situation. In essence, Reagan gave the Defense Department a blank check, telling the secretary of defense to "spend what you need." Over the next five years, the administration would spend some $1.2 *trillion* on military expenses. Something had to give.

RALLYING AGAINST REAGANOMICS A throng of more than 5,000 senior citizens staged a demonstration in downtown Detroit against Reagan's decision to cut federal budgets for Social Security and other programs to aid the elderly in 1982. **How did Reagan's actual budget cuts compare to the economic policy of his campaign?**

In the summer of 1981, Stockman warned the president, "We're heading for a crash landing on the budget." The fast-growing federal budget deficit, which helped trigger the worst economic recession since the 1930s, was Reagan's greatest failure, as he himself admitted. During 1982, 10 million Americans could not find jobs. "The stench of failure hangs over Ronald Reagan's White House," declared the *New York Times*.

> A growing federal deficit

Stockman and other worried aides finally convinced the president that the government needed "revenue enhancements" (tax increases). With Reagan's grudging support, Congress passed a tax increase bill in 1982 that would raise almost $100 billion, but the economic slump persisted for a time, with unemployment standing at 10.4 percent. In the 1982 congressional midterm elections, Democrats picked up twenty-six seats in the House of Representatives.

Yet Reagan's determination to "stay the course" in pursuing his economic program eventually began to pay off. By the summer of 1983, a major economic recovery was under way, in part because of increased government spending and lower interest rates and in part because of lower tax rates. Inflation subsided along with unemployment and "deregulation" of business, as Reagan appointed pro-business conservatives to head regulatory agencies.

> Increased military spending, lower interest rates, and lower tax rates

Reaganomics, however, was not helping balance the budget: in fact, the annual federal deficits had grown larger—so much so that the president, who in 1980 had pledged to balance the federal budget by 1983, had in fact run up an accumulated federal debt larger than that of all his predecessors *combined*. Reagan was willing to tolerate the growing budget deficits in part because he believed that they would force more responsible spending behavior in Congress and in part because he was so committed to increased military spending as a way to intimidate the Soviets.

Reagan's Anti-Liberalism

Setbacks for unions

During Reagan's presidency, organized labor suffered severe setbacks, even though Reagan himself had been a union leader. In 1981, Reagan fired members of the Professional Air Traffic Controllers Organization who had participated in an illegal strike intended to shut down air travel. Even more important, Reagan's actions broke the political power of the American Federation of Labor–Congress of Industrial Organizations (AFL-CIO), the national confederation of labor unions that traditionally supported Democratic candidates. His criticism of unions reflected a general trend in public opinion. Although record numbers of new jobs were created during the 1980s, union membership steadily dropped. By 1987, unions represented only 17 percent of the nation's full-time workers, down from 24 percent in 1979.

Reagan also went on the offensive against feminism and the enforcement of civil rights. Echoing Phyllis Schlafly, he opposed the ERA, abortion, and proposals to require equal pay for jobs of comparable worth. He did name Sandra Day O'Connor, an Arizona judge, as the first woman Supreme Court justice. Members of the Christian Right, especially Jerry Falwell and his Moral Majority followers, were furious with the president because O'Connor supported a woman's right to an abortion, but she gained the support of both Democrats and Republicans. In the days before the Senate voted on her confirmation, college students sported buttons proclaiming: "The Moral Majority Is Neither"—moral nor a majority. Reagan also cut funds for civil rights enforcement and the Equal Employment Opportunity Commission, and he opposed renewal of the Voting Rights Act of 1965.

SANDRA DAY O'CONNOR O'Connor, the first woman to serve on the Supreme Court, was confirmed in September 1981, at a hearing that was picketed by conservatives who decried her pro-abortion stance.

The Election of 1984

By 1983, prosperity had returned, the stock market was soaring, and Reagan's supply-side economic program was at last working as advertised—except for the growing federal budget deficits. By 1984, reporters had begun to speak of the "Reagan Revolution." The slogan at the Republican National Convention was "America is back and standing tall."

The Democrats' presidential nominee, Jimmy Carter's vice president, Walter Mondale, struggled to present a competing vision. Endorsed by the AFL-CIO, the National Organization for Women (NOW), and many prominent African Americans, Mondale made history by choosing as his running mate Geraldine Ferraro, a New York congresswoman.

A bit of frankness in Mondale's acceptance speech ended up hurting his campaign. "Mr. Reagan will raise taxes [to reduce budget deficits], and so will I," he told the convention. "He won't tell you. I just did." Reagan responded by vowing never to approve another tax increase (a promise he could not keep). Reagan also repeated a theme he had used against Jimmy Carter: "It's morning again in America," and record numbers of Americans were finding jobs. In the end, Reagan took 59 percent of the popular vote and lost only Minnesota (Mondale's home state) and the District of Columbia. It was the worst defeat ever for a Democratic candidate.

Reagan's Second Term

Spurred by his overwhelming reelection, Reagan called for "a Second American Revolution of hope and opportunity." He dared Democrats to raise taxes; his veto pen was ready. "Go ahead and make my day," he said, echoing a popular line from a Clint Eastwood movie.

Tax Reform Act (1986)

Through much of 1985, the president drummed up support for a tax-simplification plan. After vigorous debate that ran nearly two years, Congress passed a comprehensive Tax Reform Act that the president signed in 1986. The measure reduced the number of federal tax brackets from fourteen to two and reduced rates from the maximum of 50 percent to 15 and 28 percent—the lowest since Calvin Coolidge was president in the 1920s.

Reagan's Halfhearted Revolution

Ronald Wilson Reagan was the first president since Dwight Eisenhower to complete two full terms in office. Although in 1981 he had proclaimed his intention to "curb the size and influence of the federal establishment," he did not, in part because the Democrats controlled the House of Representatives throughout his presidency. The number of federal employees actually *grew* during the Reagan presidency. Neither the Social Security system nor Medicare, the two largest federal social-welfare programs, were overhauled during Reagan's two-term presidency. And the federal agencies that Reagan had threatened to abolish, such as the Department of Education, not only survived but saw their budgets grow. The federal budget deficit almost tripled during his two terms.

Reagan and his aides repeatedly blamed Congress for the problem, "since only Congress can spend money," but in fact the legislators essentially approved the budgets that Reagan had submitted to them (and he never submitted a balanced budget). The cost of Social Security, the most expensive government "entitlement" program, grew by 27 percent, as some

6,000 Americans each day turned 65. Moreover, Reagan failed to fulfill his campaign promises to the Christian Right, such as reinstituting daily prayer in public schools and enacting a ban on abortions.

During his two terms, Reagan was much more successful in transforming the judicial system than in ending the welfare state. He appointed 368 mostly conservative judges, three of whom were added to the U.S. Supreme Court: Sandra Day O'Connor (the Court's first woman member), Antonin Scalia, and Anthony Kennedy.

"The Great Expansion"

Martin Anderson, Reagan's domestic policy adviser, stressed that it was "a mistake to think that there ever was a Reagan Revolution, or that Reagan gave it life." It was the grassroots conservative revolution that "caused Reagan—and the same forces will continue to the end of the century."

What Reagan did accomplish was to end the prolonged period of economic "stagflation" and set in motion what economists called the "Great Expansion," an unprecedented, twenty-year-long burst of productivity and prosperity. True, Reagan's presidency left the nation with a massive debt burden that would eventually cause major problems, but the "Great Communicator" also renewed the nation's strength, self-confidence, and soaring sense of possibilities.

CORE **OBJECTIVE**

4. Explain how Reagan's Soviet strategy helped end the Cold War.

An Anti-Communist Foreign Policy

On a flight to Detroit, Michigan, to accept the Republican party's presidential nomination in the summer of 1980, Ronald Reagan was asked why he wanted to be president. He answered: "To end the Cold War." As president, Reagan systematically promoted what he called his "peace through strength" strategy. Through a series of bold steps, he would build up U.S. military strength to the point at which it would overwhelm the Soviet Union, both financially and militarily. At the same time, Reagan launched a widespread "war of ideas" against communism by charging that the Soviet Union was "the focus of evil in the modern world."

What came to be called the Reagan Doctrine revived and expanded the old notion of "containment" by pledging to combat Soviet adventurism throughout the world, even if it meant working with brutal dictatorships to do so. Reagan believed that aggressive CIA-led efforts to stalemate Soviet expansionism would eventually cause the unstable Soviet system to implode "on the ash heap of history."

A Massive Defense Buildup

The arms race and bankrupting the Soviet Union

Reagan's conduct of foreign policy reflected his belief that trouble in the world stemmed mainly from Moscow, the capital of what he called the "evil empire." Reagan had long believed that former Republican presidents Nixon and Ford—following the advice of Henry Kissinger—had been too soft on the

STRATEGIC DEFENSE INITIATIVE
President Reagan addresses
the nation on March 23, 1983,
promoting the development of
a space-age shield to intercept
Soviet missiles.

Soviets. Kissinger's emphasis on détente, he said, had been a "one-way street" favoring the Soviets.

By contrast, Reagan first wanted to convince the Soviets that they could not win a nuclear war. To do so, he and Secretary of Defense Caspar Weinberger embarked upon a major buildup of nuclear and conventional weapons. During Reagan's two presidential terms, defense spending came to represent a fourth of all federal government expenditures. Reagan claimed that such military spending would bankrupt the Soviets by forcing them to spend much more on their own military budgets.

In 1983, Reagan escalated the nuclear arms race by authorizing the Defense Department to develop the controversial **Strategic Defense Initiative (SDI)**, featuring a complex anti-missile defense system using satellites with laser weapons to "intercept and destroy" Soviet missiles in flight. The media, many scientists, and even government officials insisted that such a "Star Wars" defense system could never be built (Secretary of State George Shultz called it "lunacy"). Nevertheless, Congress approved the first stage of funding, which in turn forced the Soviets to launch an expensive research-and-development effort of their own to keep pace. As a Soviet foreign minister later admitted, Reagan's commitment to SDI "made us realize we were in a very dangerous spot."

The Americas

Reagan's foremost international concern was Central America, where he detected the most serious Communist threat. The tiny nation of El Salvador, caught up since 1980 in a brutal struggle between Communist-supported revolutionaries and right-wing militants, received U.S. economic and military assistance. Critics argued that U.S. involvement ensured that the revolutionary forces would gain public support by capitalizing on "anti-Yankee" sentiment. Supporters countered that allowing a Communist victory in

Strategic Defense Initiative (SDI) (1983) Ronald Reagan's proposed space-based anti-missile defense system, dubbed "Star Wars" by the media, which aroused great controversy and escalated the arms race between the United States and the Soviet Union.

El Salvador would lead all of Central America into the Communist camp (a new "domino" theory). By 1984, however, the U.S.-backed government of President José Napoleón Duarte had brought some stability to El Salvador.

Even more troubling to Reagan was the situation in Nicaragua. The State Department claimed that the Cuban-sponsored Sandinista socialist government, which had seized power in 1979, was sending Soviet and Cuban weapons to leftist Salvadoran rebels. In response, the Reagan administration ordered the CIA to train anti-Communist Nicaraguans, or Contras (short for counterrevolutionaries), who staged attacks on Sandinista bases from sanctuaries in Honduras.

In supporting these "freedom fighters," Reagan sought not only to impede the traffic in arms to Salvadoran rebels but also to replace the Sandinistas with a democratic government in Nicaragua. Critics accused the Contras of being mostly right-wing fanatics who killed indiscriminately. They also feared that the United States might eventually commit its own combat forces, leading to a Vietnam-like intervention. Reagan warned that if the Communists prevailed in Central America, "our credibility would collapse, our alliances would crumble, and the safety of our homeland would be jeopardized."

IRAN-CONTRA HEARINGS Admiral John Poindexter listens to a question from the investigation committee with apprehension on July 21, 1987.

Iran-Contra affair (1987)
Reagan administration scandal over the secret, unlawful U.S. sale of arms to Iran in partial exchange for the release of hostages in Lebanon; the arms money in turn was used illegally to aid Nicaraguan right-wing insurgents, the Contras.

The Iran-Contra Affair

During the fall of 1986, Democrats regained control of the Senate. They also increased their already comfortable margin in the House to 259–176. This meant that Reagan would face an oppositional Congress during the last two years of his presidency.

What was worse, reports surfaced in late 1986 that the United States had been secretly selling arms to Iran (which Reagan had called an "outlaw state") in the hope of securing the release of American hostages held in Lebanon by extremist groups sympathetic to Iran. Such action contradicted Reagan's promise that his administration would never negotiate with terrorists.

At the center of what came to be called the **Iran-Contra affair** was U.S. Marine Corps lieutenant colonel Oliver North, a swashbuckling aide to the National Security Council who specialized in counterterrorism. Working from the basement of the White House, North had been secretly selling military supplies to Iran and using the proceeds to support the Contra rebels fighting in Nicaragua at a time when Congress had voted to ban such aid.

North's illegal activities, it turned out, had been approved by Reagan's national security adviser Robert McFarlane; McFarlane's successor, Admiral John Poindexter; and CIA director William Casey. Both Secretary of State George Shultz and Secretary of Defense Caspar Weinberger criticized the arms sale to Iran, but their objections were ignored. On three occasions, Shultz threatened to resign over the "pathetic" scheme. After information about the secret dealings surfaced in the press, North and others erased incriminating computer files and destroyed documents. McFarlane attempted suicide, Poindexter resigned, and North was fired.

Under increasing criticism, Reagan appointed a three-member commission, led by former Republican senator John Tower, to investigate the scandal. The Tower Commission issued a devastating report early in 1987 that placed much of the responsibility for the bungled Iran-Contra affair on Reagan's loose management style.

The investigations led to six indictments in 1988. A Washington jury found Oliver North guilty of three relatively minor charges but innocent of nine more serious counts, apparently reflecting the jury's reasoning that he had acted as an agent of higher-ups. His conviction was later overturned on appeal. Of those involved in the affair, only John Poindexter received a jail sentence—six months for obstructing justice and lying to Congress.

THE IRAN-CONTRA COVER-UP In Paul Szep's 1987 cartoon, political figures, including President Ronald Reagan, Robert McFarlane, Lieutenant Colonel Oliver North, and Iran's Ayatollah Khomeini attempt to deflect blame for the Iran-Contra Affair. **On whom did the Tower Commission place the blame after their 1987 investigation, and how were those involved ultimately punished for their actions?**

A Historic Treaty

The most positive diplomatic achievement at the end of Reagan's second term was a surprising arms-reduction agreement with the Soviet government. Under Mikhail Gorbachev, who came to power in 1985, the Soviets pursued renewed détente with the United States so that they could reduce military spending related to the Cold War and focus on more pressing problems, especially a notoriously inefficient economy and a losing war in Afghanistan.

In October 1986, Reagan and Gorbachev met in Reykjavik, Iceland, to discuss ways to reduce the threat of nuclear war. During ten hours of intense negotiations, Reagan shocked the Soviets by saying, "It would be fine with me if we eliminated all nuclear weapons." Equally shocking was Gorbachev's reply: "We can do that." By the end of the meeting, however, the two sides remained so far apart on the details that they had given up on any agreement.

The logjam in the disarmament negotiations with the Soviet Union suddenly broke in 1987, when Gorbachev announced that he was willing to consider mutually reducing nuclear weaponry. After nine months of strenuous negotiations, Reagan and Gorbachev met amid much fanfare in Washington, D.C., on December 9, 1987, and signed the **Intermediate-Range Nuclear Forces (INF) Treaty**, an agreement to eliminate intermediate-range (300- to 3,000-mile) missiles. Reagan's steadfast show of strength against the

Intermediate-Range Nuclear Forces (INF) Treaty (1987) Agreement signed by U.S. president Ronald Reagan and Soviet premier Mikhail Gorbachev to eliminate the deployment of intermediate-range missiles with nuclear warheads.

MIKHAIL GORBACHEV Serving first as deputy chairman and later as president of the Soviet Union, Gorbachev took major strides to improve relations with the United States.

Soviets and a new kind of Soviet leader in Mikhail Gorbachev combined to produce the most sweeping reduction in nuclear weaponry in history.

The INF treaty marked the first time that the two nations had agreed to destroy a whole class of weapons systems. Under the terms of the treaty, the United States would destroy 859 missiles, and the Soviets would eliminate 1,752. Still, the reductions represented only 4 percent of the total nuclear-missile count on both sides.

Gorbachev's efforts to liberalize Soviet domestic life and improve East-West relations cheered Americans. The Soviets suddenly began stressing cooperation with the West in dealing with hot spots around the world. In the Middle East, they urged the Palestine Liberation Organization, founded in 1964 to represent the Palestinian people, to recognize Israel's right to exist and advocated a greater role for the United Nations in the volatile Persian Gulf. Perhaps the most dramatic symbol of a thawing Cold War was the phased withdrawal of 115,000 Soviet troops from Afghanistan, which began in 1988.

Reagan's Global Legacy

Reagan achieved the unthinkable by helping end the Cold War. Although his massive defense buildup almost bankrupted the United States, it did force the Soviet Union to the bargaining table. By negotiating the nuclear disarmament treaty and lighting the fuse of democratic freedom in Soviet-controlled Eastern Europe, he set in motion events that would cause the collapse of the Soviet Union. In June 1987, Reagan visited the huge concrete and barbed wire Berlin Wall and, in a dramatic speech, called upon the Soviet Union to allow greater freedom within the countries under its control. "General Secretary Gorbachev, if you seek peace, if you seek prosperity for the Soviet Union and Eastern Europe, if you seek liberalization: Come here to this gate! Mr. Gorbachev, open this gate! Mr. Gorbachev, tear down this wall!"

CORE **OBJECTIVE**

5. Characterize the social and economic issues and innovations that emerged during the 1980s.

The Changing Economic and Social Landscape

During the eighties, profound changes transformed American life. The economy went through a wrenching transformation in adapting to an increasingly interconnected global marketplace. The nations that had been most devastated by World War II—France, Germany, the Soviet Union, Japan, and China—had by the 1980s developed formidable economies with higher levels of productivity than the United States. More and more American manufacturing companies shifted their production overseas, thereby accelerating the transition of the economy from its once-dominant industrial base to a more services-oriented economy. Driving all these changes was the impact of the computer revolution and the development of the Internet.

The Computer Revolution

The idea of a programmable machine that would rapidly perform mental tasks had been around since the eighteenth century, but it took the Second World War to gather the intellectual and financial resources needed to create such a "computer." In 1946, a team of engineers at the University of Pennsylvania created ENIAC (electronic numerical integrator and computer), the first all-purpose, all-electronic digital computer.

The next major breakthrough was the invention in 1971 of the **microprocessor**—virtually a tiny computer on a silicon chip. The microprocessor chip revolutionized computing by enabling the storage of far more data in much smaller machines.

The microchip made possible the personal computer. In 1975, an engineer named Ed Roberts developed the Altair 8800, the prototype of the personal computer. Its potential excited a Harvard sophomore named Bill Gates, who improved the software of the Altair 8800, dropped out of college, and formed a company called Microsoft to sell the new system.

By 1977, Gates and others had transformed the personal computer into a mass consumer product. The development of the Internet, electronic mail (e-mail), and cell-phone technology during the 1980s and '90s allowed for instantaneous communication, thereby accelerating the globalization of the economy, dramatically increasing productivity in the workplace, and transforming the way people communicated with each other.

Carefree Consumers

During the eighties, Ronald Reagan lowered tax rates so that people would have more money to spend and thereby accelerate the growth of the economy. Americans had little trouble going on a spending spree. During the Reagan era, marketers and advertisers celebrated instant gratification. Michelob beer commercials promised that "you can have it all," and many people glorified self-indulgence. Compulsive shoppers donned T-shirts proclaiming "Born to Shop." Money—lots of it—came to define the American dream. In the hit movie *Wall Street* (1987), the high-flying land developer and corporate raider Gordon Gekko, played by actor Michael Douglas, announced that "greed . . . is good. Greed is right."

The Poor

The eighties were years of vivid contrast. Despite unprecedented prosperity, growing numbers of jobless Americans were without hope. Widespread homelessness (estimated at 400,000 people) became the most acute social issue.

A variety of causes had led to a shortage of low-cost housing. The government had given up on building public housing, urban-renewal programs had demolished blighted residential areas but provided no housing for those who

microprocessor An electronic circuit printed on a tiny silicon chip; a major technological breakthrough in 1971, it paved the way for the development of the personal computer.

Increased homelessness

were displaced, and owners had abandoned unprofitable buildings in poor neighborhoods or converted them into expensive condominiums, a process called *gentrification*.

In addition, after new medications allowed for the release of some mentally ill patients from institutions, many of them ended up on the streets because the promised mental-health services failed to materialize. Drug and alcohol abuse were rampant among the homeless, mostly unemployed single adults. A quarter of them (about 100,000 people) had spent time in mental institutions; some 40 percent had spent time in jail; a third were delusional.

The AIDS Epidemic

AIDS becomes leading cause of death for young men

Still another group of outcasts in the eighties included those suffering from a new disease called AIDS (acquired immunodeficiency syndrome). At the beginning of the decade, public health officials reported that gay men and intravenous drug users were especially at risk for developing AIDS. People contracted the human immunodeficiency virus (HIV) by coming into

AIDS MEMORIAL QUILT Composed of more than 48,000 panels, the quilt was first conceptualized by gay rights and AIDS activist Cleve Jones to commemorate those who died of AIDS-related causes. It continues to grow to this day.

contact with the blood or bodily fluids of an infected person. Those infected with the virus that causes AIDS showed signs of extreme fatigue, developed a strange combination of infections, and soon died.

The Reagan administration showed little interest in AIDS in part because it was viewed as a "gay" disease. Patrick Buchanan, the conservative commentator who served as Reagan's director of communications, said that homosexuals had "declared war on nature, and now nature [was] extracting an awful retribution."

Buchanan and others convinced Reagan not to engage the **HIV/AIDS** issue. By 2000, AIDS had claimed almost 300,000 American lives and was spreading among a larger segment of the population. Nearly 1 million Americans were carrying the deadly virus, and it had become the leading cause of death among men ages twenty-five to forty-four.

HIV/AIDS Human immunodeficiency virus (HIV) transmitted via the bodily fluids of infected persons to cause acquired immunodeficiency syndrome (AIDS), an often-fatal disease of the immune system when it appeared in the 1980s.

The Presidency of George H. W. Bush

CORE OBJECTIVE

6. Appraise the impact of the end of the Cold War and the efforts of President George H. W. Bush to create a post–Cold War foreign policy.

In his farewell address to the nation in January 1989, Ronald Reagan said with a smile: "My friends, we did it. We . . . made a difference." Over his two terms, Ronald Reagan had indeed become a transformational president. In the process of restoring the stature of the presidency, helping defuse the Cold War, and reviving the economy, he had transformed political life by accelerating the nation's shift toward conservatism and by revitalizing the Republican party after the Watergate scandal. He put the Democratic party on the defensive and forced conventional New Deal "liberalism" into a panicked retreat. For the next twenty years or so, Reagan's anti-government, anti-tax conservative agenda would dominate the national political landscape.

Reagan would prove to be a tough act to follow. His two-term vice president, George H. W. Bush, won the Republican presidential nomination in 1988. Born into a prominent New England family, the son of a U.S. senator, he enlisted at the age of eighteen in the U.S. Navy at the start of World War II, becoming America's youngest combat pilot. After his distinguished service in the war, Bush graduated from Yale University and thereafter moved with his family to west Texas, where he became a wealthy oil executive before entering government service, first as a member of the U.S. House of Representatives, then as U.S. ambassador to the United Nations, a diplomat in China, and head of the CIA before becoming vice president in 1981.

GEORGE H. W. BUSH His son, George W. Bush, would also serve as president, making them the second father-son presidential duo in history (the first was John Adams and John Quincy Adams).

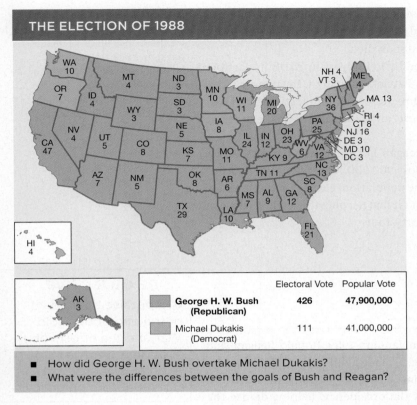

THE ELECTION OF 1988

	Electoral Vote	Popular Vote
George H. W. Bush (Republican)	**426**	**47,900,000**
Michael Dukakis (Democrat)	111	41,000,000

- How did George H. W. Bush overtake Michael Dukakis?
- What were the differences between the goals of Bush and Reagan?

In those roles, Bush had displayed intelligence, integrity, and courage. But he lacked Reagan's charm and speaking skills. One Democrat described him as a man born "with a silver foot in his mouth."

Bush was a centrist Republican who had never embraced right-wing conservatism. He promised to use the White House to fight bigotry, illiteracy, and homelessness. "I want a kinder, gentler nation," Bush said in his speech accepting the Republican nomination. His most memorable line in the speech, though, was a defiant statement ruling out any tax increases to deal with the massive budget deficits created during the Reagan years: "The Congress will push me to raise taxes, and I'll say no, and they'll push, and I'll say no, and they'll push again. And I'll say to them: Read my lips. *No new taxes.*"

Meanwhile, Massachusetts governor Michael Dukakis won the Democratic nomination, but it did little good. In the end, Bush won a decisive victory. Dukakis carried only ten states plus the District of Columbia, with clusters of support in the Northeast, Midwest, and Northwest. Bush carried the rest, with a margin of about 54 percent to 46 percent in the popular vote and 426–111 in the Electoral College, but the Democrats retained control of the House and Senate.

As the new president, George H. W. Bush felt the need to show the nation that he was his own man rather than a Reagan clone. To that end, he replaced Calvin Coolidge's portrait in the White House with one of Theodore Roosevelt, and he ordered all Reagan appointees to submit their resignation. Bush ended support for the Contras in Nicaragua and abandoned Reagan's unworkable Star Wars missile defense program.

Yet, for the most part, Bush sought to reinforce the initiatives that Reagan had put in place rather than launch his own array of programs and policies. "We don't need to remake society," he announced. As an example of his "gentler, kinder" conservatism, Bush supported the Democratic-proposed Americans with Disabilities Act (1990), which strengthened the civil rights of the physically or mentally disabled in areas such as employment, public transportation, and housing. The act also required organizations to ensure that people with disabilities could access facilities by providing mechanized doors, wheelchair ramps, and elevators.

The Federal Debt and Recession

The biggest problem facing the Bush administration was the huge national debt, which stood at $2.6 trillion in 1989, nearly three times its 1980 level. Bush's pledge not to increase taxes made it all the more difficult to reduce the annual deficit or trim the long-term debt. Likewise, Bush was not willing to make substantial cutbacks in spending on defense or social-welfare programs like Social Security, Medicare, and food stamps. As a result, by 1990 the country faced "a fiscal mess."

During the summer of 1990, Bush broke his promise and proposed several tax increases, including a spike in federal gasoline taxes. His reversal on raising taxes set off a revolt among conservative Republicans, from which he never recovered. Newt Gingrich, a Republican leader from Georgia in the House of Representatives, accused the president of "betrayal." A Republican-aligned New York newspaper expressed its views with a banner headline: "Read My Lips: I Lied."

Republicans in Congress were so angry at the president that they joined with Democrats in nixing Bush's budget proposal. A fuming Bush lashed out at Gingrich: "You're killing us. You're killing us." With Congress and the White House unable to reach agreement on the budget, the government shut down. The public was furious, and their widespread anger forced Bush to admit defeat and sign a new resolution that reopened government offices. To do so, however, he had to agree to a new budget drafted by Democrats. It replaced the president's proposed gasoline tax with an increase in the top income tax rate, from 28 to 31 percent. Only a fourth of Republicans went along with the idea, but the Democrats marshaled enough votes for it to become law in October 1990.

The budget fiasco and tax increase created a lasting divide between congressional Republicans and President Bush. Even more worrisome was that the economy barely grew during the first three years of the Bush administration—the worst record since the end of the Second World War. By 1991, the national economy was in a recession, the unemployment rate had spiked to 8 percent, and public disapproval of the president rose accordingly.

The Democracy Movement Abroad

George H. W. Bush entered the White House with more foreign-policy experience than most presidents, and like Nixon before him, he preferred to deal with international relations rather than domestic issues such as the deficit, drug abuse, and the problems of the inner cities. In the Soviet Union, amazing changes were under way. With the economy failing, Mikhail Gorbachev responded with policies of ***perestroika*** (economic restructuring) and ***glasnost*** (openness), a loosening of centralized economic planning and censorship of the press. His foreign policy sought harmony and trade with the West. Early in 1989, Soviet troops left Afghanistan after nine years. Gorbachev then renounced the right of the Soviet Union to

perestroika Russian term for economic restructuring; applied to Mikhail Gorbachev's series of political and economic reforms that included shifting a centrally planned Communist economy to a mixed economy allowing for capitalism.

glasnost Russian term for "openness"; applied to the loosening of censorship in the Soviet Union under Mikhail Gorbachev.

The end of the Soviet empire; Reunification of East and West Germany

intervene in the internal affairs of other Communist countries. Soon thereafter, the old Communist regimes in Eastern Europe were toppled with surprisingly little bloodshed. Communist rule enforced by the Soviet Union ended first in Poland and Hungary, then in Czechoslovakia and Bulgaria. In Romania, the year of peaceful revolution ended in a bloodbath when the people joined the army in a bloody uprising against Nicolae Ceauşescu, the country's brutal dictator. He and his wife were captured, tried, and then executed on Christmas Day.

The End of the Berlin Wall

The most spectacular event in the collapse of the Soviet Empire came on November 9, 1989, when Germans—using hand tools and even their bare hands—tore down the Berlin Wall, the chief symbol of the Cold War. With the borders to the West now fully open, the Communist government of East Germany collapsed, and a freely elected government came to power. On October 3, 1990, the five states of East Germany were united with West Germany.

The reform impulse that Gorbachev helped unleash in the Eastern-bloc countries sped out of control within the Soviet Union itself, however. Gorbachev had proven unusually adept at political restructuring, yielding the Communist monopoly of government but building a new presidential system that gave him, if anything, increased powers. His skills, however, could not salvage an antiquated economy that resisted change.

Communist Coup Fails

Gorbachev's popularity shrank in the Soviet Union even as it grew abroad. Communist hard-liners saw in his reforms the unraveling of their bureaucratic and political empire. Once the genie of freedom was released from the Communist lamp, however, it took on a momentum of its own. On August 18, 1991, a group of political and military leaders tried to seize the reins of power. They accosted Gorbachev at his vacation retreat in Crimea and demanded that he proclaim a state of emergency and transfer his powers to them. He replied, "Go to hell," whereupon he was placed under house arrest.

The coup was doomed from the start, however. Poorly planned and clumsily implemented, it lacked

A HAMMER TO THE SOVIET EMPIRE A West German demonstrator pounds away at the Berlin Wall on November 11, 1989, while East Berlin border guards look on. Two days later, all the crossings between East and West Germany were opened.

effective coordination. The plotters failed to arrest popular leaders such as Boris Yeltsin, the president of the Russian republic. They also neglected to close the airports or cut off telephone and television communications, and they were opposed by key elements of the military and KGB (the secret police).

On August 20, President Bush responded favorably to Yeltsin's request for support and persuaded other world leaders to join him in refusing to recognize the legitimacy of the new Soviet government. The next day, word began to seep out that the plotters had given up and were fleeing. Several committed suicide, and a newly released Gorbachev ordered the others arrested.

Yet things did not go back to the way they had been. Although Gorbachev reclaimed the title of president, he was forced to resign as head of the Communist party and admit that he had made a grave mistake in appointing the men who had turned against him. Boris Yeltsin emerged as the most popular political figure in the country.

So what had begun as a reactionary coup turned into a powerful accelerant for astonishing changes in the Soviet Union, or the "Soviet Disunion," as one journalist termed it. Most of the fifteen republics proclaimed their independence from Russia, with the Baltic states of Latvia, Lithuania, and Estonia regaining the status of independent nations. The Communist party was dismantled, prompting celebrating crowds to topple statues of Lenin and other Communist heroes.

Reducing the Nuclear Threat

The collapse of the Soviet Union accelerated efforts to reduce their stockpiles of nuclear weapons. In late 1991, President Bush announced that the United States would destroy all its tactical nuclear weapons in Europe and Asia. Bush explained that the prospect of a Soviet invasion of Western Europe was "no longer a realistic threat" and that this transformation provided an unprecedented opportunity for reducing the threat of nuclear holocaust. President Gorbachev responded by announcing similar Soviet cutbacks. The sudden end of the Cold War led many to believe that the United States could greatly reduce the vast global military responsibilities it had developed over four decades of anti-communism.

> The end of the Soviet "threat"

Panama

The end of the Cold War did not spell the end of international tensions and conflict, however. Indeed, before the end of 1989, U.S. troops were engaged in battle in Panama, where a petty tyrant provoked the first of America's military engagements under George H. W. Bush. In 1983, General Manuel Noriega had become leader of the Panamanian Defense Forces, which made him the head of the government in fact if not in title.

> Panama–U.S. "war"

In 1988, federal grand juries in Miami and Tampa indicted Noriega and fifteen others on charges of drug trafficking. The next year, the Panamanian president tried to fire Noriega, but the National Assembly ousted the

Operation Desert Storm (1991)
Assault by American-led multinational forces that quickly defeated Iraqi forces under Saddam Hussein in the First Gulf War, ending the Iraqi occupation of Kuwait.

president instead and named Noriega "maximum leader." The legislators then declared Panama "in a state of war" with the United States. On December 16, 1989, a U.S. marine in Panama was killed, whereupon President Bush ordered an invasion of Panama to capture Noriega and install a government to be headed by Guillermo Endara, who had won the presidency in a recent election nullified by Noriega.

In the early morning of December 20, U.S. troops struck at strategic targets in the country. Within hours, Noriega had surrendered. Twenty-three U.S. servicemen were killed in the action, and estimates of Panamanian casualties, including many civilians, were as high as 4,000. In April 1992, Noriega was convicted in the United States on eight counts of racketeering and drug distribution.

The Gulf War

Months later, Saddam Hussein, dictator of Iraq, focused U.S. attention back upon the Middle East when his army suddenly invaded its tiny neighbor, Kuwait, on August 2, 1990. Kuwait had recently increased its production of oil, contrary to agreements with the Organization of the Petroleum Exporting Countries. The resulting drop in global oil prices offended the Iraqi regime, which was deeply in debt and heavily dependent upon oil revenues.

President Bush condemned Iraq's "naked aggression" and dispatched planes and troops to Saudi Arabia on a "wholly defensive" mission: to protect Saudi Arabia. British forces soon joined in, as did Arab units from Egypt, Morocco, Syria, Oman, the United Arab Emirates, and Qatar. A flurry of negotiations failed, as Iraq refused to yield, leading Congress on January 12, 1991, to authorize the use of U.S. armed forces. Four days later, more than thirty nations, including ten Islamic countries, launched **Operation Desert Storm** against Iraq. The swift-moving allied ground assault began on February 24 and lasted only four days. Iraqi soldiers surrendered by the thousands.

On February 28, six weeks after the fighting began, President Bush called for a cease-fire. The Iraqis accepted, and the shooting ended. There were 137 American fatalities. The lowest estimate of Iraqi deaths, civilian and military, was 100,000. The coalition forces occupied about a fifth of Iraq, but Hussein's tyrannical regime

OPERATION DESERT STORM Allied soldiers patrol the southern Iraqi city of Salman Pak on February 27, 1991. On the side of a building is a propaganda mural of dictator Saddam Hussein in military uniform.

was intact. What came to be called the First Gulf War was thus a triumph without victory. Hussein had been defeated, but he was allowed to escape and foster greater mischief. The consequences of the brief but intense First Gulf War, the "mother of all battles," in Saddam Hussein's words, would be played out in the future in ways that no one had predicted. Arabs who felt humiliated by the lopsided American triumph began plotting revenge that would spiral into a new war of terrorism.

Bush's "New World Order"

For months after the First Gulf War in 1991, George H. W. Bush seemed unbeatable; his public approval rating soared to 91 percent. Yet the aftermath of Desert Storm was mixed, with Saddam Hussein's iron grip on Iraq still intact. The Soviet Union meanwhile stumbled on to its surprising end. On December 25, 1991, the Soviet flag over the Kremlin was replaced by the flag of the Russian Federation. The Cold War had ended with the dismemberment of the Soviet Union and its fifteen republics. As a result, the United States had become the world's only dominant military power.

Bush's "New World Order"

"Containment" of the Soviet Union, the bedrock of U.S. foreign policy for more than four decades, had suddenly become irrelevant. For all its potential horrors, the Cold War brought stability because the two superpowers, the United States and the Soviet Union, had restrained themselves from an all-out war that may well have involved the use of nuclear weapons. Now the world would witness a growing number of unresolved political crises and unstable regimes, some of which had access to weapons of mass destruction—nuclear as well as chemical and biological weapons.

Bush struggled to interpret the fluid new international scene. He spoke of a "new world order" but never defined it, admitting that he had trouble with "the vision thing." By the end of 1991, the euphoria of the Gulf War victory had worn off and a listless Bush faced a challenge in the Republican primary from the feisty conservative commentator and former White House aide Patrick Buchanan, who adopted the slogan "America First" and called on Bush to "bring home the boys."

The excitement over the allied victory in the Gulf War quickly gave way to anxiety over the depressed economy. In addressing the recession, Bush tried a clumsy balancing act, on the one hand acknowledging that "people are hurting" while on the other telling Americans that "this is a good time to buy a car." By 1991, the public approval rating of his economic policy had plummeted to 18 percent.

The Election of 1992

At the 1992 Republican Convention, Patrick Buchanan, who had won about a third of the votes in the party's primaries, blasted Bush for breaking his pledge not to raise taxes and for becoming the "biggest spender in American history." As the 1992 election unfolded, Bush's real problem was not Pat Buchanan and the conservative wing of the Republican party, however. What threatened his reelection was his own failed effort to improve the economy. A popular bumper sticker reflected the growing public frustration with the economic policies of the Bush administration: "Saddam Hussein still has his job. What about you?"

In contrast to the divided Republicans, the Democrats at their 1992 convention presented an image of centrist or moderate forces in control. For several years, the Democratic Leadership Council, led by Arkansas governor William Jefferson Clinton, had been pushing the party from the liberal left to the center of the political spectrum. Clinton called for a "third way" positioned between conservatism and liberalism.

The 1992 campaign also featured a third-party candidate, Texan H. Ross Perot, a puckish billionaire who found a large audience for his criticism of Reaganomics as "voodoo economics" (a phrase originally used in the 1980 Republican primary by then-contender George H. W. Bush before he was named the vice presidential candidate on the Reagan presidential ticket) and his warnings about the impending crisis posed by the huge federal debt.

Bill Clinton, however, attracted most of the media attention. Born in 1946 in Hope, Arkansas, he never knew his biological father, a traveling salesman who died in a car crash a few months before his son was born. Even as a teen, Clinton yearned to be a political leader on a national scale. He attended Georgetown University in Washington, D.C., won a Rhodes Scholarship to Oxford University, and then earned a law degree from Yale University, where he met his future wife, Hillary Rodham. Clinton returned to Arkansas and won election as the state's attorney general. By 1979, at age thirty-two, Bill Clinton was the youngest governor in the country. He served three more terms as Arkansas governor and in the process emerged as a dynamic young leader of the "**New Democrats**" committed to winning back the middle-class whites ("Reagan Democrats") who had voted Republican during the 1980s.

A self-described moderate seeking the Democratic presidential nomination, Clinton promised to cut the defense budget, provide tax relief for the middle class, and create a massive economic aid package for the former republics of the Soviet Union to help them forge democratic societies. Witty, intelligent, and charismatic, with an in-depth knowledge of public policy, Clinton was a superb campaigner; he projected energy, youth, and optimism, reminding many political observers of John F. Kennedy, Clinton's boyhood hero.

But beneath Clinton's charisma and public-policy expertise lurked several flaws. Self-absorbed and self-indulgent, he, like Lyndon Johnson, yearned to be loved. Biographers explained that Clinton was "emotionally needy, indecisive and undisciplined." Even more enticing to the media were charges that Clinton was a chronic adulterer. Clinton's evasive denials of both allegations could not dispel a lingering mistrust of his character.

After a series of bruising party primaries, Clinton won the Democratic presidential nomination in the summer of 1992, promising to restore the

New Democrats Centrist ("moderate") Democrats led by President Bill Clinton that emerged in the late 1980s and early 1990s to challenge the "liberal" direction of the party.

"hopes of the forgotten middle class." He chose Senator Albert (Al) Gore Jr. of Tennessee as his running mate. Gore described himself as a "raging moderate." So the Democratic candidates were two Southern Baptists from adjoining states, Arkansas and Tennessee. Flushed with their convention victory and sporting a ten-point lead over Bush in the polls, the Clinton-Gore team hammered Bush on economic issues to win over working-class voters. Clinton pledged that, if elected, he would cut the federal budget deficit in half in four years while cutting taxes on middle-class Americans.

Such promises helped Clinton win the election with 370 electoral votes and about 43 percent of the popular vote; Bush received 168 electoral votes and 39 percent of the popular vote; and Perot garnered 19 percent of the popular vote, more than any other third-party candidate since Theodore Roosevelt in 1912.

BILL CLINTON AND AL GORE The hopeful Democratic candidates round out their presidential campaign in Clinton's hometown of Little Rock, Arkansas, on November 3, 1992.

As 1992 came to an end, Bill Clinton, the "New Democrat," prepared to lead the United States through the last decade of the twentieth century. "The urgent question of our time," he said, "is whether we can make change our friend and not our enemy." During his eight years as president, Clinton would embrace many unexpected changes while ushering America into the twenty-first century.

Reviewing the
CORE OBJECTIVES |

■ **The Carter Presidency** Jimmy Carter had notable achievements, such as the 1978 *Camp David Accords*. Yet his administration suffered from legislative inexperience, a deepening economic recession, soaring inflation, and the *Iranian hostage crisis (1979)*. His sermonizing about the need for Americans to lead simpler lives compounded the public's loss of faith in his presidency.

■ **The Rise of Conservatism** Ronald Reagan's charm, coupled with the public's disillusionment over Carter's presidency, won Reagan the election in 1980. The Republican insurgency, characterized in part by a cultural backlash against the feminist movement, was dominated by the *Christian Right*. Sunbelt voters, many of whom were older transplants to southern and western states, were socially conservative and favored lower taxes and a smaller, less intrusive federal government. California passed a property-tax-lowering referendum, Proposition 13, which led to a nationwide tax revolt.

■ **Reaganomics** Reagan introduced a "supply-side" economic philosophy, commonly called *Reaganomics*, that championed tax cuts for the rich, reduced government regulation, cuts to social-welfare programs, and increased defense spending. In practice, however, Reagan was unable to cut domestic spending significantly, and the tax cuts failed to pay for themselves as promised. The result was a dramatic increase in the national debt. Reagan also did much to weaken unions and the feminist movement and to shift the political landscape away from the New Deal liberalism that had dominated American politics since 1932.

■ **The End of the Cold War** Reagan's massive military buildup, including preliminary development of the *Strategic Defense Initiative (SDI)* in 1983, brought the Soviets to agreement in 1987 on the *Intermediate-Range Nuclear Forces (INF) Treaty*—the beginning of the end of the Cold War. But Reagan's foreign policy was badly tarnished in 1987 by the *Iran-Contra affair*: members of his administration had illegally sold U.S. armaments to Iran to secure the release of American hostages. The proceeds were then secretly funneled to Nicaraguan Contras (despite a congressional ban on such aid). Reagan's loose management style, an independent commission determined, had allowed these illegal activities to flourish.

■ **America in the 1980s** The eighties brought not only unprecedented prosperity but also rising poverty and homelessness. The prevailing conservative mood condemned *HIV/AIDS* as a "gay" disease. The *microprocessor* ignited the computer revolution, which dramatically increased productivity and communications while generating new industries. Consumerism flourished all too well, resulting in massive public and private debt.

■ **A New World Order** In the late 1980s, democratic political movements erupted, failing in Communist China but succeeding in Eastern Europe. Gorbachev's steps to restructure the Soviet Union's economy (*perestroika*) and promote more open policies (*glasnost*) ultimately led to the collapse of the Soviet empire. Iraq, led by Saddam Hussein, invaded Kuwait in 1990. The U.S. led allied forces in *Operation Desert Storm (1991)*; the Iraqis soon surrendered. Despite the success of the first Gulf War, the sluggish economy led to Bush's defeat by the *New Democrats* under Bill Clinton.

KEY TERMS

Camp David Accords (1978) *p. 1130*

Iranian hostage crisis (1979) *p. 1131*

Christian Right *p. 1135*

Reaganomics *p. 1138*

Strategic Defense Initiative (SDI) (1983) *p. 1143*

Iran-Contra affair (1987) *p. 1144*

Intermediate-Range Nuclear Forces (INF) Treaty (1987) *p. 1145*

microprocessor *p. 1147*

HIV/AIDS *p. 1149*

perestroika p. 1151

glasnost p. 1151

Operation Desert Storm (1991) *p. 1154*

New Democrats *p. 1156*

CHRONOLOGY

1971	Microprocessor developed
1975	First personal computer, the Altair 8800, produced
1978	Camp David Accords
	Tax revolt in California leads to the passage of Proposition 13
1979	Jerry Falwell organizes the Moral Majority
November 1979	Iranian hostage crisis begins
1980	Ronald Reagan elected president
1981	Reagan enacts major tax cuts
1983	Strategic Defense Initiative (SDI) authorized
1987	Tower Commission issues report on Iran-Contra affair
	Reagan delivers Berlin Wall speech
October 1987	Stock market plunges 23 percent on "Black Monday"
1988	George H. W. Bush elected president
November 1989	Berlin Wall torn down
December 1989	U.S. troops invade Panama and capture Manuel Noriega
August 1990– February 1991	First Gulf War
	Soviet Union dissolves
1992	Bill Clinton elected president

🐰 INQUIZITIVE

Go to InQuizitive to see what you've learned—and learn what you've missed—with personalized feedback along the way.

YOUTH SPEAKS The Occupy Wall Street movement was born when thousands of protesters, many of them unemployed young adults, "occupied" Wall Street in downtown Manhattan to protest the "tyrannical" financial industry. The grassroots movement soon spread across the nation, then the world. Here, members of the movement stage a protest outside the New York Stock Exchange in September 2011.

Twenty-First-Century America

1993–PRESENT

The United States entered the final decade of the twentieth century triumphant. American persistence in the Cold War had brought about the shocking collapse of the Soviet Union and the birth of democracy and capitalism in Eastern Europe. During the 1990s, the U.S. economy became the marvel of the world as remarkable gains in productivity enabled by new "digital" technologies created the greatest prosperity in modern history.

Yet no sooner did the twentieth century come to an end than America's sense of physical security and material comfort was shattered by surprise terrorist attacks in 2001 on New York City and Washington, D.C., attacks that killed thousands; plunged the economy into recession; and raised profound questions about national security, personal safety, and civil liberties.

The United States thereafter led the ongoing fight against global terrorism, which embroiled the nation in long, costly, and controversial wars in Iraq and Afghanistan. Opposition to those wars would provide much of the momentum for Democrat Barack Obama to win election in 2008 as the nation's first African American president. Obama entered the White House at the same time that the United States was experiencing the Great Recession, a sharp, prolonged economic downturn that almost destroyed the global banking system, caused widespread unemployment, and ignited growing social unrest and political tensions at home and abroad.

CORE OBJECTIVES InQuizitive

1. Describe the major population trends (demographics) in the United States during the twenty-first century, and assess their impact on the nation's politics.

2. Evaluate the accomplishments and setbacks of Bill Clinton's presidency.

3. Summarize the impact of global terrorism on the United States during the presidency of George W. Bush.

4. Assess the issues and developments during Bush's second term that helped lead to Barack Obama's historic victory in the 2008 presidential election.

5. Identify President Obama's priorities at home and abroad, and assess his efforts to pursue them.

6. Explain the factors that led to Donald Trump's unexpected presidential nomination and election and assess Trump's early presidency.

CORE **OBJECTIVE**

1. Describe the major population trends (demographics) in the United States during the twenty-first century, and assess their impact on the nation's politics.

America's Changing Population

The United States in the twenty-first century witnessed dramatic social changes. By 2017, there were more than 325 million Americans, over 80 percent of whom lived in cities or suburbs.

Even more important, the nation's racial and ethnic composition was changing rapidly. The majority white population continued to decline as a proportion of the total population while the proportion represented by minority groups soared. In 1980, the population was 80 percent white. By 2015, that percentage had fallen below 63 percent. By 2060, it will be less than 44 percent.

Hispanics/Latinos represented 18 percent of the population, African Americans 13 percent, Asians about 5 percent, and Native Americans 1 percent. The rate of increase among those four groups was twice as fast as it had been during the 1980s. In 2005, Hispanics surpassed African Americans as the nation's largest minority group. In 1980, Hispanics were 6 percent; in 2017, that number had tripled to 19 percent and was growing rapidly; a third of them were under the age of eighteen. Yet the fastest-growing group in the nation were the nearly 10 million who described themselves as "multiracial," representing over 3 percent of the entire population.

> Population growth among Hispanics, African Americans, Asians, and Native Americans

The primary cause of this dramatic change in the nation's ethnic mix during the twenty-first century was a surge of immigration. In 1992, the Republican presidential candidate Pat Buchanan warned that the United States was experiencing "the greatest invasion in its history, a migration of millions of illegal aliens a year from Mexico." While Buchanan and others wanted to close the border with Mexico, many Americans believed that embracing immigrants remained one of the nation's essential ideals.

In 2017, the United States had more foreign-born residents than ever before, more than 46 million Americans, 11 million of whom were undocumented immigrants (formerly classified as "illegal aliens"). In the first decade of the twenty-first century, the United States became home to more than twice as many immigrants as *all* other countries in the world combined. For the first time in the nation's history, the majority of immigrants came not from Europe but from other parts of the world: Asia, Latin America, and Africa. Mexicans made up the largest share of Hispanics, followed by Puerto Ricans and Cubans. (Americans now consume more salsa than ketchup each year.)

> Rising immigration from Asia, Latin America, and Africa

The changing ethnic composition of American society has had an increasingly significant impact on social life. In 1980, Hispanic Americans lived mainly in five states: California, Arizona, New Mexico, Texas, and Florida. By 2017, *every* state had a rapidly growing Hispanic population. "These are big demographic changes," said Mark Mather, a population analyst. "There is going to be some culture shock, especially in communities that haven't had high numbers of immigrants or minorities in the past."

Immigration also had significant political effects. In 1980, there were six Hispanic Americans serving in the U.S. Congress. By 2010, there were more than thirty. In 1992, Hispanics constituted only 2 percent of American voters; by 2017, they were more than 12 percent. Asian Americans increased their numbers at a faster rate than any other ethnic group, largely because of a surge in Chinese immigrants. Such new voters represented an increasing share of America's future, and politicians could no longer ignore them, as had often happened in the past.

As the population was becoming more racially and ethnically diverse, the Republican party nationwide was becoming more and more white. In 2017, the Pew Research Center reported that the Republican party was 89 percent white. A Republican campaign consultant recognized that "we need to do better in minority communities." The rapidly changing ethnic and racial mix of the nation's population would become a major factor in the shifting social and political life of the twenty-first century.

OVER THE QUOTA, UNDER THE RADAR Increasing numbers of Chinese people were willing to risk their lives to gain entry to the United States. A freighter carrying undocumented immigrants ran aground near Rockaway Beach, New York, in June 1993, forcing its undocumented passengers to swim ashore.

The Clinton Presidency

CORE **OBJECTIVE**
2. Evaluate the accomplishments and setbacks of Bill Clinton's presidency.

Bill Clinton brought extraordinary gifts and oversized weaknesses to the presidency. He embraced politics as a civic duty and brought to public office impeccable academic training. Wickedly smart and politically shrewd, he genuinely loved and painstakingly learned the technical details of major policies and programs. And he mastered the personal touch: he relished mingling with crowds, up close and face-to-face, reassuring struggling people, "I feel your pain."

Yet while graced with charm and a common touch, as well as a commitment to fulfilling his campaign pledges, Clinton was also prone to self-absorption, self-deception, and self-inflicted wounds. A sucker for flattery with a compulsion to please and to be loved, he often formed his stances on issues by finding out what others believed through studying focus group interviews and public opinion surveys. A creature of both inspired leadership abilities and unruly passions, he at times seemed less a president than a flawed good ol' boy capable of self-righteous sleaziness and shameless misbehavior (he would later dismiss his impeachment as "just a political deal."). In sum, Clinton was a bundle of warring impulses whose faults often confounded his talents. Yet he displayed legendary energy and "slick" resilience. (His nickname was the "Comeback Kid"). He thrived amid storms and setbacks. One of his advisers predicted that Clinton would make every mistake possible, "but he will only make it once."

Early setbacks: "Don't ask, don't tell" (DADT) and abandonment of middle-class tax relief

Clinton's inexperience in international affairs and congressional maneuvering led to several missteps in his first year as president. Like George H. W. Bush before him, he reneged on several campaign promises. After a bruising battle with Congress, he abandoned his proposed middle-class tax cut in order to keep another campaign promise, to reduce the federal deficit. Then he dropped his promise to allow gays to serve in the armed forces after military commanders expressed strong opposition. Instead, he later announced an ambiguous new policy concerning gays in the military called "don't ask, don't tell" (DADT), which allowed gays, lesbians, and bisexuals to serve in the military only if they kept their sexual orientation secret. "I got the worst of both worlds," Clinton later confessed. "I lost the fight, and the gay community was highly critical of me for the compromise." In Clinton's first two weeks in office, his approval rating dropped 20 percent, a faster descent than any other modern president. Throughout his presidency, however, Clinton displayed a remarkable ability to manage crises and rebound from adversity.

The Economy

As a candidate, Clinton had pledged to reduce the federal deficit without damaging the economy or hurting the nation's most vulnerable people. To this end, the new president proposed $241 billion in higher taxes for corporations and for the wealthiest individuals (the top personal tax rate rising from 33 to 39.6 percent) over four years and $255 billion in spending cuts over the same period. The congressional vote on the hotly contested bill was so close that Vice President Al Gore had to provide the tie-breaking vote. For virtually the first time since 1945, Congress had passed a major bill without a single Republican vote, a troubling indication of the nation's growing partisan divide. Clinton's deficit-reduction effort worked as planned, however. It led to lower interest rates, which along with low energy prices, helped spur dramatic economic growth throughout the nineties.

NAFTA PROTESTERS A group of protesters going to a rally against NAFTA, the controversial free-trade agreement for North America.

Equally difficult was gaining congressional approval of the **North American Free Trade Agreement (NAFTA)**, which the Bush administration had already negotiated with Canada and Mexico. Clinton urged approval of NAFTA, which would make North America the largest free-trade zone in the world. Opponents of the bill favored tariffs to discourage the importation of cheaper foreign products, especially from Mexico. Yet Clinton prevailed with solid Republican support while losing a sizable minority of Democrats, mostly labor unionists and southerners, who feared that many textile mills would lose business (and millions of jobs) to "cheap labor" countries—as they did.

Successes: NAFTA, higher taxes for the wealthy, and an economic stimulus package

North American Free Trade Agreement (NAFTA) (1994) Agreement eliminating trade barriers that was signed in 1994 by the United States, Canada, and Mexico, making North America the largest free-trade zone in the world.

Health-Care Reform

Clinton's major public-policy initiative was an ambitious plan to overhaul the nation's health-care system. "If I don't get health care," he declared, "I'll wish I didn't run for president." Public support for government health insurance spread as annual medical costs skyrocketed and some 37 million Americans, most of them poor or unemployed, went without any medical insurance. The Clinton administration argued that making medical insurance available to everyone, regardless of income, would reduce the costs of health care to the nation as a whole, but critics in Congress questioned the savings as well as the ability of the federal government to manage such a huge program efficiently.

Clinton's plan called for everyone to be enrolled in a qualified health insurance plan, either through their individual initiative or through their employer. Those too poor to afford coverage were to receive government subsidies to enable them to enroll. All large businesses (over 5,000 employees) must pay for most of the medical insurance expenses of their employees while small businesses would be required to form "health alliances" so that they, too, could provide subsidized health insurance to their workers.

By the summer of 1994, Clinton's bulky 1,364-page health-insurance plan, developed by a 500-person task force of "experts" headed by the First Lady, Hillary Rodham Clinton, rather than congressional leaders, was doomed, in part because the president opposed any changes to his wife's plan and in part because the report was impossibly complicated. As one of the First Lady's aides confessed, the "ludicrously complex report . . . had something in it to piss everybody off. So by the time it goes up to the Hill, it's dead on arrival." Strenuously opposed by Republicans and health-care interest groups, especially the pharmaceutical and insurance industries, Clinton's prized health-care bill, officially called the Health Security Act, lost in Congress in August 1994. As the president lamented, "We . . . took too long and ended up achieving nothing."

| Failed health-care reform |

Landslide Republican Victory

The health-care bill disaster influenced the 1994 midterm elections, when the Democrats suffered a humbling defeat. It was the first election since 1952 in which Republicans captured both houses of Congress. The Republicans also won 32 governorships, including the largest states of California, New York, and Texas, where George W. Bush, the son of the former president and a future president himself, won handily. "We got the living daylight beat out of us," Clinton admitted. He accepted much of the blame, noting that he had allowed his new presidency to "be defined by gays in the military; by failing to concentrate on the campaign until it was too late; and by trying to do too much too fast." But he warned Republicans that he was like the inflated rubber clown doll "you had as a kid, and every time you hit it, it bounces back. That's me—the harder you hit me, the faster I come back up."

| Midterm Elections: Republicans win the majority in the House and the Senate |

A feisty Georgia conservative named Newton (Newt) Leroy Gingrich orchestrated the Republican victory. In early 1995, he became the first Republican Speaker of the House in forty-two years. Gingrich, a former history

NEWT GINGRICH Joined by 160 of his fellow House Republicans, Speaker of the House Newt Gingrich promotes the Contract with America in April 1995.

Republican opposition: Contract with America

Contract with America (1994)
List of conservative promises in response to the supposed liberalism of the Clinton administration; drafted by Speaker of the House Newt Gingrich and other congressional Republicans as a campaign tactic for the 1994 midterm elections.

professor with a lust for controversy and an unruly ego, had helped mobilize religious and social conservatives associated with the Christian Coalition. The Christian Coalition, organized by television evangelist Pat Robertson in 1989 to replace Jerry Falwell's Moral Majority (which had disbanded that year), chose the Republican party as the best vehicle for promoting its pro–school prayer, anti-abortion, anti-feminist, and anti–gay rights positions. Ralph Reed, a born-again Christian activist who would head the Christian Coalition, declared that Christians needed "to take back this country." In many respects, the Christian Right did take control of the political and social landscape in the nineties.

In 1994, Gingrich and other Republican candidates for Congress rallied conservative voters by lambasting Clinton as "the enemy of normal Americans" and promising a **Contract with America**, a pledge to dismantle the "corrupt liberal welfare state" created by Democrats eager to serve the "undeserving" poor.

The ten-point anti-big-government "contract" featured lower taxes, less regulation of businesses, less environmental protection, term limits for members of Congress, reductions in social-welfare programs, and a constitutional amendment requiring a balanced budget. As Texan Tom DeLay, a leading Republican in the House of Representatives, explained, "You've got to understand, we are ideologues. We have an agenda. We have a philosophy." In early 1995, *Time* magazine named Gingrich its "Man of the Year."

Yet the much-trumpeted Contract with America quickly fizzled. The new conservatives pushed their agenda too hard and too fast, realizing only too late that their slim majority in Congress could not launch a Republican revolution. Even with their control of Congress, the Republicans could only pass four minor elements of their "Contract." Gingrich's heavy-handed methods had backfired. Republican senator Bob Dole said Gingrich was "a one-man band who rarely took advice." He was too ambitious, too abrasive, too divisive.

When Clinton refused to go along with Republican demands for a balanced-budget pledge, Gingrich twice shut down the federal government during the fall of 1995, sending 800,000 employees home. That meant Social Security checks were not mailed, and passports were not approved. All national parks closed. The tactic backfired. By 1996, Gingrich had higher negative ratings in public surveys than the president.

The Supreme Court and Race

The conservative mood during the mid-1990s also revealed itself in Supreme Court rulings that undermined affirmative-action programs created by colleges in the 1960s to give African American students special consideration in admissions and financial aid awards. Between 1970 and 1977, African American enrollment in colleges and universities had doubled, even as white students and their parents complained about "reverse discrimination" against them.

In 1996, two major steps challenged affirmative action in college admissions. In *Hopwood v. Texas*, a federal court outlawed race as a consideration for admission. Later that year, the state of California passed Proposition 209, an initiative that ruled out any preferential treatment based on race, sex, ethnicity, or national origin. In 1995, the Court in *Adarand Constructors, Inc. v. Peña* declared that affirmative-action programs affecting businesses had to be "narrowly tailored" to serve a "compelling national interest." The implication of such vague language was clear: the Court had called into question the value and legitimacy of race-based benefit programs.

Legislative Breakthrough

After the surprising 1994 Republican takeover of Congress, Bill Clinton shrewdly resolved to save his presidency by showing that he was a "centrist," not a liberal. He co-opted much of the energy of the growing conservative movement when he reformed the federal system of welfare payments to the poor created during the 1930s under the New Deal.

> Welfare reform

In 1996, the Republican Congress passed a comprehensive welfare-reform measure that Clinton signed after some revisions. The **Personal Responsibility and Work Opportunity Act of 1996 (PRWOA)** illustrated the president's efforts to move the Democratic party away from the old liberalism it had promoted since the 1930s. PRWOA abolished the Aid to Families with Dependent Children program, which provided poor families with almost $8,000 a year in support and replaced it with the Temporary Assistance for Needy Families program, which limited the duration of welfare payments to two years in an effort to encourage unemployed people to get jobs.

Liberal Democrats bitterly criticized Clinton's "welfare reform" deal with Republicans. Yet the new federal approach to supporting the poor was a statistical success. The number of welfare recipients and poverty rates both declined during the late nineties, leading the editors of the left-leaning *the New Republic* to report that the PRWOA had "worked much as its designers had hoped."

The 1996 Campaign

The Republican takeover of Congress in 1994 gave Republicans hope that they could prevent Clinton's reelection. After clinching the Republican presidential nomination in 1996, Senate majority leader Bob Dole resigned his seat in order to devote his attention to defeating Bill Clinton. Clinton, however, maintained a large lead in the polls, in large part because he portrayed himself as a centrist. "The era of big government," he declared, "is over." There is not a "program for every problem." With an improving economy and no major foreign-policy crises, cultural and personal issues again surged into prominence. Concern about Dole's age (seventy-three) and his gruff public

Personal Responsibility and Work Opportunity Act of 1996 (PRWOA) Comprehensive welfare-reform measure aiming to decrease the size of the "welfare state" by limiting the amount of government unemployment aid to encourage its recipients to find jobs.

personality, as well as tensions within the Republican party between economic conservatives and social conservatives over volatile issues such as abortion and gun control, hampered Dole's efforts to generate widespread support.

On November 5, 1996, Clinton won a second term as president, with an electoral vote victory of 379–159 and 49 percent of the popular vote. Dole received only 41 percent of the popular vote, and third-party candidate Ross Perot got 8 percent.

MACINTOSH In 1984, Apple launched its personal computer, the Macintosh, with the tagline "For the rest of us," marketing it as an affordable and easy-to-use computer designed for the average user.

The "New Economy"

Bill Clinton's presidency benefited from a prolonged period of unprecedented prosperity. During his last three years in office (1998–2000), the federal government generated record budget *surpluses*. At the end of the twentieth century, what came to be called the "**new economy**" featured high-flying electronics, computer, software, telecommunications (cellular phones, cable TV, etc.), and e-commerce Internet firms called "dot-com" companies. These dynamic new enterprises helped the economy set records in every area: low inflation, low unemployment, and dizzying corporate profits and personal fortunes. People claimed that the new high-tech economy defied the boom-and-bust cycles of the previous hundred years. Alan Greenspan, the Federal Reserve Board chairman, suggested "that we have moved 'beyond history'"—into an economy that seemed only to grow. He would be proven wrong.

Globalization

Another major feature of the new economy in the nineties was **globalization**. The end of the Cold War and the disintegration of the Soviet Union opened up many new opportunities for U.S. companies in international trade. In addition, new globe-spanning communication technologies and massive new container-carrying ships and cargo jets shortened time and distance, enabling multinational companies to conduct a growing business abroad as more and more nations lowered trade barriers.

Bill Clinton accelerated the process of globalization. "The global economy," he said, "is giving more of our own people, and billions around the world, the chance to work and live and raise their families with dignity." He especially welcomed the World Wide Web, which opened up the Internet not just to the elite community of scientists but to everyone, and, by doing so, greatly accelerated U.S. dominance of the international economy.

By 2000, over a third of the production of U.S. multinational companies was occurring abroad, compared with only 9 percent in 1980. In 1970, there were 7,000 American multinational companies; by 2000, the number had

new economy Period of sustained economic prosperity during the 1990s marked by federal budget surpluses, the explosion of dot-com industries, low inflation, and low unemployment.

globalization An important and controversial transformation of the world economy led by the growing number of multinational companies and the Internet, whereby an international marketplace for goods and services was created.

soared to 63,000. Many U.S. multinational companies pursued controversial "outsourcing" strategies by which they moved their production "offshore" to nations such as Mexico and China to take advantage of lower labor costs and fewer workplace and environmental regulations. At the same time, many European and Asian companies, especially automobile manufacturers, built large plants in the United States to reduce the shipping expenses required to get their products to American markets.

> "Outsourcing" jobs abroad and foreign manufacturers at home

Foreign Policy in the Nineties

Unlike his predecessor George H. W. Bush, Bill Clinton had little interest in global politics. "Foreign policy is not what I came here to do," he admitted. Untrained and inexperienced in international relations, he had hoped that the post–Cold War era would create opportunities around the world for U.S. business expansion. Yet as the international analyst Leslie Gelb cautioned the new president, "A foreign economic policy is not a foreign policy, and it is not a national security strategy."

The Middle East

President Clinton continued George H. W. Bush's policy of orchestrating patient negotiations between the Arabs and the Israelis. A new development was the inclusion of the Palestinian Liberation Organization (PLO) in the negotiations. In 1993, secret talks between Israeli and Palestinian representatives in Oslo, Norway, resulted in a draft agreement between Israel and the PLO. This agreement provided for the restoration of Palestinian self-rule in the occupied Gaza Strip and in Jericho, on the West Bank, in a "land for peace" exchange as provided in UN Security Council resolutions. A formal signing occurred at the White House on September 13, 1993. With President Clinton presiding, Israeli prime minister Yitzhak Rabin and PLO leader Yasir Arafat exchanged handshakes, and their foreign ministers signed the agreement.

> Arab-Israeli peace negotiations

CLINTON AND THE MIDDLE EAST
President Clinton presides as Israeli prime minister Yitzhak Rabin (left) and PLO leader Yasir Arafat (right) agree to a pathbreaking peace accord between Israel and the Palestinians in September 1993.

The Middle East peace process suffered a terrible blow in early November 1995, however, when an Israeli zealot assassinated Prime Minister Rabin because of his efforts to negotiate with the Palestinians. Some observers feared that the assassin had killed the peace process as well when seven months later conservative hard-liner Benjamin Netanyahu narrowly defeated the U.S.-backed Shimon Peres in the Israeli national elections. Yet in October 1998, Clinton brought Arafat, Netanyahu, and King Hussein of Jordan together at a conference in Maryland, where they reached an agreement. Under the Wye River Accords, Israel agreed to surrender land in return for security guarantees by the Palestinians.

The Balkans

> U.S.-NATO intervention in the Balkans

President Clinton also felt compelled to address violent turmoil in the Eastern European nations that had freed themselves from Soviet domination. In 1991, Yugoslavia had disintegrated into ethnic warfare as four of its six multiethnic republics declared their independence. Serb minorities, backed by the new Republic of Serbia, stirred up civil wars in neighboring Croatia and Bosnia. In Bosnia, the conflict involved systematic efforts to eliminate Muslims. Clinton decided that the situation was "intolerable" because the massacres of tens of thousands of people "tore at the very fabric" of human decency. He ordered food and medical supplies sent to besieged Bosnian Muslims and dispatched warplanes to stop the massacres.

In 1995, U.S. negotiators finally persuaded the foreign ministers of Croatia, Bosnia, and Yugoslavia (by then only a loose federation of the republics of Serbia and Montenegro) to agree to a comprehensive peace plan. Bosnia would remain a single nation divided into two states: a Muslim-Croat federation controlling 51 percent of the territory and a Bosnian-Serb republic controlling the remaining 49 percent. Elections would appoint a parliament and joint president. To enforce the agreement, NATO sent 60,000 troops to Bosnia.

McRUBBLE Pro-Milošević residents of Belgrade, Yugoslavia, destroy the storefront of a McDonald's fast-food restaurant in 1999 to protest NATO and the United States' air strikes on their homeland.

In 1998, the Balkan tinderbox flared up again, this time in the Yugoslav province of Kosovo, long considered sacred ground by Christian Serbs, although 90 percent of the 2 million Kosovars were in fact Albanian Muslims. In 1998, Yugoslav president Slobodan Milošević began a program of **"ethnic cleansing,"** whereby Yugoslav troops burned Albanian villages, murdered men, raped women, and displaced hundreds of thousands of Muslim Kosovars.

ethnic cleansing Systematic removal of an ethnic group from a territory through violence or intimidation in order to create a homogeneous society; the term was popularized by the Yugoslav policy brutally targeting Albanian Muslims in Kosovo.

On March 24, 1999, NATO, relying heavily upon U.S. military resources and leadership, launched air strikes against Yugoslavian military targets.

"Ending this tragedy is a moral imperative," explained President Clinton. After seventy-two days of bombardment, Milošević sued for peace on NATO's terms, in part because his Russian allies had finally abandoned him. An agreement was reached on June 3, 1999. President Clinton pledged extensive U.S. aid in helping the Yugoslavs rebuild their war-torn economy.

The Scandal Machine

For a time, Clinton's preoccupation with foreign crises helped deflect public attention from a growing number of investigations into his personal conduct. During his first term, the president faced old charges revolving around investments that he and his wife, Hillary, had made in Whitewater, a planned resort development in Arkansas. The project turned out to be a fraud and a failure, and people accused the Clintons of conspiring with the developer. In 1994, Kenneth Starr, a former judge and a conservative Republican, was appointed as independent counsel to investigate the Whitewater case.

Starr found no evidence that the Clintons were directly involved in the Whitewater fraud, but in the course of another investigation, he happened upon evidence of a White House sex scandal. Between 1995 and 1997, Clinton had a sixteen-month-long sexual affair with an unpaid twenty-two-year-old White House intern, Monica Lewinsky (he later called it succumbing to his "old demons"). Even more disturbing, he had pressed her to lie about their relationship, even under oath.

Clinton initially denied the charges, telling the nation in late January 1998, "I did *not* have sexual relations with that woman, Miss Lewinsky." Yet the scandal would not disappear. Nebraska Democratic senator Bob Kerry recalled his reaction to the news: "Oh, my God, an intern. He's toast." A former aide, David Gergen, warned that if the president was lying, "he has betrayed the public trust and is a scoundrel." A desperate Clinton went to extraordinary lengths to camouflage the truth, even drawing his secretary into his web of deceit.

For the next thirteen months, the media circus surrounding the "Monicagate" or "Zippergate" affair captured public attention like a daily soap opera. In August, however, the bottom fell out of Clinton's denials when Lewinsky provided a federal grand jury with a detailed account of her relationship with the president.

Soon thereafter, knowing that he was about to be proven a liar, Clinton confessed to his wife and daughter before becoming the first president in history to testify before a grand jury. On August 17, the self-pitying, defiant Clinton admitted in a televised address to having had "inappropriate, intimate physical contact" with Lewinsky but insisted that he had done nothing illegal.

The Impeachment of President Clinton

On September 9, 1998, Starr, the special prosecutor, submitted to Congress thirty-six boxes of documents that included a lengthy, graphic account of the Lewinsky episode, claiming that there was "substantial and credible"

The Starr Report

IMPEACHMENT Representative Edward Pease, a member of the House Judiciary Committee, covers his face during the vote on the third of four articles of impeachment charging President Clinton with "high crimes and misdemeanors" in December 1998. **What was the public's reaction to Clinton's scandals and impeachment?**

evidence of presidential wrongdoing (committing perjury, obstructing justice, and abusing his presidential powers). The Starr Report led the Republican-dominated House of Representatives on October 8 to begin a wide-ranging impeachment inquiry of the president's behavior. Thirty-one Democrats joined the Republicans in supporting the investigation.

On December 19, 1998, the House of Representatives impeached William Jefferson Clinton, charging him with lying under oath to a federal grand jury and obstructing justice.

The Senate impeachment trial began on January 7, 1999. Five weeks later, on February 12, the Senate acquitted Clinton, largely on a party-line vote. A majority of senators, both Democrats and a few Republicans (55–45), decided that Clinton's adultery and lies about it were not the "high crimes and misdemeanors" required to remove a president from office. Most Americans agreed. As historian Steven Gillon observed, "The only thing most Americans disliked more than a devious middle-aged man lying about sex was moralizing, self-righteous hypocrites telling other people how to lead their lives."

CORE **OBJECTIVE**

3. Summarize the impact of global terrorism on the United States during the presidency of George W. Bush.

A New Century

The United States—and the world—greeted with great fanfare the new century, in a new millennium. Wild celebrations ushered in the year 2000, but the joyous mood did not last. Powerful new forces were destabilizing the post–Cold War world, the most dangerous of which were global networks of high-tech terrorists eager to disrupt and destroy Western values and institutions. As Americans decided on a new president in the fall of 2000, none suspected that the United States would soon experience the first major foreign attack on American soil since the Japanese bombed Pearl Harbor in December 1941.

A Disputed Election

The presidential election of 2000 proved to be one of the closest and most controversial in history. The two major-party candidates for president, Vice President Albert Gore Jr., the Democrat, and Texas governor George W. Bush, the son of the former Republican president, offered contrasting views on the role of the federal government, tax cuts, environmental policies, and the best way to preserve Social Security and Medicare.

Gore, a Tennessee native and Harvard graduate whose father had been a prominent senator, favored an active federal government that would do much more to protect the environment. Bush, on the other hand, campaigned on a theme of "compassionate conservatism" at home, promising to restore "honor and dignity" to the White House after the Clinton scandal and proposing, as previous Republican presidents had done, to transfer power from the federal government to the states.

A "born-again" Christian with degrees from Yale University and Harvard Business School, Bush also urged a more "humble" foreign policy, one that would end U.S. efforts to install democratic governments in undemocratic societies ("nation building"). The increasingly bitter tone of party politics (called *polarization*) inspired candidates at the extremes to run as third-party candidates. Two independent candidates added zest to the 2000 presidential campaign: the colorful conservative commentator Patrick Buchanan and the liberal consumer activist Ralph Nader, representing the Green party.

The November election results created high drama. The television networks initially reported that Gore had narrowly won the state of Florida and its decisive twenty-five electoral votes. Later in the evening, however, the networks reversed themselves, now saying that Florida was too close to call. In the chaotic early-morning hours, the networks declared that Bush had won the decisive state by the narrowest of margins, but state law required a recount. For the first time in 125 years, the results of a presidential election remained in doubt for weeks.

As a painstaking hand count of ballots proceeded in Florida, supporters of Bush and Gore sparred in the state courts and the U.S. Supreme Court; each side accused the other of trying to "steal" the election. The political drama lasted for five weeks. At last, on December 12, 2000, a bitterly divided Supreme Court handed down its decision in the case known as *Bush v. Gore*, and with a bare 5–4 majority ordered that the Florida recount be halted. This time, Bush won Florida by only 537 votes. Although Gore had amassed a 540,000-vote lead nationwide, he lost in the Electoral College by five votes when he lost Florida. Although Al Gore "strongly disagreed" with the Supreme Court's decision, he asked voters to rally around President-elect Bush and move forward. "Partisan rancor," he urged, "must be put aside."

THE RECOUNT In yet another recount on November 24, 2000, Judge Robert Rosenberg examines a ballot with a magnifying glass. That Florida's voting machines had limited accuracy introduced a great margin of doubt in a close election.

A Change of Direction

George W. Bush had promised during the campaign to cut taxes for the wealthy, increase military spending, oppose strict environmental regulations, and "privatize" Social Security by investing workers' retirement pension funds in the stock market.

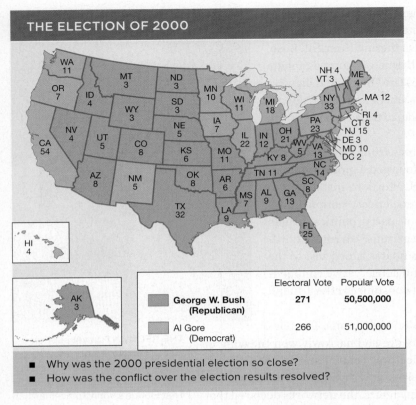

THE ELECTION OF 2000

		Electoral Vote	Popular Vote
	George W. Bush **(Republican)**	**271**	**50,500,000**
	Al Gore (Democrat)	266	51,000,000

■ Why was the 2000 presidential election so close?
■ How was the conflict over the election results resolved?

First, however, the new president had to deal with a sputtering economy and a falling stock market. By March 2001, the economy was in recession for the first time in over a decade. Bush decided that cutting taxes was the best way to boost economic growth. On June 7, 2001, he signed the Economic Growth and Tax Relief Act, which cut $1.35 trillion in taxes—even more than the famous Reagan tax cuts. Instead of paying for themselves in renewed economic growth, however, the Bush tax cuts led to a sharp drop in federal revenue, producing in turn a fast-growing budget deficit as the Clinton surpluses ran out. Huge increases in the costs of Medicare and Medicaid, the federal health-care programs, resulting from the aging of the baby-boom generation, contributed to the soaring budget deficits, as did unexpected military expenditures resulting from an unexpected war.

As had happened so often with presidents during the twentieth century, President Bush soon found himself distracted by global issues and foreign crises. Islamic militants around the world fiercely resented the "imperial" globalization of U.S. culture and power. With increasing frequency, they used brutal terrorism, including suicide bombings, to gain notoriety, exact vengeance, and generate fear and insecurity, making the world vulnerable to chaos and violence. Throughout the nineties, the United States had fought a losing struggle against global terrorist groups, in part because terrorism thrives in impoverished nations with weak governments overwhelmed by rapid population growth, scarce resources, widespread poverty, and huge numbers of unemployed young men. The ineffectiveness of U.S. intelligence agencies in tracking the movements and intentions of militant extremists became tragically evident in the late summer of 2001.

9/11—A New Day of Infamy

9/11: Terrorist attacks

At 8:45 A.M. on sunny September 11, 2001, Islamist terrorists hijacked a U.S. airliner in Boston. They flew it to New York City, where they slammed into the north tower of the World Trade Center. Eighteen minutes later, a second hijacked jumbo jet crashed into the south tower. The twin towers, 110 stories tall and filled with 50,000 workers, burned out of control, the inferno forcing hundreds of desperate people to jump to their deaths as thousands more, on floors below the points of impact, struggled to evacuate the skyscrapers. Quickly, though, the steel structures collapsed from the intense heat, destroying surrounding buildings. Nearly 3,000 people died, including more than 400 firefighters and police officers who had rushed into the burning towers. The southern end of Manhattan—"ground zero"—became a hellish scene of twisted steel, broken concrete, suffocating smoke, wailing sirens, and panicked people.

While the catastrophic drama in New York City was unfolding, a third hijacked plane crashed into the Pentagon in Washington, D.C. A fourth airliner, probably headed for the White House, missed its mark when passengers—who had heard reports of the earlier hijackings via their cell phones—assaulted the hijackers in order to prevent the plane from being used as a weapon. During the struggle in the cockpit, the plane went out of control and plummeted into the ground near Shanksville, Pennsylvania, killing all aboard.

Within hours of the hijackings, officials identified the nineteen dead terrorists as members of al Qaeda (Arabic for "the Base"), a well-financed network of Islamic extremists led by a wealthy Saudi renegade, Osama bin Laden. Years before, bin Laden had declared *jihad* (holy war) on the United States, Israel, and the Saudi monarchy in his effort to create a single Islamist *caliphate* (global empire). To foster his clash of civilizations by organizing global Islamist terrorism, he used remote bases in Sudan and war-torn Afghanistan as training centers for *jihadist* fighters recruited from around the world. Collaborating with bin Laden's terrorist network was Afghanistan's ruling Taliban, a coalition of ultraconservative Islamists who provided bin Laden with a safe haven.

SEPTEMBER 11 Smoke pours out of the north tower of the World Trade Center as the south tower bursts into flames after being struck by a second hijacked airplane. Both would collapse within an hour.

The "War on Terror"

The 9/11 assault on the United States, like the Japanese attack on Pearl Harbor on December 7, 1941, changed the course of modern life. The falling World Trade Center towers symbolized the shocking collapse of one era and the start of a new one. Numbed by the terrible events, people were initially paralyzed by grief, fear, and anger. The U.S. economy, already in decline, went into free fall. President Bush was thrust into the role of commander in chief of a wounded nation eager for vengeance. The new president told the world that he was going to launch a global **war on terror** "to answer these attacks and rid the world of evil," as if he were launching a religious crusade,

war on terror Global crusade to root out anti-Western and anti-American Islamist terrorist cells launched by President George W. Bush as a response to the 9/11 attacks.

WAR FEVER President George W. Bush addresses the Special Forces in July 2002 as part of an appeal to Congress to increase defense spending after the September 11 attacks. **How did President Bush lead in the wake of the terrorist attacks?**

War on terror abroad: Operation Enduring Freedom in Afghanistan (2001)

warning other nations, "Either you are with us or you are with the terrorists." A wave of patriotic fervor rolled across the nation. "United We Stand" became the motto for Americans determined to rebuild what had been lost in the rubble of the fallen towers and to defeat the fanatics responsible for such destruction and suffering.

Bush acted swiftly. He demanded that Afghanistan's Taliban government surrender the al Qaeda terrorists or risk military attack. On October 7, 2001, after the Taliban refused to turn over bin Laden, the United States and its allies launched a military campaign—called "Operation Enduring Freedom"—to punish terrorists or "those harboring terrorists." American and British cruise missiles and bombers destroyed Afghan military installations and al Qaeda training camps, followed by an American-led invasion working with Afghan opponents of the Taliban. Taliban forces were routed in just two months. On December 9, the Taliban regime collapsed. The war in Afghanistan then transitioned into a high-stakes manhunt for the elusive Osama bin Laden, who escaped into the mountains of Pakistan.

The "war on terror" at Home

While the military campaign continued in Afghanistan, officials in Washington worried that terrorists might attack the United States with biological, chemical, or even nuclear weapons. To address the threat and to help restore public confidence, President Bush created a new federal agency, the Office of Homeland Security. Another new federal agency, the Transportation Security Administration, assumed responsibility for screening all airline passengers for weapons and bombs. At the same time, President Bush and a supportive Congress created the **USA Patriot Act**, which gave government agencies the right to eavesdrop on confidential conversations between prison inmates and their lawyers and permitted suspected terrorists to be

USA Patriot Act (2001) Wide-reaching congressional legislation, triggered by the war on terror, which gave government agencies the right to eavesdrop on confidential conversations between prison inmates and their lawyers and permitted suspected terrorists to be tried in secret military courts.

tried in secret military courts. Civil liberties groups voiced grave concerns that the measures jeopardized constitutional rights and protections, but the superheated atmosphere after 9/11 led most people to support these extraordinary steps.

War on terror at home: Homeland Security and the USA Patriot Act

What the public did not know was that Vice President Richard Cheney, Secretary of Defense Donald Rumsfeld, and others convinced the president to authorize the use of torture ("enhanced interrogation techniques") in the CIA and FBI's treatment of captured terrorist suspects, tactics that violated international law. When asked about such activities, the shadowy Cheney scoffed that America sometimes had to work "the dark side": "We've got to spend time in the shadows in the intelligence world. . . ." Former president George H. W. Bush later reflected that Cheney had built "his own empire" within the White House and exerted too much "hard-line" influence within his son's inner circle.

The Bush Doctrine

Bush Doctrine: Preemptive military action

In the fall of 2002, President Bush unveiled a dramatic new national security policy. The **Bush Doctrine** said that the growing menace posed by "shadowy networks" of terrorist groups and unstable rogue nations with "weapons of mass destruction" (WMD) required that the United States at times must abandon diplomacy and use preemptive military action. "If we wait for threats to fully materialize" or wait for allies to join America, he explained, "we will have waited too long. In the world we have entered, the only path to safety is the path of action. And this nation will *act*."

The Iraq War

War on terror abroad: United States invades Iraq (2003)

During 2002 and 2003, Iraq emerged as the focus of the Bush administration's new policy of "preemptive" military action. Three of the president's most influential advisers, Vice President Cheney, Secretary of Defense Rumsfeld, and Deputy Defense Secretary Paul Wolfowitz, convinced Bush that the dictatorial regime of Saddam Hussein represented a "grave and gathering danger" because of its supposed possession of biological and chemical WMD.

On March 17, 2003, President Bush, eager to finish what his father had started, issued an ultimatum to Saddam Hussein: he and his sons must leave Iraq within forty-eight hours or face a U.S.-led invasion. Hussein refused. Two days later, on March 19, American and British forces attacked Iraq. Despite U.S. diplomatic attempts to assemble an international coalition similar to that of the First Gulf War a decade earlier, France and Germany refused to participate in what they viewed as unnecessary American aggression.

"Operation Iraqi Freedom" began with a massive bombing campaign intended to provoke "shock and awe," followed by a fast-moving invasion across the Iraqi desert from bases in Kuwait. On April 9, after three weeks of intense fighting amid sweltering heat and blinding sandstorms, U.S. forces captured Baghdad, the capital of Iraq. Saddam Hussein's regime and his inept, demoralized army collapsed a week later.

Bush Doctrine National security policy launched in 2002 by which the Bush administration claimed the right to launch preemptive military attacks against perceived enemies, particularly outlaw nations or terrorist organizations believed to possess WMD.

The six-week war came at a cost of fewer than 200 combat deaths among the 300,000 allied troops. Over 2,000 Iraqi soldiers were killed; civilian casualties were higher. President Bush donned a pilot's flight suit to stage a celebration on a U.S. aircraft carrier at which he announced victory in Iraq under a massive banner proclaiming "MISSION ACCOMPLISHED." Without consulting either the State Department or Defense Department, he announced his intention to bring American-style democracy to Iraq. But he declared victory much too soon; the initial military triumph carried with it the seeds of disappointment and disaster, for no WMD were found in Iraq. In the end, the American-led invasion of Iraq was one of the worst foreign-policy decisions in American history. Bush later said that the absence of WMD in Iraq left him with a "sickening feeling," for he knew that his primary justification for the war had evaporated.

Rebuilding Iraq

Growing insurgency in Iraq

It proved far easier to win the brief war than to rebuild authoritarian Iraq in America's image. Unprepared U.S. officials faced the daunting task of restoring order and installing a democratic government in an Iraq fractured by ancient religious feuds and ethnic tensions—made worse by the breakdown in law and order caused by the allied invasion. Looting and violence immediately engulfed the war-torn country, large parts of which fell under the control of local warlords and criminal gangs. Within weeks, vengeful Islamic radicals from around the world streamed into the crippled nation to wage a merciless campaign of terror, sabotage, and suicide bombings against the U.S. forces. Bush's macho reaction to the insurgency in Iraq—"Bring 'em on!"—revealed how uninformed he was about the fast-deteriorating situation. The leader of the new Iraqi government, Prime Minister Nouri al-Maliki, quickly imposed his own authoritarian, Shiite-dominated regime that discriminated against the Sunnis, the Kurds, and other ethnic and religious minorities.

Ignoring the advice of Defense Department analysts and some of his top generals, Secretary Rumsfeld greatly underestimated the difficulty and expense of occupying, pacifying, and reconstructing postwar Iraq. By the fall of 2003, President Bush admitted that substantial numbers of American troops (around 150,000) would have to remain in Iraq much longer than anticipated. He also acknowledged that rebuilding the splintered nation amid its religious

FREEDOM FOR WHOM? The American torture of Iraqi prisoners in Abu Ghraib prison only exacerbated the anger and humiliation that Iraqis experienced since the First Gulf War. In response to America's incessant promises of peace and autonomy, a Baghdad mural fires back: "That Freedom For B[u]sh."

and ethnic civil wars would take years and cost almost a *trillion* dollars. Victory on the battlefields of Iraq did not bring victory in the "war on terror." Militant Islamist groups seething with hatred toward the United States remained a constant global threat. Among Americans, the thrill of a quick battlefield victory turned to dismay as the number of casualties and the expense of the military occupation in Iraq soared.

In the face of mounting criticism, President Bush urged Americans to "stay the course," insisting that a democratic Iraq would bring stability to the volatile Middle East and thereby blunt the momentum of Islamic terrorism. Although Saddam Hussein was captured in December 2003 and later hanged by the new Iraqi authorities, Iraq seemed less secure than ever to anxious Americans worried about the

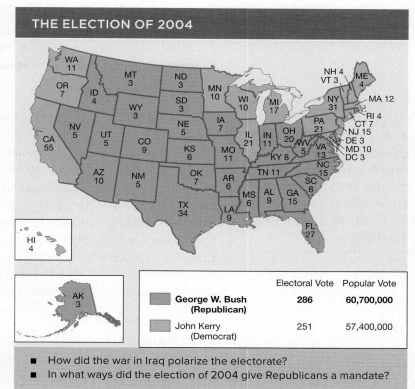

THE ELECTION OF 2004

	Electoral Vote	Popular Vote
George W. Bush (Republican)	**286**	**60,700,000**
John Kerry (Democrat)	251	57,400,000

■ How did the war in Iraq polarize the electorate?
■ In what ways did the election of 2004 give Republicans a mandate?

rising cost of an open-ended occupation. By the beginning of 2004, a thousand Americans had died in the conflict and more than 10,000 had been wounded. And the ethnic and religious tensions embroiling Iraq only worsened as violent Sunni *jihadists* allied with al Qaeda to undermine the new Iraqi government and assault U.S. forces.

The Election of 2004

Growing public concern about Iraq complicated George W. Bush's campaign for a second presidential term in 2004. The Democratic nominee, Senator John Kerry of Massachusetts, condemned the Bush administration for misleading the nation about WMD in Iraq and for its slipshod handling of the reconstruction of postwar Iraq. Kerry also highlighted the record budget deficits occurring under the Republican administration. Bush countered that the tortuous efforts to create a democratic government in Iraq would enhance America's long-term security.

On Election Day, November 2, 2004, the exit polls suggested a Kerry victory, but in the end, the election hinged on the crucial swing state of Ohio. No Republican had ever lost Ohio and still won the presidency. Despite early returns from Ohio indicating a Kerry victory there, late returns appeared to tip the balance slightly toward Bush, even as rumors of electoral "irregularities" began to circulate. Nevertheless, Kerry conceded the election. "The outcome," he stressed, "should be decided by voters, not a protracted legal battle."

By narrowly winning Ohio, Bush captured 286 electoral votes to Kerry's 251. Yet in some respects the close election was not so close. Bush received 3.3 million more votes nationwide than Kerry, and Republicans increased their majority control of both houses of Congress.

CORE **OBJECTIVE**

4. Assess the issues and developments during Bush's second term that helped lead to Barack Obama's historic victory in the 2008 presidential election.

A Resurgent Democratic Party

George Bush stumbled in his second term as he confronted thorny political problems, a sluggish economy, and continuing turmoil and violence in Iraq. In 2005, he pushed through Congress an energy bill and a Central American Free Trade Act. But his effort to privatize Social Security retirement accounts, enabling individuals to invest their accumulated pension dollars themselves, went nowhere, and soaring budget deficits made many fiscal conservatives feel betrayed by the supposedly "conservative" Bush. The editors of the *Economist,* an influential conservative newsmagazine, declared that Bush had become "the least popular re-elected president since Richard Nixon."

Hurricane Katrina

In 2005, President Bush's eroding public support suffered another blow, this time when a natural disaster turned into a political crisis. In late August, a killer hurricane named Katrina slammed into the Gulf coast, devastating large areas of Alabama, Mississippi, and Louisiana. Katrina's awful wake left over a thousand people dead in the three states and millions homeless and hopeless, especially in New Orleans. The devastation caught local political officials and the Federal Emergency Management Agency (FEMA) unprepared as the catastrophe unfolded. Disaster plans were incomplete; confusion and incompetence abounded. In the face of blistering criticism, President Bush accepted responsibility for the balky federal response to the disaster and accepted the resignation of the FEMA director.

In the November 2006 congressional elections, the Democrats capitalized on widespread public disapproval of the Bush administration to win control of the House of Representatives, the Senate, and a majority of governorships and state legislatures. Former Texas Republican congressman Dick Armey grumbled that "the Republican Revolution of 1994 officially ended" with the 2006 election. "It was a rout." The transfor-

THE AFTERMATH OF KATRINA Two men paddle through high water with wooden planks in a devastated New Orleans. **How did the federal government fail to offer immediate and long-term support to the victims of Hurricane Katrina?**

mational election also included a significant milestone: Californian Nancy Pelosi, the leader of the Democrats in the House of Representatives, became the highest-ranking woman in the history of the U.S. Congress upon her election as House Speaker in January 2007.

The "Surge" in Iraq

George W. Bush bore the brunt of public indignation over the bungled federal response to the Katrina disaster and the continuing cost and casualties of the war in Iraq. Senator Chuck Hagel, a Nebraska Republican, declared in 2005 that "we're losing in Iraq." Throughout the fall of 2006, the violence in Iraq spiraled upward. Bush eventually responded to declining public and political support for the Iraq War by creating the Iraq Study Group, a bipartisan task force whose final report recommended that the United States withdraw its combat forces from a "grave and deteriorating Iraq" by the spring of 2008.

President Bush disagreed with the study group and others, including key military leaders, who urged a phased withdrawal. On January 10, 2007, he announced that he was sending a "surge" of 20,000 (eventually 30,000) additional troops to Iraq, bringing the total to almost 170,000. From a military perspective, the "surge" strategy succeeded. By the fall of 2008, the convulsive violence in Iraq had declined dramatically, and the U.S.-supported Iraqi government had grown in stature and confidence. Still, by 2008, over 60 percent of Americans said that the war in Iraq had been a mistake.

NANCY PELOSI The first female Speaker of the House, pictured here at a news conference on Capitol Hill, Pelosi's success coincided with the mounting public disapproval of the Republican party.

Economic Shock

After the intense but brief 2001 recession, the boom/bust capitalist economy had begun another period of prolonged expansion. Between 1997 and 2006, home prices in the United States, especially in the fast-growing Sun Belt states, rose 85 percent, leading to a frenzy of irresponsible mortgage lending for the purchase of homes—and a debt-financed consumer spending spree. Tens of millions of people bought houses they could not afford, refinanced their mortgages, or tapped home-equity loans to make discretionary purchases. The irrational confidence in soaring housing prices also led government regulatory agencies and mortgage lenders to ease credit restrictions so that unqualified people could buy homes.

Financial collapses typically follow real estate bubbles, rising indebtedness, and prolonged budget deficits. The housing bubble burst in 2007, when home values and housing sales began a sharp decline. During 2008, the loss of trillions of dollars in home values set off a seismic shock across the economy. Record numbers of borrowers defaulted on their mortgage payments. Foreclosures and bankruptcies soared. Banks lost billions, first on the shaky mortgages, then on most other categories of debt: credit

RIO VISTA, CALIFORNIA With an $816,000 deficit, this northern California city filed for bankruptcy and pulled the plug on its massive 750-home housing development in November 2008. Here, model homes stand eerily in a blank landscape of sidewalks and cul-de-sacs.

cards, car loans, student loans, and an array of commercial mortgage-backed securities.

The sudden contraction of corporate spending and consumer purchases pushed the economy into a deepening recession in 2008. The scale and suddenness of the slump surprised economic experts and business leaders. Some of the nation's most prestigious banks, investment firms, and insurance companies went belly-up. The price of food and gasoline spiked. Unemployment soared. What had begun as a sharp decline in home prices became a panicky global economic meltdown. No investment seemed safe.

The economic crisis demanded decisive action to stem the panic and restore confidence. On October 3, 2008, just before the presidential election, President Bush signed into law a bank bailout fund called the Troubled Asset Relief Program (TARP), which called for the Treasury Department to spend $700 billion to keep big banks and other large financial institutions from collapsing.

Yet the passage of the bill did little to restore confidence. In early October, stock markets around the world began to crash with the onset of what came to be called the **Great Recession**, which technically lasted from December 2007 to January 2009 and forced almost 9 million people out of work. Its effects, however, would last long thereafter. The economic recovery that began in June 2009 would be the weakest since the end of the Second World War. "The Age of Prosperity is over," announced the prominent Re-

Great Recession (2007–2009) Massive, prolonged economic downturn sparked by the collapse of the housing market and the financial institutions holding unpaid mortgages; resulted in 9 million Americans losing their jobs.

publican economist Arthur Laffer in 2008. Taken together, the endless wars in Afghanistan and Iraq coupled with a slumping economy shattered public support for the Bush administration. During his last year in office, Bush's public approval rating was an abysmal 25 percent, just one point higher than Richard Nixon's during the Watergate investigations.

A Historic New Presidency

George Bush's unpopularity excited Democrats about regaining the White House in the 2008 election. The early front-runner for the Democratic nomination was New York senator Hillary Rodham Clinton, the spouse of ex-president Bill Clinton. Like her husband, she displayed an impressive command of policy issues and mobilized a well-funded campaign team. Moreover, as the first woman with a serious chance of gaining the presidency, she had widespread support among voters eager for female leadership.

In the end, however, an overconfident Clinton lost in the Democratic primaries and caucuses to little-known first-term senator Barack Obama of Illinois. Young, handsome, and intelligent, Obama was an inspiring speaker who attracted huge crowds by promising a "politics of hope." He mounted an innovative Internet-based campaign directed at grassroots voters, donors, and volunteers. In early June 2008, he gained enough delegates to secure the Democratic nomination alongside Senator Joseph Biden of Delaware as his vice presidential running mate.

Obama was the first African American presidential nominee of either party, the gifted biracial son of a white mother from Kansas and a black Kenyan father who left the household and returned to Africa when Barack was a toddler. Obama made the most of his abilities, eventually graduating from Columbia University in New York before earning a law degree from Harvard. The forty-seven-year-old senator presented himself to voters as a leader who could inspire and unite a diverse people and forge bipartisan collaborations.

Obama radiated poise, confidence, and energy. By contrast, his Republican opponent, seventy-two-year-old Arizona senator John McCain, was the oldest presidential candidate in history. As a twenty-five-year veteran of Congress and a leading Republican senator, he had developed a reputation as a bipartisan "maverick" willing to work with Democrats to achieve key legislative goals.

BARACK OBAMA The president-elect and his family wave to the crowd of supporters in Chicago's Grant Park.

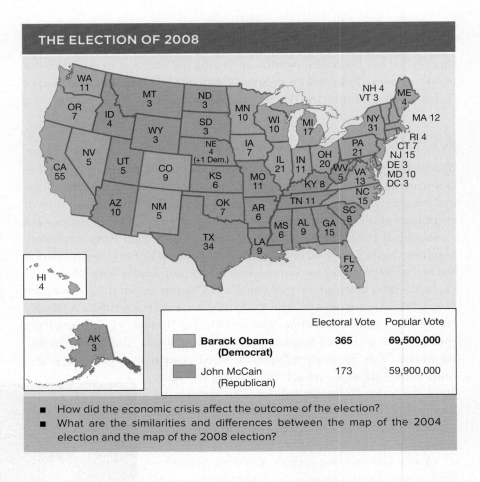

THE ELECTION OF 2008

		Electoral Vote	Popular Vote
	Barack Obama (Democrat)	365	69,500,000
	John McCain (Republican)	173	59,900,000

- How did the economic crisis affect the outcome of the election?
- What are the similarities and differences between the map of the 2004 election and the map of the 2008 election?

On November 4, 2008, Barack Obama made history by becoming the nation's first person of color elected president. He won the popular vote by 53 percent to 46 percent. His margin in the Electoral College was even more impressive: 365–173. Obama also helped the Democrats win solid majorities in both houses of Congress.

CORE **OBJECTIVE**
5. Identify President Obama's priorities at home and abroad, and assess his efforts to pursue them.

New Priorities at Home and Abroad

The new Obama administration inherited two unpopular wars, in Iraq and Afghanistan, and the worst economic collapse in eighty years. His most pressing challenge was to keep the Great Recession from becoming a prolonged depression. Unemployment in early 2009 had passed 8 percent and was still rising. The financial sector remained paralyzed, while public confidence plummeted.

Obama's First Term

To enable banks to start lending again, the new administration continued the TARP program created by the outgoing Bush administration, providing massive government bailouts to save the largest banks and financial institutions. The big bank bailouts were highly controversial, attacked by both the left and the right as deeply unfair to most struggling Americans. As Treasury secretary Timothy Geithner later explained, "We had to do whatever we could to help people feel their money was safe in the [banking] system, even if it made us unpopular." Had they not saved the big banks, Obama and Geithner argued, the whole economy would have crashed.

> Wall Street bank bailouts

Preserving the banking system did not create new jobs, however. To do so, in mid-February 2009, after a prolonged debate, Congress passed, and Obama signed, an $832 billion economic stimulus bill called the American Recovery and Reinvestment Act. The bill included cash distributions to the states for construction projects to renew the nation's infrastructure (roads, bridges, levees, government buildings, and the electricity grid), money for renewable-energy systems, and $212 billion in tax reductions for individuals and businesses, as well as additional funds for food stamps and unemployment benefits. It was the largest government infusion of cash into the economy in history. In the end, however, it was not large enough to generate a robust economic recovery.

> Economic Stimulus: American Recovery and Reinvestment Act (2009)

Health-Care Reform

The economic crisis merited Obama's full attention, but he chose as his top legislative priority a controversial federal health-insurance program that had been one of his key campaign pledges. From his first day in office, Obama stressed his intention to reform a health-care system so broken that it was "bankrupting families, bankrupting businesses, and bankrupting our government at the state and federal level." America was the only rich nation without a national health-care program. Since 1970, the proportion of uninsured people had been steadily rising along with health-care costs. In 2010, roughly 50 million Americans, 16 percent of the population, had no health insurance, most of them being either poor or young, or people of color.

> A national health-care program: The Affordable Care Act (2010)

The president's goal in creating the Patient Protection and **Affordable Care Act (ACA)**, which many people referred to as "Obamacare," was to make health insurance more affordable and make health care accessible for everyone, regardless of income. The $940 billion health-care law, proposed in 2009 and debated bitterly for a year, centered on the so-called *individual mandate*, which required uninsured adults to purchase an approved *private* insurance policy made available through state-run exchanges (websites where people could shop for insurance). Lower-income Americans were provided with federal subsidies to help pay for their coverage. Insurance companies could no longer deny coverage to people with pre-existing illnesses. Employers who did not offer health insurance would also have to pay

Affordable Care Act (ACA) (2010) Vast health-care-reform initiative championed by President Obama and widely criticized by Republicans that aimed to make health insurance more affordable and make health care accessible to everyone, regardless of income or prior medical conditions.

GO OBAMA GO A Democrat holds up a sign in support of the Affordable Care Act, more commonly known as Obamacare, in a march in Washington, D.C., in 2010. **What were some of the core features of the ACA that Democrats supported and Republicans opposed?**

higher taxes, and drug companies as well as manufacturers of medical devices would have to pay annual government fees. Everyone, but especially the wealthy, would pay higher Medicare payroll taxes to help fund the changes.

The individual mandate was designed to ensure that all Americans had health insurance so as to reduce the skyrocketing costs of hospitals providing "charity care" for the uninsured poor. The idea of forcing people to buy such insurance flew in the face of the principle of individual freedom and personal responsibility. Critics questioned not only the individual mandate but also the administration's projections that the new program would reduce federal expenditures over the long haul.

Republicans quickly mobilized to defeat the ACA. "If we're able to stop Obama on this, it will be his Waterloo. It will break him," predicted South Carolina senator Jim DeMint. Despite heated Republican opposition, however, the ACA passed with narrow party-line majorities in both houses of Congress. President Obama signed the new legislation on March 23, 2010. Its complex provisions, implemented over a four-year transition period, would bring health insurance to 32 million people, half of whom would be covered by expanded Medicaid and the other half by the individual mandate. In its scope and goals, the ACA was a landmark law in the history of health and social welfare—and in the expansion of the federal government.

Obamacare and the Courts

No sooner had Obama pushed his controversial health-care plan through Congress than Republican opponents began challenging its constitutionality. On June 28, 2012, the Supreme Court issued a much-awaited decision in the case of *National Federation of Independent Business v. Sebelius*. The landmark 5–4 ruling surprised Court observers by approving most of the new federal law. John G. Roberts, the philosophical conservative chief justice who had never before voted with the four "liberal" justices on the Court, upheld the ACA's individual mandate that required people to buy private health insurance or else pay a tax. He argued that it was within the Congress's power to impose taxes as outlined in Article 1 of the Constitution. Many conservatives, including the four dissenting justices, felt betrayed by Roberts's unexpected decision. The surprising verdict led the *New York Times* to predict that the ruling "may secure Obama's place in history."

Regulating Wall Street

The near collapse of the nation's financial system beginning in 2008 prompted calls for overhauling the financial regulatory system. On July 21, 2010, Obama signed the Wall Street Reform and Consumer Protection Act, called the Dodd-Frank bill after its two congressional sponsors. It was the most comprehensive reform of the financial system since the New Deal in the thirties. The 2,319-page law required government agencies to exercise greater oversight over complex financial transactions and protected consumers from unfair practices in loans and credit cards by establishing a new consumer financial-protection agency.

> Wall Street Reform and Consumer Protection Act (2010)

The Obama Doctrine and Iraq

President Obama had more success in dealing with foreign affairs than in reviving the American economy. His foremost concern was the overextension of U.S. power abroad. What journalists came to call the Obama Doctrine was very much like the Nixon Doctrine (1970), stressing that the United States could not afford to continue to police the world.

The Obama Doctrine reflected the president's efforts to end two complex and expensive wars, one in Iraq and the other in Afghanistan. On February 27, 2009, Obama announced that he would withdraw all 142,000 U.S. troops from Iraq by the end of 2011. True to his word, the last U.S. combat troops left Iraq in December 2011. Their exit marked the end of a bitterly divisive war that had raged for nearly nine years.

The U.S. intervention in Iraq had cost over 4,500 American lives, 30,000 wounded (many grievously so), more than 110,000 Iraqi lives, and $2 trillion. Perhaps the greatest embarrassment was that the government that the United States left behind in Iraq was inept and not even friendly to American interests.

A "Surge" in Afghanistan

At the same time that President Obama was reducing U.S. military involvement in Iraq, he dispatched 21,000 additional troops to Afghanistan. While doing so, however, he narrowed the focus of the

HOME FROM IRAQ U.S. troops returned from Iraq to little celebration. **What legacy did Americans leave behind after withdrawing from Iraq?**

U.S. mission to suppressing terrorists rather than what George W. Bush had called "nation building"—the idea of transforming strife-torn Afghanistan into a stable capitalist democracy.

End of U.S. military presence in Iraq and Afghanistan

The military surge worked as hoped. By the summer of 2011, President Obama announced that the United States had largely achieved its goals in Afghanistan, setting in motion a substantial withdrawal of forces between 2011 and 2014. In April 2014, Afghans turned out in huge numbers to choose a new president to lead them into the post-American era. But it was an expensive outcome for America's longest war. In the thirteen years since the United States invaded Afghanistan in 2001, America had spent over a trillion dollars there and had lost 2,300 military personnel.

The Death of Osama bin Laden

The crowning achievement of Obama's anti-terrorism efforts was the discovery, at long last, of Osama bin Laden's hideout. Ever since the attacks of 9/11, bin Laden had eluded an intensive manhunt after crossing the Afghan border into Pakistan. His luck ran out in 2011, however, when U.S. intelligence analysts discovered his sanctuary in a walled residential compound outside of Abbottabad, Pakistan. On May 2, 2011, President Obama authorized a daring night raid by a U.S. Navy SEAL team of two dozen commandos. After a brief firefight, the SEAL team killed bin Laden and then dropped his body into the sea. Bin Laden's death was a watershed moment, but it did not spell the end of Islamist terrorism.

The "Arab Awakening"

In late 2010 and early 2011, spontaneous democratic uprisings erupted throughout much of the Arab world, as long-oppressed peoples rose up against authoritarian regimes. One by one, corrupt Arab tyrants were forced out of power by a new generation of young activists inspired by democratic ideals and connected by social media on the Internet. Dubbed the "Arab Awakening," it sent waves of unrest rippling across Tunisia, Algeria, Bahrain, Jordan, Morocco, Egypt, Oman, Yemen, Libya, Saudi Arabia, and Syria during the Arab Spring of 2011. The remarkable uprisings heralded a new era in the history of the Middle East struggling to be born.

For all the excitement about "people power" emerging in the Middle East, however, the work of building new democratic governments proved much harder than expected. Grassroots democratic movements in most Arab nations stumbled and stalled by 2014, lurching from crisis to crisis usually triggered by their unwillingness to allow for freedom of religion. As the dream of greater democracy evaporated, many in the Arab world succumbed to apathy or despair.

ARAB AWAKENING Thousands of protesters converge in Cairo's Tahrir Square to call for an end to President Hosni Mubarak's rule.

Libya Ousts Gaddafi

The pro-democracy turmoil in North Africa engulfed oil-rich Libya, long governed by the mercurial dictator Colonel Muammar Gaddafi, the Arab world's most violent despot. Anti-government demonstrations began on February 15, 2011, prompting Gaddafi to order Libyan soldiers and mercenaries (paid foreign soldiers) to suppress the rebellious "rats." By the end of February, what began as a peaceful pro-democratic uprising had turned into a full-scale civil war that provided the first real test of the Obama Doctrine.

True to his word, the president refused to act alone in helping the Libyan rebels. Instead, he encouraged European allies to take the lead. On March 19, France and Great Britain, with American support, launched a bombing campaign against Gaddafi's military strongholds. In late August, rebel forces captured the capital of Tripoli, scattering Gaddafi's government and marking the end of his forty-two-year dictatorship. On October 20, rebel fighters captured and killed Gaddafi. But the rebel militias that removed Gaddafi soon started shooting at one another, and stability has remained elusive.

Polarized Politics

At the same time that Arabs were rebelling against entrenched political elites, grassroots rebellions were occurring in the United States as well. Barack Obama had campaigned in 2008 on the promise of bringing dramatic change to the federal government in an evenhanded way that would reduce the partisan warfare between the two national parties.

> Polarized politics: Conservative resurgence (the Tea Party)

By the end of Obama's first year in office, however, a Gallup poll found that he had become the most polarizing president in modern history. It was not solely his fault. His Republican opponents had no interest in negotiating compromises with him. American political culture in the twenty-first century suffered from a crisis of mutual resentment, so polarized that it resembled two separate nations. Each faction had its own political party, its own cable-news station and rabidly partisan commentators, its own newspapers, its own think tanks, and its own billionaire activists.

No sooner was Obama sworn in than anti-government conservatives mobilized against him and the "tax-and-spend" liberalism he represented in their eyes. In January 2009, a New York stock trader named Graham Makohoniuk sent an e-mail message urging people to send tea bags to their congressional representatives to symbolize the famous Boston Tea Party of 1773 when American colonists protested British tax policies.

Within a year or so, the tax revolt had become a national **Tea Party** movement, with groups spread across the fifty states. The Tea Party is not so much a cohesive political organization as it is a mood, an attitude, and an ideology, a diverse collection of self-described "disaffected," "angry," and "very conservative" activists, mostly white, male, married middle-class Republicans over forty-five, boiling mad at the massive government bailouts of huge banks and corporations that had come in the wake of the 2007-2008 economic meltdown.

Tea Party Right-wing populist movement, largely made up of middle-class, white male conservatives, that emerged as a response to the expansion of the federal government under the Obama administration.

OCCUPY WALL STREET The Manhattan-born grassroots movement grew rapidly from rallies to massive marches in financial districts worldwide, like this demonstration in downtown Los Angeles.

To the grassroots anti-tax rebels, the federal bailouts ordered by Bush and Obama were a form of "crony capitalism" whereby elected officials of both parties (the "elite") rewarded the big corporations that had funded their campaigns. Tea Party members demanded a radically smaller federal government (although most of them supported Social Security and Medicare, the two most expensive federal social-welfare programs). Democrats, including President Obama, initially dismissed the Tea Party as a fringe group of extremists, but the 2010 election results proved that they were a formidable political force.

Entrenched Democratic House and Senate candidates (as well as moderate Republicans) were defeated in droves when conservative Republicans, many of them aligned with the Tea Party, gained sixty-three seats to recapture control of the House of Representatives and won a near majority in the Senate as well. It was the most lopsided midterm election since 1938. "We've come to take our government back," declared one Republican congressional winner.

In an age of polarized political extremism, the Tea Party was mirrored on the far left wing of the political spectrum by the Occupy Wall Street (OWS) movement, mobilized in the fall of 2011 when a call went out over the Internet: "Occupy Wall Street. Bring tent." Dozens, then hundreds, then thousands of people, mostly young adults, many of them unemployed, converged on Zuccotti Park in Lower Manhattan. They constructed tent villages and gathered in festive groups to "occupy" Wall Street, protesting the "tyrannical" power of Wall Street banks and investment companies. The protesters described themselves as the voice of the 99 percent of Americans who were being victimized by the 1 percent of the wealthiest and most politically connected Americans. Unlike the Tea Party, however, OWS did not have staying power. Within a year, its energies and visibility had waned, in part because of mass arrests, in part because it was an intentionally "leaderless" movement more interested in saying what it was *against* than explaining what it was *for*.

Failure of bipartisanship

American politics has always been chaotic and combative; its raucous energy is one of the strengths of a democracy. During Obama's presidency, however, the emergence of the Tea Party and Occupy Wall Street symbolized how political combat had become so fierce that bipartisan *compromise* and *moderation* were abandoned. Rarely before had Democrats and Republicans viewed each other with greater venom and less respect.

Bold Decisions

For all the angry political sniping and congressional stalemate, however, attitudes toward "hot-button" cultural values were slowly changing. In December 2010, Congress repealed the DADT military policy that, since 1993, had resulted in some 9,500 men and women being discharged from the armed forces. A year after the repeal was enacted, an army task force concluded that the repeal of DADT "has had no overall negative impact on military readiness or its component dimensions, including cohesion, recruitment, retention, assaults, harassment, or morale."

In May 2012, President Obama jumped headfirst into the nation's simmering cultural wars by endorsing the right of gay and lesbian couples to marry. While asserting that it was the "right" thing to do, Obama also knew that endorsing **same-sex marriage** would ignite a firestorm of criticism. No sooner had Obama made his pathbreaking announcement than polls showed that voters for the first time split half and half on the charged issue.

The following month, in June 2012, Obama again provoked controversy by issuing an executive order (soon labeled the DREAM Act) that allowed 1.5 million undocumented immigrants who had been brought to the United States as children to remain in the country as citizens. His unanticipated decision thrilled Hispanic supporters who had lost heart over his failure to

same-sex marriage Legal right for gay and lesbian couples to marry; the most divisive issue in the culture wars of the early 2010s as increasing numbers of court rulings affirmed this right across the United States.

> The DREAM Act

REFUGEES FROM GANGLAND Braving hundreds of miles on foot, Honduran and Salvadorian children are sent off by their parents for a better life in the United States, away from the drugs and violence of Central America. Here, border guards stop a group of child refugees in Granjeno, Texas.

convince Congress to support a more comprehensive reform of immigration laws. Republicans in Congress steadfastly opposed Obama's proposal to give all undocumented immigrants, an estimated 12 million people, 80 percent of whom were Latinos, a "pathway to citizenship," without first ensuring that the U.S.-Mexican border was secured.

The DREAM Act, however, had unexpected consequences. It excited the dreams of masses of Central Americans willing to endure enormous risks to live in America. Panicked parents in El Salvador, Guatemala, and Honduras, worried about widespread drug-related gang violence, sent their children on a dangerous journey through Mexico to the United States in hopes of connecting with relatives and being granted citizenship. During 2014, officials caught some 57,000 young migrants trying to cross the nearly 2,000 mile-long border with Mexico.

At the same time, the Obama administration was deporting record numbers of undocumented immigrants (over 2 million by the end of 2014), some of whom had been working in the nation for decades while others were Central American gang members. Obama, called the "Deporter in Chief" by critics, claimed that he was only following the laws written by anti-immigration Republicans. Others suggested that the president's harsh deportation policy was part of his "grand strategy" to force Congress to pass a comprehensive immigration reform bill. Either way, the immigrants were caught in the middle.

The Supreme Court in the Twenty-First Century

Supreme Court overturns the Defense of Marriage Act (DOMA) of 1996

The Supreme Court surprised observers in 2013 by overturning the Defense of Marriage Act (DOMA) of 1996, signed by President Bill Clinton, which had denied gay and lesbian couples who married in states allowing such unions the right to federal benefits. In *United States v. Windsor* (2013), the Court by a 5–4 vote ruled that the federal government could not withhold spousal benefits from same-sex couples who had been legally married. While restoring federal benefits, the Court did not rule that same-sex marriage is a *right* guaranteed under the U.S. Constitution. Each state, therefore, decided whether to allow such marriages. During 2014, however, federal courts repeatedly overturned state laws banning same-sex marriages, arguing that the Constitution guaranteed the right to marry.

Supreme Court dismantles the 1965 Voting Rights Act (2013)

While the Supreme Court disappointed social conservatives with its ruling in the *Windsor* case, the five conservatives on the Supreme Court continued to make rulings that restricted the powers of the federal government. In June 2013, in *Shelby County v. Holder* (2013), the Court gutted key provisions of the 1965 Voting Rights Act. The majority opinion declared that in five of the six southern states originally covered by the act, black voter turnout now exceeded white turnout. Soon after the Court's ruling, counties and states in the South pushed through new laws that had the effect of making it more difficult for minorities and poor people to vote by reducing voting hours or requiring that driver's licenses or other official forms of identification be shown on voting days.

The 2012 Election

As the November 2012 presidential election approached, one thing was certain: it would be the most expensive election ever, in part because the U.S. Supreme Court ruled in *Citizens United v. Federal Elections Committee* (2010) that corporations could spend as much as they wanted in support of candidates.

After a divisive battle in the primaries that included twenty televised debates with nearly a dozen other candidates, Mitt Romney won the Republican presidential nomination primarily because he promised, as a former corporate executive and Massachusetts governor, to accelerate economic growth.

Two things injured Romney's candidacy toward the end of the most expensive ($6 billion) campaign in history. First, he sought to please right-wing voters by opposing immigration reforms that might allow undocumented immigrants a pathway to citizenship. Second, journalists revealed late in the campaign that Romney had privately told a group of wealthy contributors that he "did not care" about the 47 percent of poor Americans who failed "to take personal responsibility and care for their lives." The Obama campaign seized on the impolitic statement, demonizing the wealthy Romney as an uncaring elitist. On Election Day, the president won with 66 million votes to Romney's 61 million, and 332 electoral votes to 206.

Embedded in the election returns were some striking statistics. Nearly 60 percent of white voters chose Romney. But the nation's fastest-growing groups—Hispanics, Asian Americans, and African Americans—voted overwhelmingly for Obama, as did college-educated women, white and nonwhite.

> Obama elected to a second term (2012)

Obamacare on the Defensive

President Obama's proudest achievement, the ACA, was so massive in its scope and complicated in its implementation that it took four years of preparation before it was ready to "roll out." In the fall of 2013, the federal online health insurance "exchange" where people without insurance, mostly the working poor, could sign up, opened with great fanfare. Obama assured Americans that using the new online registration system would be "real simple."

It was not. On October 1, millions tried to sign up for Obamacare online; few succeeded. The government website crashed. At the same time, it became evident that Obama had misled the nation about key elements of his health-care plan. In campaigning for its passage in 2010, he had repeatedly told voters that if they liked their current health insurance plan, they could, under Obamacare, "keep that insurance. Period. End of story." As it turned out, however, many saw their policies canceled by insurers. Nor did Obamacare fulfill its promise of making health insurance affordable to all.

A frantic effort to repair the ACA website bore fruit. By August 2014, over 9 million people, well above the original target number, had signed up for the new health insurance. "The Affordable Care Act is here to stay," President Obama assured a nation still uncertain of its benefits. Yet with each passing year, the ACA experienced setbacks. For too many people, the medical insurance grew too expensive and more inaccessible as companies dropped out of the marketplaces. In 2016, Obama admitted that "more work to reform the health care system [was] necessary" as health care in the United States remained the most expensive in the world and coverage remained out of reach for millions of Americans. Repealing Obamacare became the Republican battle cry as the party geared up for the 2016 elections.

New Global Challenges in an Age of Insecurity

> A limited nuclear negotiation with Iran

In 2013, the United States held its first high-level talks with Iran since 1979, when Iranian militants in Tehran stormed the U.S. embassy and took its employees hostage. On November 23, Secretary of State John Kerry, who succeeded Hillary Clinton in that role that year, reached a multinational agreement with Iran to scale back its nuclear development program for six months as a first step toward a more comprehensive agreement not to develop nuclear weapons that might threaten Israel or Iran's Arab neighbors.

> Russians avert U.S. intervention in Syria

At the same time that the United States was trying to reduce Iran's nuclear threat, an increasingly bloody civil war in Syria that had so far claimed 150,000 lives unleashed major international repercussions. In 2013, U.S. intelligence analysts confirmed that the Syrian government on August 21 had used chemical weapons to kill 1,400 people, many of them children. President Obama had repeatedly warned that the use of such WMD was a "red line" that would trigger international military intervention. In late August, he (and the French government) hesitantly began preparations for a military strike, although a war-fatigued Congress and most Americans opposed such action. On September 9, Secretary of State John Kerry defused the crisis by signing an agreement with Russia to dispose of Syria's chemical weapons.

By the end of October, the chemical weapon stockpiles at twenty-three locations had been destroyed or dismantled, but the ferocious civil war raged on, and there was no guarantee that Assad's regime had eliminated all its chemical weapons. Obama's reluctance to use force in Syria illustrated his reluctance to order another U.S. military intervention in the fractious and complex Middle East, especially after twelve years of inconclusive warfare in Iraq and Afghanistan that had cost more than 2,000 U.S. troops, 20,000 wounded, and almost $3 *trillion*.

Obama broke new ground by reestablishing formal diplomatic relations with Cuba in 2016. In March the U.S. president flew to Havana for meetings with the Castro regime. He was the first U.S. president to visit Cuba since Calvin Coolidge in 1928. As he told the Cuban people, "My lifetime has spanned a time of isolation between us. I have come here to bury the last remnant of the Cold War in the Americas."

As the Syrian civil war continued, a civil uprising occurred in Ukraine, the former Soviet republic of 46 million people that had gained its independence in 1991. For years, Russian president Vladimir Putin, who viewed the humiliating disintegration of the

VLADIMIR PUTIN President of Russia and former Soviet secret service agent, Putin led the Russian charge to take control of Crimea, in Ukraine.

Soviet Union as the "greatest geopolitical catastrophe of the century," had been trying to exert economic and political control over the republics of the former Soviet Union.

On February 27, Putin sent troops into the Crimea, a disputed part of the Ukraine. A week later, the Crimean parliament voted to become part of the Russian Federation. Putin, claiming that Crimea had "always been an inseparable part of Russia" even as he lied about the role of Russian troops in Crimea, quickly made the illegal annexation official.

The speed and ruthlessness with which Putin seized control of Crimea, mobilized 40,000 Russian troops on the Ukrainian border, and cut off Ukraine's crucial access to natural gas surprised President Obama and European leaders. It may not have been the start of a new Cold War, but it put an end to hope that Russia would become a trusted partner of the Western democracies. The United States and the European Union refused to recognize the legitimacy of Russia's annexation of Crimea, warned Russia not to invade eastern Ukraine, and announced economic sanctions against Russia while pledging financial assistance to struggling Ukraine. "If Russia continues to interfere in Ukraine, we stand ready to impose further sanctions," Obama said. By a vote of 100–11, the UN General Assembly also opposed Russia's annexation of Crimea.

CIVIL WAR IN UKRAINE A protester in the Ukrainian capital of Kiev throws a Molotov cocktail during violent clashes with police on January 22, 2014. A month later, Russian president Vladimir Putin would use the unrest as an excuse to seize control of the Crimean region.

In April 2014, heavily armed pro-Russian separatists, as many as a third of whom were in fact Russian soldiers and agents, seized control of several cities in eastern Ukraine, declared a "people's republic," and called for secession from Ukraine.

Pressure mounted on the United States and Europe to impose even more sanctions against Russia when a Malaysian passenger jet flying across eastern Ukraine was shot down by a Russian-made rocket in July 2014, killing all 298 on board, most of them Dutch citizens. The missile launcher was quickly spirited back into Russia. The United States and its allies slammed Russia with more severe economic sanctions, but the coldly calculating Putin showed no sign of backing away from his adventurism in Ukraine.

Sanctions over Russian aggression in Ukraine

Events overseas during the summer of 2014 gave Obama the opportunity to take decisive action. In June, the volatile Middle East took a sudden turn for the worse when Sunni jihadists from around the world (including the United States and Great Britain) who had been fighting in the civil war in

Syria against the Assad government invaded northern Iraq and announced the creation of their own nation ("caliphate"), called the Islamic State of Iraq and Syria (ISIS).

The Islamic State had become the largest, best equipped, and most brutal of the many Islamist terrorist groups, financing its far-flung operations and 40,000 fanatical fighters by selling oil and ransoming hostages.

In the face of the ISIS advance, many Iraqi government soldiers that the United States had spent billions of dollars training and equipping simply fled, leaving to ISIS their valuable weapons and vehicles. The bloodthirsty ISIS fighters seized huge tracts of territory in Syria and Iraq while gleefully enslaving, terrorizing, raping, massacring, crucifying, or beheading thousands who refused to embrace their ruthless version of the Sunni faith.

In August 2014, after ISIS terrorists gruesomely beheaded two captured Americans, President Obama ordered "systematic" air strikes in Iraq—and later Syria—to prevent genocide as well-armed and financed ISIS fighters assaulted Christians, Yazidis, and Kurds in the region. The U.S. president scored a diplomatic coup by building a broad coalition of Arab and European partners to avoid "going it alone" against the "cancer" of the Islamic State, but there was no doubt that American warplanes would bear the brunt of the action. Obama assured Americans that he would not "get dragged into another ground war." Although some criticized Obama's actions, he characterized the effort to stop the mass murder and mayhem by the Islamic State as "American leadership at its best." Still, Obama took no comfort from the fact that he would be the only president in history to have served two full terms with the nation at war.

The Rise of Populism

CORE **OBJECTIVE**

6. Explain the factors that led to Donald Trump's unexpected presidential nomination and election and assess Trump's early presidency.

In 2016, Peggy Noonan, a prominent Republican commentator who earlier had served as Ronald Reagan's speechwriter, observed, "Our country is stressed to the point of fracture—culturally, economically, politically, spiritually. We find it hard to hold together on a peaceful day, never mind a violent one." Her gloomy assessment was all too accurate. The toxic polarization of American society and politics was on full display during the 2016 presidential campaign in which hating the other side seemed to be the highest virtue.

The 2016 Presidential Primaries

The contest began early in the spring of 2015, driven largely by a seething sense of anger at the federal government among many voters fed up with cultural liberalism, bureaucratic incompetence, and the self-serving focus of party leaders. "Both parties have failed us," observed a lifelong conservative.

Economic grievances of "blue-collar" whites

Working-class ("blue-collar") whites felt they had legitimate grievances. Many had been left behind by the economic recovery and by globalization, their wages stagnant, their prospects limited, their hopes crushed. The real median income of white males in 2017 was less than what it had been in 1970. Blue-collar workers blamed their troubles on an unfair economic system that favored the wealthy, government-subsidized racial minorities, "job-stealing illegal immigrants," and the self-serving political "elite" in Washington. Two thirds of wage-earning Americans believed that the modern high-tech economy conspired against them and that politicians did not care.

By 2016, such shared economic anxieties and social resentments had coalesced into a grassroots "lily-white" nationalist backlash against Obama's presidency. The idiosyncratic New Yorker Donald Trump brilliantly stoked that frustration and rage to fuel his unconventional campaign for the Republican nomination. Never having run for elected office, he was the only candidate who knew that campaigning in the twenty-first century was above all a performance, and he offered his receptive audiences political theater at its best—and worst.

The Democratic Ticket

A handful of Democrats emerged as presidential candidates in 2015, but the race soon narrowed to two: Hillary Rodham Clinton, the former First Lady who had served as a New York U.S. senator and as secretary of state in the Obama administration, and seventy-four-year-old Vermont U.S. senator Bernard (Bernie) Sanders. The policy-fluent Clinton, a supreme political insider, represented the party establishment while Sanders, a rumpled socialist and grandfather of seven, known for his baggy suits and unruly white hair, excited progressive young Democrats who viewed the passionless Clinton as too conservative and too scripted, a lifelong politician whom a

> Democratic candidates: Clinton and Sanders

DEMOCRATIC CAMPAIGNS, 2016 Democrats in the 2016 primary election had two very different candidates to choose between. (Left) Hillary Rodham Clinton, the first woman ever to be nominated by a major political party, was saddled with a long history of establishment politics. (Right) Bernie Sanders, in contrast, was viewed as an outsider who represented a progressive, socialist platform.

majority of voters neither trusted nor liked. "She tries so hard to be real she just seems false," said an Ohio college student.

Sanders also savaged Clinton for pretending to be a friend of the common folk while hobnobbing with the rich and famous; she promised to protect American jobs but in fact boosted free-trade pacts (NAFTA) that ended up shutting down many plants and factories in the Rust Belt. In a bruising series of primaries, Clinton won thirty-four states while Sanders carried twenty-three, thereby becoming the first female major-party nominee in history. The party fight left permanent scars, however. Sanders's supporters believed that the leadership of the Democratic National Committee had conspired against their candidate, and many of them would withhold their vote for Clinton in the general election.

The Changing Republican Party

The Republican contest was more a carnival than a campaign. Seventeen men and women competed for the nomination—governors, senators, corporate executives—but one was both unlikely and unique: Donald Trump, a brash billionaire real estate developer and reality TV star who had never held elected office and had changed his party affiliation at least four times. Unlike the other candidates, however, he had *national* name recognition as a self-worshipping self-promoter. As he himself bragged, "There's nobody like me. Nobody."

> Trump's rhetoric and disregard for facts

In his best-selling promotional book, *The Art of the Deal* (1987), Trump celebrated political demagoguery when he argued that "truthful hyperbole" was the best way to be successful. That meant saying "what people wanted to hear"—whether it was true or not. He intentionally "played to people's fantasies. . . . People want to believe that something is the biggest and the greatest and the most spectacular." Exaggeration, in other words, was to him "a very effective form of promotion."

Trump's populist nationalism, anti-immigrant rhetoric, disregard for facts, and penchant for lying infuriated many traditional Republicans and divided the party during the primaries. "He's playing to people's prejudices and fears. It is no deeper than that," said Republican senator Lindsey Graham. Peggy Noonan spoke for many Republicans when she warned that candidate Trump lacked the "skill set" needed to be president: "discretion, carefulness, generosity, judgment. There's a clueless quality about him."

> Republicans against Trump

Initially, political analysts dismissed Trump as a buffoon rather than a serious candidate, full of brag and bluster. Yet his entertaining shoot-from-the-hip candor and volatile combativeness appealed to many voters. As his grassroots support grew, mainstream Republicans began to panic. Senator Marco Rubio of Florida expressed the consternation felt by many Republicans when he said that "we're on the verge of having someone take over the conservative movement and the Republican party who is a con artist."

Such concerns led the *National Review*, a leading Republican magazine, to center its January 2016 issue on a symposium titled "Against Trump." The editors explained that "Donald Trump is a menace to American conservatism who would take the work of generations and trample it underfoot in behalf of a populism as heedless and as crude as the Donald himself."

Yet such criticism from the party elite only validated Trump's popularity among disaffected voters attracted to the Tea Party. They tolerated his excesses and falsehoods because he spoke to their greatest concern: America was in decline and needed fixing—fast. They considered his volatile spontaneity refreshing and authentic, and they welcomed his outsider candidacy as a sharp contrast to traditional politicians.

The wealthiest of all the contenders yet the only one who refused to disclose his tax returns, Trump came across as an unrelenting business dynamo, a charismatic if crude and impulsive showman who displayed the ruthless skill to skewer his opponents and the mainstream media, claiming that most journalists produced "fake news." As a presidential candidate, he effectively portrayed himself as the ultimate "outsider" eager to "drain the swamp" of corruption in Washington, D.C. and "Make America Great Again," a slogan borrowed from Ronald Reagan.

> Trump as a political outsider

Trump viewed politics as a bruising battle of us versus them, the strong and the weak. His devoted followers relished the idea of a political crusade committed to throwing the rascals out of political power. To attend a Trump rally was to indulge in a ritual of hyped-up anger and brooding vengeance, at times accompanied by violence against protesters ("I'd like to punch him in the face," Trump assured his supporters who clashed with a demonstrator. "Get him outta here!") Supporters saw in Trump a leader who would eagerly exercise power, at home and abroad, someone not afraid to be politically *incorrect*. That Trump displayed admiration for the "tough guy," autocratic Russian ruler Vladimir Putin, whom he labeled a much more effective leader than Obama, perplexed traditional Republicans but did not faze his grassroots supporters.

A Campaign Like No Other

Americans had never seen a candidate as unconventional, unpredictable, thin-skinned, and inexplicable as Donald John Trump. Born in 1946 in Queens, a borough of New York City across the East River from Manhattan, he attended Fordham University for two years before transferring to the Wharton School of Business at the University of Pennsylvania, where he earned a degree in economics in 1968. After a medical exemption (bone spurs in his heels) enabled him to avoid military service during the Vietnam War, Trump followed his father, Fred, into commercial real estate development. His dad impressed upon Donald the importance of relentless self-promotion, the appearance of being tough, and the waging of total war against opponents. The younger Trump parlayed a large loan from his father into his own successful business, called the Trump Organization.

One of his major namesake projects, the gaudy fifty-eight-story Trump Tower, opened on Madison Avenue in Manhattan in 1982, replete with a three-story princely penthouse. Before meeting with investors in the project, "the Donald" told Der Scutt, Trump Tower's architect: "Give them

> Trump's business empire and brand

REPUBLICAN RALLY Donning his "Make America Great Again" baseball cap, Donald Trump speaks at a rally in Orlando, Florida, six days before the presidential election.

the old Trump bullshit. Tell them it is going to be a million square feet, sixty-eight stories." Scutt declined: "I don't lie, Donald." A few years later, Scutt explained that "when you hear a figure quoted by Trump, divide by two and then by four, and you're probably closer to the real answer."

After opening the iconic Tower, Trump expanded his business empire into the casino-gambling industry and later acquired numerous golf resorts around the world. His many projects were not without controversy. Several of them went bankrupt and others became the target of various legal disputes. All the while, Trump focused on building his name brand. He let everyone know that he was "really, really rich," which led the outsized celebrity developer to star in a popular NBC reality show called *The Apprentice*, in which contestants competed for a management position within the Trump Organization. The hit series proved to be a commercial for Trump himself, featuring him telling losing contestants, "You're fired!"

"Birther" movement

As early as 1999, Trump had flirted with the idea of running for president, but his interest did not grow serious until 2012, when he publicly announced his aspirations for the White House. At the start, however, his maverick candidacy was sidetracked by his ongoing efforts leading the "birther" movement, claiming that President Barack Obama was born in Kenya and therefore was an illegitimate president. Trump's frequent references to the groundless charges finally led Obama to provide his birth certificate to the media in 2011, but Trump persisted in his claims that the president was illegitimate. Only in 2016, after Trump realized he needed African American voters, did he concede that Obama was indeed American-born.

A negative vision of America

A master at the use of social media, especially infamous late-night Twitter rants, Trump fed upon and reinforced the anger felt by so many Americans left out of the economic recovery. He was one of the few candidates to discuss the terrible problems confronting Americans in the left-behind parts of the country, including the opioid drug epidemic, declining manufacturing jobs, and the rising cost of health care. He depicted a declining America besieged by Muslim terrorists and illegal immigrants ("bad hombres"), police killers, and self-serving liberal "elites" championing an unconstrained diversity at the expense of national security.

Bored or confused by the complexity of policies and issues, Trump instead offered simplistic solutions to complex problems. On the campaign trail, he preferred spontaneous remarks sprinkled with profanity over pre-pared speeches written by others, and he became justly famous for his fre-quent exaggerations, half-truths, vulgarity, outright falsehoods, and defiant demeanor. Lindsey Graham told a reporter that he did not think Trump was a racist but accused him of "playing the race card."

While campaigning on the slogan "Make America Great Again" through what he described as his "beautiful" record of business "deal-making," Trump headed a freewheeling campaign organization that often seemed in a state of perpetual disorder. His contradictory statements, absurd claims, and false charges occurred so frequently that fact-checkers could not keep up with them. Yet his strategy of making outrageous statements, then defending them, then explaining that he was just kidding, before finally confessing that he really did mean what he said, succeeded in capturing the daily headlines and dominating TV coverage.

Trump focused his appeal on the concerns of his supporters ("Trump-sters"), especially working-class whites with less than a college education in the South and in the crucial Midwest Rust Belt industrial states—Ohio, Michigan, Pennsylvania, West Virginia, and Wisconsin. "I love the poorly educated," he proudly affirmed at one campaign stop. "The hell with political correctness."

With each passing week, Trump grew more convinced that his emphasis on the fears of working-class whites would result in a "big crossover" of in-dependents, Democrats, and non-voters to his side. As a Trump supporter in New Hampshire explained, "He tells us what we all think but are afraid to say." The "country's spiraling downwards, people are not getting pay raises, and we're not the superpower we think we are."

In pledging to make America great again, Trump made an array of often outlandish promises that he would accomplish within months of taking of-fice: to repeal and replace Obamacare, appoint conservatives to the Supreme Court, cut income and corporate taxes, greatly increase the military budget, ban all Muslim immigrants and refugees, roll back government regulations, abandon the "unfair" NAFTA and TPP (Trans-Pacific Partnership) trade deals for taking away American jobs, "bomb the shit out of" ISIS, reinstate the use of torture on captured terrorists and torture their families as well, and reverse the Obama administration's environmental protections.

> Trump's platform

He repeatedly lashed out at "illegal immigrants," vowing to deport 11 million undocumented migrants and to build a "beautiful" wall along the entire 2,000-mile-long border with Mexico—and make the Mexican govern-ment pay for it—all in an effort to keep the "bad hombres" and "rapists" from flooding into America. When a skeptical journalist reminded Trump that America had never had Superman presidents, the cocksure candidate re-plied: "You will if you have Trump. You watch." Trump promised voters that he would "give you *everything*. Every dream you've ever dreamed for your country will come true."

To the surprise of pundits and the chagrin of party leaders, the bombastic Trump went from dark horse to front-runner. During the spring and

> Winning the Republican nomination

summer of 2016, he leapfrogged over his conventional rivals and won the Republican nomination in July, proclaiming, "I alone can fix" the many problems facing Americans. It was a truly stunning outcome. The raucous outsider and his populist insurgency had overturned the Republican party establishment and fractured the conservative movement.

Many leading Republicans, including former presidents George H. W. Bush and George W. Bush and former presidential nominees John McCain and Mitt Romney, were so alienated by Trump's unruly behavior and mean-spirited treatment of them that they refused both to attend the Republican nominating convention and to campaign for him. Texas senator Ted Cruz, who opposed Trump in the Republican primaries, spoke for many when he castigated the victorious Trump as "a pathological liar, utterly amoral, a narcissist at a level I don't think this country's ever seen, and a serial philanderer."

A Tumultuous Presidental Campaign

A mean-spirited campaign

In August 2015, Trump stressed that "this [was] not going to be an election on niceness." He fulfilled his pledge. The contest between Donald Trump and Hillary Clinton, the two most unpopular nominees in modern history, was thoroughly negative and nasty, a campaign more memorable for its soap-opera drama and playground insults than its policy issues or compelling proposals.

Trump dismissed "Crooked Hillary" as a "nasty woman," calling her the "most corrupt person ever to seek the presidency." He lampooned Clinton as a creature of the Wall Street financial elite who masqueraded as a friend of the people while raking in millions of ill-gotten dollars, including $675,000 paid to her by the world's largest investment bank, Goldman Sachs, for three speeches, none of which she was willing to share publicly. Her service as secretary of state, he charged, had produced only "death, destruction, terrorism, and weakness." If elected president, Trump promised, he would "put her in jail," leading his supporters to don "Lock Her Up" T-shirts.

For her part, Clinton portrayed Trump as manifestly unfit for the highest office in the land, labeling him a dangerous and unpredictable leader incapable of exercising the mature and stable judgment demanded of the modern presidency. Yet she hurt her cause when amid a fit of frustration she claimed, "You could put half of Trump's supporters into what I call the basket of deplorables" because they are "racist, sexist, homophobic, xenophobic, Islamophobic—you name it."

The most unconventional campaign in history led presidential historian Douglas Brinkley to describe it as both "tacky and tawdry." Even Paul Ryan, the Republican Speaker of the House, called Trump's slurs against a Mexican American federal judge "a textbook case of racism." To be sure, Trump's populist bigotry, like that of maverick Republican candidate Pat Buchanan in 1992 and 1996, played well with those who felt bypassed by globalization, but it also fostered a sense of us-against-them politics that further splintered an American electorate already sundered by class, creed, education, gender, religion, and race.

Scandals on All Sides The fall presidential campaign featured one startling surprise after another. On October 7, 2016, just two days before the second televised debate with Clinton, the *Washington Post* released a videotape from 2005 that showed a married Trump lewdly describing his unsolicited kissing and groping of women he had met during his frequent business trips. The taped comments ignited a media furor. Some leading Republicans dropped their support of Trump's candidacy. Others, like Paul Ryan, confessed that they could not in good conscience campaign for him.

A few prominent Republicans called for Trump to bow out of the race. Former Republican secretary of state Condoleezza Rice declared, "Donald Trump should *not* be president. He should withdraw." Yet Trump barreled on, dismissing his crude and controversial comments as simply "locker room talk." That he seemed to get away with anything during the campaign led him to believe in his own invincibility. "I could stand in the middle of Fifth Avenue and shoot people, and I wouldn't lose [my] voters," Trump boasted.

Hillary Clinton confronted her own scandals and skepticism. Only 30 percent of voters considered her "honest." For years, people had questioned how she and her husband, Bill, had channeled huge donations to the Clinton Foundation from foreign and domestic corporations and individuals. Then, in March 2015, the *New York Times* reported that Clinton, as secretary of state between 2009 and 2013, had used her family's e-mail server rather than the secure State Department server for her official communications. Her doing so violated departmental protocols, created a security risk that confidential ("classified") diplomatic e-mails might be hacked and monitored by foreign agents, and prevented the State Department from archiving her 62,000 messages. After an exhaustive investigation, the FBI director, **James B. Comey**, concluded that Clinton had been "extremely careless" in handling her e-mail but saw no point in prosecuting her.

Clinton confessed that her decision to use a personal server was a "mistake" resulting from her desire for "personal convenience," but Republican critics used the issue to call into question Clinton's honesty and reliability. Donald Trump charged that Clinton's use of a personal e-mail server was "worse than Watergate."

Then came more surprises. During the summer of 2016, agents of the Russian government "hacked" into the computer system of the Democratic National Committee and forwarded the data to WikiLeaks, which released tens of thousands of confidential Democratic messages intended to embarrass and burden the Clinton campaign. Even more bizarre was Donald Trump's response to the news. He urged the Russian government to

James B. Comey FBI director fired by President Donald Trump in 2017

Clinton's email scandal

JAMES COMEY IN CONGRESS FBI Director James Comey swears an oath before the House Oversight Committee on July 7, 2016, two days after announcing that he would not recommend pressing criminal charges against Hillary Clinton, after all. **How might Comey have changed the course of the 2016 Presidential Election?**

continue its efforts to influence the election: "Russia, if you're listening, I hope you're able to find the 30,000 e-mails that are missing."

On October 28, 2016, just eleven days before the presidential election, FBI director Comey publicly informed Congress that "in connection with an unrelated case, the FBI has learned of the existence of e-mails that appear pertinent to the investigation" of Hillary Clinton's use of her personal e-mail server. He added that the FBI was in the process of determining the relevance of those newly discovered messages to its ongoing investigation.

"October surprise"

This revelation was like a bomb hitting the Clinton campaign. It raised new questions about her presidential fitness and revealed that the ongoing investigation into her e-mails would continue beyond Election Day. Clinton would later claim that Comey's revelation ("October surprise") cost her the election. Perhaps it did, but Clinton also struggled throughout the fall to articulate a unifying vision or theme—or even a compelling explanation for *why* she should be the next president.

Trump wins the electoral college, Clinton wins the popular vote

Still, Clinton's narrow loss to Trump on November 8 surprised virtually everyone. Most observers believed that she had won the three televised debates, and the major polls had predicted a narrow Democratic victory. Yet Trump ended up with 304 electoral votes to her 227, leaving much of the country in a state of stunned disbelief. True, Clinton won 3 million more votes than Trump out of the 136 million ballots cast, garnering the largest total ever by a losing candidate, but she lost—by 78,000 votes—the crucial swing states of Michigan, Pennsylvania, and Wisconsin. Their electoral votes gave Trump the edge he needed.

Clinton's totals fell far short of Obama's numbers in 2012. Surveys revealed that voters by a 2–1 margin cared most about which candidate could bring change to Washington politics. Clinton struck many voters as offering more of the same. Her failure to win over white working- and lower middle-class males in the Rust Belt states was her downfall, along with the fact that many minority voters did not go to the polls.

While Trump positioned himself as the candidate of change, Clinton struggled as a lackluster defender of the status quo. At the close of her campaign, she could only offer a limp promise, "I'm not *him*." Voters wanted more. Shannon Goodin, a twenty-four-year-old first-time voter in Michigan, explained that Trump won her vote by being a "big poster child for change." She added that traditional "politicians don't appeal to us. Clinton would go out of her way to appeal to minorities, immigrants, but she didn't really care for everyday Americans."

A Populist President

Trump's triumph sent tremors and aftershocks across the world. His unexpected win toppled the political establishment of both parties and thrilled his supporters. Traditionally, the wealthiest Americans vote for Republican presidential candidates, but in the 2016 election, Trump's primary support was among the white working class. "The forgotten men and women of our country will be forgotten no longer," he said in his victory speech.

The reaction to Trump's victory

The chest-thumping president-elect, however, caused great anxiety among many seasoned observers of the political scene. An editorial in the *Los Angeles Times* expressed the concerns of many that the new president would lead the nation into uncharted waters: "Trump is a man so unpredictable, so reckless, so petulant, so full of blind self-regard . . . it is impossible to know where his presidency will lead or how much damage he will do to our nation."

Trump, moreover, would preside over a deeply divided nation. Millions of stunned Americans viewed his victory with unprecedented foreboding. Some talked of moving to Canada. The two Democratic leaders of the California legislature released a joint statement that reflected the feelings of most Democrats: "Today, we woke up feeling like strangers in a foreign land." New York's governor, Andrew Cuomo, felt the need in the aftermath of the election to assert that "we won't allow a federal government that attacks immigrants to do so in our state."

Women concerned about Trump's election organized mass demonstrations in January 2017 on behalf of women's rights, immigrants and refugees, improved healthcare, reproductive rights, LGBT (lesbian, gay, bisexual, transgender) rights, racial equality, freedom of religion, and workers' rights. Although a worldwide phenomenon, the Women's March was the largest one-day demonstration in U.S. history, encompassing demonstrations in some 400 American cities. The Women's March on Washington, D.C., which included a half million protesters, was designed to "send a bold message to our new administration on their first day in office, and to the world that women's rights are human rights." One of the speakers, feminist leader Gloria Steinem, directed her comments at President Trump: "Our Constitution does not begin with 'I, the President.' It begins with, 'We, the People.'"

At the same time, however, Trump's devoted voters relished a future of unconventional presidential action designed to end their alienation and bitterness. In his inaugural address, he assured the nation that his swearing-in ceremony would be "remembered as

WOMEN'S MARCH ON WASHINGTON On January 21, 2017, demonstrators flooded the National Mall in support of women's rights and reproductive justice, health-care and immigration reform, racial justice, LGBTQ rights, and other interconnected issues. The Washington demonstration was grounded in the nonviolent ideology of the civil rights movement, and went down as the largest coordinated protest in U.S. history; along with hundreds of global counterparts, it drew 5 million participants.

the day the people became the rulers of this nation again." He told his ecstatic working-class supporters that "you will never be ignored again," for he would uproot the political "establishment." An unapologetic and aggressive hypernationalism would be the theme of his administration: "From this day forward, it is going to be only America first—*America first.*"

A Chaos President

In December 2015, Florida Republican Jeb Bush made a prediction about then-candidate Trump. "Donald, you know, is great at the one-liners," Bush quipped at the final GOP presidential debate. "But he's a chaos candidate. And he'd be a chaos president." Indeed, Trump had promised his supporters that he would be a "disruptive" president from day one, and during his first hundred days in office, he more than fulfilled his pledge "to shake things up."

| Rocky beginnings: staffing the cabinet

Chaos and disruption followed in President Trump's wake as the oldest president (seventy), and the first with no experience in government or the military, forged a cabinet dominated by family members and wealthy loyalist ideologues, bankers, businessmen, and billionaires, mostly older white men with little government experience—or expertise.

Some of his closest aides, such as Steve Bannon, the White House chief strategist, and senior policy adviser Stephen Miller, were leaders of "alt-right" (alternative right) hypernationalist organizations that promoted white supremacy, anti-immigrant nativism, and America First trade policies while rejecting multiculturalism and political correctness.

| Early staffing changes in Trump's administration

Andy Puzder, Trump's nominee for labor secretary, withdrew after reporters discovered that he had employed an undocumented immigrant as his housekeeper for several years. More troubling for the new president was the forced resignation of his national security adviser, Michael Flynn, a former army lieutenant general who had led the Defense Intelligence Agency. Flynn, it turned out, had misled Vice President Mike Pence about secret conversations he had with the Russian ambassador. Flynn had claimed that they had discussed nothing of importance. In fact, however, he had mentioned the possibility of lifting U.S. sanctions against Russia. He had also violated protocols and laws by failing to disclose huge payments in 2015 from foreign companies linked to Russia and Turkey.

In 2017, Flynn offered to testify to congressional committees investigating Russian efforts to influence the presidential election in exchange for immunity from prosecution. Even more worrisome for the Trump administration was the news that the FBI was investigating the possibility that people associated with the Trump campaign had secretly collaborated with Russian efforts to torpedo Hillary Clinton's campaign.

| Trump's continued disregard for the truth

Trump vigorously denied that his untested new administration was anything but perfect. "I turn on the TV, open the newspapers, and I see stories of chaos" at the White House, he grumbled. "Chaos! This administration is running like a fine-tuned machine." In truth, however, as political journalist

Timothy Noah explained, "the Trump administration in its infancy [was] creating enough blunders, scandals, and controversies to strain the resources" of the White House press corps.

Even as president, Trump continued his compulsive issuance of sulfurous, defensive, misleading, inaccurate, or simply false "tweets" from his Twitter account as he waged a war of incendiary words and unfounded charges against "the fake news press" and his political opponents. In rapid succession, the tweeter-in-chief falsely claimed that the crowd at his inauguration was the largest ever, that President Obama had authorized wiretaps of him in Trump Tower, and that Hillary Clinton outpolled him in the 2016 election only by mobilizing millions of fraudulent voters.

That there was no evidence to support these and other charges did not faze Trump, who later told an interviewer, *I don't stand by anything.* As his White House counselor, Kellyanne Conway, explained, the president had access to "alternative facts." A *New York Times* columnist offered an alternative explanation. Trump, Charles M. Blow opined, "is a pathological liar." Indeed, Trump lied so often that websites kept count of his falsehoods (see, for example, www.politifact.com). "We've never seen anything this bizarre in our lifetimes, where up is down and down is up," noted Charles Lewis, founder of the Center for Public Integrity.

The President Tries to Take Action

In an effort to appear decisive and generate a sense of momentum for his presidency, Trump during his early months in the White House declared a freeze on most federal hiring, pressured several U.S. companies to abandon plans to build plants or factories overseas, and signed thirty-two executive orders reversing many of Obama's presidential directives regulating businesses and protecting the environment. (Trump saw nothing wrong with governing by executive orders even though he had been a vocal critic of Obama's doing so.)

The most controversial of Trump's executive orders was a temporary ban on immigrants and refugees from seven Muslim-majority nations. Within days, however, federal judges brusquely dismissed it as unconstitutional. A furious Trump scorned the "ridiculous" court ruling and pledged that it "will be overturned!" The president had not even shared the hastily written immigrant ban with his cabinet. Even Republicans called it a disaster. The editors of the *Wall Street Journal* described Trump's immigration order as "so poorly explained and prepared for, that it has produced fear and confusion at airports, an immediate legal defeat, and political fury at home and abroad."

Trump then told the Justice Department to prepare a revised travel ban, only to see it too overturned in June 2017 by the 9th U.S. Circuit Court of Appeals. The three federal judges unanimously ruled that Trump's latest ban on immigrants unconstitutionally discriminated against particular nationalities.

Unconstitutional "Muslim ban"

MUSLIM BAN A crowd of protesters gather at the Los Angeles International Airport on January 29, 2017, speaking out against President Trump's Executive Order to ban immigrants from certain Muslim-majority countries from entering the United States. **Why was the immigration ban deemed unconstitutional by certain federal judges?**

Appointing Gorsuch to the Supreme Court

Trump's greatest success early in his presidency was the appointment of a conservative justice to the Supreme Court. Although most Democrats opposed the nomination of Neil Gorsuch, a federal court of appeals judge with a sterling reputation, the Republican majority revised the Senate rules to push through his confirmation.

Tackling healthcare

Eventually, however, the novice president could not govern simply by issuing executive orders; he had to negotiate the passage of legislation. Throughout the presidential campaign, Trump had lambasted Obamacare, promising to replace it "on Day One" with a much better health-care program. "You're going to have such great health care at a tiny fraction of the cost, and it is going to be so easy," Trump pledged at a Florida rally in October 2016. To that end, he and Paul Ryan unveiled in early 2017 a new health-care proposal, called the American Health Care Act (AHCA). It would have removed many of the pillars of Obamacare, including the phasing out of Medicaid subsidies that had enabled millions of people to gain coverage for the first time.

Yet surveys showed that only 17 percent of voters liked the new bill. For that reason and others, Trump and Ryan could not get the Republican majority in the House to support "Trumpcare." Most members of the Freedom Caucus, a group of about thirty-five Tea Party Republicans, refused to

TRUMPCARE Speaker of the House Paul Ryan holds up a copy of the American Health Care Act in March 7, 2017. The Republican's bill to replace the Affordable Care Act was supremely unpopular.

support the president's plan because it retained too many elements of Obamacare. The powers of persuasion that Trump had displayed as a campaigner had not carried over to his presidency. Having spent so much energy claiming that Obamacare was a failure, Trump and Republicans could not agree on a cure.

The devastating failure of Trumpcare led Paul Ryan to acknowledge that the Republicans had yet to become a "governing party" even though they controlled the Congress and the White House. Trump, the self-described wizard at "deal-making," had been unable to strike a deal with members of his own party. Without making a speech to the nation in support of his plan, he instead demanded a quick vote on Trumpcare—and lost. Afterward, he meekly admitted to being surprised "that health care could be so complicated."

A similar fate befell Trump's other showcase campaign promise: building a "huge" wall along the Mexican border and forcing Mexico to pay for it. In late April 2017, the president acknowledged that he could not convince the Congress that "Trump's Wall" was worth the over $20 billion it was estimated to cost.

> Another failure: Trump's promised wall

Forging Foreign Policies

In foreign affairs, Trump's early actions were equally minimal, in part because he, like Harry Truman, had so little preparation for global leadership. Other than hosting several foreign dignitaries, talking tough toward rogue nations North Korea and Iran, and launching a volley of cruise missiles at a Syrian air base in retaliation for a chemical attack by the Syrian government on civilians, the president's view of America's role in the world remained muddled. In 2013, when Syria had first used chemical weapons against its opponents, killing a thousand people, Trump had urged President Obama: "Do not attack Syria. There is no upside and tremendous downside." Similarly, during his campaign against Clinton, he told Reuters news service that "we should not be focusing on Syria. You're going to end up in World War III over Syria if we listen to Hillary Clinton." He saw no need to explain his change of heart as president.

Equally remarkable were many other instances in which Trump reversed his stance on issues. To be sure, most presidents engage in such flip-flopping, but Trump was remarkable for the frequency of his about-faces. During the campaign, he had suggested that NATO was "obsolete," only to reverse his opinion as president. Likewise, he had called China a "currency manipulator" only to decide that China was not manipulating its money supply. And he changed course on the "awful" deal negotiated by Obama's administration to freeze Iran's efforts to develop nuclear weapons. In April 2017, he decided that the deal was working well. He also pledged to remove the United States from NAFTA but announced on April 27 that America would stay. When asked about his many flip-flops, Trump lamely answered that he was "capable of changing to anything I want to change to."

The Hundred-Day Mark

By the end of his first hundred days in office, Trump was floundering as a result of his self-inflicted wounds, clumsy missteps and numerous contradictions, and naive understanding of the political process. At times, the Trump administration seemed overwhelmed by the tasks facing it. Of the 556 executive branch positions requiring Senate confirmation, Trump had filled only a few dozen by the summer of 2017, in part because he insisted on personally approving every nominee.

| An ineffective first hundred days |

During the campaign, Trump had pledged to generate ten significant pieces of legislation by the end of April 2017. In fact, however, he had no major legislation to his credit and the lowest public approval rating (37 percent) of any first-term president, in part because he had reversed himself on five of his campaign pledges.

The deal-making president who had promised to outdo Franklin Roosevelt in his first hundred days was unable to garner enough support in Congress to launch his agenda and spent much of his time defending himself from attacks coming from all sides. In an early assessment of the Trump presidency, Jennifer Rubin, a conservative columnist, saw "nothing much of substance" accomplished because of "an unhinged president, too many weak aides, and an administration that cannot control itself." Trump, in her view, had overpromised and underdelivered on his most important campaign promises. He had become "all flash and big talk, with very little substance."

Yet Trump defiantly issued the patently false claim that "no administration has accomplished more in the first 100 days." Within the White House, aides abided by the president's claim of infallibility. There would be no admission of errors, much less apologies. True, every new president and administration make mistakes early on, when they are least experienced, but Trump refused to accept responsibility for any shortcomings. "I think the man who came [to the White House] to drain the swamp might have become the creature from the black lagoon," said Mark Meckler, co-founder of the Tea Party Patriots and a vocal Trump supporter during the 2016 campaign. "Trump is separating himself from his own base [of support]." One of those alienated supporters complained of "getting tired of [Trump's promises of] 'biggest wall,' 'biggest bomb,' 'biggest tax cut.' How about something that can actually happen?"

At the end of his first hundred days, as political commentators rushed to evaluate the new president's performance, Trump confessed to a Reuters reporter that he was not enjoying his presidential duties: "I loved my previous life. I had so many things going." Being president, however, was much "more work than in my previous life. I thought it would be easier." In fact, during the 2016 campaign, he had repeatedly claimed how "easy" it would be for him to make fundamental changes in federal policies and legislative programs.

The Russia Scandal

Nothing came easy for the new Trump administration. However, on May 9, 2017, the president stunned the nation by summarily firing James Comey, the FBI director, who was leading the agency's investigation into contacts between the Trump campaign and Russia. White House aides had initially claimed that Trump had let Comey go because of the way he had "mishandled" the Hillary Clinton e-mail investigation, only to have the president contradict them the next day when he acknowledged that he had grown frustrated by Comey's ongoing investigation of Russian involvement in the campaign.

Only days later, the *New York Times* reported that Comey, afraid that the president "might lie" about their conversations, had created detailed summaries of his meetings with the president. Comey's notes revealed that Trump, just days after his inauguration, had inappropriately demanded the FBI director's "loyalty" during a private White House dinner. Then, on February 14, the president had ordered all aides to leave the Oval Office before privately asking Comey to drop the investigation into Michael Flynn's illegal interactions with Russian officials, pleading with him to "let this go."

Trump denied the story, but on the face of it, the bombshell revelations about his interactions with the FBI director suggested that the president may have engaged in obstruction of justice, a criminal offense. "The country is being tested in unprecedented ways," said Senate minority leader Chuck Schumer on the Senate floor. "I say to all of my colleagues in the Senate:

history is watching" how legislators would respond to the constitutional crisis emerging within the Trump administration.

During the spring and summer of 2017, several leading Republicans expressed alarm about the president's erratic behavior. Senate Foreign Relations Committee chair Bob Corker, a Tennessee Republican, said the Trump White House was "in a downward spiral." Senator John McCain compared the mushrooming scandal to Watergate in its "size and scale." John Boehner, the former Speaker of the House, remarked that Trump's young presidency had mostly been "a disaster."

Organizing a Russian Investigation

On May 18, 2017, Rod Rosenstein, the deputy attorney general, felt compelled to appoint a special counsel, Robert Mueller III, a former FBI director, to organize a criminal investigation of Russian involvement in the 2016 presidential campaign. In a TV interview, Trump admitted that he fired Comey because the investigation into Russia's efforts to influence the 2016 election was frustrating him, virtually admitting that he had engaged in obstruction of justice. Even Steve Bannon, Trump's chief strategist, lambasted the president's decision to fire Comey, calling it the "biggest mistake in modern political history."

A drop in public opinion

As the numerous investigations continued, public perceptions of Trump plummeted. By June 2017, an Associated Press poll revealed that nearly two thirds of Americans disapproved of the new president's job performance, and a similar number did not think that Trump embraced the nation's democratic principles and institutions.

Trump's response to such embarrassing news was consistently combative and self-pitying. On May 18, he tweeted that his administration was the victim of the greatest "witch hunt" in history. Witch hunt or not, Trump now faced the prospect of a prolonged criminal investigation shrouding the White House and playing havoc with his fumbling efforts to fulfill his campaign promises.

The Trump Presidency

Still, Trump continued to claim that he was more effective than virtually any previous presidents. The cavernous gap between his presidential performance and his self-congratulatory boasts led a growing number of observers, both Democrats and Republicans, to wonder if voters had been conned by a man expert at selling illusions and turning politics into spectacle. While Trump's most ardent supporters claimed that they would vote for him again, others doubted that he would ever become the president he had pledged to be.

That was Trump's greatest concern, too, for no president had sought public acclaim more than he did. On June 12, 2017, the praise-addicted president hosted his first televised cabinet meeting at which he shocked reporters and humiliated his cabinet officers by asking them one-by-one to pay tribute to him for the cameras. Their craven toadyism appalled many observers. John Harwell, a veteran CNBC journalist who had spent thirty years covering the

White House, had "never seen such an extended public display of flattery for a president from his chosen subordinates. At moments it resembled the kind of fawning that some of the strongmen rulers Trump has praised . . . might receive from their deputies."

Trump's brutish narcissism led Senator Graham to tell the president: "You are your own worst enemy." He characterized Trump as "a bull in a china shop, crude and rude." Yet the president largely ignored such criticism from within his own party. Careless in his treatment of America's closest allies and inconsistent in his foreign policies, often indifferent or bored by the substance of issues, the leader of the free world needed to display greater statesmanship and deeper knowledge of international affairs—and a certain generosity of spirit and humility.

During his first year in office, however, President Trump seemed unable to summon up those qualities of leadership. The White House remained a weekly soap opera featuring constant turmoil, infighting, and backbiting as the wounded administration lurched from one self-inflicted crisis to another. By September 2017, most of Trump's inner circle of aides and advisers had resigned or been fired, including the national security adviser, the chief strategist, the chief of staff, and press secretary. In just eight months, Trump appointed four communications directors. "I can't even think of a presidency which controls both houses of Congress getting off to such a weird, unpredictable, chaotic start," said David Gergen, who had served as a White House adviser to four presidents, both Democrats and Republicans.

The buffeted president for once acknowledged his missteps. "This has to go better," Trump muttered in frustration. On that point, the nation—and the world—agreed.

Reviewing the
CORE OBJECTIVES |

■ **Changing Demographics** From 1980 to 2010, the U.S. population grew by 25 percent, to 306 million, and was more racially and ethnically diverse. Because of a wave of immigration from Latin America, Hispanics surpassed African Americans as the nation's largest minority. The rate at which the nonwhite population increased had quadrupled since the 1970s. By 2012, the U.S. population included more foreign-born and first-generation residents than ever before.

■ **Divided Government** Just two years into the presidency of "New Democrat" Bill Clinton, Republican Speaker of the House Newt Gingrich crafted his *Contract with America (1994)* against the "corrupt liberal welfare state" and achieved a Republican landslide in the 1994 midterm elections. The *North American Free Trade Act (NAFTA) (1994)* and the *Personal Responsibility and Work Opportunity Act of 1996 (PRWOA)* were bipartisan successes. The prosperous high-tech *new economy* helped Clinton balance the federal budget. Yet Clinton's personal scandals tarnished his presidency, and in 1998 he was impeached, though ultimately acquitted by the Senate.

■ **Global Terrorism** The 9/11 terrorist attacks led President George W. Bush to declare a *war on terror*. The United States invaded Afghanistan (Operation Enduring Freedom). Congress also authorized the Office of Homeland Security and the *USA Patriot Act (2001)*. In 2003, the Bush administration invoked the *Bush Doctrine* against Saddam Hussein, the leader of Iraq. The Second Iraq War succeeded in removing Hussein from power but turned up no weapons of mass destruction. The administration was unprepared to establish order in postwar Iraq, which was soon wracked by sectarian violence. Americans became bitterly divided over the war and whether the Bush Doctrine enhanced U.S. security.

■ **A Historic Election** The 2008 Democratic primaries became a contest between two senators, Hillary Clinton and Barack Obama. In the end, Obama won. The Republicans nominated Senator John McCain, the oldest candidate in history. Obama won the popular vote and a landslide victory in the Electoral College, becoming the nation's first African American president. His victory resulted from public dismay about the *Great Recession (2007–2009)* and weariness with Bush's policies, especially the ongoing wars in Iraq and Afghanistan.

■ **Obama's Priorities** Obama's first priority was shoring up the failing economy through controversial Wall Street bailouts and a huge economic stimulus package: the American Recovery and Reinvestment Act. Economic recovery remained sluggish and unequal, widening the economic divide and spawning the Occupy Wall Street movement. Obama's legacy legislation, the 2010 *Affordable Care Act (ACA),* incited bitter opposition from the *Tea Party*. Obama reduced the U.S. military abroad, removing all combat troops from Iraq in 2011, downsizing their presence in Afghanistan, and refusing to make broad military commitments in the Arab Awakening.

■ **2016 Election** The 2016 election was a historic one in many respects. The Democrats nominated the first female candidate for the presidency, Hillary Clinton, and the Republicans nominated a brash billionaire developer, Donald Trump, who had no political experience. Trump won a close race because of his appeal to "angry" working-class white voters eager for real change in Washington. Change was what they got, for President Trump proved to be the most unpredictable chief executive in history.

KEY TERMS

North American Free Trade Agreement (NAFTA) (1994) *p. 1164*

Contract with America (1994) *p. 1166*

Personal Responsibility and Work Opportunity Act of 1996 (PRWOA) *p. 1167*

new economy *p. 1168*

globalization *p. 1168*

ethnic cleansing *p. 1170*

war on terror *p. 1175*

USA Patriot Act (2001) *p. 1176*

Bush Doctrine *p. 1177*

Great Recession (2007–2009) *p. 1182*

Affordable Care Act (ACA) (2010) *p. 1185*

Tea Party *p. 1189*

same-sex marriage *p. 1191*

James Comey *p. 1203*

CHRONOLOGY

1991	Ethnic conflict explodes in Yugoslavia
1994	NAFTA goes into effect
	Contract with America
1996	Congress passes welfare reform
1998	President Clinton impeached
2000	Supreme Court issues *Bush v. Gore* decision
Sept. 11, 2001	9/11 Terrorist attacks
October 2001	Operation Enduring Freedom begins
2003	Iraq War begins
August 2005	Hurricane Katrina
2007	Great Recession begins
2008	Barack Obama elected president
	Tea Party movement begins
2010	Congress passes the Affordable Care Act (ACA)
2011	Occupy Wall Street, Arab Awakening
August 2011	Osama bin Laden killed
2013	Defense of Marriage Act (DOMA) overturned
2014	Islamic State of Iraq and Syria (ISIS) established
January 2017	Donald Trump begins presidency

⚙ INQUIZITIVE

Go to InQuizitive to see what you've learned—and learn what you've missed—with personalized feedback along the way.

DEBATING Contemporary Immigration and the Uses of History

The study of history informs how we think about society today. Comparisons with the past are an essential part of how policy makers and citizens debate key issues. For instance, one of the most controversial topics in American society is immigration, and many arguments hinge on comparisons to past generations of immigrants and how they were perceived at the time. For Part 7, *"The American Age,"* the issue of Latino immigration demonstrates how history influences contemporary political debates. For this exercise, you will be taking on the role of historian, and thus you should focus on evaluating the uses of history, not current immigration policy.

For this exercise you have two tasks:

PART 1: Compare the ways that history is used in the two secondary sources on contemporary Latino immigration.

PART 2: Using primary sources, evaluate the arguments of the two secondary sources.

PART I Comparing Secondary Sources

Each of the following secondary sources was written by a scholar of contemporary immigration politics. In these selections, the authors draw comparisons between the issues surrounding past generations of immigrants and the issues surrounding immigrants today. The first is from Dr. Jason Richwine, a contributing writer at the *National Review* and former senior policy analyst at the Heritage Foundation. The second text is from Leo Chavez, a professor of anthropology at the University of California–Irvine. While Richwine is interested in assimilation, immigration, and national culture, Chavez is concerned with how immigrant groups are represented in contemporary discourse.

Compare the views of these two scholars by answering the following questions. Be sure to find specific examples in the selections to support your answers.

■ What issues that surround Latino immigration to America does each author address?

■ What comparisons does each author make to historical immigration groups?

■ In what ways might these authors respond to each other's work?

■ Based on what you have learned, what examples from American history can you think of that would support or refute each author's argument?

Secondary Source 1

Jason Richwine, "The Congealing Pot" (2009)

They're not just like the Irish—or the Italians or the Poles, for that matter. The large influx of Hispanic immigrants after 1965 represents a unique assimilation challenge for the United States. Many optimistic observers have assumed—incorrectly, it turns out—that Hispanic immigrants will follow the same economic trajectory European immigrants did in the early part of the last century. Many of those Europeans came to America with no money and few skills, but their status steadily improved. Their children outperformed them, and their children's children were often indistinguishable from the "founding stock." The speed of economic assimilation varied somewhat by ethnic group, but three generations were typically enough to turn "ethnics" into plain old Americans.

This would be the preferred outcome for the tens of millions of Hispanic Americans, who are significantly poorer and less educated on average than native whites. When immigration skeptics question the wisdom of importing so many unskilled people into our nation at one time, the most common response cites the remarkable progress of Europeans a century ago. "People used to say the Irish or the Poles would always be poor, but look at them today!" For Hispanics, we are led to believe, the same thing will happen.

But that claim isn't true. Though about three-quarters of Hispanics living in the U.S. today are either immigrants or the children of immigrants, a significant number have roots here going back many generations. We have several ways to measure their intergenerational progress, and the results leave little room for optimism about their prospects for assimilation....

First, the second generation still does not come close to matching the socioeconomic status of white natives. Even if Hispanics were to keep climbing the ladder each generation, their assimilation would be markedly slower than that of other groups. But even that view is overly optimistic, because of the second, larger problem with Hispanic assimilation: It appears to stall after the second generation. We see little further ladder-climbing from the grandchildren of Hispanic immigrants. They do not rise out of the lower class....

So why do Hispanics, on average, not assimilate? Theories abound. Popular explanations from the left include the legacy of white racism, labor-market discrimination, housing segregation, and poor educational opportunities. Those on the right tend to cite enforced multi-culturalism, ethnic enclaves, and a self-perpetuating culture of poverty.... [T]he lack of Hispanic assimilation is likely to create ethnic tensions that threaten our cultural core. Human beings are a tribal species, and this makes ethnicity a natural fault line in any society. Intra-European ethnic divisions have been largely overcome through economic assimilation—Irish and Italian immigrants may have looked a bit different from natives, but by the third generation their socioeconomic profiles were similar. Hispanic Americans do not have that benefit.

Persistent ethnic disparities in socioeconomic status add to a sense of "otherness" felt by minorities outside the economic mainstream. Though it is encouraging that Hispanics often profess a belief in the American creed, an undercurrent of this "otherness" is still apparent. For example, a Pew Hispanic Center Survey in 2002 asked American-born Hispanics "which terms they would use first to describe themselves." Less than half (46 percent) said "American," while the majority said they primarily identified either with their ancestral country or as simply Hispanic or Latino....

It is difficult to see how a unifying national culture can be preserved and extended in that environment.

Source: Richwine, Jason. "The Congealing Pot." *National Review* August 24, 2009, pp. 37–39.

Secondary Source 2
Leo Chavez, *The Latino Threat* (2008)

This book grew out of my attempt to unpack the meanings of ... [negative] views about Latinos. Rather than considering them in isolation, I began to see them as connected, as part of a larger set of concerns over immigration, particularly from Mexico and other parts of Latin America; the meaning of citizenship; and the power of media spectacles in contemporary life. The Latino Threat Narrative provides the raw material that weaves these concerns together.

The Latino Threat Narrative posits that Latinos are not like previous immigrant groups, who ultimately became part of the nation. According to the assumptions and taken-for-granted "truths" inherent in this narrative, Latinos are unwilling or incapable of integrating, of becoming part of the national community. Rather, they are part of an invading force from south of the border that is bent on reconquering land that was formerly theirs (the U.S. Southwest) and destroying the American way of life....

The contemporary Latino Threat Narrative has its antecedents in U.S. history: the German language threat, the Catholic threat, the Chinese and Japanese immigration threats, and the southern and eastern European threat. In their day, each discourse of threat targeted particular immigrant groups and their children. Each was pervasive and defined "truths" about the threats posed by immigrants that, in hindsight, were unjustified or never materialized in the long run of history. And each of these discourses generated actions, such as alarmist newspaper stories (the media of the day), anti-immigrant riots, restrictive immigration laws, forced internments, and acrimonious public debates over government policies. In this sense, the Latino Threat Narrative is part of a grand tradition of alarmist discourse about immigrants and their perceived negative impacts on society....

Latinos have been in what is now the United States since the late sixteenth and early seventeenth centuries, actually predating the English colonies. Since the Mexican-American War, immigration from Mexico and other Latin countries has waxed and waned, building in the early twentieth century, diminishing in the 1930s, and building again the post-1965 years. These migrations paralleled those of other immigrant groups. But Mexicans in particular have been represented as the quintessential "illegal aliens," which distinguishes them from other immigrant groups. Their social identity has been plagued by the mark of illegality, which in much public discourse means that they are criminals and thus illegitimate members of society undeserving of social benefits, including citizenship. Latinos are an alleged threat because of this history and social identity, which supposedly make their integration difficult and imbue them, particularly Mexicans, with a desire to remain socially apart as they prepare for a reconquest of the U.S. Southwest.

Source: Chavez, Leo. *The Latino Threat: Constructing Immigrants, Citizens, and the Nation.* Redwood City, Calif.: Stanford University Press, 2008. 3–4.

PART II Using Primary Sources to Evaluate Secondary Sources

When historians confront competing interpretations of the past, they often look at primary-source material to help evaluate the different arguments. Below is a selection of primary source materials relating to some of the historical issues surrounding immigration and assimilation raised by the two authors. The first document is excerpted from a short essay, one of the first works on demography, by Benjamin Franklin in 1751. The second document is an 1878 statement from the California State Senate to Congress requesting that Chinese immigration to the United States be restricted. The third document is an article by Republican senator Henry Cabot Lodge of Massachusetts, a leading immigration restrictionist who was instrumental in the passage of such legislation in the 1920s. The final document is from the 1963 book *Beyond the Melting Pot: The Negroes, Puerto Ricans, Jews, Italians, and Irish of New York City* by sociologist Nathan Glazer and future U.S. senator Daniel Patrick Moynihan. This book appeared just prior to the liberalization of U.S. immigration policy in 1965 and explores the assimilation of various ethnic groups in New York City.

Carefully read each of the primary sources and answer the following questions. Decide which of the primary source documents support or refute the authors' arguments on immigration and assimilation. You may find that some documents do both but for different parts of each author's interpretation. Be sure to identify which specific components of each author's argument the documents support or refute.

■ How does each document address the issue of assimilation and identity?

■ Based on these documents, what pattern do you see in how Americans historically have responded to the arrival of new immigrant groups?

■ Which of the primary sources do you think Richwine and Chavez would find most useful, and how might they use them to support their arguments?

■ Which of the secondary sources do you think is best supported by the primary source evidence?

Primary Source 1

Benjamin Franklin, *Observations Concerning the Increase of Mankind, Peopling of Countries, etc.* (1755)

And since detachments of English from Britain sent to America, will have their places at home so soon supply'd and increase so largely here; why should the Palatine Boors [Germans] be suffered to swarm into our settlements, and by herding together establish their languages and manners to the exclusion of ours? Why should Pennsylvania, founded by the English, become a colony of Aliens, who will shortly be so numerous as to Germanize us instead of our Anglifying them, and will never adopt our language or customs, any more than they can acquire our complexion? Which leads me to add one remark: That the number of purely white people in the world is proportionally very small. All Africa is black or tawny. Asia chiefly tawny. America (exclusive of the new comers) wholly so. And in Europe, the Spaniards, Italians, French, Russians, and Swedes are generally of what we call a swarthy complexion; as are the Germans also, the Saxons only excepted, who with the English make the principal body of white people on the face of the earth. I could wish their numbers were increased. And while we are, as I may call it, scouring our planet, by clearing America of woods, and so making this side of our globe reflect a brighter light to the eyes of inhabitants in Mars or Venus, why should we in the sight of superior beings, darken its people? Why increase the sons of Africa, by planting them in America, where we have so fair an opportunity, by excluding all blacks and tawneys, of increasing the lovely white and red? But perhaps I am partial to the complexion of my Country, for such kind of partiality is natural to Mankind.

Source: Franklin, Benjamin. *Observations Concerning the Increase of Mankind, Peopling of Countries, etc.* Boston: Printed and Sold by S. Kneeland in Queen Street, 1755. 224.

Primary Source 2

Senate of California to the Congress, "Memorial of the Senate of California to the Congress of the United States" (1878)

The State of California has a population variously estimated at from seven hundred thousand to eight hundred thousand, of which one hundred and twenty-five thousand are Chinese. The additions to this class have been very rapid since the organization of the State, but have been caused almost entirely by immigration, and scarcely at all by natural increase. . . .

The pious anticipations that the influence of Christianity upon the Chinese would be salutary, have proved unsubstantial and vain. Among one hundred and twenty-five thousand of them, with a residence here beneath the elevating influences of Christian precept and example, and with the zealous labors of earnest Christian teachers, and the liberal expenditure of ecclesiastical revenues, we have no evidence of a single genuine conversion to Christianity, or of a single instance of an assimilation with our manners, or habits of thought or life. . . . Neither is there any possibility that in the future education, religion, or the other influences of our civilization can effect any change in this condition of things. . . .

Above and beyond these considerations, however, we believe, and the researches of those who have most attentively studied the Chinese character confirm us in the consideration, that the Chinese are incapable of adaptation to our institutions. The national intellect of China has become decrepit from sheer age. It has long since passed its prime and is waning into senility. . . . Their code of morals, their forms of worship, and their maxims of life are those of the remotest antiquity. In this aspect they stand a barrier against which the elevating tendency of a higher civilization exerts itself in vain. And, in an ethnological point of view, there can be no hope that any contact with our people, however long continued, will ever conform them to our institutions, enable them to comprehend or appreciate our form of government, or to assume the duties or discharge the functions of citizens.

During their entire settlement in California they have never adapted themselves to our habits, modes of dress, or our educational system, have never learned the sanctity of an oath, never desired to become citizens, or to perform the duties of citizenship, never discovered the difference between right and wrong, never ceased the worship of their idol gods, or advanced a step beyond the musty traditions of their native hive. Impregnable to all the influences of our Anglo-Saxon life, they remain the same stolid Asiatics that have floated on the rivers and slaved in the fields of China for thirty centuries of time.

We thus find one-sixth of our entire population composed of Chinese coolies, not involuntary, but, by the unalterable structure of their intellectual being, voluntary slaves. This alien mass, constantly increasing by Immigration, is injected into a republic of freemen, eating of its substance, expelling free white labor, and contributing nothing to the support of the government. All the physical conditions of California are in the highest degree favorable to their influx. Our climate is essentially Asiatic in all its aspects. And the Federal Government by its legislation and treaties fosters and promotes the immigration. What is to be the result? Does it require any prophetic power to foretell? Can American statesmen project their vision forward for a quarter of a century and convince themselves that this problem will work out for itself a wise solution? In that brief period, with the same ratio of increase, this fair State will contain a Chinese population outnumbering its free men. White labor will be unknown, because unobtainable, and then how long a period will elapse before California will, nay must, become essentially . . . lesser Asia, with all its deathly lethargy?

Source: "Memorial of the Senate of California to the Congress of the United States." *Chinese Immigration; Its Social, Moral, and Political Effect. Report to the California State Senate of Its Special Committee on Chinese Immigration*. Sacramento, Calif.: State Office, F. P. Thompson, Supt. State Printing, 1878. 60, 62–64.

Primary Source 3

Henry Cabot Lodge, "The Restriction of Immigration" (1891)

The nations of Europe which chiefly contributed to the upbuilding of the original thirteen colonies were the English, the Scotch-Irish, so called, the Dutch, the Germans, and the Huguenot French. With the exception of the last they were practically all people of the same stock. During this century and until very recent years these same nations, with the addition of Ireland and the Scandinavian countries, have continued to furnish the chief component parts of the immigration which has helped to populate so rapidly the territory of the United States. Among all these people, with few exceptions, community of race or language, or both, has facilitated the work of assimilation. In the last ten years, however, as appears from the figures just given, new and wholly different elements have been introduced into our immigration, and what is more important still the rate of immigration of these new elements has risen with much greater rapidity than that of those which previously had furnished the bulk of the population of the country. The mass of immigration, absolutely speaking, continues, of course, to come from the United Kingdom and from Germany, but relatively the immigration from these two sources is declining rapidly in comparison with the immigration from Italy and from the Slavic countries of Russia, Poland, Hungary, and Bohemia, the last of which appears under the head of Austria. . . .

Thus it is proved, first, that immigration to this country is increasing, and, second, that it is making its greatest relative increase from races most alien to the body of the American people and from the lowest and most illiterate classes among those races. In other words, it is apparent that, while our immigration is increasing, it is showing at the same time a marked tendency to deteriorate in character. . . . As one example of the practical effect of unrestricted immigration the committee [of the Fiftieth Congress to investigate immigration] cite the case of the coal-mining country: "Generally speaking, the class of immigrants who have lately been imported and employed in the coal regions of this country are not such, in the opinion of the committee, as would make desirable inhabitants of the United States. They are of a very low order of intelligence. They do not come here with the intention of becoming citizens; their whole purpose being to accumulate by parsimonious, rigid, and unhealthy economy a sum of money and then return to their native land. They live in miserable sheds like beasts; the food they eat is so meagre, scant, unwholesome, and revolting that it would nauseate and disgust an American workman, and he would find it difficult to sustain life upon it. Their habits are vicious, their customs are disgusting, and the effect of their presence here upon our social condition is to be deplored. . . . [I]n the opinion of the committee, no amount of effort would improve their morals or 'Americanize' this class of immigrants."

Source: Lodge, Henry Cabot. "The Restriction of Immigration," *North American Review* 152, no. 410 (January 1891): 28, 30, 32–33.

Primary Source 4

Nathan Glazer and Daniel Patrick Moynihan, *Beyond the Melting Pot* (1963)

Perhaps the meaning of ethnic labels will yet be erased in America. But it has not yet worked out this way in New York. It is true that immigrants to this country were rapidly transformed, in comparison with immigrants to other countries, that they lost their language and altered their culture. It was reasonable to believe that a new American type would emerge, a new nationality in which it would be a matter of indifference whether a man was of Anglo-Saxon or German or Italian or Jewish origin, and in which indeed, because of the diffusion of populations through all parts of the country and all levels of the social order, and because of the consequent close contact and intermarriage, it would be impossible to make such distinctions. This may still be the most likely result in the long run. After all, in 1960 almost half of New York City's population was still foreign-born

or the children of foreign-born. Yet it is also true that it is forty years since the end of mass immigration, and new processes, scarcely visible when our chief concern was with the great masses of immigrants and the problems of their "Americanization," now emerge to surprise us. The initial notion of an American melting pot did not, it seems, quite grasp what would happen in America. At least it did not grasp what would happen in the short run, and since this short run encompasses at least the length of a normal lifetime, it is not something we can ignore.

It is true that language and culture are very largely lost in the first and second generations, and this makes the dream of "cultural pluralism"—of a new Italy or Germany or Ireland in America, a League of Nations established in the New World—as unlikely as the hope of a "melting pot." But as the groups were transformed by influences in American society, stripped of their original attributes, they were recreated as something new, but still as identifiable groups. Concretely, persons think of themselves as members of that group, with that name; they are thought of by others as members of that group, with that name; and most significantly, they are linked to other members of the group by new attributes that the original immigrants would never have recognized as identifying their group, but which nevertheless serve to mark them off, by more than simply name and association, in the third generation and even beyond.

The assimilating power of American society and culture operated on immigrant groups in different ways, to make them, it is true, something they had not been, but still something distinct and identifiable. The impact of assimilating trends on the groups is different in part because the groups are different—Catholic peasants from southern Italy were affected differently, in the same city and the same time, from urbanized Jewish workers and merchants from Eastern Europe. . . .

Conceivably the fact that one's origins can become only a memory suggests the general direction for ethnic groups in the United States—toward assimilation and absorption into a homogeneous American mass. And yet, as we suggested earlier, it is hard to see in the New York of the 1960s just how this comes about. Time alone does not dissolve the groups if they are not close to the Anglo-Saxon center. Color marks off a group, regardless of time; and perhaps most significantly, the "majority" group, to which assimilation should occur, has taken on the color of an ethnic group, too. To what does one assimilate in modern America? The "American" in abstract does not exist, though some sections of the country, such as the Far West, come closer to realizing him than does New York City.

Source: Glazer, Nathan and Daniel Patrick Moynihan. *Beyond the Melting Pot: The Negroes, Puerto Ricans, Jews, Italians, and Irish of New York City*. Cambridge, Mass.: Massachusetts Institute of Technology Press and Harvard University Press, 1963. 12–14, 20.

Glossary

36°30′ According to the Missouri Compromise, any part of the Louisiana Purchase north of this line (Missouri's southern border) was to be excluded from slavery.

54th Massachusetts Regiment After President Abraham Lincoln's Emancipation Proclamation, the Union army organized all black military units, which white officers led. The 54th Massachusetts Regiment was one of the first of such units to be organized.

Abigail Adams (1744–1818) As the wife of John Adams, she endured long periods of separation from him while he served in many political roles. During these times apart, she wrote often to her husband, and their correspondence has provided a detailed portrait of life during the Revolutionary War.

abolition In the early 1830s, the anti-slavery movement shifted its goal from the gradual end of slavery to the immediate end or abolition of slavery.

abolitionism Movement that called for an immediate end to slavery throughout the United States.

John Adams (1735–1826) He was a signer of the Declaration of Independence and a delegate to the First and Second Continental Congresses. A member of the Federalist Party, he served as the first vice president and the second president of the United States. As president, he passed the Alien and Sedition Acts and endured a stormy relationship with France, which included the XYZ affair.

John Quincy Adams (1767–1848) As secretary of state, he urged President Monroe to issue the Monroe Doctrine, which incorporated his belief in an expanded use of federal powers. As the sixth president, Adams's nationalism and praise of European leaders caused a split in his party, causing some Republicans to leave and form the Democrat party.

Samuel Adams (1722–1803) A genius of revolutionary agitation, he believed that English Parliament had no right to legislate for the colonies. He organized the Sons of Liberty as well as protests in Boston against the British.

Jane Addams (1860–1935) She founded and ran of one of the best known settlement houses, the Hull House. Active in the peace and suffragist movements, she established child care for working mothers, health clinics, job training, and other social programs.

affirmative action Programs designed to give preferential treatment to women and people of color as compensation for past injustices.

Affordable Care Act (ACA) (2010) Vast health-care reform initiative signed into law and championed by President Obama, and widely criticized by Republicans, that aims to make health insurance more affordable and make health care accessible to everyone, regardless of income or prior medical conditions.

Agricultural Adjustment Act (1933) Legislation that paid farmers to produce less in order to raise crop prices for all; the AAA was later declared unconstitutional by the U.S. Supreme Court in the case of *United States v. Butler* (1936).

Emilio Aguinaldo (1869?–1964) He was a leader in the Filipino struggle for independence. During the war of 1898, Commodore George Dewey brought Aguinaldo back to the Philippines from exile to help fight the Spanish. However, after the Spanish surrendered to Americans, America annexed the Philippines and Aguinaldo fought against the American military until he was captured in 1901.

Alamo, Battle of the Siege in the Texas War for Independence of 1836, in which the San Antonio mission fell to the Mexicans. Davy Crockett and Jim Bowie were among the courageous defenders.

Albany Plan of Union (1754) A failed proposal by the seven northern colonies in anticipation of the French and Indian War, urging the unification of the colonies under one Crown-appointed president.

Alien and Sedition Acts of 1798 Four measures passed during the undeclared war with France that limited the freedoms of speech and press and restricted the liberty of non-citizens.

Allied Powers The nations fighting the Central Powers during the First World War, including France, Great Britain, and Russia; later joined by Italy and, after Russia quit the war in 1917, the United States.

American Anti-Imperialist League Coalition of anti-imperialist groups united in 1899 to protest American territorial expansion, especially in the Philippine Islands; its membership included prominent politicians, industrialists, labor leaders, and social reformers.

American Colonization Society Established in 1817, an organization whose mission was to return freed slaves to Africa.

American Federation of Labor Founded in 1881 as a national federation of trade unions made up of skilled workers.

American Indian Movement (AIM) Fed up with the poor conditions on Indian reservations and the federal government's unwillingness to help, Native Americans founded the American Indian Movement (AIM) in 1963. In 1973, AIM led 200 Sioux in the occupation of Wounded Knee. After a ten-week standoff with the federal authorities, the government agreed to reexamine Indian treaty rights and the occupation ended.

American Recovery and Reinvestment Act Hoping to restart the weak economy, President Obama signed this $787-billion economic stimulus bill in February of 2009. The bill included cash distributions to states, funds for food stamps, unemployment benefits, construction projects to renew the nation's infrastructure, funds for renewable-energy systems, and tax reductions.

American System Economic plan championed by Henry Clay of Kentucky that called for federal tariffs on imports, a strong national bank, and federally-financed internal improvements—roads, bridges, canals—all intended to strengthen the national economy and end American dependence on Great Britain.

American Tobacco Company Business founded in 1890 by North Carolina's James Buchanan Duke, who combined the major tobacco manufacturers of the time, ultimately controlling 90 percent of the country's cigarette production.

Anaconda Plan The Union's primary war strategy calling for a naval blockade of major southern seaports and then dividing the Confederacy by gaining control of the Tennessee, Cumberland, and Mississippi Rivers.

Annapolis Convention In 1786, all thirteen colonies were invited to a convention in Annapolis to discuss commercial problems, but only representatives from five states attended. However, the convention was not a complete failure because the delegates decided to have another convention in order to write the constitution.

Battle of Antietam (1862) Turning-point battle near Sharpsburg, Maryland, leaving over 20,000 soldiers dead or wounded, in which Union forces halted a Confederate invasion of the North.

anti-Federalists Opponents of the Constitution as an infringement on individual and states' rights, whose criticism led to the addition of a Bill of Rights to the document.

Many anti-Federalists later joined Thomas Jefferson's Democratic-Republican party.

Anti-Masonic party This party grew out of popular hostility toward the Masonic fraternal order and entered the presidential election of 1832 as a third party. It was the first party to run as a third party in a presidential election as well as the first to hold a nomination convention and announce a party platform.

Appomattox Court House Virginia village where Confederate general Robert E. Lee surrendered to Union general Ulysses S. Grant on April 9, 1865.

Arab Awakening A wave of spontaneous democratic uprisings that spread throughout the Arab world beginning in 2011, in which long-oppressed peoples demanded basic liberties from generations-old authoritarian regimes.

Benedict Arnold (1741–1801) A traitorous American commander who planned to sell out the American garrison at West Point to the British; his plot was discovered before it could be executed and he joined the British army.

Articles of Confederation The first form of government for the United States, ratified by the original thirteen states in 1781; weak in central authority, it was replaced by the U.S. Constitution in 1789.

Atlanta Compromise (1895) A speech by Booker T. Washington that called for the black community to strive for economic prosperity before attempting political and social equality.

Atlantic Charter (1941) Joint statement crafted by Franklin D. Roosevelt and British prime minister Winston Churchill that listed the war goals of the Allied Powers.

Aztec Empire A network of more than 300 city-states and upward of 30 provinces, established in the fourteenth century under the imperialistic Mexica, or Aztecs, in the valley of Mexico.

Crispus Attucks (1723–1770) During the Boston Massacre, he was supposedly at the head of the crowd of hecklers who baited the British troops. He was killed when the British troops fired on the crowd.

Stephen F. Austin (1793–1836) He established the first colony of Americans in Texas, which eventually attracted 2,000 people.

"Axis" alliance Military alliance formed in 1937 by the three major fascist powers: Germany, Italy, and Japan.

Aztec Empire Mesoamerican people who were conquered by the Spanish under Hernando Cortés, 1519–1528.

baby boom Markedly high birth rate in the years following World War II, leading to the biggest demographic "bubble" in U.S. history.

Bacon's Rebellion Unsuccessful 1676 revolt led by planter Nathaniel Bacon against Virginia governor William Berkeley's administration, which, Bacon charged, had failed to protect settlers from Indian raids.

Bank of the United States (1791) National bank responsible for holding and transferring federal government funds, making business loans, and issuing a national currency.

Bank War Political struggle in the early 1830s between President Jackson and financier Nicholas Biddle over the renewing of the Second Bank's charter.

Barbary pirates North Africans who waged war (1801–1805) on the United States after President Thomas Jefferson refused to pay tribute (a bribe) to protect American ships.

Bay of Pigs Failed CIA operation that, in April 1961, deployed a band of Cuban rebels to overthrow Fidel Castro's Communist regime.

Battle of the Bulge On December 16, 1944, the German army launched a counterattack against the Allied forces, which pushed them back. However, the Allies were eventually able to recover and break through the German lines. This defeat was a great blow to the Nazi's morale and their army's strength. The battle used up the last of Hitler's reserve units and opened a route into Germany's heartland.

Bear Flag Republic On June 14, 1846, a group of Americans in California captured Sonoma from the Mexican army and declared it the Republic of California whose flag featured a grizzly bear. In July, the commodore of the U.S. Pacific Fleet landed troops on California's shores and declared it part of the United States.

Beats Group of bohemian, downtown New York writers, artists, and musicians who flouted convention in favor of liberated forms of self-expression.

beatnik A name referring to almost any young rebel who openly dissented from the middle-class life. The name itself stems from the Beats.

Berlin airlift (1948–1949) Effort by the United States and Great Britain to deliver massive amounts of food and supplies flown to West Berlin in response to the Soviet land blockade of the city.

Berlin Wall Twenty-seven-mile-long concrete wall constructed in 1961 by East German authorities to stop the flow of East Germans fleeing to West Berlin.

Bessemer converter Apparatus that blasts air through molten iron to produce steel in very large quantities.

Nicholas Biddle (1786–1844) He was the president of the second Bank of the United States. In response to President Andrew Jackson's attacks on the bank, Biddle curtailed the bank's loans and exchanged its paper currency for gold and silver. In response, state banks began printing paper without restraint and lent it to speculators, causing a binge in speculating and an enormous increase in debt.

Bill of Rights First ten amendments to the U.S. Constitution, adopted in 1791 to guarantee individual rights and to help secure ratification of the Constitution by the states.

Osama bin Laden (1957–2011) The Saudi-born leader of al Qaeda, whose members attacked America on September 11, 2001. Years before the attack, he had declared *jihad* (holy war) on the United States, Israel, and the Saudi monarchy. In Afghanistan, the Taliban leaders gave bin Laden a safe haven in exchange for aid in fighting the Northern Alliance, who were rebels opposed to the Taliban. Following the Taliban's refusal to turn over bin Laden to the United States, America and a multinational coalition invaded Afghanistan and overthrew the Taliban. In May 2011, bin Laden was shot and killed by American special forces during a covert operation in Pakistan.

birth rate Proportion of births per 1,000 of the total population.

black codes Laws passed in southern states to restrict the rights of former slaves; to combat the codes, Congress passed the Civil Rights Act of 1866 and the Fourteenth Amendment and set up military governments in southern states that refused to ratify the amendment.

black power movement Militant form of civil rights protest focused on urban communities in the North and led by Malcolm X that grew as a response to impatience with the nonviolent tactics of Martin Luther King, Jr.

James Gillepsie Blaine (1830–1893) As a Republican congressman from Maine, he developed close ties with business leaders, which contributed to him losing the presidential election of 1884. He later opposed President Cleveland's efforts to reduce tariffs, which became a significant issue in the 1888 presidential election. Blaine served as secretary of state under President Benjamin Harrison.

Bleeding Kansas (1856) A series of violent conflicts in the Kansas territory between anti-slavery and pro-slavery factions over the status of slavery.

blitzkrieg (1940) The German "lightning war" strategy characterized by swift, well-organized attacks using infantry, tanks, and warplanes.

Bolsheviks Under the leadership of Vladimir Lenin, this Marxist party led the November 1917 revolution against the newly formed provisional government in Russia. After seizing control, the Bolsheviks negotiated a peace treaty with Germany, the Treaty of Brest-Litovsk, and ended their participation in World War I.

Bonus Expeditionary Force (1932) Protest march in Washington, D.C. by thousands of World War I veterans and their families, calling for immediate payment of their service bonuses certificates; violence ensued when President Herbert Hoover ordered their tent villages cleared.

boomtown Town, often in the West, that developed rapidly due to the sudden influx of wealth and work opportunities; often male-dominated with a substantial immigrant population.

Daniel Boone (1734–1820) He found and expanded a trail into Kentucky, which pioneers used to reach and settle the area.

John Wilkes Booth (1838?–1865) He assassinated President Abraham Lincoln at the Ford's Theater on April 14, 1865. He was pursued and killed.

Boston Massacre Violent confrontation between British soldiers and a Boston mob on March 5, 1770, in which five colonists were killed.

Boston Tea Party Demonstration against the Tea Act of 1773 in which the Sons of Liberty, dressed as Indians, dumped hundreds of chests of British-owned tea into Boston Harbor.

Bourbons In post–Civil War southern politics, the opponents of the Redeemers were called Bourbons. They were known for having forgotten nothing and learned nothing from the ordeal of the Civil War.

***bracero* program (1942)** System created in 1942 that permitted seasonal farm workers from Mexico to work in the United States on year-long contracts.

Joseph Brant (1742?–1807) Mohawk leader who led the Iroquois against the Americans in the Revolutionary War.

brinksmanship Secretary of State John Foster Dulles believed that communism could be contained by bringing America to the brink of war with an aggressive Communist nation. He believed that the aggressor would back down when confronted with the prospect of receiving a mass retaliation from a country with nuclear weapons.

John Brown (1800–1859) In response to a pro-slavery mob's sacking of the free-state town of Lawrence, Kansas, Brown went to the pro-slavery settlement of Pottawatomie, Kansas, which led to a guerrilla war in the Kansas territory. In 1859, he attempted to raid the federal arsenal at Harpers Ferry, hoping to use the stolen weapons to arm slaves, but he was captured and executed.

***Brown v. Board of Education* (1954)** Landmark Supreme Court case that struck down racial segregation in public schools and declared "separate-but-equal" unconstitutional.

William Jennings Bryan (1860–1925) He delivered the pro-silver "cross of gold" speech at the 1896 Democratic Convention and won his party's nomination for president. Disappointed pro-gold Democrats chose to walk out of the convention and nominate their own candidate, which split the Democratic party and cost them the White House. Bryan's loss also crippled the Populist movement that had endorsed him.

"Bull Moose" Progressive party *See* Progressive party

Bull Run, Battles of (First and Second Manassas) First land engagement of the Civil War took place on July 21, 1861, at Manassas Junction, Virginia, at which surprised Union troops quickly retreated; one year later, on August 29–30, Confederates captured the federal supply depot and forced Union troops back to Washington.

Martin Van Buren (1782–1862) During President Jackson's first term, he served as secretary of state and minister to London. In 1836, Van Buren was elected president, and he inherited a financial crisis. He believed that the government should not continue to keep its deposits in state banks and set up an independent Treasury, which was approved by Congress after several years of political maneuvering.

General John Burgoyne (1722–1792) He was the commander of Britain's northern forces during the Revolutionary War. He and most of his troops surrendered to the Americans at the Battle of Saratoga.

burial mounds A funeral tradition, practiced in the Mississippi and Ohio Valleys by the Adena-Hopewell cultures, of erecting massive mounds of earth over graves, often in the designs of serpents and other animals.

burned-over district Area of western New York strongly influenced by the revivalist fervor of the Second Great Awakening; Disciples of Christ and Mormons are among the many sects that trace their roots to the phenomenon.

Aaron Burr (1756–1836) Even though he was Thomas Jefferson's vice president, he lost favor with Jefferson's Republican supporters. He sought to work with the Federalists and run as their candidate for the governor of New York. Alexander Hamilton opposed Burr's candidacy and his stinging remarks on the subject led to Burr challenging him to duel in which Hamilton was killed.

George H. W. Bush (1924–) He served as vice president during the Reagan administration and then won the presidential election of 1988. His presidency was marked by raised taxes in the face of the federal deficit, the creation of the Office of National Drug Control Policy, and military activity abroad, including the invasion of Panama and Operation Desert Storm in Kuwait. He lost the 1992 presidential election to Bill Clinton.

George W. Bush (1946–) In the 2000 presidential election, Texas governor George W. Bush won as the Republican nominee against Democratic nominee Vice President Al Gore. After the September 11 terrorist attacks, he launched his "war on terrorism." President Bush adopted the Bush Doctrine, and United States invaded Afghanistan and Iraq with unclear outcomes leaving the countries divided. In September 2008, the nation's economy nose-dived as a credit crunch spiraled into a global economic meltdown. Bush signed into law the bank bailout fund called Troubled Asset Relief Program (TARP), but the economy did not improve.

Bush v. Gore (2000) The close 2000 presidential election came down to Florida's decisive twenty-five electoral votes. The final tally in Florida gave Bush a slight lead, but it was so small that a recount was required by state law. While the votes were being recounted, a legal battle was being waged to stop the recount. Finally, the case, *Bush v. Gore*, was presented to the Supreme Court who ruled 5–4 to stop the recount and Bush was declared the winner.

Bush Doctrine National security policy launched in 2002 by which the Bush administration claimed the right to launch preemptive military attacks against perceived enemies, particularly outlaw nations or terrorist organizations believed to possess weapons of mass destruction.

buying (stock) on margin The investment practice of making a small down payment (the "margin") on a stock and borrowing the rest of the money needed for the purchase from a broker who held the stock as security against a down market. If the stock's value declined and the buyer failed to meet a margin call for more funds, the broker could sell the stock to cover his loan.

Cahokia The largest chiefdom and city of the Mississippian Indian culture located in present-day Illinois, and the site of a sophisticated farming settlement that supported up to 15,000 inhabitants.

John C. Calhoun (1782–1850) He served in both the House of Representatives and the Senate for South Carolina before becoming secretary of war under President Monroe and then John Quincy Adams's vice president. Though he started his political career as an advocate of a strong national government, he eventually believed that states' rights, limited central government, and the power of nullification were necessary to preserve the Union.

California gold rush (1849) A massive migration of gold hunters, mostly men, who transformed the economy of California after gold was discovered in the foothills of northern California.

campaign of 1828 Bitter presidential contest between Democrat Andrew Jackson and National Republican John Quincy Adams (running for reelection), resulting in Jackson's victory.

Camp David Accords (1978) Peace agreement between Prime Minister Menachem Begin of Israel and President Anwar Sadat of Egypt, the first Arab head of state to officially recognize the state of Israel.

"Scarface" Al Capone (1899–1947) The most successful gangster of the Prohibition era whose Chicago-based criminal empire included bootlegging, prostitution, and gambling.

Andrew Carnegie (1835–1919) A steel magnate who believed that the general public benefited from big business even if these companies employed harsh business practices. This philosophy became deeply ingrained in the conventional wisdom of some Americans. After retiring, he devoted himself to philanthropy in hopes of promoting social welfare and world peace.

Carnegie Steel Company Corporation under the leadership of Andrew Carnegie that came to dominate the American steel industry.

Carolina colonies English proprietary colonies comprised of North and South Carolina, whose semitropical climate made them profitable centers of rice, timber, and tar production.

carpetbaggers Northern emigrants who participated in the Republican governments of the reconstructed South.

Jimmy Carter (1924–) Elected president in 1976, Jimmy Carter was an outsider to Washington. He created the departments of Energy and Education and signed into law several environmental initiatives. In 1978, he successfully brokered a peace agreement between Israel and Egypt called the Camp David Accords. However, his unwillingness to make deals with legislators caused other bills to be either gutted or stalled in Congress. His administration was plagued with a series of crises: a recession and increased inflation, a fuel shortage, the Soviet invasion of Afghanistan, and the overthrow of the Shah of Iran, leading to the Iran Hostage Crisis. Carter struggled to get the hostages released and was unable to do so until after he lost the 1980 election to Ronald Reagan. He was awarded the Nobel Peace Prize in 2002 for his efforts to further peace and democratic elections around the world.

Jacques Cartier (1491–1557) He led the first French effort to colonize North America and explored the Gulf of St. Lawrence, reaching as far as present day Montreal on the St. Lawrence River.

Fidel Castro (1926–) In 1959, his Communist regime came to power in Cuba after two years of guerrilla warfare against the dictator Fulgenico Batista. He enacted land redistribution programs and nationalized all foreign-owned property. The latter action as well as his political trials and summary executions damaged relations between Cuba and America. Castro was turned down when he asked for loans from the United States. However, he did receive aid from the Soviet Union.

Central Intelligence Agency (CIA) Intelligence-gathering government agency founded in 1947; under President Eisenhower's orders, secretly undermined elected governments deemed susceptible to communism.

Central Powers One of the two sides during the First World War, including Germany, Austria-Hungary, the Ottoman Empire (Turkey), and Bulgaria.

Carrie Chapman Catt (1859–1947) She was a leader of a new generation of activists in the women's suffrage movement who carried on the work started by Elizabeth Cady Stanton and Susan B. Anthony.

Cesar Chavez (1927–1993) He founded the United Farm Workers (UFW) in 1962 and worked to organize migrant farm workers. In 1965, the UFW joined Filipino farm workers striking against corporate grape farmers in California's San Joaquin Valley. In 1970, the strike and a consumer boycott on grapes compelled the farmers to formally recognize the UFW. As the result of Chavez's efforts, wages and working conditions improved for migrant workers. In 1975, the California state legislature passed a bill that required growers to bargain collectively with representatives of the farm workers.

child labor The practice of sending children to work in mines, mills, and factories, often in unsafe conditions; widespread among poor families in the late nineteenth century.

Chinese Exclusion Act (1882) Federal law that barred Chinese laborers from immigrating to America.

Christian Right Christian conservatives with a faith-based political agenda that includes allowing prayer in public schools and prohibition of abortion.

Church of Jesus Christ of Latter-day Saints / Mormons Founded in 1830 by Joseph Smith, the sect was a product of the intense revivalism of the burned-over district of New York; Smith's successor Brigham Young led 15,000 followers to Utah in 1847 to escape persecution.

Winston Churchill (1874–1965) The British prime minister who led the country during the Second World War. Along with Roosevelt and Stalin, he helped shape the postwar world at the Yalta Conference. He also coined the term "iron curtain," which he used in his famous "The Sinews of Peace" speech.

citizen-soldiers Part-time non-professional soldiers, mostly poor farmers or recent immigrants who had been indentured servants, who played an important role in the Revolutionary War.

"city machines" Local political party officials used these organizations to dispense patronage and favoritism amongst voters and businesses to ensure their loyal support to the political party.

Civil Rights Act of 1957 First federal civil rights law since Reconstruction; established the Civil Rights Commission and the Civil Rights Division of the Department of Justice.

Civil Rights Act of 1964 Legislation that outlawed discrimination in public accommodations and employment, passed at the urging of President Lyndon B. Johnson.

civil service reform An extended effort led by political reformers to end the patronage system; led to the Pendleton Act (1883), which called for government positions to be awarded based on merit rather than party loyalty.

Henry Clay (1777–1852) In the first half of the nineteenth century, he was the foremost spokesman for the American system. As Speaker of the House in the 1820s, he promoted economic nationalism, "market revolution," and the rapid development of western states and territories. A broker of compromise, he formulated the "second"

Missouri Compromise and the Compromise of 1850. In 1824, Clay supported John Quincy Adams, who won the presidency and appointed Clay to secretary of state. Andrew Jackson claimed that Clay had entered into a "corrupt bargain" with Adams for his own selfish gains.

Clayton Anti-Trust Act (1914) Legislation that served to enhance the Sherman Anti-Trust Act (1890) by clarifying what constituted "monopolistic" activities and declaring that labor unions were not to be viewed as "monopolies in restraint of trade."

Bill Clinton (1946–) The governor of Arkansas won the 1992 presidential election against President George H. W. Bush. In his first term, he pushed through Congress a tax increase, an economic stimulus package, the adoption of the North America Free Trade Agreement, welfare reform, a raise in the minimum wage, and improved public access to health insurance. His administration also negotiated the Oslo Accord and the Dayton Accords. After his re-election in 1996, he was involved in two high-profile scandals: his investment in the fraudulent Whitewater Development Corporation (but no evidence was found of him being involved in any wrongdoing) and his sexual affair with a White House intern. His attempt to cover up the affair led to a vote in Congress on whether or not to begin an impeachment inquiry. The House of Representatives voted to impeach Clinton, but the Senate found him not guilty.

Hillary Rodham Clinton (1947–) In the 2008 presidential election, Senator Hillary Clinton, the spouse of former President Bill Clinton, initially was the front-runner for the Democratic nomination, which made her the first woman with a serious chance to win the presidency. However, Senator Barack Obama's Internet-based and grassroots-orientated campaign garnered him enough delegates to win the nomination. After Obama became president, she was appointed secretary of state. In 2016, Clinton ran again and won the Democratic nomination for the presidency. Although she won the popular vote, she lost the election to Donald Trump.

clipper ships Tall, slender, mid-nineteenth-century sailing ships that were favored over older merchant ships for their speed, but ultimately gave way to steamships because they lacked cargo space.

Coercive Acts (1774) Four parliamentary measures that required the colonies to pay for the Boston Tea Party's damages, imposed a military government, disallowed colonial trials of British soldiers, and forced the quartering of troops in private homes.

coffin ships Irish immigrants fleeing the potato famine had to endure a six-week journey across the Atlantic to reach America. During these voyages, thousands of passengers died of disease and starvation, which led to the ships being called "coffin ships."

Columbian Exchange The transfer of biological and social elements, such as plants, animals, people, diseases, and cultural practices, among Europe, the Americas, and Africa in the wake of Christopher Columbus's voyages to the "New World."

Christopher Columbus (1451–1506) The Italian sailor who persuaded King Ferdinad and Queen Isabella of Spain to fund his expedition across the Atlantic to discover a new trade route to Asia. Instead of arriving at China or Japan, he reached the Bahamas in 1492.

James B. Comey (1960–) FBI director fired by President Donald Trump in 2017.

Committee of Correspondence Group organized by Samuel Adams in retaliation for the *Gaspée* incident to address American grievances, assert American rights, and form a network of rebellion.

Committee on Public Information During the First World War, this committee produced war propaganda that conveyed the Allies' war aims to Americans as well as attempted to weaken the enemy's morale.

Committee to Re-elect the President (CREEP) During Nixon's presidency, his administration engaged in a number of immoral acts, such as attempting to steal information and falsely accusing political appointments of sexual improprieties. These acts were funded by money illegally collected through CREEP.

***Common Sense* (1776)** Popular pamphlet written by Thomas Paine attacking British principles of hereditary rule and monarchical government, and advocating a declaration of American independence.

Compromise of 1850 A package of five bills presented to the Congress by Henry Clay intended to avoid secession or civil war by reducing tensions between North and South over the status of slavery.

Compromise of 1877 Deal made by a special congressional commission on March 2, 1877, to resolve the disputed presidential election of 1876; Republican Rutherford B. Hayes, who had lost the popular vote, was declared the winner in exchange for the withdrawal of federal troops from the South, marking the end of Reconstruction.

Comstock Lode Mine in eastern Nevada acquired by Canadian fur trapper Henry Comstock that between 1860 and 1880 yielded almost $1 billion worth of gold and silver.

Conestoga wagons These large horse-drawn wagons were used to carry people or heavy freight long distances, including from the East to the western frontier settlements.

Congressional Reconstruction Phase of Reconstruction directed by Radical Republicans through the passage of three laws: the Military Reconstruction Act, the Command of the Army Act, and the Tenure of Office Act.

conquistadores Spanish term for "conquerors," applied to Spanish and Portuguese soldiers who conquered lands held by indigenous peoples in central and southern America as well as the current states of Texas, New Mexico, Arizona, and California.

consumer culture A society in which mass production and consumption of nationally advertised products comes to dictate much of social life and status.

containment U.S. cold war strategy that sought to prevent global Soviet expansion and influence through political, economic, and, if necessary, military pressure as a means of combating the spread of communism.

Continental army Army authorized by the Continental Congress, 1775–1784, to fight the British; commanded by General George Washington.

Contract with America (1994) A list of conservative promises in response to the supposed liberalism of the Clinton administration, that was drafted by Speaker of the House Newt Gingrich and other congressional Republicans as the GOP platform for the 1994 midterm elections. More a campaign tactic than a practical program, few of its proposed items ever became law.

contrabands Slaves who sought refuge in Union military camps or who lived in areas of the Confederacy under Union control.

Contras The Reagan administration ordered the CIA to train and supply guerrilla bands of anti-Communist Nicaraguans called Contras. They were fighting the Sandinista government that had recently come to power in Nicaragua. The State Department believed that the Sandinista government was supplying the leftist Salvadoran rebels with Soviet and Cuban arms. A cease-fire agreement between the Contras and Sandinistas was signed in 1988.

Calvin Coolidge (1872–1933) After President Harding's death, his vice president, Calvin Coolidge, assumed the presidency. Coolidge believed that the nation's welfare was tied to the success of Big Business, and he worked to end government regulation of business and industry as well as reduce taxes. In particular, he focused on the nation's industrial development.

Copperhead Democrats Democrats in northern states who opposed the Civil War and argued for an immediate peace settlement with the Confederates; Republicans labeled them "Copperheads," likening them to venomous snakes.

Hernán Cortés (1485–1547) The Spanish conquistador who conquered the Aztec Empire and set the precedent for other plundering conquistadores.

General Charles Cornwallis (1738–1805) He was in charge of British troops in the South during the Revolutionary War. His surrender to George Washington at the Battle of Yorktown ended the Revolutionary War.

Corps of Discovery Meriwether Lewis and William Clark led this group of men on an expedition of the newly purchased Louisiana territory, which took them from Missouri to Oregon. As they traveled, they kept detailed journals and drew maps of the previously unexplored territory. Their reports attracted traders and trappers to the region and gave the United States a claim to the Oregon country by right of discovery and exploration.

"corrupt bargain" Scandal in which presidential candidate and Speaker of the House Henry Clay secured John Quincy Adams's victory over Andrew Jackson in the 1824 election, supposedly in exchange for Clay being named secretary of state.

cotton gin Hand-operated machine invented by Eli Whitney in the late eighteenth century that quickly removed seeds from cotton bolls, enabling the mass production of cotton in nineteenth-century America.

cotton kingdom Cotton-producing region, relying predominantly on slave labor, that spanned from North Carolina west to Louisiana and reached as far north as southern Illinois.

cotton White fibers harvested from cotton plants, spun into yarn, and woven into textiles that made comfortable, easy-to-clean products, especially clothing; the most valuable cash crop driving the economy in the United States and Great Britain during the nineteenth century.

counterculture Unorganized youth rebellion against mainstream institutions, values, and behavior that more often focused on cultural rather than political activism.

court-packing plan President Franklin D. Roosevelt's failed 1937 attempt to increase the number of U.S. Supreme Court justices from nine to fifteen in order to save his Second New Deal programs from constitutional challenges.

covenant theory A Puritan concept that believed true Christians could enter a voluntary union for the common worship of God. Taking the idea one step further, the union could also be used for the purposes of establishing governments.

crop-lien system Credit system used by sharecroppers and share tenants who pledged a portion ("share") of their future crop to local merchants or land owners in exchange for farming supplies and food.

"Cross of Gold" Speech In the 1896 election, the Democratic Party split over the issue of whether to use gold or silver to back American currency. Significant to this division was the pro-silver "Cross of Gold" speech that William Jennings Bryan delivered at the Democratic convention, which was so well received that Bryan won the nomination to be their presidential candidate. Disappointed pro-gold Democrats chose to walk out of the convention and nominate their own candidate.

Cuban missile crisis Thirteen-day U.S.-Soviet standoff in October 1962, sparked by the discovery of Soviet missile sites in Cuba; the crisis was the closest the world has come to nuclear war since 1945.

cult of domesticity A pervasive nineteenth-century ideology that urged women to celebrate their role as manager of the household and nurturer of the children.

George A. Custer (1839–1876) He was a reckless and glory-seeking Lieutenant Colonel of the U.S. Army who fought the Sioux Indians in the Great Sioux War. In 1876, he and his detachment of soldiers were entirely wiped out in the Battle of Little Bighorn.

***Dartmouth College v. Woodward* (1819)** Supreme Court ruling that enlarged the definition of *contract* to put corporations beyond the reach of the states that chartered them.

Daughters of Liberty Colonial women who protested the British government's tax policies by boycotting British products, such as clothing, and who wove their own fabric, or "homespun."

Dawes Severalty Act of 1887 Federal legislation that divided ancestral Native American lands among the heads of each Indian family in an attempt to "Americanize" Indians by forcing them to become farmers working individual plots of land.

D-day June 6, 1944, when an Allied amphibious assault landed on the Normandy coast and established a foothold in Europe from which Hitler's defenses could not recover.

Jefferson Davis (1808–1889) He was the president of the Confederacy during the Civil War. When the Confederacy's defeat seemed invitable in early 1865, he refused to surrender. Union forces captured him in May of that year.

Bartolomé de Las Casas (1484–1566) A Catholic missionary who renounced the Spanish practice of coercively converting Indians and advocated their better treatment. In 1552, he wrote *A Brief Relation of the Destruction of the Indies*, which described the Spanish's cruel treatment of the Indians.

death rate Proportion of deaths per 1,000 of the total population; also called *mortality rate*.

Eugene V. Debs (1855–1926) Founder of the American Railway Union, which he organized against the Pullman Palace Car Company during the Pullman strike. Later he organized the Social Democratic party, which eventually became the Socialist Party of America. In the 1912 presidential election, he ran as the Socialist party's candidate and received more than 900,000 votes.

Declaration of Independence Formal statement, principally drafted by Thomas Jefferson and adopted by the Second Continental Congress on July 4, 1776, that officially announced the thirteen colonies' break with Great Britain.

Declaration of Sentiments Document based on the Declaration of Independence that called for gender equality, written primarily by Elizabeth Cady Stanton and signed by Seneca Falls Convention delegates in 1848.

Declaratory Act Following the repeal of the Stamp Act in 1766, Parliament passed this act which asserted Parliament's full power to make laws binding the colonies "in all cases whatsoever."

Deism Enlightenment thought applied to religion, emphasizing reason, morality, and natural law rather than scriptural authority or an ever-present God intervening in human life.

détente Period of improving relations between the United States and Communist nations, particularly China and the Soviet Union, during the Nixon administration.

George Dewey (1837–1917) On April 30, 1898, Commodore George Dewey's small U.S. naval squadron defeated the Spanish warships in Manila Bay in the Philippines. This quick victory aroused expansionist fever in the United States.

John Dewey (1859–1952) He is an important philosopher of pragmatism. However, he preferred to use the term *instrumentalism*, because he saw ideas as instruments of action.

Ngo Dinh Diem (1901–1963) Following the Geneva Accords, the French, with the support of America, forced the Vietnamese emperor to accept Dinh Diem as the new premier of South Vietnam. President Eisenhower sent advisors to train Diem's police and army. In return, the United States expected Diem to enact democratic reforms and distribute land to the peasants. Instead, he suppressed his political opponents, did little or no land distribution, and let corruption grow. In 1956, he refused to participate in elections to reunify Vietnam. Eventually, he ousted the emperor and declared himself president.

Distribution Act (1836) Law requiring the distribution of the federal budget surplus to the states, creating chaos among state banks that had become dependent on such federal funds.

Dorothea Lynde Dix (1802–1887) She was an important figure in increasing the public's awareness of the plight of the mentally ill. After a two-year investigation of the treatment of the mentally ill in Massachusetts, she presented her findings and won the support of leading reformers. She eventually convinced twenty states to reform their treatment of the mentally ill.

Dixiecrats Breakaway faction of southern Democrats who defected from the national Democratic party in 1948 to protest the party's increased support for civil rights and to nominate their own segregationist candidates for elective office.

"dollar diplomacy" Practice advocated by President Theodore Roosevelt in which the U.S. government fostered American investments in less developed nations and then used U.S. military force to protect those investments

Donner party Forty-seven surviving members of a group of migrants to California were forced to resort to cannibalism to survive a brutal winter trapped in the Sierra Nevadas, 1846–1847; highest death toll of any group traveling the Overland Trail.

Stephen A. Douglas (1812–1861) As a senator from Illinois, he authored the Kansas-Nebraska Act. Running for senatorial reelection in 1858, he engaged Abraham Lincoln in a series of public debates about slavery in the territories. Even though Douglas won the election, the debates gave Lincoln a national reputation.

Frederick Douglass (1818–1895) He escaped from slavery and become an eloquent speaker and writer against the institution. In 1845, he published his autobiography entitled *Narrative of the Life of Frederick Douglass* and two years later he founded an abolitionist newspaper for blacks called the *North Star*.

dot-coms In the late 1990s, the stock market soared to new heights and defied the predictions of experts that the economy could not sustain such a performance. Much of the economic success was based on dot-com enterprises, which were firms specializing in computers, software, telecommunications, and the internet. However, many of the companies' stock market values were driven higher and higher by speculation instead of financial success. Eventually the stock market bubble burst.

Dred Scott v. Sandford **(1857)** U.S. Supreme Court ruling that slaves were not U.S. citizens and therefore could not sue for their freedom and that Congress could not prohibit slavery in the western territories.

W. E. B. Du Bois (1868–1963) He criticized Booker T. Washington's views on civil rights as being accommodationist. He advocated "ceaseless agitation" for civil rights and the immediate end to segregation and an enforcement of laws to protect civil rights and equality. He promoted an education for African Americans that would nurture bold leaders who were willing to challenge discrimination in politics.

John Foster Dulles (1888–1959) As President Eisenhower's secretary of state, he institutionalized the policy of containment and introduced the strategy of deterrence. He believed in using brinkmanship to halt the spread of communism. He attempted to employ it in Indochina, which led to the United States' involvement in Vietnam.

Dust Bowl Vast area of the Midwest where windstorms blew away millions of tons of topsoil from parched farmland after a long drought in the 1930s, causing great social distress and a massive migration of farm families.

Eastern Woodlands Peoples Various Native American peoples, particularly the Algonquian, Iroquoian, and Muskogean regional groups, who once dominated the Atlantic seaboard from Maine to Louisiana.

Peggy Eaton (1796–1879) The wife of John Eaton, President Jackson's secretary of war, was the daughter of a tavern owner with an unsavory past. Supposedly her first husband had committed suicide after learning that she was having an affair with John Eaton. The wives of members of Jackson's cabinet snubbed her because of her lowly origins and past, resulting in a scandal known as the Eaton Affair.

Economic Opportunity Act (1964) Key legislation in President Johnson's "War on Poverty" which created the Office of Economic Opportunity and programs like Head Start and work-study.

Jonathan Edwards (1703–1758) New England Congregationalist minister who began a religious revival in his Northampton church and was an important figure in the Great Awakening.

election of 1800 Presidential election between Thomas Jefferson and John Adams; resulted in the first Democratic-Republican victory after the Federalist administrations of George Washington and John Adams.

election of 1864 Abraham Lincoln's successful re-election campaign, capitalizing on Union military successes in Georgia, to defeat Democratic opponent, former general George B. McClellan, who ran on a peace platform.

election of 1912 The presidential election of 1912 featured four candidates: Wilson, Taft, Roosevelt, and Debs. Each candidate believed in the basic assumptions of progressive politics, but each had a different view on how progressive ideals should be implemented through policy. In the end, Taft and Roosevelt split the Republican party votes and Wilson emerged as the winner.

Queen Elizabeth I of England (1533–1603) The protestant daughter of Henry VIII, she was Queen of England from 1558–1603 and played a major role in the Protestant Reformation. During her long reign, the doctrines and services of the Church of England were defined and the Spanish Armada was defeated.

General Dwight D. Eisenhower (1890–1969) During the Second World War, he commanded the Allied Forces landing in Africa and was the supreme Allied commander as well as planner for Operation Overlord. In 1952, he was elected president on his popularity as a war hero and his promises to clean up Washington. His administration sought to cut the nation's domestic programs and budget, ended the fighting in Korea, and institutionalized the policies of containment and deterrence. He established the Eisenhower doctrine, which promised to aid any nation against aggression by a Communist nation.

Ellis Island Reception center in New York Harbor through which most European immigrants to America were processed from 1892 to 1954.

Emancipation Proclamation (1863) Military order issued by President Abraham Lincoln that freed slaves in areas still controlled by the Confederacy but did not free the 500,000 slaves in the four border states that remained in the Union.

Embargo Act (1807) A law promoted by President Thomas Jefferson prohibiting American ships from leaving for foreign ports, in order to safeguard them from British and French attacks. This ban on American exports proved disastrous to the U.S. economy.

Ralph Waldo Emerson (1803–1882) As a leader of the transcendentalist movement, he wrote poems, essays, and speeches that discussed the sacredness of nature, optimism, self-reliance, and the unlimited potential of the individual. He wanted to transcend the limitations of inherited conventions and rationalism to reach the inner recesses of the self.

encomienda A land-grant system under which Spanish army officers (*conquistadores*) were awarded large parcels of land taken from Native Americans.

Enlightenment A revolution in thought begun in Europe in the seventeenth century that emphasized reason and science over the authority and myths of traditional religion.

enumerated goods According to the Navigation Act, these particular goods, like tobacco or cotton, could only be shipped to England or other English colonies.

Environmental Protection Agency (EPA) (1970) Federal environmental agency created by Nixon to appease the demands of congressional Democrats for a federal environmental watchdog agency.

Erie Canal (1817) Most important and profitable of the barge canals of the 1820s and 1830s; stretched from Buffalo to Albany, New York, connecting the Great Lakes to the East Coast and making New York City the nation's largest port.

ethnic cleansing The systematic removal of an ethnic group from a territory through violence or intimidation in order to create a homogenous society; the term was popularized by the Yugoslav policy brutally targeting Albanian Muslims in Kosovo.

Exodusters African Americans who migrated west from the South in search of a haven from racism and poverty after the collapse of Radical Republican rule.

Fair Deal (1949) President Truman's proposals to build upon the New Deal with national health insurance, the repeal of the Taft-Hartley Act, new civil rights legislation, and other initiatives; most were rejected by the Republican-controlled Congress.

Fair Employment Practices Commission Created in 1941 by executive order, the FEPC sought to eliminate racial discrimination in jobs; it possessed little power but represented a step toward civil rights for African Americans.

"falling domino" theory Theory that if one country fell to communism, its neighboring countries would follow suit.

Farmers' Alliances Like the Granger movement, these organizations sought to address the issues of small farming communities; however Alliances emphasized more political action and called for the creation of a Third Party to advocate their concerns.

fascism A radical form of totalitarian government that emerged in Italy and Germany in the 1920s in which a dictator uses propaganda and brute force to seize control of all aspects of national life.

field hands Slaves who toiled in the cotton or cane fields in organized work gangs.

Federal-Aid Highway Act (1956) Largest federal project in U.S. history that created a national network of interstate highways and was the largest federal project in history.

Federal Deposit Insurance Corporation (1933) Independent government agency, established to prevent bank panics, that guarantees the safety of deposits in citizens' savings accounts.

Federal Reserve Act (1913) Legislation passed by Congress to create a new national banking system in order to regulate the nation's currency supply and ensure the stability and integrity of member banks who made up the Federal Reserve System across the nation.

Federal Trade Commission (1914) Independent agency created by the Wilson administration that replaced the Bureau of Corporations as an even more powerful tool to combat unfair trade practices and monopolies.

Federal Writers' Project During the Great Depression, this project provided writers, such as Ralph Ellison, Richard Wright, and Saul Bellow, with work, which gave them employment and a chance to develop as artists.

federalism Concept of dividing governmental authority between the national government and the states.

The Federalist Papers Collection of eighty-five essays, published widely in newspapers in 1787 and 1788, written by Alexander Hamilton, James Madison, and John Jay in support of adopting the proposed U.S. Constitution.

Federalists Proponents of a centralized federal system and the ratification of the Constitution. Most Federalists were relatively young, educated men who supported a broad interpretation of the Constitution whenever national interest dictated such flexibility. Notable Federalists included Alexander Hamilton and John Jay.

Geraldine Ferraro (1935–) In the 1984 presidential election, Democratic nominee, Walter Mondale, chose her as his running mate. As a member of the U.S. House of Representatives from New York, she was the first woman to be a vice-presidential nominee for a major political party. However, she was placed on the defensive because of her husband's complicated business dealings.

Fifteenth Amendment (1870) This amendment forbids states to deny any person the right to vote on grounds of "race, color or pervious condition of servitude." Former Confederate states were required to ratify this amendment before they could be readmitted to the Union.

"final solution" The Nazi party's systematic murder of some 6 million Jews along with more than a million other people including, but not limited to, gypsies, homosexuals, and handicap individuals.

First New Deal (1933–1935) Franklin D. Roosevelt's ambitious first-term cluster of economic and social programs designed to combat the Great Depression.

First Red Scare Outbreak of anti-Communist hysteria that included the arrest without warrants of thousands of suspected radicals, most of whom (mainly Russian immigrants) were deported.

flappers Young women of the 1920s whose rebellion against prewar standards of femininity included wearing shorter dresses, bobbing their hair, dancing to jazz music, driving cars, smoking cigarettes, and indulging in illegal drinking and gambling.

Food Administration After America's entry into World War I, the economy of the home front needed to be reorganized to provide the most efficient means of conducting the war. The Food Administration was a part of this effort. Under the leadership of Herbert Hoover, the organization sought to increase agricultural production while reducing civilian consumption of foodstuffs.

"Force Bill" (1833) Legislation, sparked by the Nullification Crisis in South Carolina, that authorized the president's use of the army to compel states to comply with federal law.

Gerald Ford (1913–2006) He was appointed to the vice presidency under President Nixon after the resignation of Spiro Agnew, and assumed the presidency after President Nixon's resignation. He resisted congressional pressure to both reduce taxes and increase federal spending, which sent the American economy into the deepest recession since the Great Depression. Ford retained Kissinger as his secretary of state and continued Nixon's foreign policy goals. He was heavily criticized following the collapse of South Vietnam.

Fort Laramie Treaty (1851) Restricted the Plains Indians from using the Overland Trail and permitted the building of government forts.

Fort Necessity After attacking a group of French soldiers, George Washington constructed and took shelter in this fort from vengeful French troops. Washington eventually surrendered to them after a day-long battle. This conflict was a significant event in igniting the French and Indian War.

Fort Sumter First battle of the Civil War, in which the federal fort in Charleston (South Carolina) Harbor was captured by the Confederates on April 14, 1861, after two days of shelling.

"forty-niners" Speculators who went to northern California following the discovery of gold in 1848; the first of several years of large-scale migration was 1849.

Fourteen Points President Woodrow Wilson's proposed plan for the peace agreement after the First World War that included the creation of a "league of nations" intended to keep the peace.

Fourteenth Amendment (1866) Guaranteed rights of citizenship to former slaves, in words similar to those of the Civil Rights Act of 1866.

alliance with France Critical diplomatic, military, and economic alliance between France and the newly independent United States, codified by the Treaty of Amity and Commerce and the Treaty of Alliance (1778).

Franciscan Missions In 1769, Franciscan missioners accompanied Spanish soldiers to California and over the next fifty years established a chain of missions from San Diego to San Francisco. At these missions, friars sought to convert Indians to Catholicism and make them members of the Spanish empire. The friars stripped the Indians of their native heritage and used soldiers to enforce their will.

Benjamin Franklin (1706–1790) A Boston-born American, who epitomized the Enlightenment for many Americans and Europeans, Franklin's wide range of interests led him to become a publisher, inventor, and statesman. As the latter, he contributed to the writing of the Declaration of Independence, served as the minister to France during the Revolutionary War, and was a delegate to the Constitutional Convention.

Free-Soil party A political coalition created in 1848 that opposed the expansion of slavery into the new western territories.

Freedmen's Bureau Reconstruction agency established in 1865 to protect the legal rights of former slaves and to assist with their education, jobs, health care, and landowning.

Freedom Riders Activists who, beginning in 1961, traveled by bus through the South to test federal court rulings that banned segregation on buses and trains.

John C. Frémont "the Pathfinder" (1813–1890) He was an explorer and surveyor who helped inspire Americans living in California to rebel against the Mexican government and declare independence.

French and Indian War (Seven Years' War) (1754–1763) The last—and the most important—of four colonial wars fought between England and France for control of North America east of the Mississippi River.

French Revolution Revolutionary movement beginning in 1789 that overthrew the monarchy and transformed France into an unstable republic before Napoleon Bonaparte assumed power in 1799.

Sigmund Freud (1865–1939) He was the founder of psychoanalysis, which suggested that human behavior was motivated by unconscious and irrational forces. By the 1920s, his ideas were being discussed more openly in America.

frontier revivals Religious revival movement within the Second Great Awakening, that took place in frontier churches in western territories and states in the early nineteenth century.

Fugitive Slave Act (1850) Part of the Compromise of 1850, a provision that authorized federal officials to help capture and then return escaped slaves to their owners without trials.

fundamentalism Anti-modernist Protestant movement started in the early twentieth century that proclaimed the literal truth of the Bible; the name came from *The Fundamentals,* published by conservative leaders.

William Lloyd Garrison (1805–1879) In 1831, he started the anti-slavery newspaper *Liberator* and helped start the New England Anti-Slavery Society. Two years later, he assisted Arthur and Lewis Tappan in the founding of the American Anti-Slavery Society. He and his followers believed that America had been thoroughly corrupted and needed a wide range of reforms, embracing abolition, temperance, pacifism, and women's rights.

Marcus Garvey (1887–1940) He was the leading spokesman for Negro Nationalism, which exalted blackness, black cultural expression, and black exclusiveness. He called upon African Americans to liberate themselves from the surrounding white culture and create their own businesses, cultural centers, and newspapers. He was also the founder of the Universal Negro Improvement Association.

Citizen Genet (1763–1834) As the ambassador to the United States from the new French Republic, he engaged American privateers to attack British ships and conspired with frontiersmen and land speculators to organize an attack on Spanish Florida and Louisiana. His actions and the French radicals excessive actions against their enemies in the new French Republic caused the French Revolution to lose support among Americans.

Geneva Accords In 1954, the Geneva Accords were signed, which ended French colonial rule in Indochina. The agreement created the independent nations of Laos and Cambodia and divided Vietnam along the 17th parallel until an election in 1956 would reunify the country.

Battle of Gettysburg (1863) A monumental three-day battle in southern Pennsylvania, widely considered a turning point in the war, in which Union forces successfully countered a second Confederate invasion of the North.

Ghost Dance movement A spiritual and political movement among Native Americans whose followers performed a ceremonial "ghost dance" intended to connect the living with the dead and make the Indians bulletproof in battles to restore their homelands.

GI Bill of Rights (1944) Provided unemployment, education, and financial benefits for World War II veterans to ease their transition back to the civilian world.

***Gibbons v. Ogden* (1824)** Supreme Court case that gave the federal government the power to regulate interstate commerce.

Newt Gingrich (1943–) He led the Republican insurgency in Congress in the mid 1990s through mobilizing religious and social conservatives. Along with other Republican congressmen, he created the Contract with America, which was a ten-point anti-big government program. However, the program fizzled out after many of its bills were not passed by Congress.

Gilded Age (1860–1896) An era of dramatic industrial and urban growth characterized by widespread political corruption and loose government oversight of corporations.

The Gilded Age Mark Twain and Charles Dudley Warner's 1873 novel, the title of which became the popular name for the period from the end of the Civil War to the turn of the century.

glasnost Russian term for "openness"; applied to the loosening of censorship in the Soviet Union under Mikhail Gorbachev.

globalization An important, and controversial, transformation of the world economy whereby the Internet helped revolutionize global commerce by creating an international marketplace for goods and services. Led by the growing number of multinational companies and the Americanization of many foreign consumer cultures, with companies like McDonald's and Starbucks appearing in all of the major cities of the world.

Glorious Revolution (1688) Successful coup, instigated by a group of English aristocrats, which overthrew King James II and instated William of Orange and Mary, his English wife, to the British throne.

Barry Goldwater (1909–1998) A leader of the Republican right whose book, *The Conscience of a Conservative*, was highly influential to that segment of the party. He proposed eliminating the income tax and overhauling Social Security. In 1964, he ran as the Republican presidential candidate and lost to President Johnson. He campaigned against Johnson's war on poverty, the tradition of New Deal, the nuclear test ban and the Civil Rights Act of 1964 and advocated the wholesale bombing of North Vietnam.

Samuel Gompers (1850–1924) He served as the president of the American Federation of Labor from its inception until his death. He focused on achieving concrete economic gains such as higher wages, shorter hours, and better working conditions.

"good neighbor" policy Proclaimed by President Franklin D. Roosevelt in his first inaugural address in 1933, it sought improved diplomatic relations between the United States and its Latin American neighbors.

Mikhail Gorbachev (1931–) In the late 1980s, Soviet leader Mikhail Gorbachev attempted to reform the Soviet Union through his programs of *perestroika* and *glasnost* and pursued a renewal of détente with America, signing new arms-control agreements with President Reagan. Gorbachev allowed the velvet revolutions of Eastern Europe to occur without outside interference. Eventually the political, social, and economic upheaval he had unleashed would lead to the break-up of the Soviet Union.

Albert Gore Jr. (1948–) He served as a senator of Tennessee and then as President Clinton's vice president. In the 2000 presidential election, he was the Democratic candidate against Governor George W. Bush. The close election came down to Florida's electoral votes. While the votes were being recounted as required by state law, a legal battle was being waged to stop the recount. Finally, the case, *Bush v. Gore*, was presented to the Supreme Court who ruled 5–4 to stop the recount and Bush was declared the winner.

Jay Gould (1836–1892) As one of the biggest railroad robber barons, he was infamous for buying rundown railroads, making cosmetic improvements and then reselling them for a profit. He used corporate funds for personal investments and to bribe politicians and judges.

gradualism This strategy for ending slavery involved promoting the banning of slavery in the new western territories and encouraging the release of slaves from slavery. Supporters of this method believed that it would bring about the gradual end of slavery.

Granger movement Began by offering social and educational activities for isolated farmers and their families and later started to promote "cooperatives" where farmers could join together to buy, store, and sell their crops to avoid the high fees charged by brokers and other middle-men.

Ulysses S. Grant (1822–1885) After distinguishing himself in the western theater of the Civil War, he was appointed general in chief of the Union army in 1864. Afterward, he defeated General Robert E. Lee through a policy of aggressive attrition. Lee surrendered to Grant on April 9th, 1865 at the Appomattox Court House. His presidential tenure suffered from scandals and fiscal problems, including the debate on whether or not greenbacks, paper money, should be removed from circulation.

Great Awakening Fervent religious revival movement that swept the thirteen colonies from the 1720s through the 1740s.

Great Compromise (Connecticut Compromise) Mediated the differences between the New Jersey and Virginia delegations to the Constitutional Convention by providing for a bicameral legislature, the upper house of which would have equal representation and the lower house of which would be apportioned by population.

Great Depression (1929–1941) Worst economic downturn in American history; it was spurred by the stock market crash in the fall of 1929 and lasted until the Second World War.

Great Migration Mass exodus of African Americans from the rural South to the Northeast and Midwest during and after the First World War.

Great Railroad Strike of 1877 A series of demonstrations, some violent, held nationwide in support of striking railroad workers in Martinsburg, West Virginia, who refused to work due to wage cuts.

Great Recession (2007–2009) Massive, prolonged economic downturn sparked by the collapse of the housing market and the financial institutions holding unpaid mortgages; it lasted from December 2007 to January 2009 and resulted in 9 million Americans losing their jobs.

Great Sioux War Conflict between Sioux and Cheyenne Indians and federal troops over lands in the Dakotas in the mid-1870s.

Great Society Term coined by President Lyndon B. Johnson in his 1965 State of the Union address, in which he proposed legislation to address problems of voting rights, poverty, diseases, education, immigration, and the environment.

Horace Greeley (1811–1872) In reaction to Radical Reconstruction and corruption in President Ulysses S. Grant's administration, a group of Republicans broke from the party to form the Liberal Republicans. In 1872, the Liberal Republicans chose Horace Greeley as their presidential candidate who ran on a platform of favoring civil service reform and condemning the Republican's Reconstruction policy.

greenbacks Paper money issued during the Civil War. After the war ended, a debate emerged on whether or not to remove the paper currency from circulation and revert back to hard-money currency (gold coins). Opponents of hard-money feared that eliminating the greenbacks would shrink the money supply, which would lower crop prices and make it more difficult to repay long-term debts. President Ulysses S. Grant, as well as hard-currency advocates, believed that gold coins were morally preferable to paper currency.

Greenback party Formed in 1876 in reaction to economic depression, the party favored issuance of unsecured paper money to help farmers repay debts; the movement for free coinage of silver took the place of the greenback movement by the 1880s.

General Nathanael Greene (1742–1786) He was appointed by Congress to command the American army fighting in the South during the Revolutionary War. Using his patience and his skills of managing men, saving supplies, and avoiding needless risks, he waged a successful war of attrition against the British.

Sarah Grimké (1792–1873) and **Angelina Grimké (1805–1879)** These two sisters gave anti-slavery speeches to crowds of mixed gender that caused some people to condemn them for engaging in unfeminine activities. In 1840, William Lloyd Garrison convinced the Anti-Slavery Society to allow women equal participation in the organization.

Half-Way Covenant Allowed baptized children of church members to be admitted to a "halfway" membership in the church and secure baptism for their own children in turn, but allowed them neither a vote in the church, nor communion.

Alexander Hamilton (1755–1804) His belief in a strong federal government led him to become a leader of the Federalists. As the first secretary of the Treasury, he laid the foundation for American capitalism through his creation of a federal budget, funded debt, a federal tax system, a national bank, a customs service, and a coast guard. His "Reports on Public Credit" and "Reports on Manufactures" outlined his vision for economic development and government finances. He died in a duel against Aaron Burr.

Alexander Hamilton's economic reforms Various measures designed to strengthen the nation's economy and generate federal revenue through the promotion of new industries, the adoption of new tax policies, the payment of war debts, and the establishment of a national bank.

Warren G. Harding (1865–1923) In the 1920 presidential election, he was the Republican nominee who promised Americans a "return to normalcy." Once in office, Harding's administration dismantled many of the social and economic components of progressivism and pursued a pro-business agenda. Harding appointed four pro-business Supreme Court Justices, cut taxes, increased tariffs, and promoted a lenient attitude towards regulation of corporations. However, he did speak out against racism and ended the exclusion of African Americans from federal positions.

Harlem Renaissance The nation's first self-conscious black literary and artistic movement; it was centered in New York City's Harlem district, which had a largely black population in the wake of the Great Migration from the South.

Hartford Convention A series of secret meetings in December 1814 and January 1815 at which New England Federalists protested American involvement in the War of 1812 and discussed several constitutional amendments, including limiting each president to one term, designed to weaken the dominant Republican Party.

Haymarket Riot (1886) Violent uprising in Haymarket Square, Chicago, where police clashed with labor demonstrators in the aftermath of a bombing.

headright A land-grant policy that promised fifty acres to any colonist who could afford passage to Virginia, as well as fifty more for any accompanying servants. The headright policy was eventually expanded to include any colonists—and was also adopted in other colonies.

Patrick Henry (1736–1799) He inspired the Virginia Resolves, which declared that Englishmen could only be taxed by their elected representatives. In March of 1775, he met with other colonial leaders to discuss the goals of the upcoming Continental Congress and famously declared "Give me liberty or give me death." During the ratification process of the U.S. Constitution, he became one of the leaders of the anti-federalists.

Hiroshima (1945) Japanese port city that was the first target of the newly developed atomic bomb on August 6, 1945. Most of the city was destroyed.

Alger Hiss (1904–1996) During the second Red Scare he had served in several government departments and was accused of being a spy for the Soviet Union and was convicted of lying about espionage. The case was politically damaging to the Truman administration because the president called the charges against Hiss a "red herring."

Adolph Hitler (1889–1945) The leader of the Nazis who advocated a violent anti-Semitic, anti-Marxist, pan-German ideology. He started World War II in Europe and orchestrated the systematic murder of some 6 million Jews along with more than a million others.

HIV/AIDS Human immunodeficiency virus (HIV) transmitted via the bodily fluids of infected persons to cause acquired immunodeficiency syndrome (AIDS), an often-fatal disease of the immune system when it appeared in the 1980s.

holding company A corporation established to own and manage other companies' stock rather than to produce goods and services itself.

Holocaust Systematic racist attempt by the Nazis to exterminate the Jews of Europe, resulting in the murder of more than 6 million Jews and more than 5 million other "undesirables."

Homestead Act (1862) Legislation granting "homesteads" of 160 acres of government-owned land to settlers who agreed to work the land for at least five years.

Homestead Steel Strike (1892) Labor conflict at the Homestead steel mill near Pittsburgh, Pennsylvania, culminating in a battle between strikers and private security agents hired by the factory's management.

Herbert Hoover (1874–1964) Prior to becoming president, Hoover served as the secretary of commerce in both the Harding and Coolidge administrations. As president during the Great Depression, he believed that the nation's business structure was sound and sought to revive the economy through boosting the nation's confidence. He also tried to restart the economy with government constructions projects, lower taxes and new federal loan programs, but nothing worked.

horizontal integration The process by which a corporation acquires or merges with its competitors.

horse A tall, four-legged mammal (*Equus caballus*), domesticated and bred since prehistoric times for carrying riders and pulling heavy loads. The Spanish introduced horses to the Americas, eventually transforming many Native American cultures.

House Committee on Un-American Activities (HUAC) Committee of the U.S. House of Representatives formed in 1938; it was originally tasked with investigating Nazi subversion during the Second World War and later shifted its focus to rooting out Communists in the government and the motion-picture industry.

Sam Houston (1793–1863) During Texas's fight for independence from Mexico, Sam Houston was the commander in chief of the Texas forces, and he led the attack that captured General Antonio López de Santa Anna. After Texas gained its independence, he was named its first president.

How the Other Half Lives In this book, early muckraking journalist Jacob Riis exposed the slum conditions in New York City.

General William Howe (1729–1814) As the commander of the British army in the Revolutionary War, he seized New York City from Washington's army, but failed to capture it. He missed several more opportunities to quickly end the rebellion, and he resigned his command after the British defeat at Saratoga.

Saddam Hussein (1937–2006) The former dictator of Iraq who became the head of state in 1979. In 1980, he invaded Iran and started the eight-year-long Iran-Iraq War. In 1990, he invaded Kuwait, which caused the Gulf War of 1991. In 2003, he was overthrown and captured when the United States invaded. He was sentenced to death by hanging in 2006.

Anne Hutchinson (1591–1643) The articulate, strong-willed, and intelligent wife of a prominent Boston merchant, who espoused her belief in direct divine revelation. She quarreled with Puritan leaders over her beliefs; and they banished her from the colony.

Immigration Act of 1924 Federal legislation intended to favor northern and western European immigrants over those from southern and eastern Europe by restricting the number of immigrants from any one European country to 2 percent of the total number of immigrants per year, with an overall limit of slightly over 150,000 new arrivals per year.

Immigration and Nationality Services Act of 1965 Legislation that abolished discriminatory quotas based upon immigrants' national origin and treated all nationalities and races equally.

imperialism The use of diplomatic or military force to extend a nation's power and enhance its economic interests, often by acquiring territory or colonies and justifying such behavior with assumptions of racial superiority.

impressment The British navy used press-gangs to kidnap men in British and colonial ports who were then forced to serve in the British navy.

indentured servitude A defined period of labor (often four to seven years) which settlers consented to in exchange for having their passage to the New World paid by their "master."

Independent Treasury Act (1840) System created by President Martin Van Buren and approved by Congress in 1840 whereby the federal government moved its funds from favored state banks to the U.S. Treasury, whose financial transactions could only be in gold or silver coins of paper currency backed by gold or silver.

"Indian New Deal" This phrase refers to the reforms implemented for Native Americans during the New Deal era. John Collier, the commissioner of the Bureau of Indian Affairs (BIA), increased the access Native Americans had to relief programs and employed more Native Americans at the BIA. He worked to pass the Indian Reorganization Act. However, the version of the act passed by Congress was a much-diluted version of Collier's original proposal and did not greatly improve the lives of Native Americans.

Indian Removal Act (1830) Law permitting the forced relocation of Indians to federal lands west of the Mississippi River in exchange for the land they occupied in the East and South.

Indian wars Bloody conflicts between U.S. soldiers and Native Americans that raged in the West from the early 1860s to the late 1870s, sparked by American settlers moving into ancestral Indian lands.

Indochina This area of Southeast Asia consists of Laos, Cambodia, and Vietnam and was once controlled by France as a colony. After the Viet Minh defeated the French, the Geneva Accords were signed, which ended French colonial rule. The agreement created the independent nations of Laos and Cambodia and divided Vietnam along the 17th parallel until an election would reunify the country. Fearing a Communist take over, the United States government began intervening in the region during the Truman administration, which led to President Johnson's full-scale military involvement in Vietnam.

Industrial Revolution Major shift in the nineteenth century from hand-made manufacturing to mass production in mills and factories using water-, coal-, and steam-powered machinery.

industrial war A new concept of war enabled by industrialization that developed from the early 1800s through the Atomic Age. New technologies, including automatic weaponry, forms of transportation like the railroad and airplane, and communication technologies such as the telegraph and telephone, enabled nations to equip large, mass-conscripted armies with chemical and automatic weapons to decimate opposing armies in a "total war."

Industrial Workers of the World (IWW) A radical union organized in Chicago in 1905, nicknamed the Wobblies; its opposition to World War I led to its destruction by the federal government under the Espionage Act.

infectious diseases Also called contagious diseases, illnesses that can pass from one person to another by way of invasive biological organisms able to reproduce in the bodily tissues of their hosts. Europeans unwittingly brought many such diseases to the Americas, devastating the Native American peoples.

***The Influence of Sea Power upon History, 1660–1783* (1890)** Historical work in which Rear Admiral Alfred Thayer Mahan argues that a nation's greatness and prosperity comes from the power of its navy; the book helped bolster imperialist sentiment in the United States in the late nineteenth century.

Intermediate-Range Nuclear Forces (INF) Treaty (1987) Agreement signed by U.S. president Ronald Reagan and Soviet premier Mikhail Gorbachev to eliminate the deployment of intermediate-range missiles with nuclear warheads.

internal improvements Construction of roads, bridges, canals, harbors, and other infrastructural projects intended to facilitate the flow of goods and people.

internationalists Prior to the United States' entry in World War II, internationalists believed that America's national security depended on aiding Britain in its struggle against Germany.

Interstate Commerce Commission (ICC) (1887) An independent federal agency established to oversee businesses engaged in interstate trade, especially railroads, but whose regulatory power was limited when tested in the courts.

interstate highway system In the late 1950s, construction began on a national network of interstate superhighways for the purpose of commerce and defense. The interstate highways would enable the rapid movement of military convoys and the evacuation of cities after a nuclear attack.

Iran-Contra affair (1987) Reagan administration scandal over the secret, unlawful U.S. sale of arms to Iran in partial exchange for the release of hostages in Lebanon; the arms money in turn was used illegally to aid Nicaraguan right-wing insurgents, the Contras.

Iranian hostage crisis (1979) Storming of the U.S. embassy in Tehran by Iranian revolutionaries, who held fifty-two Americans hostage for 444 days, despite President Carter's appeals for their release as well as a botched rescue attempt.

Irish Potato Famine In 1845, an epidemic of potato rot brought a famine to rural Ireland that killed over 1 million peasants and instigated a huge increase in the number of Irish immigrating to America. By 1850, the Irish made up 43 percent of the foreign-born population in the United States; and in the 1850s, they made up over half the population of New York City and Boston.

iron curtain Term coined by Winston Churchill to describe the cold war divide between western Europe and the Soviet Union's Eastern European satellites.

Iroquois League An alliance of the Iroquois tribes, originally formed sometime between 1450 and 1600, that used their combined strength to pressure Europeans to work with them in the fur trade and to wage war across what is today eastern North America.

Andrew Jackson (1767–1837) As a major general in the Tennessee militia, he had a number of military successes. As president, he worked to enable the "common man" to play a greater role in the political arena. He vetoed the re-chartering of the Second National Bank and reduced federal spending. When South Carolina nullified the Tariffs of 1828 and 1832, Jackson requested that Congress pass a "force bill" that would authorize him to use the army to compel the state to comply with the tariffs. He forced eastern Indians to move west of the Mississippi River so their lands could be used by white settlers. Groups of those who opposed Jackson come together to form a new political party called the Whigs.

Thomas "Stonewall" Jackson (1824–1863) A Confederate general who was known for his fearlessness in leading rapid marches, bold flanking movements, and furious assaults. He earned his nickname at the Battle of the First Bull Run for standing courageously against Union fire. During the battle of Chancellorsville, his own men accidentally mortally wounded him.

William James (1842–1910) He was the founder of Pragmatism and one of the fathers of modern psychology. He believed that ideas gained their validity not from their inherent truth, but from their social consequences and practical application.

Jay's Treaty (1794) Agreement between Britain and the United States, negotiated by Chief Justice John Jay, that settled disputes over trade, prewar debts owed to British merchants, British-occupied forts in American territory, and the seizure of American ships and cargo.

Jazz Age Term coined by writer F. Scott Fitzgerald to characterize the spirit of rebellion and spontaneity among young Americans in the 1920s, a spirit epitomized by the hugely popular jazz music of the era.

Thomas Jefferson (1743–1826) He was a plantation owner, author, the drafter of the Declaration Independence, ambassador to France, leader of the Republican party, secretary of state, and the third president of the United States. As president, he purchased the Louisiana territory from France, withheld appointments made by President Adams leading to *Marybury v. Madison*, outlawed foreign slave trade, and was committed to a "wise and frugal" government.

Jeffersonian Republicans Political party founded by Thomas Jefferson in opposition to the Federalist Party led by Alexander Hamilton and John Adams; also known as the Democratic-Republican Party.

Jesuits A religious order founded in 1540 by Ignatius Loyola. They sought to counter the spread of Protestantism during the Protestant Reformation and spread the Catholic faith through work as missionaries. Roughly 3,500 served in New Spain and New France.

"Jim Crow" laws In the New South, these laws mandated the separation of races in various public places that served as a way for the ruling whites to impose their will on all areas of black life.

Andrew Johnson (1808–1875) He was elevated to the presidency after Abraham Lincoln's assassination. In order to restore the Union after the Civil War, he issued an amnesty proclamation and required former Confederate states to ratify the Thirteenth Amendment. After disagreements over the power to restore states rights, the Radical Republicans attempted to impeach Johnson but fell short on the required number of votes needed to remove him from office.

Lyndon B. Johnson (1908–1973) Former member of the House of Representatives and the former Majority Leader of the Senate, Vice President Lyndon B. Johnson assumed the presidency after President Kennedy's assassination. During his presidency, he passed the Civil Rights Act of 1964, declared a "war on poverty" promoting his own social program called the Great Society, and signed the Immigration and Nationality Service Act of 1965. Johnson greatly increased America's role in Vietnam.

Johnson's Restoration Plan Plan to require southern states to ratify the Thirteenth Amendment, disqualify wealthy ex-Confederates from voting, and appoint a Unionist governor.

joint-stock companies Businesses owned by investors, who purchase shares of companies' stocks and share all the profits and losses.

Kansas-Nebraska Act (1854) Controversial legislation that created two new territories taken from Native Americans, Kansas and Nebraska, where residents would vote to decide whether slavery would be allowed (popular sovereignty).

Florence Kelley (1859–1932) As the head of the National Consumer's League, she led the crusade to promote state laws to regulate the number of working hours imposed on women who were wives and mothers.

George F. Kennan (1904–2005) While working as an American diplomat, he devised the strategy of containment, which called for the halting of Soviet expansion. It became America's choice strategy throughout the cold war.

John F. Kennedy (1917–1963) He was elected president in 1960. Despite the difficulties he had in getting his legislation through Congress, he established the Alliance for Progress programs to help Latin America, the Peace Corps, the Trade Expansion Act of 1962, and funding for urban renewal projects and the space program. His foreign political involvement included the failed Bay of Pigs invasion and the missile crisis in Cuba, as well as support of local governments in Indochina. In 1963, he was assassinated by Lee Harvey Oswald in Dallas, Texas.

Kent State During the spring of 1970, students on college campuses across the country protested the expansion of the Vietnam War into Cambodia. At Kent State University, the National Guard attempted to quell the rioting students. The guardsmen panicked and shot at rock-throwing demonstrators. Four student bystanders were killed.

Kentucky and Virginia Resolutions (1798–1799) Passed in response to the Alien and Sedition Acts, the resolutions advanced the state-compact theory that held states could nullify an act of Congress if they deemed it unconstitutional.

Francis Scott Key (1779–1843) During the War of 1812, he watched British forces bombard Fort McHenry, but fail to take it. Seeing the American flag still flying over the fort at dawn inspired him to write "The Star-Spangled Banner," which became the American national anthem.

Martin Luther King, Jr. (1929–1968) A central leader of the civil rights movement, he urged people to use nonviolent civil disobedience to demand their rights and bring about change. He successfully led the Montgomery bus boycott. While in jail for his role in demonstrations, he wrote his famous "Letter from Birmingham City Jail," in which he defended his strategy of nonviolent protest. In 1963, he delivered his famous "I Have a Dream Speech" from the steps of the Lincoln Memorial as a part of the March on Washington. A year later, he was awarded the Nobel Peace Prize. In 1968, he was assassinated.

King Philip's War A bloody, three-year war in New England (1675–1678), resulting from the escalation of tensions between Indians and English settlers; the defeat of the Indians led to broadened freedoms for the settlers and their dispossessing the region's Indians of most of their land.

King William's War (War of the League of Augsburg) First (1689–1697) of four colonial wars between England and France.

Henry Kissinger (1923–) He served as the secretary of state and national security advisor in the Nixon administration. He negotiated with North Vietnam for an end to the Vietnam War, but the cease-fire did not last; South Vietnam fell to North Vietnam. He helped organize Nixon's historic trips to China and the Soviet Union. In the Middle East, he negotiated a cease-fire between Israel and its neighbors following the Yom Kippur War and solidified Israel's promise to return to Egypt most of the land it had taken during the 1967 war.

Knights of Labor A national labor organization with a broad reform platform; reached peak membership in the 1880s.

Know-Nothing party Nativist, anti-Catholic third party organized in 1854 in reaction to large-scale German and Irish immigration.

Ku Klux Klan Organized in Pulaski, Tennessee, in 1866 to terrorize former slaves who voted and held political offices during Reconstruction; a revived organization in the 1910s and 1920s stressed white, Anglo-Saxon, fundamentalist Protestant supremacy; the Klan revived a third time to fight the civil rights movement of the 1950s and 1960s in the South.

Marquis de Lafayette (1757–1834) A wealthy French idealist excited by the American cause, he offered to serve in Washington's army for free in exchange for being named a major general. He overcame Washington's initial skepticism to become one of his most trusted aides.

laissez-faire An economic doctrine holding that businesses and individuals should be able to pursue their economic interests without government interference.

Land Ordinance of 1785 Directed surveying of the Northwest Territory into townships of thirty-six sections (square miles) each, the sale of the sixteenth section of which was to be used to finance public education.

League of Nations Organization of nations formed in the aftermath of the First World War to mediate disputes and maintain international peace; despite President Wilson's intense lobbying for the League of Nations, Congress did not ratify the treaty and the United States failed to join.

Mary Elizabeth Lease (1850–1933) She was a leader of the farm protest movement who advocated violence if change could not be obtained at the ballot box. She believed that the urban-industrial East was the enemy of the working class.

Robert E. Lee (1807–1870) Even though he had served in the United States Army for thirty years, he chose to fight on the side of the Confederacy. Lee was excellent at using his field commanders and his soldiers respected him. However, General Ulysses S. Grant eventually wore down his army, and Lee surrendered to Grant at the Appomattox Court House on April 9, 1865.

Lend-Lease Bill (1941) Legislation that allowed the president to lend or lease military equipment to any country whose own defense was deemed vital to the defense of the United States.

Levittown First low-cost, mass-produced development of suburban tract housing built by William Levitt on Long Island, New York, in 1947.

Lewis and Clark Expedition (1804–1806) Led by Meriwether Lewis and William Clark, a mission to the Pacific coast commissioned for the purposes of scientific and geographical exploration

Battle of Lexington and Concord The first shots fired in the Revolutionary War, on April 19, 1775, near Boston; approximately 100 Minutemen and 250 British soldiers were killed.

Liberator William Lloyd Garrison started this anti-slavery newspaper in 1831 in which he renounced gradualism and called for abolition.

Queen Liliuokalani (1838–1917) In 1891, she ascended to the throne of the Hawaiian royal family and tried to eliminate white control of the Hawaiian government. Two years later, Hawaii's white population revolted and seized power with the support of American Marines.

Abraham Lincoln (1809–1865) Shortly after he was elected president in 1860, southern states began seceding from the Union, and in April of 1861 he declared war on the seceding states. On January 1, 1863, Lincoln signed the Emancipation Proclamation. At the end of the war, he favored a reconstruction strategy for the former Confederate states that did not radically alter southern social and economic life. He was assassinated by John Wilkes Booth at Ford's Theater on April 14, 1865.

Lincoln-Douglas debates (1858) During the Illinois race between Republican Abraham Lincoln and Democrat Stephen A. Douglas for a seat in the U.S. Senate, a series of seven dramatic debates focusing on the issue of slavery in the territories.

John Locke (1632-1704) An English philosopher whose ideas were influential during the Enlightenment. He argued in his *Essay on Human Understanding* (1690) that humanity is largely the product of the environment, the mind being a blank tablet, *tabula rasa*, on which experience is written.

Henry Cabot Lodge (1850–1924) He was the chairman of the Senate Foreign Relations Committee who favored limiting America's involvement in the League of Nations' covenant and sought to amend the Treaty of Versailles.

de Lôme letter (1898) Private correspondence written by the Spanish ambassador to the U.S., Depuy de Lôme, that described President McKinley as "weak"; the letter was stolen by Cuban revolutionaries and published in the *New York Journal*, deepening American resentment of Spain and moving the two countries closer to war in Cuba.

Lone Star Republic After winning independence from Mexico, Texas became its own nation that was called the Lone Star Republic. In 1836, Texans drafted a constitution, legalized slavery, banned free blacks, named Sam Houston president, and voted for the annexation to the United States. However, quarrels over adding a slave state and fears of instigating a war with Mexico delayed Texas's entrance into the Union until December 29, 1845.

Huey P. Long (1893–1935) He began his political career in Louisiana where he developed a reputation for being an unscrupulous reformer. As a U.S. senator, he became a critic of President Roosevelt's New Deal Plan and offered his alternative called the Share-the-Wealth program. He was assassinated in 1935.

Louisiana Purchase (1803) President Thomas Jefferson's purchase of the Louisiana Territory from France for $15 million, doubling the size of U.S. territory.

Lowell system Model New England factory communities that during the first half of the nineteenth century provided employees, mostly young women, with meals, a boardinghouse, and moral discipline, as well as educational and cultural opportunities.

Loyalists Colonists who remained loyal to Great Britain before and during the Revolutionary War.

Lusitania British ocean liner torpedoed and sunk by a German U-boat; the deaths of nearly 1,200 of its civilian passengers, including many Americans, caused international outrage.

Martin Luther (1483–1546) A German monk who founded the Lutheran church. He protested abuses in the Catholic Church by posting his Ninety-five Theses, which began the Protestant Reformation.

General Douglas MacArthur (1880–1964) During World War II, he and Admiral Chester Nimitz dislodged the Japanese military from the Pacific Islands they had occupied. Following the war, he was in charge of the occupation of Japan. After North Korea invaded South Korea, Truman sent the U.S. military to defend South Korea under the command of MacArthur. Later in the war, Truman expressed his willingness to negotiate the restoration of prewar boundaries which MacArthur attempted to undermine. Truman fired MacArthur for his open insubordination.

James Madison (1751–1836) He participated in the Constitutional Convention during which he proposed the Virginia Plan. He believed in a strong federal government and was a leader of the Federalists. However, he also presented to Congress the Bill of Rights and drafted the Virginia Resolutions. As secretary of state, he withheld a commission for William Marbury, which led to the landmark *Marbury v. Madison* decision. During his presidency, he declared war on Britain in response to violations of American shipping rights, which started the War of 1812.

U.S. battleship *Maine* American warship that exploded in the Cuban port of Havana on January 25, 1898; though later discovered to be the result of an accident, the destruction of the *Maine* was attributed by war-hungry Americans to Spain, contributing to the onset of the War of 1812.

maize (corn) The primary grain crop in Mesoamerica yielding small kernels often ground into cornmeal. Easy to grow in a broad range of conditions, it enabled a global population explosion after being brought to Europe, Africa, and Asia.

Malcolm X (1925–1964) The most articulate spokesman for black power. Originally the chief disciple of Elijah Muhammad, the black Muslim leader in the United States, Malcolm X broke away and founded his own organization committed to establishing relations between African Americans and the nonwhite peoples of the world. Near the end of his life, he began to preach a biracial message of social change. In 1964, he was assassinated by members of a rival group of black Muslims.

Manchuria incident The northeast region of Manchuria was an area contested between China and Russia. In 1931, the Japanese claimed that they needed to protect their extensive investments in the area and moved their army into Manchuria. They quickly conquered the region and set up their own puppet empire. China asked both the United States and the League of Nations for help and neither responded.

manifest destiny The widespread belief that America was "destined" by God to expand westward across the continent into lands claimed by Native Americans as well as European nations.

Horace Mann (1796–1859) He believed the public school system was the best way to achieve social stability and equal opportunity. As a reformer of education, he sponsored a state board of education, the first state-supported "normal" school for training teachers, a state association for teachers, the minimum school year of six months, and led the drive for a statewide school system.

***Marbury v. Madison* (1803)** First Supreme Court decision to declare a federal law—the Judiciary Act of 1801—unconstitutional.

March on Washington Civil rights demonstration on August 28, 1963, on the National Mall, where Martin Luther King, Jr. gave his famous "I Have a Dream" speech.

market economy Large-scale manufacturing and commercial agriculture that emerged in America during the first half of the nineteenth century, displacing much of the pre-market subsistence and barter-based economy and producing boom-and-bust cycles while raising the American standard of living.

George C. Marshall (1880–1959) As the chairman of the Joint Chiefs of Staff, he orchestrated the Allied victories over Germany and Japan in the Second World War. In 1947, he became President Truman's secretary of state and proposed the massive reconstruction program for western Europe called the Marshall Plan.

Chief Justice John Marshall (1755–1835) During his long tenure as chief justice of the supreme court (1801–1835), he established the foundations for American jurisprudence, the authority of the Supreme Court, and the constitutional supremacy of the national government over states.

Marshall Plan (1948) Secretary of State George C. Marshall's post–World War II program providing massive U.S. financial and technical assistance to war-torn European countries.

Massachusetts Bay Colony English colony founded by English Puritans in 1630 as a haven for persecuted Congregationalists.

"massive resistance" White rallying cry disrupting federal efforts to enforce racial integration in the South.

"massive retaliation" Strategy that used the threat of nuclear warfare as a means of combating the global spread of communism.

Mayflower Compact A formal agreement signed by the Separatist colonists aboard the *Mayflower* in 1620 to abide by laws made by leaders of their own choosing.

Senator Joseph R. McCarthy (1908–1957) In 1950, this senator became the shrewdest and most ruthless exploiter of America's anxiety of communism. He claimed that the United States government was full of Communists and led a witch hunt to find them, but he was never able to uncover a single communist agent.

McCarthyism Anti-Communist hysteria led by Senator Joseph McCarthy's "witch hunts" attacking the loyalty of politicians, federal employees, and public figures, despite a lack of evidence.

George B. McClellan (1826–1885) In 1861, President Abraham Lincoln appointed him head of the Army of the Potomac and, later, general in chief of the U.S. Army. He built his army into well trained and powerful force. After failing to achieve a decisive victory against the Confederacy, he was removed from command in 1862.

Cyrus Hall McCormick (1809–1884) In 1831, he invented a mechanical reaper to harvest wheat, which transformed the scale of agriculture. By hand a farmer could only harvest a half an acre a day, while the McCormick reaper allowed two people to harvest twelve acres of wheat a day.

McCormick reaper Mechanical reaper invented by Cyrus Hall McCormick in 1831 that dramatically increased the production of wheat.

***McCulloch v. Maryland* (1819)** Supreme Court ruling that prohibited states from taxing the Bank of the United States.

William McKinley (1843–1901) As a congressman, he was responsible for the McKinley Tariff of 1890, which raised the duties on manufactured products to their highest level ever. Voters disliked the tariff and McKinley, as well as other Republicans, lost his seat in Congress the next election. However, he won the presidential election of 1896 and raised the tariffs again. In 1898, he annexed Hawaii and declared war on Spain. The war concluded with the Treaty of Paris, which gave America control over Puerto Rico, Guam, and the Philippines. Soon America was fighting Filipinos, who were seeking independence for their country. In 1901, McKinley was assassinated.

Robert McNamara (1916–) He was the secretary of defense for both President Kennedy and President Johnson and a supporter of America's involvement in Vietnam.

Medicare and Medicaid Health-care programs designed to aid the elderly and disadvantaged, respectively, as part of President Johnson's Great Society initiative.

Andrew W. Mellon (1855–1937) As President Harding's secretary of the Treasury, he sought to generate economic growth through reducing government spending and lowering taxes. However, he insisted that the tax reductions mainly go to the rich because he believed the wealthy would reinvest their money. In order to bring greater efficiency and nonpartisanship to the government's budget process, he persuaded Congress to created a new Bureau of the Budget and a General Accounting Office.

mercantilism Policy of Great Britain and other imperial powers of regulating the economies of colonies to benefit the mother country.

James Meredith (1933–) In 1962, the governor of Mississippi defied a Supreme Court ruling and refused to allow James Meredith, an African American, to enroll at the University of Mississippi. Federal marshals were sent to enforce the law which led to clashes between a white mob and the marshals. Federal troops intervened and two people were killed and many others were injured. A few days later, Meredith was able to register at the university.

Merrimack* (ship renamed the *Virginia*) and the *Monitor First engagement between ironclad ships; fought at Hampton Roads, Virginia, on March 9, 1862.

Metacomet or King Philip (?–1676) The chief of the Wampanoages, who the colonists called King Philip. He resented English efforts to convert Indians to Christianity and waged a war against the English colonists in which he was killed.

Mexica Otherwise known as "Aztecs," a Mesoamerican people of northern Mexico who founded the vast Aztec Empire in the fourteenth century, later conquered by the Spanish under Hernán Cortés in 1521.

microprocessor An electronic circuit printed on a small silicon chip; a major technological breakthrough in 1971, it paved the way for the development of the personal computer.

Middle Passage The hellish and often deadly middle leg of the transatlantic "Triangular Trade" in which European ships carried manufactured goods to Africa, then transported enslaved Africans to the Americas and the Caribbean, and finally conveyed American agricultural products back to Europe; from the late sixteenth to the early nineteenth centuries, some 12 million Africans were transported via the Middle Passage, unknown millions more dying en route.

militant nonviolence After the success of the Montgomery bus boycott, people were inspired by Martin Luther King, Jr.'s use of this nonviolent form of protest. Throughout the civil rights movement, demonstrators used this method of protest to challenge racial segregation in the South.

Militia Act (1862) Congressional measure that permitted freed slaves to serve as laborers or soldiers in the United States Army.

Ho Chi Minh (1890–1969) He was the Vietnamese communist resistance leader who drove the French and the United States out of Vietnam. After the Geneva Accords divided the region into four countries, he controlled North Vietnam, and ultimately became the leader of all of Vietnam at the conclusion of the Vietnam War.

minstrelsy A form of entertainment that was popular from the 1830s to the 1870s. The performances featured white performers who were made up as African Americans or blackface. They performed banjo and fiddle music, "shuffle" dances and lowbrow humor that reinforced racial stereotypes.

Minutemen Special units organized by the militia to be ready for quick mobilization.

Miranda v. Arizona **(1966)** U.S. Supreme Court decision required police to advise persons in custody of their rights to legal counsel and against self-incrimination.

Mississippi Plan (1890) Series of state constitutional amendments that sought to severely disenfranchise black voters and were quickly adopted by other southern states.

Missouri Compromise (1820) Legislative decision to admit Missouri as a slave state and abolish slavery in the area west of the Mississippi River and north of the parallel 36°30′.

Model T Ford Henry Ford developed this model of car so that it was affordable for everyone. Its success led to an increase in the production of automobiles which stimulated other related industries such steel, oil, and rubber. The mass use of automobiles increased the speed goods could be transported, encouraged urban sprawl, and sparked real estate booms in California and Florida.

moderate Republicanism Promise to curb federal government and restore state and local government authority, spearheaded by President Eisenhower.

modernism An early-twentieth-century intellectual and artistic movement that rejected traditional notions of reality and adopted radical new forms of artistic expression.

monopoly A corporation so large that it effectively controls the entire market for its products or services.

"money question" Late-nineteenth-century national debate over the nature of U.S. currency; supporters of a fixed gold standard were generally money lenders, and thus preferred to keep the value of money high, while supporters of silver (and gold) coinage were debtors, they owed money, so they wanted to keep the value of money low by increasing the currency supply (inflation).

James Monroe (1758–1831) He served as secretary of state and war under President Madison and was elected president. As the latter, he signed the Transcontinental Treaty with Spain which gave the United States Florida and expanded the Louisiana territory's western border to the Pacific coast. In 1823, he established the Monroe Doctrine. This foreign policy proclaimed the American continents were no longer open to colonization and America would be neutral in European affairs.

Monroe Doctrine (1823) U.S. foreign policy that barred further colonization in the Western Hemisphere by European powers and pledged that there would be no American interference with any existing European colonies.

Montgomery bus boycott Boycott of bus system in Montgomery, Alabama, organized by civil rights activists after the arrest of Rosa Parks.

Moral Majority Televangelist Jerry Falwell's political lobbying organization, the name of which became synonymous with the religious right—conservative evangelical Protestants who helped ensure President Ronald Reagan's 1980 victory.

J. Pierpont Morgan (1837–1913) As a powerful investment banker, he would acquire, reorganize, and consolidate companies into giant trusts. His biggest achievement was the consolidation of the steel industry into the United States Steel Corporation, which was the first billion-dollar corporation.

J. Pierpont Morgan and Company An investment bank under the leadership of J. Pierpont Morgan that bought or merged unrelated American companies, often using capital acquired from European investors.

Mormons Members of the Church of Jesus Christ of Latter-day Saints, which dismissed other Christian denominations, emphasizing universal salvation and a modest lifestyle; Mormons were often persecuted for their secrecy and clannishness.

Morrill Land-Grant College Act (1862) Federal statute that allowed for the creation of land-grant colleges and universities, which were founded to provide technical education in agriculture, mining, and industry.

Samuel F. B. Morse (1791–1872) In 1832, he invented the telegraph and revolutionized the speed of communication.

mountain men Inspired by the fur trade, these men left civilization to work as trappers and reverted to a primitive existence in the wilderness. They were the first white people to find routes through the Rocky Mountains, and they pioneered trails that settlers later used to reach the Oregon country and California in the 1840s.

muckrakers Writers who exposed corruption and abuses in politics, business, consumer safety, working conditions, and more, spurring public interest in progressive reforms.

Mugwumps Reformers who bolted the Republican party in 1884 to support Democratic Grover Cleveland for president over Republican James G. Blaine, whose secret dealings on behalf of railroad companies had brought charges of corruption.

mulattoes Mixed-race people who constituted most of the South's free black population.

Benito Mussolini (1883–1945) The Italian founder of the Fascist party who came to power in Italy in 1922 and allied himself with Adolf Hitler and the Axis powers during the Second World War.

National Association for the Advancement of Colored People (NAACP) Organization founded in 1910 by black activists and white progressives that promoted education as a means of combating social problems and focused on legal action to secure the civil rights supposedly guaranteed by the Fourteenth and Fifteenth Amendments.

North American Free Trade Agreement (NAFTA) (1994) Agreement eliminating trade barriers that was signed by the United States, Canada, and Mexico, making North America the largest free-trade zone in the world.

North Atlantic Treaty Organization (NATO) Defensive political and military alliance formed in 1949 by the United States, Canada, and ten Western European nations to deter Soviet expansion in Europe.

National Banking Act (1863) The U.S. Congress created a national banking system to finance the enormous expense of the Civil War. It enabled loans to the government and established a single national currency, including the issuance of paper money ("greenbacks").

National Industrial Recovery Act (1933) Passed on the last of the Hundred Days; it created public-works jobs through the Federal Emergency Relief Administration and established a system of self-regulation for industry through the National Recovery Administration, which was ruled unconstitutional in 1935.

National Labor Union A federation of labor and reform leaders established in 1866 to advocate for new state and local laws to improve working conditions.

National Recovery Administration (1933) Controversial federal agency that brought together business and labor leaders to create "codes of fair competition" and "fair labor" policies, including a national minimum wage.

National Security Act (1947) Congressional legislation that created the Department of Defense, the National Security Council, and the Central Intelligence Agency.

National Socialist German Workers' Party (Nazi) Founded in the 1920s, this party gained control over Germany under the leadership of Adolf Hitler in 1933 and continued in power until Germany's defeat at the end of the Second World War. It advocated a violent anti-Semitic, anti-Marxist, pan-German ideology. The Nazi party perpetrated the Holocaust.

National Trades' Unions Formed in 1834 to organize all local trade unions into a stronger national association, only to be dissolved amid the economic depression during the late 1830s.

nativism Reactionary conservative movement characterized by heightened nationalism, anti-immigrant sentiment, and the enactment of laws setting stricter regulations on immigration.

natural rights An individual's basic rights that should not be violated by any government or community.

Navigation Acts (1650–1775) Restrictions passed by the British Parliament to control colonial trade and bolster the mercantile system.

Negrophobia A violent new wave of racism that spread in the late nineteenth century largely spurred by white resentment for African American financial success and growing political influence.

new conservatism The political philosophy of those who led the conservative insurgency of the early 1980s. This brand of conservatism was personified in Ronald Reagan who believed in less government, supply-side economics, and "family values."

First New Deal Franklin D. Roosevelt's campaign promise, in his speech to the Democratic National Convention of 1932, to combat the Great Depression with a "new deal for the American people;" the phrase became a catchword for his ambitious plan of economic programs.

New Democrats Centrist ("moderate") Democrats led by President Bill Clinton that emerged in the late 1980s and early 1990s to challenge the "liberal" direction of the party.

"new economy" Period of sustained economic prosperity during the nineties marked by budget surpluses, the explosion of dot.com industries, low inflation, and low unemployment.

New France The name used for the area of North America that was colonized by the French. Unlike Spanish or English colonies, New France had a small number of colonists, which forced them to initially seek good relations with the indigenous people they encountered.

New Freedom Program championed in 1912 by the Woodrow Wilson campaign that aimed to restore competition in the economy by eliminating all trusts rather than simply regulating them.

New Frontier Proposed domestic program championed by the incoming Kennedy administration in 1961 that aimed to jump-start the economy and trigger social progress.

"new immigrants" Wave of newcomers from southern and eastern Europe, including many Jews, who became a majority among immigrants to America after 1890.

New Jersey Plan The delegations to the Constitutional Convention were divided between two plans on how to structure the government: New Jersey wanted one legislative body with equal representation for each state.

New Left Term coined by the Students for a Democratic Society to distinguish their efforts at grassroots democracy from those of the 1930s Old Left, which had embraced orthodox Marxism.

New Mexico A U.S. territory and later a state in the American Southwest, originally established by the Spanish, who settled there in the sixteenth century, founded Catholic missions, and exploited the region's indigenous peoples.

New Nationalism Platform of the Progressive party and slogan of former President Theodore Roosevelt in the presidential campaign of 1912; stressed government activism, including regulation of trusts, conservation, and recall of state court decisions that had nullified progressive programs.

"New Negro" In the 1920s, a slow and steady growth of black political influence occurred in northern cities where African Americans were freer to speak and act. This political activity created a spirit of protest that expressed itself culturally in the Harlem Renaissance and politically in "new Negro" nationalism.

New Netherland Dutch colony conquered by the English in 1667 and out of which four new colonies were created—New York, New Jersey, Pennsylvania, and Delaware.

Battle of New Orleans (1815) Final major battle in the War of 1812, in which the Americans under General Andrew Jackson unexpectedly and decisively countered the British attempt to seize the port of New Orleans, Louisiana.

New South *Atlanta Constitution* editor Henry W. Grady's 1886 term for the prosperous post–Civil War South: democratic, industrial, urban, and free of nostalgia for the defeated plantation South.

New York Journal In the late 1890s, William Randolph Hearst's *New York Journal* and its rival, the *New York World*, printed sensationalism on the Cuban revolution as part of their heated competition for readership. The *New York Journal* printed a negative letter from the Spanish ambassador about President McKinley and inflammatory coverage of the sinking of the *Maine* in Havana Harbor. These two events roused the American public's outcry against Spain.

New York World In the late 1890s, Joseph Pulitzer's *New York World* and its rival, the *New York Journal*, printed sensationalism on the Cuban revolution as part of their heated competition for readership.

Admiral Chester Nimitz (1885–1966) During the Second World War, he was the commander of central Pacific. Along with General Douglas MacArthur, he dislodged the Japanese military from the Pacific Islands they had occupied.

Nineteenth Amendment (1920) Constitutional amendment that granted women the right to vote.

Richard M. Nixon (1913–1994) He first came to national prominence as a congress-man involved in the investigation of Alger Hiss, and later served as vice president during the Eisenhower administration. After being elected president in 1968, he slowed the federal enforcement of civil rights and appointed pro-Southern justices to the

Supreme Court. He began a program of Vietnamization of the war. In 1973, America, North and South Vietnam, and the Viet Cong agreed to end the war and the United States withdrew. However, the cease-fire was broken, and the South Vietnam fell to North Vietnam. In 1970, Nixon declared that America was no longer the world's policeman and he would seek some partnerships with Communist countries, historically traveling to China and the Soviet Union. In 1972, he was reelected, but the Watergate scandal erupted shortly after his victory; he resigned the presidency under threat of impeachment.

No Child Left Behind President George W. Bush's education reform plan that required states to set and meet learning standards for students and make sure that all students were "proficient" in reading and writing by 2014. States had to submit annual reports of students' standardized test scores. Teachers were required to be "proficient" in their subject area. Schools who failed to show progress would face sanctions. States criticized the lack of funding for remedial programs and noted that poor school districts would find it very difficult to meet the new guidelines.

nonviolent civil disobedience Tactic of defying unjust laws through peaceful actions championed by Dr. Martin Luther King, Jr.

Lord North (1732–1792) The first minister of King George III's cabinet whose efforts to subdue the colonies only brought them closer to revolution. He helped bring about the Tea Act of 1773, which led to the Boston Tea Party. In an effort to discipline Boston, he wrote, and Parliament passed, four acts that galvanized colonial resistance.

North Atlantic Treaty Organization (NATO) Defensive alliance founded in 1949 by ten western European nations, the United States, and Canada to deter Soviet expansion in Europe.

Northwest Ordinance (1787) Land policy for new western territories in the Ohio valley that established the terms and conditions for self-government and statehood while also banning slavery from the region.

NSC-68 (1950) Top-secret policy paper approved by President Truman that outlined a militaristic approach to combating the spread of global communism.

nullification The right claimed by some states to veto a federal law deemed unconstitutional.

Nuremberg trials At the site of the annual Nazi party rallies, twenty-one major German offenders faced an international military tribunal for Nazi atrocities. After a ten-month trial, the court acquitted three and sentenced eleven to death, three to life imprisonment, and four to shorter terms.

Barack Obama (1961–) In the 2008 presidential election, Senator Barack Obama mounted an innovative Internet based and grassroots orientated campaign. As the nation's economy nose-dived in the fall of 2008, Obama linked the Republican economic philosophy with the country's dismal financial state and promoted a message of "change" and "politics of hope," which resonated with voters. He decisively won the presidency and became America's first person of color to be elected president. In 2012, Obama successfully won re-election to serve as president for a second term.

Occupy Wall Street A grassroots movement protesting a capitalist system that fostered social and economic inequality. Begun in Zuccotti Park, New York City, during 2011, the movement spread rapidly across the nation, triggering a national conversation about income inequality and protests of the government's "bailouts" of the banks and corporations allegedly responsible for the Great Recession.

Sandra Day O'Connor (1930–) She was the first woman to serve on the Supreme Court of the United States and was appointed by President Reagan. Reagan's critics charged that her appointment was a token gesture and not a sign of any real commitment to gender equality.

Ohio gang In order to escape the pressures of the White House, President Harding met with a group of people, called the "Ohio gang," in a house on K Street in Washington D.C. Members of this gang were given low-level positions in the American government and they used their White House connection to "line their pockets" by granting government contracts without bidding, which led to a series of scandals, most notably the Teapot Dome Scandal.

Old Southwest Region covering western Georgia, Alabama, Mississippi, Louisiana, Arkansas, and Texas, where low land prices and fertile soil attracted hundreds of thousands of settlers after the American Revolution.

Frederick Law Olmsted (1822–1903) In 1858, he constructed New York's Central Park, which led to a growth in the movement to create urban parks. He went on to design parks for Boston, Brooklyn, Chicago, Philadelphia, San Francisco, and many other cities.

Open Door policy (1899) Official U.S. insistence that Chinese trade would be open to all nations; Secretary of State John Hay unilaterally announced the policy in hopes of protecting the Chinese market for U.S. exports.

open shop Business policy of not requiring union membership as a condition of employment; such a policy, where legal, has the effect of weakening unions and diminishing workers' rights.

open range Informal system of governing property on the frontier in which small ranchers could graze their cattle anywhere on unfenced lands; brought to an end by the introduction of barbed wire, a low-cost way to fence off one's land.

Operation Desert Shield After Saddam Hussein invaded Kuwait in 1990, President George H. W. Bush sent American military forces to Saudi Arabia on a strictly defensive mission. They were soon joined by a multinational coalition. When the coalition's mission changed to the retaking of Kuwait, the operation was renamed Desert Storm.

Operation Desert Storm (1991) Assault by American-led multinational forces that quickly defeated Iraqi forces under Saddam Hussein in the First Gulf War, ending the Iraqi occupation of Kuwait.

Operation Overlord The Allies' assault on Hitler's "Atlantic Wall," a seemingly impregnable series of fortifications and minefields along the French coastline that German forces had created using captive Europeans for laborers.

J. Robert Oppenheimer (1904–1967) He led the group of physicists at the laboratory in Los Alamos, New Mexico, who constructed the first atomic bomb.

Oregon Country The Convention of 1818 between Britain and the United States established the Oregon Country as being west of the crest of the Rocky Mountains and the two countries were to jointly occupy it. In 1824, the United States and Russia signed a treaty that established the line of 54°40′ as the southern boundary of Russia's territorial claim in North America. A similar agreement between Britain and Russia finally gave the Oregon Country clearly defined boarders, but it remained under joint British and American control.

"Oregon Fever" The lure of fertile land and economic opportunities in the Oregon Country that drew thousands of settlers westward, beginning in the late 1830s.

Osceola (1804?–1838) He was the leader of the Seminole nation who resisted the federal Indian removal policy through a protracted guerilla war. In 1837, he was treacherously seized under a flag of truce and imprisoned at Fort Moultrie, where he was left to die.

Overland Trails Trail routes followed by wagon trains bearing settlers and trade goods from Missouri to the Oregon Country, California, and New Mexico, beginning in the 1840s.

Pacific Railway Act (1862) Congress provided funding for a transcontinental railroad from Nebraska west to California.

A. Mitchell Palmer (1872–1936) As the attorney general, he played an active role in the government's response to the Red Scare. After several bombings across America, including one at Palmer's home, he and other Americans became convinced that there was a well-organized Communist terror campaign at work. The federal government launched a campaign of raids, deportations, and collecting files on radical individuals.

Panic of 1819 A financial panic that began a three-year-long economic crisis triggered by a reduced demand of American imports, declining land values, and reckless practices by local and state banks.

Panic of 1873 A financial calamity in the United States brought on by a dramatic slowdown in the British economy and exacerbated by falling cotton prices, failed crops, high inflation, and reckless state banks.

Panic of 1893 A major collapse in the national economy after several major railroad companies declared bankruptcy, leading to a severe depression and several violent clashes between workers and management.

panning A method of mining that used a large metal pan to sift gold dust and nuggets from riverbeds during the California gold rush of 1849.

Rosa Parks (1913–2005) In 1955, she refused to give up her seat to a white man on a city bus in Montgomery, Alabama, which a local ordinance required of blacks. She was arrested for disobeying the ordinance. In response, black community leaders organized the Montgomery bus boycott.

Parliament Legislature of Great Britain, composed of the House of Commons, whose members are elected, and the House of Lords, whose members are either hereditary or appointed.

party "boss" A powerful political leader who controlled a "machine" of associates and operatives to promote both individual and party interests, often using informal tactics such as intimidation or the patronage system.

paternalism A moral position developed during the first half of the nineteenth century which claimed that slaves were deprived of liberty for their own "good." Such a rationalization was adopted by some slave owners to justify slavery.

Patriots Colonists who rebelled against British authority before and during the Revolutionary War.

patronage An informal system (sometimes called the "spoils system") used by politicians to reward their supporters with government appointments or contracts.

Alice Paul (1885–1977) She was a leader of the women's suffrage movement and head of the Congressional Committee of National Women Suffrage Association. She instructed female suffrage activists to use more militant tactics, such as picketing state legislatures, chaining themselves to public buildings, inciting police to arrest them, and undertaking hunger strikes.

Norman Vincent Peale (1898–1993) He was a champion of the upbeat and feel-good theology that was popular in the 1950s religious revival. He advocated getting rid of any depressing or negative thoughts and replacing them with "faith, enthusiasm and joy," which would make an individual popular and well liked.

Pearl Harbor (1941) Surprise Japanese attack on the U.S. fleet at Pearl Harbor on December 7, which prompted the immediate American entry into the war.

"peculiar institution" A phrase used by whites in the antebellum South to refer to slavery without using the word slavery.

Pennsylvania English colony founded by William Penn in 1681 as a Quaker commonwealth, though it welcomed people of all religions.

Pentagon Papers Informal name for the Defense Department's secret history of the Vietnam conflict; leaked to the press by former official Daniel Ellsberg and published in the *New York Times* in 1971.

People's party (Populists) Political party largely made up of farmers from the South and West that struggled to gain political influence from the East. Populists advocated a variety of reforms, including free coinage of silver, a progressive income tax, postal savings banks, regulation of railroads, and direct election of U.S. senators.

Pequot War Massacre in 1637 and subsequent dissolution of the Pequot Nation by Puritan settlers, who seized the Indians' lands.

perestroika Russian term for "economic restructuring"; applied to Mikhail Gorbachev's series of political and economic reforms that included shifting a centrally planned Commmunist economy to a mixed economy allowing for capitalism.

Commodore Matthew Perry (1794–1858) In 1854, he negotiated the Treaty of Kanagawa, which was the first step in starting a political and commercial relationship between the United States and Japan.

John J. Pershing United States general sent by President Wilson to put down attacks on the Mexican border led by Francisco "Pancho" Villa.

Personal Responsibility and Work Opportunity Act of 1996 (PRWOA) Comprehensive welfare-reform measure, passed by a Republican Congress and signed by President Clinton, that aimed to decrease the size of the "welfare state" by limiting the amount of government aid provided the unemployed so as to encourage recipients to find jobs.

"pet banks" During President Andrew Jackson's fight with the national bank, Jackson resolved to remove all federal deposits from it. To comply with Jackson's demands, Secretary of the Treasury Taney continued to draw on government's accounts in the national bank, but deposit all new federal receipts in state banks. The state banks that received these deposits were called "pet banks."

Pilgrims Puritan Separatists who broke completely with the Church of England and sailed to the New World aboard the *Mayflower*, founding Plymouth Colony on Cape Cod in 1620.

Dien Bien Phu Cluster of Vietnamese villages and site of a major Vietnamese victory over the French in the First Indochina War.

Gifford Pinchot (1865–1946) As the head of the Division of Forestry, he implemented a conservation policy that entailed the scientific management of natural resources to serve the public interest. His work helped start the conservation movement.

Elizabeth Lucas Pinckney (1722? –1793) One of the most enterprising horticulturists in colonial America, she began managing her family's three plantations in South Carolina at the age of sixteen. She had tremendous success growing indigo, which led to many other plantations growing the crop as well.

Pinckney's Treaty Treaty with Spain negotiated by Thomas Pinckney in 1795; established United States boundaries at the Mississippi River and the 31st parallel and allowed open transportation on the Mississippi.

Francisco Pizarro (1478?–1541) In 1531, he lead his Spanish soldiers to Peru and conquered the Inca Empire.

"plain white folk" Yeoman farmers who lived and worked on their own small farms, growing a food and cash crops to trade for necessities.

plantation mistress Matriarch of a planter's household, responsible for supervising the domestic aspects of the estate.

planters Owners of large farms in the South that were worked by twenty or more slaves and supervised by overseers.

political "machine" A network of political activists and elected officials, usually controlled by a powerful "boss," that attempts to manipulate local politics

James Knox Polk "Young Hickory" (1795–1849) As president, his chief concern was the expansion of the United States. Shortly, after taking office, Mexico broke off relations with the United States over the annexation of Texas. Polk declared war on Mexico and sought to subvert Mexican authority in California. The United States defeated Mexico; and the two nations signed the Treaty of Guadalupe Hidalgo in which Mexico gave up any claims on Texas north of the Rio Grande River and ceded New Mexico and California to the United States.

Pontiac's Rebellion (1763) An Indian attack on British forts and settlements after France ceded to the British its territory east of the Mississippi River, as part of the Treaty of Paris, without consulting France's Indian allies.

popular sovereignty Legal concept by which the white male settlers in a new U.S. territory would vote to decide whether or not to permit slavery.

Populist/People's party Political success of Farmers' Alliance candidates encouraged the formation in 1892 of the People's party (later renamed the Populist party); active until 1912, it advocated a variety of reform issues, including free coinage of silver, income tax, postal savings, regulation of railroads, and direct election of U.S. senators.

Pottawatomie Massacre In retaliation for the "sack of Lawrence," John Brown and his abolitionist cohorts hacked five men to death in the pro-slavery settlement of Pottawatomie, Kansas, on May 24, 1856, triggering a guerrilla war in the Kansas Territory that cost 200 settler lives.

Powhatan Confederacy An alliance of several powerful Algonquian tribes under the leadership of Chief Powhatan, organized into thirty chiefdoms along much of the Atlantic coast in the late sixteenth and early seventeenth centuries.

Chief Powhatan Wahunsonacock He was called Powhatan by the English after the name of his tribe, and was the powerful, charismatic chief of numerous Algonquian-speaking towns in eastern Virginia representing over 10,000 Indians.

pragmatism William James founded this philosophy in the early 1900s. Pragmatists believed that ideas gained their validity not from their inherent truth, but from their social consequences and practical application.

professions Occupations requiring specialized knowledge of some field; the Industrial Revolution and its new organization of labor created an array of professions in the nineteenth century.

Progressive party In the 1912 election, Theodore Roosevelt was unable to secure the Republican nomination for president. He left the Republican party and formed his own party of progressive Republicans, called the "Bull Moose" party (later Progressive Party). Roosevelt and Taft split the Republican vote, which allowed Democrat Woodrow Wilson to win.

Prohibition National ban on the manufacture and sale of alcohol that lasted from 1920 to 1933, though the law was widely violated and proved too difficult to enforce effectively.

proprietary colonies A colony owned by an individual, rather than a joint-stock company.

Protestant Reformation Sixteenth-century religious movement initiated by Martin Luther, a German monk whose public criticism of corruption in the Roman Catholic Church, and whose teaching that Christians can communicate directly with God, gained a wide following.

public schools Elementary and secondary schools funded by the state and free of tuition.

pueblos The Spanish term for the adobe cliff dwellings of the indigenous people of the southwestern United States.

Pullman Strike (1894) A national strike by the American Railway Union, whose members shut down major railways in sympathy with striking workers in Pullman, Illinois; ended with intervention of federal troops.

Puritans English religious dissenters who sought to "purify" the Church of England of its Catholic practices.

Quakers George Fox founded the Quaker religion in 1647. They rejected the use of formal sacraments and ministry, refused to take oaths and embraced pacifism. Fleeing persecution, they settled and established the colony of Pennsylvania.

race-based slavery Institution that uses racial characteristics and myths to justify enslaving a people.

Radical Republicans Senators and congressmen who, strictly identifying the Civil War with the abolitionist cause, sought swift emancipation of the slaves, punishment of the rebels, and tight controls over the former Confederate states after the war.

railroads Steam-powered vehicles that improved passenger transportation, quickened western settlement, and enabled commercial agriculture in the nineteenth century.

Raleigh's Roanoke Island Colony English expedition of 117 settlers, including Virginia Dare, the first English child born in the New World; colony disappeared from Roanoke Island in the Outer Banks sometime between 1587 and 1590.

A. Philip Randolph (1889–1979) He was the head of the Brotherhood of Sleeping Car Porters who planned a march on Washington D.C. to demand an end to racial discrimination in the defense industries. To stop the march, the Roosevelt administration negotiated an agreement with the Randolph group. The demonstration would be called off and an executive order would be issued that forbid discrimination in defense work and training programs and set up the Fair Employment Practices Committee.

range wars In the late 1800s, conflicting claims over land and water rights triggered violent disputes between farmers and ranchers in parts of the western United States.

Ronald Reagan (1911–2004) In 1980, the former actor and governor of California was elected president. In office, he reduced social spending, cut taxes, and increased defense spending. During his presidency, the federal debt tripled, the federal deficit rose, programs such as housing and school lunches were cut, and the HIV/AIDS crisis grew to prominence in the United States. He signed an arms-control treaty with the Soviet Union in 1987, authorized covert CIA operations in Central America, and in 1986 the Iran-Contra scandal was revealed.

Reaganomics President Reagan's "supply-side" economic philosophy combining tax cuts with the goals of decreased government spending, reduced regulation of business, and a balanced budget.

Reconstruction Finance Corporation (1932) Federal program established under President Hoover to loan money to banks and other corporations to help them avoid bankruptcy.

Red Power Activism by militant Native American groups to protest living conditions on Indian reservations through demonstrations, legal action, and, at times, violence.

First Red Scare Fear among many Americans after the First World War of Communists in particular and noncitizens in general, it was a reaction to the Russian Revolution, mail bombs, strikes, and riots.

redeemers Post–Civil War Democratic leaders who supposedly saved the South from Yankee domination and preserved the primarily rural economy.

Dr. Walter Reed (1851–1902) His work on yellow fever in Cuba led to the discovery that the fever was carried by mosquitoes. This understanding helped develop more effective controls of the worldwide disease.

Reform Darwinism A social philosophy developed by Lester Frank War that challenged the ruthlessness of social Darwinism by asserting that humans were not passive pawns of evolutionary forces. Instead, people could actively shape the process of evolutionary social development through cooperation, innovation, and planning.

Reformation European religious movement that challenged the Catholic Church and resulted in the beginnings of Protestant Christianity. During this period, Catholics and Protestants persecuted, imprisoned, tortured, and killed each other in large numbers.

religious right Christian conservatives with a faith-based political agenda that includes prohibition of abortion and allowing prayer in public schools.

reparations As a part of the Treaty of Versailles, Germany was required to confess its responsibility for the First World War and make payments to the victors for the entire expense of the war. These two requirements created a deep bitterness among Germans.

Report on Manufactures First Secretary of the Treasury Alexander Hamilton's 1791 analysis that accurately foretold the future of American industry and proposed tariffs and subsidies to promote it.

republican ideology Political belief in representative democracy in which citizens govern themselves by electing representatives, or legislators, to make key decisions on the citizens' behalf.

republican simplicity Deliberate attitude of humility and frugality, as opposed to monarchical pomp and ceremony, adopted by Thomas Jefferson in his presidency.

Republicans First used during the early nineteenth century to describe supporters of a strict interpretation of the Constitution, which they believed would safeguard individual freedoms and states' rights from the threats posed by a strong central government. The idealist Republican vision of sustaining an agrarian-oriented union was developed largely by Thomas Jefferson.

"return to normalcy" Campaign promise of Republican presidential candidate Warren G. Harding in 1920, meant to contrast with Woodrow Wilson's progressivism and internationalism.

Paul Revere (1735–1818) On the night of April 18, 1775, British soldiers marched toward Concord to arrest American Revolutionary leaders and seize their depot of supplies. Paul Revere famously rode through the night and raised the alarm about the approaching British troops.

Roaring Twenties The 1920s, an era of social and intellectual revolution in which young people experimented with new forms of recreation and sexuality. The Eastern, urban cultural shift clashed with conservative and insular Midwestern America, which increased the tensions between the two regions.

Jackie Robinson (1919–1972) In 1947, he became the first African American to play major league baseball. He won over fans and players and stimulated the integration of other professional sports.

rock-and-roll music Alan Freed, a disc jockey, noticed white teenagers were buying rhythm and blues records that had been only purchased by African Americans and Hispanic Americans. Freed began playing these records, but called them rock-and-roll records as a way to overcome the racial barrier. As the popularity of the music genre increased, it helped bridge the gap between "white" and "black" music.

John D. Rockefeller (1839–1937) In 1870, he founded the Standard Oil Company of Ohio, which was his first step in creating his vast oil empire. He perfected the idea of a holding company.

***Roe v. Wade* (1973)** Landmark Supreme Court decision striking down state laws that banned abortions during the first trimester of pregnancy.

Roman Catholicism The Christian faith and religious practices of the Roman Catholic Church, which exerted great political, economic, and social influence on much of Western Europe and, through the Spanish and Portuguese Empires, on the Americas.

Romanticism Philosophical, literary, and artistic movement of the nineteenth century that was largely a reaction to the rationalism of the previous century; Romantics valued emotion, mysticism, and individualism.

Eleanor Roosevelt (1884–1962) She redefined the role of the presidential spouse and was the first woman to address a national political convention, write a nationally syndicated column and hold regular press conferences. She travelled throughout the nation to promote the New Deal, women's causes, organized labor, and meet with African American leaders.

Franklin Delano Roosevelt (1882–1945) Elected during the Great Depression, Roosevelt sought to help struggling Americans through his New Deal programs that created employment and social programs, such as Social Security. After the bombing of Pearl Harbor, he declared war on Japan and Germany and led the country through most of the Second World War before dying of cerebral hemorrhage.

Theodore Roosevelt (1858–1919) As the assistant secretary of the navy, he supported expansionism, American imperialism, and war with Spain. He led the Rough Riders in Cuba during the war of 1898 and used the notoriety of this military campaign for political gain. As President McKinley's vice president, he succeeded McKinley after his assassination. His forceful foreign policy became known as "big stick diplomacy." Domestically, his policies on natural resources helped start the conservation movement. Unable to win the Republican nomination for president in 1912, he formed his own party of progressive Republicans called the "Bull Moose" party.

Roosevelt Corollary (1904) President Theodore Roosevelt's revision of the Monroe Doctrine (1823) in which he argued that the United States could use military force in Central and South American nations to prevent European nations from intervening in the Western Hemisphere.

Rough Riders The First U.S. Volunteer Cavalry, led in the War of 1898 by Theodore Roosevelt; they were victorious in their only engagement, the Battle of San Juan Hill near Santiago, Cuba, and Roosevelt was celebrated as a national hero, bolstering his political career.

Royal Proclamation of 1763 Proclamation drawing a boundary along the Appalachian Mountains from Canada to Georgia in order to minimize occurrences of settler–Indian violence; colonists were forbidden to go west of the line.

Nicola Sacco (1891–1927) In 1920, he and Bartolomeo Vanzetti were Italian immigrants who were arrested for stealing $16,000 and killing a paymaster and his guard. Their trial took place during a time of numerous bombings by anarchists and their judge was openly prejudicial; many liberals and radicals believe that their conviction was based on their political ideas and ethnic origin rather than the evidence against them.

Sacco and Vanzetti case 1921 trial of two Italian immigrants that occurred at the height of Italian immigration and against the backdrop of numerous terror attacks by anarchists; despite a lack of clear evidence, the two defendants, both self-professed anarchists, were convicted of murder and were executed in 1927.

saloons Bars or taverns where mostly men would gather to drink, eat, relax, play games, and, often, to discuss politics.

salutary neglect Informal British policy during the first half of the eighteenth century that allowed the American colonies considerable freedom to pursue their economic and political interests in exchange for colonial obedience.

same-sex marriage The legal right for gay and lesbian couples to marry; it became the most divisive issue in the culture wars of the early 2010s as more and more court rulings affirmed this right in states and municipalities across the United States. The 2015 Supreme Court case *Obergefell v. Hodges* affirmed the right to same-sex marriage, also known as marriage equality, nationally.

Sand Creek Massacre (1864) Colonel Chivington's unprovoked slaughter of the Cheyennes and Arapahos in Colorado, initially reported as a justified battle but soon exposed for the despicable massacre it was.

Sandinista Cuban-sponsored government that came to power in Nicaragua after toppling a corrupt dictator. The State Department believed that the Sandinistas were supplying the leftist Salvadoran rebels with Cuban and Soviet arms. In response, the Reagan administration ordered the CIA to train and supply guerrilla bands of anti-Communist Nicaraguans called Contras. A cease-fire agreement between the Contras and Sandinistas was signed in 1988.

Sandlot Incident Violence occurring during the Great Railroad Strike of 1877, when mobs of frustrated working-class whites in San Francisco attacked Chinese immigrants, blaming them for economic hardship.

General Antonio López de Santa Anna (1794–1876) In 1834, he seized political power in Mexico and became a dictator. In 1835, Texans rebelled against him and he led his army to Texas to crush their rebellion. He captured the mission called the Alamo and killed all of its defenders, which inspired Texans to continue resistance and Americans to volunteer to fight for Texas. The Texans captured Santa Anna during a surprise attack and he bought his freedom by signing a treaty recognizing Texas's independence.

Battles of Saratoga Decisive defeat of 5,000 British troops under General John Burgoyne in several battles near Saratoga, New York, in October 1777; the American victory helped convince France to enter the war on the side of the Patriots.

scalawags White southern Republicans—some former Unionists—who served in Reconstruction governments.

Phyllis Schlafly (1924–) A right-wing Republican activist who spearheaded the anti-feminism movement. She believed feminists were "anti-family, anti-children, and pro-abortion." She worked against the equal-rights amendment for women and civil rights protection for gays.

Scopes Trial Highly publicized 1925 trial of a high school teacher in Tennessee for violating a state law that prohibited the teaching of evolution; the trial was seen as the climax of the fundamentalist war on Darwinism.

Winfield Scott (1786–1866) During the Mexican War, he was the American general who captured Mexico City, which ended the war. Using his popularity from his military success, he ran as a Whig party candidate for President.

Sears, Roebuck and Company By the end of the nineteenth century, this company dominated the mail-order industry and helped create a truly national market. Its mail-order catalog and low prices allowed people living in rural areas and small towns to buy products that were previously too expensive or available only to city dwellers.

secession Shortly after President Abraham Lincoln was elected, southern states began dissolving their ties with the United States because they believed Lincoln and the Republican party were a threat to slavery.

Second Bank of the United States Established in 1816 after the first national bank's charter expired; it stabilized the economy by creating a sound national currency, by making loans to farmers, small manufacturers, and entrepreneurs, and by regulating the ability of state banks to issue their own paper currency.

Second Great Awakening Religious revival movement that arose in reaction to the growth of secularism and rationalist religion; spurred the growth of the Baptist and Methodist churches.

Second Industrial Revolution Beginning in the late nineteenth century, a wave of technological innovations, especially in iron and steel production, steam and electrical power, and telegraphic communications, all of which spurred industrial development and urban growth.

Second New Deal (1935–1938) Expansive cluster of legislation proposed by President Roosevelt that established new regulatory agencies, strengthened the rights of workers to organize unions, and laid the foundation of a federal social welfare system through the creation of Social Security.

Securities and Exchange Commission (1934) Federal agency established to regulate the issuance and trading of stocks and bonds in an effort to avoid financial panics and stock market "crashes."

Seneca Falls Convention (1848) Convention organized by feminists Lucretia Mott and Elizabeth Cady Stanton to promote women's rights and issue the pathbreaking Declaration of Sentiments.

"separate but equal" Principle underlying legal racial segregation, which was upheld in *Plessy v. Ferguson* (1896) and struck down in *Brown v. Board of Education* (1954).

separation of powers Strict division of the powers of government among three separate branches (executive, legislative, and judicial) which, in turn, check and balance each other.

September 11 On September 11, 2001, Islamic terrorists, who were members of the al Qaeda terrorist organization, hijacked four commercial airliners. Two were flown into the World Trade Center, a third into the Pentagon, and a fourth plane was brought down in Pennsylvania. In response, President George W. Bush launched his "war on terrorism." His administration assembled an international coalition to fight terrorism, which invaded Afghanistan after the country's government would not turn over Osama bin Laden. Bush and Congress passed the U.S.A. Patriot Act, which allowed government agencies to try suspected terrorists in secret military courts and eavesdrop on confidential conversations.

settlement houses Product of the late nineteenth-century movement to offer a broad array of social services in urban immigrant neighborhoods; Chicago's Hull House was one of hundreds of settlement houses that operated by the early twentieth century.

Seventeenth Amendment (1913) Constitutional amendment that provided for the direct election of senators rather than the traditional practice allowing state legislatures to name them.

Shakers Founded by Mother Ann Lee Stanley in England, the United Society of Believers in Christ's Second Appearing settled in Watervliet, New York, in 1774 and subsequently established eighteen additional communes in the Northeast, Indiana, and Kentucky.

share tenants Poor farmers who rented land to farm in exchange for a substantial share of the crop, though they would often have their own horse or mule, tools, and line of credit with a nearby store.

sharecroppers Poor, mostly black farmers who would work an owner's land in return for shelter, seed, fertilizer, mules, supplies, and food, as well as a substantial share of the crop produced.

Share-the-Wealth program Huey Long offered this program as an alternative to the New Deal. The program proposed to confiscate large personal fortunes, which would be used to guarantee every poor family a cash grant of $5,000 and every worker an annual income of $2,500. This program promised to provide pensions, reduce working hours, pay veterans' bonuses, and ensures a college education to every qualified student.

Shays's Rebellion (1786–1787) Storming of the Massachusetts federal arsenal by Daniel Shays and 1,200 armed farmers seeking debt relief from the state legislature through issuance of paper currency and lower taxes.

Sherman's "March to the Sea" (1864) The Union army's devastating march through Georgia from Atlanta to Savannah led by General William T. Sherman, intended to demoralize civilians and destroy the resources the Confederate army needed to fight.

"silent majority" Term popularized by President Richard Nixon to describe the great majority of American voters who did not express their political opinions publicly— "the non-demonstrators."

Sixteenth Amendment (1913) Constitutional amendment that authorized the federal income tax.

slave codes Ordinances passed by a colony or state to regulate the behavior of slaves, often including brutal punishments for infractions.

Alfred E. Smith (1873–1944) In the 1928 presidential election, he won the Democratic nomination, but failed to win the presidency. Rural voters distrusted him for being Catholic and the son of Irish immigrants as well as his anti-Prohibition stance.

Captain John Smith (1580–1631) A swashbuckling soldier of fortune with rare powers of leadership and self-promotion, he was appointed to the resident council to manage Jamestown.

Joseph Smith (1805–1844) In 1823, he claimed that the Angel Moroni showed him the location of several gold tablets on which the Book of Mormon was written. Using the Book of Mormon as his gospel, he founded the Church of Jesus Christ of Latter-day Saints, or Mormons. In 1839, they settled in Commerce, Illinois, to avoid persecution. In 1844, Joseph and his brother were arrested and jailed for ordering the destruction of a newspaper that opposed them. While in jail, an anti-Mormon mob stormed the jail and killed both of them.

social Darwinism The application of Charles Darwin's theory of evolutionary natural selection to human society; Social Darwinists used the concept of "survival of the fittest" to justify class distinctions, explain poverty, and oppose government intervention in the economy.

social gospel Protestant movement that stressed the Christian obligation to address the mounting social problems caused by urbanization and industrialization.

social justice An important part of the Progressive's agenda, social justice sought to solve social problems through reform and regulation. Methods used to bring about social justice ranged from the founding of charities to the legislation of a ban on child labor.

Social Security Act (1935) Legislation enacted to provide federal assistance to retired workers through tax-funded pension payments and benefit payments to the unemployed and disabled.

Sons of Liberty First organized by Samuel Adams in the 1770s, groups of colonists dedicated to militant resistance against British control of the colonies.

Hernando de Soto (1500?–1542) A conquistador who explored the west coast of Florida, western North Carolina, and along the Arkansas river from 1539 till his death in 1542.

Southern Christian Leadership Conference (SCLC) Civil rights organization formed by Dr. Martin Luther King, Jr., that championed nonviolent direct action as a means of ending segregation.

"southern strategy" This strategy was a major reason for Richard Nixon's victory in the 1968 presidential election. To gain support in the South, Nixon assured southern conservatives that he would slow the federal enforcement of civil rights laws and appoint pro-southern justices to the Supreme Court. As president, Nixon fulfilled these promises.

Spanish Armada A massive Spanish fleet of 130 warships that was defeated at Plymouth in 1588 by the English navy during the reign of Queen Elizabeth I.

Spanish flu Unprecedentedly lethal influenza epidemic of 1918 that killed more than 22 million people worldwide.

Herbert Spencer (1820–1903) As the first major proponent of social Darwinism, he argued that human society and institutions are subject to the process of natural selection and that society naturally evolves for the better. He was against any form of government interference with the evolution of society, like business regulations, because it would help the "unfit" to survive.

spirituals Songs with religious messages sung by slaves to help ease the strain of field labor and to voice their suffering at the hands of their masters and overseers.

spoils system The term—meaning the filling of federal government jobs with persons loyal to the party of the president—originated in Andrew Jackson's first term; the system was replaced in the Progressive Era by civil service.

Square Deal Roosevelt's progressive agenda of the "Three C's": control of corporations, conservation of natural resources, and consumer protection.

"stagflation" Term coined by economists during the Nixon presidency to describe the unprecedented situation of stagnant economic growth and consumer price inflation occurring at the same time.

Joseph Stalin (1879–1953) The Bolshevik leader who succeeded Lenin as the leader of the Soviet Union in 1924 and ruled the country until his death. During his totalitarian rule of the Soviet Union, he used purges and a system of forced labor camps to maintain control over the country, and claimed vast areas of Eastern Europe for Soviet domination.

Stalwarts Conservative Republican party faction during the presidency of Rutherford B. Hayes, 1877–1881; led by Senator Roscoe B. Conkling of New York, Stalwarts opposed civil service reform and favored a third term for President Ulysses S. Grant.

Stamp Act (1765) Act of Parliament requiring that all printed materials (e.g., newspapers, bonds, and even playing cards) in the American colonies use paper with an official tax stamp in order to pay for British military protection of the colonies.

Stamp Act Congress Twenty-seven delegates from nine of the colonies met from October 7 to 25, 1765 and wrote a Declaration of the Rights and Grievances of the Colonies, a petition to the King and a petition to Parliament for the repeal of the Stamp Act.

Standard Oil Company Corporation under the leadership of John D. Rockefeller that attempted to dominate the entire oil industry through horizontal and vertical integration.

Elizabeth Cady Stanton (1815–1902) A prominent reformer and advocate for the rights of women, she helped organize the Seneca Falls Convention to discuss women's rights. The convention was the first of its kind and produced the Declaration of Sentiments, which proclaimed the equality of men and women.

staple crop A profitable market crop, such as cotton, tobacco, or rice that predominates in a given region.

state constitutions Charters that define the relationship between the state government and local governments and individuals, and also protects their rights from violation by the national government.

steamboats Ships and boats powered by wood-fired steam engines. First used in the early nineteenth century, they made two-way traffic possible in eastern river systems, creating a transcontinental market and an agricultural empire.

Thaddeus Stevens (1792–1868) As one of the leaders of the Radical Republicans, he argued that the former Confederate states should be viewed as conquered provinces, which were subject to the demands of the conquerors. He believed that all of Southern society needed to be changed, and he supported the abolition of slavery and racial equality.

Adlai E. Stevenson (1900–1965) In the 1952 and 1956 presidential elections, he was the Democratic nominee who lost to Dwight Eisenhower. He was also the U.S. Ambassador to the United Nations and is remembered for his famous speech in 1962 before the UN Security Council that unequivocally demonstrated that the Soviet Union had built nuclear missile bases in Cuba.

Stono Rebellion (1739) A slave uprising in South Carolina that was brutally quashed, leading to executions as well as a severe tightening of the slave code.

Stonewall riots (1969) Violent clashes between police and lesbian, gay, bisexual, transgender, and queer (LGBTQ) patrons of New York City's Stonewall Inn, seen as the starting point of the modern LGBTQ rights movement.

Strategic Arms Limitation Talks (SALT I) (1972) Agreement signed by President Nixon and Secretary Brezhnev prohibiting the development of missile defense systems in the United States and Soviet Union and limiting the quantity of nuclear warheads for both.

Strategic Defense Initiative (SDI) (1983) Ronald Reagan's proposed space-based anti-missile defense system, dubbed "Star Wars" by the media, that aroused great controversy and escalated the arms race between the United States and the Soviet Union.

Levi Strauss (1829–1902) A Jewish tailor who followed miners to California during the gold rush and began making durable work pants that were later dubbed blue jeans or Levi's.

Student Nonviolent Coordinating Committee (SNCC) Interracial organization formed in 1960 with the goal of intensifying the effort to end racial segregation.

Students for a Democratic Society (SDS) Major organization of the New Left, founded at the University of Michigan in 1960 by Tom Hayden and Al Haber.

suburbia Communities formed from mass migration of middle-class whites from urban centers.

Suez crisis (1956) British, French, and Israeli attack on Egypt after Nasser's seizure of the Suez Canal; President Eisenhower interceded to demand the withdrawal of the British, French, and Israeli forces from the Sinai peninsula and canal.

Sunbelt The label for an arc that stretched from the Carolinas to California. During the postwar era, much of the urban population growth occurred in this area.

"surge" In early 2007, President Bush decided he would send a "surge" of new troops to Iraq and implement a new strategy. U.S. forces would shift their focus from offensive operations to the protection of Iraqi civilians from attacks by terrorist insurgents and sectarian militias. While the "surge" reduced the violence in Iraq, Iraqi leaders were still unable to develop a self-sustaining democracy.

Taft-Hartley Labor Act (1947) Congressional legislation that banned "unfair labor practices" by labor unions, required union leaders to sign anti-Communist "loyalty oaths," and prohibited federal employees from going on strike.

Taliban A coalition of ultraconservative Islamists who rose to power in Afghanistan after the Soviets withdrew. The Taliban leaders gave Osama bin Laden a safe haven in their country in exchange for aid in fighting the Northern Alliance, who were rebels opposed to the Taliban. After they refused to turn bin Laden over to the United States, America invaded Afghanistan.

Tammany Hall The "city machine" used by "Boss" Tweed to dominate politics in New York City until his arrest in 1871.

tariff A tax on goods imported from other nations, typically used to protect home industries from foreign competitors and to generate revenue for the federal government.

Tariff of 1816 A cluster of taxes on imports passed by Congress to protect America's emerging iron and textile industries from British competition.

Tariff of 1832 This tariff act reduced the duties on many items, but the tariffs on cloth and iron remained high. South Carolina nullified it along with the tariff of 1828. President Andrew Jackson sent federal troops to the state and asked Congress to grant him the authority to enforce the tariffs. Henry Clay presented a plan of gradually reducing the tariffs until 1842, which Congress passed and ended the crisis.

"Tariff of Abominations" (1828) Tax on imported goods, including British cloth and clothing, that strengthened New England textile companies but hurt southern consumers, who experienced a decrease in British demand for raw cotton grown in the South.

tariff reform (1887) Effort led by the Democratic party to reduce taxes on imported goods, which Republicans argued were needed to protect American industries from foreign competition.

Troubled Asset Relief Program (TARP) In 2008 President George W. Bush signed into law the bank bailout fund called Troubled Asset Relief Program (TARP), which required the Treasury Department to spend $700 billion to keep banks and other financial institutions from collapsing.

Zachary Taylor (1784–1850) During the Mexican War, he scored two quick victories against Mexico, which made him very popular in America. He used his popularity from his military victories to be elected president as a member of the Whig party, but died before he could complete his term.

Taylorism Labor system based on detailed study of work tasks, championed by Frederick Winslow Taylor, intended to maximize efficiency and profits for employers.

Tea Party Right-wing populist movement, largely made up of middle-class, white male conservatives, that emerged as a response to the expansion of the federal government under the Obama administration.

Teapot Dome (1923) Harding administration scandal in which Secretary of the Interior Albert B. Fall profited from secret leasing of government oil reserves in Wyoming to private oil companies.

Tecumseh (1768–1813) He was a leader of the Shawnee tribe who tried to unite all Indians into a confederation that could defend their hunting grounds. He believed that no land cessions could be made without the consent of all the tribes since they held the land in common. His beliefs and leadership made him seem dangerous to the American government and they waged war on him and his tribe. He was killed at the Battle of the Thames.

Tecumseh's Indian Confederacy A group of Native Americans under leadership of Shawnee leader Tecumseh and his prophet brother Tenskwatawa; its mission of fighting off American expansion was thwarted in the Battle of Tippecanoe (1811), when the confederacy fell apart.

Tejanos Texas settlers of Spanish or Mexican descent.

telegraph system System of electronic communication invented by Samuel F. B. Morse that could be transmitted instantaneously across great distances (first used in the 1840s).

Teller Amendment Addition to the congressional war resolution of April 20, 1898, which marked the U.S. entry into the war with Spain; the amendment declared that the United States' goal in entering the war was to ensure Cuba's independence, not to annex Cuba as a territory.

temperance A widespread reform movement, led by militant Christians, focused on reducing the use of alcoholic beverages.

tenements Shabby, low-cost inner-city apartment buildings that housed the urban poor in cramped, unventilated apartments.

Tenochtitlán The capital city of the Aztec Empire. The city was built on marshy islands on the western side of Lake Tetzcoco, which is the site of present-day Mexico City.

Tet offensive (1968) Surprise attack by Viet Cong guerrillas and the North Vietnamese army on U.S. and South Vietnamese forces that shocked the American public and led to widespread sentiment against the war.

Texas Revolution (1835–1836) Conflict between Texas colonists and the Mexican government that resulted in the creation of the separate Republic of Texas in 1836.

textile industry Commercial production of thread, fabric, and clothing from raw cotton in mills in New England during the first half of the nineteenth century, and later in the South in the late nineteenth century.

Thirteenth Amendment (1865) Amendment to the U. S. Constitution that freed all slaves in the United States.

Battle of Tippecanoe (1811) Battle in northern Indiana between U.S. troops and Native American warriors led by Tenskwatawa, the brother of Tecumseh, who had organized an anti-American Indian confederacy to fight American efforts to settle on Indian lands.

tobacco A cash crop grown in the Caribbean as well as the Virginia and Maryland colonies, made increasingly profitable by the rapidly growing popularity of smoking in Europe after the voyages of Columbus.

Gulf of Tonkin incident On August 2 and 4 of 1964, North Vietnamese vessels attacked two American destroyers in the Gulf of Tonkin off the coast of North Vietnam. President Johnson described the attacks as unprovoked. In reality, the U.S. ships were monitoring South Vietnamese attacks on North Vietnamese islands that America advisors had planned. The incident spurred the Tonkin Gulf resolution.

Tonkin Gulf Resolution Congressional action that granted the president unlimited authority to defend U.S. forces abroad, passed in August 1964 after an allegedly unprovoked attack on American warships off the coast of North Vietnam.

Tories Term used by Patriots to refer to Loyalists, or colonists who supported the Crown after the Declaration of Independence.

Townshend Acts Parliamentary measures to extract more revenue from the colonies; the Revenue Act of 1767, which taxed tea, paper, and other colonial imports, was one of the most notorious of these policies.

Trail of Tears The Cherokees' eight-hundred mile journey (1838–1839) from the southern Appalachians to Indian Territory (in present-day Oklahoma); four thousand died people along the way.

transcendentalism Philosophy of a small group of New England writers and thinkers who advocated personal spirituality, self-reliance, social reform, and harmony with nature.

Transcontinental railroad First line across the continent from Omaha, Nebraska, to Sacramento, California, established in 1869 with the linkage of the Union Pacific and Central Pacific railroads at Promontory, Utah.

Transcontinental Treaty (1819) (Adams-Onís Treaty) Treaty between Spain and the United States that clarified the boundaries of the Louisiana Purchase and arranged the transfer of Florida to the United States in exchange for cash.

triangular trade A network of trade in which exports from one region were sold to another region, which sent its exports to a third region, which exported its own goods back to the first country or colony.

Treaty of Ghent (1814) Agreement between Great Britain and the United States that ended the War of 1812, signed on December 24, 1814.

Treaty of Guadalupe Hidalgo (1848) Treaty between United States and Mexico that ended the Mexican-American War.

Treaty of Paris (1763) Settlement between Great Britain and France that ended the French and Indian War.

Treaty of Versailles Peace treaty that ended the First World War, forcing Germany to dismantle its military, pay immense war reparations, and give up its colonies around the world.

trench warfare A form of prolonged combat between the entrenched positions of opposing armies, often with little tactical movement.

Harry S. Truman (1884–1972) As President Roosevelt's vice president, he succeeded him after his death near the end of the Second World War. After the war, Truman wrestled with the inflation of both prices and wages, worked with Congress to pass the National Security Act, and banned racial discrimination in the hiring of federal employees and ended racial segregation in the armed forces. In foreign affairs, he established the Truman Doctrine to contain communism, developed the Marshall Plan to rebuild Europe, and sent the U.S. military to defend South Korea after North Korea invaded.

Truman Doctrine (1947) President Truman's program of "containing" communism in Eastern Europe and providing economic and military aid to any nations at risk of Communist takeover.

Donald J. Trump (1946–) The 45th President of the United States.

trust A business arrangement that gives a person or corporation (the "trustee") the legal power to manage another person's money or another company without owning those entities outright.

Sojourner Truth (1797?–1883) She was born into slavery, but New York State freed her in 1827. She spent the 1840s and 1850s travelling across the country and speaking to audiences about her experiences as slave and asking them to support abolition and women's rights.

Harriet Tubman (1820–1913) She was born a slave, but escaped to the North. She then returned to the South nineteen times and guided 300 slaves to freedom.

Frederick Jackson Turner An influential historian who authored the "Frontier Thesis" in 1893, arguing that the existence of an alluring frontier and the experience of persistent westward expansion informed the nation's democratic politics, unfettered economy, and rugged individualism.

Nat Turner (1800–1831) He was the leader of the only slave revolt to get past the planning stages. In August of 1831, the revolt began with the slaves killing the members of Turner's master's household. Then they attacked other neighboring farmhouses and recruited more slaves until the militia crushed the revolt. At least fifty-five whites were killed during the uprising and seventeen slaves were hanged afterwards.

Nat Turner's Rebellion (1831) Insurrection in rural Virginia led by black overseer Nat Turner, who killed slave owners and their families; in turn, federal troops indiscriminately killed hundreds of slaves in the process of putting down Turner and his rebels.

Tuskegee Airmen U.S. Army Air Corps unit of African American pilots whose combat success spurred military and civilian leaders to desegregate the armed forces after the war.

Mark Twain (1835–1910) Born Samuel Langhorne Clemens in Missouri, he became a popular humorous writer and lecturer and established himself as one of the great American satirists and authors. His two greatest books, *The Adventures of Tom Sawyer* and *The Adventures of Huckleberry Finn*, drew heavily on his childhood in Missouri.

"Boss" Tweed (1823–1878) An infamous political boss in New York City, Tweed used his "city machine," the Tammany Hall ring, to rule, plunder and sometimes improve the city's government. His political domination of New York City ended with his arrest in 1871 and conviction in 1873.

Twenty-first Amendment (1933) Repealed prohibition on the manufacture, sale, and transportation of alcoholic beverages, effectively nullifying the Eighteenth Amendment.

two-party system Domination of national politics by two major political parties, such as the Whigs and Democrats during the 1830s and 1840s.

Underground Railroad A secret system of routes and safe houses through which runaway slaves were led to freedom in the North.

Unitarians Members of the liberal New England Congregationalist offshoot, often well-educated and wealthy, who profess the oneness of God and the goodness of rational man.

United Farm Workers (UFW) Organization formed in 1962 to represent the interests of Mexican American migrant workers.

United Nations Security Council A major agency within the United Nations which remains in permanent session and has the responsibility of maintaining international peace and security. Originally, it consisted of five permanent members, (United States, Soviet Union, Britain, France, and the Republic of China), and six members elected to two-year terms. After 1965, the number of rotating members was increased to ten. In 1971, the Republic of China was replaced with the People's Republic of China and the Soviet Union was replaced by the Russian Federation in 1991.

Universalists Members of a New England religious movement, often from the working class, who believed in a merciful God and universal salvation.

USA Patriot Act (2001) Wide-reaching Congressional legislation, triggered by the War on Terror, which gave government agencies the right to eavesdrop on confidential conversations between prison inmates and their lawyers and permitted suspected terrorists to be tried in secret military courts.

U-boat German military submarine (*Unterseeboot*) used during the First World War to attack enemy naval vessels as well as merchant ships of enemy and neutral nations.

utopian communities Ideal communities that offered innovative social and economic relationships to those who were interested in achieving salvation.

Valley Forge American military encampment near Philadelphia, where more than 3,500 soldiers deserted or died from cold and hunger in the winter of 1777–1778.

Cornelius Vanderbilt (1794–1877) In the 1860s, he consolidated several separate railroad companies into one vast entity, New York Central Railroad.

Bartolomeo Vanzetti (1888–1927) In 1920, he and Nicola Sacco were Italian immigrants who were arrested for stealing $16,000 and killing a paymaster and his guard. Their trial took place during a time of numerous bombings by anarchists and their judge was openly prejudicial. Many liberals and radicals believe that their conviction was based on their political ideas and ethnic origin rather than the evidence against them.

vertical integration The process by which a corporation gains control of all aspects of the resources and processes needed to produce and sell a product.

Amerigo Vespucci (1455–1512) Italian explorer who reached the New World in 1499 and was the first to suggest that South America was a new continent. Afterward, European mapmakers used a variant of his first name, America, to label the New World.

Battle of Vicksburg (1863) A protracted battle in northern Mississippi in which Union forces under Ulysses Grant besieged the last major Confederate fortress on the Mississippi River, forcing the inhabitants into starvation and then submission.

Viet Cong Communist guerrillas in Vietnam who launched attacks on the Diem government.

Vietnamization Nixon-era policy of equipping and training South Vietnamese forces to take over the burden of combat from U.S. troops.

Vikings Norse people from Scandinavia who sailed to Newfoundland about a.d. 1001.

Francisco Pancho Villa (1877–1923) While the leader of one of the competing factions in the Mexican civil war, he provoked the United States into intervening. He hoped attacking the United States would help him build a reputation as an opponent of the United States, which would increase his popularity and discredit Mexican President Carranza.

Virginia Company A joint stock enterprise that King James I chartered in 1606. The company was to spread Christianity in the New World as well as find ways to make a profit in it.

Virginia Plan The delegations to the Constitutional Convention were divided between two plans on how to structure the government: Virginia called for a strong central government and a two-house legislature apportioned by population.

Virginia Statute of Religious Freedom A Virginia law, drafted by Thomas Jefferson in 1777 and enacted in 1786, that guarantees freedom of, and from, religion.

virtual representation The idea that the American colonies, although they had no actual representative in Parliament, were "virtually" represented by all members of Parliament.

Voting Rights Act of 1965 Legislation ensuring that all Americans were able to vote; the law ended literacy tests and other means of restricting voting rights.

Wagner Act (1935) Legislation that guaranteed workers the right to organize unions, granted them direct bargaining power, and barred employers from interfering with union activities.

George Wallace (1919–1998) An outspoken defender of segregation. As the governor of Alabama, he once attempted to block African American students from enrolling at the University of Alabama. He ran as the presidential candidate for the American Independent party in 1968, appealing to voters who were concerned about rioting anti-war protestors, the welfare system, and the growth of the federal government.

war hawks In 1811, congressional members from the southern and western districts who clamored for a war to seize Canada and Florida were dubbed "war hawks."

War of 1812 (1812–1815) Conflict fought in North America and at sea between Great Britain and the United States over American shipping rights and British efforts to spur Indian attacks on American settlements. Canadians and Native Americans also fought in the war.

war on terror Global crusade to root out anti-American, anti-Western Islamist terrorist cells launched by President George W. Bush as a response to the 9/11 attacks.

War Powers Act (1973) Legislation requiring the president to inform Congress within 48 hours of the deployment of U.S. troops abroad and to withdraw them after 60 days unless Congress approves their continued deployment.

War Production Board Federal agency created by President Roosevelt in 1942 that converted America's industrial output to war production.

"war relocation camps" Detention camps housing thousands of Japanese Americans from the West Coast who were forcibly interned from 1942 until the end of the Second World War.

Warren Court The U.S. Supreme Court under Chief Justice Earl Warren, 1953–1969, decided such landmark cases as *Brown v. Board of Education* (school desegregation), *Baker v. Carr* (legislative redistricting), and *Gideon v. Wainwright* and *Miranda v. Arizona* (rights of criminal defendants).

Booker T. Washington (1856–1915) He founded a leading college for African Americans in Tuskegee, Alabama, and become the foremost black educator in America by the 1890s. He believed that the African American community should establish an economic base for its advancement before striving for social equality. His critics charged that his philosophy sacrificed educational and civil rights for dubious social acceptance and economic opportunities.

George Washington (1732–1799) In 1775, the Continental Congress named him the commander in chief of the Continental Army which defeated the British in the American Revolution. He had previously served as an officer in the French and Indian War. In 1787, he was the presiding officer over the Constitutional Convention, but participated little in the debates. In 1789, the Electoral College chose Washington to be the nation's first president. Washington faced the nation's first foreign and domestic crises, maintaining the United States' neutrality in foreign affairs. After two terms in office, Washington chose to step down; and the power of the presidency was peacefully passed to John Adams.

Watergate (1972–1974) Scandal that exposed the criminality and corruption of the Nixon administration and ultimately led to President Nixon's resignation in 1974.

Daniel Webster (1782–1852) As a representative from New Hampshire, he led the New Federalists in opposition to the moving of the second national bank from Boston to Philadelphia. Later, he served as representative and a senator for Massachusetts and emerged as a champion of a stronger national government. He also switched from opposing to supporting tariffs because New England had built up its manufactures with the understanding tariffs would protect them from foreign competitors.

Webster-Ashburton Treaty Settlement in 1842 of U.S.–Canadian border disputes in Maine, New York, Vermont, and in the Wisconsin Territory (now northern Minnesota).

Webster-Hayne debate U.S. Senate debate of January 1830 between Daniel Webster of Massachusetts and Robert Hayne of South Carolina over nullification and states' rights.

Western Front The contested frontier between the Central and Allied Powers that ran along northern France and across Belgium.

Whig party Political party founded in 1834 in opposition to the Jacksonian Democrats; Whigs supported federal funding for internal improvements, a national bank, and high tariffs on imported goods.

Whigs Another name for revolutionary Patriots.

Whiskey Rebellion (1794) Violent protest by western Pennsylvania farmers against the federal excise tax on corn whiskey, put down by a federal army.

Eli Whitney (1765–1825) He invented the cotton gin which could separate cotton from its seeds. One machine operator could separate fifty times more cotton than worker could by hand, which led to an increase in cotton production and prices. These increases gave planters a new profitable use for slavery and a lucrative slave trade emerged from the coastal South to the Southwest.

Wilderness Road Originally an Indian path through the Cumberland Gap, it was used by over 300,000 settlers who migrated westward to Kentucky in the last quarter of the eighteenth century.

Roger Williams (1603–1683) Puritan who believed that the purity of the church required a complete separation between church and state and freedom from coercion in matters of faith. In 1636, he established the town of Providence, the first permanent settlement in Rhode Island and the first to allow religious freedom in America.

Wendell L. Willkie (1892–1944) In the 1940 presidential election, he was the Republican nominee who ran against President Roosevelt. He supported aid to the Allies and criticized the New Deal programs. Voters looked at the increasingly dangerous world situation and chose to keep President Roosevelt in office for a third term.

Wilmot Proviso (1846) Proposal by Congressman David Wilmot, a Pennsylvania Democrat, to prohibit slavery in any land acquired in the Mexican-American War.

Woodrow Wilson (1856–1924) In the 1912 presidential election, Woodrow Wilson ran under the slogan of New Freedom, which promised to improve of the banking system, lower tariffs, and break up monopolies. At the beginning of the First World War, Wilson kept America neutral, but provided the Allies with credit for purchases of supplies; however, the sinking of U.S. merchant ships and the Zimmerman telegram caused him to ask Congress to declare war on Germany. Wilson supported the entry of America into the League of Nations and the ratification of the Treaty of Versailles, but Congress would not approve the entry or ratification.

John Winthrop Puritan leader and Governor of the Massachusetts Bay Colony who resolved to use the colony as a refuge for persecuted Puritans and as an instrument of building a "wilderness Zion" in America.

woman suffrage Movement to give women the right to vote through a constitutional amendment, spearheaded by Susan B. Anthony and Elizabeth Cady Stanton's National Woman Suffrage Association.

Women Accepted for Voluntary Emergency Services (WAVES) During the Second World War, the increased demand for labor shook up old prejudices about gender roles in the workplace and in the military. Nearly 200,000 women served in the Women's Army Corps or its naval equivalent, Women Accepted for Volunteer Emergency Service (WAVES).

Women's Army Corps Women's branch of the United States Army; by the end of the Second World War nearly 150,000 women had served in the WAC.

women's movement Wave of activism sparked by Betty Friedan's *The Feminine Mystique* (1963); it argued for equal rights for women and fought against the cult of domesticity of the 1950s that limited women's roles to the home as wife, mother, and housewife.

women's work The traditional term referring to routine tasks in the house, garden, and fields performed by women. The sphere of women's occupations expanded in the colonies to include medicine, shopkeeping, upholstering, and the operation of inns and taverns.

Woodstock In 1969, roughly a half a million young people converged on a farm near Bethel, New York, for a three-day music festival that was an expression of the flower children's free spirit.

Works Progress Administration (1935) Government agency established to manage several federal job programs created under the New Deal; it became the largest employer in the nation.

Battle of Wounded Knee Last incident of the Indians Wars took place in 1890 in the Dakota Territory, where the U.S. Cavalry killed over 200 Sioux men, women, and children who were in the process of surrender.

XYZ affair French foreign minister Tallyrand's three anonymous agents demanded payments to stop French plundering of American ships in 1797; refusal to pay the bribe led to two years of sea war with France (1798–1800).

Yalta Conference (1945) Meeting of the "Big Three" Allied leaders, Franklin D. Roosevelt, Winston Churchill, and Joseph Stalin, to discuss how to divide control of postwar Germany and eastern Europe

yellow journalism A type of news reporting, epitomized in the 1890s by the newspaper empires of William Randolph Hearst and Joseph Pulitzer, that intentionally manipulates public opinion through sensational headlines, illustrations, and articles about both real and invented events.

yeomen Small landowners (the majority of white families in the South) who farmed their own land and usually did not own slaves.

Battle of Yorktown Last major battle of the Revolutionary War; General Cornwallis along with over 7,000 British troops surrendered to George Washington at Yorktown, Virginia, on October 17, 1781.

Brigham Young (1801–1877) Following Joseph Smith's death, he became the leader of the Mormons and promised Illinois officials that the Mormons would leave the state. In 1846, he led the Mormons to Utah and settled near the Salt Lake. After the United States gained Utah as part of the Treaty of Guadalupe Hidalgo, he became the governor of the territory and kept the Mormons virtually independent of federal authority.

youth culture The youth of the 1950s had more money and free time than any previous generation which allowed a distinct youth culture to emerge. A market emerged for products and activities that were specifically for young people such as transistor radios, rock records, *Seventeen* magazine, and Pat Boone movies.

Zimmermann telegram Message sent by a German official to the Mexican government in 1917 urging an invasion of the United States; the telegram was intercepted by British intelligence agents and angered Americans, many of whom called for war against Germany.

Appendix

The Declaration of Independence (1776)

When in the Course of human events, it becomes necessary for one people to dissolve the political bands which have connected them with another, and to assume among the powers of the earth, the separate and equal station to which the Laws of Nature and of Nature's God entitle them, a decent respect to the opinions of mankind requires that they should declare the causes which impel them to the separation.

We hold these truths to be self-evident, that all men are created equal, that they are endowed by their Creator with certain unalienable Rights, that among these are Life, Liberty and the pursuit of Happiness. —That to secure these rights, Governments are instituted among Men, deriving their just powers from the consent of the governed, —That whenever any Form of Government becomes destructive of these ends, it is the Right of the People to alter or to abolish it, and to institute new Government, laying its foundation on such principles and organizing its powers in such form, as to them shall seem most likely to effect their Safety and Happiness. Prudence, indeed, will dictate that Governments long established should not be changed for light and transient causes; and accordingly all experience hath shewn, that mankind are more disposed to suffer, while evils are sufferable, than to right themselves by abolishing the forms to which they are accustomed. But when a long train of abuses and usurpations, pursuing invariably the same Object evinces a design to reduce them under absolute Despotism, it is their right, it is their duty, to throw off such Government, and to provide new Guards for their future security.— Such has been the patient sufferance of these Colonies; and such is now the necessity which constrains them to alter their former Systems of Government. The history of the present King of Great Britain is a history of repeated injuries and usurpations, all having in direct object the establishment of an absolute Tyranny over these States. To prove this, let Facts be submitted to a candid world.

He has refused his Assent to Laws, the most wholesome and necessary for the public good.

He has forbidden his Governors to pass Laws of immediate and pressing importance, unless suspended in their operation till his Assent should be obtained; and when so suspended, he has utterly neglected to attend to them.

He has refused to pass other Laws for the accommodation of large districts of people, unless those people would relinquish the right of Representation in the Legislature, a right inestimable to them and formidable to tyrants only.

He has called together legislative bodies at places unusual, uncomfortable, and distant from the depository of their public Records, for the sole purpose of fatiguing them into compliance with his measures.

He has dissolved Representative Houses repeatedly, for opposing with manly firmness his invasions on the rights of the people.

He has refused for a long time, after such dissolutions, to cause others to be elected; whereby the Legislative powers, incapable of Annihilation, have returned to the People at large for their exercise; the State remaining in the mean time exposed to all the dangers of invasion from without, and convulsions within.

He has endeavoured to prevent the population of these States; for that purpose obstructing the Laws for Naturalization of Foreigners; refusing to pass others to encourage their migrations hither, and raising the conditions of new Appropriations of Lands.

He has obstructed the Administration of Justice, by refusing his Assent to Laws for establishing Judiciary powers.

He has made Judges dependent on his Will alone, for the tenure of their offices, and the amount and payment of their salaries.

He has erected a multitude of New Offices, and sent hither swarms of Officers to harrass our people, and eat out their substance.

He has kept among us, in times of peace, Standing Armies without the Consent of our legislatures.

He has affected to render the Military independent of and superior to the Civil power.

He has combined with others to subject us to a jurisdiction foreign to our constitution, and unacknowledged by our laws; giving his Assent to their Acts of pretended Legislation:

For quartering large bodies of armed troops among us:

For protecting them, by a mock Trial, from punishment for any Murders which they should commit on the Inhabitants of these States:

For cutting off our Trade with all parts of the world:

For imposing Taxes on us without our Consent:

For depriving us in many cases, of the benefits of Trial by Jury:

For transporting us beyond Seas to be tried for pretended offences

For abolishing the free System of English Laws in a neighbouring Province, establishing therein an Arbitrary government, and enlarging its Boundaries so as to render it at once an example and fit instrument for introducing the same absolute rule into these Colonies:

For taking away our Charters, abolishing our most valuable Laws, and altering fundamentally the Forms of our Governments:

For suspending our own Legislatures, and declaring themselves invested with power to legislate for us in all cases whatsoever.

He has abdicated Government here, by declaring us out of his Protection and waging War against us.

He has plundered our seas, ravaged our Coasts, burnt our towns, and destroyed the lives of our people.

He is at this time transporting large Armies of foreign Mercenaries to compleat the works of death, desolation and tyranny, already begun with circumstances of Cruelty & perfidy scarcely paralleled in the most barbarous ages, and totally unworthy the Head of a civilized nation.

He has constrained our fellow Citizens taken Captive on the high Seas to bear Arms against their Country, to become the executioners of their friends and Brethren, or to fall themselves by their Hands.

He has excited domestic insurrections amongst us, and has endeavoured to bring on the inhabitants of our frontiers, the merciless Indian Savages, whose known rule of warfare, is an undistinguished destruction of all ages, sexes and conditions.

In every stage of these Oppressions We have Petitioned for Redress in the most humble terms: Our repeated Petitions have been answered only by repeated injury. A Prince whose character is thus marked by every act which may define a Tyrant, is unfit to be the ruler of a free people.

Nor have We been wanting in attentions to our Brittish brethren. We have warned them from time to time of attempts by their legislature to extend an unwarrantable jurisdiction over us. We have reminded them of the circumstances of our emigration and settlement here. We have appealed to their native justice and magnanimity, and we have conjured them by the ties of our common kindred to disavow these usurpations, which, would inevitably interrupt our connections and correspondence. They too have been deaf to the voice of justice and of consanguinity. We must, therefore, acquiesce in the necessity, which denounces our Separation, and hold them, as we hold the rest of mankind, Enemies in War, in Peace Friends.

We, therefore, the Representatives of the united States of America, in General Congress, Assembled, appealing to the Supreme Judge of the world for the rectitude of our intentions, do, in the Name, and by Authority of the good People of these Colonies, solemnly publish and declare, That these United Colonies are, and of Right ought to be Free and Independent States; that they are Absolved from all Allegiance to the British Crown, and that all political connection between them and the State of Great Britain, is and ought to be totally dissolved; and that as Free and Independent States, they have full Power to levy War, conclude Peace, contract Alliances, establish Commerce, and to do all other Acts and Things which Independent States may of right do. And for the support of this Declaration, with a firm reliance on the protection of divine Providence, we mutually pledge to each other our Lives, our Fortunes and our sacred Honor.

Georgia
Button Gwinnett
Lyman Hall
George Walton

North Carolina
William Hooper
Joseph Hewes
John Penn

South Carolina
Edward Rutledge
Thomas Heyward, Jr.
Thomas Lynch, Jr.
Arthur Middleton

Massachusetts
John Hancock

Maryland
Samuel Chase
William Paca
Thomas Stone
Charles Carroll
    of Carrollton

Virginia
George Wythe
Richard Henry Lee
Thomas Jefferson
Benjamin Harrison
Thomas Nelson, Jr.
Francis Lightfoot Lee
Carter Braxton

Pennsylvania
Robert Morris
Benjamin Rush
Benjamin Franklin
John Morton
George Clymer
James Smith
George Taylor
James Wilson
George Ross

Delaware
Caesar Rodney
George Read
Thomas McKean

New York
William Floyd
Philip Livingston
Francis Lewis
Lewis Morris

New Jersey
Richard Stockton
John Witherspoon
Francis Hopkinson
John Hart
Abraham Clark

New Hampshire
Josiah Bartlett
William Whipple

Massachusetts
Samuel Adams
John Adams
Robert Treat Paine
Elbridge Gerry

Rhode Island
Stephen Hopkins
William Ellery

Connecticut
Roger Sherman
Samuel Huntington
William Williams
Oliver Wolcott

New Hampshire
Matthew Thornton

Articles of Confederation (1787)

To ALL TO WHOM these Presents shall come, we the undersigned Delegates of the States affixed to our Names send greeting.

Whereas the Delegates of the United States of America in Congress assembled did on the fifteenth day of November in the Year of our Lord One Thousand Seven Hundred and Seventy-seven, and in the Second Year of the Independence of America agree to certain articles of Confederation and perpetual Union between the States of Newhampshire, Massachusetts-bay, Rhodeisland and Providence Plantations, Connecticut, New York, New Jersey, Pennsylvania, Delaware, Maryland, Virginia, North-Carolina, South-Carolina and Georgia in the Words following, viz.

Articles of Confederation and perpetual Union between the States of Newhampshire, Massachusetts-bay, Rhodeisland and Providence Plantations, Connecticut, New-York, New-Jersey, Pennsylvania, Delaware, Maryland, Virginia, North-Carolina, South-Carolina and Georgia.

ARTICLE I. The stile of this confederacy shall be "The United States of America."

ARTICLE II. Each State retains its sovereignty, freedom and independence, and every power, jurisdiction and right, which is not by this confederation expressly delegated to the United States, in Congress assembled.

ARTICLE III. The said States hereby severally enter into a firm league of friendship with each other, for their common defence, the security of their liberties, and their mutual and general welfare, binding themselves to assist each other, against all force offered to, or attacks made upon them, or any of them, on account of religion, sovereignty, trade or any other pretence whatever.

ARTICLE IV. The better to secure and perpetuate mutual friendship and intercourse among the people of the different States in this Union, the free inhabitants of each of these States, paupers, vagabonds and fugitives from justice excepted, shall be entitled to all privileges and immunities of free citizens in the several States; and the people of each State shall have free ingress and regress to and from any other State, and shall enjoy therein all the privileges of trade and commerce, subject to the same duties, impositions and restrictions as the inhabitants thereof respectively, provided that such restrictions shall not extend so far as to prevent the removal of property imported into any State, to any other State of which the owner is an inhabitant; provided also that no imposition, duties or restriction shall be laid by any State, on the property of the United States, or either of them.

If any person guilty of, or charged with treason, felony, or other high misdemeanor in any State, shall flee from justice, and be found in any of the United States, he shall upon demand of the Governor or Executive power, of the State from which he fled, be delivered up and removed to the State having jurisdiction of his offence.

Full faith and credit shall be given in each of these States to the records, acts and judicial proceedings of the courts and magistrates of every other State.

ARTICLE V. For the more convenient management of the general interests of the United States, delegates shall be annually appointed in such manner as the legislature of each State shall direct, to meet in Congress on the first Monday in November, in every year, with a power reserved to each State, to recall its delegates, or any of them, at any time within the year, and to send others in their stead, for the remainder of the year.

No State shall be represented in Congress by less than two, nor by more than seven members; and no person shall be capable of being a delegate for more than three years in any term of six years; nor shall any person, being a delegate, be capable of holding any office under the United States, for which he, or another for his benefit receives any salary, fees or emolument of any kind.

Each State shall maintain its own delegates in a meeting of the States, and while they act as members of the committee of the States.

In determining questions in the United States, in Congress assembled, each State shall have one vote.

Freedom of speech and debate in Congress shall not be impeached or questioned in any court, or place out of Congress, and the members of Congress shall be protected in their persons from arrests and imprisonments, during the time of their going to and from, and attendance on Congress, except for treason, felony, or breach of the peace.

ARTICLE VI. No State without the consent of the United States in Congress assembled, shall send any embassy to, or receive any embassy from, or enter into any conference, agreement, alliance or treaty with any king, prince or state; nor shall any person holding any office of profit or trust under the United States, or any of them, accept of any present, emolument, office or title of any kind whatever from any king, prince or foreign state; nor shall the United States in Congress assembled, or any of them, grant any title of nobility.

No two or more States shall enter into any treaty, confederation or alliance whatever between them, without the consent of the United States in Congress assembled, specifying accurately the purposes for which the same is to be entered into, and how long it shall continue.

No State shall lay any imposts or duties, which may interfere with any stipulations in treaties, entered into by the United States in Congress assembled, with any king, prince or state, in pursuance of any treaties already proposed by Congress, to the courts of France and Spain.

No vessels of war shall be kept up in time of peace by any State, except such number only, as shall be deemed necessary by the United States in Congress assembled, for the defence of such State, or its trade; nor shall any body of forces be kept up by any State, in time of peace, except such number only, as in the judgment of the United States, in Congress assembled, shall be deemed requisite to garrison the forts necessary for the defence of such State; but every State shall always keep up a well regulated and disciplined militia, sufficiently armed and accoutred, and shall provide and constantly have ready for use, in public stores, a due number of field pieces and tents, and a proper quantity of arms, ammunition and camp equipage.

No State shall engage in any war without the consent of the United States in Congress assembled, unless such State be actually invaded by enemies, or shall have received certain advice of a resolution being formed by some nation of Indians to invade such State, and the danger is so imminent as not to admit of a delay, till the United States in Congress assembled can be consulted: nor shall any State grant commissions to any ships or vessels of war, nor letters of marque or reprisal, except it be after a declaration of war by the United States in Congress assembled, and then only against the kingdom or state and the subjects thereof, against which war has been so declared, and under such regulations as shall be established by the United States in Congress assembled, unless such State be infested by pirates, in which case vessels of war may be fitted out for that occasion, and kept so long as the danger shall continue, or until the United States in Congress assembled shall determine otherwise.

ARTICLE VII. When land-forces are raised by any State of the common defence, all officers of or under the rank of colonel, shall be appointed by the Legislature of each State respectively by whom such forces shall be raised, or in such manner as such State shall direct, and all vacancies shall be filled up by the State which first made the appointment.

ARTICLE VIII. All charges of war, and all other expenses that shall be incurred for the common defence or general welfare, and allowed by the United States in Congress assembled, shall be defrayed out of a common treasury, which shall be supplied by the several States, in proportion to the value of all land within each State, granted to or surveyed for any person, as such land and the buildings and improvements thereon shall be estimated according to such mode as the United States in Congress assembled, shall from time to time direct and appoint.

The taxes for paying that proportion shall be laid and levied by the authority and direction of the Legislatures of the several States within the time agreed upon by the United States in Congress assembled.

ARTICLE IX. The United States in Congress assembled, shall have the sole and exclusive right and power of determining on peace and war, except in the cases mentioned in the sixth article—of sending and receiving ambassadors—entering into treaties and alliances, provided that no treaty of commerce shall be made whereby the legislative power of the respective States shall be restrained from imposing such imposts and duties on foreigners, as their own people are subjected to, or from prohibiting the exportation or importation of and species of goods or commodities whatsoever—of establishing rules for deciding in all cases, what captures on land or water shall be legal, and in what manner prizes taken by land or naval forces in the service of the United States shall be divided or appropriated—of granting letters of marque and reprisal in times of peace—appointing courts for the trial of piracies and felonies committed on the high seas and establishing courts for receiving and determining finally appeals in all cases of captures, provided that no member of Congress shall be appointed a judge of any of the said courts.

The United States in Congress assembled shall also be the last resort on appeal in all disputes and differences now subsisting or that hereafter may arise between two or more States concerning boundary, jurisdiction or any other cause whatever; which authority shall always be exercised in the manner following. Whenever the legislative or executive authority or lawful agent of any State in controversy with another shall present a petition to Congress, stating the matter in question and praying for a hearing, notice thereof shall be given by order of Congress to the legislative or executive authority of the other State in controversy, and a day assigned for the appearance of the parties by their lawful agents, who shall then be directed to appoint by joint consent, commissioners or judges to constitute a court for hearing and determining the matter in question: but if they cannot agree, Congress shall name three persons out of each of the United States, and from the list of such persons each party shall alternately strike out one, the petitioners beginning, until the number shall be reduced to thirteen; and from that number not less than seven, nor more than nine names as Congress shall direct, shall in the presence of Congress be drawn out by lot, and the persons whose names shall be so drawn or any five of them, shall be commissioners or judges, to hear and finally determine the controversy, so always as a major part of the judges who shall hear the cause shall agree in the determination: and if either party shall neglect to attend at the day appointed, without reasons, which Congress shall judge sufficient, or being present shall refuse to strike, the Congress shall proceed to nominate three persons out of each State, and the Secretary of Congress shall strike in behalf of such party absent or refusing; and the judgment and sentence of the court to be appointed, in the manner before prescribed, shall be final and conclusive; and if any of the parties shall refuse to submit to the authority of such court, or to appear or defend their claim or cause, the court shall nevertheless proceed to pronounce sentence, or judgment, which shall in like manner be final and decisive, the judgment or sentence and other proceedings being in either case transmitted to Congress, and lodged among the acts of Congress for the security of the parties concerned: provided that every commissioner, before he sits in judgment, shall take an oath to be administered by one of the judges of the supreme or superior court of the State where the case shall be tried, "well and truly to hear and determine the matter in question, according to the best of his judgment, without favour, affection or hope of reward:" provided also that no State shall be deprived of territory for the benefit of the United States.

All controversies concerning the private right of soil claimed under different grants of two or more States, whose jurisdiction as they may respect such lands, and the states which passed such grants are adjusted, the said grants or either of them being at the same time claimed to have originated antecedent to such settlement of jurisdiction, shall on the petition of either party to the Congress of the United States, be finally determined as near as may be in the same manner as is before prescribed for deciding disputes respecting territorial jurisdiction between different States.

The United States in Congress assembled shall also have the sole and exclusive right and power of regulating the alloy and value of coin struck by their own authority, or by that of the respective States—fixing the standard of weights and measures throughout the United States—regulating the trade and managing all affairs with the Indians, not members of any of the States, provided that the legislative right of any State within its own limits be not infringed or violated—establishing and regulating post-offices from one State to another, throughout all of the United States, and exacting such postage on the papers passing thro' the same as may be requisite to defray the expenses of the said office—appointing all officers of the land forces, in the service of the United States, excepting regimental officers—appointing all the officers of the naval forces, and commissioning all officers whatever in the service of the United States—making rules for the government and regulation of the said land and naval forces, and directing their operations.

The United States in Congress assembled shall have authority to appoint a committee, to sit in the recess of Congress, to be denominated "a Committee of the States," and to consist of one delegate from each State; and to appoint such other committees and civil officers as may be necessary for managing the general affairs of the United States under their direction—to appoint one of their number to preside, provided that no person be allowed to serve in the office of president more than one year in any term of three years; to ascertain the necessary sums of money to be raised for the service of the United States, and to appropriate and apply the same for defraying the public expenses—to borrow money, or emit bills on the credit of the United States, transmitting every half year to the respective States an account of the sums of money so borrowed or emitted,—to build and equip a navy—to agree upon the number of land forces, and to make requisitions from each State for its quota, in proportion to the number of white inhabitants in such State; which requisition shall be binding, and thereupon the Legislature of each State shall appoint the regimental officers, raise the men and cloath, arm and equip them in a soldier like manner, at the expense of the United States; and the officers and men so cloathed, armed and equipped shall march to the place appointed, and within the time agreed on by the United States in Congress assembled: but if the United States in Congress assembled shall, on consideration of circumstances judge proper that any State should not raise men, or should raise a smaller number of men than the quota thereof, such extra number shall be raised, officered, cloathed, armed and equipped in the same manner as the quota of such State, unless the legislature of such State shall judge that such extra number cannot be safely spared out of the same, in which case they shall raise officer, cloath, arm and equip as many of such extra number as they judge can be safely spared. And the officers and men so cloathed, armed and equipped, shall march to the place appointed, and within the time agreed on by the United States in Congress assembled.

The United States in Congress assembled shall never engage in a war, nor grant letters of marque and reprisal in time of peace, nor enter into any treaties or alliances, nor coin money, nor regulate the value thereof, nor ascertain the sums and expenses necessary for the defence and welfare of the United States, or any of them, nor emit bills, nor borrow money on the credit of the United States, nor appropriate money, nor agree upon the number of vessels to be built or purchased, or the number of land or sea forces to be raised, nor appoint a commander in chief of the army or navy, unless nine States assent to the same: nor shall a question on any other point, except for adjourning from day to day be determined, unless by the votes of a majority of the United States in Congress assembled.

The Congress of the United States shall have power to adjourn to any time within the year, and to any place within the United States, so that no period of adjournment be for a longer duration than the space of six months, and shall publish the journal of their proceedings monthly, except such parts thereof relating to treaties, alliances or military operations, as in their judgment require secrecy; and the yeas and nays of the delegates of each State on any question shall be entered on the Journal, when it is desired by any delegate; and the delegates of a State, or any of them, at his or their request shall be furnished with a transcript of the said journal, except such parts as are above excepted, to lay before the Legislatures of the several States.

ARTICLE X. The committee of the States, or any nine of them, shall be authorized to execute, in the recess of Congress, such of the powers of Congress as the United States in Congress assembled, by the consent of nine States, shall from time to time think expedient to vest them with; provided that no power be delegated to the said committee, for the exercise of which, by the articles of confederation, the voice of nine States in the Congress of the United States assembled is requisite.

ARTICLE XI. Canada acceding to this confederation, and joining in the measures of the United States, shall be admitted into, and entitled to all the advantages of this Union: but no other colony shall be admitted into the same, unless such admission be agreed to by nine States.

ARTICLE XII. All bills of credit emitted, monies borrowed and debts contracted by, or under the authority of Congress, before the assembling of the United States, in pursuance of the present confederation, shall be deemed and considered as a charge against the United States, for payment and satisfaction whereof the said United States, and the public faith are hereby solemnly pledged.

ARTICLE XIII. Every State shall abide by the determinations of the United States in Congress assembled, on all questions which by this confederation are submitted to them. And the articles of this confederation shall be inviolably observed by every State, and the Union shall be perpetual; nor shall any alteration at any time hereafter be made in any of them; unless such alteration be agreed to in a Congress of the United States, and be afterwards confirmed by the Legislatures of every State.

And whereas it has pleased the Great Governor of the world to incline the hearts of the Legislatures we respectively represent in Congress, to approve of, and to authorize us to ratify the said articles of confederation and perpetual union. Know ye that we the undersigned delegates, by virtue of the power and authority to us given for that purpose, do by these presents, in the name and in behalf of our respective constituents, fully and entirely ratify and confirm each and every of the said articles of confederation and perpetual union, and all and singular the matters and things therein contained: and we do further solemnly plight and engage the faith of our respective constituents, that they shall abide by the determinations of the United States in Congress assembled, on all questions, which by the said confederation are submitted to them. And that the articles thereof shall be inviolably observed by the States we respectively represent, and that the Union shall be perpetual.

In witness thereof we have hereunto set our hands in Congress. Done at Philadelphia in the State of Pennsylvania the ninth day of July in the year of our Lord one thousand seven hundred and seventy-eight, and in the third year of the independence of America.

The Constitution of the United States (1787)

We the People of the United States, in Order to form a more perfect Union, establish Justice, insure domestic Tranquility, provide for the common defence, promote the general Welfare, and secure the Blessings of Liberty to ourselves and our Posterity, do ordain and establish this Constitution for the United States of America.

Article. I.

Section. 1. All legislative Powers herein granted shall be vested in a Congress of the United States, which shall consist of a Senate and House of Representatives.

Section. 2. The House of Representatives shall be composed of Members chosen every second Year by the People of the several States, and the Electors in each State shall have the Qualifications requisite for Electors of the most numerous Branch of the State Legislature.

No Person shall be a Representative who shall not have attained to the Age of twenty five Years, and been seven Years a Citizen of the United States, and who shall not, when elected, be an Inhabitant of that State in which he shall be chosen.

Representatives and direct Taxes shall be apportioned among the several States which may be included within this Union, according to their respective Numbers, which shall be determined by adding to the whole Number of free Persons, including those bound to Service for a Term of Years, and excluding Indians not taxed, three fifths of all other Persons. The actual Enumeration shall be made within three Years after the first Meeting of the Congress of the United States, and within every subsequent Term of ten Years, in such Manner as they shall by Law direct. The Number of Representatives shall not exceed one for every thirty Thousand, but each State shall have at Least one Representative; and until such enumeration shall be made, the State of New Hampshire shall be entitled to chuse three, Massachusetts eight, Rhode-Island and Providence Plantations one, Connecticut five, New-York six, New Jersey four, Pennsylvania eight, Delaware one, Maryland six, Virginia ten, North Carolina five, South Carolina five, and Georgia three.

When vacancies happen in the Representation from any State, the Executive Authority thereof shall issue Writs of Election to fill such Vacancies.

The House of Representatives shall chuse their Speaker and other Officers; and shall have the sole Power of Impeachment.

Section. 3. The Senate of the United States shall be composed of two Senators from each State, chosen by the Legislature thereof for six Years; and each Senator shall have one Vote.

Immediately after they shall be assembled in Consequence of the first Election, they shall be divided as equally as may be into three Classes. The Seats of the Senators of the first Class shall be vacated at the Expiration of the second Year, of the second Class at the Expiration of the fourth Year, and of the third Class at the Expiration of the sixth Year, so that one third may be chosen every second Year; and if Vacancies happen by Resignation, or otherwise, during the Recess of the Legislature of any State, the Executive thereof may make temporary Appointments until the next Meeting of the Legislature, which shall then fill such Vacancies.

No Person shall be a Senator who shall not have attained to the Age of thirty Years, and been nine Years a Citizen of the United States, and who shall not, when elected, be an Inhabitant of that State for which he shall be chosen.

The Vice President of the United States shall be President of the Senate, but shall have no Vote, unless they be equally divided.

The Senate shall chuse their other Officers, and also a President pro tempore, in the Absence of the Vice President, or when he shall exercise the Office of President of the United States.

The Senate shall have the sole Power to try all Impeachments. When sitting for that Purpose, they shall be on Oath or Affirmation. When the President of the United States is tried, the Chief Justice shall preside: And no Person shall be convicted without the Concurrence of two thirds of the Members present.

Judgment in Cases of Impeachment shall not extend further than to removal from Office, and disqualification to hold and enjoy any Office of honor, Trust or Profit under the United States: but the Party convicted shall nevertheless be liable and subject to Indictment, Trial, Judgment and Punishment, according to Law.

Section. 4. The Times, Places and Manner of holding Elections for Senators and Representatives, shall be prescribed in each State by the Legislature thereof; but the Congress may at any time by Law make or alter such Regulations, except as to the Places of chusing Senators.

The Congress shall assemble at least once in every Year, and such Meeting shall be on the first Monday in December, unless they shall by Law appoint a different Day.

Section. 5. Each House shall be the Judge of the Elections, Returns and Qualifications of its own Members, and a Majority of each shall constitute a Quorum to do Business; but a smaller Number may adjourn from day to day, and may be authorized to compel the Attendance of absent Members, in such Manner, and under such Penalties as each House may provide.

Each House may determine the Rules of its Proceedings, punish its Members for disorderly Behaviour, and, with the Concurrence of two thirds, expel a Member.

Each House shall keep a Journal of its Proceedings, and from time to time publish the same, excepting such Parts as may in their Judgment require Secrecy; and the Yeas and Nays of the Members of either House on any question shall, at the Desire of one fifth of those Present, be entered on the Journal.

Neither House, during the Session of Congress, shall, without the Consent of the other, adjourn for more than three days, nor to any other Place than that in which the two Houses shall be sitting.

Section. 6. The Senators and Representatives shall receive a Compensation for their Services, to be ascertained by Law, and paid out of the Treasury of the United States. They shall in all Cases, except Treason, Felony and Breach of the Peace, be privileged from Arrest during their Attendance at the Session of their respective Houses, and in going to and returning from the same; and for any Speech or Debate in either House, they shall not be questioned in any other Place.

No Senator or Representative shall, during the Time for which he was elected, be appointed to any civil Office under the Authority of the United States, which shall have been created, or the Emoluments whereof shall have been encreased during such time; and no Person holding any Office under the United States, shall be a Member of either House during his Continuance in Office.

Section. 7. All Bills for raising Revenue shall originate in the House of Representatives; but the Senate may propose or concur with Amendments as on other Bills.

Every Bill which shall have passed the House of Representatives and the Senate shall, before it become a Law, be presented to the President of the United States; If he approve he shall sign it, but if not he shall return it, with his Objections to that House in which it shall have originated, who shall enter the Objections at large on their Journal, and proceed to reconsider it. If after such Reconsideration two thirds of that House shall agree to pass the Bill, it shall be sent, together with the Objections, to the other House, by which it shall likewise be reconsidered, and if approved by two thirds of that House, it shall become a Law. But in all such Cases the Votes of both Houses shall be determined by yeas and Nays, and the Names of the Persons voting for and against the Bill shall be entered on the Journal of each House respectively. If any Bill shall not be returned by the President within ten Days (Sundays excepted) after it shall have been presented to him, the Same shall be a Law, in like Manner as if he had signed it, unless the Congress by their Adjournment prevent its Return, in which Case it shall not be a Law.

Every Order, Resolution, or Vote to which the Concurrence of the Senate and House of Representatives may be necessary (except on a question of Adjournment) shall be presented to the President of the United States; and before the Same shall take Effect, shall be approved by him, or being disapproved by him, shall be repassed by two thirds of the Senate and House of Representatives, according to the Rules and Limitations prescribed in the Case of a Bill.

Section. 8. The Congress shall have Power To lay and collect Taxes, Duties, Imposts and Excises, to pay the Debts and provide for the common Defence and general Welfare of the United States; but all Duties, Imposts and Excises shall be uniform throughout the United States;

To borrow Money on the credit of the United States;

To regulate Commerce with foreign Nations, and among the several States, and with the Indian Tribes;

To establish an uniform Rule of Naturalization, and uniform Laws on the subject of Bankruptcies throughout the United States;

To coin Money, regulate the Value thereof, and of foreign Coin, and fix the Standard of Weights and Measures;

To provide for the Punishment of counterfeiting the Securities and current Coin of the United States;

To establish Post Offices and post Roads;

To promote the Progress of Science and useful Arts, by securing for limited Times to Authors and Inventors the exclusive Right to their respective Writings and Discoveries;

To constitute Tribunals inferior to the supreme Court;

To define and punish Piracies and Felonies committed on the high Seas, and Offences against the Law of Nations;

To declare War, grant Letters of Marque and Reprisal, and make Rules concerning Captures on Land and Water;

To raise and support Armies, but no Appropriation of Money to that Use shall be for a longer Term than two Years;

To provide and maintain a Navy;

To make Rules for the Government and Regulation of the land and naval Forces;

To provide for calling forth the Militia to execute the Laws of the Union, suppress Insurrections and repel Invasions;

To provide for organizing, arming, and disciplining, the Militia, and for governing such Part of them as may be employed in the Service of the United States, reserving to the States respectively, the Appointment of the Officers, and the Authority of training the Militia according to the discipline prescribed by Congress;

To exercise exclusive Legislation in all Cases whatsoever, over such District (not exceeding ten Miles square) as may, by Cession of particular States, and the Acceptance of Congress, become the Seat of the Government of the United States, and to exercise like Authority over all Places purchased by the Consent of the Legislature of the State in which the Same shall be, for the Erection of Forts, Magazines, Arsenals, dock-Yards, and other needful Buildings;—And

To make all Laws which shall be necessary and proper for carrying into Execution the foregoing Powers, and all other Powers vested by this Constitution in the Government of the United States, or in any Department or Officer thereof.

Section. 9. The Migration or Importation of such Persons as any of the States now existing shall think proper to admit, shall not be prohibited by the Congress prior to the Year one thousand eight hundred and eight, but a Tax or duty may be imposed on such Importation, not exceeding ten dollars for each Person.

The Privilege of the Writ of Habeas Corpus shall not be suspended, unless when in Cases of Rebellion or Invasion the public Safety may require it.

No Bill of Attainder or ex post facto Law shall be passed.

No Capitation, or other direct, Tax shall be laid, unless in Proportion to the Census or enumeration herein before directed to be taken.

No Tax or Duty shall be laid on Articles exported from any State.

No Preference shall be given by any Regulation of Commerce or Revenue to the Ports of one State over those of another; nor shall Vessels bound to, or from, one State, be obliged to enter, clear, or pay Duties in another.

No Money shall be drawn from the Treasury, but in Consequence of Appropriations made by Law; and a regular Statement and Account of the Receipts and Expenditures of all public Money shall be published from time to time.

No Title of Nobility shall be granted by the United States: And no Person holding any Office of Profit or Trust under them, shall, without the Consent of the Congress, accept of any present, Emolument, Office, or Title, of any kind whatever, from any King, Prince, or foreign State.

Section. 10. No State shall enter into any Treaty, Alliance, or Confederation; grant Letters of Marque and Reprisal; coin Money; emit Bills of Credit; make any Thing but gold and silver Coin a Tender in Payment of Debts; pass any Bill of Attainder, ex post facto Law, or Law impairing the Obligation of Contracts, or grant any Title of Nobility.

No State shall, without the Consent of the Congress, lay any Imposts or Duties on Imports or Exports, except what may be absolutely necessary for executing it's inspection Laws: and the net Produce of all Duties and Imposts, laid by any State on Imports or Exports, shall be for the Use of the Treasury of the United States; and all such Laws shall be subject to the Revision and Controul of the Congress.

No State shall, without the Consent of Congress, lay any Duty of Tonnage, keep Troops, or Ships of War in time of Peace, enter into any Agreement or Compact with another State, or with a foreign Power, or engage in War, unless actually invaded, or in such imminent Danger as will not admit of delay.

Article. II.

Section. 1. The executive Power shall be vested in a President of the United States of America. He shall hold his Office during the Term of four Years, and, together with the Vice President, chosen for the same Term, be elected, as follows:

Each State shall appoint, in such Manner as the Legislature thereof may direct, a Number of Electors, equal to the whole Number of Senators and Representatives to which the State may be entitled in the Congress: but no Senator or Representative, or Person holding an Office of Trust or Profit under the United States, shall be appointed an Elector.

The Electors shall meet in their respective States, and vote by Ballot for two Persons, of whom one at least shall not be an Inhabitant of the same State with themselves. And they shall make a List of all the Persons voted for, and of the Number of Votes for each; which List they shall sign and certify, and transmit sealed to the Seat of the Government of the United States, directed to the President of the Senate. The President of the Senate shall, in the Presence of the Senate and House of Representatives, open all the Certificates, and the Votes shall then be counted. The Person having the greatest Number of Votes shall be the President, if such Number be a Majority of the whole Number of Electors appointed; and if there be more than one who have such Majority, and have an equal Number of Votes, then the House of Representatives shall immediately chuse by Ballot one of them for President; and if no Person have a Majority, then from the five highest on the List the said House shall in like Manner chuse the President. But in chusing the President, the Votes shall be taken by States, the Representation from each State having one Vote; A quorum for this purpose shall consist of a Member or Members from two thirds of the States, and a Majority of all the States shall be necessary to a Choice. In every Case, after the Choice of the President, the Person having the greatest Number of Votes of the Electors shall be the Vice President. But if there should remain two or more who have equal Votes, the Senate shall chuse from them by Ballot the Vice President.

The Congress may determine the Time of chusing the Electors, and the Day on which they shall give their Votes; which Day shall be the same throughout the United States.

No Person except a natural born Citizen, or a Citizen of the United States, at the time of the Adoption of this Constitution, shall be eligible to the Office of President; neither shall any Person be eligible to that Office who shall not have attained to the Age of thirty five Years, and been fourteen Years a Resident within the United States.

In Case of the Removal of the President from Office, or of his Death, Resignation, or Inability to discharge the Powers and Duties of the said Office, the Same shall devolve on the Vice President, and the Congress may by Law provide for the Case of Removal, Death, Resignation or Inability, both of the President and Vice President, declaring what Officer shall then act as President, and such Officer shall act accordingly, until the Disability be removed, or a President shall be elected.

The President shall, at stated Times, receive for his Services, a Compensation, which shall neither be increased nor diminished during the Period for which he shall have been elected, and he shall not receive within that Period any other Emolument from the United States, or any of them.

Before he enter on the Execution of his Office, he shall take the following Oath or Affirmation:—"I do solemnly swear (or affirm) that I will faithfully execute the Office of President of the United States, and will to the best of my Ability, preserve, protect and defend the Constitution of the United States."

Section. 2. The President shall be Commander in Chief of the Army and Navy of the United States, and of the Militia of the several States, when called into the actual Service of the United States; he may require the Opinion, in writing, of the principal Officer in each of the executive Departments, upon any Subject relating to the Duties of their respective Offices, and he shall have Power to grant Reprieves and Pardons for Offences against the United States, except in Cases of Impeachment.

He shall have Power, by and with the Advice and Consent of the Senate, to make Treaties, provided two thirds of the Senators present concur; and he shall nominate, and by and with the Advice and Consent of the Senate, shall appoint Ambassadors, other public Ministers and Consuls, Judges of the supreme Court, and all other Officers of the United States, whose Appointments are not herein otherwise provided for, and which shall be established by Law: but the Congress may by Law vest the Appointment of such inferior Officers, as they think proper, in the President alone, in the Courts of Law, or in the Heads of Departments.

The President shall have Power to fill up all Vacancies that may happen during the Recess of the Senate, by granting Commissions which shall expire at the End of their next Session.

Section. 3. He shall from time to time give to the Congress Information of the State of the Union, and recommend to their Consideration such Measures as he shall judge necessary and expedient; he may, on extraordinary Occasions, convene both Houses, or either of them, and in Case of Disagreement between them, with Respect to the Time of Adjournment, he may adjourn them to such Time as he shall think proper; he shall receive Ambassadors and other public Ministers; he shall take Care that the Laws be faithfully executed, and shall Commission all the Officers of the United States.

Section. 4. The President, Vice President and all civil Officers of the United States, shall be removed from Office on Impeachment for, and Conviction of, Treason, Bribery, or other high Crimes and Misdemeanors.

Article. III.

Section. 1. The judicial Power of the United States shall be vested in one supreme Court, and in such inferior Courts as the Congress may from time to time ordain and establish. The Judges, both of the supreme and inferior Courts, shall hold their Offices during good Behaviour, and shall, at stated Times, receive for their Services a Compensation, which shall not be diminished during their Continuance in Office.

Section. 2. The judicial Power shall extend to all Cases, in Law and Equity, arising under this Constitution, the Laws of the United States, and Treaties made, or which shall be made, under their Authority;—to all Cases affecting Ambassadors, other public Ministers and Consuls;—to all Cases of admiralty and maritime Jurisdiction;—to Controversies to which the United States shall be a Party;—to Controversies between two or more States;— between a State and Citizens of another State,—between Citizens of different States,—between Citizens of the same State claiming Lands under Grants of different States, and between a State, or the Citizens thereof, and foreign States, Citizens or Subjects.

In all Cases affecting Ambassadors, other public Ministers and Consuls, and those in which a State shall be Party, the supreme Court shall have original Jurisdiction. In all the other Cases before mentioned, the supreme Court shall have appellate Jurisdiction, both as to Law and Fact, with such Exceptions, and under such Regulations as the Congress shall make.

The Trial of all Crimes, except in Cases of Impeachment, shall be by Jury; and such Trial shall be held in the State where the said Crimes shall have been committed; but when not committed within any State, the Trial shall be at such Place or Places as the Congress may by Law have directed.

Section. 3. Treason against the United States, shall consist only in levying War against them, or in adhering to their Enemies, giving them Aid and Comfort. No Person shall be convicted of Treason unless on the Testimony of two Witnesses to the same overt Act, or on Confession in open Court.

The Congress shall have Power to declare the Punishment of Treason, but no Attainder of Treason shall work Corruption of Blood, or Forfeiture except during the Life of the Person attainted.

Article. IV.

Section. 1. Full Faith and Credit shall be given in each State to the public Acts, Records, and judicial Proceedings of every other State. And the Congress may by general Laws prescribe the Manner in which such Acts, Records and Proceedings shall be proved, and the Effect thereof.

Section. 2. The Citizens of each State shall be entitled to all Privileges and Immunities of Citizens in the several States.

A Person charged in any State with Treason, Felony, or other Crime, who shall flee from Justice, and be found in another State, shall on Demand of the executive Authority of the State from which he fled, be delivered up, to be removed to the State having Jurisdiction of the Crime.

No Person held to Service or Labour in one State, under the Laws thereof, escaping into another, shall, in Consequence of any Law or Regulation therein, be discharged from such Service or Labour, but shall be delivered up on Claim of the Party to whom such Service or Labour may be due.

Section. 3. New States may be admitted by the Congress into this Union; but no new State shall be formed or erected within the Jurisdiction of any other State; nor any State be formed by the Junction of two or more States, or Parts of States, without the Consent of the Legislatures of the States concerned as well as of the Congress.

The Congress shall have Power to dispose of and make all needful Rules and Regulations respecting the Territory or other Property belonging to the United States; and nothing in this Constitution shall be so construed as to Prejudice any Claims of the United States, or of any particular States.

Section. 4. The United States shall guarantee to every State in this Union a Republican Form of Government, and shall protect each of them against Invasion; and on Application of the Legislature, or of the Executive (when the Legislature cannot be convened), against domestic Violence.

Article. V.

The Congress, whenever two thirds of both Houses shall deem it necessary, shall propose Amendments to this Constitution, or, on the Application of the Legislatures of two thirds of the several States, shall call a Convention for proposing Amendments, which, in either Case, shall be valid to all Intents and Purposes, as Part of this Constitution, when ratified by the Legislatures of three fourths of the several States, or by Conventions in three fourths thereof, as the one or the other Mode of Ratification may be proposed by the Congress; Provided that no Amendment which may be made prior to the Year One thousand eight hundred and eight shall in any Manner affect the first and fourth Clauses in the Ninth Section of the first Article; and that no State, without its Consent, shall be deprived of its equal Suffrage in the Senate.

Article. VI.

All Debts contracted and Engagements entered into, before the Adoption of this Constitution, shall be as valid against the United States under this Constitution, as under the Confederation.

This Constitution, and the Laws of the United States which shall be made in Pursuance thereof; and all Treaties made, or which shall be made, under the Authority of the United States, shall be the supreme Law of the Land; and the Judges in every State shall be bound thereby, any Thing in the Constitution or Laws of any State to the Contrary notwithstanding.

The Senators and Representatives before mentioned, and the Members of the several State Legislatures, and all executive and judicial Officers, both of the United States and of the several States, shall be bound by Oath or Affirmation, to support this Constitution; but no religious Test shall ever be required as a Qualification to any Office or public Trust under the United States.

Article. VII.

The Ratification of the Conventions of nine States, shall be sufficient for the Establishment of this Constitution between the States so ratifying the Same.

The Word, "the," being interlined between the seventh and eighth Lines of the first Page, the Word "Thirty" being partly written on an Erazure in the fifteenth Line of the first Page, The Words "is tried" being interlined between the thirty second and thirty third Lines of the first Page and the Word "the" being interlined between the forty third and forty fourth Lines of the second Page.

Attest William Jackson Secretary

Done in Convention by the Unanimous Consent of the States present the Seventeenth Day of September in the Year of our Lord one thousand seven hundred and Eighty seven and of the Independance of the United States of America the Twelfth In witness whereof We have hereunto subscribed our Names,

G°. Washington
Presidt and deputy from Virginia

Delaware
{
Geo: Read
Gunning Bedford jun
John Dickinson
Richard Bassett
Jaco: Broom
}

Maryland
{
James McHenry
Dan of St Thos. Jenifer
Danl. Carrol
}

Virginia
{
John Blair
James Madison Jr.
}

North Carolina
{
Wm. Blount
Richd. Dobbs Spaight
Hu Williamson
}

South Carolina
{
J. Rutledge
Charles Cotesworth Pinckney
Charles Pinckney
Pierce Butler
}

Georgia
{
William Few
Abr Baldwin
}

New Hampshire
{
John Langdon
Nicholas Gilman
}

Massachusetts
{
Nathaniel Gorham
Rufus King
}

Connecticut
{
Wm. Saml. Johnson
Roger Sherman
}

New York
{
Alexander Hamilton
}

New Jersey
{
Wil: Livingston
David Brearley
Wm. Paterson
Jona: Dayton
}

Pennsylvania
{
B Franklin
Thomas Mifflin
Robt. Morris
Geo. Clymer
Thos. FitzSimons
Jared Ingersoll
James Wilson
Gouv Morris
}

Amendments to the Constitution

The Bill of Rights: A Transcription

The Preamble to The Bill of Rights

Congress of the United States
begun and held at the City of New-York, on
Wednesday the fourth of March, one thousand seven hundred and eighty nine.

THE Conventions of a number of the States, having at the time of their adopting the Constitution, expressed a desire, in order to prevent misconstruction or abuse of its powers, that further declaratory and restrictive clauses should be added: And as extending the ground of public confidence in the Government, will best ensure the beneficent ends of its institution.

RESOLVED by the Senate and House of Representatives of the United States of America, in Congress assembled, two thirds of both Houses concurring, that the following Articles be proposed to the Legislatures of the several States, as amendments to the Constitution of the United States, all, or any of which Articles, when ratified by three fourths of the said Legislatures, to be valid to all intents and purposes, as part of the said Constitution; viz.

ARTICLES in addition to, and Amendment of the Constitution of the United States of America, proposed by Congress, and ratified by the Legislatures of the several States, pursuant to the fifth Article of the original Constitution.

Note: The first ten amendments to the Constitution were ratified December 15, 1791, and form what is known as the "Bill of Rights."

Amendment I

Congress shall make no law respecting an establishment of religion, or prohibiting the free exercise thereof; or abridging the freedom of speech, or of the press; or the right of the people peaceably to assemble, and to petition the Government for a redress of grievances.

Amendment II

A well regulated Militia, being necessary to the security of a free State, the right of the people to keep and bear Arms, shall not be infringed.

Amendment III

No Soldier shall, in time of peace be quartered in any house, without the consent of the Owner, nor in time of war, but in a manner to be prescribed by law.

Amendment IV

The right of the people to be secure in their persons, houses, papers, and effects, against unreasonable searches and seizures, shall not be violated, and no Warrants shall issue, but upon probable cause, supported by Oath or affirmation, and particularly describing the place to be searched, and the persons or things to be seized.

Amendment V

No person shall be held to answer for a capital, or otherwise infamous crime, unless on a presentment or indictment of a Grand Jury, except in cases arising in the land or naval forces, or in the Militia, when in actual service in time of War or public danger; nor shall any person be subject for the same offence to be twice put in jeopardy of life or limb; nor shall be compelled in any criminal case to be a witness against himself, nor be deprived of life, liberty, or property, without due process of law; nor shall private property be taken for public use, without just compensation.

Amendment VI

In all criminal prosecutions, the accused shall enjoy the right to a speedy and public trial, by an impartial jury of the State and district wherein the crime shall have been committed, which district shall have been previously ascertained by law, and to be informed of the nature and cause of the accusation; to be confronted with the witnesses against him; to have compulsory process for obtaining witnesses in his favor, and to have the Assistance of Counsel for his defence.

Amendment VII

In Suits at common law, where the value in controversy shall exceed twenty dollars, the right of trial by jury shall be preserved, and no fact tried by a jury, shall be otherwise re-examined in any Court of the United States, than according to the rules of the common law.

Amendment VIII

Excessive bail shall not be required, nor excessive fines imposed, nor cruel and unusual punishments inflicted.

Amendment IX

The enumeration in the Constitution, of certain rights, shall not be construed to deny or disparage others retained by the people.

Amendment X

The powers not delegated to the United States by the Constitution, nor prohibited by it to the States, are reserved to the States respectively, or to the people.

Amendment XI

Passed by Congress March 4, 1794. Ratified February 7, 1795.

Note: Article III, section 2, of the Constitution was modified by amendment 11.

The Judicial power of the United States shall not be construed to extend to any suit in law or equity, commenced or prosecuted against one of the United States by Citizens of another State, or by Citizens or Subjects of any Foreign State.

Amendment XII

Passed by Congress December 9, 1803. Ratified June 15, 1804.

Note: A portion of Article II, section 1 of the Constitution was superseded by the 12th amendment.

The Electors shall meet in their respective states and vote by ballot for President and Vice-President, one of whom, at least, shall not be an inhabitant of the same state with themselves; they shall name in their ballots the person voted for as President, and in distinct ballots the person voted for as Vice-President, and they shall make distinct lists of all persons voted for as President, and of all persons voted for as Vice-President, and of the number of votes for each, which lists they shall sign and certify, and transmit sealed to the seat of the government of the United States, directed to the President of the Senate; — the President of the Senate shall, in the presence of the Senate and House of Representatives, open all the certificates and the votes shall then be counted; — The person having the greatest number of votes for President, shall be the President, if such number be a majority of the whole number of Electors appointed; and if no person have such majority, then from the persons having the highest numbers not exceeding three on the list of those voted for as President, the House of Representatives shall choose immediately, by ballot, the President. But in choosing the President, the votes shall be taken by states, the representation from each state having one vote; a quorum for this purpose shall consist of a member or members from two-thirds of the states, and a majority of all the states shall be necessary to a choice. [And if the House of Representatives shall not choose a President whenever the right of choice shall devolve upon them, before the fourth day of March next following, then the Vice-President shall act as President, as in case of the death or other constitutional disability of the President. —]* The person having the greatest number of votes as Vice-President, shall be the Vice-President, if such number be a majority of the whole number of Electors appointed, and if no person have a majority, then from the two highest numbers on the list, the Senate shall choose the Vice-President; a quorum for the purpose shall consist of two-thirds of the whole number of Senators, and a majority of the whole number shall be necessary to a choice. But no person constitutionally ineligible to the office of President shall be eligible to that of Vice-President of the United States.

*Superseded by section 3 of the 20th amendment.

Amendment XIII

Passed by Congress January 31, 1865. Ratified December 6, 1865.

Note: A portion of Article IV, section 2, of the Constitution was superseded by the 13th amendment.

Section 1.
Neither slavery nor involuntary servitude, except as a punishment for crime whereof the party shall have been duly convicted, shall exist within the United States, or any place subject to their jurisdiction.

Section 2.
Congress shall have power to enforce this article by appropriate legislation.

Amendment XIV

Passed by Congress June 13, 1866. Ratified July 9, 1868.

Note: Article I, section 2, of the Constitution was modified by section 2 of the 14th amendment.

Section 1.
All persons born or naturalized in the United States, and subject to the jurisdiction thereof, are citizens of the United States and of the State wherein they reside. No State shall make or enforce any law which shall abridge the privileges or immunities of citizens of the United States; nor shall any State deprive any person of life, liberty, or property, without due process of law; nor deny to any person within its jurisdiction the equal protection of the laws.

Section 2.
Representatives shall be apportioned among the several States according to their respective numbers, counting the whole number of persons in each State, excluding Indians not taxed. But when the right to vote at any election for the choice of electors for President and Vice-President of the United States, Representatives in Congress, the Executive and Judicial officers of a State, or the members of the Legislature thereof, is denied to any of the male inhabitants of such State, being twenty-one years of age,* and citizens of the United States, or in any way abridged, except for participation in rebellion, or other crime, the basis of representation therein shall be reduced in the proportion which the number of such male citizens shall bear to the whole number of male citizens twenty-one years of age in such State.

Section 3.
No person shall be a Senator or Representative in Congress, or elector of President and Vice-President, or hold any office, civil or military, under the United States, or under any State, who, having previously taken an oath, as a member of Congress, or as an officer of the United States, or as a member of any State legislature, or as an executive or judicial officer of any State, to support the Constitution of the United States, shall have engaged in insurrection or rebellion against the same, or given aid or comfort to the enemies thereof. But Congress may by a vote of two-thirds of each House, remove such disability.

Section 4.

The validity of the public debt of the United States, authorized by law, including debts incurred for payment of pensions and bounties for services in suppressing insurrection or rebellion, shall not be questioned. But neither the United States nor any State shall assume or pay any debt or obligation incurred in aid of insurrection or rebellion against the United States, or any claim for the loss or emancipation of any slave; but all such debts, obligations and claims shall be held illegal and void.

Section 5.

The Congress shall have the power to enforce, by appropriate legislation, the provisions of this article.

Changed by section 1 of the 26th amendment.

Amendment XV

Passed by Congress February 26, 1869. Ratified February 3, 1870.

Section 1.

The right of citizens of the United States to vote shall not be denied or abridged by the United States or by any State on account of race, color, or previous condition of servitude—

Section 2.

The Congress shall have the power to enforce this article by appropriate legislation.

Amendment XVI

Passed by Congress July 2, 1909. Ratified February 3, 1913.

Note: Article I, section 9, of the Constitution was modified by amendment 16.

The Congress shall have power to lay and collect taxes on incomes, from whatever source derived, without apportionment among the several States, and without regard to any census or enumeration.

Amendment XVII

Passed by Congress May 13, 1912. Ratified April 8, 1913.

Note: Article I, section 3, of the Constitution was modified by the 17th amendment.

The Senate of the United States shall be composed of two Senators from each State, elected by the people thereof, for six years; and each Senator shall have one vote. The electors in each State shall have the qualifications requisite for electors of the most numerous branch of the State legislatures.

When vacancies happen in the representation of any State in the Senate, the executive authority of such State shall issue writs of election to fill such vacancies: *Provided,* That the legislature of any State may empower the executive thereof to make temporary appointments until the people fill the vacancies by election as the legislature may direct.

This amendment shall not be so construed as to affect the election or term of any Senator chosen before it becomes valid as part of the Constitution.

Amendment XVIII

Passed by Congress December 18, 1917. Ratified January 16, 1919. Repealed by amendment 21.

Section 1.

After one year from the ratification of this article the manufacture, sale, or transportation of intoxicating liquors within, the importation thereof into, or the exportation thereof from the United States and all territory subject to the jurisdiction thereof for beverage purposes is hereby prohibited.

Section 2.

The Congress and the several States shall have concurrent power to enforce this article by appropriate legislation.

Section 3.

This article shall be inoperative unless it shall have been ratified as an amendment to the Constitution by the legislatures of the several States, as provided in the Constitution, within seven years from the date of the submission hereof to the States by the Congress.

Amendment XIX

Passed by Congress June 4, 1919. Ratified August 18, 1920.

The right of citizens of the United States to vote shall not be denied or abridged by the United States or by any State on account of sex.

Congress shall have power to enforce this article by appropriate legislation.

Amendment XX

Passed by Congress March 2, 1932. Ratified January 23, 1933.

Note: Article I, section 4, of the Constitution was modified by section 2 of this amendment. In addition, a portion of the 12th amendment was superseded by section 3.

Section 1.

The terms of the President and the Vice President shall end at noon on the 20th day of January, and the terms of Senators and Representatives at noon on the 3rd day of January, of the years in which such terms would have ended if this article had not been ratified; and the terms of their successors shall then begin.

Section 2.

The Congress shall assemble at least once in every year, and such meeting shall begin at noon on the 3d day of January, unless they shall by law appoint a different day.

Section 3.

If, at the time fixed for the beginning of the term of the President, the President elect shall have died, the Vice President elect shall become President. If a President shall not have been chosen before the time fixed for the beginning of his term, or if the President elect shall have failed to qualify, then the Vice President elect shall act as President until a President shall have qualified; and the Congress may by law provide for the case wherein neither a President elect nor a Vice President shall have qualified, declaring who shall then act as President, or the manner in which one who is to act shall be selected, and such person shall act accordingly until a President or Vice President shall have qualified.

Section 4.

The Congress may by law provide for the case of the death of any of the persons from whom the House of Representatives may choose a President whenever the right of choice shall have devolved upon them, and for the case of the death of any of the persons from whom the Senate may choose a Vice President whenever the right of choice shall have devolved upon them.

Section 5.

Sections 1 and 2 shall take effect on the 15th day of October following the ratification of this article.

Section 6.

This article shall be inoperative unless it shall have been ratified as an amendment to the Constitution by the legislatures of three-fourths of the several States within seven years from the date of its submission.

Amendment XXI

Passed by Congress February 20, 1933. Ratified December 5, 1933.

Section 1.

The eighteenth article of amendment to the Constitution of the United States is hereby repealed.

Section 2.

The transportation or importation into any State, Territory, or Possession of the United States for delivery or use therein of intoxicating liquors, in violation of the laws thereof, is hereby prohibited.

Section 3.

This article shall be inoperative unless it shall have been ratified as an amendment to the Constitution by conventions in the several States, as provided in the Constitution, within seven years from the date of the submission hereof to the States by the Congress.

Amendment XXII

Passed by Congress March 21, 1947. Ratified February 27, 1951.

Section 1.
No person shall be elected to the office of the President more than twice, and no person who has held the office of President, or acted as President, for more than two years of a term to which some other person was elected President shall be elected to the office of President more than once. But this Article shall not apply to any person holding the office of President when this Article was proposed by Congress, and shall not prevent any person who may be holding the office of President, or acting as President, during the term within which this Article becomes operative from holding the office of President or acting as President during the remainder of such term.

Section 2.
This article shall be inoperative unless it shall have been ratified as an amendment to the Constitution by the legislatures of three-fourths of the several States within seven years from the date of its submission to the States by the Congress.

Amendment XXIII

Passed by Congress June 16, 1960. Ratified March 29, 1961.

Section 1.
The District constituting the seat of Government of the United States shall appoint in such manner as Congress may direct:

A number of electors of President and Vice President equal to the whole number of Senators and Representatives in Congress to which the District would be entitled if it were a State, but in no event more than the least populous State; they shall be in addition to those appointed by the States, but they shall be considered, for the purposes of the election of President and Vice President, to be electors appointed by a State; and they shall meet in the District and perform such duties as provided by the twelfth article of amendment.

Section 2.
The Congress shall have power to enforce this article by appropriate legislation.

Amendment XXIV

Passed by Congress August 27, 1962. Ratified January 23, 1964.

Section 1.
The right of citizens of the United States to vote in any primary or other election for President or Vice President, for electors for President or Vice President, or for Senator or Representative in Congress, shall not be denied or abridged by the United States or any State by reason of failure to pay poll tax or other tax.

Section 2.
The Congress shall have power to enforce this article by appropriate legislation.

Amendment XXV

Passed by Congress July 6, 1965. Ratified February 10, 1967.

Note: Article II, section 1, of the Constitution was affected by the 25th amendment.

Section 1.
In case of the removal of the President from office or of his death or resignation, the Vice President shall become President.

Section 2.
Whenever there is a vacancy in the office of the Vice President, the President shall nominate a Vice President who shall take office upon confirmation by a majority vote of both Houses of Congress.

Section 3.
Whenever the President transmits to the President pro tempore of the Senate and the Speaker of the House of Representatives his written declaration that he is unable to discharge the powers and duties of his office, and until he transmits to them a written declaration to the contrary, such powers and duties shall be discharged by the Vice President as Acting President.

Section 4.
Whenever the Vice President and a majority of either the principal officers of the executive departments or of such other body as Congress may by law provide, transmit to the President pro tempore of the Senate and the Speaker of the House of Representatives their written declaration that the President is unable to discharge the powers and duties of his office, the Vice President shall immediately assume the powers and duties of the office as Acting President.

Thereafter, when the President transmits to the President pro tempore of the Senate and the Speaker of the House of Representatives his written declaration that no inability exists, he shall resume the powers and duties of his office unless the Vice President and a majority of either the principal officers of the executive department or of such other body as Congress may by law provide, transmit within four days to the President pro tempore of the Senate and the Speaker of the House of Representatives their written declaration that the President is unable to discharge the powers and duties of his office. Thereupon Congress shall decide the issue, assembling within forty-eight hours for that purpose if not in session. If the Congress, within twenty-one days after receipt of the latter written declaration, or, if Congress is not in session, within twenty-one days after Congress is required to assemble, determines by two-thirds vote of both Houses that the President is unable to discharge the powers and duties of his office, the Vice President shall continue to discharge the same as Acting President; otherwise, the President shall resume the powers and duties of his office.

Amendment XXVI

Passed by Congress March 23, 1971. Ratified July 1, 1971.

Note: Amendment 14, section 2, of the Constitution was modified by section 1 of the 26th amendment.

Section 1.
The right of citizens of the United States, who are eighteen years of age or older, to vote shall not be denied or abridged by the United States or by any State on account of age.

Section 2.
The Congress shall have power to enforce this article by appropriate legislation.

Amendment XXVII

Originally proposed Sept. 25, 1789. Ratified May 7, 1992.

No law, varying the compensation for the services of the Senators and Representatives, shall take effect, until an election of representatives shall have intervened.

PRESIDENTIAL ELECTIONS

Year	Number of States	Candidates	Parties	Popular Vote	% of Popular Vote	Electoral Vote	% Voter Participation
1789	11	**GEORGE WASHINGTON**	No party			69	
		John Adams	designations			34	
		Other candidates				35	
1792	15	**GEORGE WASHINGTON**	No party			132	
		John Adams	designations			77	
		George Clinton				50	
		Other candidates				5	
1796	16	**JOHN ADAMS**	Federalist			71	
		Thomas Jefferson	Democratic-Republican			68	
		Thomas Pinckney	Federalist			59	
		Aaron Burr	Democratic-Republican			30	
		Other candidates				48	
1800	16	**THOMAS JEFFERSON**	Democratic-Republican			73	
		Aaron Burr	Democratic-Republican			73	
		John Adams	Federalist			65	
		Charles C. Pinckney	Federalist			64	
		John Jay	Federalist			1	
1804	17	**THOMAS JEFFERSON**	Democratic-Republican			162	
		Charles C. Pinckney	Federalist			14	
1808	17	**JAMES MADISON**	Democratic-Republican			122	
		Charles C. Pinckney	Federalist			47	
		George Clinton	Democratic-Republican			6	
1812	18	**JAMES MADISON**	Democratic-Republican			128	
		DeWitt Clinton	Federalist			89	
1816	19	**JAMES MONROE**	Democratic-Republican			183	
		Rufus King	Federalist			34	
1820	24	**JAMES MONROE**	Democratic-Republican			231	
		John Quincy Adams	Independent			1	

Year	Number of States	Candidates	Parties	Popular Vote	% of Popular Vote	Electoral Vote	% Voter Participation
1824	24	**JOHN QUINCY ADAMS**	Democratic-Republican	108,740	30.5	84	26.9
		Andrew Jackson	Democratic-Republican	153,544	43.1	99	
		Henry Clay	Democratic-Republican	47,136	13.2	37	
		William H. Crawford	Democratic-Republican	46,618	13.1	41	
1828	24	**ANDREW JACKSON**	Democratic	647,286	56.0	178	57.6
		John Quincy Adams	National-Republican	508,064	44.0	83	
1832	24	**ANDREW JACKSON**	Democratic	688,242	54.5	219	55.4
		Henry Clay	National-Republican	473,462	37.5	49	
		William Wirt	Anti-Masonic	101,051	8.0	7	
		John Floyd	Democratic			11	
1836	26	**MARTIN VAN BUREN**	Democratic	765,483	50.9	170	57.8
		William H. Harrison	Whig	⎱ 739,795	⎱ 49.1	73	
		Hugh L. White	Whig			26	
		Daniel Webster	Whig			14	
		W. P. Mangum	Whig	⎰	⎰	11	
1840	26	**WILLIAM H. HARRISON**	Whig	1,274,624	53.1	234	80.2
		Martin Van Buren	Democratic	1,127,781	46.9	60	
1844	26	**JAMES K. POLK**	Democratic	1,338,464	49.6	170	78.9
		Henry Clay	Whig	1,300,097	48.1	105	
		James G. Birney	Liberty	62,300	2.3		
1848	30	**ZACHARY TAYLOR**	Whig	1,360,967	47.4	163	72.7
		Lewis Cass	Democratic	1,222,342	42.5	127	
		Martin Van Buren	Free Soil	291,263	10.1		
1852	31	**FRANKLIN PIERCE**	Democratic	1,601,117	50.9	254	69.6
		Winfield Scott	Whig	1,385,453	44.1	42	
		John P. Hale	Free Soil	155,825	5.0		

Year	Number of States	Candidates	Parties	Popular Vote	% of Popular Vote	Electoral Vote	% Voter Participation
1856	31	**JAMES BUCHANAN**	Democratic	1,832,955	45.3	174	78.9
		John C. Frémont	Republican	1,339,932	33.1	114	
		Millard Fillmore	American	871,731	21.6	8	
1860	33	**ABRAHAM LINCOLN**	Republican	1,865,593	39.8	180	81.2
		Stephen A. Douglas	Democratic	1,382,713	29.5	12	
		John C. Breckinridge	Democratic	848,356	18.1	72	
		John Bell	Constitutional Union	592,906	12.6	39	
1864	36	**ABRAHAM LINCOLN**	Republican	2,206,938	55.0	212	73.8
		George B. McClellan	Democratic	1,803,787	45.0	21	
1868	37	**ULYSSES S. GRANT**	Republican	3,013,421	52.7	214	78.1
		Horatio Seymour	Democratic	2,706,829	47.3	80	
1872	37	**ULYSSES S. GRANT**	Republican	3,596,745	55.6	286	71.3
		Horace Greeley	Democratic	2,843,446	43.9	66	
1876	38	**Rutherford B. Hayes**	Republican	4,036,572	48.0	185	81.8
		Samuel J. Tilden	Democratic	4,284,020	51.0	184	
1880	38	**JAMES A. GARFIELD**	Republican	4,453,295	48.5	214	79.4
		Winfield S. Hancock	Democratic	4,414,082	48.1	155	
		James B. Weaver	Greenback-Labor	308,578	3.4		
1884	38	**GROVER CLEVELAND**	Democratic	4,879,507	48.5	219	77.5
		James G. Blaine	Republican	4,850,293	48.2	182	
		Benjamin F. Butler	Greenback-Labor	175,370	1.8		
		John P. St. John	Prohibition	150,369	1.5		
1888	38	**BENJAMIN HARRISON**	Republican	5,477,129	47.9	233	79.3
		Grover Cleveland	Democratic	5,537,857	48.6	168	
		Clinton B. Fisk	Prohibition	249,506	2.2		
		Anson J. Streeter	Union Labor	146,935	1.3		

Year	Number of States	Candidates	Parties	Popular Vote	% of Popular Vote	Electoral Vote	% Voter Participation
1892	44	**GROVER CLEVELAND**	Democratic	5,555,426	46.1	277	74.7
		Benjamin Harrison	Republican	5,182,690	43.0	145	
		James B. Weaver	People's	1,029,846	8.5	22	
		John Bidwell	Prohibition	264,133	2.2		
1896	45	**WILLIAM MCKINLEY**	Republican	7,102,246	51.1	271	79.3
		William J. Bryan	Democratic	6,492,559	47.7	176	
1900	45	**WILLIAM MCKINLEY**	Republican	7,218,491	51.7	292	73.2
		William J. Bryan	Democratic; Populist	6,356,734	45.5	155	
		John C. Wooley	Prohibition	208,914	1.5		
1904	45	**THEODORE ROOSEVELT**	Republican	7,628,461	57.4	336	65.2
		Alton B. Parker	Democratic	5,084,223	37.6	140	
		Eugene V. Debs	Socialist	402,283	3.0		
		Silas C. Swallow	Prohibition	258,536	1.9		
1908	46	**WILLIAM H. TAFT**	Republican	7,675,320	51.6	321	65.4
		William J. Bryan	Democratic	6,412,294	43.1	162	
		Eugene V. Debs	Socialist	420,793	2.8		
		Eugene W. Chafin	Prohibition	253,840	1.7		
1912	48	**WOODROW WILSON**	Democratic	6,296,547	41.9	435	58.8
		Theodore Roosevelt	Progressive	4,118,571	27.4	88	
		William H. Taft	Republican	3,486,720	23.2	8	
		Eugene V. Debs	Socialist	900,672	6.0		
		Eugene W. Chafin	Prohibition	206,275	1.4		
1916	48	**WOODROW WILSON**	Democratic	9,127,695	49.4	277	61.6
		Charles E. Hughes	Republican	8,533,507	46.2	254	
		A. L. Benson	Socialist	585,113	3.2		
		J. Frank Hanly	Prohibition	220,506	1.2		
1920	48	**WARREN G. HARDING**	Republican	16,143,407	60.4	404	49.2
		James M. Cox	Democratic	9,130,328	34.2	127	
		Eugene V. Debs	Socialist	919,799	3.4		
		P. P. Christensen	Farmer-Labor	265,411	1.0		

Year	Number of States	Candidates	Parties	Popular Vote	% of Popular Vote	Electoral Vote	% Voter Participation
1924	48	CALVIN COOLIDGE	Republican	15,718,211	54.0	382	48.9
		John W. Davis	Democratic	8,385,283	28.8	136	
		Robert M. La Follette	Progressive	4,831,289	16.6	13	
1928	48	HERBERT C. HOOVER	Republican	21,391,993	58.2	444	56.9
		Alfred E. Smith	Democratic	15,016,169	40.9	87	
1932	48	FRANKLIN D. ROOSEVELT	Democratic	22,809,638	57.4	472	56.9
		Herbert C. Hoover	Republican	15,758,901	39.7	59	
		Norman Thomas	Socialist	881,951	2.2		
1936	48	FRANKLIN D. ROOSEVELT	Democratic	27,752,869	60.8	523	61.0
		Alfred M. Landon	Republican	16,674,665	36.5	8	
		William Lemke	Union	882,479	1.9		
1940	48	FRANKLIN D. ROOSEVELT	Democratic	27,307,819	54.8	449	62.5
		Wendell L. Willkie	Republican	22,321,018	44.8	82	
1944	48	FRANKLIN D. ROOSEVELT	Democratic	25,606,585	53.5	432	55.9
		Thomas E. Dewey	Republican	22,014,745	46.0	99	
1948	48	HARRY S. TRUMAN	Democratic	24,179,345	49.6	303	53.0
		Thomas E. Dewey	Republican	21,991,291	45.1	189	
		J. Strom Thurmond	States' Rights	1,176,125	2.4	39	
		Henry A. Wallace	Progressive	1,157,326	2.4		
1952	48	DWIGHT D. EISENHOWER	Republican	33,936,234	55.1	442	63.3
		Adlai E. Stevenson	Democratic	27,314,992	44.4	89	
1956	48	DWIGHT D. EISENHOWER	Republican	35,590,472	57.6	457	60.6
		Adlai E. Stevenson	Democratic	26,022,752	42.1	73	
1960	50	JOHN F. KENNEDY	Democratic	34,226,731	49.7	303	62.8
		Richard M. Nixon	Republican	34,108,157	49.5	219	
1964	50	LYNDON B. JOHNSON	Democratic	43,129,566	61.1	486	61.9
		Barry M. Goldwater	Republican	27,178,188	38.5	52	
1968	50	RICHARD M. NIXON	Republican	31,785,480	43.4	301	60.9
		Hubert H. Humphrey	Democratic	31,275,166	42.7	191	
		George C. Wallace	American Independent	9,906,473	13.5	46	

Year	Number of States	Candidates	Parties	Popular Vote	% of Popular Vote	Electoral Vote	% Voter Participation
1972	50	**RICHARD M. NIXON**	Republican	47,169,911	60.7	520	55.2
		George S. McGovern	Democratic	29,170,383	37.5	17	
		John G. Schmitz	American	1,099,482	1.4		
1976	50	**JIMMY CARTER**	Democratic	40,830,763	50.1	297	53.5
		Gerald R. Ford	Republican	39,147,793	48.0	240	
1980	50	**RONALD REAGAN**	Republican	43,901,812	50.7	489	52.6
		Jimmy Carter	Democratic	35,483,820	41.0	49	
		John B. Anderson	Independent	5,719,437	6.6		
		Ed Clark	Libertarian	921,188	1.1		
1984	50	**RONALD REAGAN**	Republican	54,451,521	58.8	525	53.1
		Walter F. Mondale	Democratic	37,565,334	40.6	13	
1988	50	**GEORGE H. W. BUSH**	Republican	47,917,341	53.4	426	50.1
		Michael Dukakis	Democratic	41,013,030	45.6	111	
1992	50	**BILL CLINTON**	Democratic	44,908,254	43.0	370	55.0
		George H. W. Bush	Republican	39,102,343	37.4	168	
		H. Ross Perot	Independent	19,741,065	18.9		
1996	50	**BILL CLINTON**	Democratic	47,401,185	49.0	379	49.0
		Bob Dole	Republican	39,197,469	41.0	159	
		H. Ross Perot	Independent	8,085,295	8.0		
2000	50	**GEORGE W. BUSH**	Republican	50,455,156	47.9	271	50.4
		Al Gore	Democrat	50,997,335	48.4	266	
		Ralph Nader	Green	2,882,897	2.7		
2004	50	**GEORGE W. BUSH**	Republican	62,040,610	50.7	286	60.7
		John F. Kerry	Democrat	59,028,444	48.3	251	
2008	50	**BARACK OBAMA**	Democrat	69,456,897	52.9	365	63.0
		John McCain	Republican	59,934,814	45.7	173	
2012	50	**BARACK OBAMA**	Democrat	65,915,795	51.1	332	57.5
		Mitt Romney	Republican	60,933,504	47.2	206	
2016	50	**DONALD TRUMP**	Republican	62,979,636	46.1	304	60.2
		Hillary Rodham Clinton	Democrat	65,844,610	48.2	227	

Candidates receiving less than 1 percent of the popular vote have been omitted. Thus the percentage of popular vote given for any election year may not total 100 percent. Before the passage of the Twelfth Amendment in 1804, the electoral college voted for two presidential candidates; the runner-up became vice president.

ADMISSION OF STATES

Order of Admission	State	Date of Admission	Order of Admission	State	Date of Admission
1	Delaware	December 7, 1787	26	Michigan	January 26, 1837
2	Pennsylvania	December 12, 1787	27	Florida	March 3, 1845
3	New Jersey	December 18, 1787	28	Texas	December 29, 1845
4	Georgia	January 2, 1788	29	Iowa	December 28, 1846
5	Connecticut	January 9, 1788	30	Wisconsin	May 29, 1848
6	Massachusetts	February 7, 1788	31	California	September 9, 1850
7	Maryland	April 28, 1788	32	Minnesota	May 11, 1858
8	South Carolina	May 23, 1788	33	Oregon	February 14, 1859
9	New Hampshire	June 21, 1788	34	Kansas	January 29, 1861
10	Virginia	June 25, 1788	35	West Virginia	June 30, 1863
11	New York	July 26, 1788	36	Nevada	October 31, 1864
12	North Carolina	November 21, 1789	37	Nebraska	March 1, 1867
13	Rhode Island	May 29, 1790	38	Colorado	August 1, 1876
14	Vermont	March 4, 1791	39	North Dakota	November 2, 1889
15	Kentucky	June 1, 1792	40	South Dakota	November 2, 1889
16	Tennessee	June 1, 1796	41	Montana	November 8, 1889
17	Ohio	March 1, 1803	42	Washington	November 11, 1889
18	Louisiana	April 30, 1812	43	Idaho	July 3, 1890
19	Indiana	December 11, 1816	44	Wyoming	July 10, 1890
20	Mississippi	December 10, 1817	45	Utah	January 4, 1896
21	Illinois	December 3, 1818	46	Oklahoma	November 16, 1907
22	Alabama	December 14, 1819	47	New Mexico	January 6, 1912
23	Maine	March 15, 1820	48	Arizona	February 14, 1912
24	Missouri	August 10, 1821	49	Alaska	January 3, 1959
25	Arkansas	June 15, 1836	50	Hawaii	August 21, 1959

POPULATION OF THE UNITED STATES

Year	Number of States	Population	% Increase	Population per Square Mile
1790	13	3,929,214		4.5
1800	16	5,308,483	35.1	6.1
1810	17	7,239,881	36.4	4.3
1820	23	9,638,453	33.1	5.5
1830	24	12,866,020	33.5	7.4
1840	26	17,069,453	32.7	9.8
1850	31	23,191,876	35.9	7.9
1860	33	31,443,321	35.6	10.6
1870	37	39,818,449	26.6	13.4
1880	38	50,155,783	26.0	16.9
1890	44	62,947,714	25.5	21.1
1900	45	75,994,575	20.7	25.6
1910	46	91,972,266	21.0	31.0
1920	48	105,710,620	14.9	35.6
1930	48	122,775,046	16.1	41.2
1940	48	131,669,275	7.2	44.2
1950	48	150,697,361	14.5	50.7
1960	50	179,323,175	19.0	50.6
1970	50	203,235,298	13.3	57.5
1980	50	226,504,825	11.4	64.0
1985	50	237,839,000	5.0	67.2
1990	50	250,122,000	5.2	70.6
1995	50	263,411,707	5.3	74.4
2000	50	281,421,906	6.8	77.0
2005	50	296,410,404	5.3	77.9
2010	50	308,745,538	9.7	87.4
2015	50	321,931,311	4.3	91.1

IMMIGRATION TO THE UNITED STATES, FISCAL YEARS 1820–2015

Year	Number	Year	Number	Year	Number	Year	Number
1820–1989	55,457,531	1871–80	2,812,191	1921–30	4,107,209	1971–80	4,493,314
1820	8,385	1871	321,350	1921	805,228	1971	370,478
1821–30	143,439	1872	404,806	1922	309,556	1972	384,685
1821	9,127	1873	459,803	1923	522,919	1973	400,063
1822	6,911	1874	313,339	1924	706,896	1974	394,861
1823	6,354	1875	227,498	1925	294,314	1975	386,914
1824	7,912	1876	169,986	1926	304,488	1976	398,613
1825	10,199	1877	141,857	1927	335,175	1976	103,676
1826	10,837	1878	138,469	1928	307,255	1977	462,315
1827	18,875	1879	177,826	1929	279,678	1978	601,442
1828	27,382	1880	457,257	1930	241,700	1979	460,348
1829	22,520	1881–90	5,246,613	1931–40	528,431	1980	530,639
1830	23,322	1881	669,431	1931	97,139	1981–90	7,338,062
1831–40	599,125	1882	788,992	1932	35,576	1981	596,600
1831	22,633	1883	603,322	1933	23,068	1982	594,131
1832	60,482	1884	518,592	1934	29,470	1983	559,763
1833	58,640	1885	395,346	1935	34,956	1984	543,903
1834	65,365	1886	334,203	1936	36,329	1985	570,009
1835	45,374	1887	490,109	1937	50,244	1986	601,708
1836	76,242	1888	546,889	1938	67,895	1987	601,516
1837	79,340	1889	444,427	1939	82,998	1988	643,025
1838	38,914	1890	455,302	1940	70,756	1989	1,090,924
1839	68,069	1891–1900	3,687,564	1941–50	1,035,039	1990	1,536,483
1840	84,066	1891	560,319	1941	51,776	1991–2000	9,090,857
1841–50	1,713,251	1892	579,663	1942	28,781	1991	1,827,167
1841	80,289	1893	439,730	1943	23,725	1992	973,977
1842	104,565	1894	285,631	1944	28,551	1993	904,292
		1895	258,536	1945	38,119	1994	804,416
		1896	343,267	1946	108,721		

Year	Number	Year	Number	Year	Number	Year	Number
1843	52,496	1897	230,832	1947	147,292	1995	720,461
1844	78,615	1898	229,299	1948	170,570	1996	915,900
1845	114,371	1899	311,715	1949	188,317	1997	798,378
1846	154,416	1900	448,572	1950	249,187	1998	660,477
1847	234,968					1999	644,787
1848	226,527	**1901–10**	**8,795,386**	**1951–60**	**2,515,479**	2000	841,002
1849	297,024	1901	487,918	1951	205,717		
1850	369,980	1902	648,743	1952	265,520	**2001–10**	**10,503,454**
		1903	857,046	1953	170,434	2001	1,058,902
1851–60	**2,598,214**	1904	812,870	1954	208,177	2002	1,059,356
1851	379,466	1905	1,026,499	1955	237,790	2003	705,827
1852	371,603	1906	1,100,735	1956	321,625	2004	957,883
1853	368,645	1907	1,285,349	1957	326,867	2005	1,122,373
1854	427,833	1908	782,870	1958	253,265	2006	1,266,129
1855	200,877	1909	751,786	1959	260,686	2007	1,052,415
1856	200,436	1910	1,041,570	1960	265,398	2008	1,107,126
1857	251,306					2009	1,130,818
1858	123,126	**1911–20**	**5,735,811**	**1961–70**	**3,321,677**	2010	1,042,625
1859	121,282	1911	878,587	1961	271,344		
1860	153,640	1912	838,172	1962	283,763	**2011–15**	**5,356,671**
		1913	1,197,892	1963	306,260	2011	1,062,040
1861–70	**2,314,824**	1914	1,218,480	1964	292,248	2012	1,031,631
1861	91,918	1915	326,700	1965	296,697	2013	523,000
1862	91,985	1916	298,826	1966	323,040	2014	1,360,000
1863	176,282	1917	295,403	1967	361,972	2015	1,380,000
1864	193,418	1918	110,618	1968	454,448		
1865	248,120	1919	141,132	1969	358,579		
1866	318,568	1920	430,001	1970	373,326		
1867	315,722						
1868	138,840						
1869	352,768						
1870	387,203						

Source: U.S. Department of Homeland Security.

IMMIGRATION BY REGION AND SELECTED COUNTRY OF LAST RESIDENCE, FISCAL YEARS 1820–2015

Region and country of last residence	1820 to 1829	1830 to 1839	1840 to 1849	1850 to 1859	1860 to 1869	1870 to 1879	1880 to 1889	1890 to 1899
Total	128,502	538,381	1,427,337	2,814,554	2,081,261	2,742,137	5,248,568	3,694,294
Europe	99,272	422,771	1,369,259	2,619,680	1,877,726	2,251,878	4,638,677	3,576,411
Austria-Hungary	—	—	—	—	3,375	60,127	314,787	534,059
Austria	—	—	—	—	2,700	54,529	204,805	268,218
Hungary	—	—	—	—	483	5,598	109,982	203,350
Belgium	28	20	3,996	5,765	5,785	6,991	18,738	19,642
Bulgaria	—	—	—	—	—	—	—	52
*Former Czechoslovakia	—	—	—	—	—	—	—	—
Denmark	173	927	671	3,227	13,553	29,278	85,342	56,671
Finland	—	—	—	—	—	—	—	—
France	7,694	39,330	75,300	81,778	35,938	71,901	48,193	35,616
Germany	5,753	124,726	385,434	976,072	723,734	751,769	1,445,181	579,072
Greece	17	49	17	32	51	209	1,807	12,732
Ireland	51,617	170,672	656,145	1,029,486	427,419	422,264	674,061	405,710
Italy	430	2,225	1,476	8,643	9,853	46,296	267,660	603,761
Netherlands	1,105	1,377	7,624	11,122	8,387	14,267	52,715	29,349
Norway-Sweden	91	1,149	12,389	22,202	82,937	178,823	586,441	334,058
Norway	—	—	—	—	16,068	88,644	185,111	96,810
Sweden	—	—	—	—	24,224	90,179	401,330	237,248
Poland	19	366	105	1,087	1,886	11,016	42,910	107,793
Portugal	177	820	196	1,299	2,083	13,971	15,186	25,874
Romania	—	—	—	—	—	—	5,842	6,808
Russia	86	280	520	423	1,670	35,177	182,698	450,101
Spain	2,595	2,010	1,916	8,795	6,966	5,540	3,995	9,189
Switzerland	3,148	4,430	4,819	24,423	21,124	25,212	81,151	37,020
United Kingdom	26,336	74,350	218,572	445,322	532,956	578,447	810,900	328,759
*Former Yugoslavia	—	—	—	—	—	—	—	—
Other Europe	3	40	79	4	9	590	1,070	145

Asia	34	55	121	36,080	54,408	134,128	71,151	61,285
China	3	8	32	35,933	54,028	133,139	65,797	15,268
Hong Kong	—	—	—	—	—	—	—	102
India	9	38	33	42	50	166	247	102
Iran	—	—	—	—	—	—	—	—
*Israel	—	—	—	—	—	—	—	—
Japan	—	—	—	—	138	193	1,583	13,998
Jordan	—	—	—	—	—	—	—	—
*Korea	—	—	—	—	—	—	—	—
Philippines	—	—	—	—	—	—	—	—
Syria	—	—	—	—	—	—	—	—
Taiwan	—	—	—	—	—	—	—	—
Turkey	19	8	45	94	129	382	2,478	27,510
Vietnam	—	—	—	—	—	—	—	—
Other Asia	3	1	11	11	63	248	1,046	4,407
North America	9,655	31,905	50,516	84,145	130,292	345,010	524,826	37,350
Canada and Newfoundland	2,297	11,875	34,285	64,171	117,978	324,310	492,865	3,098
Mexico	3,835	7,187	3,069	3,446	1,957	5,133	2,405	734
Caribbean	3,061	11,792	11,803	12,447	8,751	14,285	27,323	31,480
Cuba	—	—	—	—	—	—	—	—
Dominican Republic	—	—	—	—	—	—	—	—
Haiti	—	—	—	—	—	—	—	—
Jamaica	—	—	—	—	—	—	—	—
Other Caribbean	3,061	11,792	11,803	12,447	8,751	14,285	27,323	31,480
Central America	57	94	297	512	70	173	279	649
Belize	—	—	—	—	—	—	—	—
Costa Rica	—	—	—	—	—	—	—	—
El Salvador	—	—	—	—	—	—	—	—
Guatemala	—	—	—	—	—	—	—	—
Honduras	—	—	—	—	—	—	—	—
Nicaragua	—	—	—	—	—	—	—	—
Panama	—	—	—	—	—	—	—	—
Other Central America	57	94	297	512	70	173	279	649

Region and country of last residence	1820 to 1829	1830 to 1839	1840 to 1849	1850 to 1859	1860 to 1869	1870 to 1879	1880 to 1889	1890 to 1899
South America	405	957	1,062	3,569	1,536	1,109	1,954	1,389
Argentina	—	—	—	—	—	—	—	—
Bolivia	—	—	—	—	—	—	—	—
Brazil	—	—	—	—	—	—	—	—
Chile	—	—	—	—	—	—	—	—
Colombia	—	—	—	—	—	—	—	—
Ecuador	—	—	—	—	—	—	—	—
Guyana	—	—	—	—	—	—	—	—
Paraguay	—	—	—	—	—	—	—	—
Peru	—	—	—	—	—	—	—	—
Suriname	—	—	—	—	—	—	—	—
Uruguay	—	—	—	—	—	—	—	—
Venezuela	—	—	—	—	—	—	—	—
Other South America	405	957	1,062	3,569	1,536	1,109	1,954	1,389
Other America	—	—	—	—	—	—	—	—
Africa	15	50	61	84	407	371	763	432
Egypt	—	—	—	—	4	29	145	51
Ethiopia	—	—	—	—	—	—	—	—
Liberia	1	8	5	7	43	52	21	9
Morocco	—	—	—	—	—	—	—	—
South Africa	—	—	—	—	35	48	23	9
Other Africa	14	42	56	77	325	242	574	363
Oceania	3	7	14	166	187	9,996	12,361	4,704
Australia	2	1	2	15	—	8,930	7,250	3,098
New Zealand	—	—	—	—	—	39	21	12
Other Oceania	1	6	12	151	187	1,027	5,090	1,594
Not Specified	19,523	83,593	7,366	74,399	18,241	754	790	14,112

Region and country of last residence	1900 to 1909	1910 to 1919	1920 to 1929	1930 to 1939	1940 to 1949	1950 to 1959	1960 to 1969	1980 to 1989
Total	8,202,388	6,347,380	4,295,510	699,375	856,608	2,499,268	3,213,749	6,244,379
Europe	7,572,569	4,985,411	2,560,340	444,399	472,524	1,404,973	1,133,443	668,866
Austria-Hungary	2,001,376	1,154,727	60,891	12,531	13,574	113,015	27,590	20,437
Austria	532,416	589,174	31,392	5,307	8,393	81,354	17,571	15,374
Hungary	685,567	565,553	29,499	7,224	5,181	31,661	10,019	5,063
Belgium	37,429	32,574	21,511	4,013	12,473	18,885	9,647	7,028
Bulgaria	34,651	27,180	2,824	1,062	449	97	598	1,124
*Former Czechoslovakia	—	—	101,182	17,757	8,475	1,624	2,758	5,678
Denmark	61,227	45,830	34,406	3,470	4,549	10,918	9,797	4,847
Finland	—	—	16,922	2,438	2,230	4,923	4,310	2,569
France	67,735	60,335	54,842	13,761	36,954	50,113	46,975	32,066
Germany	328,722	174,227	386,634	119,107	119,506	576,905	209,616	85,752
Greece	145,402	198,108	60,774	10,599	8,605	45,153	74,173	37,729
Ireland	344,940	166,445	202,854	28,195	15,701	47,189	37,788	22,210
Italy	1,930,475	1,229,916	528,133	85,053	50,509	184,576	200,111	55,562
Netherlands	42,463	46,065	29,397	7,791	13,877	46,703	37,918	11,234
Norway-Sweden	426,981	192,445	170,329	13,452	17,326	44,224	36,150	13,941
Norway	182,542	79,488	70,327	6,901	8,326	22,806	17,371	3,835
Sweden	244,439	112,957	100,002	6,551	9,000	21,418	18,779	10,106
Poland	—	—	223,316	25,555	7,577	6,465	55,742	63,483
Portugal	65,154	82,489	44,829	3,518	6,765	13,928	70,568	42,685
Romania	57,322	13,566	67,810	5,264	1,254	914	2,339	24,753
Russia	1,501,301	1,106,998	61,604	2,463	605	453	2,329	33,311
Spain	24,818	53,262	47,109	3,669	2,774	6,880	40,793	22,783
Switzerland	32,541	22,839	31,772	5,990	9,904	17,577	19,193	8,316
United Kingdom	469,518	371,878	341,552	61,813	131,794	195,709	220,213	153,644
*Former Yugoslavia	—	—	49,215	6,920	2,039	6,966	17,990	16,267
Other Europe	514	6,527	22,434	9,978	5,584	11,756	6,845	3,447

Region and country of last residence	1900 to 1909	1910 to 1919	1920 to 1929	1930 to 1939	1940 to 1949	1950 to 1959	1960 to 1969	1980 to 1989
Asia	299,836	269,736	126,740	19,231	34,532	135,844	358,605	2,391,356
China	19,884	20,916	30,648	5,874	16,072	8,836	14,060	170,897
Hong Kong	—	—	—	—	—	13,781	67,047	112,132
India	3,026	3,478	2,076	554	1,692	1,850	18,638	231,649
Iran	—	—	208	198	1,144	3,195	9,059	98,141
*Israel	—	—	—	—	98	21,376	30,911	43,669
Japan	139,712	77,125	42,057	2,683	1,557	40,651	40,956	44,150
Jordan	—	—	—	—	—	4,899	9,230	28,928
*Korea	—	—	—	—	83	4,845	27,048	322,708
Philippines	—	—	—	391	4,099	17,245	70,660	502,056
Syria	—	—	5,307	2,188	1,179	1,091	2,432	14,534
Taiwan	—	—	—	—	—	721	15,657	119,051
Turkey	127,999	160,717	40,450	1,327	754	2,980	9,464	19,208
Vietnam	—	—	—	—	—	290	2,949	200,632
Other Asia	9,215	7,500	5,994	6,016	7,854	14,084	40,494	483,601
North America	277,809	1,070,539	1,591,278	230,319	328,435	921,610	1,674,172	2,695,329
Canada and Newfoundland	123,067	708,715	949,286	162,703	160,911	353,169	433,128	156,313
Mexico	31,188	185,334	498,945	32,709	56,158	273,847	441,824	1,009,586
Caribbean	100,960	120,860	83,482	18,052	46,194	115,661	427,235	790,109
Cuba	—	—	12,769	10,641	25,976	73,221	202,030	132,552
Dominican Republic	—	—	—	1,026	4,802	10,219	83,552	221,552
Haiti	—	—	—	156	823	3,787	28,992	121,406
Jamaica	—	—	—	—	—	7,397	62,218	193,874
Other Caribbean	100,960	120,860	70,713	6,229	14,593	21,037	50,443	120,725
Central America	7,341	15,692	16,511	6,840	20,135	40,201	98,560	339,376
Belize	77	40	285	193	433	1,133	4,185	14,964
Costa Rica	—	—	—	431	1,965	4,044	17,975	25,017
El Salvador	—	—	—	597	4,885	5,094	14,405	137,418
Guatemala	—	—	—	423	1,303	4,197	14,357	58,847
Honduras	—	—	—	679	1,874	5,320	15,078	39,071

Nicaragua	31,102	10,383	7,812	4,393	405	—	—	—
Panama	32,957	22,177	12,601	5,282	1,452	—	—	—
Other Central America	—	—	—	—	2,660	16,226	15,652	7,264
South America	399,862	250,754	78,418	19,662	9,990	43,025	39,938	15,253
Argentina	23,442	49,384	16,346	3,108	1,067	—	—	—
Bolivia	9,798	6,205	2,759	893	50	—	—	—
Brazil	22,944	29,238	11,547	3,653	1,468	4,627	—	—
Chile	19,749	12,384	4,669	1,320	347	—	—	—
Colombia	105,494	68,371	15,567	3,454	1,027	—	—	—
Ecuador	48,015	34,107	8,574	2,207	244	—	—	—
Guyana	85,886	4,546	1,131	596	131	—	—	—
Paraguay	3,518	1,249	576	85	33	—	—	—
Peru	49,958	19,783	5,980	1,273	321	—	—	—
Suriname	1,357	612	299	130	25	—	—	—
Uruguay	7,235	4,089	1,026	754	112	—	—	—
Venezuela	22,405	20,758	9,927	2,182	1,155	—	—	—
Other South America	61	28	17	7	4,010	38,398	39,938	15,253
Other America	83	22,671	60,314	25,375	25	29	—	—
Africa	141,990	23,780	13,016	6,720	2,120	6,362	8,867	6,326
Egypt	26,744	5,581	1,996	1,613	781	1,063	—	—
Ethiopia	12,927	804	302	28	10	—	—	—
Liberia	6,420	841	289	37	35	—	—	—
Morocco	3,471	2,880	2,703	879	73	—	—	—
South Africa	15,505	4,360	2,278	1,022	312	—	—	—
Other Africa	76,923	9,314	5,448	3,141	909	5,299	8,867	6,326
Oceania	41,432	23,630	11,353	14,262	3,306	9,860	12,339	12,355
Australia	16,901	14,986	8,275	11,201	2,260	8,404	11,280	11,191
New Zealand	6,129	3,775	1,799	2,351	790	935	—	—
Other Oceania	18,402	4,869	1,279	710	256	521	1,059	1,164
Not Specified	305,406	119	12,472	135	—	930	488	33,493

Region and country of last residence	1990 to 1999	2000 to 2009	2010	2011	2012	2013	2014	2015
Total	9,775,398	10,299,430	1,042,625	1,062,040	1,031,631	779,929	653,416	730,259
Europe	1,348,612	1,349,609	95,429	90,712	86,956	80,333	71,325	78,074
Austria-Hungary	27,529	33,929	4,325	4,703	3,208	1232	1,114	1148
Austria	18,234	21,151	3,319	3,654	2,199	248	223	207
Hungary	9,295	12,778	1,006	1,049	1,009	984	891	941
Belgium	7,077	8,157	732	700	698	513	408	505
Bulgaria	16,948	40,003	2,465	2,549	2,322	2,646	2,226	2,336
*Former Czechoslovakia	8,970	18,691	1,510	1,374	1,316	232	303	371
Denmark	6,189	6,049	545	473	492	127	129	243
Finland	3,970	3,970	414	398	373	300	274	301
France	35,945	45,637	4,339	3,967	4,201	2,534	2,589	2,784
Germany	92,207	122,373	7,929	7,072	6,732	4,066	4,375	4,380
Greece	25,403	16,841	966	1,196	1,264	938	780	867
Ireland	65,384	15,642	1,610	1,533	1,694	1,295	1,413	1,375
Italy	75,992	28,329	2,956	2,670	2,946	2,355	2,313	2,760
Netherlands	13,345	17,351	1,520	1,258	1,294	786	665	778
Norway-Sweden	17,825	19,382	1,662	1,530	1,441	863	816	965
Norway	5,211	4,599	363	405	314	80	92	80
Sweden	12,614	14,783	1,299	1,125	1,127	783	724	885
Poland	172,249	117,921	7,391	6,634	6,024	8,697	8,304	7,886
Portugal	25,497	11,479	759	878	837	1,585	1,587	1,690
Romania	48,136	52,154	3,735	3,679	3,477	4,050	3,267	3,478
Russia	433,427	167,152	7,502	8,548	10,114	8,222	6,824	6,552
Spain	18,443	17,695	2,040	2,319	2,316	1,367	1,326	1,414
Switzerland	11,768	12,173	868	861	916	452	388	411
United Kingdom	156,182	171,979	14,781	13,443	13,938	9,459	8,906	10,095
*Former Yugoslavia	57,039	131,831	4,772	4,611	4,488	4,445	—	—
Other Europe	29,087	290,871	22,608	20,316	16,865	17,839	—	—

Asia	2,859,899	3,470,835	410,209	438,580	416,488	275,700	233,163	261,374
China	342,058	591,711	67,634	83,603	78,184	35,387	30,284	31,241
Hong Kong	116,894	57,583	3,263	3,149	2,642	2,093	1,801	1,716
India	352,528	590,464	66,185	66,331	63,320	49,897	37,854	42,213
Iran	76,899	76,755	9,078	9,015	8,955	11,623	9,620	10,344
*Israel	41,340	54,081	5,172	4,389	4,640	3,466	3,015	3,182
Japan	66,582	84,552	7,100	6,751	6,581	1,837	1,635	1,858
Jordan	42,755	53,550	9,327	8,211	7,014	2,816	2,427	2,461
*Korea	179,770	209,758	22,022	22,748	—	—	—	—
Philippines	534,338	545,463	56,399	55,251	55,441	43,489	34,591	40,815
Syria	22,906	30,807	7,424	7,983	6,674	2,196	1,832	2,004
Taiwan	132,647	92,657	6,785	6,206	5,295	5,255	4,326	4,420
Turkey	38,687	48,394	7,435	9,040	7,362	3,990	2,925	3,150
Vietnam	275,379	289,616	30,065	33,486	27,578	24,277	18,837	21,976
Other Asia	637,116	745,444	112,320	122,417	122,000	107,232	—	—
North America	5,137,743	4,441,529	426,981	423,277	409,664	271,807	222,547	247,492
Canada and Newfoundland	194,788	236,349	19,491	19,506	—	—	—	—
Mexico	2,757,418	1,704,166	138,717	142,823	145,326	99,385	94,889	105,958
Caribbean	1,004,687	1,053,357	139,389	133,012	126,615	121,349	—	—
Cuba	159,037	271,742	33,372	36,261	32,551	30,482	24,092	25,770
Dominican Republic	359,818	291,492	53,890	46,036	41,535	39,590	23,775	26,665
Haiti	177,446	203,827	22,336	21,802	22,446	23,480	13,676	14,053
Jamaica	177,143	172,523	19,439	19,298	20,300	16,442	13,547	16,566
Other Caribbean	181,243	113,773	10,352	9,615	9,783	9,384	—	—
Central America	610,189	591,130	43,597	43,249	39,837	44,056	—	—
Belize	12,600	9,682	997	933	875	966	773	851
Costa Rica	17,054	21,571	2,306	2,230	2,152	1,661	1,461	1,633
El Salvador	273,017	251,237	18,547	18,477	15,874	18,401	15,598	16,930
Guatemala	126,043	156,992	10,263	10,795	9,857	9,530	8,549	9,344
Honduras	72,880	63,513	6,381	6,053	6,773	5,462	4,433	5,039
Nicaragua	80,446	70,015	3,476	3,314	2,943	5,064	3,775	3,951
Panama	28,149	18,120	1,627	1,447	1,363	1,598	1,277	1,412
Other Central America	—			—	—		—	—

Region and country of last residence	1990 to 1999	2000 to 2009	2010	2011	2012	2013	2014	2015
South America	570,624	856,508	85,783	84,687	77,748	76,167	60,665	67,927
Argentina	30,065	47,955	4,312	4,335	4,218	4,177	3,683	3,886
Bolivia	18,111	21,921	2,211	2,113	1,920	1,961	1,527	1,689
Brazil	50,744	115,404	12,057	11,643	11,248	9,565	8,625	10,516
Chile	18,200	19,792	1,940	1,854	1,628	1,649	1,435	1,486
Colombia	137,985	236,570	21,861	22,130	20,272	22,196	16,478	17,207
Ecuador	81,358	107,977	11,463	11,068	9,284	9,470	6,952	7,664
Guyana	74,407	70,373	6,441	6,288	5,282	6,295	4,327	5,162
Paraguay	6,082	4,623	449	501	454	331	256	338
Peru	110,117	137,614	14,063	13,836	12,414	11,782	9,572	10,701
Suriname	2,285	2,363	202	167	216	160	127	183
Uruguay	6,062	9,827	1,286	1,521	1,348	933	812	902
Venezuela	35,180	82,087	9,497	9,229	9,464	7,648	6,871	8,192
Other South America	28	2	1	2	—	1	—	—
Other America	37	19	4	—	—	1	—	—
Africa	346,416	759,734	98,246	97,429	103,685	71,872	62,175	71,492
Egypt	44,604	81,564	9,822	9,096	10,172	6,213	5,094	5,693
Ethiopia	40,097	87,207	13,853	13,985	15,400	8,323	7,002	8,312
Liberia	13,587	23,316	2,924	3,117	3,451	3,923	3,035	3,042
Morocco	15,768	40,844	4,847	4,249	3,534	3,768	3,538	3,805
South Africa	21,964	32,221	2,705	2,754	2,960	2,283	2,083	2,538
Other Africa	210,396	494,582	64,095	64,228	68,168	61,455	—	—
Oceania	56,800	65,793	5,946	5,825	5,573	3,849	3,399,	3,811
Australia	24,288	32,728	3,077	3,062	3,146	1,296	1,159	1,379
New Zealand	8,600	12,495	1,046	1,006	980	482	453	514
Other Oceania	23,912	20,570	1,823	1,757	1,447	1,505	—	—
Not Specified	25,928	211,930	5,814	6,217	9,265	10,127	—	—

— Represents zero or not available.

*Note that a) Korea split into North Korea and South Korea in 1945; b) Czechoslovakia separated into the Czech Republic and the Slovak Republic in 1993; c) Former Yugoslavia, beginning in the 1990s, broke into the six nations of Serbia, Montenegro, Slovenia, Croatia, Macedonia, and Kosovo; d) and due to the way United States immigration statistics are recognized and collected, immigrants from the Occupied Palestinian Territories are grouped together with immigrants from Israel.

PRESIDENTS, VICE PRESIDENTS, AND SECRETARIES OF STATE

	President	Vice President	Secretary of State
1.	George Washington, Federalist 1789	John Adams, Federalist 1789	Thomas Jefferson 1789 Edmund Randolph 1794 Timothy Pickering 1795
2.	John Adams, Federalist 1797	Thomas Jefferson, Dem.-Rep. 1797	Timothy Pickering 1797 John Marshall 1800
3.	Thomas Jefferson, Dem.-Rep. 1801	Aaron Burr, Dem.-Rep. 1801 George Clinton, Dem.-Rep. 1805	James Madison 1801
4.	James Madison, Dem.-Rep. 1809	George Clinton, Dem.-Rep. 1809 Elbridge Gerry, Dem.-Rep. 1813	Robert Smith 1809 James Monroe 1811
5.	James Monroe, Dem.-Rep. 1817	Daniel D. Tompkins, Dem.-Rep. 1817	John Q. Adams 1817
6.	John Quincy Adams, Dem.-Rep. 1825	John C. Calhoun, Dem.-Rep. 1825	Henry Clay 1825
7.	Andrew Jackson, Democratic 1829	John C. Calhoun, Democratic 1829 Martin Van Buren, Democratic 1833	Martin Van Buren 1829 Edward Livingston 1831 Louis McLane 1833 John Forsyth 1834
8.	Martin Van Buren, Democratic 1837	Richard M. Johnson, Democratic 1837	John Forsyth 1837
9.	William H. Harrison, Whig 1841	John Tyler, Whig 1841	Daniel Webster 1841

President	Vice President	Secretary of State
10. John Tyler, Whig and Democratic 1841	None	Daniel Webster 1841 Hugh S. Legaré 1843 Abel P. Upshur 1843 John C. Calhoun 1844
11. James K. Polk, Democratic 1845	George M. Dallas, Democratic 1845	James Buchanan 1845
12. Zachary Taylor, Whig 1849	Millard Fillmore, Whig 1848	John M. Clayton 1849
13. Millard Fillmore, Whig 1850	None	Daniel Webster 1850 Edward Everett 1852
14. Franklin Pierce, Democratic 1853	William R. King, Democratic 1853	William L. Marcy 1853
15. James Buchanan, Democratic 1857	John C. Breckinridge, Democratic 1857	Lewis Cass 1857 Jeremiah S. Black 1860
16. Abraham Lincoln, Republican 1861	Hannibal Hamlin, Republican 1861 Andrew Johnson, Unionist 1865	William H. Seward 1861
17. Andrew Johnson, Unionist 1865	None	William H. Seward 1865
18. Ulysses S. Grant, Republican 1869	Schuyler Colfax, Republican 1869 Henry Wilson, Republican 1873	Elihu B. Washburne 1869 Hamilton Fish 1869
19. Rutherford B. Hayes, Republican 1877	William A. Wheeler, Republican 1877	William M. Evarts 1877

	President	*Vice President*	*Secretary of State*
20.	James A. Garfield, Republican 1881	Chester A. Arthur, Republican 1881	James G. Blaine 1881
21.	Chester A. Arthur, Republican 1881	None	Frederick T. Frelinghuysen 1881
22.	Grover Cleveland, Democratic 1885	Thomas A. Hendricks, Democratic 1885	Thomas F. Bayard 1885
23.	Benjamin Harrison, Republican 1889	Levi P. Morton, Republican 1889	James G. Blaine 1889 John W. Foster 1892
24.	Grover Cleveland, Democratic 1893	Adlai E. Stevenson, Democratic 1893	Walter Q. Gresham 1893 Richard Olney 1895
25.	William McKinley, Republican 1897	Garret A. Hobart, Republican 1897 Theodore Roosevelt, Republican 1901	John Sherman 1897 William R. Day 1898 John Hay 1898
26.	Theodore Roosevelt, Republican 1901	Charles Fairbanks, Republican 1905	John Hay 1901 Elihu Root 1905 Robert Bacon 1909
27.	William H. Taft, Republican 1909	James S. Sherman, Republican 1909	Philander C. Knox 1909
28.	Woodrow Wilson, Democratic 1913	Thomas R. Marshall, Democratic 1913	William J. Bryan 1913 Robert Lansing 1915 Bainbridge Colby 1920
29.	Warren G. Harding, Republican 1921	Calvin Coolidge, Republican 1921	Charles E. Hughes 1921
30.	Calvin Coolidge, Republican 1923	Charles G. Dawes, Republican 1925	Charles E. Hughes 1923 Frank B. Kellogg 1925

	President	Vice President	Secretary of State
31.	Herbert Hoover, Republican 1929	Charles Curtis, Republican 1929	Henry L. Stimson 1929
32.	Franklin D. Roosevelt, Democratic 1933	John Nance Garner, Democratic 1933 Henry A. Wallace, Democratic 1941 Harry S. Truman, Democratic 1945	Cordell Hull 1933 Edward R. Stettinius, Jr. 1944
33.	Harry S. Truman, Democratic 1945	Alben W. Barkley, Democratic 1949	Edward R. Stettinius, Jr. 1945 James F. Byrnes 1945 George C. Marshall 1947 Dean G. Acheson 1949
34.	Dwight D. Eisenhower, Republican 1953	Richard M. Nixon, Republican 1953	John F. Dulles 1953 Christian A. Herter 1959
35.	John F. Kennedy, Democratic 1961	Lyndon B. Johnson, Democratic 1961	Dean Rusk 1961
36.	Lyndon B. Johnson, Democratic 1963	Hubert H. Humphrey, Democratic 1965	Dean Rusk 1963
37.	Richard M. Nixon, Republican 1969	Spiro T. Agnew, Republican 1969 Gerald R. Ford, Republican 1973	William P. Rogers 1969 Henry Kissinger 1973
38.	Gerald R. Ford, Republican 1974	Nelson Rockefeller, Republican 1974	Henry Kissinger 1974
39.	Jimmy Carter, Democratic 1977	Walter Mondale, Democratic 1977	Cyrus Vance 1977 Edmund Muskie 1980

	President	*Vice President*	*Secretary of State*
40.	Ronald Reagan, Republican 1981	George H. W. Bush, Republican 1981	Alexander Haig 1981 George Schultz 1982
41.	George H. W. Bush, Republican 1989	J. Danforth Quayle, Republican 1989	James A. Baker 1989 Lawrence Eagleburger 1992
42.	William J. Clinton, Democratic 1993	Albert Gore, Jr., Democratic 1993	Warren Christopher 1993 Madeleine Albright 1997
43.	George W. Bush, Republican 2001	Richard B. Cheney, Republican 2001	Colin L. Powell 2001 Condoleezza Rice 2005
44.	Barack Obama, Democratic 2009	Joseph R. Biden, Democratic 2009	Hillary Rodham Clinton 2009 John Kerry 2013
45.	Donald J. Trump, Republican 2017	Michael R. Pence, Republican 2017	Rex W. Tillerson 2017

Further Readings

Chapter 15

The most comprehensive treatment of Reconstruction is Eric Foner's *Reconstruction: America's Unfinished Revolution, 1863–1877* (1988). On Andrew Johnson, see Hans L. Trefousse's *Andrew Johnson: A Biography* (1989) and David D. Stewart's *Impeached: The Trial of Andrew Johnson and the Fight for Lincoln's Legacy* (2009). An excellent brief biography of Grant is Josiah Bunting III's *Ulysses S. Grant* (2004). For accounts of everyday life, see Daniel E. Sutherland, *The Expansion of Everyday Life, 1860–1876* (1989).

Scholars have been sympathetic to the aims and motives of the Radical Republicans. See, for instance, Herman Belz's *Reconstructing the Union: Theory and Policy during the Civil War* (1969) and Richard Nelson Current's *Those Terrible Carpetbaggers: A Reinterpretation* (1988). The ideology of the Radicals is explored in Michael Les Benedict's *A Compromise of Principle: Congressional Republicans and Reconstruction, 1863–1869* (1974). On the black political leaders, see Phillip Dray's *Capitol Men: The Epic Story of Reconstruction through the Lives of the First Black Congressmen* (2008).

The intransigence of southern white attitudes is examined in Michael Perman's *Reunion without Compromise: The South and Reconstruction, 1865–1868* (1973) and Dan T. Carter's *When the War Was Over: The Failure of Self-Reconstruction in the South, 1865–1867* (1985). Allen W. Trelease's *White Terror: The Ku Klux Klan Conspiracy and Southern Reconstruction* (1971) covers the various organizations that practiced vigilante tactics. On the massacre of African Americans, see Charles Lane's *The Day Freedom Died: The Colfax Massacre, the Supreme Court, and the Betrayal of Reconstruction* (2008).

The difficulties former slaves had in adjusting to the new labor system are documented in James L. Roark's *Masters without Slaves: Southern Planters in the Civil War and Reconstruction* (1977). Books on southern politics during Reconstruction include Michael Perman's *The Road to Redemption: Southern Politics, 1869–1879* (1984), Terry L. Seip's *The South Returns to Congress: Men, Economic Measures, and Intersectional Relationships, 1868–1879* (1983), and Mark W. Summers's *Railroads, Reconstruction, and the Gospel of Prosperity: Aid under the Radical Republicans, 1865–1877* (1984).

Numerous works study the freed blacks' experience in the South. Start with Leon F. Litwack's *Been in the Storm So Long: The Aftermath of Slavery* (1979). The Freedmen's Bureau is explored in William S. McFeely's *Yankee Stepfather: General O. O. Howard and the Freedmen* (1968). The situation of freed slave women is discussed in Jacqueline Jones's *Labor of Love, Labor of Sorrow: Black Women, Work and the Family, from Slavery to the Present* (1985).

The politics of corruption outside the South is depicted in William S. McFeely's *Grant: A Biography* (1981). The political maneuvers of the election of 1876 and the resultant crisis and compromise are explained in Michael Holt's *By One Vote: The Disputed Presidential Election of 1876* (2008).

Chapter 16

For masterly syntheses of post–Civil War industrial development, see Walter Licht's *Industrializing America: The Nineteenth Century* (1995) and Maury Klein's *The Genesis of Industrial America, 1870–1920* (2007). On the growth of railroads, see Richard

White's *Railroaded: The Transcontinentals and the Making of Modern America* (2011) and Albro Martin's *Railroad Triumphant: The Growth, Rejection, and Rebirth of a Vital American Force* (1992).

On entrepreneurship in the iron and steel sector, and Thomas J. Misa's *A Nation of Steel: The Making of Modern America, 1865–1925* (1995). The best biographies of the leading business tycoons are Ron Chernow's *Titan: The Life of John D. Rockefeller, Sr.* (1998), David Nasaw's *Andrew Carnegie* (2006), and Jean Strouse's *Morgan: American Financier* (1999). Nathan Rosenberg's *Technology and American Economic Growth* (1972) documents the growth of invention during the period.

For an overview of the struggle of workers to organize unions, see Philip Bray's *There Is Power in a Union: The Epic Story of Labor in America* (2010). On the 1877 railroad strike, see David O. Stowell's *Streets, Railroad, and the Great Strike of 1877* (1999). For the role of women in the changing workplace, see Alice Kessler-Harris's *Out to Work: A History of Wage-Earning Women in the United States* (1982) and Susan E. Kennedy's *If All We Did Was to Weep at Home: A History of White Working-Class Women in American* (1979). On Mother Jones, see Elliott J. Gorn's *Mother Jones: The Most Dangerous Woman in America* (2001). To trace the rise of socialism among organized workers, see Nick Salvatore's *Eugene V. Debs: Citizen and Socialist* (1982). The key strikes are discussed in Paul Arvich's *The Haymarket Tragedy* (1984) and Paul Krause's *The Battle for Homestead, 1880–1892: Politics, Culture, and Steel* (1992).

Chapter 17

The classic study of the emergence of the New South remains C. Vann Woodward's *Origins of the New South, 1877–1913* (1951). A more recent treatment of southern society after the end of Reconstruction is Edward L. Ayers's *Southern Crossing: A History of the American South, 1877–1906* (1995). A thorough survey of industrialization in the South is James C. Cobb's *Industrialization and Southern Society, 1877–1984* (1984).

On race relations, see Howard N. Rabinowitz's *Race Relations in the Urban South, 1865–1890* (1978). Leon F. Litwack's *Trouble in Mind: Black Southerners in the Age of Jim Crow* (1998) treats the rise of legal segregation, while Michael Perman's *Struggle for Mastery: Disfranchisement in the South, 1888–1908* (2001) surveys efforts to keep African Americans from voting. An award-winning study of white women and the race issue is Glenda Elizabeth Gilmore's *Gender and Jim Crow: Women and the Politics of White Supremacy in North Carolina, 1896–1920* (1996). On W. E. B. Du Bois, see David Levering Lewis's *W. E. B. Du Bois: Biography of a Race, 1868–1919* (1993). On Booker T. Washington, see Robert J. Norrell's *Up from History: The Life of Booker T. Washington* (2009).

For stimulating reinterpretations of the frontier and the development of the West, see William Cronon's *Nature's Metropolis: Chicago and the Great West* (1991), Patricia Nelson Limerick's *The Legacy of Conquest: The Unbroken Past of the American West* (1987), Richard White's *"It's Your Misfortune and None of My Own": A New History of the American West* (1991), and Walter Nugent's *Into the West: The Story of Its People* (1999). An excellent overview is James M. McPherson's *Into the West: From Reconstruction to the Final Days of the American Frontier* (2006). For insights into everyday life in the West, see Candy Moulton, *The Writer's Guide to Every Day Life in the Wild West* (1999).

The role of African Americans in western settlement is the focus of William Loren Katz's *The Black West: A Documentary and Pictorial History of the African American*

Role in the Westward Expansion of the United States, rev. ed. (2005), and Nell Irvin Painter's *Exodusters: Black Migration to Kansas after Reconstruction* (1977).

The best account of the conflicts between Indians and whites is Robert M. Utley's *The Indian Frontier of the American West, 1846–1890* (1984). For the Sand Creek massacre, see Ari Kellman's *A Misplaced Massacre: Struggling over the Memory of Sand Creek* (2013). On the Battle of the Little Bighorn, see Nathaniel Philbrick's *The Last Stand: Custer, Sitting Bull, and the Battle of the Little Bighorn* (2010). On Crazy Horse, see Thomas Powers's *The Killing of Crazy Horse* (2010).

For a presentation of the Native American side of the story, see Peter Nabokov's *Native American Testimony: A Chronicle of Indian-White Relations from Prophecy to the Present, 1492–2000,* rev. ed. (1999). On the demise of the buffalo herds, see Andrew C. Isenberg's *The Destruction of the Bison: An Environmental History, 1750–1920* (2000).

Chapter 18

For a survey of urbanization, see David R. Goldfield's *Urban America: A History* (1989). Gunther Barth discusses the emergence of a new urban culture in *City People: The Rise of Modern City Culture in Nineteenth-Century America* (1980). John Bodnar offers a synthesis of the urban immigrant experience in *The Transplanted: A History of Immigrants in Urban America* (1985). See also Roger Daniels's *Guarding the Golden Door: American Immigration Policy and Immigrants since 1882* (2004). Walter Nugent's *Crossings: The Great Transatlantic Migrations, 1870–1914* (1992) provides a wealth of demographic information and insight. Efforts to stop Chinese immigration are described in Erika Lee's *At America's Gates: Chinese Immigration during the Exclusion Era* (2003).

On urban environments and sanitary reforms, see Martin V. Melosi's *The Sanitary City: Urban Infrastructure in America from Colonial Times to the Present* (2000), Joel A. Tarr's *The Search for the Ultimate Sink: Urban Pollution in Historical Perspective* (1996), and Suellen Hoy's *Chasing Dirt: The American Pursuit of Cleanliness* (1995).

For the growth of urban leisure and sports, see Roy Rosenzweig's *Eight Hours for What We Will: Workers and Leisure in an Industrial City, 1870–1920* (1983) and Steven A. Riess's *City Games: The Evolution of American Urban Society and the Rise of Sports* (1989). Saloon culture is examined in Madelon Powers's *Faces along the Bar: Lore and Order in the Workingman's Saloon, 1870–1920* (1998). On everyday life, see Thomas J. Schlereth, *Transformations in Everyday Life, 1876–1915* (1991).

On the impact of Darwin's theory of evolution, see Barry Werth's *Banquet at Delmonico's: Great Minds, the Gilded Age, and the Triumph of Evolution in America* (2009). On the rise of realism in thought and the arts during the second half of the nineteenth century, see David E. Shi's *Facing Facts: Realism in American Thought and Culture, 1850–1920* (1995). The rise of pragmatism is the focus of Louis Menand's *The Metaphysical Club: A Story of Ideas in America* (2001).

Two good overviews of the Gilded Age are Sean Cashman's *America in the Gilded Age: From the Death of Lincoln to the Rise of Theodore Roosevelt* (1984) and Mark Summers's *The Gilded Age or, The Hazard of New Functions* (1996). Nell Irvin Painter's *Standing at Armageddon: The United States, 1877–1919* (1987) focuses on the experience of the working class.

For a stimulating overview of the political, social, and economic trends during the Gilded Age, see Jack Beatty's *Age of Betrayal: The Triumph of Money in America, 1865–1900* (2007). On the development of city rings and bosses, see Kenneth D. Ackerman's *Boss Tweed: The Rise and Fall of the Corrupt Pol Who Conceived the Soul of Modern New York* (2005). Excellent presidential biographies include Hans L. Trefousse's *Rutherford B. Hayes* (2002), Zachary Karabell's *Chester Alan Arthur* (2004), Henry F. Graff's *Grover Cleveland* (2002), and Kevin Phillips's *William McKinley* (2003). On the political culture of the Gilded Age, see Charles Calhoun's *Minority Victory: Gilded Age Politics and the Front Porch Campaign of 1888* (2008).

A balanced account of Populism is Charles Postel's *The Populist Vision* (2007). The election of 1896 is the focus of R. Hal Williams's *Realigning America: McKinley, Bryan, and the Remarkable Election of 1896* (2010). On the role of religion in the agrarian protest movements, see Joe Creech's *Righteous Indignation: Religion and the Populist Revolution* (2006). The best biography of Bryan is Michael Kazin's *A Godly Hero: The Life of William Jennings Bryan* (2006).

Chapter 19

An excellent survey of the diplomacy of the era is Charles S. Campbell's *The Transformation of American Foreign Relations, 1865–1900* (1976). For background on the events of the 1890s, see David Healy's *U.S. Expansionism: The Imperialist Urge in the 1890s* (1970). The dispute over American policy in Hawaii is covered in Thomas J. Osborne's *"Empire Can Wait": American Opposition to Hawaiian Annexation, 1893–1898* (1981).

Ivan Musicant's *Empire by Default: The Spanish-American War and the Dawn of the American Century* (1998) is the most comprehensive volume on the conflict. A colorful treatment of the powerful men promoting war is Evan Thomas's *The War Lovers: Roosevelt, Lodge, Mahan, and the Rush to Empire, 1898* (2010). For the war's aftermath in the Philippines, see Stuart Creighton Miller's *"Benevolent Assimilation": The American Conquest of the Philippines, 1899–1903* (1982). On the Philippine-American War, see David J. Silbey's *A War of Frontier and Empire: The Philippine-American War, 1899–1902* (2007).

A good introduction to American interest in China is Michael H. Hunt's *The Making of a Special Relationship: The United States and China to 1914* (1983). John Taliaferro's *All the Great Prizes: The Life of John Hay* (2013) examines the role of this key secretary of state in forming policy.

For U.S. policy in the Caribbean and Central America, see Walter LaFeber's *Inevitable Revolutions: The United States in Central America,* 2nd ed. (1993). David McCullough's *The Path between the Seas: The Creation of the Panama Canal, 1870–1914* (1977) presents an admiring account of how the United States secured the Panama Canal. A more sober assessment is Julie Greene's *The Canal Builders: Making America's Empire at the Panama Canal* (2009). For a detailed treatment of TR's diplomacy as president, see James Bradley's *The Imperial Cruise: A Secret History of Empire and War* (2009).

Chapter 20

Splendid analyses of progressivism can be found in John Whiteclay Chambers II's *The Tyranny of Change: America in the Progressive Era, 1890–1920,* rev. ed. (2000), Steven J. Diner's *A Very Different Age: Americans of the Progressive Era* (1997), Maureen A. Flanagan's *America Reformed: Progressives and Progressivisms, 1890–1920* (2006), Michael McGerr's *A Fierce Discontent: The Rise and Fall of the Progressive Movement in America* (2003) and David Traxel's *Crusader Nation: The United States in Peace and the Great War, 1898–1920* (2006). On Ida Tarbell and the muckrakers, see Steve Weinberg's *Taking on the Trust: The Epic Battle of Ida Tarbell and John D. Rockefeller* (2008).

The evolution of government policy toward business is examined in Martin J. Sklar's *The Corporate Reconstruction of American Capitalism, 1890–1916: The Market, the Law, and Politics* (1988). Mina Carson's *Settlement Folk: Social Thought and the American Settlement Movement, 1885–1930* (1990) examines the social problems in the cities. Robert Kanigel's *The One Best Way: Frederick Winslow Taylor and the Enigma of Efficiency* (1997) highlights the role of efficiency and expertise in the Progressive Era.

An excellent study of the role of women in progressivism's emphasis on social justice is Kathryn Kish Sklar's *Florence Kelley and the Nation's Work: The Rise of Women's Political Culture, 1830–1900* (1995). On the tragic fire at the Triangle Shirtwaist Company, see David Von Drehle's *Triangle: The Fire That Changed America* (2003). The best study of the settlement house movement is Jean Bethke Elshtain's *Jane Addams and the Dream of American Democracy: A Life* (2002). On everyday life, see Harvey Green, *The Uncertainty of Everyday Life, 1915–1945* (2000).

On Theodore Roosevelt and the conservation movement, see Douglas Brinkley's *The Wilderness Warrior: Theodore Roosevelt and the Crusade for America* (2009) The pivotal election of 1912 is covered in James Chace's *1912: Wilson, Roosevelt, Taft, and Debs—The Election That Changed the Country* (2004) and Sidney M. Milkis's *TR, the Progressive Party, and the Transformation of Democracy* (2009). Excellent biographies include Kathleen Dalton's *Theodore Roosevelt: A Strenuous Life* (2002) and A. Scott Berg's *Wilson* (2013). The racial blind spot of Progressivism is assessed in David W. Southern's *The Progressive Era and Race: Reform and Reaction, 1900–1917* (2006).

Chapter 21

A lucid overview of international events in the early twentieth century is Robert H. Ferrell's *Woodrow Wilson and World War I, 1917–1921* (1985). For a vivid account of U.S. intervention in Mexico, see Frederick Katz's *The Life and Times of Pancho Villa* (1999). On Wilson's stance toward war, see Robert W. Tucker's *Woodrow Wilson and the Great War: Reconsidering America's Neutrality, 1914–1917* (2007). An excellent biography is John Milton Cooper, Jr.'s *Woodrow Wilson: A Biography* (2010).

For the European experience in the First World War, see Adam Hochschild's *To End All Wars: A Story of Loyalty and Rebellion, 1914–1918* (2011) and Margaret MacMillan's *The War That Ended Peace* (2013). Edward M. Coffman's *The War to End All Wars: The American Military Experience in World War I* (1968) is a detailed presentation of America's military involvement. See also Gary Mead's *The Doughboys: America and the First World War* (2000).

For a survey of the impact of the war on the home front, see Meirion Harries and Susie Harries's *The Last Days of Innocence: America at War, 1917–1918* (1997). Maurine Weiner Greenwald's *Women, War, and Work: The Impact of World War I on Women Workers in the United States* (1980) discusses the role of women in the war effort while Sara Hunter Graham's *Woman Suffrage and the New Democracy* (1996) traces the movement during the war to give women the vote. Ronald Schaffer's *America in the Great War: The Rise of the War Welfare State* (1991) shows the effect of war mobilization on business organization. Richard Polenberg's *Fighting Faiths: The Abrams Case, the Supreme Court, and Free Speech* (1987) examines the prosecution of a case under the 1918 Sedition Act. See also Ernest Freeberg's *Democracy's Prisoner: Eugene V. Debs, the Great War, and the Right to Dissent* (2009).

How American diplomacy fared in the making of peace has received considerable attention. Thomas J. Knock connects domestic affairs and foreign relations in his explanation of Wilson's peacemaking in *To End All Wars: Woodrow Wilson and the Quest for a New World Order* (1992). See also John Milton Cooper, Jr.'s *Breaking the Heart of the World: Woodrow Wilson and the Fight for the League of Nations* (2002).

The problems of the immediate postwar years are chronicled by a number of historians. The best overview is Ann Hagedorn's *Savage Peace: Hope and Fear in America, 1919* (2007). On the Spanish flu, see John M. Barry's *The Great Influenza: The Epic Story of the Deadliest Plague in History* (2004). Labor tensions are examined in David E. Brody's *Labor in Crisis: The Steel Strike of 1919* (1965) and Francis Russell's *A City in Terror: Calvin Coolidge and the 1919 Boston Police Strike* (1975). On racial strife, see Jan Voogd's *Race Riots and Resistance: The Red Summer of 1919* (2008). The fear of Communists is analyzed in Robert K. Murray's *Red Scare: A Study in National Hysteria, 1919–1920* (1955).

Chapter 22

For a lively survey of the social and cultural changes during the interwar period, start with William E. Leuchtenburg's *The Perils of Prosperity, 1914–32*, 2nd ed. (1993). Even more comprehensive is Michael E. Parrish's *Anxious Decades: America in Prosperity and Depression, 1920-1941* (1992). The best introduction to the culture of the 1920s remains Roderick Nash's *The Nervous Generation: American Thought, 1917–1930* (1990). See also Lynn Dumenil's *The Modern Temper: American Culture and Society in the 1920s* (1995). The focus is on everyday life in Mary Jo Clark and Jack Clark, *On the Home Front: Everyday American Life from Prohibition to World War II* (2012).

John Higham's *Strangers in the Land: Patterns of American Nativism, 1860–1925*, 2nd ed. (2002) details the story of immigration restriction. The controversial Sacco and Vanzetti case is the focus of Moshik Temkin's *The Sacco-Vanzetti Affair: America on Trial* (2009). For analysis of the revival of Klan activity, see Thomas R. Pegram's *One Hundred Percent American: The Rebirth and Decline of the Ku Klux Klan in the 1920s* (2011). The best analysis of the Scopes trial is Edward J. Larson's *Summer for the Gods: The Scopes Trial and America's Continuing Debate over Science and Religion* (1997). On Prohibition, see Daniel Okrent's *Last Call: The Rise and Fall of Prohibition* (2011).

The impact of woman suffrage is treated in Kristi Anderson's *After Suffrage: Women in Partisan and Electoral Politics before the New Deal* (1996). The best study of the birth-control movement is Ellen Chesler's *Woman of Valor: Margaret Sanger and the Birth Control Movement in America* (1992).

On the African American migration from the South, see James N. Gregory's *The Southern Diaspora: How the Great Migrations of Black and White Southerners Transformed America* (2005). See Charles Flint Kellogg's *NAACP: A History of the National Association for the Advancement of Colored People* (1967) for his analysis of the pioneering court cases against racial discrimination. Nathan Irvin Huggins's *Harlem Renaissance* (1971) assesses the cultural impact of the Great Migration on New York City. The emergence of jazz is ably documented in Burton W. Peretti's *The Creation of Jazz: Music, Race, and Culture in Urban America* (1992). Scientific breakthroughs are analyzed in Manjit Kumar's *Quantum: Einstein, Bohr, and the Great Debate about the Nature of Reality* (2010). The best overview of cultural modernism in Europe is Peter Gay's *Modernism: The Lure of Heresy from Baudelaire to Beckett and Beyond* (2009). On southern modernism, see Daniel Joseph Singal's *The War Within: From Victorian to Modernist Thought in the South, 1919–1945* (1982). Stanley Coben's *Rebellion against Victorianism: The Impetus for Cultural Change in 1920s America* (1991) surveys the appeal of modernism among writers, artists, and intellectuals. See also Charles J. Shindo's *1927 and the Rise of Modern America* (2010).

On Harding, see Robert K. Murray's *The Harding Era: Warren G. Harding and His Administration* (1969). On Coolidge, see Amith Shlaes's *Coolidge* (2013). On Hoover, see Martin L. Fausold's *The Presidency of Herbert C. Hoover* (1985). The influential secretary of the Treasury during the 1920s is ably analyzed in David Cannadine's *Mellon: An American Life* (2006).

On the stock market crash in 1929, see Maury Klein's *Rainbow's End: The Crash of 1929* (2000). Overviews of the depressed economy are found in Charles P. Kindleberger's *The World in Depression, 1929–1939,* rev. and enlarged ed. (1986) and Peter Fearon's *War, Prosperity, and Depression: The U.S. Economy, 1917–1945* (1987). On the removal of the Bonus Army, see Paul Dickson and Thomas B. Allen's *The Bonus Army: An American Epic* (2004).

Chapter 23

Two excellent overviews of the New Deal are Ira Katznelson's Fear Itself: The New Deal and the Origins of Our Time (2013) and David M. Kennedy's *Freedom from Fear: The American People in Depression and War, 1929–1945* (1999). A lively biography of Roosevelt is H. W. Brands's *Traitor to His Class: The Privileged Life and Radical Presidency of Franklin Delano Roosevelt* (2009). The Roosevelt marriage is well described in Hazel Rowley's *Franklin and Eleanor: An Extraordinary Marriage* (2011).

The busy first year of the New Deal is ably detailed in Anthony J. Badger's *FDR: The First Hundred Days* (2008). Perhaps the most successful of the early New Deal programs is the focus of Neil M. Maher's *Nature's New Deal: The Civilian Conservation Corps and the Roots of the American Environmental Movement* (2008). On the political opponents of the New Deal, see Alan Brinkley's *Voices of Protest: Huey Long, Father Coughlin, and the Great Depression* (1982). Roosevelt's battle with the Supreme Court is detailed in Jeff Shesol's *Supreme Power: Franklin Roosevelt vs. The Supreme Court* (2010). The actual effects of the New Deal on the economy are detailed in Elliot A. Rosen's *Roosevelt, the Great Depression, and the Economics of Recovery* (2005).

A critical assessment of Roosevelt and the New Deal is Amity Schlaes's *The Forgotten Man* (2007). James N. Gregory's *American Exodus: The Dust Bowl Migration and Okie Culture in California* (1989) describes the migratory movement. The dramatic Scottsboro court case is the focus of James Goodman's *Stories of Scottsboro* (1995). On the environmental and human causes of the dust bowl, see Donald Worster, *Dust Bowl: The Southern Plains in the 1930s* (1979). On cultural life during the 1930s, see Morris Dickstein's *Dancing in the Dark: A Cultural History of the Great Depression* (2009).

The best overview of diplomacy between the world wars remains Selig Adler's *The Uncertain Giant, 1921–1941: American Foreign Policy between the Wars* (1965). Robert Dallek's *Franklin D. Roosevelt and American Foreign Policy, 1932–1945* (1979) provides a judicious assessment of Roosevelt's foreign policy initiatives during the 1930s.

On Roosevelt's war of words with isolationists, see Lynne Olsen's *Those Angry Days: Roosevelt, Lindbergh, and America's Fight over World War II, 1939–1942* (2013), and David Kaiser's *No End Save Victory: How FDR Led the Nation into War* (2014). See also David Reynolds's *From Munich to Pearl Harbor: Roosevelt's America and the Origins of the Second World War* (2001). For the Japanese perspective, see Eri Hotta's *Japan 1941: Countdown to Infamy* (2014). On the surprise attack on Pearl Harbor, see Gordon W. Prange's *Pearl Harbor: The Verdict of History* (1986). Japan's perspective is described in Akira Iriye's *The Origins of the Second World War in Asia and the Pacific* (1987).

Chapter 24

For a sweeping survey of the Second World War, consult Anthony Roberts's *The Storm of War: A New History of the Second World War* (2011). The best detailed treatment of U.S. involvement is Rick Atkinson's multi-volume Pulitzer-prize winning series, *An Army at Dawn* (2007), *The Day of Battle* (2008), and *The Guns at Last Light* (2013). Roosevelt's wartime leadership is analyzed in Eric Larrabee's *Commander in Chief: Franklin Delano Roosevelt, His Lieutenants, and Their War* (1987).

Books on specific European campaigns include Anthony Beevor's *D-Day: The Battle for Normandy* (2010) and Charles B. MacDonald's *A Time for Trumpets: The Untold Story of the Battle of the Bulge* (1985). On the Allied commander, see Carlo D'Este's *Eisenhower: A Soldier's Life* (2002). Richard Overy assesses the controversial role of air power in *The Bombing War: Europe, 1939–1945* (2013).

For the war in the Far East, see John Costello's *The Pacific War, 1941–1945* (1981), Ronald H. Spector's *Eagle against the Sun: The American War with Japan* (1985), John W. Dower's award-winning *War without Mercy: Race and Power in the Pacific War* (1986), and Dan van der Vat's *The Pacific Campaign: The U.S.-Japanese Naval War, 1941–1945* (1991).

An excellent overview of the war's effects on the home front is Michael C. C. Adams's *The Best War Ever: America and World War II* (1994). On the transformation to the wartime economy, see Arthur Herman's *Freedom's Forge: How American Business Produced Victory in World War II* (2012) and Maury Klein's *A Call to Arms* (2013). Susan M. Hartmann's *The Home Front and Beyond: American Women in the 1940s* (1982) treats the new working environment for women. Kenneth D. Rose tells the story of problems on the home front in *Myth and the Greatest Generation: A Social History of Americans in World War II* (2008). Neil A. Wynn looks at the participation of blacks in *The Afro-American and the Second World War* (1976). The story of the oppression of Japanese Americans is told in Greg Robinson's A Tragedy for Democracy: Japanese Confinement in North America (2009). On the development of the atomic bomb, see Jim Baggott's *The First War of Physics: The Secret History of the Atomic Bomb* (2010). For the controversy over America's policies towards the Holocaust, see Richard Breitman and Alan J. Lichtman's *FDR and the Jews* (2013).

A detailed introduction to U.S. diplomacy during the conflict can be found in Gaddis Smith's *American Diplomacy during the Second World War, 1941–1945* (1965). To understand the role that Roosevelt played in policy making, consult Warren F. Kimball's *The Juggler: Franklin Roosevelt as Wartime Statesman* (1991). The most important wartime summit meeting is assessed in S. M. Plokhy's *Yalta: The Price of Peace* (2010). The issues and events that led to the deployment of atomic weapons are addressed in Martin J. Sherwin's *A World Destroyed: The Atomic Bomb and the Grand Alliance* (1975).

Chapter 25

The cold war remains a hotly debated topic. The traditional interpretation is best reflected in John Lewis Gaddis's *The Cold War: A New History (2005)*. Both superpowers, Gaddis argues, were responsible for causing the cold war, but the Soviet Union was more culpable. The revisionist perspective is represented by Gar Alperovitz's *Atomic Diplomacy: Hiroshima and Potsdam: The Use of the Atomic Bomb and the American Confrontation with Soviet Power*, 2nd ed. (1994). Also see H. W. Brands's *The Devil We Knew: Americans and the Cold War* (1993) and Melvyn P. Leffler's

For the Soul of Mankind: The United States, the Soviet Union, and the Cold War (2007). On the architect of the containment strategy, see John L. Gaddis, *George F. Kennan: An American Life* (2011).

Frank Constigliola assesses Franklin Roosevelt's role in the start of the cold war in *Roosevelt's Lost Alliances: How Personal Politics Helped Start the Cold War* (2013). Arnold A. Offner indicts Truman for clumsy statesmanship in *Another Such Victory: President Truman and the Cold War, 1945–1953* (2002). For a positive assessment of Truman's leadership, see Alonzo L. Hamby's *Beyond the New Deal: Harry S. Truman and American Liberalism* (1973) and Robert Dallek's *The Lost Peace: Leadership in a Time of Horror and Hope, 1945-1953* (2010). The domestic policies of the Fair Deal are treated in William C. Berman's *The Politics of Civil Rights in the Truman Administration* (1970), Richard M. Dalfiume's *Desegregation of the U.S. Armed Forces: Fighting on Two Fronts, 1939–1953* (1969), and Maeva Marcus's *Truman and the Steel Seizure Case: The Limits of Presidential Power* (1977). The most comprehensive biography of Truman is David McCullough's *Truman* (1992).

For an introduction to the tensions in Asia, see Akira Iriye's *The Cold War in Asia: A Historical Introduction* (1974). For the Korean conflict, see Callum A. MacDonald's *Korea: The War before Vietnam* (1986) and Max Hasting's *The Korean War* (1987).

The anti-Communist crusade is surveyed in David Caute's *The Great Fear: The Anti-Communist Purge under Truman and Eisenhower* (1978). Arthur Herman's *Joseph McCarthy: Reexamining the Life and Legacy of America's Most Hated Senator* (2000) covers McCarthy himself. For a well-documented account of how the cold war was sustained by superpatriotism, intolerance, and suspicion, see Stephen J. Whitfield's *The Culture of the Cold War*, 2nd ed. (1996).

Chapter 26

Two excellent overviews of social and cultural trends in the postwar era are William H. Chafe's *The Unfinished Journey: America since World War II*, 6th ed. (2006), and William E. Leuchtenburg's *A Troubled Feast: America since 1945,* rev. ed. (1979). For insights into the cultural life of the 1950s, see Jeffrey Hart's *When the Going Was Good! American Life in the Fifties* (1982) and David Halberstam's *The Fifties* (1993).

The baby boom generation and its impact are vividly described in Paul C. Light's *Baby Boomers* (1988). The emergence of the television industry is discussed in Erik Barnouw's *Tube of Plenty: The Evolution of American Television,* 2nd rev. ed. (1990), and Ella Taylor's *Prime-Time Families: Television Culture in Postwar America* (1989).

On the process of suburban development, see Kenneth T. Jackson's *Crabgrass Frontier: The Suburbanization of the United States* (1985). Equally good is Tom Martinson's *American Dreamscape: The Pursuit of Happiness in Postwar Suburbia* (2000). For insights into TV and everyday life, see *Karal Ann Marling, As Seen on TV: The Visual Culture of Everyday Life in the 1950s* (1996).

The middle-class ideal of family life in the 1950s is examined in Elaine Tyler May's *Homeward Bound: American Families in the Cold War Era,* rev. ed. (2008). Thorough accounts of women's issues are found in Wini Breines's *Young, White, and Miserable: Growing Up Female in the Fifties* (1992). For an overview of the resurgence of religion in the 1950s, see George M. Marsden's *Religion and American Culture,* 2nd ed. (2000).

The origins and growth of rock and roll are surveyed in Carl Belz's *The Story of Rock,* 2nd ed. (1972). The colorful Beats are brought to life in Steven Watson's *The Birth of the Beat Generation: Visionaries, Rebels, and Hipsters, 1944–1960* (1995).

Scholarship on the Eisenhower years is extensive. A balanced treatment is Jean Edward Smith's *Eisenhower in War and Peace* (2012). For the manner in which

Eisenhower conducted foreign policy, see Evan Thomas's *Ike's Bluff: President Eisenhower's Secret Battle to Save the World* (2012).

The best overview of American foreign policy since 1945 is Stephen E. Ambrose and Douglas G. Brinkley's *Rise to Globalism: American Foreign Policy since 1938* 9th ed. (2011). For the buildup of U.S. involvement in Indochina, consult Fredrik Logevall's *Embers of War: The Fall of an Empire and the Making of America's Vietnam* (2012). The Cold War strategy of the Eisenhower administration is the focus of Chris Tudda's *The Truth Is Our Weapon: The Rhetorical Diplomacy of Dwight D. Eisenhower and John Foster Dulles* (2006). To learn about the CIA's secret activities in Iran, see Ervand Abrahamian's *The Coup: 1953, the CIA, and the Roots of Modern U.S.-Iranian Relations* (2013).

The impact of the Supreme Court during the 1950s is the focus of Archibald Cox's *The Warren Court: Constitutional Decision as an Instrument of Reform* (1968). A masterly study of the important Warren Court decision on school desegregation is James T. Patterson's *Brown v. Board of Education: A Civil Rights Milestone and Its Troubled Legacy* (2001).

For the story of the early years of the civil rights movement, see Taylor Branch's *Parting the Waters: America in the King Years, 1954–1963* (1988), Robert Weisbrot's *Freedom Bound: A History of America's Civil Rights Movement* (1990), and David A. Nicholas's *A Matter of Justice: Eisenhower and the Beginning of the Civil Rights Revolution* (2007). On Rosa Parks, see Jeanne Theoharis's *The Rebellious Life of Mrs. Rosa Parks* (2013). On the testy relationship of Eisenhower and his vice president, Richard Nixon, see Jeffrey Frank's *Ike and Dick: Portrait of a Strange Political Marriage* (2013).

Chapter 27

A superb analysis of John Kennedy's life is Thomas C. Reeves's *A Question of Character: A Life of John F. Kennedy* (1991). The 1960 campaign is detailed in Gary A. Donaldson's *The First Modern Campaign: Kennedy, Nixon, and the Election of 1960* (2007). The best study of the Kennedy administration's domestic policies is Irving Bernstein's *Promises Kept: John F. Kennedy's New Frontier* (1991). See also Robert Dallek's *Camelot's Court: Inside the Kennedy White House* (2013), Thurston Clarke's *JFK's Last Hundred Days* (2013), and Ira Stoll's *JFK, Conservative* (2013). For details on the still swirling conspiracy theories about the assassination, see David W. Belin's *Final Disclosure: The Full Truth about the Assassination of President Kennedy* (1988).

On LBJ, see the magisterial multi-volume biography by Robert Caro's titled *The Years of Lyndon Johnson*. On the Johnson administration, see Vaughn Davis Bornet's *The Presidency of Lyndon B. Johnson* (1984).

Among the works that interpret liberal social policy during the 1960s, John E. Schwarz's *America's Hidden Success: A Reassessment of Twenty Years of Public Policy* (1983) offers a glowing endorsement of Democratic programs. For a contrasting perspective, see Charles Murray's *Losing Ground: American Social Policy, 1950–1980* (1994).

On foreign policy, see *Kennedy's Quest for Victory: American Foreign Policy, 1961–1963* (1989), edited by Thomas G. Paterson. To learn more about Kennedy's problems in Cuba, see Mark J. White's *Missiles in Cuba: Kennedy, Khrushchev, Castro and the 1962 Crisis* (1997). See also Aleksandr Fursenko and Timothy Naftali's *"One Hell of a Gamble": Khrushchev, Castro and Kennedy, 1958–1964* (1997).

American involvement in Vietnam has received voluminous treatment from all political perspectives. For an excellent overview, see Larry Berman's *Planning a Tragedy: The Americanization of the War in Vietnam* (1983) and *Lyndon Johnson's*

War: The Road to Stalemate in Vietnam (1989), as well as Stanley Karnow's *Vietnam: A History,* 2nd rev. ed. (1997). An analysis of policy making concerning the Vietnam War is David M. Barrett's *Uncertain Warriors: Lyndon Johnson and His Vietnam Advisors* (1993). A fine account of the military involvement is Robert D. Schulzinger's *A Time for War: The United States and Vietnam, 1941–1975* (1997). On the legacy of the Vietnam War, see Arnold R. Isaacs's *Vietnam Shadows: The War, Its Ghosts, and Its Legacy* (1997).

Many scholars have dealt with various aspects of the civil rights movement and race relations in the 1960s. See especially Carl M. Brauer's *John F. Kennedy and the Second Reconstruction* (1977), David J. Garrow's *Bearing the Cross: Martin Luther King, Jr., and the Southern Christian Leadership Conference* (1986), and Adam Fairclough's *To Redeem the Soul of America: The Southern Christian Leadership Conference and Martin Luther King, Jr.* (1987). William H. Chafe's *Civilities and Civil Rights: Greensboro, North Carolina, and the Black Struggle for Freedom* (1980) details the original sit-ins. An award-winning study of racial and economic inequality in a representative American city is Thomas J. Sugrue's *The Origins of the Urban Crisis: Race and Inequality in Postwar Detroit* (1996).

Chapter 28

An engaging overview of the cultural trends of the 1960s is Maurice Isserman and Michael Kazin's *America Divided: The Civil War of the 1960s,* 3rd ed. (2007). The New Left is assessed in Irwin Unger's *The Movement: A History of the American New Left, 1959–1972* (1974). On the Students for a Democratic Society, see Kirkpatrick Sale's *SDS* (1973) and Allen J. Matusow's *The Unraveling of America: A History of Liberalism in the 1960s* (1984). Also useful is Todd Gitlin's *The Sixties: Years of Hope, Days of Rage*, rev. ed. (1993). For a focused study, see James T. Patterson's *The Eve of Destruction: How 1965 Transformed America* (2013). On the popularity of folk music and the role of Greenwich Village, see Stephen Petrus and Ronald D. Cohen's *Folk City* (2015). A good social history is David Farber, *The Age of Great Dreams: America in the 1960s* (1994).

For insights into the black power movement, see Peniel E. Joseph's *Stokely: A Life* (2014), and Joshua Bloom and Waldo E. Martin, Jr.'s *Black against Empire: The History and Politics of the Black Panther Party* (2013).

Two influential assessments of the counterculture by sympathetic commentators are Theodore Roszak's *The Making of a Counter-Culture: Reflections on the Technocratic Society and Its Youthful Opposition* (1969) and Charles A. Reich's *The Greening of America: How the Youth Revolution Is Trying to Make America Livable* (1970). A good scholarly analysis that takes the hippies seriously is Timothy Miller's *The Hippies and American Values* (1991).

The best study of the women's liberation movement is Ruth Rosen's *The World Split Open: How the Modern Women's Movement Changed America,* rev. ed. (2006). The organizing efforts of Cesar Chavez are detailed in Ronald B. Taylor's *Chavez and the Farm Workers* (1975). The struggles of Native Americans for recognition and power are sympathetically described in Stan Steiner's *The New Indians* (1968).

The best overview of the 1970s and 1980s is James T. Patterson's *Restless Giant: The United States from Watergate to Bush v. Gore* (2005). On Nixon, see Melvin Small's thorough analysis in *The Presidency of Richard Nixon* (1999). A good slim biography is Elizabeth Drew's *Richard M. Nixon* (2007). For an overview of the Watergate scandal, see Stanley I. Kutler's *The Wars of Watergate: The Last Crisis of Richard Nixon* (1990). For the way the Republicans handled foreign affairs, consult Tad Szulc's *The Illusion of Peace: Foreign Policy in the Nixon Years* (1978). The Nixon

White House tapes make for fascinating reading. See *The Nixon Tapes* (2014), ed. by Douglas Brinkley and Luke Nichter. Rick Perlstein traces the effects of Nixon's career on the Republican party and the conservative movement in two compelling books: *Nixonland: The Rise of a President and the Fracturing of America* (2007) and *The Invisible Bridge: The Fall of Nixon and the Rise of Reagan* (2014).

The Communist takeover of Vietnam and the end of American involvement there are traced in Larry Berman's *No Peace, No Honor: Nixon, Kissinger, and Betrayal in Vietnam* (2001). William Shawcross's *Sideshow: Kissinger, Nixon and the Destruction of Cambodia*, rev. ed. (2002), deals with the broadening of the war, while Larry Berman's *Planning a Tragedy: The Americanization of the War in Vietnam* (1982) assesses the final impact of U.S. involvement. The most comprehensive treatment of the anti-war movement is Tom Wells's *The War Within: America's Battle over Vietnam* (1994).

A comprehensive treatment of the Ford administration is contained in John Robert Greene's *The Presidency of Gerald R. Ford* (1995). The best overview of the Carter administration is Burton I. Kaufman's *The Presidency of James Earl Carter, Jr.,* 2nd rev. ed. (2006). A work more sympathetic to the Carter administration is John Dumbrell's *The Carter Presidency: A Re-evaluation,* 2nd ed. (1995). Gaddis Smith's *Morality, Reason, and Power: American Diplomacy in the Carter Years* (1986) provides an overview. Background on how the Middle East came to dominate much of American policy is found in William B. Quandt's *Decade of Decisions: American Policy toward the Arab-Israeli Conflict, 1967–1976* (1977). For a biography of Carter, see Randall Balmer, *Redeemer: The Life of Jimmy Carter* (2014).

Chapter 29

The rise of modern political conservatism is well told in Patrick Allitt's *The Conservatives: Ideas and Personalities throughout American History* (2009) and Michael Schaller's *Right Turn: American Life in the Reagan-Bush Era, 1980–1992* (2007).

On Reagan, see John Patrick Diggins's *Ronald Reagan: Fate, Freedom, and the Making of History* (2007), Richard Reeves's *President Reagan: The Triumph of Imagination* (2005), and Sean Wilentz's *The Age of Reagan: A History, 1974–2008* (2008). The best political analysis is Robert M. Collins's *Transforming America: Politics and Culture during the Reagan Years* (2007). For insights into the 1980 election, see Andrew E. Busch's *Reagan's Victory: The Presidential Election of 1980 and the Rise of the Right* (2005). On Reaganomics, see David A. Stockman's *The Triumph of Politics: Why the Reagan Revolution Failed* (1986).

For Reagan's foreign policy in Central America, see James Chace's *Endless War: How We Got Involved in Central America—and What Can Be Done* (1984) and Walter LaFeber's *Inevitable Revolutions: The United States in Central America*, 2nd ed. (1993). On Reagan's second term, see Jane Mayer and Doyle McManus's *Landslide: The Unmaking of the President, 1984–1988* (1988). For a masterly work on the Iran-Contra affair, see Theodore Draper's *A Very Thin Line: The Iran Contra Affairs* (1991). Several collections of essays include varying assessments of the Reagan years. Among these are *The Reagan Revolution?* (1988), edited by B. B. Kymlicka and Jean V. Matthews; *The Reagan Presidency: An Incomplete Revolution?* (1990), edited by Dilys M. Hill, Raymond A. Moore, and Phil Williams, and *Looking Back on the Reagan Presidency* (1990), edited by Larry Berman.

The 41st president is the focus of Timothy Naftali's *George H. W. Bush* (2007). On the 1988 campaign, see Sidney Blumenthal's *Pledging Allegiance: The Last Campaign of the Cold War* (1990). For a social history of the decade, see John Ehrman's

The Eighties: America in the Age of Reagan (2005). On the Persian Gulf conflict, see Lester H. Brune's *America and the Iraqi Crisis, 1990–1992: Origins and Aftermath* (1993).

Chapter 30

Analysis of the Clinton years can be found in Joe Klein's *The Natural: The Misunderstood Presidency of Bill Clinton* (2002). Clinton's impeachment is assessed in Richard A. Posner's *An Affair of State: The Investigation, Impeachment, and Trial of President Clinton* (1999). The conflict between Clinton and Gingrich is explained in Elizabeth Drew's *The Struggle between Gingrich and the Clinton White House* (1996).

On changing demographic trends, see Sam Roberts's *Who We Are Now: The Changing Face of America in the Twenty-First Century* (2004). For a textured account of the exploding Latino culture, see Roberto Suro's *Strangers Among Us: How Latino Immigration Is Transforming America* (1998). On social and cultural life in the 1990s, see Haynes Johnson's *The Best of Times: America in the Clinton Years* (2001). Economic and technological changes are assessed in Daniel T. Rogers's *Age of Fracture* (2011). The onset and growth of the AIDS epidemic are traced in *And the Band Played On: Politics, People, and the AIDS Epidemic,* 20th anniversary ed. (2007), by Randy Shilts.

On the religious right, see George M. Marsden's *Understanding Fundamentalism and Evangelicalism,* new ed. (2006) and Ralph E. Reed's *Politically Incorrect: The Emerging Faith Factor in American Politics* (1994).

On the invention of the computer and the Internet, see Paul E. Ceruzzi's *A History of Modern Computing,* 2nd ed. (2003), Janet Abbate's *Inventing the Internet* (1999), and Michael Lewis, *The New New Thing: A Silicon Valley Story* (1999). The booming economy of the 1990s is well analyzed in Joseph E. Stiglitz's *The Roaring Nineties: A New History of the World's Most Prosperous Decade* (2003).

For further treatment of the end of the cold war, see Michael R. Beschloss and Strobe Talbott's *At the Highest Levels: The Inside Story of the End of the Cold War* (1993) and Richard Crockatt's *The Fifty Years War: The United States and the Soviet Union in World Politics, 1941–1991* (1995).

On the transformation of American foreign policy, see James Mann's *Rise of the Vulcans: The History of Bush's War Cabinet* (2004), Claes G. Ryn's *America the Virtuous: The Crisis of Democracy and the Quest for Empire* (2003), and Stephen M. Walt's *Taming American Power: The Global Response to U.S. Primacy* (2005).

The disputed 2000 presidential election is the focus of Jeffrey Toobin's *Too Close to Call: The Thirty-Six-Day Battle to Decide the 2000 Election* (2001). On the Bush presidency, see *The Presidency of George W. Bush: A First Historical Assessment*, edited by Julian E. Zelizer (2010). See also Fred H. Israel and Jonathan Mann's *The Election of 2000 and the Administration of George W. Bush* (2003). Also see Dick Cheney's illuminating, if self-serving, account of his service as Bush's vice president in *In My Time: A Personal and Political Memoir* (2011).

On the attacks of September 11, 2001, and their aftermath, see *The Age of Terror: America and the World after September 11,* edited by Strobe Talbott and Nayan Chanda (2001). For a devastating account of the Bush administration by a White House insider, see Scott McClellan's *What Happened: Inside the Bush White House and Washington's Culture of Deception* (2008). On the historic 2008 election, see Michael Nelson's *The Elections of 2008* (2009). The best biography of Obama is David Maraniss's *Barack Obama: The Story* (2012). A conservative critique is provided in Edward Klein's *The Amateur: Barack Obama in the White House* (2012).

The Great Recession is explained in Alan S. Blinder's *After the Music Stopped: The Financial Crisis, the Response, and the Work Ahead* (2013). The Tea Party movement is assessed in Theda Skocpol and Vanessa Williamson's *The Tea Party and the Remaking of Republican Conservatism* (2012) and Elizabeth Price Foley's *The Tea Party: Three Principles* (2012). The partisan gridlock in Congress is the focus of Thomas E. Mann and Norman J. Ornstein's *The Broken Branch: How Congress Is Failing America and How to Get it Back on Track* (2012). The tension between the conservative majority on the U.S. Supreme Court and the Obama administration is examined in Jeffrey Toobin's *The Oath: The Obama White House and the Supreme Court* (2012). On the growing economic inequality in America, see Joseph Stiglitz's *The Price of Inequality: How Today's Divided Society Endangers Our Future* (2013).

On the 2016 election, see Hillary Rodham Clinton, *What Happened* (2017); Larry Sabato, Kyle Kondik, and Geoffrey Skelley, *Trumped: The 2016 Election That Broke All the Rules* (2017); and, Thomas Lake and Jodi Enda, *Unprecedented: The Election that Changed Everything* (2016).

Credits

Text Credits

Bernard Bailyn: Excerpts reprinted by permission of the publisher from *The Ideological Origins of the American Revolution* by Bernard Bailyn, pp. xx–xxiii, Cambridge, Mass.: Harvard University Press, Copyright © 1992 by Bernard Bailyn.

Richard Breitman and Allan J. Lichtman: Excerpts reprinted by permission of the publisher from *FDR and the Jews* by Richard Breitman and Allan J. Lichtman, pp. 2, 6–7, Cambridge, Mass.: Harvard University Press, Copyright © 2013 by Richard Breitman and Allan J. Lichtman.

Leo Chavez: Excerpts from *The Latino Threat: Constructing Immigrants, Citizens, and the Nation, Second Edition*, by Leo Chavez. Copyright © 2008, 2014 By the Board of Trustees of the Leland Stanford Jr. University. All rights reserved. With the permission of Stanford University Press, www.sup.org

Paul Finkelman: Excerpts from "Jefferson and Slavery," in *Jeffersonian Legacies*, edited by Peter S. Onuf. pp. 181–183, 210–211. © 1993 by the Rector and Visitors of the University of Virginia. Reprinted by permission of the University of Virginia Press.

Eric Foner: Excerpt from *The Story of American Freedom*. Copyright © 1998 by Eric Foner. Reprinted by permission of W. W. Norton & Company, Inc., the author, and the Sandra Dijkstra Literary Agency.

Nathan Glazer & Daniel Moynihan: From *Beyond The Melting Pot*, excerpts from pp. 12–14, 20, © 1963 Massachusetts Institute of Technology, used by permission of The MIT Press.

Gary B. Nash: Excerpts from "Social Change and the Growth of Prerevolutionary Urban Radicalism," by Gary B. Nash. From *The American Revolution: Explorations in History of American Radicalism*, by Alfred F. Young (ed.). Copyright © 1976 by Northern Illinois University Press. Used with permission of Northern Illinois University Press.

Jason Richwine: "The Congealing Pot," by Jason Richwine from National Review, August 24, 2009. © 2009 by National Review, Inc. Reprinted by permission.

Douglas L. Wilson: Excerpts from "Thomas Jefferson and the Character Issue," by Douglas L. Wilson. Originally published in *The Atlantic Monthly*, November 1992. Used by permission the author.

Photo Credits

Front Matter

Page v: Minnesota Historical Society; p. xii: The Rapalje Children, 1768 (oil on canvas), Durand, John (1731-1805)/© Collection of the New-York Historical Society/Bridgeman Images; p. xiii: Granger, NYC — All rights reserved; p. xiv: Private Collection/Peter Newark American Pictures/Bridgeman Images; p. xv: Library of Congress; p. xvi: Library of Congress; p. xvii: Wikimedia, public domain; p. xviii: Wikimedia, public domain; p. xix: Adoc-photos/Art Resource, NY; p. xx: Bettmann/Getty Images; p. xxi: AP Photo/ Jae C. Hong.

Chapter 15

Page 532: Smithsonian American Art Museum/Art Resource; p. 535: Granger, NYC — All rights reserved; p. 537: Library of Congress; p. 538: Photo Researchers, Inc/Alamy Stock Photo; p. 539: Library of Congress; p. 540: Granger, NYC — All rights reserved; p. 543: Library of Congress; p. 545: Library of Congress; p. 548: Bettmann/Corbis/Getty Images; p. 549: Library of Congress; p. 550: Library of Congress; p. 552: Granger, NYC — All rights reserved; p. 553: Library of Congress; p. 555: John Kraljevich/John Kraljevich Americana; p. 556: Chronicle/Alamy Stock Photo; p. 558: akg-images/Fototeca Gilardi; p. 561: Library of Congress.

Chapter 16

Page 570 (Chief Joseph): Library of Congress; (Maine headline) Wikimedia, public domain; (Mulberry St): Library of Congress; (boxing painting): *Stag at Sharkey's*, 1909 (oil on canvas), Bellows, George Wesley (1882-1925)/Cleveland Museum of Art/Hinman B. Hurlbut Collection/Bridgeman Images; (Booker T Washington): Library of Congress; p. 572: David J. & Janice L. Frent/Corbis via Getty Images; p. 574: Granger, NYC — All rights reserved; p. 578: Granger, NYC — All rights reserved; p. 579: Granger, NYC — All rights reserved; p. 580: Bettmann /Corbis/Getty Images; p. 582: National Archives; p. 585: Wikimedia Commons, pd; p. 586: from John J. McLaurin 1902 *Sketches in Crude-Oil* www.archive.org, pd; p. 587: Library of Congress; p. 589: Library of Congress; p. 590: Special Collections Research Center, Earl Gregg Swem Library, The College of William & Mary; p. 591: Private Collection/Peter Newark American Pictures/Bridgeman Images; p. 592: © Museum of the City of New York, USA/Bridgeman Images; p. 594: Special Collections, Vassar College Libraries. Archives 08.07.05; p. 595: Library of Congress; p. 596: Bettmann/ Corbis/Getty Images; p. 598: Peter Newark American Pictures/ Bridgeman Images; p. 599: T.V. Powderly Photographic Collection, The American Catholic History Research Center University Archives, The Catholic University of America, Washington, D.C.; p. 601: Library of Congress; p. 602: Bettmann/Corbis/Getty Images; p. 604: Library of Congress; p. 605: PhotoQuest/Getty Images; p. 606: Bettmann/Corbis/Getty Images.

Chapter 17

Page 610: Granger, NYC — All rights reserved; p. 614: The New York Public Library/Art Resource, NY; p. 616: Library of Congress; p. 619: Granger, NYC — All rights reserved; p. 620: Corbis/Getty Images; p. 621: Corbis/Getty Images; p. 622: Everett Collection Historical/Alamy Stock Photo; p. 623: Library of Congress; p. 624: Library of Congress; p. 625: Library of Congress; p. 628: Kansas State Historical Society; p. 631: Library of Congress; p. 633: Library of Congress; p. 636: Kansas State

p. 925: Art Resource; p. 927: Gamma-Keystone/Getty Images; p. 929: National Archives; p. 931: Bettmann/Getty Images; p. 932: John van Hasselt/Sygma via Getty Images.

Chapter 25
Page 944: (black student): Bettmann/Getty Images; (airlift): Bettmann/Getty Images; (9/11): Sean Adair/Reuters/Newscom; (soldiers): Bettmann/Getty Image; (Dylan): Michael Ochs Archives/Getty Images; p. 946: Everett Collection Historical/Alamy Stock Photo; p. 947: STR/Reuters/Newscom; p. 950: Bettmann/Getty Images; p. 952: Bettmann/Getty Images; p. 954: © McNeely Image Services/The Image Works; p. 955: AP Photo/John Rooney; p. 957: Sarin Images/The Granger Collection; p. 958: Hulton-Deutsch Collection/Corbis via Getty Images; p. 959: Bettmann/Getty Images; p. 963: National Archives; p. 965: Bettmann/Corbis/Getty Images; p. 967: Bettmann/Getty Images; p. 968: Bettmann/Getty Images; p. 969: Francis Miller/The LIFE Picture Collection/Getty Images; p. 971: Hulton-Deutsch Collection/Corbis via Getty Images; p. 972: Pictorial Parade/Getty Images; p. 974: Bettmann/Corbis/Getty Images; p. 977: Granger, NYC — All rights reserved; p. 979: Martha Holmes/Getty Images; p. 981: J. T. Vintage/Bridgeman Images.

Chapter 26
Page 986: GraphicaArtis/Getty Images; p. 988: National Archives; p. 991: Everett Collection Inc/Alamy Stock Photo; p. 993: John Dominis/Time Life Pictures/Getty Images; p. 994: Heritage Image Partnership Ltd/Alamy Stock Photo; p. 996: Hulton Archives/Getty Images; p. 998: Library of Congress; p. 999 (left): Everett Collection Historical/Alamy Stock Photo; (right): Mondadori/Getty Images; p. 1001: Three Lions/Getty Images; p. 1002: Bernard Gotfryd/Getty Images; p. 1003: Allan Grant/The LIFE Picture Collection/Getty Images; p. 1005: Don Wright/The LIFE Images Collection/Getty Images; p. 1007: Mondadori/Getty Images; p. 1008: Bruce Davidson/Magnum Photos; p. 1010 (left): AP Photo/Gene Herrick (right): Charles Moore/Getty Images; p. 1012: Bettmann/Getty Images; p. 1015: A 1956 Herblock Cartoon, © Herb Block Foundation; p. 1017: Bettmann/Getty Images; p. 1018: AFP/Getty Images; p. 1021: Rue des Archives/The Granger Collection; p. 1024: Granger, NYC — All rights reserved; p. 1025: Sovfoto/Universal Images Group/REX/Shutterstock.

Chapter 27
Page 1030: Art © Robert Rauschenberg Foundation/Licensed by VAGA, New York, NY *Skyway*, 1964 (oil & silkscreen on canvas), Rauschenberg, Robert (1925-2008)/Dallas Museum of Art, Texas/Bridgeman Images; p. 1033: Granger, NYC — All rights reserved; p. 1035: Bettmann/Getty Images; p. 1036: Granger, NYC — All rights reserved; p. 1038: Bettmann/Getty Images; p. 1039: John F. Kennedy Library; National Archives; p. 1042: Carl Mydans/The LIFE Picture Collection/Getty Images; p. 1043: Granger, NYC — All rights reserved; p. 1044: Granger, NYC — All rights reserved; p. 1046: AP Photo; p. 1048: AFP/Getty Images; p. 1050: AP Photo; p. 1051: AP Photo; p. 1052: Bettmann/Getty Images; p. 1053: Bettmann/Getty Images; p. 1055: National Archives; p. 1057: AP Photo; p. 1058: Everett Collection Historical/Alamy Stock Photo; p. 1059 (top): David J. & Janice L. Frent/Corbis via Getty Images; (bottom): Imaged by Heritage Auctions, HA.com; p. 1062: Hulton Archive/Getty Images; p. 1064: Tim Page/Corbis Historical/Getty Images; p. 1065: Bettmann/Getty image; p. 1069: Jack Kightlinger, Lyndon Baines Johnson Library and Museum.

Chapter 28
Page 1076: Bettmann/Getty Images; p. 1079: Ted Streshinsky/Corbis Historical/Getty Images; p. 1080: Leif Skoogfors/Corbis Historical/Getty Images; p. 1081: AP Photo; p. 1082: Henry Diltz/Corbis via Getty Images; p. 1083: Ted Streshinsky/Corbis Historical/Getty Images; p. 1084: Michael Ochs Archive/Getty Images; p. 1087: © Globe Photos/ZUMASPRESS.com; p. 1089 (left): Eugene Gordon/The New-York Historical Society/Getty Images; (right): Bettmann/Getty Images; p. 1090: H. William Tetlow/Getty Images; p. 1092: Michael Rougier/The Life Picture Collection/Getty Images; p. 1093: Bettmann/Getty Images; p. 1094: Fred W. McDarrah/Getty Images; p. 1097: Everett Collection Historical/Alamy Stock Photo; p. 1099: Lee Lockwood/The Life Images Collection/Getty Images; p. 1100: AP Photo; p. 1101: Environmental Protection Agency/National Archives; p. 1105: Howard Ruffner/Getty Images; p. 1107: Bettmann/Corbis/Getty Images; p. 1110: John Dominis/The Life Picture Collection/Getty Images; p. 1113: AP Photo; p. 1117: MPI/Getty Images; p. 1118: Corbis/Getty Images; p. 1120: Dirck Halstead/Time Life Pictures/Getty Images.

Chapter 29
Page 1124: Wally McNamee/CORBIS/Corbis via Getty Images; p. 1127: Corbis/Getty Images; p. 1130: AP Photo; p. 1131: Bettmann/Getty Images; p. 1132: Mohsen Shandiz/Sygma/Getty Images; p. 1133: Francois Lochon/Getty Images; p. 1135: Bettmann/Getty Images; p. 1139: Bettmann/Getty Images; p. 1140: Wally McNamee/Corbis/Getty Images; p. 1143: National Archives; p. 1144: Bettmann/Getty Images; p. 1145: © Paul Szep; p. 1146: Peter Turnley/Corbis/VCG via Getty Images; p. 1148: Richard Ellis/ZUMAPRESS.com/Alamy Live News; p. 1149: Wally McNamee/Corbis via Getty Images; p. 1152: STR/REUTERS/Newscom; p. 1154: Mike Nelson/Getty Images; p. 1157: AP Photo/Susan Ragan.

Chapter 30
Page 1160: Brendan McDermid/REUTERS/Newscom; p. 1163: AP Photo/Mike Albans; p. 1164: AP Photo/James Finley; p. 1166: Richard Ellis/AFP/Getty Images; p. 1168: Image Courtesy of The Advertising Archives; p. 1169: AP Photo/Ron Edmonds; p. 1170: STR/REUTERS/Newscom; p. 1172: AP Photo/Doug Mills; p. 1173: Robert King/Getty Images; p. 1175: STR/REUTERS/Newscom; p. 1176: Kevin Lamarque/Reuters/Newscom; p. 1178: Ali Jasim/REUTERS/Newscom; p. 1180: Mario Tama/Getty Images; p. 1181: AP Photo/Pablo Martinez Monsivais; p. 1182: Justin Sullivan/Getty Images; p. 1183: AP Photo/Jae C. Hong; p. 1186: Jewel Samad/AFP/Getty Images; p. 1187: AP Photo/Erich Schlegel, File; p. 1188: Jeff J. Mitchell/Getty Images; p. 1190: AP Photo/Ringo H.W. Chiu; p. 1191: AP Photo/Eric Gay; p. 1194: Photo by Kremlin.ru: https://creativecommons.org/licenses/by/3.0/deed.en p. 1195: AP Photo/Efrem Lukatsky, file; p. 1197 (left): Spencer Platt/Getty Images; (right): David McNew/Getty Images; p. 1200: The Photo Access/Alamy Stock Photo; p. 1203: Xinhua/Bao Dandan via Getty Images; p. 1205: Amy Sussman/REX/Shutterstock; p. 1208 Brian van der Brug/LA Times via Getty Images; p.1209: Jeff Malet/Newscom.

Index

Page numbers in *italics* refer to illustrations.